T0399161

THE OXFORD HANDBOOK OF

MUSIC
COMPOSITION
PEDAGOGY

THE OXFORD HANDBOOK OF

MUSIC COMPOSITION PEDAGOGY

Edited by

MICHELE KASCHUB

OXFORD
UNIVERSITY PRESS

Oxford University Press is a department of the University of Oxford. It furthers the University's objective of excellence in research, scholarship, and education by publishing worldwide. Oxford is a registered trade mark of Oxford University Press in the UK and certain other countries.

Published in the United States of America by Oxford University Press
198 Madison Avenue, New York, NY 10016, United States of America.

Library of Congress Cataloging-in-Publication Data
Names: Kaschub, Michele, 1967– author.
Title: The Oxford handbook of music composition pedagogy /
[edited by] Michele Kaschub.
Description: [1.] | New York : Oxford University Press, 2024. |
Series: Oxford handbooks series | Includes bibliographical references and index.
Identifiers: LCCN 2022054443 (print) | LCCN 2022054444 (ebook) |
ISBN 9780197574874 (hardback) | ISBN 9780197574904 |
ISBN 9780197574898 (epub)
Subjects: LCSH: Composition (Music)—Instruction and study. |
Music—Instruction and study.
Classification: LCC MT40 .O94 2024 (print) | LCC MT40 (ebook) |
DDC 781.3071—dc23/eng/20221221
LC record available at https://lccn.loc.gov/2022054443
LC ebook record available at https://lccn.loc.gov/2022054444

DOI: 10.1093/oxfordhb/9780197574874.001.0001

Printed by Sheridan Books, Inc., United States of America

To my father, David J. Pressley, a middle school math and science teacher, commercial sardine weir fisherman, and country music lover, and my mother, Juanita R. Pressley, a high school business teacher and self-taught, accomplished church pianist, for suggesting to my brother and me—and to all of their students—that almost any goal is achievable with the investment of the time and effort needed to attain it.

I hope that the readers of this handbook—once a distant goal—will pass this idea of investing time and effort to the students in their classrooms and rehearsal halls who brim with musical imagination and artistic curiosity.

For we, music educators, have the distinct and special privilege of sharing music's boundless potentials with those who will bring forth its continued evolution.

Contents

SECTION III: UNDERSTANDING COMPOSITIONAL PROCESSES

SECTION IV: APPROACHES TO COMPOSITION PEDAGOGY

SECTION V: NURTURING YOUNG COMPOSERS

SECTION VI: COMPOSING IN CLASSROOM MUSIC

SECTION VII: COMPOSING IN SCHOOL ENSEMBLE SETTINGS

SECTION VIII: INTERNATIONAL PERSPECTIVES ON COMPOSITION PEDAGOGY

SECTION IX: SHAPING THE FUTURE OF COMPOSITION IN MUSIC EDUCATION

Contributors

Taichi Akutsu, Okayama Prefectural University, Japan

Daniel J. Albert, University of Massachusetts–Amherst

Judy Bond, University of Wisconsin–Stevens Point

Elizabeth Bucura, Kunstuniversität Graz, Austria

Pamela Burnard, University of Cambridge, United Kingdom

Suzanne L. Burton, University of Delaware

Marla A. Butke, Otterbein University

Kelly Bylica, Boston University

Patricia Shehan Campbell, University of Washington, Seattle

Bruce Allen Carter, New York University and National Council on the Arts

Ann Clements, Penn State

Carolyn Cooke, The Open University, United Kingdom

Lisa A. Crawford, Los Angeles County High School for the Arts

Renée Crawford, Monash University, Australia

Daniel Deutsch, NYSSMA Composition & Songwriting Committee

Matthew R. Doiron, Western Connecticut State University, School of Visual and Performing Arts

Jashen Edwards, Don Wright School of Music, The University of Western Ontario

John Erős, California State University–East Bay

R. J. David Frego, Penn State

Gena R. Greher, University of Massachusetts–Lowell

Maud Hickey, Northwestern University

Lamont Holden, University of Illinois, School of Music

Michael Hopkins, University of Michigan, School of Music, Theatre & Dance

Micheál Houlahan, Millersville University

Michele Kaschub, University of Southern Maine, Dr. Alfred and Suzi D. Osher School of Music

Jody L. Kerchner, Oberlin College/Conservatory of Music

Benon Kigozi, Makerere University, Kampala, Uganda

Alexander Koops, Azusa Pacific University, Azusa Conservatory of Music

John Kratus, Independent Scholar

Adam J. Kruse, University of Illinois, School of Music

Christopher Mena, University of Washington–Seattle

Elizabeth A. Menard, Bowling Green State University, College of Musical Arts

Douglas T. Owens, Old Dominion University, F. Ludwig Diehn School of Music

Heidi Partti, Finland

Sarah Genevieve Burghart Rice, Penn State

Patricia Ajamie Riley, University of Vermont

Christian Rolle, Universität zu Köln, Institut für Musikpädagogik, Germany

Patrick Schmidt, Teachers College, Columbia University

Ana Luísa Veloso, Centro de Investigação em Psicologia da Música e Educação, Portugal

Janice Smith, Queen's College, CUNY, Aaron Copland School of Music

Neil Thomas Smith, Maastricht University, The Netherlands

Sandra L. Stauffer, Arizona State University, Herberger Institute for Design and the Arts

Katherine Strand, Appalachian State University, Hayes School of Music

David A. Stringham, James Madison University, Center for Inclusive Music Engagement

Philip Tacka, Millersville University

Cynthia Van Maanen, Interlochen Arts Academy, Interlochen Center for the Arts

Heather Wadler, University of Delaware

Julia Weber, Universität zu Köln, Institut für Musikpädagogik, Germany

Peter R. Webster, University of Southern California, Thornton School of Music

Rachel Whitcomb, Duquesne University, Mary Pappert School of Music

Betty Anne Younker, Don Wright School of Music, University of Western Ontario

Vít Zouhar, Univerzita Palackého v Olomouci, Czech Republic

Preface

BETTY ANNE YOUNKER

From philosophical, psychological, sociological, and cultural considerations to inclusion at all levels and contexts as found in music education programs internationally, this handbook is rich in information with practical examples that typically are from students' works. Theory and practice are interwoven in each chapter, each supporting the other. It is the most comprehensive and inclusive publication to date about composition pedagogy. It *is* time, given that thinking about the inclusion of composition began in the 1960s with seminal conversations occurring at Tanglewood and writings by John Paynter and R. Murray Schafer being introduced. We now have research and resources and have had time for reflection. Inclusion of composition can enhance the profession's commitment to supporting each person's musical potential across the multi-faceted ways of knowing in and with music.

What follows is a brief summary of each chapter in each of the nine sections.

SECTION 1: FOUNDATIONS FOR COMPOSITION IN MUSIC EDUCATION

With a focus on the impact of social, economic, political, psychological, and educational marginalization, *Michele Kaschub* offers strategies that cultivate students' metacognizing about how they think and feel while utilizing what they know and do through composition. Based on personal narrative and rooted in anthropological, psychological, and philosophical literature, *John Kratus* justifies the inclusion of composition, and outlines and provides impediments to teaching composition and ways to overcome such impediments. *Peter Webster* includes music teaching philosophy, learning theory, and methodology and offers ideas to consider when building a pedagogy that blends knowledge and skills with spaces for creativity to occur. The ideas are applicable to elementary and secondary teachers, and music educators teaching pre-service teachers. *Neil Thomas Smith* focuses on the "vocabularies" of genius in artistic practice and pedagogy. With a historical overview of the concepts of genius and creativity, Smith provides three dilemmas of pedagogy and the role of the educator when imparting knowledge or evoking students' creativity, the canon, and genre. *Sandra L. Stauffer* explores the geneses of motivation and ideas, how composers compose, and how they "learned" to compose. Through the stories of 12 composers, insights about their processes and how they honed their craft are offered.

SECTION II: FINDING IDENTITY AND FOSTERING INCLUSION IN MUSIC COMPOSITION

Rachel Whitcomb focuses on vulnerability and authenticity, which are intimately linked, and uses teaching and songwriting as lenses through which to examine hopes, regrets, relationships, triumphs, struggles, fears, desires, and memorable stories. Autoethnographic stories reflect the journey from being a music student of the conservatory tradition to that of a country-song-writing professor and reveal vulnerable and authentic moments that shaped the author's experiences. *Alexander Koops* notes the gap between the inclusion of music composition and improvisation in National Arts Standards, at professional conferences, and in professional publications, *and* the absence in music education degree experiences, thus revealing the lack of confidence and knowledge to include composition. Offered are ideas and suggestions for inclusion of composition and improvisation in the music classroom. *Daniel Albert* provides insights about how music-making through composition can spark student agency and includes "messiness" and "space" in classrooms that are often focused and concentrated on mastery of learning goals. Albert offers how a culture can be strategically constructed for agency to be sparked and supported through composition. *Christopher Mena* and *Patricia Shehan Campbell* describe how Culturally Sustaining Pedagogy includes the understanding of the complexity of student identity features. A culture of inclusion is impacted by the choice of pedagogical strategies as musical inventions of students of diverse cultural communities are invited. With a focus on collaboration, descriptions of collective songwriting are provided and differentiated from the notion of the individual composer.

SECTION III: UNDERSTANDING COMPOSITIONAL PROCESSES

Acknowledging the centrality of listening in each music-making experience, the meaning assigned at the individual level, and music listening as creative thinking, *Jody L. Kerchner* considers the role listening plays as students compose. Expanding that role as a metacognitive process, Kerchner provides questions that guide critical, reflective, and creative thinking skill development, and offers student-centered music listening experiences. *Bruce Carter* unfolds what musicianship skills and understanding are utilized in the practices of two songwriters/music producers. With those data, Carter maps musical skills and understanding that would be of benefit to young developing musicians and questions the relevancy of practices of music theory teaching and learning. *Lisa Crawford* offers an organic, student-centered approach (INSPIRE) to composition activities with four points of understanding to be considered. The focus is on students' personalities, ways of learning, musical growth, and necessary support as they interact musically through composition. The creative process as it connects to product intentions provides a lens for each of the offered projects. *Patricia Riley* examines how revising and editing can reveal students' creative intentions through examining and discussing two student compositions at different levels of skill who participated in an online music composition community, Music-COMP. Revealed are students' processes to realize their intentions, and the role of the teacher as mentor. *Gena R. Greher* provides insights about how various forms of music technology can provide access to music composition and support the acquisition of theoretical knowledge and skills through active engagement. Strategies are included that clarify the role technology can play as students compose. *Maud Hickey* focuses on assessing students' creative products by offering thoughts based on research about (un)assessing students' original works. She presents cautions about the notion of assessing product and process because if not done thoughtfully a child's comfort and freedom to create could be crushed. Included are descriptions of assessing products and processes of original works.

Section IV: Approaches to Composition Pedagogy

Based on the value of developing all potential capacities, including the ability to create music, *Michele Kaschub* and *Janice Smith* offer a capacities-based approach to teaching and learning composition. Specifically, music capacities (compositional bases) are identified through universal experiences of feeling (feelingful intention), perception from bodily knowing as humans (musical expressivity), and interactions with music (artistic craftsmanship). Students' autonomy during the process and over the (unknown) product is critical. This autonomy requires a different pedagogy, which informs the teacher's role and allows for students to develop their understanding of music, self, and others. *Marla A. Butke* and *R. J. David Frego* provide the basis of the Dalcroze philosophy with a connection of its framework to the process of musical composition, specifically the rooted characteristics of risk-taking, creativity, and freedom to express. Building on the philosophy, explanations and examples of how the configuration of eurhythmics can lend to the goals of sensitivity and expressivity through movement are offered. *Michaél Houlahan* and *Philip Tacka* acknowledge the role of folk music, and contemporary and commercial music as we learn how to teach students sound before symbol, and as performed in authentic and culturally appropriate ways. Three organic models (Performance Through Sound Analysis, Houlahan and Tacka Model of Learning and Instruction, and Performance Through Sound Analysis and Notation) are offered for learning repertoire through audiation, with one end goal being students' development of improvisation and composition. Acknowledging that music composition is a critical component of students' music education, *John Eros* examines the pedagogy of music composition via Music Learning Theory as developed by Edwin Gordon. Eros advocates for acquisition of MLT when interacting with students via music composition in K–12 settings. *Judy Bond*, with sample lessons by *Brian Burnett*, examines music composition through the lens of Orff's composition pedagogy. Noted is the compatibility of the Orff-Schulwerk philosophy and composition, and the inclusion of improvisation by Orff and Gunild Keetman. Included are examples and lessons with references reinforcing the inclusion of all styles of music through the Schulwerk approach.

Section V: Nurturing Young Composers

Recognizing the ongoing challenge of teachers' uncomfortableness and lack of knowledge to interact with students via composition, *Pamela Burnard* and *Carolyn Cooke* set out to challenge the notion that composing must be a solo adventure and offer ways that teachers can gain confidence when interacting with students through music composition. To dismantle the soloistic notion, they examine "transdisciplinary and improvisational creativities" while embracing the reciprocity between teachers and young composers, and their relationships with materials and environments. Based on the premise that music composition is a problem-solving process—one process that is integral to creative and critical thinking—*Elizabeth A. Menard* acknowledges the challenges perceived by music teachers when engaging students in music composition. One approach to dismantling the challenge is to re-think teaching as mentorship, which opens spaces for reciprocity during collaboration. Menard provides examples and strategies noting the benefits of a collaborative mentorship between teachers and students. *Daniel Deutsch* examines student composition festivals and showcases as opportunities for young composers and their teachers, which can offer recognition of students' works, spaces to interact with peer composers and mentors, and valuable feedback to evolving composers and mentors. Strategies are offered for developing such programs that eliminate a competitive focus. *Cynthia Van Maanen* offers beneficial skills for pre-collegiate music educators as part of their preparation for university-based music studies in music composition. Topics include skill growth, discipline required to study and practice composition, the need for score study, and a recognition of challenges young composers face and the strengths they possess.

Section VI: Composing in Classroom Music

Within the framework of how music learning through composition is unique from other interactions in music, *Elizabeth Bucura* advocates for experiences that involve brainstorming and exploration. Recognizing that music educators feel tentative about engaging students through music education, Bucura draws from the literature and identifies curricular and pedagogical approaches that have been offered, aspects of child development, processes identified while composing, feedback, and the role of creativity. *Suzanne L. Burton* and *Heather Wadler* recognize children's natural inclination to make songs and examine the development and refinement of those songs. Utilizing a project in which songwriting can be facilitated and encouraged amongst middle elementary-aged students, they consider peer collaboration, reflection, revision, and self-assessment strategies, and offer a songwriting-based curriculum that is considered as developmentally appropriate. Within the framework of criticality and creativity, *Kelly Bylica* reflects on how those two constructs can achieve a balance with craftsmanship in composition as students explore musical development and engage in creating music "as a form of social response." This perspective addresses the misguided notion that composition exists to help students acquire skills that benefit performance, and positions criticality and creativity as primary values developed as students engage in composition. Bylica situates these ideas in general music settings and advocates for the fostering of critical, creative, and artistic dispositions. *Sarah Genevieve Burghart Rice* and *Ann Clements* provide ways to foster skills needed to become soundcrafters and to engage in digital recording, and cover the basics of music production and roles music producers experience. The focus of the approach for younger students shifts for older levels in terms of how students are engaged with certain processes. Sample lesson ideas, software suggestions, and a recording equipment list are provided. *Lamont Holden* and *Adam Kruse* advocate for the inclusion of hip-hop as a foundation for transformative music experiences for students. Offered are cultural, musical, and pedagogical considerations for meaningful engagements, and analysis and explanations of hip-hop lyrics and stylistic considerations.

Section VII: Composing in School Ensemble Settings

Matthew R. Doiron provides guidance for instrumental music teachers when including music composition and a rationale for such inclusion, and addresses the challenges that teachers may face as inclusion is attempted. Guidelines are provided for a safe and productive "composition-based" space, as are activities with examples of student work and suggestions for assessing students' compositions. *Katherine Strand* shares ideas of contemporary choral composers that reflect their processes. From that, Strand creates a series of musical explorations and composing projects for choir classes. Through these series students can learn about their voices and their peers' voices as well as various aspects of music. Goals include developing each student's musical ear, their creative mind, and their understanding about choral music. *Michael Hopkins* provides an overview of the orchestra teaching profession that includes surveys of thoughts about composition. Benefits and challenges of including composition with student examples of varying levels are offered with answers to common questions about the role of the teacher and planning and implementing composition projects. Hopkins lists benefits that have been experienced by those who have interacted with students through composition. *Douglas T. Owens* provides an overview of styles and practices embedded in the instrumental jazz ensemble, styles that are inclusive, and practices that include improvisation. Owens advocates for composition to be part of the practice as well, starting with beginner jazz ensembles. Guided and independent listening is viewed as a critical part of the process. Owens offers insights about the multifarious aspects of jazz style as well as instrument-specific information.

SECTION VIII: INTERNATIONAL PERSPECTIVES ON COMPOSITION PEDAGOGY

Renée Crawford interrogates what is considered essential and non-essential learning and turns to Australian and international-based research for support of music education. Focusing the lens on composition and pedagogy, a series of case studies based on Crawford's multi-dimensional/non-linear teaching and learning model are examined. Centered on research and professional literature, *Vít Zouhar* provides insights about composition pedagogy at the individual and group level as situated in the Czech Republic. Determining two core streams of Czech composition pedagogy and the roles and functions of music education, Zouhar offers an expanded meaning of composition based on the methodology of the Different Hearing program. *Heidi Partti* includes the aims and practices of composing in Finland's music education programs, as well as rationales for the inclusion of composition and the preparation of music educators. Partti concludes with positioning composing as a creative activity that should be accessible to everyone; the potential for cultural participation in addition to musical meaning-making is significant. *Christian Rolle* and *Julia Weber* describe composition pedagogy from a historical perspective as found in German music programs and compare that to current common practices and related discussions. An analysis of the practices across primary and secondary grades and an overview of current research in German speaking countries is provided. To examine how creative music-making in Japan is implemented, *Taichi Akutsu* presents data from interviews with Professor Yukiko Tsubonou who is a leading scholar of creativity in music education and contributed to the design of the Japanese curriculum with *ongakudukuri*. Explicit connections between creative music-making and composition pedagogy are provided with examples of *ongakudukuri* in Japan. *Benon Kigozi* provides insights about music composition in Africa, which views music as an academic skill and a cultural practice. Acknowledged is the composer as performer who portrays their full intention and contextual significance through the composition. Core is the oral tradition that is reflective of the African philosophy as rooted in direct experiences in music-making. Kigozi evaluates music composition through the lens of the oral tradition within formal school environments and offers experiences and strategies based on music-making. *Ana Luísa Veloso* describes music composition in Portuguese music classrooms with a historical and political perspective of education as contextualized. Included are examples from the author's experiences as a teacher and researcher. The author concludes by advocating for the expansion of music composition pedagogy into general education.

Section IX: Shaping the Future of Composition in Music Education

This section begins with an explanation of who uses what criteria as music educators and school music programs are evaluated. With the criteria as identified, *David A. Stringham* notes the rarity of assessment tools for teachers or curricula when evaluating students' skills in creating music, and their original products. In response, Stringham offers ideas for music teacher assessment and music program evaluation, ones that are compatible with state and national frameworks as articulated by professional organizations. He concludes with strategies for conversations with various stakeholders who may have some autonomy over curriculum. *Patrick Schmidt* and *Jashen Edwards* address the compatibility between music education policy and music composition, particularly when considered through a lens of critical and progressive practice. One alignment is perceived hesitations about policy and composing that speak to who decides what is done, how and by whom. The authors advocate for voices, agency, and social change within music education spaces and investigate pathways that differ from "conveyer belt" approaches. Offered are three field cases that reflect invocation and critiques of music teacher education programs in relation to the United States–based accrediting body—NASM. *Michele Kaschub* offers final thoughts about moving forward with an eye on recognizing the identity of the composer-educator, as we do with choral and instrumental educators, and curricular changes that embody composition. In terms of the distinct identity of composer-educator, music educators will view themselves as teachers who interact with students through composition and who interact with music as composers, practicing and honing their craft. With the inclusion of possible strategies for curricular changes, Kaschub reminds us that any change must be rooted in a philosophical stance that grounds us as we face the realities of constraints embedded in institutions—ones that can challenge the philosophy or provide a sense of freedom for change to occur.

Acknowledgments

THIS volume could not have been assembled without the help of family, friends, students, and colleagues. To Alan Kaschub, my husband, thank you for your patience and taking on many additional life and household tasks at key moments. To my children, David, Katie, and Daniel, thank you for understanding that writing and editing are happy pursuits that occupy my time, but are never equal to the joy you bring me every day. To Norm Hirschy, my editor at Oxford University Press, my thanks for your guidance and continuing support of this project from the first "what if" email through to the review and publication process. To colleagues contributing to this volume, whose capacity to juggle personal and professional concerns in the midst of a pandemic has allowed us to bring the valuable content of this handbook to teachers around the globe, my sincerest thanks and unending appreciation. And to my students and colleagues who have likely endured too many conversations extolling the virtues of composition, my sincere apologies, and my many thanks for your support of my passion. You have all brightened this journey.

SECTION I

FOUNDATIONS FOR COMPOSITION IN MUSIC EDUCATION

CHAPTER 1

....

MARGINALIZED NO MORE

Composition in Music Education

....

MICHELE KASCHUB

YOUNG people become part of society when they are given opportunities to discover what they think, feel, and believe across a variety of situations and contexts, and then act in a manner that reflects their dispositions. Likewise, young musicians benefit from opportunities to explore and exercise the full breadth of their musicality as they join musical communities. Composition, as a form of direct engagement with music, provides a space for such contextual evaluations of self (Kaschub & Smith, 2016a). In a well-designed composing experience students advance their artistic autonomy and develop skills for working with other musicians. Thus, composing can offer experiences that welcome and join students of diverse backgrounds and varied interests in meaningful artistic actions that inform their individual and collective perspectives.

For students to benefit from the unique opportunities that composing offers, composition needs to play a central role in music education. Some might find this an odd argument given that compositions form the very foundation of music study for much of the world's population. Though it is true that children study and often perform the compositions of others, they are far less frequently invited to create compositions of their own in formal education settings. Indeed, composition as an educative artistic endeavor to be undertaken by children did not appear in public school music education curriculum documents anywhere in the world until the latter third of the 20th century. This is due, in part, to the myths (see Figure 1.1) that surround who composers are, how they work, and what they must know to compose.

Composition presents an opportunity to welcome new and diverse voices to a continually evolving practice thought nearly as old as humanity itself. The music made by composers, songwriters, and producers reflects and projects unique perspectives tied to, and sometimes transcending, time and place. Therefore, the people inventing the music must represent the full breadth of the human spectrum if the tale of humanity's grand

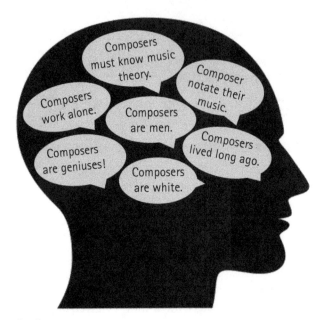

FIGURE 1.1. Myths about composers

adventure is to be accurate. As music educators, we can make space in the center of music education for every child to compose their music—just like they tell their stories and draw their pictures—so that they may sonify their understanding of what it means to live and be human in their experience.

RECOGNIZING FORMS OF MARGINALIZATION

The experience of marginalization is unique to each marginalized group and individual within that group. When children encounter negative messages about themselves or the absence of any message at all, they can develop feelings of shame and self-loathing that can lead to the dismantling of their self-identity (Umaña-Taylor & Rivas-Drake, 2021). In society, and by extension in schools, marginalization can be social, economic, political, psychological, and/or educational in nature. Marginalization can also be found in music studies when composition is ignored while all manner of performance-based instruction is presented. As examination of the full array of complex variables that enable and sustain marginalization are beyond the scope of this chapter, this section provides an overview, painted in broad strokes, of the difficulties that children may carry to school or that they may experience within schools as part of their education. Understanding how marginalization finds root and takes shape can help teachers avoid furthering such practices in music curriculum design and implementation.

Social Marginalization

Anyone who appears to deviate from the norms of the population they inhabit may be subjected to exclusionary practices and relegated to the fringes of society. The problem of social marginalization is sharply experienced by the most vulnerable members of society—the young. Children's social exclusion in school settings can take many forms and is a serious threat to social sustainability. The outcomes of experiencing social alienation can include addiction, criminal behavior, mental health issues, and suicide. Most recently, alienation has been tied to an increase in peer-on-peer violence including school-related homicides (Baird, Roellke, & Zeifman, 2017; Raitanen, Sandberg, & Oksanen, 2019).

Social marginalization in music may be an extension of any of the previous descriptors, but also may evidence itself in musical preferences. Adolescents compare their social standing, whether they belong to or are excluded from groups, along the lines of musical preference (North, Hargreaves, & O'Neill, 2000). This may included preference for different types of musical engagement. The outcome of comparisons can contribute to the maintenance of a positive social identity when children see themselves as belonging to a particular group or through preferred exclusion from other groups (Tarrant, North, & Hargreaves, 2001). Applied differently, absence of group affiliation or peer assignment to groups deemed socially or personally undesirable can have negative effects on self-esteem. Whether group association is positive or negative, preference constitutes a prominent dimension of social identity as well as grounds for acceptance or exclusion in peer groups. When young songwriters do not find their preferred form of engagement in their music classes or see a group of students who are like themselves, they can feel isolated and disconnected.

Students' musical preferences are shaped and influenced by the models and activities that teachers present. If the cultural heritages of all of the students participating in the class are presented to the class, student feel valued. Conversely, exclusion of some musics and music making activities in favor of others can constitute a threat to student identity and suggest a hidden curriculum (McPhail, Rata, & Siteine, 2018; Pratt, 2019; Wasiak, 2017) of perceptions and values. Composing offers teachers an entry point for learning with students as different musical heritages and interests can become focal points in learning about the tools and techniques of composers across a variety of cultures and practices.

Economic Marginalization

People who do not have the same opportunities as others to contribute to or benefit from participation in the trade of goods and services may be described as economically marginalized. Such marginalization is often viewed in terms of poverty. At present, more than 11% of the population of the United States lives in some form of poverty (Shrider, Kollar, Chen, & Semega, 2021) while 9.2% of world's population lives in extreme poverty

(Peer, 2021). Despite a wide range of interventions designed to target poverty and its root causes, children experiencing poverty are known to enter adulthood with different levels of confidence, expectations, knowledge, and future opportunities than their more advantaged peers.

Four types of economic marginalization impact how young people view themselves and others.

- *Generational poverty.* Families experiencing generational poverty have likely not experienced home ownership. They may not know of anyone who has benefited from education or seen job promotion as part of their work experience. These families tend to be highly mobile and may have high rates of illiteracy. Their focus is often on day-to-day survival, and they may not value education (Desmond & Western, 2018).
- *Immigrant poverty.* Immigrant families often have few resources or experience barriers in accessing the resources that may be available to them. They frequently encounter language and cultural barriers as they settle into and continue to reside in communities where they are in the minority. The adult members of immigrant families may have a strong sense of self, likely developed in their country of origin, but children are caught in a cultural divide between family traditions and their daily experiences beyond the home. Shen (2013) notes that these families view poverty as a problem caused and maintained by systems that they cannot participate in, change, or overcome.
- *Working-class poverty.* Many working-class families do not own property and live paycheck-to-paycheck without the means to absorb additional expenses. They often have limited access to health care and fear the financial devastation that illness or injury might bring to their family. Kendall (2011) observes that children raised in these circumstances tend to internalize poverty as a personal deficiency that becomes part of their lifelong identity.
- *Situational poverty.* Families with educated parents who work stable jobs and have access to health care sometimes experience temporary financial crises. These families often view their experience of poverty as temporary and not tied to a personal failing or flaw. Given time, these families often regain middle-class status. It has also been found that people who experience temporary financial upheaval may have little sympathy for those experiencing other types of poverty (Ng & Rury, 2006).

Students experiencing poverty may face an additional set of challenges if they seek to participate in school music programs. *If,* is a key concern. If families do not value education, then music as a part of education does not rank high in survival-focused priorities. Many school music programs feature offerings that require fees. Whether students are asked to purchase a $5 recorder, an $100 ukulele, a $200 keyboard, or a $800 trumpet, families may not be able to absorb the cost. For the student interested in composition, the desire to use smart devices and apps also presents economic challenges. Even when students join vocal groups where the instrument is free, they are often asked to purchase special clothing or uniforms which places an additional burden on family budgets. There are, of course, schools and programs that offer financial support to assist students in addressing concerns raised by participation fees, but students still must make requests and perhaps submit paperwork that may add to the student's or their parents'/guardians' sense of personal failure or inadequacy.

Teachers can learn about their students through composition activities that invite students to tell their personal, cultural, and musical stories. Many such projects can be undertaken using school-owned instruments, using voices, or using found sounds. Projects based on children's literature, art representative of a particular culture, or student experiences are strong entry points for helping children feel seen and valued. As students engage with musical models and create their compositions, teachers can ask open-ended questions and encourage students to share their views using statements like "In my opinion . . .," "What I sense . . .," or other forms that center the student's voice. This practice validates and empowers students (Gay, 2010). Similarly, when students share their musical products, they can be invited to describe their artistic intentions and what they value about their work. These practices help students internalize the idea that what they compose, say, and do is important.

Political Marginalization

Political marginalization involves the withholding of economic, social, and other rights as an outgrowth and extension of oppression. Examples of political marginalization include voting prohibitions and more subtle disenfranchisements that steer people to avoid participation in democratic decision-making resulting in a denial of their right to the social, economic, and political benefits experienced by a majority.

Throughout the world, women, ethnic minorities, migrants, persons with mental health or physical disabilities, members of the LGBTQIA+ community, children, the elderly, and others lack political empowerment. While women are minimized throughout much of the world of politics, men hold power through elected offices, party leadership, and appointments. This is particularly true in the Third World where male-oriented social cultures and religions are dominant. These situations are not lost on the young as their books, music, cartoons, and television shows portray a mix of "commercialism, globalization, [and] privatization" (Lemish, 2015, p. 6) that steers them toward "independence rather than interdependence" (Wells, 2014, p. 21).

For young children, political marginalization is evident from the very first day of school when they discover that what they want can be easily overridden by the teacher— the primary source of in-school power experienced by children. As children grow older, they bear witness to the results of law and policy that provide services for some, but not all. They see who is helped and who is ignored. They also come to understand the relationship that their parents or guardians have with teachers and other school officials. These and other observations allow children to ascertain how their social and cultural identities are positioned in relation to the main curricular narrative and can result in a sense of separation.

These in-school experiences are echoed in music offerings. Students may find that their music—the music they experience with their families and within their communities—is absent from their classes (Doyle, 2014). They may never sing a song in their familial language. The instruments central to their cultural experience may be completely absent. From these observations, students infer that their music—and the things they find familiar and enjoyable—are not of value. By extension, they feel unvalued and unwelcome in these settings. Music education often becomes just one more setting for political marginalization. Likewise, if emphasis is placed on products and rules of music that are, at best, unfamiliar to the students, composition can easily be one more place where different voices are not welcome. As the data analyzed by Elpus and Abril (2011) suggests, it is hard for young people to choose to participate in elective music classes and ensembles when their present and prior experiences suggest that their absence is expected.

Psychological Marginalization

The experience of marginalization carries the risk of ideological threats, particularly in reference to identity formation. While globalization and multiculturalization (Cooper & Seginer, 2018) have brought forth some celebration of diversity, youth from non-dominant backgrounds may experience prejudice and other forms of injustice. In work underpinning much of the modern understanding of identity formation, Erikson (1968) posits that most people build identities with a balance of positive and negative aspects. However, members of marginalized groups are often judged more harshly than their societally privileged counterparts. Children regularly witness indications of their casting in socially negative roles (Way & Rogers, 2015). Barraged by these messages, some children may find it easier to adopt the perceptions forced upon them by others than to embrace their positive attributes. This places them at risk of forming negative identities as their primary or dominant identity.

The ability to recognize and honor diversity in group settings requires individuals to have a positive self-identity and a positive group identity. Building this positive view of self begins with children seeing others with similar identities and backgrounds being appreciated, valued, and treated with respect. Ideally, this happens at home, but it also needs to be experienced in school. In the context of the United States, approximately 80% of teachers are white despite a more diversified student demographic (Schaeffer, 2021). Music teacher-educators are working to change the demographics of the workforce but recognize that the process will take time and may require significant shifts in the policies and practices of higher education (Kallio & Westerlund, 2020).

In settings where students compose music, teachers can update their materials to include the music of composers representing diverse backgrounds and communities.

It is important that students not only hear the music but that they see pictures of the composer. Students will find it hard to imagine themselves in the role of composer when the examples they are given are depersonalized or do not feature composers who "look like me."

Educational Marginalization

The right to education should be universal and not limited by any form of exclusion or discrimination, yet children around the world struggle to gain access to formal education. National education policies often set the tone for local practices. In some countries, such policies deny some children the right to education based on factors beyond their control. These children often reside at the intersection of multiple types of marginalization and thus experience layers of discrimination as those in power regulate education with prejudice (Freire, 1996) to retain their power and maintain the status quo.

Beyond the challenge of access, students from marginalized populations are often absent from, tokenized in, or mischaracterized through educational materials. The curriculum they experience is a construction advanced by the majority, sometimes blindly and too often intentionally devised to ignore, or erase their presence. These practices, characterized as *curriculum violence*, involve the presentation of academic programming in a manner that "ignores or compromises the intellectual and psychological well-being of learners" (Ighodaro & Wiggan, 2011, p. 2). This definition does not limit violence to brutality; rather, it considers violence relative to the whole child and highlights how normalized educational practices can constitute violent pedagogy. While curriculum violence is often considered in relation to students whose identities position them within marginalized groups, violence is also committed against students of the majority as they internalize images, messages, and beliefs that position discriminatory practices as socially and morally acceptable. Through these experiences, some children are diminished while others are emboldened to continue abuse and oppression.

It is easy to view the global picture of education to see that some children are denied access to education while at the same time perpetuating acts within music education that also bar students from entry. Schools that offer beginning instrumental instruction in upper elementary grades but not thereafter have established an exclusionary gate. Programs that offer music ensembles but not studies focused on other areas of music-making or participation fail to meet the needs of those who prefer engagements other than taking the stage to perform (Williams, 2019). The right to education, and by extension music education, should be considered absolute rather than conditioned on historic institutional practices or programmatic convenience (Kratus, 2007).

Addressing Marginalization through Music Composition Pedagogy

The complex challenges of marginalization cannot fully be solved in music classrooms, but a thoughtful approach to teaching and learning can serve to counter some of its negative effects. Music composition teaching, for example, can be tailored to focus on the unique background, needs, and interests of each student. This approach, conceived of as a bespoke pedagogy, allows teachers to engage in an emergent curriculum and to honor the different ways that students communicate how they think and feel alongside what they know and can do. In this work, teachers "study" their students. This enables teachers to fine-tune their knowledge of each student, by noticing and seeking to understand ways of communicating meaning, cultural references, and traditions that may differ from their own.

To practice this pedagogical approach, teachers can begin by striving to expand their musical knowledge and experiences beyond what is familiar and well-known to them. Teachers can then help young composers by:

- being perceptive listeners willing to offer encouraging feedback about what they hear
- offering their skills as performers to play or sing student compositions and offering the performer's perspective about things that work well or things that are difficult for performers to do
- composing both with and alongside students to model a process filled with both challenges and joy
- developing and purposefully applying pedagogical skills featuring a range of techniques and strategies to guide students as they develop their compositional capacities (Kaschub & Smith, 2016a).

Every teacher can begin with the first two bullets as they draw on skills that most music teacher training programs emphasize. Joining students in the act of composing may require a little more bravery as many teachers have not experienced composition beyond the étude assignments offered in music theory classes. And finally, the last bullet point reflects a deeper level of study and expertise, which teachers can attain through engagement in workshops and courses, or through immersion in the trove of readily available books, book chapters, and journal articles focusing on music composition.

The other key task for teachers involves making space for students to practice and develop their musical artistry. The first component of space is environmental. Students must feel comfortable in asking questions that address their need-to-know moments. They need to feel supported and nurtured as they try new things. A classroom atmosphere that welcomes new ideas and compositional risk-taking is an environment in which young composers can thrive.

The second facet of space lies in artistic autonomy. Horton, Kohl, and Kohl (1998) argue that "You provide people with opportunities to learn for themselves by making decisions" (p. 137). Teachers can help students by asking them to make decisions about how music might sound, what ideas they wish to pursue, what ideas they think should be discarded, how they will know when their piece is "right," or finished, and much more. Further, composers need to practice conceiving composition projects and managing the steps necessary to bring their ideas to sound with minimal teacher input. These processes require teachers to step back and allow students to take charge of their artistry. However, teachers still play a critical role. Their guidance fosters the growth of each composer's musical work and sense of personal identity. They facilitate formal acts of composition that can expand each composer's musical horizons. (Verhoeven, Poorthuis, & Volman, 2019). This work is especially important considering the challenges presented by different types of marginalization.

Strategies for Addressing Social Marginalization

Music teachers committed to addressing social marginalization can create composition communities (Kaschub & Smith, 2009; Stringham, 2016) in which every student has an opportunity to grow and develop at their own pace. Such environments foster a sense of belonging (Pendergast, Allen, McGregor, & Ronksley-Pavia, 2018) that allows students to become active contributors to group efforts and to be appreciated by their classmates. Some students, however, may need additional support to find entry into working groups or the larger communal mainstream. Strategies that teachers may find helpful include identifying social strugglers, planning partnerships, and social skills coaching.

Identifying Strugglers

Establishing an open and welcoming compositional community requires finding ways to make everyone feel included. While teachers may be able to quickly "read the room" and note which students seem to be ostracized from their peers, acts of social marginalization can be subtle and additional information may be required. To gain access to what students think about their classmates, give each student a class list and ask them to draw a circle around the names of the peers with whom they would like to work with on a class project. If language is a potential barrier, it may be possible to substitute photos of each student. Collect the responses and notice who is absent or indicated just a few times across the datasheets.

Next, create a series of composition activities that will allow everyone in the class to practice welcoming and inclusive behaviors. Young children will benefit from exploring a common experience through cultural variation. For example, the books *Throw Your Tooth on the Roof: Tooth Traditions from Around the World* by Selby Beeler (1998) and *Don't Throw My Teeth on the Roof!* by Sujatha Fernandes (2013) presents examples of a cross-cultural tradition and how crossing cultures can lead to misunderstanding. Students could create musical accompaniments to support the narration of short tooth tradition stories or might discover through class discussion other common areas of daily life where classmates practice different family or cultural traditions. Accompaniments might be "lightly composed/slightly improvised" in response to the narration.[1]

With slightly older children, guide the entire class in composing an "I greet you" song.[2] Once composed, future class meetings might begin with students singing the song and using different physical greetings (e.g., wave, handshake, bow, foot tap, etc.) as they signal an "I see you" to each classmate. As Merrell and Gueldner (2010) have noted, this simple acknowledgment of presence can have a big impact on students' sense of well-being and academic success.

Students in middle and high school music classes may be able to share cultural traditions through musical storytelling. Students might compose an original ballad or other narrative song that shares a traditional story. They may retell the story from their point of view or add other twists or innovations that allow them to put their own spin on tradition. Comparison and analysis of compositional products across the class will allow students to discover similarities and differences in songwriting styles as well as the special content of each story.

Partnerships and Pals

Every student needs a friend who has similar interests and with whom they can share new experiences. To help students discover potential pals, ask students to create a list of activities, hobbies, and music that they enjoy. Gather the lists and create composition teams or small groups based on a common interest. Students might write songs about a shared sports interest, score an excerpt from a film they admire, or create new music for a video game they love to play. These and similar activities can create common ground for learning about music composition and may provide a stepping-stone toward new friendships.

Social Coaching

Some students struggle to develop the social skills needed to comfortably join their classmates in learning activities. Teachers can approach this situation in a few different ways. First, consider if there are cultural behaviors, like talking over peers or not speaking until being invited to do so, that may be impacting interactions. Address these differences directly so that students can collaborate more easily. Second, observe students who are having a hard time fitting in. Note where they might benefit from a few pointers. For example, students may need to learn to take turns, or they might learn to acknowledge a peer's contribution to a project before suggesting a change to that musical idea. Model these behaviors and then discreetly encourage each student to try their emerging skills with classmates who are likely to be receptive. Once students have tried their new skills, offer feedback concerning behaviors that need to be modified. Be sure to explain why you are suggesting a behavioral change as students may not know how to reflect on social interactions to learn from unsuccessful encounters. Finally, some students may benefit from a referral to a guidance counselor or social worker to participate in groups specifically designed to foster the development of social skills.

Developing the Skills of Hope

The issues surrounding poverty-driven marginalization are complex and without singular solution. Yet, there are actions that teachers can take to help students position themselves for success. Dixson, Worrell, and Mello (2017) have found that hope—having something to look forward to and tangibly work toward—is associated with better engagement and curiosity in the classroom and higher academic achievement among students experiencing poverty. Similarly, Seligman, Railton, Baumeister, & Sripada (2016) argue the importance of anticipating and evaluating future possibilities as a means for guiding thought and action, going so far as to describe the practice as the cornerstone of human success.

Brown (2010) defines hope as a way of thinking or a cognitive process. In this definition, hope is not an emotion but a set of action steps wherein students learn to set realistic goals, figure out how to achieve those goals, and learn to persist despite challenges (Snyder, 2000). In many ways, these processes parallel those used by composers as they engage in creating new music. As such, music teachers can help students learn the strategies that contribute to the development of hope as they engage in composition projects.

Identifying and Prioritizing Goals

Goal identification and prioritization are strategies that students can use to discern what is important to them and what they wish to achieve. The practice of naming and numbering goals can feel empowering to students as they are situated within educational institutions where goals are typically controlled by adults through predetermined curricula and practices that focus on students as a collective. Composition provides teachers with an opportunity to respond to each student's musical goals. Centering the student in this partnership is mission-critical as many students are highly motivated to achieve goals that they establish for themselves, but quickly lose interest in the goals set by others.

Teachers can help students become drivers of their own success by inviting them to create a list of "I want" goals. These might include, "I want to write a country song" or "I want to create beats for my friends," or similar goals that are positive and forward-looking. Students can then be invited to prioritize their goals. This process helps students focus on what they want to achieve and limits potential distractions from stealing their focus and energy. Students also benefit from considering sub-goals. Ask them to think about what they will need to do to accomplish each goal.

Goal Analysis and Prioritization

It may be very easy for some students to create a lengthy wish list of goals. Such lists can be overwhelming and exhaust students before they set to work. Adding to this sense of overload may be the impression that goals are all-or-nothing propositions that must be accomplished all-at-once. This type of thinking is the result of the have-or-have-not dichotomy of despair. To address these misconceptions, teachers can guide students to consider their number 1 goal in detail. Students can be encouraged to consider what skills they might need to learn to achieve their goal and how the goal might be approached over several smaller steps. Students should also identify how they will know when each step toward their goal has been successfully completed and when their goal has been achieved. This allows students to acknowledge small victories and maintain the motivation needed for forward momentum.

Obstacle Framing

Like life itself, composition lessons often feature challenges and obstacles that can be frustrating. To remain engaged when work becomes hard, students need to learn that there may be multiple approaches to tackling problems and challenges. This counters the notion that encountering an obstacle signals defeat.

In creating music, composers often wrestle with finding, and then developing, their central idea. Without the tools to move forward, they may become stuck in a cycle of repetition that leaves them dissatisfied. The solution to this challenge lies in a combination of brainstorming and radical editing. Students can be encouraged to take their initial idea and sing it, play it, or write it in as many different ways as they can imagine (see Figure 1.2). Once they have amassed several or even dozens of ideas, they can try each one within the context of the music they have already made up. This process helps students learn that the barriers they encounter are not signs that they lack talent, but opportunities to think differently, see things anew, and try other options. From this process, they learn that success is not found in avoiding challenges, but in figuring out how to address the challenge and move on.

Balancing Help and Self-Reliance

It is tempting for teachers to step in and offer quick fix solutions when students experience frustration in the composition process. While it is certainly appropriate for teachers to offer multiple solutions for students to test as a pathway forward, the teacher-as-fixer model tends to insert the teacher's artistry into the student's work. Ultimately, this disempowers and possibly disenfranchises the student composer. What may most benefit students in their moment of frustration is a strategy for discovering problem-solving tools.

FIGURE 1.2. Idea development

In the composition classroom, music educators can set the stage for the discovery by including projects that feature the teacher facilitating compositions by the whole class. This setting allows teachers to engage students in the processes of idea generation, testing, and selection. They also can invite students to evaluate the affective potential of musical gestures and ask questions that guide revision. Within this collaborative setting students directly experience the enactment of a successful composition process. These experiences then become stories that students can revisit when they are stuck. Students might be prompted with questions such as, "How did we decide which idea to use?" or "How did we transition from the beginning to the middle section of the piece?" Revisiting previous successes to discover process strategies prepares students to be self-reliant, which in turn builds their self-confidence.

Positive Self-Talk

Self-talk is a powerful tool that students can use to acknowledge their progress. Physical educators have noted how the use of positive self-talk can motivate students and lead to higher levels of achievement (Ada, Comoutos, Karamitrou, & Kazak, 2019). Recently, Ohki (2020) researched similar strategies in music training and found that musicians who reinforce achievement with self-talk attain higher levels of success. Similar findings have been noted for students with learning disabilities (Feeney, 2022) and found to improve motivational resilience for middle school learners, too (Flanagan & Symonds, 2021).

As students compose, it is important that they acknowledge to themselves both minor victories (e.g., "I found the right note to end this line") and milestones (e.g., "I finished this verse"). Teachers can help students develop check sheets to facilitate this practice. Lists might include items such as: outlined the form of the piece, completed the A-section, built the beat for the chorus, created a melodic theme and three variations, and so on. Each milestone is an opportunity for students to recognize the completion of one step toward their goal. As Brown (2010) notes, taking time to note achievements is critical in the development of hope as students who use positive self-talk are more likely to reach their goals than students who loop negative messages.

Promoting the Skills of Activism through Artistic Action

Though young students rarely possess the vocabulary to name what they sense, political marginalization resonates as unfair. Young people who feel oppressed and who internalize the hopelessness it brings believe that there is nothing they can do to change their situation or the injustices they observe in the experience of others. Yet, there are actions that can be taken to identify, call out, and address political marginalization.

Throughout the world, music has a long history of being at the center of political movements, calling out injustices, and inviting/demanding change. No Doubt's 1995 "Just a Girl," featuring the line "I'm just a girl in the world, That's all that you'll let me be!," called out sexism, while James Brown's "Say It Loud (I'm Black and I'm Proud)" of

1968 defied white oppression as it became an anthem of Black Power. Bringing attention to child labor practices proliferating across the African continent, Angélique Kidjo released "We We" in 1992 while Dolma Kyab sang "Gangchampa" as a show of strength against Chinese rule through the presentation of lyrics that extol the characteristics of Tibetan identity "in grand and epic terms" (Morcom, 2018, p. 134). More recently, Dinner Party released "Freeze Tag" in 2020 to highlight the troubling relationship between police and black communities. Each of these songs and the thousands of others like them provide models for students eager to understand how they can shape and share their own messages about the injustices they see and experience in their own lives and communities.

Teachers of composition, songwriting, and production can introduce students to tools of social critique and invite them to pursue artistic social action related to issues that are important in their lives (Hess, 2019; Kaschub, 2009). At every age in public schooling, students can identify situations they deem unfair. These observations provide entry to discussions where students may find ideas for songs that name and describe the social injustices they wish to address.

Very young songwriters might create songs about the problems of having too much homework (and research would back them up!) and older students might focus on what it is like to be an immigrant in their community (Kaschub, 2009). As part of their research, students might seek the viewpoints of others by interviewing teachers, peers, family members, and local politicians about their chosen topic to expand their understanding of complex social situations. Students tend to be passionate about causes that concern them and the resulting songs could provide new insights into students' lives and experiences. Perhaps most importantly, their fledgling attempts at artistic activism prepare them to advocate for themselves or others in the future.

Building a Positive Composer Identity

Identity formation is best achieved in a welcoming and supportive environment. In the music classroom, this environment is one where students feel they can take musical risks without fear of comparison or judgment. Composition is an activity well-suited to provide this environment as lessons can be tailored to capitalize on individual students' interests and working styles as they progress in the development of their compositional capacities (Kaschub & Smith, 2009). Within this process, students will likely experience the emergence of their "compositional voice"—the characteristic sound choices and features that signal the work of a particular composer (Stauffer, 2001; Kaschub & Smith, 2009). The development of compositional voice, viewed as one dimension of the personal identity of the composer, requires that students engage in projects that are authentic to the work of composers. While the facets of this work are likely innumerable, there are key experiences that teachers can provide to help students refine their artistic goals, compositional practices, and self-concept.

Establishing Artistic Goals

Composers define their artistic goals. Even when accepting commissioned work, composers must define for themselves exactly what they will create within the parameters provided by their employer. To develop this skill with very young composers, teachers might offer choices within a composing activity (e.g., "Should we use pitched instruments or unpitched instruments to make the ostinato?") as a stepping-stone to broader autonomy. Older students can practice compositional reframing as they re-view teacher-created composition project guidelines and then discuss how they envision the final product. This shared vision then serves to guide and to unify group efforts as students undertake the composing process together. As composers gain experience, they eventually will be able to self-design and define the parameters of their projects. This is one of the final steps toward compositional independence.

In all cases, it is important that the teacher serves as a guide by asking questions and helping students refine their goals in ways that increase the likelihood of success as the composer or compositional team defines it. As one might expect, this can be a delicate task. Student composers can often imagine music of far greater complexity than they have the current skills to achieve. In such cases, the teacher serves as both a guardrail and a sounding board to help the students balance imagination and reality. As students practice decision-making and see the results of their efforts—both positive and negative—they refine their skills of definition. Guiding students to reflect on their growth over time can contribute positively to their evolving self-image.

Connecting Compositional Capacities

Kaschub and Smith (2009 & 2016b) have identified and described the musical capacities that students may develop by focusing on the feelingful, body-based sonic perception, and elemental aspects of music. The three capacities central to the role of composer are *feelingful intention, musical expressivity, and artistic craftsmanship*. With respect to identity formation, students exercise the capacity of feelingful intention by considering their own feelings and/or the feelings of others in relation to musical sounds. The former consideration requires self-knowledge while the latter requires empathy; composers must put themselves in the place of others, consider their experience, and then decide how to address the feelings that arise through the sounds of music. Composers then build these sound-feeling relationships by assembling the elements of music (artistic craftsmanship) in ways that invite perception (musical expressivity) so that others can experience music-inspired emotion and draw meaning from their encounters with the composer's music. Each composition builds upon an awareness of self and others to inform the composer's self-concept as well as their conception of social position.

Solo and Collaborative Work

Composers at all stages of experience and development benefit from opportunities to work alone and with other composers. While certainly not a requirement, it may be helpful for students to experience composing in teams or small groups before undertaking solo work. As composers work together, they can offer their ideas to the group, explain their thinking, and hear why their peers agree or disagree with their thinking. Similarly, students have an opportunity to hear the ideas of others and respond to their questions. When properly scaffolded by a teacher, within-group discussions can help students develop respect for the thoughts, ideas, and feelings of others while also sensing the value they add to the team.

These within-group exchanges form the foundation for self-critique (Beynon, 2016). When students with prior group experience work on their own, they internally mirror the dialogues shared with peers. The questions they once heard from the co-composers become the questions they ask and answer themselves. This ability to think critically about their composing processes serves to build confidence in their decision-making skills and ultimately results in greater self-assurance. Similarly, for students accustomed to working on their own, perhaps outside of school, the feedback provided by peers and others can provide new ways of thinking about and creating their compositions.

Social Grace in Giving and Receiving Feedback

One of the hardest tasks faced by composers is the challenge of listening to and processing what others think and feel about their work. Composition, even when undertaken with collaborators, is an activity that exposes the self. Meaningful compositions are an extension of what students think, feel, and believe. They are personal. For this reason, teachers should always tell students if there is an expectation of sharing. A student may feel the need to write a song about the death of their pet, but they may not want to cry in class when that song is performed. Knowing that there is an expectation that their work will be shared may help them choose to focus on a different topic or concept.

Above all, the sharing of compositions must take place in an environment where all participants feel safe, nurtured, and supported. This requires composers to meld their skills of music perceptions with a degree of social grace. Before being invited to share thoughts and opinions about other's music, composers should be invited to consider: How might my observations help another composer? What is the best way to say what I am thinking? What type of information will be valuable to the composer as they continue to develop their work or move on to their next project?

As students prepare to share their work and hear comments from their peers, they should be encouraged to think beyond "I like" and "I don't like" comments. The thoughts they share must reflect the nature of the composition which is not to be confused with the composer's performance of the work.[3] For example, a student might offer, "I hear that you have used two trumpets at the beginning and then a trumpet and trombone together when the theme repeats. I think the trumpet and trombone combination is more effective because the two timbres are easy to hear." This comment reflects the preference of the listener and provides the composer with information about audience experience that may inform their revision process. Conversely, a similar thought reduced to "The two trumpets at the beginning don't sound very good," does not provide the composer with useful information, nor does "You didn't play the theme very well."

Composers who are guided to consider how they would like to hear feedback become more empathetic and gentler with their comments. They also begin to recognize the value they can add to their peers' compositional experience. These observations contribute to their growth as composers, to their sense of value within the composing community, and to their sense of self-identity. These skills may also transfer to their work as deep listeners and close readers when they engage with stories, poems, visual art, and other art forms.

Self-Compassion

Composers need a great deal of self-compassion to return, time and time again, to a process that is built of continuous challenges and hurdles. Self-compassion is a practice in which students can accept that they are feeling frustrated by a challenge or disappointed that something is not working in their piece while recognizing that the situation is likely temporary. Acting with kindness towards oneself and remembering that imperfection is part of the journey is a critical skill equivalent in value to mastering any compositional technique.

Students struggling with self-compassion often express their feelings through frustration or anger. They may become so emotionally charged that they cannot make progress with their work. Others may become paralyzed by their need for perfection and seek to abandon their pieces to begin other work.

Teachers can help students develop self-compassionate responses by introducing a way to externalize the problem. Begin by inviting the student to imagine a fellow composer who is experiencing the exact same problem. Ask the student what advice they would offer to the friend. Then ask them if they can apply that same piece of advice to their situation. This strategy, simple as it may be, often works but is best when students have taken a few moments to step away from the intensity of their current challenge. When students develop strategies to solve their own problems and experience success, they come to believe that maybe they can develop strategies to solve other problems as well. Developing self-belief is an act of empowerment that allows students to think positively about their abilities and positions them for future success.

Practicing Educational Inclusion in Music Education

Kelly-McHale (2013) has established that teachers' curricular beliefs and practices play a significant role in welcoming or isolating students. The "include/exclude" choices that teachers make contribute to the role that music plays in students' emerging identities and the identity that students share in music. Ranging from the posters that hang on the walls, to the music distributed in ensemble folders, to the behaviors deemed acceptable/unacceptable as students make or listen to music, teachers present both explicit and hidden curricular messages.

Too often, music composition is approached through the lens of European art music, where music theory is positioned as the gate through which students must enter. This is an unfortunate curricular choice, indeed an act of curriculum violence already evidenced in music education in the United States and in many nations around the globe where indigenous music and music-making practices are threatened.[4] A more enlightened approach is possible.

Music teachers can enact culturally sustaining pedagogical practices[5] as they design and present opportunities for students to compose. This means that teachers purposefully center students' cultural backgrounds, experiences, and interests by honoring their musical practices as part of composition study. In this way, students can work within their cultural frames and comfort zones as well as explore other compositional practices. This approach reinforces the value of students' musical heritages while expanding the range of sonic possibilities that may eventually become part of their personal composition landscape.

From Marginalization to Opportunity

For the strategies presented in this chapter to be fully implemented, one more area of exclusion must be addressed: the ongoing curricular marginalization of composition in music education. Research clearly indicates that teachers believe it is important for students to experience composing, but many remain perplexed about how to bring it into their curriculums (Menard, 2015; Shouldice, 2014; Strand, 2006; Orman, 2002). This is not surprising, as globally many music teachers are trained within the performance-dominated conservatory model (Campbell, Myers, & Sarath, 2016; Kratus, 2015), and therefore they graduate underprepared to embrace the potentials that composition offers for the education of students.

Marginalization is not only present in teacher preparation, but also in national curriculum documents. Drawing on the United States as an example, the 1994 National Standards for Arts Education identifies "Composing and arranging music within specified guidelines"[6] as standard #4 within a set of nine standards.[7] In response to composition's appearance in equal positioning with singing and playing instruments, teachers voiced their discomfort and decried their lack of preparation (Bell, 2003; Byo, 1999). This perhaps influenced the subsequent standards revision in 2014.

In the latter document, composition and improvisation—two separate and unique musical experiences—are merged under the heading "Creating" at the K–8 level[8] while composition is partnered with music theory at the secondary level.[9] Where the 1994 document sparked interest in composition and set forth the pursuit of scholarly work to advance knowledge and support evolving practices, the 2014 document tucked composition out of sight at the elementary level and visually implied music theory to be a precursor to composing for secondary students with a subsection titling of "Theory/Composition." Fortunately, the work initiated in response to the 1994 standards has yielded numerous books, book chapters, and articles—even this handbook—to advance pedagogical knowledge and practice in the teaching and learning of composition so that every child can have the opportunity to compose.

Given the wealth of resources now available to music teacher-educators, practitioners, and pre-service teachers, it is time to bring composition fully inside the margins of music education. We can no longer look away from the students who are eager to compose—whether they be enrolled in our present offerings or situated beyond the bounds of our current classroom rosters. Every student deserves the opportunity to exercise the full range of their musical potentials in every direct experience—singing, playing, composing, improvising, and listening—of music. Within this frame, composition provides a unique opportunity for students to find themselves and define their artistic voice. As they compose, they explore their understandings of self, others, and the world around them through music.

Empowered young composers may not be content with being situated at the margins of education, society, or politics once they have found their compositional voices and know how to use them to explore their understandings of themselves, others, and the world around them. They may use their artistry to help create the changes they would like to see—as composers so often do.

Notes

1. A wonderful set of models for accompanying narrations can be found on Ken Nordine's album, *Colors*.
2. Strategies and models for teaching songwriting to elementary students can be found in Jackie Wiggins' 1990 *Composition in the classroom: A Tool for Teaching*, R&L Education, and Michele Kaschub & Janice P. Smith's *Experiencing music composition in grades 3–5*, Oxford University Press, 2016.
3. It is common in school settings for young composers to also be the performers of their pieces.
4. See Section VIII: International Perspectives on Composition Pedagogy, in this handbook.
5. See in this handbook, "Creating Culturally Sustaining Spaces in the Compositional Process," by Christopher Mena and Patricia Shehan Campbell.
6. The 1994 National Standards for Arts Education can be viewed at https://nafme.org/my-classroom/standards/national-standards-archives/
7. Ibid.
8. See https://nafme.org/wp-content/uploads/2014/11/2014-Music-Standards-PK-8-Strand.pdf
9. See https://nafme.org/my-classroom/standards/core-music-standards/

References

Ada, E. N., Comoutos, N., Karamitrou, A., & Kazak, Z. (2019). Relationships between dispositional flow, motivational climate, and self-talk in physical education classes. *Physical Educator, 76*(2), 357–384.

Baird, A. A., Roellke, E. V., & Zeifman, D. M. (2017). Alone and adrift: The association between mass school shootings, school size, and student support. *Social Science Journal, 54*(3), 261–270.

Beeler, S. B. (1998). *Throw your tooth on the roof: Tooth traditions from around the world.* Houghton Mifflin Harcourt.

Bell, C. L. (2003). Beginning the dialogue: Teachers respond to the national standards in music. *Bulletin of the Council for Research in Music Education* (1), 31–42.

Beynon, M. (2016, November). *Mindstorms revisited: Making new construals of Seymour Papert's legacy.* International Conference EduRobotics 2016 (pp. 3–19). Springer.

Brown, B. (2010). *The gifts of imperfection: Let go of who you think you're supposed to be and embrace who you are.* Hazelden Publishing.

Byo, S. J. (1999). Classroom teachers' and music specialists' perceived ability to implement the national standards for music education. *Journal of Research in Music Education, 47*(2), 111–123.

Campbell, P. S., Myers, D. E., & Sarath, E. W. (2016). Transforming music study from its foundations: A manifesto for progressive change in the undergraduate preparation of music majors. In *Redefining music studies in an age of change* (pp. 59–99). Routledge.

Cooper, C. R., & Seginer, R. (2018). Introduction: Navigating pathways in multicultural nations: Identities, future orientation, schooling, and careers. *New Directions for Child and Adolescent Development, 160,* 7–13.

Desmond, M., & Western, B. (2018). Poverty in America: New directions and debates. *Annual Review of Sociology, 44,* 305–318.

Dixson, D. D., Worrell, F. C., & Mello, Z. (2017). Profiles of hope: How clusters of hope relate to school variables. *Learning and Individual Differences, 59,* 55–64.

Doyle, J. L. (2014). Cultural relevance in urban music education: A synthesis of the literature. *Update: Applications of Research in Music Education, 32*(2), 44–51.

Elpus, K., & Abril, C. R. (2011). High school music ensemble students in the United States: A demographic profile. *Journal of Research in Music Education, 59*(2), 128–145.

Erikson, E. H. (1968). *Identity: Youth and crisis.* Norton.

Feeney, D. M. (2022). Positive self-talk: An emerging learning strategy for students with learning disabilities. *Intervention in School and Clinic, 57*(3), 45–49.

Fernandes, S. (2013). *Don't throw my teeth on the roof.* Create Space Independent Publishing.

Flanagan, R. M., & Symonds, J. E. (2021). Self-talk in middle childhood: A mechanism for motivational resilience during learning. *Psychology in the Schools, 58*(6), 1007–1025.

Freire, P. (1996). *Pedagogy of the oppressed* (Revised). Continuum.

Gay, G. (2010). *Culturally responsive teaching: Theory, research, and practice* (2nd ed.). Teachers College Press.

Hess, J. (2019). *Music education for social change: Constructing an activist music education.* Routledge.

Horton, M., Kohl, J., & Kohl, H. (1998). *The long haul: An autobiography.* Teachers College Press.

Ighodaro, E., & Wiggan, G. (2011). *Curriculum violence: America's new civil rights issue.* Nova Science Publishers.

Kallio, A. A., & Westerlund, H. (2020). The discomfort of intercultural learning in music teacher education. In H. Westerlund, S. Karlsen, & H. Partti (Eds.), *Visions for intercultural music teacher education* (pp. 47–61). Springer.

Kaschub, M. (2009). Critical pedagogy for creative artists: Inviting young composers to engage in artistic social action. In Gould, E., Morton, C., Countryman, J., & Stewart Rose, L. (Eds.).

Exploring Social Justice: How Music Education Might Matter. Waterloo, ON: Canadian Music Educators' Association/L'Association canadienne des musiciens éducateurs.

Kaschub, M., & Smith, J. (2009). *Minds on music: Composition for creative and critical thinking.* R&L Education.

Kaschub, M., & Smith, J. (2016a). *Experiencing music composition in grades 3–5.* Oxford University Press.

Kaschub, M., & Smith, J. P. (2016b). The big picture: Developing musical capacities. *Music Educators Journal, 102*(3), 33–40.

Kelly-McHale, J. (2013). The influence of music teacher beliefs and practices on the expression of musical identity in an elementary general music classroom. Journal of Research in Music Education, 61(2), 195–216.

Kendall, D. E. (2011). *Framing class: Media representations of wealth and poverty in America.* Rowman & Littlefield.

Kratus, J. (2007). Music education at the tipping point. *Music Educators Journal, 94*(2), 42–48.

Kratus, J. (2015). The role of subversion in changing music education. In C. Randles (Ed.), *Music education: Navigating the future* (pp. 340–350). Routledge.

Lemish, D. (2015). *Children and media: A global perspective.* Wiley Blackwell.

McPhail, G., Rata, E., & Siteine, A. (2018). The changing nature of music education. In G. McPhail, V. Thorpe, & S. Wise (Eds.), *Educational change and the secondary school music curriculum in Aotearoa, New Zealand* (pp. 74–91). Routledge.

Menard, E. A. (2015). Music composition in the high school curriculum: A multiple case study. *Journal of Research in Music Education, 63*(1), 114–136.

Merrell, K. W., & Gueldner, B. A. (2010). *Social and emotional learning in the classroom: Promoting mental health and academic success.* Guilford Press.

Morcom, A. (2018). The political potency of Tibetan identity in pop music and dunglen. *HIMALAYA, the Journal of the Association for Nepal and Himalayan Studies, 38*(1), 126–144.

Ng, J. C., & Rury, J. L. (2006). Poverty and education: A critical analysis of the Ruby Payne phenomenon. *Teachers College Record, 18*(50), 370–396.

North, A. C., Hargreaves, D. J., & O'Neill, S. A. (2000). The importance of music to adolescents. *British Journal of Educational Psychology, 70,* 255–272.

Ohki, M. (2020). *Mental training in music: Comparative systematizing of methodic approaches under integration of sport psychology.* In A. Creech (Ed.), 34th World Conference on Music Education.

Orman, E. K. (2002). Comparison of the national standards for music education and elementary music specialists' use of class time. *Journal of Research in Music Education, 50*(2), 155–164.

Peer, A. (2021, August 23). *Global poverty: Facts, FAQs, and how to help.* World Vision. https://www.worldvision.org/sponsorship-news-stories/global-poverty-facts

Pendergast, D., Allen, J., McGregor, G., & Ronksley-Pavia, M. (2018). Engaging marginalized, "at-risk" middle-level students: A focus on the importance of a sense of belonging at school. *Education Sciences, 8*(3), 138.

Pratt, A. B. (2019). Curriculum in conflict: how African American and Indigenous educational thought complicates the hidden curriculum. *Curriculum Journal,* 1–17.

Raitanen, J., Sandberg, S., & Oksanen, A. (2019). The bullying–school shooting nexus: Bridging master narratives of mass violence with personal narratives of social exclusion. *Deviant Behavior, 40*(1), 96–109.

Schaeffer, K. (2021, December 10). *America's public school teachers are far less racially and ethnically diverse than their students*. Pew Research Center. https://www.pewresearch.org/fact-tank/2021/12/10/americas-public-school-teachers-are-far-less-racially-and-ethnically-diverse-than-their-students/

Seligman, M. E., Railton, P., Baumeister, R. F., & Sripada, C. (2016). *Homo prospectus*. Oxford University Press.

Shouldice, H. N. (2014). Teachers' beliefs regarding composition in elementary general music: Definitions, values, and impediments. *Research Studies in Music Education, 36*(2), 215–230.

Shen, L. (2013). Out of information poverty: library services for urban marginalized immigrants. *Urban Library Journal, 19*(1), 4.

Shrider, E. A., Kollar, M., Chen, F., & Semega, J. (2021). Income and poverty in the United States: 2020. *Current Population Reports. US Census Bureau*, 60–273.

Snyder, C. R. (Ed.) (2000). Hypothesis: There is hope. In C. R. Snyder, *Handbook of hope* (pp. 3–21). Academic Press.

Stauffer, S. L. (2001). Composing with computers: Meg makes music. *Bulletin of the Council for Research in Music Education* (1), 1–20.

Strand, K. (2006). Survey of Indiana music teachers on using composition in the classroom. *Journal of Research in Music Education, 54*(2), 154–167.

Stringham, D. A. (2016). Creating compositional community in your classroom. *Music Educators Journal, 102*(3), 46–52.

Tarrant, M., North, A. C., & Hargreaves, D. J. (2001). Social categorization, self-esteem, and the estimated musical preference of male adolescents. *Journal of Social Psychology, 141*, 565–581.

Umaña-Taylor, A. J., & Rivas-Drake, D. (2021). Ethnic-racial identity and adolescents' positive development in the context of ethnic-racial marginalization: Unpacking risk and resilience. *Human Development, 65*(5–6), 293–310.

Verhoeven, M., Poorthuis, A. M., & Volman, M. (2019). The role of school in adolescents' identity development. A literature review. *Educational Psychology Review, 31*(1), 35–63.

Wasiak, E. (2017). Unmasking the hidden curriculum in Canadian music education. *Canadian Music Educator, 58*(4), 19–28.

Way, N., & Rogers, L. O. (2015). "[T]hey say black men won't make it, but I know I'm gonna make it": Ethnic and racial identity development in the context of cultural stereotypes. In K. C. McLean & M. Syed (Eds.), *The Oxford handbook of identity development* (pp. 269–285). Oxford University Press.

Wells, K. (2014). *Childhood in a global perspective*. Polity Press.

Williams, D. A. (2019). *A different paradigm in music education: Re-examining the profession*. Routledge.

CHAPTER 2

....

THE MUSIC NO ONE HAS HEARD YET

....

JOHN KRATUS

THE purpose of this chapter is to provide music educators potential answers to the question, "Why learn to compose?" and its corollary, "Why teach composition?" It is understandable that in most performing arts education, the re-creation of the art form through performance takes precedence over the original creation of the art form. In most schools, performing music, acting, and dancing take priority over composing music, playwriting, and choreographing. Yet, the future of performing arts is dependent on composers, playwrights, and choreographers. As Stephens (2013) writes, "Without creation, there would be no re-creation by performers, or recreation for audiences" (p. 85). Is there a place in a predominantly performance-based music education to foster students' original music-making? In this essay, I wish to make the case that creation and re-creation are not mutually exclusive musical behaviors in music education. Rather they are jointly reinforcing, leading to a more significant and sustainable form of music education. First, I present three brief narratives.

I. When I was a teenager and throughout my 20s, I played bass guitar in a series of amateur rock bands. From the time I was 13, the bands I performed in played cover songs as well as original songs by my bandmates and me in high school gymnasiums, church basements, dive bars, and even bowling alleys. Our audiences preferred to listen to cover songs like Steppenwolf's "Born to Be Wild," Spencer Davis Group's "Gimmie Some Lovin'," and Otis Redding's "Sittin' on the Dock of the Bay." We played those songs, but we also played our original songs that the audiences had never heard. Today, I ask myself why we performed those original songs, knowing that paying customers and our employers would rather hear us play familiar songs that they knew well. After much thought, I think that the reason is that the original songs expressed who we were, not only as creative musicians but as sentient beings. We took pleasure in performing cover songs, but we felt 100 times more satisfaction in performing the music we had created ourselves. Our very essence was in every phrase, lyric, harmony, and rhythm. We felt those vibrations in our blood and bones. It was music no one had heard yet.

II. Over 30 years later, I was a professor at Michigan State University and founded the Michigan Honors Composition concert, a statewide competition to identify and promote the best music composed by K–12 and special education students. The winners performed on a concert at the state's annual music education conference, which was held in Grand Rapids. One year, an eighth grader living in the Upper Peninsula of Michigan submitted a beautifully complex piece for percussion ensemble, titled, "Who Knows?" Her piece was accepted, and her music teacher arranged to transport the 12-member percussion ensemble and chaperones to Grand Rapids for the concert. The trip took over eight hours each way in the dead of winter, and the student performers and their chaperones had to stay overnight in hotels. At the concert, the young composer conducted the piece dressed in a tuxedo and smiling. The music lasted four minutes, and the audience applauded wildly. After the performance, the girl's mother gave me a pillow on which her daughter had embroidered the words, "Who Knows?" I have it today in a place of honor in my home office. The tuxedo and pillow showed how much this performance meant to the composer. Furthermore, a middle school instrumental music teacher cared enough to arrange for such an extensive trip with her students whose parents provided financing for transportation and housing to perform a four-minute piece that no one in the audience had ever heard before.

III. Several years ago, I invited a talented music educator from Oakland, Michigan, to Zoom his sixth-grade music class into my general music methods class. His classes fostered his students' creativity, and I thought that my students would benefit by learning from his students' experiences. Under his guidance, the students composed their own music, which they performed and recorded. Their recordings were sold as CDs, and the proceeds were given to Detroit-area schools that could otherwise not afford to purchase classroom instruments. My students and his students questioned each other about their musical experiences. The sixth graders spoke enthusiastically about their joy in creating their own music and sharing it with others for a good cause. For them, that is what music education was all about, and they were proud of their creative accomplishments. Then, one of the sixth graders asked my college students, "How cool is it to make up and perform your own music every day?" There was a lengthy, awkward silence, and none of my students had an answer, knowing that their collegiate music study had nothing to do with creating their own music. Their education was all about performing cover songs.

Three elements that underscore these (true) narratives are pride, joy, and passion: pride in being able to create something personally meaningful that had not existed before, joy in sharing these creations with others, and passion in the desire to overcome whatever obstacles necessary. These concepts may be summarized as a kind of personal and collective musical ownership. We rarely see words like "pride," "joy," or "passion" in curriculum documents. But why else would young people choose to make music: to win a trophy? to please a teacher? If that is the case, what happens when the trophies stop coming and the teacher is no longer present? The human impulse to create music that no one has heard before comes from a place more profound than a curriculum guide.

Looking toward the future, music educators may examine the relative merits of preserving the glorious and established musical works of the past or fostering the creative but uncertain musical potential of the future. To what extent is the purpose of music education (a) to teach students to perform renditions of previously composed music, whether those "cover songs" are folk songs for elementary students, or band, choir, and orchestra arrangements written by professionals for older students, or even popular music, or (b) to foster the creative muse that exists in all students and that defines them as musically creative beings? There may be space in this diverse (but, unfortunately, not diverse enough) field of practice to accomplish both ends. In many school music programs, option "a" is leaving little room for option "b," as noted by Williams (2011).

In this chapter, the author attempts to define "composition," examine various anthropological and psychological explanations for why humans compose music, answer the question, "Can children compose?," outline the obstacles to teaching composition, explain the means to overcome these obstacles, and reframe the teaching of music.

What Is (a) Composition?

To understand the value of composition in students' music education, it is necessary to recognize what composition is. The word "composition" can refer to the process of creating music or the resulting product of those actions. Composition as a process is the act of making music that no one had heard yet. Bits and pieces of music are explored—some are rejected, and some are developed and extended, but the music is not in a replicable form. It is under construction. At this point in the act of composing, the bits and pieces of emerging music would not be called "a composition," because the composer did not think of the song as a completed product. Composition as a product reflects closure on a compositional problem. This definition describes a composition as a relatively *fixed idea* of a musical product. That idea can exist only in the mind of the composer, and does not require a physical manifestation, such as notation or a recording.

To effectively guide students' composition, educators should be clear on what constitutes music creativity. All humanly made sounds are not musical. Nor are they creative. The sound of a hammer hitting a nail or a basketball dribbling down a court may be rhythmic, percussive, and humanly created, but they are not musical. Two concepts that can elucidate the difference between musical sounds and other sounds are "intentionality" and "orientation."

Intentionality. Music compositions are planned; they are not random or accidental. A composition has been planned to sound the way that it does, and the sounds are intentionally designated as music (Kratus, 1991). Furthermore, the sounds heard in the performance of a composition bear a strong relationship to the sounds imagined by the composer. Certain forms of improvisation by novices or younger children, as discussed below, do not possess intentionality. All music compositions do possess intentionality.

There are some special instances in music in which this notion of intentionality requires further explanation. Aleatoric music contains sounds that occur in sequence or combination by chance, but they are *planned* to occur by chance, designated as such by the composer. The chance element in the music is intentional.

The tones and timbres of music can be as varied as human imagination, but they are *planned* tones and timbres. Even sounds that primarily occur in non-musical contexts can be used by composers as intentional elements in a composition. The canon at the end of Tchaikovsky's *1812 Overture* and the audience noises in the Beatles' *Sgt. Pepper's Lonely Hearts Club Band* serve musical functions, because the composers intended for those sounds to be heard as music. Someone playing a riff with a pen on a desk is creating music, because the sounds are intended to be musical. Someone nervously and unconsciously tapping a pen on the desk is not creating music, even though the resulting sounds in the two instances are similar. Musical sounds are intended to be heard as music—they are "tones for us," regardless of their origin or sophistication (Sparshott, 1987). Music is intentionally created to be heard as music, and the composer intentionally plans the music to sound the way it does.

Orientation. The concept of orientation relates to the conscious or unconscious goal of a person engaged in a creative act. Adults generally assume that the result of a creative act is the creation of some product. In fact, some definitions of "creativity" require the production of a tangible product. But this is not always the case, especially with novices and younger children. An example from visual art may clarify. A preschool child engaged in the act of painting often does so for the joy of the act of painting. The creation of colors and shapes and the movement of the brush on the paper are what draw the child's attention. Once the painting is created, the child's attention may wander to another painting or to something else. The created object loses its value. Adults, on the other hand, tend to value paintings as objects, as products, as the things that have been created. A parent is likely to tape a young child's finger painting to the refrigerator as a created object, but for the child the value is in the making, not in the thing that is made. Young children tend to think of painting as the *act of painting*, as a process or an action, rather than as the *act of creating a painting*, a product.

One can think of these differences in creativity as a process orientation or a product orientation (Kratus, 1995). With a process orientation one does an activity for the sake of engaging in the activity. With a product orientation one does an activity for the sake of achieving some particular, if unspecified, result. One can improvise with either a process or product orientation. Adults tend to be oriented to improvisation as a product, that is, as something to be shared with others and that conveys some musical sense (i.e., is non-random). Young children tend to be oriented to improvisation as a process and engage in improvisation for the pure joy of making musical sounds in the moment.

A product orientation requires three capabilities in the creator. First is the ability to audiate (hear inwardly with meaning), so that the physical actions required to make the musical sounds match the mental images of those sounds. That means that music created with a product orientation has intentionality; the sounds heard in the music match the creator's intent.

Second is an understanding of musical syntax, which is musical structure (e.g., pulse, tempo, meter, tonality, phrasing). This understanding need not be formalized or verbal. It is learned, as is linguistic syntax, primarily through experience within a practice.

The first and second abilities enable a third: audience awareness. Those who can audiate (hear inwardly) and have an understanding of musical syntax and an awareness of an audience can choose to create *an* improvisation for an audience (product orientation) or can choose to improvise for their own pleasure (process orientation). Those people without those capabilities can only improvise with a process orientation. The act of composition requires both intentionality and a product orientation.

Peter Webster (1987) developed a comprehensive model of creative thinking in music. According to the model, the nature of the creative process depends upon certain enabling skills (e.g., musical aptitudes, conceptual understanding, craftsmanship, and aesthetic sensitivity) and enabling conditions (e.g., motivation, subconscious imagery, supportive environment, and various personality traits). Webster believes that the creative process alternates between two types of thought: divergent thinking, the generation of multiple ideas or possible solutions, and convergent thinking: the selection of a single, "best" solution based on the evaluation of known possibilities. This model presupposes that the composer is working with intentionality and has a product orientation. After understanding what composition is, one may wonder why humans compose music.

WHY DO PEOPLE COMPOSE?

The question of "why do people compose?" cannot be answered from a single perspective or even a single discipline. In this section, I review various perspectives from anthropology and psychology.

Perspectives from Anthropology

The earliest human creations in dance, painting, sculpture, and music almost surely had their roots in the imitation of the natural world and the human form. The prehistoric animal paintings found in French and Spanish caves and the Cro-Magnon stone figurines from Austria and New Guinea provide evidence to support the human desire to re-create the forms of life in their earliest visual art. It is also likely that the first dances borrowed movements from animals and that the first music derived from the sounds of nature. The Kwakiutl, a First Nations indigenous people who lived along the Pacific coast from present-day Alaska to northern California, tell ancient stories of songcatchers, who composed songs based on the sounds of running water, wind, birds, and animals (Ackerman, 1999). Performance of the songs infused those who heard them with the spirit of the natural world (Hawthorn, 1988). It is unknown whether this early artistic creativity was intended to connect to the natural world, chronicle the natural world, or impose mastery over the natural world.

Numerous theories have been postulated regarding the role and value of music in the evolution of early *homo sapiens* (Wallin, Marker, & Brown, 2000). These theories range from mother-infant bonding, to sexual attraction and selection, to communication of danger, to creation of altered states of consciousness. Ellen Dissanayake (1980 & 1982) provides evidence that over the last 250,000 years humans have responded to aesthetic qualities in their environment and have created products (e.g., paintings, songs, dances) using those qualities, a process she calls "the propensity for making special" (1982, p. 148). It is in the making of art, Dissanayake believes, that the behaviors of "making special" (e.g., curiosity, dexterity, pattern-making, imagining) become highly developed. These more highly developed skills gradually pass on to the population, strengthening it and making it more likely to succeed.

At the present point in human evolution, it may be unlikely that the creation of new music still contributes to the survival of the species. But the "propensity of making special" through the creation of music may be reflective of the quality of human existence. The extent to which humans value beauty and imagination in the musical sounds they surround themselves with may well be indicative of the cultural health of the population.

Perspectives from Psychology

The three classic schools of psychology—psychoanalytic, behavioral, and humanist— each offer unique reasons to explain the human desire to create music and art. According to Sigmund Freud (1908/1959), the founder of the psychoanalytic school of psychology, artistic creativity is a product of the self's coping mechanism for managing unfulfilled desires and tensions. In childhood one is able to escape an unpleasant reality through daydreams or fantasy, but in later life that becomes less feasible. The adult artist, said Freud, has the ability to transform that fantasy into a work of art, something that can be shared with others, and in so doing, the artist is able to release the inner tensions. Creation of an artistic work, then, can be seen as a form of therapy to combat emotional distress. Without the release provided by artistic creation, the artist could descend into neurosis or psychosis.

According to this position, the borderline between artistry and mental illness is a thin one. As a theory to explain why humans compose, the psychoanalytic view falls short, though, because it requires that in all cases a composer must first be dissatisfied, needing to escape unpleasantness through the creative process.

The behaviorist view of artistic creativity is exemplified by B. F. Skinner's essay, "A Lecture on 'Having' a Poem" (1972). The title of Skinner's essay makes reference to Samuel Butler: "A poet writes a poem as a hen lays an egg, and both of them feel better afterwards." Skinner posits that it is the environment acting on an individual that leads one to create particular works of art in inevitable ways. Neither free will nor personal desire enter into the creative process. The unconscious mind rearranges the psychic remnants of previous experiences, and the result appears to be a newly created work of art. But in reality, behaviorists believe, the composer has no choice but to apply and recombine learned knowledge in this way. The previously learned musical aspects (e.g., patterns, timbres, textures) are recombined rather than created afresh. Hence, a composer will "have" a composition rather than "create" a composition.

Undeniably, humans are products of their environment. The music that one composer or songwriter creates is certainly influenced by the vast ongoing musical cultures created by others. But to say that humans are no more than the sum of their experiences is to deny not only free will but also innovation and change. The difficulty with behaviorist view of artistic creativity is that it cannot explain breakthroughs for which no previous experience prepared the creator. As examples, Beethoven's use of sonata form in his Third Symphony, Stravinsky's use of rhythm in *Rite of Spring*, and John Coltrane's seemingly illogical chord changes with an inner symmetry in "Giant Steps" had no precedents. Composition does include but is not limited to merely reassembling previously heard patterns.

In both psychoanalytic and behavioral psychologies, the composer has little choice but to respond to the demands of influences, either internal (psychoanalytic) or external (behavioral), beyond the composer's control. The psychoanalytic view is that artistic creativity is a *casting off* or avoidance of internal strife, and the behavioral view is that it is an inevitable response to lived experience. Neither position accounts for the anthropological views of composition, which was that artistic creation was seen as a *seeking out* or attraction to the outside world.

Gestalt psychologist Ernest Schachtel's (1959) writings exemplify the humanist view of artistic creativity. Schachtel wrote that the primary motivation for creativity is the desire to relate to the world outside of the self. He believed that artistic creativity can be observed in a young child's play and in an "artist's lifelong effort to grasp and render something which he has envisaged in his encounter with the world" (p. 245). Both the child and the artist display an openness to the qualities of things around them, and this openness provides for a richer, more complex life. The humanist view is that creativity is not an *avoidance* of emotional distress nor a *response to* environmental influences, but an active *seeking out* of a greater engagement with the world.

One can see echoes of Schachtel's ideas in Abraham Maslow's concept of self-actualization (1968), Howard Gardner's theory of arts and human development (1973), Mihaly Csikszentmihalyi's seminal idea of flow (1990), and Ken Robinson's TED talk, "Do schools kill creativity?" (2006). The humanist view of creativity is also reinforced by Dissanayake's (1982) position that art-making stems from humans' "propensity for making special."

Each of the three psychological schools provide suggestions for the teaching of composition. According to the psychoanalytic school, the act of music creation serves to release pent up emotion. Music composition, primarily through songwriting, as used in some forms of music therapy and with at-risk populations, is designed to function in this way. Teaching adolescents to compose could be one way to provide students with a positive creative outlet to negotiate the emotional transition from childhood to adulthood.

From this author's own experience as a collegiate songwriting teacher, he often observed students singing original songs about such personal issues as sexual abuse, the death of a loved one, and mental illness. Their music-making helped them work through their internal tensions.

An application of behavioral views would suggest that student compositions reflect their learned understanding of how music functions and is structured in various styles. Providing students with syntactic knowledge of music (e.g., tonality, meter, form, texture, timbre) through performing, listening, and creating activities could enhance their ability to implement those characteristics in their own compositions. Students' compositions could be used as windows to the students' syntactic understanding of music. Student projects could include composing "in the style of . . ." or could be structured to focus on certain musical characteristics (e.g., "compose using only so-mi-la," "compose a song with the verse in triple meter and the chorus in duple meter."

The teaching implications from the humanist position of composing are more diffuse than from the other two schools of psychology. What the humanist position does provide teachers is a rationale for teaching composition, in that the process of being open to one's environment and acting upon it can lead students to a richer, more fulfilling life. In the psychoanalytic and behavioral positions, the student composer is simply creating in accordance with internal emotional needs or external environmental stimuli. The student composer's satisfaction in creating something new is limited, because it is either an escape from strife (psychoanalytic) or an imitation of something created by others (behavioral).

The humanist position takes into consideration the personality and lived experience of the student, as well as the desire of the student to reach out to connect with others. These two quotations from high school students in a "School of Rock" class illustrate the humanist view.

> I am so sick of hearing songs that are about having sex and partying all the time. I've been through a lot of rough stuff in my life, and I want to use those things as inspiration to write songs that will help others. I want people to be able to reach for my songs for comfort when they are in distress.
>
> I want to write songs that inspire and motivate people. I want to be the voice for those who can't be heard, and I want to expose the injustices in the world.

None of the anthropological or psychological studies are relevant if school-aged children are incapable of authentic composition. In the following section, the scholarship on children's composition is reviewed, with an emphasis on the earliest known research.

CAN CHILDREN REALLY COMPOSE?

While few would doubt that all children can create drawings, and paintings, and stories, and play act, and dance, there may be some who question whether children can actually create music. Perhaps this is due to the false assumption that composition requires a knowledge of music notation and music theory. It wasn't until the 1940s that children's original music was taken seriously as an object of research. Two series of studies in the 1940s held promise for understanding children as authentic composers. In one series of studies, educator Gladys Moorhead and composer Donald Pond published a series of four monographs from 1941 to 1951 describing the music made by children, 1½ to 8½ years old, performing freely on available classroom instruments in the Pillsbury School in Santa Barbara, California (Moorhead & Pond, 1942/1978). Moorhead created an environment in which young children could explore a variety of classroom instruments, and Pond notated the students' creations. Their collaboration resulted in the detailed documentation of the rhythms, melodic patterns, chants, movements, and instrument choices used in the children's creations.

In the same time period, psychologist Dorothea Doig published a series of three articles (Doig, 1941, 1942a, & 1942b) regarding the musical characteristics of songs composed by the students she worked with in the Saturday Morning Music Classes at the Cleveland (Ohio) Museum of Art. The classes were designed to give children "a better understanding of the arts through familiarity with available materials and by encouraging them to express themselves in music" (Doig, 1941, p. 265). The ages of the children studied ranged from six to 16 years old. Doig noted the musical characteristics of the songs created by the children, such as scalar or chordal melody, phrase structure, mode, and cadences. She also made note of differences between younger and older children in the use of these structures.

Apparently, neither Moorhead and Pond nor Doig were aware of each other's contemporaneous work. The Santa Barbara and Cleveland researchers made use of mixed methods, including frequency counts of various musical aspects used, as well as rich musical examples of the children's compositions. The verbal descriptions of children's creations and activities were especially striking:

> Both younger and older children showed a strong tendency to prefer scalewise melodies, but older children used three types of melodies, namely, scalewise, chordal, and combinations of the two, while younger children scarcely used any except scalewise melodies (Doig, 1942a, p. 354–355).

> Dance, as expressive movement, goes on continuously. A child does not move with the restricted decorum of an adult. His progress across a room is primarily an energetic propulsion of his body weight, a long flow with the head, arms and legs used in free balancing postural change (Moorhead & Pond, 1978/1942, p. 36).

These research results could have led to an understanding of the children's development of musical syntax and the genesis of a research-based pedagogy for teaching children to compose. Sadly, this line of research was never pursued further in the authors' lifetimes. Perhaps the exigencies of World War II intervened, or possibly the community of music educators was not ready to embrace students as potential composers.

In the 1960s and '70s, American educator Ronald Thomas's Manhattanville Music Curriculum Project (1970) and Canadian composer's R. Murray Schafer's (1979) soundscapes provided curricular approaches for teaching children to compose, primarily through the use of found sounds and other non-traditional means. Neither approach was research-based but both had their proponents in their day. Unfortunately, they fell short by expecting students to make the abstract mental leap between tapping and clapping, "oooohs" and "aaaahs" and the musical sounds familiar to children.

It wasn't until the mid-1980s that the formal study of children's original music was continued. Kratus (1985) studied music composed by children between the ages of five and 13 who had had no prior composition experience. This research analyzed music composed by children between the ages of five and 13. He reported that between the ages of five and 11, children's compositions become more highly structured in term of pitch range, tonality, meter, and use of melodic and rhythmic patterns, and that 13-year-olds's compositions were less highly structured that those of 11-year-olds. One year later, Swanwick and Tillman (1986) found that the compositions of over 700 children between the ages of three and 15 developed in an invariant eight-step spiral of development of increasing sophistication. In 1987, Brian Loane's research reported in great depth the musical characteristics of music composed by 11- to 14-year-olds. These studies, describing the characteristics of music composed by children, built upon the work of Moorhead and Pond and Doig 40 years previously.

In the late 1980s, research in children's composition turned from an examination of children's compositional products (compositions) toward children's compositional processes (the act of composing). DeLorenzo (1989) examined the qualitative processes of sixth grade students composing in small groups. She found that highly involved problem solvers considered the expressive potential of musical sounds, whereas less involved problem solvers rarely considered musical concern. In the same year, Kratus (1989) studied the quantitative processes of nine- to 11-year-old students exploring, developing, repeating, and being silent while composing. He reported that repetition while composing is necessary for composing replicable music. Both Delorenzo and Kratus suggested that sixth graders or 11-year-olds are capable of composing in a manner similar to reports of adult composers' compositional processes. Like Moorhead and Pond (1978/1942) and Doig (1941a, 1941b, & 1942) 47 years earlier, these authors were unaware of each other's work prior to publication.

Since the 1980's, research on children's composition (as product and process) has broadened and been embraced by an ever-expanding group of scholars from around the world. To provide the reader with an understanding of the breadth of the research on children's composing since the 1980s, here is a sampling of the research: Myung-Sook Auh and Robert Walker (1999) on factors contributing to children's compositional ability; Pamela Burnard (1999) on children's bodily intentions while composing; Louis Daignault (1996) on children's computer-aided composition; Coral Davies (1992) on structural characteristics of music by five- to seven-year-olds; Michele Kaschub (1997) on composer-guided composition with sixth graders and high school choir students; Kathryn Strand (2009) on action research for teaching children to compose; Jackie Wiggins (1994) on children's strategies while composing with peers; and Sarah Wilson and Roger Wales (1995) on the melodic and rhythmic characteristics of music by seven- and nine-year-olds. The large and growing body of research on children's composition provides ample evidence that children can authentically compose music. Given that young students can compose music as well as perform it, one may ask why so many music educators do not encourage their students to compose.

Extrinsic Impediments to Teaching Composition

The interest in teaching composition varies in different countries. In the United States, both the 1994 National Standards[1] in Music and the revised 2014 Music Standards[2] designate composition to be included in the education of all music students. But that has not necessarily resulted in the widespread adoption of teaching creative music-making in music classes and ensembles. A study of music teachers' views of the nine 1994 National Standards indicated that teachers felt least able to address the standards of improvisation and composition (Byo, 1999).

Two factors commonly cited by teachers for why composition does not have a more prominent role in the music curriculum are time and money: composing takes too long, and the equipment costs too much (Byo, 1999; Shouldice, 2014). These are extrinsic factors relative to the teacher, and they are beyond the teacher's control. Time is a precious commodity in education, and music budgets are limited.

Neither of these reasons holds up under scrutiny. Yes, in most cases it takes longer for students to compose a piece than it takes for them to learn to sing or play a piece with scores or by rote. But, so what? Music educators can learn a lesson in this regard from language teachers. It takes longer to teach students to write a sentence or a poem or an essay than it takes to read either of those. However, language teachers use class time to educate students to compose with language, because writing is an essential component of literacy and enables students to express themselves linguistically.

The factor of time is, in reality, a matter of priorities. Many things that students learn in music classes and ensembles take time. Consider the time spent teaching students to read music. Most classroom and ensemble teachers value music reading and invest precious class time teaching it. That time could have been spent teaching one more piece for the next concert. But those teachers value music reading and consider the trade-off to be worth it in terms of educating their students musically.

Regarding the issue of money, many composing techniques can be done with pencil and paper, and can be performed via homemade instruments, inexpensive ukuleles, body percussion, singing, and rapping. In instrumental ensembles, the students already have access to the instruments they would need to perform their small-group or solo compositions. For those teachers interested in using keyboards, computers, and recording technology, the cost is typically less than the per-student expense for woodwind, brass, or string instruments.

In addition to the extrinsic rationales for not teaching composition, time and money, can be added the idea that students in ensembles are there to perform music, not create music. If music teachers were preparing students for careers in professional orchestras and concert bands, that might be a reasonable argument. But since the vast majority of students in school ensembles discontinue their music performance after graduation from high school (Kratus, 2019), it may be worthwhile to provide students with the tools to continue making music in less formal settings, without conductors, scores, and 50 other musicians. A study of 77 high school band students (Randles, 2010) found that high school band students who took advantage of opportunities to compose on GarageBand during band class had a significantly stronger perception of their musical ability than students who did not. Students with a greater perception of their musical ability are more likely to remain musically active.

Intrinsic Impediments to Teaching Composition

The intrinsic rationales for not teaching composition are: (1) musical, (2) pedagogical, (3) psychological, and (4) sociological. Each of these are learned behaviors, and each can be overcome.

Musical Impediment

Teachers cannot teach what they cannot do themselves. No textbook, workshop, or methods course can prepare someone who has never composed to teach composition. The accrediting organization for collegiate music schools in the United States and Canada, the National Association of Schools of Music (NASM), requires that all music majors have opportunities to compose. The reality is that in many colleges these creative experiences are merely technical exercises in a music theory class. Without authentic, meaningful composing experience, music education majors would be less likely to realize the value of composition for their own students.

There are colleges that prepare pre-service music teachers in a more authentic way. The University College of Music Education in Stockholm, for example, offers popular music genres as a major and teaches songwriting to music education majors. The University of Southern California allows singer-songwriters to become music educators.

To understand how the emphasis on large ensemble performance and relative lack of composition and chamber music in college music curricula came about, it is necessary to look at a 200-year-old paradigm. In the early 19th century, orchestras and opera companies were spreading rapidly throughout Europe, due to a burgeoning middle class. Secular conservatories were established in many European cities to meet the need for large numbers of classically trained musicians. The music curriculum in those conservatories was designed to prepare graduates to take their place in the growth industry of classical music. The primary educational emphasis was on orchestral and opera experiences, with small group instruction on a primary instrument or voice, music theory and sight-singing using solfege, some piano, and 19th-century European music literature.

The musical world of the 21st century has certainly changed, but the core curriculum for most music majors, including music education majors, has been surprisingly resistant to conversion. Many colleges are still preparing music majors to take their place in a nonexistent music world in which positions in large ensembles and opera companies are plentiful.

Audition requirements for collegiate music students vary widely regarding students' compositional ability. In the United States, it would be a rare college, indeed, that would ask students auditioning to be music majors to compose a simple melody. By contrast, in England, the "A-Level" music tests for entrance to most collegiate music study require potential music majors to compose two pieces: one four and one-half minute composition in response to given guidelines, and one free composition (AQA, 2019).

Pedagogical Impediment

A second reason for not teaching composition in music classes and ensembles is a lack of pedagogical knowledge. A teacher with experience composing may not have strategies for teaching composition to others. This is a problem that I faced myself. I have composed songs since I was 13, and I had included guided composition activities for my music students from middle school through college aged. But when one of my college students in 2000 asked me if I could teach songwriting class, I did not know where to begin, because I had no pedagogical models. The class had 18 students enrolled, and I learned how to teach songwriting as the semester progressed.

Collegiate music methods courses are increasingly emphasizing the teaching of composition and other forms of creativity, such as improvisation and arranging. The obstacles of musicianship and pedagogy may be the easiest to overcome in the education of music teachers through updated curricula. However, there are other, more potent, causes for some music educators' resistance to teaching composition: psychological and sociological.

Psychological Factor

Possessing a high degree of creativity is not necessarily a positive characteristic. It simply is what it is: some people are very creative, some are very uncreative, and most are moderately creative. Creativity is domain-specific, meaning that a creative mathematician is not necessarily a creative chef. Creativity is learned and not genetic. Some people are more creative in certain domains and other certain conditions than are other people. Some may assume that all music educators possess a high degree of music creativity, given the subject they teach. But this is not necessarily so.

The Field Theory of creativity says that human behavior is a function of the individual and the environment (Selby, Shaw, & Houtz, 2005). In other words, one's creativity is determined by interaction with other people, the presence or lack of stimulation, and the rules and expectations of the domain in which the person functions. Creativity is not stimulated when another person directs one's action toward a predetermined end.

Let us apply Field Theory to large ensemble performance. In most settings, the music teacher studies a score and develops a mental map of how the piece should sound. Students' performance is then guided toward a particular goal, with the teacher stopping performances to eliminate errors, clarify instructions, and occasionally praise the performers. Given Field Theory, this is not the way to develop students' musical creativity. If music educators do not necessarily value creativity, it is not because they are poor musicians. It may well be that the ways they were taught to be musical required them to follow directions rather than be creative themselves.

An analogy may explain my point. In high school, I took three art courses: drawing and painting, advertising, and photography. Making art (and music) was my passion, to the point of my spending two months in art class capturing the details of a rutabaga in a large charcoal drawing. I also enrolled in a class in mechanical drawing to fulfill a high school requirement in vocational education. The contemporary equivalent to mechanical drawing is cad-cam, computer-generated drawings to illustrate complex designs. In the late 1960s, these drawings were done by hand while working over a tilted desk with protractors, rulers, and compasses. Students were given models to recreate.

I enjoyed the exacting precision of mechanical drawing class, but it in no way was like an art class to me. My teacher in mechanical drawing class would walk past our rows of desks, deducting three points if the angle of a line we drew was imprecise or five points if our lettering was not ¼-inch high using all caps. Looking back at the experience, the class was more about following directions and avoiding errors than it was about creating anything that reflected me personally. I could not imagine my art teacher deducting three points because I did not use enough blue in a painting or five points for drawing my rutabaga too large. Art was about something more personal and significant than avoiding errors.

My concern is that what is taught in large ensembles and other music settings is similar to what I was taught in my mechanical drawing class. The experience can be enjoyable for the precision required, but it is not exactly music as an art form. The question I am asking is: are we teaching music as the aural equivalent of mechanical drawing? Is it the music teacher's job to inspire their students' musicality in ways that are personally meaningful and expressive or to aim their students toward technical perfection in accordance with pre-established rules? Avoiding errors is not particularly inspirational. I have never used mechanical drawing even once after completing that course. The theme of "mechanical music" will be reprised in the conclusion of this chapter.

Sociological Factor

In most classrooms, music teachers control the flow of information from teacher to students. Teachers select the music, they distribute the music, they organize the rehearsals, and they decide when the music is ready for performance. In elementary classrooms, this music is often taught by rote; in secondary ensembles the music is passed out with scores. This flow is disrupted when students themselves are the creators of music.

Levin and Nolan (2014) describe several types of teacher authority in the classroom that enable teachers to guide student learning. Expert authority stems from the teacher being perceived by students as having superior knowledge of the subject. Referent authority derives from teachers being perceived by students as a decent person, one who cares about them and has the students' best interest in mind. Expert authority is especially valued by students at the secondary level. The expertise that music teachers bring to the classroom is, at least theoretically, derived from their years of performance on a single instrument or voice type, in large ensembles and through private instruction.

In most music learning settings, students respond in various ways to music provided by their teachers. In a composition or songwriting class, this situation is reversed. The teacher responds to the original music students provide. When I started teaching songwriting, I needed to readjust my teaching to provide an environment for nurturing creativity rather than guiding students toward a predetermined set of curricular objectives. The flow of information from students to teacher may be perceived as undermining the teacher's expert authority. Some educators have worried that the loss of the music teacher's control through superior expertise in classical traditions "may be sowing the seeds of our own demise" (Allsup, 2008, p. 5).

The obstacles presented in this section may be explained as educators' fears: I fear that my musicality does not include composition (musical), I fear that I do not know how to teach composing (pedagogical), I fear that I am personally not very creative (psychological), and I fear that my control of the class/ensemble may falter if I am not perceived as the musical expert in the room (sociological). These unspoken fears are certainly not universal among music teachers, by any means. But they are learned behaviors, based on being musically educated in a system based on a 200-year-old paradigm.

OVERCOMING THE OBSTACLES

Psychologists understand that these obstacles can be overcome. A study by Jarymowicz and Bar-Tal (2006) concluded that individuals and organizations "can overcome their fear with much determination and establish an orientation of hope which allows change in situations dominated by fear" (p. 367). Two of the obstacles—musical and pedagogical—can be addressed with curriculum revision at the collegiate level.

The other two obstacles—psychological and sociological—will be more difficult to overcome.

It is unlikely that musical deficiencies regarding composition will soon be the norm in collegiate classes for applied music and music theory. Hope may be on the horizon, however. The College Music Society, an organization of thousands of college music professors from the United States and Canada, recently noted in a manifesto that the collegiate music school has been "resistant, remaining isolated and, too frequently, regressive rather than progressive in its approach to undergraduate education. While surface change has occurred to some extent through additive means (that is, simply providing more courses, more requirements, and more elective opportunities), fundamental change (that is, in priorities, values, perspectives, and implementation) has not occurred" (Task Force on the Undergraduate Music Major [TFUMM], 2016). The report added, "TFUMM takes the position that creativity (defined for purposes of this report as rooted in the ability to improvise and compose) provides a stronger basis for educating musicians than does interpretation (the prevailing model of training performers in the interpretation of existing works)" (TFUMM, 2016). That is quite a remarkable statement! It remains to be seen whether the College Music Society's manifesto will result in a greater emphasis on composition and improvisation in the college curriculum. But at least there is a recognition that change needs to occur.

Until then, it may be necessary to teach prospective music teachers to compose in music education methods classes. In many collegiate methods classes, students are now learning music by ear, arranging music, composing music, and employing the technological tools for composing and recording music. In-service sessions and summer classes can help current music teachers to develop these skills.

Regarding pedagogical deficiencies, there are a variety of new resources that explain how to teach composition in various settings. Certainly, this book is an important resource (Kaschub, 2021), as are *Musicianship: Composing in band and orchestra* (Randles & Stringham, 2013), *Music outside the lines: Ideas for composing in K–12 music classrooms* (Hickey, 2012), and *Composing our future: Preparing music educators to teach composition* (Kaschub & Smith, 2013). In addition, *Music Educators Journal* has published special issues on composition (2016), creativity (2017), and popular music education (2019) to provide new pedagogical approaches to teaching composition.

The musical and pedagogical obstacles can be addressed through curriculum reform at the college level, additional sessions after graduation, and published and online resources. The psychological and sociological obstacles will be more difficult to overcome. Consider the psychological issues regarding the development of student musicians. Student visual artists usually create their works individually. Their teacher offers minimal guidance and instead offers a nurturing environment for individual development. Student musicians in a large ensemble are directed by a teacher to perform as a member of a large group, all contributing to a single music product. There is no wonder that music students who have experienced six to 10 years of being directed by others may be lacking in their own creativity.

One solution would be to create more opportunities for music learners to think creatively in music on their own and with other learners. One approach toward this end would be the inclusion of more chamber music, with the teacher acting as a resource rather than as a director. Large ensembles could also break into smaller groups for the purpose of composing their own music.

The sociological obstacle is that the teacher's control will be diminished if the teacher is no longer the person in control of the music. From my own experiences teaching songwriting classes, I can say that when a teacher allows the class to assess each other's work, the teacher's role is strengthened, not weakened.

The work of Austrian philosopher Martin Buber can offer some guidance in this regard. In his 1924 book, *Ich und Du* (I and Thou), he described two type of relations that we have with people and things around us: I-It and I-Thou. The more common of the two is I-It, in which we consider the objects and even people around us to have a particular function in relation to us. This is a chair; I can sit in it. This is a book; I can read it. These are my students (or trombones or sopranos); I can teach them. I-Thou relations involve more of a mutual regard for the intentions and uniqueness of each other. To apply this to education: an I-It approach would reward achievement, and an I-Thou approach would reward growth. I-It would regard the learning space as a classroom or rehearsal room; It-Thou would consider it to be a community. I-It has assignments; I-Thou has growth opportunities. I-It is more subject-centered; I-Thou is more learner-led. Certainly, the teacher and student have different roles and responsibilities, but the respect that teachers may fear they would lose in an I-Thou setting is increased, not diminished.

Applying Buber's ideas to ensemble performance would require teachers to ask students more questions about the music being performed and to include students in more of the decision-making. What repertoire should be studied? How fast should the allegro tempo be? To what extent should student compositions be performed?

Mechanical Drawing, Composition, and Music Education

I want to conclude with another reference to my high school days. I kept every major artwork I ever created in my art classes. Those artworks reflected who I was at the time and also reflected the times I was living through. One work of mine from those days was a photographic essay. I had taken my camera to a Vietnam War protest at the University of Buffalo and took pictures of the students around me, resisting police brutality and tear gas. Back in my safe suburban school, I painstakingly cut the photos I developed into shapes fitting the shapes of the 50 United States. I then glued each photo into a collage of a map of the United States. That artwork meant a great deal to me.

As mentioned previously in this chapter, I also created mechanical drawings in high school in a vocational education class. I saved none of them, even though I took pleasure in learning in such a rule-bound environment. So, what was the difference? Both my artworks and my mechanical drawings required precision and technique. The mechanical drawings of gears required meticulous precision, as did the fastidious cutting of photographic states. Both mechanical drawing and visual art required a knowledge of technique (e.g., ways of labeling aspects of a mechanical drawing correctly and ways of developing a photograph correctly). But there was one essential difference. In my mechanical drawing class, I followed someone else's rules. In my art classes, I followed my own. In addition to the precision and technique my art teachers taught me, I also needed to develop my own muse, which was something that mechanical drawing did not do. The art teacher's job was to create a stimulating environment that encouraged students to create something that no one had seen before. The mechanical drawing teacher's job was to encourage all students to draw something the same way in according to pre-established conventions.

It is not difficult to translate this analogy to music education. In many music ensembles and classes, students are taught music selected by the teacher and performed in accordance with musical conventions and the teacher's expectations. Music performance requires precision (e.g., correct rhythms) and technique (e.g., proper embouchure), whether it is music given to students by the teacher or music created by the students themselves. In many music classes and ensembles, the music performed follows someone else's rules. Dare I call this form of music education "mechanical music"? The learning that occurs in many music classes is not dependent on students' desires but rather on those of the teacher. What is missing is the fostering of the students' muse. They do not own the music they perform.

While in junior and senior high school, I wrote songs for my fledgling rock band. Not once did I think of myself as a composer, perhaps because the word "composer" carries a lot of baggage. "Composer" too often connotes the use of standard notation, performance in formal concert halls, and an orientation of antiquated seriousness, as exemplified in the phrase "dead white composers."

The word "composition" may well be inhibiting the interest that students exhibit in learning to create their own music. Perhaps music teachers should stop trying to teach their students to "compose." The word "songwriting" may be more appropriate, given that many young people consider all music to be songs. But not all compositions are songs. Another possibility is that music teachers could discuss with their students performing a combination of music created by someone else, along with music that they create themselves: the music no one has heard yet. Music teachers may well find that "the music no one has heard yet" will be of greater interest to students than their interest in performing cover songs.

Performance will continue to be the heart of music classes and ensembles. But the students in those classes and ensembles are also capable of creating some of the music they perform. As exemplified in the three opening vignettes, the music students create themselves is more meaningful to them than the music created by others. Consider the words of Jean-Jacques Rousseau (1779/2003), a philosopher who influenced the revolutions in the United States and France and an important French composer. He wrote 240 years ago that "to understand music, it is not sufficient to be able to play or sing; we must learn to compose at the same time, or we shall never be masters of this science." The students performing music made by themselves and their classmates will be passionate in their music-making. An audience hearing music that is not only performed by students but also created by them will respond enthusiastically. The teachers fostering their students' compositional ability will be the first lucky listeners of the music no one has heard yet.

NOTES

1. The 1994 National Standards for Music can be in the National Standards Archives at https://nafme.org/my-classroom/standards/national-standards-archives/
2. The 2014 *National Core Arts Standards* are available from State Education Agency Directors of Arts Education (SEADAE) at https://www.nationalartsstandards.org.

REFERENCES

Ackerman, D. (1999). *Deep play*. Random House.

Allsup, R. E. (2008). Creating an educational framework for popular music in public schools: Anticipating the second-wave. *Visions of Research in Music Education, 12*(1), 1–12.

AQA. (2019, August 29). A-Level music. https://filestore.aqa.org.uk/resources/music/specifications/AQA-7272-SP-2016.PDF

Auh, M.-S., &Walker, R. (1999). Compositional strategies and musical creativity when composing with staff notations versus graphic notations among Korean students. *Bulletin of the Council for Research in Music Education, 141*, 2–9.

Buber, M. (1924/1970). *I and Thou*. Simon & Schuster.

Burnard, P. (1999). Bodily intention in children's improvisation and composition. *Psychology of Music, 27*(2), 159–174.

Byo, S. J. (1999). Classroom teachers' and music specialists' perceived ability to implement the national standards for music education. *Journal of Research in Music Education, 47*(2), 111–123.

Csikszentmihalyi, M. (1990). *Flow: The psychology of optimal experience*. Harper & Row.

Daignault, L. (1996). *Children's creative musical thinking within the context of a computer-supported improvisational approach to composition*. [Unpublished doctoral dissertation]. Northwestern University.

Davies, C. (1992). Listen to my song: A study of songs invented by children aged 5 to 7 years. *British Journal of Music Education, 9*(1), 19–48.

DeLorenzo, L. C. (1989). A field study of sixth-grade students' creative music problem-solving processes. *Journal of Research in Music Education, 37*(3), 188–200.

Dissanayake, E. (1980). Art as a human behavior: Toward an ethological view of art. *Journal of Aesthetics and Art Criticism, 38*(4), 397–406.

Dissanayake, E. (1982). Aesthetic experience and human evolution. *Journal of Aesthetics and Art Criticism, 41*(2), 145–155.

Doig, D. (1941) Creative music I: Music composed for a given text. *Journal of Educational Research, 35*(4), 263–275.

Doig, D. (1942a). Creative music II: Music composed on a given subject. *Journal of Educational Research, 35*(5), 344–355.

Doig, D. (1942b). Creative music III: Music composed to illustrate given musical problems. *Journal of Educational Research, 36*(4), 241–253.

Freud, S. (1908/1959). Creative writers and day-dreaming. In J. Strachey (Ed.), *The standard edition of the complete psychological works of Sigmond Freud* (Vol. 9, pp. 141–154). Hogarth Press.

Gardner, H. (1973). *The arts and human development: A psychological study of the artistic process.* Wiley.

Hawthorne, A. (1988). *Kwakiutl art.* University of Washington Press.

Hickey, M. (2012). *Music outside the lines: Ideas for composing in K–12 music classrooms.* Oxford University Press.

Jarymowicz, M., & Bar-Tal, D. (2006). The dominance of fear over hope in the life of individuals and collectives. *European Journal of Social Psychology, 36*(3), 367–392.

Kaschub, M. (1997). A comparison of two composer-guided large group composition projects. *Research Studies in Music Education, 8*(1), 15–28.

Kaschub, M., & Smith, J. (Eds.). (2013). *Composing our future: Preparing music educators to teach composition.* Oxford University Press.

Kaschub, M. (Ed.). (2021). *The Oxford handbook on composition pedagogy.* Oxford University Press.

Kratus, J. K. (1985). *Rhythm, melody, motive, and phrase characteristics of original songs by children aged five to thirteen* [Unpublished doctoral dissertation]. Northwestern University.

Kratus, J. (1989). A time analysis of the compositional processes used by children ages 7 to 11. *Journal of Research in Music Education, 37*(1), 5–20.

Kratus, J. (1991). Orientation and intentionality as components of creative musical activity. *Research Perspectives in Music Education, 2,* 4–8.

Kratus, J. (1995). A developmental approach to teaching music improvisation. *International Journal of Music Education, 26*(1), 27–38.

Kratus, J. (2019). A return to amateurism in music education. *Music Educators Journal, 106*(1): 31–37.

Levin, J., & Nolan, J. F. (2014). *Principles of classroom management: A professional decision-making model* (7th ed.). Pearson.

Loane, B. (1987). *Understanding children's music.* [Unpublished doctoral dissertation]. University of York.

Maslow, A. H. (1968). Music education and peak experience. *Music Educators Journal, 54*(6), 72–171.

Moorhead, G., & Pond, D. (1942/1978). *Music of young children.* Pillsbury Foundation for the Advancement of Music Education.

National Core Arts Standards. (2014). State Education Agency Directors of Arts Education (SEADAE) at https://www.nationalartsstandards.org.

Randles, C. (2010). The relationship of compositional experiences of high school instrumentalists to music self-concept. *Bulletin of the Council for Research in Music Education, 184,* 9–20.

Randles, C., & Stringham, D. A. (Eds.). (2013). *Musicianship: Composing in band and orchestra.* GIA.

Rousseau, J.-J. (1779/2003). *Emilius* (W. H. Payne, Trans.). Prometheus Books.

Schachtel, E. (1959). *Metamorphosis: On the development of affect, perception, attention, and memory*. Basic Books.

Selby, E. C., Shaw, E. J., & Houtz, J. C. (2005). The creative personality. *Gifted Child Quarterly, 49*(4), 300–314.

Schafer, R. M. (1979). *Creative music education*. Schirmer Books.

Shouldice, H. N. (2014). Teachers' beliefs regarding composition in elementary general music: Definitions, values, and impediments. *Research Studies in Music Education, 36*(2), 215–230.

Skinner, B. F. (1972). A lecture on "having" a poem. In B. F. Skinner (Ed.), *Cumulative record: A selection of papers* (3rd ed., pp. 345–355). Prentice-Hall.

Sparshott, F. (1987). Aeshtetics of music: Limits and grounds. In P. Alperson (Ed.), *What is music?* (pp. 33–98). Pennsylvania State University Press.

Stephens, J. (2013). Artistic knowledge in practice. In E. Georgii-Hemming, P. Burnard, & S.-E. Holgersen (Eds.), *Professional knowledge in music teacher education* (pp. 73–96). Ashgate.

Strand, K. D. (2009). A narrative analysis of action research on teaching composition. *Music Education Research, 11*(3), 349–363.

Swanwick, K., & Tillman, J. (1986). The sequence of musical development: A study of children's composition. *British Journal of Music Education, 3*(3), 305–339.

Task Force on the Undergraduate Music Major. (2016.) *Transforming music study from its foundations: A manifesto for progressive change in the undergraduate preparation of music majors*. https://www.music.org/pdf/pubs/tfumm/TFUMM.pdf

TED. (February, 2006). Do schools kill creativity? | Sir Ken Robinson [Video]. YouTube. https://www.ted.com/talks/sir_ken_robinson_do_schools_kill_creativity?language=en

Thomas, R. B. (1970). Manhattanville Music Curriculum Program. Final Report. https://files.eric.ed.gov/fulltext/ED045865.pdf

Wallin, N. L., Merker, B., & Brown, S. (Eds.). (2000). *The origins of music*. MIT Press.

Webster, P. R. (1987). Conceptual basis for creative thinking in music. In J. C. Peery, I. W. Peery, & T. W. Draper (Eds.), *Music and child development* (pp. 158–174). Springer-Verlag.

Wiggins, J. H. (1994). Children's strategies for solving compositional problems with peers. *Journal of Research in Music Education, 42*(3), 232–252.

Williams, D. A. (2011). The elephant in the room. *Music Educators Journal, 98*(1): 51–57.

Wilson, S. J., & Wales, R. J. (1995). An exploration of children's musical compositions. *Journal of Research in Music Education, 43*(2): 94–111.

CHAPTER 3

....

REFINING AND EXPANDING MUSIC COMPOSITION PEDAGOGIES

....

PETER R. WEBSTER

> To teach a child to think in music is the way to teach that child crea-
> tivity. The new model for American music education should be based on
> teaching for creativity. Creativity is authentic thought. The way to teach
> creativity in music is to train the mind to think musically. That leads me
> to ask: "What, now, is the real mission of music education in America?"
> Libby Larsen
>
> (Strand & Larsen, 2011, p. 64)

CONSIDER the following short vignettes as models of practice for teachers and their
learners:

- Small groups of third graders are huddled in the corner of Mr. Henderson's music
  classroom. Each group works separately with a collection of xylophones, resonator
  bells, percussion instruments, and soprano and tenor wind recorders. Their task
  is to create a short, accompanied song to commemorate the heroic work of some
  health care workers in a local hospital. They are encouraged to notate the composition in any way they wish, record it, and then perform it for the class. After
  each group shares and discusses their music, the class seems eager for more time to
  create on their own. The students ask for opportunities like this and ask for help in
  how to do it better.
- Jill, a seventh grade trumpet student, finished composing a short fanfare to precede
  an important event. She is using an online notation program on a tablet computer
  as part of Ms. Sanchez's middle school band activities. Jill's excitement is palpable as
  the composition is shared with the family at home and Jill asks if they can help find
  a composition teacher to provide private lessons during the summer. Jill hopes to
  write a larger piece for brass ensemble.

- Darin, a 10th grader who is new to music classes, has just finished an online song-writing class. The course was offered by Mr. Epstein, a choral music educator, as part of the 2020–2021 COVID remote music curriculum. The experience has been transformative for Darin, who, for the first time, feels the intense enjoyment of creating music that has personal meaning beyond written words. Darin is excited and eager to learn more.
- Sarah, a 12th grade pianist, has been asked to join a group of friends in forming a popular music group. Sarah has extensive experience with classical piano performance, but there is a lingering secret love for popular music that has not been addressed in private instruction. Upon learning about the group, Sarah's piano teacher, Mr. Riker, has begun to blend into Sarah's lessons some experiences with a digital piano and some sequencing software that supports live music performance. Sarah hopes that Mr. Riker might provide some guidance for the popular music group.
- Ron is a first semester college music education major. During college orientation, Ron tested out of much of the basic theory content contained in the first semester course and was placed in an advanced section. The theory professor, Dr. Cruz—an accomplished composer—has created an entirely new approach to second semester theory that makes extensive use of music composition. After several weeks in the course, Ron has discovered a whole new world of music understanding that will play a role in his future teaching.

These enthusiastic and motivated students are experiencing music teachers who seem to be working differently than many before them. These teachers have stressed the technical aspects of music theory, history, and performance—as many have so rightly done before. But these teachers also do something equally as important: they offer a chance for learners to *create their own music* using the knowledge and skills so necessary for music learning.

CHANGING LANDSCAPE OF MUSIC EDUCATION PEDAGOGY

The blend of technical understanding with opportunities for personally constructed, creative work is an important aspect of a changing landscape of music education pedagogy writ large across methodologies, cultural settings, and levels of instruction (J. Barrett & Webster, 2014; Lewis, 2020; Webster, 2014).

This chapter and the many other chapters in this Handbook join the hundreds of other theoretical, practical, and empirical writings in the last century and a half that have encouraged teachers to stress the personal, generative work of music learners as much as possible. This is one of many "big ideas" in music teaching and learning that challenge us to make pedagogies more effective for a musically diverse world far different than previous music educators may have experienced or considered.

The music teachers in the short vignettes that start the chapter may also be influenced by other building blocks in this changing landscape that support the construction of creative experiences. For example:

1. Learner-centered approaches that offer chances for projects and personal exploration to support differentiated instruction (Williams & Kladder, 2019).
2. Multiple genres of music, including more popular styles of music and music of other cultures (Anderson & Campbell, 2011; Burnard, 2012; Green, 2008).
3. Interdisciplinary content both within the traditional music subdivisions (e.g., history, theory, performance, education) and outside of music (e.g., "hard" sciences, social sciences, humanities, related arts) (Abril & Gault, 2016; J. Barrett, 2001).
4. Diverse approaches to assessment of learning that include portfolios of work, parental and teacher collaboration, and learner self-assessment of progress (Brophy, 2019; Hebert, 2001).
5. Diverse types of music often rendered with technological affordance online or from phones and tablets (Bamberger, 2013; Bauer, 2020; Dorfman, 2013; Freedman, 2013; Greher & Burton, 2021; Ruthmann & Mantie, 2017; Williams & Webster, 2023).
6. Public face of music teaching and learning that not only features polished performances of others' music but *also* student-created music presented in and outside of the concert hall (Dobson & Pitts, 2011)
7. Students not typically engaged in band, orchestra, and choir ensembles experiencing music creatively and in diverse ways (Williams, 2012).

In this context, the purpose of the chapter is to offer music educators clear reasons to expand their engagement of students in compositional activities and to do so with clearly reasoned, contemporary pedagogy. To help with this, the chapter offers historical and more recent writings that bolster the rationales for why this might be done. Teachers of elementary and secondary education are the focus, however much of what is summarized here holds enormous significance for music teachers in higher education, especially those responsible for teacher preparation. This chapter is offered with an eye toward blending knowledge and skills with creative affordance.

BROAD CONTEXT OF MUSIC PEDAGOGY

Just what is a "pedagogy," and how might it relate to "music teaching philosophy," "learning theory," and "methodology"? In music teacher discourse, these terms are often conflated. One way of unpacking them is to consider a hierarchy that moves from philosophy through to the practice.

Philosophy

Philosophical discourse about the nature of learning falls traditionally under the realm of epistemology (Fumerton, 2009). One way to think about and understand this branch of philosophy is to imagine the quest for what is knowledge and justification. To seek the personal answers to what music pedagogy to practice is to start with epistemological questions that music education philosophers face.

In the opening pages of Bowman and Frega's (2012) *Oxford handbook of philosophy of music education*, the purpose of education philosophy as it is practiced in this contemporary era is explained as:

> Not so much to identify timeless or universal truths as to develop and refine theoretical perspectives that are provisionally useful: hypothesized relationships between beliefs and actions. The validity of such orientations must be continuously tested and revised in light of emerging (and often unforeseen) circumstances. Philosophy's truths are contingent and contextual—for the time being, under present circumstances, until further notice. That may be all philosophy can reasonably aspire to achieve; but perhaps it is all we really need. (p. 22)

Music education philosophy and the scholars that form it take on the big picture of teaching and learning, often drawing on the work of the major thinkers who proceeded them. Many of our finest philosophers have contributed greatly to the endorsement of creative music experiences, especially music composition (e.g., Reimer, 2003/2022; Jorgensen, 2003; Elliott & Silverman, 2014; and Allsup, 2016). Each has positioned creativeness and its consequence in slightly different ways but always as a primary concern.

Learning Theories

Learning theories,[1] growing in part from a philosophical base and epistemological roots, provide a strong foundation for effective teaching strategies. Taetle and Cutietta (2002) offered a review of broad-based learning theories that included the perspective of behaviorist, cognitive, and constructivist approaches. Highlighted were specific contributions by Edwin Gordon, Howard Gardner, and Jeanne Bamberger among others.

In more recent work, Senyshyn and O'Neill (2011) contributed a detailed orientation to selected learning theories. Stressed was the important role of a psychological orientation in helping to define learning strategies and the importance of a pluralistic and "reflexive" approach to understanding learning theory—meaning an engagement of our own experiences teaching music and our awareness of the changing landscape of music and culture. They characterized music learners and their relation to learning theory as a likely combination of the following: (1) a skilled performer (behaviorism), (2) a collaborator (constructivism), (3) an explorer (pragmatism), and (4) an authentic music being (existentialism) (pp. 18–28).

Both general and music-specific learning theories support creative engagement in music experiences (especially those related to constructivism, pragmatism, and existentialism).

> In a broad sense, learning theories aim to achieve some form of understanding about how learners gain knowledge, understanding, and skills and how educational structures and practices evolve or develop particular perceptions, visions, or strategies for the transfer of communication of knowledge. In educational contexts, learning theories are especially concerned with discovery and invention (i.e., recognizing, creating, or exploring new knowledge; manipulating knowledge and understanding to generate new ideas or concepts; facilitating changes in behavior). (Senyshyn & O'Neill, 2011, p. 5)

Methodologies

Most educators would agree that philosophy and learning theory are powerful conceptual frames that help to guide a teacher's chosen methodology to the point where a solid pedagogy (see below) of instruction can be realized. For example, the notion of blending knowledge and skills with personal creative experiences in music may be seen as a meaningful methodical activity leading from chosen philosophies and learning theories. Precious class time is devoted to making a methodology of this sort work. However, for some, this pathway from theory to practice is less clear and decisions about methods are not always systematically considered in planning. There are likely others who are aware of the pathway from theory to practice but have not decided to endorse pedagogies that feature creative work because of concerns related to unpredictability, risky outcome, time, or personal skill in leading such activities.

There are some reasons why this diversity exists that may be traceable in part to how we prepare music teachers. In many teacher education programs, a set of traditional "methods courses"[2] may or may not be designed to make the connection with theory and practice. Widely known methodologies for general music instruction for grades pre-K to middle school are summarized by Mark and Madura (2014, pp. 97–133). Some of these are founded by famous pedagogues such as Dalcroze, Orff, Kodály, and Gordon. Some may be associated with significant curriculum projects such as Manhattanville and Comprehensive Musicianship. These methodologies and their collegiate instruction may result in meaningful connections to philosophy and learning theory including creative work blended with knowledge and skills, but many may not.

Instrumental/choral teacher education instruction is anchored by student methods books exemplars.[3] Use of these traditional and highly regarded publications may or may not contain or have been constructed with a philosophical base or learning theory in mind.

Complicating the picture further are private instrumental and voice instruction, together with music theory and history classes that are often engineering by well-meaning instructors that follow long-established approaches for knowledge about music and technical mastery. The master-apprentice model that is often at work may or may not be informed by philosophy or learning theory.

All of this points to teaching practices that may not be consistent with carefully crafted teaching philosophy, well-chosen theories of learning, and culturally relevant methods of teaching today's youth who experience a world of music that is multi-dimensional.

Pedagogies

Classic, dictionary-like definitions of pedagogy often include such ideas as "science of teaching," "theory and practice of teaching," or "didactical thinking." Pedagogies represent the sum total of what teachers **do** on a daily basis to help students acquire knowledge and skills. It is the act of teaching itself on a daily basis over time that involves decisions about teaching strategies influenced by methodologies "in action" that are formed by learning theories and philosophies. For examples of pedagogies in action, return to the opening vignettes that start this chapter and the building blocks of the changing landscape that support the construction of creative experiences.

Murphy (2008) offers some nuance about "pedagogy" from a postmodern perspective:

> The redefinition of pedagogy as an art follows from the view that pedagogy is about the *integrations between teachers, students and the learning environment and learning tasks.* . . . Pedagogy cannot be disembedded from the wider educational system. So, in order to address what is effective pedagogy, we must be agreed on the goals of education. [italics in original, p. 35]

The notion of pedagogy as an "art" underscores the dynamic process of designing teaching structures that are flexible and responsive to the students themselves, the times in which students live, and—in the case of music teaching and learning—a sensitivity to the power of music as an expressive medium coming from the blend of the technical with the creative. For example, the recognition of pedagogies that endorse the "teaching moment" and other techniques of carefully managed improvisation (Sawyer, 2011) are highly valued in this context.

Informed pedagogies that are reassessed and recalibrated routinely by teachers in working with students in today's contemporary world of music-making move us closer to what is often referred to as "culturally-responsive" and "critical-based" approaches to teacher action leading on from philosophy and theory (Abrahams, 2005); Lind and McCoy, 2016). Allsup's (2016) powerful notions of remixing music education combined with Jorgensen's (2003) pleas for transformation and Schmidt and Colwell's (2017) collected essays on the importance of informed policy all help to construct a new level of pedagogical thinking.

This chapter argues for an emphasis to be placed on student compositional voice to understand music better and to complement other music experiences such as music improvisation, performance of others' music, and active engagement in music listening

(Kerchner, 2013). The blend of the technical with the creative in this context can help to form a more grounded pedagogy. Put another way, we should consider moving away from uninterrogated methodology to a more dynamic and artful pedagogy that is supported by theory and philosophy.

Exemplars for a Music Composition Pedagogy

What follows are brief overviews of selected literature that may help teachers at all levels of instruction build a composition pedagogy that is carefully crafted and richly designed in terms of philosophy and learning theory. Exemplars are organized in two sections: one devoted to larger conceptual frames and the other to more detailed examples of application. They are carefully chosen for their compelling meaning for today's teaching environment and usefulness in expanding time devoted to creative activities—particularly music composition.

Conceptual Frame Exemplars

Five groups of writing are considered: (1) an historical account of music composition pedagogy, (2) two works that address philosophy/learning theory as a base for music composition, (3) writings on creativity broadly viewed in the psychology literature, (4) writings on creativity specifically relevant to music education and composition teaching, and (5) teacher/composers' own powerful words and actions.

Composition Pedagogy: An Historical Account

In the opening pages of one of the only extensive studies of music composition pedagogy, Williams (2010) proposed that

> a pedagogy of musical composition be adopted that would reunite *technique* and *creativity* in a common field of study. Modifications to the pedagogical approach toward the teaching of both Music Theory and Composition are proposed in order to ensure that neither pursuit would remain isolated from its interrelated counterpart. By combining the "details, methods or skills which are applied to [music composition]" with the "capacity for, or state of, bringing [music] into being" a pedagogy emerges that can address all aspects of learning to compose. [italics and quotation marks in original, pp. 2–3]

This notion of technical understanding joined with creative composition process is at the heart of many accounts of music composition pedagogy as it relates to western art music and can be found in modern accounts of composition pedagogy in popular music as well (Clauhs, Powell, & Clements, 2020).

The study by Williams (2010) provided an historical account of the growth of composition as an improvisational experience before the eighteenth century and based on the study of conventions in treatises such as those noted, by Zarlino and others (pp. 24–25). This tradition continued into the eighteenth century and became more codified by the emergence of rules of species counterpoint by Fux, the notion of thoroughbass, and the systematic study of harmony by Rameau. This would dominate studies of music in the nineteenth century (Williams, 2010, p. 39). Also of note were composers' attention to melody as noted by the writings of Mattheson and the memorization of the "stock melodic schemata for the realization of thoroughbass, or *partimenti*, in a stylistically appropriate manner" (p. 44).

Amidst this historical/technical background in the development of what might be thought of as today's field of music theory, came the nineteenth century conservatoire that established music theory as the important landmark of music instruction as it exists today. The beginnings of pedagogy for music composition were likely embedded into the instruction of music theory. Attention to the emergence of the great composers of western art music in the eighteenth and nineteenth centuries was often attributed to the mastery of historically defined technical skills together with the romantic "mystery of genius" attribution. This "mystery of genius" is one of the major "myths" that has been inaccurately used to explain creative achievement (Sawyer, 2012).

As time passed, it became clear that the mastery of technique and the "genius" notion were not enough to explain compositional achievement. "The idea that studies in Fuxian counterpoint and Harmony could—or at least should—no longer serve as preludes to studies in composition led to a divide between the fields of music theory and composition at the turn of the twentieth century" (Williams, 2010, p. 56). By mid-century the separation of music theory and composition was complete as schools of music established both closely related but separate courses of study, especially at the graduate level.

Williams (2010) ended his work with an analysis of selected books on music composition designed for higher education, noting strengths and weaknesses with an eye toward the balance of technique and creativity.[4] Williams also noted that the National Association of Schools of Music (NASM) guidelines for undergraduate and graduate programs in composition are purposefully vague and are of no help in understanding contemporary composition pedagogy. In fact, even to this day, the lines between music theory and composition may not always be clear.

Perhaps to improve this, Williams proposed competencies that might be considered when framing music composition pedagogy, as well as providing hints toward some instructional techniques for guidance. These are displayed in Figure 3.1.

Although crafted as recommendations for collegiate instruction, these competencies and techniques may be useful for compositional pedagogy at any level and appear in various forms in other exemplars to follow.

Philosophy and Learning Theory as a Base for Music Composition

Webster (2010) focused on the many complicated facets of constructivism as a philosophy and learning theory. The author reviewed generally accepted tenants of

Coherency	Demonstrating orderly, logical, and aesthetically consistent relationship of the parts to the whole.
Idiomatic Writing	Using, containing, or denoting expressions that are natural to an instrument/voice
Orchestration	Arranging, manipulating, or coordinating multiple instruments/voices
Creative Competencies	
Conceptual Fluency:	Forming ideas, plans or sets of intentions from original or found sources.
Originality:	Employing a relatively unique, individualized approach
Instructional Techniques	
<ul><li>encouragement of self-criticism: formulating and expressing a sophisticated judgement regarding one's own work</li><li>constructive criticism from mentor</li><li>problem design</li><li>instructional discourse</li><li>deliberate practice of composition competencies</li><li>encouragement of a personal voice</li><li>class/group composition lessons</li></ul>	

FIGURE 3.1. Technical/creative competencies and instructional techniques for music composition Pedagogy (adapted from Williams, 2010, pp. 107–143)

constructivism as frequently characterized in the psychology and general education literatures. These are seen as being supportive of student-centered approaches, independence of thought, creative thinking encouragement, and culturally relevant pedagogy. Implications for music learning and a précis of the many music education scholars who have made the case for a constructivist approach to creativity in music learning are included. Possible weaknesses are also addressed, and the chapter is followed by another chapter (Colwell, 2010) that focuses on direct instruction, critical thinking, and transfer that provides an interesting comparison.

The Webster (2010) chapter ends with an extensive review of empirical research evidence in music teaching and learning that used constructivism as a base for studying generative behavior in a wide variety of music learners. These writings support student-centered learning and the vital need for recognizing student voice.

Kratus (2012) presented a number of philosophical and culturally rich conceptual frames for composition pedagogy and student composers (songcatchers). Issues of definition, origins of originality, and pedagogical concerns are provided. He noted that intentionality may be a key to the meaning of musical sounds and their creative use by learners in compositional and improvisational ways. For example, students should have an intentionality to their work by having the ability to hold music ideas in their heads (audiate) and command some sense of musical syntax such as meter and tonality, and rhythmic and tonal patterns. Traditional or invented notation may or may not be needed for composition to occur.

In his consideration of implications from philosophy and psychology, Kratus suggested that the psychoanalytic, behavioral, and humanist perspectives offer foundations for pedagogy (see Taetle & Cutietta, 2002, and Senyshyn & O'Neill, 2011). Behaviorism may help to explain the role of the environment and other human experiences in terms of the creative process. Humanism may help to understand an individual's drive to share creatively with the world around us—to help self-actualization and optimal experience.

Kratus noted that the perspective of composers themselves are a source of insight—especially in understanding the creative process as it merges with technical understanding.[5] However, such reports need to be approached with caution:

> In applying the accounts of composers to an educational setting, one must be cognizant of the potential unreliability of their reports. Educators should also be aware that the work habits of professionals may not always provide the best guidance to novices. . . . Nevertheless, the words of composers cannot be easily dismissed, especially when so many of their accounts have a great deal in common. (Kratus, p. 378)

In concluding pages, Kratus provided vital perspectives on the role of the teacher:

> In many traditional music-teaching settings, the teacher provides the music, either through model or notation, and students respond in accordance with the teacher's instructions. In a composition classroom, the music comes from the students, and the teacher responds in accordance with the needs of the students and the qualities of their music. In such a changed paradigm, the teacher's role becomes one of establishing guidelines for student composition, fostering a supportive environment, and providing assessment of student work. (pp. 380–381)

The Webster and Kratus work may help teachers to develop strong philosophical and learning theory statements to support expanded attention to composition pedagogy.[6]

Perspectives of Creativity from Psychology

As one might expect, the treatment of "creativity" as found in the modern psychological literature from the middle of the last century is vast and complex and touches multiple disciplines and their interconnections. But if studied carefully, a general understanding of the major facets is possible and can help frame instructional pedagogies for teaching. An excellent perspective on this can be found in the second edition of the *Cambridge Handbook of Creativity* (Kaufman & Sternberg, 2019). It contains the writings of eminent scholars from many related fields and includes chapters on assessment (3), divergent thinking (11), theory (16), classrooms (27), play (28), aesthetics (33) and imagination (34). Each is especially meaningful for pedagogical content in music. A separate, shorter, and perhaps more accessible publication based on much of this same content has been recently published (Kaufman & Sternberg, 2021).

The book by Sawyer (2012) is an especially good summary of the scholarship on creativity. The author's background as a jazz pianist as well as an education and psychology scholar is a strong foundation for this book. His historical structure of three "waves" of research that focus on individual difference and socio-cultural influence[7] is useful as are the many dimensions of the creativity literature identified to help summarize both personal and social attributes. These include individual difference, incremental and consistent hard work, motivation, persistence, risk-taking, self-efficacy, social interaction, collaboration, formal and informal settings for learning, agency, and personal identity, among others.

Saywer also places the historic notions of preparation, incubation, illumination, and verification—often attributed to Wallas (1926)—in context with several other theories that offer more detailed explanations that include problem finding, generating and combining ideas, and network building. Sawyer's chapters on computer simulation, education, and neuroscience might be important for music teachers in building a foundation for their work.

Feldman, Csikszentmihalyi, & Gardner (1994), published a short collection of chapters providing a meaningful perspective on creativity research stressing the role of social and cultural contexts. The opening chapter, co-authored by all three scholars, conceptualized three primary subsystems interacting: the *person* with cognitive and affective processes, the *domain* consisting of organized bodies of knowledge about a specific topic, and the *field* made up of people that arbitrate the structure of the domain such as critics, historians, and curators. This "systems approach" is then explained in detail by each author in subsequent chapters. Although the intention may seem focused on the explanation of the highest levels of creative achievement, the so called "Big-C," this same conceptualization might be applied to work with emerging creative learners.

Much of the writing in the recent psychology literature underscores the power of creativity across an entire schools' curriculum. For example, Gardner's powerful theory of multiple intelligence is important:

> I have defined the creative individual in ways paralleling my definition of intelligence. Specifically, the creative individual is one who regularly solves problems or fashions products in a domain, and whose work is considered both novel and acceptable by knowledgeable members of a field. (Gardner, 2011, p. xxxvi)

This may be of great interest to those on school-wide committees that may be charged with reforming curricula in many disciplines and in bolstering interdisciplinary understanding. Decisions to adopt a school-wide perspective using learning philosophies and theories of learning might be powerful way to support a music teacher's methodology and pedagogy.

Music Educators Perspectives on Composition Pedagogy

Interest among music teachers and researchers in composition pedagogy emerged as early as 1922 with the writings of Satis Coleman (1922). Coleman's ground-breaking work as documented in part by Volk (1996) is worth a careful read. Coleman's work is also noted by Dallman (1970), who wrote one of the very first dissertations on creativity and music composition in schools, predated by several music education studies on the subject during the 1960s. Reviews of these and other historical work by music educators can be found in Running (2008).

Creativity and music education (Sullivan & Willingham, 2002) includes these words in the Foreword by Mihaly Csikszentmihalyi and Lori Custodero for this volume of edited chapters:

> Teaching with creativity as a goal changes the nature of instruction in music classrooms. The editors and contributors of this important book have created a mandate for such change through their collective vision of a new musicianship. Multiple voices, spanning the roles of research, teacher, teacher/educator, and composer/improviser, tell convincing stories regarding how and why music education might be best practiced. (p. xv)

In a similar vein, the chapter by Cohen is notable for its thoughts on musical creativity and teacher training and an early contribution by Wiggins on the importance of children's meaningful music thinking foreshadowed her later work. The book also included a more refined version of Webster's model of creative thinking in music. The Webster model attempted to place divergent and convergent thinking at the core of processes often cited in the creativity literature. Influences of both enabling skills and conditions and product intention and resultant products were stressed. Webster placed the model in context with a more practical twist in a special issue of the *Music Educators Journal*[8] (Webster, 1990) years earlier.

Another collection of important contributions that serve as exemplars for music composition pedagogy can be found in an edited volume by Odena (2012). This collection featured well known contemporary scholars from the United Kingdom including Burnard, M. Barrett, Welch, Seddon, and Odena himself. Included in this collection is a case study (Webster, 2012) focused on teacher-guided revision by of a middle school student working to revise a composition with the aid of a adult composer who specializes in the teaching of composition to children. Here is a portion of the interview with this composer/teacher who in working from an informed pedagogy:

> On the subject of revision specifically, my first approach with young students (and many older ones) tends to be leading them through a process of discovery: what details about the music are they hearing mentally, or playing for me, that have not yet made it onto the page? Do they need more dynamics, articulations, etc. to make the page match what they hear? By posing revision first as the process of realizing their ideas more fully on paper, of making the work more individuated and more "theirs," students realize that revision does not threaten the initial creation. From there I often ask students to imagine, play or sing various possible ways of changing certain elements of the piece. The process is playful and improvisatory rather than corrective. I always let the student be the final judge of which version they like best, but I find that by leading them through this exploratory process and posing multiple

suggestions, they usually arrive at a revision that demonstrates greater musical so-phistication and are able to articulate good reasons for their choices. Once a student is comfortable with this sort of process, I feel I can begin to use diagnostic language to identify possible weaknesses in their work or question larger assumptions about music that their work demonstrates. (Webster, 2012, pp. 107–108)

A major contribution by Burnard in the same year (2012) extended focus beyond the traditional school settings to the "creativies" that mark music-making in our society in a variety of contexts. This book established a convincing argument that creativeness and its understanding is deeply influenced by social and cultural contexts—a theme echoed in much of the writings by creativity scholars from history and today (see Sawyer, 2012). Burnard's own words in the book's introduction made this clear:

I put forward a framework for understanding multiple musical creativities and the development of socially responsive teaching and learning practices. It explores how the field of music in education might relate a little closer to industry experi-ence, at least in awareness of how musicians create in real world practices. Ways for operationalizing an expanded concept of musical creativity in the world of the Internet, e-learning, and virtual fields are discussed. (p. 4)

One might begin their reading of Burnard by considering an earlier chapter in an-other publication (Burnard, 2011) in which she exposes the richness of children's meaning making as composers with descriptions of four case studies of children's con-ception of what composing is. Such study of the voices of people engaged in the doing and teaching of composition adds greatly to our pedagogical understanding.

Teacher/Composer Voice

Reflecting on his time as a student of famed composition pedagogue Nadia Boulanger[9], Ward-Steinman, reinforced the importance of craft/technique in composition (Ward-Steinman, 2011).[10] He noted that counterpoint was deeply valued by Boulanger as was inner hearing and melodic development. But also valued in the mind of Ward-Steinman, as he reflected on his own experience as a composition teacher, was the student's "flame" and "creative spark":

Is craft something separate from the art of composing? Are counterpoint and theory the tools of craft? These tools can indeed by taught, but they are only kin-dling material—the flame must come from within the student. . . . The teacher's job is to help the student express him- or herself musically and nurture whatever artistic spark or talent may be present. (p. 9)

Ward-Steinman also stressed Boulanger's concern for revision and self-criticism of one's work, which was also noted by Williams (2010). Ward-Steinman reflected on time at San Diego State University and his engagement with the famed Comprehensive Musicianship Project (Mark & Madura, pp. 25–28) that encouraged, among other things, *group* composition classes to supplement individual instruction. In this context, Ward-Steinman wrote:

> Why shouldn't all musicians compose, not just the composition majors? I think they should. There are really only three things to be done with music: compose it, play it, or listen to it. Everything else we do in music is a spin-off from this triangle of fundamental activities. It follows, then, that *a musician's training should emphasize equally all three activities*, which is the underlying philosophy of comprehensive musicianship. [italics added, p. 17]

Content analysis studies of student and teacher interactions in music composition study are remarkably rare. M. Barrett (2006) used a case study approach to investigate composition instruction between an eminent teacher/composer and a student composer. Video recordings were captured for a series of lessons and interviews conducted to probe the findings. Twelve teaching strategies were identified (pp. 201–202) wherein the teacher:

1. extended thinking, provided possibilities
2. referenced work to and beyond the tradition (signposting)
3. set parameters for identity as a composer
4. provoked the student to describe and explain
5. questioned purpose, probed intention
6. shifted back and forth between micro and macro levels
7. provided multiple alternatives from analysis of student work
8. prompted the student to engage in self-analysis
9. encouraged goal-setting and task identification
10. engaged in joint problem finding and problem solving
11. provided reassurance
12. gave license to change

The article included detailed transcriptions of interviews between teacher and student and themes were identified—all helpful for developing a perspective on pedagogy. M. Barrett and Gromko (2007) published a similar case study the following year.

A Socratic dialogue between Katherine Strand and Libby Larsen on music, musical experience in American culture, and music education was particularly meaningful (Strand & Larsen, 2011). This dialog revealed important aspects of music education from the vantage point of a noted composer, including the meaningful epigraph that starts this chapter. Strand is a music education professor and Larsen a professional composer with a strong interest in music education. Among the many topics covered were Larsen's views on the mismatch between music and its teaching in schools, the scope of reach to all students, and culturally relevant teaching approaches.

> I firmly believe we are at a crossroads in music and we have got to take a close look at how we prepare future music teachers. We use methodologies for codifying/notating

rhythmic motion that were developed in another time. . . . We have built our ideas about theory, composition, and music education on the parameters derived from a narrow band of Western classical music. Now we must rethink our theoretical systems based on how we truly hear each other if we wish to regain our relevance. (pp. 58–59)

Preparing teachers to help children think creatively in sound was another topic.

I was offered a commission to compose a work for a high school band program. In talking with the director of the ensemble, I asked if every kid in the band could be part of the process and compose along with me. He was intrigued to build a process that was both open and structured at the same time—a project in which his kids could practice their creativity within the sphere of their technical abilities. So I borrowed a culturally known form of an egg carton (because we all know what cartons are) along with poetry and imagery about the moon. I created a musical work in this structure, with nine sections mine and eight sections blank. The band members had to re-organize themselves into small groups to fill in the empty sections with their own music, working through the basic elements of music: pitch, motion, architecture, and emotional impact, in whatever way they chose. They simply had to invent a piece that flowed in the carton structure. The only direction I gave them was that they had to be able to explain their choices for pitch, motion, architecture, and emotional impact. It worked really well. (pp. 63–64)

Application Exemplars

This second section features several writings that include practical strategies for teaching composition to beginning learners and are selected to be matches for the changing landscape of music pedagogy today. Historical books from the latter twentieth century are included, followed by recent publications of major significance.

Historical Landmark Books

The noted Canadian composer, writer, and educator, R. Murray Schafer, had a passion for teaching music. Starting in 1965, Schafer began writing short "booklets" that captured that passion. Five were created, published separately, then pulled together in a combined volume in 1976 that is referenced here (Schafer, 1976). Growing up in school, Schafer described his personal experience with formal music education as a troubled one; the set of teaching strategies and suggested approaches found in these booklets presumably might have been preferred. For example, the first booklet, *The Composer in the Classroom*, is based on dialogs Schafer had with elementary and secondary students on topics like music's definition, what a composer does, and how music is formed. The author described experiments with sounds played by the students to encourage discussions and used music improvisational exercises like strategies used by lecturer/ writer Nachmanovitch (1990) today.

Another booklet experimented with *Ear Cleaning* exercises that were Shafer's approach to aural skills. Music elements such as melody, silence, texture, and timbre were used in experiments and complete "soundscape" compositions were created. In the booklet, *When Words Sing*, experiments with vocal sounds are described in some detail, together with graphic scores of created compositions. Consciousness of the sonic landscape was stressed. The collection of booklets ends with a set of statements about music education reimagined. Fifty years later, these readings still feel fresh and stimulating.

Books by (Paynter & Aston, 1970) and (Paynter, 1992) revealed wisdom about music and its teaching by way of creative thinking in sound . They share Schafer's approach to project description and graphic displays. Paynter and Aston were college teaching colleagues and developed *Sound and Silence* as an extension of their beliefs as educators. A conceptual introduction is followed by 36 projects sequenced by difficulty and based on contemporary music of the time. They are designed for learners at a variety of levels, and many involve found objects in nature. For example, Project 11 starts with the isolation of a found object in nature, a study of its structure, a drawing of the object, and its instantiation in sound with attention to patterns; collaborative work is encouraged and a musical score of some sort was expected. Study of others' music that follow a similar approach was encouraged. The authors held sacred the interaction of sound and silence:

> It is in ways like this, developed over several lesson periods, that we would aim to give children and young people a genuine experience of what music is really about; to help them feel its expressive power and enable them to use it to say something. (Paynter & Aston, 1970, p. 23)

Paynter's second book (Paynter, 1992), some 20 years later, upped the ante a bit in terms of complexity and is organized around 16 projects with multiple parts and a set of concluding teaching points. One of the interesting aspects of many projects in each book was the use of a concrete object and its design to organize a composition. A favorite from *Sound and Structure* is Project 8, which uses the structure of a pyramid as a focus of design " . . . by putting musical sounds together that resembles as closely as possible the way in which stones were put together to make the ancient Egyptian pyramids" (p. 97). A building up of complex textures is imagined, perhaps by using cornerstones as guides and filling in the rest layer by layer. Can the layers be made to sound different but still be perceived as related layers? Might there be something to be done with the layers to support a volcanic eruption through the layers? Paynter relies on the imagination to fathom a kind of implied motion—a sense of movement in time but in a restricted space. These ideas are presented as starting points for structure and are not meant to be programmatic renderings of what a pyramid might sound like per se. The student is really creating a kind of private grammar of sounds and textures in an effort to create a personal voice. Again, the technical is married to an imaginative spark of uniqueness. Interestingly, traditional notation is used often to demonstrate how this might be crafted—a difference between Schafer and Paynter.

Modern Landmark Books

The 21st century began in a strong way for exemplars that inspire composition peda-gogy. Hickey's important collection of writings (Hickey, 2003) celebrated a gathering of national and international scholars on the topic of why and how to teach music compo-sition. In terms of foundational work, M. Barrett's opening chapter (M. Barrett, 2003) on children's meaning-making through composition is predictive of Burnard's (2011) work. Moore's chapter (Moore, 2003) on the nature of style and the music experience and the turn to the world of digital realizations of music underscores the vignettes of teachers and student vignettes portrayed in the opening of the current chapter. Hickey's own chapter (2003) in this edited edition adds perspectives to Amabile's componen-tial model of creativity and its relation to composition in schools; Hickey's conceptual scheme for musical composition curriculum, endorsement of consensual assessment, and sequential notions for teaching composition would appear again in the author's important 2012 book (Hickey, 2012). Espeland and Wiggins offered chapters on com-position processes featuring models[11] important to consider. Espeland also noted the importance of considering children's composition processes as not always identical with those of adults and Wiggins[12] underscored the vital importance of social context. Stauffer and Gromko each provided glimpses into the importance of student voice in composition and provide exemplars for student engagement. Finally, the chapters contributed by Webster, Stephens, Reese, and Younker represented an important col-lection of exemplars on how teachers might best assess student composition in order to encourage growth.

The work of the writing team of Kaschub and Smith, taken separately and together, represents an impressive number of exemplars for composition pedagogy. *Minds on Music Composition for Creative and Critical Thinking* (Kaschub & Smith, 2009) is noted here because of its blending of conceptual frames and examples for practical application organized by level of instruction. Many of the conceptual bases explained elsewhere in this chapter are found in the first two parts of this book in expanded form and many newer ones added. Sections on preparing for composing and composing communities were both notable.

Beginning with Part III, several exemplars for working with various levels of ed-ucation were presented. Sample lessons were proposed and accompanying etudes for teachers in preparation or in-service were included. Touchpoint summaries were used as well as teaching scenarios. In suggesting lessons, a balance was made between prescriptive versus vague descriptions. Much is left to the creative teacher to craft approaches that fit student and teacher circumstances. The last chapter focused on the establishment of a unified composition program in schools that continues in an organ-ized way across grades.

Designed with a similar intent to Kaschub and Smith, Hickey (2012) offered support of composition pedagogy with an "Issues" chapter that should be required reading for all those interested in this topic. Presented were reasons for open versus closed composi-tion assignments, group versus individual composition, traditional notation versus less traditional, and practical approaches to technology use and assessment. Composition in ensembles was celebrated. What followed are chapters on listening and exploration of sound with suggested activities such as the use of listening journals. A special approach using an innovative curriculum model was also included.

A chapter on getting started with composition with various prompts that draw on learners' music experiences provided moving and genuine circumstances for why one writes music. Examples of activities were offered that touch on related arts, soundscapes, personal memories, and many more. A concluding chapter also offered a composition program across grades as an essential core of the music program.

A few years later, two volumes were published that offered a treasure trove of exemplars for band, orchestra, and choir (Randles & Stringham, 2013; Kerchner, Strand, & DiOrio, 2016). Over 40 lessons across both books are portrayed and documented by nationally known researchers and teachers. The editors chose introductory, conceptual chapters with multiple references that set the stage for coming applications. All sample lessons are clearly described, and all come from real practice in today's school ensembles.

Riley (2016) documented composition activities internationally. Students from China, Ireland, Mexico and the United States were represented improvising and composing music deeply influenced by their own social contexts. Children interviewed and observed creating underscored the notions of cooperative learning and community music-making. The author introduced the children and their imaginations—planning, making, refining, and presenting their music. Concluding chapters contextualized the children's work and provide powerful exemplars that fit well for written standards in many countries.

Considered as a whole, the exemplars on application noted here are remarkable. From the early writings of Schafer and Paynter to the most current publications by Hickey, Kaschub, and Smith, and Randles and colleagues, the case has never been stronger for developing composition pedagogies in PreK–12 education.

Concluding Thoughts

Throughout the history of writings that have addressed the pedagogy of composition, the notion of blending knowledge and skills of music with creative opportunities for learners to create their own music with teacher guidance and encouragement seems to be clear. This rather simple but profoundly important way to help construct a pedagogy of composition (or any creative endeavor) that can be justified by philosophical and learning theory principles is worthy of consideration. The vignettes of teachers and learners in the opening of this chapter should not be considered as unusual but central to how we all should be thinking about music teaching and learning.

Such pedagogical thinking may require some recalibration of time-honored traditional approaches, a dedication to learning new music teaching competencies, and some risk-taking and willingness to give up control—characteristics often cited as important attributes for a contemporary teacher working in todays' schools. Doing so, by nearly all accounts, leads to rather amazing results that do not sacrifice but deeply enhance our hopes for significant musical understanding across multiple music styles and musical traditions.

One final thought, one that might have occurred to the reader after considering this chapter and the many others in this Handbook: Those of us in charge of music teacher preparation need desperately to recalibrate what we do. We too ought to be risk-takers and be willing to give up some control in order to prepare our music teachers for the social and cultural context that is today and will undoubtably be tomorrow. It is time to make this happen.

> "What, now, is the real mission of music education in America?"—Libby Larsen
>
> (Strand & Larsen, 2011, p. 64)

Notes

1. One interesting accounting of learning theories: https://www.educationcorner.com/learning-theories-in-education/
2. In fact, the choice of the term "methods course" may well be avoided by many recent scholars in teacher preparation since it is so often associated with static views of teaching not informed by contemporary philosophy and theories of learning dedicated to today's youth and their diverse musical cultures.
3. One listing of these can be found at https://pacificu.libguides.com/c.php?g=1023491&p=7535131
4. A study of such books (i.e., Russo & Stevenson, 2012) may be useful for clues to PreK–12 curricular.
5. Another exemplar of composers' perspectives can be found in Lapidaki (2007).
6. Also of interest is the study by Schultz (2000) on the role of John Dewey's philosophical perspective in terms of compositional pedagogy.
7. The socio-cultural influence on contemporary work on creativeness in education and the arts is underscored by Amabile (1983) and work on consensual assessment which, in turn, has implications for how teachers can approach evaluating creative work in music (Hickey, 2001).
8. In addition to this issue, the March 2016 special issue of *Music Educators Journal* (Kaschub, 2016) contains important articles by Webster, Kaschub, & Smith, Deemer, Stringham, Deutsch, Kratus, Strand, and Jorgensen that help to ground composition pedagogy.
9. Bomberger (1998) provided additional accounts of Boulanger's pedagogy.
10. Biró (2020) reflected more recently on the practice of teaching composition in a pluralistic world with group and individual lessons, music analysis, performance, and the use of technology.
11. In addition to the models of composition process offered by Webster, Hickey, Wiggins, and Espeland, also consider the one presented by Sloboda (1986, p. 119, & 2001).

12. Wiggins's volume (2015) on teaching for musical understanding is another exemplar for serious study, providing numerous examples of work with children withing the frame of a constructivist philosophy.

REFERENCES

Abrahams, F. (2005). The application of critical pedagogy to music teaching and learning: A literature review. *Update: Applications of Research in Music Education, 23*(2), 12–22. https://doi.org/10.1177/87551233050230020103

Abril, C. R., & Gault, B. M. (2016). *Teaching general music: Approaches, issues, and viewpoints.* Oxford University Press. https://doi.org/10.1093/acprof:oso/9780199328093.001.0001

Allsup, R. E. (2016). *Remixing the classroom: Toward an open philosophy of music education.* Indiana University Press.

Amabile, T. (1983). *The social psychology of creativity.* Springer-Verlag.

Anderson, W. M., & Campbell, P. S. (2011). *Multicultural perspectives in music education* (3rd ed.). Rowan & Littlefield.

Bamberger, J. S. (2013). *Discovering the musical mind: A view of creativity as learning.* Oxford University Press.

Barrett, J. (2001). Interdisciplinary work and musical integrity. *Music Educators Journal, 87*(5), 27–31. https://doi.org/10.2307/3399705

Barrett, J. & Webster, P. (2014). *The musical experience: Rethinking music teaching and learning.* Oxford University Press. https://doi.org/10.1093/acprof:oso/9780199363032.001.0001

Barrett, M. (2006). "Creative collaboration": An "eminence" study of teaching and learning in music composition. *Psychology of Music, 34*(2), 195–218. https://doi.org/10.1177/0305735606061852

Barrett, M. S., & Gromko, J. E. (2007). Provoking the muse: A case study of teaching and learning in music composition. *Psychology of Music, 35*(2), 213–230. https://doi.org/10.1177/0305735607070305

Bauer, W. (2020). *Music learning today: Digital pedagogy for creating, performing, and responding to music.* (2nd ed.). Oxford University Press.

Biró, D. P. (2020). The practice of teaching composition. *Revista Vórtex, 8*(1), 1–12.

Bomberger, E. D. (1998). Rheinberger, Boulanger, and the art of teaching composition. *Journal of Music Theory Pedagogy, 12*, 53–64.

Bowman, W., & Frega, A. (2012). What should the music education profession expect of philosophy? In W. Bowman & A. Frega (Eds.), *The Oxford handbook of philosophy in music education* (pp. 17–36). Oxford University Press. https://doi.org/10.1093/oxfordhb/9780195394733.013.0002

Brophy, T. S. (Ed.) (2019). *The Oxford handbook of assessment policy and practice in music education.* Volume 1. Oxford University Press.

Burnard, P. (2006). Understanding children's meaning-making as composers. In *Musical creativity* (pp. 127-149). Psychology Press.

Clauhs, M., Powell, B., & Clements, A. C. (2020). *Popular music pedagogies: A practical guide for music teachers.* Routledge.

Coleman, S. N. (1922). *Creative music for children.* G. P. Putnam's Sons.

Colwell, R. (2010). Roles of direct instruction, critical thinking, and transfer in the design of curriculum for music learning. In R. Colwell & P. Webster (Eds.), *MENC handbook of research on music learning* (pp. 35–83). Oxford University Press.

Dallman, R. M. (1970). A survey of creativity in music through composition in the elementary schools of Colorado (Ed.D). Available from ProQuest Dissertations & Theses Global. (302442364)

Dobson, M. C., & Pitts, S. E. (2011). Classical cult or learning community? exploring new audience members' social and musical responses to first-time concert attendance. *Null*, *20*(3), 353–383. https://doi.org/10.1080/17411912.2011.641717

Dorfman, J. (2013). *Theory and practice of technology-based music instruction* (2nd ed.). Oxford University Press.

Elliott, D. J. & Silverman, M. (2014). *Music matters: A philosophy of music education*. Oxford University Press.

Feldman, D. H., Csikszentmihalyi, M., & Gardner, H. (1994). *Changing the world: A framework for the study of creativity*. Praeger.

Freedman, B. (2013). *Teaching music through composition a curriculum using technology*. Oxford University Press.

Fumerton, R. (2009). *Epistemology*. John Wiley & Sons.

Gardner, H. (2011). *Frames of mind the theory of multiple intelligences* (3rd ed.). Basic Books.

Green, L. (2008). *Music, informal learning and the school: A new classroom pedagogy*. Ashgate.

Greher, G. R., & Burton, S. L. (2021). *Creative music making at your fingertips: A mobile technology guide for music educators*. Oxford University Press.

Hebert, E. A. (2001). *The power of portfolios: What children can teach us about learning and assessment*. Jossey-Bass.

Hickey, M. (2001). An application of Amabile's consensual assessment technique for rating the creativity of children's musical compositions. *Journal of Research in Music Education*, *49*(3), 234–244.

Hickey, M. (Ed.). (2003). *Why and how to teach music composition: A new horizon for music education*. MENC: The National Association for Music Education.

Hickey, M. (2012). *Music outside the lines: Ideas for composing in K–12 music classrooms*. Oxford University Press.

Jorgensen, E. R. (2003). *Transforming music education*. Indiana University Press.

Kaschub, M. (Ed.). (2016). Special focus: Composition. *Music Educators Journal*, *102*(3), 1–74.

Kaschub, M., & Smith, J. (2009). *Minds on music: Composition for creative and critical thinking*. Rowman & Littlefield Education.

Kaufman, J. C., & Sternberg, R. J. (2019). *The Cambridge handbook of creativity*. Cambridge University Press.

Kaufman, J. C., & Sternberg, R. J. (2021). *Creativity: An introduction*. Cambridge University Press.

Kerchner, J. L. (2013). *Music across the senses: Listening, learning, and making meaning*. Oxford University Press. https://doi.org/10.1093/acprof:oso/9780199967612.001.0001

Kerchner, J. L., Strand, K., & DiOrio, D. (2016). *Musicianship: Composing in choir*. GIA Publications.

Kratus, J. (2012). Nurturing the songcatchers: Philosophical issues in the teaching of music composition. In W. Bowman & A. Frega (Eds.), *The Oxford handbook of philosophy in music education* (pp. 367–385). Oxford University Press. https://doi.org/10.1093/oxfordhb/9780195394733.013.0020

Lapidaki, E. (2007). Learning from masters of music creativity: Shaping compositional experiences in music education. *Philosophy of Music Education Review*, *15*(2), 93–117. https://doi.org/10.2979/PME.2007.15.2.93

Lewis, J. (2020). How children listen: Multimodality and its implications for K–12 music education and music teacher education. *Null, 22*(4), 373–387. https//doi.org/10.1080/14613808.2020.1781804

Lind, V. R., & McKoy, C. (2016). *Culturally responsive teaching in music education: From understanding to application.* Routledge. https://doi.org/10.4324/9781315747279

Mark, M. L., & Madura, P. D. (2014). *Contemporary music education.* Schirmer Cengage Learning.

Murphy, P. (2008) Defining pedagogy. In K. Hall, P. Murphy, & J. Soler (Eds.), *Pedagogy and practice: Culture and identities* (pp. 28–39). Sage.

Nachmanovitch, S. (1990). *Free play: Improvisation in life and art.* Putnam.

Odena, O. (2012). *Musical creativity: Insights from music education research: Insights from music education research.* Taylor & Francis Group.

Paynter, J. (1992). *Sound & structure.* Cambridge University Press.

Paynter, J., & Aston, P. (1970). *Sound and silence: Classroom projects in creative music.* Cambridge UP.

Randles, C., & Stringham, D. (Eds.). (2013). *Musicianship: Composing in band and orchestra.* GIA.

Reimer, B. (2022). *A philosophy of music education* (3rd ed.). SUNY Press. (Original work published 2003, Prentice-Hall.)

Riley, P. E. (2016). *Creating music: What children from around the world can teach us.* Rowman & Littlefield.

Running, D. J. (2008). Creativity research in music education: A review (1980–2005). *Update: Applications of Research in Music Education, 27*(1), 41–48. https://doi.org/10.1177/8755123308322280

Russo W. Ainis J. & Stevenson D. (19881983). *Composing music: a new approach.* University of Chicago Press.

Ruthmann, A., & Mantie, R. (Eds.). (2017). *The Oxford handbook of technology and music education.* Oxford University Press.

Sawyer, R. K. (2011). *Structure and improvisation in creative teaching.* Cambridge University Press.

Sawyer, R. K. (2012). *Explaining creativity: The science of human innovation* (2nd ed.). Oxford University Press.

Schafer, R. M. (1976). *Creative music education: A handbook for the modern music teacher.* Schirmer Books.

Schmidt, P., & Colwell, R. (2017). *Policy and the political life of music education.* Oxford University Press.

Schultz, M. S. H. (2000). *A study to investigate John Dewey's process of inquiry and the development of an inquiry-based method for teaching composition to middle school music students* (D.M.A.). Available from ProQuest Dissertations & Theses Global. (304673539).

Senyshyn, Y., & O'Neill, S. A. (2011). How learning theories shape our understanding of music learners. In R. Colwell & P. Webster (Eds.), *MENC handbook of research on music learning* (pp. 3–34). Oxford University Press.

Sloboda, J. A. (1986). *The musical mind: The cognitive psychology of music.* Oxford University Press. https://doi.org/10.1093/acprof:oso/9780198521280.001.0001

Strand, K., & Larsen, L. (2011). A socratic dialogue with Libby Larsen on music, musical experience in American culture, and music education. *Philosophy of Music Education Review, 19*(1), 52–66. https://doi.org/10.2979/philmusieducrevi.19.1.52

Sullivan, Timothy, & Willingham, L. (Eds.). (2002). *Creativity and music education.* Canadian Music Educators' Association.

Taetle, L., & Cutietta, R. (2002). Learning theories as roots of current musical practice and research. In R. Colwell & C. Richardson (Eds.), *The new handbook of research on music teaching and learning: A project of the music educators national conference* (pp. 279–298). Oxford University Press.

Volk, T. M. (1996). Satis Coleman's "creative music." *Music Educators Journal, 82*(6), 31–47. https://doi.org/10.2307/3398949

Wallas, G. (1926). *The art of thought.* Harcourt, Brace, and Company.

Ward-Steinman, D. (2011). On composing: Doing it, teaching it, living it. *Philosophy of Music Education Review, 19*(1), 5–23. https://doi.org/10.2979/philmusieducrevi.19.1.5

Webster, P. R. (1990). Creativity as creative thinking. *Music Educators Journal, 76*(9), 22–28. https://doi.org/10.2307/3401073

Webster, P. R. (2010). Construction of music learning. In R. Colwell & P. Webster (Eds.), *MENC handbook of research on music learning* (pp. 35–83). Oxford University Press.

Webster, P. R. (2012). Towards pedagogies of revision: Guiding a student's music composition. In O. Odena (Ed.), *Musical creativity: Insights from music education research: Insights from music education research* (pp. 93–112). Taylor & Francis Group.

Webster, P. R. (2014). 2014 Senior researcher award acceptance address: Cautious optimism for the future of research in music teaching and learning. *Journal of Research in Music Education, 62*(3), 203–214.

Williams, B. J. (2010). *Music composition pedagogy: A history, philosophy and guide* (Doctoral dissertation, The Ohio State University).

Williams, D. A., & Kladder, J. R. (2019). *The learner-centered music classroom: Models and possibilities.* Routledge.

Williams, D. B. (2012). The non-traditional music student in secondary schools of the United States: Engaging non-participant students in creative music activities through technology. *Journal of Music, Technology & Education, 4*(2), 131–147. https://doi.org/10.1386/jmte.4.2-3.131_1

Williams, D., & Webster, P. (2023). *Experiencing music technology* (4th ed.). Oxford University Press.

Wiggins, J. (2015). *Teaching for musical understanding.* Oxford University Press.

CHAPTER 4

VOCABULARIES OF GENIUS AND DILEMMAS OF PEDAGOGY

Originality, Imagination, and Creativity

NEIL THOMAS SMITH

THERE is little sign of the narrative of genius abating in popular culture, particularly in the world of publishing. If swathes of books are to be believed, its presence is felt in the military, the arts, science, sports, as well as amongst animals, places, and nations. Indeed, there appears to be a renewed swell of genius in the shape of tech entrepreneurs, most notably around such figures as Steve Jobs. Genius in music education may appear like the preserve of a few gifted individuals and prodigies (Sternberg & Davidson, 2005). Yet, it is argued here that the concept of genius is in fact part of a network of ideas—a "vocabulary" (Lyas, 1998, p. 168)—that is deeply embedded at all levels of education. This network includes terms such as imagination, creativity, and the canon. After all, there are few greater compliments than to say that a piece is original and few qualities that are sought as keenly by many professional artists. As argued below, originality is for school students an implicit ideal to strive toward, while the means of getting there are hotly debated. In tertiary studies there is a more obvious sense of duty to train the next generation of artists and originality begins to be felt as an increasingly explicit criterion.

That originality, creativity, and imagination comprise a network of meanings is attested to by numerous authors. Timothy Gould argues that the "rise to theoretical pre-eminence of the concept of genius is inseparable from [a] demand for originality" (1998, p. 159); while Colin A. Lyas states that the "genius vocabulary" is "related" to the vocabularies of "creativity" and "originality" (1998, p. 168). Wordsworth's contention that "[g]enius is the introduction of a new"—presumably original—"element into the intellectual universe" is matched by the view of Vlad P. Glăveanu and James C. Kaufman who write that "to create means to bring new ideas or things into existence." The latter authors believe that the "older incarnations" of the idea of creativity can be found in "genius, talent, invention discovery and imagination" (2019, p. 9). Lucy Green goes further in connecting the notation of classroom creativity with history, contending that the privileging of notated music "occurs in the celebration of the composer's genius and of the music's transcendent greatness" (1997, p. 82). This means that it is difficult to tackle any one of these terms in isolation and that all are culturally and historically specific ways of understanding human creativity.

That this is of relevance to the classroom setting throughout a child's education must be established. For it would be an ambitious educator indeed who expected composition students to show "genius" or wholly original contributions to their field. Assessment criteria rarely mention originality explicitly, but its partners "creativity" and "imagination" appear regularly. In many ways they are still at the heart of composition pedagogy. Two brief but entirely typical examples of assessment rubrics from the UK are informative here. The Scottish Qualifications Authority (SQA) states that in their Advanced Higher course (taken at the end of high school), pupils should experiment and use a "range of music concepts and compositional methods in sophisticated and creative ways to develop, refine and create original music" (Scottish Qualifications Authority, 2013). "Original" here refers more to the music not having existed previously rather than a significant contribution to its field but evidently "creative" requires more than this. The AQA A-Level scheme of assessment uses similar vocabulary in the criteria for its highest marks column, where "musical elements are used with flair and imagination" and "imaginative use of the brief" is praised (AQA, n.d.). Genius may not feature, but its vocabularies remain in some of the most important policy documents that teachers and students use to define their school music activities.

This chapter is split into two sections, the first offering a brief history of genius and its critiques, the second exploring how certain "dilemmas" of pedagogy[1] can be seen to relate back to these same debates. The former considers the presence of vocabularies of genius in both scholarship and practice, with a particular emphasis on literature.[2] As Glăveanu and Kaufman also argue, a historical overview is vital to understand where and when the foundations of our understanding of artistic practice were laid so that they can "paradoxically, shed light on the future" (2019, p. 21). The genius vocabularies will be seen as historically contingent rather than *how it must be*.

In the second half of the chapter it is argued that the best way to achieve creativity and originality is still very much a contested issue in contemporary education, as demonstrated by the three "dilemmas" that are explored with reference to composition: imparting knowledge versus inspiring creativity; flexible canons versus destroying them altogether; and genre hierarchies.[3] It is also maintained that the classroom is a key site in the continued perpetuation of ideas of what creativity means and how it should be approached. Normative constructs—who "should" be seen to compose and what music they "should" write—act in a similar and related way to the "[g]endered musical meanings" that Green identifies as "not only handed down through history" but persisting "in the organization of musical production and reception in present-day society at large" and "re-enacted daily in the life of the music classroom" (1997, p. 229).

A Short History of Genius

The first important thing to understand about the concept of genius is that it has a history. Indeed, Laura C. Ball describes a long history of use that has led to it acquiring "multiple meanings over time, each describing vastly different phenomena" (2014, p. 4). An early-modern monk or nun, preparing devotional music for their religious establishments, would likely not talk of their work as a unique expression of their individual essence but an attempt to praise God within a particular tradition (Hanchett Hanson, 2015, p. 2).[4] Originality, therefore, is the result of particular cultural currents and not a necessary way of understanding human creative activity. For example, there is a strong argument to be made that the cult of genius has links with the rise of capitalism: it masks structural inequalities by positing a level playing field and relies on modern conceptions of individualism. Marcia Citron sees the nineteenth-century conceptions of creativity celebrating "individual achievement, including economic fulfillment, in a climate of free enterprise" (1993, p. 201), ideas that are vital to capitalist expansion.

Humanization of Creativity

Vlad P. Glăveanu and James C. Kaufman argue that there is something of a standard historical narrative around the history of genius, with its emergence in the Renaissance, solidification in the Enlightenment, and take-off with Romanticism (2019). For Oli Mould the critical juncture for the term "creativity" comes in the Enlightenment. Before this, the "power" of the creative process had been "beyond human agency," usually the result of some kind of divine intervention, or at least devoted to its service (2018, p. 11). The growth of humanism allowed a different perspective to emerge: that humans themselves might be responsible for their own powerful acts of creativity. Christine Battersby states that the 18th century gave rise to the belief that "[i]t was creativity, not reason or talent, that made man resemble god" while genius "was supposed to make the Art (with a capital 'A') that European civilization produced different from the 'crafts' (with a small 'c') produced by primitives and other lesser human types" (1989, p. 3). Genius and originality were, therefore, created as powerful tools of distinction, creating hierarchies between genres and freezing out those without economic means.

The humanization of creativity did not lead to a sense that just anyone could be an original, rather this is the beginning of the cult of genius that continues to hold significant sway on musical imaginaries. Indeed, the 18th century saw a change in meaning of "genius" as a spirit possessed, potentially, by all to genius as the precious preserve of a few.[5] Mihaly Csikszentmihalyi argues that this idea persists today, with geniuses being seen as the "lucky heir to some unknown strand of DNA that made them in some respects super-human" (2014, p. 534). As seventeenth-century English poet John Dryden comments, in eminently quotable fashion, "[g]enius must be born and never can be taught" (1885, p. 60). For those without the special strand there is, it seems, little to be done.[6]

Genius and Aesthetics

Kant and Hegel, who produced some of the most influential works in aesthetics during the 18th and 19th centuries, advanced this attitude to the fine arts and to the special status of genius. Kant states that "fine arts must necessarily be regarded as arts of genius," while genius is the "innate productive faculty of the artist" rather than following some kind of scientific rule (2007, p. 136). He also argues that undirected genius is not enough and that "[g]enius can only furnish rich material for products of beautiful art; its execution and form require talent cultivated in the schools [. . .]" (2007, p. 115). The connections between genius and the privilege of training and education, therefore, are sown early on. Richard T. Eldridge believes that Kant has had a lasting influence, stating that "[f]or generations, teachers of poetry painting, music, acting, and dance have worked in this way, hoping for that magical moment when precursor work is all at once fully internalized, taken up, and actively transformed by the student as nascent successor" (2014, p. 120). This is the hope for the pastiche composition exercises that persist in much music education.

Hegel shares some common ground with Kant but adds that the context of the work of art, as well as the conscious work of the artist, is paramount. For Hegel, the work of art relates to something other than the subjective creativity of the artist genius. Artistic content, in the words of Eldridge, must "represent and express attitudes toward what a significant number of people who share a significant stretch of culture most deeply care about in common: romantic love, honor, family" (2014, p. 121). This brief comparison of Kant and Hegel brings forth a key tension in conceptions of genius, labeled by Thomas McFarland the "originality paradox," which concerns the relationship between the individual genius and wider culture and tradition (1974): are the "great masters" sustenance for the artist, or a debilitating inheritance? That the debate persisted is demonstrated by T. S. Eliot's "Tradition and the Individual Talent," written in 1919 (1932), and debates around the "Anxiety of Influence" (see Straus, 1991, and Whittall, 2003).

The Romantic Individualist

By the late 19th century, the figure of the towering genius taming the powers of their rampant creative impulses becomes the dominant image of the romantic artist. Samuel Taylor Coleridge argues that poetry is the shaping of "deep feeling" in words with a "sense of novelty and freshness" (1906, p. 166); Percy Bysshe Shelley describes inspiration as "original purity and force," directed by "labor and study," thereby taking a middle road between the individual and tradition (1991, p. 228). Composers became more autonomous during this period, relying less on noble patronage, at the same time as the modern notion of the autonomous individual was cemented.[7] This is no coincidence if the aforementioned connections between genius and capitalism are taken seriously. At the same time, "geniuses were deemed more individual than ordinary human beings, less likely to think and act by established conventions and norms, genuinely original and soft tone eccentric, or even mad" (Chaplin & McMahon, 2016, p. 3). For an intriguing number, becoming a composer was in itself a kind of rebellion, one against the wishes of their artisan or professional families (Plantinga, 1984, p. 5). The romantic notions of the artist present a very different beast from the composer apprentice learning a particular musical language through careful imitation of exemplars. Rather, the creative process is one of passion and the violent eruption of creative energy, finding its complete expression in the "Promethean" figure of Beethoven (Plantinga, 1984, p. 16).

Individualism certainly continued into the 20th century, as did the sense of the past as a burden, most notably theorized by Frankfurt School philosopher Theodor W. Adorno. For him, being a composer meant engaging with the contemporary state of the "musical material" and is, therefore, dependent on the state of this material at a particular time. Importantly, Adorno does not expect artists to reproduce the past but to engage with it, to tease out its contradictions, in order to find some kind of artistic truth. This leads to statements such as: "Art must turn against itself, in opposition to its own concept, and thus become uncertain of itself, right into its innermost fiber" (1997, p. 2). This is no cozy relationship with the past but a constant self-questioning and struggle. The results of this, alongside the philosopher's critique of what he saw as the dehumanizing effects of popular culture, are some true artistic heroes and villains in his writings (Mould, 2018, p. 16).

The Artistic Hero

The artist hero, therefore, continues with the advent of modernism, though now engaging—or even vanquishing—the titanic forces of history and, in some conceptions, holding fast to the idea of musical progress. In music, key figures often towed a perilous line between narratives of revolutionary fresh starts and statements that encouraged a view of them as the next in a line of canonic figures. Arnold Schoenberg is particularly revealing in this respect, as is French composer Pierre Boulez. The former is well known for stating that his serial technique—a radical, though not unprepared, break with traditional compositional method—would "ensure the dominance of German music for the next hundred years" (in Danuser, 2004, p. 280). He looked to the future, therefore, but he was also keen to point out continuity with great figures of German art, such as Bach and Brahms.[8] Boulez famously called for the destruction of the opera houses as inert bastions of tradition, though he quickly became a cornerstone of French bourgeois society.

Genius and Myth

Originality and genius, therefore, are an inheritance from centuries of artistic practice and, to some extent, artistic myth-making. Conflicting discourses of revolutionary new ideas and century-old artistic lineages are fused together, with the idea of the canon figuring extensively. Such discourses have not gone uncontested, though it took until the late 20th century for scholars to problematize these notions in depth. These more recent positions will be the focus of the next section. Before moving on, however, it is important to highlight the cultural specificity of this historical narrative of genius. It is, after all "fundamentally Western and, to a large extent, European and American." Control over what constitutes creativity is a power to potentially dismiss whole cultures of artistic practice. Western societies "deliberately depicted other people and other cultures as noncreative, traditional, or stuck in time" (Glăveanu & Kaufman, 2019, p. 14). Creativity as a "power" to be conferred may no longer be said to come from God but its application is still highly unequal.

Critiques of Genius

While the latter part of the 20th century saw many critiques of genius, it is notable how many of its trappings are still taken for granted in, particularly classical, music practice. The figure of the composer, or the "maestro" conductor, still looms large, both in the consumption and marketing of classical music and in the portrayal of—even contemporary—musicians. So, while this section focuses on critiques of genius, it is worth bearing in mind the persistence of ideas from the 19th century. In 1994 Tia DeNora and Hugh Mehan argued that the "ideology of genius . . . remains, in spite of attempts to deconstruct, powerful and persuasive" (p. 167). There have only recently been serious efforts to open up what kind of person the composer might be, resulting in various schemes championing women and composers of color, yet questioning of the value of individual creative energy that the composer represents has had far less coverage.

The Need for Originality

Starting with the more recent manifestation of genius, that within modernist discourses, there has been criticism from a number of angles that questions its originary expression and its relationship with history. In 1978 Rosalind Krauss famously railed against the apparent omnipresence of the "grid" in contemporary visual art (1985), pointing to its presence in a diverse range of artists: Mondriaan, Sol de Witt, Josef Albers, Agnes Martin, etc.[9] The implication is that the grid is almost a placeholder for original artistic contribution, even when so many artists make use of it. At the same time, more recent research on the rituals of acceptance into creative fields—and their poor representation of society—have pointed to the various, supposedly non-artistic, skills and networks required for success as an artist in contemporary society (El-Ghadban, 2009; Smith & Thwaites, 2017; Brook, O'Brien, & Taylor, 2020).

The concept of genius received further criticism from currents often understood as postmodern: collage, the mixing of high and low art, and interdisciplinary practice. Originality suffers here because of a wholesale critique of authorial intention. It appears not only as a myth in this understanding but essentially irrelevant, as attempts at new expression may seem doomed before they have begun. When any "text" is only ever made up of other texts and the author is "dead," artistic intention is fundamentally problematized (see Barthes, 1977). More immediately damaging, however, have been the critiques that come from gender, race, and postcolonial perspectives, relating to the cultural specificity of genius. These argue that the figure of the genius is inherently male and Eurocentric with inbuilt prejudices against others and presuming stringent hierarchies within the arts. Indeed, the concept of "the arts" has itself come under fire (Gaztambide-Fernández, 2020).

Gendered Genius

Christine Battersby's *Gender and Genius* (1989) is an early and sustained exploration of the way that the concept of genius is tied up with all kinds of exclusions. She points to the curious way in which romantic geniuses were praised for having many supposedly feminine qualities, yet at the same time excluded women almost completely. Battersby writes that the "genius was *like* an animal, a primitive, a child or a women; but, of course, this likeness was deceptive" for the "genius's instinct, emotion, sensibility, intuition, imagination—even his madnesses—were different from those of ordinary mortals" (1989, p. 4, emphasis in original).[10] Almost like the "uncanny valley" of contemporary artificial intelligence, the closer women came to genius, the more unnatural and disturbing it became. In the Romantic period in particular, the idea of human creativity becoming a violent eruption, rather than a slow and careful nurturing, was reflected in language that directly linked creativity with male sexuality. Friedrich Nietzsche, for example, defined the creative impulse "physiologically" as the "creative instinct of the artist and the distribution of semen in his blood" (1968, p. 424).

It is a mistake, however, to think that artists and public were bound irreparably to the language they inherited. Exclusions required rigid policing. The stories of active female composers and the moralizing backlash they faced against their compositional efforts from within and outwith compositional practice has now been well documented (see, for example, Battersby, 1989, and Beer, 2016), while there is white bias and gendered exclusions baked into the philosophies of some of the chief aestheticians. Kant, for example, admits that the "fair sex has just as much understanding as the male," yet—fatally for the female genius—it "is a beautiful understanding" while male understanding should be "deeper" (1960, p. 78).

Creativity and Economics

Finally, there is a criticism of the term "creativity" in relation to neoliberal economic models that place the emphasis of "success" onto individuals and their apparent ability, or inability, to adapt to changing economic conditions. The present status of Western capitalist societies, it is argued, is directly reflected in our view of creativity. Mould argues that the "system that causes homelessness—and other related injustices: precariousness, racism and the emboldening of fascism, massive inequality, global health epidemics and the rest—is the very same system that tells us we must be 'creative' to progress" (2018, p. 10). This is seen most notably in the burgeoning quasi-self-help creativity literature. A book like Adam H. Grant's *Originals* (2017)—which seeks to analyze the way that creative individuals in business and technology operate so that we might learn from them—is for Mould just a symptom of the "language of creativity" being "subsumed by capitalism" in a vision that sees everything in the world as monetizable (2018, p. 23). The blurb of the book *Normal Genius* makes this more or less explicit: "The fact is that we live in a world of competitive job applications, zero-hour contracts, institutionalized 'self-employment,' career insecurity, startups and constant exhortations to be entrepreneurial. People are increasingly left without support and having to fend for themselves in a brutal and intimidating market." Mould does not argue that there is nothing to be retrieved from notions of creativity, merely that genuinely creative, resistive practices can all too easily be ignored and suppressed.

Transforming Originality

Thus far, critiques of the originality principle have been heard from various sources, such as art and literature criticism, education, and aesthetics. Yet it is worth highlighting that there has been a current in artistic practice that has questioned the enlightenment, romantic, and modernist notions of who an artist should be and what they should produce. This group contains all manner of site-specific experiments, socially interventionist art, work that problematizes the work concept and single authorship, and work that involves the audience as a core part of its "material." Birgit Eriksson, Carsten Stage, and Bjarki Valtysson claim that "since the social turn in art and aesthetics in the 1990s," there has been a "strong interest in participatory art practices that both transform the role of the recipient and engage art more directly in society" (2019, pp. 2–3). In *Artificial Hells* (2012) Claire Bishop presents an overview of such artistic maneuvers, from the public and extreme to the private and almost—from the point of view of an audience—unknowable. Bishop summarizes the approach of the works she explores, in which "the artist is conceived less as an individual producer of discrete objects than as a collaborator and producer of *situations*; the work of art as a finite, portable, commodifiable product is reconceived as an ongoing or long-term *project* with an unclear beginning and end" (2012, p.2, emphasis in original). That these efforts are (still) rarely seen as mainstream artistic activity is an indication of the power that concepts of originality still hold in contemporary art worlds.

Only a few composers feature in Bishop's story, though some do quite spectacularly such as the "Hooter Symphonies" that "aimed to turn the whole city into an auditorium for an orchestra of new industrial noise" (2012, p. 65). Yet, in recent years there have been many pieces that were written in community settings, that rearranged the orchestral set-up to create immersive musical spaces, that engaged the audience in the manner of a debate or game show or have had other dramatic or participative elements.[11] What is important to grasp is that the critiques of originality and genius have been reflected in artistic practice for some time and that their effect may have even greater impact in the future. Though music is somewhat late to the party, collaborative and socially-embedded models are finding growing traction amongst funders, in Europe at least.[12] If it is the job of teachers to prepare students for the future then it should be borne in mind how different it might look and sound.

Summary

As this section has shown, criticisms of genius are well established in scholarship and in practice. Yet, it is clear that artistic judgement has not simply disappeared: for individuals there are still aesthetic experiences of greater and lesser value, and artistic figures given platforms to assume more prominent profiles. There are still innovations in artistic practice that are discussed and disputed. "[E]xceptionality" is a trait that Keith Negus and Michael Pickering argue has been overlooked in sociological studies of art, stating that the "fact that the great praise and attention accorded to various individuals, and the artworks or products associated with them, may have served certain ideological interest in the past, does not mean that they or their achievements are utterly subsumed by these interests" (2002, p. 182). Yet, the very notion of who and what is exceptional are articulated in terms and language that was established with the concepts of genius, originality and creativity. That this is a difficult challenge points to the way in which such conceptions are integrated so deeply into music practice. For example, do we seek to elevate composers of color and composers who are women so that they can take their rightful place in the pantheon, or is it time to deconstruct the pantheon because music making under such conditions cannot ever be non-exclusionary, let alone emancipatory? This is one of the dilemmas discussed below.

These issues do not need to be resolved here, indeed cannot be resolved here as it is for teachers to take their own stances in these debates, but it is vital that the dilemmas are understood because they have far-reaching consequences for pedagogy. Though few teachers would demand entirely "original" works, from their high school students at least, there is a significant overlap between concepts of "imagination" and "creativity," particularly in their individualist overtones, which are very much prevalent in educational settings. These will be explored in the next section, which examines how three particular pedagogical debates are informed by this scholarly and historical background: whether pedagogy involves imparting knowledge or unlocking students" creativity; whether the canon can be elastically broadened or must be dispensed with; and the question of genre.

DILEMMAS OF PEDAGOGY: KNOWLEDGE TO IMPART OR CREATIVITY TO UNLEASH?

That the debates over genius and the nature of creative endeavor explored in section 1 are not limited to the 18th and 19th centuries but are very much a twenty-first-century concern, is illustrated by disputes between two prominent pedagogical North American philosophies, those of David J. Elliott and Randall E. Allsup. These approaches diverge significantly in their priorities and methods and in how they believe originality can be fostered.

Elliott is keen to distinguish acts of creation from child's play or undirected thought. He argues that all creative acts are "*intentional*" (1995, p. 222, emphasis in original), even if the precise product at the end is unclear. For Elliott, "music educators must be honest with students about what counts as musical and what counts as musically creative in relation to past and present attainment in musical practices" (1995, p. 222). He encourages creativity to be developed within particular artistic domains in which excellence can be achieved. Creativity is, he states, a "congratulatory term that singles out a concrete accomplishment that knowledgeable people judge to be especially important in relation to a specific context of doing and making" (1995, p. 216). There is more than a little residue here of a Kantian focus on exemplary artistic works within particular domains of artistic practice, though Elliott does also offer a more Hegelian nod to a "set of social institutions, or field, that selects from the variations produced by individuals those that are worth preserving" (1995, p. 217). The canon, or canons for he does not mandate the particular musical "domain," are very much still in action.

Allsup, in his *Remixing the Classroom*, characterizes Elliott's approach as being complicit in a "Master-apprentice" relationship (2016, p. 16; c.f. Lamb, 1999), an accusation Elliott has attempted to refute (Elliott & Silverman, 2017). There is a residue in Elliott of an approach Margaret Wilkins labels old-fashioned, in which "[y]oung composers were expected to thrive on a diet of weekly exercises in which the styles of the classical composers of the past (Palestrina, Bach, Mozart, Schubert) were imitated." Once these techniques were "mastered, young composers were 'allowed' to compose freely, though by then they were nearing the end of their higher education" (2006, p. 4). Taking inspiration from radical pedagogies of such thinkers as bell hooks and Elizabeth Gould, Allsup looks for a different way of conceiving creativity and the educational process that should encourage it. He searches for tools to create different relationships between students and teachers in which teachers do not have all the answers, "outcomes are as unpredictable as they are (currently) certain" (2016, p. ix), and to distance pedagogy from a model in which "initiates must learn the rules before they are allowed to break the rules" (2016, p. 16).

Elliott's argument that teaching should strive for excellence in a single domain comes in for particular criticism from Allsup. He states that "[w]hen education is tradition-based, rather than focused on the reordering and remaking (and rereading) of past and present realities, practitioners are always starting with another person's frame or the outlines of a tradition one must earn entrance into" (2016, p. 32). He encourages teachers and students to "put together their own frames as often as not—or look for new ones" (2016, p. 32). Rosalind Krauss might agree here, exhorting students to find their own grid. Rather than clarity of expertise and prior knowledge, Allsup wants pedagogy to be "willfully hybrid, the open-sourced and appropriated, the interdisciplinary and the weird, our wondrous and unholy muddle" (2016, p. 33).

Certainly, there is issue to be taken with Elliott's conception of original products being recognized by those with expertise as "worth preserving." The history of art is littered with marginalized figures whom the tastemakers ignored. Allsup makes similar critiques to those of genius above in terms of what people, what bodies are more "in place" within particular spaces (Ahmed 2007, p. 153). He argues that "closed" pedagogical forms, in which "norms are preestablished, expertise is objectively recognized" (2016, p. 67), are "commonsense definitions as to who can do what and how—who can play the tenor saxophone, who can direct a college band, and so on" (2016, p. 28). A fixed attitude to these roles is detrimental to students for Allsup as "[t]here is no master without an apprentice" (2016, p. 29).[13]

A move to facilitation of learning is important and logical if originality is conceived as self-expression given space to breathe. The teacher cannot teach originality because they do not—and cannot—know what students' originality would sound like. Originality, in this view, can seem like heightened individuality, i.e., that the road to original expression is to find out more about the self. It is important, however, to stress (as does Allsup) that few educators would see the encouragement of self-expression and encountering the new and strange as mutually exclusive. Constructivist views of the self see it as an ongoing narrative, into which many diverse streams feed, not least our encounters with the outside world. The classical tradition—implicit in much of what Elliott describes—can play a key part in this construction of the self, but teachers cannot necessarily decide on its role.

Crudely characterized, then, there is a question here about whether the teacher is an expert with knowledge to impart or a facilitator engaged in a process of exchange with their students that has the potential to allow both to find their voice. In fact, in this formulation it begins to assume the form of venerable question regarding whether composition can be taught or is "innate." For the composition teacher, however, it is important to break down this pedagogical binary: there are (classed, gendered) routes to self-realization within more traditional music pedagogy—why would so many teachers, performers, and composers be here if there were not?—while Allsup is not advocating a learning environment in which teachers have no expertise and students are only confronted with what they know—quite the opposite in fact.[14] Rather, the tendency in more recent pedagogical literature is to help students come up with responses to their own particular position in their world and to learn skills that will help them express themselves more fully (e.g., hooks, 1994).

The implementation in practice of such a position is less simple than it might first appear. Students do not arrive as blank slates but with particular ideas of what music is and should be, while, at the same time, as Michele Kaschub and Janice Smith write, "[i]mitative works are often the first to emerge" (2013, p. 7). The response to these works is usually both to provide technical feedback that might make these pieces more like their models, while also facilitating a process of expansion and discovery so that students have a wider world of music to choose from. The latter includes being exposed to different kinds of music, trying out new composition techniques and contexts, and experimenting with instruments. I am often reminded of a fellow student who was perfectly happy creating music that resembled its models with—to me—incredible accuracy. For most of a music education this should be unproblematic, though issues may arise in later tertiary study, which is geared further toward the training of future artists. This example is useful in that it points out that music education, even in the empowering and diverse recent literature, is still invested in a sense of unique selfhood. That a self might be completely happy to submit to previous models is so rarely considered shows the level to which we are still invested in the idea that we are all unique,[15] that the idea of genius as individual spirit lingers.

Gender and the Canon: Making Room or Breaking Down the Walls?

It is helpful to situate the power and reach of vocabularies of genius in a more concrete setting: the UK classroom. Lucy Green's 1997 exploration of music, composition, and gender is an often disturbing example of how networks of meaning concerning genius, originality, and creativity impact children. She describes marked differences in the way that teachers articulate the compositional efforts of "boys" and "girls" and, poignantly, in the way that they describe themselves. Though this binary division may give us pause today, the dominant discourses around femininity and masculinity Green identifies are still prevalent. Green describes certain "delineations" associated with musical practices and gender, in which "[m]asculinity is characterized by a confident, rational approach to composition based on creativity and genuine attainment through natural talent" and "femininity is constructed as lacking confidence in composition, as bound up with feelings on one hand and rules on the other, as conservative, traditional and attaining success only through hard work" (1997, p. 215).

The mention of "hard work" may sound like a compliment but this is misleading. Within the context of this masculine/feminine divide this is a deficient attribute when compared with the spontaneous and confident creativity of the boys. In a teacher questionnaire the boys were credited with "imagination, exploratory inclinations, inventiveness, creativity, improvisatory ability and natural talent" as opposed to the girls, who were "conservative, traditional and reliant on notation" (1997, p. 195). In assessing the work of girls not one was described "inspired, creative, imaginative or brilliant" (1997, p. 218). Green's argument is not that schools have taken a conscious decision to limit female creativity, rather they take part in the "wider field of gender and sexual politics" (1997, p. 192).

It is easy to observe in Green's discussion that vocabularies of genius and originality are brought to bear on this gender binary, a vocabulary that has been valuing masculinity over femininity since at least the 18th century. Race is not Green's primary focus here, but it would be valuable indeed to consider similar issues with such a lens. In particular, her discussion of the split Susan McClary (and Citron, 1993, p. 53) identify between the mind and body in Western classical music speaks to the racist discourses around supposedly "primitive" and physical—rather than cerebral—African cultures, not to mention other indigenous cultural practices and products *within* Europe. The move to present classical music, in McClary's words, as "rational" and by "laying claim to such virtues as objectivity, universality, and transcendence" presents both a racialized and gendered discourse (1991, p. 17). This same claim to universality in higher music education has recently been robustly challenged by Philip Ewell (2021), who argues that music theory operates within an exclusionary "white racial frame" (c.f. Bradley, 2007).

Such criticisms have potentially deep consequences for the canon of works that are used as exemplars for composers learning their craft. DeNora and Mehan criticize Battersby's attempts to "sensitize us to a hitherto unrecognized proportion of 'gifted' or 'genius' women" through arguing for greater recognition. There is a link here to what has been labeled the "add-women-and-stir" approach (Lamb et al., 2002, p. 666). The problem is that this is trying to funnel women—and people of color—into a template designed for white men. For DeNora and Mehan "this position does not consider the ways in which the ability to recognize hitherto overlooked instances of the category of 'genius' (in this case women) is simultaneously transforming the shape of that category to add to the canon is also to transform it" (1994, p. 170). For example, celebrating epic artistic gestures with huge forces and long durations already excludes the many who were never able to access such resources. Allsup advocates for the "idea that public education is supposed to prepare us for *what might be*—that schools and universities are expected to transform a culture, to innovate, reimagine, and liberate" (2016, p. 40). The classroom, for him, can be part of this transformation, finding new ways of conceptualizing creativity outside of canon, outside of racialized and gendered hierarchies, outside of "the work" as we know it. Co-composition is already something of a resistive act against singular conceptions of creativity, though anyone who has run or participated in a class that makes use of co-composition will know that this can bring significant challenges for students and teachers alike.

There has been some response from scholars working within higher music education who, through their focus on musical literacy, analysis, music theory, and score-based music composition, make the argument that there are still aspects of the canon to be preserved. Much of this debate was in response to an article in the *Guardian* newspaper by Charlotte C. Gill that described an emphasis on teaching music notation as elitist, and notation itself as a "cryptic, tricky language—rather like Latin" (Gill, 2017). Julian Horton, in response, argues for the continuing value of music analysis and theoretical understanding against those who would see it as ahistorical and "solipsistic" (2020, p. 2).

One of the epiphenomena of this movement is a move toward the defense of canons, if not *the* canon. Horton and Ian Pace argue for canons as a means of resisting the presence of late capitalism in all forms of human interaction: musical autonomy and the canon as a collection of works honored for their artistic rather than market value in this view becomes a perpetual source of inspiration in an otherwise drab and market-driven world (Pace, 2016a).[16] There is more than a little hint of Adornian superstition of popular culture, as well as the feeling that there is a tension between classical music's "dominant" position within traditional music curricula and its seeming irrelevance to the course of much wider society. The questions of canons and their elasticity will be picked up again in the conclusion, but this question of genre is important and requires further discussion.

Genre Trouble: Genius as a Classical Preserve?

Underlying much of the criticism around vocabularies of genius is the question of genre and with it what the role of a music education should be. A key site of this has already been explored in the notion of the canon, which is characterized both as a tool of oppression and a weapon against neoliberalism. The latter conception relies on a view of popular music—or at least that which is most prevalent in social and retail spaces—as the unmediated agent of the market. Such a view is unlikely to hold out much hope for the analysis and deeper understanding of this music as it is seen as a placeholder for the pursuit of capital. While this can be a source of interest from a sociological point of view, it does not satisfy the desire of those who wish to engage with music's autonomy, i.e., how it sounds and is structured.

This links in with a debate that seems about as old as popular music studies itself, whether such music is "worthy" of study, particularly in higher education, and in relation to this, what kinds of music are "dominant" in society. In 2002, David Hesmondhalgh and Keith Negus described an increasing, though sometimes grudging, acceptance of popular music studies (2002, p. 1), a trend that has only continued, though unevenly throughout nations, regions, and particular institutions. The school music classroom has not traditionally been the nursery for the hip-hop artist or DJ, which some would see as a missed opportunity to inform children's creativity, others as a vindication that, in these cases, the "market will provide."

Ian Pace argues in this vein when he offers a parodic vision of Western musical exposure: "Personally, I can rarely go into a bar without being barraged by Japanese gagaku music, cannot go shopping without a constant stream of Stockhausen, Barraqué, mid-period Xenakis" (Pace, 2016b). Pace also argues another point, which seeks to turn the "diversification" debate on its head. This relates again to literacy and primary and secondary education. He states that "removal of core musical skills from state education can only reinforce the privilege that is already fostering elitism in music" (2017). Any relinquishing of the duty of schools to teach staff notation can be argued, then, as a step back for class diversification, particularly if that is a necessary skill for university music study. This view is complicated by the very real contributions of private musical education to supposed "school-taught" literacy but can also be criticized for a narrow view of what musical literacy means (Benedict, 2012).

Yet there is no binary decision to be made on classical versus pop. There are many musical cultures to explore, including the traditional music of the ethnic groups making up the student cohort and the traditions of wherever the school is situated. Moreover, aligning popular music study with a lack of literacy is an elision that is by no means unavoidable: reading notation, knowledge of instruments and scoring, and significant music technological know-how could all be important parts of a popular musician's toolkit. The "lack" of skills in music literacy is also regularly seen as simply a transferal of skills to other domains, particularly knowledge of recording and digital technologies.

Questions of genre are linked to vocabularies of genius by an—often reflex—evaluative process: genius can only take place in genres that are worthy of the name. In many high school classrooms this evaluative framework has already been dispensed with and popular, traditional, and classical genres already coexist. In higher education, the situation is still contested, with doctorates in the composition of, for example, popular song still not mainstream. Horton and Pace would see the academy as one of the last bastions—already breached to a degree—against encroaching marketization. For all practitioners there is a great deal at stake.

Conclusion

There will be no ultimate resolution to the dilemmas of pedagogy outlined here. The "problem" of vocabularies of genius is as difficult to solve as it is deeply embedded in musical—and wider—culture. This may make addressing the issues of distinction an insurmountable challenge, dispersed to places and people elsewhere, yet there are steps educators can take to halt the negative perpetuation of hierarchies in music genres, gender, and race. Green argues that an "awareness of gendered musical meaning and of its influential presence within our musical experiences" is the best place to begin (1997, p. 257). Such awareness is more about reflexive questioning than knowledge of "the answers." Practitioners may wish to ask themselves certain questions in their daily practice:

1. Do you use the same language to describe the work of all your students?
2. Do your compositional exercises give students the space to radically reframe and recontextualize?

3. Does your teaching imply that certain musical activities have greater value than others?
4. What do you mean when you tell students to be original?

These questions, and the current chapter, are an effort to bring awareness to the surface, while answers will be reached through the collaborative work of students and teachers.

In 1853 John Stuart Mill made the point that "[o]riginality is the one thing which un-original minds cannot feel the use of. They cannot see what it is to do for them: how should they? If they could see what it would do for them, it would not be originality" (1978, p. 62). This problematizes the image of the teacher as guardian of a tradition or the arbiter of excellence. Rather it suggests we should strengthen the ability of teachers to teach what they do not know. No student comes to composition "knowing it all" so there must be a sense in which the new and strange is encountered in compositional classes, but there nevertheless should be a dialogue, particularly later in compositional studies, between student and teacher about what the course of study might be. The Kantian no-tion of exemplary forerunners can perhaps be resuscitated here, with some important caveats. Artists regularly shape a world of creative endeavor, almost a personal my-thology of origins and precursors: their own personal canon. Student and teacher can work together to create this for each individual from a wide variety of sources. Rather than seeing Kant's exemplars as teleological and unitary, they can be split open to re-veal a myriad of threads and influences. For those not wishing to pursue compositional studies, this process can still be enlivening and, dare one say, pleasurable.

The role of the teacher is an important theme to emerge from the three dilemmas considered here. In Elliott's case, there is a sense of an expert encouraging excellence within a particular musical domain, while Allsup's teacher is a "loving facilitator" (2016, p. 34), who encourages co-authorship and interdisciplinary experimentation. There are a number of radical challenges to standard classical music education present in Allsup, covering a similar range of issues to recent discussions around decolonization of the music curriculum. Yet, it can be easy to misunderstand the contrast between these two approaches—more traditional versus "critical" pedagogy—as the difference between a viewpoint that believes there is "something" to teach that is beyond the experience of the student, and one that believes students already have everything they need.

It is not glib but realistic to say that from the contradictions of these pedagogical contrasts—imparting knowledge versus facilitating exploration, learning from the best versus not experimenting with failure—that a diversity and flexibility of pedagogical ap-proach is vital. As Kaschub and Smith state, there are "as many approaches to teaching composition as there are potential composers waiting to be taught" (2013, p. 11). Finding the right way must be a negotiation between students and teachers. Yet, it is clear no music teacher can profess deep expertise in all areas of music-making. To engage as many students as possible, however, it is important that types of music that fall outwith the teacher's expertise are valued rather than dismissed and that exhortations to engage with the sound of music itself, its artistic autonomy, is not used as a cloak to conceal deep-seated genre hierarchies.

The historical survey of notions of originality, genius, and originality also presents the opportunity to consider that views of human creative endeavor are always in flux and that major societal, cultural, and technological upheavals can have significant effects. In science, the notion of the individual genius making breakthroughs is being seriously troubled by artificial intelligence and the networked nature of so many contemporary projects. Hanchett Hanson argues that the "current trends in creativity research point to an emerging participatory synthesis, which goes beyond assigning creativity to a single person with an idea and now includes a wide variety of roles that people take-up in bringing about change" (2015, p. 17). If such a change were to become widespread in the arts, the participatory thread of practice described in the first section would not be just an intriguing historical niche but an indication of where things might be headed. Creative work and exchange amongst classroom groups takes on increasing importance in light of this and should be valued, even if it presents difficulties in assessment, perhaps indeed *because* it does this.

Finally, a word on the classical tradition. There is a sense in these binary arguments that it and the motivations and desires of students are opposed, and indeed that it is a static entity without sense of development. Provision for art and culture is thin indeed in many Western democracies, yet the practice of Western Art music is not so very fragile that it is endangered by the inclusion of other perspectives. Indeed, it may stand to be revivified by them. Charles Rosen states that a "tradition is often most successfully sustained by those who appear to be trying to attack or to destroy it" (2012, p. 17). Relinquishing standard narratives of genius—who is worth listening to—and of artistic production—what art *should* look and sound like—may encourage not just the engagement of a wider range of students but the invigoration of the traditions about which many educators care so deeply.

NOTES

1. With thanks to the staff of the National Library of Scotland, whose work during a global pandemic made this research possible.
2. Though (instrumental) music was regularly seen as a paradigmatic "romantic" art (Hoffman in Strunk, 1981, p. 775–76), it was literature and aesthetics that cemented early romantic thought (Longyear, 1969, p. 7).
3. The huge range of psychological studies of genius are not covered here. For artistic creativity, it is argued, the concept of genius as a cultural phenomenon is far more important. As Mihaly Csikszentmihalyi argues, "Looking for creativity in the head of an individual could never lead to an understanding of the phenomenon" (2014, p. 535).
4. Though, as Keith Negus and Michael Pickering point out, the idea of the creator as a "medium" or "vessel" for a larger being, consciousness, or spirit has remained (2002, pp. 179–180).
5. Scholars often point to the merging of the Latin *genio*, meaning individual spirit, with that of *ingenium*, meaning innate talent (Lyas, 1998, p. 163)
6. That this was written in the 17th century, i.e., rather early in the story of genius as innate talent, points toward the overlapping uses of the term. The words are written in praise of

his close associate William Congreve, who had some success as a playwright. That his career was short (he produced little after 1700 until his death in 1729) shows that "genius" is not all that is required to be a successful artist long term.

7. Chaplin and McMahon also make the point that modern notion of the celebrity arose at this time and that the two concepts can be closely intertwined (2016, p. 3).

8. See, for example, "Brahms the Progressive," in *Style and Idea* (1950).

9. See McClary (1989) for a critique of modernism in music.

10. There is, incidentally, also a body of literature on this link between genius and mental illness. See, for example, Kaufman, 2017.

11. See in particular works concerned with the "new discipline" or *diesseitigkeit* groups, e.g., Jennifer Walshe. Both Johannes Kreidler and Philip Venables have experimented with TV-style participatory events as pieces.

12. The specific funding models will have a major impact here, providing another link to the socio-economic situation of the arts. The North American philanthropic model may move more slowly in this direction due to being defined more completely by societal elites. European social-democracies, with their attempts at transparency and value for money for taxpayers, may see the move toward participative models as expanding the reach of their arts funding.

13. This point is reminiscent of French philosopher Jacques Rancière's *The Ignorant Schoolmaster* (1987), which discusses the maverick 19th-century educator Joseph Jacotot. Jacotot was renowned for teaching subjects of which he himself was ignorant, most notably in this context, the piano.

14. For further discussion on what it means to give students power in the classroom, see hooks, 1994 (p. 151).

15. Allsup does mention the "curious novitiate who knocks on the door of a great and worthy tradition and freely elects to abide by the norms that govern the execution of its context-specific practices may not find inordinate satisfaction in submission to its rule" (2016, p. 83).

16. The position of popular music within the market has, however, long been a source of interest for scholars of popular music (e.g., Frith, 1981, p. 11).

REFERENCES

Adorno, T. W. (1997). *Aesthetic theory* (R. Hullot-Kentor, Trans.). University of Minnesota Press.

Ahmed, S. (2007). A phenomenology of whiteness. *Feminist Theory, 8*(2), 149–168.

Allsup, R. E. (2016). *Remixing the classroom: Toward an open philosophy of music education.* Indiana University Press.

AQA. (n.d.). Scheme of assessment. AQA website https://www.aqa.org.uk/subjects/music/as-and-a-level/music-7272/scheme-of-assessment [Accessed December 9, 2020]

Ball, L. C. (2014). The genius in history: Historiographic explorations. In D. K. Simonton (Ed.), *The Wiley handbook of genius* (pp. 3–19). Wiley-Blackwell.

Barthes, R. (1977). *Image, music, text* (S. Heath, Trans.). Fontana.

Battersby, C. (1989). *Gender and genius: Towards a feminist aesthetics.* London: Women's Press.

Beer, A. (2016). *Sounds and sweet airs: The forgotten women of classical music.* Oneworld.

Benedict, C. L. (2012). Critical transformative literacies: Music and general education. *Theory into Practice, 51*(3), 152–158.

Bishop, C. (2012). *Artificial hells: Participatory art and the politics of spectatorship*. Verso.

Bradley, D. (2007). The sounds of silence: Talking race in music education. *Action, Criticism, and Theory for Music Education, 6*(4), 132–162.

Brook, O., O'Brien, D. & Taylor, M. (2020). *Culture is bad for you*. Manchester University Press.

Chaplin, J. E., & McMahon, D. M. (2016). Introduction. In J. E. Chaplin & D. M. McMahon (Eds.), *Genealogies of genius* (pp. 1–10). Palgrave MacMillan.

Citron, M. J. (1993). *Gender and the musical canon*. Cambridge University Press.

Coleridge, S. T. (1906). *Biographia literaria*. J. M. Dent & Co.

Csikszentmihalyi, M. (2014). The systems model of creativity and its applications. In D. K. Simonton (Ed.), *The Wiley handbook of genius* (pp. 533–545). Wiley-Blackwell.

Danuser, H. (2004). Rewriting the past: Classicisms of the inter-war period. In A. Pople & N. Cooke (Eds.), *The Cambridge history of twentieth-century music* (pp. 260s–285). Cambridge University Press.

DeNora, T., & Mehan, H. (1994). Genius: A social construction, the case of Beethoven's initial recognition. In T. R. Sarbin & J. I. Kitsuse (Eds.), *Constructing the social* (pp. 157–173). Sage.

Dryden, J. (1885). Epistle to congreve. In W. Scott and G. Saintsbury (Eds.), *The works of John Dryden* (Vol. 11, pp. 57–60). Paterson.

Eldridge, R. T. (2014). *An introduction to the philosophy of art* (2nd ed.). Cambridge University Press.

El-Ghadban, Y. (2009). Facing the music: Rituals of belonging and recognition in contemporary Western art music. *American Ethnologist, 36*(1), 140–160.

Eliot, T. S. (1932). Tradition and the individual talent. In *Selected Essays 1917–1932* (pp. 3–11). Harcourt, Brace and Company.

Elliott, D. J. (1995). *Music matters: A new philosophy of music education*. Oxford University Press.

Elliott, D. J., & Silverman, M. (2017). On the "truthiness" of *Remixing the classroom*: A reply to Randall Allsup. *Action, Criticism, and Theory for Music Education, 16*(1), 124–167.

Eriksson, B., Stage, C., & Valtýsson, B. (Eds.). (2019). *Cultures of participation: Arts, digital media and cultural institutions*. Routledge.

Ewell, P. (2021). Music theory's white racial frame. *Music Theory Spectrum 2021*, 1–6. https://doi.org/10.1093/mts/mtaa031

Frith, S. (1981). *Sound effects: Youth, leisure, and the politics of rock 'n' roll*. Pantheon.

Gaztambide-Fernández, R. (2020). The orders of cultural production. *Journal of Curriculum Theorizing, 35*(3), 5–27.

Gill, C. C. (2017). Music education is now only for the white and the wealthy. *Guardian*. https://www.theguardian.com/commentisfree/2017/mar/27/music-lessons-children-white-wealthy [accessed December 9, 2020].

Glăveanu, V. P., & Kaufman, J. C. (2019). Creativity: A historical perspective. In J. C. Kaufman & R. J. Sternberg (Eds.), *The Cambridge handbook of creativity* (2nd ed., pp. 9–26). Cambridge University Press.

Gould, T. (1998). Genius. In M. Kelly (Ed.), *Encyclopedia of aesthetics* (2nd ed., pp. 156–163). Oxford University Press.

Grant, A. H. (2017). *Originals: How non-conformists change the world*. W. H. Allen.

Green, L. (1997). *Music, gender, education*. Cambridge University Press.

Hanchett Hanson, M. (2015). *Worldmaking: psychology and the ideology of creativity*. Palgrave Macmillan.

Hesmondhalgh, D., & Negus, K. (2002). Popular music studies: Meaning, power and value. In D. Hesmondlagh & K. Negus (Eds.), *Popular music studies* (pp. 1–10). Arnold.

hooks, b. (1994). *Teaching to transgress: Education as the practice of freedom*. Routledge.

Horton, J. (2020). On the musicological necessity of musical analysis. *Musical Quarterly, 103*(1–2), 62–104.

Kant, I. (1960). *Observations on the feeling of the beautiful and the sublime* (J. T. Goldthwait, Trans.). University of California Press.

Kant, I. (2007). *Critique of judgement* (J. C. Meredith, Trans.). Oxford University Press.

Kaschub, M., & Smith, J. (2013). *Composing our future: Preparing music educators to teach composition*. Oxford University Press.

Kaufman, J. C. (Ed.). (2017). *Creativity and mental illness*. Cambridge University Press.

Krauss, R. E. (1985). *The originality of the avant-garde and other modernist myths*. MIT Press.

Lamb, R. (1999). "I never really thought about it": Master/apprentice as pedagogy in music. In K. Armatage (Ed.), *Equity and how to get it: Rescuing graduate studies* (pp. 213–238). Inanna Publications and Education.

Lamb, R., Dolloff, L.-A., & Wieland Howe, S. (2002). Feminism, feminist research, and gender research in music education: a selective review. In R. Colwell & C. P. Richardson (Eds.), *The new handbook of research on music teaching and learning: A project of the Music Educators National Conference* (pp. 648–674). Oxford University Press.

Longyear, R. M. (1969). *Nineteenth-century romanticism in music*. Prentice-Hall.

Lyas, C. A. (1998). Genius and feminism. In M. Kelly (Ed.), *Encyclopedia of aesthetics* (2nd ed.), pp. 163–169. Oxford University Press.

McClary, S. (1989). Terminal prestige: The case of avant-garde music composition. *Cultural Critique, 12*, 57–81.

McClary, S. (1991). *Feminine endings*. University of Minnesota Press.

Mcfarland, T. (1974). The originality paradox. *New Literary History, 5*(3), 447–476.

Mill, J. S. (1978). *On liberty*. Hackett.

Mould, O. (2018). *Against creativity*. Verso.

Negus, K., & Pickering, M. (2002). Creativity and musical experience. In D. Hesmondlagh & K. Negus (Eds.), *Popular music studies* (pp. 178–190). London: Sage.

Nietzsche, F. (1968). *The will to power*. W. Kaufmann (Ed.). (W. Kaufmann & R. J. Hollingdale, Trans.). Vintage.

Pace, I. (2016a). Deskilling and musical education—Response to Arnold Whittall's 80th birthday celebrations. *Blog: Desiring Progress*. https://ianpace.wordpress.com/2016/08/21/deskilling-and-musical-education-response-to-arnold-whittalls-80th-birthday-celebrations/ [Accessed December 9, 2020]

Pace, I. (2016b). On canons (and teaching *Le Sacre du Printemps*). *Blog: Desiring Progress*. https://ianpace.wordpress.com/2016/11/23/on-canons-and-teaching-le-sacre-du-printemps/

Pace, I. (2017). The insidious class divide in music teaching. *Conversation*. https://theconversation.com/the-insidious-class-divide-in-music-teaching-77574 [Accessed December 9, 2020]

Plantinga, L. (1984). *Romantic music: A history of musical style in nineteenth-century Europe*. Norton.

Rancière, J. (1987). *Le mâitre ignorant: Cinq leçons sur l'émancipation intellectuelle*. Fayard.

Rosen, C. (2012). Culture on the market. In *Freedom and the arts: Essays on music and literature*. Harvard University Press, (pp. 15–23).

Schoenberg, A. (1950). *Style and idea*. Philosophical Library.

Scottish Qualifications Authority. (2013). Advanced higher unit specification: Music: composing skills (Advanced Higher) Unit. https://www.sqa.org.uk/files_ccc/AHUnitMusicComposingSkills.pdf [Accessed December 9, 2020]

Shelly, P. B. (1991). A defence of poetry. In A. D. F. MacRae (Ed.), *Shelley selected poetry and prose*. Routledge, (pp. 204–233).

Smith, N. T., & Thwaites, R. (2017). Narratives of originality in competitive opportunities for "emerging composers." *TEMPO, 72*(283), 45–55.

Sternberg, R., & Davidson, J. E. (2005). *Conceptions of giftedness*. Cambridge University Press.

Straus, J. N. (1991). The "anxiety of influence" in twentieth-century music. *Journal of Musicology, 9*(4), 430–447.

Strunk, W. O. (1981). *Source readings in music history [5]: The romantic era*. Faber.

Whittall, A. (2003). James Dillon, Thomas Adès, and the pleasures of allusion. In P. O'Hagan (Ed.), *Aspects of British music in the 1990s* (pp. 3–27). Routledge.

Wilkins, M. L. (2006). *Creative music composition: The young composer's voice*. Routledge.

CHAPTER 5

....

MUSIC CREATORS ON CREATING MUSIC

....

SANDRA L. STAUFFER

WHAT does it mean to create music, and how do people who create music come to do so? What motivates composers? Why do they create, and how does their composing process unfold? What are their earliest memories of creating music? How did they learn to compose? And what advice do they have for young people who want to compose or who are already creating music, and for teachers who work with them?

These questions guided interviews[1] with twelve composers during the closing months of 2020 and the first months of 2021—a time of pandemic and lockdowns, when all of them were living and working in unexpected ways and still creating music. They represent different genres of music, different ways of working, and different generations. They have had diverse experiences in music and taken sometimes unexpected pathways to their careers as composers. Following brief introductions, the sections of this chapter interweave their reflections about when and how they started to create music, the experiences and people who helped them along the way, descriptions of their working processes, and advice for students and teachers.

INTRODUCTIONS

....

John Adair, composer, songwriter, producer, and performer, has created music for the television shows *Just Shoot Me*, *Alaska: The Last Frontier*, and *The Wizards of Waverly Place*, and for films such as *Bridge Walkers* and *Gilbert*. He has also written music for television commercials. https://www.wildox.com/

Peter Bernstein, composer and conductor, has scored music for numerous films and television series. His credits include music for the films *The Ewok Adventure*, *Planet*

Raptor, and *American Black Beauty*, and for episodes of *Honey, I Shrunk the Kids*, *Chicago Hope*, and *21 Jump Street*. https://www.imdb.com/name/nm0003367/

Steven Bryant composes for bands and wind ensembles at both beginning and advanced levels, for instrumentalists with piano, and for chamber ensembles and orchestra. His *Ecstatic Waters* for wind ensemble and electronics has become one of the most performed works of its kind. https://www.stevenbryant.com/

Connor Chee, Navajo pianist and composer, combines his classical piano training with his Native American heritage to create piano works and music for videos and films. His music is inspired by traditional Navajo chants and songs and references elements of Navajo culture. https://www.connorchee.com/

Miriam Cutler has created music for independent films, particularly documentaries, and for television, as well as two circuses. She wrote the scores for the films *RBG* and *Love, Gilda* (both CNN) and *Dark Money* (PBS), as well as *Ghosts of Abu Graib* and *Pandemic: Facing Aids*. https://www.miriamcutler.com/

Steve Hampton has created music for television, film, commercials, and the occasional polka. His credits include music for television shows *Alaska: The Last Frontier* and *Jessie*, films such as *Gilbert* and *Jonathan Scott's Power Trip*, and national advertisements for Adidas, GE, and Pepsi. https://www.stevehamptonmusic.com/

Jennifer Jolley writes for beginning and advanced bands, and for orchestras, vocalists, chamber groups, and electronics. She is co-founder of NANOWorks Opera, which supports emerging artists. Her music engages political subjects such as climate change and the #MeToo movement. https://www.jenniferjolley.com/

Anne McGinty is a prolific composer of concert band music, with compositions for beginner as well as advanced ensembles. An expert in wind instruments, she has also written for solo instruments, solo instruments with piano, and chamber music for brass and woodwinds. https://mcgintymusic.com/

Jessie Montgomery, a composer, violinist, and educator, interweaves classical music with elements of vernacular music, improvisation, language, and social justice in her works. Her compositions include works for solo string instruments as well as chamber and orchestra music. https://www.jessiemontgomery.com/

Daniel Bernard Roumain composes chamber, orchestral, and operatic works, as well as site-specific music events for public spaces. One of his recent works is *We Shall Not Be Moved* with dancer/choreographer Bill T. Jones and writer/spoken-word artist Marc Bamuthi Joseph. https://www.danielroumain.com/

Mari Esabel Valverde has composed choral works for different voice combinations and music for high and low solo voice with piano and various instrumental accompaniments. She has also written for solo piano, for woodwind, brass and string chamber groups, and band and orchestra. https://marivalverde.com/

Eric Whitacre, best known as composer of choral music, has also written for orchestra, band, and musical theater. He has collaborated with artists and ensembles throughout the US and abroad. In 2010, he pioneered Virtual Choirs, an experiment in social media and digital technologies. https://ericwhitacre.com/

BEGINNINGS, PLAY, AND CURIOSITIES

How does the creative life in music begin? Children are spontaneous music-makers, and the impulse to create for these twelve composers was often rooted in early experimentation with sound and song. Jennifer Jolley remembered "messing around on the piano" as a child. Conner Chee recalled making up music on a small Yamaha keyboard his father had received as a gift. Jessie Montgomery began violin lessons early, and at age five or six she participated in *Creative Ability Development*[2]—a program that emphasized improvisation. Daniel Bernard Roumain also began violin when he was five and recalled "making up little tunes" as a child. Anne McGinty's first composition was a song about an unfortunate incident involving a parakeet and a red sweater, and Eric Whitacre's first song was about baseball cards. By his early teens, John Adair was jotting melodies for his rock band in a book of manuscript paper. Steven Bryant, whose father was a music educator and an accomplished trumpet player and arranger, remembered being fascinated with notation and "actually physically writing the notes, even before I could read music. As soon as I could I was just writing things down."

Messing around or playing with sound is now part of what these composers do as adults. "Playing is an essential component of making progress and actual work," Steven Bryant noted. Connor Chee described improvising at a digital keyboard as part of his current composition process. He encouraged experimentation as the way to begin creating with sound:

> Start right away with any sounds that you hear. Create new sounds out of non-traditional ways of playing instruments and also things you wouldn't think of as an instrument. That's a great way to get the ball rolling, and that's empowerment—when students see that they can do it from the beginning. That's when they'll come to you with questions: "I want to do this. How do I do it?"

Other composers, too, encouraged exploration and play as a means of engaging young people in the impulse to create music. "Think of ways to make it fun for kids," Miriam Cutler advised. "Let them explore and get excited without any expectations. Give them a computer program, like GarageBand, and mini keyboards so that they can play different patches and hear different sounds. And also acoustic instruments. Listen to things and try them out. Keep it wide open."

OF ROCK BANDS, SCHOOL BANDS
(AND OTHER ENSEMBLES), AND
MUSICAL DIVERSITY

I was one of the millions and millions of ships launched by the Beatles.
—John Adair

Musical diversity pervades the lives of these twelve composers, although that diversity came about in different ways. Daniel Bernard Roumain played violin throughout his public school education, however, he attributes his experience with popular music to becoming a multi-instrumentalist. He explained:

> By fourth grade, I had already been in different bands. We all had bands in our garages. In this garage there was a rock band and then we had a funk band over there. I just started picking up other instruments. In the rock band I played bass. In the funk band I played keyboards. If somebody got grounded or didn't show up—you know, the drummer—then you played drum kit that day. We would all just switch. It was kind of a lab.

For some composers, rock bands and popular music forms were places for experimentation and pathways to composition. Peter Bernstein, who took piano lessons in his youth, also played bass and toured with various rock and roll bands and singer-songwriters. His composing career evolved from there:

> I produced records, I became an arranger and orchestrator, then composer, and now composer and conductor. A lot of people in film composing go that route because it's become an offshoot of popular music. Fewer people have gone the full classical route, and even if they've done that, they've also done the other. I was a bit of both. Part of my rock and roll days were borne of knowing in some inchoate corner of my soul that I was a musician, but not wanting to be anywhere where my dad (Elmer Bernstein) was. Big shoes—and who wants to be like their parents anyway?

John Adair, who also had diverse musical interests early in life, made a bargain with his parents:

> They would allow me to learn the guitar as long as I also learned a *real* instrument. For me, that was the clarinet. I knew what they meant. They meant if you want to do this, we would like you to know how to read and understand music. I think my interest in popular music is where my motivation to try to *write* music came from, but music instruction is what gave me the tools to do it. Somewhere around age 12 or 13 I started messing with writing melodies, and then I'd write a lead sheet.

Adair played guitar in rock and bluegrass bands in the Washington, DC, area during high school and "started doing some writing there too, getting interested in how things were arranged and put together." He continued playing clarinet and saxophone in high school ensembles but was "not really indulging any creative impulses on that side of things" until his family moved to Olympia, Washington, and his high school band director invited an advertising composer as a guest speaker. Adair was fascinated but continued into college as a clarinet performance major and later switched to composition.

Steve Hampton, "a rock and roller from the beginning," played classical guitar in college because that was the only option for guitarists to be admitted as music majors at the time. He graduated with a music theory and composition degree, but, he explained:

> I had no idea what I was going to do. Meanwhile, a friend who had a studio called me and said, "Hey, I have a friend who has a business and he needs music for a radio commercial." I knew nothing about it, but I did it, and I thought, "Well that was kind of fun." The other thing that happened in college was that I had been into a real recording studio with a band. We'd record super late at night because nobody was there, and it completely changed my world. It was like, *this* is where I want to be. I'd love to write music and be in a studio, and I have no idea how I'm going to do that. Then this little commercial came along, then another one . . .

Miriam Cutler's first instrument was piano, and while she longed to play cello, her parents had other ideas. She played clarinet during her school years, but her musical pathway traveled through dance. She commented:

> I started by playing folk music. I was a folk dancer, so I learned a lot about world music that way. When they found out I played clarinet, they asked, "Why don't you play in the band?" I've never played legit clarinet. I played the blues, I played ethnic music, swing. I knew early on that I was never going to be a virtuosic musician.

Cutler started college as a music major but changed to anthropology after one semester in music theory, explaining, "It gets in the way of the way my brain works." She left graduate school to work as a research investigator for public interest lawyers, which she loved, however:

> I was very young—23 or something. I was working on really heavy stories—corruption, graft, murder, unnecessary surgeries—and I thought, "I can do this when I'm older. I'm just going to be a kid now." I ended up in bands like Oingo Boingo. I was in a feminist band,[3] and I did my own stuff. Little by little, I was a songwriter. That's how I got started. I put together a little recording studio for my songwriting.

That home studio became the base for what is now Cutler's career as a leading documentary film composer.

While Miriam Cutler was absorbing folk music, swing, and the blues, Daniel Bernard Roumain grew up in a family and in a neighborhood rich with musical diversity:

> At the time in south Florida, my neighborhood, even though it was kind of segregated—we were the first black family in our neighborhood—was still very diverse. You could walk down the street and hear music from Jamaica, the Bahamas, Israel, the Middle East, Spain, Italy. My parents were from Haiti, so a lot of Haitian music, and my father was very eclectic. You might hear Jackson Five, then it was von Karajan and the Vienna Philharmonic on Time Life Records.

Roumain identifies this diverse "listening palette" as part of his pathway to composing.

Some composers had in-school experiences that supported their interest in composition. Steven Bryant wrote brass quintets and pieces for the basketball pep band. Jennifer Jolley attended an arts high school in Orange County, California, where she took a composition class that included "some assignments—definitely a piano variation." She continued:

> A group of students were asked to participate in an LA opera outreach. They were premiering Tobias Picker's opera, *The Fantastic Mr. Fox*, and we got to write pieces as a group based on the story. I learned that sometimes group composition can be a little fraught. You're dealing with high school egos. But I was very proud that I wrote one section of this collaborative piece.

Even when music composition classes or experiences were not available, the recognition and support of teachers affirmed these composers' early creative inclinations. Mari Esabel Valverde explained:

> In eighth grade I had little chicken scratches that I would take to my choir director. In retrospect, she really helped me get on track. I almost want to cry remembering it . . . the fact that she would play through my things, which sounds really silly when it's just two or four bars of 4/4 and it's all quarter notes and I don't know what I'm doing. But she was playing something I wrote and I felt really proud of it.

Connor Chee described a similar experience:

> My elementary school music teacher really encouraged me to do what I was doing— to play piano and write my own music. She helped me write things down before I could really write the notes, and she submitted it to some local competitions. I think what I liked about it was that it was purely what I felt and what I wanted to do.

LEARNING: MUSIC THEORY (OR NOT), COUNTERPOINT, AND ORCHESTRATION

> If you want to write music, then you need to write music, and you need to do it now, and you need to do a lot of it. Don't wait. You don't need music theory. It's great to take music theory, later on, if you want to, sure. But you don't need to wait until you have music theory to write music. Try to dispel that myth.
>
> —Steven Bryant

> If you want to be a composer, then the most important thing to do is compose.
>
> —Jessie Montgomery

During their interviews, these twelve composers emphasized repeatedly that they learned how to compose by creating music—by experimenting, trying things, and learning along the way. In effect, they were learning to compose by composing, not by studying how to compose or mastering music theory. When they did encounter music theory, what they learned (usually) made sense because they were already creating music. Theoretical studies gave them labels, strategies, insights, or confidence in what they were doing. Conversely, learning theory first, or encountering teachers who emphasized theory prior to composing, could actually thwart the creative impulse.

The combination of critique and an overemphasis on theory discouraged Connor Chee during his teenage years and throughout college:

> As I got older and focused more on the piano, I did try writing things, but my teachers would critique it and tell me, "That's great, but it needs to have form and needs to have structure and needs to have" all these things that I hadn't studied. So, I backed off for a long time. It was a total turnaround from when I was younger. I thought, "Wait, there's a right way to do this. I'm not doing it correctly. I don't know enough to be composing music." It held me back because that thought stuck in my mind: You just don't know enough. You have to be super educated to be composing music or it's not right.

Chee went to college for piano performance and took a broad spectrum of theory courses and composition electives, including computer and electronic music creating and score engraving, but he did not consider any of that activity composition. He "accidentally started composing again" when a project aimed at preserving the songs of his Navajo grandfather turned into a suite for piano.

Miriam Cutler, who changed majors from music to anthropology because of music theory, commented, "My brain cannot process music in that way. I know the circle of fifths, but don't make me say it. I hear chords. I know what they are. I know I can recreate them. I just can't think of music that (theory) way." And while Steve Hampton finished his degree in music theory and composition, he was skeptical about the value of two years of common practice music theory. "I did well in it," Hampton said, "but I didn't really like it. I wished there were other classes, but I didn't have access to them."

Peter Bernstein wished for a class in high school that would have helped him "understand more what was inside the music. I knew I, IV, V from piano. I wanted to know *why* it worked the way it did, what's underneath it all that holds it together." Mari Esabel Valverde pointed to the value of experience prior to theory. An avid school choir member, she liked to "sing through all the parts and put different colors and different qualities with chords. So, when I took music theory, it gave a name to the organization of sound that I was already perceiving." In other words, for these composers, labels are secondary while creating. Steve Bryant explained, "As I compose, I try *not* to think, 'This is what I'm doing. This is over an altered bass.' I don't *want* to think about that. It's a sense of density and sound moving forward. The more word-less and label-less it can be, the more fun it is and the easier it is to do."

Counterpoint studies in college or graduate school made a difference for some of these composers. Mari Esabel Valverde found value in "understanding how a contrapuntal voice resolves and relates to other lines, or, if I cross voices, then how and why and what that sounds like." She recalled, "One of our assignments was to compose in the style of a Bach Invention. While that's not something that I aspire my music to be like, understanding that convention helped me to connect to the wires in my brain of how things are guided musically, melodically, horizontally . . . and to be more assertive about decisions in terms of crafting the music."

Similarly, some of the composers, including Valverde, pointed to orchestration studies as important to their learning. She explained, "Up until that point I had a crayon box with 12 colors, and I was really good with them. I knew how to do all the combinations of those colors. I found things that I loved and was confident about. But when I took orchestration and learned how to listen to symphonic music, those 12 colors turned into 64." Still, learning orchestration often occurred in action rather than in study. Jennifer Jolley explained, "Yes, I read an orchestration book, but I didn't really have that connection until I had to actually do it."

The learning experience that many of these composers valued most, however, was listening to music, often with a score in hand and sometimes with a mentor beside them. Jennifer Jolley explained, "I learn most in a concert setting when I can actually see the physicality of what's going on. I learned *way* after the fact that actually having the score in front of you while listening to the music was immensely helpful." Eric Whitacre described a similar experience in lessons with composer John Corigliano:

> He'd sit with me with either his own scores or maybe Stravinsky or Bartok. We'd listen and occasionally he'd stop and just point things out. "You see this? How this is happening? How this is connected to this?" He taught me about the idea of structure, deep structure, and how important it was. I look back now and realize he completely altered the way I think about music and the way that I make music.

In Process: Intuition, Ideas, and Intentions

Just noodle and play and listen until you find something.
—Steven Bryant

Early in their lives, some of these composers wrote music just for themselves or for friends in school ensembles or bands outside of school. Some wrote songs about things that interested them or to send messages to people such as "girls that I was too shy to talk to." Now, as adult composers with vibrant careers, the creative projects they enjoy most are those that align well with their own motivations and priorities and their own musical and aesthetic sensibilities. As Steve Hampton explained,

> There are two layers to it. One is, "Here's the job I have to do, and hopefully I'm going to do it well." The other layer is, "What is it for me that makes this rewarding? Why do I want to do this?" And *that* layer touches the place way down in me that makes it all worth it.

"The most successful pieces I've written have been based on images or stories or some kind of personal connection to a topic," Jessie Montgomery explained, "or when I have a very clear image of something—the performance of an act or a beautiful geometric object." Social justice themes animate Daniel Bernard Roumain, Jennifer Jolley, Jessie Montgomery, and Miriam Cutler. Imagery in poetic texts fascinates Mari Esabel Valverde. Events, narrative, dance, art, film, theater, sculpture, satellites space, snow—all of these and more are motivation to create for these twelve composers. And sometimes, the motivation is a commission, an invitation from an ensemble, or a contract for a film or television project.

So how do they get started? Where do their musical ideas come from? Steve Bryant described the beginning stages of composing as "finding a way in. I think of it more *that* way than 'Where's my idea?' Instead, I think, 'Where's my way into this piece? What is my reason to write anything at all?' It's different with every piece." Bryant and other composers talked about cultivating a mindset for creating. "It's not so clear cut as, 'I want to write a piece, this is what I'm going to do,' and it just happens," Connor Chee explained, "There's definitely some fostering of creativity. When I'm in the right mindset, then usually something will come."

The "right mindset," for Chee, involves setting aside anxieties and negative messages from early teachers about a "right way" to compose. Miriam Cutler confessed, "Every time I have a job, I'm scared, even now. One of the most important things I've learned is how to get out of my own way. I need to create the atmosphere for success by freeing my mind. Do yoga or meditate. Just trust your own creativity." Eric Whitaker described "moving through the world with what I call beginner's mind. When I'm seeing everything for the first time again, then the ideas are there."

While they consciously cultivate a mindset for creating, these composers are not sitting around waiting for inspiration to strike. They experiment, research, question, and listen to music to generate ideas. "Sometimes finding a way in involves a lot of noodling at the keyboard," Steven Bryant explained, "It doesn't even feel like work necessarily; I'm just messing around playing, maybe scrolling through patches on the synthesizer and . . . 'Oh that sounds cool.'" Similarly, several of the composers described the value of noodling on acoustic instruments. Miriam Cutler was keenly aware that physically touching instruments and making sounds, even on instruments she doesn't play, could trigger her imagination.

Listening, too, can generate ideas. "I can inspire myself by listening to my Navajo grandfather sing songs and by turning to other musicians, other genres of music, other art, and seeing other people create," Connor Chee explained. Steven Bryant described multiple variations of the generative value of listening, such as

> listening to music and thinking, "Oh. I don't really like this piece. I wish it did *this* instead of what it does." Listening to music you *don't* like can be just as helpful: "Okay, what would you change then?" Or sometimes I'll listen to things that aren't related at all to what I'm writing. I love Nine Inch Nails and some electronic music when I'm writing for orchestra. What's their sound world like? How can I replicate the way that music makes me *feel*, but with *these* noise making devices?

Listening to reference music supplied by clients is particularly important for film, television, and advertising composers, because reference music provides parameters. Miriam Cutler explained, "I may have a blank page of music, but I have lots of ideas, and oftentimes the filmmakers have their own ideas too."

Sometimes idea generation involves conversation with clients, musicians, conductors, and teachers—a process that Jennifer Jolley referred to as "personalizing" a piece. When writing for school bands, Anne McGinty asks those who commissioned her, "Who can be featured? Who do you want me to bury? What are your students' ranges?" Steven Bryant also thinks about what might interest the players. "I try to remember what it is like to that age, to be in band or orchestra," he said, "What would have blown my mind? What would I have really enjoyed playing at that age?" For composers working in the film and television industry, conversations with clients are tremendously important and can also pose a different kind of challenge. "A *huge* part of learning to become a successful scoring musician is learning how to understand human beings and their psychology as it relates to music," John Adair explained, "because what they're really looking for when they say something about the music you've created and it's not precise. Not everybody speaks music fluently."

Jennifer Jolley elaborated on the multifaceted nature of her listening and research explorations for a single piece:

> I was doing some space research for a piece eventually called *Questions to Heaven*, which is the name of the Chinese poem *Tianwen* and the Chinese satellite to Mars. So I downloaded some Mars sounds. At the same time I was listening to David Bowie's *Space Oddity* album and trying to get some different ideas of what space would sound like, which is nothing because it's a vacuum. I was also listening to sounds from the NASA Mars rover Perseverance. I was going on websites and looking up articles and seeing if that inspired some kind of melody or form. I did research on the soundtrack to the film *2001: A Space Odyssey* because it's amazing. I listened to some Strauss, some Ligeti. And I ended up including an electric organ part, because why not?

IN PROCESS: BRICKS AND DETAILS, STRUCTURES AND FORMS

> I start with an idea, and some of them are really, really brief.
> —Anne McGinty

For many of these composers, once a piece is underway, their work tacks back and forth between small ideas—bricks and blocks, and large ideas—forms or structures. "Everything's basically building blocks," Miriam Cutler explained, "A building block can be an instrument, a melody or a harmony. I love chords and chord progressions. It can be a style. It can be anything," perhaps a problem. "I come up with some very specific problem and think small," Steven Bryant commented. Thinking small can be very pragmatic. Anne McGinty revealed, "Sometimes, especially with the beginning band music, I would base a piece on a motif that I was determined they had to learn in their lifetime, like dotted quarter and eighth." At the same time, "even the easier pieces have to have a form to them, some sort of shape," she explained, and experimenting with those forms and shapes could make the music interesting for both composer and performer.

In the spirit of "less is more," Steven Bryant described the way in which working with small ideas develops into larger pieces:

> Take as little a bit as possible and build everything out of it. It's similar to writing a paper: the more focused you are, the less material you throw in, the more discipline you have, the easier it is to build something that feels like it belongs together. I tell people, "Restrict what you're doing. Take all that other stuff out. Those four notes and that one rhythm—that's enough to build an entire piece." Learning how to develop a motive is an incredible skill and a way of constructing something that all belongs together. And that's very important to me—music that really is lean.

For Mari Esabel Valverde and Eric Whitacre, structure might evolve from a poem. "I usually print out the text on two sheets of paper," Valverde explained, "On one sheet, I record my gut reactions to the text. The second page I'll use for analysis on the structure, where the shifts are, if there's any rhyme or imagery." Jennifer Jolley also noted that form is important, regardless of genre or ensemble. "I try to map out a form first," she explained, "Usually I know how long the piece is supposed to last, and then a form dictates kind of what I want to say about the piece." Jessie Montgomery also felt that she worked best "when there's already a form in place," though that form could be inspired by art, sculpture, or a narrative.

Eric Whitacre described his creative process as "the focusing of ideas and intentions," beginning with what he calls *emotional architecture* and *the golden brick*. "I actually make pictures before I write anything," he said, showing drawings that included geometric forms, descriptive and aspirational words, and a few notes of music. "I draw what I'm hoping the piece will be, what I call emotional architecture," he said. "I map out the emotional journey I hope the audience and the performers take as the piece unfolds." And then:

> I spend a lot of time looking for my golden brick. It's different than just a musical motive or an *idée fixe*. For me the golden brick is a chord, a note that just hums with possibility, or a couple of notes that contain all of the DNA for the entire piece. It's got within it some meta material, that golden brick idea. And then there's the structural idea. If I don't have a structure, like from a poem, I spend a lot of time building the structure.
>
> For me, the creative process has two parts. There's the lightning bolt or the jumping down the rabbit hole part, and there's the learning how to swim part. The learning how to swim part is an endless series of tiny revelations, over and over and over. It's one thing to imagine building a cathedral; it's a whole other thing to build a cathedral. Building the cathedral is where the little inspirations come, and that has to do with the focusing of ideas and intentions. You start, and you have a sense of what you want it to be, and then it becomes about little decisions. Those are the two parts—the macro part and the painting the house with the Q tip part.

In Process: Conscious and Unconscious, Embodied Knowledge and Being in Flow

Historical and contemporary accounts of creative experiences in many disciplines include multiple examples of moments when an idea or solution seems to appear out of nowhere. Graham Wallas (1926/2014), one of the earliest creativity writers, encouraged the practice of working hard on a problem or project and then stepping away to let the mind continue to make connections, which was when creative ideas would occur. Peter Webster's model of creative thinking in music (http://peterrwebster.com/pubs/model.jpg) includes *time away* as part of the core creative process.

These twelve composers described moments when solutions to compositional conundrums occurred during time away. Mari Esabel Valverde explained, "When I'm writing music, sometimes I obsess about something that I can't figure out. It's like a Rubik's cube. I'll go to bed, and then I'll wake up and (snaps fingers) I'll know it." Anne McGinty described a similar phenomenon, "There have been pieces where I get up in the middle of the night and change something. It's all in [my head] and playing back like it's on a loop. I could hear a rhythm that was wrong while I was sleeping."

Several composers consciously leverage the power of the unconscious to generate ideas. Jessie Montgomery described a journaling process, noting, "Ideas come when I have time to sit and reflect. I do a lot of writing . . . my own version of theorizing." Anne McGinty noted, "I think my backyard has produced most of my pieces. I'm just fussing around pruning a plant or watching the clouds and I'll just start whistling or singing something. And I go, '*Oh*, there's a motif I can work with.'" Eric Whitaker advised:

> Fill your head with all kinds of different things—not just pieces of music, but poetry and art and science and math and food and whatever you can experience. Then find someplace and get very bored. I mean *really* bored. You can't have a phone, you can't have a computer, walks are good, but there can be no input. Then the mind starts to wander. It takes an idea here and an idea there, and suddenly a connection gets made. That's where the truly original ideas come from, though it's hard to manufacture that moment.

Some composers described a sense of not being in control at times, or of different compositions coming to fruition in different ways. "I've written pieces that were not easy to write, that I feel as though I went through hell with," Mari Esabel Valverde recalled, "And then there are other pieces that I wrote quickly—like the piece composed itself." Anne McGinty described a similar sense: "Every time I sat down to write I didn't know the notes were in there until they started coming out. I don't think they're just mine. I don't think that I'm in control of everything." Eric Whitacre also described a sense of being led by the music:

> There's this very delicate part of the process . . . I've got the perfect analogy: Somebody told me once that when your child is born you have about a year to figure out who they are, and then you raise the kid you've got and not the kid you wanted. It's exactly the same thing with a composition. You start to dance with the material. You can force it somewhat, but frankly, when you're doing it well it feels more like guiding or a tango. It's a dance between the two of you. Maybe you're leading, but you've also got to listen to it.

Some of what these composers experience is similar to Csikszentmihalyi's (1990/2008) description of flow—experiences of working hard on a project, being unconscious of the passage of time, and reveling in the feeling of what happens as well as what they produce. Peter Bernstein described it this way:

> There would be moments where I'd start at eight in the morning, and now it's six in the evening and I had barely gotten up except to use the bathroom and have a sandwich. Those 10 hours would go by unnoticed. I would stop to have dinner. And after dinner, I would go over what I had written and sometimes the light bulb moment would happen. I would think, "Wow, I wrote that? Really?" Because you're so in flow, which is an interesting thing about composition. I don't know how you teach this, but you have to balance consciousness and unconsciousness in this process. You have to be able to go back and forth to assess, and then let something flow, and then assess, and it's not necessarily an easy thing.

While these composers are conscious of their flow experiences and the power of their minds, they also described the power of embodied knowing—the knowledge they held in their bodies as music-makers and how that physicality might help, or hinder, their creative work. "I'm a violinist first," Jessie Montgomery explained, "And the tactile response of playing an instrument and hearing sound is something that I've always had." She described learning the tools of composing by composing—physically getting ideas into one's body by writing or drawing or moving, similar to the way in which a violinist learns the physical techniques of playing the violin.

Mari Esabel Valverde is aware of how her sensibilities as vocalist and pianist inform her creative work. "If I have a keyboard in front of me and I put my fingers down, I'm going to think of harmonic ideas," she explained, "So if I'm trying to focus on a single line, having easy access to vertical sonority is a distraction. When I'm trying to write a vocal line, I want to be *away* from the keyboard. It just feels different. When I'm away from the keyboard I'm literally feeling the breath move past my voice." For her, this sense of embodied knowing applies to writing for instruments as well. "I sing all the time when I'm composing, even if there's not a vocal part," she explained. "If it's a bassoon I will make sounds to help me understand what I'm hearing in my head. I need to know where I'm breathing and where my bassoonist is breathing. I need to sing it, because I need it to be human."

In Process: Collaborators and Co-Creators

Somewhere in the public imaginary is an idea that composers are solitary people working alone to bring forth their next pieces. These twelve composers may indeed work by themselves, but they are also highly collaborative, open to ideas from fellow musicians, dancers, artists, and others. Other people impact these composers' work in two important ways: by playing their music for them and by contributing ideas.

"Pester your friends into playing passages for you," Steven Bryant advised. "When you hear somebody bring expression to a simple line of quarter notes, you realize, 'Oh, I need to get out of the way of the musicians, and let them do some stuff.' There are lessons that viscerally come from hearing other people your play music." Connor Chee also commented that hearing a musician's interpretation can be "surprising, because you'd think if you wrote it, you would know how it's going to sound. But I'm not of the idea that there's one right way to play a piece of music. What's exciting for me is listening to somebody else and what they come up with or what they find." Eric Whitaker explained, "Usually if a musician makes a suggestion, especially an instrumentalist, they're right; it's better. They know their instrument better than I ever will. And occasionally conductors will do something different to a piece that I wouldn't do and it's illuminating." Anne McGinty advised a direct approach: "If I have a question about how to write something, I ask someone who plays the instrument." While asking questions and having their music performed can be validating for composers, whether beginners or seasoned professionals, writing for their friends and having their music played can have practical learning implications. Jennifer Jolley explained:

> I can talk with student composers till I'm blue in the face—"Hey, you might not want to give the sopranos those high notes. A singular soprano can do that. Multiple sopranos? They will hurt you. I care for your safety, please." A student laughed at me, and I said, "No, seriously. Your midi playback, that's a tool. Do you know any sopranos? Think." So yeah, write for your friends.

Jolley also advised thinking about the lives of musicians and respecting them and their instruments. "In grad school, I was friends with a lot of percussionists. I know what angers them," she explained. "I know to make sure that I really need that instrument, because they have to schlep it. Do you *really* need that piccolo timpano? Think real hard. Do you really need it? *Maybe* you need it. Be conscious of those decisions."

For composers of ensemble music, collaboration with musicians sometimes involves making edits in rehearsals leading up to premieres. For composers in film, television, and advertising, suggestions from studio musicians about voicings, doublings, microphone placements, and more were key learning experiences. Collaborations with musicians during recording sessions could be crucial to a successful outcome. Steve Hampton explained:

> Sometimes clients would change their minds midstream and say, "This isn't really working for us. Can you try something else?" There you are, on the spot. So you walk out into the studio and make sure the engineer has the mics down so nobody in the control room can hear you, and you say, "Look, this isn't working and I don't know what to do. I was thinking maybe . . ." and you start brainstorming with the musicians. Now everybody's contributing their creative ideas and energy to it; and one way or another we usually made it work.

SOUNDS, SAMPLES, AND STUDIOS

> My career is a study in the history of recording, the introduction of computer technology, and the home recording boom.
>
> —Miriam Cutler

> If you're teaching music these days, there's no way to avoid including technology.
>
> —Steve Hampton

All twelve composers use digital keyboards and computers as they create music, though they also work with acoustic instruments in hand. Some experimented with technologies early in their creative lives. Eric Whitacre played with synthesizers and drum machines as a teenager. Daniel Bernard Roumain's high school had a

Fairlight system—an early digital workstation that included a keyboard and computer.[4] Roumain's experience became useful during an internship with what was then Skyywalker Records led by Luther Campbell of 2 Live Crew.

The composers with careers in film, television, and advertising have seen tremendous changes in technologies they use, the ways that they work, and the people with whom they work. John Adair described the transformation:

> Early in my career there was the composer, then there was the arranger, and then the orchestrator, who was not necessarily the same person. Then there were the performers, different people altogether. Then there was a recording engineer and a mastering engineer. Now all this has to be done by one person with a computer in their home studio. It may not sound like a dramatic change but consider the fact that all of those roles were hugely developed specialties and now they've been collapsed into a situation where one person like me needs to understand what an engineer does, the nuances of performance—whether it's live instruments or samples, synthesize it, put it together, and turn out something that sounds real and believable.

While these composers worked with musicians on sounds stages, and sometimes still do, their practices have changed. Steve Hampton, Adair's long-time creative and business partner, commented, "Now we all have home studios and we have gazillions of great sample libraries. The players come to our home studios, whereas 20 years ago, we would have booked one of the many LA recording studios and met there."

Home studios have also changed as well. "There were no computers or anything when I started," Miriam Cutler explained. She moved from recording decks and mixers, to consoles and tape machines, to synthesizers and samplers, to her current set-up of computers and keyboards. Anne McGinty has also "pared it down over the years to a computer and keyboard synthesizer." Conversely, Jennifer Jolley collects mini and modular synthesizers, even learning how to build them for use in her pieces for acoustic musicians and electronics.

Computers, sample libraries, and other technologies, including notation programs, offer advantages for creating music. Steven Bryant, who also writes for acoustic ensembles and electronics, described scrolling through patches on the synthesizer to explore sounds as part of his working process. Connor Chee commented on the affordance of capturing and retaining ideas via technology: "I can hit the record button as I'm improvising or coming up with things. If I'm at the acoustic piano, I might play something and within seconds it's gone. If I'm at the computer, I can rewind and listen, or cut that little piece out and save it for what I'm working on."

On the other hand, over-reliance on technology can be misleading. Jessie Montgomery described a sense of getting "stuck in the score" and needing to step away from the computer. Steven Bryant noted that midi sounds can be misleading. "The number one thing you need as a composer is to hear the music played by humans, if it's for human beings, for instruments," he said. "You can render it, you can hear the computer play it, but that really lies to you. Have someone play an eight-bar melody, for example on a flute, and then you really learn, 'Oh that feels so much higher than it did.' You get a visceral sense of it. Those are the *real* orchestration lessons." Similarly, John Adair cautioned that "some composers have, let's say, a trumpet patch on their computer. But what they don't understand, because they haven't worked with real trumpet players, is that tessitura matters. If you write everything on the ledger lines, their lips are gonna bleed." He explained a similar but more subtle problem brought about over-reliance on technology in his own creative practice:

> When sample libraries started to become effective for computer composition, I got lazy and started to write from my samples. In other words, I would call up my orchestral template and start building a piece that way. Boom. Off I'd go. Well, one day I had an epiphany. I listened to some of the things that I had done earlier and setting aside the comparison between live musicians and sampled music, I noticed that the more re-cent stuff was less impactful, kind of cloudy and less focused. And I realized what was happening. I was doubling things that I otherwise never would have doubled—just slathering on trombone and cello parts. Yeah, it worked, but it was kind of mush. And I finally realized, I'm letting the technology lead me. It needs to be the other way around.

Technologies for creating will continue to evolve. Steve Hampton advocated that teachers "blend traditional instruction with new technologies and resources." Similarly, Eric Whitacre suggested that "if you can get students who are already playing instruments in front of synthesizers, then a single note is a whole world and can un-lock a direction in a way that a typical instrument can't." Anne McGinty suggested having students "play around with GarageBand." And, once students are using digital technologies, John Adair advocated learning "how to prioritize and what to purchase out of the *bazillions* of sample libraries out there."

While none of composers in this chapter work specifically in the popular music in-dustry, they pointed to ways in which popular music genres, particularly hip-hop, evolved concurrently with digital technologies and sampling. "It's a completely different discipline," John Adair explained, "I had to dig deeply into the computer world to un-derstand how things were put together and how to create a sense of movement, build, and release when you are working with pre-existing electronic artifacts." Peter Bernstein noted that "what holds today's popular music together might be technological in nature. So there's a lot to learn. Where did it come from? Why is the way it is? Who used it? What is there to know about it? And the answer is, *a lot*."

PROJECTS AND POSSIBILITIES FOR FUTURE CREATORS AND THEIR TEACHERS

When asked about suggestions they might have for young people who are creating music or their teachers, all twelve composers expressed gratitude for past and present music educators and offered the following ideas in that spirit.

John Adair elaborated on ideas for elementary and secondary ensembles:

At the elementary school level, if the kids are playing a tune together with their instruments, even on a recorder, say, "Hey, do you want to make up a different melody?" Then help them get that melody into a place where it can be repeated reliably so it's actually a thing. Then work with them. Ask them, "Okay, if you're doing this and Emily is playing the glockenspiel, what do you think Emily should play along with your melody? *When* do you think she should play?"

Those kinds of experiences could happen in middle school too. It's vitally important to have spontaneity and encourage them to express themselves, and there's huge value in collaborative music-making. So break up the band into smaller ensembles and let them be creative within those ensembles, even if it's at an arranging or orchestrating level. What happens if you do an arrangement of a Mozart string quartet for a four-piece woodwind ensemble? What happens if the parts get flipped? What if the flute does the clarinet part? Flip that around so they can start to have that creating experience.

In high school, where they are more specialized and skilled, do projects. Break them into smaller ensembles. Take a piece of music that interests them so that they're working with the stuff they're actually listening to and that they love. Maybe one ensemble is working on a jazz composition, maybe another one is doing a hip-hop piece, maybe another one is doing Southern fried rock and roll. Whatever it is, charge each group with pulling it apart, dissecting it, just like they do in science class with a frog. Figure out how it's built. Why does it work? What about it makes it work? What happens if you do it at a slower tempo? What happens if you do it at a much faster tempo? What happens if you change the key? What happens if you add a singer? How do you talk to each other to accomplish what it is that you want to accomplish? In pulling it apart, they're understanding innately how it's built. By the end of the term, the goal would be to build their own piece in a way that is informed by what they learned from pulling apart the composition that was the focus of their study.

Peter Bernstein pointed to the value of imitating other composers and focused listening:

Start out creating something that is *like* something you've heard before, and then do something with it to take it to another level or another place. It's great to get into another composer's head, learn what they did, and then make it your own. And then, really learn how to hear. In other words, you might hear a kick drum and a snare drum doing something, but just because you've heard them doesn't mean you've *really* heard what they are. What are they doing? What makes them good and unique? Close is okay, but figure out what's *really* going on, which requires conscious listening.

Steven Bryant challenged instrumental ensemble teachers to listen to students and engage their interests:

If somebody loves to lay down beats on their laptop but they also play trombone in the band, do something with that. Yes, I understand, there's limited rehearsal time, but have them bring it in. Have it played through the sound system and have the band improvise over it. Find a way to meld those worlds. Band does not need to sound like band has always sounded. Orchestra does not need to sound like orchestra always has. None of that really matters. We're not going to destroy the canon. There's no danger. Playing and expanding the boundaries of what music can mean is so much more engaging. And the kids, I imagine, will be on fire. If I were a band director, I would do that. Probably we would never compete, but we would play together all the time.

Connor Chee also focused on identifying student interests and asking questions:

Find out what students want as a starting point. They might want to write songs or do singer-songwriter-type things, or they might want to compose for an orchestra or a movie. Identify what it is that they like most or what drew them in. From there, encourage them to listen to more music or watch music performances that are similar to what interests them. If one of my students was to say, "I want to start composing for movies," then I'd ask, "What are some of your favorite movie scores? Bring me some of your favorites and let's talk about them." That gets them excited, and once they have that starting point, it's a much more natural conversation about what to do next.

Miriam Cutler also emphasized excitement and the fundamental value of exploration and play:

You know what the most important thing is? Excitement. One of the most amazing experiences I ever had was opening up my new clarinet and smelling it. I'm not kidding. Every time I picked up a different instrument, I wanted to play it. I still get excited when I see real instruments. So have kids play more instruments early on instead of trying to become virtuosic at one of them. Don't limit them when they're young, because the excitement is so raw for kids. Have kids touch instruments and make noise on them and see which one feels like them. They will pick one or two or maybe three. They'll find their own thing, and maybe some of them will go, "Man, this guitar is really cool. I really like the computer. What happens if I play guitar *and* use computer sounds?" Give them all the options. It teaches them to see the world.

Steve Hampton advocated for technology and for finding one's place as learner and creator:

For a kid who wants to be a composer, the resources are unending. Think of something you want to learn, then do a Google search on it and find the YouTube video that shows you how. All those resources are an amazing opportunity for students, and they're doing that anyway. Then, if you choose to study music in college, choose a place that fits how you are musically. And obviously, whether it's old school or new school, develop your abilities. If you're in the tech end of things, great, you've got to learn everything. If you're a violinist, great, you've got to practice. Raw talent blended with all this new technology and resources makes for a very powerful opportunity. If you're teaching, you've got to be comfortable with that and try to incorporate it into your method.

Jennifer Jolley emphasized improvisation:

Encourage improvisation in every class and ensemble. As my friend (composer) Omar Thomas says, we're not talking about capital "I" improvising at the Blue Note with a spotlight. We're talking about little ditties and incorporating improvisation in different ways, such as adding notes or rearranging familiar tunes. I understand there's a curriculum and there's a lot going on, but improvisation teaches listening, you're learning about music, and you're creating music in real time.

Anne McGinty argued for student composers to be heard:

Have their music played. Not criticized—*played*, and then talk about it. How do you feel? Does this work for you? Are there finger problems? What kind of instrumentation is it? Good feedback can help. Negative feedback can destroy them and the whole idea. If they've got a piano around, work with that, or a guitar, or a synthesizer, or a flute—whatever they've got. Or just sing.

Jessie Montgomery emphasized collaboration and honoring the journey of discovery:

Give them projects to do. I might say, "Find your cello friend, and write something for them. Get your friend to help you with the notation and ask you questions about what you wrote. And then let me know how it goes." Then do it again with a violinist or a flutist. And make sure there are opportunities for the kids to work in groups. I like the idea of instilling early on that composing can be a collaborative experience. The act of composing and sharing ideas about music back and forth is something that can enhance their experience. Ask them to imagine a portfolio of their works. What would you put in that portfolio? And remember that in composition, unlike learning an instrument, there are no wrong answers. The student is on a journey of discovering their own music. Think about it as walking with them as they make their mistakes. Take a mentorship approach. I would say that's fundamental.

Daniel Bernard Roumain offered a three-part strategy for encouraging young creators, and a three-island metaphor for teachers:

When a kid says, "I want to be a composer," I say three things. The first is, "I agree with you. I think it's fantastic. I think you can do it. I think you *will* do it. I want to help you, and if I was 10 years old right now, here's what I would do." It's not just positive reinforcement, it's *I agree*. I'm trying to reinforce their choice and partner with them. Then they know they're not alone. Second, if they want to be like another composer, I say, "You should listen to all of their music and should learn everything you can about them—where they were born, where they grew up. Listen and learn. Then share that with the people you love—your parents, your family, your dog." I'm challenging them to get into the research and go deep. The third thing is, "*You* start creating your own scores, your own music, your own tracks, if you're not doing that already. Use your phone. Make your own movie and then create your music to it. Dive into that pool of creativity and keep going. Falter through. If you have a teacher, share it with your teacher. Just start." It's about affirmation of their choice, it's about biography and re-search, and it's about the actualization of their creative practice. Don't wait. Do it.

For teachers, the analogy I would use is, you're trying to build bridges between three islands. The first island is *their* island. What are they listening to? What are they wearing? What is their cultural practice—the totality of it? Every one of your students has their own island. Then, what's *my* island? This is what I'm listening to, this is what I like. Once that is shared—not exchanged yet, just shared—the bridge starts to happen. Then, third, where can we go together? What are all the things that are in common between our musics? They're going to say things we can't imagine. I've been in a class and played a minute of Bach and a minute of Eminem and asked, "Okay, what are the differences?" Easy. "What do they share in common?" It's incredible. Nine times out of ten they start to realize there's far more in common between those two composers than differences. That's the bridge building I'm talking about, and that's *so* exciting.

Mari Esabel Valverde spoke directly to students:

If you have a piece of music inside of you, do your best to get it out. Write the whole thing. Try getting it on staff paper. You don't have to have all the answers. Just try. And then, get somebody to *do* your music, perform your music. It's so validating and so important, no matter what. Do that as early as possible, honestly.

Eric Whitacre offered a one-day creative project:

I've stumbled on something that I'm calling the four-note challenge. You wake up in the morning and choose four notes, any four from a chromatic scale. Choose four notes that have some meaning to you. They might spell out your own name or your parent's or someone you love or your phone number. Then, your piece has to use only those four notes, be less than one minute long, and it must be finished by midnight, no matter what. The idea is to upload it to social media, like TikTok. Built into that that lesson are massive constraints, and those constraints cause you to use a different part of your brain. You become adaptive and clever and constructive. And you also have less judgment on yourself, because you've only got four notes, so how inter-esting can this possibly be? Too often creativity and composition is taught as this wide open field where anything is possible, and that's absolutely paralyzing, espe-cially if you've never done it before.

Coda

Throughout the interviews, these twelve composers told small stories with huge meaning for their own lives and perhaps for the lives of young people everywhere who yearn to compose or who are already creating music—on their own, with their friends, on their computers or their phones, with their voices and instruments. For some young people, creating music may be how they choose to be in the musical in the world. Mari Esabel Valverde explained:

> I was fortunate to know right out of high school that I wanted to pursue a degree in composition. There's an extra aspect that I've learned retroactively, which is, because I'm transgender, because I struggled to understand what that meant and what to do about it as a young person, I knew going down the road of composition would allow me to participate in music without having to be seen and without having to perform. Yes, I sang in choirs, but at a certain point I didn't want to be a performer because I struggled with how the world perceived my gender. The reason that's important is, I knew that by being a composer I could work in the background and still be in music.

Creating music can be an act of affirming identity, a means of responding to the present moment, a chance to make a difference, a way to engage with others. Jennifer Jolley put it this way:

> I also know that I exist, personally, as a composer, and that I best articulate how I'm feeling and how I'm reacting to the world through my music. There was a time in my life that I had a bit of an existential crisis: "What good is being a composer when bad things happen?" Well, I'm here to create music. There's nothing wrong with that. If there's one thing we've learned from this pandemic, it's that we need music. We crave it. Music has purpose and meaning and function. And I've learned that through my music I can still make a difference. Maybe not on a big global level, but I know that I can write pieces with social justice themes, or, my purpose right now is, maybe we just need a bop.

So, from Miriam Cutler to young musicians and composers everywhere:

> Maybe you have this idea: "I'm a fan of this musician, this composer. I want to be just like them." Well, whoa, guess what? You can be just like *you*. That's what *they* are. They are just like them, and you can be just like you. Here's how you do it. Find your world. Find what turns you on. And then just do it.

NOTES

1. Thank you to Herberger Institute for Design and the Arts staff members Larissa Stucki for assistance with contacting composers, first edits of Zoom transcripts, and wrangling permissions, and Shelly Laug Wilsterman for the not-so-small feat of scheduling the interviews.
2. Creative Ability Development is a program developed by Alice Kanack in Rochester, New York. See http://kanack.org/
3. Miriam Cutler's feminist band was the New Miss Alice Stone Ladies Society Orchestra. Videos of the band can be found on YouTube.
4. In fact, the inventors of the Fairlight system, Kim Ryrie and Peter Vogel, coined the term *sample* (Wildman, 1999).

References

Csikszentmihalyi, M. (1990/2008). *Flow: The psychology of optimal experience*. HarperPerennial.

Wallas, G. (1926/2014). *The art of thought*. Solis Press.

Wildman, J. (1999). Electronic music. In L. Stacy & L. Henderson (Eds.), *Encyclopedia of music in the 20th century* (pp. 187–192). Routledge.

SECTION II

FINDING IDENTITY AND FOSTERING INCLUSION IN MUSIC COMPOSITION

....

CHAPTER 6

FROM VULNERABLE TEACHER TO VULNERABLE SONGWRITER

A Reflective Journey toward Authenticity

....

RACHEL WHITCOMB

Have you ever felt afraid to show parts of your musical self to other musicians, fellow teachers, or music students?

Do you long to share discoveries you have made about yourself as a musician and teacher that revealed you—a you that you wished you could have embraced sooner?

Have you deliberately separated the musician you are in your personal life from the musician you show to your students?

What are you hiding?

Why are you hiding?

THIS chapter provides a descriptive timeline of experiences that have shaped my thinking about vulnerability and authenticity in both teaching and songwriting, and how the collision and gradual merging of those identities has provided frightening, rewarding, and informative moments in my musical and pedagogical journey. This autoethnographic account aims to briefly relate these personal experiences to literature within the music education profession and related fields, provide music teachers with opportunities to reflect upon the vulnerabilities they and their students may bring to the learning environment, and consider ideas for addressing and overcoming challenges associated with those vulnerabilities. Each story concludes with a life lesson and a list of questions to ponder as we all strive to discover ways to develop welcoming, creative, and authentic learning spaces for songwriting endeavors.

Vulnerability and Authenticity: Meanings and Context for Music Educators

In my view, vulnerability and authenticity are inextricably linked. Without authenticity, one cannot truly be vulnerable, and one usually feels vulnerable in part because the authentic self is at the forefront of the endeavor. In scholarly literature, there are many definitions for both vulnerability and authenticity from which to choose. This chapter is not designed to provide an exhaustive literature review that cites hundreds of years of writing and research from philosophers, scientists, and scholars in an effort to whittle it all down to a comprehensive definition of vulnerability. In an effort to avoid feeling more vulnerable about successfully writing that type of background, in addition to preventing readers from feeling vulnerable while reading it for fear of having to recall all of that information, I will instead share ideas from the literature that I have found the most relevant to my experiences and the experiences of the many music teachers with whom I have worked in the hope that these ideas will resonate with readers and not do too much damage to my professional credibility. I do hope that the personal stories I share later will be received with mercy, as well. The remainder of this section includes a professional context for vulnerability and authenticity in order for readers to recognize themselves and their students in the personal stories that follow.

In *Daring Greatly* (2012), Brené Brown defines vulnerability as "uncertainty, risk, and emotional exposure" (p. 34). Of particular interest to musicians and teachers is how Brown describes actions, thoughts, or feelings that illustrate her definition of vulnerability:

> To put our art, our writing, our photography, our ideas out into the world with no assurance of acceptance or appreciation—that's also vulnerability. To let ourselves sink into the joyful moments of our lives even though we know that they are fleeting, even though the world tells us not to be too happy lest we invite disaster—that's an intense form of vulnerability. (p. 34)

Her words *let ourselves* in the above description connect with the word *willingness* in the following definition of vulnerability: "willingness to show emotion or to allow one's weakness to be seen or known; willingness to risk being hurt or attacked" (Dictionary. com, n.d.). As songwriters and teachers, it seems that the nature of what we do lends itself or even requires us to possess a willingness to engage in vulnerable artistic and interpersonal experiences. Karen Salvador (2019) directly states, "Teaching music is an act of vulnerability" (p. 28) due in part to the stressful working environments, cognitive distortions, perfectionist tendencies, and numbing behaviors that accompany the emotion-filled connections we make with our students and with music itself on a daily basis. Mara Culp and Sara Jones (2020) point out that music educators can also face uncomfortable moments when disagreeing with others in the profession by stating, "It is not the belief or behavior that is scrutinized but the individuals themselves. Disagreements of philosophy can sometimes devolve into personal attacks that call a person's ability, character, and value as a person into question" (p. 77). Although Salvador, Culp, and Jones have begun to discuss the vulnerabilities of teacher-musicians and student-musicians and the challenges that vulnerabilities present in classrooms, we are apparently still collectively feeling, well, vulnerable. Lauren Kapalka Richerme (2016) states, "Despite the pervasive potential for teachers and students to experience vulnerability during musically educative endeavors, vulnerability remains almost completely absent from music education philosophy and discourse" (p. 28).

Vulnerability connects with authenticity because, as I stated earlier, I believe that when we feel vulnerable, we are usually sharing parts of our true selves that may have been hidden. To be authentic, one is "true to one's own personality, spirit, or character" (Merriam-Webster.com, n.d.). Regarding the meaning of authenticity in relation to teaching, Patricia Cranton and Ellen Carusetta (2004) state, "Authenticity is a multifaceted concept that includes at least four parts: being genuine, showing consistency between values and actions, relating to others in such a way as to encourage their authenticity, and living a critical life" (p. 7). When music teachers consider authenticity, they may feel the need to make room for musical identities as well as teacher identities. Kristen Pellegrino (2009) indicates that music teachers have the added challenge of "teacher versus performer identity conflict" (p. 40). So, who we are and what we do as musicians may be in contrast to who we are and what we do as teachers, and that requires careful personal reflection to determine which parts of our musicianship are the most authentic and how those parts are demonstrated and modeled in our teaching. We must be careful to create environments where are our students can discover their authentic musical identities without losing our own!

STORIES AND LESSONS

I learned from [director] Mike Nichols that you don't have to tell someone what to do. You can tell them a story instead, engage them. And by the end of the story, they'll know what to do.

(Cher, 1998, p. 262)

Songwriting is a personal and vulnerable endeavor. In the spirit of soul-baring songwriting, I chose an autoethnographic approach to this chapter because it "acknowledges and accommodates subjectivity, emotionality, and the researcher's influence on research, rather than hiding from these matters or assuming they don't exist" (Ellis, Adams, & Bochner, 2011, p. 274). To illustrate ways that vulnerable and authentic moments can inform instructional decisions when working with young songwriters, I will divulge moments of risk and truth in my own musical and professional life. Each story I share contains a life lesson that has emerged in my work as a music teacher, researcher, and songwriter as I have taught, studied, discussed, created, listened, and reflected over the years. Throughout the discussion, I will apply these life lessons to teaching song-writing or fostering creative music environments sometimes directly and through inference. One sincere goal in this personal narrative approach is, as Carolyn Ellis (2004) describes, for readers to "take a more active role as they are invited into the author's world, aroused to a feeling level about the events being described, and stimulated to use what they learn there to reflect on, understand, and cope with their own lives" (p. 46) as musicians and teachers. The lesson learned from each story is indicated upon its conclusion, followed by questions music teachers may wish to ponder when investigating their own vulnerabilities.

Story #1: Self-Stifled Graduate Student, June 1995

It is the spring of 1995 and I'm outside my apartment in Evanston, Illinois, a few blocks from the Northwestern University campus where I will complete my oral exam and present a reflective portfolio of artifacts representing various endeavors in teaching and music-making from the past year. The exam and presentation are the final requirements for the Master of Music in Music Education. Professors Bennett Reimer and Peter Webster, internationally known and widely respected musician-teacher-scholars in the music education profession, will preside. I attempt to pack my car with a pile of turquoise binders that comprise the portfolio, hard copies being the norm at the time. The backseat of my car does not have the depth to hold the binders securely. In order to fit the four huge binders onto the front passenger seat safely for the drive to the Reimer/Webster extravaganza, I will need to move my cherished plastic container of country music CDs down to the floor. Emotionally, this is almost too much to ask. It was, after all, the height of the Garth Brooks era. I then say defiantly, aloud yet only to myself, "This is the last time!"

Although I could not articulate it fully back then, I still remember the many things I meant by that statement 25 years later: This is the last time I will put my music to the side to follow the rules. This is the last time I will postpone my true musical self. This is the last time I will invalidate the music I choose to sing and long to write by keeping it from my teachers and colleagues. This is the last time I will allow self-doubt to triumph over vulnerability and authenticity. This is the last time I will be safe in my choices instead of taking musical, emotional, and social risks. Sadly, it was not the last time for any of those things.

When I arrived at the exam, I safely answered questions about philosophy, curriculum, research, and technology in music education. I presented domain projects within my portfolio, which had never been done in the program before. These projects were meant to be developed individually based on the interests and career goals of each student at the master's level. Dr. Webster indicated early on that the faculty would not provide samples of these types of projects because that would be the antithesis of the creative freedom they hoped to foster. I would love to be able to report here that one of my projects focused on country music, but that would not have been the safe choice! What would the faculty have thought of me? Instead, I presented a series of upper elementary general music listening lessons for Dvorak's *New World Symphony* and detailed plans for creating and maintaining a successful voice studio. While I was proud of my projects, I did not connect my personal musicianship with my professional musicianship because I was afraid and embarrassed. I was bitter that I had to symbolically (and in the car, literally) move my beloved music to the side to make room for these projects. I realize now that my professors created an environment with endless possibilities and that I created the stifling rules myself! I was in my own way. I hindered my own path to creative glory.

I must clarify that neither the late, great Bennett Reimer or the wonderfully influential Peter Webster knew of my internal dialogue or struggle. At that time, I'm quite certain they were unaware that I listened to or enjoyed country music because I worked very hard to hide it. My commitment to keep my musical preferences hidden stemmed from many years of being told by music teachers when to breathe, what vowel sound to make, and how to sit. When I vocally ventured into bluegrass straight-tone territory, I was told by my high school choir director to sing prettier. She and many other music teachers never asked me what music I preferred, and country music was only mentioned during class as part of disparaging jokes.

Of course, this goes beyond vulnerability and authenticity into inclusivity and diversity. It would have been helpful to have even one outspoken supporter of country music within the music education profession at the time, but I would have to wait quite a long time for that. Vincent C. Bates, Jason B. Gossett, and Travis Stimeling (2020) state, "In more than a century of *Music Educators Journal*, there have been no articles devoted specifically to country music, reflecting a history of American school music that grew out of efforts to preserve and perpetuate European classical music—to bring 'high culture' to common folk" (p. 29). At Northwestern in 1995, I chose to use the isolation I felt within the profession and my previous music teachers' lack of acknowledgment of country music as evidence that Drs. Webster and Reimer would be in agreement with my former teachers.

In retrospect, perhaps one promising way to reconcile and ultimately combine the worlds of traditional/school music with my real-life music was to tell these thoughtful, considerate professors about my predicament. Unfortunately, youth and fear prevailed. In 2018, while Dr. Webster was virtually visiting my class of undergraduate music education majors, I fessed up. He had no idea until then. We had a nice laugh about it. I wish I had the opportunity to tell Dr. Reimer before he passed away. He was always delighted by my blunt honesty when discussing philosophical issues in class. He never knew that the context for those discussions in my mind were aesthetic experiences I had with songs written by John Denver, Dolly Parton, or Clint Black instead of orchestral repertoire composed by Brahms or Stravinsky. I saved my papers from his class and when reviewing them to write this chapter, I can see his positive handwritten comments in the margins. I would like to think that he would have written them regardless of the style of music of which I wrote.

Lesson #1: Get out of your own way.

Questions to Ponder:

- What rules from your former teachers are you still following? How do those rules assist or inhibit your authentic musical self?
- How have you gotten in your own way as a musician?
- What are you telling yourself about how your musical preferences are perceived by others and how will that inner voice affect you as a teacher?

Story #2: Pedagogical Risk-Taker, Songwriting Scaredy-Cat, September 2001

While teaching elementary general music in a suburb of Nashville, Tennessee, I developed a step-by-step, Kodály-based approach to teaching vocal improvisation (Whitcomb, 2003). My students were improvising solfège patterns regularly and I was pleased with their achievements in both singing technique and improvisation. Although improvisation is considered a creative endeavor within the profession, the approach that I developed was rather prescriptive and yet at that time it may have been considered by some in the profession to be rebellious. Six years after my work with Drs. Reimer and Webster, I was still intent on following rules but I was now confident enough to have a hand in creating those rules, with the help of Zoltan Kodály, of course. It felt like a creative endeavor for me and for the students, although I sometimes worried that I was going against the foundations of the Kodály method by incorporating improvisation into the prepare-present-practice sequence.

When I published the approach and presented demonstrations about the improvisational endeavors in the years that followed, my ideas were received favorably by music teachers in part because of the inherent and careful balance of creativity and teacher control within the sequence. I dare say that other music teachers were feeling the same inner turmoil with which I struggled! Perhaps we wanted to foster creativity within our students, but we had not fully embraced it in our own musical endeavors because we were too busy following the rules or preferences of our former teachers. Maybe we had only experienced musical vulnerability when we failed to play the music that someone else created and had never even been invited to share our own musical creations. My later research (Whitcomb, 2005 & 2007; Gruenhagen & Whitcomb, 2014) would confirm that factors inhibiting teachers from incorporating improvisation into their teaching included a lack of experience improvising as musicians. It seems reasonable to consider that this could be true for songwriting, as well.

Back in my suburban Nashville classroom in 2001, my instructions to elementary students during improvisational activities included supportive phrases such as, "Create something new!" or "Don't be afraid to make a mistake!" I did my best to create a welcoming environment for them to try out their musical ideas. On the surface, that sounds rather admirable. However, I had been living in Nashville for over a year to fulfill my dream of becoming a country singer-songwriter and had not yet written a country song. Ever. As Val Kilmer's Doc Holliday says to Kurt Russell's Wyatt Earp in the movie *Tombstone*, "It appears my hypocrisy knows no bounds" (Cosmatos & Jarre, 1993). Although I was willing to listen to my own instructions to create something new within my teaching, I was still stuck in a crippling state of vulnerability as a musician, which ultimately affected my authenticity as both a teacher and a musician.

My few attempts at songwriting while living in Nashville were rather academic in that I tried to approach songwriting the way I had approached music theory homework during my undergraduate studies. It was difficult to connect the emotional and expressive elements that occurred regularly when I sang country music to my creative endeavors within the style. This difficulty reminds me of how Sam Reese (1980) connected Polanyi's theory of tacit knowing to music. Reese summarizes a portion of the theory by stating, "*We can know more than we can tell*" (p. 77, emphasis in original). In my case, I could feel more than I could compose.

I was much more willing to interpret the music and lyrics from other songwriters than to express my own thoughts and feelings. One strength in my singing was the ability to connect with individual audience members through facial expressions and eye contact during performances. When meeting audience members after performances, they regularly told me that as I sang, they could tell how I was feeling and relate to those feelings, and they expressed how my performance allowed them to listen closely to the meaning of the song. I was touched by these comments. At that time, it was as if I was safely hiding behind other songwriters. I was in the spotlight literally but at the same time I had no need take ownership of any less-than-perfect lyrical stories or melodic choices that had been made within the songs I sang. Certainly, there are many positive aspects of performing the musical works of others. At that time, however, I was starting to realize that I had different things to say lyrically and musically, but I was not yet willing or able to authentically express them. A small songwriter identity was starting to emerge, but it was not in harmony (literally or figuratively) with my performer identity.

Teaching continued to bring me a great deal of joy, and I wanted to further my studies in music education and become a music teacher-educator. The decision to enroll in a doctoral program was one of the five best decisions I have made in my career, and I would not wish it away. However, I am convinced that part of the timing of that decision had to do with running toward the comfort of rules and structure and running away from the vulnerability of the songwriting process. My teacher identity was in conflict with my performer identity (Pellegrino, 2009), and both were in conflict with my newly developing songwriter identity. There were too many of us, and I hoped that eventually only the most genuine of us would be permitted to stay.

Lesson #2: Get real.

Questions to Ponder:

- What advice do you give your students that you avoid taking yourself? Why?
- In what ways are you embracing or ignoring your true musician identities and teacher identities? In what ways are those identities in harmony or in conflict? What do you think about that? What will you do about it?

- What risks have you taken as a musician or teacher? What risks should you take in the future?

Story #3: Safe Scholar, Terrified Teachers, 2005

By the time I began writing my dissertation on improvisation, I was much more confident in my abilities to contribute to the profession as a teacher and scholar. This confidence stemmed primarily from the fact that I had more diverse teaching experiences and had become more familiar with how others in the field were approaching improvisation. Timing within the profession was also in my favor. In 2005, teachers were aware of the expectation that improvisation and composition be part of music instruction due to the inclusion of these creative endeavors within the United States' (voluntary) National Standards for Music Education (Consortium of National Arts Education Associations, 1994[1]), but I had a sense that these things were still not happening everywhere despite the fact that it had been over ten years since the standards were published. Ever the rule follower, I did an exhaustive literature review focusing on improvisation in elementary general music classrooms. I was pleased that my article on Kodály-based vocal improvisation was well received by teachers and had become part of that literature. The more I read, the more confident I became in my own abilities to design more creative opportunities for music students in the future and contribute to the profession in meaningful ways. In their book, *The Confidence Code* (2014), Katty Kay and Claire Shipman state, "Confidence occurs when the insidious self-perception that you aren't able is trumped by the stark reality of your achievements" (p. 48).

My dissertation developed into a descriptive study on the status of improvisation in elementary general music classrooms in the state of Illinois (Whitcomb, 2005). This was an old-school survey study in which questionnaires were mailed to the participants who then completed them with a pen and mailed them back to me in a postage-paid envelope. Data from paper questionnaires does not automatically enter itself into a spreadsheet like today's online survey tools, so my husband (Dave, not a music teacher) and I decided to make data entry a bonding experience for us and our cats. We regularly drove together to pick up the returned questionnaires from our post office box. Dave read the results to me aloud and I entered them into my electronic spreadsheet while the cats did their best to distract us.

In the questionnaire, I asked respondents to indicate the kinds of improvisational activities occurring in their classrooms by circling "yes" or "no" for each activity within a comprehensive list, inquired about the instructional time allotted to improvisational activities (again, primarily yes/no questions), and asked teachers to provide background information such as years of teaching experience. Data for these types of questions was easily entered into the spreadsheet (e.g., 1 for yes, 2 for no), to be analyzed in more detail later. One question required teachers to rank 10 activities—singing, playing instruments, notating, listening, evaluating, improvising, composing, connecting music to history and culture, moving to music, and connecting music to the arts and disciplines outside the arts—based on the amount of instructional time allotted, with 1 indicating the activity that received the most instructional time and 10 indicating the activity that received the least amount of instructional time (p. 147). I also asked teachers to indicate factors that assisted and inhibited them in including improvisation in instruction and gauged teachers' attitudes regarding improvisation. As Dave read the results, we both developed an understanding of what was happening in elementary general music classrooms in Illinois related to improvisation. Entering the 1s and 2s was rather straightforward.

The last question on the survey was the only open-ended question, where I provided a few blank lines for respondents to share additional handwritten information related to teaching improvisation. A common theme within the data for that question was a low confidence level on the part of the teachers to include improvisation due to a lack of improvisational experiences as musicians, with comments such as the vulnerable yet honest, "I would like improvisation to play a bigger role in my instruction, but because I feel inexperienced myself, it is difficult to incorporate" (p. 114). Although the last question was the only official opportunity for respondents to share thoughts in their own words, some did not hesitate to use any available blank space on any page to share their views. The rule follower side of me did not report any of the information that respondents added this way, but in my opinion, the information they shared illustrated the stronghold that self-doubt and vulnerability had on these teachers.

Approximately 10 years after the study was completed, in a quest to downsize my file cabinet collection, I discarded the paper surveys and therefore cannot directly quote respondents' editorial comments from the margins. I can, however, recall the humorous, fictional voice that my husband used in between recitations of 1s and 2s to express the "How *dare* you!" sentiment that teachers launched toward my study and me. Some teachers were appalled that I would care at all about creative endeavors when there are more important things to accomplish in music class with the limited instructional time available. The page with the question requiring teachers to rank the activities based on instructional time was particularly popular for respondents to vent about the unfairness of it all, most likely because they could no longer safely circle "yes" when asked if improvisation and composition were important. Once they ranked the activities, perhaps they felt vulnerable that the evil researcher would use it against them. Out of the 10 activities, improvisation ranked ninth and composition ranked 10th (p. 102). It seemed to be angry vulnerability, as if I were their professor and I was expecting them to do something that they were unprepared or unable to do. Alyson J. Bond, Laura Ruaro, and Janet Wingrove (2006) state:

> When people perceive a threat to the ego, they are likely to feel hurt. In order to avoid these negative feelings, they may use defence mechanisms, resulting in the externalising of these feelings as anger towards the source of threat. A negative evaluation of the perpetrator, whether the threat was intentional or not, reduces disturbing feelings of vulnerability. (p. 1088)

At first, I regressed and felt vulnerable in my abilities as a researcher—so I was angry right back! But as I talked it through with Dave and the cats, I heard myself saying that I wished these teachers would realize that through this study I was simply trying to gauge what was happening, why it was happening, and the factors that contributed to it. I was not in judgment mode, nor was I a threat to their teaching in the ways they might have perceived. Ultimately, my goal was to first understand and then, if possible, assist. Although they were throwing angry vulnerability at me, I still intended to be on their team.

Lesson #3: Find a support system and be a support system.

Questions to Ponder:

- How might students express angry vulnerability during the songwriting process and how can music teachers address it productively?
- How and where can music teachers find support systems for their own creative musical endeavors?
- What do music teachers and their students have in common and how can that affect songwriting processes?
- How can music teachers productively break down the defensiveness that students display when presented with new musical challenges or ideas in order to foster creative learning?
- What can music teachers do or say to become a support system for young songwriters?

Story #4: Withholder of Playlists, Summer 2011

After my sixth year of collegiate teaching, I thought it might finally be time to get a smartphone. Noticing an undergraduate student using one during an on-campus summer event, I asked him to give me a tutorial. As I held the phone for the first time, I instantly saw the icon for the iTunes app and was delighted with my aging self for recognizing anything! When I verbalized this delight and touched the icon, the student ripped the phone out of my hand with a quickness. I was shocked and asked why he did this, and he said that he did not want his professor to know the type of songs he had on his phone. That's right. An undergraduate studying to be a music teacher did not want his music education professor to know the music that he liked. This turn of events made me want to see it even more. With my curiosity piqued, I tried to remain as professional as possible in my unsuccessful attempt to grab the phone back. I asked nicely to see just one playlist, again without success. I made a strong case for why it was vital that I know the go-to music of my students' generation, and I asked philosophical questions about our current situation and how it might negatively affect his future students. He gave up nothing.

When the fall semester began, I still had not purchased a smartphone but was the happy owner of a new tablet. I always need help with new technology, so I consulted the experts (also known as the undergraduates hanging around down the hall from my office in between methods classes and ensemble rehearsals). It just so happened that the very same student who refused to show me the music on his phone the previous summer was willing to help me set up my tablet. As he showed me how to transfer data from my laptop to the tablet, he came across my music library. As soon as I realized this, I reached in desperation to grab the device away from him. It was too late. In my heart, all was officially lost. He spotted a Flo Rida song.

A number of interesting things happened in those moments. I realized that even though I had been appalled that this student refused to share his music with me just months earlier, I had the same reflex to hide my music from him. Perhaps he did not want to be vulnerable in this way because up until that point I was not willing to be vulnerable. If my music library had remained hidden from him, I would have reinforced his image of me as an ivory tower, out-of-touch professor whose music had no connection to his music. I would have missed the magical way his facial expressions changed as he scrolled through my downloaded songs. What started out as a look of playful rebellion morphed into looks of confusion, appreciation, disgust, acknowledgment, and intrigue as he made his way through songs by Bon Jovi, Bruno Mars, Destiny's Child, Eminem, Lee Ann Womack, and Peter, Paul, and Mary. The look of relief, however, had the most enduring effect on my relationship with this student and perhaps with all students from that moment on. He seemed relieved that he had heard of some of these artists because that made me more relatable and less intimidating. Perhaps he assumed that I would only be listening to Schubert art songs or symphonic works, which were mixed in as well. It seemed that by hiding important parts of my personal, musical self, I was withholding the very things that would allow me to best reach my students. While the student scrolled, he obliterated the distance between us that had created his own trepidations about sharing his musical preferences. Although I was sweating profusely, I was relieved as well. Only in retrospect have I realized that it took more energy and became much more difficult to hide my authentic musical self than to share it. Later that semester within our music school, I performed an Orff-instrument-arranged Eminem rap along with this student and his cohort. I knew every word of my part long before we started rehearsing.

Lesson #4: Get over yourself. Or, in the true spirit of Eminem, *lose yourself.*

Questions to Ponder:

- How has the mutual appreciation and/or shared understanding of songs connected you to other musicians, other teachers, or your students? How might you describe the value of those connections?
- What about your musicianship makes you feel vulnerable and why?
- What aspects of your musicianship feel authentic and why?

Story #5: Reluctant Songwriter, Amateur Professor, 2012–2013

I enthusiastically welcome Dr. John Kratus to take credit for anything positive that has resulted from the events in this next story. With a caring and humorous heart, I also blame him entirely. In Greensboro, North Carolina, Dr. Kratus presented the conference session, "Developing Students' Vernacular Musicianship in a Music Methods Course" (2011) to a national audience of music teacher-educators, and I was pleased to attend. By this time, I was quite familiar with his work on vernacular musicianship. Kratus provided the following description of vernacular musicianship and how it relates to music teacher education:

> The type of music-making that most people outside of formal school settings engage in is called vernacular musicianship, which can be defined as "native or indigenous musicianship." Aspects of vernacular musicianship include, but are not limited to, arranging, learning by ear, improvising, and composing. None of these aspects is given serious and sustained attention in the collegiate education of music teachers. [Abstract]

It was exciting to learn about Kratus's efforts to stretch the musicianship capabilities of the undergraduates enrolled in his secondary methods course when he added three small-group Musicianship Development Projects, as described below:

> The three projects were: (1) learn by ear and perform a cover of a song, (2) arrange and perform a song in a style different from the original, and (3) compose (as a group) and perform an original song. Students were given one week to prepare each project. I offered no instruction in how to accomplish the projects, preferring to find what the students developed on their own. The performances were held in class during the regularly scheduled class time. [Abstract]

Upon learning of these projects, I was enthusiastic to incorporate them into my methods class as soon as possible. While still on a high from our Eminem performance, I decided to incorporate these projects into my fall 2012 methods class. Around this time, my students began to repeat back to me semi-philosophical phrases I would use in class, such as, "If you are uncomfortable, you are probably learning something." While I was happy that they took these types of ideas to heart, I also felt the need to live by my own words in order to embrace authenticity. I felt strongly that I should not ask students to do anything in class that I had not previously attempted. The three projects that Kratus designed were new to me and to my students, and it seemed appropriate and helpful for me to demonstrate them prior to expecting the students to complete them, just as I had regularly done for years with elementary general music activities. Again, I thank and blame Dr. Kratus for what would become the most exhilarating and terrifying moments of my professional life.

Learning a country song by ear as a vocalist was something I had done regularly, so that aspect of the first project did not put me in a vulnerable position. In order to be authentic to my musical preferences, I chose *The King of Broken Hearts*, a traditional country song written by Jim Lauderdale. My undergraduate country band consisted of a combination of music education and music technology majors, and I initially felt confident in guiding them to learn the song by ear. The two music technology majors had each learned to play their major instruments (guitar and bass) primarily by ear in their basements, and they taught me more than I taught them about learning music by ear (more on that later). The music education majors in the newly-formed country band felt the need to write things down, but since I prohibited them from using standard notation on behalf of Dr. Kratus, they created charts for their own use. Although the arrangement developed nicely, the most vulnerable aspect of the first project for me was performing a country song in a classroom that typically served as the setting for applied classical lessons and chamber ensemble rehearsals. Nevertheless, I literally dusted off my cowboy boots and demonstrated the first Musicianship Development Project for my methods class. I shared the video with Dr. Kratus and in return received positive comments about my efforts. So far, so good.

For the second project, I enlisted undergraduate musicians from the Tamburitzans, a Pittsburgh-based multicultural song and dance company "dedicated to perpetuating international cultural heritage through entertaining performance" (Tamburitzans, n.d.). Many of the instrumentalists within the Tamburitzans work together in small groups regularly and have learned their instruments by ear from family members, so when I asked them to work with me on a bluegrass version of "Welcome to the Jungle," they did not hesitate. I would like to think Axl Rose and Slash were proud of our efforts. The silliness of this endeavor created a very low level of vulnerability on my part, and the methods students were seeing more of my authentic musical self. After all, one must truly love Guns N' Roses to do this sort of thing. My risk-taking, combined with the high level of vernacular musicianship on the part of the Tamburitzans and levity from the music itself, earned me credibility among my methods students while creating an environment of acceptance and mutual understanding. By this time, students were facing the reality that they would all soon be completing these projects, so they were hopeful that the acceptance and kindness they extended to me during my demonstrations would be reciprocated when it was their turn to perform. Things were still going well.

It was time for the third project, which was to compose an original song. I had written a number of developmentally appropriate children's songs for elementary general music purposes, but this was something much different. In my regular communication with Dr. Kratus, he indicated that his expectations for this particular project had been clarified for his students over time and, in turn, for me. The song must be in a style that would be conducive to radio play now or in the past. He was basically telling me not to hide behind Orff or Kodály, but to actually create a song that I might want to hear on a country station. As I thought about this last project, a few things were going on in my inner dialogue alongside the sheer terror I had experienced in past vulnerable moments. The bluegrass Guns N' Roses situation had me leaning toward a rogue, country professor identity and I felt more comfortable in it than I had anticipated. Perhaps that comfort came from being on the tenure track at an institution where I could envision a long and enjoyable future. At the age of 40, staying employed at a place that did not embrace my creative sides no longer appealed to me. I believed that my colleagues at Duquesne University welcomed creativity and also expected rigor within my teaching and scholarly work as I continued on the road to tenure and promotion. It was now or never. The rule-follower part of my identity felt there was no choice in the matter because Dr. Kratus told me to do it. He put me in a position where I did not have the option not to be creative. See? Credit and blame.

Time was running out. In order for me to demonstrate an original song for my methods students, I had to write one far enough in advance that I could rehearse with a guitarist and perform it at least 10 days before the students' performances would occur, giving them time to write and rehearse in their groups. My guitar skills were good enough for the writing process, but not quite at performance level. That would mean I would need to first share the song with the guitarist, which would be the first vulnerable moment of the third project. That moment was softened by the fact that I had become acquainted with the guitarist (Matt) from our *The King of Broken Hearts* performance and he was very kind and extremely patient. We had also had a humorous conversation about his recent dating experience, and I remember thinking about the differences between what he said and the ways my female students described dating.

As the third project swiftly approached, I was driving to a student teaching observation and decided that the best way to get started with the songwriting process without distraction was to avoid listening to music in my car. I thought about my students and myself. I thought about my favorite country songs and how most of them have to do with relationships. With that recent conversation I had with Matt in mind, I reflected on the relationships I had in college and wondered how I would describe who I was at that time to my current students. And then, as the clouds parted and sun burst through the car windows, I sang out, "Lonely, lonely, lonely girl" to an improvised melody. Not bad. In fact, good enough to take out my portable audio recorder (still no smartphone) and sing it again. I kept singing! I used no solfège. I had no visual representation because I was driving. I remembered that when I lived in Nashville, most of my rehearsals were in the car. I would improvise vocal ornamentations, revise them until I liked what I heard, and then repeat them over and over to work on technique. The songwriting process turned out to be very similar, only I was creating much more than ornamentation. Even though I needed to get this song written quickly in terms of available days, I had lots of available driving time built into my schedule. With its many bridges and tunnels, Pittsburgh and its challenging traffic patterns added hours to my workweek, particularly because of the large number of student teachers I was observing at the time. I wrote the song by ear in multiple sessions while driving and eventually sat down at home with my guitar and laptop to confirm the chords and lyrics. I created my first chart and made an appointment with Matt for the day before the big methods class performance. Before he arrived, I was lying on the floor of my office short of breath with butterflies in my stomach, wondering (a) how bad my song really was, (b) why I decided to write about something so personal instead of choosing a horribly stereotypical country topic like trucks or whiskey, and (c) how Dr. Kratus could do this to me. I eventually managed to invite Matt in and summoned the courage to sing my first original country song, *Lonely Girl*, for him. I made no eye contact, and my voice was shaking during the first run-through. The song starts with the following lyrics:

> Lonely, lonely, lonely girl
> Trapped inside your hopeless world
> No confidence, no self-esteem
> You're losing sight of all your dreams (Whitcomb, 2014)

The lyrics at the end are more uplifting:

> Lonely, lonely, lonely girl
> You have the strength to change your world
> You'll find your joy when you decide
> To share the beauty that's inside
> So love yourself enough to see
> The special girl you're meant to be (Whitcomb, 2014)

Matt approached my first sing-through with his usual kindness and continued with positive reinforcement throughout the remainder of the rehearsal. We had a short discussion of the overall mood I wanted to convey with the song, but most of the rehearsal was a matter-of-fact give-and-take about chord choices, dynamics, and moments of schmaltzy rubato. Gradually, vulnerability gave way to authentic musical decision-making.

During the class session, I indicated that the song was dedicated to the female students in the class and was inspired by my own relationships in college. Before the performance, I told the students how nervous I was and while I procrastinated for what seemed like years, they good-naturedly laughed at me for not starting the song. The song begins with a strum of the tonic chord and then I have an a cappella vocal pickup, with the guitar coming back in on the downbeat. Matt must have played the first chord eight times before I had the nerve to start singing, but in a hesitant voice, I eventually did. In the middle of the performance, I vividly remember being shocked by the fact that I genuinely wanted it to last forever. I felt truly authentic for the first time in my professional life. It took 40 years, but my identities of rule-follower, country music fan, creator, musician, researcher, and teacher merged. I have a video recording of the performance and I can recognize that moment of merging identities when I watch it. The students were kind once again and I could tell from their facial expressions during the performance that they were listening to the lyrics. One female student came to my office later that day to tell me how much the lyrics touched her. In the weeks that followed, the students' projects were memorable and I believe that the vulnerability and authenticity we experienced together through those projects is one of the reasons we are all still in touch with each other today.

The moment of merging identities was instantly addictive, and I immediately threw myself into performing country and bluegrass music as often as possible on campus. The bass player (Keith) from *The King of Broken Hearts* performance was an accomplished student in our music technology program and was the first student in that program with whom I worked. I asked Keith about his musical journey leading up to college and most of what he told me was reminiscent of the informal music learning principles I read about in *Music, Informal Learning, and the School: A New Classroom Pedagogy* by Lucy Green (2008, pp. 9–10). For example, Keith learned to play bass by listening to and copying recordings of songs that he enjoyed. He shared a song with me that he had written while alone over Thanksgiving break. In addition to his music school responsibilities, he played in a band with his friends. When we worked together on our arrangement of *The King of Broken Hearts*, he went to and from listening, playing, and improvising with such speed that, try as I might with all of my prior formal music education, I could not keep up. I recognized that I needed to continue to learn from him, so I asked him to be the musical director for the very first full-length country concert on campus.

The dean of the music school was extremely supportive of the concert and my colleagues encouraged me with positivity. The preparations created culture shock at times, such as how the performance was consistently referred to as a faculty recital, evoking visions of me standing in the crook of the piano singing an aria. I decided to go all in, despite familiar moments of fear and vulnerability. I watched and learned as Keith directed the many accomplished classical musicians who were learning how to play in a country music style for the very first time. It was evident and embarrassing that the rehearsals would have run much more smoothly if I had not been a part of them. Two of my new original songs were on the program, and during rehearsals, Keith would ask me my thoughts on the arrangements and I became paralyzed, unable to make musical decisions about songs I wrote because I was convinced that the mostly 20-years-younger-than-me musicians in the room must know better than me. Imposter syndrome at its finest. After one particularly brutal rehearsal, Keith sent me an email of encouragement that contained the following:

> When I left today, I was reminded of when we first started working together, in that you were nervous as hell about your performance as a singer. . . . If you can . . . back up the things that you do, why would you or anyone have the authority or the gall to question that. . . . I'm tired of you questioning yourself because it reminds me of me. Confidence, belief, joy, timidness, nerves, stress, intimidation. Pick which ones you want people to leave with. This will be an experience where you are allowed to do what you want. Own it. (personal communication, January 10, 2013)

In one email, this 21-year-old called me out on my vulnerability, admitted that he suffered from it as well, alluded to the fact that this is nothing new for those pursuing creative endeavors, and gave me an authenticity directive.

For the remaining rehearsals, I listened to Keith and shut out the voices in my head telling me that I was an imposter. The only time I wavered was the night of the performance when the band began the first song and I was just about to go on stage. I stood alone in a red dress thinking that I was seconds away from committing career suicide. This was not the type of music or performance practice that had any type of credibility in higher education. In fact, I had never heard of any music education faculty colleague in any institution citing performances or compositions as scholarly or creative output. Articles, chapters, presentations, and books were scholarly. Singing country songs was not. In that moment, I knew there was something wrong with that. What did I want my students to know and be able to do? My fear of not going through with this performance and having to answer to myself was worse than any repercussions I might face within the profession. I took a deep breath and walked out on stage.

Earlier that day as I drove to campus, I left my beloved CDs (still no smartphone) on the front passenger seat of my car as a symbol of victory over my former self from 1995. The program consisted mostly of country song covers from the 1990s. *Lonely Girl* had its world premiere, and the female student who had previously shared her admiration of my lyrics sang background vocals. The red dress was one of three outfits for the performance. Months later, after my husband had complimented me on many aspects of my musical efforts, he suggested that I probably only needed one outfit for the next concert because, contrary to what I might think, I was not Reba McEntire. Apparently, I did not suffer from vulnerability when it came to my wardrobe. Little victories.

A little over one year later, I performed a second on-campus concert that included two new original country songs mixed in with a collection of classic country and bluegrass covers (and only two outfits this time). Shortly after that performance, as I was preparing for class with my back turned to my open office doorway, I heard an unfamiliar voice: "Excuse me, are you the country songwriter?" I turned around, a bit confused and delightfully surprised. I thought about it for a moment. "Well," I said with a surprised laugh, "I suppose I am!" This polite stranger introduced himself as a junior jazz guitar performance major who had always wanted to develop his mandolin playing so he could become more involved in country and folk music. He gave me his newly printed business card and courageously told me that he still considered himself a beginner on the mandolin but hoped we could work together in the future. As I assured him I would include him in our next gig, I hoped he had room on the front passenger seat of his car for his mandolin.

Lesson #5: Tell your story and others will follow.

Questions to Ponder:

- What story have you been reluctant to share about your personal relationship with music?
- What stories from your own life might inspire your students during their songwriting process?
- What story do you want to tell in the future about your musical journey?
- What can we learn from our students about vulnerability and authenticity? What can they learn from us?

Closing Thoughts

> When we hear someone else sing about the jagged edges of heartache or the unspeakable nature of grief, we immediately know we're not the only ones in pain. The transformative power of art is in this sharing. Without connection or collective engagement, what we hear is simply a caged song of sorrow and despair; we find no liberation in it. It's the sharing of art that whispers, "You're not alone." (Brown, 2017, p. 30)

The lessons presented in this chapter invite us to pursue the valuable lessons that are hidden within ourselves and within our interactions with our students: (1) Get out of your own way. (2) Get real. (3) Find a support system and be a support system. (4) Get over yourself. (5) Tell your story and others will follow. As music teachers, we have the joy and challenge of modeling musicality, creativity, songwriting, confidence, vulnerability, interpretation, and authenticity. We can certainly try to avoid vulnerable moments in teaching and songwriting. However, if we can instead embrace those moments, fully experience them, and thoughtfully reflect upon them, we can ultimately provide our students with the gift of our authentic selves so that we may then be invited into their musical worlds. Let us accept this precious invitation.

Note

1. The 1994 National Standards for Music can be in the National Standards Archives at https://nafme.org/my-classroom/standards/national-standards-archives/

References

Bates, V. C., Gossett, J. B., & Stimeling, T. (2020). Country Music Education for Diverse and Inclusive Music Classrooms. Music Educators Journal, 107(2), 28–34. https://journals.sagepub.com/doi/10.1177/0027432120956386

Bond, A. J., Ruaro, L., & Wingrove, J. (2006). Reducing anger induced by ego threat: Use of vulnerability expression and influence of trait characteristics. *Personality and Individual Differences, 40*(6), 1087–1097. https://doi.org/10.1016/j.paid.2005.12.002

Brown, B. (2012). *Daring greatly: How the courage to be vulnerable transforms the way we live, love, parent, and lead.* Gotham Books.

Brown, B. (2017). High lonesome. *Psychotherapy Networker, 41*(6), 30–35, 55.

Cher. (As told to Coplon, J.) (1998). *The first time.* Simon & Schuster.

Consortium of National Arts Education Associations (1994). *National standards for arts education.* MENC.

Cosmatos, G. P., & Jarre, K. (1993). *Tombstone* [Film]. Buena Vista Pictures.

Cranton, P., & Carusetta, E. (2004). Perspectives on authenticity in teaching. *Adult Education Quarterly, 55*(1), 5–22.

Culp, M., & Jones, S., (2020). Shame in music education: Starting the conversation and developing resilience. *Music Educators Journal, 106*(4), 36–42. https://journals.sagepub.com/doi/10.1177/0027432120906198

Dictionary.com, LLC (n.d.). Vulnerability. In *Dictionary.com dictionary*. Retrieved January 15, 2021, from https://www.dictionary.com/browse/vulnerability?s=t

Ellis, C. (2004). *The ethnographic I: A methodological novel about autoethnography*. AltaMira.

Ellis, C., Adams, T., & Bochner, A. (2011). Autoethnography: An overview. *Historical Social Research/Historische Sozialfoschung, 36*(4 [138]), 273–290. https://doi.org/10.17169/fqs-12.1.1589

Green, L. (2008). *Music, informal learning and the school: A new classroom pedagogy*. Routledge. https://doi.org/10.4324/9781315248523

Gruenhagen, L. M., & Whitcomb, R. (2014). Improvisational practices in elementary general music classrooms. *Journal of Research in Music Education, 61*(4), 379–395. https://journals.sagepub.com/doi/10.1177/0022429413508586

Kapalka Richerme, L. (2016). Vulnerable Experiences in Music Education: Possibilities and Problems for Growth and Connectivity. *Bulletin of the Council for Research in Music Education, 209,* 27–42. https://doi.org/10.5406/bulcouresmusedu.209.0027

Kay, K., & Shipman, C. (2014). *The confidence code: The science and art of self-assurance—what women should know*. HarperBusiness.

Kratus, J. (2011, September 16). *Developing students' vernacular musicianship in a music methods course* [Conference session]. Symposium on Music Teacher Education, Greensboro, North Carolina. Abstract retrieved from http://smte.us/wp-content/uploads/2011/08/1B-Kratus.htm

Merriam-Webster.com, Inc. (n.d.). Authentic. In *Merriam-Webster.com dictionary*. Retrieved May 15, 2021, from https://www.merriam-webster.com/dictionary/authentic

Pellegrino, K. (2009). Connections between performer and teacher identities in music teachers: Setting an agenda for research. *Journal of Music Teacher Education, 19*(1), 39–55. https://journals.sagepub.com/doi/10.1177/1057083709343908

Reese, S. (1980). Polanyi's tacit knowing and music education. *Journal of Aesthetic Education, 14*(1), 75–89. https://doi.org/10.2307/3332452

Salvador, K. (2019). Sustaining the flame: (Re)Igniting joy in teaching music. *Music Educators Journal, 106*(2), 28–36. https://journals.sagepub.com/doi/10.1177/0027432119873701

Tamburitzans. (n.d.). *About us: Our story*. Retrieved January 14, 2021, from https://www.thetamburitzans.org/about/ourstory

Whitcomb, R. (2003). Step by step: Using Kodály to build vocal improvisation. *Teaching Music, 10*(5), 34–38.

Whitcomb, R. (2005). A description of improvisational activities in elementary general music classrooms in the state of Illinois (Doctoral dissertation, University of Illinois at Urbana-Champaign, 2005). *Dissertation Abstracts International, 66,* 12A.

Whitcomb, R. (2007). Elementary improvisation in New York state: Survey results. The School Music News: The Official Publication of the *New York State School Music Association, 71*(2), 31–33.

Whitcomb, R. (2013). Teaching improvisation in elementary general music: Facing fears and fostering creativity. *Music Educators Journal, 99*(3), 43–50. https://journals.sagepub.com/doi/10.1177/0027432112467648

Whitcomb, R. (2014). Lonely Girl [Song]. On *Navigate the pain*. Rachel Whitcomb.

CHAPTER 7

....

BECOMING A COMPOSITION TEACHER

....

ALEXANDER KOOPS

THERE are many ways to enter composition teaching. Some teachers may find world music as a place to start, while others might dive in with improvisatory warm-ups, explore technology as a tool for composing, or begin songwriting. In this chapter, teachers are invited to think about pathways to develop as composition teachers through vignettes and a variety of entry points. For example, consider this vignette describing a middle school band director exploring Australian Aboriginal music as a pathway to creativity.

> The band students' eyes grew big with wonder as they heard their teacher performing multiphonics and circular breathing on her P-bone, imitating a didgeridoo player's kangaroo dance performance. She then showed a short YouTube of a didgeridoo player in Australian playing the piece she had just imitated. "What animal is being imitated?" she asked, and students quickly responded "rabbit? . . . Kangaroo?" "Yes, kangaroo! And now it's your turn!" she exclaimed, challenging the class to imitate an animal of their own choice on their own instrument. The class erupted in creative cacophony as they experimented with various non-traditional approaches to playing their instruments. Sounds and movements representing sloths, bumblebees, and gorillas eventually emerged during the collaborative animal music composition that ensued.

Music teachers can imagine themselves in the stories and examples and consider how their individual teaching situation might be able to include creativity lessons. This chapter begins by defining creativity and discussing why it is important to include in music education. It then proceeds to topics for developing composition lessons including workshops, mentors, books, journal articles, repertoire, and more. Each music teacher's journey will be varied, sometimes starting from their own upbringing, but often developing during their career. Composition pathways can be discovered in all types of music classes, from before-school jazz combos, to online classes, and from Orff ensembles to steel drum bands, but no class should be devoid of creativity!

What Is Creativity and Why Is It Important to Include in Music Education?

It is essential that any music teacher considering incorporating composition and improvisation into their curriculum understand why they are doing so. Many music education researchers and practitioners emphasize the value and importance of including creativity in all music classes (Kaschub & Smith, 2009a; Koops, 2009; Riley, 2006; Taft, 2019; Webster, 2016), but teachers have varying ideas of what creativity is. While no music teacher disputes that musicians are expected to make basic musical decisions that require some creative thinking, such as adding dynamics, rubato, and articulation when performing a musical phrase, it must be clarified that those aspects of musicianship don't equate to the general concept of creativity by most standard definitions. Piirto (1998) defines creativity as "a basic human instinct to make that which is new" (p. 41), while Crawford (2016) defines creativity as "the generation of a product that is judged to be novel and also to be appropriate, useful, or valuable by a suitably knowledgeable social group" (p. 7). In other words, creativity is seen or heard when students develop and perform, or produce a piece of music, that is an original composition or improvisation. Historically, many K–12 and collegiate music education programs have focused primarily on performance, reserving composition only for advanced students, but Webster (2016) has pointed out that "all children are not only capable of music composition but that they thrive on it as a way to deeply enhance their musical understanding" (p. 27). He emphasized that music teachers must offer comprehensive music education including composition on a regular basis.

While composition is recognized and valued as a significant way that students are creative in music, improvisation is an equally important aspect of creativity in music education. *Grove Music* defines improvisation as "the creation of a musical work, or the final form of a musical work, as it is being performed" and also states that "in virtually all musical cultures there is music that is improvised" (Nettl et al., 2001). Many people associate improvisation with jazz, and it has been widely researched in that area (Fisher, 1981; Kearns, 2011; Rummel, 2010; Warner, 2014), but it should be incorporated into all music classes. An examination of internationally recognized pedagogical approaches as well as the music of various cultures around the world provide numerous examples of improvisation. Chandler (2018) pointed out research showing improvisation pedagogy in Orff Schulwerk (Beegle, 2001), Kodály's concepts (Whitcomb, 2007), Dalcroze Eurhythmics (Anderson, 2012), and Gordon's Music Learning Theory (Azzara, 1993). The Routledge

World Music Pedagogy Series[1] features a chapter on composition and improvisation in each of its volumes, reflecting the underlying value of creativity in music from all parts of the world.

Pathways to Composition and Improvisation

Creativity, as expressed through composition and improvisation, should be a core component of all levels of music education. Teachers need to understand and promote the concept that creative products are new and unique, as opposed to added ornaments or shaped phrases of others' music. To foster this idea in practice, teacher can present a variety of pathways that allow students to explore their musical creativity in they compose and improvise.

World Music Cultures as a Pathway to Composition and Improvisation

Katie Noonan, a school music teacher in New York, is featured by Montemayor et al. (2018) for her journey into creativity through world music. She traveled to Ghana one summer and studied Ewe dance and drumming, and upon returning she arranged two Ewe songs she had learned for her fifth grade concert band. She taught the songs by rote to the students, reflecting Ghanaian music pedagogy. She also involved her students in making creative decisions about the arrangement. Noonan explains:

> Originally, I wrote the arrangement. But after the band played it, some things didn't seem to work, so I asked for feedback from the students. Originally, we weren't going to sing the songs in the arrangement, but then someone suggested, "Why don't we sing it and then play it after?" and everyone said, "Yes! Absolutely, let's do that!" I also think I originally wrote an accompaniment part for the low brass, and they said, "We want the melody! We don't want to play this part." So, we decided to have everyone play the melody in unison, which was fine, because that is the way they sing it Ghana anyway." (Montemayor et al., 2018, p. 133)

While not every teacher can travel to Ghana, the availability of world music resources including YouTube videos, books, and online materials like the Smithsonian Folkways Recordings and lesson plans is phenomenal. Recognizing that composition and improvisation are a central part of diverse styles of music from around the world is an important step toward opening pathways to creativity in music education classes. Webster (2016) notes that "music of other cultures, particularly in India, Iran, China, and West

Africa, were shown to rely heavily on improvisation within established boundaries" (p. 28). Around the world, in many cultures composition and improvisation are valued as core activities in music. Montemayor et al. (2018) explain that "many cultures embrace the belief that anyone is capable of creating original music of exceptional quality" (p. 109). Campbell (2004) makes it clear that culture-bearers have regularly endorsed creating and re-creating world music. She explains that:

> When music is treated respectfully, with ample time given to its study, it is often a source of pride for people from a culture to hear their traditions—or new expressions reminiscent of their traditions—performed by those who have given their time and energy to it. (p. 193)

Relationships are at the heart of teaching, and approaching literature this way connects both cultural heritage and the creative process in a way that exposes the class community to the possibilities of deep and meaningful learning through a student-centered approach. Students come from diverse backgrounds and cultures and studying music from cultures that are represented by the class itself is an incredible way to connect with students and their families. Teachers should examine, sing, and play songs from diverse cultures and, as a part of teaching those songs, may open the door for students to create within the cultures of the given literature.

It can be daunting for a teacher to face the myriad cultures that are unfamiliar, but this shouldn't be a cause for alarm. Instead, one can start with just a single culture that is somewhat familiar or particularly interesting and develop a lesson plan or two around that culture. A place to start could be a song like "Kye Kye Kule,"[2] a game song from Ghana that can be adapted to any age and used in instrumental classes. After learning to sing the original song by rote, students and teachers can start to improvise other melodic ideas and use vocables or play on any instrument to develop or extend the original game song in new ways. For those interested in pursuing this pathway at a deeper level, each volume in the World Music Pedagogy Series from Routledge contains a chapter devoted to improvisation and composition in the context of world music. The Smithsonian Folkways Learn website[3] also offers lesson plans on music from around the world.

Another interesting aspect of studying music from non-Western cultures is that many of them do not use notation. When introducing composition to students, teachers should remember that notation does not need to be a core aspect of the lesson. In fact, leaders in the field of teaching composition, like Wiggins (2001), suggest that when young composers are required to notate a score, they are likely to be less creative, so if a teacher really wants to emphasize creativity, it is better to not require traditional notation. Focusing on composing without the worry of writing it down can be freeing and result in more creativity and authenticity. This could be accomplished by simply performing an idea enough times to remember how it goes, or by audio recording an idea, but it could also involve written words and graphic symbols to help remember the piece.

Books Featuring Creative Music Making Projects and Activities

In recent years, more and more information has been published on teaching musical creativity in books, journal articles, research publications, and online resources. While reading about how to teach music composition and improvisation is not as ideal as observing sample lesson, it provides a viable pathway to begin or delve deeper into this topic. General resources covering all areas of music education, as well as some specific recommendations for general, instrumental, and vocal music will be discussed.

For those looking for a single resource for teaching music composition in any music education class, *Music outside the lines: Ideas for composing in K–12 Classrooms* (Hickey, 2012) is a top choice. Hickey offers a clear pathway for teachers of all backgrounds and types of music classes to start including improvisation and composition. She begins by presenting a view of what composition is and why it is so important, and goes on to cover some significant issues, such as "open versus closed," settings and parameters, composition assignments, notation, use of technology, assessment, and composing in ensembles. She also offers her definition of composition and provides ideas for listening and exploring, which are key central components of composition. The "meat" of the book includes engaging compositional prompts, studying form in music, and presenting composition through an "elements of music" approach.

Other books on teaching music composition that are more general in approach include the "classic" *Sound and Silence: Classroom Projects in Creative Music* (Aston & Paynter, 1973), which stands out as one of the earlier books pioneering the way for music teachers to include composition; *Minds on music: Composition for creative and critical thinking* (Kaschub & Smith, 2009b); *Creative and critical projects in classroom music* (Finney, Philpott, & Spruce, 2020); and *Composing our future: Preparing music educators to teach composition* (Kaschub & Smith, 2013). Aston and Paynter (1973) feature 36 projects developed from real classroom experiences and include lots of examples, photographs, and diagrams. Kaschub and Smith (2009b) begin with rationale and research, but then really dig into the important aspects of developing composition pedagogy and explain how to do that with students from early childhood through high school age. One notable feature of this book is that it includes an online webpage that lists many supplemental resources such as full color templates for student Sketchpages. Finney, Philpott, and Spruce (2020) build on Aston and Paynter's book and include 16 creative classroom projects designed and enacted by real classroom music teachers offering updated research and plans that are relevant to 21st century teachers and students.

Finally, Kaschub and Smith (2013) have targeted those working to prepare future music teachers. This book should be essential reading for all college music education professors, but it also offers practicing music education professionals an incredible resource full of well-researched information on teaching composition in a wide variety of settings. After a significant introduction to the topic with foundational elements presented by Peter Webster, Maud Hickey, and Randall Allsup, the book covers model practices in teaching music composition for K–12 general music, gifted learners, instrumental and choral settings, and working with special needs students. There are also chapters on using digital composition tools, incorporating composition in university courses, and a visionary chapter on "Strategic Administrative Practices for Including Composition in Music Education."

Some music teachers may want more specifics for their area of teaching. For elementary and general music teachers, Kaschub and Smith's (2016) *Experiencing music composition in grades 3–5* is a top resource, as well as Wiggins' (1990) *Composition in the classroom: A tool for teaching*, and Burnard and Murphy's (2017) *Teaching music creatively*. For instrumental teachers, several recent books have been published, including *Composition concepts for band and orchestra* (Koops & Whitener, 2020), *Musicianship: composing in band and orchestra* (Randles & Stringham, 2013), and *Musicianship: Improvising in band and orchestra* (Stringham, Bernard, & Randles, 2019). Agrell's (2007) *Improvisation games for classical musicians: A collection of musical games with suggestions for use* is also a great resource for instrumental teachers, though many of the games can be used in general music and vocal settings as well. For choral directors, *Musicianship: Composing in choir* (Kerchner & Strand, 2016) is a great resource, as well as the multitude of books available on songwriting. Musical Futures from the UK offers an excellent songwriting curriculum guide in the form of a free booklet.[4] *Songwriting: Strategies for musical self-expression and creativity* (Hauser, Tomal, & Rajan, 2017) is another great resource for vocal teachers. Wilkins (2006), a composer herself, offers *Creative music composition* as a significant resource for those wanting to support emerging high school and collegiate composers on their journey.

For digital technology and curricular ideas, Freedman's (2013) *Teaching music through composition: A curriculum using technology*, is highly recommended and includes practical lesson plans and assignments that have all been field tested, as well as an extensive companion website of audio, MIDI, and video files. Freedman's book is great for beginners to technology as well as those with experience looking for ways to expand. Several other recommended books include Watson's (2011) *Using technology to unlock musical creativity*, Bell's (2020) *The music technology cookbook: Ready-made recipes for the classroom*, Bauer's (2020) *Music learning today: Digital pedagogy for creating, performing, and responding to music*, and Dammers and LoPresti's (2020) *Practical music education technology*. Watson's book comes with 29 detailed, teacher-tested lesson plans for creative musical activities and includes a companion website. Bell offers 56 lessons by 49 music technology experts from around the world, organized in five parts, starting with beat-making and performance, and then diving into composition, multimedia and interdisciplinary projects, production, and ending with programming and design. Bauer (2020) takes a standards-based approach covering the topics of creating, performing, and responding and his companion website has excellent resources and links making this a helpful resource for much more than just composition or technology! Dammers and LoPresti's (2020) book is broader than just composing, including topics such as audio recording and sequencing, loop libraries, and accompaniment and practice software.

Randles (2020) provides a moving philosophical argument for including composition in *To create: Imagining the good life through music*. He shares experiences in his own life and teaching that shine light on the importance and relevance of music creativity and how that contributes to "The Good Life." Another inspirational book for teaching composing is Adolphe's (2020) *The mind's ear: Exercises for improving the musical imagination for performers, composers, and listeners*, which includes exercises and stories that can be used in teaching composition to individuals or groups. Adolphe's ideas include concepts such as hearing in silence and dialoguing through music. He challenges teachers in the preface by giving three examples of ways to present the same composition. Two of the examples are quite inspirational and motivational, while the third is completely boring and non-musical. Here is the second:

> Imagine you are in the audience of a courtroom trial. A man who has just been wrongly convicted of a serious crime suddenly turns to the jury and makes an impassioned speech, trying to convince them of his innocence. His voice rises higher and higher until he is screaming at them, and then suddenly he collapses and is silent. The court is stunned. The man stands up and quietly asks for their mercy and understanding. No one speaks. Take this and use it to create a short violin solo. (Adolphe, 2020, pp. xv–xvi)

Adolphe concludes: "The point is clear: the way we teach can inspire creativity or dull it." (p. vxii). One of his goals with this book is to "break down the barriers that prevent some musicians from improvising and composing, to make it fun to engage in creative exploration" (p. xxii).

There are more and more books as well as online resources on composition and improvisation coming out, so this is a great time to really "take the plunge" and start trying ideas out in this field. Some of the books are focused on a specific type of class or age, while others are more general music education books that contain great advice on teaching composing. Any one of them will work to facilitate, support, and enhance music learning and creation in music students' lives.

Assessment

Imagine a middle school music teacher starting her career with modern band and choir classes. First, her passion and goals focused on making her choir a top-rated ensemble, which she did very well! She knew the National Standards[5] and realized she should include composing but struggled to justify taking time away from preparing for performances. However, she realized she could use composition assignments as a way of assessing her students' understanding of music concepts in a way that would directly help them be better performers. This led to her including more composing assignments and gradually realizing the value of students' creative development was equally important to their performance development. Eventually, songwriting and other creative activities became a standard part of her curriculum.

Teachers all want to know if their students learned the concepts that were presented, and music composition is the ultimate way to do that. Music teachers can give a formative assignment such as performing a certain scale and add a short composition assignment that includes using the required scale to compose and play or sing a four- to eight-measure melody that uses all the notes of the scale and is mostly stepwise in motion. Another formative composition lesson would be to take a short challenging rhythm from the repertoire that is currently being worked on and ask students to compose new notes to go with the same rhythm. This would give the teacher evidence that students really understood the rhythm and be creative at the same time! On the other hand, a summative end-of-year assessment using composition could be composing a piece that uses ABA form, modeled from a performance piece that the ensemble worked on with ternary form, but using a contrasting narrative idea to shape the emotion of the piece. It is worth noting that Anderson and Krathwohl (2001) suggested a new version of Bloom's taxonomy that places creating as the top level representing higher order thinking. Figure 7.1 shows an example of how Anderson and Krathwohl's taxonomy can be adapted to music.

For those wishing to help music students reach their full potential, composing and improvising offer students a capstone opportunity to showcase their music learning. As teachers consider using composing to assess musical concepts their students are learning, it is important to remember that it is not a choice of whether composing is used just to see if the students really understand a concept, or if composing is used in and of itself to support student creativity. Both are worthwhile objectives and facilitate deeper understanding and learning.

Lower order thinking skills ━━━━━━━━━━━━▶ Higher order thinking skills					
Remember	Understand	Apply	Analyze	Evaluate	Create
Recognizing Recalling	Interpreting Exemplifying Classifying	Executing Implementing	Differentiating Organizing Attributing	Checking Critiquing	Generating Planning Producing
Music Examples					
Know your note names Identify an interval by sound and sight	Noting similarities between two different pieces	Performing dynamics correctly	Analyzing the form of a piece of music	Critiquing how one performance is better than another	Composing a piece of music Producing an album

FIGURE 7.1. Hierarchy of thinking skills (Adapted from Anderson & Krathwohl, 2001, pp. 67–68)

Songwriting

There was once a boy who attended a public school where he started trombone in the beginning band and continued in music through high school and college, pursuing a career in music teacher education. During his K–12 experience, he never did anything with composition because the opportunity to compose was never presented and he didn't know that it was really a thing to do. As he reflected during a graduate degree on the state of music education, he was struck by the fact that band, orchestra, and choir classes reached relatively few students in an average middle school or high school, and this led him to launching a songwriting class open to all students in the high school where he was teaching. Having a class specifically designed for teaching creativity and reaching students that were not in the traditional ensembles was an exciting leap forward for the former trombone player.

Songs are a part of every one's life and are particularly good ways for general music, choir, and modern band students to delve into composition. Whether a teacher has composing experience or not really doesn't matter! What is important is the commitment to opening the door for students to express themselves. This can include creative lyric/poetry writing, melody writing, chord exploration on piano, guitar, and ukulele, and can be done in a variety of styles to engage students. An easy entry-point is to start with a simple arrangement or cover of a student's favorite song, and then develop a small original B section, or compose a new version that uses some contrasting styles or new harmonies.

Warm-Ups as a Pathway to Composing and Improvising

Warm-up exercises are common in many types of music classes, and often involve activities that are very specific to the subject, such as breathing exercises for wind players, bowing exercises for string players, or vocalises for singers, but there are many ways to incorporate student creativity into warm-ups regardless of the particular discipline. Trying out creative warm-ups offers a step into composing and improvising without feeling like it takes away time required for upcoming performances or necessary technical development. Exercises may be composed by the teacher first and then imitated and carried on in new ways by students. This section will cover call-and-response warm-ups, conducted improvisations, the tuning meditation, McAllister's *Urban Groove*,[6] repertoire specific warm-ups, and an animal charades game.

Call-and-response rhythms or melodies are fun and engaging and are common warm-up exercises in all music classes. One creative warm-up that can be done is to model a rhythm in common time for one measure and have students clap it back, followed by a new one-measure improvised rhythm that is again repeated by the students. After several improvised rhythms have been demonstrated, the teacher can hand off the leader role to a student. Students can improvise a short one-measure rhythm and then the class copies the new rhythm. A non-stop rotation can be set up where each individual student takes a turn improvising a rhythm and the class can copy the rhythm. This same concept can be used with pitch sets as well, so students can improvise a short one-measure motive or melody using a predetermined number of pitches, and the rest of the class will echo and imitate the newly improvised music. The great thing about these warm-up exercises is that they can be adapted to any level, and they reinforce inner hearing, performance skills, confidence, self-worth, and creativity all simultaneously!

The *Tuning Meditation*[7] is a peaceful slow-paced musical exercise that is published as part of *Four Meditations for Orchestra* by Pauline Oliveros (1996/1971). It can be adapted to be used in any size group with any instruments or voices and with any age. Basically, the directions are for musicians to begin by playing or singing a pitch that they hear in their imagination, and then after contributing a pitch, listening for another player's pitch and tuning in unison to the pitch as exactly as possible. Listen again and play or sing a pitch that no one else is playing. The duration of pitches is determined by the duration of a comfortable breath or bow. The dynamic level is soft throughout the piece. This is a very slow improvisation, but it can result in some beautiful sounds, in free time, and provide a total contrast to everything else in a typical rehearsal.

Conducting improvised soundscapes is another warm-up activity that students enjoy and can lead to a new composition or simply be a one-time sound exploration. A simple way to start is by having students play or sing high notes when the leader's hands are high in the air, and low notes when the hands are low. If the leader's hands jab or swell, students should try to represent that gesture with their playing. Additionally, if the leader cues a specific player, singer, or section, those people will be featured and can improvise until the leader stops them. After the teacher demonstrates some basic types of visual communications that are possible, student conductors can take turns leading the class. No verbal communication is needed, so it also really develops students' skills in watching and reacting to a conductor. The soundscape can be totally random, but as students become comfortable with the process, it can be fun to imagine pictures or stories as a guide to the soundscape, as well as exploring different instrument and voice color combinations in high and low, loud and soft, solo or group, etc. Gestures for pulsating notes, ostinatos, jabs, swells, and decrescendos are fun for the teacher as well as the students to try out.

Using the left hand for the left side of the ensemble and right hand for the right side can provide exciting mixes, blends, and dialogues, and can be done in free time or with steady rhythm.

As part of leading an improvised conducted soundscape, teachers can introduce specific grooves or ostinatos that can lay a groundwork for improvising solos by individuals. Composer and educator John McAllister has shared his composition *Urban Groove* for free through his website and it offers five different "grooves" that can be played by an instrumental ensemble in any order and in any combination. While this piece is explicitly written for concert band, the music and the concept could easily

FIGURE 7.2. Know your stuff for *Earthshine*—A five minute makeover.
Change the notes with an "X" to any other note listed in No. 1. Then add two slurs and one tie. Play it and listen. Do you like your makeover?

be applied to any type of music class and adapted to various skill levels. McAllister says of this work:

> *Urban Groove* is a fantastic way to get young (or even mature) musicians to get to be creative within a full band setting. I made this tune up on the fly with a group of students specifically to have "looped" music that we could play at a pep rally. If you have fun with this, kids will absolutely love it. I've never had a group that didn't go crazy the first few times we did this! (johnmcallistermusic.com)

Of the five grooves, some of them are easy and some are a little harder, so if teachers have a group of mixed ability, the less advanced students can easily play the simple grooves. In addition to the written grooves, students can improvise solos on top of the groove, and any student, whether a beginner or and advanced player can take a turn improvising. This type of warm-up is fun and offers a lot of flexibility for focusing on creativity, or rhythm work, or harmonies as needed on any given rehearsal.

Often, music teachers will need a warm-up that can help students prepare for a specific piece of repertoire coming up in the rehearsal. Most pieces don't have pre-composed warm-ups, but teachers and students can compose their own. Jodie Blackshaw is a great example of a composer and educator that has modeled this in many of her pieces. Her middle school band piece *Earthshine* (2014) comes with a published warm-up that is composed of fragments of the main melody that are introduced in short exercises to help students learn how to play, count, and sing the melody. Figure 7.2 shows an excerpt from the student warm-up for *Earthshine*, which can be accessed from the composer's website.[8]

Repertoire

Repertoire is viewed as the meat and potatoes of many music classes, and naturally musical compositions can be a gateway to student creativity. Imagine a teacher leading a rehearsal:

> Did you hear the way those dissonant chords brought out the emotional pain we all sense upon losing a loved one? That is good composing! I believe the composer put that harmony in there just at the right moment and we should really lean into it, and

then back away as it resolves to best communicate the message of this music. (Koops vignette)

This rehearsal comment reflects a teacher connecting with a composer's ideas to address an aspect of performance that might otherwise have been simply delivered as "Please crescendo and decrescendo." Whenever teachers work on a piece of music in a rehearsal or engage students in listening and responding to music, a great way for them to set the stage for future composing is by presenting the music from the composer's perspective. Ruthmann (2007) brilliantly suggests reading books about writer's workshops to get ideas for teaching composition, and when reading those books to simply substitute "composing" when the author uses "writing" and substitute "listening" when one sees "reading" (p. 43). For example, in chapter 6 of her book on writing workshops, Katie Wood Ray (2002) suggests teachers should "Read Like a Teacher of Writing." She explains that:

> The world is full of ~~writing~~ [composing] that makes us slam on our brakes when we're ~~reading~~ [listening] and think, Ooo . . . ~~look at~~ [listen to] that. I need to show that to my students. That's really good ~~writing~~ [composing] (p. 90) . . . As teachers of ~~writing~~ [composing], over time we develop a sort of general habit of mind that always asks of the well-written ~~texts~~ [compositions] we encounter, "Okay, now how's this ~~written~~ [composed]?" (p. 93)

Ray's book as well as other writing workshop books are packed with great ideas like this that can be directly applied to teaching music composition in a school setting. In today's world, access to diverse music from all styles and cultures is phenomenal, and music teachers should stay active with listening and learning and share what they find to be exciting with their students. As teachers present, listen to, and rehearse repertoire with students, they should do it from the composer's perspective and consider how that can evoke deeper music-making from their students and inspire further student-created projects.

While any repertoire could lead to composing, some repertoire is particularly great for inspiring students to compose, such as a piece that has variations on a theme, which can lead to students composing new variations or working on a ternary form piece and then having students compose a piece with the same form. The BandQuest[9] and ChoralQuest[10] pieces from the American Composers Forum offer a free curriculum guide that includes composing or improvising lesson plans directly related to the pieces—though the plans can easily be adapted to any type of music class and are highly recommended.

In contrast to the more standard repertoire in music education, there are some "project pieces" being published that require students and teachers to compose in order to perform the piece. Composer Jodie Blackshaw published *13 moons: A project piece for band* in 2018. While targeted at concert bands of any level, it could easily be adapted to orchestras, or any type of instrumental ensemble. The basic materials include a main melody, the scale on which the melody is built, several contrasting melodic exemplars, and a harmony idea. Students then organize the materials and develop them into actual compositions. Similarly, Libby Larsen published *Introduction to the moon: A concert piece with eight improvisational sections for symphonic winds, tuned water glasses, and amplified voice* in 2005. The work challenges students to improvise and play by ear in response to eight poems about the moon in between nine pre-composed sections[11].

In addition to traditional ensemble repertoire, students' favorite music styles, including anything from hip-hop and video game music to EDM (Electronic Dance Music), can be used as a gateway to creativity. Students enjoy the chance to create a cover of their favorite song, and that, in turn, can lead to writing an original song. One of the most fascinating and exciting things about teaching composing and improvising is seeing how students combine various styles of music, whether consciously or not, into unique new works.

Collaboration with a Professional Composer

Imagine a music teacher who experienced a high-level performance-focused experience during her own high school and college years. After starting to teach high school choir, she was invited to have her students be part of a large collaborative concert featuring a guest film composer, who worked with all the participating students on a group composition project. The culminating concert included individual student compositions as well as a world premiere of the collaboration that the composer put together based on the students' collaborative composition work. As part of the rehearsal process, students participated in circle singing with improvisation as well as working on individual and group compositions. A couple of the individual student compositions were selected and performed on the final concert in addition to the large collaborative work and the overall experience was positive for the entire high school choir. This event opened the door to include more composing projects in the future.

Partnering with a professional composer can be an exciting way to begin composing with students. The ideal situation involves a composer who is willing to work in a collaborative style that opens the door for students to be creative as part of the process, though this can be done in many ways. Some composers will write something for the students and then get feedback from them while other composers might engage with students to come up with musical ideas that are completely the students' original materials.

Utilitarian Approaches, Notation, and the General Study of Music

Another teacher's pathway to including composition in his curriculum was utilitarian. He felt a need to vary his five-day weekly rehearsal schedule to include something other than simply rehearsing the same music over and over. To hold individual students accountable for their musical progress, he began requiring students to perform playing assignments in a small room next to the main rehearsal room. While students were waiting their turn to perform individually, he created some short assignments to keep everyone engaged. He started by creating worksheets with basic music theory and then added music history projects. This eventually led to some brief composition assignments within clear parameters. While the assignments filled time, and students were learning notation and theory, the composition results were quite boring.

To make things more interesting, students were then required to perform their own compositions as part of their playing assignments, which helped them think and reflect about their own compositions: another step forward! One thing led to another, and the original composition assignment of 20 to 30 seconds became the cumulative end-of-the-semester project. The teacher was inspired to develop more creative composition assignments. He kept offering new challenges each semester, such as picking a story and telling it in music. As the students took on each challenge, the teacher realized he could tie his composition assignments directly to performance-related elements of his program, such as learning tonality, or modes in the repertoire that the ensemble was preparing. More assignment ideas continued to develop including animal compositions inspired by Saint-Saens' *Carnival of the Animals*, and compositions inspired by paintings, as Mussorgsky did with *Pictures at an Exhibition*. The students performed their compositions in class for each other and enjoyed listening to not only the music, but also the numerous compliments that always ensued. The teacher gradually realized that creative aspects of musicianship were far more important and rewarding than technical theory assignments, and students developed a deeper understanding of theory as a by-product of the emphasis on composition.

While it must be emphasized that that composition does not require notation, as can be easily observed by many non-Western cultures around the world, it remains that notation can be used as a pathway to composition. In days of old, famous composers like Mozart would spend time copying older famous composers' music by hand, and through that exercise study the process of composing. The process of writing by hand can be a helpful step in the process of learning to compose, but certainly need not be a requirement. Computer notation programs are readily available and keep getting better with both quality of sounds as well as ease of entering notation. It is an invaluable asset for young composers to enter notes in a notation software program and immediately listen back to simulated music to get a sense of what they are inputting.

There are several solutions to the notation barrier that many grade-school students face. An alternative to notation for young composers is to work with non-notation-based computer programs like Chrome Music Lab, Bandlab, Soundtrap, or GarageBand, or simply audio record their pieces. Professional composers as well as young students also use graphic notation to keep track of their ideas. Finally, having teachers help notate composition ideas from students is a great way to progress as well if the teacher has time. It is a rewarding experience to see students' composition ideas spring to life!

Programmatic Music

Composers in many cultures build their work around a programmatic element such as a tall tale, a historical character, and other story-like influence, including films. Australian Aboriginal musicians playing the didgeridoo will tell the tale of a kangaroo, while a Chinese composer might write a song about a beautiful evening on the prairie, with starlight shimmering down. The Romantic-era composer Richard Strauss is famous for his large orchestra tone poems such as *Till Eulenspiegel's merry pranks*, and Howard Shore's scores for the *Lord of the rings* films features diverse programmatic music from epic battle scenes to the idyllic hobbit theme music reminiscent of the hymn "This Is My Father's World."

For young students, using a story book or picture book is a great way to start the composing process. Stories offer not only a creative inspiration but can also connect with the cultural background of students, and social justice issues. Examples of children's stories that can connect well to composition assignments include *Where the wild things are* by Maurice Sendak, *The tale of Peter Rabbit* by Beatrix Potter, *Chicka Chicka Boom Boom* by Bill Martin Jr., and John Archambault, *Ingri and Edgar Parin d'Aulaires book of Greek myths*, and *Esperanza rising* by Pam Muñoz Ryan. Stories can be illustrated with music page-by-page or students can simply represent the spirit or mood of the overall story. Stories about animals can be particularly fun to use for compositions because the actual sounds the animals make can be imitated as part of the music. For example, *Why mosquitoes buzz in people's ears* by Verna Aardema and illustrated by Leo and Diane Dillon (1975), can start with students creating buzzing sounds, and using hand claps to imitate the real-life scenario of trying to slap a mosquito. Stories can also connect with students drawing and painting as a cross discipline form of creativity. *Tuesday*, by David Wiesner (1991), can appeal to children's visual imagination in a way that can be transferred to creative compositions. Students could create soundscapes that represent the eerie flotilla of frogs flying on lily pads through the air. This could be created on synthesizers, or iPad or phones with instrument apps including world music instruments like the erhu or thumb piano, but it could also be created by voices and body percussion making interesting creative sounds, not just singing sounds, or classroom instruments like Orff instruments, ukuleles, or recorders.

In a secondary level music classroom, stories dealing with culture or social justice might be considered as inspiration for new compositions. In *Esperanza rising*, (2002) by Pam Muñoz Ryan, Esperanza and her mother flee their privileged lives in Mexico and find refuge in the migrant camps of Southern California during the Great Depression. Sounds of mariachi could be mixed with sounds of American folk music, or minor and diminished chords could be explored to represent the sadness of leaving a place one loves and arriving at a new and challenging environment one has never experienced before.

Films and video games are popular among students of all ages and can provide an exciting and motivating experiences for younger composers. They can also be very short and therefore a positive gateway to the beginning of composition in the classroom. Note that, for film music composing, teachers could start by asking students to find music samples from YouTube or other digital music sources and put their choice of music together, based on existing music, like a "temp track" that real life film makers often create. That could then lead to a short original music composition project. The National Association for Music Education (NAfME) has shared a free exemplary curriculum model with embedded lesson plans on composing, and their "Composition/Theory Responding Unit, Advanced Level" example[12] includes a set of six lessons using old black and white silent films that are available for free and can be downloaded from the Library of Congress (USA). While targeting advanced level student composers, the ideas could be adapted to any level, and there are also free published curriculum examples for introductory level students. One film example to check out as a starting point is *Little Mischief*.[13] Lasting just 44 seconds, it was produced by Edison Manufacturing Co. in 1899.

Technology

Imagine an elementary music teacher who had explored songwriting and popular music in high school, but mainly focused on classical piano in college. Her preservice training did include a small amount of work in creative music-making, but she found composition was difficult to include in her classes as she started her career. However, she developed a strong interest in music technology and started to have students create projects in Flat, BandLab, and other online music programs. Through her commitment to teaching the national standards and her exploration of technology she found more and more ways to include composition as a core part of her classes.

Technology can be used in countless ways and continues to develop every year. Composer Alex Shapiro offers an exemplary instrumental composition curriculum[14] on her website that focuses on creativity and has no required notational component. Her plans are available for beginners through advanced levels and start with students making up their own 10-second motive performed over a drone. In her lessons, students develop their ideas by actually playing them and recording them, so the focus is on creativity, not notation. Students then work in small groups to combine and develop their motives collaboratively. Students can use free programs like Audacity, GarageBand, Bandlab, or Soundtrap to record themselves, so there is not any cost involved with this type of project. Phones, iPads and synthesizers can be used as both composing tools and as instruments to explore new sounds, and students can have the option to mix electronic and acoustic instrument sounds.

There are countless digital programs now available for creativity, though it is important to explore how and if programs work on various devices. For younger students, Chrome Music Lab Experiments, Buttonbass, Beepbox, Groove Pizza, and AQWERTYon are just a few programs to consider. Hyperscore is a composing program that is great for elementary students, because it uses a drawing feature to compose instead of traditional notation but it is only available for PC's (see Crawford, 2016). For notation, the most commonly used programs include Sibelius, Finale, Logic Pro X, Noteflight, Flat, MuseScore, Notion, and Dorico, and electronic based music production programs include GarageBand, BandLab, Soundtrap, Soundation, Adobe Audition, FL Studio, Magic ACID Pro, Zulu DJ, Ableton Live, and Bitwig Studio. Interesting musical instruments continue to be created as apps available on phones and tablets, whether imitating existing acoustic instruments or creating new electronic instruments. Examples of current world music instrument apps include Djembe!, Tabla!, Doumbek!, Darbuka, Guzheng, Kalimba, and Mouth Harp. The key is for teachers to have fun with the technology and try it out themselves, and then not to be afraid to open it up to students, regardless of the teacher's expertise or lack thereof. Generally, the students will figure it out pretty quickly, and help each other as well.

PLANNING COMPOSITION INTO YOUR CURRICULUM

Imagine a middle school music teacher who directs orchestra, band, and guitar ensemble classes. He began incorporating composition after being challenged with the prospect of doing so during his graduate degree in music education. Initially he used plans from other teachers, and then eventually started designing his own composition lessons. His key to success was not simply the lesson ideas, but the actual planning of the composition sessions into his monthly teaching schedule. Teachers can read books, attend workshops, and compose pieces as preparation for teaching composition, but none of those will matter if the key elements of the times and dates are not put on the calendar.

There are as many ways to include composition lessons into a music curriculum plan as there are teachers. Some teachers like to plan a four-week composition unit during January and February each year, and as a follow up, selected students participate in a young composer festival at the end of the school year. This plan gives students time to establish social relationships, build trust and gain the requisite skills and knowledge during the fall semester. Composing requires students to be brave enough to share ideas that their peers might be critical of, so an atmosphere of collegiality and respect is important to have established. January also seems ideal because it is before the busy spring festival season or performance pressure build-up, and compositions can even be used for solo and ensemble festivals, not to mention composition festivals. Other teachers prefer to plan a short lesson once a week and spread the creative projects throughout the entire year. Additionally, using the last few weeks of school to work on composing projects can be ideal if there is down time after performances, and students are ready to try out something different and creative. Another consideration is to put some dedicated lesson time in at the beginning of the year, and then, offer short composition assignments throughout the year. A final consideration is to identify a young composer festival or showcase or plan one for the school district and plan your composing lessons to culminate in time for the festival.

CONCLUSION

There are many pathways that may be taken to reach the ideal of a creative classroom. Music teachers looking to walk this path may find it helpful to consider the checklist in Figure 7.3, which summarizes many of the ideas presented in this chapter.

Assessment, books, songwriting, music technology, and other approaches represent a few of the pathways we have at present—and more options will follow. Regardless of the pathway that teachers select, the key is to take the first step. Try one or two small creative music-making activities, and then continue to purposefully schedule composition into classes so it becomes a normal part of teaching and learning. There

☐   Know why composition and improvisation are important to include in all music classes

☐   Read articles/books or view webinars/conference sessions on teaching composition and improvisation to get ideas

☐   Try out music composition and improvisation yourself

☐   Analyze some musical works from your class repertoire (past, present, or future) and prepare them for use as examples to lead to student composing projects

☐   Compose warm-ups that prepare students for specific repertoire challenges

☐   Listen to some of your students' favorite music and prepare excerpts for use as examples to lead to student composing projects

☐   Invite students to compose for their own ensemble or chamber groups (all styles welcome)

☐   Support student compositions by playing through the compositions with the full ensemble or class, and consider performing student compositions

☐   Explore world music/popular music repertoire and pedagogy as a way to incorporate composition and improvisation
Try out technology options, like Chrome Music Lab, BandLab and Noteflight

☐   Collaborate with a friend on composing/song-writing with an online program like BandLab

☐   Plan some assessments that use music composition as a way to see if students fully understand the material

☐   Plan time into your teaching/lesson schedule to support composition and improvisation

FIGURE 7.3. Checklist for starting music composition

is no "one" way that music teachers journey into the areas of teaching composing, just like there is no "one" way that composers begin composing. What is important is opening the door for both teachers and students to begin their creative adventure. Music curricula that provide students with opportunities to explore and develop composition and improvisation skills and interests can produce life-long learners and musical artists who think creatively and empathetically, no matter what career field they may choose to pursue.

NOTES

1. *Early Childhood Education, Elementary Music Education, Secondary School Innovations, Instrumental Music Education, Choral Music Education,* and *School-Community Intersections.*
2. Smithsonian Folkways Recordings can be found at https://folkways.si.edu/
3. https://music.si.edu/learn
4. A free PDF booklet from Musical Futures may be found at http://www.musicalfuturesinternational.org/free-guide-to-songwriting.html
5. Information about the 2014 *National Core Arts Standards* is available from State Education Agency Directors of Arts Education (SEADAE) at https://www.nationalartsstandards.org.
6. Information and examples may be found at https://www.johnmcallistermusic.com/uploads/2/4/7/2/24727629/urban_groove.pdf
7. To learn more about this work see Oliveros, P. (2011). Pauline Oliveros: The world-wide tuning meditation. *Leonardo Music Journal,* p. 85.
8. See   https://www.jodieblackshaw.com/earthshine-conductors-notes   for   warm-up examples.
9. Information and examples of instrumental works may be found at https://composersforum.org/bandquest/
10. Information and examples of choral works may be found at https://composersforum.org/choralquest/
11. Additional information can be obtained at https://libbylarsen.com/works/an-introduction-to-the-moon/
12. Visit   https://nafme.org/wp-content/uploads/2020/04/Composition-Music-Theory-Responding-Unit-Advanced-Level.pdf to access this lesson material.
13. *Little Mischief* can be accessed at https://www.loc.gov/item/00694128/
14. E-ensemble composing syllabus/curriculum by Alex Shapiro is available at https://www.alexshapiro.org/Shapiro-E-ensemble_Syllabus.html

REFERENCES

Aardema, V., Dillon, L., Dillon, D. (1975). Why mosquitoes buzz in people's ears: a West African tale. Dial Press.

Adolphe, B. (2020) *The mind's ear: Exercises for improving the musical imagination for performers, composers, and listeners.* Oxford University Press.

Agrell, J. (2007) *Improvisation games for classical musicians: A collection of musical games with suggestions for use.* GIA Publications.

Anderson, L. W., & Krathwohl, D. R. (2001). *Taxonomy for learning, teaching, and assessing: A revision of bloom's taxonomy of educational objectives, Abridged edition*. Pearson.

Anderson, W. T. (2012). The Dalcroze approach to music education: Theory and applications. *General Music Today, 26*(1), 27–33.

Aston, P., & Paynter, J. (1973). *Sound and silence: Classroom projects in creative music*. Cambridge University Press.

Azzara, C. D. (1993). Audiation-based improvisation techniques and elementary instrumental students' music achievement. *Journal of Research in Music Education, 41*(4), 328–342.

Bauer, W. (2020). *Music learning today: digital pedagogy for creating, performing, and responding to music*. Oxford University Press.

Beegle, A. C. (2001). *An examination of Orff-trained general music teachers' use of improvisation with elementary school children*. (Catalog number 05A 2026). Master's thesis, University of St. Thomas. Master's Thesis International.

Bell, A. P. (2020) *The music technology cookbook: Ready-made recipes for the classroom*. Oxford University Press.

Blackshaw, J. (2014) *Earthshine*. Notes to the Conductor. Wallabac Music. https://13071e95-4bdd-97a4-0fb3-f67f59071d85.filesusr.com/ugd/b8e057_5ad2b1af57af48d6978458d865ce8e73.pdf

Burnard, P., Murphy, R., (2017). *Teaching music creatively*. Taylor & Francis.

Campbell, P. S. (2004). *Teaching music globally: Experiencing music, expressing culture*. Oxford University Press.

Chandler, M. D. (2018). Improvisation in elementary general music: A review of the literature. *Update: Applications of Research in Music Education, 37*(1), 42–48. https://doi.org/10.1177/8755123318763002

Crawford, L. A. (2016). *Composing in groups: Creative processes of third and fifth grade students* (Order No. 10195571). Available from ProQuest Central; ProQuest Dissertations & Theses Global. (1868501124). Retrieved from http://o-search.proquest.com.patris.apu.edu/docview/1868501124?accountid=8459

Dammers and LoPresti (2020). *Practical music education technology*. Oxford University Press.

Freedman, B. (2013). *Teaching music through composition: A curriculum using technology*. Oxford University Press.

Finney, J., Philpott, C., & Spruce, G. (2020) *Creative and critical projects in classroom music: Fifty years of sound and silence*. Routledge.

Fisher, L. F. (1981). *The Rationale for and development of jazz courses for the college music education curriculum* (Order No. 8129159). Available from ProQuest Dissertations & Theses Global. (303122233). Retrieved from http://o-search.proquest.com.patris.apu.edu/dissertations-theses/rationale-development-jazz-courses-college-music/docview/303122233/se-2?accountid=8459

Hauser, C., Tomal, D. R., & Rajan, R. S. (2017). *Songwriting: Strategies for musical self-expression and creativity*. Rowman and Littlefield.

Hickey, M. (2012). *Music outside the lines: Ideas for composing in K–12 music classrooms*. Oxford University Press.

Kaschub, M., & Smith, J. P. (2009a). A principled approach to teaching music composition to children. *Research and Issues in Music Education, 7*, 1–15.

Kaschub, M., & Smith, J. (2009b). *Minds on music: Composition for creative and critical thinking*. R&L Education.

Kaschub, M., & Smith, J. (Eds.). (2013) *Composing our future: Preparing music educators to teach composition*. Oxford University Press. DOI: 10.1093/acprof:oso/9780199832286.001.0001

Kaschub, M., & Smith, J. (2016). *Experiencing music composition in grades 3–5*. Oxford University Press.

Kearns, J. M. (2011). *Thinking about jazz education in Canada: A comparative case study of collegiate educators regarding pedagogy, administration, and the future of jazz education* (Order No. 3453011). Available from ProQuest Central; ProQuest Dissertations & Theses Global. (867263617). Retrieved from http://o-search.proquest.com.patris.apu.edu/dissertations-theses/thinking-about-jazz-education-canada-comparative/docview/867263617/se-2?accountid=8459

Kerchner, J. L., & Strand, K. (Eds.), (2016). *Musicianship: Composing in choir*. GIA Publications.

Koops, A. (2009). *Incorporating music composition in middle school band rehearsals*. (Order No. 3389504). Available from ProQuest Dissertations & Theses Global. (304996481). Retrieved from http://o-search.proquest.com.patris.apu.edu/docview/304996481?accountid=8459

Koops, A. and Whitener, J. L. (2020). *Composition concepts for band and orchestra*. R&L Education.

Montemayor, M., Coppola, W. J., & Mena, C. (2018). World music pedagogy, Volume IV: Instrumental music education. [VitalSource Bookshelf 9.3.0]. Retrieved from vbk://9781351704311

Nettl, B., Wegman, R., Horsley, I., Collins, M., Carter, S., Garden, G., Seletsky, R., Levin, R., Crutchfield, W., Rink, J., Griffiths, P., & Kernfeld, B. (2001). Improvisation. Grove Music Online. Retrieved January 2, 2021, from https://www.oxfordmusiconline.com/grovemusic/view/10.1093/gmo/9781561592630.001.0001/omo-9781561592630-e-0000013738

Oliveros, P. (2011) Pauline Oliveros: *The World Wide Tuning Meditation*. *Leonardo Music Journal* 2011; 21 85. doi: https://doi.org/10.1162/LMJ_a_00076

Oliveros, P. (1996/1971). *Four meditations for orchestra*. Deep Listening Publications, ASCAP.

Piirto, J. (1998). *Understanding those who create* (2nd ed.). Great Potential Press.

Randles, C. (2020). *To create-imagining the good life through music*. GIA Publications.

Randles, C., & Stringham, D. (2013). *Musicianship: Composing in band and orchestra*. GIA Publications.

Ray, K. W. (2002). *What you know by heart: How to develop curriculum for your writing workshop*. Heinemann.

Riley, P. E. (2006). Including composition in middle school band: Effects on achievement, performance, and attitude. *Update: Applications of Research in Music Education, 25*(1), 28–38.

Rummel, J. R. (2010). *Perceptions of jazz improvisation among Pennsylvania music educators* (Order No. 3411771). Available from ProQuest Dissertations & Theses Global. (578526292). Retrieved from http://o-search.proquest.com.patris.apu.edu/dissertations-theses/perceptions-jazz-improvisation-among-pennsylvania/docview/578526292/se-2?accountid=8459

Ruthmann, A. (2007). The composers' workshop: An approach to composing in the classroom. *Music Educators Journal, 93*(4), 38–4. https://doi.org/10.1177/002743210709300416

Ryan, P. M. (2000). *Esperanza rising* (First). Scholastic Press.

Stringham, D., Bernard, C., & Randles, C. (Eds.). (2019). *Musicianship: Improvising in band and orchestra*. GIA Publications.

Taft, S. A. (2019). Composition in the ensemble classroom: Ideas from eight researcher-designed methods. *Update, 38*(1), 25–33. National Association for Music Education.

Warner, M. E. (2014). *Paradox, problem, and potential in secondary school jazz education* (Order No. 3581112). Available from ProQuest Dissertations & Theses Global. (1545997025).

Retrieved from http://o-search.proquest.com.patris.apu.edu/dissertations-theses/paradox-problem-potential-secondary-school-jazz/docview/1545997025/se-2?accountid=8459

Watson, S. (2011). *Using technology to unlock musical creativity*. Oxford University Press.

Webster, P. (2016). Creative thinking in music: Twenty-five years on. *Music Educators Journal, 102*(3), 26–32.

Whitcomb, R. (2007). Improvisation in elementary general music: A survey study. *Kodály Envoy, 34*(1), 5–10.

Wiesner, D., & Goldenberg, C. (1991). *Tuesday*. Clarion Books, an imprint of HarperCollins.

Wiggins, J. H. (2001). *Teaching for musical understanding*. McGraw-Hill.

Wiggins, J. (1990). *Composition in the classroom: A tool for teaching*. Music Educators National Conference.

Wilkins, M. L. (2006). *Creative music composition: The young composer's voice*. Routledge. https://doi.org/10.4324/9780203036204

CHAPTER 8

....

CULTIVATING STUDENT AGENCY IN THE PREK−12 COMPOSITION CURRICULUM

....

DANIEL J. ALBERT

STUDENTS have rich musical lives outside of the formal music classroom. Some perform in garage bands and other music groups with peers. Others participate in culturally relevant ensembles, listen to music that moves them, or write songs as a means of expressing thoughts that cannot be fully articulated (Green, 2002 and 2008a; Hewitt, 2018; Kratus, 2016; Lind & McCoy, 2016). Creating a classroom culture that honors students' musical lives can be a powerful way to build trust and mutual respect (Wiggins, 2015). Furthermore, incorporating composition experiences based on their musical lives can enable student agency (Kaschub & Smith, 2009), broadly defined as "students' ability to define and act on their own goals" (Vaughn, 2018, p. 63). The feeling of relevance in our classrooms can fuel student motivation, empowerment, and ownership. What music educator doesn't want that?

There are, however, several items to consider. Educators need to adhere to their district's curriculum, some of which might be overly prescriptive (McMurrer, 2007; Onosko, 2011). Also, for compositional endeavors, educators need to foster a classroom culture that encourages "messiness," space for exploration, and employment of agency (Hickey, 2003 and 2012; Partti & Westerlund, 2013; Webster, 2003). Learning how to facilitate that type of classroom culture *and* satisfy instructional goals can be intimidating for educators (Conway & Hibbard, 2020; Hickey, 2013; Randles & Smith, 2012; Regelski, 2002; Smith, 2014; Stauffer, 2013; Strand, 2006). Many music educators are "trained" during our teacher education programs to be teacher-centered classroom managers who direct students to replicate, rather than create or invent (Conway & Hibbard, 2020; Regelski, 2002; Smith, 2014). Also, what exactly is "agency"? What does it look like in the music classroom? Why should music educators concern themselves with this concept?

The purpose of this chapter is to explore the phenomenon of student agency in the composition classroom and provide strategies as to how the music educator can harness that student agency to satisfy curricular and teacher-designed goals and objectives. After a brief review of social constructivist principles, I will discuss three types of agency germane to music composition classes: personal, learner, and musical. I then will explore the concept of classroom culture and its relevance in fostering agency within students, as well as review research studies that explore how learner and musical agency are elements in the creation of a classroom culture conducive to music learning via composition. Finally, I will provide instructional strategies for creating a classroom culture that empowers students to develop their agency and express it via compositional processes in the music classroom.

Three Dimensions of Agency: Personal, Learner, and Musical

Learning is a socially constructive process. In other words, we construct meaning through both formal experiences (e.g., school and school-related) and informal experiences (e.g., out-of-school) by interacting with and building upon the ideas of others (Rogoff, 1990; Vygotsky, 1978; Wenger, 1998). Social constructivists believe that learning is, fundamentally, a socially situated process. The learning process is initiated when the learner chooses to engage with the activity at hand—employing their agency—and make meaning of the experience. Three types of agency must be present for learning to occur and are of particular interest for music education contexts: personal, learner, and musical.

Personal Agency

While there are differences across disciplines, scholars largely define *personal agency* as having the power to influence one's life and control one's circumstances during a particular situation or moment in time. Individuals are not "bystanders." Rather, they influence their lives within contexts to which they have a vested interest in and contribute to the outcome (Bandura, 2006; Bruner, 1996; Dewey, 1916).

Albert Bandura, a psychologist who wrote extensively on the nature and function of agency in social cognitive theory, posited that personal agency is a dynamic force that is influenced by the interaction of behavioral, intrapersonal, and environmental determinants (Bandura, 1986). It is composed of four main factors (Bandura, 2006):

- Intentionality: having the intention to instigate change and be proactive by devising action plans and strategies to realize those plans.
- Forethought: using cognitive representation to visualize the future and provide motivation to be intentional with one's action toward the manifestation of goals and provide forward momentum with one's life.

- Self-reactiveness: having the ability to self-regulate and motivate oneself to follow through with action plans. *Creating* the action plan is not enough. The effectiveness of one's personal agency is heavily dependent on self-efficacy, which Bandura (1989) defined as "capacity to exercise control over one's own thought processes, motivation, and action" (p. 1175).
- Self-reflectiveness: having the ability to reflect on the appropriateness of one's actions and thoughts vis-à-vis their action plans toward achieving goals and making adjustments as necessary.

Exercising personal agency plays a critical role in the development of student composers. Generating a work of art based on uniquely lived experiences is a deeply personal act. Students need to feel that they have freedom to exercise their personal agency and make artistic choices that have their compositions reflect who they are. This is not to say that music educators should not employ scaffolding practices to assist their students. This topic will be discussed throughout the chapter.

Learner Agency

A subset of personal agency, *learner agency* allows students to have the self-motivation to learn and feel that their ideas emanating from interactions with others are recognized and valued (Bruner, 1996; Wiggins, 2015 and 2016). Interactions situated within a caring learning community that values student choice (autonomy) and incorporates authentic learning tasks provide a catalyst for intrinsic motivation (Kohn, 1999), thus strengthening learner agency. Students' intentional efforts with agency can lead to a sense of flow (Csikszentmihalyi, 1990), which occurs when the "body or mind is stretched to its limits in a *voluntary* effort to achieve something difficult and worthwhile" (p. 3, emphasis mine).

Lev Vygotsky's (1978) zone of proximal development, defined as "the distance between the actual developmental level as determined by independent problem solving and the level of potential development as determined through problem solving under adult guidance, or in collaboration with more capable peers" (p. 86), has particular significance for supporting learning agency. If one teaches above a learner's zone of proximal development, the student does not possess the prerequisite skill or conceptual knowledge to execute or understand. Conversely, teaching below one's zone of proximal development means that the learner already has the prerequisite skill or conceptual knowledge to execute or understand the topic at hand.

Vygotsky advocated for educators to plan for instruction to take place within the zone of proximal development: while the learner's skill level or conceptual knowledge lies just below what is needed for execution or competency (i.e., working just outside one's "comfort zone"), the learner can succeed with the support of a teacher or knowledgeable peer. Scaffolding is a key complementary concept. Teachers (or any other knowledgeable other, including a peer) can employ scaffolding practices, allowing them to support students by having them assume responsibilities for tasks that are within their reach *with proper support* (Bruner, 1986; Lave & Wenger, 1991). However, a crucial piece of this scenario is the willingness of the learner to believe in their capabilities and take risks in participating in a circumstance that requires working above their competence at that moment.

Learning involves risk taking, initiative, responsibility, and vulnerability. It cannot occur unless the student exercises personal agency (Rogoff, 2003). Therefore, it is incumbent upon music educators to help create a learning environment that encourages risk taking and fosters students' personal and learning agency (Wiggins, 2011b).

Musical Agency

In her analysis of how *musical agency* is employed in music education contexts, Sidsel Karlsen (2011) noted that researchers largely share the belief that it can be conceived of as "an individual's *capacity for action* in relation to music or in a music-related setting" (p. 110, Karlsen's emphasis). Scholars across related fields, including ethnomusicology, psychology, philosophy, and sociology, have examined musical agency and the role that it plays in musical experiences and identity development (Barone, 2000; DeNora, 2000; Green, 2008a; Hargreaves et al., 2002; Woodford, 2005). David Hargreaves, Dorothy Miell, and Raymond MacDonald (2002) posited that musical agency can be employed as part of the expression of one's self-identity (the overall view that we have of ourselves), as the agent uses their choice of musical material to communicate their membership to cultural sub-groups. Furthermore, employing musical agency through interactions with music (e.g., singing, playing, listening, creating, movement to music by oneself or with others) empowers individuals and helps to create and express individual and collective identities (Green, 2011; Westerlund, 2002). Musical agency influences not only actions, but also future behaviors (DeNora, 2000; Karlsen, 2013).

In regard to music education contexts, several researchers have encouraged educators to facilitate learning experiences in which students employ their agency as a means of building musical skills and extending their understandings about music. Students then can feel empowered to engage in self-directed music learning and performance outside of the formal music classroom and throughout their lifetimes (Blair, 2009; Green, 2008a; Karlsen, 2009; O'Neill, 2012).

AGENCY AND CLASSROOM CULTURE IN THE COMPOSITION CLASSROOM

The culture of a music classroom is a major determinant in how students employ their agency during compositional experiences (Albert, 2020; Allsup, 2003; Green, 2008b;

Wiggins, 2005 and 2015). For the purposes of this chapter, classroom culture is defined as the common and patterned practices of classroom members (students and teacher) shaped by the values and ideas that reflect the societal norms and mores of a community (Geertz, 1983; Prentiss, 1998). Every classroom has a unique culture due to the expectations and suppositions that students and the teacher bring to new contexts based on their lived experiences (Prentiss, 1998) and knowledge constructed via processes of social constructivism (Bruner, 1996; Rogoff, 1990; Vygotsky, 1978; Wenger, 1998).

Music education researchers have encouraged music educators to employ democratic learning principles in music classrooms, particularly those with learning based in creative processes (Allsup, 2003, 2011, and 2016; Cremata, 2017; Jaffurs, 2004; Partti & Westerlund, 2013; Sætre, 2011, Snell, 2009). Teachers who seek to create a democratic-based approach provide students the opportunity to share authority of the classroom rather than teachers being the locus of power and control (Bruner, 1996). Students also serve as distributors of knowledge to all (including teachers). In turn, students feel encouraged to assert their agency and risk-taking. Both actions are important for compositional activities to flourish (Albert, 2020; Muhonen, 2016; Odena, 2012; Ruthmann, 2012; Ruthmann & Dillon, 2012; Wiggins, 2015; Wiggins & Medvinsky, 2013), as is recognizing them for their efforts. Student agency also helps to shape the classroom culture in which they interact, thus influencing how students learn and participate in musical activities. This phenomenon produces a synergistic cycle: student agency fueling the desire to learn more, which, in turn, creates an increase in student agency.

Teacher Influences on Classroom Culture and Student Agency

The teacher plays an important role in the creation of a classroom culture and community, as well as in the facilitation of student agency. Teachers bring beliefs grounded in lived experiences, such as their own experiences as students and their relationships with current and past students and colleagues, that can strongly influence classroom proceedings (Fairbanks & Broughton, 2003; Sturtevant, 1996). Teachers also guide students in more overt ways. They determine how students will use their lived experiences to inform use of agency in present and future situations, model reflection techniques and feedback delivery for students to scaffold musical growth and use amongst their peers and recognize students for their efforts and contributions to the community (Albert, 2020; Deutsch, 2013; Kaschub & Smith, 2009 and 2017; Wiggins, 2011a and 2015; Wiggins & Medvinsky, 2013). Teachers also play an important role with the development of a classroom's physical climate—resources and physical layout of the room; intellectual climate—programming activities which provide students an appropriate level of challenge commensurate with their skill level; and emotional climate—students feeling safe to take risks without fear of failure (Odena, 2012; Odena et al., 2005). All three play an influential role with the successful implementation of composition in the music classroom.

Part of the work of constructing such an environment includes teachers being facilitators (Cremata, 2017; Green, 2002 and 2008a; Watson, 2011), as well as learning how to get out of students' way and providing them with space so that students feel empowered to employ their agency. As a result, they feel that they can have control over their situation, feel capable of learning and that their ideas are valued, and can take risks and be vulnerable (Albert, 2020; Kaschub & Smith, 2009 and 2017; Stauffer, 2013; Wiggins, 2015; Wiggins & Medvinsky, 2013). Teachers sharing their own composed works also can challenge students' conceptions of creativity (Burnard et al., 2013) and help facilitate a collaborative and mutually respectful environment (King, 2012).

Representative Studies of Student Agency in Action

Randall Everett Allsup (2003) undertook an ethnographic study of informal music learning (Green, 2002 and 2008a) with high school band students who self-selected into a "garage band model" of music-making. He purposefully placed himself in the role of facilitator, rather than an authority figure. By enabling students to utilize their learner and musical agency, participants learned from each other, utilized respectful dialogue, and negotiated power dynamics through shared decision-making. Allsup related these actions to the democratic learning environment and noted how it assisted students' use of agency and reflected their identities:

> When students are given space to explore freely, to work democratically, they will create (from one of *their* musical worlds) a context about which they are familiar, conversant, or curious. We might refer to context as a workable space, a landscape for exploring the curiosities of a given genre. Context, thus, may take the form of a popular tradition like progressive rock, a contemporary brass ensemble, or the reimagining of 1930s swing music. The materials that students choose to explore will represent a world that is theirs, a world they understand, a world that defines who they are. (p. 35)

In their studies of the influences of classroom culture on students' agency and compositional processes and how to construct a classroom environment conducive for such practices, researchers have found that teacher and peer-to-peer criticism and feedback processes help to challenge students' musical beliefs and ideas during creative endeavors (Albert, 2020; Burnard et al., 2013; Lapidaki et al., 2012; Ruthmann, 2012). For example, Deborah Blair (2009) studied how her fifth-grade music students utilized musical maps while listening to music to enable their musical understanding. Two particularly insightful findings related to learner agency emerged: students' desire to enable and further their own understanding by taking initiative to make discoveries for themselves and have ownership of that process. In the music classroom, this was manifested in the students' desire to function as musicians—to participate with others as composers, listeners, and performers. Blair found that this mapping process provided students with opportunities to employ their learner agency as young musicians and share their understandings via the music listening process. Students seemed to have learned a great deal through problem-solving experiences that imitate real-world "everyday" contexts and provide meaningful learning (Dewey, 1938). These feelings of success, fueled by learner agency, increased their levels of confidence, encouraged them to participate in additional experiences (Wiggins & Espeland, 2012), and helped them apply their new-found understandings to new musical experiences with the expansion of their zones of proximal development (Wiggins et al., 2006). Blair also found that students used their agency to communicate their desire to be respected as members of the learning community who had valid musical ideas to be valued. Respecting students' agency and the knowledge that they are creating by using that agency is an important attribute of a successful learning community that influences the classroom culture.

Daniel Albert (2020) undertook an ethnographic study of the culture of a middle school music technology classroom based in musical composition, seeking to understand how the classroom culture was co-created between the educator and students and how that classroom culture influenced participation in musical composition activities. Through individual interviews and a focus group discussion with students, as well as through multiple observations of the class, Albert found that the educator, Gerard,[1] encouraged use of student agency through his active participation in the creation and sustainment of classroom culture.

Gerard employed a strategy recommended by multiple scholars (Burnard et al., 2013; Lapidaki et al., 2012; Ruthmann, 2012; Shouldice, 2019) and affirmed students' efforts using positive and constructive feedback. He also encouraged further creative growth through utilization of specific feedback and constructive criticism (e.g., "Yeah, that's cool. Maybe think of this . . .", "OMG, that's so awesome!"; "Uh, that's okay, try this sound over here. . . . yeah, I like that more") to create a sense of support in the classroom culture and have students feel comfortable with creative explorations, as well as feeling comfortable composing music that has meaning for them. Students, in turn, were observed employing similar feedback techniques as Gerard. This suggests that the teacher was modeling actions he deemed appropriate with the students incorporating these techniques learned in the social constructivist classroom. Gerard also composed his own musical works as students were composing themselves, further demonstrating that he, as his students, is also a composer and a learner. He also made sure to share his work when it was time for students to share with each other.

Also, rather than utilizing direct, whole-class instructional techniques, Gerard utilized musical and social scaffolding practices (Wiggins, 2011a, 2015) to foster student creativity and agency. He provided his students with individual and group time to compose, as well as space to work in various parts of the rehearsal room and surrounding

---

[1] A pseudonym chosen by the educator.

environs that gave them "room" during class to create and refine ideas for their compositions. In this sense, students felt free to experiment and explore their creative selves, enhancing the synergy that contributed to the classroom culture and students' use of their agency for creative endeavors. However, Albert (2020) noticed several moments of tension between students as well as off-task behaviors, demonstrating the "messiness" of social life (Greener, 2011; Murchinson, 2010) undergirded by a classroom culture that supported learning, another "messy" process (Davis-Seaver, 2000; Stauffer, 2013). Indeed, tension and conflict are to be expected during the learning process (Argyris & Schon, 1978; Delamarter, 2018; Osterman & Kottkamp, 2004). Gerard helped to create an environment sustained by students' sense of agency within an overarching and supportive framework in which "messiness" was permitted, as Gerard recognized that it is a necessary part of learning and the creative process (Kaschub & Smith, 2009; Stauffer, 2013).

S. Alex Ruthmann's (2008) study presents another angle of the influence the teacher and the nature of their feedback have on students' use of their agency. Using a multi-faceted qualitative approach (Denzin & Lincoln, 2000), Ruthmann explored the relationship between learner agency and the nature of feedback and compositional intent through the lived experiences of the teacher of a music technology class (Mary), a student composer (Ellen), and Ellen's peers with whom she interacted. Ruthmann attended and collected data from all 43 class sessions of a general music class based in technology for students ages 10 and 11. A focus of Ruthmann's analysis was what transpired during a movie soundtrack project and the tension between Ellen's interpretation of her work and Mary's vision for the piece. Throughout their interactions, Mary provided feedback that communicated an agenda to conform to her interpretation of the work, assuming the role as "expert." Rather, Ellen was looking for Mary to be a "guide."

Ruthmann and others (Calkins, 1994; Wiggins, 2003) advocated for educators to discover the student's vision for the piece, ascertaining their reason(s) for asking for feedback, and providing scaffolding feedback that is appropriate for the *student-as-composer*. While Ruthmann freely admits that the descriptive and interpretive sections of his study are reflective of his own biases, his findings demonstrate the importance of music educators putting personal agendas for students' compositions aside. In helping students attain both personal and educational goals, teachers should seek and understand their students' musical intentions.

IMPLICATIONS AND SUGGESTIONS FOR THE COMPOSITION CLASSROOM

For our students to desire employing their personal and musical agency in the composition classroom, we first need to develop our own personal and musical agency with composition so that we may be effective role models and facilitators of composition-based experiences (Randles & Smith, 2012; Wiggins & Medvinsky, 2013). As Sandra Stauffer (2013) stated, "Overcoming personal, professional, and political constraints and moving toward a pedagogical practice that nurtures children's creative musical abilities requires the courage to take risks and to cultivate one's own curiosity, wonder, and interest in creating" (p. 100). Throughout this section, I will offer suggestions as to how both in-service and preservice educators can help foster a classroom culture that allows student agency to flourish, as well as how teacher agency can be leveraged for student learning via composition.

"Do I Consider Myself a Composer?": The Importance of Composition Experience

Researchers have found that in-service educators are hesitant to employ composition in their classes due to lack of preparation to teach composition in their teacher preparation programs (Menard, 2015; Strand, 2006). Similarly, Carlos Abril and Brent Gault (2006, 2008) have noted that preservice educators might have been less likely to engage in composition experiences in their own K–12 music education. They also might feel less confident about their identities as composers, self-efficacy with composition, and their ability to teach composition in part due to performance-based activities being the primary means of music education in the United States (Abril & Gault, 2006 and 2008; Randles & Smith, 2012). How, then, can music educators develop new skills to improve their assistance to their students?

Quite simply, to develop comfort in the role of composer and, by extension, composition teacher, music educators should compose! Our beliefs about composition in music education are directly related to our experiences and self-efficacy with composition (Jaffurs, 2004; Odena & Welch, 2007 and 2009; Randles, 2009; Randles & Smith, 2012). Whenever time allows, create works that are meaningful to you and reflect—learn from—the process. When students are composing during class, balance composing with them and providing feedback to students when requested. Also, there are many print and online resources on how to go about teaching students to compose.

For preservice educators, music teacher educators should consider scaffolding and implementing activities throughout the teacher education course sequence (e.g., courses, units, etc.) that place preservice educators in the role of composer, as well as discuss how to implement composition activities in a K–12 music education program as part of a comprehensive curriculum addressing state curricular standards and district-mandated curricula. Fieldwork experiences (observing educators who implement composition in their instruction and/or preservice educators teaching music through composition) can be powerful moments that "bridge" discussions from methods classes into the real-world classroom. Additionally, music composition faculty might consider creating seminars on composition pedagogy and arranging for music education majors.

Composition faculty also could collaborate with music teacher educators for classes addressing composition pedagogy.

Teachers provide role models for children in the composition environment. Their feelings on composition in a music education curriculum, as well as their personal experience with composition, are reflected in their pedagogy (Csikszentmihalyi et al., 1993; Randles, 2009). Teachers who demonstrate genuine excitement about composition and show interest in furthering their own abilities as a composer have greater potential to pique students' interest and develop their intrinsic motivation. This type of "modeling" also encourages use of personal and musical agency to engage in composition activities (Csikszentmihalyi et al., 1993; Odena & Welch, 2007).

Compositional Style

Educators' preservice musical foundation is largely built on the Western classical "canon," but compositional style need not reside solely within the Western classical realm (Odena & Welch, 2007). Practitioners should endeavor to compose in a breadth of styles similar to what one might teach in K–12 schools, including jazz, hip-hop, rock, pop, and R&B. For example, the Modern Band curriculum (Little Kids Rock, 2020) includes working with composition through popular music styles. Working with improvisation, learning music by ear, and undertaking types of open-ended experiences that have a sense of "play" to them (Koops & Taggart, 2011) will serve as catalysts that broaden students' conceptions of creativity (Koops & Taggart, 2011; Odena & Welch, 2009), as well as increase students' confidence and build composition skills.

Additionally, if preservice educators have worked with composition in their teacher preparation programs, they should continue engaging in composition activities once they begin their in-service careers. This will help to continue deepening their identities as composers and feel more comfortable with teaching composition in the classroom. Educators sharing finished compositions or works-in-progress can help to create a culture of creativity in the classroom, strengthen relationships, and establish credibility with students (Kratus, 2016). As a result, the trust between students and educator is strengthened and students feel more encouraged to employ their personal, learner, and musical agency.

Scaffolding

"Letting Go," Providing Space, and Developing Trust in the Learning Community

As educators explore the craft of composition themselves, they soon gain an appreciation for the time and space that is needed so that one has "room" to consider the state of their composition and how to refine it. Gerard (Albert, 2020) demonstrated how purposeful use of time and space provides "room" for students to think, experiment, and refine ideas for their compositions. Gerard's classroom also exuded the "messiness" of the creative process with students inventing, evaluating, and refining musical ideas in a very non-linear fashion. "Letting go" and providing students with this freedom can enable students' agency for creative endeavors, but it can also be a challenge for both preservice and in-service educators (Robbins, 1999; Schmidt, 2012; Wright-Maley, 2015). In addition to the lack of composition background or study of composition pedagogy (Menard, 2015; Strand, 2006), educators might fear a loss of control in part due to their "training" (this word used purposefully) to be teacher-centered managers/directors (Conway & Hibbard, 2020; Regelski, 2002; Smith, 2014). In-service educator participants in Cory Wright-Maley's (2015) study noted that " 'stepping back and letting go' of controlling student participation is 'not natural' " (p. 222) and requires "trust that [students are] going to do what you want them to do. And that can be really hard" (p. 221).

One of the hallmarks of a learning community is a shared sense of reliance and trust among its members (Blanchard et al., 2011; Kensler et al., 2009; West & Williams, 2017). Others have characterized "trust" as feeling "safe" and respected within the community (Lichtenstein, 2005). Educators who wish to provide students with a sense of personal agency within a learning community would be advised to co-create a classroom culture of trust in which students feel that they can take risks and be vulnerable and yet feel safe and supported by the educator and peers. Making space for all in the community (including the educator) to share their creative works, as well as establishing meaningful positive relationships with all students, being genuine, and modeling appropriate interactions for students to employ in their own interactions with each other (such as peer feedback) are strategies that must be present in the composition classroom. Educators may wish to engage their students in discussion at the beginning of the academic year to determine what type of environment they, as a learning community, would like to create together and what rules and parameters they would like to establish (Koops & Taggart, 2011). With these guidelines in place, students can feel safer to share their compositions with their peers.

The Role of Feedback and Sharing

Making time for students and teachers to share their compositions with each other should be a priority, as those experiences are the most valuable learning opportunities for students (Wiggins, 2015). The songs that students generate as part of a learning community could very well serve as generative material for future compositions: adapting and borrowing ideas from each other as they work together and are exposed to new means of expressing emotions and thoughts via the musical medium. While compositions could be finished products, students should be encouraged to share works-in-progress to receive feedback not only for the sake of improvement, but to receive positive comments that can further encourage students' use of agency. Sharing works-in-progress with each other and receiving feedback within a community also serves as a visceral reminder that composing is an ongoing process that requires time, space, and "room."

Indeed, one of the most important tasks an educator must consider is what feedback is appropriate at a certain point in a student's development as a composer and how that feedback should be delivered. As with any descriptive feedback procedure (Hickey & Reese, 2001; Shaw, 2018), educators and peers should provide age-appropriate specific information as to *why* something is considered particularly well done and why something could be improved and *how*, all while being affirming and supportive. Michele Kaschub and Janice Smith (2017) stated that not only is the content of the feedback important, but how the feedback is delivered is, oftentimes, more important. They suggested that elementary educators have their students envision what type of feedback they hope to receive and practice providing and receiving that feedback with a sample composition. Additionally, "Composers' Circles" provide the opportunity for students to offer and receive praise and constructive criticism in a balanced format: two praise comments for each comment of constructive criticism. Similarly, MacLeod (2013) suggested a "critique sandwich" (a term coined by fifth graders) structure of providing feedback following presentation of the composition:

- Begin with a comment supporting the student's efforts and something positive about the composition.
- Then, provide a "rich filling" to the "sandwich" with clear, specific, and substantive comments, but take care not to "overstuff it" with comments that would make the experience difficult to remember.
- The final and "top layer" comment should encourage the student with their endeavors.

For older students, John Kratus (2016) provided similar strategies and stressed that educators will need to be mindful of class discussions/feedback sessions. Students can be extremely vulnerable when sharing original songs with their peers that address issues of identity, significant life moments, and traumatic events. While he specifically referenced sharing and feedback in a songwriting course, his suggestions for types of feedback throughout the course of a class could be applicable to multiple types of composition settings:

- Supportive: This phase includes generally supportive feedback that is non-specific in nature with the objective of providing students with a sense of security and confidence in their efforts, as well as increasing the level of trust in peers and the educator. The guiding question about a student's performance: "What specifically did you like in the song?"
- Descriptive: The educator asks the student audience questions on specific musical and lyrical characteristics of the performed song. The purpose of this phase is to affirm to the composer that their song is worthy of critique and analysis, as well as point out interesting musical and lyrical characteristics that other class members might wish to employ in their own songs.
- Prescriptive: Here, students provide the composer with suggestions for improvement, taking on a "master class" feel with all students commenting, rather than one "featured" individual. Composers will need to have a sufficient level of confidence

and self-efficacy in their skills, as well as trust in their peers and the educator, at this stage. Kratus (2016) warned that arriving at this level will take time and should not be rushed.

Regardless of the chosen strategy, respect of the composer is paramount in feedback sessions and criticism of performance or composition skills should not be allowed.

Teachers should take care to make themselves available for individual consultations with students. However, as part of respectful scaffolding (Wiggins & Medvinsky, 2013), feedback should be provided when it is solicited on students' own volition, rather than imposed on students. Furthermore, teachers should seek to understand students' intent behind their composition and not impose their own musical conception of the work, or what they think is "musically correct," on the student. As we read earlier in this chapter with Mary (the educator) and Ellen (Mary's student), such interactions could have negative implications for student agency and diminish the motivation to engage further in composition (Ruthmann, 2008). Educators, rather, need to understand that students might have a reasonably formed conception of their composition in their head. The role of the educator is to listen to the composer's vision and help them refine the work to become the desired aural product.

Logical Sequencing and the Zone of Proximal Development

When considering how to structure a class to be conducive to compositional processes, educators should reference social constructivist learning theories and remember that learner construction of knowledge is the product of social interaction, interpretation, and understanding (Vygotsky, 1962). To this end, educators can design activities that are grounded in these learning theories and provide opportunities for students to explore and experience musical concepts that will maximize their readiness to engage in composition. Additionally, educators will need to design and implement an assessment of students' prior knowledge and skills at the beginning of instruction to determine what initial learning tasks, or "entry points" (Wiggins, 2015), are at the appropriate challenge level for students' skill levels. Educators can then design compositional activities according to students' progress with their learning.

Educators should also consider how scaffolding can be structured to accommodate students' various zones of proximal development and how scaffolding can be purposefully structured to assist students with reaching a new level of understanding. Scaffolding does not necessarily only have to originate from the educator; rather, knowledgeable peers may also provide scaffolding for their less knowledgeable colleagues (Bruner, 1986; Green, 2002 and 2008a). Under this arrangement, students can be paired with more knowledgeable peers and transition from an observer-type role to one that is more active. Mindfulness of and responsiveness to a student's pace shows respect for students, which is essential for co-creating a classroom culture that encourages them to employ their agency. Educators will, however, need to monitor how students engage with classroom activities as they could continually choose to silently disengage or even present disruptive behaviors due to fear of failure with creative activities (Burnard, 2012).

Additionally, educators need to consider how learning activities can be differentiated to accommodate students' various zones of proximal development. They should take the care to foster opportunities that have students learn, experience, and manipulate musical concepts in some depth prior to composing, to maximize their readiness to engage in composition. Learning of skills and concepts should be logically sequenced so they can be built upon and provide students with the best opportunities for success. Finally, modeling, scaffolding, feedback, and encouragement, all of which are important in the creativity-based classroom, will need to be thoughtfully employed.

Designing Appropriate Tasks

Getting to know students' musical histories can be a powerful connection point for determining students' knowledge about music and providing them with appropriate assignments that engage them at an appropriate skill and challenge level to enable their success and growth, also while affirming their musical interests and identities (Kaschub & Smith, 2009 and 2017). There has been considerable debate surrounding the structure of composition assignments, as well as the number of freedoms and constraints within those assignments (Kratus, 1989; Wiggins, 2015). Issues include providing

Compose!	• Compose works both during class with students and outside of class to deepen your self-efficacy and identity as a composer. • Compose in multiple styles (e.g., jazz, rock, pop, hip-hop, etc.).
"Let Go" and Provide "Space"	• Embrace the fact that composition is, like all creative endeavors, a "messy" process. • Co-create a classroom culture in which students feel that they can take risks and be vulnerable, yet feel safe and supported.
Feedback and Sharing	• Educators *and* peers should provide age-appropriate specific information as to *why* something is considered particularly well done and why something could be improved and *how*, all while being affirming and supportive. • Teachers should seek to understand the intent behind the student's composition and not impose any teacher conceptions of the work, or what they think is "musically correct," on the student.
Application of Learning Theories	• Educators *and* knowledgeable peers can provide scaffolding to accommodate students' various zones of proximal development.
Designing Appropriate Tasks	• Provide students with a "point of entry": an educator-imposed requirement of including a musical element students have studied to be included in a work, with the remainder of the artistic decisions to be made by the student.

FIGURE 8.1. Key ideas to promote student agency

students with tasks matched with outcome goals that they believe are attainable, as well as having an appropriate balance between freedoms and constraints. Too much freedom might overwhelm students with choices, while too much constraint might stifle imagination and focus on satisfying the parameters of the assignment rather than creating a unique product. Jackie Wiggins (2015) provides somewhat of a middle ground and suggests that educators provide students a "point of entry": an educator-imposed requirement of a musical element students have studied and understand to be included in a work, with the remainder of the artistic decisions to be made by the student. This solution provides students with the opportunity to employ their agency to create a work of personal and artistic significance for them, as well as satisfies teachers' curricular and assessment objectives. Examples of approaches that capture these ideas are found in Figure 8.1.

CONCLUSION

Composition is a means through which thoughts, emotions, and identities can be expressed and can be an especially useful outlet when students cannot articulate them through the written and spoken word. Educators should consider how students can be encouraged to use their agency in their classrooms to not only satisfy curricular aims and objectives via composition, but also help them make choices that provide them with a sense of empowerment that assist them with creating a fulfilling and meaningful life with realized potential. They deserve nothing less, and the possibilities are endless.

REFERENCES

Abril, C., & Gault, B. (2006). The state of music in the elementary school: The principal's perspective. *Journal of Research in Music Education, 54*(1), 6–20. https://doi.org/10.1177/002 242940605400102

Abril, C., & Gault, B. (2008). The state of music in secondary schools: The principal's perspective. *Journal of Research in Music Education, 56*(1), 68–81. https://doi.org/10.1177/002242940 8317516

Albert, D. J. (2020). The classroom culture of a middle school music technology class. *International Journal of Music Education, 38*(3), 383–399. https://doi.org/10.1177/025576141 9881483

Allsup, R. E. (2003). Mutual learning and democratic action in instrumental music education. *Journal of Research in Music Education, 51*(1), 24–37. https://jstor.org/stable/3345646

Allsup, R. E. (2011). Popular music and classical musicians: Strategies and perspectives. *Music Educators Journal, 97*(3), 30–34. https://doi.org/10.1177/0027432110391810

Allsup, R. E. (2016). *Remixing the classroom: Toward an open philosophy of music education.* Indiana University Press. https://www.jstor.org/stable/j.ctt1d9npqk

Argyris, C., & Schon, D. A. (1978). *Theory in practice: Increasing professional effectiveness.* Jossey-Bass.

Bandura, A. (1986). *Social foundations of thought and action: A social cognitive theory.* Prentice-Hall.

Bandura, A. (1989). Human agency in social cognitive theory. *American Psychologist, 44*(9), 1175–1184. https://doi.org/10.1037/0003-066X.44.9.1175

Bandura, A. (2006). Toward a psychology of human agency. *Perspectives on Psychological Science, 1*(2), 164–180. https://doi.org/10.1111/j.1745-6916.2006.00011.x

Barone, T. (2000). Breaking the mold. In T. Barone, *Aesthetics, politics, and educational inquiry* (pp. 119–134). Peter Lang.

Blair, D. V. (2009). Learner agency: To understand and to be understood. *British Journal of Music Education, 26*(2), 173–187. https://doi.org/10.1017/S0265051709008420

Blanchard, A. L., Welbourne, J. L., & Boughton, M. D. (2011). A model of online trust: The mediating role of norms and sense of virtual community. *Information, Communication & Society, 14*(1), 76–106. https://doi.org/10.1080/13691181003739633

Bruner, J. (1986). *Actual minds, possible worlds.* Harvard University Press.

Bruner, J. (1996). *The culture of education.* Harvard University Press.

Burnard, P. (2012). *Musical creativities in practice.* Oxford University Press. https://doi.org/10.1093/acprof:oso/9780199583942.001.0001

Burnard, P., Boyack, J., & Howell, G. (2013). Children composing: Creating communities of musical practice. In P. Burnard & R. Murphy (Eds.), *Teaching music creatively* (pp. 37–54). Routledge.

Calkins, L. (1994). *The art of teaching writing.* Heinemann.

Conway, C., & Hibbard, S. (2020). Pushing the boundaries from the inside. In C. Conway, K. Pellegrino, A. M. Stanley, & C. West (Eds.), *The Oxford handbook of preservice music teacher education in the United States* (pp. 3–22). Oxford University Press. https://doi.org/10.1093/oxfordhb/9780190671402.013.1

Cremata, R. (2017). Facilitation in popular music education. *Journal of Popular Music Education, 1*(1), 63–82. https://doi.org/10.1386/jpme.1.1.63_1

Csikszentmihalyi, M. (1990). *Flow: The psychology of optimal experience.* Harper & Row.

Csikszentmihalyi, M., Rathunde, K., & Whalen, S. (1993). *Talented teenagers: The roots of success and failure.* Cambridge University Press.

Davis-Seaver, J. (2000). *Critical thinking in young children.* Edwin Mellen Press.

Delamarter, S. (2018). Archaeology of an online course: Teaching and learning as social engineering. *Teaching Theology & Religion, 21*(3), 213–227. https://doi.org/10.1111/teth.12445

DeNora, T. (2000). *Music in everyday life.* Cambridge University Press.

Denzin, N. K., & Lincoln, Y. S. (2000). The discipline and practice of qualitative research. In N. K. Denzin & Y. S. Lincoln (Eds.), *Handbook of qualitative research* (pp. 1–28). Sage.

Deutsch, D. (2013). Teaching gifted learners in composition. In M. Kaschub & J. P. Smith (Eds.), *Composing our future: Preparing music educators to teach composition* (pp. 127–148). Oxford University Press. https://doi.org/10.1093/acprof:oso/9780199832286.003.0007

Dewey, J. (1916). *Democracy and education.* Macmillan.

Dewey, J. (1938). *Experience and education.* Kappa Delta Pi.

Fairbanks, C. M., & Broughton, M. A. (2003). Literary lessons: The convergence of expectations, practices, and classroom culture. *Journal of Literacy Research, 34*(4), 391–428. https://doi.org/10.1207/s15548430jlr3404_2

Geertz, C. (1983). *Local knowledge.* Basic Books.

Green, L. (2002). *How popular musicians learn: A way ahead for music education.* Ashgate.

Green, L. (2008a). *Music, informal learning, and the school: A new classroom pedagogy.* Ashgate.

Green, L. (2008b). Group cooperation, inclusion, and disaffected pupils: Some responses to informal learning in the music classroom. Presented at the RIME Conference 2007, Exeter, UK. *Music Education Research*, *10*(2), 177–192. https://doi.org/10.1080/1461380080 2079049

Green, L. (Ed.). (2011). *Learning, teaching, and musical identity: Voices across cultures*. Indiana University Press.

Greener, I. (2011). *Designing social research: A guide for the bewildered*. Sage.

Hargreaves, D. J., Miell, D., & MacDonald, R. A. R. (2002). What are musical identities, and why are they important? In R. A. R. MacDonald, D. J. Hargreaves, & D. Miell (Eds.), *Musical identities* (pp. 1–20). Oxford University Press.

Hewitt, D. (2018). Constructing informal experiences in the elementary general music classroom. *Music Educators Journal*, *104*(3), 46–53. https://doi.org/10.1177/0027432117745361

Hickey, M. (2003). Creative thinking in the context of music composition. In M. Hickey (Ed.), *Why and how to teach music composition: A new horizon for music education* (pp. 31–53). MENC: The National Association for Music Education.

Hickey, M. (2012). *Music outside the lines: Ideas for composing in K–12 music classrooms*. Oxford University Press. https://doi.org/10.1093/acprof:osobl/9780199826773.001.0001

Hickey, M. (2013). What pre-service teachers can learn from composition research. In M. Kaschub & J. P. Smith (Eds.), *Composing our future: Preparing music educators to teach composition* (pp. 33–56). Oxford University Press. https://doi.org/10.1093/acprof:oso/978019 9832286.003.0003

Hickey, M., & Reese, S. (2001). The development of a rating scale for judging constructive feedback for student compositions. *Journal of Technology in Music Learning*, *1*(1), 10–19. http://www.atmimusic.com/wp-content/uploads/2013/05/JTML.1.1c_HickeyReese_The-deve lopment-of-a-rating-scale-for-judging-constructive-feedback-for-student-compositi ons.pdf

Jaffurs, S. E. (2004). The impact of informal music learning practices in the classroom, or how I learned how to teach from a garage band. *International Journal of Music Education*, *22*(3), 189–200. https://doi.org/10.1177/0255761404047401

Karlsen, S. (2009). Access to the learnable: Music education and the development of strong learners within informal arenas. In E. Gould, J. Countryman, C. Morton, & L. S. Rose (Eds.), *Exploring social justice: How music education might matter* (pp. 240–251). Canadian Music Educators' Association.

Karlsen, S. (2011). Using musical agency as a lens: Researching music education from the angle of experience. *Research Studies in Music Education*, *33*(2), 107–121. https//doi.org/10.1177/ 1321103X11422005

Karlsen, S. (2013). Immigrant students and the "homeland music": Meanings, negotiations and implications. *Research Studies in Music Education*, *35*(2), 161–177. https://doi.org/10.1177/ 1321103X13508057

Kaschub, M., & Smith, J. (2009). *Minds on music: Composition for creative and critical thinking*. Rowman and Littlefield.

Kaschub, M., & Smith, J. (2017). *Experiencing music composition in grades 3–5*. Oxford University Press.

Kensler, L. A. W., Caskie, G. I. L., Barber, M. E., & White, G. P. (2009). The ecology of democratic learning communities: Faculty trust and continuous learning in public middle schools. *Journal of School Leadership*, *19*(6), 697–735. https://doi.org/10.1177/10526846090 1900604

King, A. (2012). The student prince: Music-making with technology. In G. E. McPherson & G. F. Welch (Eds.), *The Oxford handbook of music education* (Vol. 2, pp. 476–491). Oxford University Press. https://doi.org/10.1093/oxfordhb/9780199928019.013.0031

Kohn, A. (1999). *Punished by rewards.* Houghton Mifflin.

Koops, L. H., & Taggart, C. C. (2011). Learning through play: Extending an early childhood music education approach to undergraduate and graduate music education. *Journal of Music Teacher Education, 20*(2), 55–66. https://doi.org/10.1177/1057083710373578

Kratus, J. (1989). A time analysis of the compositional processes used by children ages 7 to 11. *Journal of Research in Music Education, 37*(1), 5–20. https://doi.org/10.2307/3344949

Kratus, J. (2016). Songwriting: A new direction for secondary music education. *Music Educators Journal, 102*(3), 60–65. https://doi.org/10.1177/0027432115620660

Lapidaki, E., de Groot, R., & Stagkos, P. (2012). Communal creativity as sociomusical practice. In G. E. McPherson & G. F. Welch (Eds.), *The Oxford handbook of music education* (Vol. 2, pp. 371–388). Oxford University Press. https://doi.org/10.1093/oxfordhb/9780199928019.013.0025

Lave, J., & Wenger, E. (1991). *Situated learning: Legitimate peripheral participation.* Cambridge University Press.

Lichtenstein, M. (2005). The importance of classroom environments in the assessment of learning community outcomes. *Journal of College Student Development, 46*(4), 341–356. https://doi.org/10.1353/csd.2005.0038

Lind, V. R., & McCoy, C. (2016). *Culturally responsive teaching in music education: From understanding to application.* Routledge.

Little Kids Rock. (n. d.) *Modern band.* Little Kids Rock. Retrieved December 1, 2020, from https://www.littlekidsrock.org/the-program/modernband/

MacLeod, S. (2013). The Vermont MIDI Project: Fostering mentorships in multiple environments. In M. Kaschub & J. P. Smith (Eds.), *Composing our future: Preparing music educators to teach composition* (pp. 211–225). Oxford University Press. https://doi.org/10.1093/acprof:oso/9780199832286.003.0012

McMurrer, J. (2007). *NCLB year 5: Choices, changes, and challenges: Curriculum and instruction in the NCLB era.* Center on Education Policy.

Menard, E. A. (2015). Music composition in the high school curriculum: A multiple case study. *Journal of Research in Music Education, 63*(1), 114–136. https://doi.org/10.1177/0022429415574310

Muhonen, S. (2016). *Songcrafting practice: A teacher inquiry into the potential to support collaborative creation and creative agency within school music education* [Doctoral dissertation, University of the Arts Helsinki, the Sibelius Academy]. HELDA – Digital Repository of the University of Helsinki. http://urn.fi/URN:ISBN:978-952-329-024-2

Murchinson, J. M. (2010). *Ethnography essentials: Designing, conducting, and presenting your research.* Jossey-Bass.

Odena, O. (2012). Creativity in the secondary general classroom. In G. E. McPherson & G. F. Welch (Eds.), *The Oxford handbook of music education* (Vol. 1, pp. 512–528). Oxford University Press. https://doi.org/10.1093/oxfordhb/9780199730810.013.0031_update_001

Odena, O., & Welch, G. F. (2007). The influence of teachers' backgrounds on their perceptions of musical creativity: A qualitative study with secondary school music teachers. *Research Studies in Music Education, 28*(1), 71–81. https://doi.org/10.1177/1321103X070280010206

Odena, O., & Welch, G. (2009). A generative model of teachers' thinking on musical creativity. *Psychology of Music, 37*(4), 416–442. https://doi.org/10.1177/0305735608100374

Odena, O., Plummeridge, C., & Welch, G. (2005). Towards an understanding of creativity in music education: A qualitative exploration of data from English secondary schools. *Bulletin of the Council for Research in Music Education*, *163*, 9–18. http://www.jstor.org/stable/40311590

O'Neill, S. A. (2012). Becoming a music learner: Toward a theory of transformative music engagement. In G. E. McPherson & G. Welch (Eds.), *The Oxford handbook of music education* (Vol. 1, pp. 163–186). Oxford University Press. https://doi.org/10.1093/oxfordhb/9780199730810.013.0010

Onosko, J. (2011). Race to the Top leaves children and future citizens behind: The devastating effects of centralization, standardization, and high stakes accountability. *Democracy & Education*, *19*(2), Article 1. https://democracyeducationjournal.org/home/vol19/iss2/1/

Osterman, K., & Kottkamp, R. (2004). *Reflective practice for educators: Professional development to improve student learning* (2nd ed.). Corwin Press.

Partti, H., & Westerlund, H. (2013). Envisioning collaborative composing in music education: Learning and negotiation of meaning in *operabyyou.com*. *British Journal of Music Education*, *30*(2), 207–222. https://doi.org/10.1017/S0265051713000119

Prentiss, T. (1998). Teachers and students mutually influencing each other's literacy practices: A focus on the student's role. In D. E. Alvermann, K. A. Hinchman, D. W. Moore, S. F. Phelps, & D. W. Waffe (Eds.), *Reconceptualizing the literacies in adolescents' lives* (pp. 103–128). Lawrence Erlbaum.

Randles, C. (2009). "That's my piece, that's my signature, and it means more . . .": Creative identity and the ensemble teacher/arranger. *Research Studies in Music Education*, *31*(1), 52–68. https://doi.org/10.1177/1321103X09103631

Randles, C., & Smith, G. D. (2012). A first comparison of pre-service music teachers' identities as creative musicians in the United States and England. *Research Studies in Music Education*, *34*(2), 173–187. https://doi.org/10.1177/1321103X12464836

Regelski, T. (2002). On "methodolatry" and music teaching as critical and reflective praxis. *Philosophy of Music Education Review*, *10*(2), 102–123. https://muse.jhu.edu/article/408680/summary

Robbins, J. (1999). Getting set and letting go: Practicum teachers' in-flight decision-making. Mountain Lake Reader (Spring), 26–32.

Rogoff, B. (1990). *Apprenticeship in thinking: Cognitive development in social context*. Oxford University Press.

Rogoff, B. (2003). *The cultural nature of human development*. Oxford University Press.

Ruthmann, S. A. (2008). Whose agency matters? Negotiating pedagogical and creative intent during composing experiences. *Research Studies in Music Education*, *30*(1), 43–58. https://doi.org/10.1177/1321103X08089889

Ruthmann, A. (2012). Engaging adolescents with music and technology. In S. L. Burton (Ed.), *Engaging musical practices: A sourcebook for middle school general music* (pp. 177–192). Rowman & Littlefield.

Ruthmann, S. A., & Dillon, S. C. (2012). Technology in the lives and schools of adolescents. In G. E. McPherson & G. F. Welch (Eds.), *The Oxford handbook of music education* (Vol. 1, pp. 529–547). Oxford University Press. https://doi.org/10.1093/oxfordhb/9780199730810.013.0032

Sætre, J. H. (2011). Teaching and learning music composition in primary school settings. *Music Education Research*, *13*(1), 29–50. https://doi.org/10.1080/14613808.2011.553276

Schmidt, M. (2012). Transition from student to teacher: Preservice teachers' beliefs and practices. *Journal of Music Teacher Education*, 23(1), 27–49. https://doi.org/10.1177/10570 83712469111

Shaw, B. P. (2018). *Music assessment for better ensembles*. Oxford University Press. https://doi. org/ 10.1093/oso/9780190603144.001.0001

Shouldice, H. N. (2019). "Everybody has something": One teacher's beliefs about musical ability and their connection to teaching practice and classroom culture. *Research Studies in Music Education*, 41(2), 189–205. https://doi.org/10.1177/1321103X18773109

Smith, J. (2014). Entrepreneurial music education. In M. Kaschub & J. Smith (Eds.), *Promising practices in 21st century music teacher education* (pp. 61–78). Oxford University Press. https:// doi.org/10.1093/acprof:oso/9780199384747.003.0004

Snell, K. (2009). Democracy and popular music in music education. In E. Gould, J. Countryman, C. Morton, & L. S. Rose (Eds.), *Exploring social justice: How music education might matter* (pp. 166–183). Canadian Music Educators' Association.

Stauffer, S. L. (2013). Preparing to engage children in musical creating. In M. Kaschub & J. P. Smith (Eds.), *Composing our future: Preparing music educators to teach composition* (pp. 75–108). Oxford University Press. https://doi.org/10.1093/acprof:oso/9780199832 286.003.0005

Strand, K. (2006). Survey of Indiana music teachers on using composition in the classroom. *Journal of Research in Music Education*, 54(2), 154–167. https://doi.org/10.1177/00224294060 5400206

Sturtevant, E. G. (1996). Lifetime influences on the literacy-related instructional beliefs of experienced high school history teachers: Two comparative case studies. *Journal of Literacy Research*, 28(2), 227–257. https://doi.org/10.1080/10862969609547920

Vaughn, M. (2018). Making sense of student agency in the early grades. *Phi Delta Kappan*, 99(7), 62–66. https://doi.org/10.1177/0031721718767864

Vygotsky, L. S. (1962). *Thought and language*. MIT Press.

Vygotsky, L. S. (1978). *Mind in society: The development of higher psychological processes* (M. Cole, V. John-Steiner, S. Scribner, & E. Souberman, Eds. & Trans.). Harvard University Press.

Watson, S. (2011). *Using technology to unlock musical creativity*. Oxford University Press.

Webster, P. R. (2003). Conference keynotes: Asking music students to reflect on their creative work: Encouraging the revision process. *Music Education Research*, 5(3), 243–248. https:// doi.org/10.1080/1461380032000126337

Wenger, E. (1998). *Communities of practice: Learning, meaning, and identity*. Cambridge University Press.

West, R. E., & Williams, G. (2017). "I don't think that work means what you think": A proposed framework for defining learning communities. *Educational Technology Research and Development*, 65, 1569–1582. https://doi.org/10.1007/s11423-017-9535-0

Westerlund, H. (2002). *Bridging experience, action, and culture in music education*. [Doctoral dissertation, University of the Arts Helsinki, the Sibelius Academy]. HELDA – Digital Repository of the University of Helsinki. http://urn.fi/URN:ISBN:952-9658-98-2

Wiggins, J. (2003). A frame for understanding children's compositional processes. In M. Hickey (Ed.), *Why and how to teach music composition: A new horizon for music education* (pp. 141–166). MENC.

Wiggins, J. (2005). Fostering revision and extension in student composition. *Music Educators Journal*, 91(3), 35–42. https://doi.org/10.2307/3400074

Wiggins, J. (2011a). When the music is theirs: Scaffolding young songwriters. In M. S. Barrett (Ed.), *A cultural psychology of music education* (pp. 83–113). Oxford University Press. https://doi.org/10.1093/acprof:oso/9780199214389.003.0005

Wiggins, J. (2011b). Vulnerability and agency in being and becoming a musician. *Music Education Research, 13*(4), 355–367. https://doi.org/10.1080/14613808.2011.632153

Wiggins, J. (2015). *Teaching for musical understanding* (3rd ed.). Oxford University Press.

Wiggins, J. (2016). Musical agency. In G. E. McPherson (Ed.), *The child as musician: A handbook of musical development* (2nd ed., pp. 102–121). Oxford University Press. https://doi.org/10.1093/acprof:oso/9780198744443.003.0006

Wiggins, J., Blair, D., Ruthmann, A., & Shively, J. (2006). A heart-to-heart about music education practice. *Mountain Lake Reader, 4,* 82–91.

Wiggins, J., & Espeland, M. (2012). Creating in music learning contexts. In G. E. McPherson & G. Welch (Eds.), *The Oxford handbook of music education* (Vol. 1, pp. 341–360). Oxford University Press. https://doi.org/10.1093/oxfordhb/9780199730810.013.0021

Wiggins, J., & Medvinsky, M. (2013). Scaffolding student composers. In M. Kaschub & J. P. Smith (Eds.), *Composing our future: Preparing music educators to teach composition* (pp. 109–125). Oxford University Press. https://doi.org/10.1093/acprof:oso/9780199832286.003.0006

Woodford, P. G. (2005). *Democracy and music education: Liberalism, ethics, and the politics of Practice.* Indiana University Press.

Wright-Maley, C. (2015). On "stepping back and letting go": The role of control in the success or failure of social studies simulations. *Theory & Research in Social Education, 43*(2), 206–243. https://doi.org/10.1080/00933104.2015.1034394

CHAPTER 9

....

CREATING CULTURALLY
SUSTAINING SPACES IN THE
COMPOSITIONAL PROCESS

....

CHRISTOPHER MENA AND
PATRICIA SHEHAN CAMPBELL

HUMAN creativity, and its musical manifestations in processes of composition and improvisation, is a cross-cultural phenomenon of considerable intrigue to those who wonder about human invention, imagination, and individuality within a given realm of collective cultural understandings. Because music reflects culture, musicians quite naturally draw from their cultural experiences in expressing themselves—both in compositions that are formulated over long periods of time and in moments of spontaneous improvisation (Swanson & Campbell, 2016; Kohfeld et al., 2019; Shao et al., 2019). Student musicians who compose will quite naturally lean in the direction of music acquired at home, through experiences in the family and among friends, and from 'round-the-clock media exposure, in their crafting of songs, instrumental works, and mixed media expressions. Given the diverse expanse of cultural communities that students call "home," it is then the responsibility of music educators to know their students, to learn of their interests and influences, and to step aside to make space for the music their students will compose. The task of creating cultural spaces in the compositional process is not so much a release of teaching duties to students to "do whatever" but rather a shaping by teachers of a sensitivity to the complexities of student identities and cultural values that students call their own. In honoring the cultures and communities of students whose creativity can be kindled in school music programs, the trade-off of top-down "teaching" control for the fine-honed teaching qualities of listening and facilitating is essential for ensuring the rights of all students to making music that reverberates to, from, and through them in meaningful ways.

The aim of this chapter is to offer perspective on the pedagogy of creative composition as it interfaces with issues of culture, and as it relates to honoring the agency of diverse learners in making music they can own, that entices and energizes them, and that expresses their cultural identities and interests. Attunement to cultural sensitivity in fostering the creative impulses of a diversity of students requires deciphering and decolonializing school music practices that extend from the music itself to the teacher's facilitation. It requires the embrace of an amalgam of music and musicians as potential influences of the music that they will compose, including music shared by students from their communities and from mediated sources, and as suggested by teachers as likely models of melodies, rhythms, textures, and forms. In shifting from the head of the class to the role of "guide-by-the-side," teachers can nonetheless steer students to a rich reserve of musically creative possibilities. With recognition of the critical component of culture in the creative process, and a sensitivity to student voice and cultural values, creative composition then becomes a successful endeavor for students of every community. While recognizing the social and educational inequities that have characterized schooling, this chapter probes theoretical models and methods that ensure that the creative composition process is an experience that honors a spectrum of influential musical possibilities while also exercising student agency in formulating the new music that they can call their own.

CREATIVITY AND CULTURE

International Perspectives

Creativity is a pan-human phenomenon, and yet it is differently defined and demonstrated from one culture to the next. From Germany to Japan, and from Canada to Kenya, references to creativity are frequently accompanied by descriptions of creative people and processes as "original," "imaginative," "curious," "flexible," "open-minded," and "intelligent" (Campbell, 1991; Amabile, 1988; Torrance, 1988). Creativity spans a spectrum of cultural allowances, from a reinterpretation of tradition to an invention that completely breaks with tradition. As well, a creative product, be it a new poem, a painting, or a piece of music, does not emerge out of "thin air," disconnected from all that came before. It operates within a set of cultural understandings, or "rules."

Whether at the meta- or micro-level, creativity is bound to culture. In music, there are broad regional distinctions of approach to creativity, such as the preference by sub-Saharan African cultures to create collectively in groups as opposed to adhering to Western ideals of individualist creativity. A collectivist approach is apparent across the African diaspora, where, for example, co-creative musical productions in the form of spontaneously expressed improvisation is shared and supported by all members of a musical group—be it African American–inspired jazz, Afro-Brazilian samba, or Afro-Cuban salsa. The individualist composer, by contrast, is the honored one in Western art music, where European and Euro-American works for orchestra, opera, and chamber music groups are attributed to a sole creator.

There are also discrete facets that influence creative processes and products, such that local culture, and even the model of a particular artist, can significantly impact a newly emergent work. Consider, for example, "schools," styles, and movements such as Claude Monet's wide-scale influence on the development of decades of French Impressionist paintings, the contributions of Langston Hughes in the intensely creative time of the Harlem Renaissance of the 1920s, and the impact of the Beatles on the development of guitar bands in the UK and US in the second half of the 20th century. The artistic styles were sparked by creative forces that led to the development of cultures all their own, in which shared beliefs and values inspired a particular expressive way.

Perspectives on the act of musical composition appeal to an interdisciplinary mix of scholars inside and outside the field of music and are held also by the composers themselves (and by performing musicians and those who are responsible for teaching them, mentoring them, and inspiring them). These perspectives may be emic, that is, coming from musicians themselves, or etic, arising from others who are intrigued with various manifestations of human creativity but are not themselves engaged in the compositional process. Taken together, the various views are frames of mind for understanding the musically creative process.

Interdisciplinary Perspectives

The process of defining and conceptualizing creativity, exploring and experimenting with it, theorizing and modeling it, and assessing and evaluating it has been an interdisciplinary one (Wallas, 1926). From the musically distant social sciences, especially psychology (Glaveanu, 2010; Sternberg, 1985) and sociology (Weiner, 2000), has come an external yet thoroughly provocative set of empirical studies (MacDonald, Byrne, & Carlton, 2006; Goncy & Waehler, 2006), many of which have led to an intellectualization of artistic creativity as a manifestation of the human propensity for original expressions to be steered by the rules of a given cultural system. Based upon observations, interviews, score study, and deliberation, theories have arisen that thoughtfully underscore the critical components of cultural beliefs and behaviors as core to the compositional process, as well as the processes of improvisation and interpretation (Berliner, 1994; Hill, 2018).

Within the field of music alone, composers have written of the process (Craft, 2006), as have musicologists (Bent, 1984; Blackburn, 1987) and ethnomusicologists (Nettl, 1974, 1998). In cracking the mysteries of the compositional process, research by Garrido, Bernard, and Davidson (2013) revealed that composers tend toward autonomy, impulsivity, and cognitive originality, even as they are tuned to the cultural norms of the musical works they invent. Composers seek to craft compositions as sounding newly unusual, original, and often edgy, and they tend to recognize that their listeners are coming from a culture of standards, rules, and regularities. They generally accept that there is a tipping point beyond which composers may not go if they expect to relate to and be accepted by a listening audience. The cultural norms that composers attend to are coming from their formal and focused musical study as well as from the "ambient" or informal experiences that govern their expressions.

For practicing musicians, many of whom are insiders to the creative process (although perhaps more in ways of improvisation and interpretation rather than through the compositional process itself), creative invention is embraced as vital to the performance art itself. A violinist will work up ideas for a virtuosic cadenza at the close of a concerto, a saxophone player will emit a riveting improvisation that launches from the "head" of the jazz tune, a singer of North Indian Hindustani *khyal* will strive for a novel expression within the parameters of *raga* and *tala*, and a classical pianist will closely follow the score of a work by Brahms and Ravel but with the potential for the nuanced shaping of dynamics and tempo. Depending upon the instrument, the repertoire, the practice, and the culture, creativity will manifest itself variously as to what one does "in the course of performance" (Nettl, 1998). Performing musicians on the inside track of creative invention will adhere to the standards of their culture in determining the nature and extent of their creative work. They may engage in a stepwise progression that typifies the compositional process or express themselves spontaneously through the immediacy of the improvisational experience, or even maintain the substance of the pre-composed music even while they provide subtle shadings of tempo, dynamics, melodic nuances, and ornamentations, too.

Music Education Particularities

The phenomenon of creativity has long captivated the attention of music educators, and composing and improvising figure prominently in contemporary K–12 curricular standards. Likewise, questions of culture have surfaced in the field via movements of multiculturalism, social justice, and efforts in education at large on matters of diversity, equity, inclusion, and access. Yet the realms of composition and diversity issues, though weighty with promise for integration, are more frequently found moving on parallel rather than intersecting tracks. In music education, "creative thinking in music," as advanced by Peter Webster, launched a full attention to the possibilities of creative musical expression in the curriculum (Webster, 2009). Research led to policy and practice, and fueled a concerted effort to probe the intellectual process of musical invention as naturally evolving from children as well as teachable through a pedagogical sequence. An impressive extent of published research is available on developmental levels of increasingly sophisticated musical invention, as is a host of practical articles that describe, deconstruct, and provide practical exercises in the fostering of the creative musical impulse. "Musical creativities" have turned up within the processes of composition, improvisation, songwriting, and even the art of personal interpretation (Burnard, 2012), and pronouncements of classroom creative music-making experiences send the message that all students can compose when given the opportunity to do so.

While most music educators graduate from performance-based degree programs with limited, if any, study of composition, they nonetheless assert the importance of creativity within the music education curriculum. In fact, they are at the heart of creative music-making ventures in schools, in that they provide the pedagogical models and sequences. Creative musical experiences abound: Young children in "rhythm bands" with sticks and drums, pint-sized players of Orff-styled wood xylophones in a Schulwerk exercise intended to draw out the soloistic expressions of individual students between "tutti" sections, middle schoolers at work in programs fashioned after professional digital audio workstations (DAW), secondary school jazzers with impressive performance chops to enable them to join in the process of taking solos and "trading fours." Music educators value the compositional process as a means of engaging students in divergent ways of musical thinking as well as in understanding music through direct manipulation and exploration of its elements. Through their efforts, students deepen their knowledge of melody and rhythm, phrasing and form, and texture through carefully constructed curricular opportunities to explore new musical designs.

Yet efforts in the pedagogy of composition in American music education have all too seldom given attention to culture, whether to offer global examples of compositional efforts, or experiences in compositional processes from diverse cultures, or opportunities to develop musical works that emanate from students' own families, local communities, or mediated musical forms. Instead, composition in music education has tilted toward the ideals of Western-oriented Euro-American (or European) musical expressions, upholding standards of Western-styled art, folk, and popular music as models to emulate in both content and process. Conceptualizations of composition pedagogy are frequently associated with white culture, given that the preponderance of music educators are white, their conservatory trainings are rooted in Western-oriented white art music, and the music education curricular standards continue to perpetuate the music, pedagogies, and ideals of Western-white culture. Little attention has been given to the impact of culture on composition, nor has there been a thorough-going effort to reach to the values of black, brown, and indigenous students, their cultural communities, and their musical identities. Whose music should stand as models of composition? Which teaching-learning approaches could be put into play to allow students' own musical voices and values to be expressed? How can students of marginalized communities be brought headlong into compositional experiences? Moreover, can creativity and culture converge in school music classrooms, so that all learners can be enticed and encouraged to express themselves in ways that are at the core of who they are?

Asset Pedagogies as a Post-Colonial Framework for the Compositional Process

It is widely maintained that the American educational system has functioned to preserve white cultural hegemony (Alim & Paris, 2017; Darder, 2012; Banks, 2004). A hegemonic system has long been evident in the development of curriculum, pedagogies, and policies whose purpose is to devalue the experiences, contributions, and epistemologies of marginalized groups while upholding those of dominant white culture. In response to the commonly held view that Black, Brown, and Indigenous students maintain a deficit of skills and knowledge to successfully navigate educational spaces, educationists such as James Banks, Gloria Ladson Billings, Geneva Gay, and Django Paris have developed theories to challenge this harmful thinking. Rather than viewing the cultural backgrounds of marginalized students as an impediment to educational achievement, scholars draw on this knowledge as an asset and resource to increase student engagement. These approaches are generally referred to as *asset pedagogies*, which serve to reposition "the linguistic, literate, and cultural practices of working-class communities, specifically poor communities of color, as resources and *assets* to honor, extend, and explore in accessing white middle-class dominant cultural norms of acting and being that are demanded in schools" (Alim & Paris, 2017, p. 4). Asset pedagogies emerged in the 1990s as a result of decades of research that began in the late 1970s when student responses were studied as to their assimilative influences in their learning environments. Noteworthy, too, were *deficit pedagogies* that sought to denigrate students' cultural backgrounds so that they could be shed and supplanted with values that were congruent with *Whitestream* learning spaces and institutions (Urrieta, 2010). Descriptions follow of three notable asset pedagogies—*culturally relevant pedagogy, culturally responsive teaching, and funds of knowledge*, each of which have been recognized as relevant to music education practices.

Culturally Responsive Pedagogy

The concept of Culturally Responsive Pedagogy (CRP) was first introduced by Gloria Ladson-Billings in her pioneering article, "Toward a theory of culturally relevant pedagogy" (1995). In this grounded theory study, she examined classrooms where African American students were experiencing success to document how pedagogical practices that provided encouragement and guidance to these students related to the central elements of CRP including student achievement, cultural competence, and cultural critique. Ladson-Billings was able to deduce three overlapping characteristics of Culturally Responsive Pedagogy that teachers demonstrate: (1) the conceptions of self and others held by culturally relevant teachers, (2) the manner in which social relations are structured by culturally relevant teachers, and (3) the conceptions of knowledge held by culturally relevant teachers (p. 478). In essence, CRP challenges notions of assimilation, and asserts that pedagogical practices "must provide a way for students to maintain their cultural integrity while succeeding academically" (p. 476).

Successful teachers whose pedagogy was grounded in the tenets of CRP demonstrated their belief-in-action, that all students are capable of success in academic pursuits (Ladson-Billings, 2009). As well, successful teachers viewed themselves as part of the community and, thus are invested in the success of students to "give back" and improve their community. This perception of oneself as a contributing member of the community is then passed on to their students through activities that help "students make connections between their community, national, and global identities" (Ladson-Billings, 2009, p. 38).

Being attendant to CRP requires that teachers focus much of their efforts in the classroom on demonstrating *authentic caring* (Valenzuela, 1999). This concept defines the ways that teachers seek to develop relationships that are grounded in equity and reciprocity as a means for creating an academic environment conducive to learning. CRP teachers encourage positive peer relationships as a means to develop as a community of learners where students are encouraged to "learn collaboratively and be responsible for another" (Ladson-Billings, 1995, p. 480). Teachers succeeding in the precepts of Culturally Responsive Pedagogy demonstrate a tendency to conceptualize knowledge in ways that allowed for all students to feel that their contributions to the learning community are valued and essential to the construction of shared knowledge within it. One way that this can be achieved is to develop students' belief that they are independent learners and capable of viewing all knowledge critically. In essence, this decenters the teacher as the sole producer of knowledge and situates them as another member of the learning community (albeit, a facilitator) that is invested in the success of the group. An additional characteristic of efficacy in this domain is that CRP teachers view assessments not as a measure of dichotomized demonstrations of right or wrong but, rather, as a means to allow students to demonstrate multiple forms of excellence that are congruent with their valued modes of learning.

Culturally Responsive Teaching

Culturally Responsive Teaching (CRT) is the concept widely connected to educationist Geneva Gay. In her book *Culturally Responsive Teaching* (2000), she provides an exploration of the principles of CRT, as well as a synthesis and comparison of similar ideas from various scholars. The concept of "cultural blindness" in education is discussed, the four critical aspects of culturally responsive teaching are described, and three major categories of responsibility of CRT teachers are examined.

According to Gay, the foundational belief of Culturally Responsive Teaching is that it "validates, facilitates, liberates, and empowers ethnically diverse students by simultaneously cultivating their cultural integrity, individual abilities, and academic success" (2000, p. 44). She offers a direct challenge to an educational system that she maintains to have largely ignored the skills and strengths of ethnically diverse students. As a central tenet of her argument for CRT, she presents five points of cultural blindness upon which systems of schooling are built:

1. The belief that education has no connection to heritage.
2. The reality that the majority of teachers do not possess an adequate understanding of how their practice is rooted in middle-class white values.

3. The assumption that treating students differently based on their racial, ethnic, and cultural identities is fundamentally racial discrimination.
4. The idea that *good* teaching is immutable and somehow transcends all cultural differences, world views, and epistemologies.
5. The understanding that the goal of education is to provide an effective pathway to assimilation for all students. (2000, p. 21)

To overcome the harmful impact an unquestioned adherence to beliefs in cultural blindness can have on ethnically diverse students, Gay posits that teachers implementing curriculum rooted in CRT must consider the four fundamental aspects of *caring, communication, curriculum, instruction.* "Caring" in CRT refers to the authentic relationships that teachers develop with their students in ways that "honor their humanity, hold them in high esteem, expect high performance from them, and use strategies to fulfill their expectations" (p. 46). To demonstrate caring, teachers must exhibit certain behaviors (i.e., academic, social, personal, moral) toward their students in ways that clearly convey a deep respect for them as complete and complex beings, as well as an investment in their academic success. The hope is that students will eventually begin to emulate these behaviors as they navigate educational spaces. This ultimately allows for the achievement of culturally congruent success in schools.

Communication refers to the deep relationship between culture and communication in educational spaces, such that "languages and communication styles are systems of cultural notations and the means through which thoughts and ideas are expressively embodied" (p. 81). In essence, all learning experiences of students are inevitably bound by language and thus are subjected to the cultural expectations with which the language used in educational settings is imbued. Moreover, the languages and communication styles that each student brings to the classroom maintain their own set of cultural expectations that is either congruent or in conflict with the dominant mode of discourse in the classroom. Gay argues that it is precisely this relationship that teachers need to be made aware of in order to understand the profound implications for student engagement in the classroom.

The third aspect of CRT refers to curriculum and the way that it promotes and honors racially, ethnically, and culturally diverse perspectives. The main goal of CRT is to empower ethnically diverse students and that "knowledge in the form of curriculum content is central to this empowerment" (p. 111). Fundamentally, curriculum constructed in a culturally responsive manner must focus on representing the histories, cultures, and contributions of ethnically diverse groups as a means to engage all students with meaningful learning moments regardless of their membership in a minoritized group. Moreover, a curriculum grounded in culturally responsive precepts connects with the lived experiences of all students, in intercultural exchange and through equalizing the long-held asymmetrical power dynamics that occur through these between-group interactions. Gay suggests that by diversifying the perspectives shared in curricular sources (e.g., textbooks, literature, news samples) and increasing community connections (i.e., using community spaces and members as valid sources of knowledge production), student learnings will be grounded in positive representations of different cultural groups.

The final aspect of CRT, instruction, encompasses the "interactional processes" between teachers and students in learning environments that lead to the students' acquisition of knowledge. Gay suggests that viewing instruction through the lens of CRT provides for the understanding that modes of knowledge transmission is culturally influenced. Moreover, students who enter mainstream education (typically at five years of age) have already "internalized rules and procedures for acquiring knowledge and demonstrating their skills" (p. 148). Instruction in this context is often referred to as the *praxis* of CRT in that it "combines all other components into coherent configurations and puts them into practice to expedite learning" (p. 148). As such, the central focus of instruction is to develop an understanding of the *learning styles* of ethnically diverse students. While the learning styles of various groups should not be viewed as monolithic (as they are influenced by ethnic identification and affiliation, socioeconomic status, orientation toward traditionalism), they should be seen as patterns and thus tools to provide "more cultural congruity in teaching/learning processes" (p. 148). Certainly, instruction grounded in CRT is a complex and dynamic endeavor that is context-dependent, and yet there are methods that exemplify the principles: providing space for cooperative learning, incorporating multimodal learning experience (i.e., using music and movement), and creating learning environments that are centered on ethnic worldviews.

Funds of Knowledge

Another asset pedagogy, the concept of Funds of Knowledge (González, Moll, & Amanti, 2005) refers to the cultural artifacts and strategies that students acquire as members of their complex cultural and community assemblages and use to negotiate learning environments they encounter in life. However, Funds of Knowledge also refers to an inquiry-based approach that requires teachers to conduct interviews grounded in participatory ethnography of parents, relatives, and other community stakeholders. These interviews, observations, and insights are essential to growing robust understandings of the knowledge and other adaptational strategies that have been developed and passed on to students. Another important aspect of the Funds of Knowledge approach is the collaboration between cohorts of teachers and facilitators who are actively engaged in examining their students and local communities. Through the sharing of data, observations, and insights, these teachers can collectively produce broad understandings that more effectively allow them to theorize their practice as well as develop more effective pedagogical strategies.

Funds of Knowledge is largely based on the Vygotskian concept of *mediation*, which posits that our interactions in the world are influenced and, in many ways, bound by culture (González, Moll, & Amanti, 2005). As we negotiate these spaces, we use cultural artifacts as "tools for thinking through which we interact with our social worlds" (p.

18). Essentially, this means that all human actions are mediated through these cultural artifacts. The cultural artifacts, or funds of knowledge, that students possess are important for teachers to understand, because these are the tools that students use to negotiate both formal and informal learning spaces. In line with this thinking, teachers do well to develop community relationships that provide for authentic, compassionate, and in-depth exploration of the cultural artifacts that students have acquired from their home environments. In turn, these understandings then become cultural artifacts for teachers to develop learning environments that allow for student success to be demonstrated in ways that are congruent with their own strategies for exploration.

Emerging Asset Pedagogies in Music Education

The previous section presented notable asset pedagogies that first emerged in the field of education and were then utilized by music educators seeking to situate their teaching within the principles of these asset-based pedagogies. Music-specific asset pedagogies have also been developed and used in various education settings, for learners of various ages and experiences. These approaches embrace the virtues of Culturally Relevant Pedagogy, Culturally Responsive Teaching, and Funds of Knowledge, but are shaped as well by the particularities of selected musical practices, the artist-musicians, and the communities to which they belong. Two approaches that focus on using aspects of various musical cultures as foundational to the instructional practice are Hip-Hop Pedagogy and World Music Pedagogy.

Hip-Hop Pedagogy for Developing Social Consciousness

Although Hip-Hop Pedagogy is a relatively recent framework that has been implemented in music education, the emphasis of drawing on the *community cultural wealth* (Yosso, 2005) of students in urban settings provides great potential for "creating engaging and inclusive classrooms, increasing cultural relevance, and developing students' critical social consciousness" in music education spaces (Kruse, 2014).

The term Hip-Hop Pedagogy is widely believed to have been coined by rhetoric scholar Jeff Rice (2003). However, this first iteration focused more on using hip-hop techniques such as sampling to develop alternative modes of composition (i.e., written essays) for college students and less on engaging minoritized students in urban schools. The practice of using Hip-Hop Pedagogy as a tool to engage minoritized students specifically was developed by Marc Lamont Hill (2009) as a means to introduce a "more expansive vision of pedagogy that reconsiders the relationships among students, teachers, texts, schools, and the broader social world" (p. 120).

Through examination of the urban youth context from which hip-hop emerged, Hill situates hip-hop as a "rich site for complex forms of identity work" (p. 1) that maintains profound possibilities for engaging marginalized (particularly Black and Brown) student populations. This occurs through the creation of culturally congruent learning spaces, providing opportunities to engage in alternative modes of academic discourse, and expanding the criteria for what is considered valid knowledge and cultural production. In his conceptualization of Hip-Hop Pedagogy, Hill (2009) presents three main classification for educators to consider when implementing this framework into their classrooms: pedagogies *of* hip-hop (i.e., understanding how knowledge is validated in hip-hop), pedagogies *about* hip-hop (i.e., analyzing, critiquing, and reproducing hip-hop), and pedagogies *with* hip-hop (i.e., using hip-hop to navigate traditional subject matter).

World Music Pedagogy as Pathway to a Broader Sonic Pallette

The academic recognition of music as a world phenomenon arose in the second half of the 19th century when musicologists began to stretch their ears to music beyond the Western world and began to recognize the different but equally logical expressions that emanate from villages across the African continent and out of the royal courts of Asian kingdoms. They were "comparative musicologists," paving the way for ethnomusicology to develop as a field in study of music as cultural behavior (Nettl, 2015). A century later, music educators saw that the study of world music cultures could serve as a pathway to intercultural understanding and global competence. It became clear that a pedagogical approach would need to be developed that would honor the logic and beauty of music from beyond the West, and that could develop a respect for people through the music that they make. In fact, it also seemed that the study of some previously neglected expressive forms might provide opportunities for marginalized students to find themselves in the music of cultures that had been dismissed at some earlier time as "unfit" for school curricular studies.

In her development of World Music Pedagogy, Patricia Shehan Campbell positioned it to recognize the value of music in every community and culture (Campbell 2004; 2018). It recognizes music as a badge of cultural identity and a means of bonding people together through experiences in listening, singing, and playing the music, dancing to the music, creating in the style of the music, and understanding the cultural meaning of music in its place of origin. Situated midway between the fields of ethnomusicology and music education, World Music Pedagogy embraces art, folk, and popular music practices of diverse cultural communities, both local and global, that are distinguished by such facets of identity as color, creed, socioeconomic status, gender-sexuality, lifestyle, and geographic region. It is a method that embraces both music and culture, and is intent on moving learners beyond the exclusive study of Western European Art Music (WEAM), and music that is historically of the white middle-class dominant culture that is the standard practice historically in school music programs. World Music Pedagogy takes into account the widespread process of orality-aurality, of learning music by ear rather than via notation, and of learning music through multiple lenses, and of knowing music through an interdisciplinary experience that combines insights to music and culture through language, politics, history, geography, and the related arts. It asserts the importance of invention by students of new music in the style of a musical model through composition, thus "enhancing the skills and understanding of a strong musicianship" (Campbell & Lum, 2019, p. 106). Critical to World Music Pedagogy is the attention to music as cultural expression, and the potential students have of tapping into music that is close and far from them for the ways that it can help to shape identity as well as make people-to-people connections.

CULTURALLY SUSTAINING PEDAGOGY AS FRAMEWORK FOR CREATIVE MUSICAL COLLABORATION

Although Culturally Sustaining Pedagogy (CSP) exists under the umbrella of asset pedagogies, it expands on the purpose, function, and scope of previous conceptions of other asset approaches in education at large and in music education in particular. To begin, educationists Django Paris and Samy Alim, who initiated Culturally Sustaining Pedagogy as an alternative or development of earlier pedagogies, provide three main critiques of earlier education pedagogies. First, they suggest that the concepts such as *culturally relevant* and *culturally responsive* do not "do enough to support the goals of maintenance and social critique" (Alim & Paris, 2017, p. 4). They assert that while curriculum and pedagogical strategies might be *relevant* or *responsive* to student needs when using these frameworks, the power structures that persist to alienate Black, Brown and Indigenous students remain unexamined and, in many ways, concealed. When re-envisioning curriculum to be in line with the goals of Culturally Sustaining Pedagogy, Alim and Paris (2017) suggest that teachers expand the question from first asking *what to include* to "for what purposes and what outcomes" (p. 4). Similar to the *social action* approach to multicultural curriculum reform (Banks, 2004), CSP focuses on engaging students by encouraging them to become active agents of change by examining the power dynamics that affect their lives.

The second critique by Alim and Paris (2017) of other asset pedagogies is that culture is presented as static and based on scholars and educators' abstract understandings of culture. Instead, Alim and Paris suggest that the lives that contemporary youth live need to be viewed as "emerging, intersectional, and dynamic" (p. 9). This means that all aspects of education need to be rooted in the lived experiences of students as *people* rather than in monolithic understandings of their cultures as abstractions that obscure the "racialized, gendered, classed, dis/abilitied, language (and so on) bodies of the [students] enacting them" (p. 9).

Alim and Paris (2017) offer a third critique, in that previous asset pedagogies did not focus enough on providing individuals with the tools to critically examine certain practices within Black, Brown, and Indigenous communities. They further suggest that educators have too often uncritically embraced these practices as "positive or progressive" (p. 10) simply because they emerged in non-Whitestream spaces. As such, the goal of Culturally Sustaining Pedagogy is to forward practices challenging discourses within these communities that perpetuate marginalization of its members.

The landscape of educational equity is constantly being refined and, as a moral imperative, it thus becomes necessary for music educators to stay abreast of these developments. New methods of musical engagement must also be sought that will allow students to be honored in all of their complexity while providing moments where true creative collaboration can occur. Moreover, these methods must provide a space where asymmetric power structures can be critiqued while simultaneously allowing for students to be positioned as active agents of change in their communities. We advocate for using the Collective Songwriting Process as a compositional tool that can help educators to develop creative spaces that are in line with the tenets of Culturally Sustaining Pedagogy.

TESTIMONIO AND COLLECTIVE SONGWRITING

The Collective Songwriting Process (CSP) is a collaborative composition protocol that has roots in Zapatista communities in Chiapas, Mexico. The Zapatistas are an autonomous group in Mexico that is composed of various Mayan cultures that speak a variety of languages (Gonzalez, 2020). While the roots of these communities extend generations into the past, this group gained global exposure due their popular uprising against the signing of the North American Free Trade Agreement in 1994 (Khansnabish, 2012). The shared principle that guides interactions within this group is called *Zapatismo*. This philosophy is based on Indigenous world views and focuses largely on the principle of "participatory horizontality," which is a method that allows for a diffusion of power in a particular practice in an effort to maximum community participation (Figueroa Hernandez, 2007). Additionally, Zapatismo has also incorporated pedagogical techniques from urban *guerilleros* that helped to organize this group against government forces. These include developing a profound understanding of Indigenous epistemologies, critiquing their own revolutionary values that were steeped in Euro-Enlightenment assumptions, subjugating their own political desires to the needs of the communities they serve, and embracing to power of collective decision-making (Khansnabish, 2012).

The Collective Songwriting process (CSW) was brought to the United States and developed for community projects by scholar/organizer/activist musicians Martha Gonzalez and Quetzal Flores. After studying these techniques with musician/activist Rosa Marta Zarate in Chiapas, Gonzalez and Flores further refined this approach for use in a variety of community-based settings including juvenile detention centers, community music and education forums, and transnational musical collaborations (Gonzalez, 2020). The process itself is imbued with this philosophy of Zapatismo in several ways. First, the process provides space for all participants to share their lived experiences and community concerns as well as participate in a collective decision-making process that will allow for their ideas to be incorporated into a final musical artifact. This relates to the notion of participatory horizontality in that all members are allowed to participate in ways that honor their specific skill set. Whether they are instrumentalists, vocalists, lyricists, dancers, or even visual artists, all participants are provided with an opportunity to contribute. Second, the Collective Songwriting process provides a space where individuals can theorize on their community needs and develop these thoughts and perspectives into "sung theories" (Gonzalez, 2020, p. 94). Through their sharing of narrative developments of lived experiences and perspectives, or *testimonios* (Reyes & Curry Rodríguez, 2012), participants reimagine new ways of engaging community issues that are in line with their specific modes and conceptualizations of action. Additionally, these testimonios also serve to document community world views thus allowing for a more thorough understanding of the ways in which they make sense of their specific contexts. Lastly, the Collective Songwriting process challenges Eurocentric notions of knowledge validation. Rather than focusing on mechanical composition procedures that prioritize specific musical techniques and theory, the principal epistemologies that guide the creative process in CSP are "*convivencia* [coexistence], testimonio, trust, healing, and knowledge production" (Gonzalez, 2020, p. 94). This allows for the creative process to always be grounded in community needs and modes of artistic expression.

Songwriting as Classroom Process

As a compositional process, CSW is a flexible approach that has several entry points. As such, there is no sequence that must be followed but rather, there is a loose framework that allows for the community of participants to guide the creative process. The compositional activity begins with an educator facilitating community conversations that serve to draw out from students their testimonios or views on community needs, concerns, and desires. These testimonios are then crafted into verses and choruses through a collective decision-making process. Concurrently, while the testimonios developed by one group of students form a collage of expressed thoughts into a pastiche of words, phrases, and sentences that emerge as song lyrics, a second group of students begin to generate chord progressions, melodies, and rhythms that amplify the tone that these testimonios have taken. Music educators are there to provide questions and comments as prompts for the development of lyrics and music, and to facilitate and encourage ideas to flow, even while students engage one another in creating the spirit of the song, the poetic images, the musical matter. When music educators join with the students on instruments, they may suggest initial musical ideas, and yet all members of the community are welcomed in as contributors to musical ideas regardless of their proficiency with voice or instrument.

After elements of the collective song are finalized, the two groups of students rehearse the musical artifact, be it the lyrical or the instrumental component. Opportunities for performing on an instrument, or singing the newly fashioned lyrics into a melody, or dancing to the song are extended to the entire student group. This provides opportunities, too, for students to switch groups, or to help one another out across the aisle, where an instrumentalist may offer a vocal line or a member of the lyrics group may take up the cajón or conga drum. The focus of the rehearsal is not about presenting a perfect performance but, rather, on maximizing participation from all group members. The final performance, whether for one another or to the public, a group of friends, or family members, is documented and shared with the group. This performance and its recording is an important step in the process because it allows the final product to serve as an artifact of a collectively mediated expression of new possibilities, or what Holland et al. (2003) would refer to as a "figured world" (p. 41). The experience of repeated listening to these "sung theories" (Gonzalez, 2020) is what compels the participants toward action by allowing them to "*pivot* or shift into the frame of a different world" (Holland et al., 2003, p. 51).

Entre Mujeres: Collective Songwriting in a Mexican Community

To illustrate their experience with the Collective Songwriting, Martha Gonzalez (2020) provides an in-depth account of a collaboration where both she and musician Quetzal Flores engaged in this process. As a part of a Fulbright-García Robles sponsored scholarship project called *Entre Mujeres*, Gonzalez and Flores relocated to Xalapa, Mexico, to collaborate with women participating in another participatory musical culture called *son jarocho*. Their goal was to create musical artifacts that expressed the women's experiences as participants in this tradition as well as their concerns regarding the effects of transnationalism on their lives. Through moments of participation in community musical events called *fandangos*, extended *jam sessions* captured on portable recording equipment, and conversations that focused on generating collective expression and chronicling the essence of the shared testimonios through lyricism, Gonzalez and the other participants were able to create a musical artifact that documented their "experiences as women, life lessons, and general life philosophies" (Gonzalez, 2020, p. 97). As described in the above section, the testimonios that were produced through these vulnerable, emotionally charged, and hopeful conversations set the tone for the music that eventually emerged. Below are the lyrics to the song "Sobreviviendo" that this group created (Gonzalez, 2020, g. 98):

> The people live in struggle
> Without knowing what is to come
> As they walk their journeys
> New roads emerge
> They don't know if there will be a tomorrow
> But nevertheless they depart
> **Surviving, survive**
> **Just moving, without sensing**
> Despite the strongest winds
> The palm tree will always be
> I bend to the sadness
> I stand tall for the loving
> The root is what matters
> For all humanity

In essence, the process of creating the lyrics is the foundational activity of Culturally Sustaining Pedagogy, mainly because "testimonio centers firsthand knowledge and experience as an invaluable resource and a place from which knowledge can be formulated" (Gonzalez, 2020, p. 101). This knowledge is not limited only to socio-historical understandings of the world but also extends to the negotiated synthesis of musical knowledge that results from the sharing of musical contributions from each participating member. For example, the final musical artifact contained elements of *son jarocho*, the extended harmonies of vocal jazz, Afro-Peruvian cajón rhythms (particularly *zamacueca*), a soaring violin melody, and musical stylings that are similar to the South African choir tradition. In line with the indigenous element of participatory horizontality introduced earlier (Figueroa Hernandez, 2007), all participants were able to contribute based on the particular skill sets and perspectives that they brought to the collaboration.

Atawit: Collective Songwriting at the Yakama Nation Tribal School

Another illustration of the Collective Songwriting process as a direct manifestation of Culturally Sustaining Pedagogy is a project within a program of music educators with students of the Yakama Nation Tribal School. This "Atawit" project, which resulted in the composition of the song, "Atawit Nawa Wakishwit" (Our Sacred Lives), featured a group of university-associated students and faculty music educators with youth enrolled in a Native American tribal school in Washington state. In an ongoing partnership known as Music Alive! In the Yakama Valley, the long-standing program shifted gears several years ago from the provision of fundamental applied lessons by university students for

Yakama Nation students to a compositional effort that would engage adolescent students, ages 13 to 18 years, in expressing their views, in their words, with their preferred melodies, harmonies, and rhythms (Campbell, Mena, Gestsson, & Coppola, 2019; Igari, Vita, Flesher, Armstrong, Gestsson, & Campbell, 2020). The project was aimed at honoring student voices, community values, and principles of indigenous pedagogy, and was intended to address social issues among marginalized youth in their rural and remote community on the Yakama Reservation as they could be expressed in musically artistic ends.

Over a period of four months, the visiting music educators facilitated the process of determining which issues were emerging as important to the Yakama youth, and that they themselves saw as important to express in a musical form. The conversation initiated with student talk about preferred listening choices, then graduated to academic and social challenges at the tribal school, and finally extended to student concerns for health, education, employment, and their own future prospects on and off the reservation. Several teachers and staff of the tribal school, as well as visiting tribal elders, were present in the spaces in which the conversations emerged, observing and only occasionally interjecting a thought (sometimes in the language of the Yakama, Sahaptan, or Ichishkin). In a series of one-day sessions, poetry was shared, recordings were exchanged, and basic skills of poetry writing, guitar-playing, and percussion techniques were developed. A three-day period then ensued, in which a full-fledged collective songwriting workshop transpired. Students found their ways into core groups of lyric-writers and instrumentalists, where with continued encouragement by the university team of music educators (as well as modeling, or "prompting," or suggestions of trialing one idea and then another), there arose a workable set of lyrics, melodies, chords, and rhythms that students found satisfying. Yakama teachers and elders were present, too, and students looked to them for translations and pronunciations of Sahaptan/Ishishkin words that would communicate the sacred images of Yakama culture. A portion of the song, partly sung, partly rapped in rhythmic fashion, appears below. A violin, synthesizer, cajón drum, guitars, and the Yakama drum were called in to envelop the lyrics.

> We believe and perceive.
> We will not grieve or leave.
> One nation that's alive:
> We stand for our land tonight!
> Land is our pride and joy.
> Our land is scared and
> Is not to be destroyed.
> Natives don't want to be hated.
> WALK TALL, THINK STRONG.
> Atawit nawa wakishwit.
> We love our lives.
> Forgiveness to those who don't see us thrive.

The university team musically engaged the students of the Yakama Nation Tribal School in listening, vocalizing, employing body percussion and movement, and the playing of instruments. The music took on a combination of sounds emanating from the experiences of students, with the creation of a conglomerate of sounds that mixed current popular music idioms of their choosing with Yakama musical (and lyrical) sensibilities. Over the course of the Atawit project, students grew in their functional capacity to play instruments and to sound out their ideas in ways that were expressive, colorful, poetic, and deeply significant to them. They recognized the power of their music to fully connect to the meaning of the text, and that they could musically express their native pride and sense of Yakama identity in the collective song they had made.

Cultural Sensitivity in the Facilitation of Creative Composition

Students deserve opportunities in our music education programs to exercise their agency. If music is an expressive art form, then composition is a process into which they can be invited to express their values, influences, and experiences. The coinciding of the issues of creativity and culture are natural and even expected phenomenon. Yet they are largely overlooked by music educators, even when the compositional process can quite credibly embrace the cultural identities of students, the culturally-honed musical models that offer students ideas for the content and processes of creative musical expression, and pedagogical techniques that acknowledge the complexities of young student composers who warrant the teacher as facilitator rather than top-down absolute autocrat. Facilitation requires an off-the-podium guide-on-the-side approach, and a respect by music educators for students, particularly those in marginalized groups, whose experiences differ from teachers' own experience and education. The creative musical expressions of students are traceable to their identities, which frequently include membership in global youth culture as well as the cultural heritage of the communities in which they live. For composition to be relevant and meaningful to students "across the board," music educators will need to embrace the concept of culture and an understanding of the potential for the creative process to validate and empower students to express themselves in ways that allow them to represent their culture histories and their emerging and intersectional identities. That can happen through the reform of university teacher education programs and professional organizations that acknowledge and present pathways that move past colonial and white-dominated structures to an embrace of local and global perspectives of the composition process as manifestation of culture.

References

Alim, S. H. and Paris, A. (2017). What is Culturally Sustaining Pedagogy and why does it matter? In A. Paris & S. H. Alim (Eds.), *Culturally sustaining pedagogies: teaching and learning for justice in a changing world* (pp. 1–25). Teachers College Press.

Amabile, T. M. (1988). A model of creativity and innovation in organizations. In B. M. Staw, & L. L. Cummings (Eds.), *Research in organizational behavior* (pp. 123–167). JAI Press.

Banks, J. A. (2004). Approaches to multicultural curriculum reform. In J. A. Banks & C. A. McGee (Eds.), *Multicultural education: Issues and Perspectives*. Wiley & Sons.

Bent, M. (1984). Diatonic ficta. *Early Music History, 4*, 1–48. Doi: 10.1017/S0261127900000413

Berliner, P. (1994). *Thinking in jazz: The infinite art of improvisation*. University of Chicago Press.

Blackburn, B. J. (1987). On compositional process in the fifteenth century. *Journal of the American Musicological Society, 40*(2), 210–284. Doi: 10.1525/jams.1987.40.2.03a00020.

Burnard, P. (2012). *Musical creativities in practice*. Oxford University Press.

Campbell, P. S. (2004). *Teaching music globally: Experiencing music, expressing culture*. Oxford University Press.

Campbell, P. S. (1991). *Lessons from the world*. Schirmer Books.

Campbell, P. S. (2018). *Music, education, and diversity: Bridging cultures and communities*. Teachers College Press.

Campbell, P. S. (2019). *World music pedagogy: School-community intersections*. Routledge.

Campbell, P. S., Mena, C., Gestsson, S., and Coppola, W. (2019). "Atawit nawa wakishwit": Collective songwriting with Native American youth. *Journal of Popular Music Education, 3*(1), 11–28.

Craft, R. 2006. *Down a path of wonder*. Naxos.

Darder, A. (2012). *Culture and power in the classroom: Educational foundations for the schooling of bicultural students*. Paradigm Publishers.

Figueroa Hernández, R. (2007). *Son jarocho: Guia histórico-musical*. Conaculta, Fonca.

Garrido, S., Bernard, S., & Davidson, J. (2013). The creative personality: Composers of music, their inspirations and working methods. Proceedings of the 9th ACM Conference on Creativity & Cognition.

Glăveanu, V. P. (2010). Principles for a cultural psychology of creativity. *Culture and Psychology* (16), 147–163. Doi: 10.1177/1354067X10361394.

Goncy, E. A., and Waehler, C. A. (2006). An empirical investigation of creativity and musical experience. *Psychology of Music, 34*(3), 307–321.

Gonzalez, M. (2020). *Chican@ artivistas: Music, community, and transborder tactics in East Los Angeles*. University of Texas Press.

Gonzalez, N., Moll, L. C., & Amanti, C. (2005). *Funds of knowledge: Theorizing practices in households, communities and classrooms*. Erlbaum. Doi: 10.4324/9781410613462

Hill, J. (2018). *The creative musician*. Oxford University Press.

Hill, M. L., (2009). *Beats, rhymes, and classroom life: hip-hop pedagogy and the politics of identity*. Teachers College Press.

Holland, D., Lachicotte, W., Jr., Skinner, D., & Cain, C. (2001). *Identity and agency in cultural worlds*. Harvard University Press.

Igari, K., Vita, J. C., Flesher, J., Armstrong, C. Gestsson, S., and Campbell, P. S. (2020). "Let's stand together, rep my tribe forever": Teaching toward equity through Collective Songwriting at the Yakama Nation Tribal School. *Journal of Folklore and Education, 7*, 65–78.

Khasnabish, A. (2012). "To walk questioning": Zapatismo, the radical imagination, and a transnational pedagogy of liberation. In R. H. Haworth (Ed.), *Anarchist pedagogies: Collective action, theories, and critical reflection on education* (pp. 220–242). Oakland: PM Press.

Kohfeld, M., Coppola, W., Mena, C., Shakerifard, S., & Campbell, P. S. (2019). Culture-specific cases of a cross-cultural musical act. In B. G. Johansen et al. (Eds.), *Expanding the space for improvisation pedagogy in music* (pp. 17–33). Routledge.

Kruse, A. J. (2016). Toward hip-hop pedagogies for music education. *International Journal of Music Education, 34*(2), 247–260. Doi: 10.1177/0255761414550535.

Ladson-Billings, G. (1995). Toward a theory of culturally relevant pedagogy. *American Educational Research Journal, 32*(3), 465–491. Doi: 10.2307/1163320.

Ladson-Billings, G. (2009). *The dreamkeepers: Successful teachers of African American children* (2nd ed.). Jossey-Bass Publishers.

MacDonald, R., Byrne, C., & Carlton, L. (2006). Musical creativity and flow in musical composition: An empirical investigation. *Psychology of Music, 34*(3), 292–306.

Nettl, B. (1974). Thoughts on improvisation: A comparative approach. *The Musical Quarterly, 60*(1), 1–19. Doi: 10.1093/mq/LX.1.1.

Nettl, B. (1998). Arrows and circles: An anniversary talk about fifty years of ICTM and the study of traditional music. *Yearbook for Traditional Music, 30*, 1–11. Doi:10.2307/768550.

Nettl, B. (2015). *Issues in ethnomusicology (or Encounters with ethnomusicology).* University of Illinois Press.

Reyes, K. B., & Curry Rodríguez, J. E. (2012). Testimonio: origins, terms, and resources. *Equity & Excellence in Education, 45*(3), 525–538. Doi: 10.1080/10665684.2012.698571.

Rice, J. (2003). The 1963 hip-hop machine: Hip-hop pedagogy as composition. *College Composition and Communication, 54*(3), 453–471. Doi: 10.2307/3594173.

Shao, Y., Zhang, C., Zhou, J., Gu, T., & Yuan, Y. (2019). How does culture shape creativity? A mini-review. *Frontiers in Psychology, 10*, 1219.

Sternberg, R. J. (1985). Implicit theories of intelligence, creativity, and wisdom. *Journal of Personal Social Psychology 49*(3), 607–627. Doi: 10.1037/0022-3514.49.3.607.

Swanson, M., and Campbell, P. S. (2016). Informed by children: Awakening improvisatory impulses in schools and communities. In A. Heble & M. Laver (Eds.), *Improvisation and education: Beyond the classroom.* Routledge.

Torrance, E. (1988). The nature of creativity as manifest in its testing. In R. Sternberg (Ed.), *The nature of creativity* (pp. 43–73). Cambridge University Press.

Urrieta, L. (2010). Whitestreaming: Why some Latinas/os fear bilingual education. *Counterpoints, 371*, 47–55.

Valenzuela, A. (1999). *Subtractive schooling: U.S.-Mexican youth and the politics of caring.* State University of New York Press.

Wallas, G. (1926). *The art of thought.* Watts.

Webster, P. R. (2009). Children as creative thinkers in music. In S. Hallam, I. Cross, & M. Thaut (Eds.), *The Oxford handbook of music psychology* (pp. 421–428). Oxford University Press.

Weiner, R. P. (2000). *Creativity and beyond: Cultures, values, and change.* State University of New York Press.

Yosso, T. J. (2005). Whose culture has capital? A critical race theory discussion of community cultural wealth. *Race, Ethnicity and Education, 8*(1), 69–91. Doi: 10.1080/1361332052000341006.

UNDERSTANDING COMPOSITIONAL PROCESSES

....

CHAPTER 10

LISTENING TO COMPOSE, COMPOSING TO LISTEN

Music Listening as Foundational Musical Behavior

....

JODY L. KERCHNER

MUSIC listening is foundational to every generative musical behavior—composing, improvising, and performing. For example, singers in a choral setting learn to listen not only to their own vocal contributions, but also to surrounding singers, in part, to synchronize dynamics, staggered breathing, vowel sounds, and tone color. A pianist in a jazz combo listens to ensure their vision for an improvisation matches the pitches and rhythms produced by their fingers, while also listening for and incorporating into their own product ideas performed by other musicians in the group. A composer listens voraciously to diverse musics, such that the sounds, styles, and feelingful impressions inform their own compositional style.

Kaschub (2016) called for music students to actively engage in each of three primary music-making roles (i.e., composing, performing, listening), acknowledging that "the very nature of music demands the interaction of all three" (p. 58). Kaschub and Smith (2016) suggested that these roles share complementary "musical capacities"—innately human potentials, or possibilities, for "knowing" music and fully experiencing these generative musical roles in purposeful and meaningful ways. Because of the intersections of the musical capacities, it is difficult for people to assume only one of these roles as they engage in musical activity. For example, performers consider the composer's articulated ideas, listeners experience performers' interpretations of the composer's visions, and composer's listen for ways that performers and composers craft musical sounds as models for conveying musical and feelingful impressions.

Kaschub and Smith (2016) proposed capacities specific to music listeners: (1) purposeful attention to the music, (2) musical impressivity, and (3) artistic perception. Listeners have agency to determine the reasons for listening, the amount of attention given to the music listening task, and the attention afforded to specific musical events related to the composition and/or performance. Listeners have the capacity to become aware of how the composer (as mediated by performers) created and organized sounds and communicated musical impressions—musical representations—of emotions by provoking feelingful states. Listeners are mindful of how these sounds make them feel according to sociocultural aesthetic norms and within the physical spaces in which the music is heard. Listeners also have the capacity to become sensitive to, perceive, process, and interpret the skillful and artistic ways that composers employ compositional tools and techniques to create music that invites feelingful responses by listeners and performers alike. Listeners enlist these musical capacities as they intentionally choose to engage with musical sounds, embody connections between those sounds and the feelings they invite, and, ultimately, create uniquely personal meaning from the sounds that are perceived, prioritized, and processed.

Each music-making role not only involves a person's musical capacities, but also creative thinking that leads to a product experienced as a composition, an improvisation, and/or a performance. Webster (2002) defined creative thinking as "the engagement of the mind in the active structured process of thinking in sound for the purpose of producing some product new for the creator" (p. 26). He marked music listening as a creative endeavor since it provokes listeners to engage in creative thinking that enables them to make aesthetic decisions, spend time with the music, and have intentions for purposeful listening.

While music listening engages students' critical and creative thinking, music educators in the United States often situate music listening as a passive, "responsive" activity in comparison to music performance experiences. This disposition minimizes the creative enterprise that is irrefutably involved, whether a listener is barely aware of the music or the listener is keenly attuned to what is being heard. Unfortunately, music listening is typically interpreted as "purposeful" only if it involves tacit listening followed by discourse regarding music theoretical attributes or historical and cultural contexts. There are many everyday reasons for listening to music, however, most which do not involve intentional analytical listening. To be clear, information about music theory, history, and cultural contexts are important knowledge bases for students to possess, but teaching these constructs alone disregards the reciprocal relationship of person (listener) and the music, at the heart of which is artistic and emotional connection. We miss opportunities in music classes and rehearsal settings when we prioritize academic musical deconstruction over personal experience that is (or is not) created as a result of listening to music.

Like performing, composing, and improvising, music listening is a personally creative process, resulting in externalized and observable physical responses *and* internal, less obvious physiological, cognitive, and affective responses unique unto each individual (Dunn, 2006; Kerchner, 2014; Morrison, 2009; Peterson, 2006). In the aggregate, these tangible and intangible (even ineffable) music listening responses comprise the music *experience*, and it is this experience that is the resultant creative product of music listening. The intersections of "old" and "new" cognitive structures and, more holistically, the feelings, socio-cultural contexts, and associations bound to the music listening experience lead to a uniquely-created, personal musical experience. This "new" experience, in turn, becomes the "prior experience" that influences and is foundational for future music experiences.

Refined musical meaning is crafted as one listens to music that moves them beyond their currently held mental models, brain mappings, and embodied emotions. These integrated body-mind-spirit-feelingful processes and products are inherently linked to one's memory of prior musical and non-musical experiences, the strength of emotions attached to these experiences, and the listener's imagination employed during the creation (production) of personally novel music listening experiences (Kerchner, 2021).

Music Listening and the Compositional Process

Having considered the role and musical capacities of the music listener and the creative nature of music listening itself, let us consider music listening as a generative experience that directly contributes to and influences other generative musical experiences—in this case, composition. More than ever before, the accessibility and affordability of technology has expanded music listeners' (and composers') soundscapes beyond their immediate personal socio-cultural environs. Many of our students bring vibrant prior music listening experiences into our classrooms and ensembles, and as educators, we can continue to expand all students' musical horizons as they craft their musical and personal identities, musical preferences, and affective sensitivities. How might music teachers capitalize on their students' personal playlists as they guide students' compositional activity? What are the rationales teachers might promote as they help student composers realize the inherent connections between listening and their compositional processes and products?

Prior Listening

Prior music listening experiences are essential in stocking personal cognitive and musical reservoirs with compositional possibilities. Attentive music listening encounters provide an array of soundscapes, stylistic idioms, melodic and rhythmic ideas, and potential musical tools for arranging sounds that provoke artistic, musical, and affective impressions. Students might not be fully aware, however, of specific trends surrounding their personal soundscapes. Enculturation and the transmission of expectations regarding sound organization and aesthetic norms determine what listeners "know" about music and its elemental interactions, even if listeners are not yet aware of the role their own socio-cultural contexts play in defining their music listening habits. This information is deeply connected to the memory of listeners' prior musical experiences which are embodied in their body-mind-spirit-feelingful selves. Student composers should be encouraged to reflect on their personal soundscapes and listening habits, for they directly influence the decisions they make about their own compositions. To that end, students might identify musical works, sounds, patterns, and genres that have particular meaning to them, and subsequently explore "what about these musical sounds" embodies that meaning.

Wiggins and Medvinsky (2013) referred to music listening—in and outside of school music programs—as laying the groundwork for music composition, serving as concrete prior knowledges and prior experiences upon which students can draw and inform their own compositions. The authors wrote, "To be able to conceive of original material, learners need to have a solid understanding of the framework and possibilities *before* they are asked to engage in the process" (p.116). Music listeners create meaning of their present musical encounters in light of their past musical experiences. These "old" and "new" musical sounds and the personal meanings students ascribe to them form the deep reservoirs of musical and expressive possibilities that are transformed into personal expressions made manifest within students' musical compositions.

Emotional Inspiration

Composers listen to an array of musical styles and genres that serve as musical and emotional inspirations. Strand (2013) noted that, similar to any creative activity, composition requires inspiration. When composers listen to music, they are reminded of the many other composers who have created musical and affective impressions that connect and communicate with others in meaningful ways. Therefore, listening to music is an act that inspires composers to enlist music as a medium to convey thoughts, feelings, experiences, and creativity.

Other inspirations might take the form of a poem, event, person/character, artwork, natural scene, or another piece of music (Kennedy, 2002; Kerchner, 2016; Koops, 2013). Listening to someone else's music can serve as a "force" that drives creative thinking (Webster, 2002, p. 28) and inspires problem-solving that seeks resolution. As student composers embark on their compositional projects, they are faced with a "problem": How do I organize and relate musical sounds so that they convey the musical and affective impressions that I wish to communicate? In the prior section, music listening was positioned as foundational in creating cognitive "*prior* musical experiences" that composers use to frame their subsequent works. However, music listening is effective when used as a consultative agent throughout the compositional process.

Student composers can explore others' compositions for solutions that inform specific compositional "problems" they are facing during the compositional process. Students might consult their listening library, maybe even their peers' listening playlists, in order to glean sounds and idiomatic figures that fulfill musical and affective purposes within their own compositions. Kennedy (2002) found her choral student composers to benefit from listening to compositions (including their peers' compositions) as a way to build their repertoire of ideas and impressions that ultimately affected the nature of their compositional products. Furthermore, she found that music listening acted as an "aural tutor of form, theory, and harmony" (p. 103).

Student composers, therefore, benefit from listening to an array of diverse musics, because they serve as concrete models for their own compositions. Music teachers can expand students' musical models by bringing music listening examples that are obvious in their demonstration of specific forms, moods, programmatic narrative, chord progressions, melodic contour, rhythms, dynamics, articulations, and tempi. Similarly, teachers can invite students to listen to examples of compositions that effectively and less effectively demonstrate artistry and affective connection to listeners. This comparative conversation might also include the topic of listening subjectivity and personal interpretation of compositional effectiveness.

Teachers cannot assume that students will automatically understand composers' tools and strategies for creating a work simply by listening to their music. Intentional critical listening calls on teachers to draw students' attention to specific characteristics in the music listening example, followed by students and teacher describing the processes the composer utilized. Asking questions before and after students listen to musical excerpts can facilitate the discussion of how composers create musical relationships in order to convey a programmatic theme, create emotional moments in the music, and organize sounds amidst expressive qualities, essentially determining how the composer's organizational scheme "works" for the listener.

Emotional Affirmation

Composers listen to an array of musical styles and genres that serve as musical and emotional affirmations. The process of creating music demands composers to explore musical possibilities and, ultimately, commit to ordering musical sounds, creating musical relationships, and employing compositional strategies for sharing musical and affective impressions with their audiences. Students' problem-solving strategies are affirmed when they recognize that other composers have made similar organizational decisions, used similar compositional tools and strategies, or even used the same or similar sources of compositional inspiration.

Teachers and students can collaboratively research music that uses similar programs, styles, compositional tools, or affective impressions that are similar to inspirations that arise from the student composers' work. Together they can discuss how a composer approached compositional tasks, while learning about the student composer's intentions and approaches to a similar compositional "problem."

Imagine a student composer whose composition was to include a loud, "disruptive" sound in the midst of an otherwise mellow melody. This student could listen to Haydn's "Surprise Symphony" (Symphony no. 94 in G Major) in order to hear how that composer used dynamics, accents, and instrumentation to create a similar surprise and how it fit into the overall musical puzzle. Imagine another student composer for whom an historical event was an inspiration. Listening to Julie Giroux's "To Walk with Wings" might provide the student composer with affirmation that others, too, have found historical accounts such as the evolution of flight and exploration of space, to be inspirational. The composition would also model musical and emotional possibilities for developing a musical form and program based on the depiction of a fanfare, trial and error of flying machines, tragedies of space exploration failure, and resilience of the human spirit. Theoretical analyses and personal reflection on the music listening experience could provoke the student composer to further reflect on their own compositional action, i.e., reflection-on-action (Schön, 1992). This, in turn, could inform the composer's level of personal satisfaction with the compositional effect they created, and potentially inspire and suggest ways for editing the current version of their composition.

Listening to Self-Composed Works

Composers listen to their own compositional products as they organize musical sounds into a larger composition. Composing is analogous to an intricate dance between the critically thinking brain and the intuitive musical self. On the one hand, composers enlist their musical and aural discrimination and critical thinking skills as they listen to their own compositions, in order to determine the effectiveness of their composition in communicating meaningful musical and affective impressions. On the other hand, composers listen to their compositions and enlist their intuitive musical sensitivities to assess the degree to which their vision for the composition is coming to musical fruition from an aesthetic perspective.

Listening to one's own music and reflecting on its musical and emotional impacts leads to necessary revision, both intentional (Webster, 2012) and intuitive. "In-flight" decision-making (i.e., reflection-in-action, Schön, 1992) occurs as composers perform chunks of their compositions and edit something that does not quite fit aurally or emotionally in the moment, seeking to explore other "best" possibilities, before continuing the compositional process. After a certain point in the compositional process, however, composers must step back from the real-time composing process and listen to the performance of larger segments of the composition and engage in reflection-on-action (Schön, 1992), i.e., what worked and what does not yet work musically and affectively. Reflection-on-action leads composers to pose questions such as, "Is this musical product what I want? If not, why?" This type of reflective thinking is important in taking inventory of "what is" within a composition, but it is not enough. Subsequent editorial action must be taken. Therefore, reflection-for-action (Killion and Todnem, 1991)—reflexive practice during which composers identify possible pathways forward in revising and expanding their compositions—completes the inherent listening-reflecting-editing cycle that defines the compositional process.

As student composers listen to their compositions, they may also wish to consider guidelines for reflecting on their "in-process" work. Kaschub and Smith (2016) suggested the acronym "M.U.S.T.S." (i.e., Motion-stasis, Unity-variety, Sound-silence, Tension-release, and Stability-instability) as considerations in building relationships between the musical features. Students should be encouraged to critically listen for and reflect on the M.U.S.T.S. word-pairs as they occur in their compositions. Reflective questions might include, "To what extent is each component of a word pair present?" and "How might I change the balance between word pair(s) in order to provoke sensation and then feeling?"

Hickey (2012) crafted the acronym "SCAMPER": Substitute, Combine, Adapt, Magnify/Modify/Minify, Put to other use, Eliminate, Reverse/Rearrange (p. 46) as a device for student composers as they puzzle how to use their shorter compositional ideas to form larger compositional chunks. For example, a student composer might have created a melodic or rhythmic idea, yet they do not yet know the various options for using it to expand their composition. The student could explore placing the musical idea elsewhere within the composition, combining it with other musical ideas, varying an aspect of the idea, changing the rhythmic duration of the idea, giving the idea a different function within the composition, eliminating the idea completely (not likely if the student is really attached to the idea!), or using the reverse order of the pitches or rhythms of the idea.

The SCAMPER and M.U.S.T.S. strategies cannot work, however, without the student composer employing critical listening, critical thinking, and reflective thinking skills. The composer must listen in order to determine the efficacy of how the musical puzzle pieces occur within the larger compositional context, and then editing according to whether or not the composition decisions are musically and affectively compelling. The SCAMPER strategy and M.U.S.T.S. word-pairs provide student composers with ample suggestions for editing and expanding, but they must constantly listen to their compositional edits to determine if they align with their compositional vision, or if additional edits are needed.

Listening to Others, Inviting Others to Listen

Composers listen to others for feedback and constructive criticism and think critically about how to facilitate others to listen to their creative products. Until this point of the chapter, listening to music has been the focus of the discussion. We shift direction now to another crucial form of listening that also provides valuable information to composers. It involves listening to others—performers and listeners (e.g., critics, peers, and teachers)—about their perceptions and responses to the composers' compositions. Listening to others, truly listening and being open to how other people experience the compositions, encourages another layer of the composers' continued reflection and revision. Inviting critical dialog can seem daunting, especially since composers' work involves personal attachment, investment of time, dedication, and creativity. Criticism, even if it is presented in a constructive manner, can cause angst as student composers listen to others' opinions.

Initiating discussion and asking key questions that solicit observational feedback are skills for student composers to develop, but this requires teacher modeling and student practice. While it is ultimately up to the composers to determine which bits of criticism to receive and act on, listening and responding to musical consumers seems a valuable habit to develop, so that the composers can better teach, conduct, discuss, and connect their musical ideas to other people.

What questions might student composers pose to spark conversational feedback? Composers will want to learn if the concept they hold for their composition coincides with the listeners' and performers' reception of the musical work. In other words, did the general musical scheme for their work—the basic musical and affective impressions for the composition—have the effect that the composer intended? Asking others what worked or did not yet work in light of the composer's intent can foster the reframing and recrafting of musical ideas to achieve what was originally intended by the composer. This conversation can also inform the performers' interpretation of the composer's work.

Composers might ask performers questions regarding the level of difficulty experienced in performing the music, the accessibility of the composition in relation to the instrumentation or voicing, and the level of engagement required to maintain performers' interest in performing the composition (think about the bass drum player performing one measure in a 15-minute composition). For songs, student composers will want to listen to the performance of the composition and subsequently ask the performers about the extent to which the melody "sings" within the vocal timbre and range. Student composers will want to listen to the performer's ease of singing the text setting in relation to open vowels and their placement within specific pitch ranges. Performers could provide information about the clarity of the notation used in the score of the composition. How might the score be more effectively notated so that performers can interpret the composer's intent?

FACILITATING ENGAGED MUSIC LISTENING

Thus far, we have considered ways in which music listening can serve as the foundation and inspiration for students generating compositional products. Student composers internalize models of pitch and rhythm patterns, harmonic and formal structures, and style-specific idiomatic features simply by listening to musics in their surrounding environments, with or without teacher guidance. Focused listening, however, can facilitate student composers gaining insight into the artistic music elemental relationships that lead to feelingful responses. As music educators, we have the opportunity to scaffold music listening experiences that deliberately draw students' attention to ways in which composers organize sounds and create artistic and feelingful impressions. What then are examples of specific pedagogical strategies that teachers might implement in order to lead students toward personal soundscape development and expansion, such that music listening directly leads to informed, inspired, and thoughtful compositions that are not only musically and artistically formed but are also emotionally engaging? How might teachers facilitate engaged music listening?

Much of my pedagogical and research work has focused on observing and analyzing students' verbal, visual, and kinesthetic responses to music listening as means for driving student-centered pedagogy that facilitates music listening skill development (Kerchner, 1996, 2000, 2009). By considering what I have learned from music student learners, I offer the following pedagogical strategies as starting points for teachers to consider and adapt according to their specific music teaching and learning contexts.

Questioning and Offering Feedback

It can be challenging for teachers, who are typically highly trained and knowledgeable musicians, to remember that what they perceive and process musically is not necessarily what students recognize as obvious features of a music listening example. Similarly, what draws students into a music listening example may be completely different from teachers' aesthetic and musical values developed throughout their accumulated (and presumably varied) music listening experiences. Therefore, it is important to select musical examples that clearly demonstrate a musical element, compositional tool, or emotional impression and to guide the music listening experiences for the purposes of engaged instructional listening. Students' compositions might also serve as illustrative examples. While students listen to musical examples in order to inform their own compositional work, they can also learn from listening to, analyzing, and reflecting on their own work.

To add awareness to the music listening experience, teachers are encouraged to provide students with focus directives or questions that lead them to discover something specific in music listening examples—a pattern, a rhythm, an instrumental or vocal interaction, a theme, a melodic contour, or a feeling impression. Students bring these options into their own awareness as possibilities for their own compositions. Otherwise, teachers can assume that individual students will each focus their attention on a variety of musical features during classroom or ensemble music listening experiences. Both directives and questions are presented prior to the listening and serve to focus students' attention. Debriefing about what the students noticed relative to the point of guided focus immediately follows listening to the musical example. These discussions, in turn, lead to another listening of the same musical excerpt to either listen for a different musical feature or to listen again for the original musical feature brought to the students' attention, but perhaps missed in the plethora of musical information that moves rapidly through time and space.

A focus directive is a statement with which the teacher invites students to do something during the music listening, often as a way of gauging their listening discrimination skills. Sample directives include: "When you hear this theme (students learn to sing the theme before the question is posed), stand up." "Raise your hand when you hear the music begin to move faster (accelerate)." "Hold up your pointer finger when you hear the trombone, and hold up your pinky finger when you hear the flute." "As you listen to the music, think about how the composer created the image of a fast machine as we listen to John Adams' *Short Ride in a Fast Machine.*" The teacher gives the students a direction regarding what they should do or consider as they listen to the music. No question is actually posed, however.

Teachers' carefully-worded focus questions posed prior to musical listening experiences can encourage students to imagine, think in musical sound, dream, predict, compare, contrast, anticipate, speculate, critique, reflect, and pose their own questions (Kerchner, 2014). A focus question is a prompt for the students to consider during the act of music listening. For example, "As we listen, which instruments do you hear? We'll discuss after the music ends." Notice this particular focus question asks a "closed question" and converges on a correct response, usually offered verbally by students.

Another type of question is a "guided question" that points the students' focus of attention toward something specific about the music. An example might be: "As we listen to the music, what do you notice about the way the different instruments play the theme when it returns in the conclusion of the composition?" This question focuses the students' attention on the musical instruments and a repeated musical theme, but there is also room for students' personal interpretations about the relationship between the instruments and the theme. Teachers pose "open-ended focus questions" prior to listening to a musical excerpt in order to intentionally prime cognitive and emotional wells. These questions solicit a variety of diverse student responses, certainly not limited to a single accurate response. Open-ended questions can also be crafted to be intentionally vague when teachers want to engage students' imaginations and cast the net wide to see what they are thinking, feeling, and hearing as they listen to a composition. These open-ended questions might include: "What did you notice about the musical mood?" or "What did you notice or experience as you listened to this piece?"

Providing focus directives and posing focus questions require teachers to reflect on what specifically they want the students to glean from the music listening excerpt. In addition to asking an array of questions—closed, guided, and open-ended—teachers are also encouraged to pose questions that engage the cognitive skills reflected in each of the six levels of Benjamin Bloom's et al. (1956) *Cognitive Taxonomy.* Anderson and Krathwohl (2001) reimagined this taxonomy by reversing the synthesis and evaluation levels within the taxonomy and using verbs (instead of nouns) to depict the how humans demonstrate the various levels of thinking.

Bloom's hierarchical levels include foundational, concrete levels of thinking (knowledge, comprehension, and application) and move to the levels that represent higher-order thinking (analysis, synthesis, and evaluation). Asking questions that engage the type of thinking indicative of each level of the taxonomy helps students become cognitively flexible. Varied questioning moves students beyond lower-level memorization and recall of facts and into higher-level application and analysis. Developing these higher-order thinking skills results in the capacity to generate ideas, problem-solve, reflect, and develop personal preferences. Examples of questions and directives for each of Bloom's taxonomic levels are found in Figure 10.1; Anderson and Krathwohl's taxonomic descriptors are in parentheses.

Bloom's Taxonomy (Anderson & Krathwohl's Taxonomy, 2001)	Focus Directive	Focus Question
Knowledge (remembering)	Name a famous jazz performer.	What is the definition of this symbol as it appears in the music?
Comprehension (understanding)	Count how many times you hear the flute playing the melody.	How did the composer change the pattern in order to add interest to the music?
Application (applying)	Raise your hand when you hear a big shift in dynamics in the music.	What would the music sound like if we used "forte" in this section of the music?
Analyze (analyzing)	Raise your hand when you hear the primary theme. Stand when you hear the secondary theme.	How does the first phrase of the musical excerpt compare to the second phrase in terms of texture?
Synthesis (evaluating)	Create a summary charts of the vocal styles we heard, showing what they have in common and how they are different.	How might the composer rearrange the sections of the music to create x effect?
Evaluation (creating)	Jot down three questions you would ask the composer. List three suggests for alternative endings to the piece of music we listened to.	How would the composer possibly justify the inclusion of found-sounds and natural sounds in the recorded composition?

FIGURE 10.1. Focus directives and questions based on Bloom's Taxonomy (1956)

Teachers are encouraged to model how to articulate guided and open-ended questions and how to provide specific observational feedback on students' compositional processes and products. Observational feedback statements ("I noticed that _____") are especially useful to student composers, since they remove personal judgement and state directly what the peers (and teachers) have heard and experienced by listening to the composition. Peer comments such as, "This composition is good" or "I like it" provide the composer little detail for improving or taking alternative pathways toward crafting intended musical, artistic, or feelingful impressions. Instead, teachers might prompt peer reviewers to add the word "because" to complete the statement with description: "This composition is good, *because* _____" or "I like this composition, *because* _____." With these observational and descriptive statements, student composers receive specific feedback, and peer reviewers develop their critical thinking skills by articulating the reasons for the feedback they offer the composer.

Engaging Students' Verbal, Visual, and Kinesthetic Responses

A preponderance of teachers' pedagogical strategies rely on verbal interactions between their students and themselves. This is the case with discussions that ensue at the conclusion of music listening experiences, when students are invited to respond to a focus question that the teacher had posed. Teachers use student verbal descriptors to gauge the degree of students' musical understanding and perceptual acuity. Likewise, music teachers spend substantial energy helping students refine their written musical descriptions (i.e., standard musical notation and vocabulary).

The education profession values students' linguistic abilities because of its link to the rational, logical mind. Yet written words and spoken language are mere metaphors for the vastness and depth of thinking (Vygotsky, 1986). Words and symbols cannot convey the nuanced emotion and the repleteness of understanding embedded within them. Furthermore, student speakers consciously or unconsciously determine the extent of that which they verbally share about their music listening experience. Therefore, relying only on verbal musical description, especially when asking children to describe what they are thinking, feeling, and hearing during music listening, warrants caution. What other forms of description, in addition to verbal descriptors and standard music notation, could encourage students to be actively engaged during music listening?

Student composers might try drawing music listening maps—graphs, pictures, shapes, words, and lines—to represent that which they are thinking, hearing, and feeling as they listen to musical examples, including their own compositions. In addition to describing verbally "what about the music" they have depicted in the representations included in their music listening maps, it is beneficial for teachers to observe students "perform" their maps (i.e., pointing to the mapping symbols while they listen to the music). In that way, teachers witness the performance and can infer musical understandings that are not apparent in students' verbal descriptions.

Students might wish to create the scores for their compositions using alternative music notation as well, using representational markings similar to those included in their music listening maps. As student composers seek to invent the form of notation most effective in communicating and preserving their compositional ideas, they might consult musical scores using alternative notation created by Cathy Berberian's ("Stripsody"), John Cage ("Fontana Mix") or Brian Eno ("Ambient 1: Music for Airports"), Pauline Oliveros ("Sonic Meditations"), or Nelson Howe ("Fur Music") as inspirations. An interesting activity would be for students to listen to these pieces while viewing their musical scores and discussing what about the music was evident in the score. While learning standard musical notation can be an important skill to learn, the process of using an unfamiliar, standard symbol system can also be intimidating and cumbersome to people who want to perform and compose.

Implementing another mode of response, student composers might create physical gestures, or movement, to represent what they are thinking, feeling, and hearing during music listening. Movement provides students the opportunity to demonstrate not only what they hear perceptually, but it is especially effective in conveying affective responses that defy verbal description (Ebie, 2004; Kerchner, 2000, 2009, and 2014). Again, teachers will want to observe students "perform" these movements as the students listen to the musical excerpt in order to extract meaning that might not have otherwise been described verbally in spoken descriptions or visually in the listening maps.

Whether describing musical excerpts or their own compositions verbally, visually, or kinesthetically (i.e., physical movements), teachers must meet the students "where they are" in terms of the vocabulary they use to convey information about their music listening experiences. Having observed students coordinate their movement or mapping performances to the music to which they are listening, teachers can try to determine what about the music students are describing, and then offer students alternative words (inclusive of musical vocabulary) to describe those musical events or characteristics. The manner in which students describe their music listening experiences is valid, as it is their personalized representation of musical and experiential meaning. It is up to their teachers, then, to try to understand inferentially what students are trying to convey.

Repeated Listening

Focusing students' attention during music listening experiences by posing questions or directives brings the opportunity for enhanced musical awareness and expansion of cognitive constructs. Yet, music moves quickly throughout time and space, making it impossible to experience in a single music listening occasion all that the music has to offer. Leonard Meyer (1956) wrote:

> Because listening to music is a complex art involving sensitivity of apprehension, intellect, and memory, many of the implications of an event are missed on first hearing. It is only after we come to know and remember the basic, axiomatic events of a work . . . that we begin to appreciate the richness of their implications." (46)

Therefore, repeated exposure to a piece of music, perhaps even their own compositions, facilitates familiarity. With repeated opportunities to listen to a piece of music, people listen from different cognitive perspectives, find musical sounds and elemental relationships they might not have heard before and, accordingly, allow for new body-mind-feeling-spirit responses (Kerchner, 1996). These different responses to the experience prompt listeners to reformulate, reshape, and revise their prior musical mental representations. Students' initial impressions and neural mappings during music listening become more sophisticated and replete during repeated listenings. Similarly, repeated listening and its concomitant familiarity can lead to increased enjoyment. Therefore, repeated, and focused listening are essential in helping students develop "deep" music listening skills (Shehan Campbell, 2005).

Along with listening to diverse styles and genres of music, students practice their critical thinking skills by listening to multiple performances of the same piece of music. Inviting student composers to compare and contrast the different versions opens their eyes to possibilities for variation and stylistic nuance, and the subsequent musical and affective effects, within their own compositions. For example, students might initially consult a recording of "My Funny Valentine," sung by Frederica von Stade. To explore other arrangers' and performers' musical choices, students might also listen to "My Funny Valentine" performed by Miles Davis, Sting, Kristin Chenowith, and Ella Fitzgerald. For a different comparison, students might listen to Frank Sinatra's 1953 and 1962 recordings of "My Funny Valentine" and compare these iterations to his duet of "My Funny Valentine" with Lorrie Morgan (1994). To encourage critical thinking and potential composer application, teachers might ask students questions indicative of the "analysis" level of the Bloom's Taxonomy (see Figure 10.1) to engage students in considering composers'/arrangers'/performers' choices for musical interpretation, including the comparison of the song performed by singers in comparison to instrumental-only arrangements.

Listening in the compositional process must include diverse styles and genres of music created by underrepresented composers and performers, particularly people of color. Jenkins (2020) stated that while African-Americans' influence on jazz and the blues has been well documented, "the history and aesthetics of 'classical' music compositions by African-American composers have enjoyed less robust inquiry" and that there is "no single description [that] could adequately capture the variety represented in this canon" (p. 1). Composers and performers of color have always been a part of music history, yet their stories and contributions to music have remained intentionally oppressed and concealed throughout the centuries. Student composers must have the opportunity to see themselves in composers and performers having the same color skin. This, too, is an inspiration and affirmation for budding composers who are exploring how to express their own personal creativity through music.

Music listening examples must also move students to encounter music beyond Western musical paradigms. Three of many free online resources that are particularly useful resources for finding popular and global soundscapes are the Smithsonian Folkways Recordings (https://folkways.si.edu/), the Rock & Roll Hall of Fame (https://www.rockhall.com/education), and Carnegie Hall's Resources for Music Educators (https://www.carnegiehall.org/Explore/Learn/Music-Educators). Encourage students to explore recordings of global musical performances, focusing on timbres of indigenous instruments and voices, rhythms, melody construction, and tonalities. Have students note particularly interesting moments in the recordings. As a class or in small groups, discuss why these moments of interest have captured the students' attention and how the composer/performer created those moments of interest. Prompt student composers to consider how those identified points of interest might inspire and inform their own compositions. In order to facilitate musical and cultural sensitivities, teachers are encouraged to nurture collaborative investigations and discussions of the performers' and composers' cultural contexts, the spaces in which the music might be performed, and the everyday functions of the music when encountering unfamiliar musics.

LISTENING TO COMPOSE

This chapter began with a discussion about the musical capacities of listeners that essentially situated music listening as a creative musical behavior that results in listeners generating novel products that include tangible and intangible responses indicative of the music listening experience. We examined strategies for incorporating music listening into students' composing processes, such that music listening examples serve as models, inspirations, and affirmations for student composers as they organize musical sounds in artistic and expressive ways. Following this, we explored ways to facilitate guided music listening by incorporating repeated listenings to musics that are diverse in style, genre, and culture. To lead students "into" the music example or student composition, teachers and peers formulate questions and offer feedback that potentially guide student composers to discover pathways for expressing themselves through music while simultaneously connecting to others who experience their compositions.

In addition to suggestions for teachers and student composers already offered in this chapter, this chapter concludes with two final examples that demonstrate "listening to compose." The first deals with student-generated music listening maps based on their compositions, cutting the map apart and recombining the written notation that results in a re-composed piece. The second example involves adapting a familiar song by incorporating a musical feature or impression found in a recording of a different piece of music. In each example, notice the interaction of the three primary music-making roles—composer, listener, and performer. Sample directives and closed, guided, and open-ended questions are provided as models for possible ways to engage students' critical, creative, and reflective thinking.

Re-composing Music

In pairs, small groups, or as a full class:

1. Student composers collaboratively create a one-minute composition.
2. Student composers create music listening maps (i.e., non-standard, alternative notation that includes drawings, words, graphs, icons, etc.) for their compositions.

   Directive: "As you listen to your composition, create a music listening map of drawings, words, graphs, and/or icons that capture specific musical elements, events, and impressions in your composition."

3. As the compositions are performed (recorded versions are best), the composer "performs" their music listening map. Project the maps onto a screen (i.e., Prometheus or Smartboard); the composer points to the markings on the music listening map as they occur in the music performance. As the composer "performs" the score, the other students try to determine "what about the music is represented" in the music listening map.

   Focus Question (prior to listening): "As you listen to the composition and watch the composer perform the music listening map, what about the music is captured on the written music listening map?"

4. At the completion of the performance, students discuss each notational marking on the listening map and its relationship to the music.

   Open-Ended Question: "What about the music do you think is represented on the map?"

5. A partner or member of the group (not the composer) takes a paper version of the music listening map and cuts it into large sections (or even into small pieces for individual markings on the map). Original markings should remain intact. For example, if there is a circle on the map, students would not cut the circle in half.

   Guided Question: "Where are the natural sections written on the music listening map?"

   Closed Question: "Do you want to cut the map into larger chunks, small pieces of individual representations/markings, or some combination?"

6. The partner or group members (including the composer) reassemble the music listening map into a new music listening map for a re-composed piece of music.

   Open-Ended Question: "What do you imagine the music to sound like with the re-arrangement of the listening map pieces?"

7. The composer and peers create musical sounds, maybe even segments of the original composition, indicative of the new arrangement of the visual music listening map notation.

   Guided Question: "What musical sounds or ideas will you keep from the original composition, but repurpose them in the new composition?"

   Open-Ended Question: "How else might you arrange these sounds? What are other possibilities?"

8. Students listen to recordings of the original and re-composed pieces in order to compare and contrast how the reorganization of sections, ideas, and sounds maintained or changed the composer's original musical, artistic, and feelingful impressions.

   Directive: "As you listen to the recordings of both pieces, jot down what remained similar and what changed."

   Reflective Question: "How did this recomposed piece change your [the composer's] original vision?"

Reflective Question: "What about the recomposed piece worked effectively musically and affectively?"

Finding "Something Interesting"

As an individual student composer or small group of composers:

1. Student(s) listens to a recording of and learn to sing the song, "Swing Low, Sweet Chariot." Student(s) then listens to a recording of Florence Price's "Swing Low, Sweet Chariot" for string quartet (*Five Folk Songs in Counterpoint*).
   Closed Question: "Which instruments played the main melody?"
   Guided Question: "What was something interesting that you found in Price's setting of the familiar song?"
2. Student composer(s) brings a recording of music that highlights "something interesting" (i.e., a rhythmic or melodic pattern, a mood, instrumentation, expressive vocal or instrumental quality, changes in tempi or dynamics, harmonic progressions, etc.).
   Reflective Question: "Why did you select this particular recording/music/song?"
   Guided Question: "What is the feature of this music that you found interesting?"
3. Student composer(s) shares their recordings and describe the "something interesting" that is highlighted in the musical examples.
4. Student composer(s) finds a familiar piece of music (i.e., a folk song, part of a piece of music being rehearsed in school or community ensemble, etc.) that they can perform vocally or instrumentally.
5. Student composer(s) takes a "something interesting" from the recordings they just listened to and find ways to incorporate it into the familiar piece of music.
   Directive: "Find three different ways for incorporating your 'something interesting' into the familiar piece."
   Directive: "Describe the effect that the 'something interesting' has on each version of the familiar piece."
6. Student composer(s) perform both the original and adapted versions of the music for the class.
   Open-Ended Question: "What did you notice?"
   Guided Question: "What compositional strategies did the composer use in incorporating the 'something interesting' into the familiar song?"
7. Following the performances, students discuss what was similar and different in the two versions of the music. Discuss the effect of adding the "something interesting" into the familiar song.
   Guided Question: "How did the incorporation of 'something interesting' change the musical and affective impressions of the music?"
   Open-Ended Question: "What are other ways that the composer might have used the 'something interesting' in the familiar piece of music?"

References

Anderson, L. W., & Krathwohl, D. R. (Eds.). (2001). *A taxonomy for learning, teaching, and assessing: A revision of Bloom's Taxonomy of Educational Objectives.* Allyn & Bacon.

Bloom, B. S. Furst, E. J., Hill, W. H., Krathwohl, D. R. (Eds.). (1956). *Taxonomy of educational objectives, Handbook I: The cognitive domain.* David McKay Co. Inc.

Dunn, R. (2006). Teaching for lifelong, intuitive listening. *Arts Education Policy Review, 107*(3), 33–38.

Ebie, B. (2004). The effects of verbal, vocally modeled, kinesthetic, and audio-visual treatment conditions on male and female middle-school vocal music students' abilities to expressively sing melodies. *Psychology of Music, 32*(4), 405–17.

Hickey, M. (2012). *Music outside the lines: Ideas for composing in K–12 music classrooms.* Oxford University Press.

Jenkins, C. (2020). *Exploring the aesthetics of African-American classical musics.* American Society for Aesthetics. Retrieved from https://cdn.ymaws.com/aesthetics-online.org/resou rce/resmgr/files/diversity/Jenkins_African_American.pdf

Kaschub, M. (2016). Comprehensive choral artistry: Developing musical intelligence through empathetic, creative, and artistic practice (pp. 45–62). In J. L. Kerchner & K. Strand (Eds.), *Musicianship: Composing in choir.* GIA Publications.

Kaschub, M. & Smith, J. P. (2016). The big picture: Developing musical capacities. *Music Educators Journal, 102*(3), 33–40.

Kennedy, M. A. (2002). Listening to the music: Compositional processes of high school composers. *Journal of Research in Music Education, 50*(2), 94–110.

Kerchner, J. L. (1996). *Perceptual and affective components of the music listening experience as manifested in children's verbal, visual, and kinesthetic representations.* Unpublished doctoral dissertation, Northwestern University.

Kerchner, J. L. (2000). Children's verbal, visual, and kinesthetic responses: Insight into their music listening experience. *Bulletin of the Council for Research in Music Education, 146*, 31–50.

Kerchner, J. L. (2016). Contemporary a cappella ensembles: Social and musical interactions during song arranging. In J. L. Kerchner & K. Strand (Eds.), *Musicianship: Composing in choir* (pp. 167–186). GIA Publications.

Kerchner, J. L. (2009). Drawing middle-schoolers' attention to music (pp. 183–198). In J. L. Kerchner & C. Abril (Eds.), *Music experience in our lives: Things we learn and meanings we make.* Rowman & Littlefield Education.

Kerchner, J. L. (2014). *Music across the senses: Listening, learning, making meaning.* Oxford University Press.

Kerchner, J. L. (2021). Music listening: An evolution of craft. In K. Holdhus, R. Murphy, & M. Espeland (Eds.), *Music education as craft: Reframing theories and practices* (pp. 105–116). Springer.

Killion, J. P., & Todnem, G. R. (1991). A process for personal theory building. *Educational Leadership, 48*(6), 14–17.

Koops, A. P. (2013). Facilitating composition in instrumental settings. In M. Kaschub & J. P. Smith (Eds.), *Composing our future: Preparing music educators to teach composition* (pp. 149–166). Oxford University Press.

Meyer, L. B. (1956). *Emotion and meaning in music.* University of Chicago Press.

Morrison, C. D. (2009). Music listening as music making. *The Journal of Aesthetic Education, 43*(1), 77–91.

Peterson, E. M. (2006). Creativity in music listening. *Arts and Education Policy Review, 107*(3), 15–21.

Schön, D. (1992). *The reflective practitioner: How professionals think in action.* Basic Books.

Shehan Campbell, P. (2005). Deep listening to the musical world. *Music Educators Journal, 92*(1), 30–36.

Strand, K. (2013). Guiding compositions in choral settings. In M. Kaschub & J. P. Smith (Eds.), *Composing our future: Preparing music educators to teach composition* (pp. 167–184). Oxford University Press.

Vygotsky, L. S. (1986). *Thought and language* (A. Kozulin, Ed.). M.I.T. Press.

Webster, P. (2002). Creative music thinking: Advancing a model. In T. Sullivan & L. Willingham (Eds.), *Creativity and music education* (pp. 16–33). Canadian Music Educators' Association.

Webster, P. (2012). Towards pedagogies of revision: Guiding a student's composition. In O. Odena (Ed.), *Musical creativity: Insights from music education research* (pp. 93–112). Taylor & Francis Group.

Wiggins, J., & Medvinsky, M. (2013). Scaffolding student composers. In M. Kaschub & J. P. Smith (Eds.), *Composing our future: Preparing music educators to teach composition* (pp. 109–126). Oxford University Press.

CHAPTER 11

SKILLS SUCCESSFUL SONGWRITERS AND PRODUCERS UTILIZE AND WHY IT MATTERS TO MUSIC EDUCATORS

BRUCE ALLEN CARTER

THERE is currently an ongoing debate among musician theorists, largely on social media platforms, concerning the appropriateness of teaching music theory in its current, centuries-old form.[1] Much of the discussion has centered on the cultural implications of solely valuing a tonal system embedded in a white European tradition. Additionally, many have contemplated the appropriateness of promoting older musical traditions embedded in most music theory training through AP testing and college music major programs. It seems to be an inflection point for music theory educators as they interrogate why many are teaching music systems embedded so deeply in the past. Moreover, the imminent difficulty remains, just what is required to sustain the musical life of today's musician, what is relevant, and what is taught simply out of tradition? For music educators, specifically those who teach composition and songwriting, the question might be extended to ask, what exactly do current music producers and songwriters say they require to be successful?

In this chapter, I investigate the ways two very prominent songwriters/music producers discuss their process to question: what types of music skills are they utilizing? Second, what role did their musical training play in forming their musical output in their day-to-day work? Working backward, or perhaps from a top-down perspective, I hope to gain insight into the skills most needed by successful music professionals engaged in songwriting and song production. In this way, music educators can begin to map musical skills that merit continued emphasis when

engaging young people in the educative musical experience. For music educators focused on the pedagogy of songwriting, it is perhaps time we ask ourselves, just like
the music theorists, what matters and how can we better guide the next generation of
musical creatives. Last, this chapter features two musicians who define themselves as
songwriters and producers in the electronic dance and rap genres. When I requested
the two participants define what they do, what the term producer means to them, they
both acknowledged that the producer role is complex, multifaceted, and requires a
wide range of skills. A definition of producer or songwriter is not provided in this
paper because the participants use these terms in a myriad of ways to represent the
complexity of their music-making. The dissonance between their definitions of the
terms, and the way music educators typically denote composing or songwriting is detailed later in the chapter.

I begin by introducing the reader to Chris Leacock, one of the most successful and
prominent songwriters and DJs in the United States and beyond. Next, I unpack the
ways Chris describes his approach to the creative process and what he states most valuable. Last, I connect the themes presented by Chris to current streams of research
of music education with an emphasis on extending this work in more detailed and
nuanced ways. Next, I introduce Cody Colacino, a record producer, musician, branding
expert, entrepreneur, and founder of Pure Sinners Entertainment. Similarly, I explicate
the ways Cody describes his creative process and the ways his early formative musical
experiences shape his current aesthetic.

An Introduction to
Christopher Leacock

Better known by his stage name, Jillionaire, Christopher Leacock (born April 3, 1978)
is a Trinidadian DJ and music producer. Chris's work has been performed at the largest
venues and most successful EDM festivals in the world. He is better known for being a
past member of the American electronic music group Major Lazer, along with Diplo
and Walshy Fire. In 2014 he released then EP *Fresh* along with Salvadore Ganacci on
the Universal Music label. Jillionaire is recognized for developing a unique mix of indie
dance and big room house together the Caribbean rhythms and harmonies. I asked
Chris if I could interview him for this work and his perspective as a working musi-
cian/songwriter/DJ. Chris and I met on several occasions and discussed the two central questions of this chapter via Zoom in January 2021. After completing the chapter,
I asked Chris to review the work as a member checking technique to ensure his words
were not taken out of context and his intentions were best expressed. Additionally, before our call I asked Chris about the research topics I was exploring in an attempt to provide him ample time to reflect meaningfully on the topics.

Confronting Bias

One of the primary questions guiding this paper is, what exactly do current music producers and songwriters say they require to be successful? Although most of my interactions with Chris were informal, I asked this question in a way, and tone, that allowed him to be a bit more clinical about his answer. This is the first of many occasions during the interview where the answer I anticipated was far from correct. I prepared to hear stories of early musical training, although that did occur later, followed by the other markers of the typical trajectory of music majors. It was then I began to realize the preconceived notions that were guiding my thought process and the interview. It was clear that Chris thought of the creative musician in ways that were outside of the canon of typical composition in the academy, or even singer/songwriter tropes of education and professional development. My bias also extended to the ways Chris delivered his thoughts on the musical process. While his dance music is extremely successful due to the high energy and fast-paced chords, lyrics, and tonal shifts, his approach to our discussion was measured, low key, and slow-paced. It is not just what Chris said that startled me, it was the levels of metaphor and consistent presentation of intersections of all forms of arts modalities to describe his work that I found inspiring and mesmerizing. It was clear from the beginning that nothing about his work was happenstance. His approach was liberating, brilliantly thoughtful, and examined with a lens of self-critique that was profound and illuminating.

How to Be a Successful Songwriter/DJ

When asked this question, Chris's response was unequivocal and assured: "The most important skills required are critical thinking and ability to collaborate with others." Chris emphasized the need to critically examine one's work, to not simply follow typical archetypes of those you view as successful, but meaningfully question all aspects of both the process and the product you are creating.

> I have a curatorial overview of what I want to people to feel, whether it's walking into my house . . . eating a meal . . . what it should taste like. I take the time to consider the art as experience. Imagery and metaphors are everything. It is paramount to be a jack of all trades, master of none. You can make a parallel between any of the arts. You may not have an understanding of the technique but you can capture emotion in food or pictures, or film study. I am not a painter, but I know what I like. I have a strong sense of what I am after and work aggressively to make sure that approach is received by others in ways that inspire the emotion I have in mind.

On numerous occasions Chris mentioned the need for musicians to be more critical of their decisions and decision-making process. He states that this is important due to the ineffable nature of the musical craft and the ethereal ways music is received. Chris believes that musical creation is one of the most difficult art forms to express because the technical elements can be difficult to learn and exact effectively. He further states that visual artists and filmmakers are able to rely on strong emotional response from pictures and other stimuli that help them more easily convey something quickly with little background or context. For this reason, critical thinking is a paramount skill for musicians of any genre to adequately express their ideas in emotion through a logical detailed form.

The use of form and its importance in constructing music was also overriding in Chris's approach to critical thinking and music-making. The architecture of a song should be clear and concise, with deliberate delineations between the intro, verse, chorus, break/bridge, riser, and outro. Chris states that a musician needs to have a clear view of what they are constructing and what forms and structures are required to articulate their work to an audience. In sum, Chris states that critical thinking as it relates to self-awareness, openness for revision, and mindful and deliberate approaches to structure are important parts of the creative process.

> It is sometimes difficult to walk into a room, even a room of familiar and trusted people, and present your ideas only to have them critique your work. At the same time, I do not want to be surrounded by yes-men either, in my professional or personal life. That said, sometimes changing or revising something, removing the idea that took you hours, can be extremely frustrating and a downer that's tough to rebound from. I just keep asking myself: Am I remaining true to my vision? Does this revision make the song better or just more line with what people expect? I do find myself falling into the typical artist's trap of believing my current work is far better than anything I've done before, then at the end realizing it wasn't so great after all. So much of music is not the notes, but the way the beat or hook is introduced, the organization of it all.

Just as Chris reiterates the value of revision and structure, he also addresses the role of his emotions while creating, something in my experience, rarely discussed in music education settings. Chris repeatedly stated that his emotional being or mindset was important to his ability to provide good music.

Collaboration

Although Chris mentioned critical thinking as important, the larger emphasis was placed on collaboration. The collaborative process is important to Chris for two reasons. First, a good collaborator brings energy and passion to a project, a quest to find a sound or communicate a message. Second, collaborating means addressing areas of the songwriting process you need help with or just finding people to help make the work stronger due to their technical knowledge or musical skill. I asked Chris to elaborate on what he describes as a good collaborator:

They need to be passionate. If you are passionate, you are driven to have a strong work ethic. I look for those with passion to work with and alongside, because I know the drive will follow. Sometimes someone can approach you with an idea, but they do not have the technical knowledge to make it happen. That is where I believe I can assist. Technical knowledge and knowhow are easy, passion is not. I can teach people; if they are excited, they will learn what I need for them to learn. I always tell people that technical people or knowledge is great, but give me passion all day, every day. The passion translates to good music.

Chris described a recent song and his collaborative process:

[For] the process of songwriting, first, I say, "Send song references, what you want it to sound like." Align expectations. If they say, "I want to make a record that sounds like this," I can reach out to the people I need to help the aesthetics happen. I ask: "Do you have a writer? Do we need to find a writer? Are you performing it? Who is the intended audience?"

The last project in Trinidad [was] two collaborations, actually, one a singer-songwriter, one a producer. I said, "This is a great song; we should get a female voice on this." We brought it to a woman who does music in Trinidad, a legend in the Caribbean music community. She said, "I love this; I want to perform it." She came into the studio, she recorded it—it was tear-jerking. I then went to other friends who play flute and sax, and said, "I need additional instrumentation." Then we went to a female poet on the island and she recorded a little piece. So, we took this idea as a sketch, and we were able to pull people in to help pull the vision off and tighten us in the mix and the production. Alignment of expectations is first and always important. You say, "Hey, this is my vision; we are working together."

Chris was adamant in expressing that the myth of creating alone and in isolation is indeed a myth. All of the major producers and teams of writers that they know all work in teams. Further, Chris identified some of the major singer-songwriters of our time and how their work is the direct result of working with someone, volleying ideas back and forth to create a piece of music. We both lamented the ways musical credit is still largely assigned to one artist, with little emphasis or knowledge of the multiple people it requires to realize a song or album.

I began the chapter describing my bias in the ways I approach composition and how that impacted the ways I thought Chris would describe his musical journey. I found it fascinating to note what he did *not* describe. In our discussions there was never a mention of talent, or innate music skills. Everything, in his perspective, has to be worked on as a craft. Also, there was no discussion of formal training. From Chris's perspective the pedigree of one's education was not important. What mattered was the passion and specific skills brought to the creative process. Finally, when Chris read this chapter before it was sent to press, he stated that his belief that passion supersedes education was a thought he never made note of before this interview. However, when seeing it on paper he felt the need to stress the importance of personal drive to any formative musician and their development.

Culture

One theme that arose time and again throughout our discussions was Chris's attachment to Caribbean culture and his ties to his family and culture of Trinidad. Chris grew up in a home surrounded by music. It was his father's interest in music equipment and music technology that informed his musical language. Chris was taught early on that the aural experience—the technical components of sound engineering—were crucial to the quality of experience for the listener. Chris describes venturing into his father's record collection, hearing Prince, Santana, Trinidadian music from the 1970s and 1980s, and how it informed his perspectives on music, cuisine, and fine art. These experiences formed his basic aesthetic underpinnings.

For Chris, his music-making is about creating context for Caribbean culture and bridging the gap between Western music and Caribbean music. Formal musical training was not provided to Chris as a child, but by the music and cultural environment of the musical experience. His mother was in the church choir that sang the seminal hymns he can easily recollect. His grandfather played the organ and keyboard and encouraged everyone in the family to engage with music. Without question the role of family informed Chris's perspective toward music production and the ways he would eventually craft his own musical vernacular. Chris reflects:

> It is important to speak to the intersection of social mores and music. It's very important because of representation; it is important to represent. It's important [that] I represent my culture in its most authentic form. It is important to make sure an outsider looking in can get it right, that they understand a Trinidadian visual artist, or tech or I.T. guru. For future generations this is important, that they can see themselves in these different roles.

For Chris, there is an emphasis on bringing an authentic representation to Trinidadian culture in an effort to both express the culture in an appropriate outward-facing way, but also provide an inward-facing effort to serve as a role model for younger generations from the islands.

An Introduction to Cody Colacino

At the young age of 27, Cody Colacino is a successful record producer, musician, and entrepreneur residing in Los Angeles. His credits include Lil Xan, Trippie Redd, Tyla Yaweh, Lil Keed, Ski Mask the Slump God, Blac Youngsta, Tee Grizzley, FaZe Clan, and Bad Neighbors. Cody is recognized for pushing boundaries within the rap and trap music ecologies, encouraging musicians to move into more complex melodic and rhythmic motives than typically found within the genre. I spent an afternoon with Cody via Zoom to address the central questions being addressed in this chapter. Before speaking with Cody, I provided an outline of the chapter and explained the purpose of my call and for interviewing him. Like I did with Chris, after completing the chapter I asked Cody to review the work to make sure I was presenting his stories in ways that were authentic. Lastly, I was asked to speak with Cody's agent to address how this work might be amplified through social media.

Confronting Bias, Again

Just as I described my bias when interviewing Chris, I also address my own issues and shortcomings when approaching an interview with Cody. Before my interview I had heard of Cody and his work as a musician and record producer. Cody and most of the artists he represents are tattooed and surrounded with images that are aggressive. I worried about my ability to connect Cody's story to the field of composition and creativity as codified within this book. However, knowing that I am a music teacher-educator, Cody began the interview describing his music education experience, and I realized how wrong I had been in presuming the lack of connection to music education. His mother placed him in piano lessons at the age of three, and he began playing other instruments in band during elementary school. He enjoyed learning various brass instruments and also the violin during middle school. Music in his household was valued and he was appreciative of the access to lessons and to his early musical training.

Cody was overt and passionate about his support for music education in schools, which was highlighted by his successful early exposure to piano lessons and band. However, when Cody left middle school for high school he was placed in a school that offered no opportunities for arts education. This shift, moving from a school that fostered his musician training to a high school that provided no arts education, was profoundly jarring and upsetting to Cody as a young man. The absence of an outlet for his artistic identity created so much dissonance in his life that Cody rebelled and began to get into trouble at school and at home. Cody was so distraught by his lack of artistic space he left home during his freshman year and lived on the streets. Cody described himself as a very angry and upset young man who struggled with a life on the streets where every day was a battle. In his late teens he found his way to Los Angeles, and began working various jobs at coffee houses and bars to improve his quality of life.

It was during this time he began reflecting on his real passions of making music. After driving by a school that focused on recording and sound engineering every day, he decided perhaps he should attend, or at least begin a few classes, to see if the fit was right. Within the first few weeks Cody realized that making music was indeed his passion and life mission. He applied to the school's four-year program in recording, sound engineering, and music business and was accepted. During these four years Cody described how his teachers were able to introduce him to various studios through internships. I asked if all the students received the same opportunity for dynamic internships, having a feeling that this could not be possible. He sheepishly replied, "No, very few got internships," which led to my following question: "Why you?" Cody explained that his life on the streets taught him to be assertive and seek out the things he wants in powerful ways. In school, he described himself as hard-working and a self-starter, skills that were quickly noticed by the faculty. Additionally, he asked questions, a lot of questions. So much so faculty members would sometimes confuse his interest and questions as being cross. Cody mentioned that it was during this time he decided that no one would work harder than him in school. He wanted to know every detail the teacher knew about the topic being presented. He was mesmerized by the possibilities of creating and mastering music in ways no one else had thought of or could complete due to the technical knowledge required.

It was during his last internship at Universal during his senior year that Cody had a pivotal point in his career. Cody had already started recruiting musical talent in his early 20s and would invite clients to record at the studio at a discounted rate. He brought so many musicians into the work room during his brief tenure that Universal made more than $40,000 from their recording fees. Impressed with Cody's ability to bring in and work with talent, they hired him at the studio full-time. At his age, to be given that job and that much responsibility was something unique, and he cherished the opportunity. It was during this job in his early 20s that Cody really learned the music business and gained experiences in the wide array of jobs involved in the multifaceted music industry. In 2018, Cody began his own label, Pure Sinners Ent., as producer and founder. This venture was possible due to experience Cody had gained in recruiting musicians, building brands, mastering recordings, and marketing their work.

Before interviewing Cody, I began listening to the songs he produced, to get a better understanding of him and his aesthetic. The group he recently signed—Bad Neighbors—has already produced a music video and song that is gaining traction on social media. The artists themselves have an aggressive look, but their rapping style is quite different from what one might typically hear. These artists are singing the lines as much as they are speaking them. There are moments of just talking over a beat, but the main hook and chorus are complex lyrically. I asked Cody about the music and why his music stood out.

> I constantly draw on my formative skills of music-making at the piano and elsewhere when I am writing and producing. The rappers I am working with aren't using the standard language of "crescendo or decrescendo," so I communicate my musical wants differently. Without question my experience as a musician in my early years shapes my approach and provided me with the technical language needed to make good music.

Two themes are often present when Cody is discussing his music making—good music, and technical skill. I pressed him to define good music, the markers he believes are required for some rap or trap songs to sound or better. He explained that a lot of rap music has been boiled down to an extremely simple formula, sometimes just simple words over a beat. He likes to hear more complex combinations lyrically and rhythmically when his artists are in the studio. Technical proficiency was also of paramount importance, as a musician but especially as the person mastering the records. The technical skill Cody gathered in school is a source of pride, but also a source of confidence that draws artists to his label.

Last, Cody spoke with authority and sense of assuredness when speaking about creating his own style in the studio. When he signs an artist, they understand they are expected to make at least 500 songs in the studio within the first six months.

> If you only make three songs, there is no way to know what you sound is like. You have to work and work to get at what you are as a musician. In the beginning, I want them to try everything, be fearless, and throw as much paint on the wall as possible. Later, after a period of months, we start zooming in on what themes keep happening, what sounds work and what is authentic.

Without question Cody's work ethic is present at every part of the music-making venture. This drive and attention to detail is no doubt one of the attributes that has led to his success in establishing his own label.

How to Be Successful

When I asked Cody about what it takes to be a successful musician/producer in Los Angeles his demeanor changed to one that was buoyant.

> Look, there are people that might know more. But no one is going to out-work me. I tell young people all the time, if you are not willing to work 24/7 . . . every day, and sacrifice everything you have, do something else. Being in this industry in Los Angeles is one of the hardest things anyone could ever do. Being a musician is hard.

Cody also stated that the difficult part of his job was having to be proficient at so many areas of the music business. According to Cody, you cannot cheat and hire out the work you do not want to do or doesn't come easy. Everyone must learn the job before giving it to someone else. Being a musician also meant being able to write, mix, record, manage talent, master, produce, execute contracts, create engaging social media, and more. While Cody is adamant that hard work and a diverse knowledge base are essential, he also described the importance of knowing one's own voice and staying true to what you know.

> When people approach me and want to work with me, I have to be honest with them and myself. If it is not a genre that I know, then it isn't right.

Cody further explained that sometimes artists engage the wrong producer for their work and aesthetic, and the product of that mismatch is often a source of consternation for all involved.

Last, Cody stated that he has worked hard to develop his "critical listening" and states that you can passively listen to music or you can critically listen to music, and those two very different roles have to be defined when working. According to Cody, a critical ear is one of the most difficult things to develop and often the most overlooked. Knowing the sound you want and how to achieve it through mixing and mastering is critical to his work.

Finding His Voice and Niche

Cody defines himself as a producer but also very involved in the contractual and marketing side of the music business. In the beginning of Cody's recording career, he produced for a lot of artists who were just starting out and learning the trade.

> What I learned, though, was my passion—was helping others finding their voice, their sound. I was helping people make beats and helping them with recordings, engineering, mastering.

To find your voice you have to help understand the importance of recording, mixing, mastering and then working on the composition itself. Cody states that without those four components working together you cannot be successful. Your voice, he asserts, is the combination of all those principles, and that is why you have to be a good engineer to be a successful producer. Also, he posits that the best producers have the technical musical training required to help others develop their own style. According to Cody, every musical genre is a language, and we all speak a language to help us connect to those around us. Music is no different; every genre is it is own language, and you have to deeply immerse yourself to understand and make a difference.

Collaboration

For Cody, collaboration is one of the most essential elements of music-making. When he signs an artist, one of the things he looks for is their willingness to respond positively to critique. Furthermore, he states there is a direct correlation between inexperienced musicians and their inability to respond to feedback. The best artists, the ones with the most experience in the studio, seek out advice; they understand the need to get differing opinions. He further states, those kinds of artists walk into a studio with a strong sense of their abilities yet are willing to flex and push themselves to find the new.

> My expertise is working with others to help them understand their brand and to help them find their niche. You have to help them find what works for them, what brings them energy and joy.

For Cody, he begins at the end. He helps artists design their own goals for distribution and performance then helps them identify the road map needed to achieve this goal. Sales and social media presence are of paramount importance to him and to his clients.

The Artist's Mindset

One of the topics Cody spoke about with intensity was the need for music programs in schools. His reasoning for music education was slightly different than what I had heard before. For Cody, music is an emotional outlet and he believes that students need to be taught how to be artists, that music programs should focus on the mental preparation required to express oneself and subsequently the emotional ups and downs and that often follow the creative process. Cody's value of music education focused on providing an outlet for artistic expression, but more importantly emphasizing the sociological and psychological aspects of the creative process. Last, he stated that the best thing we can do for young people is to prepare them for the difficult moments in creating, to help students self-assess and diagnose their frustrations. Cody states that if he had been given these opportunities to be musical and express himself, much of the angst and difficulties he experienced as a teenager could have been avoided.

Connections to Research
Music Education

The three primary themes that emerged from my discussions with Chris and Cody were the importance of critical thinking, collaboration, and role of culture. In this section I connect these themes to work often cited within the music education ecology.

Critical Thinking

Pogonowski (1987) writes that within the musical experience, critical thinkers engage in both cognitive and affective thought processes concurrently in dynamic and unique ways to music. She writes that "critical thinking is the result of experiential learning that embraces the learner's affective and cognitive domains" (p. 34). To further stimulate critical thinking as an active endeavor in the music process, she emphasized the need to highlight experiences in musical expression to connect to making meaning. Pogonowski (1989) further states that the teacher has a critical role in fostering a critical thinking mindset in developing musicians. The call to critical thinking extends into music education associations. For example, the National Association for Music Education has numerous references addressing critical thinking[2] as an important part of the educative process for young people. Duong (2014) questions whether our current music education approach invites critical thinking, and whether we should reconsider teaching practices that enhance the autonomy and decision-making skills of students. Woodford (1996) also highlights the importance of critical thinking, but emphasizes that for critical thinking skills to be reinforced, teachers must make connections across disciplines to inspire students to engage dynamically and differently. Woodford's detailed description of the need to reinforce creative intentions across modalities was certainly mirrored in Chris's approach to creative thinking. Chris described his approach as a curatorial overview that ran through his music, but more importantly through all of his interactions with the arts: design, architecture, cuisine, art, and more. For Cody, critical thinking was described as the important part of what allowed him to gain success as a producer and own his own label. Additionally, his hypercritical approach was noted in all facets of the music business, from songwriting to marketing.

Collaboration

Next, collaboration has been addressed by numerous music education researchers, with numerous studies conducted examining the role of collaboration in the creative process. Some academicians have focused on the ways students collaborate (Wood, 2010), while others have addressed the differences with composing in community or collaborative environments (Younker, 2003; Wiggins & Espeland, 2012). Gaunt and Westerlund (2013) describe the need for music educators to abandon the apprenticeship model of music education often modeled in university settings and call for a reframing of the music education approach that emphasizes collaboration as the most needed and utilized skill for performers and composers. Chris and Cody consistently mentioned the importance of collaboration in their work insisting that fostering a group that works together is the most important thing you can do as a musician or producer. They both spurn the notion of the singular artist working toward creating a successful song and highlight that even the most talented musicians need mixing and masters so their work is received well.

Role of Culture and Identity

Chris's description of his family and his connections to Trinidad are in line with one of the most popular research trends—identity research—in relation to music-making and understanding. Much of the identity research is explicated through a psychological or sociological lens and questions how one's understanding or self-awareness of identity informs their musical selves (Hargreaves, Marshall, & North, 2003). Additionally, there has been extensive research into the role of family in creating and developing a young person's approach to the musical experience (Hargreaves & North, 1999). The various strands of one's interpersonal and intrapersonal life and their relation to the ways they view themselves have become a cornerstone of identity research and are frequently cited throughout music education research literature (Macdonald et al., 2002). For Chris, his early exposure to Caribbean life and music had a profound impact on his value systems as a person and a musician. For Chris, leaving home at an early age and finding what he describes as his "chosen family" allowed him to create an identity with people believed and maintained similar values. For both men, cultures and identity are clearly paramount in their creative lives, and help ground them in every part of the decision-making. Last, this cultural assuredness is what has provided a sense of aesthetic that shapes their music into a sound that is received as authentic and marketable.

SUMMARY

The topics of collaboration, critical thinking, and role of culture in relation to the musical experience are not new to music education academicians. However, perhaps it is time we view these important parts of the creative process not just as ancillary components or soft skills, but rather as essential components required for developing musicians. Chris Leacock's and Cody Colacino's perspectives as highly successful songwriters and producers highlight the skills musicians call upon on a day-to-day basis within the creative experience. So, the question to further ask is, what is the role and responsibility of music educators to help develop and foster these skills? Should music educators focus solely on the technical and leave the other elements of critical thinking and collaboration to students to learn in other ways or other modalities? One could easily state that an educator cannot teach everything required for success, but perhaps we should open the aperture to the ways we approach musical creativity and what is required for success. In the next section, I provide ideas for music educators to consider within their classrooms.

Research to Practice

Collaboration, one of the primary themes among the participants, has already been researched and addressed within music education. Kondo and Wiggins (2019) described the importance of giving the learner agency in the music education classroom while highlighting the importance of group activities when asking students to be creative. For music educators, perhaps an even more systemic change is needed in the classroom to promote collaboration. In a band, orchestra, or chorus class, what would the classroom look like if decision-making and responsibilities for a performance were assigned to students as opposed to be given by the director? The intent would be to not only ask students to draw on their musical abilities and knowledge to help the group, but more importantly, begin the process of encouraging students to work in groups to problem solve issues. Chris and Cody approached the music experience from this perspective: You do what you need to do to get the song recorded and noticed. This type of thinking could be utilized in the classroom as a first step toward creating a classroom culture of personal initiative—a self-starting mindset. Additionally, this type of classroom might create an environment that encourages students to not only accept more agency, but also more risk. Classroom teachers are often heard lamenting the difficulty of getting students to be more creative in the classrooms. One reason for this might be that the classroom is not felt to be a safe place for exploration and play. Collaboration, encouraging students to work together at all facets of the music education experience, could be democratized to help students understand the diversity of knowledge and skills required to see a performance to fruition.

Critical Thinking

Critical thinking was another theme discussed by the participants. For music educators, developing critical thinking and collaboration skills within the classroom should be concurrent. Autonomy and decision-making could be more easily achieved by asking students to work within small groups and engage in group projects outside the norm of performance. Lucy Green (2002) described this combination of critical thinking and collaboration in her study of popular musicians and how they approached musical performance. Green lamented the lack of encouragement of aural imitation, improvisation, and experimentation, as well as commitment and passion, in most music education classrooms. She calls for music educators to engage students in ways that promote more social and dynamic play, and to watch how popular musicians gain musical insight. She further described how some ensemble directors intentionally removed themselves from the classroom and required students to figure out how to play a song in small groups. As a music teacher-educator working in the academy, I have adopted this strategy almost every year within a methods course. Every year, the students would all agree that the week I placed them in small groups and insisted they work together to figure out how to play a song was the most impactful part of the seminar. Even for college music majors, the act of being told to learn a song, and not from a conductor or a given methodology, was jarring. Perhaps it is time for music educators to reconsider the method book approach that has made some facets of music teaching easier, and adopt a more dynamic and open-framed view of their classrooms. This paper is far from the first call for more inclusive curricula in music education classrooms, but Chris and Cody's stories as highly successful musicians continue to add to the growing body of evidence that suggest music education should change.

At many higher education institutions, there is a growing trend to include entrepreneurial classes in the curriculum to help students prepare for future careers and to open their minds to different possibilities for arts engagement. This type of reframing needs to occur in the music education field as well. It is time music educators address what many of these institutions already know: the world is changing fast, and to adapt, a major curricular overhaul is required. Music teachers must go beyond ancillary approaches to composition and creativity and adjust their teaching to help students adapt to changes and expectations occurring in the field. By observing the stories of Chris Leacock and

Cody Colacino, it is obvious that the role of formative musical training and exposure is important, but there are ways we can further help music students evolve musically and creatively.

Notes

1. https://www.insidehighered.com/news/2020/08/07/music-theory-journal-criticized-symposium-supposed-white-supremacist-theorist
2. See https://nafme.org for resources connecting critical thinking and music education

References

Duong, T. M. (2014). EFL teachers' perceptions of learner autonomy and their classroom practices: A case study. *International Journal of Education and Management Engineering, 4*(2), 9–17.

Gaunt, H. & Westerlund, H. (2013). *Collaborative learning in music education*. Routledge.

Green, L. (2002). *How popular musicians learn: A way ahead for music education*. Routledge.

Hargreaves, D. J. & North, A. C. (1999). The functions of music in everyday life: redefining the social in music psychology. *Psychology of Music, 27*, 71–83.

Hargreaves, D. J., Marshall, N. & North, A. C. (2003). Music education in the 21st century: A psychological perspective. *British Journal of Music Education, 20*, 1–17.

Kondo, S., & Wiggins, J. (2019). Learner agency in musical creative process and learning. In Tsubonou, Y., Tan, A.-G., & Oie, M. (Eds.), *Creativity in music education* (pp. 17–33). Springer Nature Singapore.

Macdonald, R. A. R., Hargreaves, D. J., & Miell, D. E. (Eds.). (2002). *Musical identities*. Oxford University Press.

Pogonowski, L. (1987). Developing skills in critical thinking and problem solving. *Music Educators Journal, 73*(6), 37–41.

Pogonowski, L. (1989). Critical thinking and music listening. *Music Educators Journal, 76*(1), 35–38.

Wiggins, J., & Espeland, M. I. (2012). Creating in music learning contexts. In G. E. McPherson, & G. F. Welch (Eds.), *Oxford handbook of music education*, Vol. 1, (pp. 341–360). Oxford University Press.

Wood, E. (2010). Developing integrated pedagogical approaches to play and learning. In P. Broadhead, J. Howard, & E. Wood (Eds.), *Play and learning in the early years: From research to practice* (pp. 9–26). Sage.

Woodford, P. (1996). Developing critical thinkers. *Music Educators Journal, 83*(1), 27–32.

Younker, B. A. (2003). The nature of feedback in a community of composing. In M. Hickey (Ed.), *Why and how to teach music composition: A new horizon for music education* (pp. 233–242). MENC: The National Association for Music Education.

CHAPTER 12

··

COMPOSITIONAL
IDEA SELECTION AND
DEVELOPMENT

··

LISA A. CRAWFORD

ALL children can compose music. Some seem naturally inclined to compose, with and without invitation from music teachers; some only respond to opportunities to compose in class. A student may feel surprised to discover that they can sing a song they have written, or that they can compose a piece that others enjoy hearing or performing. Students enjoy working together in groups to create music and write songs with themes of social justice, personal experiences, and humor. Presenting work to peers can provide inspiration. This chapter presents a philosophy for placing music composition at the forefront of music teaching and learning.

For educators, idea generation, idea selection, and idea development are organizational parts of the musical knowledge-building process. Generation and selection of ideas come from an educator's experiences, training, and style of approach. Idea development comes from the strength of original ideas, experience of student response, and reorganizing expectations of students' interests and capabilities. Re-generation, re-selection, and re-development are also integral parts of this process for educators as extension and revision.

Hickey (2003 & 2012), Webster (1977, 1987, & 1988), and Kaschub (2009) present compelling ideas for teaching music composition in K–12 classrooms. While research has not extensively considered compositional idea selection and development, there are useful articles about "creative music" with young children from the early and mid-20th century (Coleman, 1922; see also Volk, 1996; Snyder, 1957; and Pierce, 1959). These authors present good ideas for music educators in presenting opportunities for students to compose.

More recently, music education scholars continue to write about creating music with K–12 students (Barrett, 1995, 1996, 2006, & 2012; Glover, 2002; Hickey, 1999, 2003, & 2013; Kaschub & Smith, 2009; Kratus, 1989; Paynter, 2000; Upitis, 1989 & 1990, and 1992;

Staufer, 2002; Webster, 2012 & 2013; and Wiggins, 1990, 2005, & 2007). Studies have been developed for band directors (Koops & Whitener, 2020), orchestra ensembles (Love & Barrett, 2019), choir directors (Childs et al., 2007; Mulholland & Walker, 2007), and elementary-level general music (Kaschub & Smith, 2013). Research supports working at all levels with popular music (Smith et al., 2016), jazz (Sarath, 2013), rock music (Little Kids Rock, 2017), and technology and music production (Freedman, 2013; Oswinsky, 2017; Ruthmann & Mantie, 2017; Williams & Webster, 2002, 2020, 2022; Wise, 2016). International support of these from the National Association for Music Education (2014), South African Department of Basic Education (de Villiers, 2015), The Arts—Australian Curriculum (2020) and England Department for Education (2021) have renewed and updated music education standards that include application for music composition.

Compositional idea selection and development across the music teaching and learning landscape may find materials written for educators of all musical subjects, grade levels, and musical disciplines (Webster, 2016a, 2016b). Extending beyond the Western canon, resources for working compositionally with young students may be found about integrating popular music (Waksman and Bennett, 2014): new journals, for example, *Journal of Popular Music Education* (Intellect Books, 2021); dissertations focusing on composition through group work in elementary and secondary classrooms with technology (Crawford, 2016; Preston, 2010); and articles about songwriting for student teachers working with K–12 students (Kratus, 2013). Additionally, digital applications early musical learners, such as Chrome Music Lab, Musicfirst (Noteflight, and Soundtrap), and industry-standard music production software such as ProTools, Logic, Bandlab, and others have influenced deeper understanding from perspectives such as equipment, or "gear" basics, to composing with digital devices, and issues of compositional devices and style (Tobias, 2017).

Inclusion of composition in music education for some may be challenged by dis-comfort or perceived elements of "time." Crawford (2004) completed a national survey of music education professors finding that 1) time, 2) focus on Western ensembles and performance, and 3) relatively limited experience with presenting compositional lesson plans are the primary reasons for not presenting opportunities to compose with students. Students in college environments may also feel challenged, as identified in Dammers' (2007) study considering composing during band. Here, students' compositional output and understanding of their project seemed limited. Ackles (2018) has written about creating opportunities for students to think and respond musically (p. 34), student-centered music education. I communicate frequently that I am not the "boss," that I am not a judge, that students are the creators who make choices and decisions I could never think of. Student-centered education where self-assessment is part of the educational process is well-supported through beginning with composition in music teaching and learning.

These many studies have set the stage for this chapter by advancing discussion toward specific goals and objectives leading to compositional idea selection and development for creating and composition projects with students. It is promising, with certain effort, that the challenges music educators may experience when first interested in composing with K–12 or tertiary environments can be eliminated. Project ideas provided in this chapter are available to try and then expand. Your personal experience and creative ideas will go a long way to formulate, extend, and further develop composition experiences for your students that may be shared with other music educators. Composition ideas presented here will transfer to any group of students, no matter a student's age, musical interests, instrument, ability level, or past musical experience.

Beginning with Composing

Educator Focus: Musical Experience Transfer

Scholars continue to look deeply at early musical experience of students. However, deeper reflection on *educators'* personal musical beginnings may play a vital role in teaching young students how to compose music. Personally, as a child of six, while mystified by it at first, I experienced a natural unfolding of myself as a musician when I started to create my own music, and I tried it repeatedly to see if the new musical ideas would continue to happen. They did. My personal world as a young musician was to begin chording on my music educator father's piano at the age of three, then to begin composing about two years into my piano lessons, develop a relationship with performance, that was less than comfortable, all during my K–12 education. I taught piano and composition privately beginning at the age of 12 and my early career in the music industry included composing and producing music. These experiences are not excluded from my current teaching, and in fact, support it. I am genuinely driven to learn about music educators' experiences though my workshops, sessions, and scholarly work because of my personal beginnings with music.

Beginning creating and composition is less related to age or musical knowledge, and more related to the shift we may choose to make toward music teaching and learning through creating and composition. As students work together independently or in groups, aspects of this idea include knowing "who is in the room," the relationships students share in groups, and the balance of their ability to move forward with creating and composing that evolves for each student individually. Music teaching and learning can begin with composing through presentation of introductory musical concepts, for example, rhythm, and introduction to various types of notation, invented and Western, as students learn about rhythm through creating it. Development of template outlines that may inspire students to innovate creative work through extensions of their *own* idea selection and development is effective as inspiration arrives in different moments and for different reasons. As music teaching and learning includes opportunities to explore working together, students may work both independently and in groups to discover their composing selves. Students may be invited to present everything they compose to build their experience of personal confidence, whether it is rhythms and drumming or a piece for mariachi band also independently or in groups.

The route to completing compositional projects is most often developed through extensions of initial ideas such as adding more challenge to material, inclusion of technology and development of music production skills, through positive critique from other students, and finally, presentation of all compositions for each other in class or for school and community events. Revision most frequently comes through "next projects" to support students' process and moving specific elements of the product they create forward. If the outline for each composition project is met, students' compositional work can receive full points and students move forward with a feeling of success in the social classroom environment.

Social-emotional aspects of learning are primary to creative and composition projects. Students' feelings expressed through educator questions and comments can be checked consistently throughout students' process. Students experience anxiety at times when beginning creative projects, but more often "flow," and excitement that builds—in reality, sometimes slowly, but sometimes also very quickly, in my observations, are more frequent. Differing experiences of students (private lessons, performance, music production, and technology) also augment classroom dynamics and outcomes of completed projects as well as lead to next projects. Listening to the ideas of everyone in the room is essential and creating a cohesive atmosphere is fundamental. Through all of this, composing becomes a favored music experience for students, with and without technology.

Personalities of Young Composers

Students offer surprises with their compositional ideas and over time I have considered students, both K–12 and university level, from a variety of composing personality types. It is important to understand students' compositional perspective when providing creative opportunities. Overall, the expression or intuitive recognition of children's *feelings* holds the greatest importance when beginning with composing. Part of a music educator's work is learning about interest held by students for writing music of their own.

Consistently asking students questions about their thinking may create new ideas and new development, the ideas of which can be examined, shifted, reimagined, and built upon throughout your process. And yet, reflections on observations of music educators' *understanding* of what children are experiencing during creating and composition remains limited. While it is through their abundant communication that my conceptualization of idea selection and development has been assembled and developed over time, to both students and educators, my gratitude is highlighted (see Figure 12.1).

The *Crawford Conceptual Framework of Musical Productivity: Types of Young Composers* (Crawford, 2016) considers student productivity. Students 1) with little or no interest in composing, 2) who may enjoy composing projects but exhibit no further

Crawford Conceptual Framework of Musical Productivity

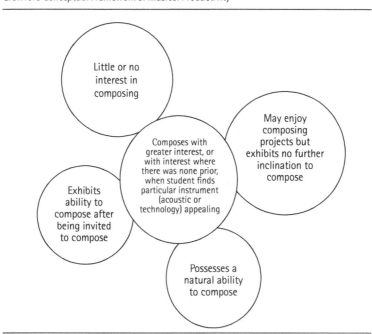

FIGURE 12.1. Crawford conceptual framework of musical productivity: Types of young composers

inclination to compose, 3) who exhibit ability to compose after having been invited to do so, 4) who compose with greater interest, or where there was none prior, when student finds a particular instrument (acoustic or technology) appealing, and 5) who possesses a natural ability to compose may be grouped to support clearer thinking for teachers. An aspect of awareness of young composer characterization is that each of these young composer "types" appear at the same time, in the same class, and compositional teaching and learning still happens.

In other words, during compositional work, a place is created for everyone in the room no matter who is in the room. All student personality types work together. As well, students' ability for writing text or lyrics may be unseen, and when visibility is created, there comes a realization that everyone has different areas of expression and realization may be brand new. As an example of 3), 4), or 5) in the framework above, suddenly, one group has the text for a remarkable new song related to social justice.

Educators may be able to add to this framework from earned experience. As an example, students may use music they find on the internet for a piece they are creating even though they are aware they are to create original music. What about the student who never discusses in my surveys their private lesson experience and composes music similar to genres from the pieces they learn through private lessons? That may be yet another group.

Compositional Devices: Idea Selection through Compositional Elements

Digital options provide engaging ways for students to learn Western notation, listening examples of major and minor intervals and triads, and other elements of music theory. However, the work of creating and composition is related to direct experience of "doing." We work with compositional elements that may otherwise be overlooked when approaching compositional work that has premium effectiveness for inspiring learning about not only notation, but elements of music theory through how a young composer wants something to sound. I identify these for students through a digital handout titled, "Sequence," with a staff for trying each idea next to each element (see Figure 12.2).

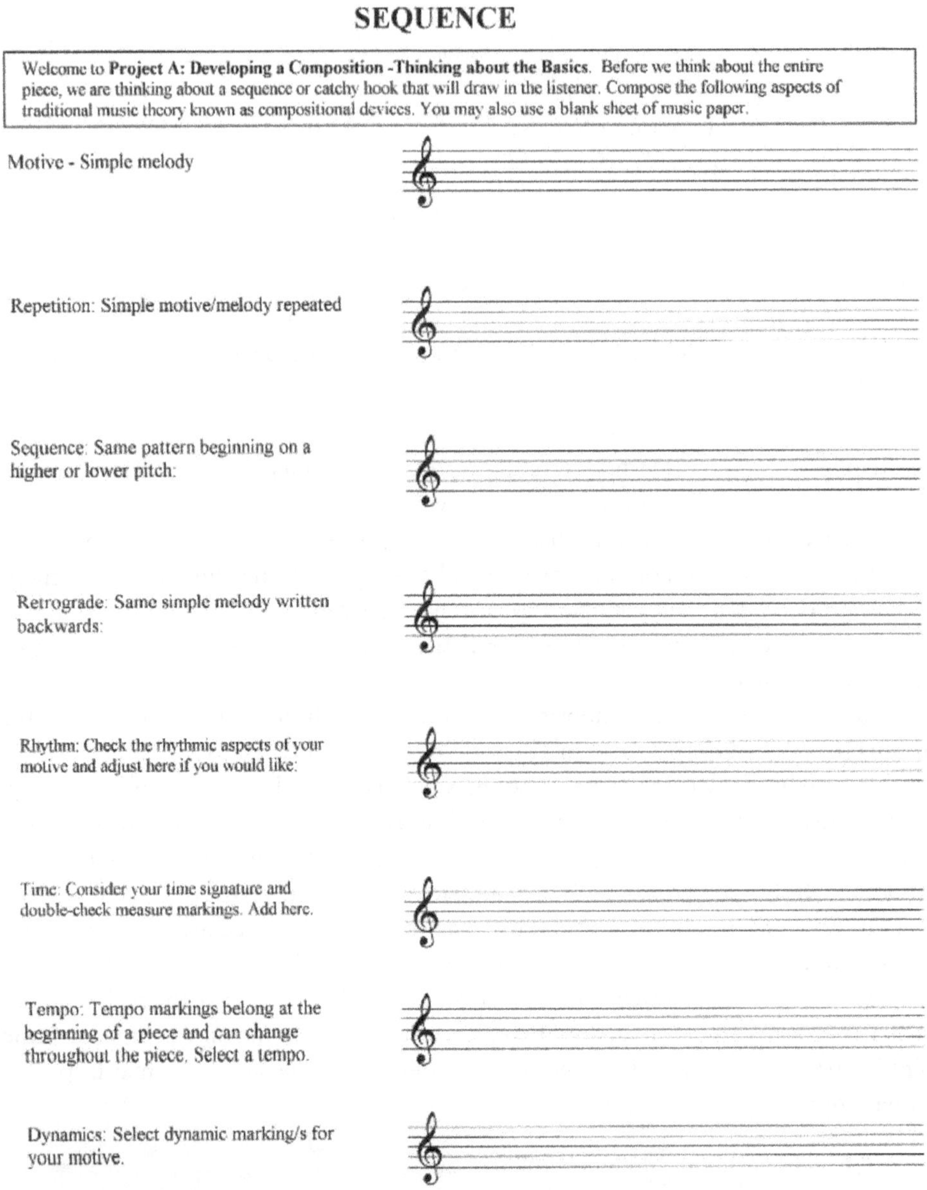

SEQUENCE

Welcome to **Project A: Developing a Composition -Thinking about the Basics**. Before we think about the entire piece, we are thinking about a sequence or catchy hook that will draw in the listener. Compose the following aspects of traditional music theory known as compositional devices. You may also use a blank sheet of music paper.

Motive - Simple melody

Repetition: Simple motive/melody repeated

Sequence: Same pattern beginning on a higher or lower pitch:

Retrograde: Same simple melody written backwards:

Rhythm: Check the rhythmic aspects of your motive and adjust here if you would like:

Time: Consider your time signature and double-check measure markings. Add here.

Tempo: Tempo markings belong at the beginning of a piece and can change throughout the piece. Select a tempo.

Dynamics: Select dynamic marking/s for your motive.

FIGURE 12.2. Sequence

Idea selection is a careful process. Your project ideas may be selected through your belief that you, as the teacher, know what will come next. This has rarely happened for me. Additionally, my ideas are merely a starting point. Educators have toolkits. Mine includes several headliner projects—the ones I have found that students absolutely love to compose and develop. These include *Box Comps, Birds on a Wire, Imagine Writing a Song about Social Justice, Composer Pauline Oliveros and Deep Listening, Composing without Melody, Happy Sappy Theme: Where Am I?*, and *Suspense Film Intro*. One capstone project I use is creating a video that uses a student/group-written script and added music. Generally, this is not a music video for a song. It is from these ideas that other projects often develop.

Considering a way of evaluating student work, two rubrics are included. I maintain awareness of rubrics however I find that observation of student process is what matters most to me. The first (see Figure 12.3) can be used as a potential outline for music educators to focus on compositional aspects and develop different points of view than mine.

Introductory	Intermediate	Advanced
Listening: Black Violin; John Cage; Pauline Oliveros; OkGo; Alma Deutscher; Young Mozart	Listening: Tin Pan Alley; You Smile in My Head; OkGo; Student compositions	Listening: Jazz; Beginning of Each Century Unit; Contemporary Music of Each Century Unit; Avenue Q
Discussion: What do you picture when thinking of the word "composer"; Does music require melody? Why or why not?; What music have you created?	Discussion: What do you picture when thinking of yourself as a composer?	Discussion: What do you picture when you think of your peers as composers?
Composition Units: Invented Notation-Box Comps; Deep Listening; Indigenous Cultures; World Music; Child Composers; Birds on a Wire; Braille Music; Compositional Elements	Composition Units: Box Comps Review; Composing Without Melody; Songwriting; Script Development; Compositional Elements 2	Compose Music for Short Script (Sound designs, Songs, Cues); Capstone Project
Technology: Exploratorium: Science of Music; Chrome Music Lab; Noteflight Introduction; Soundtrap Introduction	Technology: External sounds imported into cloud software tracks; Developing your ears as a producer of music through effects; Create Video-Add Music & Spoken Text;	Technology: Theater/Music; VR/Music; Album Development; Music Video
Reading, Writing, Music Theory, Music History: Notation Types; Indigenous Map Projects; Essay Projects; Form for Hip Hop and Popular Music; Major-Minor Ear Training; Interval & Triad types, Intro to Theme through Underscoring for Video	Reading, Writing, Music Theory, Music History: Form-Comparing Songs and Compositions; Development of Theme	Reading, Writing, Music Theory, Music History: Script writing; Thematic considerations;

FIGURE 12.3. Curriculum overview: Introductory–Intermediate–Advanced

Music educators may wish to analyze and evaluate compositional work through a lens of groups of students who work together (see Figure 12.4). This rubric is an index that considers the work students accomplish when composing together and accounts for the unexpected and the unforeseen, focusing less on final notes but more on the work process of students. The index also places value on the formidable musical experience of individual teachers.

PROCESS & PRODUCT RUBRIC	Beginning Learner	Developing Learner	Proficient Learner	Advanced Learner
Melodic Content				
Use of Compositional Devices				
Originality				
Collaboration: Interaction, Communication, Product Completion				
Creative Process & Innovation				

FIGURE 12.4. Evaluation rubric for composing

Student Focus: Idea Selection

The basics of being human are found in every music classroom. Students emerge with ego and competitive feelings as composing experience grows and perhaps receives consecutive and resounding positive feedback about creative projects. This is where the "work" of including creating and composition in the classroom begins. For example, students (age 12) may say to their group, "but I'm the one who has production experience so listen to me." Again, development of compositional projects occurs because of who is in the room, personal interests of students, proclivities students hold for acoustic instruments or technology, and competition. As students learn about the projects completed by older students, their focus toward outcome may override their process, which returns us to the most important objective of compositional work—ensuring the aspect of "process" through communication, both personally and musical, as the strongest outcome for students through compositional teaching.

Following the introduction of a new project, students complete composition assignments by a deadline and present their compositions in class. Students give positive critique following in-class presentations in response to hearing their peers' compositions. In this formal presentation, students identify ideas they have used for the development of the composition or creative project. Also requested through the presentation is, "Tell us about the effects you developed. What do you appreciate about the voices you selected?" "What might be improved for this composition?" or "What do you find remarkable about your composition?" As students set and follow through with basic norms, learning about compositional devices, and values of giving positive comments to others, their ability to give positive critique for peers becomes extraordinarily strong. What students learn from their own experiences of "receiving" that support from others is imperative. Students become comfortable speaking without being called upon, even in introductory courses, less related to a student's grade or fear of not giving responses, but because of the learned feel-good elements of providing positive musical feedback to another student about their compositional work.

Ability to present well is an important skill development area through compositional music teaching and learning. Throughout a class, students discuss the social-emotional values of preparing and presenting compositions. Beginning a presentation with the words "so," "uhm," or "well" sends the student back to restarting the presentation. A student's ability to craft these presentations becomes extraordinarily strong by the end of a course of study. Students' ability to discuss the details of their work in front of others also strengthens remarkably student understanding of music. While positive critique from the class develops self-appreciation, discussions develop about how all humans must learn how to manage nerves and, although not novel for music educators, the more we practice something with frequency, the better we may do it. Leadership and knowledge-building becomes evidentiary through the practice of presentation.

Again, early compositional learning environments, when well presented, establish a place for every student. As development of identity becomes more visible and students learn more about the basics of kindness to themselves and others, students also learn about checking aggrandizement at the door, yet bringing their self-love. Solid preparational teaching, time given during class to compose, personal time wherein students may decide they want to spend more time composing, and that final step where all compositions are presented in class to receive a grade are interdependent. Grades are given for meeting the requirements outlined for a project and the presentation of it, but instead of being based on qualities of a creative work, my grading is most often found in a student's reflection on feedback given and discussion about a completed composition with peers as each composition must be presented to the class with three feedback comments given by other students.

Developmental Aspects of Ideas for Composition Projects

In the classroom, we utilize both group projects as well as independent work using both teacher- and self-selected groups. Over time, students appreciate thematic work that is clear and well-constructed. Discussions related to a variety of ethnic and world music pedagogies, cultural exchange in class, and development of how these relate to everyone consider that creativity is the development of something new. For example, much of the listening in my elementary classes are found on the *Smithsonian Folkways Recordings*. John Cage's *4'33"*, Black Violin's *Showoff*, and Pauline Oliveros's *Deep Listening*, are included as listening examples at the secondary level, plus a fantastic array of many composers who have tried "something new," or who have become well known for innovative compositional elements that broke barriers of one or all of many types—cultural, melody and harmony, voicings, style, and innumerable other musical elements. Students become skilled at discussion of these.

Methods for developing, using, and expanding your creating and composition curriculum are similar to other musical areas yet, unlike teaching a simple song, the development of each section for classes or ensembles may be different every time. While important to keep future coursework in mind, there may be 1) overlaps (back and forth) of your presentations due to less experienced students, 2) fewer or greater numbers of more advanced students in a class that shift the timbre of all of your lessons, 3) greater numbers of less musically-experienced students that shift lessons entirely, and, 4) less interested or more deeply interested students in compositional learning that change the landscape for the whole class. Your way of extending or transferring music teaching and learning becomes significant in this area (see Figure 12.5).

Beginning	Use any of the sections of an introductory music cloud app selected to introduce creating
Completion	Students present projects with a description of what is included in their "creation". Students respond with positive critique. Revision is used only when the foundational instructions are incomplete. Teacher response may be given but the importance of it is reduced purposefully. Students' personal ideas are not "judged" by the teacher but by their following the template and personal feeling about their creativity/composition.
Extension 1	Extension 1 invites students to resume a piece or begin a new one that does something different because of the technology itself, i.e., effects, instrument choices, and/or sequential revisions
Extension 2	Extension 2 invites students to consider how others may perform the new composition. This may mean students (having used box comps) may create graphic notation or use Western notation to communicate with performers.

FIGURE 12.5. Extending beginning compositional experience with music apps

Standardization of foundational specifics of the composition projects (lesson plans) presented works well as these can present starting places that easily open up for students more than originally designed or in ways only the composer will think of. This is as much uniformity as there may ever be in my development of compositional assignments. As well, if challenged, students may adjust their process while still meeting the template overview for the project (see Figure 12.6).

Having identified many aspects of classroom presentation, creative and compositional projects are not random or developed from a "whatever happens" perspective. An educator's availability for each student through completion of a creative music

Crawford Index of Quality for Composing Groups (CIQCG)					
Process Scoring Rubric for Composing Groups	**1**	**2**	**3**	**4**	**5**
Interaction	Group is challenged by working together and may not overcome the challenge. (1)	Group is challenged by working together but may overcome the challenge at times. (2)	Group is able to work together and even if challenged at times, they improve over time. (3)	Group works together well and experience few challenges. (4)	Group works together in a unique way that supports successful outcome of the composition. (5)
Communication	Communication techniques are not improved over the course of the project. (1)	Communication techniques are somewhat developed over the course of the project. (2)	Communication techniques are improved over the course of the project. (3)	Communication techniques work well amongst most/all members of the group and support development of a strong project with rehearsal and revision of the project. (4)	Communication techniques are at a high level and rehearsal, revision, rehearsal, additional revisions are unchallenging. (5)
Leadership/ Innovation	Leadership remains unexplored generally by this group. (1)	Leadership is explored but at a low level. (2)	Leadership is found in at least one member of the group and group effort and project development are improved because of this. (3)	Leadership is explored well by more than one member of the group; group effort and project development are high because of this. (4)	Leadership is explored well by each/most members of the group; group effort and project development are at highest level. (5)
Creative Process	Creativity is limited or missing from the group effort and in their project development. (1)	Creativity is found at times in group effort and/or in project development. (2)	Creativity is found in group effort and/or in project development. (3)	Creativity is evidenced through working relationships and process. (4)	Creativity is evidenced through working relationships, process and final product. (5)
Product Completion	Composition remains incomplete or brief. (1)	Composition is incomplete or complete but brief. (2)	Composition is nearly completed or is completed for this project. (3)	Composition is complete or completed for this project. (4)	Composition is completed and perhaps additional work is begun. (5)
(Scoring note: Scores may be produced by following each column for one overall score, or, one section from any column (totaling five) may be selected with score noted in parentheses.)					

(Crawford, 2016)

FIGURE 12.6. Crawford Index of Quality for Composing in Groups assignment is important to student process. As projects become more extensive, or students begin to compose independently with greater frequency, learned student follow-through becomes something that may be transferred throughout other academic work.

One of my favorite introductory creative music projects is "Box Comps" (shortened from Box Compositions). These are simply empty boxes in 1 x 4, 2 x 4, or 4 x 4 format. You also may wish to model box comps found in *Voiceworks: A Handbook for Singing* (Hunt, 2001). Box Comps support integrating student learning of graphic, iconic, and Western notation, including note values (perhaps one beat per square), time signatures, and beginning ensemble performance where students eventually may choose to perform more than one part simultaneously. Students may initially choose body percussion, found objects, use of text and vocal sounds, and world instruments. Students may eventually develop thematic sequences. Students create a "key" to guide classroom peers as a map for the performance of Box Comps. Teachers support further development of parts with added boxes (see Figure 12.7). Students will stop anything and everything to do the next Box Comp, perform them, or listen to another group Box Comp creation.

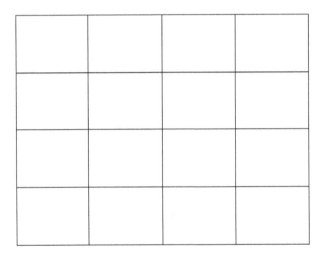

FIGURE 12.7. Box Comp

Through creating and composition projects, music educators train ears! Suggesting that silence is an important aspect of music assists with creating atmosphere in a piece rather than simple sounds. Complete projects may be recorded as they are performed and highlight the outcomes of learning what a beat is, singing, playing drums and handheld instruments, arranging, listening, revision, and overall, communication.

Develop next composition projects based upon who is in the room, with careful observation of new ideas and discussion that have just occurred. Teaching about compositional devices throughout your curriculum leads to expanding your project ideas and introduction of motive, sequence, dynamics, tempo, and form. Taking careful note of each student's process,

Composing with Technology

Creating and composition pedagogy can include technology and advance understanding of compositional devices, notation applications, digital audio workstations, pad controller devices, and software and production experience. This relies on building students' capacity for inquiry. In order to begin students' use of these tools, I invite them to explore cloud applications that are fun to use. More importantly, offering introductory support highlighting appreciation for inquiry ("figuring stuff out yourself as you would your video games") assists with engagement when learning about technology. As well, enter here the familiar feeling of nerves when students are new to working with technology.

Exploration is a keyword for the experience of learning about music composition while developing capacity for working toward completion of technology-based projects. Several cloud applications (Exploratorium, Chrome Music Lab, Learning Music-Ableton, GarageBand, Soundation, Musicfirst Soundtrap, and BandLab) are wonderful for introduction and may be used to start conversations throughout compositional experience. Students may work with any one of the above examples and sometimes may consider that there are relatively few areas in their experience that actually support their knowing what they are doing. This exploration creates a wonderful beginning place for creating and composition learning. While other internet applications may be used for preparatory work, my appreciation for Soundtrap has to do with its similar setup to ProTools, a digital audio workstation (DAW). While the exploration students initially complete with the use of pre-made loops, my concern is that these may challenge composing development for some students (see Figure 12.8)

Learning about music composition begins independently of Western notation. In my forthcoming curriculum, we listen to music or songs that have created change, for countless reasons, at introductory, intermediate, and advanced levels. There are numerous ideas for developing musicality without relying on Western ensembles. In fact, the more I work compositionally with students, the more I see that the road to "getting there" is not about arriving to knowledge of facts about the history or theory of music, but inspiration, what lights imagination, joy that can be found in learning about music around the world, from all cultures, of styles unlike one another, and finding what a student may wish to say with music that is of their own voice, created by individuals or groups of students. This is the foundation of my approach to beginning music teaching and learning with composition.

Ideas for educators primarily reflect a "work with what sticks" approach as "time" can work against me, too, even when classes are fundamentally focused toward composing. Students work in groups to rehearse before performing them in class. Because performance of compositions is a strong aspect of this curriculum, performance of original works is a fun way to begin work with groups of four, and maybe more, students. As composers, we are communicators, and therefore the process of creating the key and titling the piece, adding the names of the composer or a group of composers, and performance, are all aspects of introductory assignments. There are endless extensions for

Creating & Composition Project	Idea (Template Overview)	Development (Extension)
Box Comps	Teacher modeling: Perform two examples of box comp pieces using examples found in *Voiceworks: A Handbook for Singing, Bk. 1 and 2*, Hunt, P. (2001). Note: Modeling is less utilized in my teaching for student creativity. Use paper or digital handout of 4x4 boxes to invent graphic notation and performance key. Box Comps create an interactive rhythm or an atmosphere that an audience will be able to recognize. Perform Box Comp as group or independently.	Invite others to perform your Box Comp. Discuss what was successful. What needs more refinement to communicate your ideas more fully?
Drumming Circle- Arranging Rhythms	As a class, create six 8-measure rhythms together for each group. These will repeat during performance Design what instruments (pitched and non-pitched instruments (drums, world instruments) will be used for each part Select student groups for the six rhythms Introduction-A-B-A-B-C-Ending Rehearse arrangement, revise, rehearse, perform	Select a student to conduct this piece and perform live Video a performance of this piece Understand interlocking rhythms and consider adding sections utilizing these
Spoken Poem with Composition - Video	Students write a four-verse poem (may have longer length) Students compose underscoring to support poem Videotape performance Share with school event	Notate the score you compose for your poem Identify voices first (choral, instrumental) Create a score that is publish-ready
Imagine Writing a Song about Social Justice	Share song *Imagine* (John Lennon; Pentatonix) As a class, find words to describe our world, ending homelessness, ending racism and add to a list accessible to everyone Work in self- or teacher-selected groups to write text related to issues of social justice Share text in class (1st draft) before continuing process of adding music Work with digital audio workstation or cloud applications to create music (I use this project as an introductory project after first time logging in to MusicFirst) Work with groups to ensure they have needed support for developing compositions	Students can be invited to consider that writing a song has to do with the feeling developed between both text and music Invite students to work with instruments that they already play and write text at the same time as "feeling" the music Add effects to the music to create atmosphere for the music overall Audiences, or listeners of music, find certain aspects of songs that make them want to listen over and over. Where is your hook? "Feel" your music in order to write unique aspects of verse, chorus, bridge, and hooks that make listeners want to hear something over and over again

FIGURE 12.8. Idea selection and project development examples

Birds on a Wire	Through whatever the length of time I work with students, they are invited to consider that not all music must have melody but can have other elements such as repeating sounds that make listening a remarkable experience. Students review photos of birds on a wire Students may take pictures of birds on a wire and share with class Using a cloud application for Western notation, notate the pitches as seen in a photo of birds on a wire	Share the video "Birds on a Wire – For the Birds" Study this video: Ask students to watch a second time listening for all of the sound effects; watch again without sound; listen without seeing video; invite comments about what students have discovered about sound and music in film
Composer Pauline Oliveros & Deep Listening	Review the bio of composer Dr. Pauline Oliveros. Highlight for students what is of interest to you Discuss the types of music she composed (electronic music over fifty years) and listen to three pieces you find that are different I use *Panaiotis*-Deep Listening and ask students to spend time with the recording over a period of a week Using a DAW of any type (cloud-based, keyboard, or program) students work independently to develop a composition without melody This composition may have form but I don't require it Presentation in class of composition with clear overview given of how student composed the piece Potential teacher questions for students: 1. Tell us how you developed the atmosphere of your piece 2. Tell us what you visualized during your composing process 3. (Related to aspect of the composition) How did you select [aspect] as your main theme without melody? 4. Tell us about the external sounds you selected 5. What added effects did you use for external tracks	Students may be assigned the task of learning four details about Dr. Oliveros separate from music Students record an external sound and import into DAW as a track External sounds (vocal/instrumental) may have effects added
Composing With or Without Melody, Underscoring for a Video about Animals in Nature	Select two or three videos that students may choose from to add instrumental underscoring Students will learn how to remove sound from an already produced video through importing into a video editing application Student selects section of video to add underscoring Student sets up timing for underscoring segments Student understand that music is not required for every second of a video; teach about musical silence Student adds music to sections of video to support activity of video	Student creates video of animal/s in nature Student adds music and edits with formal introduction and closing; melody or sound effect and effects on sound Independent and student groups shift outcomes Can be capstone project for groups

FIGURE 12.8. Continued

Happy Sappy Theme: Where Am I?	Students compose music with an "over-the-top" happy feel yet must directly communicate a place in the world Must be :30 length in order to demonstrate student can utilize application for timings Student composed interesting element that listener first hears and must repeat again in the work Student may not use loops May manipulate sounds found in sound bank	Students may record external sounds and upload into tracks
You Smile in My Head	Introduction to Western notation through cloud app or notation software Student transcribes 4–8 measures of notation given digitally into notation application or software Student adds harmony to first voice Presents to class Student reviews You Smile in My Head and adds one voice and percussion in notation application or software	Student adds greater number of tracks to piece Student records several voices singing You Smile in My Head externally and imports into DAW Student mixes tracks Presents in class
Suspense Film Intro	Students create a sound design that might be used to introduce a suspense film Student-selected length Variations of sounds but may not use loops Greater use of effects for this project	External sounds imported into track/s
QR Codes & My Composition	Using QR coding application, students learn how to integrate MP3 into a QR code Student learns how to place link into website Student learns how to print out a QR code or share a QR code	Student learns how to create materials for sharing QR codes Student presents QR code in performance space
Capstone Video with Script and Music	Students may work independently, with a partner, or in groups Student/s write a script about one of five areas provided by teacher (I like "humor", but there are many) – Turn in for review Student/s video their performance of script (may be completed in sections and edited later) Student/s create edited version of video Student composes 8 measures of pitches/notes – May use two staves only – Notate both voices (also referred to as parts) – Upload into DAW as one track Title project Student/s use variations of sounds and must meet 1:30 length requirement Student/s develop and mix score (underscoring, composition, song) in DAW Student/s edit music with video in video editing application Presentation in class	

FIGURE 12.8. Continued

compositional assignments as music educators observe where transfer may be made for students. As we want "flow" to be part of each assignment undertaken, movement between all projects is most well-received when it feels seamless to students. Goals include students looking forward to coming back to class for more compositional experience, developing an interest in doing it in their own time, and presenting compositions through school and community programming.

Early in compositional work, I invite students to compose without melody (Cage, Oliveros are two of our favorites for listening) and there is great response from students reviewing old videos of John Cage's *Water Walk* or *4′33″*. As students gain experience, there are many experimental and 'new music' composers to choose from through global repertoire. Smithsonian Folkways Recordings, Black Violin, OKGo, the Piano Guys, and Alma Deutscher have been well-received resources; no matter the examples you select for your students, the purpose is to inspire curiosity, culturally relevant and responsive music teaching and learning, and creative thinking.

Inspiration: The Feelings of Children as Composers

We listen closely for responsiveness of students in music education. We may find creativity that is cultural, social-emotional, demonstrates musical knowledge, and shares performance capacities. As a kid, I did not know that most kids feel the same way I did about being visible as young students and even adults must work to improve their experience of performing an original work, singing, or playing an instrument. Perhaps there was limited instruction about how to work with nerves. This is an important element of providing opportunities to compose. Over the years, I have not found much difference amongst students of any age responding to my questions about performance of their compositions. Children communicate what they think and feel about aspects of musical performance of their own work with responses most often identifying increased comfort over time. Noteworthy is that tertiary students are sometimes less certain of their ability to compose than elementary students. Shifts may come after having experienced varied opportunities to compose.

Observing student experiences when composing is a remarkable aspect of my own learning experience. When students are invited to communicate about their creative work, they communicate their feelings. Determining how students feel about their creative work is important to me, enough so that I ask students to communicate.

When music educators are invited to communicate about their thoughts and experiences about teaching creative work in my workshops and sessions, they communicate their own feelings and also often communicate about the feelings of their students. This is the aspect of working compositionally with educators I might love the most. I pose similar questions to most groups of educators I work with and responses that are offered with considerable frequency. Figure 12.9 offers a brief set of student comments representative of shared students experiences.

Student Grade	Response: Tell me about your composing experience.
University	Rehearsing *Birth Announcement* was fun. I enjoyed working with my group to create and interpret the score. One thing that I felt frustrated by was my group's literal reading of the score. Our first instinct was to read from left to right and top to bottom. We also took the number of markings literally. For example, if there were seven "stomp" symbols, we stomped seven times. Part of me wished that we wouldn't view the score so literally. I wish there was a way I could sometimes forget the musical training I have had and experience these types of scores with no knowledge of conventional music notation.
	I had a really fun time rehearsing and performing this. I like that we had the flexibility to determine who would perform the parts and if we would take repeats. I was somewhat self-conscious of my screaming as I realized it was intended to be the screams of birthing, and I have not had much experience in that area before. I liked my performing partners and felt that we really clicked. I felt that I could have connected with my "primal" side a bit more to offer up a more authentic performance. I was not nervous or embarrassed at any time and felt very supported by my classmates!
	When I was performing the piece I was concentrated on my entrances, but when I watched the other group I was able to observe the piece in its entirety. I also enjoyed seeing the different decisions about performance made by the other group, such as the difference in screams and hollers, and not repeating the lower stanza or stomping all together.
High School	Music is different from most subjects like math & science. I came to class every time not worrying about homework or extremely bored, but looking forward to the next music piece I could write. We had lots of different options in songwriting, and we were able to express ourselves even though it was just classwork. I think that's what I liked the most about it. Music didn't feel like a 'class' anymore, it felt like something I'd do in my spare time. I know some students don't really like music, but I'd ask them to at least give it a try. Even if you're not looking to compose later on in life, doing a little music here and there is going to make you feel better.
	I had a lovely time composing in our class. It was a space where I really felt comfortable. I love any class that encourages me to write in new and interesting styles. I also really benefited from being in a small class, because it kept me from feeling too overwhelmed. I've always loved composing, and being in this group helped foster my songwriting skills.

FIGURE 12.9. Secondary and tertiary responses to composing

Middle School	I think music was a great experience! I had so much fun.
	You make my classmates and I feel so special and talented. I am really going to miss this.
	Thank you for making music class something I want to go to instead of avoid. This was the first class where I really enjoyed and learned how to create music instead of just parroting songs like at my old school.
	Music is AMAZING! I love creating music...and all of the projects we have done have really helped me to learn how to create music.
	Thank you for always being so encouraging with our music compositions. It's really nice to know that you're so supportive in the music we create.
	Thank you for creating such a welcoming learning environment.
	It is really fun to be in music class when I get to express my creativity and I know you will support me with whatever I do!
	Thank you. You give us the best prompts and really give awesome and instructive feedback in order for us to have the best time in your class.

FIGURE 12.9. Continued

Kelly & Veronee (2019) report students' perceptions of nontraditional music classes. Just because you introduce composition projects to your students does not mean that all students will adequately understand each project or even understand each one in the same way. As teachers, our job is to ensure that we know how each student individually approaches the concept of creating music, most importantly their individual process in class composition projects. We undertake this aspect of music education, creating and composition, with careful approach to the prompts we give and the order in which they are given. This, I think, makes the difference for students.

Final Thought – INSPIRE Approach

Kratus (2012) tells the story of the Songcatchers, an indigenous culture of North America living along the coast of the Pacific Northwest and concludes with the idea that "every generation in every culture has its songcatchers." I believe these songcatchers are also children. As we approach some shift in thinking required to work compositionally with students of all ages with different musical experiences, the INSPIRE approach shares related teaching concepts for providing creative musical opportunities with strategic highlights you may want to take with you to support your inspiration of students (see Figure 12.10).

Music educators can develop their own path for compositional work with students making creativity a prominent feature of classroom music teaching and learning. I find gratitude for remarkable music teaching and observe that music in our world becomes stronger because of educators who provide opportunities for creative thinking with young people. Kratus is right. Every generation, in every culture, has its songcatchers. You are one of them, too.

1) Imagine new creative ideas that are of interest to you, the educator. Notice first, response to these ideas from your students. Carry these forward as you refine your remarkable presentation designs.

2) Nurturing each student's process is managed through development of effective tasks that you appreciate as much as students do. All we need to do is identify what these are for our many different groups of students. Provide your basic template and take yourself out of the decisions made by students in their creative process of extension.

3) Special recognition for creative work is not my focus. Even for all the times that I have been remarkably impressed by a student's composition, recognition is given by providing excellent, thoroughly thought-through, "next" projects. Opportunity to discuss, perform, or share works in some way is always valuable. Each class has different student types. All student groups provide positive feedback to their classmates about what they heard, what they loved, and what adjustments can be considered for the future. Student voice is special and much greater to hear than my voice.

4) Pride in one's compositional work is built through your strong teaching and discussion supports and through questions such as "do you know why this is an outstanding piece," or, "do you think this is an outstanding composition?", or, "what compositional elements might work in the next piece you compose", or "can you identify what you might revise".

5) Integration of musical knowledge *and feeling* is an exceptional combination. Work with students to determine their increasing capacity for centering themselves with their work enough to develop expression of emotion as an imperative contribution. This changes most creating and composition efforts.

6) Relevance is determined by students not teachers. Teachers may invite students to compose a *Suspense Film Intro* identifying that, "screams" do not necessarily create suspense. Students still use screams in their pieces.

7) Ears. Everyone hears everyone's compositions in our classes. This does not mean that they hear compositions in the same way. While no student has a hearing requirement, an educator's presentation of listening and responding are imperative to every students' compositional process.

FIGURE 12.10. INSPIRE

REFERENCES

Ackles, B. O. (2018). Agile development instructional framework (ADIF): A new strategy for student-centered music education. *The Choral Journal, 59*(2), 22–36.

Barrett, M. (1995). Children composing: What have we learnt? In *Honing the craft: Improving the quality of music education*. Conference Proceedings of the Australian Society for Music Education, 10th National Conference. Bloomsbury, London: Artemis Publishing.

Barrett, M. (1996). Children's aesthetic decision-making: An analysis of children's musical discourse as composers. *International Journal of Music Education, 22*, 37–62. https://doi.org/10.1177/025576149602800104

Barret, M. (2006). "Creative collaboration": An "eminence" study of teaching and learning in music composition. *Society for Education, Music and Psychology Research, 34*(2), 195–218. https://doi.org/10.1177/0305735606061852

Barrett, M. (2012). Preparing the mind for musical creativity: Early music learning and engagement. In O. Odena (Ed.), *Musical creativity: Insights from music education research* (pp. 51–72). Ashgate Publishing Co. https://doi.org/10.4324/9781315596952

Childs, E. (2007). ICAD 2006: Global Music—The World by Ear. *Computer Music Journal, 31*(1), 95–96. DOI: https://doi.org/10.1162/comj.

Coleman, S. N. (1922). *Creative music for children: A plan of training based on the natural evolution of music, including the making and playing of instruments, dancing—singing—poetry.* G. P. Putnam's Sons.

Crawford, L. A. (2004). *Leadership in curricular change: A national survey of music education faculty perceptions regarding music composition in teacher training* (Doctoral dissertation, Master's thesis, University of the Pacific, Stockton, CA. What Pre-Service Teachers Can Learn from Composition Research 53).

Crawford, L. (2016). *Composing in groups: Creative processes of third and fifth grade students.* (University of Southern California ProQuest Dissertations Publishing, 10195571.)

Crawford, L. (*Forthcoming*). *Beginning with composition: Strategies for integrating music teaching and learning through composition in elementary, secondary, & tertiary music education.*

Dammers, R. (2007). A survey of technology-based music classes in New Jersey High Schools. *Contributions in Music Education, 36*(2), 25–43.

de Villiers, A. (2015). The transformation of music education: A South African case study. *British Journal of Music Education, 32*(3), 315–322. DOI: 10.1017/S0265051715000376.

Freedman, B. (2013). Teaching music through composition: A curriculum using technology. Oxford University Press.

Glover, J. (2002). *Children composing, 4–14.* Routledge Falmer. https://doi.org/10.4324/978020 3134412

Hunt, P. (2001). *Voiceworks: A handbook for singing, Bk. 1.* Oxford University Press.

Hickey, M. (1999). Assessment rubrics for music composition. *Music Educators Journal, 85*(4), 26–34.

Hickey, M. (Ed.). (2003). *Why and how to teach music composition: A new horizon for music education.* MENC: The National Association for Music Education.

Hickey, M. (2012). *Music outside the lines: Ideas for composing in K–12 music classrooms.* Oxford University Press. https://doi.org/10.1093/acprof:osobl/9780199826773.001.0001

Hickey, M. (2013). What pre-service teachers can learn from composition research. In M. Kaschub & J. P. Smith (Eds.), *Composing out future: Preparing music educators to teach composition* (pp. 33–56). Oxford University Press. https://doi.org/10.1093/acprof:oso/978019 9832286.003.0003

Kaschub, M., & Smith, J. (2009). A principled approach to teaching music composition to children. *Research & Issues in Music Education, Article 5, 7*(1), 1–13.

Kaschub, M., & Smith, J. (2009). *Minds on music: Composition for creative and critical thinking.* Rowman & Littlefield.

Kaschub, M., & Smith, J. (Eds.). (2013). *Composing our future: Preparing music educators to teach composition.* Oxford University Press.

Kelly, S., & Veronee, K. (2019). High school students' perceptions of nontraditional music classes. *Bulletin of the Council for Research in Music Education,* (219), 77–89.

Koops, A., & Whitener, J. (2020). *Composition concepts for band and orchestra: Incorporating creativity in ensemble settings.* Rowman & Littlefield.

Kratus, J. (1989) A time analysis of the compositional processes used by children ages 7 to 11. *Journal of Research in Music Education, 37*(1), 5–20. https://doi.org/10.2307/3344949

Kratus, J. (2012). Nurturing the songcatchers: Philosophical issues in the teaching of music composition. In W. Bowman & A. L. Frega (Eds.), *The Oxford handbook of philosophy in music education* (pp. 367–385). Oxford University Press. https://doi.org/10.1093/oxfordhb/ 9780195394733.013.0020

Kratus, J. (2013). Preparing music educators to facilitate songwriting. In M. Kaschub & J. Smith, (Eds.), *Composing our future: Preparing music educators to teach composition* (pp. 267–283). Oxford University Press.

Love, K. G., & Barrett, M. S. (2019). Signature pedagogies for musical practice: A case study of creativity development in an orchestral composers' workshop. *Psychology of Music, 47*(4), 551–567.

Mulholland, J., & Walker, G. (2007). *Composers on composing for choir.* GIA Publications.

For the National Core Arts Standards State Education Agency Directors of Arts Education. (2014). National Core Arts Standards. Dover, DE: State Education Agency Directors of Arts Education.

Oswinsky, B. (2017). *The recording engineer's handbook* (4th ed.). Bobby Oswinsky Media Group.

Paynter, J. (2000). Making progress with composing. *British Journal of Music Education, 17*(1), 5–31.

Pierce, A. E. (1959). Teaching music in the elementary school. *Music Educators Journal, 46*(2), 76. https://doi.org/10.2307/3389215

Preston, C. A. (2010). *An investigation into the nature and quality of children's experiences of group composing in the secondary classroom based on the concept of flow.* Open University (United Kingdom).

Ruthmann, S. E., & Mantie, R. (Eds.). (2017). *The Oxford handbook of technology and music education.* Oxford University Press. https://doi.org/10.1093/oxfordhb/9780199372133.001.0001

Sarath, E. W. (2013). Improvisation, creativity, and consciousness: Jazz as integral template for music, education, and society. SUNY Press.

Smith, G. D., Moir, Z, Brennan, M., Kirkman, P., & Rambarran, S. (2016). *The Routledge research companion to popular music education.* Routledge Taylor & Francis Group. https://doi.org/10.4324/9781315613444

Snyder, A. M. (1957). *Creating music with children.* Mills Music.

Staufer, S. (2002). Connections between the musical and life experiences of young composers and their compositions. *Journal of Research in Music Education, 50*(4), 301–332. https://doi.org/10.2307/3345357

Tobias, E. (2017). Re-situating technology in music education. In S. A. Ruthmann & R. Mantie (Eds.), *The Oxford handbook of technology and music education* (pp. 291–308). Oxford University Press. https://doi.org/10.1093/oxfordhb/9780199372133.013.27

Upitis, R. (1989). The craft of composition: Helping children create music with computer tools. *Psychomusicology, 8*(2), 151–162. https://doi.org/10.1037/h0094241

Upitis, R. (1990). *This too is music.* Heinemann Educational Books.

Upitis, R. (1992). *Can I play you my song: The compositions and invented notations of children.* Heinemann Educational Books.

Volk, T. M. (1996). Satis Coleman's "Creative Music": Hands-on music education for children was the goal of the innovative music educator Satis Coleman. *Music Educators Journal, 82*(6), 31–47.

Waksman, S., & Bennett, A. (2014). *The Sage handbook of popular music.* SAGE Publications.

Webster, P. R. (1977). *A factor of intellect approach to creative thinking in music.* (Unpublished doctoral dissertation, University of Rochester.)

Webster, P. R. (1987). Conceptual bases for creative thinking in music. In C. Peery (Ed.), *Music and child development* (pp. 158–174). Springer-Verlag. https://doi.org/10.1007/978-1-4613-8698-8_8

Webster, P. R. (1988). Creative thinking and music education. *Design for Arts in Education, 89*(5), 33–37. https://doi.org/10.1080/07320973.1988.9935522

Webster, P. (2012). Children as creative thinkers in music: Focus on composition. In S. Hallam, I. Cross, & M. Thaut (Eds.), *The Oxford handbook of music psychology* (pp. 421–428). Oxford University Press https://doi.org/10.1093/oxfordhb/9780199298457.013.0039

Webster, P. R. (2013). Music composition intelligence and creative thinking in music. In M. Kaschub & J. P. Smith *Composing our future: Preparing music educators to teach composition* (pp. 19–32). Oxford University Press. https://doi.org/10.1093/acprof:oso/9780199832 286.003.0002

Webster, P. R. (2016a). Creative thinking in music: Twenty-five years on. *Music Educators Journal, 102*(3), 26–32. https://doi.org/10.1177/0027432115623841

Webster, P. R. (2016b). Pathways to the study of music composition by preschool to precollege students. In Hallam, Cross, & Thaut (Eds.), *Oxford handbook of music psychology* (2nd ed., pp. 681–202). Oxford University Press. https://doi.org/10.1177/0027432115623841

Wiggins, J. (1990). *Composition in the classroom: A tool for teaching.* MENC: The National Association for Music Education.

Wiggins, J. (2005). Fostering revision and extension in student composing. *Music Educators Journal, 91*(3), 35–42. https://doi.org/10.2307/3400074

Wiggins, J. (2007). Compositional process in music. In L. Bresler (Ed.), *International handbook of research in the arts, Vol. 16.* Springer Science & Business Media.

Williams, D., & Webster, P. (2002; 2020; 2022). *Experiencing music technology* (4th ed.). Oxford University Press.

Wise, S. (2016). Secondary school teachers' approaches to teaching composition using digital technology. *British Journal of Music Education, 33*(3), 283–295. https://doi.org/10.1017/s0265051716000309

Wish, D., Speicher, C., Zellner, R., & Hejna, K. (2015). *Music as a second language & the modern band movement.* Little Kids Rock.

CHAPTER 13

·····································

ADDRESSING CREATIVE INTENTIONS THROUGH REVISION AND EDITING

·····································

PATRICIA AJAMIE RILEY

HELPING children achieve their creative intentions is one of the most rewarding aspects of teaching music. As children strive to express themselves musically, they compose in individually unique ways but also using common processes. Once initial ideas are developed, an essential next step in the music composition process is revision and editing.

The United States' National Music Standards (NCCAS, 2014) focus on artistic processes that students should engage in as they interact with music—creating, performing, responding, and connecting. The process components, or steps, for creating are imagine, plan and make, evaluate and refine, and present (nafme.org/standards). Researchers have also identified processes that include steps, phases, cycles, or stages of the music composition process. Ashby (1995), Fautley (2005), Kratus (1989), Levi (1991), Perconti (1996), and Wiggins (1994) write that children progress through phases as they compose. Marsh (1995) writes of cycles, Swanwick and Tillman (1986) of stages, and van Ernst (1993) of steps. Kratus (1989) identifies four phases: 1) children prepare to explore problems and solutions; 2) possible solutions are considered and ideas developed; 3) children arrive at tentative solutions; and 4) final compositions are evaluated and refined. Levi (1991) outlines a five-phase process that consists of exploring, focusing, rehearsing, composing, and editing. Younker (2000) describes a process of composing with technology in which students explored, recorded, listened, evaluated, and edited. Although called by different names, the common element to these processes is a step, phase, cycle, refinement, or stage of revision and/or editing.

Considering Revision

Revision is a step that could include (a) changing, (b) eliminating, (c) adding, (d) expanding, or (e) contracting musical ideas. Kaschub (1997) characterizes revision as "a return to exploration in which composers test ideas that they previously accepted against new ideas while refining their finished product" (p. 24). According to Webster (2012):

> Revision is the active consideration of new material in the face of old with the idea of improving a final product. It is based on the notion that the first gestures of musical ideas are worthy of change by expanding, extending, or otherwise altering the musical ideas beyond the initial form. Revision can take many forms and can take place in countless ways. (p. 95)

Wiggins (2005) asserts that students view revision as integral to the music composition process. While engaged in the process, students seem to welcome suggestions to revise, but once they feel their piece is finished, they do not necessarily welcome such suggestions (p. 41). Stauffer (2013) writes that whether and how children revise their compositions is affected by differences in their "individual and group abilities, learning styles, experiences, and stages of cognitive, emotional, and social development" (p. 95). Kaschub and Smith (2017) state the importance of teachers' respecting students' stages of development when suggesting possible revisions, and that students "may be more open to suggestions for revisions if those suggestions further their own artistic intensions" (p. 41).

Webster (2003) supports encouraging children to "work beyond their first ideas and to think more deeply about sound formed to express feeling" (p. 58). He presents a model of creative thinking in music that includes revision as a central component and recommends that teachers devise ways to promote revision so that children view it as a natural part of the composition process. He asserts that if children see revision not as an attempt to fix something that is wrong with their original ideas, but as a way of "taking the initial ideas further for the sake of a deeper musical experience, the whole idea of revision and extension will seem logical and important" (p. 61). Hickey (2003) also presents a model of creativity that includes revision—specifically, a musical creativity model having to do with music composition. This model is an adaptation of the Amabile (1996) componential model of creativity. According to Hickey, if students are sufficiently motivated, they will be more likely to want to revise or compose again.

Matt LaRocca, executive director of Music-COMP (https://music-comp.org), the online music composition mentoring program for students in grades three through 12 that pairs student composers with professional composers as they create original work, writes,

> Revision is one of the most important steps in the creative process because it encourages students to think carefully about their music and fully identify their

musical goals. Composing is a dynamic process. Revision encourages musical growth in young composers (and indeed composers of all ages) as well as personal growth. By thinking critically about their music, students adapt their current version of a piece to better fulfill their creative intentions. (personal correspondence, December 14, 2020)

Kaschub (1997) explores group-composition processes of sixth-grade general music students and high school chorus students that were paired with professional composers. The professional composers assisted the students with crafting group compositions re-flective of their musical thinking, but not limited to their previous music knowledge and skills. Kaschub found that throughout the revision process, "students challenge each other's musical ideas and often new musical concepts emerge as students defend their original ideas or seek to reach compromise" (p. 15).

Webster (2012) shares conversations with 12-year-old composer, Carson. Regarding revision, Carson states,

> I get the ideas down that I like and then I go back and sort of make it better, like adding dynamics and stuff. I like the different timbres in Sibelius. I figure out where the problems are and I fix them. I like lots of contrast, but I also like to make things kind of different but similar." (p. 94)

In a 2001 case study, Stauffer (2001) describes the evolving composition strategies of third-grader, Meg as she composed using a computer program that was non-notation-based. According to Stauffer, Meg started *Tweety Bird*, her second composition, "by writing a short melodic fragment, listening to it, then revising (changing) or adding to what she had just written and listening again" (p. 6). Stauffer characterizes Meg's three-phase composition process as consisting of exploration, development, and ending—with revision occurring during the development and/or ending stages.

Ruthmann (2008) examines student agency during the revision stage of the compo-sition process in a case study regarding teaching and learning in a technology-based environment. Participants were Ellen, a fourth-grade student composer, and Mary, the teacher. According to Ruthmann,

> What was particularly striking to me about the help that Mary gave was that she did not ask Ellen her intent before providing [revision] comments. Instead, during both teacher feedback sessions, Mary tried to help Ellen express an interpretation of the movie scene that Mary assumed was held in common. This process excluded Ellen from meaningful engagement in the discussion. Nearly all of Mary's feedback was geared toward teaching and improving the *composition* through the imposition of her own interpretation and musical ideas, rather than helping Ellen express her com-positional intent. (p. 51)

Ruthmann concludes that had Mary asked Ellen about her creative intentions at the beginning of their feedback sessions, the sessions might have been more successful. "Through adopting a pedagogy of composing that begins with the practice of seeking and understanding their students' musical intentions, teachers may be more successful at supporting their students' development as composers" (2008, p. 56).

Similarly, Allsup (2003) investigates the interactions between students and teacher as the students composed in self-directed small groups in an instrumental music setting in which the teacher served mostly as facilitator.

> When students are given space to explore freely, to work democratically, they will create (from one of *their* musical worlds) a context about which they are familiar, conversant, or curious. . . . The materials that students choose to explore will represent a world that is theirs, a world they understand, a world that defines who they are. (p. 35)

Wiggins (2003) writes "students are more apt to understand and relate to teacher and peer help with the details of their compositions if it is presented in a way that indicates that the helper understands the big picture and the intent" (p. 162).

> Students use music as a means of personal expression. In order to scaffold their work, an outsider needs to understand what they are trying to express. A teacher trying to scaffold student composers needs to start by asking questions, seeking information about what they are trying to do. (Wiggins, 2005, p. 41)

Deutsch (2016) also encourages revision and recommends asking questions throughout the composition teaching and learning process aimed at understanding the student's intentions. According to Deutsch, "when the teacher emphasizes and respects the student's intentions, the chances are much greater that the composition will have expressive power" (p. 57).

REVISION IN PRACTICE

This chapter explores how to address student creative intentions through the compositional step of revising and editing. It is examined through the lens of both student composer and teacher mentor within the context of the online music composition community, Music-COMP. Two student compositions at different levels of compositional skill are shared, analyzed, and discussed. They exemplify students revising and editing their pieces to more closely achieve their creative intentions, as well as teacher mentors working to help the students achieve those intentions, develop their compositions, and further their compositional skill.

Gracie's Composition

The first piece, *The Weather Outside*, was written by 11-year-old Gracie. According to Gracie, she plays violin, ukulele, guitar, and piano. The following is Gracie's description of her composition in its final (revised and edited) form (to hear the work, visit https://www.music-comp.org/).

> *The Weather Outside* is a piece that shows the changes of weather. The piece plays for a string quartet. There are several places in my piece that gradually get louder, softer, slower, and faster. The weather outside mostly will sound like it is raining. This piece connects to Vermont because of course, weather! In this piece I decided to do something different instead of having one boring part and a completely awesome one, I decided to give each instrument equal playing parts. There are so many emotions throughout the piece, from sad to angry and even happy.

Gracie's creative intentions evolved throughout her revision and editing process. Originally, Gracie's composition was titled *the sunset* and had to do with two opposing ideas: day and night. The first version of Gracie's composition appears in Figure 13.1.

(a)

the sunset

FIGURE 13.1. Gracie's first version

FIGURE 13.1. Continued

A pre-service music educator, Jake, served as Gracie's composition mentor for this piece via Music-COMP (the online music composition mentoring program for students in grades three through 12). Jake was a student of mine in the music education program at the University of Vermont, and within this program, he earned a music composition concentration. During his time in this concentration, Jake took courses in classical and jazz composition, as well as mentoring for three semesters within Music-COMP. Jake guided Gracie's revisions and editing with suggestions focused on helping Gracie achieve her creative intention and also on developing her composition and compositional skill. The following mentoring guidelines offered by Music-COMP informed Jake's mentoring:

- offer two or three suggestions without overwhelming young composers
- comments should be designed to help a student revise and improve, not to completely re-do a piece
- encourage development of material with specific suggestions
- comments should first deal with broader issues and as pieces near "completion," the finer tuning takes place
- ask questions to focus thinking

- make suggestions in language rather than changing their music for them
- use phrases like: "Have you considered . . ." and "I wonder if . . ." rather than being directive
- lead students to discover what their piece can be
- be sensitive to "letting go" of a piece when the student is ready to move on
- too much flowery praise is not useful, nor is it seen to be sincere.

(S. MacLeod, personal correspondence, January 6, 2016, cited from Riley, [2016] p. 248)

Excerpts of the conversation between Jake and Gracie as she revised and edited her piece are shared below. The full conversation between Jake and Gracie, as well as more versions of Gracie's piece as it developed, can be found in the chapter *Mentoring Student Creations* in Riley (2016).

Jake to Gracie:

Hi Gracie! My name is Jake and I will be your composition mentor. I think you're off to a fantastic start! There are some really lovely harmonies in your piece, and your home tone is very firmly established. I think there are a lot of really great ideas in your piece. So, the next thing to work on with this section would be to add dynamics and articulations. You use slurs to create a feeling of *legato*, which means smooth and connected, in the beginning of your piece. Have you considered using that effect again? *Legato* is a great sound! Now, with dynamics, you'll be establishing loud and soft. Your piece is about the sun setting, so is there a certain volume you would associate with the sun setting? Should the music soften, signifying a feeling of calm, or should it get loud, signifying something more triumphant? Do whatever speaks to you!

From your description, it sounds to me like your piece will have two distinct sections. If this is the "day" section, what will "night" sound like? Will the key change? These are things to think about as you progress with your composition. Another thing to think about is, a lot of the time, your harmonies use two pitches split between the instruments you're using. Have you considered trying three- or four-note harmonies? If done effectively, the result could be quite beautiful!

Gracie to Jake:

Hi Jake. I have been working on adding dynamics daily, and I actually am changing the name of my piece to "I don't know what to feel," because I kept listening to my piece and it didn't go right with the title. It sounded like mixed emotions to me so yeah, and I do intend for my piece to have *legato* at the middle.

Jake to Gracie:

Hello again, Gracie. I want to clarify that with Opus 30 [Opus 30 was the live performance opportunity for which Gracie was creating her piece—students within Music-COMP competitively submit work for performance consideration, and mentoring is provided to help students not only achieve their creative intentions in their composition, but also to help them do well in the competition and progress with their compositional skill], we're asking that each piece have some sort of Vermont theme to signify the importance of Music-COMP's 20th year. Can you think of some sort of Vermont theme to tie into your piece? Sunset would have been a good theme, but it's perfectly fine if you don't want to title it that. Another thing to keep in mind is that if you find inspiration in a certain Vermont concept, such as the Winooski River or

Mount Mansfield, you may find that centering your piece on that concept will help inspire you to compose things you may not have otherwise!

The next thing I would recommend is to keep composing more material for the C section. I like the sudden change in instruments that you use, and your use of rhythm is really interesting. Measure 24 has a sort of confusing sound to it, but I think it's really neat! Other than that, I just want to mention dynamics again, but I know you're working on it!

One more thing to consider—the second violin never really has its own unique melody. It's either doubling a melody or playing a harmony. It might be nice to give violin II the melody at some point. While it won't affect the sound on the *Noteflight* playback, it will make a difference if performed live. And a second violinist would always appreciate having the melody! This isn't something you necessarily have to implement, but it's just something to think about. Thanks for all your hard work, Gracie. I'm looking forward to your next update!

Gracie to Jake
I actually just changed to *The Weather Outside* so it has a Vermont theme. I intend to have the violin part 2 play a melody and I will add more to the C section.

Jake to Gracie
Sounds good, Gracie. I'm glad you have ideas for where to go next in your piece. Now that you've selected a title, how do you want the music to reflect that title? The weather in Vermont is unpredictable, as I'm sure you know! One day there could be a blizzard, one day could be sunny and warmer out, one day could be rainy. How might you use music to reflect that unpredictability in weather?

Gracie to Jake
I was thinking that the music could be more and less dense as the seasons change.

Jake to Gracie
That sounds like a great idea! I look forward to seeing it in action!

Gracie to Jake
I'm not making it change through seasons anymore. Instead, it's going to show how boring it is to stay inside on a rainy day.

Jake to Gracie
I like the revisions you've made. The piece has a certain intensity and darkness to it. I think with using certain dynamics and articulations, you could make this effect even more pronounced. Your melodies are great and I like the interaction between the instruments with the melody line.

You talk about writing about how "boring" it is to be stuck inside on a rainy day. I would recommend trying to think of different emotions to also convey. Music has the power to convey emotions in a clear way, and to move people to different emotional states.

Gracie to Jake
I will try to mix in other emotions like you said, and I will add in dynamics.

Jake to Gracie
Sounds good, Gracie. The important thing is really how the music makes you feel. If you feel the music conveys what you want it to, then you've done what you're supposed to! :)

Gracie to Jake

I have been working on adding other emotions to the piece. I'm just wondering if you think there should be anything changed in the piece so it will be more improved.

Jake to Gracie

Wow! What a great update. Your piece feels very substantial and between different melodies, harmonies, dynamics and articulations, you clearly put in a lot of time and took much care in your composing. I just have a few suggestions for things to tinker with or try out. Could you try giving the viola or cello a solo at some point, for the sake of contrast? If you find anywhere in the piece that you could utilize one of those instruments for a solo, I would try to do so and see if you like the sound. I would also experiment with softer dynamic markings such as *piano* or *pianissimo* at some point in the piece. The C or D sections seem like they would work well with a softer volume at times. I think those sections also may benefit from using a slur to create a feeling of *legato*, or smoothness.

Gracie to Jake

I gave the viola and cello a small duet, and I will add a feeling of *legato* in there soon. I added *piano* in part D.

Jake to Gracie

Again, I just have suggestions for little changes. I think using slurs to connect the notes the instruments play in your D section would be really effective. It will make every note transition sound smooth. Also, I was wondering about the very last measure. Right now, you use a repeat with a first and second ending, but the second ending hasn't been composed yet, so right now the piece feels like it ends abruptly. I would think about how you want the very end of your piece to sound and then compose something for that second ending.

Gracie to Jake

I added that second ending. I am going to end my piece now because it can only be three minutes long for the Opus concert, and it's starting to limit me. I will work on adding more crescendos and decrescendos. I also added some slurs in section D, but not too many because I was going into a section that had more volume to it.

Jake to Gracie

Thanks for the quick update. I think your use of slurs in D is really great. I think the amount you used was perfect. As for the amount of minutes, I think 3 minutes is excellent! If you feel done as far as working on the melody, you can take the next few weeks to tinker with different aspects of the piece.

Gracie to Jake

I just changed my piece a little. I added those dots that make the notes shorter—I don't know what they're called, but I added them in places that I thought would be good. I'm not really sure about them, I might take some out—what do you think?

Jake to Gracie

Those dots are called *staccato*, and as you can hear through listening to your piece, it tells the performer to make the note short. I think they all work well in your piece and you found good spots to use them. To my ear, I think I actually like the sound of measures 15 to 18 without the staccatos, but if you prefer that sound, I wouldn't change a thing.

Gracie to Jake

I thought so too—I took them out in measures 15 to 18 and it sounds good. Any other suggestions???

Jake to Gracie

The only thing I would consider adjusting is the decrescendo in the second ending at the end of the piece. That entire phrase that you end the piece with has a ton of energy and to me, it feels weird to end it by getting softer. I think it would make sense to keep the volume and sustain that energy to the end. What do you think?

Gracie to Jake

I took out the decrescendos there. I liked your idea of having a nice and strong ending, so is that all?

Jake to Gracie

I think if you feel like your piece is complete at this point, then we can call it complete. Thanks for your tremendous work!

Gracie to Jake

Hi Jake—Okay then! I guess we are done here. Fingers-crossed, hopefully this gets in Opus 30. Thanks for helping me.

Jake to Gracie

Hi Gracie. I really enjoyed working with you and I think your piece is fantastic! Regardless of what happens, know that you did a great job!

Gracie to Jake

Hi Jake—I just wanted to let you know that I won opus!!! I'm very happy, and I can't stop smiling!!!!

The final (revised and edited) version of Gracie's composition appears in Figure 13.2 through 13.5. Analytical comments and comparisons between versions follow.

Gracie revised her opening phrase, that previously had a melody line in the first violin doubled in the viola, and a harmony line in the second violin doubled in the cello, ending with a solo whole-note in the first violin. In her revised opening phrase, Gracie has four distinct lines with mostly three-part harmonies, ending with all four instruments playing a three-part chord. In the second phrase (starting in measure 6), Gracie has a motif in the first violin, that two measures later is mostly repeated in the first violin but is also accompanied by a harmonizing cello part with the same intervals and rhythm. In her revised final version, Gracie has a one-measure motive that is passed down between all four instruments, top to bottom. The A section in her first version is 12 measures in length, and in her revised version is 14 measures in length, with the last measure being silent. Gracie's first version has no measures of complete silence until the not-yet-composed beginning of the C section. On the first page, Gracie has also added dynamic markings, including crescendos and decrescendos, articulations (accents, staccatos, and marcato marks), and an expression marking, "sadly." She continued to add dynamics and articulation markings throughout the revised and extended piece.

The B section in Gracie's first version is also quite different from the final revised version. Rather than having all four parts playing in all but one measure of the first version,

FIGURE 13.2. Gracie's final version

she alternates between the violins playing two measures and the viola and cello playing two measures, followed by one measure for each pair, then two measures of all four parts playing together. There is much more rhythmic variety in the revised version. There are many more measures in the first version that contain only one type of rhythmic value, with the revised version having more measures with rhythmic variety within measures. The first version is seven measures in length, and the revised version is 10 measures in length.

Gracie extended the earlier versions of her composition to include C and D sections in this final revised version. While there are no words indicating the mood, articulations, or tempos in the original version, Gracie includes the words "smoothly," "very marcato,"

FIGURE 13.3. Gracie's final version, mm. 11–19

"smooth," and "lively" in the final version (as well as the previously mentioned "sadly"). I believe these words assisted Gracie substantially in achieving her creative intent.

The C section is quite different than the other sections, and consists entirely of quarter and half notes, except for a pair of eighth notes in the violins and viola on the four beat of measure 29, whole rests in the violin 2, viola, and cello parts in measures 34–37, and a whole note and whole rest in all four parts to end the section. This section is characterized by contrasting articulations and tempos. It is first marked "smoothly," then "very marcato," then "smooth," and ending with "lively."

In the D section, Gracie returns to the articulation from the opening phrase of her first version, slurs. She also uses the dynamic markings *piano* and *mezzo piano* for the

(a)

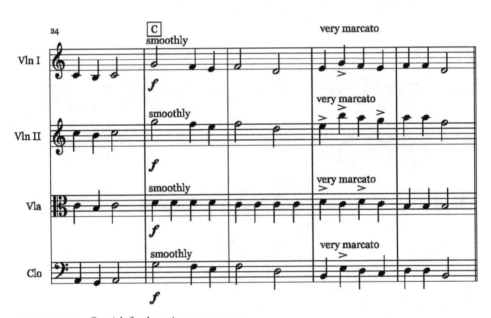

FIGURE 13.4. Gracie's final version, mm. 20–39

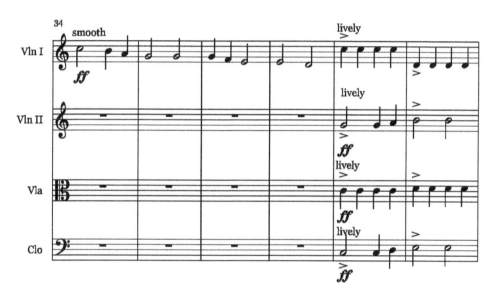

FIGURE 13.4. Continued

first time, before returning to *forte* to end the piece. Additionally, Gracie includes a *ritar-dando* in the last two measures. This D section is characterized by changes in texture. It starts with a solo, followed by a duet, another solo and duet, and ultimately ends with all four parts playing together.

I feel that Gracie's revisions and editing did help her achieve her creative intentions for *The Weather Outside*. I believe that her piece does communicate Vermont weather, specifically what it feels like to be inside on a rainy day. As Gracie intended, the instrument parts are mostly equal, the second violin part does include some melody, there is a *legato* section, and there are a variety of emotions expressed, including sad, angry, and happy.

FIGURE 13.5. Gracie's final version, mm. 40–end

FIGURE 13.5. Continued

Ethan's Composition

The second piece, *St. Albans, 1864* was composed by 13-year-old Ethan, who at the time played piano and euphonium. The following is his description of his composition in its final (revised, extended, and edited) form:

> The song envisions the sequential series of events of the St. Albans Raid of 1864, the most northerly land action of the American Civil War. The song starts with the Confederates crossing the Canadian border into Vermont. Afterward, it tells of a scene from the town, a small but lively place. Then, we go back to the raiders entering the town and preparing for the raid. The town sleeps for the night and the robberies begin. Afterward, the raiders escape into Canada. A total of $88,000 (today over $3 million) was stolen from three St. Albans banks. I wanted to have the feeling of angst at first, followed by the depiction of the town, which was quiet and peaceful

beforehand, followed by the same angst-driven melody that would eventually build into the song's climax, the raid itself. (https://www.music-comp.org/)

Like Gracie's, Ethan's creative intentions evolved throughout his revising and editing process. Originally, his composition was titled *Crusade* and depicted a battle between Vikings and the English, but Ethan quickly changed it to the St. Albans Raid once he was made aware of the Vermont theme that was required for his piece to be considered for the Music-COMP 20th Anniversary live-music performance event "Opus 30." An early version of Ethan's composition appears in Figure 13.6.

(a)

St. Albans, 1864

Ethan Duncan

FIGURE 13.6. Ethan's first version

(b)

FIGURE 13.6. Continued

FIGURE 13.6. Continued

(d)

FIGURE 13.6. Continued

Pre-service music educator Will served as Ethan's primary composition mentor for this piece. Like Jake, Will was a student of mine in the music education program at the University of Vermont, and within this program earned a music composition concentration. During his time in this concentration, Will, took courses in classical and jazz composition, as well as mentored within Music-COMP.

According to Ethan,

> The mentoring process for this song was less about planting ideas into my head about different melodies or notations, but more about finding the best ways to

"convey" different parts of the story musically using dynamics, tone, articulations, etc. This piece specifically helped me grow as a composer because it introduced me to the idea that music is conveyed not only through the notes/rhythms/melodies/harmonies/etc. but also through tone, tempo, articulations, and these more intricate details that go beyond the listener's surface-level view. (personal correspondence, December 4, 2020)

Will guided Ethan's revisions and editing with suggestions focused on helping him achieve his creative intentions and also on developing his composition and compositional skill. The mentoring guidelines offered by Music-COMP, shared previously, informed Will's mentoring. Excerpts of the conversation between Will and Ethan as he revised and edited his piece (via Music-COMP) are shared below.

Will to Ethan
Thank you for submitting your first draft! My name's Will and I'll be your mentor while you develop this new piece. I think you're off to a great start with "Crusade"! You have a lot of really interesting ideas happening in this piece. I love your use of seven-measure phrases in the A section (mm. 1–14) and your reinforcement of the key (G minor) with the F-sharp in m. 14. Your four-bar transition into the B section (mm. 19–34) is effective and sets up a nice modulation into B-flat major. One small suggestion I have is to use slurs to connect notes, particularly when you have multiple adjacent notes with tenuto articulations (violin m. 3). The performers will instinctively connect the notes and make them more *legato*. Slurs may also work well for the flute in the B section—play around with them and see what you think.

Now that you have some initial themes down, consider a few big picture ideas. 1) What form will the piece have when it's finished? 2) What tonalities (keys) will be used in each section? 3) What kind of story will the piece tell? You've already done a good job of outlining the storyline of the piece in your description. Continue to think about how you will shape the music to reinforce the battle between the Vikings and the English you described.

Ethan to Will
Will, thanks for choosing my piece to mentor. I appreciate everything you guys do to help out with our pieces. I have been told that my piece is supposed to have something to do with Vermont, so I changed it from the Viking battle to the St. Albans Raid in the Civil War. I'm changing the dynamics of the piece to suit the situation. The beginning is more quiet now, representing the Confederates sneaking across the Canadian border. I also closed out the first section picturing the town, now St. Albans, instead of some English town. I'm hoping that I stopped the pizzicato at the right time. If not, surely you would tell me.

Will to Ethan
I think you've done a great job introducing a Vermont theme to your piece and the music complements the storyline you've chosen quite well. Regarding the pizzicato—it certainly starts in the correct spot but I would write "arco" on the downbeat of m. 39, as that's where the strings begin their long-held notes once

again. I would also experiment with ways to make your transition back into the A section (mm. 43–46) a little more dramatic, especially since you change from a major to minor tonality here. Play around with these measures, perhaps with a *ritardando* and/or another fermata, or perhaps dynamic contrast (for example, a crescendo into m. 47?) This is totally your call. Last but not least, I would recommend experimenting with the second A section (mm. 47–60) to see if you can vary it even more from the first A section, perhaps rhythmically or harmonically (the chords). You've already varied it slightly with the new long-held notes in the strings in mm. 54–57. I'm sure you can find other ways to make this reiteration of the A section even more interesting and dramatic.

Ethan to Will

I changed a few things with this next A section; I created a new second violin and viola pattern in the second part of the section to add a little bit of variety and movement behind the melody of the first violin. I also moved the arco to the spot you suggested, on the downbeat of m. 37. This next section, I think, is when the Confederates are just reaching the town, and sneaking their way in. I'll work more on this section and see where it goes.

Will to Ethan

You are doing an excellent job developing this composition and realizing the storyline. I assume that measure 69 begins the C section in which the town sleeps for the night, just before the robberies begin. Keep in mind that the long-held bass and cello notes in this section will be extremely quiet as they are in a low register as well as marked at a *piano* dynamic. I would strongly consider introducing them at *mezzo piano*, but the choice is yours. This is a balance concern that can be easily taken care of in performance.

Your decision to slow down the tempo of the A section was certainly beneficial—the *staccato*, syncopated eighth-note parts sound much more clear and will be much easier to coordinate and hear during performance. I like that you used them again during the C section of the piece. Make sure to go back and consider using more articulations for the flute part throughout the piece. Using slurs during the B section to add more of a "flowing," *legato* quality to the flute part may be helpful in communicating your storyline, if you see fit. How do you think you will continue to vary the A section when it makes its third appearance in measure 87? Don't be afraid to play with the phrasing a little bit as the listener is accustomed to hearing 7-bar phrases during the A section up until this point. Keep on composing and let me know your thoughts for the remainder of the piece and if you have any questions. Once again, excellent work and I look forward to seeing more.

Ethan to Will

I've added some articulations that should make a difference to the sections where it's involved. I also added a cool sort of "D" section at the end before the final A section. I think it represents the run to the border after they robbed the banks.

Will to Ethan

Nice work using and expanding on pre-existing melodic and rhythmic material in the new D section, especially in flute part mimicking the transition in mm. 15–18. I would recommend adding some articulations to the flute part during mm. 109–114 to add clarity to the moving eighth-note part. You did a nice job adding a *legato* feel to the flute part in mm. 69–83 using slurs. How do you feel about the final four measures? Do you think you'd like the piece to end here on a quiet, mysterious note? Or do you think you'll end the piece with more of a "bang"?

Ethan to Will
I have added some accents and a few staccatos to the flute at mm. 109–114. It defines the important notes and makes the part easier to listen to. I also added to the D section, which now has a C minor part to it and a transition back to G minor, where the piece finishes. I also added a part into the last 32 bars and gave the flute a pretty regular resting point in the higher sections.

Will to Ethan
I just wanted to drop in and congratulate you alongside Erik for having *St. Albans, 1864* chosen for performance at the Opus 30 concert! [Erik is senior mentor with Music-COMP and graciously stepped in to help out with some mentoring on this piece while Will was ill.] I believe you have a unique, outstanding final product that the audience and performers will thoroughly enjoy.

The final (revised and edited) version of Ethan's composition appears in Figures 13.7 through 13.15. Analytical comments and comparisons between versions follow.

The opening section remains unchanged from the early version to the final revised and edited version.

In the A section, the rhythms are unchanged and pitches mostly unchanged between versions. Ethan has, however has added some articulations (slurs and staccatos) and moved the arco marking to four measures earlier.

The piece's opening melody and harmony return in the B section. Except for the tempo change from quarter note = 220 to 192, the first seven measures of this section are unchanged between the early and final versions. In the second seven measures, while the flute, first violin, and double bass parts remain unchanged, the second violin and viola parts were changed to have a more interesting, syncopated rhythm. The early version ends in measure 60, while the final version extends the B section to measure 68 with a restatement of measures 15–18.

The final version continues to include C, D, E, and F sections. The C section can be characterized as consisting mostly of a *mezzo forte* quarter- and eighth-note flute melody that includes slurs and staccatos, accompanied by softer longer notes in the cello and bass parts, later joined by a syncopated rhythm in the second violin and viola parts (reminiscent of the B section).

Starting in measure 83, there is a dramatic crescendo to louder dynamic levels and some accents are added. In measure 87, the melody (a restatement of the B section melody) is passed to the first violin part and the flute rests for the remainder of the section. There is another dramatic crescendo to end the C section.

The D section begins quite loudly and is generally characterized by more accents, more rhythmic activity within the parts, and more interplay between parts.

St. Albans, 1864

Ethan Duncan

FIGURE 13.7. Ethan's final version, mm. 1–14

The E section continues with a key change, loud dynamic levels, abundant accents, interplay between parts and active rhythms. There is a dramatic buildup of rhythmic activity and intensity to end the section.

In the F section, the melody from the B section is again restated (as it was toward the end of the C section), but this time, it is repeated. On the repeat, the flute part joins in

FIGURE 13.8. Ethan's final version, mm. 15–45

FIGURE 13.8. Continued

with a new countermelody. The dynamic level in this section starts at *mezzo forte* and builds in the second ending to an accented *fortissimo* to end the piece.

I believe that Ethan's revisions, extensions, and editing did help him achieve his creative intentions for this piece. I feel that *St. Albans, 1864* does communicate the story he intended, not only through the melody, harmony, rhythm, and form, but also through the articulations, dynamics, and texture. Ethan stated that the mentoring for his piece "was less about planting ideas into my head about different melodies or notations, but more about finding the best ways to 'convey' different parts of the story musically using dynamics, tone, articulations, etc.," and I believe that these elements contributed substantially to Ethan's achieving his creative intentions.

FIGURE 13.9. Ethan's final version, mm. 46–60

RECOMMENDATIONS FOR MENTORING
STUDENTS AS THEY REVISE AND EDIT

In order to encourage and facilitate student revision of compositions so that creative intentions are achieved and compositional skills developed, I recommend using the mentoring guidelines offered by Music-COMP, shared earlier in this chapter.

FIGURE 13.10. Ethan's final version, mm. 61–72

The mentoring Jake and Will provided adhered to these guidelines and I believe that Gracie and Ethan's success in achieving their creative intentions was in large part due to this adherence to the guidelines. Providing specific suggestions and asking questions (not only to focus thinking, but also to ascertain creative intention) figure prominently in the mentoring, and in my view, were most helpful.

Deutsch (2016), Ruthmann (2008), and Wiggins (2005) also recommend asking questions to determine creative intention. Some of the questions Jake and Will asked Gracie and Ethan, designed to ascertain their creative intentions were as follows:

FIGURE 13.11. Ethan's final version, mm. 73–83

FIGURE 13.12. Ethan's final version, mm. 84–110

FIGURE 13.12. Continued

FIGURE 13.13. Ethan's final version, mm. 111–122

FIGURE 13.14. Ethan's final version, mm. 123–148

FIGURE 13.14. Continued

FIGURE 13.15. Ethan's final version, mm. 149–end

Jake to Gracie

- Your piece is about the sun setting, so is there a certain volume you would associate with the sun setting? Should the music soften, signifying a feeling of calm, or should it get loud, signifying something more triumphant?
- From your description, it sounds to me like your piece will have two distinct sections. If this is the "day" section, what will "night" sound like?
- Now that you've selected a title, how do you want the music to reflect that title? The weather in Vermont is unpredictable, as I'm sure you know! One day there

could be a blizzard, one day could be sunny and warmer out, one day could be rainy. How might you use music to reflect that unpredictability in weather?

Will to Ethan

- Now that you have some initial themes down, consider a few big picture ideas. 1) What form will the piece have when it's finished? 2) What tonalities (keys) will be used in each section? 3) What kind of story will the piece tell? You've already done a good job of outlining the storyline of the piece in your description. Continue to think about how you will shape the music to reinforce the battle between the Vikings and the English you described.
- Using slurs during the B section to add more of a "flowing" *legato* quality to the flute part may be helpful in communicating your storyline, if you see fit. How do you think you will continue to vary the A section when it makes its third appearance in measure 87?
- How do you feel about the final four measures? Do you think you'd like the piece to end here on a quiet, mysterious note? Or do you think you'll end the piece with more of a "bang"?

Asking questions is also among the recommendations Webster (2012) offers for designing revision experiences for students:

- Ask children about how they are or have been revising. Composition students may be revising as they go. We can never presume that when a composition is presented to us as teachers, that there has not been much thinking about sound already. Try to establish what the process of composition has been in order to figure out how to help improve the work.
- Have children discover on their own. Ask the questions necessary for students to discover what might be profitable for revision. Let them be the final decision-maker, but be sure that as many sonic possibilities have been considered as makes sense. Feel comfortable with challenging ideas but never dictate. (pp. 109–110)

These recommendations are congruent with the Music-COMP guidelines and I highly recommend that they be combined as teachers work to mentor students as they revise, extend, and edit their compositions.

Another area that I recommend teachers focus on as they mentor student revision is the five compositional principles of "sound/silence, motion/stasis, unity/variety, tension/release, and stability/instability" (Kaschub & Smith, 2009, p. 15).

Music's expressive power relies on our ability to perceive the continually shifting balances within and between motion and stasis, unity and variety, sound and silence, tension and release, and stability and instability. These five musical principles, which we term "MUSTS," correspond directly to the way we perceive changes in our condition and environment through the complex array of our internal and external senses. When children understand this connection, they learn to reference their own intuitive understandings and can draw on a personal bank of feelings that have arisen in their own experiences to consider how sound might be shaped to invite similar feelings. This skill allows composers to strategically select and shape how feelings are *sonified*—expressed in sound. (Kaschub & Smith, 2017, p. 16)

I believe that focusing on these principles will not only assist students in developing their compositions and compositional skill but will also help students achieve their creative intentions. Students drawing on their own feelings and experiences informs creative intentions and should be encouraged, valued, and honored. Revision and editing are vital components of the music composition process. The primary focus of such revisions should be addressing and furthering students' creative intentions.

References

Allsup, R. (2003). Mutual learning and democratic action in instrumental music education. *Journal of Research in Music Education, 51*(1), 24–37.

Amabile, T. M. (1996). *Creativity in context: Update to the social psychology of creativity.* Westview Press.

Ashby, C. L. (1995). An analysis of compositional processes used by children. *Masters Abstracts International, 34*(01), 0040. (UMI No. 1375862)

Deutsch, D. (2016). Authentic assessment in music composition: Feedback that facilitates creativity. *Music Educators Journal, 102*(3), 53–59.

Fautley, M. (2005). A new model of the group composing process of lower secondary school students. *Music Education Research, 7*(1), 39–57.

Hickey, M. (2003). Creative thinking in the context of music composition. In M. Hickey (Ed.), *Why and how to teach music composition: A new horizon for music education* (pp. 31–54). MENC.

Kaschub, M. (1997). A comparison of two composer-guided large group composition projects. *Research Studies in Music Education, 8,* 15–28.

Kaschub, M., & Smith, J. (2009). *Minds on music: Composition for creative and critical thinking.* Rowman & Littlefield.

Kaschub, M., & Smith, J. (2017). *Experiencing music composition in grades 3–5.* Oxford University Press.

Kratus, J. (1989). A time analysis of the compositional processes used by children ages 7–11. *Journal of Research in Music Education, 37*(1), 5–20.

Levi, R. (1991). A field investigation of the composition processes used by second-grade children creating original language and music pieces. *Dissertation Abstracts International, 52* (08), 2853A. (UMI No. 9202227)

Marsh, K. (1995). Children's singing games: Composition in the playground? *Research Studies in Music Education, 4,* 2–11.

NCCAS (2014). *National core music standards.* https://www.nationalartsstandards.org/

Perconti, E. S. (1996). Learning to compose and learning through composing: A study of the composing process in elementary general music. *Dissertation Abstracts International, 57*(10), 4301A. (UMI No. 9710259)

Riley, P. E. (2016). *Creating music: What children from around the world can teach us.* Rowman & Littlefield.

Ruthmann, S. A. (2008). Whose agency matters?: Negotiating pedagogical and creative intent during composing experiences. *Research Studies in Music Education, 30*(1), 43–58.

Stauffer, S. L. (2001). Composing with computes: Meg makes music. *Bulletin of the Council for Research in Music Education, 150*, 1–20. https://www.jstor.org/stable/40319096

Stauffer, S. L. (2013). Preparing to engage children in musical creating. In M. Kaschub & J. Smith (Eds.), *Composing our future: Preparing music educators to teach composition* (pp. 75–108). Oxford University Press.

Swanwick, K., & Tillman, J. (1986). The sequence of musical development: A study of children's composition. *British Journal of Music Education, 3*, 305–339.

van Ernst, B. (1993). A study of the learning and teaching processes of non-naïve music students engaged in composition. *Research Studies in Music Education, 1*, 22–39.

Webster, P. (2003). "What do you mean, make my music different?": Encouraging revision and extensions in children's music composition. In M. Hickey (Ed.), *Why and how to teach music composition: A new horizon for music education* (pp. 55–68). Music Educators National Conference.

Webster, P. (2012). Towards pedagogies of revision: Guiding a student's music composition. In O. Odena (Ed.), *Musical creativity: Insights from music education research* (pp. 93–112). Ashgate.

Wiggins, J. H. (1994). Children's strategies for solving compositional problems with peers. *Journal of Research in Music Education, 42*(3), 232–252.

Wiggins, J. H. (2003). A frame for understanding children's compositional processes. In M. Hickey (Ed.), *Why and how to teach music composition: A new horizon for music education* (pp. 453–69). MENC: Music Educators National Conference.

Wiggins, J. H. (2005). Fostering revision and extension in student composing. *Music Educators Journal, 91*(3), 35–42.

Younker, B. (2000). Thought processes and strategies of students engaged in music composition. *Research Studies in Music Education, 14*, 24–39.

CHAPTER 14

....

THE ROLE OF TECHNOLOGY
IN LEARNING TO COMPOSE

....

GENA R. GREHER

> The computer can simulate any number of musical possibilities in a non-destructive way allowing the musician to try different ideas and explore a vast range of musical possibilities.
>
> (Brown, 2007, p. 9)

MUSIC technology, such as notation software and digital audio workstations (DAW), as well as the development of MIDI instruments and a host of other music creation tools and apps, allows for more inclusive access to music creation for anyone with an interest in music. What this means for the average student is the potential for an increased ability to explore, play with, and manipulate sound to create new sonic experiences, as well as imitate and recreate music they hear in their lives both in and out of school. At its most basic level, whether students are using computers or mobile devices, music technology allows students to become sound explorers.

Being a *sound explorer* is a trait we want to instill in our students, specifically with regard to composing. Since most of us do not necessarily have the skill of Mozart or Beethoven, who could put to paper the music in their mind's ear, music technology affords anyone at any age the ability to "play with sound." Music creators at any level of ability or expertise can immediately determine what sounds good or interesting to them through the act of manipulating the musical elements. When one thinks of the term "play," one is generally more apt to think of infants and toddlers discovering and exploring the vast array of objects and sounds that encompass their young, new, and exciting world. For many teachers of older students, the term "play" in educational settings brings to mind games, and other less serious off-task endeavors (Pegrum et al., 2013). The research on open-ended play and interest driven learning allows for the generation of new ideas and inventions. As suggested by Howell (2017), "open-ended, exploratory, imaginative play . . . plays an important role in the feedback loops between technology, context, informal learning and innovation" (p. 252). With regard to music, allowing students to play and tinker with the materials of music and sound can accommodate multiple ways of thinking for a diversity of students (Resnick, 2017; Resnick & Rosenbaum, 2013; Turkle, 1995). Wohlwend (2017) points out, "Players play while they learn and learn while they play, creating a balanced, bidirectional relationship between play and learning" (p. 597).

As students enter the upper grades, the focus in many school music classes generally shifts away from the visceral aural sensation that made music a pleasurable experience for them in the first place, toward a more visual and abstract endeavor. Learning to play music in a school setting typically has more to do with learning the symbol system surrounding the study of music than with the actual musical sound itself. Often, students are learning "about" music in the abstract rather than feeling and experiencing music through sonic explorations. Rather than learning the principles of music as theoretical concepts of Roman numerals and rules, music technology can turn abstract mental exercises into concrete active listening and doing experiences, allowing students to actually hear and most importantly, manipulate chords, chord progressions, melodies, rhythm, timbre, form, dynamics, and expressivity. Whereas many music teachers have shied away from incorporating music composition in their classes until their students learn some music fundamentals such as traditional notation and basic music theory, music technology makes possible an approach to music composition that is more intuitively oriented. This approach allows students to begin exploring musical ideas before they know all the formal rules of composing. In fact, growing up with the ability to hear a diversity of musical genres anywhere and anytime, today's students, as suggested by Bamberger (2003), have some highly developed musical intuitions for music teachers to tap into. Peppler (2017b) believes music technology can help serve as a bridge between what our students intuitively know, and the formal understandings we wish to impart.

Brown (2007) views the computer as having three distinct musical roles: he sees it as a tool, a medium, and an instrument. As a musical tool it makes tasks more efficient and allows the user to accomplish goals that otherwise might be more difficult or in some instances not even possible. As a medium, Brown writes,

> When using the computer as a musical medium, the musician acts as an explorer. The possibilities of musical and sound transformations afforded by the computer can be depicted as a vast landscape. The computer as medium represents that terrain and various software applications or computational functions are vehicles for the musician to explore that terrain. (Brown, 2007, p. 10)

According to Brown, its role as an instrument, as with any instrument, allows the musician a means for communicating musical ideas. He also discusses the bond that develops between a musician and their instrument, where the instrument almost becomes an extension of the musician. Unfortunately for many music teachers, the perception exists that making music with and through technology is "not quite real music," which they believe can only be created with and through traditional instruments.

Williams (2014; 2021) suggests in his writings and discussions regarding the iPad as a musical instrument, that much like any musical instrument, the iPad or in fact any other computing device, requires the "human touch." That is to say, the sounds a traditional acoustic instrument or technologically enhanced device produces, along with expressive qualities and other aspects of musicality, are entirely dependent on human input and interaction. As with playing an instrument, without the human factor, whether it's in the programming of a computing device or the actual playing of a laptop or mobile device, no sound or music will be produced.

I would be remiss however for not pointing out that music technology in the form of hardware and software is neither neutral nor a blank slate. Even with algorithmically created music, there exists a human programmer somewhere in the background helping to determine the outcome. What we can do with the technology is oftentimes affected by the intent and limitations imposed by the technology's designers (Brown, 2007; Peppler, 2017b). Of course choosing the proper hardware and software environments for your compositional objectives is crucial, and the design of new music technologies can have the inadvertent effect of favoring some ways of music knowing over others (Peppler, 2017b) This is all to say, if the goal is to have students create music with and through technology as a composition tool in a school or afterschool setting, one needs to choose music technology that allows students to explore their musical intuitions without too many technological barriers. Ease of entry, a low price point, and choosing software that allows for the teaching of broad concepts should be the major considerations for music technology choices (Greher & Heines, 2014).

In this chapter I will provide strategies for employing a variety of music software applications and platforms for developing an understanding and ability to compose music with both novice and advanced students. There will be a focus on how students can use technology to manipulate sounds and organize their musical thoughts through a range of approaches for lesson activities and considerations on choosing the right tools for one's learning objectives. From easy entry points for young musicians such as the use of looping software, to more advanced approaches to music composition involving recording, editing, and mixing within a DAW, readers will gain an overview of the role technology can play in engaging students. Simple music coding, through a program such as Scratch,[1] which is a visual programming language developed by the Lifelong Kindergarten group at MIT's Media Lab under the direction of Mitchel Resnick, can be employed to aid students in learning about and manipulating musical form, as well as teach students the basics of algorithmic music composition. Learning about timbre and lessons on layering and combining sounds will be discussed through the use of MIDI instruments and the role that notation software can play in music teaching. Teachers will ultimately gain an understanding of the benefits and constraints of the types of platforms one can use to access music technology in their classroom, such as whether to use cloud-based or desktop-specific applications, as well as digital apps that can be used if teaching in a bring-your-own-device (BYOD) classroom.

Pedagogical Underpinnings for Music Technology

The ultimate goal of this chapter is to provide the pedagogical and technological foundation for engaging students in music creation and composition. With a focus on informal and non-formal learning, I will suggest approaches similar to those of Computer Clubhouses, developed by researchers from MIT's Lifelong Kindergarten group. These clubhouses were developed to facilitate students' interests in computing by allowing students to set their own goals. Embedded in this framework is an emphasis on project-based, informal, and participatory approaches to learning at its core, involving sharing and collaboration with few obstacles to artistic expression. In *Lifelong Kindergarten*, Resnick (2017) discusses his philosophy of technology creation with regard to what Papert[2] refers to as high ceilings and low floors. What this means is designing the technology to allow novice users easy entry into working with the software. In other words, the low floors metaphor is about creating user-friendly technology without a steep learning curve. Yet the high ceilings is the technology's ability to provide a structure for users to develop greater sophistication and complexity in their work as they become more experienced. With regard to the Computer Clubhouses, Resnick adds the caveat of also including wide walls in the design of technology. Resnick (2017) states the objective of the wide walls comparison is to design the technology to encompass a wide range of interests and pathways to achieving one's goals. The potential for growth and complexity within this environment is limited only by one's imagination, and as suggested by Peppler (2017b), allows for the development of interest driven expertise through exploration, trial and error, peer-to-peer collaboration, feedback, and mentoring. With a minimum of technological expertise and expense, setting up a class environment that allows for open ended excursions into playing with and manipulating sound as entry points into composition will yield higher levels of student engagement and interest.

The computer clubhouse supports project-based learning to connect students to learning through activities they find personally meaningful (Brennan et al., 2010; Peppler, 2017b; Resnick, 2017; Rusk et al., 2009). Another feature is the collaborative, open-ended approach that is less teacher-directed and is framed by a more constructivist approach to education (Jones, 2017). This approach supports the development of critical thinking and problem-solving skills and encourages students to not just consume and interact with technology, but to be creators. As with music teachers who wait until their students know traditional notation before letting them compose, Resnick (2017), believes many educators are wary of project-based learning, fearing that one needs to first teach the basics before students can work on projects. Yet his research emphasizes that project-based learning can provide meaningful contexts for students to interact with concepts and apply what they are learning in other areas as well.

Teachers who adopt a clubhouse approach to student engagement and interaction, would need to employ informal and non-formal learning approaches that are participatory in nature, allowing students to investigate and explore their creative ideas more in depth and build on the social interactions that are ever present in students' lives (Jenkins et al., 2009; Martin, 2017; Peppler, 2017b; Turino, 2008). In addition to learning to code in Scratch, which is web-based, (Brennan et al., 2010; Resnick, 2017; Rusk et al., 2009), there is a very robust online community. The Scratch website is set up much like a social-networking site so that students all over the world can share their ideas and their projects, as well as give and receive feedback on their work. The peer-to-peer mentoring that takes place in music clubhouses and within the online Scratch community, along with the access to music and media technology, supports the goals of today's students for sharing and creating music with one's peers (Kenny, 2016; Tobias, 2015; Waldron, 2012). Music technology, whether it's as a tool, medium, or instrument, makes it possible for students to pursue the music that interests them, lets them connect with their peers on a social level, and provides a sense that what they are doing matters (Jenkins et al., 2009; Tobias, 2015).

Informal learning practices in music, popularized by Lucy Green in the United Kingdom through the Musical Futures Project is based on the intuitive practices employed by popular musicians (Green, 2001, 2006, 2008) and (Peppler 2017a). Students decide what music they want to learn using their ears and intuitive music knowledge, without much outside intervention or reliance on formal notation. With a non-formal approach, the programming is a bit more structured by adults, though students can help to determine their individual goals. The role of an adult in this approach is to be more of a facilitator (Peppler, 2017a; Smith, 2017). In the Musical Futures model students are tackling the learning of the actual music they are hearing out in the world, as opposed to the often-simplified compositions that are the stock and trade of many school music classes and ensembles (Peppler, 2017a). Composing with music technology is a way for students to get really close to replicating the music they are growing up with. With its ability to provide instant aural feedback along with many of the effects processors and tools artists use, students can easily alter instruments, harmonies, and melodic versions, based on what sounds good them. Green's (2001, 2006, 2008) research suggests the informal learning approach utilized in the Musical Futures project helps increase school engagement of disaffected youth through participation in music study. It should be noted, as Green points out, that in a typical informal, out-of-school context, students work at learning the music at their own pace without the pressure of formal assessments.

One of the earliest developments in music technology for young children was based on the underlying premise of Jeanne Bamberger's groundbreaking work in music cognition, and her research into musical intuition, particularly with regard to musical hierarchy and form. (Bamberger, 1979, 1995, 1996, and 2000). Her research into students' perceptions of how music works, how melodies are structured, and what gives music coherence began with the creation of a game through a Logo Music[3] project she called Tuneblocks (Bamberger, 1979). It is one of the earliest interactive computer programs for young children that allowed them to manipulate the materials of music, rather than drill them about music. It helped students make sense of the music, not as notes but as motives, figures, and phrases, and provided immediate aural feedback.

Her work with Logo eventually led to the creation of Impromptu[4] in 1999, as a digital music platform that encourages students to actively build their knowledge base through analyzing simple tunes and creatively developing their own musical understandings. This software is divided into five discrete "playrooms" for melody, rhythm, harmonization, four-part harmony, and rounds. The two most prominent ones are Tuneblocks for melody, and Drummer for rhythm. In the Tuneblocks playroom, students are asked to reconstruct simple folk melodies by putting the blocks containing musical phrases in the correct sequence, in order to reconstruct the tune. They are then asked to think about how the tune is constructed, which blocks are repeated and why, as well as the function of each block; which is a beginning, middle, or end (Bamberger, 2000 and 2003).

Students can open the individual blocks to see and learn about pitch and duration properties. They edit them based on a variety of scales and modes. In addition to traditional folk tunes, there are several melody playrooms that feature music from a variety of cultures,[5] as well as ones that feature music with no tonal center. The program also allows students to remix melody notes and rhythms within the blocks, as well as altering the tonal system for each block. The Drummer playroom allows users to employ everyday mathematics to understand the structures that organize music rhythmically through ratios and proportions. Another feature of this program is its ability to let users access multiple representations of detail such as pitch contour, piano roll, rhythm bars, or rhythm roll (see examples in Figure 14.1 for the tune "Lassie"). There are many activities that can be accomplished with the Impromptu software, which can be found on the software's website at: http://www.tuneblocks.com and at https://makingmusicco unt.org.

The concepts embedded in Jeanne Bamberger's Impromptu will be further expanded upon in this chapter with the Interactive Puzzle Card Activity, which helps students to think about and explore how music is structured.

While these more exploratory informal and non-formal approaches to learning and assessing are often at odds with the way in which school-based classes are structured, the benefit of these approaches is that students are composing, improvising, and immersing themselves in a great deal of deep listening and musical analysis. Perhaps through

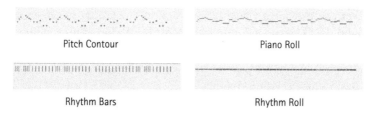

FIGURE 14.1. Graphic representation of the tune "Lassie" in Impromptu

the development of open-ended projects that are personally meaningful to students, teachers can find the right balance for engaging students, while including some form of peer and self-assessment in the grading mix. Would they share their creation with their friends or post it on YouTube or SoundCloud? Why or why not?

MUSIC SOFTWARE 101 BASICS

In aligning technology choices to teaching objectives, it is important to understand all the capabilities and limitations of hardware and software choices. In many instances, the hardware may be predetermined by the school district, in terms of using traditional PC's or Mac OS computers, Chromebooks, or mobile devices. Each type of hardware will often dictate the software options that are available to use. There are software platforms that are web-based, inexpensive, or free, and not platform-specific. These web-based platforms have the advantage of allowing students to work from anywhere at any time, not just in the school's computer lab. For instance, though my college students have access to an up-to-date computer lab equipped with a variety of music software options, I have gravitated over the years to using software that is more web-based. The software programs in our lab, which are often costly, have computer-specific site licenses. Web-based software in general is licensed to each student as a registered user, allowing students access to the software, wherever and whenever they want. This option generally has a lower cost-per-student price point and also doesn't involve a great deal of maintenance or upgrades. The major negative is when there's an internet failure or a power outage, which means unless there's the ability to save a project to a desktop rather than the cloud, students would be unable to work on their project until their internet service is up and running. Many schools have also adopted Chromebooks as their device of choice, which means that web-based products would be the best option. Many of the web-based programs will function on a mobile device, plus there are many mobile apps for music-making that are available for both iOS and Android devices. Some of them are operating-system-specific, yet there are generally similar functioning apps that can be found.

In thinking about the types of software that would typically be used for music composition, at the top of the list would be a good all-purpose digital audio workstation (DAW), which can facilitate composing, recording, editing, arranging, and mixing music. DAWs will often but not always include looping software and music sequencers. The sequencer can provide a visual representation of a composition, generally in the form of a piano roll as shown in Figure 14.2. Most DAWs have the capability of working with MIDI (musical instrument digital interface) files or audio files such as .mp3, .wav, or .aiff. MIDI is how various keyboard controllers, electronic instruments, and computers communicate with each other.

There are numerous options, from introductory prosumer versions that are free, such as Apple GarageBand, which comes with Mac OS, to web-based licensed subscription

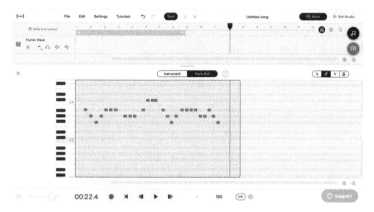

FIGURE 14.2. Piano roll view in Soundtrap

versions such as Soundtrap. More advanced options, which can be purchased outright or with a monthly subscription, are Ableton Live, Apple Logic Pro, Avid Pro Tools, Steinberg Cubase, Image-Line FL Studio, and Reason Many of these DAWs even have mobile apps.

Working with Young Students and Music Technology

Starting with the youngest sound explorers, there are a number of graphically oriented software apps. Google Chrome Music Lab (https://musiclab.chromeexperiments.com) has several visually oriented apps to allow students to explore melody and song creation. Both Song Maker (https://musiclab.chromeexperiments.com/Song-Maker/) and *Melody Maker* (https://musiclab.chromeexperiments.com/Melody-Maker/) use an interface that is similar to graph paper so that when each graph square is clicked, a note will play with a specific color associated with that note. The pitch colors are aligned with the colors of Boomwhackers[6] that many music teachers use in the early grades. The pitch changes move along a vertical axis while the rhythmic duration is on a horizontal axis. Morton Subotnick's Pitch Painter app for iOS devices is a finger-painting app that allows young children to literally draw and explore sounds in much the same way along a vertical and horizontal axis. This Pitch Painter app also introduces young children to several different scale tunings from different world regions.

Looping Basics

Looping software is another user-friendly way for students to enter into music creation that builds on their musical intuitions and preferences. Loops are short, pre-recorded phrases that allow for endless repetition. Loop libraries contain extensive assortments of sounds that can consist of multiple musical genres and eras, acoustic and electronic instruments, and a variety of moods and atmospheres. There are loops that are melodic, rhythmic, or simple sound effects. These loops can be put together in an infinite range of patterns and can be edited and layered into a variety of original compositions. DAWs such as GarageBand, which is MacOS and iOS based, generally come bundled with Apple products. However, there are several web-based inexpensive or freeware DAWs geared for educational purposes, such as Soundtrap (https://www.soundtrap.com) and BandLab (https://www.bandlab.com). In addition to providing loop libraries, these programs are great all-purpose DAWs for sequencing, recording, editing, and mixing music. Students can input their own vocals and MIDI instruments, and upload external audio tracks and MIDI files, as well as manipulate the audio parameters of each track through an assortment of effects processors, allowing for a great deal of creative input from the user. One of the features in Soundtrap that is particularly suited for participatory music-making is the collaboration feature, which makes it possible for multiple users to simultaneously enter the same Soundtrap studio to record, edit, and mix. For teachers using a learning management system or Google Classroom, both Soundtrap and BandLab have the capability of being integrated into them for ease of distributing and assessing assignments.

Notation Basics

Once students are at the point of working with traditional music notation, a notation software program will allow students to turn their musical ideas into printable transcriptions for any number of instruments, with the added benefit of letting students hear what their composition sounds like, with any combination of acoustic and electronic instruments. While using a stand-alone notation program will require familiarity with traditional music notation, some sequencers have the ability to print out a score in either traditional notation or in piano roll format. There are any number of excellent software platforms to choose from that are available for computers and mobile devices, ranging from entry-level to professional quality use, with a range of price points. For educational purposes, Noteflight is low-cost, web-based, and cross-platform, with the ability for students to work alone or collaboratively with their peers and share their work. Students can input any number of instruments, as well as print out individual parts and scores. As with BandLab and Soundtrap described above, Noteflight can be integrated into a learning management system where music teachers can upload scores to share with students and provide feedback. Noteflight will even allow users to export their scores into Soundtrap. If budget allows, it may also make sense to invest in MIDI keyboard controllers, though all of the software will work from a computer keyboard, or in the case of a mobile device, the normal touch interface. Becoming familiar with audio platforms that allow students to upload and share their creations, such as SoundCloud and YouTube, and understanding the issues of copyrighted material as well as privacy concerns regarding making files public, should also be investigated and discussed with students.

Makey Makey Basics

In addition to the programs mentioned above, there are a number of hardware and software platforms and apps that allow for users to explore different sounds and different ways of putting music together that are more visually oriented. One such device is the Makey Makey Invention Kit, created by Jay Silver and Eric Rosenbaum while they were students at MIT's Media Lab (https://makeymakey.com). It was created to allow students to tinker and explore the possibilities of electrical conductivity and circuitry, yet when connected to MIDI-based software, there are endless musical possibilities as well. It is a small, relatively inexpensive microcontroller that mimics the functions of a game controller. With no additional software, the Makey Makey can be connected to a computer through a USB cable and the device will function like a keyboard controller. It is literally a plug-and-play device. Using the included alligator clips, along with any kind of material you can find that conducts electricity, students can complete an electrical circuit, to create anything they can imagine. With the students' interests in mind, this device will provide opportunities to explore the materials and plan and conceptualize the types of instruments they would like to create, as well as explore both MIDI-based sounds and their own sonic creations for an interactive improvisatory composition. The Makey Makey device supports an almost constant state of discovery and exploration, while in reality students will be learning how to work as teams, discover new uses of the technology at hand, and use basic electronic circuitry to make music.

Yes, Anyone Can Teach with Technology: Here's How to Do It!

How might these tools be used to encourage students to play with and manipulate sound while also teaching musical concepts? In this section, activities will range from using the Google Chrome Music Lab's Song Maker app to teach about musical patterns and form, to using DAWs to create hip-hop tracks. In many cases these activities will also have interdisciplinary connections into literacy development, math, and science. What follows is a variety of lesson activities and software types to help get started with some simple entry points. These activities can be employed as is, or adapted and expanded upon to suit teaching goals, students' interests, and curricular requirements.

Basic Form with Song Maker

When a group of pre-service music education students were working with a middle school music class to teach form, they developed a very extensive set of activities to teach these students using Song Maker (https://musiclab.chromeexperiments.com/

Song-Maker/). What they discovered after the first day was that the students were using the software to write messages to each other or write out their names to see what they sounded like. Building on what the students were doing, the next lesson involved having each student write their first name in the software to see what it sounded like as their A section. Given the nature of what this would involve, the texture could be quite dense. The new goal was to ask them to create a B section that had a different texture that was less dense.

Song Maker has the ability to let students choose the note to start on, choose whether it is a major, minor, or pentatonic scale; along with choosing the number of bars, beats per measure, and how to split the beat, users can also determine the number of octaves that are desired for this composition. There is a "save" button that creates a URL for students' work. The program is designed to allow users to download the file as a MIDI or .wav file and can also provide and embed code. It's always a good idea to have the students email teachers that link. This is a link for my version of the A section in the above activity: https://musiclab.chromeexperiments.com/Song-Maker/song/61366 04328984576. Of course, it can be a great ear training tool when students are provided with some simple tunes to see if they can then input the melody into Song Maker by ear.

The True Story of the Three Little Pigs, by John Scieszka

Using music technology, specifically with a looping software program such as those previously mentioned, students can create soundtracks/soundscapes for children's stories. It is a great way to engage upper elementary students in musical and creative thinking. John Sciescka's *The True Story of the Three Little Pigs*[7] is a satirical twist on the classic story that many children know. This version is told from the Wolf's perspective. A teacher can either create a read-aloud version of the book, or use the YouTube version from YouTube Kids, where the author is reading the story with the book's visuals, but without any music or sound effects. The object here is to have a discussion with students about what the mood is for specific parts of the story and what action could be supported by music and/or effects. This is also a great opportunity to discuss how this story differs from the original version they are familiar with. It would be beneficial to create a list of the various scenes, noting what is happening, what the mood or atmosphere might be, and what words or phrases could be emphasized with music. Then ask students, either individually or in pairs, to explore the software for a variety of loops they think match the moods and actions from the list.

In addition to creating moods and supporting actions, this activity would be perfect for a unit on musical motifs by asking students to create some character attributes for each of the pigs, as well as the wolf. They can then explore short motifs for each of the characters based on the attributes they came up with. Once they have gathered all the loops they think are appropriate, ask them to create a soundscape that tells the story through words, music, and sound effects. An example of a track layout is shown in Figure 14.3. A DAW such as GarageBand or Soundtrap will allow them to have a

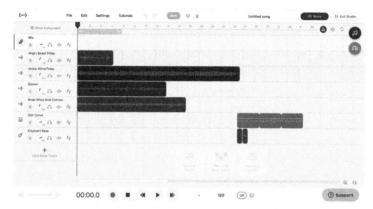

FIGURE 14.3. Example of a Soundtrap track layout

multitrack recording in order to keep narration, music loops, and sound effect loops as separate tracks for ease of layering and mixing sounds. They can then record their own narration or use either the teacher-created one or the one from the YouTube version. It should be noted that while this story is fun to explore, the activity of creating a soundtrack to a story can work with any story where it would be conducive to adding mood music, sound effects, and musical motifs for specific characters.

Hip-Hop Meets Children's Lit

This activity is great for getting middle school or even high school and college students to explore a DAW such as Soundtrap or BandLab, fueled by their interest in beat-making. Hopefully this activity will also encourage a larger discussion about how hip-hop is shaping our culture globally, and as a means of expression for students. It encompasses not just music, but visual art, dance, the written word, theater, fashion, and politics. Though it began in the very urban Bronx, New York, its influence can be felt worldwide. It is also extremely fortuitous that several well-known contemporary artists such as Ludacris (https://www.youtube.com/watch?v=PFtHeo7oMSU), Migos

(https://www.youtube.com/watch?v=zPJl2e38S4g), and Post Malone (https://www.youtube.com/watch?v=ioVAbpKCDxI) paved the way for this activity, providing fun and inspiration to students of all ages, by rapping/freestyling read-alouds to children's books. After viewing their videos created by these popular artists based on children's books and nursery rhymes, ask students to choose a nursery rhyme or children's book they are particularly fond of. Dr. Seuss books seem particularly well suited to this activity. For younger students it might be a good idea to suggest a couple of titles for students to choose from, such as: *The Cat in the Hat, Green Eggs and Ham, One Fish Two Fish Red Fish Blue Fish, Horton Hears a Who!, The Lorax,* or *Fox in Sox.* Once the text has been selected students need to first adapt the text to a rap rhyme scheme,[8] which can be a bridge for an interdisciplinary lesson on poetry. Once they have the rap lyric worked out, they will need to create a backing track to rap to by exploring the beat-making loops in whichever DAW they are working with. This activity works well by teaming students up in pairs and giving them the option of performing their rap live in class to their backing track or creating a TikTok video to present to class.

Public Service Video Announcement (PSA)

Creating a public service announcement (PSA) is great activity to do with middle school or high school students. This is a good opportunity for students to take on an issue they care about, or one that may be part of a larger school curriculum, such as anti-bullying, food insecurity, or any number of social justice or public health issues that are important to them. A well-crafted public service announcement is like an advertisement, though not for a product, but a service or message that will benefit the community and or the public good (https://en.wikipedia.org/wiki/Public_service_announcement).Download ing several old-time cartoons from https://archive.org can be an easy and fun way to find visuals to help create the message. It is best to then extract the audio from these cartoons to share with students, so they are not influenced by any existing dialog or music. The audio-free cartoons can then be uploaded to a Google Drive folder, Dropbox folder, or One Drive, to then share the links with students.

Once students have come up with an issue for their PSA and created a script with a strong memorable tag line, students can then record their narration. After reviewing the cartoons to find the most appropriate scenes to edit together to support their message, they will need to create an original music underscore or song and add titles and sound effects to create their finished Public Service Announcement. As a group project students can collectively work on this in a DAW such as Soundtrap. The length of the PSA should be 60 or 90 seconds. The musical parameters can be simple, asking students to just use loops, or they can be more complex, requiring students to create several original tracks recorded with MIDI or acoustic instruments. The sound effects should be tracks they create themselves, much like a Foley artist[9] would do in filmmaking or radio/podcast production.

A variation on this activity for elementary students would be to find a scene from a single cartoon sequence to work with, remove the audio, and discuss what might be happening in this cartoon. What sounds, dialogue and what kind of music might be needed to make this cartoon feel complete? Working in groups the students can create the soundtrack to this short cartoon sequence.

Music Arranging Activity—For Notation Novices

There are several ways to do this activity based on age and level of familiarity with traditional music notation. With upper elementary or middle school students they can listen to some simple tunes or TV or movie themes they might be familiar with and see if they can use their ears to input the melody on either some kind of keyboard or guitar. Whatever notation program they are using, such as Noteflight or Musescore, there will be options to choose from. Once they have the melody transcribed, that will be their A section. For the B section, they come up with two or three variations on the A melody to be played by different instruments and then return to the A section.

Music Arranging Activity—For Advanced Students

There are a number of websites where it is possible to obtain free MIDI files of cartoon, TV, and movie themes your students might be familiar with (see https://www.midiwo rld.com). The whole class can be assigned the same MIDI file theme to work on, or students can be given an option to choose from four or five that have been selected. It is possible to set up user groups in Noteflight to share scores, so once a MIDI file has been uploaded, that file can be shared with the class as a user group. When starting a new project there is an option of starting from a blank score sheet, allowing users to indicate a specific clef or instrument, or a project can be started by importing a MIDI or .xml file. When starting from a MIDI file users can choose the option to create parts from tracks. However, depending on the arrangement of the imported MIDI file, it is possible the score opens up with a great deal of complexity encompassing numerous ledger lines and rhythmic difficulty. For less experienced students, it may make sense to first simplify the parts before sending it out to them, and for the more experienced students it can be left for them to listen and simplify.

Once students have their MIDI file of a cartoon, TV, video game, or movie theme uploaded to a Notation program, the idea is to have the students create an arrangement for any number of small ensembles. This can include any of the following: a basic rock band, a funk band, an a capella vocal group, a percussion ensemble, a string quartet, or woodwind or brass quintets. They will need to think about what keys are appropriate for the group they are writing for, as well as what rhythmic adaptations might be needed to accommodate the type of ensemble and level of musicians they are writing for. This could be an activity for a general music class, or it could work just as easily for instrumental and/or vocal ensemble students to create these arrangements for members of their ensembles to perform.

Scratch and the Makey Makey Invention Kit: Creating Interactive Tuneblocks Puzzle Cards

It is possible to expand on the concepts embedded in the Impromptu software to encompass the music students are listening to, as a way to encourage active listening and develop their ear training and transcription skills. This will come in handy in their future compositions. Within *Impromptu* it is entirely possible to have students create a set of blocks based on a popular tune and chunk them into phrases, while developing

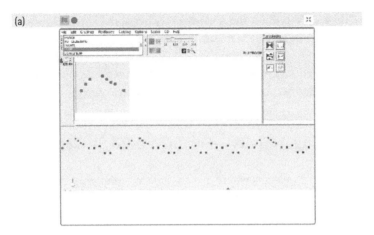

FIGURE 14.4A. Scratch Puzzle Card screen—Puzzle player view

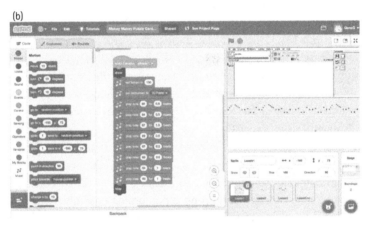

FIGURE 14.4B. Scratch Puzzle Card screen—Programming view

their ability to recognize patterns. Outside of *Impromptu* one can explore similar activities through musical puzzle cards, which is an activity many teachers employ to develop aural skills, teach about form, and introduce a form of graphic notation and/or invented notation, often in advance of teaching traditional music notation (https://musicalmaps. weebly.com/puzzle-cards.html; Wiggins, 2009). However, with traditional puzzle cards students don't get the immediate aural feedback. With a little help from technology, the Musical Puzzle Card concept can be fused with Bamberger's Tuneblocks through an interactive listening activity that can be accomplished with Scratch and a computer keyboard (See Figures 4a and 4b). For even more interactivity with a bit more of a STEAM approach, the Makey Makey Invention Kit can be integrated into this activity (See Figure 4.5).

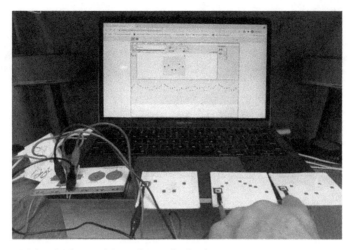

FIGURE 14.5. Makey Makey and Scratch Puzzle Card

Puzzle Card/Scratch Activity

This is an interactive puzzle card activity I created in Scratch to work with the Makey Makey as the touch interface for the actual puzzle pieces. As long as students are attached to the ground, when they touch the conductive material on each of the puzzle cards, they can play and hear the different phrases of the tune. As with Bamberger's Impromptu, the goal is to play the tune in the proper sequence, so in this case the student needs to touch each puzzle card in the proper sequence. In recreating the song "Lassie" from Impromptu, I used screenshots of the Impromptu screen as well as screenshots of the pitch contour for the tune, in order to program them into Scratch. For users to access my example of the interactive version of the "Lassie" tune puzzle card, they first need to set up an account in Scratch at https://scratch.mit.edu. This link will lead to a puzzle card activity where my example may be viewed: https://scra tch.mit.edu/projects/30037804/

Very simple programming features have been used and this link provides a template for what to do. It is important to remind students that whenever they are opening up someone else's program, they must be sure to first click on the remix button, shown in Figure 14.6, and save the work as new program with its own unique URL. When creating an interactive puzzle for students, be sure to choose a piece of music geared to the students' age and musical interests or to a particular piece of music they may be working on. A set of interactive Scratch puzzle cards can focus on either having students reconstruct a tune based on its melodic contour or based on its rhythmic map. Be sure to include a button/sprite that will play the tune in its entirety and then ask students to put the different blocks in order. If students all have access to a computer, they can save their work and then share their unique link. When working with just a teacher computer and a projector or smartboard, the Makey Makey Invention Kit can be programmed to

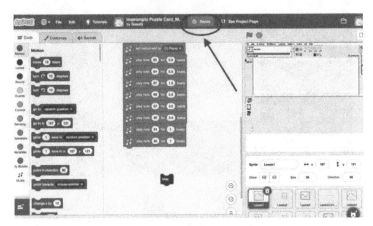

FIGURE 14.6. Scratch screen with Remix button circled

create an interactive component where students can take turns to see if they can play the tune in its proper sequence of phrases. Just make sure they are connected to a ground to complete the circuit in order for it to play.

BeatBox/Makey Makey Activity

This is an activity that can be accomplished with a variety of age groups using simple coding in Scratch. A good freeware audio recording and editing program to be familiar with is Audacity. Audacity is not as good for multitrack recording projects, but it will provide students a great many editing and effects options for this project. In this activity it is important to let students explore the variety of sounds they can make through "Mouth Percussion" and "Body Percussion." They will need to record all their sounds using either Audacity or another DAW on their computer if there's a built-in microphone, or they can use a hand-held digital device, such as their cell phone. Once their sounds are recorded, they will need to upload these sounds into Audacity and explore the various effects they can add to transform these sounds. I always ask my students to see if they can create at least two additional timbres from each sound they record. There are numerous effects to choose from. They will have the ability to reverse their sounds, pan their sounds, distort sounds and cut them up to create an entirely new sound from what was recorded.

Once they have all their sounds recorded, they will need to export them as mp3 files. They will then need to explore the Makey Makey and think of the interface they want to create to make a new musical instrument that will play these sounds. They can even create a wearable object that will in essence turn them into a human beatboxing machine. Once they have decided on the interface using a variety of conductive materials, they will need to map all their sounds to a program such as Scratch, shown in Figure 14.7.

Students can upload their individual mp3 files as audio files in Scratch and then trigger each sound through controllers mapped to their computer keyboards using the up, down, left, right arrows and space bar, which will allow students to use the al-ligator clips to connect their interface to the Makey Makey (shown in Figure 14.8a). If students are using more than five sounds, they can add additional sounds by con-necting to the Makey Makey by programming the W, A, S, D, F, and G keys in Scratch, which will connect to the Makey Makey through the white wires included in the kit (see Figure 14.8b).

They will also need to connect to a ground, which is called "earth" on the device, in order to play their sounds and perform their composition for an in-class performance.

FIGURE 14.7. Makey Makey clay and foil sound triggers connected to Scratch

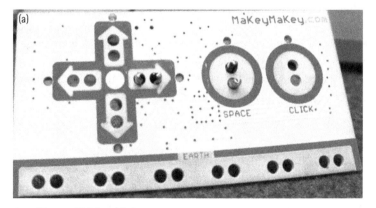

FIGURE 14.8A. Front of Makey Makey

FIGURE 14.8B. Back of Makey Makey

Wrapping It Up

Much of technology's potential in education is often narrowly focused on a more utilitarian tools-based approach, rather than technology's potential to be a creative and expressive medium. Prensky (2012) put it quite succinctly when he stated, "To create effective 21st-century learning, it is not just our tools that need to change—it is our thinking." As suggested by Papert (1987), the focus needs to shift so that children are using technology to create. To provide a technology-based learning environment that encourages students to be *sound explorers* and fully develop their intuitive understandings, however, teachers too need more opportunities to explore their own intuitions, as well as develop a comfort level with these music technology tools.

As suggested in this chapter, with just a few software options, mentioned throughout this chapter, it is possible to provide students an infinite variety of ways to explore all the musical possibilities embedded in the world around them. When given the freedom to explore their creative potential in music-making activities, we can support the innovative and creative thinking that the high-pressure, high-stakes testing environment often stifles. It is my hope that through providing this overview of some basic music technology tools along with the pedagogical framework of more informal approaches for employing them, music teachers will develop a comfort level and repertoire for supporting all the creative musicians in their classrooms.

NOTES

1. Scratch—https://scratch.mit.edu—is a visual programming language developed by the Lifelong Kindergarten group at MIT's Media Lab
2. Seymor Papert was an MIT mathematician who was one of the pioneers of constructionism and artificial intelligence and inventor of Logo. For more information see *The Children's Machine: Rethinking School in the Age of the Computer*, rev. ed., Basic Books (April 29, 1994);

and *Mindstorms: Children, Computers, and Powerful Ideas* Basic Books; Revised edition (October 6, 2020).

3. Music Logo is an offshoot of the Logo Programming language developed by Seymour Papert at the MIT Artificial Intelligence Laboratory—https://el.media.mit.edu/logo-fou ndation/what_is_logo/history.html

4. To find out more about *Impromptu* go to www.tuneblocks.com and https://makingmusicco unt.org

5. For research on how Impromptu was used to test students cultural assumptions, see Downton, M. P., Peppler, K. A., Portowitz, A., Bamberger, Lindsay, E. (2012). *Composing pieces for peace: Using Impromptu to build cross-cultural awareness.* Visions of Research in Music Education. Retrieved from https://opencommons.uconn.edu/vrme/vol20/iss1/

6. Boomwhackers are color-coded, hollow plastic tubes tuned to specific pitches. The basic set is tuned to a C major diatonic scale and there are chromatic sets as well.

7. *The True* Story *of the Three Little Pigs by a Wolf* is a children's book by John Scieszka, author, and Lane Smith, illustrator. Published by Penguin Young Readers Group.

8. See Rapping Deconstructed by Open Mike Eagle—https://www.youtube.com/watch?v= QWveXdj6oZU&feature=youtu.be

9. Foley artists create many of the sounds and sound effects heard in films. To learn about the role of a Foley artist see: https://en.wikipedia.org/wiki/Foley_(filmmaking)

References

Bamberger, J. (1979). *Logo music projects: Experiments in musical perception and design.* A. I. Memo 523/ Logo Memo 52, Issue. Cambridge, MA, Massachusetts Institute of Technology

Bamberger, J. (1995). *The mind behind the musical ear.* Harvard University Press.

Bamberger, J. (1996). Turning music theory on its ear: Do we hear what we see; Do we see what we say? *Int'l. Jrnl. of Computers for Mathematical Learning, 1*(1), 33–55. www.springerlink.com/content/w3tj41127k625313/

Bamberger, J. (2000). *Developing musical intuitions.* Oxford University Press.

Bamberger, J. (2003). The development of intuitive musical understanding: a natural experiment. *Psychology of Music, 31*(7), 7–36.

Brennan, K., Monrroy-Hernandez, A., & Resnick, M. (2010). Making projects, making friends: Online community as catalyst for interactive media creation. *New Directions for Youth Development, 128,* 75–83.

Brown, A. R. (2007). *Computers in music education: Amplifying musicality.* Routledge.

Green, L. (2001). *How popular musicians learn.* Ashgate.

Green, L. (2006). Popular music education in and for itself, and for "other" music: Current research in the classroom. *International Journal of Music Education, 24*(2), 101–118.

Green, L. (2008). *Music, informal learning and school: A new classroom pedagogy.* Ashgate.

Greher, G. R., & Heines, J. M. (2014). *Computational thinking in sound: Teaching the art and science of music and technology.* Oxford University Press.

Howell, G. (2017). Exploring intersections of technology, play, informality and innovation. In S. A. Ruthmann & R. Mantie (Eds.), *The Oxford handbook of technology and music education* (Vol. 1, pp. 247–254). Oxford University Press.

Jenkins, H., Clinton, K., Purushotma, R., Robison, A. J., & Weigel, M. (2009). *Confronting the challenges of participatory culture: Media education for the 21st century.* Cambridge, MA, Massachusetts Institute of Technology.

Jones, W. K. (2017). Project-based learning. In K. Peppler (Ed.), *The Sage encyclopedia of out-of-school learning* (Vol. 2, pp. 634–636). Sage Reference.

Kenny, A. (2016). *Communities of musical practice.* Routledge.

Martin, F. (2017). Computational thinking. In K. Peppler (Ed.), *The SAGE encyclopedia of out-of-school learning* (Vol. 1, pp. 117–119). SAGE Publications, Inc. https://doi.org/http://dx.doi.org/10.4135/9781483385198.n52

Papert, S. (1987). A critique of technocentrism in thinking about the school of the future. *Children in an Information Age: Opportunities for Creativity, Innovation, and New Activities.* Sofia, Bulgaria.

Pegrum, M., Oakley, G., & Faulkner, R. (2013). Schools going mobile: A study of the adoption of mobile handheld technologies in Western Australian independent schools. *Australasian Journal of Educational Technology, 29*(1), 66–81.

Peppler, K. (2017a). Equity and access in out-of school music making. In S. A. Ruthmann & R. Mantie (Eds.), *The Oxford handbook of technology and music education* (pp. 503–509). Oxford University Press.

Peppler, K. (2017b). Interest-driven music education: Youth, technology, and music making today. In S. A. Ruthmann & R. Mantie (Eds.), *The Oxford handbook of technology and music education* (pp. 191–202). Oxford University Press.

Prensky, M. (2012). *Before bringing in new tools, you must first bring in new thinking.* https://marcprensky.com/writing/Prensky-NewThinking-Amplify-June2012.pdf.

Resnick, M. (2017). *Lifelong Kindergarten: Cultivating creativity through projects, passion, peers and play.* The MIT Press.

Resnick, M., & Rosenbaum, E. (2013). Designing for tinkerability. In M. Honey & D. Kanter (Eds.), *Design, make, play: Growing the next generation fo stem innovators* (pp. 163–181). Routledge.

Rusk, N., Resnick, M., & Cooke, S. (2009). Origins and guiding principles of the computer clubhouse. In Y. B. Kafai, K. Peppler, & R. N. Chapman (Eds.), *The computer clubhouse: Constructionism and creattivity in youth communities* (p. 192). Teachers College Press.

Smith, G. D. (2017). Musical futures. In K. Peppler (Ed.), *The SAGE encyclopedia of out-of-school learning* (pp. 523–526). SAGE Publications.

Tobias, E. (2015). Participatory and digital cultures in practice: Perspectives and possibilities in a graduate music course. *International Journal of Community Music, 8*(1), 73–92.

Turino, T. (2008). *Music as social life: The politics of participation.* University of Chicago Press.

Turkle, S. (1995). *Life on the screen: Identity in the age of the internet.* TouchStone/Simon & Schuster.

VanderLinde, D. (n.d.). Puzzle cards. Musical Maps. https://musicalmaps.weebly.com/puzzle-cards.html.

Waldron, J. (2012). YouTube, fanvids, forums, vlogs and blogs: Informal music learning in a convergent on and offline music community. *International Journal of Music Education, 31*(1), 91–105.

Wiggins, J. H. (2009). *Teach for musical understanding* (2nd ed.). Center for Applied Research in Musical Understanding.

Williams, D. A. (2014). Another perspective: The iPad is a REAL musical instrument! *Music Educators Journal, 101*(1), 93–98.

Williams, D. A. (2021). The iPad as a musical instrument! In G. R. Greher & S. L. Burton (Eds.), *Creative music making at your fingertips: A mobile technology guide for music educators* (Vol. 1, pp. 83–97). Oxford University Press.

Wohlwend, K. E. (Ed.). (2017). *Playful learning*. SAGE Publications.

....

CHAPTER 15

(UN)ASSESSING THE PROCESSES AND PRODUCTS OF CHILDREN'S ORIGINAL MUSICAL COMPOSITION

....

MAUD HICKEY

> There should be one place in the school system where marks do not count. The art room should be a sanctuary against school regulations, where youngsters are free to be themselves and to put down their ideas and feelings and emotions without censorship, where they can evaluate their own progress toward their own goals without the imposition of an arbitrary grading system. (Lowenfeld & Brittain, 1987, p. 176)

IMAGINE if the art/music rooms in schools were indeed sanctuaries for students to create freely without the threat of grades or evaluations hanging over them. In John Dewey's fictional visit to a utopian world of schooling, assessment or grading did not exist, much less any kind of standardized curriculum for learning (Schubert, 2010). My own bias would favor such an imaginary school, or at least a music room, where evaluation didn't exist, and creative ideas sprouted forth from learners' individual paths and motivations. But alas, even though the "un-grading" idea has caught some movement in education (e.g., Blum, 2020) and writer Alfie Kohn has long advocated for schools to end grading (1999 and 2020), it is not realistic, nor practical. The current and deeply entrenched system of grading and evaluation in schools will take some great time and effort to undo. So, in that spirit I will not simply begin and end the chapter with a "Just don't do it" mantra. However, I do strongly believe (and will show that research supports) that when it comes to the *creative* educational experiences of children, evaluation—specifically external rewards such as grades—can squelch both intrinsic motivation and creative risk-taking. Grading specifically, and evaluation, more broadly, of a child's creative product, as well as process, should be done with utmost care. Assessment done thoughtlessly (even with good intentions) has the potential to squelch a child's comfort and freedom toward creative production. In this chapter I will show there *are* ways in our music classrooms that we can approach music creative activities such as composition and improvisation with a spirit of "un-grading," through thoughtful and productive assessment.

Music composition as a curricular activity, while relatively new to K–12 music classrooms in the United States, has grown gradually since its inclusion in the 1994 National Standards for Arts Education.[1] Though materials continue to be published to help teachers facilitate music composition activities in their classrooms (such as this book), the assessment part of doing so is still a bit daunting for teachers. One of the first and most common questions I get asked when talking to teachers about integrating music composition activities into in their classrooms is: "But how do we grade composition?" This is a legitimate question! Given that teachers indeed must put grades on their students' work, this chapter offers both research-based and practical ideas for approaching the assessment of music composition in the classroom so that creativity can flourish.

It is important to note here that this chapter is focused toward using composition in classrooms as a way for students to exercise creative thinking through music. While there may be other motives for utilizing composition in the music classroom, such as to learn objective facts ("closed"), the assessment consequences are far greater (and riskier) when using composition for the purpose of creative thinking ("open").

An example of a "closed" composition assignment would be one in which students have to demonstrate their understanding of the $\frac{6}{8}$ time signature. The task would be set up in a fairly structured manner: A limited number of measures, a key signature, and requirements for using only certain rhythms such as quarter, eighth, and 16th notes. The assignment would be to create a simple melodic or rhythmic composition using $\frac{6}{8}$ in a preset template. In this type of composition assignment, the purpose is to evaluate the understanding of a particular concept ($\frac{6}{8}$) through the application of it in a basic composition task. This is a musically authentic way to assess students understanding of a musical concept (as opposed to answering a question about it on a worksheet). However, while students have some room to be creative in their answer, the main purpose is *not* to enhance creativity per se, but to evaluate understanding of a factual concept. This type of task is easy to evaluate since we are looking for the correct "answer" (it is either right or wrong).

When a composition task has no right or wrong answer, such that the assignment is "open," then creativity can flourish, but the assessment stakes and consequences are much more consequential. The main purpose of this chapter is to address assessment of processes and products of music composition for which the goal is to enhance creativity.

Terms

In this section I operationalize the terms used in this chapter, specifically assessment, evaluation, and grading. While these terms can be utilized in a variety of ways, and hold a range of possible definitions, the purpose here is to clarify what I mean when using them in this chapter.

Assessment is the broadest of the three terms and the act of assessment is built into all human nature. We are constantly assessing our environment and whereabouts, as well as the people with whom we interact. When confronted with something new, we immediately go to an assessment mode of thinking: Do I like it? Is it harmful? Does it taste good? Could I use this in my wardrobe? And so on. Often, we turn to others to help us assess a situation: Does this color look good on me? Do you think I added too much salt? What do you think about this movie?

Getting more specific is the idea of evaluation, which is adding a value to our assessment. Phrases such as "I really do not like this color," "I like your recipe better than mine because mine is too salty," and "I love this book you gave me, even better than the one this author wrote previously," all have values (positive or negative) associated with the assessment. We put value on an item or situation and often compare it to similar items we are familiar with. While unambiguously adding a value to a judgment, we let others ascertain our beliefs about something—our *value* of that which is being judged. And when offering an evaluation, it is easy to influence others by swaying their own judgments. Evaluation is a central part of schooling, and teachers hold tremendous power when evaluating students' work. In a music classroom specifically, this authority can influence students' values toward their own or others' music and can either bolster or make them doubt their own creative potential.

Finally, and most relevant to the environment of school, is grading. Grading concerns putting a hard and fast "number" (or letter) on a product to provide a quantitative measure of an evaluation. By use of the term "grade," I am referring generally to a letter (the ubiquitous A, B C, D or F), or a percentage, or a number on a scale, or even a check, plus or minus. However, while a grade represents a quantitative measure, getting to that measure could be a very subjective process. It is an attempt to provide the recipient with a score of the evaluation of their product or action.

In the big picture of schooling, giving a grade is a small part of the daily assessment that teachers do, and as mentioned previously, it can be given from very subjective means. From a student's perspective, however, a GRADE looms large and can have profound effects on both their motivation and creativity. The pressure to get a good grade, from teachers, and parents, and even society, is often at the forefront of student thinking and motivation. In the next section I examine the research that shows just how intertwined rewards (e.g., evaluations) and creativity are for students.

RESEARCH RELATED TO CREATIVITY AND REWARDS

Hundreds of published investigations have revealed that the promise of a reward made contingent on task engagement often serves to undermine intrinsic task motivation and qualitative aspects of performance, including creativity. (Hennessey, 2016, p. 129)

Staunch proponents for abolishing any type of grading in schools (e.g., the authors in Blum, 2020; Kohn, 1999, 2013, 2020) posit that external rewards such as grades squelch intrinsic motivation as well as creativity. While it is generally true that the explicit evaluation or external reward for creative processes and products has the potential to squelch a person's creativity (Amabile, 1985; Amabile, Hennessey, & Grossman, 1986; Cerasoli, Nicklin, & Ford, 2014; Deci, Koestner, & Ryan, 2001; Hennessey, 2000, 2010; Kohn, 1999; Ryan & Deci, 2000), research over the years since this connection was made has shown that it is more nuanced and complicated than the simple inverse relationship (Hennessey, 2016; Gerhart & Fang, 2015).

Views have changed due to the realization of the complexity of all components related to creativity, task motivation, and rewards in that the type of task and the circumstances surrounding the task can mitigate the potential deleterious effect (e.g., see meta-analyses by Byron & Kazanchi, 2012, and Malik & Butt, 2017). The relationship between creativity and reward can be mediated by "cognitive style" (Baer, Oldham, & Cummings, 2003), learning goal orientation (Malik, Choi, & Butt, 2019), task enjoyment (Benedek, Bruckdorfer, & Jauk, 2020), task choice (Amabile, Hennessey, & Grossman, 1986) cultural expectations (Hennessey, 2016), reward contingency (Byron & Khazanchi, 2012), and gender (Baer, 1998; Conti, Collins, & Picariello, 2001). The interaction between rewards and creativity also depends on the theoretical lens of learning that one uses.[2]

In the following section I identify the salient findings from these research studies and apply them to a best practices guideline for successful assessment when evaluating students' music compositions. The framework is illustrated in Figure 15.1, with each section of the framework described in the text that follows. After this, I present two examples in different music class scenarios highlighting assessment from the practices described here.

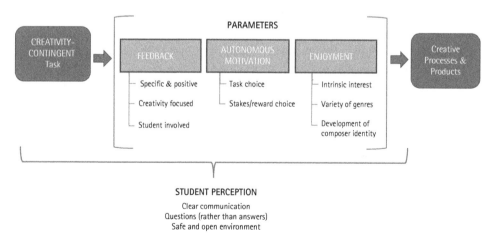

FIGURE 15.1. Best practice framework for successful assessment of creative composition processes and products

RESEARCH-BASED BEST PRACTICE
ASSESSMENTS FOR SUPPORTING CREATIVITY

Task Contingency

As mentioned previously, a composition task may be given for different reasons, such as to show understanding of a specific concept (or compositional technique), or to check off a box for completion, or to exercise creative thinking. The reward that each of these possibilities rely on can affect the intrinsic motivation and creativity of the resulting processes and products. A performance-contingent task is given to assess knowledge of a specific concept or technique—a standardized performance. This type of task has specific and "right answer" parameters as well as pre-determined standards for completion. The reward is based on meeting the objectives set up for the task (for example, the $\frac{6}{8}$ time signature activity illustrated in the introduction). A task given simply to check off the completion of an assignment would be considered a completion-contingent task, given for no other reason than adding it to a "got done" check list. The third type of task, a creativity-contingent task, is given to support and encourage creative thinking. In this type of task, creativity and risk-taking are explicit aims to be valued and encouraged. It is one in which creativity is clearly the objective. The assignment parameters should be relatively wide open, and flexibility for assignment choice is paramount. A creativity-contingent composition task should have no one correct way to complete it—no right or wrong answer. There may be some guidelines for students, but the basic premise of this type of assignment is for them to have room for their own creative interpretation and growth.

To ensure the highest level of motivation and creative output, researchers have found that rewards explicitly based on creativity and given for creativity-contingent tasks are most successful if the assessment is clearly associated with a creative outcome. When creativity is the clear outcome, then it is unlikely that the evaluation will squelch intrinsic motivation toward the task (Byron & Kazanhi, 2012; Eisenberger & Rhoades, 2001; Eisenberger & Shanock, 2003). In other words, a creativity-contingent task should be given for creativity to flourish. "Rewards increase creativity when individuals understand that rewards are contingent on creative (rather than routine) performance" (Byron & Kazanchi, 2012, p. 823).

Assessing performance-contingent or completion-contingent tasks are relatively simple, whereas assessment for a creativity-contingent music composition task must be approached in a more sensitive manner. The parameters of feedback, motivation, and enjoyment for doing so are described next.

Parameters for Assessment

Some compositions are simply not as successful as others, and children know this as well as the adults who teach them. Just as some paintings or stories show more imagination than others, so too do the musical creations of children. It would be a mistake to treat all compositions in the same way, and this is apparent to children as well as to the adults with whom they may share their works (Upitis, 1992, p. 32).

Specific and Positive Feedback

Given a creativity-contingent composition assignment does not mean that teachers (or peers) should let anything go and not give feedback to students' work. As Upitis reminds us in the quote above, students know that not all processes or products are as successful as others and they also understand that teachers and fellow students certainly have opinions about their work. Students also want to know how to improve or fix problems they sense in their compositions through peer and teacher feedback. For assessment to be most effective in a creativity-contingent task, an environment must be established so that students can hear their peers' or teacher's feedback in a way that does not shut down their willingness to experiment or lose motivation to complete the task. To do this, feedback should be specific to the purpose or issue or question at hand, positive, and creativity focused. There is absolutely no reason for giving feedback that is hurtful or negative to the composer. Continued positive support for creative ideas in the process of composition provides psychological safety and "permission" for risk-taking. In addition, the composer herself should be involved in the feedback process by given chances to ask questions and self-assess. Specific and positive feedback should be catered to the unique needs of the composer.

Motivation Orientation

Self-determination is undermined when a learner either does not feel in control or feels overly controlled by an authority figure such as a teacher (Deci & Ryan, 2008; Deci, Koestner, & Ryan, 2001; Ryan & Deci, 2000). Deci and Ryan (2008) define three types of motivation related to their self-determination theory of human growth: *controlled*, *autonomous*, and *amotivation*. Also called "causality orientations," Deci and Ryan explain these motivation types refer to "(a) the way people orient to the environment concerning information related to the initiation and regulation of behavior, and thus (b) the extent to which they are self-determined in general, across situations and domains" (p. 183).

Of the three motivation types, amotivation refers to a complete lack of intention and motivation. Controlled and autonomous motivation include both intrinsic and extrinsic types of influence, but it is the controller of the rewards that differ. In controlled motivation, it is an outside person, such as the teacher, who presents or manipulates these rewards (or is perceived to by the student). In autonomous motivation, which is most conducive to creative thinking and intrinsic motivation, the control lies with the learner. The most important concept for supporting autonomous motivation in a classroom is to allow learners to have choices in both the task and reward. This certainly does not mean letting go of all decision-making but rather providing choices. "In short, conditions that offer choice and are less controlling are likely to improve creativity-contingent rewards' effects on creative performance by increasing perceived volition, thus providing conditions that enhance intrinsic motivation to engage in the task and support creative expression" (Byron & Kazanchi, 2012, p. 813).

Within a relatively open composition assignment (creativity-contingent) students can be given choices, such as instrumentation or length or genre, or anything appropriate to the learning situation or composition circumstance. Options can also be provided for choosing to work alone or in collaboration with others. Allowing students to choose *which* composition they want to turn in for a final evaluation also allows them, as composers, to decide on what they feel is their best work. If a composition is included in an overall grading scheme, then teachers might consider providing a way for students to grade their own work in partnership with the teacher. Having choices for both task and reward puts the learner/composer in control and supports creative development and autonomous drive toward a creative task.

Enjoyment

"Whether they are three or 83 years of age, if individuals are to reach their creative potential, they must engage in an activity for the sheer pleasure and enjoyment of the task itself rather than for some extrinsic goal" (Hennessey, 2000, p. 58). Finally, and though it might seem obvious, it is critically important that the process of composition be pleasurable in order for the assessment process to be effective. The assessment of a child's original work should *not* be overly bearing or intimidating. Students should look forward to the composing time they have and be encouraged to explore a variety of genres, including genres that are intrinsically interesting to them. Encourage students to develop their composer "identity" by reflecting on their styles and their own likes and dislikes in the composing process. This gradual development of a unique composer identity can only help a student enjoy and take ownership for a composition task as a composer, as well as improve their own best self-critique skills.

Student Perception

The suggestions for sensitive and useful assessment parameters outlined previously are meaningless if the teacher's perception and student's perception of the learning environment do not align. Citing Achievement Goal Theory literature, Hennessey reminds us that "it is an individual's *interpretation* [emphasis added] of a reward or evaluation contingency and not the reward or evaluation itself that will determine whether intrinsic motivation (and creativity) will be enhanced" (2016, p. 145). The intersectionality of task-contingency, creativity, rewards, and motivation is as complex and nuanced as our students. While research has helped to clarify some understanding of how rewards affect creativity and motivation, the learners in our classroom have unique perception of themselves as learners, as well as their own unique perceptions of intrinsic and extrinsic rewards. For example, we may view asking questions about a composition, rather than giving a grade to a composition, as a way to avoid an extrinsic reward, but the learner may perceive the teacher asking questions about a composition as a threatening external reward.

As teachers we need to be constantly aware of how our students might be perceiving the assessment atmosphere. Setting up the learning environment as psychologically safe and free from negative judgment is crucial. In addition, constructing an atmosphere of clear, honest, and direct communication between teacher and learner by asking questions before assessing is also critical to aligning the student and teacher perceptions of the learning environment. There are many times I have listened to a child's composition for the first time, and they watch me intently with a proud smile on their face, waiting for me to respond, and I have to hold judgment (and control my facial expressions) when I just cannot quite understand what is going on musically. So, before I offer an initial knee-jerk reaction to what I just heard, I ask questions about the composer's intent and purpose. Nine times out of ten this has allowed me to better understand what it is they were attempting to depict in their music—and I often then realize it is incredibly creative! I always first give the student a chance to share with me what they were imagining or hoping to convey in their music. This prevents miscommunication and misjudgment at the least and is a step toward understanding students' perception of their own creations.

Following are two examples of applying assessments in music classrooms. The first is a fifth-grade general music class, and the second is a high school band. In both cases creativity is included as a component of the rubric to highlight to students that it is valued. For purposes of defining it in the rubric, I draw from the most common and agreed-upon definition from the literature: that is, a creative object is both original as well as "effective"[3] (Amabile, 1986; Mayer, 1998; Runco & Jaeger, 2012).

EXAMPLES

General Music

This composition project takes place in a grade five classroom in a small rural school district that offers music to all elementary students twice weekly. Much of the teacher's work has been composition-based throughout the K–4 curriculum, but mostly for evaluation of learned concepts and to get students slowly used to composing with relatively closed parameters (e.g., as students learn rhythms or note reading, they compose simple exercises to show proficiency). However, the fifth-grade year students are presented with their first large and open composition project that spans most of the year.

The music classroom has a large and varied inventory of Orff-type music instruments. Students are paired in groups of two to five to work together (they choose their working groups with the teacher's help). The assignment is a "commission" to provide background music for a designated space or place. The idea of a commission for this project makes it an authentic task–one which composers are often hired to do. First each group is to identify a space or location or circumstance that could benefit from background music, and then to plan and compose music for that particular space (e.g., a local business, hallway passing, library ambiance, cafeteria, playground, school bus, etc.). It is a creativity-contingent task because it is wide open and encourages students to be creative with their final product; there is no right or wrong answer.

The student composers will plan and compose the music using Orff instruments that either they play themselves or they direct their classmates to play (if they need more instrumentation than is available in their group). They ultimately will record their final composition for playback in the designated—commissioned—area. A notated score is required, but the composers may notate however they wish to convey what is to be played (traditional or graphic) by the performers for the final recording.

The final three weeks of school are dedicated to rehearsals, fine-tuning, and then recording of each groups' final compositions. The timeline of assessment (Figure 15.2)

TIME	TASK	FEEDBACK ACTIVITY	ASSESSMENT TYPE
OCTOBER	SELECT music space	Questionnaire	Check off
NOVEMBER	RESEARCH and plan for space requirements	Research Sheet and pre-planning specs	Check off
JANUARY	EXPLORE	Student begin bi-weekly practicing/ exploring. Keep notes and reflections on progress in portfolio	Teacher feedback conversations with students
FEBRUARY	PERFORM First (and rough) draft performances	Peer and teacher feedback (Liz Lerman *Critical Response Process*)	CRP feedback forms
MARCH	REFINE	Workshop: Students practice and refine their compositions based on the February feedback session.	Teacher feedback conversations with students
APRIL	PERFORM Second performance for classmates	Peer and Student feedback – comment sheets	Comment sheets
MAY	PRODUCE	All class time is dedicated to composer groups for final clean performances and recordings. Recordings are delivered to the space.	Teacher feedback conversations with students
JUNE	REFLECT/ASSESS	Composers and teachers work together to evaluate the final product	Rubric sheet

FIGURE 15.2. Timeline of assessment for the general music project

outlines the monthly steps and assessment procedures for completing this year-long task.

Looking In

It is a workshop day in March and students are practicing and refining their compositions based on their feedback session from February. The student groups are spread throughout the classroom, practice rooms, and some on the auditorium stage, creating a medium level cacophony of sounds. Ms. Jones is going around to offer her thoughts to each student group, and they are excited to have her listen in. As she comes around to each group, she looks at their scores and listens as the students practice and refine. First, she might ask, "Do you have any specific questions for me?" and if they do, she will answer them honestly. If not, she will begin to ask more questions to see if students have considered, for instance, something about the setting they may have not thought of. "This seems a bit loud if you intend it to be used in a library; how might you play your melody softer? Perhaps consider a different instrument? Or just play it softer?" Or "How long do you think this will be when finished? Have you considered adding a silent break or surprise in the middle?" She might also refer to the *Critical Response Process*[4] exercise they did in February by reminding them of the suggestions from their peers. The questions and suggestions posed by Miss Jones are honest and specific and students know they can disagree with a suggestion because she has set up this atmosphere of trust in the composition process from the beginning.

Rubric

Figure 15.3 provides an example of a final rubric sheet that might be used for the final evaluation of students' original compositions. The "pre-planned specs" the rubric refers

	Missing-in-Action	Beginning Stage (room to grow)	Still Emerging, (but close to the top)	BRAVO!
Commission Space specs.	The pre-planned specs were not turned in.	A start, but take another look at the pre-planned specs	Some of the pre-planned specs were missing.	The pre-planned specs were all met
Organization	Not finished	The organization of the performance and/or notation needs tightening.	Organization of performance and/or notation is mostly clear, with just a few issues.	This composition comes together well – in performance and notation
Creativity	N/A	This sounds like I've heard it before. Can you make it more unusual?		This was very original and interesting approach to the space!

FIGURE 15.3. Rubric for general music commission composition

to concern the planning sheet the composers created early in the process and was to be used as a guide for their final composition (e.g., desired length, tempos, dynamics, instrumentation, etc.).

High School Band

This band program is set in a suburban setting outside a large metropolitan area. The high school has three bands that meet daily: freshman, intermediate, and advanced. All students in the freshman band complete a chamber music composition project. This guided composition project prepares the students for other music composition projects that they will encounter as they move through the other bands in their high school career, including a full band collaborative composition project that is done every other year with the advanced band.

The chamber music composition project has students in teacher-arranged chamber groups (these are traditional groups such as woodwind or brass quintets, and other four to five member groups arranged as necessary based on the instrumentation of the band). Each group will collaboratively create an original chamber composition for their group using either Flat or Noteflight software (both are free and web-based). This is a fall semester-long project gearing up for the January winter chamber concert in which each group performs their original music (students also have the option to perform these compositions for the district-wide solo and ensemble contest in April).

Students first meet in their groups to determine their time signature, tempo, mood, key signature, and form (choosing from AABA, Theme and Variations, or ABA) on a detailed spec sheet. From that point, Ms. Bartell will set up basic online templates for each group—essentially a shell for their final composition. In the template she will provide chord progressions for the entire piece with the instructions that each student part must start each measure with one of the chord tones. They have an option to add an introduction as well as an extended ending. Other than the chord tone instructions, the only other parameter is that the students must be able to perform what they write. While there are some limits with the parameters for the composition (such as chord tones and the obvious note ranges for specific instruments), students will be encouraged to be creative in their effort. From October through December students begin entering the notation for their compositions. Figure 15.4 outlines the assessment timeline for the project.

Looking In

It is December and the holiday concert was presented the week after Thanksgiving. Students have the two weeks before holiday break to hone and practice their chamber music. They spend each rehearsal period practicing and refining their chamber group music (each student has a laptop where they can read their score as well as change it on

TIME	TASK	FEEDBACK ACTIVITY	ASSESSMENT TYPE
SEPTEMBER	Discuss and PLAN for final composition	Detailed spec sheet filled in	Check off
OCTOBER–NOVEMBER	Begin writing	Weekly goals for progress completion of chamber music.	Weekly check off
DECEMBER	PERFORM First (and rough) draft performances	Peer and Teacher feedback (parts of the Liz Lerman *Critical Response Process*)	CRP feedback forms
JANUARY	REFINE & PRESENT Students practice, re-fine and perform their compositions once again for classmates.	"Process" Rubric (filled out by teacher, and self-assessed by each chamber group)	Rubric
FEBRUARY	CONCERT	Chamber Music Concert. Concert Final Rubric (filled out by teacher, and self-assessed by each chamber group)	Final Rubric

FIGURE 15.4. Timeline of assessment for the high school band chamber project

the fly). Today is one of three of class periods before break where each group performs their very rough edition of their chamber music for the entire band. Ms. Bartells' job is to facilitate feedback from the "audience" (other band members) as each group performs. All students have a handout they are to fill in to when listening to each chamber group composition. This form includes two (of four) response items from Lerman's CRP: *The music was interesting to me because . . .*, and *"Why did you decide to . . .?"* Student must write at least one statement for each and Ms. Bartells will collect them and hand them to each chamber group for their consideration. They will use this feedback to continue to fine tune their original compositions.

Rubric

The rubric shown in Figure 15.5 will be used for both "process" (see January in the time-line) as well as final performance (early February). By seeing where they stand with the process rubric, students will have a clear path to working toward a polished final com-position and performance.

In general, a creativity-contingent music composition project should be given ample time to complete, with a supportive atmosphere for experimentation and risk-taking (called "stretch and explore" in the visual arts Studio Habits of Mind Framework [Hetland et al., 2015]). The assessment "space" should consist of continual dialogue and reflection between students and teacher with a variety of assessment checkpoints

	Missing-in-Action	Beginning Stage (room to grow)	Still Emerging (but close to the top)	BRAVO!
Chord tone uses	The pre-planned specs were not turned in.	Many of the chord tones are missed (where required).	Most of the chord tones have been used where required.	Every chord tone is correctly used throughout.
Overall ensemble effect	Not finished	One or more of the parts are too similar to another or missing.	At times one of the parts seems absent.	The parts blended well together.
Performance	Not performed	Need to polish the performance a bit.	The performance was close to perfection. Just a little more practice.	A very musical performance of this music!
Creativity	N/A	This sounds like I've heard it before. Can you make it more unusual?		This was very original and effective composition.
Individual Contribution	Please provide input in this space as to your individual contribution to the groups' work.			

FIGURE 15.5. Rubric for final high school band chamber music project

during the process to ensure supporting the most creative and intrinsically motivated classroom.

As one can see from the sample project assessment timelines (Figures 15.2 and 15.4), there is a combination of types of assessments to be collected, ranging from check-off completion tasks, to qualitative feedback along the way, to a final "rubric" for assessment of the finished product. While the major tasks are creativity-contingent, some parts along the way are completion contingent (e.g., turning in a planning sheet) as it allows for the process to unfold over time with appropriate guidance. Students will receive continual positive and specific feedback at points in their process, and also given plenty of choices to take or leave along the way. The "grade" is not a single thing but a collection of multiple check-ins and tasks. If used, a rubric should reflect what the teacher hopes the students focus on for a final product or process (including creativity). How the teacher uses a final rubric assessment, or any of the assessment points, in the overall grading scheme for the class is a decision she will have to make. I would encourage teachers to consider student voice in creating the rubrics and assessment points. A collaborative effort between teacher and students in the grading scheme would certainly offer students some rightful ownership in this process. Finally, in the two scenarios above, the composition is only one part of overall evaluations for students, as assessment for performance skills, notation reading, and other curricular requirements will also be collected.

MECHANISMS FOR MUSIC COMPOSITION ASSESSMENT IN THE CLASSROOMS

The tools, or "mechanisms" listed below offer some concrete ways for managing the assessment of compositions in the classroom. Portfolios provide the large "envelope" with which to organize the complex and varied assessments within a composition unit, Liz Lerman's Critical Response Process offers a clear way for teachers and peers to respond to a classmate's composition, and rubrics are suggested for providing a final evaluation of a music composition.

Portfolios

The idea of using a portfolio to collect a variety of items has been around for a long time. Professional artists keep their artworks, often in different stages, in portfolios and use them to show versatility or progress. Arts Propel first developed the idea of process and product portfolios for visual art and music educators in the 1990s. This project, begun by Howard Gardner and Steve Seidel at Harvard Project Zero, provided guidance for teachers to systematically collect, and have students reflect on, their processes of creative production over time (see http://www.pz.harvard.edu/projects/arts-propel for more information about Arts Propel). Portfolios provide an excellent way for teachers (and students) to guide, reflect on, assess, and simply keep track of the messy and complex work of music composition over time. Portfolios allow students to keep all of their processes and products in one place so they can easily make decisions and choices to submit their best work for a final evaluation or assessment. The timelines shown in Figures 15.2 and 15.4 could all be managed and utilized through a portfolio process— where students take ownership for keeping track of the processes, collecting and reflecting on their assessments along the way, and choosing what gets selected for any formal assessment points. (This could be facilitated with computer and web-managed software).

Following are three excellent resources for teachers to get started on setting up the portfolio process in their classrooms:

- The *Introductory Handbook to Arts Propel* (Winner, 1993) is free and downloadable at: http://www.pz.harvard.edu/resources/arts-propel-an-introductory-handbook
- *The Arts Propel Handbook for Music* (Myford et al., 1995) can also be downloaded for free at: http://www.pz.harvard.edu/resources/arts-propel-a-handbook-for-music
- *The Power of Portfolios: What Children Can Teach Us About Learning and Assessment* (Hebert, 2001) offers practical ideas as well as philosophical rationale for using the portfolio assessment process from a principal's perspective.

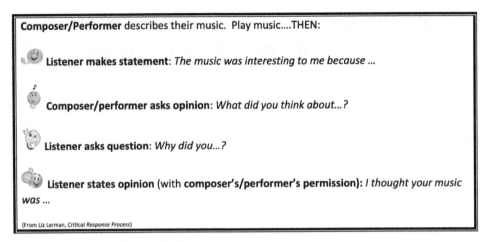

Composer/Performer describes their music. Play music....THEN:

Listener makes statement: *The music was interesting to me because ...*

Composer/performer asks opinion: *What did you think about...?*

Listener asks question: *Why did you...?*

Listener states opinion (with **composer's/performer's permission**): *I thought your music was ...*

(From Liz Lerman, *Critical Response Process*)

FIGURE 15.6. A simplified critical response process for composers

Critical Response Process

"If we prefer dialogue, we have to do more asking than telling. That means engaging in conversations (conferences) with students rather than firing off comments for them to ponder" (Kohn, 2020, p. xiv). Using questions as a technique toward assessment is a critical first step when examining a creative product (or process) such as in music composition. Choreographer Liz Lerman developed a questioning method for giving and getting feedback on creative works in a method called the *Critical Response Process* (CRP). It is a four-step process to use when responding to an artist's work. First, responders provide positive statements of what they found meaningful about the work, second, the artist asks questions of the responders, third the responders submit neutral (non-value laden) questions to the artist, and fourth, with permission, the responders offer opinions to the artists. Figure 15.6 is an example of a basic checklist of the CRP I have used with young composers as they share, as well as listen and respond to, each other's musical works. More information about the process can be found at: https://lizlerman.com/critical-response-process/.

Rubrics

As many teachers are aware, the use of rubrics for evaluation offers a more substantial assessment of a product (or process) than a single grade or score. Rubric writing, however, is not easy, and in the case of rubrics for music composition, where the categories and descriptions need to be positive and specific, even less so. Descriptors should not be negative or imply lack of skills but be encouraging and point toward potential for growth. The categories for assessment should be specific to the assignment parameters and ones that the teacher wishes to highlight. For instance, if a minimum length of time is specified for the composition, then that should be one of the categories for rating. And as discussed previously, creativity should be included as a category if indeed creativity is valued in the final product.

CONCLUSION

The purpose of this chapter was to show that less "grade-like" assessment is necessary for projects that require and enhance creative thinking in the classroom—such as music composition. The assessment, or evaluation, or even grading of a music composition process and product should not be a one-time act but should take multiple forms and consist of many dialogues between students and teacher. There may be times in the process where a completion-contingent task is required (e.g., I turned in my first draft). There are times when objective measures and performance-contingent tasks will be given and assessed along the way to see if students are learning prerequisite concepts or techniques for successful completion of a music composition. But to be certain to support creativity and intrinsic motivation for a composition task, then the assignment itself must show value for creativity. And for a creativity-contingent task, any type of feedback should be specific, positive, and always with creativity at the forefront.

A great need and real opportunity at this time in our education history is to make the music room a sanctuary for creativity. The examples I used illustrated school settings where composition was an ordinary part of the curriculum. Hopefully we can move toward this ideal. Knowing how to set up careful and organized assessment frameworks will help immensely in reaching such a goal.

Music composition in the classroom can provide a place where judgment takes a back seat to flexibility and risk-taking, and messiness and mistakes are encouraged. The more that teachers can create an atmosphere toward healthy, and value-less assessment, and ensure students that the grade is not the main point, the better our students will thrive in the creative music composition process.

NOTES

1. The 2014 National Core Arts Standards are available from State Education Agency Directors of Arts Education (SEADAE) at https://www.nationalartsstandards.org.
2. For example, there are proponents whose beliefs are based in social science theory such as Amabile (1986), Amabile, Hennessey, and Grossman, (1986) and the Self-Determination Theory of Deci and Ryan (2008), and those who come from a more behavioristic view of learning such as Eisenberger and Rhoades (2001) "Learned Industriousness Theory." These debates and differences are detailed in Hennessey (2000) as well as in Byron and Khazanchi (2012).
3. The term "effective" could be substituted with "appropriate" or "useful" or other similar terms depending on the product or circumstance.

4. This is described in detail later in the chapter.

REFERENCES

Amabile, T. M. (1985). Motivation and creativity: Effects of motivational orientation on creative writers. *Journal of Personality and Social Psychology*, *48*(2), 393.

Amabile, T. M. (1986). *Creativity in context: Update to the social psychology of creativity.* Westview Press.

Amabile, T. M., Hennessey, B. A., & Grossman, B. S. (1986). Social influences on creativity: the effects of contracted-for reward. *Journal of Personality and Social Psychology*, *50*(1), 14–23.

Baer, J. (1998). Gender differences in the effects of extrinsic motivation on creativity. *Journal of Creative Behavior*, *32*, 18–37.

Baer, M., Oldham, G. R., & Cummings, A. (2003). Rewarding creativity: When does it really matter? *Leadership Quarterly*, *14*(4–5), 569–586.

Benedek, M., Bruckdorfer, R., & Jauk, E. (2020). Motives for creativity: Exploring the what and why of everyday creativity. *Journal of Creative Behavior*, *54*(3), 610–625.

Blum, S. D. (Ed.). (2020). *Ungrading: Why Rating Students Undermines Learning (and What to Do Instead).* West Virginia University Press, *Project MUSE*. Retrieved from: muse.jhu.edu/book/78367.

Byron, K., & Khazanchi, S. (2012). Rewards and creative performance: a meta-analytic test of theoretically derived hypotheses. *Psychological Bulletin*, *138*(4), 809.

Cerasoli, C. P., Nicklin, J. M., & Ford, M. T. (2014). Intrinsic motivation and extrinsic incentives jointly predict performance: A 40-year meta-analysis. *Psychological Bulletin*, *140*(4), 980.

Conti, R., Collins, M., & Picariello, M. (2001). The impact of competition on intrinsic motivation and creativity: Considering gender, gender segregation, and gender-role identity. *Personality and Individual Differences*, *31*, 1273–1289.

Deci, E. L., & Ryan, R. M. (2008). Self-determination theory: A macrotheory of human motivation, development, and health. *Canadian Psychology*, *49*(3), 182–185.

Deci, E. L., Koestner, R., & Ryan, R. M. (2001). Extrinsic rewards and intrinsic motivation in education: reconsidered once again. *Review of Educational Research*, *71*(1), 1–29.

Eisenberger, R., & Rhoades, L. (2001). Incremental effects of reward on creativity. *Journal of Personality and Social Psychology*, *81*(4), 728.

Eisenberger, R., & Shanock, L. (2003). Rewards, intrinsic motivation, and creativity: A case study of conceptual and methodological isolation. *Creativity Research Journal*, *15*(2/3), 121.

Gerhart, B., & Fang, M. (2015). Pay, intrinsic motivation, extrinsic motivation, performance, and creativity in the workplace: Revisiting long-held beliefs. *Annual Review of Organizational Psychology and Organizational Behavior*, *2*, 489–521.

Hebert, E. (2001). *The power of portfolios: What children can teach us about learning and assessment.* San Francisco: Jossey-Bass.

Hennessey, B. A. (2010). The creativity-motivation connection. In J. C. Kaufman & R. J. Sternberg (Eds.), *The Cambridge handbook of creativity* (pp. 342–365). Cambridge University Press.

Hennessey, B. A. (2000). Rewards and creativity. In C. Sansone & J. M. Harackiewicz (Eds.), *Intrinsic and extrinsic motivation: The search for optimal motivation and performance* (pp. 55–78). Academic Press.

Hennessey, B. A. (2016). The creativity-motivation-culture connection. In V. P. Glăveanu (Ed.), *Palgrave studies in creativity and culture: The Palgrave handbook of creativity and culture research* (pp. 125–158). Springer Nature.

Hetland, L., Winner, E., Veenema, S., & Sheridan, K. M. (2015). *Studio thinking 2: The real benefits of visual arts education.* Teachers College Press.

Kohn, A. (1999). *Punished by rewards: The trouble with gold stars, incentive plans, A's, praise, and other bribes.* Houghton Mifflin Harcourt.

Kohn, A. (2013). *No contest: The case against competition.* Houghton Mifflin Harcourt.

Kohn, A. (2020). Foreword, in S. D. Blum & A. Kohn, *Ungrading: Why rating students undermines learning (and what to do instead)* (pp. xiii–xx). West Virginia University Press.

Lerman, L., & Borstel, J. (2003). *Critical Response Process: A method for getting useful feedback on anything you make, from dance to dessert.* Dance Exchange.

Lowenfeld, V. and Brittain, W. L. (1987). *Creative and mental growth* (8th ed.). Macmillan Publishing Co.

Malik, M. A. R., & Butt, A. N. (2017). Rewards and creativity: past, present, and future. *Applied Psychology, 66*(2), 290–325. doi:10.1111/apps.12080

Malik, M. A. R., Choi, J. N., & Butt, A. N. (2019). Distinct effects of intrinsic motivation and extrinsic rewards on radical and incremental creativity: The moderating role of goal orientations. *Journal of Organizational Behavior, 40*(9–10), 1013–1026.

Mayer, R. (1998). Fifty years of creativity research. In R. Sternberg (Ed.), *Handbook of creativity* (pp. 449–460). Cambridge: Cambridge University Press.

Myford, C., Plasket, D., Swinton, S., Torff, B., Waanders, J., Davidson, L., Scripp, L., & Winner, E. (1995). *Arts Propel: A handbook for music.* Educational Testing Service. Retrieved from: http://www.pz.harvard.edu/sites/default/files/Arts%20Propel%20-%20A%20Handbook%20for%20Music%5B1%5D.pdf

Consortium of National Arts Education Associations. (1994). *National standards for arts education.* Music Educators National Conference.

Runco, M. A., & Jaeger, G. J. (2012). The standard definition of creativity. *Creativity research journal, 24*(1), 92–96.

Ryan, R. M., & Deci, E. L. (2000). When rewards compete with nature: The undermining of intrinsic motivation and self-regulation. In C. Sansone & J. M. Harackiewicz (Eds.), *Intrinsic and extrinsic motivation: The search for optimal motivation and performance* (pp. 13–54). Academic Press.

Schubert, W. H. (2010). *Love, justice, and education: John Dewey and the Utopians.* Information Age Publishing.

Upitis, R. (1992). *Can I play you my song? The compositions and invented notations of children.* Heinemann.

Winner, E. (1993). *Arts Propel: An introductory handbook.* Educational Testing Service. Retrieved from: http://www.pz.harvard.edu/sites/default/files/Arts%20PROPEL%20-%20An%20Introductory%20Handbook_0.pdf

SECTION IV

APPROACHES TO COMPOSITION PEDAGOGY

CHAPTER 16

DEVELOPING COMPOSITIONAL CAPACITIES

Feelingful Intention, Musical Expressivity, and Artistic Craftsmanship

MICHELE KASCHUB AND JANICE SMITH

ONE purpose of education is to develop capacities representative of the breadth of human enterprise. Education functions optimally when ideas and skills are introduced, students are intrigued and inspired to act, and knowledge is cultivated in ways that advance human flourishing. The capacity to compose music, like all other areas of human endeavor, presents across the population through varied interests, skills, and levels of engagement. Composition allows everyone, from novice to expert, to embrace the feelingful aspects of music, explore its complex potentials, and craft music in ways that create personal and societal meaning. The approach that we will present in this chapter seeks to position feeling, body-based perceptual knowing, and compositional technique as equal contributors to the development and exercise of each student's artistic agency.

A CAPACITIES-BASED APPROACH TO MUSIC COMPOSITION

The capacities-based approach (Kaschub & Smith, 2009, 2016a) to music composition focuses on the development of *Feelingful Intention, Musical Expressivity,* and *Artistic Craftsmanship* (see Figure 16.1). *Feelingful Intention* refers to an awareness of the emotion or mood that one might experience in parallel to the sounds shaped by the composer. *Musical Expressivity* refers to how the changes in the sounds of music

Feelingful Intention	Musical Expressivity	Artistic Craftsmanship
The capacity to determine the musical potentials of an experienced or projected feeling, or extra-musical connection or connotation.	The capacity to select sounds and imagine how they can be shaped by altering the balance of Motion – Stasis, Unity – Variety, Sound – Silence, Tension – Release, (and/or) Stability – Instability, (acronymized as "MUSTS") to invite a sensory response.	The capacity to purposefully assemble and manipulate the elements of music in ways that shape musical expressivity and invite feelingful engagement.

FIGURE 16.1. Compositional capacities defined

are physically experienced within the body. Expressive potentials can be described by referencing five principle-pairs: motion-stasis, unity-variety, sound-silence, tension-release, and stability-instability. For ease of use, we refer to these by the acronym MUSTS. Each of these pairs exists on a continuum. Expressivity is achieved when a shift toward either end of the continuum is sensed or when changes in the prominence of any of the five principle-pairs is perceived. Such observances give rise to the body-based perceptual knowing that provides critical information for meaning making. The term *Artistic Craftsmanship* is used to refer to how a composer purposefully shapes the elements of music to create sounds with the potential to be experienced as expressive.

A capacities-based approach positions all three compositional capacities as being of equal importance. Rather than focus solely on imparting technique to advance the manipulation of pitch, time, form, and other musical elements, this approach draws on personal and shared experience to activate the imagination. It looks to feeling and somatic awareness as critical components in the creation of music. As the meanings that result from the composition process cannot be fully isolated from the conditions which influence its evolution, this approach recognizes composing as an artistic process situated in complex contexts that contribute to and shape both the musical product (art object) and its creator. Thus, to fully understand the compositional endeavor, we consider the musical product, the human shaped and reshaped by the process of creating, and the experiential process that develops the two, in reciprocal balance.

Children, left to their own devices, exhibit a natural, intuitive balance in their music making. Feeling, body-based perceptual knowing, and technique are all present in the work of young composers. While formal music study often favors a technique-based approach to composition activities, young composers will, if asked, offer comments that resist such limitations. They describe their music using words that highlight mood or emotion and can readily detail how they feel and sense music in their bodies as they chronicle experiences of calm, expectation, motion, repetition, surprise, tension, and so on. The breadth of these statements is important. Each observation demonstrates the multifaceted nature of the musical experience and suggests that a singular instructional focus has considerable and unfortunate confines. Why, then, has music education walked such a narrowly drawn path?

The Current Challenge

From the latter half of the 20th century through current practice, music education in the United States has focused almost exclusively on elements-focused instruction. Spurred by the Soviet Union's successful Sputnik launch in 1957, political leaders in the United States turned to science to reclaim global dominance. Other disciplines scrambled. The concept of "musical elements" appeared in *Basic Concepts in Music Education* in 1958 propelling the elements toward center-stage where they found reinforcement in the *Manhattanville Music Curriculum Project* (Kyung-Suk, 2006; Thomas, 1970). Ultimately, elements-focused methods eclipsed more open-ended and student-focused pedagogical approaches (Mark, 1996; Stewart Rose & Countrymen, 2016).

This hasty alignment with science-focused conceptions of education preserved music's place in the school curricula but failed to advance music's most important dimensions (Reimer, 2022/2003). The after-effects of this preservation-driven curricular shift still linger. Beyond the element-laden content of the 2014 *Core Music Standards*, the initial rollout by the National Association for Music Education presents four pillars— creating; performing, presenting, and producing; responding; and connecting—with graphics akin to those of the periodic table (See https://www.nationalartsstandards. org). Indeed, over the past 60 years the notion of teaching the elements has become so normalized in the curriculum that it dominates PK–12 education as well as the preparation of music teachers.

Unfortunately, this curricular approach has some unintended consequences that eclipse the development of equally important aspects of musical knowledge and artistic understanding. For example, teachers often position lower-level skills, such as identifying aspects of melodic construction, *patching* the beat, or naming instruments, as end goals rather than as steps toward developing an understanding of music's expressive value. The demand to evidence "What is it" knowledge and "How to do it" skill often positions teachers to omit instruction addressing "How music comes to have meaning" as they push their students toward benchmarks outlined in school-sanctioned curriculums. Such practices disenfranchise learners through a framework of dominance that denies diversity and individual agency. Further, music activities become atomistic in design and fail to connect with students' innate physical and emotional relationship with music. Music education conceived of in this way leaves students with a narrowed set of skills to access the meaningful interactions with music that could enrich their lives (Brown & Dillon, 2016).

So how can we reframe our curricular objectives and teaching methods to better reflect the nature and value of students' interactions with music?

Reframing Our Vision for Music Education

When we began to teach children to compose, we found they were not particularly engaged or connected to their music. We tried to ensure student success through the use of detailed project guidelines. We offered templates which would lead students to the "right" answers. We even provided checklists and rubrics detailing required expectations that specified the use of each musical element. The resulting work might be most aptly described as "cookie-cutter compositions." The products were nearly identical and lacked expressivity. Moreover, as the students had made very few artistic decisions in creating their work, they had little sense of ownership or interest in their products.

In questioning how we might help improve upon this situation, we discovered that many of the instructional tools being used to ensure student success—often the same types of tools used in performance-focused instruction—were, in practice, preventing our young composers from connecting with the music they were being asked to make. Drawing on philosophy, neuroscience, and creativity research to further understand the generative act of composition, we began to reframe our practices to shift more artistic control to students while simultaneously introducing them to ways of thinking and feeling that could enhance their work (Kaschub & Smith, 2009). In the next section we share the foundations that helped us to shape our focus on musical capacities.

THE ROOTS OF A CAPACITIES-BASED APPROACH TO MUSIC COMPOSITION PEDAGOGY

The question centering the capacities-based approach is a deceptively simple one: "How can the building blocks of music be assembled in a manner that purposefully invites feeling?" While philosophers readily acknowledge a relationship between feeling and music within the human experience and musicians seek to shape the elements of music in ways that will invite such outcomes, the exact nature of the relationship has evaded explication. Recent advances in neuroscience (Brain and Creativity Institute, 2020) offer insights that bridge the worlds of philosophical inquiry and musical practice. This work positions body-based perception as a precursor to feeling and cognition and may suggest that we can intentionally create music to invite and advance unique human understandings.

Philosophical Musings Supported by Neuroscientific Data

Some of the most prescient writing addressing the relationship between feeling and music is offered by Susanne Langer. In *Philosophy in a New Key* (1942), she writes, "There are certain aspects of the so-called "inner life"—physical or mental which have formal properties similar to those of music—patterns of motion and rest, of tension and release, of agreement and disagreement, preparation, fulfillment excitation, sudden change, etc." (p. 228). These observations correspond to the features of *musical expressivity* (Kaschub & Smith, 2009). As her work advanced in *Writing in Mind: An Essay on Human Feeling* (1967), Langer proffered a feeling-based biological theory which delineated perceptual and conceptual knowings.

More than five decades after Langer's initial ideas were published, neuroscientist Antonio Damasio published *Descarte's Error* (1994) and *The Feeling of What Happens* (1999). Drawing on data derived from technologies not available in Langer's time, he describes a theory of consciousness built upon the connections between a person, an event, a bodily-based emotional response, and a feeling that invites consciousness. The feeling, he writes, "depends on the juxtaposition of an image of the body proper to an image of something else, such as the visual image of a face or the auditory image of a melody" (Damasio, 1994, p.145). He continues to suggest that cognition begins when we realize we have sensed a movement, change, or alteration against the background of biological homeostasis. What Langer's philosophical lens identified as perceptual knowledge made possible through an "inner life," Damasio substantiates as the fundamental action required for all forms of knowing.

Making Connections

Direct experiences with music, through singing, playing, composing, listening, and improvising, evoke the background biological responses which Langer and Damasio reference. Such experiences create feeling and then consciousness. Not only does music arouse feelings that are familiar, attainable, and comfortable, but also it allows for the opportunity to explore the unfamiliar, unattainable, and uncomfortable at a body-safe distance.

Music and feeling, then, are related in two ways. First, music parallels feeling. Composers seek to invite felt responses to their music, performers craft interpretations that seek to invite particular responses, and listeners often attribute emotional meaning to the music they encounter. Second, engagement with music generates physical sensation. Music plays a causal role in producing specific body-based perceptions and that give rise to feeling and give rise to mental processes which allows music to convey emotional meaning (Sloboda, 2010; Veloso & Carvalho, 2012). Our engagements with music are acts of translation; the inner imaginative work of composers, performers, and listeners translates to an outward representation of experience, which then has the potential to become an internalized understanding.

Developing Compositional Capacities

Every child has musical potential and nascent compositional capacity. Toddlers weave their songs intuitively, expressing their state-of-being as they draw on the sounds around them. As children grow older, increased self-awareness and social expectations may lead them to engage in this behavior less frequently. However, composers—like uninhibited young children—tap into the natural desire to create music and in doing so cultivate practices that reveal their compositional capacities. With the guidance of helpful teachers, children can learn to work purposefully with these and other musical capacities (Kaschub & Smith, 2016b, 2022a, 2022b; Johnson-Green, 2020).

In the following sections, we will focus on strategies for fostering the development of *Feelingful Intention*, *Musical Expressivity*, and *Artistic Craftsmanship*, as well as the critical relationships between these capacities that give rise to music's ability to expand our understanding of what it means to be human (Brown & Dillon, 2016). We recognize that there are specific differences in what emotions are identified and how music is crafted in various cultures. However, because the foundation of musical experience is situated in the body, the capacities-based approach is flexible enough to be responsive to cultural variations.

We will present these ideas as they relate to the work of novice, intermediate, and advanced composers. These categories will be used to describe the general tendencies of students at different stages of growth. It is important to note that age is not a key factor in determining developmental level or progress. Novice, intermediate, and advanced compositional practices can appear at nearly any age or in any composition.

Compositional development varies with each student and boundaries between these experience-level categories are fluid. As each capacity develops along its own continuum, students may advance in one area without advancing in others. When this happens, it is important for teachers to make achievements explicit as they guide students to consider the role of the other capacities. This helps student come to understand the necessary interconnectedness of all capacities in fully achieving their artistic and musical goals.

Developing the Compositional
Capacities of Novice Composers

Novice composers may be generally characterized as those who have had limited experience with deliberately creating music for expressive purposes. Using processes that are
often intuitive, composers create shorter works that are closely related to their personal
experience. Novice composers usually invent pieces that exhibit simple relationships between the capacities: a single *Feelingful Intention*, musically expressed through a single
MUSTS pair, crafted using one compositional technique.

Characteristics of Novice Composers

Novice composers are often eager to play with sounds and manipulate materials. They
enjoy exploring sound sources to determine what sounds are available to them. This exploration fulfills a vital role in the creation of the sonic palette that composers will use
in their work. Exploration is an early step of the compositional process and composers
may need to engage in this work before focusing on other compositional tasks. Novices
can be very imaginative with how they use the sounds they have available and may seek
to create new sounds from familiar materials and sound sources. Most importantly, they
want their work to be successful but may lack the technical skills to compose what they
can imagine.

   Intuitive processes often influence the work of novice composers. Their ideas are
based on the music with which they are familiar and how that music has functioned
in their lives (Ohman-Rodriguez, 2004). Sometimes their compositions include
direct song quotes. Timid beginners may need assistance with getting started
and with sharing their work, but all beginners benefit from guidance and specific
feedback. At the same time, novice composers must have the freedom to utilize
their musical knowledge and skills if they are to have a sense of ownership in their
work. Too many guidelines and restrictions hamper individual voice and creativity.
Too few can stall the process before it begins. The balance between freedoms and
constraints is a delicate one that teachers must carefully consider as they establish
task guidelines.

   Novices are often proud of their work, especially when their compositions match
their product intentions and are reacted to positively by teachers, parents, and peers.
Compositions are often "about" something and may be related to play or other personal
experiences. Novices benefit from interaction with models of similar work examined
through the lens of each capacity. Analytical questions might include: 1) What might
be the composer's *Feelingful Intention*? Why do you think so? 2) Which of the MUSTS
contribute to the *Musical Expressivity* of the work? How so? and 3) What techniques of

Artistic Craftsmanship did the composer use? How did these choices serve to invite a feelingful engagement with the music?

How Novice Composers Engage Capacities

Feelingful Intention

Feeling is the "hook" that entices novices to engage in composition. Therefore, the single most important task for the teacher of novice composers is helping them identify their *Feelingful Intentions*. Well-chosen compositional prompts (i.e., stories, games, activities, or phrases like "Think of a time when . . .") can spark the imagination (Wong & Lim, 2017). Such scaffolding offers students a sense of familiarity as they undertake what may be a new musical role—that of composer. They may have personal experiences like those suggested by the prompt or may find that new ideas are within reach of their imaginations. Such starting points help novice composers begin to make the connections between feeling and sound from the very outset of their compositional experiences. They literally begin to anticipate how the sounds they imagine will feel.

Musical Expressivity

Novice composers use their intuition to make decisions about the expressive features of their music. They often do this subconsciously. They may respond to motion in their music by continuing it or shifting it toward stasis. They may sense that their music needs repetition to create unity or that it is time to introduce something new. As they make these and other decisions related to the MUSTS, they rely on how they feel—what they sense in their own bodies—as a point of information. Teachers can help novice composers move these decisions from their natural positioning in the subconscious into the realm of the explicit. Noticing and labeling how the MUSTS are used in models or in the composer's own works helps them begin to consider how they might purposefully use the principles of *Musical Expressivity* to achieve their *Feelingful Intentions*. As they gain experience, composers can think about which MUSTS likely will have the most important role in their work before and while they compose.

Artistic Craftsmanship

The term *Artistic Craftsmanship* should be considered in two parts. First, for the novice composer, the "crafting" of sounds into music is often driven by the instruments or voices most readily available to them. The ability to immediately hear musical ideas sounding externally allows the composer to verify their thinking and advance to the next step of their music-making process. "Artistry" is found in the judgment that follows as composers ask themselves the question "Do these sounds capture the feeling I want?" When the answer is "Yes," composers may experience forward momentum. When the answer is "No," they return to experimentation to seek the sounds that will fulfill their goals. Composers may also seek input from others, either the teacher or peers, to acquire the technical skills they need to match the sounds they have imagined.

Sample Projects for Developing Capacities with Novice Composers

An important aspect of composer projects for novices is that they feature something culturally familiar. While the exact nature of what constitutes familiar will vary, it remains a vital consideration in that it positions students to be comfortable within the task. As we share grade-level projects we will identify moments where teachers can encourage students to think about capacities by using "FI" to indicate *Feelingful Intention*, "ME" to indicate *Musical Expressivity*, and "AC" to indicate *Artistic Craftsmanship*. These may occur during the introduction, active composing time, or during sharing and reflection at the end of the process. These models, shown in Figures 16.2–16.5, also feature a variety of contexts including individual, partnered, small group, and whole class projects. Additionally, Figure 16.6 features a project lead sheet resulting from the lesson shown in Figure 16.5 .

COMPOSING EMOJI THEME MUSIC	
Grade Level	K–2
Composing Context	Individual
Materials	Collection of 4 – 6 emoji faces positioned where students can reference them; pitched percussion, 1 per composer
Overview	Students will compose a short piece evocative the emotion expressed by an emoji face.
Activity	■ Have each composer select an emoji. Invite composers to create music that sounds like the emoji feels. [This engages composers with feelingful intention (FI).] Encourage composers to practice playing their piece until they ready to share it. When ready, invite composers to perform their pieces for the class. Note: There is no need to specify length. Students will compose what they can recall, music of about 20-30 seconds in duration. ■ As composers share their pieces, encourage classmates to identify musical ideas that might suggest which emoji was the focus of the composer's work. Composers can also be asked to identify sounds in their composition that are particularly important in creating the feeling they associated with their emoji. [This encourages students to link FI and artistic craftsmanship (AC).] Ask composers to describe how at least one MUSTS (ME) contributed to shaping the emoji's feeling. This helps composers understand how musical expressivity serves as a bridge between feelingful intention and artistic craftsmanship.

FIGURE 16.2. A lesson for K–2 novice composers

OUR EMOJI RONDO	
Grade Level	3–5
Composing Context	Teacher-facilitated whole group and independent small groups
Materials	Many emoji from a familiar theme; pitched (one per group) and unpitched percussion
Overview	Students collaborate to compose a class rondo using a set of related emoji as organizers.
Activity	■ Engage the class in a review of what a rondo is. Help students to select a familiar theme for their rondo. (AC). For example, a "pets" theme would allow the class to create an A–section focused on how pets make us feel in general (FI) and other sections might feature specific types of pets (FI). ■ Guide the class in the creation of a four-line lyric. Ask composers to describe how the music for these lyrics might sound using MUSTS (ME). Invite composers to sing, hum, or play their ideas for the first line. Ask for volunteers to share ideas and have the whole class sing each idea to experience how it feels. When a few ideas have been shared, vote to pick the idea that works best for each line. Set other ideas aside as they might work in other spots. Repeat for remaining lines. Have students sing the completed A–section several times to internalize it. Ask composers to decide whether the other sections will have lyrics or be instrumental. ■ For the remaining sections, divide the class into small groups and encourage each team select one pet emoji (dog, cat, turtle, etc.) as their focus. Encourage students to compose music of about the same length as the A–Section. When composers have finished, invite each team to perform their section. Allow time for group members to describe *Feelingful Intention–Musical Expressivity–Artistic Craftsmanship* connections. Have the class perform the A–section with each group performing their section. Perform, revise, and repeat as time allows. When composers are satisfied with their rondo, record a performance. Listen to the recording and discuss how the sections differ from the unifying A–section (FI, ME, AC).

FIGURE 16.3. A lesson for grades 3–5 novice composers

EMOJI WORD JAZZ	
Grade Level	6–8
Composing Context	Small group
Materials	Collection of 10-12 emoji (use those without faces); varied instruments or apps; recording device, if desired
Overview	Students will compose a spoken word and music performance using an emoji as a point of inspiration.
Activity	■ Introduce composers to selections from Ken Nordine's *Colors* album. This album features the personification of a paint color presented as word jazz (spoken word with instrumental accompaniment). Divide the composers into small groups. Instruct the composers to select an emoji and to create a poem of 8 to 12 lines personifying the emoji. Encourage composers to consider what it might feel like to be the emoji (FI), how the emoji might act within its environment (ME), and what sounds might best present the experience of the emoji (AC). ■ Instruct the students to adopt roles. Each group needs a narrator to read the poem while others explore and test musical ideas to accompany the reading. Composers should repeat this process, refining their choices, until their composition emerges. Let composers know whether they will share their pieces through recordings or live performance. Allow recording time, if needed. ■ As works are shared, audience members might identify their emotional impressions (FI). Ask composers to explain what expressive gestures (ME) and crafting techniques (AC) contribute to their experience. Listeners' comments can be used to spark conversation about how music becomes expressive and how different people can have varied experiences of the same composition.

FIGURE 16.4. A lesson for grades 6–8 novice composers

EMOJI INSPIRED SONGS	
Grade Level	9–12
Composing Context	Individual or partnered
Materials	Guitar, ukulele, or apps suitable for producing chordal accompaniment with a strumming sound or close approximation; a collection of emoji; resources for creating a simple lead sheet (lyrics and chord changes, melodic notation optional)
Overview	Students work individually or in pairs to create a simple song telling a story about an emoji.
Activity	■ Invite songwriters to identify the basic formal components (intro, verse, chorus, pre-chorus, transition/middle 8, outro, etc.) of songs they know. Introduce the songwriting task and have songwriters select an emoji to feature in song lyrics that tell a story. Help songwriters focus their work by asking them to create a single sentence to describe the song's message (FI). ■ Next, encourage songwriters to consider what feeling they hope listeners will experience (FI), which of the MUSTS will be used to hold the listeners' attention (ME), and how they will use chord patterns, rhythmic strumming, melodic contour, and other techniques to shape their song (AC). Invite songwriters to explore sound and lyric options. Some will focus on chords first, others on lyrics, and some may engage with lyrics, melody, and accompaniment all at once. ■ When songs are finished, ask songwriters to offer a brief "composer's overview" describing how they used FI-ME-AC in creating their songs. Also, ask them to talk about their songwriting process as all students will benefit from hearing about different approaches to composing music.

FIGURE 16.5. A lesson for grades 9–12 novice composers

FIGURE 16.6. Example of Emoji composition

DEVELOPING THE COMPOSITIONAL
CAPACITIES OF INTERMEDIATE COMPOSERS

Intermediate composers may be generally characterized as those who have had some experience with deliberately creating music for expressive purposes and who are somewhat comfortable with creating original music. Their compositions are important to them and often very personal. They may feel a deep sense of ownership in their work. Intermediate composers can create longer works of increasing complexity and understand that intentional thinking about and use of the capacities can improve their work.

Characteristics of Intermediate Composers

Intermediate composers tend to have definite musical preferences, but they are usually curious about all kinds of music. While they are particularly interested in how familiar sounds are produced and may be crafted in ways new to them, they are also attracted to unfamiliar instruments and other sounds.

Intermediate level composers work especially well in groups based on friendship or other self-selection criteria. (Hewitt, 2008). While some composers will find working with peers helpful for generating ideas and refining their compositional thinking (Kaschub, 1999), others will lean toward individual work. Freedom and constraint in compositional contexts as well as in composition task parameters becomes increasingly important. Balancing the constraining factor of group acceptance or rejection of one's ideas with the freedom to do exactly as one wishes may mean making choices (Rolle, Weidner, Weber, & Schlothfeldt, 2018) about what context works best for the intermediate composer. At the same time, working preferences vary as tasks and contexts change.

The music created by intermediate level composers remains intuitive and reflective of their experiences. However, students are able to imagine what feelings might be felt in situations they have not directly experienced. Consequently, composers experiment with expressing these more distanced feelings in sound.

Intermediate composers create more complex works than their novice counterparts. As part of this process, they readily benefit from compositional models that they then emulate or reframe to suit their own compositional inclinations. They best acquire the required skills of *Artistic Craftsmanship* on a need-to-know basis. The influence of models and increasing complexity of their musical inclinations leads to an increasing number of student-initiated questions.

How Intermediate Composers Engage Capacities

Feelingful Intention

Activities that inspire imagination and draw on familiar feelings remain salient. Composers may work with an increasing range of *Feelingful Intentions* and may deliberately focus on a single mood throughout a piece. Their interest in how the audience responds to their work increases in importance as they seek to refine intentions with products.

Musical Expressivity

Intuition remains an important influence in compositional work, but intermediate composers are increasingly able to make deliberate choices about which of the *Musical Expressivities* (MUSTS) are likely to elicit the feelings they are attempting to sonify. In most cases, they focus on one or two *Musical Expressivities* for each *Feelingful Intention*. Individual "voice" (Stauffer, 2003) emerges and typical expressive gestures may appear in their compositions.

Artistic Craftsmanship

Intermediate composers continue to favor familiar genres and they conform to the stylistic conventions of those genres. However, some composers will use unusual sounds and atypical organizational forms as part of their endeavors in *Artistic Craftsmanship*. Composers become attentive to how the elements can be combined to influence the balance of MUSTS and to invite specific feelingful responses. They become more adept at layering sounds and an expanding collection of compositional techniques is used. They often ask many "How do I . . . ?" questions and begin to move beyond accepting their first idea as their best one (Muhonen & Väkevä, 2012).

Sample Projects for Developing Capacities with Intermediate Composers

SONIFYING PICTURE BOOKS	
Grade Level	K–2
Composing Context	Whole class
Materials	Familiar and well-like picture book. Books to consider: ■ *Abuela* by Arthur Dorros and Elisa Kleven (Puffin, 1997) ■ *The Great Big Enormous Turnip* by Aleksey Tolstoy and Helen Oxenbury (Macmillan, 1972) ■ *Hush! A Thai Lullaby* by Minfong Ho and Holly Meande (Scholastic, *1996)* ■ *The Napping House* by Audrey Wood and Don Wood (Harcourt Brace Jovanovich, 1984) ■ *Today is Monday* by Eric Carle (World of Eric Carle, 1993) ■ *Whopper Cake* by Karma Wilson and Will Hillenbrand (McElderry Books, 2006)
Overview	In this pre-film scoring activity, students will create music to enhance the portrayal of characters, places, and events in a story.
Activity	■ Begin the lesson by viewing a short cartoon with the sound turned off. Ask composers what is missing. Play the cartoon again with the sound on help the composers identify dialogue, sound effects, and background music. When composers identify background music, ask them what feeling they have and what it is about the music that suggest that feeling to them (FI, ME). ■ Select a familiar story to sonify. Almost any excellent picture book will do, but cumulative stories where characters are added as the story unfolds work well with the very young. Read the story several times or use a book that is the focus of class work outside of music. Note: Avoid stories that have well-known music as creating new music for these stories is a more advanced skill. ■ Address the story in two steps. On reading 1, ask the composers to determine where sound effects would make the story more interesting. On reading 2, read in short sections. Discuss where the story suggests feelings. Ask questions like: How does this part of the story feel (FI)? What would music sound like that also felt that way (ME)? How can we make music that sounds like that (AC)? ■ Encourage the composers to make short melodies that capture the mood of the place, character, or action of this segment. Do the same for other places in the story. Rehearse the story with the music they have composed and the sound effects. Make a recording of their work and listen to it with them. Ask the composers what worked well and what might have worked better. Decide whether any changes or additions should be made. Revise and re-record as time allows.

FIGURE 16.7. A lesson for K–2 intermediate composers

THEMATIC BOOKSCORING	
Grade Level	3–5
Composing Context	Whole class and small group
Materials	A picture book or a short chapter book, preferably with several settings. Books to consider: ■ *Imani's Moon* by JaNay Brown Wood and Hazel Mitchell (Charlesbridge, 2014) ■ *Louise, the Adventures of a Chicken* by Kate DiCamillo and Harry Bliss (Harper Collins, 2008) ■ *Riki-Tikki-Tavi* by Rudyard Kipling, adapted by Jerry Pinkney (HarperCollins, 2004) ■ *Sadako and Thousand Paper Cranes* by Eleanor Coerr and Ronald Himler (Putnam, 1977) ■ *The Gruesome Guide to World Monsters* by Judy Sierra and Henrik Drescher (Candlewick Press, 2005)
Overview	Students will create a theme for a main character and vary that theme to reflect the character's journey.
Activity	■ Read the story to the class. Ask the composers to identify what the main character does and how the character might feel (FI). Discuss how theme music for the character might sound (ME). Consider which of the MUSTS will play a prominent role the character's music (ME). As a class, create a short theme for the character using the available materials (voices, instruments, electronics). Listen to individual ideas, test ideas, select and combine ideas as guided by the students (FI-ME-AC). ■ Once the theme has been created and learned by all members of the class, discuss the feeling of the character in the major scenes or action points of the story (FI). How might the character's theme change to reflect each setting (ME)? Discuss the term variation and ask composers how a theme can change (AC). Demonstrate these techniques using a familiar tune and list variation options for composers to reference as needed. ■ Divide the class into small groups. Assign each group a section of the story. Groups may use the ideas generated by the class or their own ideas as they vary the theme to fit their section of the story. Encourage composers to make whatever artistic decisions seem right but remind them that the theme must be included and varied in some way. ■ As groups are nearing the completion point, determine the order of performance (including a statement of the theme in its original form). Have groups discuss how they will connect each statement at transition points. Ask the class if they would like to include an introduction or coda. Revise and rehearse and then record the performance. Listen to the performance and discuss: What was most interesting about each variation? What techniques did the composers use to capture the feeling in their part of the story (AC)? Which of the MUSTS (ME) was most useful in evoking the desired mood or feeling (FI)?

FIGURE 16.8. A lesson for grades 3–5 intermediate composers

CREATING A TITLE SEQUENCE	
Grade Level	6–8
Composing Context	Small group (acoustic); individual/partnered (technology)
Materials	Digital audio workstation, apps with basic production features, cameras to record video or simple animation software
Overview	Television shows have a recognizable theme that audibly establish their brand. These themes are introduced through a title sequence which serves to bridge the everyday activities of the viewers and the imagined world of the show. Filmmakers use these introductions to ease viewers into the rhythm of this alternate world. In this activity, students will create a title sequence for a show that they would like to pitch to a TV executive. Part of the pitch will include sharing a brief clip that captures the essence of the show.
Activity	<ul><li>Ask students to share the name of a favorite show. Invite them to describe how the show starts. Identify this opening as a title sequence. View a few of these together and ask students to note commonalities. For example, title sequences are usually 30 seconds in length and include the text of the opening credits delivered before or over live-action, animation, music, still images, and/or graphics. Some shows use a cold open – beginning with the action of the show – and then run the title sequence a few minutes into the storyline and before the first advertisements are shown. Once the composers have made these observations, introduce the title sequence project telling students to imagine that they use the title sequence they create to pitch their show idea to a network executive.</li><li>Encourage producers to create a description of what their show will be about, what the main characters will be like (FI), and what sort of challenges or experiences those characters will encounter. This overall concept gives direction for the creation of a title sequence.</li><li>Next, producers should decide what kind of imagery they want in their title sequence (AC). Some may choose to serve as actors and film clips to piece together, others may use a series of snapshots or other imagery to collage, and some may wish to work with animation software to create cartoon images. Note: The snapshot/collage option is most time efficient.</li><li>Once producers have their title sequences designed, they shift to the role of composer to create their theme. Encourage composers to consider what the overall tone (comedy, drama, action, adventure, scary/horror, other) of their show will be (FI). What is it about their music that will invite the audience to settle into the mood of the show (ME)? Composers will also want to consider what tools they have available to them (AC) and how they might craft music to capture the mood they wish to invite (AC). If students are unsure of how to begin, encourage watching several title sequences within their chosen genre to understand how other composers have addressed a similar challenge. They might begin by building a beat (AC) that could provide a unifying (ME) background for their title sequence. They might also consider writing themes that reflect the nature of one or more characters (FI) and explore how these themes might be woven together to hint at the overall soundtrack of the show.</li><li>When projects are pitch-ready, invite "network executives" to join the class. These executives might be people who have experience in television, theater/film directors or actors from the community, or teachers from within the school. The job of the executives is to 1) hear the pitch, 2) ask questions to uncover how FI-ME-AC contribute to the concept/brand, 3) offer praise and encouragement, and 4) playfully deliver a "We'll call you!" regarding the future production of the show.</li></ul>

FIGURE 16.9. A lesson for grades 6–8 intermediate composers

SCORE AN EXISTING SHORT FILM	
Grade Level	9–12
Composing Context	Partnered
Materials	Short film, movie clip, or cartoon (a varied collection can be found at archive.org); notation software for creating a score, or acoustic instruments for performing the composition
Overview	Students will compose a film score for a brief work. They will consider characters, places, and events, but with the additional challenge of working within the fixed time frames that have been established by a director. This may seem like a minor shift in challenge, but it can be difficult to creating a series of very brief compositions that enhance emotion without overwhelming the viewing experience.
Activity	<ul><li>As a class, view a few movie clips, shorts, or cartoons and discuss how music contributes to the experience. Divide the class into teams of 2. Distribute movie clips of 1.5 to 2.5 minutes in length to each team. Teams may use the same or different clips. Both approaches work well, but the discussion that follows sharing differs based on which approach is used.</li><li>Invite the teams to watch their clip several times noting the time codes where they think they should add music (AC). As they study their clip, encourage them to note if/when the mood or feeling of the movie changes (FI) and what brings this change about as these shifts (ME) provide guidance for the music they will create.</li><li>Next, guide composers to decide what matters most at different points in their film – characters, action, or scene? For example, in a movie featuring two characters fly fishing, it may be important to capture the serenity (FI) of the stream at the outset and then to shift to ramping up the tension (ME) as a character gets swept downstream. Composers might address the most important aspects of the film first and then return to round out their soundtracks.</li><li>Once composers have completed their work, set up a movie viewing event where they can discuss the challenges presented by their clips. If all composers have used the same clip, the discussion might center on how (AC) and why (FI/ME) interpretations varied. If different clips have been used, composers might discuss what features they prioritized and the different techniques (AC) they used to achieve their artistic vision.</li></ul>

FIGURE 16.10. A lesson for grades 9–12 intermediate composers

DEVELOPING THE COMPOSITIONAL CAPACITIES OF ADVANCED COMPOSERS

Students who have had considerable experience with intentionally creating music for expressive purposes and who are comfortable with composing original music can be characterized as advanced composers. Not unlike their novice and intermediate counterparts, the work of advanced composers may reflect personal experiences. However, advanced composers frame their work with greater objectivity and a sense of professional distance. A strong command of capacities makes the creation of highly intentional works with extremely complex or purposefully simple structures possible. Advanced composers create pieces of varied lengths and they are sensitive to the musical language of the specific genres. While they understand the importance and influence of historical practices, they bring their own ideas and musical voice forward as they extend the lines of compositional practice.

Characteristics of Advanced Composers

Advanced composers can readily identify product intentions. They may choose to deeply immerse themselves within a specific genre (i.e., string quartets) or to explore a broad range of musical genres and styles in an attempt to expand their knowledge of compositional tools, techniques, and practices. The tendency to use certain types of musical gestures often allows listeners to match composition to composer.

While advanced composers can work well with others, they may prefer to work alone. They are often eager to initiate and develop their own ideas without the need to compromise or defend their decisions. Advanced composers are able to establish their own objectives and boundaries and, in order to develop the skills necessary for artistic independence, they need practice in setting these frames for their work. At the same time, these composers may benefit discussing their plans with teachers or other mentors who may be able to tease out any gaps that may exist in the planning process.

The music created by advanced composers exhibits a balance between intention and intuition. Intuition-based decisions now occur within the framework of intentionally crafted, specific contexts. Composers have the ability to select *Feelingful Intentions* and purposefully choose compositional tools and techniques to enliven those intentions. Taking time to access and study the work of other composers remains an important tool in advancing technique and evolving personal style.

How Advanced Composers Engage Capacities

Feelingful Intention

Advanced composers address *Feelingful Intentions* on multiple levels of their works. They may consider the emotional tone of an entire work, the character of a specific section, or the subtle difference in feeling that unfolds from phrase to phrase, motive to motive, or even note to note. Advanced composers are mindful of context and can imagine the emotional implications of scenarios beyond their direct experience. Most importantly, they deliberately attend to feeling. Whether they explore a range of feelings or focus on developing the nuance of a single emotion for an extended period, their work reveals increasingly insightful connections.

Musical Expressivity

Advanced composers can shape *Musical Expressivity* in an expanding number of ways. While they possess the ability to explore different proliferations of a single MUSTS pair, they more commonly tip the balances of multiple pairs as they craft music to invite increasingly complex soundscapes rich with emotion. The choices made by advanced composers remain rooted in intuition, but intuition now underlies thoughtful decisions rather than simply presenting itself as *the* solution to compositional problems.

Artistic Craftsmanship

Advanced composers gravitate to preferred genres and styles. They employ a compositional language that can often be recognized as their "voice." Given their comfort with a particular set of tools, they often seek techniques from other genres to disturb their comfort or alter their perception. Similarly, the application of familiar tools and techniques in new ways can lead to defining points of inspiration. In this way, *Artistic Craftsmanship* develops through self-imposed challenges. Such explorations often lead composers to see their work in new ways and invites a level of revision not often observed in less experienced composers.

Sample Projects for Developing Capacities with Advanced Composers

Considering Advanced Composers in Grades K–2

Encounters with advanced composers in grades K–2 are exceedingly rare. Children from homes with musical parents or children who have studied an instrument from a very young age may exhibit the characteristics of advanced work. These very young composers are likely to have been encouraged to make up their own music and praised for their efforts to do so. They are often excited to share their music with music teachers and will benefit from questions that support their continued work. Generally, these composers consider their pieces finished and they may be unwilling to alter their work. However, they will sometimes add to their pieces to make them longer, if encouraged to do so.

When encountering these composers and their music, ask lots of questions. Begin with "Can you tell me about your song or piece?" and "Why did you compose it?" With the composer's thinking framed, begin to explore the capacities by asking, "How do you feel when you are playing your piece?" or "How do you think others feel when they hear it?" (FI).

To help composers become aware of how music becomes expressive, make observations: "I noticed how the beginning of your song came back at the end. The

A PIECE FOR MY INSTRUMENT	
Grade Level	3–5
Composing Context	Individual
Materials	An instrument the composer has some technical ability to play
Overview	Students will compose a piece that showcases their instrument and that could be performed in a recital or at a composition festival. Instruction takes place over an extended period, rather than a single class meeting, and the composers are encouraged to revise and lengthen their pieces as seems appropriate.
Activity	<ul><li>Begin by asking the composers to imagine themselves, or a friend who plays the same instrument, on a stage playing a piece that they have written. Guide them to imagine what the piece sounds like with questions such as: Can you describe the music you hear at the beginning (ME)? What happens in the middle and at the end (ME)? What is most interesting idea in this piece (AC)? What other ideas do you notice (AC)? Do the beginning, middle and end sections have the same mood (FI)? Encourage students to make some notes about what they have imagined.</li><li>Following this guided exercise, challenge the young composers to try to make up something for one section of their piece and share it at the next lesson. If that comes easily to them, have them begin work on another section. Invite composers to share their work at their next lesson, possibly in the context of a composers' circle (Kaschub & Smith, 2016b) where peers also provide feedback.</li><li>Each time composers share, guide them to think critically about their music by asking lots of questions. For example, will the piece have one or multiple feelings (FI)? How will the feeling be maintained or altered (ME)? What is the best formal arrangement of their musical ideas (AC)? Remind composers that their pieces do not have to reveal their musical ideas in the order that they were composed. Sometimes the first musical idea composed is best suited for the middle or end of their piece. Ask composers if their work needs an introduction or coda (AC). Some composers may also desire accompaniment (AC). In such cases, teachers can create keyboard arrangements for composers who lack the ability to do so. However, it is very important that teacher contributions reside within the intentions of the composer.</li><li>Repeat the above processes for several class meetings allowing students ample time to compose and prepare their works for performance. If possible, feature these composer-performed works in a public recital where composers can introduce and briefly describe what they have done.</li></ul>

FIGURE 16.11. A lesson for grades 3–5 advanced composers

COMPOSING FOR UNACCOMPANIED SOLO INSTRUMENT OR VOICE	
Grade Level	6–8
Composing Context	Individual
Materials	Access to notation software
Overview	Students of advanced compositional experience have likely composed a work for their own instrument or voice, but perhaps have not yet fully explored the potentials of other instruments. In this lesson, students will interview a peer or more advanced performer who plays a different instrument or sings a different voice part. Students will construct a profile of the instrument/voice and its performer to inform the composition of a solo work.
Activity	■ Begin this project by asking composers to identify what they need to know about an instrument or voice so that they can appropriately compose music for it. Follow-up on this idea by encouraging students to consider how specific skill level and preferences of the performer might impact the performance of a work. ■ Help composers construct a list of questions designed to learn about a specific instrument/voice and its performer. Topics might include clef, range, notes that are difficult to produce, tempo to accuracy ratios of the performer, any special sounds the instrument/voice can make, extended techniques, how often does the performer need to breathe, articulations, bowings, etc. Facilitate time for composers to interview the performers who will play their compositions. ■ As part of gathering information, encourage composers to listen to existing unaccompanied solo works for their focus instrument or voice. Guide composers to attend to the character, moods or feelings commonly attributed to the instrument (FI), the nature of the musical gestures (ME), and the most featured techniques (AC). ■ Next, encourage composers to sketch the rough form of their work. What feeling do they wish to invite (FI) at different points? What musical gestures (ME) will they use to unify their work or to create a sense of movement? As composers begin to imagine their pieces, they might draft a few melodic fragments representative of different sections of their work (AC). Composers should review this plan with the teacher as this provides an opportunity for teachers to ask questions that may help composers refine their product goals. ■ As composers work on their pieces, it will be helpful for them to have periodic "testing" meetings with their performers to make sure that the composition is singable/playable. A key lesson for composers is that artistic vision can be defeated by technical limitations. Composers might need to be reminded that while it is perfectly fine to compose music that is too hard to sing or play, it is frustrating to never hear one's work performed. ■ Once compositions are complete and have been performed, composers should be guided to reflect on their process. Prompt questions might include: What did you learn as you interviewed the performer? How did the performer's specific skills and interests shape your thinking about your piece? If you were to compose another piece for this instrument, what might you? Why?

FIGURE 16.12. A lesson for grades 6–8 advanced composers

SELF-DESIGNED PROJECTS	
Grade Level	9–12
Composing Context	Flexible
Materials	Flexible
Overview	Advanced composers need opportunities to design projects that reflect their unique musical interests and goals. Teachers, though, can still offer important support, particularly in helping composers establish a productive personal process.
Activity	■ Teachers can encourage composers to begin their self-defined projects by briefly describing their product intentions. Consideration might be given to instrumentation, form, length, and other musical parameters. Composers should contemplate capacities (FI-ME-AC) as overarching considerations and as decision-drivers at increasingly finite levels. ■ Composers and teachers should work together to determine an appropriate level of description for a pre-composition plan. Some composers will prefer to think about the "big picture" and work out the finer details as they compose. Others will plan almost to the note. Regardless of approach, the key point for the pre-composition conference should be to clarify intentions, identify any challenges that may need to be addressed, and to establish a timeline identifying key points in the process. ■ As with all composition experiences, it is important for composers to reflect on their work. In the case of self-designed projects, students may find it valuable to compare their pre-composition intentions with their final products (FI-ME-AC). Composers might consider: What stayed the same and what changed? How did the choice of instruments influence the crafting of musical ideas (AC)? What impact did specific musical gestures (ME) have on the expressive potential of the work (FI)?

FIGURE 16.13. A lesson for grades 9–12 advanced composers

repetition seemed to unify your work (ME: unity-variety)." Similarly, craftsmanship can be addressed with statements such as, "I noticed how your music started with long sounds and ended with lots of short, quick sounds (AC: half notes, eighth notes). How did you decided to do that?" Also, try to connect these students with models. Listen together and share recordings, particularly of composers who write for the student's instrument or who pursue a similar style.

Finally, encourage composers to record and share their work with private teachers, relatives, and classmates. Just as adults often place children's visual artwork on display at home, young composer's creations should be highlighted. Family social media sites can be used and so can informal performances for friends. Praise and audience feedback can be motivating and fulfilling for some very young composers.

Opportunities in Teaching Music Composition

The composition activities described in this chapter demonstrate that teaching students to compose is different from nearly every other music learning activity that teachers typically lead because the final music product does not exist at the outset. Listening lessons begin with a recording and ensemble preparation starts with a score, but with composition there is nothing.

There is no product to analyze or discuss until the young composer begins to create. The lack of access to an immediate performance, a recording, or even a score, requires music teachers to think differently about their pedagogy. But "differently" is definitely possible.

The following pedagogical pointers can be used to guide planning and interactions with students. These pointers, particularly those that address the provision of feedback, must be used with caution. Feedback is most effective when it addresses concerns that have been voiced by the composer. Conversely, teacher-driven feedback may be overwhelming if it exceeds the zone of proximal development (Vygotsky, 1978) with regard to the student's compositional capacities.

10 Pedagogy Pointers

1. Design activities that draw on the natural interests and curiosities of students. Composition can be rewarding, but it can also be frustrating in the "hard work" stages. When students are connected to the work through their interests and when they are actively engaged in solving problems that they have invented or identified, they are more likely to persist through challenges.

2. Keep composition tasks real. The activities that students experience should be similar to the compositional work undertaken by composers outside of K–12 settings. The feeling of doing real compositional work allows students to integrate "composer" into their musical identity.

3. The ability to ask probing questions that illuminate student thinking is a critical skill. When we ask questions, we learn what students are thinking and trying to do—and we are more likely to avoid making assumptions that may not fit their intentions. Some of the questions we ask simply seek details, but others must evoke imaginative responses so that students can see new possibilities.

4. Consider how music composition will be included within the music curriculum. Developing the skills and knowledge of young composers requires multiple opportunities for them to explore, create, and share their work.

5. Follow the student's lead in determining the introduction of concepts and pace of instruction. Listening to recordings as well as in-class sharing sessions often result in new interests. These are "need to know" moments where new information is more likely to be remembered and applied in future work.

6. Encourage students to explore a wide range of instruments, sound sources, and technologies. Breadth of experience allows students to identify the media that best capture their artistic aspirations.

7. Remember that notation is a tool, not a necessity. Use recordings and encourage the use of invented symbols as needed. These will serve as a gateway to the use of traditional notation if it becomes necessary for sharing or preserving student work.

8. Be an advocate for your students' work. Provide opportunities for them to share what they have created and for others to perform their works. When sufficient artistic freedom is present in the compositional tasks, students are often quite proud of their work. Having that pride affirmed by others motivates future compositional activity.

9. The definition of "musically right" is made by the composer. Honor student work by supporting their musical decisions and resisting the urge to "fix" their work.

10. Help students discover and develop their innate artistry by constantly reinforcing that music is a process. It always involves feeling, knowing within the body, and exercising creative, musical, and artistic actions.

CONCLUSION

Teachers and students can find great success—defined as growth of musical knowledge, skills, and understandings along with growth of self—when they use a capacities-focused approach to music composition. This approach allows teachers to adopt practices that facilitate and advance student work while respecting and honoring students' emerging ideas and artistic voice. In pursuing this path, music teachers can welcome diverse perspectives, include students of differing abilities, and study familiar and novel musics from a position of curiosity and vulnerability that actively embraces music's potential to enliven the human spirit. This is an invaluable and richly rewarding opportunity that every child deserves.

REFERENCES

Brain and Creativity Institute. (2020). *Music education and brain development.* Retrieved January 5, 2020, from https://dornsife.usc.edu/bci/brain-and-music.

Brown, A. R., & Dillon, S. (2016). Meaningful engagement with music composition. In D. Collins (Ed.), *The act of musical composition: Studies in the creative process* (pp. 79–110). Routledge.

Damásio, A. R. (1994). *Descartes' error: Emotion, reason, and the human brain.* Putnam Publishing.

Damásio, A. R. (1999). *The feeling of what happens: Body and emotion in the making of consciousness.* Harcourt, Inc.

Hewitt, A. (2008) Children's creative collaboration during a computer-based music task. *International Journal of Educational Research, 47*(1), 11–26.

Johnson-Green, E. (2020). Music composition as immersive learning in K–5 music education: Results of a 4-year study. *Visions of Research in Music Education, 35,* 1–41. Retrieved from http://www-usr.rider.edu/%7Evrme/v35n1/index.htm

Kaschub, M. E. (1999). *Sixth grade student's descriptions of their individual and collaborative music composition processes and products initiated from prompted and unprompted task structures*. [Unpublished doctoral dissertation]. Northwestern University.

Kaschub, M. and Smith, J. P. (2009). *A principled approach to teaching music composition to children*. RIME: Research and Issues in Music Education.

Kaschub, M., & Smith, J. P. (2016a). The big picture: Developing musical capacities. *Music Educators Journal*, *102*(3), 33–40.

Kaschub, M., & Smith, J. (2016b). *Experiencing music composition in grades 3–5*. Oxford University Press.

Kaschub, M., & Smith, J. (2022a). Experiencing music composition in grades K – 2. National Association for Music Education with R&L Education – A Division of Rowman & Littlefield Publishers, Inc.

Kaschub, M., & Smith, J. (2022b). Experiencing music composition in middle school general music. National Association for Music Education with R&L Education – A Division of Rowman & Littlefield Publishers, Inc.

Kyung-Suk M. (2006). The commencement of the Manhattanville music curriculum program: 1957–1966. *Journal of Historical Research in Music Education*, *31*(2), 71–84.

Langer, S. K. (1942). *Philosophy in a new key*. Harvard University Press.

Langer, S. K. (1967). *Mind: An essay on human feeling* (Vol. 2). John Hopkins University Press.

Mark, M. (1996). *Contemporary music education* (3rd ed.). Wadsworth/Thomson Learning.

Muhonen, S., & Väkevä, L. (2012). Seizing the dynamic moment in situation-originated learning: The origin of songcrafting examined through Dewey's theory of inquiry. *Nordic Research in Music Education, Yearbook*, *13*, 151–169. Retrieved from https://core.ac.uk/download/pdf/30847191.pdf

Ohman-Rodriguez, J. (2004). Music from inside out: Promoting emergent composition with young children. *YC Young Children*, *59*(4), 50–55.

Reimer, B. (2022). *A philosophy of music education: Advancing the vision* (3rd ed.). SUNY Press. (Original work published 2003).

Rolle, C., Weidner, V., Weber, J., & Schlothfeldt, M. (2018). Role expectations and role conflicts within collaborative composing projects. In C. Christophersen & A. Kenny (Eds.), *Musician-teacher collaborations: Altering the chord* (pp. 50–61). Routledge.

Sloboda, J. A. (2010). Music in everyday life: The role of emotions. In P. Juslin & J. Sloboda (Eds.), *Handbook of music and emotion: Theory, research, applications* (pp. 493–514). Oxford University Press.

Stauffer, S. (2003). Identity and voice in young composers. In M. Hickey (Ed.), *Why and how to teach music composition: A new horizon for music education* (pp. 91–111). Rowman & Littlefield Education.

Stewart Rose, L., & Countryman., J. (2013). Repositioning 'the elements': How students talk about music. *Action, Criticism, and Theory for Music Education*, *12*(3), 45–64.

Thomas, R. B. (1970). *Manhattanville music curriculum program*. Final Report. Manhattanville College of Sacred Heart, Purchase.

Veloso, A. L., & Carvalho, S. (2012). Music composition as a way of learning: emotions and the situated self. In O. Odena (Ed.), *Musical creativity: Insights from music education research* (pp. 73–91). Routledge.

Vygotsky, L. S. (1978). *Mind in society*. Harvard University Press.

Wong, S. S. H., & Lim, S. W. H. (2017). Mental imagery boosts music compositional creativity. *PloS One*, *12*(3), e0174009. https://doi.org/10.1371/journal.pone.0174009.

CHAPTER 17

MOVEMENT → IMPROVISATION → COMPOSITION THROUGH DALCROZE EURHYTHMICS

MARLA A. BUTKE AND R. J. DAVID FREGO

> Joy arises in the child the moment his faculties are liberated from any restraint, and he becomes conscious of his control over them, and decides on the direction in which that control shall be exercised. The joy is the product of a joint sense of emancipation and responsibility.
>
> —(Jaques-Dalcroze, 1921/1972, p. 175)

ÉMILE Jaques-Dalcroze explained music learning as multi-sensory, professing "the ear that hears, the body that feels and senses, and the brain that imagines, judges and connects" (Abramson, 1980, p. 32). This speaks to the outcome of the affective, cognitive, and kinesthetic domains being combined in the process of creating new music. Composers have been known to say, "I hear the music in my head." A Dalcroze student would say, "I feel the music in my body." The aural, visual, and kinesthetic modes can all be engaged in the construction of a piece of music. A student's immersion into the Dalcroze philosophy and process can contribute to that student's ability to be creative and to make artistic choices in composition.

BRIEF HISTORY

Swiss composer, pianist, actor, and dancer Émile Jaques-Dalcroze (1865–1950) pioneered the approach of experiencing, understanding, and demonstrating music through movement, now known as Dalcroze Eurhythmics. His mother had studied the philosophy of Heinrich Pestalozzi (1746–1827), who was an early advocate of teaching and learning through the senses and experiences separate from the printed word. Both Pestalozzian and Dalcroze philosophies center on the multi-sensory experiences that lead to a more comprehensive understanding of musicianship and in the making of music. (Collins, 1993). In the arts, young Émile was encouraged to sing, play, dance, and create (Spector, 1990).

As a young man, Jaques-Dalcroze studied at the Geneva Conservatory, the Paris Conservatory, and the Vienna Conservatory. He was influenced by the teachings of Mathis Lussy (1828–1910), who wrote on the subject of expressive musical performance and musical understanding (Caldwell, 1995). Lussy's philosophy propelled Jaques-Dalcroze to approach musical learning through scholarly inquiry and to seek solutions through a scaffolded approach (Spector, 1990).

Following composition studies with Gabriel Fauré, Adolf Prosniz, and Anton Bruckner, plus a season as assistant conductor and chorusmaster at the Théâtre des Nouveaux in Algiers, Jaques-Dalcroze returned to the Geneva Conservatory as a professor of solfège. Here he observed his students and considered the disconnect between their technical playing and their expression of nuances in music. He found that the concept of maintaining a steady beat to be a challenge for many of them. Jaques-Dalcroze turned to locomotor movement to instill steady beat. This included walking, moving expressively, singing, breathing, changing tempi, skipping, and conducting while moving (Odom, 1998). Through shared learning experiences with peers, the students were led to discover the interrelationships of time, space, and energy. With the addition of rhythmic and purposeful movement to music, the students were able to perceive the body as the first instrument of expression. Through singing, moving, and creating, Jaques-Dalcroze's holistic approach to learning began to take shape (Dutoit, 1971, p. 9).

With the encouragement of two German industrialists, Jaques-Dalcroze assisted in the development of an experimental garden city named Hellerau, being designed north of Dresden. The concept of Hellerau was a planned industrial settlement of furniture manufacturing with a school for artistic development. Between 1910 and 1914, Hellerau thrived as a cultural center for music, theater, and dance.

In partnership with theater designer Adolphe Appia (1862–1928), Jaques-Dalcroze oversaw the construction of the school, student housing, and the performance space that was noted for architectural and staging innovations. All stage components were modular and movable by the performers. There was no proscenium in front of the stage, which brought the audience closer to the performance. The side walls were covered with treated canvas that concealed recessed lighting that provided visual effects (Spector, 1990). During performances, students interchanged roles of musicians, dancers, and actors. During the summer festival season, well-known artists, writers, and teachers came to experience Hellerau. They included theater personalities Konstantin Stanislavsky, George Bernard Shaw; dancers Mary Wigman, Hanya Holm, Serge Diaghilev, and Rudolf von Laban; and musicians Darius Milhaud and Jan Paderewski (Martin et al., 1965).

Hellerau closed at the beginning of World War I and Jaques-Dalcroze returned to Geneva to establish the Institut Jaques-Dalcroze that continues to operate. An instructor training program was established that enabled others to teach his approach. Training centers and professional organizations in eurhythmics have since been established around the globe. Jaques-Dalcroze continued to refine the approach as well as compose and teach until his death in Geneva in 1950.

Today, the Dalcroze approach is applied as an instructional tool in musical training from early childhood through college experiences. It is also found in dance, acting, and music therapy approaches (Frego et al., 2008), as well as with older adult populations (Treveño et al., 2018).

Philosophy of Eurhythmics

As stated in the historical section, the body is considered to be the primary instrument. It is the body that feels rhythm and hears pitch and reacts through movement. Jaques-Dalcroze promoted the idea that every musician should strive to be sensitive and expressive, and to express music through creative and purposeful movement (Pennington, 1925, p. 9). The goal of eurhythmics is to internalize all the elements of music through kinesthetic activities, allowing the learner to experience music physically and joyfully and to perform the music artfully and thoughtfully.

Robert Abramson (1980) describes a flow of learning through the Dalcroze approach that seeks to clarify the philosophy. In this flow of learning, improvisation and performance appear at the height of musical development. Improvisation is a technique that requires the musician to create music in the moment based on a developed toolkit of musical styles and techniques. When composition is the goal, we propose that students in Dalcroze classes approach composition through improvisation. The following flow of learning allows improvisation to become the experimental period prior to composition. A comparison of the Abramson and Butke-Frego models is shown in Figure 17.1.

Abramson Model	Butke–Frego Model
Hearing to moving	Hearing to moving
Moving to feeling	Moving to feeling
Feeling to sensing	Feeling to sensing
Sensing to analyzing	Sensing to analyzing
Analyzing to reading	Analyzing to reading
Reading to composing	*Reading to improvising*
Composing to improvising	*Improvising to composing*
Improvising to performing	*Composing to performing*

FIGURE 17.1. A comparison of activity flow between Abramson and Butke-Frego

While participants in a eurhythmics class do not experience all these actions in one lesson or rehearsal, they are moving through various levels based on the musical maturity of the student and the goal of the lesson. In the second half of this chapter, we will present lesson plans and activities that prepare the student toward improvisation and composition.

Mead (1994) brings the philosophy of this approach together with four premises: 1) eurhythmics awakens the physical, aural, and visual images of music and the mind; 2) rhythmic *solfège* (sight-singing and aural skills), improvisation, and purposeful movement combine to improve expressivity and enhance intellectual understanding; 3) music may be experienced through speech, gesture, and movement. These can likewise be experienced in time, space, and energy; and 4) as humans, we learn best when learning through multiple senses. Music, then, should be taught through tactile, kinesthetic, aural, and visual senses.

Components of Eurhythmics

Music educators and music therapists often identify this approach as eurhythmics, which encompasses the four components of eurhythmics (rhythmic and purposeful movement); rhythmic *solfège* (pitch and inner hearing), improvisation (physical and musical creativity), and *plastique animée* (artistically representing music through movement). The related components are often taught as an integrated lesson, complementing the facets of each, but the components can also be taught independently.

Eurhythmics

The first is rhythmic movement, or eurhythmics itself. The term eurhythmics comes from the Greek "eu" meaning good, and "rhythmy," meaning rhythm, proportion, and symmetry. All elements of music, including pulse, beat, rhythm, meter, phrasing, dynamics, and form, can be taught through kinesthetic experiences, both through space and within space. Seitz (2005) speaks to the connections between musicality and movement and states that musical expressivity resides in the physical characteristics of the body and entails physical and social interactions with others (p. 420). In a eurhythmics class, the teacher leads the session using a hand drum, piano, or recorded music and students react physically to the elements of the music. Participants work individually, in pairs, or in small groups to physicalize what they hear. The lesson/rehearsal often flips, with students creating the movement and the teacher accompanying what is being physically created.

Rhythmic *Solfège*

Jaques-Dalcroze believed that students must learn nuanced listening skills and develop "inner hearing." Musicians should be able to hear with their eyes and sing with their ears. Music notation then becomes meaningful when realized in real performance or in the imagination. *Solfège* is often taught using the fixed-*do* approach, based on the French system. In the United States, United Kingdom, and Hungary, the naming of the pitches has evolved into a movable-*do* approach. Students develop sensitivity to pitches, the relationship of pitch to each other, and to the tonal framework. What makes rhythmic *solfège* unique is that it is combined with rhythm and movement, both locomotor and non-locomotor.

Improvisation

Improvisation skills are developed sequentially and used in many settings. A teacher might improvise at the piano while students react to the sound and create movement, react spontaneously to verbal instructions, or change in musical character. Conversely, a student might improvise movement while another student accompanies with a drum, at the piano, or vocally. Students soon develop skills to be able to improvise musically and expressively on their own instruments. According to Mead (1994), these joyful and spontaneous performance activities are designed to communicate musical intent and to improve response time.

Plastique animée

Sometimes referred to as *plastique*, it is often seen as a culminating experience or performance in a eurhythmics class. *Plastique animée* is defined as the artistic and creative embodiment of the music through individual or group movement (Butke & Frego, 2016). The students are provided with the basic musical elements and are asked to spontaneously create an interactive composition with the music. In essence, in a *plastique* experience, the students are asked to be the music. While the music may be improvised, it is often recorded music that highlights the focused skill set presented in the lesson/rehearsal.

APPLICATION OF DALCROZE EURHYTHMICS TO MUSIC COMPOSITION

In the previous section, we outlined the basic facets of the eurhythmics experience: Eurhythmics—rhythmic and purposeful movement; Rhythmic *solfège*—singing with movement; Improvisation—physical and musical improvisation; and *Plastique animée*—music represented through motion. In the Dalcroze approach, the concept of time, space, and energy permeate all of these facets. When we move, we are making decisions about speed, distance, and the energy to embody the music. When we sing, we are making decisions about tempo, duration, and dynamics. When we improvise in music, we are making all of the decisions noted above. Finally, when we engage in *plastique animée*, we are reacting to and representing the music in a purposeful and planned manner.

Looking through the lens of time, space, and energy, we propose that participants in eurhythmics may approach the compositional process through four stages: movement exploration, sound exploration, exploration to improvisation, and improvisation to composition. A description of each stage is shown in Figure 17.2.

Stage 1 Movement Exploration	This is an opportunity for the body to take the lead in creating a movement piece by experimenting with the same elements that exist in movement as exist in music; dynamics, tempo, and thematic material that develop into a form. This movement exploration may occur individually, but eurhythmics is a social experience and group development is more common. Through repetition and sharing of ideas, the movement moves towards becoming a set piece in the students' kinesthetic memory, resulting in a movement composition that can be recreated.
Stage 2 Sound Exploration	At some point when the movement is close to being set, some of the participants may move over to instruments to experiment with the soundscape of the movement. This can be accomplished by watching the movement and creating the appropriate musical response in real time. This symbiotic relationship of movement and sound also creates a non-verbal dialogue between the plastic artist and the musician. This exploration stage is aided with the knowledge of the phrases, form, and the musical elements being expressed in movement. Through exploration, these structures are added to the students' toolkits.
Stage 3 Exploration to Improvisation	As the individual and collective toolkits develop with ideas, patterns and structures, students can now select among the collected ideas and improvise fragments, phrases, or sections, while changing or recreating through repetition and recreation. While each repetition is not the same, but the structure of the work remains intact, the students have moved into improvisation.
Stage 4 Improvisation to Composition	Eventually, all plastic artists are contributing to the developing musical work. Aided by their physical memory of the movement and the experimental progression of the soundscape, a composition begins to emerge. Similar to a movement composition, this piece can be recreated close to its original intention. The composition may also include some improvisational elements, but it can now be recorded or transferred to a notational form agreed to by the group.

FIGURE 17.2. Four stages to composition

Review and Reflection of the Literature

Researchers at Coventry University incorporated Dalcroze Eurhythmics into the teaching of music composition. In this study, thirteen planned sessions of purposeful movement activities relating to the elements of music became learning strategies for composers to draw inspiration (Habron et al., 2012). In setting the design of the project, the authors wrote:

> The intention was that the participants experienced each topic bodily before beginning to compose. In order for participants to experience composition in relation to movement, four compositional tasks were set over the course of the project. The design of the project was such that participants would be asked to compose music based directly on their experiences during the sessions: two-part composition; composition involving metric changes; chord sequence with varied bass lines; and theme and variations. (p. 19)

A follow-up interview was held with the participants and four themes emerged: 1) the influence of Dalcroze Eurhythmics on the process and product of composition; 2) the influence of enhancing musical understanding from a kinesthetic perspective; 3) the experience of kinesthetic learning; and 4) the implications for incorporating Dalcroze Eurhythmics into the composition curriculum. It was interesting that the majority of the students reported a positive and somewhat joyful learning experience, but this was not unanimous. That tells us to be aware of barriers to this approach. These can include perceived body image, self-consciousness, ability to work within a group, and a willingness to take risks (p. 24). While this project involved college students, those same attitudes may exist with young learners as well. In our personal work with gifted/talented children, group work takes enormous energy among the learners and often leads to increased frustrations. Similarly, children with special needs, such as being on the autism spectrum, express challenges with group dynamics, levels of sound, and moving a task to completion. However, many children learn kinesthetically and can build new understandings through movement. Eurhythmics provides teachers with more options to reach efficacy in the music classroom.

Pamela Burnard (2004) has studied children's music-making from the perspectives of both improvisation and composition. Her research revealed three attitudes of children toward these three tasks:

1. Improvisation and composition as ends in themselves and differently-oriented activities;
2. Improvisation and composition as interrelated entities whereby improvisation is used in the service of making a composition; and
3. Improvisation and composition as indistinguishable forms which are inseparable in context and intention. (p. 38)

One of Burnard's conclusions is that the approach to teaching/facilitating improvisation may be different than teaching/facilitating composition, even though the outcomes may be indistinguishable. While improvisation is *in the moment*, using the tools developed in movement and musicianship, composition is *goal-oriented* with a product that can be replicated. This resonates with the spiral nature of the Dalcroze approach. Improvisation is often the most common activity in movement and in playing. Young children may respond in movement to a teacher's improvisation. In another case, one child may create a movement improvisation that is accompanied in real time by young musicians using percussion and/or pitched instruments. In this example, improvisation could be one of the goals of the lesson. But, where composition is the goal, a group of students work to create a piece that can be replicated by themselves or others. Students then can agree on a notation system, if needed, and map out their work.

The second approach is that improvisation is used in the service of making a composition. This is more common in a Dalcroze class as a natural progression of learning. Repetition of movement and music improvisation often leads to setting the work. In *plastique animée*, a movement representation of a piece of music, the students' movements start to become more concrete through repeated listening to the music. Similarly, the parameters of an improvisation start to become more predictable through repeated playing.

The third approach that Burnard wrote about was that improvisation and composition are inseparable in intention. The goal of a task in a Dalcroze class might be to create a movement built on a theme and variations where the variations are improvised, or a rondo form where the "A" section is composed and the sections in between are improvised. This can be realized in movement and in musical improvisation. In all cases, Burnard concluded that children compose through improvisation. However, the goal of the task leads to how improvisation and composition are experienced (Burnard, 2004).

In an earlier study, Burnard (1999) observed 12-year-old children engaged in music improvisation and composition through distinct modes of "bodily intention." Burnard found that children's experiences were determined by the interplay between body movement, instrument, and preference of instrument. While this study confirmed other studies that showed children compose through improvising, Burnard found that children involved in composing used a reflective synthesis of what was known, and improvisation involved responding with what they could do in the moment.

An additional study by Burnard (2000) concluded with a model that mapped different ways of experiencing improvisation and composition. Four categories were created to indicate that these two approaches are oriented toward: 1) time, 2) body, 3) relations, and 4) space.

These categories resonate with eurhythmics specialists in that time, space, and energy are interrelated and interdependent upon each other. Similar to eurhythmics, Burnard (2000) places the body in the center with time, relations, and space around it. Both improvisation and composition activities need to be preceded with movement activities that allow students to explore how these actions function in movement and music.

Questions often asked by teachers involve notation. Western notation is a complicated system for young children to both decode and encode. Beginning in the late 1990s, researchers looked at strategies where motion could be captured and converted to sound design (Chung et al., 2011). Szu-Ming Chung and Chih-Yen Chen (2011, p. 264) adapted the approach of Dalcroze Eurhythmics in creating an electronic game that involved rhythmic, melodic, and chord progression improvisation activities. Improvisation was designed not to follow a prescribed compositional formula, but to freely create and respond to others, whereas the compositional aspect involved rules where rhythms, melodies, and chords were conceived as teachable elements that encouraged inner hearing and developed notation skills.

The Orff Schulwerk, Kodály, and Dalcroze approaches all use some form of mapping notation for young musicians. This involves the children creating their composition, then reverse engineering to how it should look on paper. The children are able to show tempo, themes, pitch direction, articulation, and expression in their paper renderings of their works. Dalcroze teachers might give a group's composition to another group and ask them to interpret it musically. The other group's interpretation is in itself a teachable moment on interpreting a composition.

Susan Kenny (2013, p. 47) wrote an important article on mapping music through movement in a Dalcroze class. According to the author, moving to and mapping music assists with teaching the musical elements, interpreting a musical score, teaching children how to negotiate in and through space, and problem solving. The detailed musical maps presented in the article were useful in interpreting music through the children's thought process. Kenny also noted the development of self-control, awareness of surroundings, large and small motor movements, directionality, and creativity. These decision-making processes are needed as precursors for both improvisation and composition.

The Implementation of the Dalcroze Philosophy in Today's Music Classroom

The implementation of the Dalcroze philosophy begins with a culture of movement created for the students by the teacher. Students within a general music classroom, choral or instrumental rehearsal setting, or private music studio need to comprehend and value the guiding principles of what meaningful movement experiences involve in terms of behaviors and attitudes. It is also important for students to be given permission to be creative and relaxed in a supportive atmosphere. The preparation of a Dalcroze experience requires clarity in instruction, consistency in expectations, and joyful enthusiasm by the teacher. The teacher and students are intertwined in informing each other of how the movement experience will be shaped. The end goal is the strengthening the students' musicality through physical awareness and kinesthetic understanding. Once students begin to use the body to create musical meaning, they can begin to create music.

Physical Exploration

Students need to develop a movement vocabulary as part of the process in creating musical understanding and expression through physical means. Physical exploration includes how the body moves, how the body reacts to music, and what physical choices the body can make to be creative and expressive. Physical exploration can further be embodied through the countless kinesthetic possibilities involving locomotor and non-locomotor movements; various body part usage; varying amounts of energy expended in movements; speed, shape, and direction of movement; spatial levels in movement; and individual, pairs, small groups, and/or large groups of synchronous or non-synchronous movements.

Students require frequent, varied, and sequential opportunities to explore all the countless ways a body can move. For example, a teacher can provide the open-ended instruction that students simply walk through space. If there are 20 students in a class-room, there will be twenty different examples of walking. Students should be made aware of the differences in how other students move so dividing the class will allow the students to observe the many variations of how people move through space. Tempo, posture, energy, flow, and arm position are just a few of the nuances for the students to observe. The teacher would next set up a framework whereby students hear music through piano improvisation or a recording. The music will dictate tempo, energy, and flow but the students have the freedom to move various parts of their body as well as choose what shape, direction, and level to use when they are walking through space.

A teacher can create an activity called a *quick reaction* exercise to give students the oppor-tunity to react to music. It is defined as a movement change in response to a musical or verbal cue (Butke & Frego, 2016). An example of a quick reaction would be "Walking the Bass/ Clapping the Treble." The students walk the rhythm of what they hear in the bass and clap the rhythm of what they hear in the treble as the teacher improvises on the piano/keyboard. The teacher changes the rhythmic durations after several measures, so students react to the changes that occur. The exploratory aspect of this activity is in the way that the students are moving in terms of direction, energy, and shape. The amount of focus and discernment on the student's part creates a structure for developing aural skills as well as allows creativity in movement choices. By using piano improvisation, the teacher can ascertain how quickly the students are hearing the changes in the movement and adjust to their level of competency.

Plastique animée provides an opportunity for students to experience a quick reaction activity and develop that first step into a physical representation of the music. When students have assembled a large movement vocabulary, they can then begin the process of bringing the music to life through a somatic depiction of the music. The aural and physical understanding of musical concepts is realized through an expressive and accu-rate demonstration of the music through movement.

Purposeful Movement

Students engaged in movement activities begin on a continuum of exploration and end with the comprehensive *plastique animée* experience. In the middle of the continuum lies the opportunities to hear, understand, and physicalize various musical concepts. The students will create a physical and visual soundscape rooted in musical meaning because their bodies have experienced it. Once the continuum has been completed and students demonstrate aural, cognitive, and physical understandings, they can begin to create new music. If the students are entrenched in the Dalcroze philosophy, their perception of ex-pressivity and nuance can further inform their ability to create music in a more meaningful way. Sample activities (Butke & Frego, 2016) that help students physically and intellectu-ally comprehend musical concepts are shown in Figures 17.3 through 17.6.

Concepts	Activities
Steady Beat	1. Using Copland's "Hoe-Down," the students are sitting and imitating the teacher showing a steady beat in different ways/places on the body as the music is played. 2. The second time the music is played, the students discover their own ways of demonstrating a steady beat. The teacher calls out "change" when the students should find a new way.
Durations	1. Students stand in pairs facing each other. To form two parallel lines with the elastics, each student has an elastic and holds one end of the elastic wrapped around the wrist and holds the end of the partner's elastic wrapped around the other wrist. 2. Teacher plays half notes and quarter notes on the hand drum and the students pull the elastics according to the indicated note value. 3. Play "Fight Song" by Platten/Bassett, and students pull half notes on the verse and quarter notes on the refrain.
Meters	1. Students stand in self-space. 2. Each student is given a racquetball. Have the students bounce them to practice catching the ball. 3. Teacher plays a steady beat on the hand drum, accenting every other stroke to indicate duple meter. The students bounce and catch on the beat while saying "bounce, catch." 4. Teacher helps the students identify the anacrusis (preparation), crusis (point of contact), and metacrusis (follow through which turns into the anacrusis) of bouncing and catching the ball. 5. Teacher increases the tempo as the students bounce and catch the balls. 6. Teacher explains that the space and energy need to change to accurately bounce the ball on the beat at a faster tempo. The concept of time (the tempo), space, and energy is an important part of movement. 7. Teacher decreases the tempo of duple meter, and the students continue to bounce and catch the ball. Students discuss how they needed to change space and energy to bounce the ball to a slower tempo. 8. Teacher changes to triple meter. The students must show a long, melded metacrusis/anacrusis for beats two and three. 9. Teacher changes tempo in triple meter. Students respond accordingly, adjusting space and energy to bounce the balls in each tempo. 10. Add recordings with various tempi.
Syncopation	1. Students stand in self-space. 2. Using "Ivan Sings" by Khachaturian, the teacher claps the syncopated pattern in the left hand in the B section. The students imitate by clapping the rhythm. 3. Students form pairs facing each other with one student designated as "A" and the other student designated as "B." 4. Each student puts the left arm out with palm up and places the right-hand fingertips on top of the partner's left hand. 5. The "A" student taps the melodic rhythm, and the "B" student taps the accompaniment rhythm. 6. Switch tasks. 7. Teacher plays the second half of the piece and the students step to the accompaniment rhythm.

FIGURE 17.3. Rhythmic activities to develop physical and conceptual understandings

Melodic Rhythm	1. Students stand in self-space
	2. Students sing the folk song, "Rocky Mountain."
	3. Students sing the song while clapping the beat.
	4. Students sing the song while clapping the melodic rhythm.
	5. Students form partners and sing the song while tapping the beat with their right-hand fingertips into the left hand palms up of their partners.
	6. Repeat the last step while tapping the melodic rhythm into their partners' hands.
	7. In partners, students sing the song, while one student taps the beat and the other student taps the rhythm simultaneously.
	8. Switch roles and repeat the activity.
	9. Continue with the students singing the song while one student is tapping the beat and the other student is tapping the rhythm, but at the signal from the hand drum by the teacher, switch roles.
	10. Students stand in self-space.
	11. Students sing the song and walk the beat.
	12. Students sing the song and walk the melodic rhythm.
	13. Repeat the last step but at the signal from the hand drum, they switch to walking the melodic rhythm. At the next signal, they switch to walking the beat.

FIGURE 17.3. Continued

Concepts	Activities
High/Low	1. Students stand in self-space.
	2. Students walk a steady beat in a tempo indicated by the teacher.
	3. Teacher plays four different pitches on the piano as quarter notes followed by four beats of rest, then repeats the same pitch sequence and the students snap on the highest of the four pitches while walking the beat.
	4. Teacher repeats this procedure several times using different pitch sequences.
	5. Repeat process but students clap on the lowest pitch.
	6. Repeat process with students snapping on the highest pitch and clapping on the lowest pitch.
Melodic Direction	1. Students stand in a circle facing in a counter-clockwise direction.
	2. Students sing a major scale using *solfège* and walk forward during the ascending scale and backwards during the descending scale.
	3. Students sing "Frère Jacques" and walk the beat.
	4. Students repeat the song and walk the melodic rhythm.
	5. Students repeat the song phrase by phrase walking the melodic rhythm and moving in the direction of the melodic contour.
Intervals – Melodic Dictation	1. Students stand on their *do*. Students echo-step short motives and sing using *solfège* syllables.
	2. Students echo step motives with altered pitches using *solfège* syllables.

FIGURE 17.4. Melodic activities to develop physical and conceptual understandings

Concepts	Activities
Form	1. Students stand in self-space. 2. Teacher plays "Spring: *Allegro*" from *The Four Seasons* by Vivaldi and students walk the beat and change directions for each new section. 3. Students form small groups. 4. Students decide on a type of movement for each section (locomotor or non-locomotor). 5. Teacher plays the music again and students move accordingly. Have one group present at a time so the other students can observe the different movement choices.
Phrasing	1. Students stand in pairs facing each other. 2. Student "A" starts by moving the body in a flowing manner for eight beats (teacher is either playing the drum or improvising on the piano) and student "B" mirrors the movement (split-second imitation). 3. Student "B" leads the next eight beats. 4. Students continue to alternate who is leading the movement. 5. Repeat the activity with "Song for Viola" by Adams. This piece is in a slow 12/8 meter so each phrase will be twelve beats long (one measure).
Harmonic Structures	1. Students stand in self-space. 2. Teacher repeatedly plays a tonic (I) chord as quarter notes with the root in the bass. The students walk forward. 3. Teacher repeatedly plays a dominant-seventh (V7) chord as quarter notes with the root in the bass. The students walk backwards. 4. Teacher repeatedly plays a submediant (vi) chord as quarter notes with the root in the bass. Students walk in a circle. 5. Teacher repeatedly plays a subdominant (IV) chord as quarter notes with the root in the bass. The students walk sideways. 6. Teacher plays uneven phrases of the repeated chords, followed by various sequences of the four chords. The students walk in the corresponding directions. 7. Teacher improvises a melody using the four chords. The students walk in the corresponding directions.

FIGURE 17.5. Form, phrasing, and harmonic activities to develop physical and conceptual understandings

Concepts	Activities
Dynamics	1. Students stand in self-space and each student holds an elastic. 2. Teacher plays "Baba Yetu" by Tin and the students move through space, stepping the quarter note beat while stretching the material for four beats (whole note). 3. When the teacher says, "small group," the students will form small groups and join elastics together and continue to stretch the whole notes while showing the dynamics by keeping the elastics low during *piano* sections, high during *forte* sections, and stretching during crescendos. 4. When the teacher says, "large group," the students form large groups and join the elastics together while continuing to show the dynamics.
Articulations	1. Students stand in self-space. 2. Teacher improvises *legato* music on the piano and the students make painting motions in the air in a flowing manner. 3. Teacher improvises *staccato* music on the piano and the students make a flicking or light tapping motion in the air. 4. Teacher improvises *marcato* music and the students make a punching motion in the air. 5. Teacher improvises music alternating the three articulations and the students do the appropriate movements. 6. Teacher plays "Dance of the Sugar Plum Fairy" by Tchaikovsky and students do the appropriate movement (*staccato*). 7. Teacher plays "The Imperial March" by Williams and students do the appropriate movement (*marcato*). 8. Teacher plays the theme from "The Cider House Rules" by Portman and students do the appropriate movement (*legato*).

FIGURE 17.6. Expressive activities to develop physical and conceptual understandings

Within the context of purposeful movement, the music informs the movement conceptually but not in totality. Students should be given the opportunity to have as many choices in the ways to move as possible. Movement in a Dalcroze activity is not choreography. Purposeful movement entails much more than just walking the beat to a piece of music. The Dalcroze philosophy calls for the students to be aware of much more. Students are negotiating space while making decisions about their movements. Technique plays a part in the movement as well. When students are walking the beat, they need to be stepping lightly, maintaining good posture, and swinging their arms naturally. Dalcroze teachers remind students to breathe and relax during movement. The attention to nuance in the movement is paramount to fully realizing the music with the body.

Movement can also inspire the music which serves as a precursor to composition. A foundational activity uses two students where one student is the "mover" and the other student improvises on the piano (a hand drum or barred instrument can be used as well). The mover creates a short movement sequence (6 to 10 seconds) using a variety of motions that can represent melodic contour, dynamics, articulation, and/or tempo. The mover repeats the sequence and the improvisor creates music that represents the move-ment. Typically, the music will be atonal as the improvisor must watch the mover as the music is played. This activity is exploratory in nature but sets up the boundless number of choices in both movement and musical representation.

The use of notation within a Dalcroze setting is multi-dimensional. It comes later in the process as the foundation of musical understandings is set through movement. Students feel and experience the music first and are provided terminology and traditional musical notation later. This aligns with other musical approaches, specifically as Kodály has the preparation stage; the teacher adapting a Dalcroze philosophy spends much time preparing students through physical and aural activities. The use of iconic and/or visual representation is also used in both approaches (and others) as to make notation easy to grasp for younger students and to assist those students who are visual learners.

For example, students participating in the "Disappearing Beat" activity (Butke & Frego, 2016) would be taught by rote but the teacher would write a visual representa-tion of Xs and Os on the board to represent when they are walking and when they are clapping. Figure 17.7 offers an overview of the activity and an iconic representation for students who need a visual representation.

Activity Sequence	Iconic Representation	
1. Students stand in self-space.		
2. Students walk 8 beats.	PHRASE	X -WALK
3. Students walk 7 beats in a new direction		O -CLAP
and clap on beat 8.	1	XXXXXXX
4. Students walk 6 beats in another direction	2	XXXXXXO
and clap on beats 7 & 8.	3	XXXXXOO
5. Continue process until students are	4	XXXXOOO
clapping all 8 beats.	5	XXXXOOOO
6. Students clap 7 beats and walk on beat 8.	6	XXXOOOOO
7. Students clap 6 beats and walk on beats 7	7	XXOOOOOO
& 8 in a new direction.	8	XOOOOOOO
8. Continue process until students are walking	9	OOOOOOOO
all 8 beats again.	10	OOOOOOOX
	11	OOOOOOXX
	12	OOOOOXXX
	13	OOOOXXXX
	14	OOOXXXXX
	15	OOXXXXXX
	16	OXXXXXXX
	17	XXXXXXXX

FIGURE 17.7. Activity sequence and iconic representation of "disappearing beat"

The process of transforming an embodiment language to inspire and create composition can be successfully accomplished by students of all ages. The notation is derived from both recordings and scribing either iconic or traditional notation in the following three lessons. These lessons describe the process of movement-based composition and require the students to have had many eurhythmic experiences in order to fully engage and connect the body to the act of composing.

Composition Lesson Examples

Young students who have experienced purposeful movement can create a movement piece which can then be notated and lead to other students "performing" the piece of music through instrumental playing on a keyboard or barred instrument, or through movement. The act of notation can be done by another student or group of students in the role of taking a picture dictation. In any composition, the performance interpretation will be unique each time, not just because the notation might not be as definitive, but more importantly because the options in performance are varied and numerous. Figures 17.8, 17.9, and 17.10 outline three model composition lessons inspired by movement for different age levels. Additional resources for exploring Dalcroze are shown in Figure 17.11.

Composition Focusing on Dynamics

1. A group of three second graders are given the task of composing a piece showing dynamics.

2. The students decide on movements that would clearly demonstrate the dynamics of *piano*, *forte*, *crescendo*, and *decrescendo*.

3. The students explore individually moving through space showing the representative dynamics.

4. The students make group decisions as to what order to show the dynamics, consider any repetitions they want, and how long each dynamic level should occur. They could also assign one student to be the leader and that student would make the duration decisions and the other two students would do split-second reactions to imitate the appropriate dynamic levels for the moved durations.

5. The students 'perform' the composed movement piece showing dynamics for the class.

6. While the other students watch the performance, a few students should use their own mapping/notation systems to illustrate the dynamic levels as they occurred in time.

7. The performing students look at the iconic compositions to assess the congruency of the performance with the notation.

8. The notation is placed on the board and all of the students 'perform' the music with movement. The teacher could indicate the time changes through movement or cues.

9. Some students go to barred instruments and/or one or two students could be at a keyboard and play the composition using either atonal or pentatonic modalities. The other students in the class 'perform' the composition through movement.

10. Extension – students are video-recorded and then watch the performances. The students can then decide how they might want to change the composition.

FIGURE 17.8. A movement-inspired composition for early elementary students

Composition Focusing on Harmony
Previous learning – students have participated in the Harmonic Structures activity several times before doing this activity. This lesson would take place over several class periods/days.

1. Students individually create a sequence of harmonies in the key of D with I, IV, V7, and vi chords. The composition is notated with the Roman numerals. The students must start with the I chord and end with the I chord. The teacher can assign a meter and length. The chords must maintain the harmonic rhythm in quarter notes of at least two measures per chord.

2. The students form pairs and exchange compositions.

3. The students take turns walking the appropriate direction for the appropriate number of measures of each student's composition.

4. The students go to barred instruments where one student in the pair plays the root of each chord and the other student moves accordingly.

5. The students switch roles.

6. The students repeat steps #4 & #5 but improvise a melody through singing. This process is audio-recorded.

7. The students then listen to the audio and notate the melody using traditional notation or iconic notation showing melodic direction, steps and skips, and rhythm (stick notation).

FIGURE 17.9. A movement-inspired composition for upper elementary students

Composition Focusing on Melody
Previous learning – students would have experienced the Melodic Activities before doing this lesson. This lesson would take place over several class periods/days.

1. The students sing and walk a C major scale ascending and descending.

2. The students echo-step and sing melodic phrases played by the teacher.

3. The students create a 16-measure melody in 4/4 by walking to an improvised melody and rhythm. The students can be given parameters in terms of rhythms and chromatics depending on their previous knowledge.

4. The students compose the melody in four-measure phrases. This process is video-recorded.

5. The students watch the video and sing what they see.

6. The students make changes as desired.

7. The students use traditional notation to write down the composed melody.

8. Students exchange compositions for other students to walk and sing.

FIGURE 17.10. A movement-inspired composition for upper elementary students

Resources for Learning More about Dalcroze Eurythmics

Articles and Books

Butke, M. (2014). Assessing expressive movement: Measuring student learning outcomes in the general music classroom. *General Music Today, 27*(3), 23-27. This article explains the expressive movement process, including *plastique animée*, and presents a rubric used for assessing expressive movement.

Butke, M., & Frego, R. J. D. (2016). *Meaningful movement: A music teacher's guide to Dalcroze Eurhythmics.* Music is Elementary. This book contains 206 lessons incorporating Dalcroze Eurhythmics based on four levels of competency. There is access to videos of elementary and college students performing some of the activities.

Butke, M., & Frego, R. J. D. (2011). Selecting music for purposeful movement. *The Orff Echo, 44*(1), 20-22. This article contains guidelines for selecting music for eurhythmics activities, specifically *plastique animée* as well as providing lesson plan guidelines.

Frego, R. J. D. (1996). Determining personal tempo in elementary-aged children through gross motor movements. *Southeastern Journal of Music Education, 8,* 138-145. This research article provides specific data of natural tempi for different grade levels for the purpose of implementing developmentally appropriate music.

Frego, R. J. D., & Leck H. H. (2005). Creating artistry through movement: Dalcroze Eurhythmics in the choral setting [DVD]. Hal Leonard. This DVD provides video representation of foundational eurhythmics activities within the choral classroom.

Henke, H. H. (1984). The application of Émile Jaques-Dalcroze's solfège-rhythmique to the choral rehearsal. *The Choral Journal, 25*(3), 11-14. This article provides eurhythmic exercises focusing on *solfège* for the choral classroom.

Henke, H. H. (1993). Rehearsing with Dalcroze techniques. *The Instrumentalist, 47*(10), 46-53. This article provides a variety of Dalcroze exercises to be used in an orchestral or band rehearsal as well as application of the philosophy to the instrumental classroom.

Jacobi, B. S. (2019). Eurhythmics, sufficient space, and the role of environment in the child's development. *Music Educators Journal, 105*(4), 37-44. This article provides the elementary music teacher guidelines to setting up the classroom space to support a eurhythmics curriculum.

Mead, V. H. (1994). *Dalcroze Eurhythmics in today's music classroom.* Schott Music Corporation. This book contains many eurhythmics activities for elementary general music students.

Website Information

American Eurhythmics Society (AES) americaneurhythmics.org. This organization, created in 2014, serves music educators throughout the country and internationally by providing workshops and resources on eurhythmics.

Dalcroze Society of America (DSA) dalcrozeusa.org. This organization promotes the artistic and pedagogical principles of Émile Jaques-Dalcroze through educational workshops and publications.

FIGURE 17.11. Additional resources for teachers

A Note about the Piano

As discussed throughout this chapter, the role of the piano/keyboard is foundational in the philosophy. However, the expectation that all Dalcroze teachers must be master level pianists is unrealistic and restricting. The pianist must be able to play musically but has a range of options for invoking movement and reacting to the students' movement. Atonal playing can be very effective as it allows the teacher to have many choices as well as gives the teacher the ability to watch the students, which is paramount in a Dalcroze experience. Modes with white keys and the pentatonic scale with black keys are easy tools to demonstrate musical concepts for the students. Most times, simple musical examples are better for students so they can clearly hear the concept being taught.

Intimidation concerning the use of the piano has been a roadblock for some teachers considering a Dalcroze approach to music education. With some training and practice, almost any teacher will be able to successfully use the piano in the Dalcroze classroom. Other instruments can be effective teaching tools as well. The hand drum is practical because the teacher can move among the students. There are many sounds and concepts a hand drum can create. Barred instruments allow choices similar to a keyboard and therefore are viable options. Guitars and ukuleles allow the teacher to be closer to the students (like the hand drum) and can provide improvisational opportunities to teach a variety of musical concepts. String, woodwind, and brass instruments can also have a place in a eurhythmics activity. The goal is to have the improvisation or excerpt be played musically, represent the musical concept to be taught clearly, and must give the teacher the opportunity to be able to watch the students.

CONCLUSION

The role of choice, which takes place in both movement and composition processes, can be juxtaposed effectively for composers of all ages, especially children. In addition, the atmosphere of a Dalcroze setting which is rooted in risk-taking contributes to a sense of open-mindedness for generating musical options. These characteristics mirror the qualities needed in a composer. The opportunities afforded to a student in a Dalcroze musical experience provide a myriad of movement choices for increased kinesthetic insight, ultimately leading to cognitive understanding.

Physical exploration, purposeful movement, and *plastique animée* help students to become expressive, knowledgeable musicians which sets up the partnership for movement-informed composition to be established.

REFERENCES

Abramson, R. (1980). Dalcroze-based improvisation. *Music Educators Journal*, 66(5), 62–68.

Burnard, P. (1999). Bodily intention in children's improvisation and composition. *Psychology of Music, 27*(2), 159–174.

Burnard, P. (2000). Examining experimental differences between improvisation and composition in children's music-making. *British Journal of Music Education, 17*(3), 227–245.

Burnard, P. (2004). Thinking about improvising and composing and children's forms of representation. In P. Shand (Ed.), *Music Education Entering the 21st Century: History of the ISME Music in Schools and Teacher Education Commission and Papers and Workshop Descriptions from the MISTEC 2000 and 2002 Seminars* (pp. 33–40). International Society for Music Education (ISME), Nedlands, Western Australia.

Butke, M. A., & Frego, R. J. D. (2016). *Meaningful movement: A music teacher's guide to Dalcroze eurhythmics.* Music is Elementary.

Caldwell, J. T. (1995). *Expressive singing: Dalcroze eurhythmics for voice.* Prentice Hall.

Chung S.-M., & Chen C.-Y. (2011). Improvising on music composition game. In M. Chang, W.-Y. Hwang, M.-P. Chen, & W. Müller (Eds.), *Educational games and virtual reality/augmented reality applications.* Edutainment Technologies, Lecture Notes in Computer Science (Vol. 6872, pp 264–275). Springer.

Collins, D. L. (1993). *Teaching choral music.* Prentice Hall.

Dutoit, C. L. (1971). *Music movement therapy.* Institute Jaques-Dalcroze.

Frego, D., Liston, R., Hama, M., Gillmeister, G. (2008). The Dalcroze approach to music therapy. In Darrow, A. (Ed.), *Introduction to approaches in music therapy* (pp. 25–30). American Music Therapy Association.

Frego, R. J. D. (2009). Dancing inside: Dalcroze eurhythmics in a therapeutic setting. In Kerchner, J. & Abril, C. (Eds.), *Musical experience in our lives: Things we learn and meanings we make* (pp. 313–328). Rowman & Littlefield.

Habron, J., Jesuthasan, J., & Bourne, C. (2012) *Moving into composition: The experiences of student composers in higher education during a short course of Dalcroze eurhythmics.* Higher Education Academy. http://www.heacademy.ac.uk/events/detail/2012/seminars/disciplines/DW007

Jaques-Dalcroze, E. (1972). *Rhythm, music and education.* Benjamin Blom.

Kenney, S. (2013). Moving music, mapping music: Connecting children to the classics. *General Music Today, 26*(3), 44–47.

Martin, F., Dénes, T., Berchtold, A., Gagnebin, H. Reichel, B, Dutoit, C. L., & Stadler, E. (1965). *Émile Jaques-Dalcroze: L'homme, le compositeur, le créateur de la rhythmique.* Baconnière.

Mead, V. H. (1994). *Dalcroze eurhythmics in today's music classroom.* Schott.

Odom, S. L. (1998). *Jaques-Dalcroze, Émile. International encyclopedia of dance* (Vol. 3). Oxford.

Pennington, J. (1925). *The importance of being rhythmic.* Knickerbocker Press.

Seitz, J. A. (2005). Dalcroze, the body, movement and musicality. *Psychology of Music, 33*(4), 419–435.

Spector, I. (1990). *Rhythm and life: The work of Émile Jaques-Dalcroze.* Pendragon Press.

Treviño, E. N., Elizondo, J. E., & Alvarez-Bermúdez, J. A. (2018). Dalcroze eurhythmics as agents to induce a state of flow in older adults. *International Journal of Latest Research in Humanities and Social Sciences, 4*(1), 8–16.

CHAPTER 18

....

CONSTRUCTING A PEDAGOGY FOR MUSIC IMPROVISATION AND COMPOSITION

A Kodály Perspective

....

MICHEÁL HOULAHAN AND PHILIP TACKA

KODÁLY advocates that we should

> teach music and singing at school in such a way that it is not a torture but a joy
> for the pupil; instill a thirst for finer music in him, a thirst which will last for a
> lifetime. Music must not be approached from its intellectual, rational side, nor
> should it be conveyed to the child as a system of algebraic symbols or as the secret
> writing of a language with which he has no connection. The way should be paved
> for direct intuition.[1]

Teaching improvisation and composition skills also should be approached using this
philosophical perspective. But how do we develop models for teaching improvisation and composition adopting "direct intuition" or organic approaches to teaching?[2]
How can we establish a process for teaching creativity that stems from the performance and analysis of music repertoires that are also reflective of the cultural heritage of all the students we teach? To address these questions, we need to understand
how the teaching of improvisation and composition relates to the development of
musicality and musicianship within the context of a music curriculum shaped by the
Kodály philosophy.[3]

THE KODÁLY PERSPECTIVE

Kodály's views regarding the importance of developing musicianship are reflected in a speech, "Who Is a Good Musician?" given at the end of the 1953–54 academic year at the Liszt Academy, Budapest, Hungary. He summarized the characteristics of a good musician as someone who had (1) a well-trained ear, (2) a well-trained intelligence, (3) a well-trained heart, and (4) a well-trained hand. He articulated these four themes as the essential components of musicianship.

We would like to expand Kodály's definition to reflect the transformational changes in music in the twenty-first century. Using Kodály's definition of "Who Is a Good Musician?" as a frame, we define musicians as performers, cultural stewards, critical thinkers, creative beings, and informed listeners. We refer to these aspects of music as the Multiple Dimensions of Musicianship. Further description of each characteristic is offered in Figure 18.1.[4]

Positioning ourselves within this framework, we offer twelve observations in Figure 18.2 concerning the multiple dimensions of musicianship and knowledge that expert musicians possess. These observations are based on our research and practical experience in teaching and observing elementary, middle school, high school, undergraduate, and graduate students.

As a profession, we strive to create a contemporary music education curriculum that will "define an educational agenda which will synthesize indigenous culture and traditional aurality with the literary and scientific resources of modern formal education."[5] The inclusion of an increasingly expansive array of diverse "sound" repertoires such as folk music, global folk music, contemporary and commercial music coupled with "symbol" repertoires such as art music and recently composed music inform how we teach music in the twenty-first century. Creating effective pedagogical models for teaching musicianship has become a priority for music educators. The multiple dimensions of musicianship suggest that music skills are "interrelated." To develop these

Performers	Can perform "sound" or "symbol" vocal or instrumental repertoires and create gestures that enrich the performance.
Stewards of Their Cultural Heritage	Are familiar with "sound" and "symbol" repertoires.
Critical Thinkers	Can learn to perform repertoire by listening and analyzing by ear or reading from notation.
Creative Human Beings	Can improvise, compose, and arrange music. Exhibit knowledge of music literacy and technology supporting these activities.
Informed Listeners and Audience Members	Can aurally and visually identify stylistic features of repertoire and have an understanding of the music history associated with this repertoire.

FIGURE 18.1. Multidimensions of musicianship

1. Developing the multiple dimensions of musicianship can frame the best practices in music education programs for all levels of instruction.

2. It would appear that the multiple dimensions of musicianship are integrated and interconnected, and our research indicates that these competencies cannot be taught in isolation.[1]

3. Improvisation, the art of composing extemporaneously, and composition, the art of formulating and writing music, are essential components of the multiple dimensions of musicianship and cannot be viewed as activities that merely support the development of music literacy skills.

4. Imitation of rhythmic and melodic elements and stylistic devices is a useful pedagogical tool for teaching improvisation and composition and offers a clear pathway to innovation.

5. The teaching approaches associated with improvisation and composition are closely tied to learning music repertoire from both the "sound" and "symbol" traditions.

6. Singing plays a central role in music education as it promotes the development of inner hearing or audiation. The ability to audiate is an essential skill in performing, analyzing, improvising, and composing music.

7. Students learn to perform "sound" repertoires by embracing the best learning practices of commercial musicians and "symbol" repertoires by adopting classical and commercial musicians' best learning practices.

8. By applying critical thinking skills when learning and performing repertoire, students recognize the stylistic traits and the building blocks of compositions. It is this knowledge that can inspire and inform students' improvisations and compositions.

9. When creating improvisations and music compositions, students can use technology to develop, enhance, and record their artistic ideas. In a Kodály classroom, students are also expected to use their knowledge of music notation.

10. An historical perspective, biographical information concerning the composer, the reason for creating the composition, and performance practice associated with the repertoire are all aspects that inform the creative process.

11. Every music class is an opportunity for the music teacher to share their musicality and musicianship with their students. Through a carefully guided teaching process, the students take ownership of this knowledge and inform their musicianship, improvisations, and compositions.

12. In the learning process, the role of the teacher is to allow students to develop their musicality and musicianship using a discovery orientation to learning.

---

[1] Nite, S. B., Houlahan, M., Tacka, P. & Moreno, P. (2015). Improving music teachers' musicianship skills. In C. A. Shoniregun & G. A. Akmayeva. *IICE-2015 Proceedings*, Ireland International Conference on Education, Dublin, Ireland: Infonomics Society.

FIGURE 18.2. Observations concerning multidimensions of musicianship and knowledge

skills, one must adopt holistic or organic pedagogical models for teaching and learning. Therefore, the music instructor's musicality and musicianship impact students' success by developing the multiple dimensions of musicianship, focusing on improvisation and composition skills. The ability to improvise and compose are essential characteristics of what it means to be a "good" musician.[6]

An Overview of Integrated Models for Teaching Improvisation and Composition

We propose three models that promote the performance of diverse repertoire and the development of music literacy and improvisation and composition skills. We employ the *Performance Through Sound Analysis* (PTSA) model for teaching repertoire, improvisation and composition without reference to music notation. This allows students to engage with music improvisation and composition where knowledge of music theory is not a requirement. The *Houlahan & Tacka Model of Learning and Instruction* (HTM) is used to develop audiation, music literacy skills and improvisation and composition.[7] This model allows students to engage with music improvisation and composition with varying or limited knowledge of music theory. We can use the *Performance Through Sound Analysis and Notation* (PTSAN) model for learning repertoire and teaching music improvisation and composition.

These three models provide students with techniques to discern and recognize the stylistic features and musical building blocks of repertoire through performance, audiation, critical thinking, and creative activities. The PTSA and PTSAN model's effectiveness works best when students have performed and thoughtfully analyzed several music examples that use the same form, rhythmic, melodic, and harmonic components. To use the PTSAN model, students need to read new repertoire, or sections of the repertoire, using rhythm and solfège syllables. We use these models to advance students' musicality and musicianship skills at all levels. The process for teaching musicality and musicianship skills is consistent for all levels of instruction. Teachers currently use these models, and the authors have presented this research at national and international conferences.[8]

These models also provide teachers with a pedagogy for teaching students at all levels about the craft and artistry of music improvisation and composition. Teachers need to be familiar with "sound" and "symbol" repertoires and use teaching approaches that foster students' performance, critical thinking, and creative skills. Students learn to perform "sound" repertoires through listening and sound analysis and "symbol" repertoires through listening, sound analysis, and music notation. "The opposition between orality and literacy ought not to be seen as an opposition between two conditions, as a dichotomy, but rather as a continuum where cultures have different degrees (as well as types) of literacy."[9] As students engage, progress, and apply their critical thinking skills to performing repertoire, they gain essential information concerning the interaction between form and the fundamental rhythmic, melodic, and harmonic building blocks. This foundational knowledge becomes the basis for developing improvisation and composition skills through imitation that leads to innovation.

Observations about the Models

The PTSA, HTM, and PTSAN models are used at all levels of musicianship training. For example, students can learn to improvise in the style of global pentatonic folk music in elementary school. The models can also be used at the college level to explore pentatonic music in the compositions of Bartók and Debussy. They can be used in a fifth-grade class to explore modal folk songs or in a high school music theory class to study mixolydian modes in the music of the Beatles or the use of a particular mode in commercial repertoire. These models provide a way for students to create music in the style of a particular repertoire. Students can ultimately move beyond imitating the style of this repertoire to incorporating compositional techniques into their unique improvisations and compositions.

We have adopted these models for teaching musicianship skills, improvisation, and composition in our music theory classes and methods courses at the Tell School of Music, Millersville University of Pennsylvania, USA. Music theory classes begin with understanding the fundamental stylistic forms, meters, rhythm patterns, melodic patterns, and tonalities of folk music; this is accomplished primarily through an emphasis on aural skills training in Music Theory 1. This knowledge lays the groundwork for understanding all other types of music. Music Theory 2 students study modal folksongs, leading to the study of medieval and renaissance music. Students in Music Theory 3 study and sing folk songs and global folk music, including challenging rhythms, sequences, decorative notes, seventh chords, secondary dominants, and folk songs with fifth changes (real and tonal answers). This leads to examinations of Baroque music, which includes the study of seventh chords and the study of the Neapolitan chord. Students continue their work with diatonic folk songs that include triadic melodies with clear harmonic functions, chromatic notes, modulations, and 16-bar strophic forms. Classic era style includes the study and analysis of altered tonic and dominant chords and the augmented sixth chords. In Music Theory 4, students analyze global folk songs with lowered third and sixth scale degrees. This progresses to a study of modal borrowings and chromatic harmony, and more complex modulations in Schubert's and Brahms's music.

We approach 20th- and 21st-century music study by singing global folk music containing mixed meters, asymmetric meters, pentatonic music, modal melodies, and hybrid scales. This transfers to a study of post-tonal and atonal twentieth-century reading with solfège syllables and letter names. In all music theory classes, students are guided to improvise and compose in the style of the repertoire that they are studying and bring this knowledge into their songwriting and composition courses. In the music theory classes, the instructor integrates the PTSA, PTSAN, and HTM models of learning to develop musicality and musicianship skills, focusing on improvisation and composition. Students learn the philosophical foundations for these models in music education courses and practice applying the teaching techniques used in these models—based on their previous experience—in music theory classes, peer teaching, and field experiences in K–12 vocal and instrumental classrooms. From our work within these models, we offer the following observations:

1. PTSA, PTSAN, and HTM offer organic approaches to developing the multiple dimensions of musicianship.
2. Listening, the performance of diverse repertoire, critical thinking, improvisation, composing, and being an informed listener are at the core of music learning.
3. These models only work if music teachers are willing to share their musicality and musicianship skills with their students.
4. All students engage as musicians with the teacher and other students in a collaborative learning process.
5. "Sound" thinking (inner hearing) is fundamental to developing improvisation and composition skills.
6. "Sound" music theory is used to describe "sound" music repertoire. It uses the students' vocabulary to analyze sound repertoire. Standard music terms can be substituted for this vocabulary. "Symbol" music theory uses rhythm and solfège syllables and knowledge of music symbols to analyze symbol repertoire.
7. We believe that knowledge of music literacy that focuses on solfège and rhythm syllables will be of interest to all musicians.
8. These models work for vocal and instrumental styles of music.
9. The inclusion of folk music in the curriculum is important as it is a repertoire that can be used with the PTSA, HTM, and PTSAN models of instruction. Stylistic elements of classical and commercial music can be found in folk music, a repertoire that lends itself to both "sound" and "symbol" approaches to learning.
10. These models provide a framework for teaching improvisation and composition.

Developing Improvisation and Composition Skills Using the PTSA Model

The Performance through Sound Analysis (PTSA) model for learning repertoire can be used to develop "sound" improvisation and composition skills. In other words, students create music without using traditional music notation. This model can be adapted to teach both vocal and instrumental unison and multi-part music. The following steps outline the approach used in the PTSA model.

Step 1: Listening to the composition. Students listen to a live performance or a recording. The task is for students to listen and critically think about the form and construction of the piece. Therefore, the performance should be of high quality.

Step 2: Consider the history of the composition. The teacher offers some background on the composition. Learning the context for the composition provides students with a rationale for understanding the emotional content the composer was trying to convey and subsequently creating this type of repertoire.

Step 3: Engaged listening and sound analysis of the text. This helps students come to an understanding of the connection between text and music. Here they discover how the intonation and declamation of the text can initiate and inspire melodic contours. (When teaching instrumental music, we skip Step 3).

Step 4: Engaged listening and sound analysis of the musical elements. In this step students are guided to identify the piece's global characteristics. This is the students' opportunity to listen, analyze, and get a "big picture" of the score. This strengthens students' listening and analytical skills and improves their ability to memorize. Examples of activities designed to engage students with the broad features of a work are shown in Figure 18.3. and demonstrate how we introduce students to basic "sound literacy" theory concepts. Figure 18.4 provides an overview of forms that might be considered.

Step 5: Engaged listening and participation. At this point, students begin to participate in the performance of the song. Teachers might have students keep the beat using different motions for each phrase of the song that indicates the song's form. Students might also conduct or in some way show the contours of important melodies.

Step 6: Teaching the repertoire. Here, the teacher uses sound music theory concepts and form to teach the repertoire. Each style of music has its pedagogy for teaching and learning repertoire.

Step 7: Teaching improvisation and composition. Students apply the knowledge of "sound" music literacy concepts and the role and place of rhythmic, melodic, or harmonic ideas in the repertoire they have learned and subsequently use this knowledge to generate improvisations and compositions. It is important to note that within the Kodály philosophy, students learn to discern the significant "stylistic traits" of repertoire. It is this information that provides the foundation to develop student's improvisation and compositional skills. Once students have performed and analyzed an appropriate body of repertoire with similar stylistic characteristics, they can then create imitations or replicas of this repertoire in their improvisations and compositions. Later, these ideas will inform their own innovative "sound" improvisations and compositions. During this step, instructors can help students perform their compositions and offer feedback and advice.

Example 1

Students might be asked to identify the form of the composition. The understanding of form begins with an understanding of the words "same," "different," and "similar" as they relate to describing music phrases in the repertoire. This type of understanding is a prerequisite for understanding larger forms. In smaller forms, we identify phrases by using lower case letters, and in larger forms, we use capital letters. (ABA, ABBA, ABCA, etc.). The first phrase of a song begins with "A," and any other phrase that is the *same* will share the "A" label. A different phrase would receive the letter "B," and so on. If a phrase is *similar*, perhaps just a change in one or two solfège syllables, we label that as a variant: "Av." The "v" labels the phrase as different but related to the original phrase. Understanding the form of composition is linked to musical memory, reading, writing, improvisation, composition, and inner hearing skills.

A basic procedure for teaching form in smaller compositions include the instructor performing the composition, students identifying the number of phrases in the composition, further identification of whether the phrases are the "same," "similar," or "different," and students labelling the form with letters such as the AABA form. Form permits musicians to categorize and organize musical ideas. Understanding how the form and the rhythmic, melodic, and harmonic building blocks of composition create musical cohesion are important pre-improvisational and compositional skills.

Example 2

Did you hear any attention-grabbing rhythms? Here we suggest using "sound music theory" and not "symbol music theory." This allows students to use their vocabulary to describe what they hear. Of course, as student's knowledge of music literacy develops, they will incorporate more musical terms into their responses. Typical questions could include the following: Did you hear something appealing in the rhythms of the compositions? Are there any sections of the composition where the rhythm does not sound steady and even? What rhythms occur during cadences in the melody? Do phrases begin with downbeats, or are there any with upbeats? The goal here is for students to identify typical rhythmic building blocks, commonly referred to as motives or gestures, and figure their role and placement in the composition. "Sound" music theory helps students to describe the building blocks and stylistic traits of this repertoire. For example, students learn to describe the meter of the piece of music using the terms duple, triple, and quadruple. Rhythms can be described as even or uneven, syncopated, faster rhythms or slower rhythms. Figure out the duration of these rhythms, comparing them to the beat.

Example 3

Did you hear something appealing in terms of the melodies in the composition? Again, we suggest not using "symbol literacy" terms. Have students describe what they are hearing. Describe the melodic contour of each phrase. Does the melody seem to descend or ascend? Is there an arch form or an inverted arch form in the melodic line? Students will learn to describe the intervals in melodic motives as moving in step or skips. The goal here is for students to identify typical melodic building blocks or motives and figure out their role and placement in the composition.

Example 4

How might you describe the use of dynamics? Where do the dynamics change? Is there a connection between dynamics and text?

FIGURE 18.3. Discussion points to guide students in analysis

Example 5 Describe how tempo is used. Does the tempo change? Are tempo changes related to text? Are tempo changes related to form?
Example 6 Describe the texture. What is the texture of the piece? Does it remain the same throughout? If the texture changes, how so, and why?
Example 7 How would you describe the use of harmony? Is it functional? Does the composer use a fundamental chord progression?
Example 8 Does the piece remind you of any style of music?
Example 9 Do you hear a connection between the form, rhythmic and melodic building motives?

FIGURE 18.3. Continued

Step 8: This is the final step of the PTSA model. Students share their improvisation or composition with their peers and talk about the reasons and choices they made to create their music. Here, peers have the opportunity to share their observations about the composition.

SAMPLE IMPROVISATION AND COMPOSITION ACTIVITIES USING THE PERFORMANCE THROUGH SOUND ANALYSIS (PTSA) MODEL

The following improvisation and composition activities are approached from a "sound" perspective, using no symbol literacy such as rhythm or solfège syllables, or music notation. It is essential to set the parameters for improvisation and composition activities. The classroom atmosphere should be collaborative, so students feel comfortable enough to experiment and determine preferences. It is an opportunity for students to collaborate and have fun while using their musical skills easily and instinctively. We use three types of creative activities: embellishing repertoire, creating new variants, and creating a new improvisation or composition. Figure 18.5 contains sample improvisation and composition activities ranging from simple to complex.

Sound Analysis of the Musical Elements: Form	
Repetition and Repeat Sign	Repeat signs and first and second endings are components of the form. A simple way to address this is to take a folk song in ABAC form and rewrite it with repeat signs and first and second endings.
Question and Answer Form	Is encountered in forms identified as AAv or AB, where the final of the "A" phrase ends on the dominant note, and the final of the "Av" or "B" phrase ends on the tonic note. This structure creates an open (prevalent) phrase and a closed (tonic) phrase. Guided movement activities can help students identify the form.
Strophic Form	Strophic form can be introduced by using a song with a refrain. Understanding strophic form through folk song leads to studying classical music and the 32-bar form in American Popular music. Some of these melodies can also be in bar form.
Strophic folk song form: AA⁵BA	This is a typical Hungarian folk song form found also in American folk songs. One phrase is introduced and then repeated at the interval of a fifth with the same intervallic relationship, thus A and then A⁵. This type of folk song can be sung in one key throughout. But another option that emphasizes a relationship between parts is to sing the A and A⁵ sections with the same solfège syllables for each phrase. In a more advanced repertoire, this is also a helpful way to practice dominant modulations.
Verse-Chorus and Verse-Chorus-Refrain	The Verse-Chorus-Bridge Chorus form can also be explored (ABABCAB). Sometimes one finds a pre-chorus and post-chorus in these forms.
Period Structure in Classical Music	Singing folk songs with an AAv or AB question and answer form connect to singing period structures in classical music. This form is characteristic of the Viennese Classical Style. The structure consists of the antecedent phrase (question) and the consequent phrase (answer). The second phrase can be parallel (Av) or contrasting (B). Students learn that antecedent phrases sound open and consequence phrases sound closed. An initial step is to present period structures that are eight measures in length and follow the AAv model. The "A" phrase ends on the dominant note, and the "Av" phrase ends on the tonic note; later, students can identify phrases that end on either the third or the fifth of the dominant or tonic triads. The most important task is for students to identify the phrases as either "open" or "closed." This parallels the development of harmonic understanding and the ability to identify cadences aurally.
Modulating Period Structures	Students can also perform period structures that involve modulations. The easiest ones to hear and then analyze are those that involve a modulation from the minor key to the major key. Once the concept is established, the instructor and students can consider modulating period structures that move from the tonic key to the dominant key.
Larger Forms	
Binary Form	The most straightforward approach is to use a repertoire that includes two periods, where students can analyze each period and relate the two to each other. Sometimes the final cadence in the first period can be considered closed; however, it acts as a half cadence when viewed as a complete example.

FIGURE 18.4. Considering form in the sound analysis of musical elements

Ternary Form	Expressed using the letters ABA. At times, the second section in ternary form is shorter than the first section. In that case, we may use the letters AbA
Trio Form	A combination of binary and ternary forms. We usually find this form in the third movement of classical symphonies. It exists as a type of ternary form and can include mood and tempo changes.
Rondo	Consists of a "theme" and the appearance of at least two episodes, resulting in a label of ABACABA.
Variation Form	Variation form describes a theme that goes through multiple variations. Variations can include rhythmic, melodic, and harmonic alterations. Select examples that students can sing, as singing helps with the analysis and provides the basis for student improvisation and composition.
Complex Forms	These advanced forms include sonata-allegro form, fugues, concertos, and forms. Students can be guided to sing themes from these works to analyze different sections of the music aurally.

FIGURE 18.4. Continued

DEVELOPING IMPROVISATION AND COMPOSITION SKILLS USING THE HOULAHAN AND TACKA MODEL (HTM) OF LEARNING AND INSTRUCTION

We use the HTM to teach students how to aurally identify and notate rhythmic, melodic, harmonic elements and structural elements.[10] Teaching music elements using this model develops a variety of essential skills related to teaching improvisation and composition. Of particular importance is the development of inner hearing or audiation. The learning process always begins with singing and performing repertoire. We use the PTSA model for learning new repertoire and the HTM model to teach students how to aurally identify and notate typical music patterns. This is essential for developing music literacy and improvisation and composition skills.[11] For younger students, the focus is on teaching one specific rhythmic or melodic pattern. The focus could be on learning several rhythmic, melodic, or harmonic building blocks for older students. The acquisition of audiation skills is one of the most important goals in this process. This teaching approach can be used with all music styles, including 20th and 21st-century atonal music.

Preparation: Cognitive Phase of Learning

We begin by having students sing repertoire and use a kinesthetic motion to distinguish the new rhythmic, melodic, or chord concepts to be taught. Students then determine

Creative Activities in Performance through Sound Analysis
Embellishing Repertoire
■ Improvise motions that align with the form of the repertoire. For example, have students create a movement activity to reflect the form of the composition. Students walk clockwise for the "A" phrases and counterclockwise for the "B" phrases. Motions can also be assigned to selected phrases. ■ Improvise a rhythmic ostinato using body percussion or hand clapping to accompany the composition. One student or the group may generate these motions. ■ Improvise a new game to accompany a folk song. Students can create new game motions for a known composition. As in all improvisations, students can borrow motions from other games to create a new game. ■ Improvise a melodic ostinato to accompany a composition.
Circle Jam
■ Improvise using a "Circle Jam." Give students a form, number of beats per phrase, and hum one or two building blocks from a known composition. Allow them to generate their melodies and improvisations and figure out how to layer different rhythmic and melodic voice lines over each other. All of this can be created using neutral sounds. An excellent example of this technique of layering can be seen in Si Le Le" composed by Bobby McFerrin and performed by the British vocal ensemble VOCES8 (https://www.youtube.com/watch?v=M9xDt4oduYE)
Creating a New Variant
■ Improvise a different version of the newly learned composition by changing rhythms. For example, change even rhythm patterns into syncopated patterns. ■ Improvise a different version of the newly learned composition by changing the meter from duple to compound meter. ■ Improvise new text for a phrase of known composition. Change the words to simple known or unknown melodies. ■ Create a harmonization for a composition. Students create a two-part-harmonization for the folk song. Improvise using the style of a specific performer. Students improvise a song in the style of a given commercial artist. ■ Improvise in a given style. Students can improvise a song in a given classical or popular style. Students could improvise a melody in Schubert's style or sing a song in a Gospel style. ■ Create a new arrangement of a composition. Students can combine several of the improvisation techniques that they have learned to arrange a composition. Once they have decided on the final format, they can notate their arrangement and revise it to become a composition.
Creating a New Composition
■ Create a new rhythmic composition based on rhythms in a known composition. Students create a sixteen-beat rhythm composition. The composition can then be performed as a rhythmic accompaniment to a song. Students enjoy creating several of these *beat* compositions and performing them at the same time to accompany known repertoire. These rhythmic improvisations can be performed with body percussion, hand-clapping, or performing in rhythmic instruments. ■ Create a new composition. Students collaborate to create an original composition. Students can begin by establishing the rules for their composition. What is the inspiration for the composition? What form will be used? What textures and harmonies will be used? Will it be a song or an instrumental composition? Students can decide on the use of rhythmic or melodic motives to be used in the composition. These ideas will come from the building blocks analyzed in the repertoire. Students also need to determine the emotions they will want to convey through their improvisation or composition. The role of the teacher should be to "stand back, observe, diagnose, guide, suggest and model, attempt to take on pupils' perspective, and help pupils to achieve the objectives that they had set for themselves."[1] Students can then work independently to create their compositions and determine their own choices about the form of their composition and the emotions they would like to convey.
[1] Green, (2008, p. 152).

FIGURE 18.5.   Creative activities in PTSA

the "sound" characteristics of this new element. This is accomplished by answering the teacher's carefully sequenced questions that require that require students to "play back" or "audiate" in order to answer. Students then create a visual or pre-notation score representing the new concept within a phrase of the song. Once these steps have taken place, the instructor presents the musical element. The presentation takes place in two stages.

During Stage 1, students sing the song that contains the new element and are guided to simply label the new sound with rhythm syllables or with solfège syllables and hand signs for a new pitch and immediately put it into practice. To accomplish this students simply read from the instructor's hand signs or learn the name of the rhythm syllable for the newly learned element and sing. "Symbol" music theory concepts are advanced through the artful teaching of rhythm and solfège syllables. We recommend using *takadimi* rhythm syllables, and moveable-do relative solmization syllables.[12] The *takadimi* syllables can be used at all levels of musicianship training, and unlike traditional Kodály syllables, they can be used for reading very complex rhythms. Rhythm and solfège syllables facilitate the process of audiating music notation, which is central to reading, writing, improvisation/composition, and the development of musicality. In Stage 2 of the Presentation-Associative Phase, students learn how to notate the new element in several ways, including rhythmic notation and solfège syllables and how to notate the new melodic pattern on the staff.

Presentation: Associative Phase of Learning

In the Practice-Assimilative Phase of Learning, students use the new element or "building block" in reading, writing, and improvisation and composition. In terms of improvisation and composition, these building blocks or music motives can be readily incorporated into students' creative activities through imitation or transformation.[13]

This highly organized and planned pedagogical process ultimately provides students with a process for discovering new elements. It expands a student's knowledge of music literacy and prepares them to transfer this knowledge to instruments. Most importantly, in terms of developing generative skills, this process deepens a students' knowledge of the craft and artistry of improvisation and music composition.

Sample Improvisation and Composition Activities Using the HTM

The following are sample improvisation techniques used to practice rhythmic, melodic, and harmonic building blocks. The goal is for students to develop both fluency using rhythm and solfège syllables and fundamental improvisation and composition skills. The purpose of these activities is to strengthen students' knowledge of music literacy concepts and develop fundamental improvisation and composition techniques that they cause during improvisation and composition music lessons. Students integrate these skills when learning how to embellish repertoire, creating a circle jam, creating a new variant, or writing a new composition. Figure 18.6 contains sample improvisation and composition activities.

Improvisation Techniques to Practice use of Rhythmic, Melodic, and Harmonic Building Blocks
Embellishing a Composition
■ Chain improvisation rhythm game. ■ Students sit in a circle and improvise a four-beat rhythmic phrase using a newly learned rhythmic element; students chant a four-beat rhythm pattern in succession. Once the beat is established and the game begins around the class, the beat's momentum should not be interrupted for hesitation or an error. The improvisation continues until all students have had a turn. An essential aspect of this type of activity is that it compels students to make quick decisions. In many cases, these decisions are intuitive, which indicates that the musical elements in question have been completely internalized. This type of activity can also be performed with percussion instruments. ■ Improvise rhythms according to a given form. Students are given a form to follow, and students improvise chanting the rhythms. The teacher or other students can specify forms such as AABA, ABAB, A AvBBv, etc. ■ Chain improvisation melodic game. ■ One student performs a four-eight-beat melodic pattern. The next student performs this pattern and adds a four-beat pattern, and the next student repeats the new pattern and adds his or her pattern and so on.
Circle Jam
■ Create a "Circle Jam" using the new rhythmic, melodic, or harmonic building block. ■ Students create a four-to-eight beat rhythmic or melodic circle jam incorporating their knowledge of the new element. Students will use rhythmic and solfège syllables in this process. (Students improvise on neutral syllables when using the PTSA model.)
Creating a New Variant of the Composition
■ Question and answer: ■ The teacher establishes the beat. Sing a four to eight-beat melody with solfège syllables and hand signs and have students respond with a different four to the eight-beat melody. As students become more proficient, the teacher can lengthen the phrase or change the tempo. This leads to melodic conversations. Question-and-answer conversations can continue around the class. ■ First and second endings: ■ After working with question-and-answer melodies, move to songs that have first and second endings. The teacher or another student can perform a melody through the first ending. Another student performs the melody but improvises a second ending using solfège syllables and hand signs. This type of activity develops musical memory as well as the ability to improvise. It can also be done using rhythm syllables. ■ Create new versions of a folk song by incorporating the newly learned melodic elements. In this process, students create a new version by including the new rhythmic or melodic elements. For example, transform a duple meter song into a triple meter variation. Transform a major pentatonic song into a minor pentatonic song.

FIGURE 18.6. Activities using the HTM

Creating a New Composition

- Improvise/compose a melody to a given rhythmic pattern. Have students take turns improvising solfège syllables to a given rhythmic pattern.
- Improvise/compose a melody over a functional bass line. Provide a bass line to students and have them improvise a melodic line.
- Improvise/compose a melody over a chord progression. Provide a bass line to students and have them improvise a melodic line.
- Improvise/compose a canon. Provide students with typical chord progressions that they have studied. Ask three students to improvise a phrase of music using the notes of the suggested chord progression. Review the melodies and choose a melody for each line. Assign a specific voice part to each student, voice 1, voice 2, and voice 3. Perform the work; as a challenge, have each student memorize the line of the following student while they are singing their line.
- Improvise/compose an original composition.

FIGURE 18.6. Continued

DEVELOPING IMPROVISATION AND COMPOSITION SKILLS USING THE PERFORMANCE THROUGH SOUND ANALYSIS AND NOTATION MODEL (PTSAN)

The PTSAN model differs from the PTSA model in that students also use their knowledge of rhythm and solfège syllables, music theory, and notation. The following six steps outline a teaching sequence using the PTSAN model.

Step 1: Listening to the composition. Use the same process described in the PTSA model.

Step 2: Considering the history of the composition. Offer some background of the work. Learning the context for the composition's performance is important as it provides students with the rationale for creating this type of repertoire.

Step 3: Engaged listening and sound analysis of the text of the composition. Use the same process described in the PTSA model.

Step 4: Engaged listening and sound analysis of the musical elements in the composition. Students now use their knowledge of music theory to answer questions. Students identify the meter as duple or triple and the key as major or minor. Ask select students to identify essential rhythms or melodies with rhythm or solfège syllables. During this step, help students create a skeleton score for the new song. Consider indicating bar lines, double bar lines, measures, and add measure numbers.

Step 5: Engaged listening and participation. Perform the song and ask students to participate during the performance. Here they use their knowledge of reading, writing, and music theory to participate in singing parts of the folk song. For example, ask students to show the phrases, conduct the meter, demonstrate the contour of the melodic line of the song, notate with letters the sections of the composition, or create a framework for the structure of the piece of music. For example, students could create a scoring outline with the time signature, measures, phrases.

Step 6: Learn to perform the composition. As we mentioned above, in addition to the steps we use in the PTSA model, students now use their music theory skills to learn the song through notation. Depending on the students' skill level, we suggest the following notation approaches.

- *Hand signs.* Sing the text or hum a phrase of the composition and have students point to the pre-notation score. Then sing the text again and ask students to point to the contour on their own. Have students sing the work or section of the work with solfège syllables reading from the teacher's hand signs. As students learn more about staff notation, we can ask them to read from notation.
- *Reading a song from a scale written on the board.* Write the range of notes, commonly referred to as tone set, on the staff as whole notes going from the lowest note to the highest note. Then point to the notes of the melody on the staff; students read using solfège syllables and hand signs.
- *Reading the rhythmic notation of songs.* Write the song with stick notation or traditional rhythmic notation on the board. Do this if students know all of the rhythmic elements used in the song. Guide students to chant the rhythm with rhythm syllables and then count with numbers while as they conduct.
- *Reading the rhythm notation of a song with solfège syllables.* Write the song on the board in rhythm notation with solfège syllables written beneath the notation. The rhythmic and melodic elements should be familiar to the students. Guide students to sing using solfège syllables and hand signs.
- *Reading a melody from the staff.* Provide the staff notation of the melody either with or without text. Guide the students to first read through the song with rhythm syllables and then have them sing using solfège syllables and hand signs.

Step 7: Teaching improvisation and composition. This is the final step of the PTSAN model. Here, students apply their knowledge of music literacy to generate improvisations and compositions based on the rhythmic and/or melodic frameworks that formed the newly learned repertoire's content. Later, these ideas will inform their own innovative "symbol" improvisations and compositions

Step 8: This is the final step of the PTSA model. Students share their improvisation or composition with their peers and talk about the reasons and choices they made to create their music. Here, the student's peers have the opportunity to share their observations about the composition.

Sample Improvisation and Composition Activities using the PTSAN Model

The following are sample improvisation and composition activities using the PTSAN model ranging from simple to complex. Improvisation and composition activities in the PTSAN model, shown in Figure 18.7, involve the use of rhythm and solfège syllables and notation.

Performance Through Sound Analysis and Notation Activities
Embellishing Existing Repertoire
■ Improvise a rhythmic ostinato using body percussion or hand clapping to accompany the *composition*. Students can now identify the rhythmic ostinato using rhythm syllables. Use rhythms abstracted from the song material. ■ Take rhythm patterns from a composition and arrange them according to a given form. Clap this rhythm to accompany the composition. ■ Improvise a melodic ostinato to accompany a composition. Students can use melodic patterns abstracted from the known repertoire.
Circle Jam
■ Improvise using a "Circle Jam." Give students a form, number of beats per phrase, and provide them with one or two melodic patterns from a known composition. Allow them to generate their melodies and improvisations and figure out how to layer different rhythmic and melodic voice lines over each other. Students must use their knowledge of rhythm and solfège syllables.
Creating a New Variant
■ Improvise a new version of the newly learned composition by changing rhythms. For example, change even rhythm patterns into syncopated patterns. Students can do this from notation. ■ Improvise a new version of the newly learned composition by changing the meter from duple to compound meter and notating this new variant. ■ Improvise a new variant of a composition or newly learned repertoire by singing it using an asymmetric meter. ■ Improvise a new variant of the melody by changing the mode of composition. This type of activity can be accomplished using modes and twentieth-century hybrid modes. For example, students can create new variants of folk songs by using the Lydian scale with an augmented 5th, using the acoustic scale (major scale with raised 4th and lowered 7th), or the Aeolian scale with diminished 5th. ■ Create a harmonization for a composition. Students create a two-part-harmonization for the folk song. Improvise the song in the style of a singer. Students improvise a song in the style of a given commercial artist. ■ Create a new arrangement of a composition. Students can combine several of the improvisation techniques that they have learned to arrange a composition. Once they have decided on the final format, they can then notate their arrangement and revise it to become a composition.
Creating a New Composition
■ Create a new rhythmic composition based on rhythms in a known composition. Students create a sixteen-beat rhythm composition. The composition can then be performed as a rhythmic accompaniment to a song. Students enjoy creating several of these *beat* compositions and performing them at the same time to accompany known repertoire. These rhythmic improvisations can be performed with body percussion, hand-clapping, or playing it on rhythmic instruments. ■ Create a new composition. Students collaborate to create an original composition. Students can begin by establishing the rules for their composition. What is the inspiration for the composition? What form will be used? What textures and harmonies will be used? Will it be a song or an instrumental composition? Students can decide the meter, what motives to use, determine the tonality and what melodic motives to be used in the composition. These ideas will come from the building blocks analyzed in the known repertoire. Students also need to determine the emotions they will want to convey through their improvisation or composition. Students can then work independently to create their compositions and decide on their own choices about the form of their composition and the emotions they would like to convey.

FIGURE 18.7. Activities using the PTSAN

Using the PTSA, HTM, and PTSAN Models to Develop Improvisation and Composition Skills

A student's creative voice is grounded in their knowledge of diverse repertoires' performance, audiation abilities, ability to hear this music with inner hearing, and applying their critical thinking musicianship skills to analyze this repertoire. These musicianship skills help students find their creative voice and provide the music parameters for their composition. Performing and analyzing repertoire offers students a frame of reference and an understanding of the compositional process. Understanding how different modes, tempos, dynamics, and harmonies impact the listener are essential skills developed through the models offered in this paper. Experiences with these kinds of activities prepare students for individual composition lessons where their instructor can guide and mentor them using resources such as Belkin's *Musical Composition: Craft & Art* (2018) or Paul Hindemith's *The Craft of Musical Composition* (1942). We agree with Dan Trueman (2012), professor of composition at Princeton, that "good teaching is more about establishing rich contexts (or cultures) for learning than it is about the direct transmission of knowledge, skills, or ideas."[14]

In a Kodály music curriculum, students begin studying improvisation and composition by performing and analyzing folk music, global folk music, art music, contemporary music, and recently composed music. They then become acquainted with the stylistic features of different kinds of repertoire, which becomes the inspiration for students' creative activities. Carbon (1986) also believes that this approach to composition can be the basis for creating a pedagogy of composition. "The order and emphasis of these approaches and the role they play in the pre-compositional and compositional process help to determine each composer's style and method of composition and should be central to the teaching of composition" (p. 117).

One of the tenets central to our PTSA, HTM, and PTSAN models is that the instructor deconstructs the repertoire through singing, audiation, and critical listening and thinking skills so that students can reconstruct this repertoire for themselves. Using these models, students gain an understanding of the composer's compositional tools. At a more advanced level, students apply this knowledge to create their unique improvisations and compositions. This approach to teaching is echoed by Dan Trueman, who states that "an ideal composition teacher, at any level, is (1) able to help the student listen, critically, and profoundly, to his/her music, and (2) considers it a priority to develop and refine the kind of technical tools that will help the student implement his/her artistic vision. Having such tools is what allows one to imagine more" (2012, p. 4).

In the Assimilative Phase-Practice portion of HTM and Step 7 of the PTSA and the PTSAN models, students use their knowledge of rhythmic, melodic, and harmonic elements and understanding of tempo and dynamics derived from the repertoire that they have learned to perform to embellish a song or instrumental melody with rhythmic and melodic ostinatos, create a harmonization of the melody, create a new variant of folk songs, and create a new composition.

Throughout this process, students work collaboratively, they must acknowledge all participants' ideas, find ways to build upon them, filter all suggestions, and determine what makes one embellishment or improvisation more attractive. Through collaboration, they determine and select the best suggestions and techniques to create a musical score. Students should use technology and notation to revise and record their final creative activities. At its most superficial level, student improvisations might contain simple rhythmic or melodic ostinatos, new texts, or variants of specific phrases of their newly learned work. They should be encouraged to be imaginative in their text considerations, creating new melodies or melodic turns, and selecting instruments for their composition. Students may also be allowed to work on their own and create their improvisations and compositions. Because singing and performing are central to these models, students learn about the craft of music composition and develop a creative mindset. This entire process addresses John Carbon's (1986) concern that there is "a preponderance of emphasis on the intellectual side of our artistic training" (p. 113) at the expense of also developing necessary creative musicianship skills.

We propose the following pedagogical sequence for teaching improvisation and composition based on the improvisation and composition activities used in the PTSA, HTM, and PTSAN models:

1. Improvising embellishments of known repertoire through collaboration.
2. Independently improvising embellishments of known repertoire.
3. Composition through creating a variant of known repertoire through collaboration.
4. Independently creating a variant of known repertoire.
5. Co-creating a composition with other students.
6. Independently creating a composition.

These are not developmental stages but are improvisation and composition activities that inform the final steps in all three models. This approach can be used when introducing students to different types of repertoire or when students have learned new rhythmic, melodic, or harmonic concepts. Stage 6 (independently creating a composition) would typically occur in a specialized composition or songwriting class.

CONCLUSION

Our goal for this chapter was to demonstrate that teaching students how to improvise and compose is an organic process. Students learn to perform a body of repertoire that shares similar stylistic traits, learn how to analyze this repertoire from a "sound" or "symbol" process, and then use this knowledge to improvise and compose embellishments and variants of this repertoire. Once students have gained fluency in this process, they can begin to improvise and compose compositions generated by their knowledge of music literature and by their own choices and are not subjected to choices imposed by the teacher.

Understanding the role of the dimensions of musicianship skills can provide a pathway to teaching and developing improvisation and composition. The teacher's musicality, musicianship, and pedagogical expertise in 1) selecting appropriate repertoire, and 2) teaching students how to perform this repertoire, using approaches such as the PTSA and PTSAN models of learning, are essential for developing students' compositional voice.

Developing improvisation and composition skills begin by using critical thinking musicianship skills to learn and perform the repertoire. Step 7 in the PTSA and PTSAN models begins with students creating improvisation and compositions related to the performed repertoire. Using knowledge of performance, sound analysis, and music notation, with a music teacher's guidance, students can explore their innovative ideas to develop their compositional voice.

These models can also deepen the musicality, musicianship, and pedagogical skills of pre-service and in-service music teachers. In undergraduate and graduate musicianship classes, professional development workshops, pre-service, and in-service, teachers can learn how to perform diverse repertoires, learn critical thinking skills to analyze and notate this repertoire, and incorporate it into improvisations and compositions. From our experience, teachers must build their musicality and musicianship skills over time to incorporate these models effectively in their teaching. The advantages of this approach to teaching are twofold. First, it addresses the College Music Society's[15] call to action regarding educating a musician for the 21st century. Secondly, it provides a process for training music educators to teach artfully in the 21st-century classroom. Our final advice for the music educator is to "compose yourself" and try these models.

Notes

1. See Ferenc Bónis, Ed., *The selected writings of Zoltán Kodály*, trans. Halápy & Macnicol. (Budapest: Zenemikiadó Vállalat, 1964; London: Boosey & Hawkes, 1974), p. 124.
2. For a discussion of *Organic versus synthetic learning: A synopsis*, visit http://hs-survival. blogspot.com/2010/11/organic-versus-synthetic-learning.html
3. This chapter incorporates information from the authors' previous and forthcoming Kodály-related publications from Oxford University Press.
4. For a comprehensive description of The Multiple Dimensions of Musicianship, see chapter 6 of Houlahan, M., & Tacka, P. (2015). *Kodály today: A cognitive approach to music education* (2nd ed.), Oxford University Press.
5. See Flolu, 1996, p. 172.
6. See "Ki a jó zenész?" [Who is a Good Musician?], the title of a speech at the end-of-session ceremony in the Budapest Academy of Music, 1953. Kodály bases his ideas on Robert Schumann's definition of a good musician. Published in *Zenei szemle*, Budapest: Zenemikiadó, 1954: n.p. ML5.Z396. In *Visszatekintés* 1, pp. 275–277. Included in Bónis, 1964, pp. 185–200.

7. Houlahan, M. & Tacka, P. (2012). From sound to symbol: A new pitch for developing aural awareness. In *Sound musicianship: Understanding the crafts of music* (pp. 113–129). Cambridge Scholars Publishing.

8. Houlahan, M. (2017). Creating global musicians for the 21st century. China Conservatory of Music, Beijing, China; Houlahan, M. (2017). Sound advice from sound beginnings: Creating a pathway for authentic adaptations of global music pedagogies. A Global Forum Among Leaders of Higher Music Institutions, China Conservatory of Music, Beijing, China.

9. See Lilliestam, L. (2006). On playing by ear. *Popular Music*, 215(2), 197.

10. See Houlahan, M. & Tacka, P., 2012, pp. 113–129. See also From sound to symbol: A model of learning and instruction for teaching music concepts, elements, and skills, chapter 5 in Houlahan & Tacka, 2015.

11. See Karpinski, G. (2017). *Manual for ear training and sight singing* (2nd ed.), W. W. Norton & Company; Houlahan, M. & Tacka, P. (1990/1991), *Sound thinking: Music for sight-singing and ear training*, Vols. I & II, Boosey & Hawkes.

12. The takadimi system of rhythmic reading was developed by Richard Hoffman, William Pelto, and John W. White for use with college students, as detailed in Hoffman, Pelto, & White. (1996). Takadimi: A beat-oriented system of rhythm pedagogy, *Journal of Music Theory Pedagogy*, 10, 7–30. The system has been adapted and developed for use with younger learners by Houlahan & Tacka in *From sound to symbol* (2nd ed.), Oxford University Press, 2011.

13. Wiggins, J. (2015). *Teaching for Music Understanding*, Oxford University Press, p. 57.

14. See Dan Trueman's article Teaching' composition at Princeton in the *Contemporary Music Review*, 31(4), 327.

15. See Ed Sarath, David Meyers, and Patricia Shehan Campbell's *Redefining music studies in an age of change: Creativity, diversity, and integration*, Routledge Press, 2017.

REFERENCES

Belkin, A. (2018). *Musical composition: Craft and art*. Yale University Press.

Carbon, J. J. (1986, January). Toward a pedagogy of composition: Exploring creative potential. *College Music Symposium*, 26, 112–121.

Hindemith, P. (1942). *The craft of musical composition* (Vol. I). Schott & Co., Ltd., London.

Trueman, D. (2012). 'Teaching' composition at Princeton. *Contemporary Music Review*, 31(4), 323–329.

Williamson, S. (2009). Artistry through improvisation in the choral rehearsal. In J. C. Conlon, (Ed.), *Wisdom, wit, and will* (pp. 281–301). GIA Publications.

CHAPTER 19

GORDON MUSIC LEARNING THEORY

A Framework for Composition

JOHN ERŐS

MUSIC composition is viewed as an essential component of a child's music education, as evidenced in both national (National Coalition for Core Arts Standards, 2014) and state standards (California State Board of Education, 2019), as well as in research and discussion in music education (Burnard, 2010; Kaschub, 1997; Kennedy, 2002; Stringham, 2016; Viig, 2015). The purpose of this chapter is to explore the pedagogy of music composition as viewed through the lens of Music Learning Theory (MLT), an approach to music teaching and learning developed by Edwin E. Gordon (1986 & 2012). Along with the Orff approach, Kodály concept, and Dalcroze eurythmics, Gordon Music Learning Theory for decades has been recognized as one of the major approaches to music education (Shehan, 1986). As an influential framework for music teaching and learning, therefore, it behooves music educators to develop knowledge of and the capacity to utilize Music Learning Theory as a resource for teaching music composition in their K–12 curricula.

This chapter will discuss the background for Music Learning Theory, explore its tenets and organizational structure and how they relate to musical composition, and provide suggestions for how K–12 music educators might implement musical composition activities utilizing Music Learning Theory into their curricula. Although Music Learning Theory is frequently utilized within early childhood contexts (Etopio & Cissoko, 2012), it is also quite applicable to older K–12 students (Santucci, 2017; Taggart 2005). Finally, the chapter will conclude with vignettes from two current music educators in which they describe how they use MLT for composition-based activities.

Music Learning Theory

For decades, Music Learning Theory (commonly referred to as MLT) has been considered among the most prominent approaches to music teaching and learning utilized within K–12 music education in the United States (Shehan, 1986). It was developed by Edwin E. Gordon following an extensive period of research focused on musical aptitude (1965, 1979a, 1979b, & 1986). As with the Orff approach and the Kodály concept, music educators may pursue specialized training ultimately leading to certification in MLT. A thorough treatment of all relevant aspects of MLT is therefore beyond the scope of this chapter. However, a wealth of scholarship into MLT, much of it by Gordon himself (2003, 2009, & 2012) exists, as does the Gordon Institute for Music Learning (2020). As with any approach to music teaching and learning, MLT does not present a perfect solution to every conceivable scenario in K–12 music education. It can, however, be utilized as the basis for a curriculum, in addition to serving as one component contributing to a unique teaching situation.

Foundational Principles of Music Learning Theory

Music Learning Theory, as evidenced in Gordon's own as well as others' writing, is characterized by a high degree of precision as regards concepts and terminology. As the nomenclature, at times, diverges from that which is in most common parlance among music educators, there may be inconsistencies between this chapter's language and that which might be encountered in Gordon's foundational texts. I have sought to explain and implement Gordon's ideas such as is possible without the extensive treatment necessary to capture all specific nuances. Music educators in the United States are privileged to have direct access to MLT through Gordon's prodigious scholarship (books, journal articles, instructional material, all in original English), videos (Gordon, 2011), as well as his serving as a faculty member and presenter for many years in American universities, as compared to reading Kodály's writing in its original Hungarian.

Audiation

Gordon's theory has, at its core, the concept of "audiation," or inner hearing. To illustrate what is meant by audiation, I will begin with a hypothetical situation. Imagine two composers. The first composer is engaged in the process of composing a major work for chorus and orchestra. Without the use of an instrument or any other external source, the composer sings individual lines, part by part, to a scribe who writes them down in hard copy. The music flows freely from the composer's inner ear to his externalizing it in the form of writing. The second composer, tasked with creating an original composition, sits at the keyboard and experiments with different melodic ideas, making notes on staff paper along the way. Eventually, the composer finds an idea that he likes. It's a keeper! The composer takes his newly-discovered idea and uses it to write a piece for solo keyboard. What I am describing is, of course, two scenes from the film *Amadeus*, which depicts the vaguely rumored rivalry between Mozart and Salieri (courtesy more of Hollywood than of rigorous scholarship into music history). The comparison to the topic here is imperfect, as is the film from a scholarly standpoint, although it might be noted that *Amadeus* was extremely successful from the perspective of the motion picture industry. Nevertheless, the notion of creating finished music based on one's inner ear (audiating), right down to the instrumentation, versus composing music after a period of exploration on an instrument, is an important idea to consider as part of appreciating the central principle of MLT. Please note that the conclusion that one composer is demonstrating audiation, and one is not, should not be taken as a value judgment of either the composers or the music. Indeed, this is not to say that composing with an instrument or, perhaps, in a more exploratory manner will invariably yield music of lesser quality (as seems to be implied in the film). Rather, the point is to indicate that, in light of MLT's focus on audiation, the former illustrates composition while audiating while the latter does not.

Gordon (1999) further characterizes this concept as, "Audiation is to music what thought is to language" (p. 42) although again, to be precise, Gordon does not view music as a language. Gordon's concept of audiation has many facets, a comprehensive treatment of which is well beyond the scope of this chapter. For purposes of our discussion, however, I will highlight one facet in particular: rather than existing as one general concept only, audiation is considered to exist in eight different non-sequential types with numbers six through eight including creativity, identified as "creating and improvising" (p. 14).

Although the activities of MLT frequently focus more on improvisation than on composition, Gordon's writings nonetheless describe how his principles, primarily audiation, may be utilized to write and create unfamiliar music as part of the eighth, or final, type of audiation. Additionally, Gordon indicates that the types of audiation are not sequential. Hence students should be capable of utilizing audiation to write and create music at any grade level. As this chapter is intended to serve as a resource for music educators with little or no experience with MLT as well as for those with MLT experience who might or might not have utilized it in the teaching of music composition, we must take time to center audiation in our discussion of musical creativity.

Types of Audiation

As mentioned, there are eight non-sequential types of audiation (see Figure 19.1). Composition, although not mentioned specifically, is considered within the larger topic

Type 1	Listening to familiar or unfamiliar music
Type 2	Reading familiar or unfamiliar music
Type 3	Writing familiar or unfamiliar music from dictation
Type 4	Recalling and performing familiar music from notation
Type 5	Recalling and writing familiar music from memory
Type 6	Creating or improvising unfamiliar music while performing or in silence
Type 7	Reading and creating or improvising unfamiliar music
Type 8	Writing and creating or improvising unfamiliar music

FIGURE 19.1. Types of audiation

of creativity. It is located within the sixth, seventh, and eighth audiation types where the focus shifts to unfamiliar music in connection with creating. The addition of writing (notation) becomes an element in the final, eighth, type of audiation. A closer look at these is warranted.

Note further that although notation is also present earlier, via the presence of the writing of unfamiliar music (Type 5: Recalling and writing familiar music from memory), in that case it is taken from dictation and, hence has already been created by another source. Type 6 (Creating or improvising unfamiliar music while performing or in silence) focuses on student creativity, although the more specific focus is on creativity through performance, suggesting that vocal or instrumental improvisation is the greater focus of Type 6. Type 7 (Reading and creating or improvising unfamiliar music) adds notation to the element of unfamiliarity. It might, in a sense, be viewed as sight-reading, although the notation in question might take a variety of forms from the more specific (conventional notation) through the progressively less specific (i.e., figured bass or jazz chord changes, or through graphic or other indeterminate notation). Finally, in Type 8 (Writing and creating or improvising unfamiliar music), with the addition of writing, composition, in which a symbolic record will be maintained, becomes present—although the overall process of composition might involve other types of audiation. Given that they share an emphasis on written music, there is considerable overlap between Type 7 and Type 8. As has been mentioned, creativity has been both a goal and a focus for some time now, within curricula based on MLT. Furthermore, as regards Type 8 specifically, an additional form of audiation exists. It is known as notational audiation. Gordon (2012) notes that

> an eighth type of audiation takes place as we are writing both familiar and unfamiliar patterns and at the same time creating or improvising unfamiliar music. It includes notational audiation. If, however, we recall over a period of time what we have created or improvised before we write it, Type 8 could become Type 5. Processes for Types 7 and 8 are the same; the physical difference is Type 7 culminates in reading whereas Type 8 culminates in writing music we have created or improvised. (p. 29)

Hence, the types of audiation are not sequential and may be experienced even within the same learning activity.

Pedagogical Devices

Music Learning Theory makes use of specific pedagogical approaches, all of which will be utilized in preparing students to compose. These devices might fundamentally be organized into those based on pitch and those based on rhythm. Moreover, pitch and rhythm are further organized, for purposes of the delivery of content, into discrete groups of notes, known as "patterns."

Patterns: The Basis of Music Learning Theory

In the case of both pitch and rhythm, the basis for the development of audiation lies in the use and internalization of patterns as a fundamental component of musical education. Patterns refer to brief tonal and rhythmic motives, typically three or four pitches, or two beats in length. The patterns are further organized into areas based on meter, rhythmic figures, scales, and implied harmony, (i.e., *do-mi-do* as a pattern to be associated with the I chord in major). The ability to audiate is cultivated through repeated practice utilizing the patterns until students are able to audiate the patterns in a variety of settings, including different meters and tonalities. Patterns serve to aid the students in developing a musical vocabulary which may be used later as a basis for composition. Dalby (2020) observes that "in order to create or improvise, the student must have something to create or improvise with."

Tonal Materials

Topics related to pitch are referred to using the designation "tonal." The term "tonal" is often associated specifically with tonal music or tonal harmony, in which music is organized according to a hierarchy of relationships between notes and harmonies. In the case of MLT, topics that involve pitch are referred to as "tonal," even when other more specific materials (i.e., the church modes, which would more commonly be referred to as "modal music") are utilized.

Resting Tone

"Resting tone" is the tone upon which given a melody "comes to rest." Tonal materials in a given piece of music or set of patterns must be considered in reference to a resting tone. It is the tonal basis or what, in other frames of reference, might be viewed as the tonic. That is true whether the music in question is in a major/minor framework, or a church mode. It is important to be precise with terminology, however. Hence, the term tonic will not be used in reference to a specific pitch.

Tonal Solfège

Moveable-*do* solfege is utilized in curricula reflecting MLT. In this system, *do* refers to the resting tone (tonic pitch) regardless of key signature. This is in contrast to the fixed-*do* system (known as immovable-*do* in Gordon's writing), in which C is always *do*, or systems involving numbers. Additionally, MLT uses *la*-based minor, in which minor scales use *la* (the relative minor) as the resting tone, rather than *do*-based minor, in which *do* remains the resting tone and diatonic pitches must be altered. Hence, beginning in an MLT class, minor is achieved via singing from *la* to *la* without altering any syllables (the end result corresponding to the natural minor scale).

An additional, crucial element is that tonal patterns are designed in relation to their given harmonic function within a particular tonality (i.e., major, minor, Dorian). For example, it is not an accident that two of the most commonly-performed tonal patterns in major are *do-mi-do* and *ti-re-so*. The first tonal pattern indicates a tonic function and the second indicates a dominant function. Gordon organizes the tonal patterns according to major and minor tonalities, as well as the church modes (Dorian, Phrygian, Lydian, Mixolydian, Aeolian, and Locrian). Moreover, within these tonalities, a variety of functions are outlined. In major and minor, the functions that are outlined include tonic, dominant, and subdominant (there are five others). Hence, representative patterns in major would be *do-mi-so*, *so-ti-re*, and *fa-la-do*, corresponding to tonic, dominant, and subdominant respectively. Tonal patterns for other tonalities outline, at times, different functions, such as the dorian tonality which includes tonic, subtonic, and subdominant (dominant function is not present). As should be apparent, consistent practice with the tonal patterns will provide students with a harmonic vocabulary as well as a tonal vocabulary. Again, terminology in MLT varies, at times, from more customary nomenclature. The reader is encouraged to undertake more thorough research to develop a representative knowledge of the terminology.

Modes

Music Learning Theory prioritizes going beyond major and minor scales as the exclusive tonal province of music education. The church modes have a prominent role, particularly, although not limited to, Dorian and Mixolydian. In the case of the former, tonal patterns would use *re* as the resting tone and, with the latter, *so* would be the resting tone. The extensions for additional modes follow similarly. Ideally, students will audiate, and subsequently compose (at the appropriate point) in Phrygian, Locrian, etc. To be terminologically consistent, the modes are referred to as "tonalities" in Gordon's pedagogy.

Bass Line

Given Gordon's career as a professional classical and jazz bassist, it should come as no surprise that MLT places a strong emphasis on bass lines, such that melodies are typically learned, audiated, and performed with their accompanying bass line. In MLT, the bass line for a given melody is referred to as the root melody. Knowledge of the root melody plays a role in the development of harmonic knowledge, as well as the development of improvisation. By studying tonal patterns, and associating them with their harmonic functions, a root melody can be audiated in a straightforward manner. For example, the teacher might have the students sing the following patterns: *do-mi-so, do-fa-la, so-fa-re-ti, do-mi-do*. Resultingly, an accompanying root melody of *do–fa–so–do*, or tonic–subdominant–dominant–tonic from the standpoint of harmonic function, emerges.

Rhythm Materials

Music teaching and learning that utilizes MLT places a strong emphasis on the element of time. That includes the organization of time, as well as specific rhythmic figures. Topics related to rhythm, meter, etc., are referred to using the designation "rhythmic."

Macrobeat versus Microbeat

Brink (1983) characterizes Gordon's approach as referring "not to meter signatures which account for a commonly understood duple or triple grouping of pulses, but to the division of pulses" (p. 3). At the foundation of Gordon's concept of rhythm is the notion of macrobeat versus microbeat. To begin with a concrete example, in a $\frac{4}{4}$ time signature, the quarter note would represent the macrobeat and the eighth note would represent the microbeat. The number of microbeats within each macrobeat in a given meter demonstrates the metric identity; namely, if the macrobeat divides into two pulses, as in $\frac{2}{4}$ or $\frac{4}{4}$, the meter is referred to as a duple meter. If the macrobeat may be divided into three pulses, as in $\frac{6}{8}$ or $\frac{9}{8}$, the meter is referred to as triple meter. This is different from the simple/compound, duple/triple set of designations often encountered in other settings, such as where $\frac{6}{8}$ would be described as "compound duple." Rather, what is of greatest importance is for students to audiate the number of subdivisions (which they must do before giving it its "official" name), or microbeats, within a given macrobeat.

Rhythm Solfège

Music Learning Theory uses the *du-de* system, as opposed to the Cheve *ta ti-ti*, or *takadimi*, or other system (see Sletto, 2011, for a comparison of the various systems). What remains constant is that the beat (more specifically, the macrobeat) is always pronounced as "du," regardless of any further subdivision or any specific meter signature. For duple meters, the macrobeat is divided into two pulses by the syllables *du-de* (*de* rhymes with "day") and further divided into four pulses as *du-te-de-te* (*te* rhymes with "the"). The analog for triple meters, i.e. $\frac{6}{8}$ is for *du* to remain the macrobeat while the three microbeat subdivision is articulated as *du-da-di* (*da* is pronounced "dah," and *di* rhymes with "tea") and further as *du-te-da-te-di-te*. These rhythmic syllables will form the core of the rhythm patterns which students will audiate and perform at every class.

Odd Meters

Odd, or mixed meters, such as $\frac{7}{8}$ and $\frac{5}{8}$, are emphasized throughout MLT curricula. These are called "unusual meters" in MLT, as opposed to "usual meters" such as $\frac{2}{4}$ and $\frac{4}{4}$. Again, music educators will want to be familiar with MLT's nomenclature which, in the case of rhythm, diverges from that which is used more commonly. Moreover, MLT uses a different set of rhythm syllables for unusual meters, although *du* remains the syllable that identifies the macrobeat. It is to be noted that nursery rhymes and other traditional chants are a common fixture of music education, particularly within Orff- or Kodály-based curricula. Commonly, that material is in either simple/compound, duple/triple time exclusively. Rhythms in odd meters are comparatively less common, although they are still to be found in, for example, repertoire from Eastern Europe (much of it non-notated). Regardless, published MLT curricular materials, and Gordon himself, provide a wealth of odd meter material. For the purposes of this chapter, suffice it to say that compositional instruction involving the principles of MLT should strive to include a variety of meters, going beyond the more common $\frac{2}{4}, \frac{3}{4}$, and $\frac{4}{4}$, and into the darker waters of, for example, $\frac{7}{8}$ and $\frac{5}{4}$.

A Word on Notation

In addition, a brief discussion of the topic of notation is warranted. Audiation does not require notation and, in fact, maintains a distance from notation for the most part. Hence, throughout discussions of audiation there is an implicit inclination away from notation as a default component of musical education. Notation is approached deliberately, and with particular care. Given the necessity of some form of symbolic record of student work as a component in musical composition, one might conclude that MLT is at best only peripherally relevant to the teaching of music composition. That is not the case. It is, however, to be remembered that notation in and of itself is not likely to be encountered in MLT-informed practice.

Generally speaking, MLT does not emphasize symbols. That can be viewed as including both conventional notation as well as other forms, such as the stick notation commonly used in elementary music. It can also be considered in relation to the wide variety of symbols utilized in music teaching and learning, from those that are native to non-Western cultures to more contemporary graphic or indeterminate notation. The reason, in brief, is the view that symbols have limited value without accompanying audiation. Therefore, the utmost priority is to be placed on the development of secure audiation. Gordon considers the teaching of symbols without a musical context based in audiation to be of limited value. In fact, Gordon himself is quoted as saying "Get rid of notation!" (Fehr, 2015). Hence, symbols (whether traditional Western notation or otherwise), are introduced late in the process. Azzara (2005) observes that

> while learning to read is important to an individual's music education, many times
> music teachers ask their students to read the notation for music without first asking

them to think and "speak" musically. Reading music is the ability to hear and comprehend music in your head when looking at a page of notation, just as you can read and comprehend the words on this page. (p. 417)

Therefore, notation is not emphasized in the earlier stages and phases of audiation, if it is present at all. While discussing rhythm in particular, Gordon (2009) observes, "Without audiation, notation can teach us virtually nothing. Notation simply helps us remember what we have already learned and achieved through audiation" (p. 5). Music Learning Theory and notation are not, however, irreconcilable. Music composition, as a written (symbolic) record of the composition persists, depends on notation, whether traditional or otherwise. Music educators and students can create music all they want, but at some point, particularly in a K–12 setting, odds are that it will be preserved in some sort of written form (other methods of preservation are, of course, possible, i.e. recordings). Again, MLT principles indicate that students must be able to audiate their compositions after they are written down.

The consistent use of formal terminology, such as that of harmonic function, might suggest that the ultimate objective of MLT curricula is grounded in music theory and ear training as the terms are commonly used. In fact, Gordon frequently takes the field of music theory to task for placing an overemphasis on written analysis and conventional notation, rather than practical application via performance and audiation. Gordon suggests that the "value of understanding notation and music theory without audiating . . . is questionable" (2012, p. 23). Hence, lessons involving MLT must approach notation mindfully, and with proper preparation. Audiation must precede notation in MLT-based activities.

The question might arise as to the compatibility of MLT with music of a somewhat less precise nature, such as music created using environmental (and unpredictable) sound, or graphic or otherwise indeterminate notation. Suffice it to say that the focus of MLT is traditionally on the tonal and rhythmic musical materials that have been discussed thus far. Hence, at times music educators will utilize MLT and MLT-based activities as one among several approaches in the construction of their curricula. The second vignette at the end of the chapter, for example, is written by a teacher who utilizes elements of both MLT and the Orff approach in planning lessons.

UTILIZATION OF MUSIC LEARNING THEORY WITHIN MUSIC COMPOSITION

Music educators must approach composition from the proper mindset if MLT is to be utilized in a significant role in planning for instruction. It is in the preparation for musical composition that MLT is particularly well-suited, rather than necessarily providing a sequence of steps. Taggart (2005) observes that, to be precise, music learning theory is not and never was intended to be a methodology. It is not that specific or prescriptive. Rather, Music Learning Theory provides teachers with a theoretical framework to help them understand how to prepare and structure learning. (p. 185)

It is this theoretical framework that is to be utilized in structuring activities which will, ultimately, facilitate composition.

A day in which composition will be involved must, therefore, be preceded by work with tonal and rhythmic patterns as a way to prepare the students' audiation such that proper conditions for composition may exist. The emphasis, as always, is on audiation. According to MLT and the central focus on audiation within MLT curricula, if the students are audiating, then music composition is possible. Conversely, if the students are not audiating, they may still utilize symbols in a given lesson, but they will not be composing music; they will only be decoding symbols. Audiation must always be at the center of musical instruction. Students must be able to hear sound internally before they read and write symbols, a necessary element for recording and revising musical activities. Hence, there is a strong emphasis on preparation for composition. One must take the proper approach from the outset, namely that a teacher cannot "teach students how to compose," but might create the conditions such that composition becomes available to students as an outcome. Therefore, although the inclusion of composition in a music curriculum will not necessarily be postponed, an end result of original music, which the student has audiated before committing to notation, is not an inherent given.

A quick word is also warranted as regards the structure of classes and activities that represent MLT. Another central tenet of MLT is the use of a whole-part-whole format. The beginning and end of class (whole), in which formal musical skills (i.e., rhythm and tonal patterns) are studied, are considered Learning Sequence Activities, whereas Classroom Activities, in which the bulk of activities (including activities reflecting creativity, such as composition and improvisation) take place during the middle of class. Composition activities involving MLT-based practice will typically reflect these three elements, although each element need not be represented in every single learning activity.

Beginning with Patterns

Musical composition in an MLT environment necessitates the development of a vocabulary of ideas, and the building blocks of musical vocabulary are the tonal and rhythmic patterns utilized in Music Learning Theory. Gordon is clear on this point: "The students' ability to compose and improvise music in various styles in classroom music activities would be limited without previous performance of tonal patterns and rhythmic patterns" (2012, p. 220). In fact, returning to the Types 6, 7, and 8 (those within which creativity is placed), patterns are present in a foundational role, as follows, according to Gordon. Each contains, as a fundamental component, "familiar and unfamiliar patterns" (p. 29), in whichever combination of creating and improvising, reading, and writing is present. Hence, within MLT, students must work on their patterns. Ultimately, work on pre-written patterns will lead to students' development of their own patterns. These are the Learning Sequence Activities that take place at the beginning and end of class. Moveable *do* solfège (with *la*-based minor) is utilized, as is the *du-de/du-da-di* system of rhythmic performance. Azzara (2005) advocates the learning of harmonic patterns as well, identified as "two or more simultaneous sounding pitches that progress from one to the next with the tonic chord as the reference" (p. 410).

Metric Variety

Compositions representing MLT instruction should reflect meters beyond the usual $\frac{2}{4}$, $\frac{4}{4}$, or $\frac{6}{8}$. The rhythmic patterns that are performed in a given class must include, at the very least, patterns in both duple and triple meter. Ideally, the rhythmic patterns will also include at least some work in unusual meters as well. Preparation in Music Learning Theory should lead to student competence within a variety of metric forms. Commonly, music education in the United States focuses on meters such as $\frac{2}{4}$ and $\frac{4}{4}$. Such a limited vocabulary, consisting solely of usual duple meters, would be incompatible with thorough education utilizing MLT as students would have been performing and audiating in a variety of usual and unusual (as defined previously) meters from an early age. Therefore, in addition to $\frac{4}{4}$ and $\frac{6}{8}$, students would audiate, and create, music in meters such as $\frac{5}{8}$ and $\frac{7}{8}$. Music educators seeking a focus on an expanded metric pallet will find MLT to be particularly applicable in this manner.

Tonal Variety

Compositions representing MLT will reflect tonalities other than the customary major and minor. In particular, students will utilize different modes, particularly Dorian and Mixolydian modes. Modes will be performed and audiated through the logical extension of *la*-based minor, namely *re*-based Dorian in which one sings from *re* up to *re*, and the Dorian mode simply emerges, as well as *so*-based Mixolydian. The other modes emerge in similar fashion. Music composition that demonstrates instruction in MLT should therefore reflect modal variety. The combination of a thorough grounding in tonal and rhythm patterns will lead students, ultimately, beyond $\frac{4}{4}$ major compositions into the more expanded world of $\frac{5}{8}$ Dorian compositions.

Root Melody

Again, MLT emphasizes the bass line. The division of tonal patterns into corresponding harmonic functions makes the association of patterns with bass activity comparatively straightforward, at least considering the functions in root position at the outset. Composed music will therefore include an emphasis, or at least an awareness of a bass line. With the emphasis on root melody including, by extension, harmonic audiation, composition must involve a root melody.

Reading and Writing Symbols

Finally, for the reading and writing of symbols to have meaning, students must be able to audiate anything that they commit to paper (virtual or otherwise). Otherwise, the symbols are, in Gordon's view, effectively meaningless; teachers should check to make sure that students can audiate what they have written. The audiation must precede the writing. Students will not write a sequence of notes without any idea of what they will sound like, hence with no initial basis in audiation.

Music Learning Theory and Instrumental Music: A Brief Note

Extensive research, and curricula, have been written regarding the use of Music Learning Theory within instrumental music settings (Azzara, 1993; Grunow, 2005), including the recorder as well as instruments associated with wind band (and orchestra). Writers in music education have also considered MLT in relation to the Suzuki method, particularly inasmuch as both view the learning of music as similar to the learning of language (Stamou, 2005). Although the following suggested activities suggest a greater applicability for elementary, or non-performance ensembles, they may nevertheless be adapted to instrumental music (including large ensemble) settings. The principles of audiation remain constant throughout music education, regardless of specific musical settings, as Gordon notes: "An instrument is an extension of a human's audiation" (2011). Certain modifications will be necessary, based primarily on mechanical differences inherent in instrumental as opposed to vocal performance. Practicalities of fingering on given wind instruments, for example, will impact which patterns might be advisable at a particular time. Regardless of how well a beginning trumpet player can audiate a D below the staff, it will always be sharp if he doesn't have a reliable third valve slide. The important point as regards this chapter is that activities will not be presented separately for a general and instrumental music, as the common thread of audiation is present in both and an individual teacher's education will be able to make the transfer.

SUGGESTED ACTIVITIES

As stated previously, MLT is not intended to be a sequential methodology for teaching music in all settings. However, it is intended to provide a theoretical framework.

Therefore, the principles of MLT can be employed in a variety of settings in which music composition figures prominently. It is more apt to view the relationship of MLT to composition in terms of how the music teacher might approach the teaching of musical composition with representative aspects of MLT consciously present as a part of the lesson activity, rather than necessarily "composing with Music Learning Theory."

Getting Started: Development of a Vocabulary

In addition to developing the ability to audiate, consistent practice with tonal and rhythm patterns also serves to give students a "vocabulary" of musical ideas. Indeed, the development of initial musical ideas has been identified as among the most difficult aspects of musical composition, a situation shared by student and professional composers alike. Randles and Sullivan (2013) observe that, "Beginning a composition is sometimes the most daunting act. This reality is the same for students as it is for established composers" (p. 52). They go on to conclude that "helping students generate ideas that will propel their work forward is the primary goal as students begin a piece of music" (p. 52). With this in mind, music educators should realize that one important aspect of the performance of tonal and rhythmic patterns is preparation for composition.

The Beginning of Class

In a class that is utilizing MLT, lessons involving music composition will typically begin with exercises in audiation, rather than heading immediately for instruments and/or paper (virtual or otherwise). The teacher should first lead students through audiation of tonal and rhythmic patterns and, furthermore, would be well advised (depending on level) to include emphasis on root melody (i.e. bass line), before moving into activities involving composition. If the current location in the curriculum is to emphasize particular tonal or rhythmic elements, the class must begin with audiation exercises representing those particular concepts. If the day's activities call for work within the Dorian mode, the teacher would typically begin class with Dorian tonal patterns. When the teacher is confident that students are successfully audiating patterns in Dorian, the conditions will be much closer to composing music in Dorian than if students were to simply be given a sequence of written pitches.

Bass Line versus Bourdon

Music educators might opt to combine elements of MLT with elements of other approaches to music education, i.e. the Orff approach (Lange, 2005). For example, instead of approaching an Orff-based activity through bourdon, music educators might consider using root melody as the concept. Instead of a bourdon from bass xylophones and contrabass bars, students should first audiate a root melody, perform it, and notate it for purposes of revision and future performance. Removable bars lend themselves easily to an expanded modal palette. Students might also audiate a bass line to a familiar melody, and then transfer the bass line to bass xylophones or contrabass bars.

Metric Expansion

Challenge students to adapt their tonal patterns into unusual (odd) meters, such as $\frac{5}{8}$ and $\frac{7}{8}$. With exceptions, we do not typically hear unusual meters on a regular basis in the modern United States. Notating in unusual meters may be more challenging for some students than notating simple and compound meters as the groupings of notes will be less predictable. That is certainly not insurmountable. After improvising rhythm patterns and tonal patterns in a variety of unusual meters, a greater level of comfort should develop.

Tonal Expansion

The musical world is one that reaches beyond the realm of major and minor scales. Students should be encouraged to audiate modes as part of the process. After sustained practice in audiating a variety of modal contexts, a roomful of 25 major key compositions might sound a bit monotonous to students. That is precisely the time to challenge them to revisit their audiation in the modes. The preparation via audiating tonal patterns in the modes will facilitate this. Music Learning Theory does not consider tonal patterns beyond western tuning systems. However, more advanced students, or in particular contexts, might experiment with audiating musics which lie, tonally, outside of Western tuning. For example, it would be a challenge, but not an insurmountable one, to guide students towards audiating quarter tones as part of the study of Persian classical music.

Audiation Check

In curricula that reflect MLT, students should be able to audiate anything that they notate. Periodically, teachers should check with students and ask the students to perform the compositions, so as to demonstrate that they can audiate what they have written. If their performance demonstrates that what they have notated does not match their notation, the emphasis should go to the audiated original music. This would take the students from Type 8 audiation to Type 5 audiation until such time as their notated music represents what they are audiating.

Popular Music Pedagogy

Music education has witnessed a steady, if not steep, increase in the presence of popular music (Green, 2002, 2006; Tobias, 2013) and rock band pedagogy (Dorfman, 2017) in the modern K–12 music classroom. Although scholarship into popular music within school music education dates back to the days before Woodstock (Swanwick, 1968), an in-depth discussion of popular music is not to be found within scholarship into MLT. Gordon himself is dismissive of modern popular music, particularly inasmuch as he views its capacity to foster creativity through audiation (2012, p. 47) to be virtually non-existent. Regardless, at present, individual music educators are already utilizing popular music alongside MLT, demonstrating that the two are in fact perfectly compatible. It follows, then, that further explorations of popular music education, particularly such topics as songwriting, from within an audiation-based framework are warranted.

In actual fact, it should be noted that the focus on root melody makes for a natural match between MLT and popular and rock musics. This is particularly true given the emphasis on bass in much American popular music. Considering the increasing popularity of including the study of popular music, particularly insofar as learning by ear (absent notation) is emphasized, music teachers should challenge their students to audiate their favorite melodies irrespective of genre. The bemoaned "ear worm" phenomenon, in which students simply "can't get a tune out of their heads," might in fact be the perfect vehicle towards musical composition utilizing audiation. Teachers should, of course, be mindful of proper performance technique such that, for example, students maintain proper vocal health. They might audiate a given vocal tone as well as the rhythms and pitches, but their own performance must represent safe vocal technique.

Once students have audiated their melodies, they should then be challenged to audiate the root melody. Teachers should guide students towards pieces that are appropriate, that is to say attainable, within the students' current rhythmic and tonal vocabularies. Not every popular genre will be a perfect fit for MLT, nor will every specific piece within a given genre, although audiation remains constant through music.

Notational Accuracy

The role of notation must be considered. Notation, or reading and writing of symbols (conventional or otherwise), is necessary or at the very least advisable for a thorough experience in musical composition. When their aural models are in place, and audiation is secure, students must be made secure in accurate notation. Fundamentally, it would be unfortunate to discover that what students are audiating does not in fact match the notation that they are creating and viewing. Or to have other students perform the original student composers' work only to discover that the performances that they are hearing do not match the material that the student composers audiated at the outset. As one of the vignettes will discuss, the education in notation need not take a great deal of time and, one might conclude, an overemphasis on notation in the first place is a risk. Hence, the final point is simply that if students are going to notate music, their notation must accurately reflect the music that they initially audiated, and settled on as their desired musical outcome.

Vignettes

The following are two vignettes written by music educators in the Bay Area of the United States, both of whom utilize MLT in their teaching although, one might conclude, in different forms. That is consistent with Taggart's point that Music Learning Theory is not a prescriptive methodology, but a theoretical framework for structuring music teaching and learning. The first teacher describes how he builds towards musical composition through the different phases and stages of audiation, working towards the final phase (Type 8: Writing and creating or improvising unfamiliar music) in which the students compose music. The second teacher describes working towards rhythmic composition with early elementary students. The reader will note that MLT "looks different" in each setting. It is to be remembered that, as discussed earlier, MLT serves as a framework. It is incumbent upon music educators to utilize select curricular materials and techniques, i.e. the use of popular or other genres of music, to address the needs of their specific students and settings.

Teacher Vignette #1: Joshua Diamant (Oakland Unified School District, Oakland, CA)

In my Music Learning Theory–inspired classes, we start composition activities early in kindergarten. But it might not look or sound like what most people consider composition.

We have just sung a favorite song together—let's say "Five Little Speckled Frogs." It's in major tonality and duple meter. I haven't told my kids that, but having done lots of repertoire in many tonalities and meters, they are developing a sense of musical context. In a previous class meeting, between repetitions of the song, I have had students echo, both in solo and all together, short tonal patterns, e.g., "*do-so-mi*" or "*ti-re-so*," on neutral syllables. These are arpeggiated patterns using notes from the tonic or dominant chords.

This time, instead of everyone imitating the patterns, I tell them, "OK, this time, I'm going to sing a pattern and then call on one person. That person can choose whether they would like to be the same as me or different from me." I demonstrate an example of what each of those might sound like. "Then, the rest of the class will have to tell us whether that person was the same as me (two fists) or different from me (one fist and one open hand)." After four to eight students have sung, we sing the song together again, and the cycle repeats until everyone has had a turn or students begin to lose focus.

With this simple first step into improvisation (which, of course, works with rhythm patterns just as well as with tonal), we've accomplished many things. Students who feel ready to jump into spontaneous creation will choose to be different. Sometimes they have internalized the musical context and their response is a tonic or dominant pattern; sometimes they haven't and their response doesn't make musical sense. But just as we don't discourage babies who haven't figured out how to pronounce words yet from babbling, all responses are equally valid here. Some students would prefer to imitate what I just sang, and that's fine too. The "same/different" game the rest of the class plays ensures that students who choose to imitate rather than create don't feel like they've picked the lesser option. If a student doesn't sing at all, I move on without comment, but I find that since the stakes are so low, this is rare.

From this beginning, students progress smoothly over the next six years. Pattern work where all students are expected to be different from the teacher (eventually including solfège and rhythm syllables) leads to students creating their own ostinati, which in turn leads to improvising within a given chord sequence, which in turn leads to creating entire melodies and notating them. But it all starts with giving students many opportunities to musick with fluency and spontaneity.

Vignette #2: Pete Santucci (Ross Valley School District, San Anselmo, CA)

As part of a Music Learning Theory curriculum, I include composition activities as part of my K–3 sequence for teaching the performance and reading of music rhythms. I feel this is similar to a classroom teacher supporting students' English language study of vocabulary and reading by asking students to compose their own sentences that include some of the vocabulary words that are being taught. This sequence takes place throughout the year, advancing as quickly as students are able to progress. According to Music Learning Theory, students need to develop four types of vocabularies: 1) listening, 2) speaking (performing), 3) reading, and 4) writing. Listening and performing vocabularies are often learned in tandem and reinforce each other, just as reading and writing vocabularies can also support each other. In Music Learning Theory the ability to write or compose music with notation is not an isolated activity or end unto itself. Rather, it is a natural part of the learning sequence and a result of the previous learning which naturally comes after students have learned to audiate music they hear, improvise, and read.

Starting in kindergarten, students learn to echo four-beat rhythm patterns in duple meter ($\frac{2}{4}$ or $\frac{4}{4}$) and triple meter ($\frac{6}{8}$). As students progress in age and ability, I adjust the content and difficulty of the rhythm patterns. Once most students are comfortably able to echo familiar patterns accurately using rhythm solfege, I begin to ask students to volunteer if they would like to orally improvise a rhythm pattern for the class to imitate, using the same type of content that I am using.

After performing rhythms aloud, and improvising, students are introduced to reading the same four-beat rhythm patterns that they have learned aurally, using the same rhythm solfège syllables. During this process, I am writing the rhythm patterns using standard notation. The solfège syllables are not written on the board, they are only performed orally in relation to the notation. In point of fact, because the students have already learned the four-beat rhythm patterns through an aural/oral process, the students are actually just being taught to recognize the visual notation for patterns that they already know how to perform orally.

When most students have become comfortable with reading a set of patterns, I ask them to write some rhythm patterns. I give them the option of first copying the rhythms that I have written, or they may compose their own rhythms if they would like to do so. Most students quickly tire of copying the rhythms I have written on the board and begin experimenting with their own combinations of rhythms. Keep in mind that students have not been taught the words "quarter note," "eighth note," or "sixteenth note." They know them only as *du*, *du-de*, and *du-ta-de-ta*. In these early stages of writing, students freely arrange those rhythms according to their own whim or their own sense of audiation, but without using measure lines or time signatures. As students progress in understanding and age, I teach them to include measure lines and time signatures, but with only the most basic explanation so as not to distract them with theoretical names, which often get in the way of audiation. I simply explain to them that, as they may have noticed in the rhythm patterns that I write on the board for them to read, after a certain number of beats are written there is a vertical line that is drawn. This is called a measure line and the space between two measure lines is called a measure. Within each measure there is time for a certain number of macrobeats. We perform some rhythm patterns while moving to or tapping the macrobeats so that students can understand that there are the same number of beats in each measure of my examples even though there may not be the same number of written notes. Because of the use of Gordon's beat-function syllables, this is easily identified by students, as they can easily feel there are four downbeats in each measure of $\frac{4}{4}$ time, for example.

For a few students who are struggling to feel or audiate the concept, I may have to explain intellectually that they need to have four things in each measure and they can choose from either *du*, *du-de*, or *du-ta-de-ta*. Through a circular process of aural/oral imitation, exploration, improvisation, reading, writing, and then reading aloud what they have written, students gradually learn to self-correct and accurately compose their own rhythms.

CONCLUDING THOUGHTS: STUDENT OWNERSHIP AND RELEVANCE

Although MLT does not necessarily have composition as a primary goal in and of itself, Gordon nonetheless viewed composition as a means to develop student ownership of music, itself the goal of music education:

> When a teacher provides students with skills to create and improvise music, music becomes the property of students themselves. This should be the ultimate goal of all

music teaching. Relative merit of what music students create is not really important. What is important is students believe music belongs to them. (2012, p. 27)

Familiarity with and implementation of the principles of MLT, with which greater knowledge is available via focused professional development, gives the teacher tools with which to structure musical composition for students at virtually all levels. For example, with proper preparation in audiation via tonal and rhythmic patterns, original student compositions in Dorian mode within $\frac{7}{8}$ time are obtainable. Furthermore, this is the opportune moment to tap into the musical backgrounds that students bring into their classrooms, namely any traditional or culturally representative musics from their own specific home or community situations. In addition to the development of skills in tonal and rhythmic audiation as presented in class, students will likely bring a tonal and rhythmic audiational context based on their own backgrounds.

Between the greater focus on improvisation (Azzara, 1999) and the limited emphasis on notation, one is liable to come away with the sense that composition pedagogy and MLT are nearly incompatible. This is not true. Music Learning Theory can be viewed as an excellent approach for preparing students to successfully compose original music and, eventually, to take ownership of their originally-created music. Student ownership of music, particularly in a time when notions of music education in the United States continue to diversify at an ever-increasing rate, is a hugely relevant if not critical objective.

REFERENCES

Azzara, C. D. (1993). Audiation-based improvisation techniques and elementary instrumental students' music achievement. *Journal of Research in Music Education, 41*(4), 328–342. https://doi.org/10.2307/3345508

Azzara, C. D. (1999). An aural approach to improvisation: Music educators can teach improvisation even if they have not had extensive exposure to it themselves. Here are some basic strategies. *Music Educators Journal, 86*(3), 21–25. https://doi.org/10.2307/3399555

Azzara, C. D. (2005). Understanding music through improvisation. In M. Runfola & C. C. Taggart (Eds.), *The development and practical applications of music learning theory* (pp. 399–424). GIA Publications, Inc.

Brink, E. (1983). A look at Edwin E. Gordon's theories. *Bulletin of the Council for Research in Music Education, 75*, 1–13. http://www.jstor.org/stable/40317784

Burnard, P. (2010). How children ascribe meaning to improvisation and composition: rethinking pedagogy in music education. *Music Education Research, 2*(1), 7–23. https://doi.org/10.1080/14613800050004404

California State Board of Education (2019). California arts standards. Retrieved December 13, 2020 from https://www.cde.ca.gov/be/st/ss/vapacontentstds.asp

Dalby, B. (2020). About music learning theory. The Gordon Institute for Music Learning. https://giml.org/mlt/about/

Dorfman, J. (2017). Examining music teachers' experiences in a rock band performance and pedagogy professional development course. *Journal of Popular Music Education, 1*(3), 281–296. http://dx.doi.org/10.1386/jpme.1.3.281_1

Etopio, E. A. & Cissoko, K. M. (2012). The hard work of music play: Establishing an appropriate early childhood music environment. In M. Runfola & C. C. Taggart (Eds.), *The development and practical applications of music learning theory* (pp. 53–68). GIA Publications, Inc.

Fenr, R. (2015). In memoriam: Edwin E. Gordon, creator of Gordon music learning theory. National Association for Music Education. https://nafme.org/in-memoriam-edwin-e-gordon-creator-of-gordon-music-learning-theory/

Gordon, E. (1965). *Musical aptitude profile*. Houghton Mifflin.

Gordon, E. E. (1979a). Developmental music aptitude as measured by the Primary Measures of Music Audiation. *Psychology of Music, 7*(1), 42–49. https://doi.org/10.1177/030573567971005

Gordon, E. E. (1979b). *Primary measures of music audiation*. GIA Publications.

Gordon, E. (1986a). *Intermediate measures of music audiation*. GIA Publications.

Gordon, E. E. (1986b). A factor analysis of the musical aptitude profile, the primary measures of music audiation, and the intermediate measures of music audiation. *Bulletin of the Council for Research in Music Education, 87*, 17–25. https://www.jstor.org/stable/40317975

Gordon, E. E. (1999). All about audiation and music aptitudes: Edwin E. Gordon discusses using audiation and music aptitudes as teaching tools to allow students to reach their full music potential. *Music Educators Journal, 86*(2), 41–44. https://doi.org/10.2307/3399589

Gordon, E. (2003). *A music learning theory for newborn and young children*. GIA Publications.

Gordon, E. E. (2003). *Learning sequences in music*. GIA Publications.

Gordon, E. (2009). *Rhythm: Contrasting the implications of audiation and notation*. GIA Publications.

Gordon, E. (2011). "Music Learning Theory practical applications part 7." GIML Publications. https://www.youtube.com/watch?v=lJEqbAKPPao&t=215s.

Gordon, E. E. (2012). *Learning sequences in music: A contemporary music learning theory*. GIA Publications.

Gordon Institute of Music Learning. (2020). The Gordon institute for music learning. https://giml.org/

Green, L. (2002). *How popular musicians learn: A way ahead for music education*. Ashgate Publishing, Ltd.

Green, L. (2006). Popular music education in and for itself, and for "other" music: Current research in the classroom. *International Journal of Music Education, 24*(2), 101–118. https://doi.org/10.1177/0255761406065471

Grunow, R. F. (2005). Music learning theory: A catalyst for change in beginning musical instrumental instruction. In M. Runfola & C. C. Taggart (Eds.), *The development and practical applications of music learning theory* (pp. 179–200). GIA Publications, Inc.

Kaschub, M. (1997). A comparison of two composer-guided large group composition projects. *Research Studies in Music Education, 8*(1), 15–28. https://doi.org/10.1177/1321103X9700800103

Kennedy, M. A. (2002). Listening to the music: Compositional processes of high school composers. *Journal of Research in Music Education, 50*(2), 94–110. https://doi.org/10.2307/3345815

Lange, D. M. (2005). Combining Music Learning Theory and Orff in the general music classroom. In M. Runfola & C. C. Taggart (Eds.), *The development and practical applications of music learning theory* (pp. 143–156). GIA Publications, Inc.

National Coalition for Core Arts Standards (2014). National core arts standards. National Coalition for Core Arts Standards. https://www.nationalartsstandards.org/

Randles, C. & Sullivan, M. (2013). How composers approach teaching composition: Strategies for music teachers. *Music Educators Journal, 99*(3), 51–57. https://doi.org/10.1177/0027432112471398

Santucci, P. (2017). MLT, modes, meters and . . . monsters? Integrating Orff approach with an infusion of Edwin E. Gordon's music learning theory. Session presented at 2017 Bay Area Elementary Music Conference. Hayward, CA.

Shehan, P. K. (1986). Major approaches to music education: An account of method. *Music Educators Journal, 72*(6), 26–31. https://doi.org/10.2307/3401273

Sletto, T. (2011). A comparison of rhythm syllables and a recommendation. *Kodaly Envoy, 37*(3), 4–8.

Stamou, L. (2005). Music learning theory, physiology of learning, and the Suzuki philosophy: When research meets philosophy and educational practice. In M. Runfola & C. C. Taggart (Eds.), *The development and practical applications of music learning theory* (pp. 265–281). GIA Publications, Inc.

Stringham, D. A. (2016). Creating compositional community in your classroom. *Music Educators Journal, 102*(3), 46–52. https://doi.org/10.1177/0027432115621953

Swanwick, K. (1968). *Popular music and the teacher*. Pergamon Press.

Taggart, C. C. (2005). Meeting the musical needs of all students in elementary general music. In M. Runfola & C. C. Taggart (Eds.), *The development and practical applications of Music Learning Theory* (pp. 127–142). GIA Publications, Inc.

Tobias, E. S. (2013). Composing, songwriting, and producing: Informing popular music pedagogy. *Research Studies in Music Education, 35*(2), 213–237. https://doi.org/10.1177/1321103X13487466

Viig, T. G. (2015). Composition in music education: A literature review of 10 years of research articles published in music education journals. *Nordic Research in Music Education, 16*, 227–257.

CHAPTER 20

PLAYING WITH MUSIC

Composition Pedagogy with Orff Schulwerk

JUDY BOND

with sample lessons by

BRIAN BURNETT

As a musician and composer, Carl Orff sought a new way of teaching music by involving students in improvisation with music and movement, often inspired by the rhythm of speech. The Orff Schulwerk philosophy is a holistic approach involving body, mind, and spirit, the result of Orff's search for what he called "elemental"—combining music and movement through improvisation. In his words, "The starting point was an artistic rather than a purely educational one" (1978, p. 13). Later, when the Schulwerk was adapted for children, Orff declared that musical imagination could be awakened by "the building up of simple rhythms and melodies, drones and ostinati, with the inclusion of all kinds of instruments" (p. 131).

The philosophy of *Orff-Schulwerk: Music for children* is centered on what children like to do. It's all about PLAY, imagination, creativity, and fun. Play is the work of children, and the joyful, playful experiences observed in Orff music classes have drawn teachers around the world to study and implement the practices and teaching/learning processes developed by artist teachers who understand and value children's musical play. The structure of the Orff music class is designed by the teacher to enable meaningful, purposeful experiences that keep a playful spirit. There is a magical quality that emerges when the teacher introduces a simple musical idea and leads the students through a process where new ideas are encouraged and explored. As the students play with sound, rhythm, and melody, the teacher becomes a guide, encouraging and supporting, giving the students confidence in their own music-making. The focus is on group collaboration rather than individual competition.

The following statement from Wilhelm Keller's *Introduction to Music for Children* provides a concise summary of Orff-Schulwerk philosophy and practice:

> The real goal of the Schulwerk is attained in one's enjoyment of the fruitful combination of personal and interpersonal resources. Creating, reproducing, and listening to music are not separate and exclusive areas of work, but are presented as one entity in the elementary musical experience of all participants. (Keller, 1954, 1963, p. 5)

ORFF COMPOSITION PEDAGOGY IN ACTION: "EVERY MORNING WHEN I WAKE UP"

"Every Morning When I Wake Up," showing in Figure 20.1, is a short canon[1] by Avon Gillespie[2] that provides infinite possibilities for exploration, improvisation, arranging, and composition with the Orff approach. For example, students can:

Learn the canon through listening, movement, and imitation:

- Have the students move as you play or sing the melody several times, suggesting a different way to move or focus with each repetition. Ask for comments from the students. " What did you hear?" Students may talk with a partner or in a small group. Collect responses and generate ideas about musical aspects such as style, range, phrasing, repetition, patterns, rhythm, tonality. Responses will depend on developmental level and musical background of the students.
- Teach the words. Have the students sing and move, walking with the beat, performing body percussion with the beat, or pat-clapping to the beat. Encourage the students to make up new combinations, sometimes dividing the beat or making up rhythm patterns based on feeling for the beat. Do everything in canon, first 2 parts, then 4 and 8 parts, depending on size and ability of the group.

FIGURE 20.1. "Every Mornin' When I Wake Up"

Add instrumental accompaniments:

- Using barred instruments (xylophone, metallophone, glockenspiel), have the students improvise an accompaniment using only the tonic pitch, in different octaves. (Students should form small groups, based on the number of barred instruments available.) Students should listen to different possibilities, considering variety of tone color and use of silence. Design a visual representation of the final choice. This could be an iconic representation or traditional musical notation.
- Using unpitched percussion instruments, have small groups of students improvise rhythm patterns 4 beats or 8 beats long, to fit the phrase length of the melody. Through group collaboration, select an accompaniment with at least two different percussion instruments. Design a visual representation of the final choice.
- Add another layer of texture with melodic ostinati. Have the students select short motives from the song, such as "every morning" or "sing my children" or "song to sing", and practice singing and playing different possibilities as an accompaniment to the song. Consider using the motives in combination or lengthen through augmentation. Make decisions about which instruments will play each accompaniment part.

Arrange or create a new composition:

- At this point, students have experienced several kinds of composition. The next step might be to build a musical score by combining selected elements from the process outlined above, including singing, instruments, and movement. Working as a class or in small groups, students create a performance form: ABA or Rondo. A canon might be included. Students practice, discuss, and revise the composition through group collaboration and decision making.
- Students may be asked to think about their personal feelings in the morning, and to create word chains, statements, or short poems based on their own morning feelings. A student may demonstrate morning feelings in movement while another student describes the feelings in words. An artwork, another piece of music, or a book may be used for inspiration.[3] Working in small groups, using the music skills presented and practiced in the previous lesson, students compose a new piece of music. Depending on age and expertise of the students, compositions may be saved through audio recording, visually through a drawing or iconic notation, or through standard notation

FIRST STEPS IN THE EVOLUTION OF ORFF-SCHULWERK COMPOSITION PEDAGOGY

The composition pedagogy of Carl Orff is embedded in the five volumes of *Orff Schulwerk: Music for Children*, through musical examples, along with rhythmic and melodic exercises. A detailed pedagogical sequence was later provided in *Elementaria* (1974) by Gunild Keetman, Orff's closest collaborator and composer of much of the music in the Schulwerk, including the five volumes and many supplementary works.

The foundational roots of Orff Schulwerk pedagogy reach back to the 1920s, when Orff collaborated with teachers, musicians, and dancers in the 1924 founding of Dorothea Gunther's *Guntherschule*, in Munich, Germany, with a curriculum focused on gymnastics, dance, and music. In *The Schulwerk* (1978), volume 3 of Orff's eight-volume autobiography, he describes how development of his ideas began with experiments in improvisation, imagining how the elemental human activities of singing, saying, dancing, and playing could come together in spontaneous group music-making and movement to create new music. The curriculum at the *Guntherschule* integrated experiments in improvisation with training in music and movement skills.

In 1930 Orff began to realize that his philosophy of teaching and creating through improvisation would need to be published for it to be known beyond the small group at the school. He approached publisher Willy Strecker (Schott, Mainz), and they came to an agreement for the first publications, with the overall title *Orff-Schulwerk: Elementare Musikubung*. The first volume in the series was *Rhythmisch-melodische Übung*. In this volume Orff describes how he explored his memory for "rhythms and melodies that had been thought of and tried out in movement sessions" and later stated that "pieces that are found in the volumes are borderline cases for composition, as so often happens when improvisations are written down in notation" (1978, p. 115). Publication of these early works continued from 1930–1934, culminating in an invitation for Orff to create music for the opening of the 1936 Olympic Games in Berlin—a production involving more than 6,000 children as well as youth and adult musicians. On January 7, 1945, approaching the end of World War II, the *Guntherschule* was destroyed, along with many educational materials and instruments (1978, p. 211).

In 1948 Carl Orff received a phone call asking if he could write music like what the caller, Dr. Panofsky, a colleague from Bavarian State Radio, heard on a recording of music Orff had composed for the 1936 Olympic Games in Berlin.[4] Dr. Panofsky wanted music for radio broadcasts that would appeal to children, and that "they could play themselves" (Orff, 1978, p. 212). Orff was attracted to the idea because it was a new beginning for the ideas which originated at the *Guntherschule* in the 1920s. Now these ideas and the Schulwerk principles and philosophy could have a different dimension, reaching thousands of children. Orff described this new opportunity as "A music exclusively for children that could be played, sung, and danced by them but that could also in a similar way be *invented by them*—a world of their own" (p. 212). This is where the story of Orff's pedagogy of composition with children begins.

Orff accepted this challenge, and the radio programs began on September 15, 1948, with broadcasts from Munich. Remains of the instruments that survived World War II were found, and Orff's associate and fellow composer Gunild Keetman put together the materials, directing a group of children ages 8 to 12 who were the performers. "Children made music for children and with children" (Orff, 1978, p. 216). The next step was composition by the children. Long, theoretical directions were avoided. Instead, after hearing the music created by Orff and Keetman, played by the children under Keetman's direction, the children who listened to the broadcasts were simply given rhymes and told to make up their own tunes and accompaniments, to write them down, and send to the address given. Some of the compositions were then selected for the next broadcast. Prizes were given to selected composers, usually in the form of musical instruments (Orff, 1978).

The pedagogical work with children received a "gratifyingly large response" indicating that "the broadcasts were being properly understood and carried out" (p. 218). Orff expressed the philosophy as follows:

> It is not a question of unusual talent but of children who have been awakened, for whom the elemental originality of the Schulwerk way of making music has released in them musical powers, that, if their musical education remains solely reproductive, stay buried. This is by no means to say that work with Schulwerk should exclude the other. (Orff, 1978, p. 218)

The success of the radio broadcasts was followed by classes for children at the *Mozarteum* in Salzburg, Austria, with a holistic curriculum similar to that of the *Guntherschule*, but adapted for children: singing, speech, movement, and instruments, with activities including games, improvisation, and reading and writing music. The radio broadcasts to schools continued and were the basis for *Orff-Schulwerk: Music for Children*, a five-volume set of books published by Schott starting in 1950.[5]

> The introduction to *Orff Schulwerk: Music for Children* begins with a single sentence: "Music for children has grown out of work with children." This simple statement is followed by a brief but comprehensive description of the materials, instruments, organization, and focus for each of the three parts of the book. "The three parts 1) *Nursery Rhymes and Songs*, 2) *Rhythmic and Melodic Exercises*, and 3) *Instrumental Pieces* are complementary to each other and should be used together from the start. Thus, immediately after the early nursery rhymes ("Cuckoo," "Pat-a-Cake," "Tinker Tailor," etc.) the first speech exercises, clapping and ostinato exercises should be attempted. In order to achieve freedom in performance the children must play from memory. The teacher should nevertheless instruct them in musical notation right from the beginning, starting with the speech exercises where only rhythmic notation is necessary. At first musical notation should primarily be used to write down original inventions of melody and rhythm." (*Orff-Schulwerk: Music for Children: Volume I*, 1950, English translation by Margaret Murray)

The compositions in *Volume I* are conceived as "models for improvisation." Although the songs and accompaniments in *Part One* and *Instrumental Pieces* in *Part Three* are often taught as performance pieces, following the notation as written, the intent is for teachers and students to revise and adapt the pieces to fit the developmental level, skill, and musical imagination of the students.

Composition Pedagogy as Originally Presented by Orff and Keetman

Essential elements of an Orff-Schulwerk pedagogy of composition are found in *Music for Children: Volume I, Part Two: Rhythmic and Melodic Exercises*, with short, simple (elemental) patterns that provide the material for imitation, skill development, experimentation, and creation, including development of accompaniment patterns, combining rhythm and text, and question/answer improvisation, under the headings "Rhythms to be completed" (p. 64) and "Melodies to be completed" (p. 79). The "Instructions and Notes" at the end of Volume I (p. 141–143) provide teaching recommendations and explanations of the various sections. Speech exercises are fundamental to the Orff Schulwerk teaching/learning process, and Part Two begins, logically, with a variety of examples (p. 50–52).

> The speech exercise comes at the beginning of all musical practice, both rhythmic and melodic. Single words, grouped together according to sound or meaning, names, sayings and proverbs should be, as these examples show, worked out and written down in their equivalent note values. In speech exercises it becomes easy to teach duple and triple time, the meaning of bar-lines and upbeats, and sudden time-signature changes. The combination of clapping and conducting with the speech exercises will make it easier to learn musical notation. (Instructions and Notes, p. 141)

The speech exercises are to be used rhythmically and melodically in improvising and composing short pieces incorporating the use of ostinato, body percussion, canon, and making up melodies, first with two or three notes (*so, mi, la*), and later the pentatonic scale tones (*do, re, mi, so, la*). A drone bass accompaniment can be added, and vocal timbre can be varied through different combinations of solo voice, smaller and larger groups, and echo by a soloist or chorus. Use of dynamics and articulation of the text can also be explored. New word patterns and short poems created by the students and teacher provide infinite possibilities for improvisation and composition.

The next section of Volume I, Part Two, focuses on body rhythms, starting with clapping. With 25 pages of rhythmic exercises, this is by far the longest section of Part Two, beginning with *Rhythms for imitation* (pp. 53–55). Patterns in this category are to be practiced simultaneously with the speech exercises, through experiences and games with echo clapping, progressing from simple to advanced, including both duple and triple meters as well as upbeats, dotted rhythms. Following these "basic training" exercises, the rhythm section continues with the following categories: *Rhythms for clapping, melody-making and fitting words to rhythmic patterns, Rhythms for ostinato accompaniments, Rhythms over ostinato accompaniments, Rhythms to be completed (Question/Answer), Rhythmic rondos, Songs with rhythmic accompaniment, Rhythmic canons, and Exercises for knee slapping* (patting or patschen, an Orff term for thigh patting).

Examples of *Melodies to be completed* are presented on pp. 79–81. Using xylophones and glockenspiels with *fa* and *ti* bars removed, students complete a given melody by improvising an ending or create a beginning for a given melody ending. Similar exercises can be created for voice or recorder. In these exercises there are opportunities for students to develop body percussion coordination, and to learn the basics of Orff Schulwerk compositional style through creating melodies with and without text, use of ostinato, rhythmic accompaniment of songs and melodies, and canon. Through combinations of various patterns, students develop confidence in their ability to create their own music.

The last section of Volume I, Part Two, includes *Ostinato Exercises* for tuned percussion instruments, *Rondos*, and *Canon* exercises. The "Instructions and Notes" for this section of Volume I, Part Two, emphasizes in bold letters that **"This exercise represents use of the fundamentals of the entire teaching"** (p. 142).

The ostinato exercises for tuned percussion instruments (most often called Orff instruments or barred percussion) provide examples of the basic Orff accompaniment based on the tonic and fifth, called a drone or bordun. Many variations of the simple drone, single moving drone, and double moving drone are presented: 95 examples in duple meter (pp. 82–83), followed by 95 examples in triple meter (pp. 84–85). Combining or layering two drones creates a more complex texture. The examples for this possibility are designed to be played on two instruments (pp. 86–87). Rondo form provides a structure for improvisation as well as composition of longer pieces.

> From the beginning the drone supports all melodic exercises. The simple drone can be used for every melody in this volume, and at first only simple or easy moving drones should be used to accompany improvisations. (p.142)

Many experiments and explorations with rhythm and melody can be inspired by incorporating the ideas set forth in *Music for children: Volume 1, Part Two*. Through experiencing and practicing rhythm patterns with speech, body percussion, and percussion instruments, children can combine and re-arrange patterns with two or three sounds to a beat, longer note values, and rests. The rhythm patterns can be done in diminution or augmentation, patterns can be organized in various phrase lengths, and combined to create longer compositions. For melodic improvisation, starting with a rhyme, proverb, or word chain provides the rhythm. A *so-mi* chant can then be the first melodic improvisation. Additional pitches are added one by one to form the pentatonic scale: *do, re, mi, so, la.* The tonal center for melodies in Volume I is C *do*. As students advance, melodies are composed with *la* as the tonal center, creating a minor tonality. Later, students may also improvise pentatonic melodies with *re, mi,* or *so* as the tonal center, adjusting the tones of the drone accordingly, in preparation for later improvisation and composition work with Aeolian, Dorian, Phrygian, and Mixolydian modes.

Drone accompaniment gives rhythmic and tonal support for improvisation of melodies, as well as providing pathways to exploration of texture and dynamic contrast, through combining and layering the drone patterns.

Essential Contributions by Gunild Keetman

Gunild Keetman's *Rhythmische Übung* is an essential companion book to *Music for Children: Volume 1*. This delightful and treasured book has body percussion compositions sequenced in order of difficulty, starting with only *Patschen* (thigh patting) and progressing through more complex pieces for *Stampfen, Patschen, Klatschen,* and *Schnalzen* (stamp, pat, clap, snap). Each piece can serve as an interlude, an accompaniment, a rondo section, a stand-alone composition, or a pathway and inspiration to new speech and body percussion compositions. Transfers from body percussion to speech, or vice versa, provide another challenge, leading to more composition opportunities.

We turn now to Keetman's *Elementaria: First acquaintance with Orff-Schulwerk* (1970, trans. Murray, 1974). Although *Elementaria* does not address teaching composition directly, Keetman's pedagogical work provides information and helpful directions, leading students through improvisation to composition while supporting the "Instructions and Notes" given in *Music for Children: Volume I, Part Two*. The book serves as an essential handbook and guide to implementing the Orff-Schulwerk teaching process with children. Part One provides a sequence for instruction in developing music notation understanding and skills through rhythmic and melodic exercises (pp. 17–94). This is followed by a single page titled "Hints on the early stages of recorder playing" (p. 95), which reinforces the holistic nature of Schulwerk teaching, suggesting activities combining singing, speech, and movement in a recorder teaching/learning process of imitation, exploration, and improvisation.

Keetman begins *Elementaria, Part Two: Elementary movement training* with a quote from Carl Orff, "Elemental music is never music alone, but forms a unity with movement, dance, and speech" (p. 107). Here we see how children's games and play can develop skills, in an environment where freedom, acceptance and encouragement, self-expression, and independence lead to confidence in making up new music, through playing with sound and movement, and improvisation leading to composition.

As presented in *Music for Children: Volume 1, Part Two, Rhythmische Übung,* and *Elementaria*, Orff Schulwerk composition pedagogy gives students infinite opportunities to practice, explore, improvise, and compose their own music.

ORFF COMPOSITION IN PRACTICE

The following six lessons, by Brian Burnett, shown in Figures 20.2 through 20.7, are based on his understanding and interpretation of the original work of Orff

Objective	Students identify beat, parallel rhythm, and complementary rhythm.
Materials	Assorted 16-beat rhymes using rhythm patterns found in *Rhythmische Übung* (RU) #33 Schott ed. 6359; "Hugh, Hugh" in *Jelly Belly*, by Dennis Lee, Macmillan of Canada; "Rain, Rain, Go Away" traditional bordun accompaniment with melodic improvisations in *Re* Pentatonic on D, D Hexatonic, or D Mixolydian.
Activity	Rhythmic Speech with Body Percussion **Prepare:** ■ Establish a steady beat pat-clap pattern with simultaneous imitation. ■ Lead an eight-beat pattern with simultaneous imitation using the first half of RU #33 with the text "Rain, rain, go away, come again another day." Label the eight beats as a full phrase. Repeat the phrase ending on a pat instead of a clap. *Note: This is parallel rhythm since the text matches the body percussion. Performing one rhythm in two media: speech and movement.* **Present:** ■ Add a 16-beat rhyme by reading from a visual or phrase rote/echo imitation: "Hugh, Hugh" or "Pease Porridge Hot" *Hugh, Hugh at the age of two,* *Built his house in an old brown shoe.* *Hugh, Hugh, what'll you do?* *There's holes in the soles and the rain comes through!* ■ Students speak the rhyme while the teacher performs the ostinato. Then, switch. The teacher may perform both to assist the students if needed. *Note: The rhythmic speech and ostinato have some points of parallel rhythm. Children may fall into playing the rhythm of the speech when there are more than two beats of parallel rhythm in a row.* **Compose:** ■ With the class, create a new ostinato. Divide the group in two. One group performs the rhyme, while the other performs the newly created ostinato. Switch roles. ■ Repeat in small groups (and later with partners). Students select two contrasting hand percussion instruments and use one to represent rhythm of the text. For the other instrument, students create a new ostinato. Students will need time to practice the two ideas together before sharing with the class. **Analyze:** ■ Show a graphic of the two texts with notation above aligned vertically to identify where beats are parallel. Two adjacent beats are fine, but circle where the texts are parallel for more than two. *Hint: Look over the bar lines.* *Differentiated Opportunity: The students may select from two options: steady beat of pat-clap or a student-created ostinato accompaniment.* **Assess:** ■ *Students maintain a steady beat with multiple patterns.* ■ *Students perform the speech and the body percussion together.* ■ *Students' instrument timbre choices are complementary, and parts are discernible.* ■ *Students can identify parallel rhythms.*

FIGURE 20.2. Lesson 1: A Rainy Day

Objective	Students explore dynamics and longer forms through movement and found sounds. Small groups accompany movement of a student conductor.
Materials	Hand drums; rain sticks/boxes of cereal/pasta/rice; cymbals/pot lids/thunder sheet; trash cans; and other sound makers that might contribute to the creation of a musical rainstorm.
Activity	Aleatoric Sound Exploration with Movement, Dynamics, and Form: Creating a Musical Rainstorm

Prepare:
- Discuss the properties of a thunderstorm using story construction icons—beginning, middle, end—and dynamics. *Nature doesn't recognize rhythmic phrase lengths.*
- Have students work in small groups to construct a word list using paper sticky notes. Students might list rain sounds as: drip-drop, pitter-patter, thunder crash, lightning flash, wind, etc. Movement words might include: bending, flashing, flicking, floating, pressing, slashing, spinning, swaying, turning, twisting. One student from each group posts the notes on the wall to create a class "word wall." *Combine duplicates and take a photo for later review.*

Present:
- Movement Exploration: Divide the class into small groups to explore individual movement, unison group movement. Groups create a short form that contrasts unison and individual movement. Students decide how to present the contrasting pieces.
- Each group performs their choreography while the rest of the class improvises an accompaniment with found sounds. Evaluate the effectiveness of the accompaniment to match the movement.

Assess:
- *The players follow the movers.*
- *The energy of the movers demonstrates a clear dynamic contrast.*
- *The range of motion supports the dynamics of the players.*
- *There is a clear beginning, middle, and ending.*

Found Sounds Exploration:
- Students select an instrument to represent vocabulary from the student-created word wall and form small groups based on their instrument and word choices. *The teacher must limit available instruments to those that are grade appropriate and accessible. Students should play the instruments in a safe way with correct technique.*
- Demonstrate gestures to convey start/stop, and dynamics. Select a student to conduct a sound exploration. *Discuss whether the music and movement determine cadences with a resting point.*

Assess:
- *The players follow the conductor.*
- *The conductor demonstrates a clear dynamic contrast.*
- *The players support the energy of the conductor.*
- *There is a clear beginning, middle, and ending.*

Compose:
- Combine movement and sound explorations into larger forms with sections. *Performance may be enhanced through the use of props for movement improvisation: scarves, umbrellas, cardboard lightning and clouds, or puppets of woodland creatures; costumes: raincoats/slickers, rubber boots, rain hats; and staging: cardboard trees, shrubbery.* |

FIGURE 20.3. Lesson 2: Aleatoric Sound Exploration: Creating a Musical Rainstorm

Objective	Students create rhythmic phrases that function as connectors and cadences using elemental building blocks/bricks.
Materials	Building block visuals; *Rhythmische Übung* (RU) #33 Schott ed. 6359
Activity	**Prepare:** ■ Prepare a visual of five building blocks/bricks with symbols or text of your choosing. This could use simple text—"down up, down-up up," "pat clap, pat-clap clap," a rhythm syllable system, or two-line notation. For example: Visual blocks: 1 ta ta, 2 ta-di ta, 3 ta-di ta-di, 4 ta ta-di, 5 ta rest **Present:** ■ Students decode and perform the two-beat building blocks. Identify blocks ending with a strong cadence on a downbeat, and those that serve as a "connector." ■ Perform the first half of RU #33 while the students listen and analyze the patterns used. Students must identify repetition and contrast. ■ Provide a blank graph of a four-measure half phrase. Give three attempts for students to move the building blocks into the phrase visual to notate the given pattern. Have the students check by performing the phrase. **Compose:** ■ Students work alone or with a partner, *"Create an eight-beat phrase using some of the boxes."* New phrases must show both repetition and contrast and may end with a strong cadence on a downbeat, or function as a connector ending with an upbeat. ■ For notating purposes, provide students with small two-line staff building blocks on cards to place in order. Include some blank two-line measures for new patterns. *Use iPads/phones to snap a picture of their work to save for later sharing and grading.* ■ Check for phrases that have an elemental form. A memory cue could be *"They (the blocks) can't be all the same and they can't be everything different."* In other words, an elemental phrase form cannot be "aaaa," or "abcd." *Note: Phrase forms are always labeled with lower-case letters based on outline form. Full phrases use capital letters and larger sections use upper-case Roman numerals.* **Perform** ■ Students perform their phrase twice to give the listeners time to understand their form. *"It's so nice, I want to hear it twice!"* ■ Perform an expanded Rondo form as needed: A (rhyme alone, or just the last line to save time), BCD... (group sharing). ■ If time permits, have students transfer their patterns to two contrasting hand percussion instruments. Create a longer form with: *"Say it, then play it."* *Assess:* ■ *Students can create eight-beat phrases in an elemental form showing both repetition and contrast.* ■ *Students can analyze building blocks for possible function.* ■ *Students can label phrases for function: connector/cadence.* ■ *Students can accurately transfer rhythmic syllables to hand percussion.*

FIGURE 20.4. Lesson 3: Rhythmic Building Blocks

Objective	Students create a complementary speech ostinato to accompany a metric poem. Identify types of metric poetry with simple or compound rhythm. *Takadimi syllables are used in these examples. Any common system may be substituted.*
Materials	Copy of "Rig-a-Jig Jig." (This version of "Rig-a-Jig Jig" is found in McGraw-MacMillian's *Share the Music*, Grade 1, ISBN-13: 978-0022950507.)
Activity	**Speech Ostinati with Poetry** *Note on Doubling Games: "Doubling" is one of four strategies for addition in first grade. The game allows children to listen and observe before jumping in.* Prepare: ■ Engage children in a movement doubling game in a large space. ■ Children sit in large circle while the teacher sings and walks to the beat. Before the rhythm-change cue, "hi-o, hi-o, hi-o," select a partner to rise and join both hands to gallop around the perimeter with the second half of the song. ■ Repeat song with the teacher and the old partner walking to each find new partners. Continue doubling until the whole class is engaged. *Some students may pat to simulate walking and galloping if necessary. The two sections provide both simple and compound rhythm experience in a meter of two. This is a rhythm change, not a meter change. "To dot, or not to dot? That is the question." The meter is still two with a walking or galloping feel. The adult mind may perceive compound rhythm as 6/8 time, but this is an adult cognitive construct beyond elemental style for younger children.* Present: ■ Demonstrate rhythm syllables for the poetry students will be exploring. *Limit to compound or simple rhythm for any given lesson work. Much of our English poetry is in compound rhythm. This lesson will feature poetry normally spoken in compound rhythm. Prosody is the natural intonation and rhythm of language. An example:*

Let's go!	rig-a-jig jig	jig and-a jig and-a-	way we go a-	Hurry! Go!
ta-ta	ta-ki-da ta	ta-ki-da ta-ki-da	ta—da ta—da,	ta-ki ta

FIGURE 20.5. Lesson 4: Speech Ostinati

- Echo rhythm from the game with syllables to identify two-beat building blocks on visuals of the text:

- Students sort the building blocks by function with manipulatives for each pair of students where possible. Does the building block land on a downbeat to create a cadence, or an upbeat to create a connector.
- Students create four-beat half phrases with syllable cards. *"Say it, then play it."* Students transfer the patterns to hand percussion that can be played with two hands.
- Add a visual of stick notation after students are secure working with syllables. *Speech competency must proceed visual decoding.*

Compose:
- Select speech rhythms from sample poems and transfer to syllables. Students explore and list other words that would fit the theme of the poem. Identify whether the words can stand alone or need a partner to make a new building block. Sort these by function: connector/cadence.
- Students work with a partner to create a four-beat ostinato to accompany a poem. *Check for elongation of any text. If using a direct quote of text from the poem, the rhythm must remain the same.*
- Students work in partners or in small groups to perform the ostinati with poem with partners to check for parallel rhythm.
- Check for more than two consecutive beats of parallel rhythm. If present, *"slide it, flip it, or put in a rest"* to fix the parallels of more than two beats. *Note: The issue of parallel rhythm is only for the composition stage and not improvisation. "There is no rule in elemental music forbidding parallels in improvisation. Such rules would stifle the creative flow; besides, they are meaningless to a beginning student, regardless of age"* (Warner, p. 138).
- Transfer the poem and ostinato to contrasting hand percussion. Create a longer form by saying then playing.

Assessment criteria:
- *Students can accurately identify compound and simple rhymes.*
- *The ostinato is complementary to the poem. There are no more than two consecutive beats of parallel rhythm.*
- *The ostinato text has good prosody. There are no elongated text and the word stress matches the rhythm of the poem.*
- *Students can accurately transfer rhythmic syllables to hand percussion.*
- *Instrument timbre choices are complementary so that the parts are discernible.*

FIGURE 20.5. Continued

and Keetman, as found in *Music for Children: Volume I, Rhythmische Übung*; and *Elementaria*. Burnett's lessons demonstrate how composition pedagogy in the Schulwerk is integrated within the teaching process. Students learn to focus their imagination while playing with speech, movement, singing, and playing instruments, using small musical elements. Through play, the art of composition is prepared and realized. The sequence of each lesson plan is flexible based on the media being used and the experience of the students in the class. Exploration of the

Objective	Individual students create melodic improvisations using known melodic patterns on barred instruments.
Materials	Copy of "Rain, Rain, Go Away" and *Rhythmische Übung* (RU) #33 Schott ed. 6359.

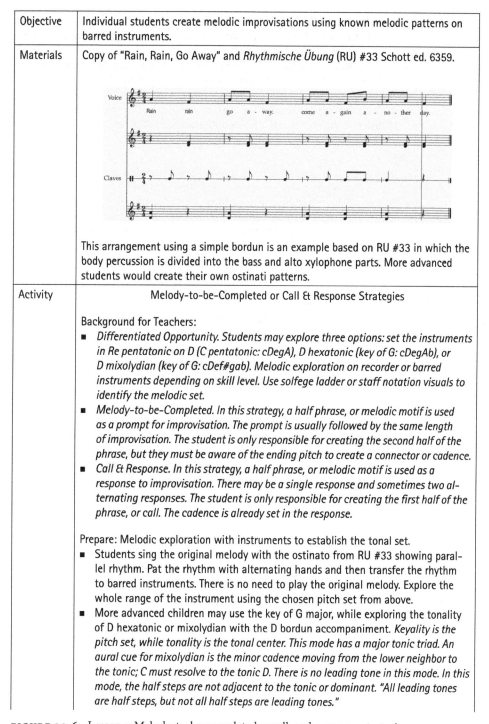

This arrangement using a simple bordun is an example based on RU #33 in which the body percussion is divided into the bass and alto xylophone parts. More advanced students would create their own ostinati patterns.

Activity	Melody-to-be-Completed or Call & Response Strategies

Background for Teachers:
- *Differentiated Opportunity. Students may explore three options: set the instruments in Re pentatonic on D (C pentatonic: cDegA), D hexatonic (key of G: cDegAb), or D mixolydian (key of G: cDef#gab). Melodic exploration on recorder or barred instruments depending on skill level. Use solfege ladder or staff notation visuals to identify the melodic set.*
- *Melody-to-be-Completed. In this strategy, a half phrase, or melodic motif is used as a prompt for improvisation. The prompt is usually followed by the same length of improvisation. The student is only responsible for creating the second half of the phrase, but they must be aware of the ending pitch to create a connector or cadence.*
- *Call & Response. In this strategy, a half phrase, or melodic motif is used as a response to improvisation. There may be a single response and sometimes two alternating responses. The student is only responsible for creating the first half of the phrase, or call. The cadence is already set in the response.*

Prepare: Melodic exploration with instruments to establish the tonal set.
- Students sing the original melody with the ostinato from RU #33 showing parallel rhythm. Pat the rhythm with alternating hands and then transfer the rhythm to barred instruments. There is no need to play the original melody. Explore the whole range of the instrument using the chosen pitch set from above.
- More advanced children may use the key of G major, while exploring the tonality of D hexatonic or mixolydian with the D bordun accompaniment. *Keyality is the pitch set, while tonality is the tonal center. This mode has a major tonic triad. An aural cue for mixolydian is the minor cadence moving from the lower neighbor to the tonic; C must resolve to the tonic D. There is no leading tone in this mode. In this mode, the half steps are not adjacent to the tonic or dominant. "All leading tones are half steps, but not all half steps are leading tones."*

FIGURE 20.6. Lesson 5: Melody-to-be-completed or call-and-response strategies

	Present: ■ Provide a graphic of the text and place letter names or solfege over the words for the prompt "Rain, rain, go away." ■ Students play the half phrase prompt of the melody and "air play" the remaining text. Prepare scale-wise motion or smaller three-pitch motifs (i.e. so-la-mi, mi-re-do) for exploration. ■ Divide the class so that half plays the prompt and the other improvises a half phrase to complete the melody. Standard practice has the text appear under the notation.
	Improvise: ■ Task students with creating two improvisations in a circle game: the first ends with a connector and the second creates a strong cadence. ■ Five or six children sit in a circle. Children sing the song while the first leader tosses a bean bag to a friend to play the improvisation either on a recorder, or a barred instrument in the circle. Everyone in the circle provides the prompt or ending response. ■ If the student is successful, they earn a point or token for the entire team. Repeat the song and toss the bean bag to a new leader. *Assessment criteria for Re pentatonic:* ■ *If using Melody-to-be-Completed strategy, the phrases alternate between connector and cadence. In Call & Response strategy the cadence is already set.* ■ *Improvisations present all five pitches of the pentatonic scale.* ■ *Improvisations establish the 're-la' bordun as the tonal center.* ■ *Improvisations include a minor cadence even though 're' pentatonic has no triad.* *Assessment criteria for Hexatonic or Mixolydian:* ■ *If using Melody-to-be-Completed strategy, the phrases alternate between connector and cadence. In Call & Response strategy the cadence is already set.* ■ *Improvisations present all six pitches of the hexatonic scale.* ■ *Improvisations present a major tonic triad or pentachord as the tonal center.* ■ *Improvisation include a minor cadence to signal mixolydian.*

FIGURE 20.6. Continued

material may come before the students discover the objective. These lessons may be adapted for use with any grade level. Teachers should consider factors such as experience, frequency of instruction, age appropriateness of material, and time for the lesson. The key experiential focus of each lesson is on student involvement and creativity.

Reflections on the *Rainy Day* Sequence of Lessons

Is Orff's vision of a music created *by* children really possible? Wolfgang Hartman (2000) states that "it will consist of a form of music-making that remains at the level of play, and

Objective	Students work with partners to create movement that shows contrast through body facing, group relationship, and/or individual versus unison movement. *This is related to the previous lesson on "Rain, Rain, Go Away."*
Materials	Additional poetry options: *Rain.* Robert Louis Stevenson (1850-1895). *Rain On the Green Grass.* Anon. *Slip On Your Raincoat.* Anon. *Who Likes The Rain?* Clara Doty Bates (1838-1895). *April Rain Song* – Langston Hughes (1902-1967). *I Like to See a Thunder Storm* – Elizabeth Coatsworth (1893-1986).
Activity	Using Movement to Explore the Relationship of Ideas Prepare: ■ Using group formations, movement shapes, and gestures, students explore various body facing relationships with a partner. ■ Change group relations or formation: random, lines, circle, double circle, squares of four. ■ Students incorporate body facing changes: front-to-front, side-to-side, back-to-back, side-to-back, etc. Present: ■ Discuss wood nymphs or woodland animal characteristics for thematic context with visuals or poetry. Students develop a word list of possible movement gestures. *Pantomime is the art of conveying emotions, actions, and thoughts by gestures without speech.* Compose ■ Divide the class into small groups to explore individual movement versus unison group movement using mirroring and exact copy. ■ Small groups of students create a short AB form. Establish a phrase length using a hand drum or wood block. ■ Provide time for small groups to discuss and evaluate their work based on the assessment criteria. Perform ■ Each group performs their choreography for the class when ready. *Possible costumes: matching-colored T-shirts with paper face masks.* Assess: ■ *Choreography presents a form through contrast.* ■ *Gestures suggest appropriate thematic characteristics matching movement words.* ■ *Students demonstrate multiple body facing changes.* ■ *Students change group formation or relationship.*

FIGURE 20.7. Lesson 6: Using movement to explore the relationship of ideas

in which the acquiring of technical skills is of less importance than in the traditional realm of the Orff approach" (p. 94). This manner of thinking about Orff's composition pedagogy conceives the role of the teacher as one of providing the environment and a stimulus, perhaps a story, a word, a poem, a piece of art, or something from nature, with space, materials, and a variety of sound makers, not limited to traditional instruments. The class time (play time) must strike a balance—it is not the freedom of "anything goes" but requires a high degree of preparation by the teacher, who must be a great listener, with the attitude and skill of making suggestions. Students explore, experiment, collaborate and communicate in small groups, make up and try out ideas, discarding and refining.

Take another look at the lessons and allow your imagination to flow beyond the words on the page. Is student creativity encouraged in a variety of ways throughout the lessons? Do you see how the framework and sequence could be implemented for different ages with appropriate choice of materials? What elements are suitable for all ages? Are there elements or activities you would change or adapt to fit your own situation? Music teachers who integrate the Orff approach typically ask questions like these as they work with students and grow as teachers. Along with questions and reflection, imagination, creativity, improvisation, and composition are central to the work.

OTHER INTERPRETATIONS OF ORFF-SCHULWERK COMPOSITION PEDAGOGY

Approaching Composition Through Recorder Playing

One pathway to understanding the Orff Schulwerk pedagogy of composition is through the work of Isabel Carley, composer, teacher, editor, and author of *Recorder Improvisation and Technique, Books 1–3* (Carley, 2011). All aspects of the Orff approach are presented in each book, with sequential lessons clearly laid out for the teacher/learner, and composition is clearly part of the process from the beginning. Recorder playing progresses as skills in reading and writing music develop organically, with students learning to notate music they create and want to save. The Carley approach to teaching recorder is unique in its emphasis on making up music as part of learning to play the instrument.

Book One of the Carley series is for soprano recorder. The students begin by making music through listening, improvisation, singing, and then playing songs, first using only two pitches. Ensemble materials include layering of rhythmic patterns with body percussion, barred instruments, and hand percussion. The resulting music is both simple and complex, and therefore challenging and interesting. Still using only two pitches, students echo patterns played by the teacher and then make up new patterns, playing an echo game with other students. With melodies using only two pitches, the students have immediately started on the pathway to making and understanding music through improvisation and composition. *Book Two*, for alto recorder, approaches mastery of the instrument with more complex material, while still emphasizing improvisation and composition.

Book Three is sub-titled "Advanced-Composing, Arranging, Analysis." Students who have proficiency with soprano and alto recorder (C and F fingerings) could start with this book. Carley has synthesized the work of Orff and Keetman, gained when she studied composition with Carl Orff in Austria. In this book she shares her deep understanding of Orff-Schulwerk, with the goal of inspiring the creativity of each student to compose original music.

Elemental Style: Theoretical Understanding of Orff's Composition Pedagogy

What does it mean to compose in Orff's "elemental style?" This chapter has addressed the question through a brief summary of the history leading to the publication of works by Carl Orff and Gunild Keetman, followed by a detailed outline of the basic principles presented in the original volumes, and practical teaching examples of how the theory and philosophy have been interpreted by teachers and students. As Orff-Schulwerk has expanded throughout music education in the U.S. and the world, teachers and students continue to explore, experiment, and create with the elemental style envisioned by Orff as the foundation of their teaching and learning. Publication of *The elemental style: A handbook for composers and arrangers* (Cribari & Layton 2019) provides a rich and essential resource for teachers interested in deeper exploration. The book will be most meaningful and useful for music teachers who have completed, or are currently enrolled in, Orff Levels courses.

Extensions and Adaptations of Orff's Composition Pedagogy

Evidence of the adaptability of Orff-Schulwerk composition pedagogy is an indication of how the approach has evolved through time, involving transfer of the basic principles to other areas of music-making and music education. A few of the many extensions and adaptations, listed in Figure 20.8, are in the areas of curriculum, jazz, late 20th century compositional styles, and world music.

- Curriculum: *Artful, Playful, Mindful: A New Curriculum for Music Making and Music Thinking,* Frazee (2012).
- Jazz: *Now's the Time: Teaching Jazz to All Ages,* Goodkin (2004).
- Late 20th century compositional styles: *Sound Alert: Diversity for Ears and Minds,* Bond (2000).
- World Music: *Orff Schulwerk: Brief History, Description, and Issues in Global Dispersal,* Shamrock, (1995).

FIGURE 20.8. Modern adaptations of Orff-Schulwerk

CONCLUDING THOUGHTS ABOUT COMPOSITION PEDAGOGY IN ORFF-SCHULWERK

Music teachers who experience an Orff class or workshop for the first time are often amazed by the creative process of elemental music-making. It starts with simple rhythmic elements drawn from speech and movement, building phrases through combining short motives and patterns, adding texture through layering, moving from exploration to improvisation, and culminating with extended musical composition. The results can be magical, building artistry and musicality, and bringing participants of any age together in a joyful community of music-makers through singing, saying, dancing, and playing instruments. The elemental approach of Orff-Schulwerk is profound in its simplicity, enabling adaptation of the structure and process to any culture or style of music.

Beyond the scope of this brief look at composition pedagogy in Orff-Schulwerk is the larger picture of Orff's philosophy of holistic education with music and movement at the center. At the opening of the Orff Institute in Salzburg, Austria, in 1963, Orff spoke about challenges in education, including stimulating the imagination, emotional development, and awakening "powers of the spirit" (Orff, 1977, p. 8). Over 50 years later, the same challenges are before us, and the elemental approach of the Orff-Schulwerk philosophy is an open door inviting those who are motivated and encouraged to take the risk of making up their own music through imagination, exploration, and creativity.

NOTES

1. *Every Mornin' When I Wake Up*, words and music by AVON GILLESPIE ©1976 (Renewed) BELWIN-MILLS PUBLISHING CORP., a Division of ALFRED MUSIC. All rights reserved. Used by Permission of ALFRED MUSIC.
2. Avon Gillespie (1938–1989) was a highly respected and beloved teacher of Orff-Schulwerk. His canon "Every mornin' when I wake up" has inspired many teachers and students around the globe. For more information about Avon, his teaching, his compositions, and his understanding of Orff-Schulwerk, see www.AOSA.org, Distinguished Service Award 2017.
3. For example, see *The way to start a day*, (1976, 77, 78), by Byrd Baylor, illustrated by Peter Parnall. Copyright under the Berne Convention. This book inspires the imagination through images of people from different times and places who greet the sun and celebrate the coming of the day.
4. The music was *Einzug und Reigen*, Schott Edition 3564.
5. The original five volumes of *Orff-Schulwerk: Musik für Kinder*, in German, were published from 1950 to 1954 by B. Schott's Söhne, Mainz.

REFERENCES

Bond, J. (2000). *Sound alert: diversity for ears and minds.* In A. deQuadros (Ed.), *Many seeds, different flowers: The music education legacy of Carl Orff* (pp. 19–27). Callaway International Resource Centre for Music Education.

Carley, I. M. (2011). *Recorder Improvisation and Technique* (2nd ed., Books 1–3). Brasstown Press.

Cribari, P. B., & Layton, R. D. (2019). *The elemental style: A handbook for composers and arrangers* (Pt. 1). Sweet Pipes Publishing.

Frazee, J. (2012). *Artful-mindful-playful: A new Orff-Schulwerk curriculum for music making and music thinking.* Schott Music.

Goodkin, D. (2004). *Now's the time: Teaching jazz to all ages.* Pentatonic Press.

Hartmann, W. (2000). *Creative playgrounds: Music by children.* In A. deQuadros (Ed.), *Many seeds, different flowers: The music education legacy of Carl Orff* (pp. 94–99). Callaway International Resource Centre for Music Education.

Keetman, G. (1970). *Rhythmische Übung.* Schott.

Keetman, G. (1974). *Elementaria: First acquaintance with Orff-Schulwerk.* London: Schott & Co. Translated from *Elementaria: Erster Umgang mit dem Orff-Schulwerk*, by M. Murray, 1970. Ernst Klett Verlag.

Keller, W. (1954; revised edition 1963). English translation by Susan Kennedy, 1970. Introduction to music for children. B. Schott's Sohne.

Lee, D. (2001). *Jelly Belly.* Macmillan: Garders Books.

Orff, C. (1977). Orff-Schulwerk: Past & future. In I. McNeill Carley (Ed.), *Re-Echoes.* American Orff-Schulwerk Association, 10–17.

Orff, C. (1978). *The Schulwerk, Carl Orff/documentation, his life and works (Vol. 3).* (M. Murray, Trans.). Schott Music.

Orff, C., & Keetman, G. (1957). *Music for children: Volume I.* (English adaptation by M. Murray). Schott & Co. Ltd.

Shamrock, M. (1995). *Orff-Schulwerk: Brief history, description, and issues in global dispersal.* American Orff-Schulwerk Association.

Warner, B. (1991). *Orff-Schulwerk: Applications for the classroom.* Prentice Hall.

SECTION V

NURTURING YOUNG COMPOSERS

....

CHAPTER 21

HOW TRANSDISCIPLINARY AND IMPROVISATIONAL CREATIVITIES CAN NURTURE YOUNG COMPOSERS AND TEACHERS AS CONFIDENT "MAKERS"

....

PAMELA BURNARD AND CAROLYN COOKE

In this chapter we (a) challenge a monodisciplinary perspective on composing, (b) dismantle the myth that composing is a solitary act, and (c) make explicit how teachers and student teachers can become confident music composition pedagogues. We explore *transdisciplinary and improvisational creativities* that challenge individualistic views of composing. We present a way to re-see young composers and teachers as entangled in material and embodied processes where they are *makers with* each other and the world.

We expand the concept of improvisational creativity from the usual understanding within the music discipline to a transdisciplinary creativity—that is, humans and non-humans pushing outward generatively to create different relationships between child, teacher, materials, and environments. Transdisciplinary creativity seeks to decouple the specific language of a discipline from its original context to open-up new possibilities for *making and becoming makers/composers*. This process may begin as a "dialogue" across disciplines in compositional/making practices. Here we present ideas developed from the analysis of two sequences of making, one involving a young composer and one involving student teachers.

Drawing on a study by Alecia Youngblood Jackson (2016) that explores the ontology of the backflip as a movement of both the greatest potential, and the greatest danger (p. 191), we take these formidable modes of musical creativity and re-see composition as "an experiment in contact with the real" where "experiment" is considered "an analytic adventure" and "real" is "more or less the process of how something is moved through" (p. 184). This repositions transdisciplinary creativity and improvisational creativity (i.e., these diverse creativities) as a potential-filled meeting between teachers, students, and the world, where movement, the body and response are seen as critical. We therefore offer you, the reader, generative points of departure for rethinking how we learn music composing and develop composition pedagogy. We invite you to engage with our ideas, images, and examples, to positively re-affirm and to rethink critically the roles and responsibilities (and response-abilities) of composers and composing, of teachers and students, and of our relationships with each other and the world.

Several studies on composition pedagogy in music education research suggest teachers are insufficiently knowledgeable about and lack confidence in composing (Burnard & Younker, 2004). For example, Strand's (2006) survey of composition practices in public schools across the state of Indiana highlighted a lack of a unified definition of composition and composing among teachers and researchers, which might exacerbate this issue. There is also overwhelming evidence of a lack of professional development in this area, suggesting the problem may be more deep-rooted (Collins, 2012; Waddington-Jones, King, & Burnard, 2019; Burnard, 2012a and 2012b; Devaney, 2018 and 2019). Perceiving *how* teachers act, understand and nurture young composers helps to fill the gap in the current literature.

The etymology of *com-position* where "com" has developed from the Latin meaning with or together, points us toward a retelling of composing as embedded in notions of community, where coming together with others, and being open to the differences that are created as a result, challenges the hegemony of Western art music.

So, what are learners' and teachers' understandings of the enactment and nature of composing? How can we explode the "myth" of the "isolated genius" composer by accepting that composing occurs in a multiplicity of social spaces in which the contexts give and incorporate a multiplicity of authorings? And finally, what can transdisciplinary and improvisational creativities contribute to the dismantling of dominant discourses and myths about what, who and where composers are and what they do?

In this chapter, we will explore some assumptions that underpin the concept and act, enactment, and experience of "music composition." We will explore how and why myth making is at work when composing is seen as a solitary act (and enactment) and how teachers and student teachers can become confident music composition pedagogues and nurture young composers by using *transdisciplinary and improvisational creativities*. As such, and to this end, we will examine the materiality of the performative "practice of practice" of composing (Britzman, 2003), which is not about representations of "reality" but rather a material articulation of the world (Barad, 2007, p. 139).

INTERROGATING MYTHS AT WORK IN COMPOSING: REVISING RESPONSE-ABILITIES

While there is no universally agreed definition of composition, most teachers and researchers distinguish between various types of practices. There are *contemporary classical composers* whose compositional creativity is guided by principles of genre mastery, genre traditions, and artistic originality. In contrast, there are *turntablist (DJ) composers* whose practice calls into question conventional understandings of the interplay between innovative sampling, audiences, and constructed socio-spatial principles. Then there are *audio or sound designers* and *film or game music composers* who work in industries where priority is given to team collaboration and technological innovation. For the most part, however, the diversity of these sites, discourses and practices of composition is anchored in cultural appropriations (for professional enactments and ends), co-optations (often for economic enactments and ends) and ideologies (for neoliberalized educational enactments and ends).

Myth-making is reinforced by public images promoting gendered, classed, and racialized notions of those who are considered, for instance, famous scientists and mathematicians, composers, and conductors. Myths are of great significance in music education. They create binaries, separating us with "yes-no" relations: yes, you are musical, you are creative, you have talent to compose, you measure up, or no, you do not. Myths also generate a version of humanism grounded in a domination by one sector of society "in accordance with its god-given civilizing mission" (Taylor & Hughes, 2016, p. 8). Myths about musical creativity tell a story and function to divide us into mutually opposed groupings of those who can and cannot compose.

When we think of a composer, we think of Wolfgang Amadeus Mozart, the famous composer and child prodigy; a classic instance of "genius." This myth and metaphor of genius is directly at odds with the notion of child makers. Children, as makers in music, are often "hidden"—only "becoming composers" once well up the mythical and metaphoric ladder. Similarly, most people think they are not composers or "not really very creative or musical," as sociologist Lucy Green (1988) argued over 30 years ago:

> Classical music has in fact maintained a hegemonic position of cultural superiority ever since the Enlightenment. Ideology immanently ratifies and maintains the dominance of an elite musical institution that, along with its reified products, is made to seem superior: and it does so by propagating the appearance that there is a musical mass which, along with its profane products, is not really very musical. (p. 2)

In the face of widening inequality and hegemonic positioning of cultural superiority, these views of dominance, division, and difference between us (as students, teachers) and them (as composers) manifests in significant ways in how we conceptualize and enact composition teaching.

In her PhD thesis on attitudes toward and practices of composing in schools in England, Birmingham-based composer and music educator Kirsty Devaney (2018) notes that 92.8% of teachers surveyed believed that some people have a natural aptitude for composing. Her work also revealed other associated myths and metaphors including that the term "composition" rarely if ever relates to the work of students and teachers, and that composing is a profession or job that is unrelated to other acts of musical creativities such as song writing, DJing, or experimenting with music creation apps. This separation, Devaney (2018) notes, can in some part be explained by the term's association with Western art music composition. It is part of the mythology that Lydia Goehr (1994) writes about in her seminal book *The imaginary museum of musical works*, where she critiques the composition, performance, and reception of classical music and how the concept of a "musical work" fully crystallized around 1800, and subsequently defined the norms, expectations, and behavioral patterns that have come to characterize classical musical practice.

In addition to myths about who or what counts as composition, there are also associated myths about the processes of becoming and being a composer. While "natural aptitude" and the notion of the child genius shape a particular narrative around being able to compose or not, the teaching of composition can take on what Philpott (2020, p. 51) calls a "conservationist creative process." This type of approach situates creativity against a backdrop of selected traditions and cultures, where individual expression is confined within pre-planned structures and languages. This can manifest in technical approaches to teaching composition, the notion of a "toolbox" of techniques that need to be mastered, and a focus on replication or stylistic imitation as compositional learning (Devaney, 2018). As Philpott (2020) argues, the conservationist approach to composition raises significant questions: "Whose culture? Whose traditions? Whose creativity?" (p. 55).

Dismantling these myths, particularly for teachers of composing in school settings, is a complex business. Images, language, and material environments keep these myths active and powerful. However, transdisciplinary and improvisational creativities offer different ways to use images, language, and environments to trouble the myths and forge new ways of being and doing. They offer a different relationship with materials and environments that generate different conceptualizations of a composer. The composer is no longer seen as alone, arising from seemingly nowhere, with a brilliant mind/ear and a toolkit of techniques at the ready, but instead is reconceptualized as a maker, *making with* materials, bodies, and sounds. This reconceptualization challenges not only how we think of composers and the composition process, but also how composers learn to become, the role of teachers in this process, and the relationships that are involved.

Reflecting on what makes a "creative musician" or a composer involves commitment to looking anew at things as they are, giving form to the idea that traditions are continually changing. Reflecting on what makes for "creative teaching" in relation to "creative learning" is only part of understanding and developing innovative practices in higher music education.

Music teachers must be creative teachers and make a conscious effort to develop both compositional and improvisational expertise. This means seeing risk-taking and learning through mistakes as effective educational practices that create improvisatory spaces and freedom for creativity. It requires a new form of relational expertise, where composing is repositioned as entangled in community partnerships, in the very broadest of senses. Ensuring that these partnerships lead to well-designed and collaborative practices may depend upon identifying who has the power over decision-making in composition.

WHY DO POSTHUMANIST TRANSDISCIPLINARY CREATIVITIES MATTER?

Late-20th-century creativity discourses in education remained, for the most part, limited by singular and individual humanist notions of creativity, such as "teaching creatively" or "teaching for creativity" (Jeffrey & Craft, 2006), "creative thinking" (Lucas & Spencer, 2017), or "creative pedagogies" (Cremin & Chappell, 2019). This includes scholarship in specific fields such as music creativity, mathematics creativity, scientific creativity, artistic creativity, computing creativity, and cross-cutting interdisciplinary and transdisciplinary creativities.

Some innovations toward more "transdisciplinary creativities" (where sciences and arts meet, where technology often plays a valuable role in crossing cultural and disciplinary boundaries in music), including those framed through the lens of STEAM (Burnard & Colucci-Gray, 2020), have helped diversify understandings and appreciation of multiplicities of creativities in education contexts. While transdisciplinarity deterritorializes creative practices and generates new ways in which musical composition can entangle with other disciplines to make new creations, posthumanism re-sees the potential of more-than-human elements within this compositional process. Shifting away from notions of materials as inert, waiting to be manipulated by human skill and control (Ingold, 2009) toward materials as active "ontological heterogeneous partners" (Haraway, 2016, p. 17), engaging with us in "materialdiscursive" practices of becoming together, where we deliberately engage in how material entanglements make a difference to the realities of practices, (Murris, 2016, pp. 6–7) challenges Western art music and educational myths about composing. This is particularly the case where compositional pedagogies focus on epistemic outcomes or compositional products as evidence of learning, commensurate with other "academic" subjects, rather than experiential, making, and exploratory/generative activity. Such generative activity does not begin and end with the human subject but includes and often features more-and-other-than-human worlds.

The 21st century and its provocations of rapid development of artificial intelligence and machine learning, alongside the accelerator of COVID-19, have produced an opportunity for seriously reconsidering the interconnectedness of practices, places, relationships, and processes that we have traditionally considered as music composition. Like Grosz (2008) we include it, along with music, dance, and performance as forms and conditions associated with the invention/creation and pedagogies of composition. It is time for something new. Posthumanist theory offers what some are calling a paradigm-shifting move toward *thinking with nature* in ways that can embed *sustainability and eco-awareness* in a new generation. By adopting posthumanism's core beliefs of *decentering the human* from its pre-eminent position in the hierarchy of planetary beings, matter, and needs, pedagogues and practitioners of music composition have the opportunity to rethink whether there is something more to "composing" music and "composing" in the general sense that might enable a surprising and provocative outcome. The interdisciplinary (and transdisciplinary) possibilities constitute a radical assault on the very notion of "composing" through a lens of *making with*, becoming with, and experiencing with, rather than "teaching" or "learning" as separate activities.

While posthumanist theory has expanded into multiple disciplines since the start of the 21st century (see, e.g., Braidotti, 2013; Braidotti & Bignall, 2018), others have applied the lens of posthumanism to early childhood and primary education contexts and investigations (e.g., Somerville & Powell, 2019). Karen Murris's (2016) seminal book *The Posthuman Child* shifts our focus from a "Western 'adultlike' knowledge basis for figurations of child as deficient (innocent, vulnerable, needy) to 'child as rich, resilient, and resourceful' " (Murris, 2016, p. 177). Kerry Chappell (2018) has introduced us to the notion of *posthumanizing creativity*. She acknowledges that, with the passage of time, and the deepening of an "emergent ethical" understanding of ecological sustainability, we need to recognize the "other-than-human actants" with whom we collaborate (2018, p. 286).

In a new book on posthumanizing creativities in practice, Burnard (forthcoming) offers an assemblage of inter- and transdisciplinary configurations and types of authorship of music that shake up the routine logic through which we conceptualize music creativity. She finds manifestations of diverse creativities that, not surprisingly, reveal a special fascination with a collective assembly (mix and muddle) of human and non-human interactions that cross the boundary between people and things. These interactions also challenge bifurcations in knowledge (and musical genres) such as those related to subject-object, classical-pop and nature-culture. As Stengers (2010) argues, ecology is the "science of multiplicities" and

> the field of ecological questions is one where the consequences of the meanings we create, the judgments we produce and to which we assign the status of "fact," concerning what is primary and what is secondary, must be addressed immediately, whether those consequences are intentional or unforeseen. (pp. 34–35)

IMPROVISATIONAL WAYS OF BEING:
MAKING WITH OTHERS

Posthumanism's challenge to decenter the human, to see ourselves as *making with* and becoming with collective assemblages, requires us to reconsider the nature of relationships in composition, how we are with others (human, and more and other than human), and how they are with us. Improvisational creativities give us a structural metaphor, a language, and ways of being, which allow us to challenge the myths of composer as genius, as self-made, and as having a toolbox of techniques and skills. They reposition a human as one of many who are involved in the processes of making. They ask us to reposition ourselves and be responsive in the moment to what we are *making with*, whether as "teacher-makers" or "student-makers." Improvisatory ways of being include us in:

- horizontal, non-hierarchical positioning of others in relation to self through shared responses and mutual support (Ross, 2014; Saladin, 2009; Giacomelli, 2012)
- the simultaneous creation and execution of plans—a conflation of process and product (Ross, 2014)
- the constant investigation in the moment of materials for their potential (Prevost, 2009)
- an openness to what will happen, accepting it for itself, staying alert to the here and now (Saladin, 2009)
- a collective dimension—group improvisation as a vehicle to probe the limits of acceptable conventions (Ross, 2014).

These improvisatory ways of being with others and *making with* others (whether human, sonic or material) shift our attention, our gaze (Masschelein, 2010) away from individualist humanism and monodisciplinary views of making to something more entangled, more together (in com-posing) and more "lived." This resonates with Nardone's (1996) notion that the lived experience of improvisation is a coherent synthesis of the body and mind engaged in socially valued conscious activity.

The emergence of improvisational forms of creative teaching, of incorporating creativities into university pedagogy classes, and of integrating creativity into the program of study for instrumental music teaching is a challenge for university teacher practice. It requires a shift in the paradigm of higher music education. Bennett Reimer (2003), a philosopher and influential advocate for music education, insists on the democratization of creativity, in both teaching and learning, as this allows it to be something all people have to some degree. He shows how creative teaching links to the co-construction of creative learning:

> Such a view of creativity as existing in degree, and as constituted of particular, identifiable ways of dealing with one's world, *provides a role for education*. Whatever the

level of one's capacity to be creative at something, that level can be better achieved by educational interventions designed to improve one's thinking and doing so as to make them "more creative." (pp. 108–109, emphasis added)

In higher music education settings, when teachers and learners collaborate, their different conceptions of teaching and different paradigms of expertise must be resolved before they can construct an effective creative learning environment. Creative teaching represents the improvisational end of the paradox, while creative learning has been shown to help professional learning communities enliven and loosen up tightly scripted ways of teaching (Burnard & Swann, 2010). As one creative practitioner put it in Maurice Galton's (2010) study on the impact of creative practitioners in schools and classrooms:

> To me being here is about several things. One important thing for me is to look at a different model of working: of the ways artists can work with schools and teachers in a much more collaborative way rather than be expected to come in and deliver and then go away again. And another important thing is with the children. What we are trying to do here is to be a person who responds to ideas that the children are coming up with and then to bring our own practice to share. (p. 365)

So, with improvisation, creative teaching moves flexibly and reflexively between scripted and unscripted moments—a kind of partly improvised and partly choreographed dance. It tends to follow constructivist traditions of learning, in dynamic interaction with all those present as well as the environment and materials available.

Another relevant dimension of improvisation that is often referred to in music and theater is "going with the flow" or "getting in the groove." These skilled performances are based on a high degree of tacit knowledge and practice, like all professional expertise. Improvised behaviors involve ideas that leap to mind and to jazz players' fingers and can be seen in the perceptual responsiveness of the teacher to the students. When teachers and students work and learn creatively together, particularly if they are undertaking digital experiments, creativity and innovation become critical competences and good practices are created. This is a reconfiguration of composing as co-constituted practices of matter, and of symbolic, sociological, material, biological and political forces. This is where we need to (re-)set our sights and pursue the desire to work in more entangled, more potential-filled relationships with humans and more than humans alike.

SUMMARIZING KEY POINTS OF DEPARTURE FOR RETHINKING MUSIC COMPOSITION PEDAGOGY

What are the generative points of departure here? What are our provocations for you, the reader, for rethinking music composition pedagogy that positively re-affirms or rethinks the roles and response-abilities of both teachers and students?

First, we need to ask what constitutes a "music composition" and music composition pedagogies that are culturally diverse and appropriate for early years, primary, and secondary, and further, into higher music education. This remains ambiguous yet particularly relevant to nurturing young composers, who are often hidden, not considered "real" composers. Are they only considered composers when they are able to notate? Does an improvised sonic exploration count? The language is confusing, and it is common for slippage to occur between the terms "teacher creativity," "student creativity," "compositional creativity," and "creative composition." In this chapter, we begin "plugging in" (Deleuze & Guattari, 1987, p. 4) to a continuous process of "making and unmaking" (Jackson & Mazzei, 2013, p. 262), allowing us to dis-assemble and re-assemble classroom narratives on composing. We know that programs that aim to foster, promote, and teach music composition (and compositional creativity) can involve re-imagining new creative ecologies in composing as manifest in creative professional contexts *and* classroom contexts. Programs that bridge the gap between education and real-world creative industries, where composers take risks, engage in imaginative activity, and do things differently, are the most successful (Kinsella & Fautley, 2020; Daubney & Tunmer, 2020; Philpott, 2020).

Second, we need to remind ourselves of the ongoing debates about composition pedagogies such as: (a) *where* the disciplinary specificity creates a binary opposition between performers and composers; (b) *when* creating "what if" questions is vital to engaging students by activating diverse creativities; and (c) *how* teachers and learners co-construct *pedagogy* involving collaboration. The act of teaching can be a collaboration between ideas, values, cultures, and collective histories that inform, shape, and redefine the domain of the 21st-century musician and what might be done differently in the future. The core of composition teaching is acts of making, where materials (physical or sonic), forms, prior experiences, and bodies are set in motion with each other, creating the potential to make new or to make differently. This requires both students and teachers to be makers. They must pay attention to what has been set in motion, what potential emerges as a result, and to be able to respond (sensorially, musically, physically) to this potential in the act of making.

Composing involves a multiplicity of creative authorship practices, modalities, and claims of authority that can be institutionally bound up in the place and space that authorize the particular practice of composing. Some artist-scholars use a more improvisational, open-ended approach in their composing, while others use a more structured style. Evidence from our research with children, student teachers, and teachers illustrates that a shift toward repositioning composition as *making with*, rooted in transdisciplinary, posthumanist, and improvisational ways of being, both challenges the myths around composition and composers, and generates different ways of *making with* children.

For many years the primary and secondary school sectors have employed visiting composers and professional musicians to work in educational partnerships with teachers in schools. The industry knowledge of professional composers (both the "know-how" of composing and "know-what" of composing) provides insights for both learners and teachers about the ability to learn from failure, and about becoming "prod-users" of disciplinary and transdisciplinary knowledge, rather than consumers of teacher knowledge. They challenge intention-directed pedagogies, with their linear routes to declarative and assessable outcomes that are predictable in advance, by creating collaborative explorations of what is possible. In educational research there is a small, but growing, body of research that identifies the pedagogical potential of partnerships led by composers or artists (Burnard & Swann, 2010; Triantafyllaki & Burnard, 2010).

Making *with* as a Transdisciplinary and Improvisational Way of Being and Authoring Change

The term "making" is often linked to a particular narrative currently used in education where it is bound to "Enlightenment" views of knowledge and learning as fixed, declarative, transferable, and ultimately as related to humans, and specifically the brain. These stories often center around three interwoven views of "making":

- *making as a "tool" to achieve understanding* (e.g., by composing a pop song melody students will understand the concept of "home key"),
- *making as a "sound demonstration" of learning* (e.g., their drumming piece showed they understood how to repeat and vary patterns),
- *making as a site of skill development* (e.g., by composing a motif for a character they can develop their skills in manipulating pitch, dynamics, and timbre).

These three views of making in education hold teachers and children in particular relationships, where teachers of composing are providers of suitable materials, spaces, opportunities, and most importantly knowledge to enable the individual student to be successful in composing, either to achieve understanding, demonstrate learning, or develop specific skills. In this way making is separated from the teacher, and the teacher is separated from the materials.

Posthumanism, transdisciplinarity, and improvisation challenge this view of making. Being entangled with and becoming with others (humans or non-humans) becomes an inevitability, where "nothing makes itself; nothing is really autopoietic or self-organizing," (Haraway, 2016, p. 58). Following this view of composing as *making with*, involving reconceptualizing roles, relationships, and forms in composition pedagogy, we offer the following evidence of *making with* experiences with a young composer, and with student teachers. Arising from a combination of a PhD project and lived practices, this evidence is not intended to exemplify or justify a particular approach. Instead, these examples are brought together in conversation with each other and with the arguments of this chapter to afford us the opportunity to "read" these experiences and ideas with each other "to engage aspects of each other in dynamic relationality" (Barad, 2007, p. 93). Diffractively playing (Haraway, 2016) with these experiences is generative. It forges new ways to consider roles, relationships, and forms. Ethical permissions were sought and granted to use the images and report on the experiences.

EVIDENCE OF "COMPOSING" AS "MAKING WITH": NEW ROLES, NEW RELATIONSHIPS, NEW FORMS

Making with Trees

It was a warm day for the north of Scotland. In the wildlife area Gregor started exploring under the hawthorn tree. After a period of climbing, and exploring the holes in the trunk for bugs, he found a stick. He sat on the ground watching the others and stripping the bark off the stick, enjoying the sensation of the very smooth surface he found below. He stated the wood that remained was "shiny new" as he held it up against the tree trunk, which was much rougher. And then he noticed the broken branch low down, just below his knee, which looked different in texture and color. He hit it with his stick. It resonated (Figure 21.1).

He started hitting it rhythmically, moving the stick (now a beater) to different places, exploring the sound. He played with the height and force needed to make the branch below resonate. And then the contrast, the scraping of the tree trunk, and the hitting of the tree trunk, finding no "giving" and no discernible resonance (Figure 21.2).

I picked up another stick, and found a different branch, negotiating through eye contact if it was OK for me to join in. I played with him [Figure 21.3], exploring the beat together, exploring the branch sounds together.

We came to a dramatic finish as he played a rapid "trill" with the stick, and then he had had enough, saw a friend, and joined them to start climbing a tree again.

This biological-botanical-sonic episode of making with materials emerged. It was not planned as we entered the wildlife area. We had no prior intention of making with the trees in this way. It was both "purposeless" and "playful." The trees, the stick and the physical accessibility of the broken branch allowed Gregor to "push out," exploring how the different materials acted, what the different textures and colors "meant" in sonic terms, how the materials changed as he played with them in different ways (peeling the bark, striking them in different ways), how the materials responded to his body (rubbing his palm, leaving bits of bark under his fingernails, bouncing in his hand as it hit the branch), and how he responded to them (changing his stance, raising his arm higher, leaning in toward my tree to hear better).

FIGURE 21.1. Finding a resonance

FIGURE 21.2. Exploring the trunk

FIGURE 21.3. Worlding with

FIGURE 21.4. Something unexpected emerges

Making with Keys

A group of student teachers were asked to get percussion instruments and start improvising together. In the middle of the improvisation, Charlotte, the course leader, reached into her pocket and pulled out a set of keys. She played the very edges of the cymbals with the keys (Figure 21.4), while the rest of the group smiled—something unexpected had emerged into the space. The movement was slow, and careful. There was space and time to watch and consider what was emerging into the improvisation.

As she played louder, pushing the key against the cymbal more strongly, Ana began to react. She looked away as well as showing discomfort on her face, with her mouth opened wide and eyes scrunched tight (Figure 21.5).

I questioned later whether she was really responding only to the sound of the key, or whether the sight of a "non-instrument" playing a musical instrument in this way was "troubling" (Haraway, 2016)—her image of music, of what was acceptable, of what was allowed. This was further explored when Charlotte dropped the keys (Figure 21.6), allowing them to fall off the cymbal and onto the floor.

Ana started to copy, lifting her cymbal up, looking at the floor, and then pretending to drop the cymbal while still holding the strap, but she stopped herself releasing completely (Figure 21.7).

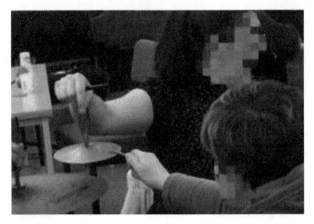

FIGURE 21.5. Annie reacts

FIGURE 21.6. Dropping the keys

For this group of music student teachers, the arrival of the keys into the making space disrupted notions of disciplinary materials. The keys were not intended to be instruments, they had not been chosen from the percussion trolley, and they were not meant to touch the cymbals. However, the students allowed them to continue in the space, they allowed them to generate different ways of being improvisatory, and they explored how the keys "played" with their bodies and other materials. In theatrical improvisation there is a well-known principle called "yes, and" (Johnstone, 1979), where moving the improvisation forward requires those involved to say "yes," accepting what

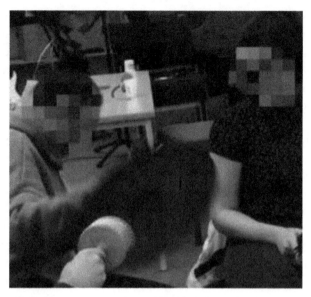

FIGURE 21.7. Pretending to copy

has been offered (in this case the keys) and then "and," involving adding to, developing, and working with what results from that acceptance. In this scenario, Charlotte as the "teacher" pushed the group to accept the keys. She saw the potential in moving across the disciplinary boundaries of what counted as "instruments," creating a transdiciplinary entanglement that was generative. Through the course of the improvisation the keys *became* instruments with the student teachers to the point that when they were dropped it was a moment of shock, so that Ana could not quite bring herself to follow through with the cymbal.

Making New Roles

In both "making with trees" and "making with keys," acceptance of what was being generated in the moment of the making forged new perceptions of who was involved in the process. These changes in perceptions of roles are illuminated by who or what is seen as able to respond (response-able) within the *making with*, and how this ability to respond manifests.

Asking who or what was response-able in "making with trees" disrupts well-trodden conceptions of the child as incapable and powerless (Murris, 2016), where the label of learner denotes a "not-yet" being (Lindgren, 2020). Gregor's response-abilities to make with incorporated the feel of the wood (of the stick and of different parts of the tree), the feel of the vibrations of different textures and resonances that were created, the emotional satisfaction of the more resonant sound, the accepting of the invitation to make with another human, the creation of a rhythm and the playing of that rhythm with another rhythm, and the ability to respond with form through the making of an ending. These response-abilities position Gregor, and children, not as incapable or powerless but as "rich, resourceful and resilient" where they "[e]merge in unbounded materialdiscursive relationships" (Murris, 2016, p. 184). This shift re-sees children, not as "yet-to-become" composers, but as already young *makers with*, intra-acting (Barad 2007, p. 141) with their socio-audio-material worlds in processes of action *with and between* each other. This view of the young as *makers with* is inherently transdisciplinary, engaged already in exploring the world not only from a disciplinary perspective, but crossing and reaching out as "able materialdiscursive meaning-makers and problem-posers" (Murris, 2016, p. 200).

However, "making with trees" does more than re-see children as transdisciplinary, improvisatory *makers with*. It also repositions the role of teacher. In both experiences binary divisions between learner-teacher, child-adult, and expert-novice were "troubled" (Haraway, 2016), creating new ways of being with. In making with trees, the teacher role was to make with what was already present. I, Carolyn, was not an instigator or facilitator, but was a co-maker, a "teacher-maker," entangling myself with all that was already in play, already in motion. We were improvising together, finding ways to make sounds in different ways, simultaneously negotiating where the making was going, allowing each of us (myself, Gregor, the materials) to have moments of leading, much like in an improvisation ensemble.

The role of the teacher in "making with keys" took on a different quality. Here the teacher introduced the keys into what was already in play. In responding to what was emerging, to the sonic, material, sensorial entanglement, she added to it, and created a role of teacher-as-entangler. That the material was "hers"—that it came from her pocket—was a material entangling of herself with the others in the group. This challenged the disciplinary boundaries and blurred the lines of personal and the professional. The boundaries of the instrument and non-instrument were also blurred. Her role of teacher-as-entangler was not one of power over "in which one body is compelled by another to behave or act in a certain way" (Bell, 2014, p. 1014) but required a different playing of status (Johnstone, 1979).

Johnstone's seminal work on theater improvisation talks of the status games played by individuals. He argues that we embody status through stance, gesture, language, and how we use and occupy materials, and these can either allow or block the continuation of improvisations (Johnstone, 1979, pp. 36–37). Therefore, Johnstone calls on improvisers to develop a fluidity of statuses, being able to move their own status (as enacted through their embodied and material roles) up and down in response to the scene to keep the improvisation going. In both "making with trees" and "making with keys," the role of "teacher-maker" involved status fluidity. In "making with trees," joining in with Gregor's making was an act of being "minoritarian" (Taguchi, 2010, p. 172), assuming a low status in relation to Gregor and his musical ideas, and allowing the materials and his making to lead. While in "making with keys" the act of bringing keys into the entanglement could be seen as fairly high status, instigating a new direction for others in the group.

The teacher remained seated, at a physical distance, and physically lower than others in the group, as she reached in toward the cymbals. This meant that reaching in toward the cymbals was significant. There was a physical and metaphorical "space" for different directions to be taken.

Making New Relationships

Both "making with trees" and "making with keys" were experiences of improvisatory, transdisciplinary making with, which "troubled" (Haraway, 2016) notions of the teacher as in control, as pre-planning a linear route of learning, or having pre-set outcomes that they were steering the experiences toward. Instead, in both experiences, there was an exploratory playfulness. The trip to the wildlife area was not intended to become a "music lesson," and in setting up the improvisation activities with student teachers, there was no intention for keys to emerge. This messy, indeterminate making with aligns strongly with what Cage calls "purposeless play":

> This play . . . is an affirmation of life—not an attempt to bring order out of chaos nor to suggest improvements in creation, but simply a way of waking up to the very life we're living, which is so excellent once one gets one's mind and one's desires out of its way and lets it act of its own accord. (Cage, as quoted in Hill, 2018, p. 59)

This awakening to living and therefore to the here and now of making shifts our attention. No longer is making only a tool for understanding, a sound demonstration of learning, or a site of skill development *for the future*. Making is not about a "world to come," a world we cannot know in advance and plan to be ready for, but instead is about *making with* as becoming with the world as it is now. As Haraway (2016) argues, shifting our attention to "worlding with" involves learning to be "truly present, not as a vanishing pivot between awful or edenic pasts and apocalyptic or salvific futures, but as mortal critters entwined in myriad unfinished configurations of places, times, matters, meanings" (p. 1).

Making with the dead wood of the tree that was gradually rotting away or *making with* the teacher's keys that were present in her pocket at that moment of time or *making with* the emotional response to the newly made instrument (keys) being dropped, was to make different relationships. This requires different ways of being "teacher-maker," with a different relationship with materials.

Both "making with trees" and "making with keys" involved allowing others to create their own material relationships, not seeing these relationships as static or achieved, but as something of the moment. In both experiences, the materials (keys and trees) were actively "doing." They were accepting our human involvement with them, allowing the bark to peel, allowing the vibrations to travel along and up the keys and cymbals, allowing the hollow branch to resonate. They were "playing" with us. This view of material play aligns with the French definition of the term which, as well as encompassing the play of children and theatrical play, also includes the idea of materials as "having a little play" in them. The closest we get in the English language is talking of a steering wheel having "too much play" in it. This notion of materials as agentic, of expressing their abilities to be played, allowing us as humans ways into playing with them, changes the nature of our material relationships in composing. We are no longer imposing ourselves onto materials (sonic or physical), but we are playing with, *making with*, what the materials allow us to do.

To re-see materials as "doing" is to change the relationship we have with them as composition teachers, where materials are no longer inert, to be used, but instead are full of potential, are actively shaping and "teaching" with us. In "making with trees," recognizing that the materials (the tree, the branch, the stick) were in relationship with Gregor and observing his exploration of their potential to "play" with him, and make with him, also repositioned my relationship with the material. In that moment my relationship was one of attentiveness to what the trees were "doing" with Gregor. This attention to material "doings" requires us as "teacher-makers" to consider our own material relationships, as was evident in "making with keys."

Supporting material play in young makers, where we are part of the making that is happening, therefore involves us being comfortable in exploring our own material play. As a discipline, music is a materially rich space. We as music teachers have a wealth of material relationships, embodied ways of being with materials, and understandings of material skill that are part of our habitual ways of being music teachers (Cooke, 2020). As McWilliam (2005) notes, habitual ways of being also characterize forms of pedagogy, where "acquisition of certain routinised patterns of thinking and behaving . . . [is] useful . . . when the conditions in which they work are predictable and stable" (pp. 3–5). However, the type of *making with* experienced in both "making with trees" and "making with keys" was far from predictable and stable. In spaces where materials, bodies, forms, sounds, and ideas were entangled and in motion, imposing habitual ways of being musical and being a music teacher might, as McWilliam (2005) also argues, have "actually become impediments to social success" (p. 5). This was most strongly felt and seen in "making with keys" where the introduction of the keys "troubled" notions of disciplinary "doing." They were not expected to emerge in this space, they were not considered "instruments," and in becoming instruments they "troubled" notions of expertise, who was the expert, and how they were to be played. They therefore "troubled" notions of skills, of right/wrong and of "habit." Together with the attentiveness of the students, they forged a new and unknown relationship that was of and in the moment. This making involved entanglements in the here and now, where habitual ways of being musical and being a music teacher were expanded by the forward motion of the purposeless and playful exploration of materials and processes of playing-with.

Concluding Thoughts on the Interplay of Transdisciplinary and Improvisatory Creativities for Nurturing Young Composers as "Makers"

To nurture our young composers as *makers with* is to allow their *making with* materials to be both improvisatory and transdisciplinary. This involves a re-seeing of material play as a core aspect of composing where, like many art forms, the maker improvises their way, exploring the possibilities their entanglements allow. This changes how we see materials, not as inert objects to be *used* but as active and mutual participants in the processes of making, where they exert influence, and can emerge unexpectedly into the compositional space. It also challenges notions of disciplinary boundaries, because being a maker is entangling with anything that has the potential to be generative. This type of entangling is not only about developing young makers' exploratory abilities, seeing the potential in materials, and saying "yes, and" (Johnstone, 1979), but is also about helping them understand their sound-material worlds. Such understandings arise from what Jackson (2016) calls "plays of forces," where movements, intensities, and exploratory making "regenerate the territory" from within and outside, "mak[ing] it newer each time and motivat[ing] it to continue" (Jackson, 2016, p. 190) in ever-changing, ever-developing relationships.

The research we have highlighted (see also Cooke, 2020) demonstrates a growing consensus that nurturing young composers necessitates them creating their own opportunities and developing skills that will enable them to become "makers." As teachers, supporting the development of young *composers-as-makers-with*, we must *also* be open to transdisciplinary and improvisational playing with materials. As with the example of the student teachers, sometimes we need someone or something to "trouble" (Haraway, 2016) our existing relationships with materials, pushing outward in a centripetal way to support young makers when they *become with* different types of entanglements.

Three Key Messages for Supporting Young Makers

First, seeing teaching composing as "making" involves being dynamic, responsive, and open to what happens in the moment or as a result of a particular coming together of materials, bodies, forms, and ideas. Composing in this sense requires allowing children malleable spaces in the present, rather than fixed habitual or historical precedents. It is about supporting children to *join in with* and *make with*, rather than being imposed on or imposing themselves onto.

Second, seeing oneself as and being a "teacher-maker" means nurturing young composers in ways that are purposefully malleable and fluid, where "interferences" and "eruptions" caused by transdisciplinary and improvisation creativities are generative and reliant on shifting tasks. Young people are thus seen as self-directed learners who are enabled by a learning community where they can make with and through meaningful and mutual relationships.

Third, nurturing young composers invites us to engage with a multiplicity of practices that are social, collaborative, and collective, and that encourage unlearning the rules and exploring a myriad compositional creativities. These creativities have the potential to be recognized and valued, and to become manifest in conversation with real-world practice. Learners have redrawn the boundaries of composing as *making with*. This requires teachers to do the same.

REFERENCES

Barad, K. (2007). *Meeting the universe halfway: Quantum physics and the entanglement of matter and meaning.* Duke University Press.

Bell, D. M. (2014). Improvisation as anarchist organization. *Ephemera: Theory and Politics in Organization, 14*(4), 1009–1030.

Braidotti, R. (2013). *The posthuman.* Polity Press.

Braidotti, R., & Bignall, S. (2018). *Posthuman ecologies: Complexity and process after Deleuze.* Rowman and Littlefield.

Britzman, D. P. (2003). *Practice makes practice: A critical study of learning to teach.* State University of New York Press.

Burnard, P. (2012a). *Musical creativities in practice.* Oxford University Press.

Burnard, P. (2012b). The practice of diverse compositional creativities. In D. Collins (Ed.), *The act of musical composition: Studies in the creative process* (pp. 111–138). Ashgate.

Burnard, P. (forthcoming). *Posthumanizing diverse creativities in music.* Brill-I-Sense.

Burnard, P., & Colucci-Gray, L. (Eds.). (2020). *Why science and arts creativities matter: (Re-) configuring STEAM for future-making education.* Brill.

Burnard, P., & Swann, M. (2010). Pupil perceptions of learning with artists: A new order of experience? *Thinking Skills and Creativity, 5*(2), 70–82.

Burnard, P., & Younker, B. A. (2004). Problem-solving and creativity: Insights from students' individual composing pathways. *International Journal of Music Education, 22*(1), 59–76.

Chappell, K. (2018). From wise humanising creativity to (posthumanising) creativity. In A. Harris, P. Thomson, & K. Snepvangers (Eds.), *Creativity policy, partnerships and practice* (pp. 279–306). Palgrave Macmillan.

Collins, D. (Ed.). (2012). *The act of musical composition: Studies in the creative process.* Ashgate.

Cooke (2020). *"Troubling" music education: (Re-)making research and music education differently* [PhD thesis]. Edinburgh University.

Cremin, T., & Chappell, K. (2019). Creative pedagogies: A systematic review. *Research Papers in Education, 36*(3), 299–331.

Daubney, A., & Tunmer, O. (2020). Rhythms, rhymes and beats in time. In C. Philpott, G. Spruce, & J. Finney (Eds.), *Creative and critical projects in classroom music: Fifty years of sound and silence* (pp. 156–162). Routledge.

Deleuze, G., & Guattari, F. (1987). *A thousand plateaus: Capitalism and schizophrenia.* Continuum International.

Devaney, K. (2018). *How composing assessment in English secondary examinations affects teaching and learning practices* [EdD thesis]. Birmingham City University.

Devaney, K. (2019). Teaching composition: Challenging the stereotypes and myths. *Primary Music Teacher Magazine, 3*(1), 27–30.

Galton, M. (2010). Going with the flow or back to normal? The impact of creative practitioners in schools and classrooms. *Research Papers in Education, 25*(4), 355–375.

Giacomelli, M. (2012). Theorizing improvisation as a form of critical pedagogy in music education. *Critical Studies in Improvisation, 8*(1).

Goehr, L. (1994). *The imaginary museum of musical works: An essay in the philosophy of music.* Oxford University Press.

Green, L. (1988). *Music on deaf ears: Musical meaning, ideology and education.* Manchester University Press.

Grosz, E. (2008). *Chaos, territory, art: Deleuze and the framing of the earth.* Columbia University Press.

Haraway, D. (2016). *Staying with the trouble: Making kin in the Chthulucene.* Duke University Press.

Hill, S. C. (2018). A "sound" approach: John Cage and music education. *Philosophy of Music Education Review, 26*(1), 46–62.

Ingold, T. (2009). The textility of making. *Cambridge Journal of Economics, 34*(1), 91–102.

Jackson, A. Y. (2016). An ontology of a backflip. *Cultural Studies: Critical Methodologies, 16*(2), 183–192.

Jackson, A. Y., & Mazzei, L. A. (2013). Plugging one text into another: Thinking with theory in qualitative research. *Qualitative Inquiry, 19*(4), 261–271.

Jeffrey, B., & Craft, A. (2006). Creative learning and possibility thinking. In B. Jeffrey (Ed.), *Creative learning practices: European experiences. Ethnography and education* (pp. 73–91). Tufnell Press.

Johnstone, K. (1979). *Impro: Improvisation and the theatre.* Routledge.

Kinsella, V., & Fautley, M. (2020). Giving value to musical creativity. In C. Philpott, G. Spruce, & J. Finney (Eds.), *Creative and critical projects in classroom music: Fifty years of sound and silence.* Routledge, 65–76.

Lindgren, T. (2020). The figuration of the posthuman child. *Discourse, 41*(6), 914–925.

Lucas, B., & Spencer, E. (2017). *Teaching creative thinking: Developing learners who generate ideas and can think critically.* Crown House Publishing.

Masschelein, J. (2010). E-ducating the gaze: The idea of a poor pedagogy. *Ethics and Education, 5*(1), 43–53.

McWilliam, E. L. (2005). Unlearning pedagogy. *Journal of Learning Design, 1*(1), 1–11.

Murris, K. (2016). *The posthuman child: Educational transformation through philosophy with picturebooks.* Routledge.

Nardone, P. (1996). *The experience of improvisation in music: A phenomenological psychological analysis.* Saybrook Institute.

Philpott, C. (2020). Conceptions of the creative process in music and arts education. In C. Philpott, G. Spruce, & J. Finney (Eds.), *Creative and critical projects in classroom music: Fifty years of sound and silence* (pp. 49–64). Routledge.

Prevost, E. (2009). Free improvisation in music and capitalism: Resisting authority and the cult of scientism and celebrity. In Mattin & A. Iles (Eds.), *Noise and capitalism* (pp. 38–60). Arteleku Audiolab.

Reimer, B. (2003). *A philosophy of music education: Advancing the vision* (3rd ed.). Prentice Hall.

Ross, D. S. (2014). "Now's the time": Improvisation-based pedagogies and the creation of coevalness. *Journal of Educational Alternatives, 3*(1), 4–22.

Saladin, M. (2009). Points of resistance and criticism in free improvisation: Remarks on a musical practice and some economic transformations. In Mattin & A. Iles (Eds.), *Noise and capitalism* (pp. 38–59). Arteleku Audiolab.

Somerville, M., & Powell, S. (2019). Researching with children of the anthropocene: A new paradigm? DOI:10.4018/978-1-5225-5317-5.ch002

Stengers, I. (2010). *Cosmopolitics I*. Minnesota University Press.

Strand, K. (2006). Survey of Indiana music teachers on using composition in the classroom. *Journal of Research in Music Education, 54*(2), 154–167.

Taguchi, H. L. (2010). *Going beyond the theory/practice divide in early childhood education: Introducing an intra-active pedagogy*. Routledge.

Taylor, C. A., & Hughes, C. (2016). *Posthuman research practices in education*. Palgrave Macmillan.

Triantafyllaki, A., & Burnard, P. (2010). Creativity and arts-based knowledge creation in diverse educational partnership practices. *UNESCO Observatory E-Journal, 1*(5).

Waddington-Jones, C., King, A., & Burnard, P. (2019, March 22). Exploring wellbeing and creativity through collaborative composition as part of Hull 2018 City of Culture. *Frontiers in Psychology: Performance Science, 10*, 1–10.

....

CHAPTER 22

MENTORING YOUNG COMPOSERS

Collaborative Pathways for Developing Musicianship

....

ELIZABETH A. MENARD

EARLY in my career as a music educator, I was hired to teach a music enrichment class for gifted musicians as a high school elective. Participating students were identified as "talented," and came from all walks of musical life. There were country music singers; classically trained pianists; students from band, choir, and orchestra programs; and even rock-and-roll guitar players. I met with these students in small groups once a week, and school administrators provided me with four primary areas of instruction that were to be included in the "talented" music curriculum: development of performance skills, music theory instruction, study of music history, and experience in *music composition*. For me, the first three areas seemed manageable. However, when considering how to approach teaching composition, I was terrified. I had absolutely no training in how to teach composition and was completely unsure about where to begin. The students in my classes came from widely varying levels of musical ability and knowledge. Some read and understood music notation, some read guitar tablature, some learned by ear and didn't read notation at all.

I was fortunate to be able to work with the students in small groups, which allowed time for *some* individual instruction. I also had piano keyboards available for each student. My first efforts in providing composition instruction often involved asking students for very specific details in their compositions—requiring a specific number of measures, asking for demonstration of musical details such as dynamic contrast, ABA form, etc. These prescriptive requirements left little room for student creativity. After many years of trying different approaches, some successful and some not, I began to allow the students much greater freedom in their choices and simply tried to offer suggestions to guide the process. I identified a few strategies that seemed to work. Even more importantly, I discovered reasons that the composition projects in these classes were a critical part of the students' musical development. First, though the students came from different areas and levels of musicianship, all seemed to be incredibly engaged in finding ways to realize and document the musical ideas and the sounds in their heads. Most students felt a sense of ownership of their music compositions and experienced pride in their accomplishments, especially when musical ideas were shared or performed. Finally, it was clear that the students developed improved levels of musicianship through the process of imagining and constructing their music compositions. The experience of music composition seemed to effectively support learning in those "other" areas of instruction that I was responsible for. I learned how to "teach" composition in a public school setting by trial and error, and by simply mentoring the students as they explored their musical ideas.

Today, there are many remarkable publications and resources available that document successful composition programs and delineate teaching strategies that will work in varied music education settings. There is clearly a powerful push, in our many music education circles, to increase opportunities for creative thinking in music through music composition. My goal for this chapter is to explore some of those strategies for teaching composition and identify simple guiding principles that will support the process of mentoring young composers as they develop their musicianship through composition experiences.

DEVELOPMENT OF ACCESSIBLE PATHWAYS TO COMPOSITION IN K–12 SCHOOLS

Participation in music composition activities provides an important and necessary opportunity for children to think musically and construct musical meaning. We can identify many resources that support the importance of music composition as an essential part of the music curriculum for every age. In a philosophical discussion of the role of composition and creativity for children, Margaret Barrett (2003) described music composition as a meaning-making process, critical to the musical, social, and emotional life of children, sharing, "If education, and by extension music education, is the development of children's capacity to construct their worlds in meaningful ways, then a view of composition as a form of meaning-making seems a worthy enterprise" (p. 115). Constructing meaning in any subject area surely is a primary goal of education.

Jackie Wiggins (2007) examined compositional process in music and identified a critical need for children to have opportunities for music expression through composition, saying, "Since all people are capable of inventing musical ideas, it would seem that all music learners should, at some time in their education, have opportunities to explore this capability as part of their learning" (p. 465). Wiggins also believes that students who compose are working "in an environment that fosters ownership and agency" (p. 466). This idea of ownership and agency is important in student identity and engagement with music and is often visible in students that participate in the composition process. One goal of all music educators should be to help students experience this sense of agency and ownership in music. Music composition experiences lead our students to explore creativity by sharing their musical ideas and help them to make meaningful connections to the musical concepts that we want them to learn.

Overcoming the Roadblocks to Composition Instruction

Developing creative pathways for musicianship through composition is clearly a necessary and valuable part of a child's music education experience. However, I also understand teachers' valid concerns about *how* to effectively include music composition activities in their traditional music classrooms. Teachers worry about issues such as the amount of time needed to implement meaningful composition instruction and how composition activities may limit time to address the more traditional performance curriculum (Kaschub, 2013; Menard, 2015; Strand, 2006). There is no doubt that creative musical thinking and composition processes take time and dedication. However, providing time and opportunity for our students to construct musical meaning through composition activities is a critical area of instruction and should be a primary goal for music educators—worth finding time for.

Often educators believe that their lack of formal training in composing or composition pedagogy may inhibit their ability to provide meaningful instruction (Menard, 2015; Reese, 2003; Stauffer, 2013; Strand, 2006). Few music teacher education programs offer courses in composition pedagogy. While resources and professional development opportunities are plentiful, the amount of time needed, and lack of comfort in the process, may cause some teachers to turn away from this important opportunity. It is interesting to note that professional composers often experience apprehension about the level of *teacher training* they receive in teaching composition to their students. Mark Applebaum (2012) shared concerns that composers are not trained to be composition teachers and that it is often assumed that since they are good composers, they will automatically be good composition teachers. He proposed a pedagogy that includes mentorship for graduate composition students and developing a "robust sense of community that helps us turn our students into teachers" (p. 262). We might take that advice as music educators. A sense of community involving teachers and students when planning and teaching composition might be a good approach. Applebaum also believes that in addition to preparing to teach others, a composer must also learn to teach oneself. This is good advice for music teachers preparing to teach composition. Finding ways to explore and validate our own musical ideas as novice composers may be an appropriate way to begin the composition mentor training process. Clint Randles and Mark Sullivan (2013) share this sentiment and advise that it may be necessary for teachers to provide initial ideas to get a student started and encourage teachers to start composing themselves. "One must first do before one can teach" (p. 15). In addition, Applebaum's (2012) idea of developing a shared community of composition may be a successful path to follow when approaching music composition experiences in K–12 schools. As a shared community—all stakeholders—teachers and students, should be involved in the process of composing and teaching.

Music teachers may also be concerned that students in their classes are not adequately equipped with the theoretical music knowledge necessary to support music composition activities in their classrooms (Hickey, 2012; Menard, 2015). If the vision for composition instruction is limited to traditional Western art music, and requires traditional harmonies and notation, composition may indeed seem to be an overwhelming layer of instruction to add to the music curriculum. It is important for teachers to identify and establish a level of shared musical knowledge, or a fundamental musical base from which to begin. This does not have to involve concepts of notation or formal training in music theory. It is possible for students with no formal training to bring creative musical ideas from their informal musical lives to the composition community. Daniel Deutsch (2013) shared: "Children can ride bicycles without knowing the laws of gyroscopic inertia; they can make up stories without learning a list of grammatical rules. So, too, children can compose before they learn theoretical concepts" (p. 131). Exploration of musical ideas with the base understanding that: notes move up, notes move down, and notes stay the same, musical sounds are short, long, loud, soft, and can be in patterns, facilitates a beginning foundation for the organization of musical ideas and the composition process.

How then, can we best eliminate the roadblocks to composition instruction that are faced by music teachers? Let me share the experience of one band director, who grudgingly agreed to add composition instruction to his band program curriculum one day a week, for seven weeks, to help with a research project I was involved in. In an interview, Mr. Lee (a pseudonym) identified his concerns about adding composition activities to his band program. He felt that composition would interfere with the traditional culture of his band program by limiting time for performance. Time is so often seen as a critical factor. He also felt that the large number of students (75 in his band), the traditional band classroom set up, and unmanageable noise levels would prohibit implementation of a meaningful experience. Mr. Lee also believed that he was not a composer, and therefore not qualified to teach composition. He felt that it was absurd to think that band directors could teach composition without training. His final concern was that his students lacked the fundamental musical knowledge necessary to compose. Mr. Lee is a wonderful example of a good teacher expressing valid concerns about how to add composition to the curriculum effectively.

After participating in the composition instruction program for seven weeks, Mr. Lee adjusted his opinions. He was surprised that the noise level was manageable, and that the large majority of students were highly engaged with the activities and often worked on the projects at home, even though this was not expected or required. The students were open to the experience and embraced the activities. He was surprised at how important it was for the students to share their ideas with classmates. After each composition activity, students were eager to share with one another and their teacher. It was apparent to Mr. Lee that some of the students who may have been his "best" and most highly accomplished musicians were not always the most creative composers. Finally, Mr. Lee realized that his personal life experiences as a musician (conductor and performer of music from many genres) provided him with the necessary foundation to teach composition effectively. He came to understand that composition was not a waste of time because his students were experiencing music in a different way. His students were *in* the music—thinking about music using a pathway that complemented their performance, and did not diminish it (Menard, 2015).

This is the story of just one teacher, and Mr. Lee's discoveries may not be applicable in every situation. However, this type of awakening to the powerful potential of creative thinking in music *is* possible for both students and teachers. Shouldn't we strive for this? Maud Hickey (2012) clearly states the call to action, saying:

> For too long, music composition has been put on a pedestal and viewed as a special skill that only an elite few could do. It is time to dispel that notion and offer classroom and studio teachers not only reasons for making music composition an integral part of their curriculum, but also provide ideas and activities for doing so. (pp. 13–14)

I propose that music educators heed this call and work to reframe the process of "teaching" composition. A more effective way to approach teaching composition may be to think of it as a necessary process of *mentorship* and musical collaboration between students and teachers. Thinking of teaching composition in this way can help to promote a composition community that provides opportunity for musical exploration and development of musicianship for *both* teachers and students.

Reframing the Composition Teaching Process as Mentorship

Is there a difference between teaching and mentoring? Varying definitions are available for these terms. The focus for this chapter is to understand the role of the teacher as composition mentor—one who provides opportunity for exploration, supports growth, offers guidance, and serves as a role model for music composition students in the classroom. This is a different path for instruction than a path providing didactic instruction or a pedagogy with a narrow focus on specific strategies. Examples of effective composition mentorship can be found in all levels of education. Mentorship can be also be recognized through other terms in the literature such as facilitation, scaffolding, and experiential and constructive learning in music composition, to mention just a few. All of these areas are worth exploring to help support this vision of collaborative mentorship as a pathway for developing musicianship in our students.

Composition Mentorship in Collegiate Settings

Shulamit Ran (2012), Pulitzer Prize–winning composer, penned an essay reflecting upon her personal development as a composer and shared beliefs about teaching composition. Ran's personal definition of a good composition teacher?

> An ideal composition teacher, at any level, is (1) able to help the student listen, critically, and in a deep way, to his/her own music, and (2) considers it a priority to develop and refine the kind of technical tools that will help the student implement his/her personal artistic vision. (p. 307)

While Ran is speaking about teaching composition on a professional level, this definition can be easily adapted for teachers in K–12 settings. If our role as composition mentors includes enabling our students to listen to their own musical ideas deeply and critically, and encourages our students to develop musical "tools" that will expand their musical and artistic vision, then I think we are on the right track. Listening critically is the first step for students to begin revision and extension of their musical ideas. Developing musical tools is indicative of gaining knowledge that will improve compositional ability. This knowledge may also transfer directly to areas of musicianship beyond the composition classroom.

Margaret Barrett (2006) conducted an "eminence study of teaching and learning in music composition" (p. 195), by studying composer-teacher interactions between an established and well-respected (eminent) university composition professor and two collegiate level composition students. After reviewing videorecorded lessons and completing interviews with both the composition teacher and students, Barrett identified 12 composition teaching strategies that were observed in the data. The eminent composer-teacher in this study:

- Extended thinking, provided possibilities
- Referenced work to and beyond the tradition (signposting)
- Set parameters for identity as a composer
- Provoked the student to describe and explain
- Questioned purpose, probed intention
- Shifted back and forth between micro and macro levels (p. 201)
- Provided multiple alternatives from analysis of student work
- Prompted the student to engage in self-analysis
- Encouraged goal setting and task identification
- Engaged in joint problem-finding and problem-solving
- Provided reassurance
- Gave license to change. (p. 202)

Barrett felt that studying the composition teaching process from an eminence perspective provided valuable information for music educators planning effective music composition instruction in K–12 school settings. These twelve strategies may help teachers to better understand the musical "tools" necessary for successful composition instruction mentioned by Ran (2012). Barret's strategies help us to define the collaborative nature of composition experienced by students and their teachers who participate meaningfully in the process. Most if not all of the 12 strategies used by the composer to guide the university level composition students are easily transferred to music composition experiences in *any* K–12 music education context. However, it is important to highlight some phrases in particular: setting parameters (giving guidance and setting accomplishable limits), engaging in joint problem-solving (working together to discover musical ideas), extending thinking (encouraging students to go beyond their initial ideas), providing possibilities and alternatives (sharing musical suggestions and choices to guide student progress), giving license to change (it is *always* possible to change an idea), and providing reassurance. These key areas are necessary in creating a climate of mentorship in K–12 composition classrooms.

In 2006, Barrett suggested that teaching and learning compositional skills is really a form of "creative collaboration" between teacher and student, finding that the "emergent view of the teaching and learning process in music composition is one of a dyad working towards shared goals in a process characterized by collaboration, joint effort, and social support" (p. 195). This view lends support to the idea that we may not need to think of teaching composition through the traditionally structured teacher-student relationship, but instead see it as a joint problem-solving process between teacher and student. We should redefine the role of composition teacher as *composition mentor, working in collaboration with the young composers* in our classrooms.

Approaches to Composition Mentorship in K–12 Settings

In schools today, there are numerous education concepts that define effective teaching. Often these concepts become important buzzwords in education circles and help to direct successful teaching strategies. It is important to stress that the process of composition mentorship does not consist of one single process. There are many ways to approach mentorship that help to define it as "good teaching!"

Scaffolding and Mentorship

There is some debate as to who is responsible for introducing the term "scaffolding" into education research literature (Shvarts & Baker, 2019). The idea is sometimes connected to Jerome Bruner, who often related scaffolding to problem solving. Wood, Bruner, and Ross (1976) explained that scaffolding done well begins with a teacher guiding a student into actions that will produce solutions that are meaningful. The teacher helps the student to understand problems and discrepancies and serves in this role until the students are ready to proceed on their own (p. 90).

In a meaningful discussion of scaffolding and its important connection to music composition instruction, Jackie Wiggins and Michael Medvinsky (2013) explain it more clearly. "Everything teachers do to support student learning can be considered scaffolding, including framing and planning the learning experience, providing appropriate groundwork to foster and enable student success in the experience, and assessing student understanding throughout the experience" (p. 111). Scaffolding is another excellent framework for consideration, as we investigate just what mentors do in the collaborative mentorship process. Wiggins and Medvinsky suggest eight areas of focus as teachers plan for music composition instruction:

- Supporting students musically
- Fostering a supportive environment
- Fostering invention and articulation of musical ideas
- Respecting and honoring the learner's voice
- Meeting learners where they are
- Laying groundwork through prior experience
- Framing compositional problems to foster success
- Providing time and space

Each of these strategies, when used in the process of composition instruction, will help to establish a safe environment for creative musical interaction between teacher and students. These suggestions also help to create a community, where collaborative mentorship is possible.

Problem-Solving and Mentorship

Problem-solving is often seen as a critical thinking skill and necessary in the process of learning how to compose. In an analysis of the composing pathways used by students when creating, Burnard & Younker (2004) determined that the many pathways characterizing students' composing processes are influenced by each individual's culture and life experience. Problem-solving by the young composer is embedded in the process of navigating the pathway. Peter Webster (2002) shared his *Model for Creative Thinking in Music*, which outlines the cognitive processes used in creative activity. At the center of the model, Webster proposed that the creative thinking process involves an interaction between four areas: *preparation, working through, time away, and verification*. These steps are informed by *divergent* and *convergent* thinking. Webster shares that "creative thinking is driven by a problem and a need for a solution" (p. 28). The process of moving between divergent and convergent thinking during the composition process is a clear illustration of critical thinking and the problem-solving process. Today, domain-specific problem–solving has been identified as a *21st-century skill* that is necessary for student education in contemporary settings (Grieff et al., 2014). The domain of music and the process of composition is an ideal setting for students to exercise these important 21st-century skills.

Young composers are asked to explore their musical ideas and make decisions about how to shape and share those ideas. It is also important to realize that creative thinking and the development of a composition occur in a social and collaborative setting. Social interaction in problem-solving is a beneficial and necessary part of the education process for students in our schools (Care et al., 2016). Esther Care and colleagues propose a framework of Collaborative Problem Solving (CPS), that stresses the importance of shared engagement in problem-solving. Activities such as asking questions, peer mentoring, and teacher feedback "can help a student to solve problems that they may otherwise not have been able to, and moves them toward higher competency" (p. 252). This is one very positive way to approach the collaborative mentorship process in music composition. Thinking about and making decisions about musical ideas is a cognitive problem-solving process that teachers must guide and support. Teachers, classmates, and each individual composer are members of a collaborative community, and all are part of the joint problem-solving process in music composition classes.

Feedback and Mentorship

As I shared at the beginning of this chapter, the music composition instruction I provided to my gifted music students in their enrichment class did not start out with great success. One of the areas I really struggled with was assessment. How would I assess learning in these projects? I tried checklists and rubrics with assessment areas such as: required number of measures, dynamic markings added, etc. This was clearly not *valid* assessment of the true process of creative thinking and composition. I found myself responding with comments like "sounds good," or "nice job," instead of offering meaningful critique. Daniel Deutsch (2016) states that *authentic* assessment is required when providing meaningful feedback for student compositions. "With authentic assessment, teachers treat student composition as meaningful musical expression, not merely as a school exercise. They accomplish this by shaping assessment and instruction in response to the musical intentions of each composer within the context of each composition" (p. 59).

I learned through the years of working with my students, that what was truly important was the *process* that the students were working through. The formative feedback that the students received from me during the composition process needed to be specific and meaningful, as well as designed to give direction on how each piece could move forward. The other area of critical feedback came from fellow students in the classroom. Sharing their compositions in class and receiving critique from their peers was perhaps the most important assessment and validation that these young composers could receive. Sam Reese (2003) shared an important point: "Teaching composition might be thought of as providing a structured environment in which students teach themselves or each other" (p. 212).

Yes, feedback is critical to the collaborative mentorship process. It is important to reflect upon how to respond to novice composers in a way that will support musical growth and creativity without overpowering or inhibiting it. Because the young composers come from such different backgrounds and levels of ability, the feedback needs to be appropriately addressed to be helpful for each individual. Sam Reese provides a general list of suggestions to guide teacher feedback for young composers:

- Acknowledge, recognize, and/or verify student work
- Encourage, motivate, and/or set expectations
- Describe salient characteristics and successful aspects of the piece. Be a "mirror" to increase awareness of what others are hearing.
- Provide explanations and definitions of unfamiliar musical material.
- Point out composers and compositions that students might find interesting based on the type of music they are composing.
- Ask students to describe their piece and to explain the feedback they are seeking and ask about student intentions.
- Facilitate critique and reflection by questioning and probing about the piece or the composing process.
- Point out musical problems and potentials in the piece.
- Encourage students to experiment—to extend, alter, and develop.
- Provide suggestions for changes, additions, or deletions to students' music.
- Play or sing musical examples and possibilities (p. 220).

There are clearly many ways to eliminate the roadblocks to implementing composition instruction in our music education classrooms. The value of composition instruction for our students is often first recognized by teachers when they actually jump in and begin mentoring their students in composition activities. It was definitely that way for me.

Examining Models of Composition
Mentorship for Young Composers

It may be helpful to learn of some existing programs in K–12 music settings where composition mentorship is flourishing and changing the lives of both the students and teachers involved. First, we'll examine a sixth-grade general music class, which provides an example of a single teacher providing mentorship in beginning composition experiences that were connected to traditional music concepts in a Music Creations class. Next, the Very Young Composers (VYC) of Central Wisconsin features pre-service music educators serving as composition mentors for fourth- and fifth-grade students in an after-school composition program. Finally, Music Plus, a university partnership with a local urban school district, tells the story of undergraduate music education majors serving as composition mentors for high school musicians (choral, band, and orchestra students) in a service learning program.

Music Creations Class

To improve the level of interest and student engagement in a general music class offered at a middle school, the principal and band director reworked the curriculum to consist almost entirely of music creation activities. They changed the name of the class from the traditional *General* music class to *Music Creations* class. It was clear to students that this class would be very different than the previous general music class offered at the school.

Sixth-grade *Music Creations* was one semester long and had approximately 18 students registered. Ms. Baldwin (pseudonym used) had over 25 years of experience as a middle school band director and general music teacher and she faced the same challenges many music educators face in trying to implement composition activities in the classroom. While she did have some band students in the class, most of her students had little previous musical experience. The only available classroom in which to hold the class was the school band room, so she had limited instruments available and no student computers to use for composition notation. She did have bucket drums and a set of drumsticks for each student in the class, one upright piano, two electronic keyboards, and a number of typical mallet percussion instruments in the band room. This was a place to start!

The semester began with exploration and echoing of rhythmic patterns on bucket drums designed to create a comfortable atmosphere and encourage students to think creatively and explore musical patterns—a theme that would be reinforced throughout the Music Creations class. Students repeated patterns they heard, created their own, and took turns leading the drum sessions. Ms. Baldwin frequently shared with the students that she was not there to teach, but simply to help them explore their musical ideas. These sixth-grade students were intrigued with that concept. To them, it seemed "cool" and perhaps even a bit strange to have a teacher that was not there to teach. The most important rule in the classroom was that all compositional ideas created by the students were important, should be respected, and shared in the classroom. The students began to think of themselves as composers, so it was important to create a safe and welcoming space in which the students could explore, create, and celebrate their musical ideas.

Baldwin began the melodic composition activities with careful instruction on how to use the instruments (xylophones, marimbas, keyboards, etc.) in the classroom appropriately. Next, a common base of musical understanding was established. Ms. Baldwin explained that musical notes can move up, move down, they can repeat, move by steps, and by leaps. There can also be silence between musical sounds. The students were given the opportunity to explore musical sounds on the various melodic percussion instruments and encouraged to create short melodic ideas of their own. They worked in small groups (two or three students at an instrument) and took turns creating and sharing their musical ideas.

Students clearly enjoyed sharing ideas and listening to the musical ideas of their classmates. As their ideas were extended, the students used graphic notation symbols, or "composition maps," to help them remember their ideas. Composition maps consisted of drawings with swirls, steps, circles, and other graphic notations to create representations of the music that helped them to remember the ideas they had composed. Students were instructed to use the "play it three times in a row rule." A musical idea was considered composed when a student could repeat that musical idea three times in a row. This number of repetitions seemed to solidify the idea for both the teacher and the student. Along with the graphic notation, Ms. Baldwin also recorded the ideas for reference, if needed. However, the reference was not needed very often. The students seemed to feel a sense of agency and ownership of their musical ideas. During one of my visits to the class, Ms. Baldwin asked a seventh-grade student who had been in the class the previous year to come in and share the composition she had created in the class. Without any hesitation, the student stepped up to the marimba and performed her composition just like it had been performed the year before. The musical ideas she shared were hers, and she had not forgotten them!

After creating opening compositional ideas, Ms. Baldwin asked students to expand their work by adding other ideas that worked well with the first one. The composition process took off! Students worked hard on their projects and extended and developed their ideas. During this part of the composition process, Ms. Baldwin first introduced the musical concept of form. This helped them to give structure to their compositions. As the compositions neared completion, students worked in groups to add accompaniment to their compositions. Students collaborated as they added non-pitched percussion instruments such as maracas, triangles, and small drums, and created rhythmic patterns to embellish their melodies. Student collaboration in the projects was important to Ms. Baldwin, so she also required the students to teach their melodies to other members of their group. This "student teaching" component surprised Baldwin with its effectiveness. It seemed to be very important to each of the young composers that the student receiving the composition instruction played the new composition correctly. The final component of this part of the class was for each composer to perform his or her work for the class, and invited guests, in its extended form with group accompaniments. This process required musical rehearsing and collaboration between students in preparation for the performance. Students in the class were very receptive to all of the compositions shared by their classmates and celebrated all of these new works with applause and smiles.

It is important to note that no musical terms other that those that defined how notes move (steps, skips, repeats, up, and down, silence) were used to begin this process. Musical learning was occurring through exploration and student creativity. During class composition sharing times, Ms. Baldwin introduced musical concepts such as dynamics, articulation, rhythm, and form using the student compositions as models. For example, the young composers worked to identify form in their own compositions and in the compositions of their classmates. They also explored how their compositions might be made more interesting by adding musical concepts such as dynamic contrasts, accents, and tempo changes.

Creative thinking in music provided a spirit of teacher and student collaboration as the students took an active part in creating the learning environment. Their compositions provided a place to apply the information they were learning—and an understanding of why it was important to learn about these concepts. (Menard, 2013, p. 64)

As was discussed earlier in the chapter, teachers often feel that the creation of musical ideas is too difficult for students who do not come from a music performance background. However, participation in these composition activities provided an excellent context for constructing musical understanding. Creating their own musical ideas gave these students important and meaningful connections to important musical concepts such as dynamics, form, texture, and even traditional notation. While the process of teaching composition may intimidate some teachers, these middle school students were intrigued by the idea of creating their own musical ideas—with a guide instead of a "teacher." Webster (2002) encouraged music educators to "design environments that help learners to construct their personal understanding of music . . . to develop a sense of musical independence." In this model for composition instruction, the students constructed their understanding of music in a general music classroom that was a safe environment for musical exploration. Ms. Baldwin facilitated and mentored the composition process for these students as they discovered musical ideas, created musical compositions, and then connected these experiences to meaningful musical learning.

Very Young Composers of Central Wisconsin

The Very Young Composers of Central Wisconsin (VYC) is an extension of the New York Philharmonic Very Young Composers program. The New York program provides an opportunity for students in grades three through five to compose and have their compositions performed by members of the New York Philharmonic. The Wisconsin program, run as a community and university partnership, involved collaboration of university students and faculty, as well as area general music teachers. Fourth- and fifth-grade students interested in composition participated in a four-week class during the January winter term. The composition class consisted of three sessions (two hours in length) each week, and ended with a public performance of student works. The young composers were mentored by undergraduate music majors, including music education, performance, and composition students. The young composers were not required to have any music theory knowledge or previous musical experience to participate in the classes.

The undergraduate composition teacher/mentors were trained by area general music teachers and university faculty serving as camp directors. These composition mentors participated in a weekend workshop that included group exercises such as: creative body movement, connecting movement and emotion (run joyfully, hop angrily) to musical ideas, expressing musical ideas in graphic notation, and role-playing (teacher/mentors and young composers) the process of documenting and notating the compositions. Throughout the training, there was intense discussion and reflection about the importance of guiding the young composers in the composition process, valuing and supporting their ideas, and offering direction; all while trying not to influence their musical ideas. This training offered a wonderful opportunity to experience the challenges and benefits of nurturing creativity through composition mentorship in a classroom setting.

In the Wisconsin VYC program, teachers first introduced musical and creative concepts to the young composers through group warm-up activities they had learned in their training. Musical instruments were introduced to the to the young composers in "instrument interviews." During the interviews, the young composers were introduced to several wind, percussion, and string instruments through teacher demonstration. After they learned what the instruments sounded like, and what special techniques might be available on the instrument, students were asked to compose their first musical ideas—one for each of the instruments they interviewed. The composers chose the instruments they wanted to compose for based on these experiences. Composers began with a story (either original or known) that had a beginning, a middle, and an end. This became the guide or framework for the piece. The young composer's musical ideas represented events in the story and were notated using a scribing process. The students shared their ideas with their mentors through: vocalization of the sounds they desired, playing patterns and melodies improvised on electronic keyboards, graphic notation (pictures that they drew); and verbal descriptions of their ideas. A few composers, with some musical background, used traditional notation for communication of ideas. When the young composer could repeat their idea multiple times and make decisions about the musical idea they wanted to include, the teacher mentor "scribed" the idea on a computer using music notation software. The teachers often had to ask for clarification of the ideas that were shared and frequently offered the young composer choices. For example, when a student drew a "basket of flowers" as a flute melody, the teacher played a group of trills and then a collection of scales to offer two choices for interpretation of what a basket of flowers sounded like. The young composer could choose one of the examples or provide more information to make sure the idea was notated the way they imagined it. They were also invited to revise their ideas throughout the composition process.

When a young composer was not working individually with the mentor, a piano lab, supervised by area general music teachers, was available to allow individual work and additional composition support. The composition teachers/mentors performed the final compositions at the concluding program with an introduction to each piece shared by its young composer. The teacher/mentors met as a group following each session to reflect upon and discuss successes and challenges faced during each day's activities.

Through observation of these classes and interviews with the teacher/mentors and young composers, I was able to understand teacher perceptions of the experience. As expected, one of the challenges that the teacher-mentors faced was the large amount of time required. The class was held during winter session at the university, and some of the teachers had jobs in the area or were taking winter session classes, which likely added to their concerns about time. It was a very intense four weeks. The teachers also shared concerns about how to validly represent ideas of the young composers. Scribing exactly what the young composer wanted could be frustrating. Sometimes the young composers knew exactly what they wanted to hear, and other times they were satisfied to just accept the teacher's idea. Related to this was the difficulty the teachers had in understanding the difference between guiding the young composers in the composition process and influencing composer ideas (Menard & Rosen, 2016). Reflection upon these discussions provides a realization that it is almost impossible not to influence the process, while also guiding it. Teachers should encourage student decisions about musical ideas, offer multiple opportunities for students to change their minds, and then do their best to validly represent those ideas. Some teacher influence may be a natural part of the learning process. For these pre-service teachers, their beliefs about the positive aspects of the composition mentoring process are important. Teacher perceptions of personal benefit in composition mentorship were identified as:

- Gaining valuable teaching experience with fourth- and fifth-grade students. This included developing positive relationships with the young composers they worked with.
- Gaining a better personal understanding of the composition process for both the young composers and for themselves.
- Gaining a personal identity as a composer and increased appreciation for composer intent.
- Developing clear visions for use of composition activities in their future classrooms. (Menard & Rosen, 2016)

School and university partnerships and service-learning projects like the VYC classes can offer important opportunities for pre-service music educators to develop composition teaching skills and would be excellent pathways for expanding music composition knowledge in the music teacher education curriculum.

Music Plus Composition Program

In a school-university partnership with a local urban high school, a midwestern university established the *Music Plus* program. School band, choir, and orchestra directors recommended students to the program who were: interested in receiving additional music training, good citizens in their music programs, and financially unable to access private music instruction outside of the school day. For 10 weeks in the fall and spring, the students were bused to the campus for two hours of music instruction each week. Instruction included private lessons on their instruments, ensemble participation, keyboard class, aural skill development, and an opportunity to share their musical ideas through composition instruction. This service learning project was administered by music education faculty members, with undergraduate and graduate music education students serving as the instructional staff for the program. This was a meaningful opportunity for music education majors to experience composition mentorship as part of their music teacher training program.

None of the music education students had experience in composition. At the beginning of the program, some were very apprehensive at the idea of having to lead composition instruction. Graduate and undergraduate students from the university composition degree program were also invited to participate in the process, giving these students the opportunity to experience *teaching* composition. The 30-minute composition classes were held in a piano lab with every student seated at their own piano with headphones available. These high school students were excited to be on the college campus and most were willing to participate in any experience that was offered. Some were fairly competent on their primary instruments, but many were not. Some basically learned much of the music they performed by ear and very few had previous piano experience. For the graduate composition majors, who were teachers in the program, the lack of theoretical training in these students was a difficult hurdle. How could one develop composition experiences for students who had such varied and sometimes limited musical ability? For the undergraduate music education majors, it was a relief to know that they didn't have to "know how" to compose to get started. Instruction began with the students creating brief musical ideas that were prompted by questions to stir their imagination. Concepts such as musical questions and answers; consonance and dissonance; and form (beginning, middle, end) were addressed. After exploration on the keyboards, the Noteflight music software program was used by the students to notate their ideas. The university provided access to a Noteflight online classroom for the Music Plus program. In this platform, the students could continue work on their compositions at home and teachers could also access student compositions to offer suggestions and encouragement during the week. Most students had only cell phones to access the website, but it was amazing what they could do with their phones!

The undergraduate students served as composition mentors and were available to assist with transferring a difficult or complicated musical idea to notation so that it could be documented in the system. They were provided with simple instructions: help with notation, try to think from the composer's perspective, honor the composer intent, and go with the creative flow. This worked well, and it did not take long for the young composers of the class to begin to notate most of their own ideas. The undergraduate composition mentors rotated around the classroom to hear ideas, give guidance, offer suggestions, and served as excellent mentors to the high school composers.

The composition majors that assisted with class instruction began to understand the need for establishing parameters for the young composers. They designed beginning activities that limited notes or intervals used by the novice composers. As the students began working on full composition projects, teachers introduced concepts such as motive, form, extending ideas, moving ideas to a different place, reversing ideas, and combining ideas. The composition majors were amused by the simple concepts, but also impressed that the concepts clearly related to processes that they used in writing their own compositions.

During the spring semester, pieces were composed for instruments that the college students played. At the final program, the compositions were performed by the undergraduate music majors, and each young composer spoke to the audience to describe their inspiration for the piece. The level of personal satisfaction and agency this composition opportunity provided for these high school musicians was clearly visible. The music education students adapted to the role of composition mentor exceptionally well. They embraced the process and overcame concerns about a lack of training. They did an exceptional job of providing guidance, and when they were not needed, many sat at a piano or computer and worked on their own compositions, and on developing their own composer identities. As with the mentors in the VYC program, the undergraduate Music Plus composition mentors developed strong relationships with the high school composers they worked with. Some were inspired to consider a future working in urban and under-resourced school settings. The power of creating music in the lives of these high school students was beneficial in so many ways. Music teacher-educators need to be creative in the process of finding opportunities for pre-service music teachers to experience the process of composition mentorship (Kaschub, 2013). The Music Plus program was an effective training opportunity as well as a nurturing community for composition and creative thinking.

GUIDELINES FOR EFFECTIVE MENTORSHIP OF YOUNG COMPOSERS

> Children have no need of adults to be creative; they are musically playful and inventive on their own. The commitment adults can make to children—what adults can do in schools and elsewhere—is to enact pedagogies that develop communities of creative musical practice, that extend children's musical capacities, and that nurture and support creative thinking as a disposition—a fundamental part of human life. (Stauffer, 2013, p. 100)

Young composers don't need composition "teachers." They do need a process of collaborative mentorship that will scaffold and support their experiences in the music composition process.

As Ms. Baldwin shared with her sixth-grade music creation class, she was not there to teach, but was really there to guide them in the exploration of musical sounds and ideas. Teacher-mentors in the Very Young Composer Program shared how the process of mentorship helped them to appreciate composer intent and begin to see themselves as composers working alongside their students. It is often the case that *both* teachers and students cultivate greater confidence in their composition skills and develop identities as composers through the collaborative mentorship process.

1. *Provide a safe environment for musical exploration and sharing.* This environment is a shared, supportive, and creative community where *all* compositional voices are honored and respected by mentor and classmates alike. Margaret Barrett (2006) suggested that providing reassurance was necessary, even for college level composers. Jackie Wiggins and Michael Medvinsky (2013) called for a supportive environment that respects and honors the learner's voice. Embrace the challenge of time in this process. Time is necessary for mentorship of the creative process and development of an accepting, open, classroom community.

2. *Establish a fundamental base of musical knowledge from which to begin.* Wiggins and Medvinsky (2013) explained this as meeting the learners where they are. Sam Reese (2003) suggests that acknowledging student work, recognizing and verifying their work will encourage growth. This requires understanding the musical learners and their backgrounds, planning a starting point, and being ready to provide simple explanations for unfamiliar material. Creative thinking in music and exploration of musical ideas can begin at *any* level of experience.

3. *Set parameters to promote success in the composition process.* Begin with simple prompts that encourage success, and then expand the young composer's range. The idea of sharing one's musical ideas in a composition can seem overwhelming. Laying groundwork by connecting to previous musical experiences, and setting clear goals and expectations (Reese, 2006) are part of this process.

4. *Engage in joint problem-solving.* Esther Care (2016) encouraged "shared engagement" in the problem-solving process. Many of our authors felt that the composition teacher should participate in *joint* problem finding and solving by providing multiple alternatives and suggestions for change. With collaborative engagement, both the mentor and classmates can share in the process of problem solving and in the development of composer identity.

5. *Encourage extension and revision.* Barrett (2006) describes this as "giving license to change." Peter Webster's (2002) concept of "working through" is also a good descriptor. Sam Reese (2003) shared that students should be encouraged to extend, alter and develop their ideas. Encouraging reflection and revision is also an area where joint problem-solving will be necessary. Teacher encouragement in critical listening to one's own compositions is the first step to extension and revision (Ran, 2012).

6. *Encourage students to describe and explain their musical ideas and process.* Many of our authors support the idea of having students discuss and describe the music, its characteristics, their inspiration, and their ideas. An extension of this process that connects to joint problem-solving is encouraging the mentor tp "mirror" student ideas to help validate them (Reese, 2006).

7. *Plan for frequent sharing of musical ideas and compositions.* Students who engage in composition develop a strong sense of ownership and agency in their products. Encouraging discussion and critique (from both mentors and classmates) with the process of sharing ideas should be a regular part of the composition community.

8. *Embrace opportunities to expand knowledge and musicianship.* It is important to bring new musical concepts to the composition process. Connecting musical learning in other areas to student compositions will promote musicianship and create opportunity for meaningful transfer of musical knowledge.

9. *Nurture development in musical identity as a composer.* Margaret Barrett (2006) shared that composer-teachers should "set parameters for identity as a composer" (p. 201). In a collaborative mentorship relationship, both teachers and students should welcome the opportunity to nurture and develop identities as composers.

FIGURE 22.1. Planning for effective mentorship

CONCLUSION

As Sandra Stauffer (2013) shares, "Overcoming personal, professional, and political constraints and moving toward a pedagogical practice that nurtures children's creative musical abilities requires the courage to take risks and to cultivate one's own curiosity, wonder, and interest in creating" (p. 223). An examination of the approaches and strategies shared in this chapter, as well as study of existing, successful composition mentorship programs, provides an opportunity to share Figure 22.1, listing nine guidelines for consideration when planning for effective mentorship of young composers in your classroom.

Making the decision to embrace the process of including composition as a primary area of instruction may require some risk but mentoring young composers as a pathway to develop their creativity *and* musicianship is a powerful way to guide student musical learning. It is profoundly *good teaching*.

REFERENCES

Applebaum, M. (2012). Existential crises in composition mentorship and the creation of agency. *Contemporary Music Review*, *31*(4), 257–268. http://doi.org/10.1080/07494 467.2012.725809

Barrett, M. (2006). "Creative collaboration": An "eminence" study of teaching and learning in music composition. *Psychology of Music*, *34*(2), 195–218. https://doi.org/10.1177/030573560 6061852

Barrett, M. S. (2003). Freedoms and constraints: Constructing musical worlds through the dialogue of composition. In M. Hickey (Ed.), *Why and how to teach music composition: A new horizon for music education* (pp. 3–27). MENC.

Burnard, P., & Younker, B. A. (2004). Problem-solving and creativity: Insights from students' individual composing pathways. *International Journal of Music Education*, *22*(1), 59–76. https://doi.org/10.1177/0255761404042375

Care, E., Scoular, C., & Griffin, P. (2016). Assessment of Collaborative Problem Solving in education environments. *Applied Measurement in Education*, *29*(4), 250–264. http://dx.doi.org/ 10.1080/08957347.2016.1209204

Deutsch, D. (2016). Authentic assessment in music composition: Feedback that facilitates creativity. *Music Educators Journal*, *102*(3), 53–59. https://doi.org/10.1177/0027432115621608

Deutsch, D. (2013). Teaching gifted learners in composition. In M. Kaschub & J. P. Smith (Eds.), *Composing our future: Preparing music educators to teach composition* (pp. 127–148). Oxford University Press. https://doi.org/10.1093/acprof:oso/9780199832286.003.0007

Greiff, S., Wustenberg, S., Csapó, B., Demetrious, A., Hautamäke, J., Graesser, A. C., & Martin, R. (2014). Domain-general problem-solving skills and education in the 21st century. *Educational Research Review*, *13*, 74–83. http://dx.doi.org/10.1016/j.edurev.2014.10.002

Kaschub, M. (2013). Advancing composition in music education through strategic professional development. In M. Kaschub & J. P. Smith (Eds.), *Composing our future: Preparing* music educators to teach composition (pp. 319–337). Oxford University Press. https://doi.org/10.1093/acprof:oso/9780199832286.003.0019

Hickey, M. (2012). Music outside the lines: Ideas for composing in K–12 music classrooms. Oxford University Press. https://doi.org/10.1093/acprof:osobl/9780199826773.001.0001

Menard, E. (2013). Creative thinking in music: Developing a model for meaningful learning in middle school music. Music Educators Journal, 100(2), 61–67. https://doi.org/10.1177/0027432113500674

Menard, E. A. (2015). Music composition in the high school curriculum: A multiple case study. Journal of Research in Music Education, 63(1), 114–136. https://doi.org/10.1177/0022429415574310

Menard, E., & Rosen, R. (2016). Preservice music teacher perceptions of mentoring young composers: An exploratory case study. Journal of Music Teacher Education, 25(2), 66–80. https://doi.org/10.1177/1057083714552679

Ran, S. (2012). On teaching composition. Contemporary Music Review, 31(4), 305–312. https://doi.org/10.1080/07494467.2012.725813

Randles, C., & Sullian, M. (2013). How composers approach teaching composition: Strategies for music teachers. Music Educators Journal, 99(3), 51–57. https://doi.org/10.1177/0027432112471398

Reese, S. (2003). Responding to student compositions. In M. Hickey (Ed.), Why and how to teach music composition: A new horizon for music education (pp. 211–230). MENC: The National Association for Music Education.

Shvarts, A., & Bakker, A. (2019) The early history of the scaffolding metaphor: Bernstein, Luria, Vygotsky, and before. Mind, Culture, and Activity, 26 (1), 4–23. https://doi.org/10.1080/10749039.2019.1574306

Stauffer, S. L. (2013). Preparing to engage children in musical creating. In M. Kaschub & J. P. Smith (Eds.), Composing our future: Preparing music educators to teach composition (pp. 75–108). Oxford University Press. https://doi.org/10.1093/acprof:oso/9780199832286.003.0005

Strand, K. (2006). Survey of Indiana music teachers on using composition in the classroom. Journal of Research in Music Education, 54(2), 154–167. https://doi.org/10.1177/002242940605400206

Webster, P. R. (2002). Creative thinking in music: Advancing a model. In T. Sullivan & L. Willingham (Eds.). Creativity in Music Education (pp. 16–34). Britannia Printers.

Wiggins, J. (2007). Compositional process is music. In L. Bresler (Ed.), Springer International handbook of research in arts education, 6, 453–469. Springer. https://doi.org/10.1007/978-1-4020-3052-9_29

Wiggins, J., & Medvinsky, M. (2013). Scaffolding student composers. In M. Kaschub & J. P. Smith (Eds.), Composing our future: Preparing music educators to teach composition. (pp. 109–125). Oxford University Press. https://doi.org/10.1093/acprof:oso/9780199832286.003.0006

Wood, D., Bruner, J. S. & Ross, G. (1976). The role of tutoring in problem solving. Journal of Child Psychology and Psychiatry (17) 89–100. https://doi.org/10.1111/j.1469-7610.1976.tb00381.x

CHAPTER 23

CREATING AND MANAGING YOUNG COMPOSER FESTIVALS AND SHOWCASES

DANIEL DEUTSCH

STUDENT composition festivals and showcases offer valuable opportunities for young composers and music educators. These events help to nurture the development of young composers by recognizing their achievement and by providing venues for them to interact with peers and mentors in educational workshop settings. In addition, these programs serve educators by demonstrating benchmarks of excellence in composition and by offering professional development sessions for teachers. All state music educators' associations have long included programs to recognize and reward student achievement in musical performance. Now that the profession has a greater awareness of the importance of *creating* music, a growing number of organizations are implementing such programs in the areas of composition and songwriting.

The content of this chapter is drawn from decades-long experience in creating and administering composition programs for schools as well as state, regional, and national music education organizations, including the New York State School Music Association (NYSSMA), the National Association for Music Education (NAfME), and the Eastern Division of NAfME. I present strategies for establishing and developing higher-level programs and offer a detailed description of program elements, all of which can be shaped to fit the needs of various organizations. The chapter includes a discussion of student composer competitions, with suggestions for "taking the competition out of competition."

The Importance of Composition
and Performance

Composition should be a vital component of every child's musical education. Just as a language arts curriculum encompasses listening, reading, writing, and speaking, so too must a complete music curriculum include not only performing and responding to music, but also composing and improvising—activities in which the students learn to create their own music. As students use the art of music to express their own ideas and emotions, they gain increasing musical mastery and understanding, and they acquire powerful tools of self-expression. Imagine if we learned as children to read, but not to write essays, stories, poems, or correspondence. We would not be fluent in our language. The same is true of music. When students compose, they enter the creative source of music and learn to appreciate the *intentionality* of music, the idea that composers are expressing *meaning* in their work. In addition to the intrinsic value of musical self-expression, this awareness increases students' abilities as performers and listeners because they learn to better understand the communicative vector of music (Deutsch, 2009).

Most compositions are meant to be performed. From the earliest stages in PreK and elementary school, music classes should include the performance of student-created music. Developed in this context, the performance of student composition and improvisation becomes a normal means of musical communication and the walls between composer, performer, and listener are transcended. Within the safety of a supportive classroom, performances of early experiments in composition and improvisation, generated by groups and individuals, help students to feel empowered as creators expressing their own musical ideas, even if quite simple at first, just as their first attempts at creative writing empower them as young authors. Even at the introductory level, as students make aesthetic choices, they join the ranks of composers. They learn that they are adding to the body of art in the world and should be told that they are making the world a more beautiful place. At the appropriate stages, the audience may be expanded by inviting other classes and/or parents, which provides a somewhat more formal setting for performance.

Expanding Venues for Performance
of Student Composition

As students make progress and gain more experience in composition, teachers should encourage them by offering wider opportunities for performance. One of the most effective ways of inspiring students to create compositions and to persevere to completion is to provide venues for performance. Scheduled performances set tangible goalposts for students. They reinforce the communicative purpose of composition because they provide a pathway from the loneliness of composition to the shared aesthetic response of a community of listeners. Even professional composers often emphasize the important role that deadlines and performance commitments play in encouraging task completion.

Elementary, middle, and high schools are all appropriate settings for student composition concerts or "young composer festivals." Close mentoring and instruction help students to make the most progress, but simply announcing a date and setting for a young composer festival is often enough to motivate students to create pieces. Planning for a young composer festival attracts the attention of the students with the strongest interest in composition and helps to build a community of young composers. If students are being mentored to develop their own unique musical ideas, the concerts will be extraordinarily varied, with music ranging among pop songs, jazz combos, "classical" solos and chamber works, and even avant-garde experimental works. Because the students are expressing their own feelings and ideas in the music, there is often a higher level of passion and emotional intensity than is usual in school concerts. A random sequence of composition titles from a festival of my fifth- and sixth-grade students from a single year hints at the diversity and emotional force of the works: *Invention 4.1*; *Gone for Good*; *Jazz Pizzazz*; *My Dream World*; *Tessellations*; *Dance of the Butterfly*; *Bittersweet*; *The Workshop of Daedalus*.

When parents, teachers, and administrators attend the concerts, they are often surprised by the high quality of many of the compositions. A frequent result is that parents and educational administrators become stronger proponents of school composition programs. The compositions can be revealing. Sometimes they seem to confirm the personality of the composer to their parents and friends, as when a perennially cheerful student creates a piece that hops along happily. But sometimes they open a new window into the audience's perception, as when a competitive athlete composes a tender piece, or a shy student composes a piece of thundering passion. As one parent wrote to me in an email after a young composer festival: "We, the parents, have learned more about our children through their work [in composition]" (A. He, personal communication, March 26, 2010).

The most highly motivated students are eager to expand their horizons beyond the school walls, which is why higher-level festivals are so important. Teachers can guide them to existing state, regional, and national programs and competitions. If their state or region lacks such programs, educators can adopt some of the ideas that follow in this chapter to create them.

Competitions

Composition competitions have a long history, dating back in the West at least as far as ancient Greece, where composer-performers competed alongside thespians and athletes in festivals such as the Pythian Games, which began in the sixth century BCE (Mathiesen, 2001). For the most ambitious composers, competitions are often important in the trajectory of their careers. From 1803 through 1968, France sponsored the Prix de Rome, which included prizes for the "best" compositions (Gilbert, 2001). (It is amusing to look at the list of winners and see such a long catalog of composers who mostly are unknown at present.) In today's music world, an internet search leads to hundreds of composition competitions. Contests such as the BMI Student Composer Awards and the ASCAP Morton Gould Young Composer Awards attract many of the most aspiring young composers in order to build their academic and professional careers. The ladder continues to rise all the way to the Pulitzer Prizes and Grawemeyer Awards.

I personally have recommended competitions to several of my most motivated students (including several winners who have pursued careers in composition), and I have helped to create, administer, and judge competitions. However, I have ambivalent feelings about them, especially when considering the purpose of composition education in general. The goal of including composition in music education is to empower all students to make music creatively, not merely to launch the compositional careers of a tiny fraction of students. Many critics of competition in education have published compelling arguments (Abramo, 2017; Kohn, 1992). As James R. Austin (1990) wrote in *Music Educators Journal*, "Competition, by definition, always produces few winners and many losers; one person's success requires another person's failure" (p.23).

When the NYSSMA young composer program began in 1990, my colleagues and I were acutely aware of this problem. One of our goals was to recognize and reward outstanding students by inviting them to present their works and participate in workshops at our state conference, which has an inherently competitive element. But we also were determined to serve the needs of a large number of students and teachers. The idea of issuing a call for compositions and then accepting 12 "winners" and rejecting 150 "losers" appalled us. As a result, we developed a composition evaluation program by enlisting a team of composers and teachers to write detailed, supportive feedback to all students and teachers who submit compositions. I helped to develop a similar evaluation program for the NAfME competitions, in which hundreds of students receive written evaluations every year. State and national programs and festivals have an unavoidable factor of competition, but we have tried to mitigate the negative effects by serving a broad base of students and teachers. These evaluation programs are discussed in detail later in the chapter.

On the other hand, selecting outstanding students for participation in higher level festivals through an inevitably competitive process has positive points. In *Developing Talent in Young People*, Lauren A. Sosniak (1985) wrote about successful young concert pianists who were studied for four years in a well-known research project headed by Benjamin S. Bloom:

> Recitals, competitions, and adjudications were also powerful means of developing actual competence and feelings of efficacy for music-making abilities. These events gave students and teachers something very specific to work for and also provided a

means of evaluating one's progress over time. They also brought the children's solitary work into a public arena. All the fanfare that went along with these activities helped the children view their work as something that was real and important in the larger world. (p.488)

At state or national conferences, it is important to bring the selected students together in workshops, seminars, and reflection sessions with supportive mentors so that they develop a sense of community and a realization that they are not merely competitors. As the students discuss their work processes with each other, the competitive barriers tend to weaken. This aligns with a point Joseph Abramo (2017) makes in an article that is highly critical of competition:

> How do educators avoid a retreat into hoarding and isolation and retain the positive aspect of convening and comparing that competition festivals provide while addressing some of the problems created by measurement and competition? Educators might exploit the opportunity to participate in the public space of competitions, but transform the practice in important ways where the term "competition" is no longer appropriate. In this new conception of competition, students and educators explicitly describe and show to other students and educators what they learned and what they struggled with through the process of preparing a performance. (p.165)

A key goal of conference sessions and workshops for young composers is to help the students think of each other as colleagues rather than competitors.

CREATING YOUNG COMPOSER FESTIVALS AND SHOWCASES

When designing and implementing young composer festivals and showcases, it is vital to base the programs on the educational needs of the students and the professional needs of educators and to respect the commitment of the composers' parents. The students will often have to travel a considerable distance to attend and will miss school time, and the parents will have to take time off from work to accompany their children. In many cases, parents will not be reimbursed for travel expenses. It is not enough to simply schedule a young composer concert, present certificates, and send the students home. Successful programs showcase student achievement at young composer concerts, but they also provide a rich offering of educational opportunities such as composition workshops, seminars, and interactions with peers, performers, and professional composers—a full day of learning activities. State music education association conferences are excellent settings for such programs because the conference venues and information infrastructure are in place, and the conferences already include statewide recognition for student excellence in performance. The young composer festival functions as a mini-conference within the state conference. Many of the program components can be adapted and implemented for smaller venues, such as schools, districts, and regional areas.

The details of the programs will vary depending upon the scale of the events and the available resources. The components of effective programs may include the following, each of which will be discussed in detail later in the chapter:

- Written evaluations with constructive feedback for all applicants
- Student composition concerts
- Composition coaching workshops
- Post-concert reflective sessions for student composers and conference attendees
- Participation of prominent composers-in-residence
- Coordination with honors ensembles to feature works by visiting composers
- Educational sessions for teachers.

Overcoming Obstacles to Innovation

Establishing state-wide programs like this can be a challenge. Large organizations often have considerable inertia and may be resistant to change. They have customs, histories, and standard procedures that new programs may seem to disrupt. Conferences are already filled with concerts and educational sessions packed into tight schedules; how can anything new be added? Associations often have many committees and chairs who are attached to their own turf and view advocates of change as interlopers in a zero-sum game trying to usurp power and resources. Colleagues may bristle at the idea of state recognition for student composers because they are not selected in exactly the same way that all-state performers are chosen, and the students may not fit neatly into band, orchestra, chorus, or jazz programs. For all of these reasons, establishing a new program often requires great perseverance and persuasion.

As more and more states create programs, however, innovators can point across state lines to illustrate models of success. For example, several state associations have invited me to consult and visit their conferences to discuss the NYSSMA program and to offer ideas on implementing new programs, and such efforts have been fruitful. Therefore, a good first step in creating a program is to reach out to other states and learn from their experiences. The NAfME Council for Music Composition is conducting an ongoing survey of state programs that it continues to update. The chair of the council is a good source for more information.

Another useful tactic for successful innovation is to assemble a team. Ideally each state should have a composition chairperson and committee. An effective committee should, if possible, include a diverse group of educators of all grade levels, from elementary school through college, with expertise in general music, performance, theory, and composition. To effect change in a resistant environment, it is useful for the committee to include some members who are esteemed particularly highly in the organization, such as well-regarded professors or former officers of the association. Fortunately, the emphasis on "creating" in the National Core Arts Standards has cast a bright light on the importance of composition and songwriting, so resistance to change may be diminishing as associations see the need to address the issue.

CALL FOR COMPOSITIONS

When a new festival program is established, it is important to get the word out to association members through journals, newsletters, and/or electronic communication. In each cycle of the program, the organization should issue a call for compositions to solicit submissions for consideration. The call includes the following information:

- A brief description of the program
- Age categories
- Rules and regulations
- Submission requirements and instructions
- Duration limit of composition
- Instrumentation limitations, if any
- Fee information
- Criteria for selection
- Information about performers
- Expectation that selected students will attend the conference
- Submission deadline

For examples of calls for compositions, visit the websites of NAfME (nafme.org) and NYSSMA (nyssma.org/composition). Both of these associations issue three separate calls, with each one seeking works in a particular category: acoustic composition (i.e., works for instruments and/or voices), electronic composition, and songwriting. The most efficient way for teachers and students to submit compositions is online, through application submission software. In all three categories, students submit audio files of recordings. NAfME and NYSSMA require PDF files of scores for the acoustic compositions and lyric sheets for songwriting.

The scope of the call for compositions will be limited by the resources of the sponsoring organization. NYSSMA, for example, accepts acoustic composition submissions without any instrumental limitations. The call states that if a composition is selected for performance at the conference, NYSSMA will attempt to recruit performers but cannot guarantee a performance. For practical reasons, NAfME limits the instrumentation for its student composers' concert to an annually rotating series of instrumentation such as string quartet, brass quintet, woodwind quintet, or saxophone quartet. But NAfME accepts submissions and supplies written evaluations of compositions for any instrumentation.

Criteria for Evaluation

Criteria for the evaluation of compositions continue to evolve, reflecting the progress currently underway in young composer festivals and showcases. Each organization will shape criteria to fit its own program. NYSSMA and NAfME have used the following three broad criteria for the evaluation of acoustic compositions: compositional technique, overall music appeal, and originality. (In 2021, NYSSMA changed the third criterion from "originality" to "creativity.") Figure 23.1 illustrates the NAfME evaluation criteria for its three competitions.

Student Composers Competition

Compositions submitted to the Student Composers Competition are evaluated according to three broad criteria:

(1) **Compositional Technique** refers to the following elements, where applicable:

- Organization of pitch elements (such as melody, harmony, and counterpoint)
- Organization of rhythmic elements
- Formal design
- Accuracy and clarity of notation
- Appropriate writing for instruments and/or voices

(2) **Overall Musical Appeal** includes the following aspects:

- Stylistic coherence (regardless of the particular style)
- Effective handling of unity/variety and tension/release
- Effective use of dynamics, articulations, and expression marks
- Interaction of all of the elements (atmosphere, mood, direction, and flow of the music)

(3) **Originality** refers to aspects of the piece that reveal the composer's individual "voice" and distinguish the piece from a musical exercise or a direct imitation of another piece.

(National Association for Music Education, 2021a)

Electronic Music Composition Competition

Entries will be judged based on their aesthetic quality, use of electronic media, and the interaction of all the elements (i.e., atmosphere, mood, direction, and flow of the music).

(National Association for Music Education, 2021b)

Student Songwriters Competition

Entries will be judged based on their originality, aesthetic quality, and the effectiveness of the music and lyrics.

(National Association for Music Education, 2021c)

FIGURE 23.1. National Association for Music Education criteria for the evaluation of compositions

These criteria from NAfME (virtually identical to the NYSSMA criteria) are intended to be receptive to a wide range of student creativity. For example, note that "[c]ompositional technique includes the following elements, where applicable." The phrase "where applicable" may apply to the trivial case in which a drum composition will not have "organization of pitch elements," but on a deeper level it leaves open the possibility that a student may challenge a conventional norm of "appropriate writing for instruments" by experimenting successfully with avant-garde instrumental technique.

The NYSSMA criteria description includes an additional statement that the criteria "are not intended as a 'checklist' that each student should go through as they compose a piece. Each piece is unique, and the committee attempts to assess each composition on its own terms" (New York State School Music Association, 2021a). This represents an attempt to promote creativity, to encourage students to develop their own inventive voices. A potential problem with competitions and rubrics is that they may incline students to reverse engineer their work to fit a conception of what they imagine the judges wish to hear, rather than trusting their own authentic ideas (Deutsch, 2016).

Selection Process

The young composer concert at a state or regional festival showcases the achievements of a group of outstanding students and illustrates benchmarks of excellence that help teachers understand the potential in the student population. Unlike in a competition, the goal of the judges is not merely to identify the "best" compositions on a unitary scale of evaluation, which is a difficult or illusory goal in any event. Rather, the goal is to showcase an attractive, aesthetically pleasing concert that spans a range of musical expression, genres, styles, and techniques. The different age categories should be represented and approximate gender equity is a good signal to both students and teachers that composition is for everyone. Student diversity is an important goal.

The number of entries will lead to different strategies for the selection process. In the NYSSMA acoustic composition program, for example, the committee usually receives between 100 and 150 submissions each year. The committee members meet to review the pieces together. In the first review, the committee listens to each piece, or at least a significant portion of it, while looking at the score. In this first listening, each member labels the piece as 1) almost surely a "winner"; 2) a contender deserving another listening; or 3) definitely not suitable for the concert. A convenient way to record these opinions is for each member to have a shared spreadsheet on his or her laptop. The spreadsheet contains the composers' names, composition titles, school grade, etc. To the right of these columns, there is a group of columns—one for each committee member. For each composition, the member selects a color to fill his or her appropriate spreadsheet cell: green for "excellent," yellow for "maybe," and red for "evaluation only." The use of colors makes it quite easy to see the aggregate opinion of the group. For example, a piece that demonstrates a high level of compositional technique, overall musicality, and creativity will have a horizontal line of green cells, while a piece with less skill in evidence will have a line of red cells. This is much easier than trying to add up numerical ratings. After the first review, the committee listens again to the more skillful pieces and gradually reduces the list, keeping track of the total duration of the remaining pieces.

There are some considerations that are not strictly related to the quality of the compositions. In practice, if the concert has varied instrumentation and set-ups, the musical duration should be little more than half of the allotted concert time. The committee also attempts to represent different geographical areas of the state, although there are usually clusters in areas where students receive more instruction in composition. Because a goal is to inspire the music teachers in the concert audience, the committee tries to include pieces that include brass, woodwinds, strings, voice, and piano in "classical," jazz, and occasionally "popular" styles. The NYSSMA conference also includes a student electronic music composition concert and a songwriters' concert. Approximately 12 compositions are selected for each concert, and several other pieces are singled out for "honorable mention."

Organizations that lack the resources to bring a committee together in person can use electronic meeting platforms, as NYSSMA did due to the pandemic in 2020. In any case, judging by a diverse team is better than having a single judge because an individual person may have blind spots and unknown prejudices. A team blends varied points of view into a consensus.

When the NYSSMA committee judges the compositions, the committee members do not go through a checklist or rubric to assign quantitative scores to compositions. Because the members are experienced composers and teachers, they have internalized the criteria for selection and consider them all in the judging process. They view these criteria as interconnected qualities, not in isolation. This is a subjective opinion the committee shares, but other programs might well use checklists and rubrics judiciously.

I have been a judge in several composition competitions in which the adjudicators were provided with grids describing aspects of compositions such as clarity and correctness of notation, appropriate writing for instruments, effective use of musical parameters, and aesthetic qualities. We were instructed to enter numerical scores in the indicated boxes for each criterion and add up the points to assign a numerical grade for each composition. Because this process uses the same numbers to measure noncomparable properties, the results were often ludicrously incorrect in ranking the value of the compositions, and the judges rebelled against using this method. One solution was merely to triple the "overall musical appeal" score. The "wow factor" that we feel when hearing a superb composition is difficult or impossible to quantify.

Pianist and professor Matti Raekallio (2012), made a similar point when discussing quantitative scoring in piano competitions: "The very concept of a precise judging of performances in music competitions is delusional at best, especially when the results of the judging are processed using an exact but inappropriate system such as numeric point scores" (p. 1).

Communicating Non-Acceptance

Many, perhaps most, students whose works are not selected for performance at the young composer concert will feel disappointed, particularly those who are passionate about composition. It can be especially disappointing for students whose pieces have been selected in prior years. When informing applicants of the results, administrators wear two hats. They are simultaneously emphasizing the outstanding achievement of the students whose works have been selected and attempting to mitigate the other students' feeling of "losing."

For ease of distribution and to avoid large postal expenses, it is practical to notify students, parents, and teachers through electronic communication. Figure 23.2 illustrates a sample letter emailed to students whose works were not selected for performance at the conference. Although this letter is an impersonal announcement sent to all applicants, each student also receives an evaluation that is highly personalized and supportive.

Even if a program is described as a festival or showcase and not as a competition, there is an undeniable competitive element, and administrators should be as compassionate as possible.

Dear Composer,

Thank you for submitting your composition to the Call for Compositions sponsored by the New York State School Music Association (NYSSMA).

A panel of composition teachers adjudicated the compositions and selected the following pieces for performance at the NYSSMA Winter Conference:

[List of selected pieces and composers]

Due to time constraints at the concert, the judges could select only 12 compositions out of the 112 pieces submitted. With 112 submissions, the odds were particularly difficult this year. The decisions were quite challenging for the judges to reach. Many truly outstanding compositions were not included in the program. The fact that your piece was not selected implies nothing bad about your composition.

The following pieces achieved the distinction of Honorable Mention. Although they were not selected for the Young Composer Honors Concert, they were reviewed more than once and were top contenders for inclusion:

[List of honorable mention pieces and composers]

All students and teachers will receive written evaluations of your compositions as attachments to separate e-mails in the very near future.

Congratulations to all of the young composers and their teachers! We hope that you continue to express yourself in your own original music! Best of luck to you!

[Chairperson signature]

FIGURE 23.2. Sample non-acceptance letter from NYSSMA

WRITTEN EVALUATIONS AND CONSTRUCTIVE FEEDBACK

A key component of a higher-level program, perhaps the most important element, is providing written evaluations to all students and teachers who submit compositions. An evaluation program delivers a reward to every student and teacher who participates. It is an opportunity to educate a large group of students and teachers. The students who submit compositions have extremely diverse backgrounds and resources. The spectrum ranges from students who are composing completely on their own, with little or no mentoring from any teacher, all the way to aspiring young professionals who are enrolled in conservatory pre-college composition programs. The background of sponsoring teachers is also quite varied, running the gamut from instrumental and vocal teachers with limited training and experience in composition to professional composition teachers. Based on many years of responses from students, teachers, and parents, it is clear that teachers and students of all levels appreciate and learn from well-written evaluations.

The NYSSMA and NAfME programs send students and teachers narrative evaluations rather than itemized checklists with numerical or letter grades. A paramount aim is to encourage each student to persevere and continue to develop as a composer. A low grade may cause a student to feel like a failure and stop composing, while a narrative evaluation can point out all of the shortcomings in a supportive and empathetic manner that motivates the student to grow and move forward. A drawback of checklists is that they imply that every composition has to illustrate every item in the checklist, but there are many musical masterpieces that do not address every element of such criteria. For example, Bach's Prelude No. 1, from *The Well-Tempered Clavier*, Book I, completely lacks the rhythmic or textural variety required by many sets of checklist criteria. A student might submit a minimalist composition that is quite accomplished, but that would similarly fail a checklist's requirement for "variety." Checklists can mislead students by suggesting that the strategy for composing a piece begins by satisfying discrete criteria, rather than springing from an expressive impulse, idea, image, process, emotion, or artistic intention (Deutsch, 2016).

GUIDELINES FOR WRITTEN EVALUATIONS

A written evaluation is a summative assessment, providing a punctuation mark in the student's growth, helping the composer to reflect on problems and successes in a given composition. Therefore, it can seem like a snapshot: A piece is finished, the evaluator rates it, and it is frozen in time. The goal of the evaluator, however, is to use comments about a piece written in the past in order to propel the student forward in his or her creative development. One of the values of an evaluation written by someone other than the student's own teacher is to provide an independent opinion that adds a different perspective and broadens the student's understanding. But the student will be much more receptive if the evaluator sounds less like a high court judge and more like a teacher sitting beside the young composer. Compositions are personal and expose feelings; the evaluator must handle them with care. It is important to recruit a team of evaluation writers who combine expertise and empathy. If possible, potential evaluators should submit sample evaluations before joining the evaluation team, and organizations should present online webinar/discussion sessions to prepare evaluators for their work. In addition, the chair should spot check evaluations by each evaluator.

In recent years, NAfME and NYSSMA have sent a list of guidelines to all of the evaluators, titled "Guidelines for Written Evaluations," shown in Figure 23.3 (New York State School Music Association, 2021b).

Examples of Evaluations

NYSSMA and NAfME evaluations are distributed as email attachments to student and teachers. They consist of a cover page that thanks, congratulates, and encourages the students and lists the criteria for evaluation. The evaluator adds a page or more of comments. Figure 23.4 shows the evaluation sent to a sixth-grade student and sponsoring teacher.

Clearly, providing the level of both constructive criticism and supportive comments in this example takes a good measure of time and thought. (NYSSMA and NAfME compensate evaluators with a small honorarium for each evaluation written.) Because the evaluations are distributed as attachments to emails, evaluators can include links to educational resources that elucidate comments. One helpful link is to the Music Notation Style Guide on the website of the Indiana University Jacobs School of Music Composition Department at https://blogs.iu.edu/jsomcomposition/music-notation-style-guide/. Evaluators can also include links to videos of musical performances to illustrate concepts raised in the evaluations or to suggest new repertoire for listening and study.

Figure 23.5 is an abridgement of evaluations sent to a very talented 10th grader selected for honorable mention. It contains links to educational resources and suggestions for listening.

The student's email response to the evaluator is shown in Figure 23.6.

Responses from Students, Teachers, and Parents

It is a good idea for the program chairperson to include a request for responses to evaluations when sending them to students and teachers. Responses can help the chair recognize potential blind spots or problems with certain evaluators. For the most part, however, they validate the effectiveness of the program.

Guidelines for Written Evaluations

The aim of written evaluations is to nurture students, affirm their achievement, provide constructive criticism, and encourage them to keep composing.

- **Use a supportive and optimistic tone of voice in assessing student work.**

  The tone should evoke the character of a person-to-person conversation, and the evaluator should seem more like a collaborative artist than a judge.

- **Remember how you felt when you were the age of the composer.**

  Composition is quite personal, and most students are very vulnerable to criticism. It is easy for students to become discouraged.

- **Begin and end with positive comments.**

  Most students begin reading their evaluations with a feeling of anxiety, so the evaluator should break the ice. Especially with very young composers, positive comments should outnumber critical points.

- **Focus on the future.**

  In most cases, the composition being evaluated feels to a student like part of his or her past, so it is helpful to spin learning toward the next composition. Particularly when serving as an outside evaluator, include statements like: "You may have already tried this, but in a future piece you could...."

- **Clearly differentiate between objective and subjective elements.**

  For example, it is an error to write outside the range of an instrument, but it is not required that a first theme return in the tonic, or even return at all. For subjective points, helpful phrases include: "you may wish to" or "you might consider."

- **Phrase comments in the form of questions sometimes.**

  This approach avoids sounding overly judgmental, and it encourages the student to think and wonder. For example, if there is no chance for a singer or wind player to take a breath in a phrase, ask the student where the best place for a breath would be.

- **Explain the terms you use.**

  Most students have a limited grasp of technical terms. If the composers are not your own students, encourage them to discuss the terms with their teacher.

- **Teach each student his or her own composition.**

  Many students compose intuitively, so it is helpful for the evaluator to embed an analysis of the form and technique of the composition within the evaluation.

- **Highlight emerging shoots of success when addressing problems.**

  For example, if the composition lacks variety, find a few examples where the student does achieve variety and explain how those techniques could be extended.

- **Include musical notation in written evaluations.**

  It is often helpful to musically illustrate comments and suggestions and to demonstrate correct notation.

- **Recognize your own spheres of expertise and limits of knowledge.**

  For example, you may not be the best judge of a hip-hop composition or big band jazz chart, so you should seek guidance when needed.

- **Suggest musical repertoire for study.**

  Guiding the students to relevant scores and recordings can effectively support the written evaluation by providing models that nurture and encourage their creative growth.

  (New York State School Music Association, 2021b)

FIGURE 23.3. Guidelines for written evaluations used by NAfME and NYSSMA

Dear Sally [Pseudonym],

Thank you for submitting a composition this year! It's obvious to me that you have put a great deal of work into this piece. Composing your own music is not easy—so you, your teacher, and your family should be proud of your work. I want to share some thoughts about your piece that I hope will give you even more great ideas for compositions you will write in the future.

You've done a fine job of notating your piece! You have been very clear about what you expect from the performers in terms of tempo and dynamics. My only suggestion for your next piece is that you be just as clear in terms of articulation and phrasing. For example, should the pianist play the triplet figures in a separated style? Connected, but without pedal? With pedal? I would encourage you to think like a performer as you write. What would you want to know if you were playing this piece for the first time?

Your form is very clear and reflects the title of your composition well. Changing key areas in the middle section helps to separate the sections of your piece. In future compositions, think about other ways that you might create variety, within or between sections of the piece. For example, you might consider changing the meter or the style in some part(s) of your composition.

You've done a great job of writing for piano and for violin. Many young composers write music that is awkward to play, but you have done a good job of composing music that works well for both instruments! I enjoyed the fact that you used a different register of the violin in the middle section of the piece—in your next composition, you might also think about places where you could use different registers of the piano.

I also really like the way that you used several motives to tie the composition together. The melodic gestures that repeat, as well as the triplet accompaniment, give the different sections a sense of unity. That said, reusing material too much could start to sound monotonous. This is my subjective opinion, but you might consider varying the accompaniment throughout the piece. You've done this in a couple of places (mm. 32-35, mm. 44-51), but you might also consider other opportunities to create more interest. Tying this together with my suggestion above about using a different register in the piano, you might consider doing something like this at measure 18:

I hope that you'll continue to write more of your own music! As you continue to compose, make a habit of listening to lots of music, in as many different styles as you can. When you hear an idea you like, figure out how the composer created it, and make it part of your own compositional "toolbox." A score can be helpful if it's available, but also try to recreate the elements you like with your voice, with your instrument, and in notation. Your compositions will become even more interesting as you expand your palette. I hope to see more of your works in the future—best wishes for a successful school year!

[Signed by evaluator]

FIGURE 23.4. Evaluation sent to a sixth-grade student and teacher-sponsor from NYSSMA

Hi Peter [Pseudonym]!!

Congratulations on this marvelous piece! It came very close to being selected for the Rochester concert. There are very few Honorable Mention compositions this year, so you, your teacher, and your family should be proud of your achievement!

If I use any terms you are not familiar with, please ask [teacher name] about them, and of course I welcome questions and comments at [evaluator email address].

The rolling texture of perpetual arpeggios in the left hand makes the title of this piece perfect. It really does spin along like a revolving planet.

The most astonishing thing to me and to others on the committee is your amazing intuitive sense of chromatic harmony. Most composers your age stick pretty close to the tonic (the home key center) and use mostly diatonic (not chromatic) harmony. You, on the other hand, start right from the beginning with a chromatically descending bassline, and you fill it in with harmonies that fit perfectly, creating evocative layers of chromatic harmony that pull the listener along.

Your harmonic palette is fluid. You move from F-sharp minor to G major, to C minor, back to F-sharp minor, to G-sharp minor, back to F-sharp minor, and finally to A minor. Some advanced theory students would have difficulty moving from F-sharp minor to C minor, because they are distantly related keys, but you do it with ease. Congrats! [clapping emojis]

It is difficult to respond fully to a composition like this through a written evaluation, because you and I cannot have a dialogue in which I ask you your intentions and provide feedback throughout the creative process. Therefore, my following points are subjective—just my opinion. But because you are so talented, I want to speak frankly about possible areas for future growth. My impression is that you composed this very intuitively. Creative intuition like yours is a precious gift. Treasure it! The next step (which you are probably already doing) is to aim it with more conscious direction. Maybe this analogy will make my thoughts clearer: It's like you are a great figure skater who can glide anywhere on the ice, forward and backward, performing great tricks and spins, but you don't know exactly where you are on the ice, so some of your best tricks may be off in the corner of the rink. The next step for the skater is to plan the big picture of the entire skating routine. The climactic triple axel should be planned to occur right in the center of the rink at just the right moment. Back to the music: Your ear seems to lead you step by step to new key areas, but the next stage in your compositional work could be to plan the moves more strategically. It is true that you keep returning to F-sharp minor, so that is a bit of strategy. Maybe you have already done this, but I suggest that you intensely study some scores of music you enjoy and analyze how the composers establish key areas and move between them. What are the proportions they use? How long do they stay in one key before moving on? How do the various key areas relate to each other? Based on your piece, I think composers like Schumann, Chopin, Liszt, and Scriabin would be good choices to study. I don't suggest that you slavishly follow their examples; just steal what works for you!

Another area for future growth is to pay more attention to the melody and melodic consistency. Again, I realize that you wrote this piece a long time ago, and you are probably doing amazing things with melodies right now. The harmony flows seamlessly throughout this composition, but the melodies seem to change subject quite a bit. It is true that melodic motives reappear, but many of the melodic fragments appear only once. The result is that the melodic dimension is not as unified as it could be. Analyze how composers you admire retain and transform their melodic ideas to create a unified and varied melodic universe. How do they use, reuse, reshape, fragment, recombine, and extend their melodic ideas? But it's not just intellectual. I recommend that you sing all of your melodies. Somehow singing aloud helps to make melodies flow more convincingly. Many of the melodic ideas in this piece sound more like arpeggiations of your harmonies than true melodies.

FIGURE 23.5. Abridgement of NYSSMA evaluation sent to an advanced 10th-grade student and teacher-sponsor

Here are some techniques of motivic development that Prof. Jono Kornfeld of San Francisco State University posted online:

http://jkornfeld.net/motive_development_1.pdf

http://jkornfeld.net/motive_development_2.pdf

If you and I were sitting in the same room, I could ask you how you hear the rhythms in your piece. Clearly there are six eighth-note pulses in each measure. When we hear groups of six eighth-notes, our brains tend to group them in one of two ways. Either they are 2+2+2, which is 3/4 meter, or we hear them as 3+3, which is 6/8. You notated your piece in 6/8, but I hear most of it in 3/4. Listen to it and clap your hands with the beat you feel. If you are clapping three times per measure (on the first, third, and fifth eighth-notes), it is in 3/4. If you clap just twice per measure (on the first and fourth eighth-notes), it is in 6/8. There are some measures that really do sound like 6/8 to me (e.g., mm. 44 and following). The metric notation gets out of whack beginning in m. 47, though. Your chords change midway through the measures, but I think they should be shifted to change on beat one. You would have to add three eighth-notes somewhere, or use a 3/8 measure.

A couple of final notes on notation: I think your piece would benefit from more dynamic markings. Also, there are some enharmonic spelling errors in the G-sharp minor section that you can clean up. For example, the leading tone should be F double sharp, not G natural.

But far more important than all of these technical details is the emotional impact of your work, which is profound and generous. Bravo!

I hope that this evaluation doesn't seem too critical to you and that you take my comments in the spirit in which I mean them. It is a sign of my great respect for you! I'm a big fan and I look forward to hearing much more of your music in the future.

I know you are listening to a wide variety of music and trying to figure out how the composers work their magic. Here are links to videos of three pieces I listened to recently:

Caroline Shaw: Partita for 8 Voices (first movement)

https://www.youtube.com/watch?v=ogu7Wfg1MLY

This is the first movement of a piece that won the 2013 Pulitzer Prize.

Water, Wine, Brandy, Brine by Viet Cuong performed by Sandbox Percussion
https://www.youtube.com/watch?v=7L_NxXX4gFM
I was at this concert! This piece is written for wine glasses!

Appalachian Spring (chamber version), by Aaron Copland
https://www.youtube.com/watch?v=ypdLLtloF1c
This is a classic of American composition.

Thanks again for submitting your composition and best of luck!

[Signed by evaluator]

FIGURE 23.5. Continued

Dear [Evaluator],

Thank so much for all your feedback on my compositions. I read it through carefully and found many crucial things I can improve on. I have been recently trying to sing my melody to help improve on it, and also reusing themes and melodies found earlier is very helpful. I am very glad to hear that you are a big fan of my music! As for more music in the future, I just recently finished a piano solo piece that will be performed soon. Thank you again for the feedback and the evaluation of my pieces.

Look forward to seeing you,

[Student signature]

FIGURE 23.6. Student response to evaluator

This is the email response of one public school teacher-sponsor of two NYSSMA submissions (with pseudonyms for the students' names):

> Please pass on my sincere thanks to the composers who took the time to evaluate and comment on Mary and John's pieces. The comments by [the evaluators] were supportive, knowledgeable, and helpful. It is clear that they took significant time to write thoughtful mentoring comments that both encourage young composers and challenge them. Mary and John will benefit tremendously. . . . Through your work, my two students have made helpful connections with mentors and with peer composers, connecting with a composition community that has inspired and informed their work. (J. Jefferis, personal communication, August 19, 2015)

A student composer who went on to study composition at Yale University responded to two evaluations:

> I wrote two solo piano pieces and submitted them to the NYSSMA Call for Compositions. I received back thorough, well thought out, sensitive, and carefully written comments that showed a depth of thought about my music that was incredibly inspiring. [The evaluator's] comments helped me take the music in new and previously unanticipated directions. (S. Feiner, personal communication, April 4, 2018)

One appreciative parent wrote this in an email about her daughter's NAfME evaluation:

> Thank you for your formal evaluation of [my daughter's] music composition. . . . We really appreciate your taking the time to formally evaluate [my daughter's] piece, and furthermore, offering details conducive to learning and supportive ways of improvement. This piece of paper is gold to [my daughter], and through your wisdom, as displayed, she will strive to continually develop and continue her composition writing. Your critique of [my daughter's] work was done with great effort, has provided a positive effect, and is thoughtful and helpful. (C. Whitehouse, personal communication, May 12, 2014)

CONFERENCE OR FESTIVAL EVENTS

Student Composition Concerts

Student composition concerts are the centerpiece of young composer festivals. The formats will differ according to the needs and resources of the sponsoring organization. The NYSSMA conference includes three concerts: the Student Composer Honors Concert, the Student Electronic Music Showcase, and the Student Songwriters Honors Concert. The 90-minute Student Composer Honors Concert features music of diverse genre, style, and instrumentation. The concerts have included solo and chamber works together with pieces for orchestra, band, chorus, and jazz band. The pieces are performed by students, teachers, school ensembles, and quite often by students and faculty from the State University of New York at Fredonia. Programming for diverse ensembles is a challenge due to difficulty in recruiting performers and complex set-up requirements, but such programming has two advantages. It produces a more varied concert, and it attracts the interest of band, orchestra, choral, and jazz teachers. Prior to the concert, there is a rehearsal session in which many of the composers meet their performers for the first time. Teacher-mentors help the students communicate effectively with the performers in the rehearsal.

NAfME responded to this challenge by reducing the number of compositions selected for performance at its conference and by limiting the instrumentation to a specific group of instruments each year. NAfME, it should be noted, hires professional performers for the concert. In recent years, the concert has included a public discussion among the NAfME president, the composition council chair, and the student composers that is integrated into the concert. An attractive feature of the NAfME event is that it has been scheduled so that there are no competing conference events in the same time slot. In a separate competition, NAfME selects a student-composed band, orchestra, or choral work to be performed by an all-national honor ensemble. In addition, NAfME sponsors annual electronic composition and songwriting competitions. Written evaluations are provided to all applicants in each of these NAfME programs.

The launching of a songwriting category by NAfME (in 2020) and NYSSMA (in 2021) illustrates the organizations' eagerness to evolve and improve. It demonstrates an attempt to reach an ever-wider range of student creators. Dynamic programs should welcome change, not resist it.

Composition Coaching Workshops

NYSSMA conducts composition coaching workshops for student composers and songwriters at the conference. In these one-hour small-group workshops, the students, usually four in number, introduce their pieces and the group listens to recordings of the works. Composition teachers, usually two per workshop, guide a discussion of each piece in what is essentially a composition master class. The audience consists of the composers' families and a small group of conference attendees. The informal format also gives students and parents the opportunity to ask for guidance about academic and career opportunities from the clinicians. Many students and parents have commented that the workshops are the highlight of the conference.

Post-Concert Reflective Sessions for Students and Conference Attendees

After the concert, it is a good idea to have some refreshments for the young composers, followed by a session for reflective conversation. One effective format is to arrange the young composers and composition teachers in a semicircle in front of the audience of families and conference attendees. The teachers facilitate a discussion in which they try to get all of the students to participate, and audience members are also invited to ask questions and share ideas. Topics are quite varied and may include the following:

- Reactions to the concert
- Responses to each other's pieces
- Students discussing what kind of teaching has helped them
- Compositional process
- Current projects
- Current favorite listening repertoire
- Writer's block and strategies to succeed

Participation of Prominent Composer-in-Residence

If the budget permits, festivals can include the participation of a prominent composer-in-residence. NYSSMA includes this role in the conference budget parallel to the roles of all-state ensemble conductors. The composer-in-residence participates in one of the composition coaching workshops and the post-concert reflection session, and the student composition concert includes a work by the visiting composer. At the NYSSMA conference, one or two of the all-state ensembles perform works by the guest composer. The composer visits rehearsals of the all-state ensembles and helps to coach the group and conductor, providing a rich educational experience for hundreds of students. The responses of the conductors and students is usually quite intense, with many students gathering around at breaks asking for autographs. After Christopher Theofanidis helped to coach the New York All-State String Orchestra, conductor David Hagy wrote in an email:

NYSSMA not only provides students of its all-state ensembles the opportunity to perform music of living composers by programming it and acquiring the music, but it also hires the composers to come to the rehearsal process and speak to the students and directors about the reasons behind the piece, the intentions of the notations, and answer any questions about the piece. What could inspire the students more than to be involved in the performance of a piece by a world-famous composer WITH HIM/HER THERE! Our experience with Chris Theofanidis was outstanding as he told us he was seeking something very positive after finishing several pieces that were darker emotionally. What a difference in the sound this made! What an experience this was! (D. Hagy, personal communication, March 13, 2014)

Diversity is a significant factor to consider when selecting a composer-in-residence. Ideally students will, over time, have the chance to experience composers of diverse gender, race, and ethnicity in this luminary role. Giving diverse students models of successful composers who resemble themselves can have lasting power as a positive motivating force.

Educational Sessions for Teachers

An advantage of having a state composition chair and committee is that it assembles an expert group to plan educational sessions for conferences. Sessions should include ideas for integrating composition into all music education specialty areas and should be relevant for all grade levels from PreK through collegiate. Further, these sessions should present an array of approaches to teaching composition to allow teachers to tailor methods and activities to meet the needs of their unique teaching and learning environments.

Responses to Higher-Level Festivals

Students, parents, teachers, and composers-in-residence have expressed enthusiastic appreciation of composition festivals and showcases. Michael Brown, a successful composer-pianist who attended several conferences as a student, emailed in 2008:

NYSSMA's Winter Conference played a significant and important role in my development as a composer and musician. As composers we're naturally isolated, and to hear all of the wonderfully talented composers from the state opened me up to new and creative possibilities. The reactions and opinions of the distinguished composers-in-residence have stayed with me and influenced my compositional growth. It was also wonderful to be introduced to their music and have the opportunity to delve into their creative thought processes. I consider myself a lucky guy to have been included in this exploratory and inspiring atmosphere. (M. Brown, personal communication, August 29, 2008)

In 2018, former composer-in-residence Libby Larsen summarized her impression of NYSSMA's young composer program:

> The program experience you've crafted to identify, nurture, and mentor young composers is such a fine way to encourage them and give them a sense of a community with their peers. When I had the pleasure of working with NYSSMA composers, I was left with the feeling that these young artists are secure in their talent and in their joy for creating music. (L. Larsen, personal communication, April 3, 2018)

CONCLUSION

A comprehensive composition program for festivals and conferences offers students, families, and teachers an exciting educational experience. Such programs showcase and reward student achievement in composition and illustrate benchmarks of excellence. Bringing the young composers together with peers and professional composers in workshops and panel discussions creates a forum in which they can share insights and gain valuable knowledge. Inviting a composer-in-residence and programming his or her music for an honors ensemble extends the educational reach of the program to include hundreds of young performers. By providing supportive written evaluations of all submitted compositions, the program makes a broad, positive educational contribution to a large number of students and teachers and mitigates the competitive aspect implicit in any selective program.

REFERENCES

Abramo, J. M. (2017). The phantasmagoria of competition in school ensembles. *Philosophy of Music Education Review*, 25(2), 150–170. doi:10.2979/philmusieducrevi.25.2.04

Austin, J. R. (1990). Competition: Is music education the loser? *Music Educators Journal*, 76(6), 21–25. https://doi.org/10.2307/3400964.

Deutsch, D. (2009). Mentoring young composers: The small-group, individualized approach. *Kansas Music Review*, 72(3), 27–32.

Deutsch, D. (2016). Authentic assessment in music composition: Feedback that facilitates creativity. *Music Educators Journal*, 102(3), 53–59.

Gilbert, D. (2001). Prix de Rome. *Grove Music Online*. https://doi.org/10.1093/gmo/9781561592 630.article.40632

Kohn, A. (1992). *No contest: The case against competition* (Revised ed.). Houghton Mifflin Harcourt.

Mathiesen, T. (2001). Pythian games. *Grove music online*. https://doi.org/10.1093/gmo/978156 1592630.article.22605

National Association for Music Education. (2021a). 2021 *NAfME student composers competition rules and entry directions*. https://nafme.org/wp-content/uploads/2021/03/2021-Stud ent-Composer-Rules-and-Entry-Directions.pdf

National Association for Music Education. (2021b). *2021 NAfME electronic music composi-tion competition rules and entry directions.* https://nafme.org/wp-content/uploads/2021/01/2021-NAfME-Electronic-Music-Composition-Competition-Rules-and-Entry-Dir ections.pdf

National Association for Music Education. (2021c). *2021 NAfME student songwriters compe-tition rules and entry directions.* https://nafme.org/wp-content/uploads/2021/01/2021-Stud ent-Songwriters-Competition-Rules-and-Entry-Directions.pdf

New York State School Music Association. (2021a). *Criteria for the evaluation of compositions.* https://www.nyssma.org/wp-content/uploads/2021/04/Criteria-for-the-evaluation-of-compositions.pdf

New York State School Music Association. (2021b). *Guidelines for written evaluations.* https://www.nyssma.org/wp-content/uploads/2021/04/Guidelines-for-written-evaluations.pdf

Raekallio, M. (2012). Music competitions: Why? *Finnish Music Quarterly.* https://fmq.fi/artic les/music-competitions-why

Sosniak, L. A. (1985). A long-term commitment to learning. In B. S. Bloom (Ed.), *Developing talent in young people* (pp. 477–506). Ballantine Books.

CHAPTER 24

....

PREPARING YOUNG
COMPOSERS FOR
COLLEGIATE STUDY

....

CYNTHIA VAN MAANEN

WHEN I was a freshman in college, my advisor met with me in the first week of school. He asked me a great many questions about my background as a musician—which I quickly came to realize was not much, in his opinion. One of the questions he asked me was "Do you play piano?" I had taken a few lessons at around age ten with a woman from our church. If we had not moved, I would have continued those lessons because I really enjoyed piano and I liked my teacher. But we did move, and circumstances changed as they often do in life. I answered his question with "no," and his pragmatic reply,—"then you will never be able to succeed at being a composer"— was burned white hot into my memory. I clearly recall the moment, the look of his office, the sound of the carillon starting on campus, the embarrassment rising within me, and my immediate reaction of feeling that I should not have the nerve to even try this thing—this composing music. All I had done up until this moment was arrange music for my friends. I had bounced into his office so excited about my composition lessons and classes, but I left his office embarrassed that I was not already better at the very things I wanted to learn.

This moment is still so easy for me to recall that writing a description brings tears to my eyes. I look back on that moment now and know some things. I know that I did become a composer. I know that this advisor had a narrow viewpoint and was wrong about what someone can or cannot do in their own life. I also know that his statement pushed me in a way that likely caused me to do better than I ever would have otherwise in my life, whether to spite him or because it ignited a drive in myself, or both. I know now that every student who wants to be a composer needs me to be a different kind of teacher for them. Some need me to drive them, some need me to stay out of their way, most need me to cheer them on. *All* of them need me to listen and to correct them. They need me to provide that correction and criticism in a manner that they can receive it. Finally, I know that my advisor (who was also a faculty member) taught all of his students using methods that did not change. He did not understand the value in developing varying paths to a goal for different individuals. Because of my experience with him, I am a different teacher for each of my students as they need me to be. It's a wonder I'm not as mad as Alice's Hatter.

I am going to start with several of the ways I have worked with high school students throughout my twenty-one years at the Interlochen Arts Academy. I will present what has and has not worked, in the hope that it helps you to nurture a young composer. I will refer to both my experience teaching private composition students and my elective class for non-composition majors. My topics will all tie back to compositional craft and will include confidence level, learning to edit, the daily discipline of composing, learning what constitutes composing, how to work smarter, score study, and some of the challenges they all face along with the strengths they already possess. We will look at the topic of college/conservatory applications through the lens of developing a stronger artist. The goal is for schools to see the students' artistic ability and vision expressed through their own words and compositions.

I know now that my younger seventeen-year-old self, sitting in that office, had the tools necessary to learn composition, because I had the most important ones in spades: the *desire* and *determination* to write. It was a passion for me, but it took me many years to believe in myself again after that moment.

It is the process of learning how to work as a composer—practicing a daily routine, learning to study scores, making observations, becoming a critical thinker about music, and learning to see and work with their strengths and limitations—that prepares a student for composition at the college or conservatory level. One does not have to be a composer or composition teacher to help students do what I will suggest, although obviously it helps. The knowledge of how much *time* it takes to compose, edit, rewrite, prepare score, and make parts is critical toward helping students realize all the elements of this process. It also helps to realize that the act of writing—whether words or notes—is a very naked act. The composer is putting their artistic vision out to the world to be accepted or possibly rejected. Imagine a situation where someone else is describing your creative effort and what you would hope to hear as feedback. Keeping that situation in mind will aid you in giving feedback that your students can accept and internalize.

THE PROBLEM OF CONFIDENCE AS RELATED TO COMPOSING

The first thing I want to address is the high school ego and adolescent psychology, and how these impact a students' realistic observation and editing of their work. The level of confidence in students greatly affects their ability to see their product realistically and make artistic changes that strengthen it. They can easily fall in love with their first draft[1] and be averse to changes for a couple of reasons. One is fear—a lack

Student bold/scared statement:	What they mean:
Yes, I know!	I've done this once before, so I know everything about it.
Let me show you what I've learned!	I've been studying! Please acknowledge my hard work!
That's not the way my previous teacher taught me.	I'm nervous that everything is about to change.
I think it would be better if we tried it my way.	I don't know how to make the changes you want from me.
It's not finished. I have to change...	Please don't judge harshly, it's not done. See my intent.
MIDI sucks!	This program isn't playing what's in my imagination!
I didn't know how to (insert issue), so I didn't.	I'm frustrated with what I don't know how to do.
I'm sorry it's not better.	I'm scared I'm a fake. I have imposter syndrome.
Which idea do *you* think is better?	My decisions aren't valid, but yours are—help me.

FIGURE 24.1. What students' bold/scared statements really mean

of self-confidence and not knowing what to do next. A second is overconfidence—imagining it is the greatest thing ever composed. Most of these students are averse to change simply because they have not had the opportunity to familiarize themselves with more possibilities (score study and knowledge of living composers for example).

I am certain that the challenges of the high school ego are familiar to anyone reading this chapter. Students of this age want to be seen as independent and able to act on their own decisions, and they like to showcase their abilities. Their confidence can be strong, weak, or hover between the two.

Because I work with teenaged artists, I find the extremes of this range are more common. Regardless of where students sit on this continuum, they need guidance that shows them what they need to learn without either bursting or exaggerating their confidence. I frequently hear the following bold/scared statements, translated in Figure 24.1 to reveal their true meaning, that help me gauge the level of confidence of my students.

Overconfidence

Sometimes a student's identity is strongly tied to "being right." This story provides an example of a situation and a strategy for working with an overly confident student so that they might grow.

A student (junior) composed an orchestra piece using Sibelius with MIDI and had altered the dynamics artificially. The harp was marked "ffff" and the mid-high ranged brass was "mp." The rest of the orchestra was situated in mid-low registers, but in full force dynamically. I began to comment that the mid-low range harp and flutes would never be heard. Before I could finish my sentence, however, this student interrupted insisting that it would be fine[2]. He said that our two harpists could play out more and all would be well. I could easily have shut him down with examples of why he was wrong, but I knew that would entrench his insistence on being seen as "right." What I recognized in this young person was that he needed to BE right. His ego and cultural background depended on it.

Rather than show him where his thinking was misguided, I took a different tactic. I asked him to describe to me the sound he wanted to hear. He is part of our orchestra, so he had direct experience with balance. As his description went on, we would stop and look at the various sections of the music in small chunks. The more he described his sound and the more he observed his work an evident change in his confidence started to take hold. He became skeptical of certain areas of the music but kept his confidence in others. Eventually he came to realize that I had walked him into the idea that "the harp and flutes will never be heard" on his own. We had a good laugh and he apologized for interrupting. This student walked out of his lesson knowing what I hoped he would learn, but more importantly kept his confidence about things that were solid.

Lack of Confidence

Students who lack confidence often seek "in-between" moments—those times that occur at the end of the day, between classes, or whenever you feel rushed to be elsewhere—to ask their questions. They murmur questions like "If you have time, would you tell me if this is good?" in tones that suggest they do not want to bother you. Hearing these, we are tempted to reply, "If you'll come back during office hours or make an appointment," or worse, we take a quick look and respond too abruptly with "Yeah, that's good but it would be better IF . . ." because we are in a hurry. For a student with plenty of confidence being put off until another time is fine. They do not take this gesture personally. For students who are lacking in confidence, however, this response is "proof" that their art is not good enough.

Lack of confidence can cause a paralyzing fear for any creative artist, including composers. Students may begin to struggle with choice of notes, rhythms, harmonies, etc. Simply spending time with these students and answering even one question can make all the difference in their confidence level as is shown in this story:

A student who had been working with me for about a year and a half was sitting across from me in my office during her lesson. We were (I thought) editing a finished piece for the layout of her score on the page. I was making comments about placement of dynamics, addition of articulation—the usual polishing notes. When I looked up, she was sitting very still, in tears. I was floored, lost. I stopped talking and sat still for a minute. She eventually started apologizing and I when I responded with "You have nothing to apologize for"—more tears.

After a little time had passed, she was able to talk, and we decided to go for a walk around campus. What eventually emerged was that she felt everything she did was wrong. She felt this way because I was always commenting on what she should change. I realized she was unaware that I thought her music was very strong, very good! She did not know, because I had not made it obvious: the reason I could make detailed comments on her work to the level I was doing was because her music was so very well written. I learned a lot that day. I learned that for everything I say that could be perceived as a negative, I needed to be sure to bolster it with what is working in the music (Marano, 2003; Zenger & Folkman, 2013).

The Craft of Composing Through Learning to Edit

Students often fall in love with their first draft. For example, if a student's melody is not good—for whatever reason—saying so can crush their spirit. They have searched long and hard and high and low for this melody, and this is IT. This is the ONE. These same students also compose eight bars and think they are automatically measures 1–8. They also assume their next four bars are measures 9–12. Once those measures are done, they must search for *new* material to follow. And, so, it goes. Because they have worked so hard, they believe these measures are set in stone. Students fear that cutting material will leave them without ideas and wonder how they will ever replace what they have cut away. Making any suggestion about altering their work is both an affront to ego ("... *but I'm amazing, how dare you suggest* . . ." or "*I knew I was never any good*") and incitation of fear about creating *more* musical material. At this point, students need to learn that editing does not mean that their musical ideas were bad. Editing and rewriting are tools that can get them even closer to their artistic ideal (Ponsot & Deen, 1982).

To teach the craft of editing, I use a concept I call "skeletonizing." It is loosely based on Schenkerian analysis, but from the point of view of creating material. Its goal is to generate musical ideas to use throughout the piece (development) that are based on the primary idea. A student takes their first product, the melody, and brainstorms through "how to develop"[3] it through the five steps shown in Figures 24.2.

Assuming the student does the work, the next lesson is one of the most fun days the teacher will have teaching high school composers! They come in excited about what they have discovered: that they have control over what they are composing. They also lose the fear concerning finding new material. They begin to understand that composing is not mystical or based on luck, but is the result of hard work, craft, and editing. Three important things will now happen: 1) they will view their first draft more objectively, 2) they will come to you with ways to improve it, and 3) they will present their music and their ideas with greater confidence.

Skeletonizing shows students they can trust themselves. They will see that there are multiple solutions in most cases and that they are not stuck with their first (or only) idea. For a high school student to be able to discuss their work through the lens of *what they changed as they edited their work* is significant growth. They understand that they have control over their work and this reinforces the right kind of confidence in their artistic choices.

Step 1. Write out the melody by hand, then sketch out the basic shape of it. For example:

Step 2. Identify the crucial notes that make up the overall shape of the melody: if these notes were altered the melody would no longer be the basic shape, above.

Step 3. Remove all other notes and focus on the remaining notes which are the skeleton of the melody—the architecture holding it up. You can keep or strip the original rhythm. It helps to see the "pillars" of melody that hold up the overall shape.

Step 4. Using only the remaining notes from step three, try the following:

- Augment/diminish the rhythm, possibly to create a bass line or counterpoint.
- Invert them and repeat the first idea.
- Use them to create a new melody either in the basic shape or inverted.
- Try all the above in retrograde/retrograde inversion.
- Try various rhythms/dynamics/articulations/phrase markings, etc.
- Try various meter shifts, sequencing, location of weak/strong beat, tempo alterations, etc.
- Take the basic shape and stretch it out to four measures, eight measures—or make it shorter than the original.
- Try out a variety of textural ideas to go with the new ideas.

Step 5. Assignment. For our next lesson, create a full, handwritten page of musical ideas using any of these concepts.

FIGURE 24.2. Skeletonizing a melody

THE DAILY DISCIPLINES THAT HELP
STUDENTS LEARN COMPOSITIONAL CRAFT

The art of composing is different in many ways from the art of learning to perform. I am a flautist. In those lessons I was given specific sections or pieces of music I should prepare for the following week, and I spent time focusing on the mechanics of playing my instrument. But I was never worried about *creating* what music I should play. It can be a rather frustrating thing to sit down to compose and walk away with . . . nothing.

Nothing done, nothing to show, nothing that can be seen or heard by another person. How do you prepare for a composition lesson if this can happen? How can your student feel they are progressing and stay inspired? In this section I will describe an approach to preparing for the weekly lesson through a daily plan. This model assumes a one-hour composition lesson each week.

Recognize What Constitutes the Work of Composing

Students often make the assumption that composing a certain number of measures equals success for the period of time they spent composing. This is only true if those measures are worth keeping in the final score. Like the flute example above, a certain amount of daily time spent working is beneficial but only when students understand what that daily work entails. Unlike the flute example, a teacher cannot assign a certain section of music or number of measures to work on weekly. The amount of music composed will vary from student to student and also in relation to how far along the new score has progressed. With that in mind, do not assign a certain number of measures to be composed each week. This is not practical and is potentially harmful. A teacher would never say out loud, "another student composed 45 measures this week, so you must not be trying very hard or spending enough time composing." Students, however, are likely to make these comparisons on their own and then develop the belief that they must spend hours working to produce the few measures assigned. It is this negative narrative of implying we are all able to produce the same amount of work each week that creates attachments to the much beloved melody mentioned earlier—the one they are unwilling to edit under any circumstances. Rather than ask that a certain amount of work be produced, teach students that *the time spent is the work*, then teach them how to spend their composition time wisely.

Learn to Work Smarter

Composers can learn to work with great efficiency. Recent brain research suggests that working for shorter bursts of time generates creative productivity with the highest retainable output (Kaufman, 2019; Beaty, 2020). The first assignment I have given my private lesson students for the past fifteen years is an adaptation of an activity featured in David Cope's *Techniques of the Contemporary Composer* (1997, p. 11). Shown in Figure 24.3, this activity engages students in a self-assessment of their work environment.

It does not matter what students compose or how much material is produced during this activity. This assignment is about empowerment. Students need to feel like they are in control of their environment which, in turn, will help them produce creative results. Once they submit this assignment, we have a group discussion and share what they learned about themselves. They are amazed at how many differences there are between

Cope's three things to experiment with when you compose:
- When you compose (time of day: morning/afternoon/evening)
- Where you compose (inside, outside, at a piano, at a desk, by a lake, etc.)
- What you compose with (computer, pencil/paper, with/without piano/instrument, etc.)

Van Maanen adaptations:
- Compose everyday, vary the time, location, and materials used.
- Compose for the same duration each day, if possible.
- Spend three weeks trying these variables.
- Keep a journal of your experiences. Make notes of how you were feeling and how productive you were during that time, in that location, with those materials.
- At the end of these three weeks add a concluding paragraph that reflects on when, where, and with what materials you think work best for you and *why*.
- Share the journal with your teacher.

FIGURE 24.3. Composer practices: A self-assessment of work environment

them all! Students discover a feeling of freedom when they realize they do not have to compose in a manner like someone else to be successful.

Establish a Routine

Self-assessment of one's work environment is just the first step toward developing a daily compositional practice routine. Students must compose every day and, if possible, compose on a schedule (Lally & Van Jaarsveld, 2010). I require students to compose five days a week—they decide which days. As many composition students are also performing musicians, they know how to use routines for practicing their own instrument, but it might not occur to the new composer that this model could be a useful tool to help them grasp the daily discipline of composing music. Figure 24.4 presents a model for dividing one hour of composition practice time into three focused activities. These form the bulk of compositional practice and when done as a routine help composers recognize their success and loosen their grip on the material that needs editing. It is worth noting that the hour of suggested time is meant only as a starting place for those students who struggle with time management. What is most important is that the amount of time be the same each day to create a sense of continuity.

This model is adaptable and should be used on a sliding scale. If, for example, a student is planning to compose a new piece, the hour might be spent fully engaged in score study for two to three *weeks* as you and the student delve into specifics about how to compose for the certain instrumentation.[4] (Score study will be addressed later in this chapter.) After this initial score study phase, students might improvise a page or two of ideas for their lesson, or two lessons if needed. This gives the student the ability to choose the ideas they are most attracted to and you an opportunity to help them

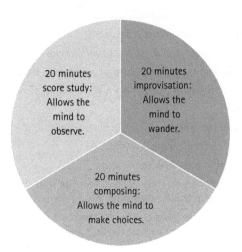

FIGURE 24.4. Model of daily compositional practice

determine which ideas show the greatest promise for longevity. You can, at this point in their development, try the skeletonizing exercise on their ideas. Be responsive to the needs of your individual students: A fast writer will be able to do more; let them. A slow writer will struggle to come up with one page—and that is fine. Acknowledge their accomplishment.

When students are in the midst of composing, the 20/20/20 breakdown is most effective. If they get writer's block, they move to score study or improvisation. If they are on a roll, they compose. The point to be made is that there is always a task they can be working on even if they are temporarily stuck. If the student is in the final section of composing the piece (meaning approximately two-thirds of the way through or more), that hour should be focused on composing as score study and improvisation may not be needed during this time. The segments of the 20/20/20 routine do not need to be completed in a single one-hour block. Students can take breaks, as these are shown to improve creativity. Walk away for five to twenty minutes in between work sessions, or work for 20 minutes in the morning on one task and return in the evening for the final 40 minutes of work. These breaks, however long, provide time for reflection.

Private Study

Composition lessons, with individuals or in classroom settings, should reflect this daily routine. Students often only want to show you their musical products but encourage them to take you through their weekly work, including material that they discarded. Ask how and why they made specific choices to keep certain ideas. Their descriptions give them practice discussing their music and will be useful in college auditions. Invite them to identify where they need help and tackle those spots. If you believe there is a problem area and they do not raise it, ask them to describe their work in that spot. Explore it together without judgment. Should students not produce enough work to fill a one-hour lesson, spend time modeling score study (discussed later in this chapter) or address other topics (i.e., counterpoint or orchestration) that may inform their work.

A Composition Challenge

I introduce my 20/20/20 model with students in a composition challenge that happens each October in my studio. I specifically choose October so that school is settled, parent conferences are behind us, and the days are rolling along nicely with routine. This challenge originated with Professor Jamie Leigh Sampson and Dr. Andrew Martin Smith, both at SUNY–Fredonia. Professor Sampson initially came up with the idea of modeling a composition challenge based on a podcast about learning to run called Couch to 5K. The challenge essentially eases students into what to do while composing and complements the daily routine I teach. I have adapted their collegiate challenge for high school students as shown in Figure 24.5.

I keep a record of both my individual students as well as the whole class for inspiration, and I send daily messages of encouragement. I also do this challenge with them and they can see my work alongside their own work. At the end of the month, I take my studio out for dinner to celebrate. There, I talk about the progress I saw in all of them and ask them what they learned from the challenge. I record and share their average number of minutes worked per day. We repeat the challenge for a "pick me up" in March, but only for two weeks, due to other academic demands. At that time, I ask each of them to strive for their personal October average per day plus ten minutes.

This challenge is amazing because it gives students a starting point each day! They begin to believe they can create new music every day, and this reinforces the idea that the music

---

Composition Challenge Rules

1. Everyone must compose for one hour a day, no more no less.
2. You should compose at the same time of day if possible, so choose wisely.
3. We will do this for four weeks, seven days a week.*
4. At the end of each week a prize will be given to celebrate various successes.
5. You will submit a daily report stating how many minutes were worked, what specific work was done during that time, and includes a picture of the progress made.

*Research suggests that it takes 66 days to build a new habit (Lally, Van Jaarsveld, Potts & Wardle, 2010). I limit this challenge to a month recognizing that educators work within a system of other classes where many demands are made of students. I discuss this research with students highlighting the psychological phases that have been used to describe the building of a new habit: Phase I: First third (22 days) you want to quit; Phase II: Second third, you are adjusting to the new routine and it is becoming easier; Phase III: Last part, you are really getting it and it is becoming progressively easier (Anderson, 2020). I encourage students to continue the challenge on their own within a reasonable scope for their schedule.

FIGURE 24.5. Composition challenge rules

composed today is dispensable because more will follow tomorrow. It empowers them to let go of their ideas without worrying about finding something new. It also separates them from the idea—an idea can be good or bad without the student feeling they are good or bad as a composer. Students become excited to engage in meaningful conversation about their work (without tears, wringing of hands, or ego-bruising). Most importantly, a deeper sense of trust develops as students realize that teacher feedback is not meant to criticize *them* but intended to instead advance their compositional skills. As a bonus, college composition faculty will be impressed by an interviewee's ability to calmly discuss the process they went through to create material, how they decided what material they would keep and why, and how they edited and developed their musical ideas.

Score Study

Helping the student find their compositional voice requires acknowledging who they are as a person, determining what they want to express through their music, and helping them figure out how to compose music that reflects just that.[5] Focused score study can help students not only strengthen their craft, but also find their own artistic, musical voice. This process takes time, even years, but with high school students it frequently means gently nudging them away from Mozart or that favorite film/video game composer they are emulating—the comfortable pieces they already know—toward an experience that introduces them to hundreds of new pieces and composers. Score study will broaden their base of musical knowledge so that new ideas which are uniquely theirs, can emerge.

Connecting students to new (to them) music is easy. The number one go-to resource for my students is YouTube. To be fair, they find some pretty amazing pieces on that site. However, they need access to physical scores, not just videos/recordings. I usually strike a bargain by saying: "I'll listen to one piece that you find on YouTube if you listen to/look at a physical score for every three pieces I suggest." They always take the deal. They like to show me what they find, so I learn with my students. They adore that part of our lesson.

Once students get into score study, they fall in love with it because they are starving for this information. The scores I choose for students fall into three categories:

- Resource: A score that is pertinent to the development of the current piece the student is composing and helps them solve a problem. Make this a score they can understand easily (draws on their knowledge of music theory or has some other familiarity).
- Exploration: A score for the sheer joy of discovering something new. There is not a specific connection to the piece they are currently composing.
- Challenge: A score where the harmonic language, texture, or other elemental usage challenges your student in some way. Consider choosing scores that are based on texture rather than melody, for example.

The score that is selected is key. As Ponsot and Deen have noted, "Observations go between the naïve and the critical response. But they also begin the analysis, the loosening of the order of the work the student is reading" (1982, p. 161). Score study should not only be concerned with traditional analysis of a musical score. It is about observing what is possible. When you suggest score study, students will want to impress you with some deeply profound psychological aspect of the work that they found on Wikipedia absent the specific knowledge of the technical workings of the piece or the reasons why the composer made the choices they made. Students do not know how to simply observe the score; you must teach them the skill.

Routine and Guidelines for Score Study

To engage in score study requires the development of the language of observation. This is particularly important in pedagogical contexts as teachers and students need a shared language to talk about music. Harvard's Project Zero[6] offers two thinking routines that advance this skill set: "See, Think, Wonder," and "Color, Symbol, Image."

Routine I: "See, Think, Wonder"

This exercise invites students to look at a page of score and simply state what they see, what they think about what they see, and what it makes them wonder (Project Zero, 2016). "I see" can be changed to "I hear" if students are listening without score. The goal is for them to state clearly what is they see/hear. You will be surprised at how many students cannot do this exercise. They would prefer to ponder the deep meaning rather than state the obvious. For these students I will start with leading questions or statements like:

- Describe the dynamics you see/hear. How/where do they change?
- What is the rhythm of the main motive you have been talking about?
- How does that rhythm change on page 1? On page 2?
- Why do you think the composer made those decisions?

Once students understand the simplicity of the process, they are able to grasp the concept. The observation that happens helps students understand (see) how *much* detail is needed in their own composition. Without you saying "add more dynamics" they will start to do just that.

Along with "See, Think, Wonder," I have students engage in score copying. On staff paper, with a pencil, they copy out one to three pages of their favorite score. They must use a ruler and line up beats, produce straight bar lines, etc. In copying the work, they engage in a sustained attention that requires quality of focus (Ponsot & Deen, 1982). This work allows them to notice everything and absorb what is on the page deeply and with true understanding.

Routine II: "Color, Symbol, Image"

After listening to a new piece of music have you ever asked a student to respond only to be met with "I liked it" or "It was pretty"? Beyond that statement, they cannot articulate further what they liked about it, what was pretty, or how the composer created the "pretty" aspect. If pushed, students become frustrated because they cannot think of any other way to describe the music. The problem is twofold: a single listening is not sufficient for the brain to process all that happens in a composition, and students need a vocabulary for describing what they have heard.

The first task in vocabulary development is identifying the terms they already know and can use. "Color, Symbol, Image" asks student to:

- Pick one section of the music and choose a color for it that best captures the essence of that idea.
- Pick a different section of music and choose a symbol for it that best captures the essence of the idea; and
- Pick a third section of music and choose an image that captures the essence of this idea.

After the initial listening, students work in pairs or small groups and describe to each other how their choices represent each musical section. "The idea is to simply find some common ground that can be used to communicate about the piece"[7] (Project Zero, 2015). Students who previously could not describe music on first hearing will now be describing detailed images of what they saw/heard as the music was being played. This exercise works best with unfamiliar pieces selected to challenge students in some way. Further listening results in deeper observations and descriptions.

Using Routines I and II

"See, Think, Wonder" and "Color, Symbol, Image" can be used for a few weeks or even months, interchangeably and together, depending on the progress of the student(s) in any composition instructional setting. Once students have gained a degree of comfort with these routines, we move on to the music-specific vocabulary shown in Figure 24.6. The discussions that happen once this music-specific vocabulary is in place will result in more detailed observation of content. Students now possess the vocabulary to describe the specifics of what a composer has chosen to do in their piece.

Routine 3: Observational Critique

Once students have reached this ability in our score studies, we are ready to add the process of sharing in-progress student works. This new activity, often taking place two to three months into the score study process, will require students to use their newly acquired vocabulary while adding the skills of giving and receiving constructive feedback. Begin by discussing what critique is and how it contributes to growth. Introduce the

Articulation	Fragmentation	Phrase
Augmentation	Harmonic language	Phrasing
Cadence	Harmonic rhythm	Row
Development	Inversion	Set
Diminution	Key	Texture
Dynamics	Melodic Shape	Theme
Effects (pizz., tremolo, etc.)	Motive	Timbre
Extended techniques	Orchestration	Tonal Center
Form	Pedaling	Retrogression

FIGURE 24.6. Vocabulary of some compositional terms for study (listed alphabetically)

"Ladder of Feedback" as a helpful tool for organizing four aspects of critique: "1) Clarify: ask questions to help you understand fully; 2) Value: Express what you liked by giving detailed examples; 3) State concerns: Kindly express your concerns; and 4) Suggest: Make suggestions for improvement."[8] Encourage students to balance each concern with an idea, suggestion, or possible solution. (Project Zero, 2018)

As students listen to each other's work, they should be tasked to consider their own compositional challenges. Ask them to focus on a single issue and consider how the presenting student handles the same challenge. If they cannot think of a challenge in their own work, encourage them to select a topic from the vocabulary list shown in Figure 24.6 and observe that topic as they listen. Students may also use the techniques from "See, Think, Wonder" or "Color, Shape, Image" to help focus their attention. Now that students have ideas they wish to express about others' work, they can use the ladder of feedback to share their thoughts constructively. In addition, Figure 24.7 provides a brief overview of how listeners can articulate observations and pose questions such that the power of choice remains with the composer.

Composers open the sharing process by introducing their pieces and presenting a problem they are currently working to address (i.e., a tough transition from the A to B idea). Students then play the work, often via MIDI playback, and invite comments. As feedback is offered, composers are encouraged to listen, not react. The goal of the exercise is to empower the composer by becoming more informed about their work so that they can make good choices as they strive to attain compositional goals. When critique sessions are properly facilitated by the teacher, students emerge excited to compose and have gained many ideas about how to solve the problem they presented to the group. Most importantly, taking time to discuss compositions-in-progress allows all composers to become more articulate concerning their music and artistic vision while they acquire the information needed to make that vision a musical reality.

Making Observations	Asking Questions
Avoid statements that begin with "I like" and try to focus on statements that begin with "I notice". For example, instead of saying, "*I like the short motives in this piece*" which could potentially stop the conversation, rephrase the observation to become, "*In this passage I'm noticing a lot of short motives. They give energy to the piece and help push this music forward.*" This response offers an observation and extends it to give the composer information about the affect of the piece. A stated observation of this nature leaves the power of choice with the composer. It moves the response from you (I like it) to the piece (neutral), which is our focus. Evaluations such as "I like it" take power away from the composer and may drive them to compose music in response to the observer's suggestions as opposed to their own artistic ideas.	Observation statements can also be combined with questions: "*You mentioned it was hard making the transition work in these measures. What would happen if you tried _____*"? This allows discussion to take place about the specific spot the composer is struggling to address. Even if a solution is not reached, the question has presented some ideas for the composer and anyone else struggling with the same issue to consider.
Sometimes it may help to simply comment on what you know about the music and then expand it to a brief analysis. For example, "*There are three main motives in this piece. Two of them are being developed using inversion and imitation. The third is developed by repetition.*"	More generalized questions can also be used. For example, "*I notice you switch (key, mode, inversion, rhythm) in this place. What affect are you after?*" and "*I notice you use the motive in sequences, but the third time you change it. How did you make that decision?*" invite the composer to reflect on their choices. You will find that you will begin paying more attention to the music as you make statements and ask questions and the composer will begin to understand their work better through this conversation.
You could stop there, or continue to offer, "*This leaves me wondering how you view the third motive. Is it as important to you?*" This response helps the composer understand what they have written and not what you want them to write.	Always keep in mind that you are commenting on choices the composer has made, not the choices you would make instead. Remember:
	▪ Accept the piece on its own terms (for example: style, melodic/harmonic choice, etc.).
	▪ Remember: This is not your work.
	▪ You are only one listener. Be thoughtful, not rigid.
	▪ Take initiative. Make an objective observation and offer respectful critique without regard to what others will think.
	▪ Respect the work, the composer, and the process we all go through as artists.
Note: The ideas used in this process were introduced to me by Anne-Marie Oomen and drawn from *Beat Not the Poor Desk Writing: What to Teach, How to Teach It, and Why* by Marie Ponsot and Rosemary Deen.	

FIGURE 24.7. How to critique a composition through observation

Some Common Challenges and
Strengths of Student Composers

Challenges

One of the most common challenges that students need to address in preparation for advanced compositional study, as might occur within college composition programs, is that of notation. Software programs can make music sound great while simultaneously producing notation that is nearly unreadable by human performers. Figures 24.8 and 24.9 sound the same in computer playback, but Figure 24.9 correctly presents the rhythm in $\frac{4}{4}$ while Figure 24.8 does not. Figures 24.10 (incorrect) and 24.11 (correct) highlight the same problem in compound meter.

DAWs and software notation programs are wonderful for many reasons, but students who begin their study using these programs need to also learn notational rules so that they can recognize errors that software can allow. I address this challenge by returning to physical notation with the following assignment: "Compose a one- to two-page piece for your own, unaccompanied instrument. Notate it by hand." If students have not yet learned to notate rhythms, this becomes a daunting task. Take time to show students how to physically notate their music by hand.[9] Another assignment that can help students recognize proper notation is to have them copy something small, perhaps a duet. Teach them to use a ruler to make bar lines, beams, and alignments of events like dynamics/lyrics/crescendo marks, etc. This process will slow them down so that they must observe all the details of the score they are copying. The resulting conversations that occur will help your students grasp rhythm (or other concepts) quickly and with greater depth of understanding.

Another common challenge is trust between student and teacher. Students want to trust their teacher, but if for some reason they do not give us that trust immediately, it can be earned by doing one thing: Talk less, listen more. Start by asking questions that encourage *them* to talk. For example, ask "What is the inspiration for your piece?" Most students want to talk for a while on this topic because they are excited to tell you

FIGURE 24.8. Incorrect version of written rhythm

FIGURE 24.9. Correct version of written rhythm

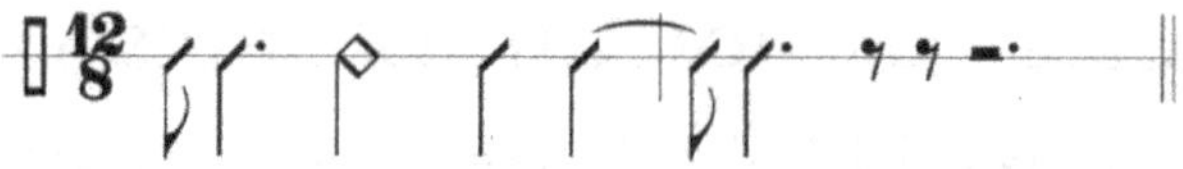

FIGURE 24.10. Incorrect version of written rhythm

FIGURE 24.11. Correct version of written rhythm

all about it. Follow up with: "How did you make the harmony/rhythm/melody choices based on this inspiration?" Then listen. Most importantly, do not explain their piece to them. It is their art, their idea! The more you listen without interrupting the more you solidify their trust because you are interested in what they have to say as an artist. Hear who they are as an artist *first*, then work out the details of the problems. The rule of 5:1 applies (Benson, 2017; Zenger & Folkman, 2013).[10] Speak five positives for every one (perceivable) negative. This will make the student willing to hear you. As more trust is earned, you can help them address more challenges in their music without their ego crumbling.

A third common challenge for students is recognizing that there are aspects of music often more important than the notes themselves. The musical gestures created by phrasing, dynamics, articulation, orchestration, etc. can have more power to create the desired musical result than choosing the exact right notes. A quick exercise I do with students to illustrate this idea is to have them draw their composition in shapes (gestures) with colored pencils. Questions that follow this exercise focus on why certain colors and shapes were chosen and lead to conversations that move beyond notes.

Strengths

A common strength is that students have limitless imagination and want to compose about every topic under the sun! They often do not have the musical language to achieve the sound they want or need, but that is part of this process. I sometimes have students literally bouncing up and down in my office, excited to tell me about their new idea. If imagination gets in the way of practicality, visit rehearsals, and let them see how performers work. How much time do percussionists need to change mallets? Why do the harpists not use their pinky fingers? How long will it take for the flute to switch to piccolo? How often do wind players need to breathe? Anything you can show rather than tell will preserve and inform their imaginations.

A second strength is that of collaboration. Students are excited to share their discipline with dance, theater, visual art, film, etc. If you can provide an opportunity for collaboration within your school community, do so! Work with students in-progress and do not wait for their piece to be finished. Review it at several stages as this will allow them to hear what is or is not working with ample time for change or revision. These changes and revisions are easier in progress because of two reasons: 1) it is easier for the student to make changes over smaller sections of their work than an entire piece; and 2) if they perceive it as complete, the problem of falling in love with their project returns. Once it is finished, read through it and give them a recording. If the work is strong enough, offer to put it on a concert.

The most important strength I have saved for last: determination. If a student wants to compose, they are going to compose, regardless of their skill level when they begin. As educators, it our privilege to nurture this potential and help it find direction. That direction, for some, may include composition study in higher education.

College Applications and Auditions for Composers

Students who are interested in studying composition in college need to make the most of their junior year by assembling a portfolio of their work for college applications. As of this writing most schools in the United States have application deadlines of November (early admit) and December 1st (regular admit). This means September and October of their senior year should be spent in the application process (essays, forms, gathering financial information, etc.) and choosing and organizing the pieces they will include in their portfolios. Fast writers may compose a piece during these two months but doing so causes a great deal of tension and stress. Remember that there needs to be time to make a recording if your plans include live recordings.

Junior and Senior Year Preparation

The focus of high school juniors must be on portfolio development. Most college programs will require the submission of three to five works in the audition process. Begin by taking stock of composed pieces and identify those suitable for inclusion in the portfolio. Next, determine what is missing. Student work should vary in instrumentation and ensemble size. Small works typically feature one to three performers, medium four to eight, and works requiring nine or more performers are considered large. Works for band, chorus, and/or orchestra are usually not required. Most collegiate composition faculty would prefer a stronger set of smaller pieces, well-composed and edited than a large ensemble work that does not highlight a composer's knowledge and strengths.[11]

During the senior year, students turn their focus to the application process. Ideally, they are not creating new materials, but revising scores, looking at the graphic layout, and reworking anything they decide to edit. If live recordings are available, even if flawed, submit them. MIDI is acceptable, too, so this should not be a point of stress for students. As mentioned, some students will want to compose one more piece, but I do not usually recommend this due to time constraints unless they are very quick writers. For students who study with me only their senior year, I focus on helping them understand there is not time to compose, edit, and potentially rehearse and record an entire portfolio from September until November. Their portfolios should be a collection of works from across multiple years. This shows growth but also relieves the pressure of composing everything within a two or three month timeframe.

Schools and Auditions

At this point, it is important to talk with your students about what schools are right for them. If they are anything like my students, they want to attend a few "name brand" schools. However, they need to consider other factors. Talk with them about what makes them most happy as an artist—what creates artistic inspiration for them? I have them consider not only the program offered at the school, but also the following: big city versus small town; large versus small studio; near versus far from home; ease of getting their music performed at that school. At the beginning of the school year, ask them to think about all of this for a few weeks and then begin having conversations about specific schools that fit *all* their interests.

With focus now on the schools that will be a good fit, make a list of things to do during the audition visit. Examples might include:

- Talk to students currently in attendance at the school. Ask: How easy it is to get performers for your pieces? Are student performers excited to be part of new music? What is the composition studio like? Do you enjoy working with the faculty?
- Pay attention to the interactions with faculty both in email and in person. Do you feel inspired by these people? Are you comfortable with them in your audition?
- Research the music faculty prior to the visit. The best composition teachers are not going to teach you to compose like them, but if you enjoy their music then you know you can be inspired by them in some way.

Finally, have composition students practice talking about their music. The more students do this, the more ready they will be to describe and discuss it using the solid music vocabulary they have learned. Put seniors on the spot in a friendly environment, using one work they have chosen themselves. Studio mates or classmates ask questions, and the composer responds. While this process will not address every question an auditioning committee might ask, it does alleviate the fear of an unfamiliar process for my students. Everything they have practiced in my studio: adjusting confidence, learning to edit, the daily discipline of compositional craft, the composition challenge, score study, and recognizing personal challenges will give them the ability to discuss their music in an empowered and knowledgeable way.

A Final Word

I will end with the same thought I shared at the beginning: any student with enough determination will find a way to compose. We should be mindful of making comments that can cause an aspiring young artist to doubt themselves and we should work to build realistic confidence in our lessons through teaching solid craft, daily routine, and by taking the mystery out of creating new music. The true craft of composition lies in its daily practice of skills and routines that can be strengthened just like any other daily practice. These tools will help your high school students feel confident in their abilities and gain authority in talking about their work with anyone, in any situation, including college audition interviews and beyond.

Notes

1. Anne-Marie Oomen, colleague from our Creative Writing Department at Interlochen, is the person I first heard use this phrase, "falling in love with your first draft."
2. Unfortunately, I have found as a woman teaching composition that my ideas and critiques are often challenged by teenage male students. I have noticed that I am interrupted by them far more often than they interrupt my male colleagues. This is fear showing itself through attempted dominance. They are afraid to be perceived as wrong. As this chapter will cover, these students will learn that criticism of their work is not personal, but that lesson takes time.
3. A wonderful tool in teaching development is an old one: Bernstein's *Young People Concerts*, "What Makes Music Symphonic," is a detailed lesson on what development is and the various ways composers use it in their music.
4. Offer a variety of pieces from different eras and different styles! If your student is the flute player who is writing her first string quartet, offer Haydn string quartets. Spend more time, however, studying current string quartets (within 20–30 years). It is wonderful as a composer of any age to identify with living, breathing human beings doing the same work as you. There are many databases at libraries that have scores online for viewing. Alexander Street Press is an excellent source as one database example. Students without direction will go to YouTube to search and not have any idea if the styles and techniques they are encountering are limited to electronic production or also suitable for live performance.
5. If a student is constantly rewriting Mozart or any other composer from long ago, steer them into listening to music that is more current. All their mimicry means is that this is what they are hearing. It can be difficult to relate to music that does not represent who you are as a person because it does not speak to what is happening now. Do not steer them away from older music if they love it but do find out if they love it because it is all they know.
6. Project Zero, located at Harvard University, is a research center founded in 1967 that explores topics in education such as deep thinking, understanding, intelligence, creativity, and ethics.

7. From "Color, Symbol, Image": A routine for distilling the essence of ideas non-verbally from the Project Zero Website. http://www.pz.harvard.edu/sites/default/files/Color%20Symbol%20Image_1.pdf

8. See http://www.makinglearningvisibleresources.org/ladder-of-feedback-see-supporting-learning-in-groups-in-the-classroom.html

9. I am not trying to subvert great computer programs. Those programs can be used much more efficiently, however, if the basic knowledge of notation is understood by students. There is a great connection between the physical, tactile act of writing music by hand and understanding the spacial relationships of rhythm and counterpoint.

10. The Gottman Institute is focused on relationships within marriage, but this concept applies to all relationships including student to teacher. "That 'magic ratio' is 5:1. This means that for every negative interaction during a conflict, a stable and happy marriage [interaction in a composition lesson] has five (or more) positive interactions." To learn more about this idea, visit https://www.gottman.com/blog/the-magic-relationship-ratio-according-science/

11. There are some schools who ask students to send fewer works or only excerpts of works showcasing their best compositional moments. These types of requests are rare. The majority of conservatory and universities request three to five completed scores.

REFERENCES

Beaty, R. E. (2020). The creative brain. Dana Foundation. dana.org/article/the-creative-brain/

Benson, K. (2017). The magic relationship ratio, according to science. The Gottman Institute. gottman.com/blog/the-magic-relationship-ratio-according-science/

Bernstein, L. (1958). *What makes music symphonic?* Young People's Concert. Leonardbernstein. com/lectures/television-scripts/young-peoples-concerts/what-makes-music-symphonic

Cope, D. (1997). *Techniques of the contemporary composer.* Schirmer.

Kaufman, S. B. (2019). The neuroscience of creativity: A Q&A with Anna Abraham. *Scientific American.* blogs.scientificamerican.com/beautiful-minds/the-neuroscience-of-creativity-a-q-a-with-anna-abraham/

Lally, P., Van Jaarsveld, C. H., Potts, H. W., & Wardle, J. (2010). How are habits formed: Modelling habit formation in the real world. *European Journal of Social Psychology, 40*(6), 998–1009.

Marano, H. E. (2003). Our brain's negative bias. *Psychology Today, 20,* 1–3.

Ponsot, M., & Deen, R. (1982). *Beat not the poor desk writing: What to teach, how to teach it and why.* Boynton/Cook.

Project Zero. (2018). Ladder of Feedback. pz.harvard.edu/resources/ladder-of-feedback

Project Zero. (2015). Thinking Routine Color, Symbol, Image. pz.harvard.edu/resources/color-symbol-image

Project Zero. (2016). Thinking Routine See, Think, Wonder. pz.harvard.edu/resources/see-think-wonder

Zenger, J., & Folkman, J. (2013). The ideal praise-to-criticism ratio. *Harvard Business Review, 15.* hbr.org/2013/03/the-ideal-praise-to-criticism

SECTION VI

COMPOSING IN CLASSROOM MUSIC

CHAPTER 25

COMPOSITION IN EARLY CHILDHOOD

ELIZABETH BUCURA

EARLY childhood tends to be a particularly musical and creative period (Marsh, 2008). Children are playfully inventive with music (Stauffer, 2013). Despite this, composition remains inconsistent in elementary and early childhood programs and may go unnoticed and underdeveloped in other places as well. Composition provides children real-world contexts for learning, applying, and practicing musical skills and understandings (Wiggins, 1990). Through composition, children can construct personal meanings and express themselves (Kaschub & Smith, 2013). Although composition has increased in schools (Kaschub & Smith, 2013), a general need for composition persists at all levels, including in early childhood (Deemer, 2016).

In this chapter I discuss relevance of early childhood composition as well as theoretical and practical considerations for the field of music education. I consider that early childhood comprises preschool through elementary children (roughly ages three through 10 years old). Throughout the chapter, I refer to this group primarily as *children* rather than *students* to reflect the broad places and spaces in which they compose music.

AN ENDURING NEED FOR VOICES AND CHOICES

Composition is an important creative musical activity among others, such as improvisation and arrangement. These activities can afford children a voice in learning music and opportunities to make choices so that music can become a reflection of their growing selves. Creative musicianship is a broad category however, comprising many activities (Oseka, 2016). As Pamela Burnard (2012) pointed out, in addition to composing, arranging, improvising, and performing activities, musical creativity might also comprise other activities like "sampling, resampling, mixing, mashing and songwriting" (p. 6). Creativity of all types can hold cultural values and provide significant learning opportunities (Robinson, 2001).

What is composition? It is both a process and an outcome (Kaschub & Smith, 2009) that can strengthen children's musical skills and interests, for instance by nurturing engaged listening and aesthetic decision-making (Barrett, 2000–2001). Composition is distinct from other kinds of music learning (Hogenes et al., 2014) and can allow musical elements to be understood and applied in a meaningful context. Researchers have also associated composition with extramusical benefits. For instance, Cynthia Colwell et al., (2005) stated that the experience of composing could improve one's self-concept. Michele Kaschub and Janice Smith (2013) noted it is a significant form of knowing that "reveals and constructs an understanding of one's self and others" (p. 7). In fact, composition can further lead to a "feelingful understanding of what it is to be human" (Kaschub & Smith, 2013, p. 7).

Through composition, children can apply and transform musical elements in their own ways. However, the types of activities children engage with informally do not tend to align with those in school settings (Burnard, 2012). Pamela Burnard (2012) and Scott Schuler (2011) have called to reduce prescriptive curricula to increase the relevancy of school music classes. Composition, which can build autonomy and ownership in children (Burnard, 2012), can certainly be one means to that end.

In the United States, traditional elementary music classes and music teacher preparation programs have inconsistently integrated composition. Nicholas Cook (1998) stated that teachers may prioritize performing over composing due to the ways they may have been prioritized in their own educational experiences. A lack of composing experience often continues into university studies. Music teacher preparation programs emphasize performance, including lessons, large ensembles, and recitals that favor Western classical art traditions. Pre-service music teachers do not typically have significant experience with composition (Deemer, 2016; Kaschub & Smith, 2013). Inexperience may extend beyond the classroom into field work and student teaching. As pre-service music teachers enter the field, they may lack confidence to lead composition tasks (Kaschub & Smith, 2013). University experiences that prioritize performance over teaching and creativity can lead to an underdeveloped sense of teaching self (Deemer, 2016), and weak composition and facilitation skills.

Music teachers' concerns may also include lack of time for creative tasks, often exacerbated by policies that emphasize standardized testing and narrowed curricula (Schuler, 2011). Administrators may emphasize the importance of creativity for children while nevertheless enacting policies that limit it (Burnard, 2012). Time to create and develop skills, however, is necessary for developing composition abilities (Bucura & Weissberg, 2016–2017; Stauffer, 2001). While inclusion of composition has increased, inconsistencies remain among elementary and early childhood music teachers and programs (Mills, 2009).

In recent years, composition has come into increasing focus in the field of music education, including not only music teacher preparation programs, but professional development, graduate coursework, publications, and conferences (Kaschub & Smith, 2013). These have broadened teachers' interests, practices, and strategies for composition (Burnard, 2012). Additionally, curriular publications have emerged that have been pivotal in shaping composition approaches (Hickey, 2012; Kaschub & Smith, 2009, 2013). In 2011, the National Association for Music Education initiated the Council for Composition (Kaschub & Smith, 2013), and in 2014, *Creating* became one of four rewritten national standards (Deemer, 2016; NAfME, 2014).

Young Composers

Prominent educational theorists such as Rousseau, Pestalozzi, and Vygotsky have influenced ideas about teaching and learning in early childhood, including in the approaches of Montessori, Reggio Emilia, and Waldorf (Miller & Pound, 2011). Often, the latter are associated with preschool-age learners if not also older learners. They contribute to cultural expectations of children's roles that may prevail into elementary grades. In the following sections, I discuss theories of child development (Piaget, 1970/2008; Erikson, 1959/1980) and curricular approaches for young children (e.g., Montessori, Reggio Emilia). I then discuss theories of creativity (Csikszentmihalyi, 1996) and scholarship specific to composition with children.

Childhood Development and Learning

Jean Piaget (1970/2008) theorized stages of cognitive development. Between ages 0 and 2, children coordinate their senses with motor responses. They explore the world through feel, touch, and sound experimentation. In preoperational thinking (ages two to seven), children begin to use syntax and grammar to express themselves. They are imaginative but do not think abstractly. When composing, children may represent and express musical ideas through pictures, imagery, and embodied movements and gestures. Erik Erikson (1959/1980) theorized stages of psychosocial development, defined by psychosocial crises. Between ages three and five, children undergo a play stage, experiencing initiative versus guilt. Children initiate their own projects and tasks and carry out plans; otherwise, they may feel guilty about a lack of independence. During this stage, children explore their own purposes and can develop resilience. Later, school children (five to 11) experience industry versus inferiority. They can develop competencies, finding satisfaction in applying themselves to tasks, otherwise potentially feeling inferior to those who do.

According to Linda Miller and Linda Pound (2011), early years education should focus on warmth and care in recognition of young learners' developmental and personal vulnerabilities. Scholars have also discussed the importance of teaching music with an ethic of care for all learners, for instance with humanity (Jorgensen, 2020) and empathy (Seddon, 2012). Miller and Pound (2011) believed care should be so prominent that "it should be impossible to educate without caring, nor care without developing and promoting children's learning" (p. 2).

Jean Piaget stressed interactions among person, environment, and actions (Rogoff, 1990), which result in one's construction of reality (Furth, 1974). Piaget theorized that learners assimilate new information in relation to prior experiences and their understandings of them (Piaget, 1964). Like Piaget, Lev Vygotsky (1934/1986) considered a relationship between individual and environment, stating that the intellectual growth of an individual cannot be considered apart from social environment (1934/1986; see also Rogoff, 1990). Piaget proposed stages of development that lead to learning, whereas Vygotsky held a constructivist view that social learning contributes to development. Vygotsky emphasized interactions with more knowledgeable members of one's society (Rogoff, 1990) and culture that contributes to a formation of values and ideas. Through interactions like guidance, mentoring, role modeling, and scaffolding, learners grow. Over time, learners internalize processes and approaches that enable them to solve increasingly intricate problems. Vygotsky described the more knowledgeable other as sensitive—one to guide but not overwhelm the learner (Cole et al., 1978). Although social interactions have the potential to result in negative outcomes, points of conflict or confusion can nevertheless produce valuable dialogue, consideration of different views, and negotiation of ideas. For both Piaget and Vygotsky, reflection is also important as inner dialogue leading to higher mental functioning (Rogoff, 1990).

Jerome Bruner (1983) was influenced by Vygotsky and similarly emphasized social support for learning. Bruner noted the learning environment and the learner's active construction of understandings. Bruner considered construction processes were helped by scaffolding, described as supported learning that enables initial success, while continually fading support in order for the learner to gradually take ownership (Bruner, 1983). Bruner also conceptualized children's processes of coding new information in stages of enactive, iconic, and symbolic representations, signifying increasing complexity and deeper understandings. Bruner highlighted not only children's abilities to learn coding systems (like language or music notation of varied sorts) but also their abilities to make use of the system.

Play is a ubiquitous theme in early childhood education, widely regarded as natural and necessary (Paley, 2004). For Montessori teachers, play and work are equivalent; therefore, practical tasks tend to be emphasized. For instance, children might play kitchen or construction as they take on imaginary roles associated with visible adult work. Paley also discussed play as work, but emphasized the importance of imaginative play, describing the open-mindedness and storytelling that can result from free association, fantasy, role-play, and imagery. Mary Kellet (2010) noted the importance of historical, cultural, and economic conditions that interact in the construction of childhood. For Montessori teachers, caregivers are essential for learning, whether as support or partners (Bruce, 2011). Lisa Huisman Koops (2020) discussed infants' communicative bonding with caregivers toward musical and relational development. Vygotsky (1934/

1986) referred to the beginning stages of communication in this way as an internal language of melody, considered the most intimate kind of thought.

Others have also emphasized the learning environment, including in nature, for instance, in Waldorf or Reggio Emilia philosophies. While not focused specifically on music, early childhood approaches can offer insightful ways to inspire, challenge, and engage children as independent learners, problem-solvers, and overall creative people. In Waldorf philosophy for example, adults structure children's time and environment—including in nature—through routines and purposeful spaces that promote independence (Miller & Pound, 2011). In the Reggio Emilia approach, the environment is considered a third teacher (Miller & Pound, 2011). Environment can involve a display of ongoing projects and an inclusion of indoor and outdoor experiences (Clark, 2007). In this approach, teachers promote creativity by mutually emphasizing both knowledge and expressivity (Anttila & Sansom, 2012) while children naturally interact with their environments. One's learning environment can be similarly considered for music composition with young children. The environment can provide fertile ground for inspiration (e.g., naturally occurring and human-created sounds, shapes, and patterns). Additionally, the organization of space, for instance tables, chairs, bookcases, and musical instruments, could promote composition. Perhaps the tables and chairs are located around the perimeter of the room, enabling a large open space in which children dance, play, and interact. Perhaps the instruments are located low on an open shelf where small children can reach them.

These varied views of child development have influenced ways educators approach learning for, perhaps *with*, children. Friedrich Froebel, who conceptualized the kindergarten, used plants as a metaphor. The (kinder)garden provides nurture for growing children (plants) (Froebel, 1889/2005). Education is therefore embedded in living, rather than considered *preparation* for living (Miller & Pound, 2011). In other words, education is not imposed on the child by adults who have decided what they should learn to become an adult. Rather, the child exists in the adult world as a person—a citizen—whose lived experiences are upheld and valued. The child should therefore make decisions, solve problems, take actions, and view themselves as strong, capable, autonomous contributors. The child themself, is therefore valued.

Creativity and Collaboration

Creativity somewhat eludes definition. To consider what constitutes creativity, J. P. Guilford (1950) discussed divergent and convergent thinking. John Baer and James Kaufman (2012) detailed categories of fluency, flexibility, originality, and elaboration in creative processes of divergent thinking, noting the importance of intrinsic motivation. E. Paul Torrance (1965) emphasized the novelty of creative products, and Teresa Amabile and Elizabeth Tighe (1993) considered the factor of usefulness. Social value influence what products are deemed useful (Mumford et al., 1994). As Margaret Barrett (2012) and Sandra Stauffer (2013) have pointed out, however, creativity scholarship tends to focus on modern Western values, though non-Western cultures often describe and value creativity differently.

Mihály Csikszentmihalyi (1996) believed children cannot attain creativity, stating that something must be widely accepted as useful before it can then be considered creative. Csikszentmihalyi therefore differentiated creativity for children, indicating that a child's creativity could be acknowledged within a particular field—for instance the field of *children's arts*. Csikszentmihalyi focused on the creative product, stating that big "C" creativity represented an idea or outcome important on a cultural level, while little "c" creativity could exist in everyday ideas and solutions important on a local level (of which children are capable). James Kaufman and Ronald Beghetto (2013) elaborated on Csikszentmihalyi's "little c" and "big C," describing four categories that included these and added two more: mini-C (personally meaningful insights), and Pro-C (professional or expert level, but without recognition as legendary). Kaufman and Beghetto explained a graduate student paper might be considered "little c" while a child's project would constitute "mini-c." Sir Ken Robinson (2001) suggested three principles to help define creativity in children and adults: Creativity involves a process of doing something within a specific domain, it has originality at some level, and it has value or worth (which can include value to the child). Robinson also noted the necessity of imagination in producing something creatively (see also Barrett, 2012).

Young children tend to feel positively about music, enjoying it and feeling confident in their creativity (Burnard, 2012). They often spontaneously make music in their homes, adapting songs, melodies, and movements (Barrett, 2012; Burnard, 2012; Koops, 2020). Their playful musicking is not random, but focused and purposeful (Stauffer, 2013). According to Ruth Butler (2008), young children view themselves as music-makers and -creators. At later stages of development, however, older children may begin to believe that only select people hold musical talents, and self-perceptions of their musical and creative abilities, may then decline (Burnard, 2012). Perceptions of rare talents may also be a notion parents reinforce (Koops, 2020), indicating the crucial period of early childhood for fostering musical creativities.

Music Composition

Music education scholars have emphasized the naturalness and importance of playful engagement and collaborative learning in early childhood years (Campbell, 2010; Marsh, 2008), including in the home environment (Koops, 2020) and online (Ruokonen & Ruismäki, 2016). Here I discuss literature comprising composition processes (Collins, 2016; Kratus, 1989), pedagogical approaches (Hickey, 2012; Kaschub & Smith, 2013), and technology considerations (Burnard, 2012; Deemer, 2016), as well as feedback (Webster, 2012).

Music education researchers have studied collaboration extensively, in particular associated with creativity and composition (e.g., Barrett, 2006; Veloso, 2017). Collaborations hold value, as Vygotsky noted, through social interactions promoting cognitive development (Cole et al., 1978). Children can successfully create music individually *and* with groups (Stauffer, 2013), although children have preferences for one or the other (Bucura & Weissberg, 2016–2017). Children's prior musical experiences differ, and they must negotiate ideas with peers. Voice and agency are not guaranteed because some children may dominate (Stauffer, 2013). Groupwork, while valuable, must involve facilitation of group-working skills; these skills cannot be assumed.

Researchers have noted that children benefit from both free and constrained composing opportunities (Barrett, 2003; Kaschub & Smith, 2009; Stauffer, 2013). Göran Folkestad (2004) stated that a composing task (different than an open-ended task) should be considered a skill-building step. Maud Hickey (2012), however, encouraged open-ended tasks first, to prompt needed techniques toward which structured tasks might then develop. Kaschub and Smith (2017) and Stauffer (2013) emphasized continued opportunities over time for composing meaningful compositions, prioritizing them over theoretical exercises.

Completely open-ended tasks may interestingly result in children imposing their own constraints (Bucura & Weissberg, 2016–2017). For others, however, open-endedness can overwhelm. Constraints can be suggested in different ways, including highly structured theoretical or technique-building tasks, or guiding principles that serve to inspire. Folkestad (2004) recommended carefully considered external conditions to protect one's "internal act of creation" (p. 88). Rather than experiencing one or the other (i.e., constraint or freedom), children should experience ongoing instructional *and* compositional opportunities, the former building skills and the latter allowing agency and expression (Burnard, 1995). Children should also help determine and define activities through which they will compose (Burnard, 2012).

Children currently grow up members of what Pamela Burnard (2012) referred to as a computerized generation. Children can access what Rob Deemer (2016) described as a "dazzling array of tools with which they can create and manipulate musical or sonic ideas" (p. 42). These include digital notation, and sequencing and looping software, as well as online tools, digital music players, and networks (Deemer, 2016). Scholars' views on the inclusion of technology for young children vary. However, changes related to the global COVID-19 pandemic that have necessitated at-home and virtual learning warrant a fresh consideration of technologies for young children and the learning possibilities they might afford.

Some music programs invest in technological tools, assuming their worth in preparation for an adult life. According to some, digital technologies can interfere with communication skills like expression and body language (Pagani et al., 2010). In Waldorf curricula, modern technologies are considered inappropriate for children (Taplin, 2011). Instead, Waldorf students use *warm technologies*, like "corn grinders, drills and whisks" (Steiner Waldorf Education, 2009, p. 28), which might compare with instruments like rachets, hand drums, and xylophones. On the other hand, Reggio Emilia teachers embrace modern technologies considered essential to modern life (Miller & Pound, 2011). Technologies used for music composition have broadened compositional approaches and can increase accessibility (Deemer, 2016). Technologies can be particularly helpful for developmental limitations that are problematic for traditional school instruments, requiring, for example fine motor skills, lung capacity, and an ability to hold and manipulate a large or heavy instrument.

Online learning and technology use can challenge collaboration. Although researchers have investigated online music learning and collaborative communities of practice (e.g., Partti & Westerlund, 2013; Waldron, 2013), these studies have not tended to involve young children. Young learners engaged in virtual learning may require aid from caregivers to manipulate tools or to resolve technology failures. Increased involvement by caregivers is likely difficult when juggling multiple demands that can also include one's own work apart from caregiving. Caregiver involvement could, however, also reinforce learning by bolstering shared musical interactions throughout a child's day (Koops, 2020). In other words, with additional musical involvement of a caring adult, music would not be relegated to music time, but instead interactively woven in small moments throughout the day. Similarly, music would not be relegated to a music teacher, but shared as a human practice with adults anywhere.

IN PRACTICE

The following sections detail practical approaches for facilitating composition with young learners. Despite an underdeveloped role in music education programs, scholars such as John Kratus (1989) have long emphasized a need for composition. Authors have described the significance of exploration and development (Kratus, 1989; Levi, 1991), which can lead to a rich musical life through playful experience, while enhancing and expanding composition skills. Children's exposure to, and experiences of music, when playfully and creatively encountered, can equip them with understandings that build a foundation of musical thinking.

Playful Music Experiences

Musical experiences, which children acquire everywhere, have potential to deeply engage children. Music teachers and caregivers can foster a broad array of experiences that, as Folkestad (2004) described, are an important component of one's creative potential and a foundation on which to build a musical identity. Piaget (1970/2008) wrote that children assimilate new information and accommodate growing understandings in relationship to previously acquired knowledge and skills. Vygotsky described psychological tools (and acquisition of them), leading to the notion of multiple literacies (Kozulin, 2003). Tools can include artifacts like signs, symbols, and texts (Kozulin, 2003), possibly representative of Bruner's (1977) sequence of representations (i.e., enactive, iconic, symbolic). Drawings, icons, and symbols, for example, have been described by music educators as ways for children to represent compositions (e.g., Barrett, 2002; Miller, 2007).

While music teachers may be concerned with their role in broadening children's musical perspectives by exposing them to unfamiliar repertoire, it is equally important to create space for already-existing musical interests. One's foundation of experience could be, in some cases, considered enculturation (Barrett, 1996), necessary in order to become acquainted with a domain (Csikszentmihalyi, 1996; Robinson, 2001). However, definitions of a musical domain can differ among children and adults. While musical experiences provide knowledge and understanding that one can use to compose, such experience can also potentially constrain one's thinking (Stauffer, 2013). This might be particularly so if unrelated to past experiences and preferences, therefore difficult to assimilate. Pedagogical approaches to composition should be considered a lived process (Stauffer, 2013). Teachers and caregivers must create space for diverse musics while also valuing ideas stemming from children's unique lived experiences.

Before and Beyond School

Prior to school age, children's growing world of musical experiences may develop from caregivers, music groups or classes, child care teachers and babysitters, television, apps, toys, siblings, films, instruments, and more (Barrett, 2012). According to Margaret Barrett (2012), the home environment plays a critical role in providing the support, exposure, practice, and formal instruction that contribute to musical understandings. Children's early musical interactions tend to be improvisatory and involve a variety of experimental sound-sources (e.g., rattles, pots and pans, forks and plates, vocalizations). Interactions with others contribute to quality of experience and might "emphasize generative and playful music- and meaning-making" (Barrett, 2012, p. 58) between child and caregiver. As Sandra Stauffer (2013) noted, every musical activity can be an opportunity for questioning, invention, and creating. With such an approach, children can be encouraged to take ownership of repertoire by applying, adapting, and transforming it.

Although music teachers may have little to say about students' musical lives prior to and outside of school, Barrett (2012) stressed the importance of access, particularly important for students who did not have musically enriching early years. Playful musical engagement in school can promote music-making within households and communities, and playful musical engagement outside of school can spark ownership and creative thinking in school music. Music teachers can create opportunities in schools intending continued playful musical engagements in home environments. Caregivers, including child care centers, may also appreciate collaborative opportunities to promote musical and creative readiness, for instance sing-alongs with school groups that encourage divergent renditions of familiar songs and cross-age collaborations that allow children to make music their own, perhaps with older siblings. A song or musical game may make its way into one setting from another, through a sibling, perhaps. Caregivers can listen, value, and potentially incorporate these moments.

Personal and Group Repertoire

Children are influenced by music that teachers may not know about or may not think to include. Repertoire commonly used in music classrooms includes folk songs, songs of varied cultures, and Western classical art music, but music educators have faced criticism for a lack of connection between school music and children's musical lives (Schuler, 2011). Schuler (2011) argued that teachers must value prior musical experiences, tastes, and interests. For young learners, this may also encompass music from toys, cartoon theme songs, and various performing artists. Children's creative work will incorporate such influences. When teachers value and encourage them, children will be more likely to share and to create with meaning.

New Music. Continuous experience of new or novel musics can also foster ownership of musical material. A one-time experience does not usually suffice for children, particularly if the style is unfamiliar. Teachers and caregivers will attest to young children's desire for familiarity through repetition. While a teacher may feel that children have sufficiently experienced repertoire after two or three listening opportunities, children may be overwhelmed with new information they cannot immediately accommodate. It can be satisfying for young learners to engage with repeated repertoire, and repetition can foster their ownership of it, thus preparing them to consider their own creative adaptations.

Shared Experiences. Collective experiences, different from collaborations, are also an important outcome of music composition that can foster shared understandings and group identity. While collaborations tend to involve group efforts toward a particular goal, collectivity is a sense of togetherness—a group who come together as community. Although composition may sometimes be an individual endeavor, social context is paramount for creativity and learning, and will also influence individual projects. A class repertoire can build mutuality and familiarity. Once repertoire is known well, children will playfully reinforce songs and activities to one another in spaces apart from a music classroom. What once was "that music" can become "our music," hummed on the playground, incorporated into play, and modified and expanded. Children will creatively adapt music. Music teachers should accept and value children's tendencies to make light of their experiences. Silly, joking renditions of class repertoire can play a powerful role in retention, understandings, and community-building. Children might take ownership through such antics, and if done in a harmless way, can positively demonstrate growing creativities. In other cases, however, teachers and caregivers may not be aware of children's adapted song forms. Children may softly hum or sing to themselves during play, and adults may not notice the ways one musical idea quietly interacts with those of peers. Intentional and responsive listening as well as recognition and reciprocation are key to teachers and caregivers understanding and fostering children's diverse creativities.

Children's Media. For online music classes or classes that incorporate virtual content, the challenge of community-building demands consideration. Children's media tend to play a significant role in their musical worlds. Children may feel comfortable expressing themselves musically at home, yet on camera or with virtual content they may appear to only passively engage. Despite what may appear to be disinterest, adults may be surprised to hear the child singing or humming the same music later while doing other things. In a similar way, teachers can role model activities that children can take outside the classroom. Young children will not always respond in obvious ways in the learning setting, even when in-person, but may do so in their own time and in their own spaces. Ideally, caregivers will take part, too, to foster music-making with senses beyond the screen (e.g., touch, movement, interaction). Media may plant musical seeds that foster person-to-person musical interactions. Synchronous interactions build young children's repertoire and skills. Although video content might engage children (Koops, 2020), its substitution for live music may be concerning. Media can nevertheless play a role in exposing children to new musical ideas, particularly when followed up on by a caring adult.

Parents and Peers. Children tend to incorporate musical ideas they learn from peers (Campbell, 2010). This may be difficult to replicate online, as on-camera learning may limit informal and personal interactions. Caregivers of all types, however, might play a key role in what Koops (2020) referred to as *parenting musically*. Different from musical parenting (e.g., organizing private lessons), Koops explained that parenting musically may involve uninhibited musical and playful interactions for a range of purposes beyond music, for instance in order to build relationships (e.g., to connect, to laugh) or to complete or enforce practical tasks (e.g., dance for brushing teeth, chant for tying shoes, song for going to bed). Peers and siblings play similar reinforcing roles when teachers and caregivers have role-modeled playful musicking for (and with) them.

Listening. Listening can influence children's creative inspirations and strategies. When trying to achieve or recreate a particular sound, children will "listen with heightened interest and attentiveness to another composer using similar approaches" (Fallin, 1995, p. 25). Interesting musical ideas they hear may also inspire them to create for themselves. While it is necessary to incorporate children's tastes and experiences, the more they create, the more they will develop a desire to understand new creative pathways that listening to diverse musics can provide.

Young children tend to have favorite repertoire (from media, pop culture, friends, church, dance practice, piano lessons, parents, or more) that they can sing, hum, dance to, or chant. Songs are appealing in that the lyrics may detail an engaging story, tell a joke, set a scene, or cultivate a mood. Lyrics help some children feel the music as concrete, important if they are to deviate from it creatively. In schools, a class can form a shared repertoire of favorite songs, particularly when serving multiple purposes, like songs-with-game, -dance, or -body percussion. Children will often change songs, sometimes accidentally, inadvertently taking ownership.

Self-Made Music. Playing one's own music can enforce coordination of one's body and mind in time. Gesturing to create specific patterned sounds on one's instrument or body, particularly when synchronized with others, is also important in building a schematic understanding of musical parts and interrelations. In the preoperational stage (see Piaget, 1970/2008) children may draw inspiration from such experiences when writing their own music. The action of playing a xylophone, for example, can be an enactment of musical understanding, and when another child joins in, a need to synchronize, take turns, or otherwise formulate a plan will likely arise, presenting a problem that children are challenged to resolve. Negotiations may then proceed.

Movement. Movement and music are deeply connected. Movement is foundational for young children as a basis of development (Anttila & Sansom, 2012); learning (Hannaford, 2007); and creativity, imagination, and knowledge (Sansom, 2007). The body and mind influence one another, building consciousness and reflectivity (Anttila & Sansom, 2012). Researchers have suggested additional purposes for movement that include development of mental operations and one's nervous system (Stevens-Smith, 2004), emotional scaffolding toward empathy and perspective (Grafton, 2009), and language development (Anttila & Sansom, 2012). Movement comprises synchronized dance as well as creativity and improvisation, often meaningful activities for young children that may be intertwined with acting, storytelling, and visual imagery. Eeva Anttila and Adrienne Sansom (2012) stated that movement allows one to make sense of their experiences and communicate interpretations to others. These "embodied processes—sensations, perceptions, gestures and movements—connect human beings to the material and social world" (Anttila & Sansom, 2012, p. 182). Movement is an important means for children's communication, improvisation, expression, and creating and shaping of musical ideas.

Literature. Poetry and stories play powerful roles in children's development of musical ideas. Teachers can use children's literature; folk tales; fables; the storylines of television, film, and other media; and children's own invented stories to provide creative activities connected to music. Poetry can enforce rhythm, flow, form, metaphor, and expression. Children's literature can "stimulate creative thinking by transferring words to sounds and by capturing feelings through sounds" (Fallin, 1995, p. 27). Representation of scene, character, or storyline through sound can provide children with strategies; understandings of representation in general; and structural concepts, including form, mood, and feeling. This may involve analyzing others' works (e.g., rhythm, repetition, forms of words in stories), adapting existing works to a different context (e.g., changing the mood, adapting the rhyme scheme), to the same context (e.g., a variation on the same theme), or creating one's own musical representations (e.g., an inspired musical idea). As Jana Fallin (1995) noted, stories can stimulate creativity and inspire through the exciting arc of a story line, rhyme scheme, rhythm of the words, characters, mood, onomatopoeia, imagery, repetition, and contrast.

Kinesthetic Connection. Body percussion can also be used as a representation of actions or sounds in a story (Fallin, 1995). Children should identify sounds that appeal to them and attempt to describe why that is so, reflecting on budding compositional ideas. Educators can emphasize process and respect for the divergent ways by which children make creative musical decisions, giving value to children's choices and encouraging their ownership. As Fallin (1995) suggested, "The sounds suggested in children's books can come alive in the music class . . . [to] accompany the story, turn into music, and even become compositions themselves" (p. 24). Children can also use music already attached to stories to analyze divergent representations of similar content, paving the way for an expanded and empathetic worldview by noting multiple interpretations. In these musical experiences, children should have opportunities to experience music in song, movement, instruments, and story; consider a variety of sound-making sources; and embody musical experiences in diverse ways. Importantly, while these experiences are fundamental building blocks of musicianship in general, the playful ways by which classes consider, improvise, experiment with, and evaluate small adaptations can lead children to make their own playful changes, setting a tone for creative musical decision-making and growing creative skills.

Brainstorming and Exploration

Beyond musical experiences and understandings, focused brainstorming and exploratory opportunities can also build ownership in adapting known music. As Patricia Sheehan Campbell (2010) mentioned, children do this naturally, and teachers can encourage it further. The lines between adapting known music and creating original music will blur, particularly for young children who may not recognize the ways known musics influence their own ideas. Regardless of the degree of originality in a child's musical creation, their feelings of originality are often empowering and deeply meaningful. According to Sir Ken Robinson (2001), the development of one's creativity can take shape in many ways. Children make use of the materials and tools in their environment and assign meanings to manipulate them (Robinson, 2001). Young children may use invented songs to communicate their feelings or to narrate their environments (Barrett, 2012) as they make meaning for themselves and of themselves (Kaschub & Smith, 2017).

The ways children interact with others impact improvisation and development of musical material (Barrett, 2012), which may not only *lead to* composition, but can exist *as* composition. Children might repeat and elaborate on rhythmic or melodic ideas and draw heavily from known musics. These adjustments and arrangements from known music demonstrate growing abilities to think divergently. Educators can task children with varied adaptations and arrangements, creating opportunities to experiment with sounds inspired by their experiences. According to Burnard (2012), young children enter the classroom as music-makers who create and bear their own cultural experiences and music educators can use this as a point of connection.

Rob Deemer (2016) noted that pre-service music teachers should work with composers to gain skills in composing. In-service music educators might also seek some composers for residencies and guest workshops, particularly if they are playful and flexible. These partnerships can take place once or over a period of time and may be fruitful depending on program goals.

In an artist collaboration project described by Julia Getino et al. (2018), students began by listening to and analyzing a professional composer's work. Following a listening analysis and guided discussion, students generated musical ideas in groups through instructional composition exercises. They then created musical ideas based on characteristics of the prior analysis. The exercises prepared students to create appealing sounds, manipulate sound sources, and consider the interactions of sounds. These activities provided pathways they could return to when composing their own works. It is important however, that when children compose, composers are aware of their support role rather than directive. Children should focus on creating the *most* possible ideas, along with *most different* ways of doing them, rather than a *best* way, in line with Baer and Kaufman (2012) and Torrance (1965) creative categories of fluency, flexibility, and originality. Brainstorming exercises should also be separate from processes of editing and refining, as brainstorming can be most fruitful with open attitude of "anything is possible."

Crafting Compositional Skills

Children grow from continuous opportunities to generate, organize, and refine musical ideas. One's accumulation of experiences can build musicianship skills. In this section I discuss continuous opportunities to compose. I also discuss structural considerations, and topics of meaning and expressivity.

Continuous Opportunities

Although music teachers may provide some opportunities for young children to compose, the time spent on composition is sometimes minimal. Stauffer (2001) noted that time, tool, and technique all interact in children's composition processes. In terms of time, children need time to compose, as well as many opportunities to practice composing over time (Bucura & Weissberg, 2016–2017). Stauffer (2001) found that time is important for several reasons that include familiarization with the medium (e.g., software, instruments), development of skills and gestures, and practice. Children need continuous opportunities to revise and develop their musical ideas; therefore, it may be important they find ways to retrieve musical ideas over time. According to Getino et al. (2018), it can be important to create a score of some kind, naming two reasons: "to help students remember tomorrow what was done today and to be able to reflect on paper what has been put together" (p. 33). The score, however, can be considered with flexibility. Standard notation will be unfamiliar to many children—it can restrain composition even among those who know and use it. Very young children may not be skilled in the coding system of language either, in which case other means of representation can be helpful. Imagery, movement, recordings, and invented notation (e.g., Barrett, 2002), however, are some methods of documenting musical ideas that can be accessible and retrievable to young children. These representations may promote expressivity as well, as children can focus on appealing sounds and expressive representations rather than focusing on a system of representation.

Structure

In addition to aforementioned experiences and competencies that can form a basis for conceptualizing music, Folkestad (2004) also noted that these interact with cultural practices, tools, instruments, and instructions. Music spaces—including in the home—can provide selections of sound sources, including a variety of musical instruments and software. Whether children have refined playing skills on these tools is mostly beside the point—children will enjoy strumming or picking guitar strings, for example, or identifying melodies on a keyboard. They may also be inspired by the timbre itself, or the gesture involved in making the sound (e.g., plucking, strumming, hitting, blowing, dragging). Such experiences may even promote an interest in further learning what sounds the instrument offers, thus inspiring skill development. Recorders are sometimes required in elementary music classes and can enable children to melodically create with a different timbre and experience from that of voice, xylophone, or the like. Yet other types of instruments, slide or tin whistles for instance, may also be appealing to children and can be interpreted as a novel and inspiring sound source. Other sound sources less commonly experienced can play similar roles, like alto recorders, accordions, harmonicas, and steel pans, which may be borrowed when purchase is not possible.

In addition to engaging sound sources made available to children, a stimulating environment in general is an important part of some early childhood education approaches, for instance in the Reggio Emilia approach (Miller & Pound, 2011). In addition to a wide array of interesting and available sound sources, displays of works-in-progress can foster dialogue about learning and creativity. Such displays may include plans in the form of maps, formulas, or iconic or symbolic representations; invented notation; imagery like photographs, collages, screenshots; or comments from peers or others. Stations, for example for listening to recordings, to gather instruments, to make music, or to dance and move, can also foster a creative environment. Displays and stations can document works and processes, promote dialogue, make space, and therefore communicate value for children's ideas. These can reinforce to children that their ideas should be taken seriously by adults and by themselves.

Compositions can draw on a wide array of additional environmental influences to spark imagination, for instance spaces outside the classroom and in nature. Children love to sing in a resonant stairwell, on an auditorium stage, or in an enclosed space all their own (e.g., under a table, in an alcove, behind a curtain). When in nature, bird song, traffic, weather, and the like can suggest musical ideas. In a classroom, natural scenes can also be evoked through pictures, video, and descriptive storytelling, for instance beach scenes, neighborhood, farmland, highway, pond, and so on. Interaction with the environment can occur through physical exploration (e.g., running, twirling, or rolling on grass; dripping water through fingers; squishing mud or slime) and exploration of sound and form (e.g., loud, soft, echo, loop, cycle). Interaction with differing spaces can be particularly inspirational, especially when children are liberated to explore the full extent of possibilities in order to draw boundaries for themselves before focusing ideas (Bucura & Weissberg, 2016–2017). It can be difficult for adults to allow children to explore such boundaries (e.g., the loudest possible sounds, the biggest possible group, the most possible instruments), but these experiences are often necessary in order for children to then mediate their own approach that they chose for themselves.

Meaning and Expressivity

Rob Deemer (2016) referred to composition as a personal act that blends both emotion and intellect. Compositions can lack emotion if children feel unsafe expressing themselves. Beyond exercises and activities intended to build compositional skills, it is important that teachers and caregivers value space and time for children to compose their own, unrestricted music. In these instances, composing can allow children to articulate their feelings and uniquely express themselves. As Michele Kaschub and Janice Smith (2017) stated:

> The act of composing transcends the limits of verbal and mathematical representations and allows children to explore sound as a means for sharing who they are, what they think, and what they feel about their experiences in the world. It invites them to draw on the full breadth of their musical skills and understanding to create music that represents their unique insights. (p. 13)

When children autonomously compose, teachers can emphasize the goals of voice and expression by providing prompting inspirations rather than skill-building directives. These may include open-ended prompts involving art, dance/movement, scenes, stories, moods, or characters meant to evoke prior experiences, interpretations, and feelings.

Teacher Role

Teachers must consider their roles sensitively in relation to children's creative works. In the Reggio Emilia approach, creativity grows when teachers refrain from prescription and are instead sensitive and attentive observers, responders, and interpreters (Anttila & Sansom, 2012). Music education scholars recommend similar facilitation approaches, particularly learner-centeredness (Huhtinen-Hildén & Pitt, 2018). Teachers must recognize children's differentiated understandings and participate in creative interactions with them (Malaguzzi, 1998).

Young children are often excited to share their work. Although some children will feel inhibited by surveillance or competition (Amabile et al., 2018), children often seek teacher approval. As an extrinsic motivator, teacher approval can congest intrinsic drive. Unspecific praise can stifle creativity and promote a fixed idea of musicianship (Dweck, 2007) or talent. The teacher-student hierarchy can result in hesitation to take risks and to trust one's own decisions. Getino et al. (2018) noted the teacher's role should allow students autonomy while being available for suggestions and reflections. According to Getino et al., this helps establish teachers' relationships to, and understandings of, students' works and can help move processes along when children feel unsure or stuck. Teachers must therefore provide sensitive, specific feedback while consciously making space for children to trust and value themselves.

Teachers should also collaborate sensitively and flexibly to aid in bringing children's intentions to sound (Kaschub & Smith, 2017). Teachers and caregivers can compose their own music (Bucura & Weissberg, 2016-17; Nagy, 2016) and welcome children's feedback on it, therefore role modeling value for composition as a human act, as well as respect and appreciation for varied perspectives. This communicates that composing music is for everyone. In this way, teachers can also disrupt the teacher–student hierarchy. According to Deemer (2016), teachers and children should collaborate as well, which can occur as a whole-class or small group activity.

Feedback, Reflection, Revision

Artistic outcomes are typically the result of long-term work to realize one's intentions through processes of revision and refinement. While musical exploration and brainstorming are important steps toward idea generation, processes of receiving feedback (even one's own), and reflecting on it with revision, are important steps for children to grow as composers.

Children should reflect on their processes and products (Barrett, 2000–2001). Reflection allows children to consider the overall effect in relationship to their intentions. Kaschub and Smith (2017) noted that before considering what revisions they might make, children should articulate reasons for them. Children can revisit their original inspirations and intentions. For instance, *Does the piece sound the way I wanted? What about it works well?* and *What would happen if . . .?* Music teachers facilitate reflection with such questions, encouraging children to experiment, elaborate, create alternate possibilities, or create anew. Children should describe their compositions and reflect on both processes and products (Barrett, 2000–2001), which they can do in a variety of ways: with teacher or peers, self-reflection (written, audio, video), in pictures, or discussion. Over time, reflective processes may become habitual and self-initiated.

As Peter Webster (2012) described, revision involves improving composition by making changes to the original. Webster believed the composer must first consider their musical ideas worthy of such feedback, which teachers can bolster by showing interest and asking questions. Young children, who experience the world in immediate ways, may also *not* choose to edit their music. Young children tend to write music and stop at a point of satisfaction without looking back. Rather than return to finished pieces, they may prefer instead to create entirely new pieces, one after another. Despite feelings of completion for each, they may unconsciously return to prior musical ideas that reoccur in subsequent compositions (Stauffer, 2013). In assessment, teachers can consider a student's many compositions, over which time a refinement of skills might be noted that are not apparent when considered individually.

Feedback should vary, including self-, peer-, and teacher-assessments with differing degrees of formality. With an end-product that is not yet realized and learning that can occur in unexpected ways, assessments must be clear yet flexible. As Pamela Burnard (2012) noted, assessments are one way by which institutions legitimize and normalize their values. Assessments will therefore communicate to children why composition is valuable and in what ways. Young children may not always skillfully consider others' perspectives. As they age and grow in composition skills, they can improve in considering others' perspectives, and may write music with intended listener interpretations (Kaschub & Smith, 2017). Younger composers, however, may be surprised or disappointed if a peer does not understand their intention or musical references. Peer feedback can provide valuable perspective to the composer if they are prepared to consider it. Children can share reflections, successes, and suggestions as well as pose challenges (Getino et al., 2018). Children must gain these skills, and such interactions can build a community of support, safety, and encouragement. Such interactions also have the potential to negatively impact the self-concept of young composers and therefore, must be carefully guided. Young children can successfully provide observational feedback that avoid opinion, for instance, "I noticed . . ." or "I heard . . . ." These comments can contribute to analytic skills for listeners while providing interpretations to the composer without the judgment of "I liked . . . ."

While reactions, questions, and impressions others have about a student's piece can influence revision, children will have varying degrees of readiness for feedback (Webster, 2012). Music teachers must consider feedback sensitively for each student, gauging their readiness to receive it, to what degree, and how so. Similarly, peer feedback involves sharing compositions. When sharing, children should have opportunities to represent their compositions in a variety of ways (e.g., visual representation of all variety, recordings, performances, embodiment of musical ideas, verbal description). While many young children will be eager to share, others may not. If a student is hesitant, they might instead explain ideas or describe their music. Sharing compositions may be especially difficult for older children, particularly if the peer group feels unsafe or is new. Sharing should not be forced but continually invited and encouraged, and role modeled as safe, respectful, and supportive.

Teachers should also be prepared for children to create in unexpected ways. When comfortable with composing processes, children may develop skills in communicating feelings (Anttila & Sansom, 2012). It is important to bear in mind that the composers are the experts of their own feelings. Children may express worrying feelings or themes that the teacher must then navigate, particularly in songwriting where lyrics might provide an explicit message, for instance trauma, neglect, or violence. Teachers must then prioritize the child's well-being while striving to maintain a safe space for creation and expression, necessitating careful consideration of children's expressions alongside their own legal and ethical responsibilities to them. Through processes of playful musical experiences, brainstorming and exploration, and crafting compositional skills, children will grow in their abilities to express themselves musically. Each process necessitates thoughtful considerations (see Figure 25.1). When grounded in an ethic of care, children will be nurtured as composers.

Playful Musical Experiences	Brainstorming and Exploration	Crafting Skills
Experimenting and interacting (personal music-making during play)	Inspiration (environment, listening, analysis, diverse sound sources)	Time (idea-generation, exploration, refinement, composing over time)
Valid representation (signs, symbols, icons, movement, stories, poetry, acting, body percussion)	Exploration (creating many and different possibilities)	Tools (instruments, technologies, mediums of representation)
Value for familiar and unfamiliar repertoire, repeatedly used, experienced together	Adaptations	Techniques (musical gestures, effects, instruments, negotiations)
Influences (caregivers, friends, siblings, toys, films), a variety of sound-sources	Arrangements	Voice, emotion, feeling, message
Playful modeling and interactions, songs to accompany tasks, or with games and dance	Improvisation	Revision, varied forms of feedback (mirroring, questioning, observing)

FIGURE 25.1. Early childhood composition processes

Conclusion

Young children can exude creativity and musicianship. Socialization into meanings of musicianship come about early and can be furthered through creative tasks like composition. Conceptions of who creates music (and how) can quickly diminish a child's confidence to articulate and share musical ideas. The early childhood stage is foundational in not only growing musical skills and understandings, but in fostering a proclivity toward creating music.

Caregivers and teachers contribute to children's musical experiences. Children make their own meanings of these experiences, and when space exists for them to bring themselves into music-making and creating, they can compose music in meaningful ways. Adults have a responsibility to respect and care for children's ideas, nurture skills toward an articulation of those ideas, and provide feedback in ways that can promote refinement of skills as they are ready.

Children's musical experiences and creative ideas extend beyond pedagogical parameters and school settings. Music teachers can play important roles in fostering musical experiences that build composition skills. Teachers can value time and space for creating as well as instructional exercises that enable possibilities, examples, and strategies. Adults in all roles, however, can also model playful, creative musicianship, including an adaptation of known musics and a generation of unique musical ideas. Children can then deepen musical thinking, gain confidence to share and receive feedback, and advance abilities to reflect, revise, and refine ideas. Children must be treated with sensitivity, flexibility, and a deep ethic of care. When adults encourage, value, and celebrate creative musical thinking, young children will gain composition skills and make meanings of their growing musicianship.

References

Amabile, T. M., Collins, M. A., Conti, R., Phillips, E., Picariello, M., Ruscio, J., & Whitney, D. (2018). *Creativity in context: Update to the social psychology of creativity*. Routledge.

Amabile, T. M., & Tighe, E. (1993). Questions of creativity. In J. Brockman (Ed.), *Creativity* (pp. 7–27). Touchstone.

Anttila, E., & Sansom, A. (2012). Movement, embodiment, and creativity: Perspectives on the value of dance in early childhood education. In O. N. Saracho (Ed.), *Contemporary perspectives on research in creativity in early childhood education* (pp. 179–204). Information Age Publishing.

Baer, J., & Kaufman, J. C. (2012). *Being creative inside and outside the classroom: How to boost your students' creativity—and your own*. ProQuest Ebook Central https://ebookcentral.proquest.com

Barrett, M. (1996). Children's aesthetic decision-making: An analysis of children's musical discourse as composers. *International Journal of Music Education*, os-28(1), 37–62. https://doi.org/10.1177/025576149602800104

Barrett, M. S. (2000–2001). Perception, description, and reflection: Young children's aesthetic decision-making as critics of their own and adult compositions. *Bulletin of the Council for Research in Music Education, 147*(Winter, 2000/2001), 22–29. http://www.jstor.org/stable/40319382

Barrett, M. S. (2002). Invented notations and mediated memory: A case-study of two children's use of invented notations. *Bulletin of the Council for Research in Music Education, 153/154* (Summer-Fall, 2002), 55–62.

Barrett, M. (2003). Freedoms and constraints: Constructing musical worlds through the dialogue of composition. In M. Hickey (Ed.), *Why and how to teach music composition: A new horizon for music education* (pp. 3–30). MENC: The National Association for Music Education.

Barrett, M. (2006). "Creative collaboration": An "eminence" study of teaching and learning in music composition. *Psychology of Music, 34*(2), 195–218. https://doi.org/10.1177/0305735606061852

Barrett, M. (2012). Preparing the mind for musical creativity: Early music learning and engagement. In O. Odena (Ed.), *Musical creativity: Insights from music education research* (pp. 51–72). Routledge.

Bruce, T. (2011). Froebel today. In L. Miller & L. Pound (Eds.), *Theories and approaches to learning in the early years* (pp. 55–70). SAGE Publications.

Bruner, J. (1977). *The process of education*. Cambridge, MA: Harvard University Press.

Bruner, J. (1983). *Child's talk*. New York: Norton.

Bucura, E., & Weissberg, J. (2016–2017). Children's musical empowerment in two composition task designs. *Research & Issues in Music Education, 13*(1), Article 4. https://commons.lib.jmu.edu/rime/vol13/iss1/4

Burnard, P. (1995). Task design and experience in composition. *Research Studies in Music Education, 5*(1), 32–46. https://doi.org/10.1177/1321103X9500500104

Burnard, P. (2012). Rethinking "musical creativity" and the notion of multiple creativities in music. In O. Odena (Ed.), *Musical creativity: Insights from music education research* (pp. 5–28). Routledge.

Butler, R. (2008). Evaluating competence and maintaining self-worth between early and middle childhood: Blissful ignorance or the construction of knowledge and strategies in context? In H. W. Marsh, R. G. Craven, & D. M. McInerney (Eds.), *Self-processes, learning and enabling human potential: Dynamic new approaches* (pp. 193–222). Information Age Publishing.

Campbell, P. S. (2010). *Songs in their heads: Music and its meaning in children's lives* (2nd ed.). Oxford University Press.

Clark, A. (2007). *Early childhood spaces: Involving young children and practitioners in the design process* (Working Paper No. 45). Bernard van Leer Foundation.

Cole, M., Jolm-Steiner, V., Scribner, S., & Souberman, E. (Eds.). (1978). *Mind in society: The development of higher psychological processes. L. S. Vygotsky*. Harvard University Press. https://doi.org/10.2307/j.ctvjf9vz4

Collins, D. (2016). *The act of musical composition: Studies in the creative process*. Routledge.

Colwell, C. M., Davis, K., & Schroeder, L. K. (2005). The effect of composition (art or music) on the self-concept of hospitalized children. *Journal of Music Therapy, 42*(1), 49–63. https://doi.org/10.1093/jmt/42.1.49

Cook, N. (1998). *Music: A very short introduction*. Oxford University Press.

Csikszentmihalyi, M. (1996). *Creativity: Flow and the psychology of discovery and invention*. HarperCollins Publishers.

Deemer, R. (2016). Reimagining the role of composition in music teacher education. *Music Educators Journal, 102*(3), 41–45. https://doi.org/10.1177/0027432115626253

Dweck, C. (2007). *Mindset: The new psychology of success*. Ballantine Books.

Erikson, E. H. (1959/1980). *Identity and the life cycle*. W. W. Norton.

Fallin, J. R. (1995). Children's literature as a springboard for music. *Music Educators Journal, 81*(5), 24–27. https://doi.org/10.2307/3398852

Folkestad, G. (2004). A meta-analytic approach to qualitative studies in music education: A new model applied to creativity and composition. *Bulletin of the Council for Research in Music Education, 161/162*, 83–90. http://www.jstor.org/stable/40319241

Froebel, F. (2005). *Autobiography of Friedrich Froebel* (E. Michaelis & H. Keatley Moore, Trans.). Syracuse, NY: Project Gutenberg. Retrieved Nov. 30, 2020, from https://www.gutenberg.org/ebooks/16434 (Original work published 1889)

Furth, H. G. (1974). Two aspects of experience in ontogeny: Development and learning. In H. W. Reese (Ed.), *Advances in child development and behavior* (Vol. 9, pp. 47–67). Academic Press. https://doi.org/10.1016/S0065-2407(08)60314-6

Getino, J., González-Martín, C., & Valls, A. (2018). The composer goes to the classroom. *Music Educators Journal, 105*(2), 28–35. https://doi.org/10.1177/0027432118805191

Grafton, S. T. (2009, October 5). What can dance teach us about learning? The Dana Foundation. https://labs.psych.ucsb.edu/grafton/scott/Papers/Grafton2009The%20Dana%20Foundation.pdf

Guilford, J. P. (1950). Creativity. *American Psychologist, 5*(9), 444–454. https://doi.org/10.1037/h0063487

Hannaford, C. (2007). *Smart moves: Why Learning is not all in your head* (2nd ed.). Great River Books.

Hickey, M. (2012). *Music outside the lines: Ideas for composing in K–12 music classrooms.* Oxford University Press. https://doi.org/10.1093/acprof:osobl/9780199826773.001.0001

Hogenes, M., van Oers, B., & Diekstra, R. F. W. (2014). Noa, a 10-year-old composer: A case study. *Journal of Arts & Humanities, 3*(12), 1–15. http://www.theartsjournal.org/index.php/site/index

Huhtinen-Hildén, L., & Pitt, J. (2018). *Taking a learner-centred approach to music education: Pedagogical pathways.* ProQuest Ebook Central https://ebookcentral.proquest.com

Jorgensen, E. R. (2020). Life, liberty, and the pursuit of happiness: Values for music education. *Bulletin of the Council for Research in Music Education, 66*(226), 66–79. https://doi.org/10.5406/bulcouresmusedu.226.0066

Kaschub, M., & Smith, J. (2009). *Minds on music: Composition for creative and critical thinking.* Rowman & Littlefield Education.

Kaschub, M., & Smith, J. (Eds.). (2013). *Composing our future: Preparing music educators to teach composition.* Oxford University Press. https://doi.org/fjm6

Kaschub, M., & Smith, J. (2017). *Experiencing music composition in grades 3–5.* Oxford University Press.

Kaufman, J. C., & Beghetto, R. A. (2013). Do people recognize the four Cs? Examining layperson conceptions of creativity. *Psychology of Aesthetics, Creativity, and the Arts, 7*(3), 229–236. Doi: 10.1037/a0033295

Kellet, M. (2010). *Rethinking children and research: Attitudes in contemporary society.* Continuum Publishing.

Koops, L. H. (2020). *Parenting musically.* Oxford University Press.

Kozulin, A. (2003). Psychological tools and mediated learning. In A. Kozulin, B. Gindis, V. Ageyev & S. Miller (Eds.), *Vygotsky's educational theory in cultural context* (pp. 15–38). New York: Cambridge University Press.

Kratus, J. (1989). A time analysis of the compositional processes used by children ages 7 to 11. *Journal of Research in Music Education, 37*(1), 5–20. https://doi.org/10.2307/3344949

Levi, R. G. (1991). *A field investigation of the composing processes used by second-grade children creating original language and music pieces* [Doctoral dissertation, Case Western Reserve University]. OhioLINK Electronic Theses & Dissertations Center. https://bit.ly/367t5l2

Malaguzzi, L. (1998). History, ideas, and basic philosophy: An interview with Lella Gandini. In C. Edwards, L. Gandini, & G. Forman (Eds.), *The hundred languages of children: The Reggio Emilia approach—Advanced reflections* (2nd ed., pp. 49–97). Ablex Publishing.

Marsh, K. (2008). *The musical playground.* Oxford University Press.

Miller, B. A. (2007). Of hot cross buns and hot dog buns: Bridging the gap between iconic and symbolic modes of understanding. *General Music Today, 20*(3), 11–18. Doi:

Miller, L., & Pound, L. (2011). *Theories and approaches to learning in the early years.* SAGE.

Mills, J. (2009). *Music in the primary school.* Oxford University Press.

Mumford, M. D., Reiter-Palmer, R., & Redmond, M. R. (1994). Problem construction and cognition: Applying problem representations in ill-defined domains. In M. A. Runco (Ed.), *Problem finding, problem solving, and creativity* (pp. 3–39). Ablex Publishing.

Nagy, Z. (2016). *Embodiment of musical creativity.* Routledge. https://doi.org/10.4324/9781315469010

National Association for Music Education. (2014). *2014 music standards (composition/theory).* https://nafme.org/wp-content/uploads/2014/11/2014-Music-Standards-Composition-Theory-Strand.pdf

Oseka, O. (2016). *Musical creativity: Insights from music education research.* Routledge.

Pagani, L. S., Fitzpatrick, C., Barnett, T. A., & Dubow, E. (2010). Prospective associations between early childhood television exposure and academic, psychosocial, and physical well-being by middle childhood. *Archives of Pediatrics and Adolescent Medicine, 164*(5), 425–431. https://doi.org/10.1001/archpediatrics.2010.50

Paley, V. G. (2004). *A child's work: The importance of fantasy play*. University of Chicago Press.

Partti, H., & Westerlund, H. (2013). Envisioning collaborative composing in music education: Learning and negotiation of meaning in *operabyyou.com*. *British Journal of Music Education*, *30*(2), 207–222. https://doi.org/10.1017/S0265051713000119

Piaget, J. (2008). Intellectual evolution from adolescence to adulthood (J. Bliss & H. Furth, Trans.). *Human Development, 51*, 40–47. https://doi.org/10.1159/000112531 (Reprinted from "Intellectual evolution from adolescence to adulthood," 1972, *Human Development, 15*, 1–12, https://doi.org/10.1159/000271225; original work published 1970)

Piaget, J. (1964). Cognitive development in children: Piaget. *Journal of Research in Science Teaching, 2*, 176–186.

Robinson, K. (2001). *Out of our minds: Learning to be creative*. Capstone.

Rogoff, B. (1990). *Apprenticeship in thinking: Cognitive development in social context*. Oxford University Press.

Ruokonen, I., Ruismäki, H. (2016). E-learning in music: A case study of learning group composing in a blended learning environment. *Procedia-Social and Behavioral Sciences, 217*, 109–115. doi:10.1016/j.sbspro.2016.02.039

Sansom, A. (2007). Rudolph von Laban. In J. Kincheloe & R. Horn, Jr. (Eds.), *The Praeger handbook of education and psychology* (pp. 231–239). Praeger.

Schuler, S. C. (2011). Building inclusive, effective twenty-first-century music programs. *Music Educators Journal, 98*(1), 8–13. https://doi.org/10.1177/0027432111418748

Seddon, F. A. (2012). Empathetic creativity in music-making. In O. Odena (Ed.), *Musical creativity: Insights from music education research* (pp. 133–148). Routledge.

Stauffer, S. L. (2001). Composing with computers: Meg makes music. *Bulletin of the Council for Research in Music Education, 150*(Fall, 2001), 1–20. http://www.jstor.org/stable/40319096

Stauffer, S. L. (2013). Preparing to engage children in musical creating. In M. Kaschub & J. Smith (Eds.), *Composing our future: Preparing music educators to teach composition* (pp. 75–108). Oxford University Press.

Steiner Waldorf Education. (2009). *Guide to the early years foundation stage in Steiner Waldorf early childhood settings*. Association of Steiner Waldorf Schools.

Stevens-Smith, D. (2004). Movement and learning: A valuable connection. *Strategies, 18*(1), 10-11.

Taplin, J. T. (2011). Steiner Waldorf early childhood education: Offering a curriculum for the 21st century. In L. Miller & L. Pound (Eds.), *Theories and approaches to learning in the early years* (pp. 86–98). SAGE.

Torrance, E. P. (1965). Scientific views of creativity and factors affecting its growth. *Daedalus, 94*(3), 663–681.

Veloso, A. L. (2017). Composing music, developing dialogues: An enactive perspective on children's collaborative creativity. *British Journal of Music Education, 34*(3), 259–276. Doi: 10.1017/S0265051717000055

Vygotsky, L. S. (1986). *Thought and language* (A. Kozulin, Ed. & Trans.; Rev. ed.). MIT Press. (Original work published 1934)

Waldron, J. (2013). YouTube, fanvids, forums, vlogs and blogs: Informal music learning in a convergent on- and offline music community. *International Journal of Music Education, 31*(1), 91–105. https://doi.org/10.1177/0255761411434861

Webster, P. (2012). Towards pedagogies of revision: Guiding a student's music composition. In O. Odena (Ed.), *Musical creativity: Insights from music education research* (pp. 93–112). Ashgate.

Wiggins, J. (1990). *Composition in the classroom: A tool for teaching*. MENC: The National Association for Music Education.

CHAPTER 26

....

FACILITATING SONGWRITING WITH CHILDREN

....

SUZANNE L. BURTON AND HEATHER WADLER

CHILDREN are natural songmakers. Effortlessly and intuitively, they take part in creating and improvising melodies, experimenting with combinations of musical fragments that have potential to be woven into song. Often occurring in informal settings, their songs may arise spontaneously during solitary or group play (Marsh, 1995).

Growing older, children's informal songmaking can lead to the intentional development of songs through songwriting. As children develop their songs, modes to capture their musical intent are accessible through video and audio recording, and graphic or approximated traditional notation. With their songs preserved, they can review their music, and make creative and impactful decisions through reflection and refinement of their songs. During the creative process of songwriting, children's musicianship flourishes as they demonstrate musical knowledge-in-action, applying musical concepts and skills through songs. During the process of songwriting, children's musicianship flourishes as they demonstrate musical knowledge-in-action, applying musical concepts and skills in songs that are uniquely theirs. As children preserve their songs, they are afforded the opportunity to make creative and impactful musical decisions through reflection, revision, and refinement.

In this chapter, we present a project where we elaborate on the idea of children as songmakers. We extend children's propensity for songmaking into an approach that acknowledges their musically creative capacities to express themselves through songwriting. Over ten weeks, students learn primary features of song construction and apply them in project activities. Throughout, students engage in reflection and self-assessment, while receiving teacher and peer feedback (Deutsch, 2016)—all of which expand their musical thinking and facilitate thoughtful shaping of their songs. The culmination of the project is an original song written in small groups, known as "bands."

Songmaking

From the youngest of ages, children are active participants in their music development (Bannan & Woodward, 2010; Barrett, 2009; Malloch & Trevarthen, 2009; Reynolds & Burton, 2017; Young & Illari, 2012). Intuitively, they absorb and respond to music in their environment, assimilating its tonal, rhythmic, and stylistic syntax (Gordon, 2013; Gruhn, 2002). Acquiring a rich sonic foundation for musical expression (Moog, 1976), they build a music vocabulary accessible for improvisation, songmaking, and songwriting (Smith, 2017).

Children vocally explore musical ideas for self-entertainment (Campbell, 1998; Young, 2002). They accompany, narrate, and punctuate their lives with spontaneous musical improvisation (Burton, 2002; Custodero, Cali, & Diaz-Donoso, 2016; Moorhead & Pond, 1978; Young, 2002). Seeking to make sense of the world around them, their improvisations take form as they mark life events and routines through songmaking (Barrett, 2009; Custodero, 2006), sometimes creating songs that are personal and intimate in nature (Barrett, 2009; Young, 2002).

Children engage in songmaking (see Figure 26.1) in any number of settings (Burton, 2002; Moorhead & Pond, 1978; Pond, 1981; Young, 2002, 2006): while waiting in line at the grocery store, doing household chores, riding in the car with parents and siblings (Harwood, 1987; Koops, 2014; Young, 2002), or just going about their day (DeNora, 2000; Moorhead & Pond, 1978; Young, 2002). Reciprocal musical participation with families and care givers supports children's songmaking (Barrett, 2009; Custodero, 2006; Custodero & Johnson-Green, 2006; Reynolds & Burton, 2017; Steever, 2015).

At preschool, during free play, a group of four children are "putting out a fire" in the playhouse. While the story is played out in improvisational style, the children are songmaking in like fashion. A musical in raw form, we observe that the owner is stranded in the house. She sings a motif of, "Fire! Fire! Fire! Help! Help!" In response, a fire fighter sings, "Here we come! Here we come!" The children continue to sing in a call and response form, changing the words as suited their play-needs.

FIGURE 26.1. Song-spotting I: Songs in free play

Children also freely, expressively, and playfully extend and expand musical ideas (see Figure 26.2) from songs previously learned (Barrett, 2009; Burton, 2002; Marsh, 1995; Niland 2009). These songs offer a platform for children to exercise their music vocabularies through imitation, improvisation, and songmaking (Burton, 2002; Young, 2002; Reynolds, Long, & Valerio, 2007; Campbell, 1998).

> *Four-year-old Rachel is playing with large cardboard bricks in the middle of the family room of her home. Building a tower, she is singing a familiar song without the lyrics. As she places block after block on top of one another, Rachel begins trying out scat-like syllables. She varies the style, dynamics, tempo, and meter as she sings. Later in the day, while picking up her toys, she returns to the song, continuing to make it uniquely her own.*

FIGURE 26.2. Song-spotting II: Extending musical ideas

For young children, learning environments tend to be informal, unstructured, and play-based. As children move on to elementary school, the educational context becomes more structured and systematic. In this formal setting, children may have fewer opportunities to express themselves musically throughout the day. Establishing an environment that is conducive to students' "meaningful discovery, experience, and knowledge of music" (Littleton, 2015, p. 88; Williams, 2014) furthers their musical curiosity and propensity for songmaking in elementary school (see Figure 26.3).

> Song-spotting III
>
> *Best friends, eight-year-old Alex and seven-year-old Chris are in the playroom of Alex's house. As they play, they trade melodic ideas, developing a theme song for their "race car show," that features their "fast and furious" remote-controlled race cars on a newly built track. Revving up their cars with loud engine noises and incorporating high speed and crash-like sound effects, the theme song captures the spirit of a NASCAR race.*
>
> *Nine-year-old Kendall is riding the bus home from school. Settled in for the 15-minute ride home, she is audiating fragments of the song she and her friends created as they jumped rope and played hand-clapping games during recess. Exiting the bus, Kendall skips home singing, improvising, and extending the song that originated on the playground.*

FIGURE 26.3. Song-spotting III: Finding time for musical expression

Facilitating Songmaking in Elementary School

Taking notice of their uninhibited and improvisatory musical approach, we can learn from the informal and playful songmaking of children. Their instinctive experiences with improvisation and songmaking should cause us to be mindful of how we construct our curriculum, the instructional approaches we use, and that we ensure an open, creative environment where all students have a musical voice (Thompson, 1980; Wiggins, 1999).

Improvisation

When improvising, children are empowered to take advantage of the freedom to make musical decisions within self-imposed musical constraints (Kratus, 1995). Creating music in the moment (Azzara, 2002; Burton & Snell, 2018; Kratus, 1995; Shouldice, 2018), improvisation enriches students' musical development as they draw upon their prior musical experiences and connect their informal and formal music learning (Campbell, 2010). Sparking their musical imaginations for songmaking and eventual songwriting, improvisation is one means for children to share the music they have "inside" (Gordon, 2003; Burton, 2011; Burton & Snell, 2018; Shouldice, 2018). Although improvisation can seem to be messy with "imperfect" results, it is a primary channel for students' to assimilate and synthesize musical concepts and skills, often leading to song (Azzara, 2002; Burton & Snell, 2018; Shouldice, 2018).

Presented are three activities to assist you as you guide students' intentional melodic improvisation in your classroom. Each one uses a song as a foundation, which sets the musical context—either informally or formally, depending on your students' ages and their musical needs. Sensitivity to their varied improvisational styles is key to supporting students' musically creative processes as they bring musical ideas together through songmaking.

Answering the Call

In this activity, you will use the form of call and response to facilitate improvisation. First, teach your students a call and response song such as "I Got a Letter" as shown in Figure 26.4.

When students are comfortable singing both the call and response, deconstruct this short, yet emotive song. Consider the lyrics and their intent. Discuss the message of the song and its implications for interpretation and expression. With the class, try out variations of the song as a means of comparison with the original, leading your students to discover how form, tonality, meter, and melodic rhythm coalesce to achieve unity and variety coupled with the tension and release within each phrase through the form of call and response.

I Got a Letter

FIGURE 26.4. "I Got a Letter"

Now, involve students in improvisation. Model how to improvise a response to the call for your students. Before inviting them to sing their improvised responses to your call, invite students to audiate possible responses. Then, ask the class to improvise their responses (as an entire group), to your call. Although cacophonous, this technique promotes a safe environment for students to improvise and gain confidence sharing their musical ideas without feeling singled out. Ask student volunteers to sing improvised responses to your call. Repeat the activity switching roles with students, where they improvise the call, and you sing the response.

Improvising Antecedent-Consequent Phrases

A technique for improvisation that is similar to that of call and response songs is to use a familiar song with clear antecedent-consequent phrases. "I Got a Letter" could be used if each call and response were conceptualized as separate phrases. Another song that could serve the same objective is "Sally Go 'Round the Sun," found in Figure 26.5.

Review the song with your class, leading them to discover the construction of the song as you did with "I Got a Letter." Next, demonstrate for the class by singing the first phrase (antecedent) with an improvised second phrase (consequent). Invite the class to audiate possible consequents and then, collectively improvise one in response to your antecedent. Follow a similar process, but this time ask students to improvise antecedents with the consequent remaining stable. As an extension, engage students in musical dialogue by inviting half of the class to sing the antecedent with the other half improvising the consequent and vice versa. Ask individual student volunteers to improvise an antecedent while the class sings the consequent or have the class sing the antecedent while a student improvises the consequent. Then, pair up students to take turns improvising antecedents and consequents using "Sally Go Round the Sun" as a reference.

Sally Go Round the Sun

Traditional

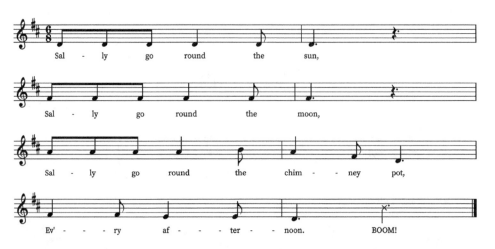

FIGURE 26.5. "Sally Go 'Round the Sun"

Songmaking through Improvisation

Continuing to use "Sally Go 'Round the Sun" as an illustration, ask students to use antecedent and consequent fragments to compose a two-phrase song to be shared with the class. Assemble students into small groups with the objective of creating a song that has two clear antecedent-consequent phrases. As they work together on their songs, move about the class to observe their progress, and offer guiding questions. At this time, suggest that your students write down or save their ideas in some way. Provide a means for doing so, leading students to songwriting.

SONGWRITING

Songwriting is a comprehensive way to guide students to think critically, aesthetically, and artistically about the music they listen to, perform, and create themselves. It sparks students' musical imaginations as they make deep and expressive connections in personally meaningful ways (Hickey, 2012; Webster, 2002). Songwriting is possible with children of any age in elementary school. Just as children participate in art-making early on, they can surely take an active part in songwriting (Johnson-Green, 2021). A developmental and constructivist approach to songwriting will give students a foundation for independent musicianship as they grow and mature musically.

Facilitating Songwriting in Elementary School

Extending students' improvisations and songmaking can function as an introduction to songwriting for elementary school students. In this 10-week project, students learn how to write an original song (Wadler, 2019). Easily adapted for students of different ages and a variety of learning environments, the project is divided into two distinct parts with a total of 10 lessons. Lessons are planned so that each day aligns with an elementary music class that meets 50 minutes, once per week. In Part One (Days 1–4) students gain a deeper understanding of the primary features of songs and songwriting. Part Two (Days 5–10) shifts to an approach through which students participate in the creative process of composing their own songs.

Part One

On Day 1, students are introduced to the concept of lyrics and provided with strategies to write them for an original song (see Figure 26.6).

What to Say?	
Grade Level	Third
Compositional Context	Teacher-led, whole class
Materials	Songs familiar to students, white board, and markers
Procedure	1. Begin class by singing examples of short 4–phrase familiar songs with words to your class. Explain to your students that the words of a song are called lyrics. 2. Sing another familiar song together as a class and discuss whether the song is singable and memorable and why. 3. Explore how the words are used by asking your students questions about the topic and if the lyrics describe an event or tell a story. 4. Point out the phrases and their form, noting that the song is 4-lines long. Together, discover whether the lyrics align with the melody with a cohesive melodic rhythm. 5. With your class, brainstorm possible topics for lyrics, such as students' interests or hobbies. As students share their ideas, write them on a white board. 6. From the ideas generated, determine a topic through a blind voting process. Ask students to close their eyes and vote for the topic of their choice by show of hands. Present the top three choices to the class. Then, ask students to vote again, narrowing the options to a single topic. 7. Brainstorm words associated with the decided upon topic, writing all students' suggestions on the board. For example, if the selected topic is *Spies* ask guiding questions such as: *What is a spy? What do they look like? What do they do? How do they act?* Give students examples of how to use the words to form short sentences or phrases such as: *I'm a spy, I'm undercover; Secret agent is my name, being sly is my game; You will never find me!* 8. Ask students to think of their own phrases and invite them to share their ideas with the class. Write their responses on the board line by line, reading each one as a class. 9. Involve students in conversation about the meaning of each phrase, phrase length, rhythmic flow, and if a rhyme scheme is important. Discuss the number and sequencing of the phrases. (Also see Step 1 of this activity plan.) 10. Next, take students' suggestions for revision and incorporate them into the lyrics. As a class, read the modified lyrics, evaluate their efficacy, and revise them accordingly. 11. Together, sing the lyrics to simple, familiar melodies such as "Frere Jacques" or "Twinkle, Twinkle Little Star." The lyrics may not align with the chosen song's melody, presenting an opportunity for you to problem solve with your students. 12. Inform students that modifying the melody, the rhythm, or lyrics are simple strategies to try. Ask for their suggestions, experimenting with them in the context of the familiar song. 13. End of class: Review the process used for the class to analyze and generate lyrics.

FIGURE 26.6. Day 1: Focus on lyrics

On Day 2, students will be introduced to the concept of *melody* as they are guided to compose a melody for a poem (see Figure 26.7). Invite your students to contribute musical ideas for the project and share your own. While you will notate the melodic ideas and the final melody for the class to read and sing, many of your students will find other ways to preserve their songs (Barrett, 2006) as they continue to work on them. Ultimately, a combination of some type of notation (e.g., traditional, invented, or iconic) and a diary of their audio recordings (Johnson-Green, 2021) will capture their compositional processes as they refine them to form the final product—an original song.

Melody Grabbing	
Grade Level	Third
Compositional Context	Teacher-led, whole class
Materials	"The Swing" poem by Robert Louis Stevenson, white board, markers
Procedure	1. Begin class by distributing a copy of a poem to each student. For this activity, "The Swing" by Robert Louis Stevenson is a good option; it has three sections, each with four lines. Read the poem out loud as a class and discuss how some poems can be used for lyrics of a song. With the class, study the form, the phrases, rhyme scheme, meter, and rhythmic flow. THE SWING by Robert Louis Stevenson How do you like to go up in a swing, Up in the air so blue? Oh, I do think it the pleasantest thing Ever a child can do! Up in the air and over the wall, Till I can see so wide, Rivers and trees and cattle and all Over the countryside— Till I look down on the garden green, Down on the roof so brown— Up in the air I go flying again, Up in the air and down! 2. Prompt your students to think about a memorable melody of a song they know or have heard. Guide their thinking around attributes such as tonality, melodic range, melodic rhythm, lyrics, phrase contour, meter, tempo, form, and expression. 3. As a class, develop a list of the discovered attributes of a memorable melody (see Steps 1 and 2) and short descriptions of those qualities. 4. From the list and descriptions generated in Step 3, make a tip sheet students can refer to throughout the project. 5. Sing a melodic example in a plain style for the class. Using the information generated for the tip sheet, prime students to listen for an attribute they hear in the next example. Repeat the melody, this time zeroing in on just one attribute without disclosing what you changed. Invite students to share what they heard. 6. Tell your students that they can create their own melodies to go with the poem. Provide the class with time to audiate and vocalize melodic ideas for the first line of text, with everyone experimenting at once. 7. Then, engage students in *melody-grabbing*. Ask a student volunteer to sing one or more of their melodic ideas. Have the class echo the melody as you notate it on the white board. Repeat this process for the remaining three lines of text until a melody for a section of the poem has been composed. Sing the entire melody as a class.

FIGURE 26.7. Day 2: Focus on melody

	8. As a class, evaluate the attributes and effectiveness of the melody, using the tip sheet as a guide. 9. Invite the students guiding questions about ways the melody could be revised to better express the theme or intent of the poet. Remind them of simple strategies for revision: modifying the melody, the rhythm, or lyrics. Add these strategies to the tip sheet. 10. Experiment with students' ideas, making deliberate revisions to the melody until the class is satisfied with the product. 11. At the end of class sing the completed melody.

FIGURE 26.7. Continued

During Day 3, students will work with a partner to combine the lyrics they created on Day 1 with an original melody. As student-pairs are creating their melodies, assist those who may be chanting or rapping, or using familiar melodies instead of composing their own. Should this occur, guide them through an improvisatory approach to songmaking, scaffolding them toward the development of a melody.

Collaborative learning allows you to move about the room to informally assess students' progress. This provides time to offer support through individualized instruction, timely feedback, and provoking students' critical thinking about their musical decisions. Through informal assessment you can also gauge your instruction to meet your students' needs, adapting the project as needed for their success (see Figure 26.8).

Better Together	
Grade Level	Third
Compositional Context	Teacher-led, whole class, student-pairs
Materials	Lyrics from Day 1, tip sheet, projector, regular and staff paper, pencils, audio recorder
Procedure	1. Provide students with a copy of the tip sheet that was developed last week. 2. Review the attributes of a memorable melody that were discovered on Day 2. 3. Remind students that, when the lyrics from Day 1 were sung with "Twinkle, Twinkle Little Star" (or another song), they learned simple strategies for revision. 4. On the white board, project the lyrics generated by the class on Day 1 and review them with your students. 5. Explain to your students that they will work in pairs to create a melody for the lyrics from Day 1. 6. Have students choose a partner. 7. Give student a clear timeframe to create and practice their melodies. 8. Invite student-pair volunteers to present their melodies to the class. After each performance, model how to give clear, specific feedback, taking care to use vocabulary specific to songwriting. 9. At the end of class, have students audio record or notate their melodies.

FIGURE 26.8. Day 3: Focus on lyrics and melody

The activities of Day 4 draw students' awareness to song structure with particular attention to verse and a refrain in Figure 26.9.

What's the Difference?	
Grade Level	Third
Compositional Context	Teacher led, whole group, student-pairs
Materials	Recording of "ABC" by the Jackson 5; speakers, white board, markers, room to move
Procedure	1. Have a song playing as your students enter the classroom. The song should clearly feature verse and refrain. One song that works well is "ABC" by the Jackson 5.
	2. Pre-write the lyrics of the first verse and refrain on the white board. Do not allow students to see the white board at this time.
	3. While the music is playing, invite students to follow your movement designed to highlight the form. One example might be tapping your shoulders to the beat for the verse and patting your thighs for the refrain. *Take care to stop the music before a new type of section, such as the bridge, is played.*
	4. Relate your movements back to the sections of the music labeling them as *verse* and *refrain*.
	5. Discuss similarities and differences between the verse and refrain, using the tip sheet as a guide.
	6. Through think-pair-share, extend students' analysis of the techniques that were used to address unity and variety within the verse and the refrain, and between the verse and refrain. Add new discoveries to the tip sheet.
	7. If time and student attention allows, repeat Step 6, this time addressing tension and release, again adding to the tip sheet.
	8. Show the pre-written lyrics on the white board. Label where the verse and refrain occur. Recall the type of movement that were used to differentiate between the two sections.
	9. Play the selection again, moving in the same way to each section as in Step 3.
	10. Repeat the activity, this time paring up students to create their own movements, one for the verse and one for the refrain. Observe whether students' movements correspond with the form.
	11. Invite student pairs to demonstrate their understanding of verse and refrain through movement. Repeat this process with other songs from different genres, having students lead the class in movement.

FIGURE 26.9. Day 4: Focus on song form

Considering the Teacher's Role

In Part One you led students to discover strategies to write a song. Now, in Part Two they have autonomy on the strategies they use to reach that goal. Provide them with time to think about their songs and to make revisions as they organize and reorganize their musical ideas to take shape in the form of a song. In this type of learning environment mistakes are okay, and students' musical ideas are welcomed, respected, and celebrated.

During Part Two, your role will become increasingly that of a facilitator (Green, 2008; Kooistra, 2016). In this capacity, you play the important part of stimulating students' musical thinking and understanding (Wiggins, 2015). Scaffold their learning with guiding, open-ended questions rather than direct answers. Invite their questions and curiosities on songwriting, encouraging them to brainstorm musical ideas. Your feedback should prompt students' critical thinking in music as they identify problems and generate solutions to refine their songs.

Part Two

With a foundation established, students will now turn their attention to the creation of an original song. Day 5 (see Figure 26.10) is devoted to beginning the songwriting process and determining the final project criteria. Students will also create songwriting journals to capture their thoughts, feelings, and new understandings, while tracking the development of their songs. To make the journals, use colorful construction paper for the cover or pocket folders with fasteners. If appealing to students, provide them with stickers or other decorative materials for the front cover. Attach plain, lined, and manuscript paper, the project expectations (see Day 5, Step 2), a tip sheet, and several forms for reflection.

On to the Finish!	
Grade Level	Third
Compositional Context	Teacher-led, whole class
Materials	Songwriting Self-Reflection form, materials for Songwriting Journal

Procedure	1. Remind students of the previous lessons and the goals they achieved as they experienced, explored, and discovered processes for (a) creating lyrics, (b) composing an original melody that supports the lyrics, (c) following a simple song form, and (d) having a sense of meter and rhythmic flow.
	2. Discuss the project criteria with the class, taking care that your expectations are age appropriate. Students should compose a song that incorporates the following:
	   ▪ *Lyrics*—Original lyrics with a clear theme/message.
	   ▪ *Melody*—Original melody.
	   ▪ *Form*—Song form: verse and refrain (chorus) with the song's title in the refrain.
	   ▪ *Rhythm*—Cohesive sense of meter and flow of the melodic rhythm.
	3. Provide each student with materials to create a songwriting journal.

FIGURE 26.10. Day 5: Focus on the final project

Figure 26.11 is an example of a Songwriting Self Reflection Form. It relates directly to the project criteria and is a way for students to assess their own progress and that of their soon to be assembled "bands." The form can be useful as a discussion prompt for band members to collectively reflect upon their song and consider areas for improvement and general progress. Be sure to review and demonstrate how to use the form to promote students' purposeful reflection on their songs and their compositional processes, giving rise to thoughtful revision. Students will also have a better understanding of the criteria and can track their progress as they move through the project to complete their original songs.

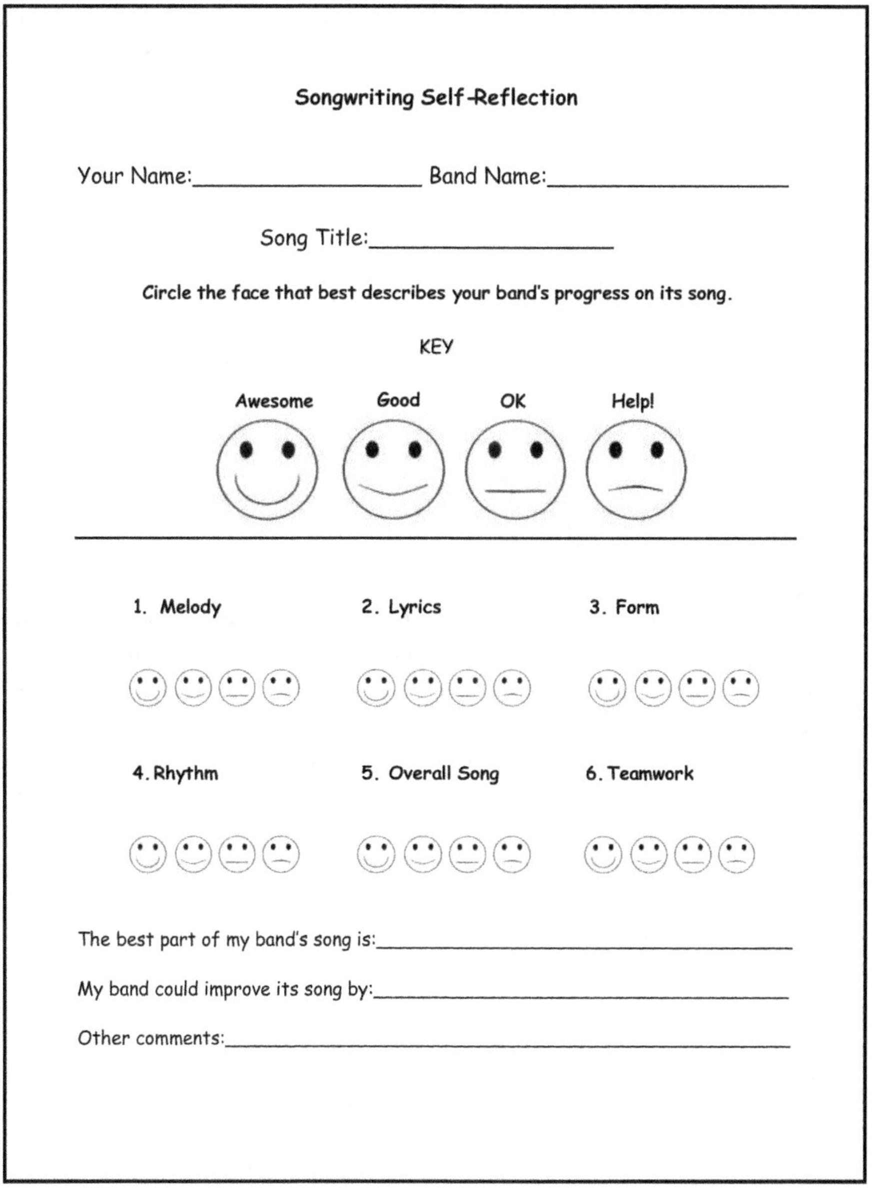

Songwriting Self-Reflection

Your Name:__________________ Band Name:__________________

Song Title:__________________

Circle the face that best describes your band's progress on its song.

KEY

Awesome **Good** **OK** **Help!**

1. Melody **2. Lyrics** **3. Form**

4. Rhythm **5. Overall Song** **6. Teamwork**

The best part of my band's song is:____________________________________

My band could improve its song by:____________________________________

Other comments:____________________________________

FIGURE 26.11. Songwriting self-reflection

Days 6–9: Focus on Collaborative Songwriting, Peer Feedback, Reflection, and Revision

After students have received their songwriting journals, explain that they will now work in small groups, or "bands" to compose an original song. Allow students to choose friendship groups of two to four students. Anticipate who might struggle with finding a group or those students who might not work well together. Consider solutions that emphasize inclusivity and lead students to making good choices. Encourage the student groups to name their bands. Have them explore ideas for their songs as the Rockers' band did. Figure 26.12 is a page taken from a band member's songwriting journal. Notice that the Rockers were already brainstorming the theme/message of their song.

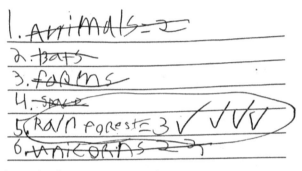

FIGURE 26.12. The Rockers' songwriting journal

On Days 6 and 7, students work collaboratively in their bands. They are given un-structured and largely uninterrupted extended periods of time to conceptualize and write their songs. Remind them to complete a songwriting self-reflection form at the end of each class. Collect these forms as they will give you insight on the extent to which students thoughtfully reflect on their songs and their overall progress. The tip sheet is also useful as a prompt for deeper reflection and a means for recalling and employing strategies learned in Part One.

On Day 8, ask students to provide peer feedback on each other's songs. By giving feed-back to each other's bands, students will be apt to mindfully contemplate their own work.

For meaningful peer feedback, model a strategy for the class, such as praise, question, and suggestion (PQS). Invite a band to volunteer for the demonstration and ask them to sing their song in its current form. Using the PQS format, first, offer *Praise*: "The change your band made to the melodic direction of your song helped focus the listener on the meaning and emotion of the lyrics." Then, ask a *Question*: "What musical decisions did your band make as you revised your melody?" and offer a *Suggestion* for revision: "Consider ways to strengthen the cohesiveness of your melody when transitioning from verse to refrain." Pair up bands to perform their songs for each other with students taking turns using the PQS strategy.

At the beginning of class on Day 9, have each student complete a songwriting self-reflection form. Today, the form is used as a discussion prompt for students to talk about their band's progress with their song—such as what they like about their song or improvements that could be made. Give the bands time to talk about each member's reflections. As you observe students' interactions, ask the bands about their next steps with their songs. Finally, have them prepare for the next class: performance day.

On Day 10 the bands will perform their songs for the class. Students are usually very excited and often a bit nervous when this day arrives (see Figure 26.13).

Sing Us Your Song!	
Grade Level	Third
Compositional Context	Teacher-led, student-led
Materials	Audio recorder, Songwriting Self-Reflection form
Preparation	Have a recording device ready to record performances so that you and your class can listen to the songs later. Listening to the performances after the unit has been completed will engender further reflection.
Procedure	1. At the start of class, welcome your students to their special performance day and give the bands a few minutes to practice their songs before they perform. 2. When the bands are ready, briefly address audience etiquette such as being positive and supportive for friends who are performing, and that each band should receive appropriate applause after each performance. 3. Have the bands come up to the front of the class one by one to present their songs. After each performance, encourage students to use the PQS format to ask the bands questions about their songwriting process and the creative decisions they made to arrive at their final product. 4. Ask each band member to complete the Songwriting Self-Reflection Form. 5. Have students hand in their songwriting journals. Review and reflect upon their understanding of the varied facets of songwriting, the effectiveness of your instructional techniques, and revisions you will make the next time students participate in a songwriting project.
Note: For such an important day, celebratory refreshments are in order! *The project need not end after the final performance. You may wish to offer the bands time to incorporate further feedback into revisions of their songs, make a class EP, or perhaps begin a new songwriting project.*	

FIGURE 26.13. Day 10: Focus on songs, performance, and reflection

WORK SAMPLES

In this 10-day songwriting project, third grade students used a variety of techniques to preserve their songs. For example, most did not use traditional or iconic notation as they wrote their songs. Handwritten lyrics were the basis by which they would recall and work out their songs. Revisions were evidenced by such things as erasures, crossing out of words, or arrows indicating the form or direction of the melody. Figure 26.14 shows the Magic band's work on their lyrics and melody. Instructions for "regler singing" helped remind the band of the desired timbre of the vocals.

Blue Fury indicated that the "coras" is to be sung two times. The only band to choose a particularly poignant and sensitive theme, Blue Fury's song (see Figure 26.15) addressed death through their heavyhearted lyrics. The Mystic Mangoes composed lyrics with a clearly labeled verse and refrain (see Figure 26.16).

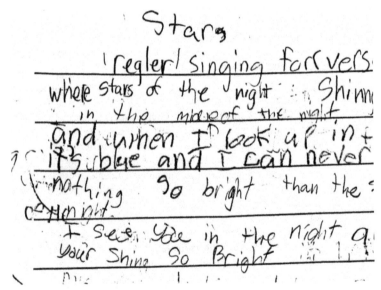

FIGURE 26.14. Magic: "Stars"

Figure 26.17 depicts the songwriting journal from the band Take Three. In their song, they included directives for their band member, Kenjie, to sing a "harmonie" part to *I'll never see you again* and the others to "repeat" *I'll run away . . . from you.*

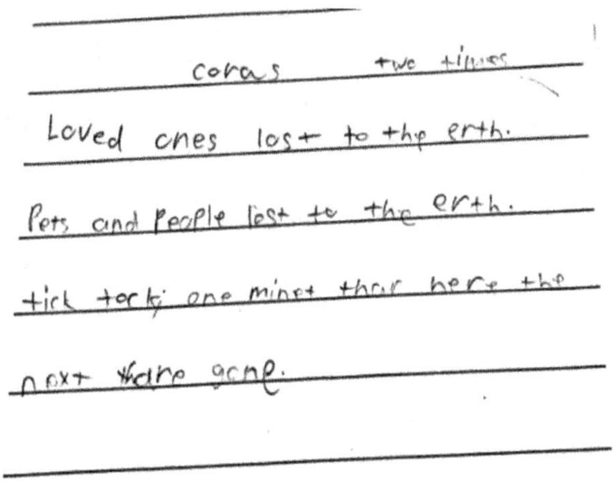

coras   twe times

Loved ones lost to the erth.

Pets and People lost to the erth.

tick tock; one minet their here the

next there gone.

FIGURE 26.15. Blue Fury: "Loved Ones Lost"

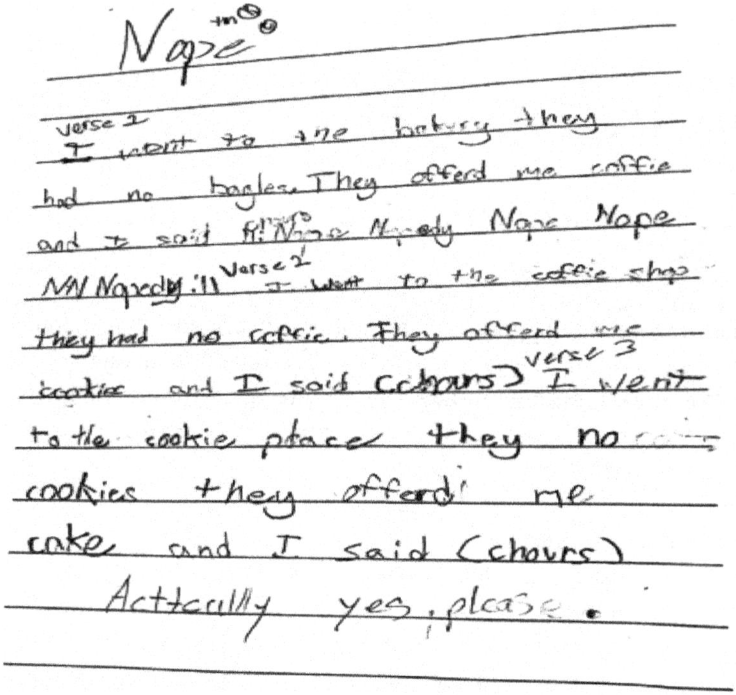

Nope

verse 1
I went to the batery they
had no bagles. They offerd me coffie
and I said fi'No Nobody Nope Nope
NN Nobody." Verse 2 I went to the coffie shop
they had no coffie. They offerd me
cookies and I said (chours) verse 3 I went
to the cookie place they no
cookies they offerd me
cake and I said (chours)
Actteally yes, please .

FIGURE 26.16. Mystic Mangoes: Songwriting journal example

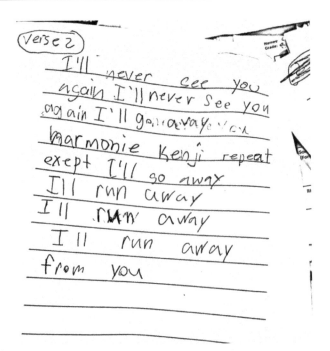

FIGURE 26.17. Take Three: "Run Away"

CONSIDERATIONS FOR MUSIC TEACHERS

Implementing a songwriting project such as the one described in this chapter takes time and careful planning. However, it is rewarding when your students synthesize and elaborate on the musical information they have acquired over time while assimilating the new through songwriting. As you incorporate songwriting into your curriculum, consider these suggestions:

- Establish an environment of acceptance, openness, and kindness. Set the tone for your classroom to be a safe space for improvisation, songmaking, and songwriting.
- Allow for flexibility. Curriculum development, assignment deadlines, length of the project, and so on, may impact the timing of the implementation of the project.
- Give students freedom. Provide students with opportunities to approach songwriting on their own terms.
- Choose relevant repertoire. In classroom activities, allow students to have a choice of the music used in class Incorporate repertoire that has personal importance and are songs that they enjoy. Use these songs as examples for students to analyze.
- Create accompaniments. Give students access to instruments (small percussion, keyboards, ukuleles, guitars, drum set, etc.) that could contribute to the realization of the songs they are writing.

- Incorporate technology[1]. Technology's role in songwriting serves a number of functions. MIDI keyboards, tablets, or apps can be used to generate accompaniments such as a simple backing track of a bass line or a rhythmic ostinato using an electronic drum patch. Audio or video recording will help students save work samples, songs-in-progress, or final products. Recordings are also useful for student reflection and self-assessment. Looping programs offer new ways to create songs and notation programs can be helpful for students who wish to use traditional notation.
- Assess students' work authentically[2]. Feedback facilitates thoughtful reflection as students think and rethink their songwriting options. Authentic assessment fosters students' musically creative growth and their understanding of musical concepts and skills. Peer feedback given and received provides students with additional options and techniques for writing their songs. Further, portfolios serve to document students' work over time charting a longitudinal course of students' progress.

CONCLUSION

Children are songmakers from a very young age, having absorbed music from their environment, even before birth (Woodward, n. d.). They come to school with an expansive foundation of musical knowledge that undergirds their improvisations, songmaking, and the songs they write . Music teachers have the distinct privilege of nurturing their students' inherent desire to engage in creative musicianship, guiding each one on their musical journey as independent musical decision-makers (Richmond, 2013) through songwriting.

NOTES

1. See Bauer, 2020 and Kaschub & Smith, 2021 for additional ways to incorporate technology.
2. See Deutsch, 2016 and Hebert, 2001 for techniques to authentically assess your students.

REFERENCES

Azzara, C. D. (2002). Improvisation. In R. Colwell & C. Richardson (Eds.), *The new handbook of research on music teaching and learning* (pp. 171–187). Oxford.

Bannan, N., & Woodward, S. (2010). Spontaneity in the musicality and music learning of children. In S. Malloch & C. Trevarthen (Eds.), *Communicative musicality: exploring the basis of human companionship*. (pp. 259–284). Oxford.

Barrett, M. S. (2006). Inventing songs, inventing worlds: the "genesis" of creative thought and activity in young children's lives. *International Journal of Early Years Education, 14*(3), 201–220.

Barrett, M. S. (2009). Sounding lives in and through music: A narrative inquiry of the "everyday" musical engagement of a young child. *Journal of Early Childhood Research, 7*, 115–134.

Bauer, W. (2020). *Music learning today: Digital pedagogy for creating, performing, and responding to music* (2nd ed.). Oxford.

Burton, S. (2002, Special edition). An exploration of preschool children's spontaneous songs and chants. *Visions of Research in Music Education, 2,* 7–16.

Burton, S. L. (2011). Language acquisition: A lens on music learning. In S. L. Burton & C. C. Taggart (Eds.), *Learning from young children: Research in early childhood music.*((pp. 23–38). Rowman & Littlefield Education. Published in partnership with National Association for Music Education.

Burton, S. L., & Snell, A. H. II. (2018). *Ready, set, improvise!: The nuts and bolts of music improvisation.* Oxford.

Campbell, P. S. (1998). The musical cultures of children. *Research Studies in Music Education 11,* 42–51.

Campbell, P. S. (2010). *Songs in their heads: Music and its meaning in children's lives* (2nd ed.). Oxford.

Custodero, L. (2006). Singing practices in 10 families with young children. *Research Studies in Music Education, 54*(1): 37–56.

Custodero, L., & Johnson-Green, E. (2006). Caregiving in counterpoint: reciprocal influences in the musical parenting of younger and older infants. *Early Childhood Development and Care, 178*(1), 15–39.

Custodero, L., Cali C., Diaz-Donoso, A. (2016). Music as transitional object and practice: Children's spontaneous musical behaviors in the subway Research. *Studies in Music Education 38*(1), 55–74. https://DOI:10.1177/1321103X15612248

DeNora, T. (2000). *Music in everyday life.* Cambridge University Press.

Deutsch, D. (2016). Authentic assessment in music composition: Feedback that facilitates creativity. *Music Educators Journal, 102*(3). https://doi.org/10.1177/0027432115621608

Gordon, E. E. (2003). *Improvisation in the music classroom.* GIA.

Gordon, E. E. (2013). *A music learning theory for newborn and young children* (Rev. ed.). GIA.

Hebert, E. A. (2001). *The power of portfolios: What children can teach us about learning and assessment.* Jossey-Bass.

Gruhn, W. (2002). Phases and stages in early music learning: A longitudinal study on the development of young children's musical potential, *Music Education Research, 4*(1), 51–71.

Harwood, E. E. (1987). *The memorized song repertoire of children in grades four and five in Champaign, Illinois* (EducatD dissertation). Available from Dissertations and Theses: A&I. (AAT 8721651)

Green, L. (2008). *Music, informal learning, and the school: A new classroom pedagogy.* Ashgate.

Hickey, M. (2012). *Music outside the lines: Ideas for composing in K–12 music classrooms.* Oxford.

Kaschub, M., & Smith, J. P. (2009). *Minds on music: Composition for creative & critical thinking.* Rowman & Littlefield Education. Published in partnership with National Association for Music Education.

Kaschub, M., & Smith, J. P. (2021). With app attention. In G. G. Greher & S. L. Burton (Eds.), *Creative music-making at your fingertips: A mobile technology guide for music educators* (pp. 67–80). Oxford.

Koops, L. (2014). Songs from the car seat: Exploring the early childhood making place of the family vehicle. *Journal of Research in Music Education, 62*(1), 52–65. https://doi-org.udel.idm.oclc.org/10.1177/0022429413520007

Johnson-Green, E. (2021). iAssess: Using mobile technology for student self-assessment in a K–5 music composition curriculum. In G. G. Greher & S. L. Burton, (Eds.), *Creative music-making at your fingertips: A mobile technology guide for music educators* (pp. 126–144). Oxford.

Kooistra, L. (2016). Informal music education: The nature of a young child's engagement in an individual piano lesson setting. *Research Studies in Music Education, 38,* 115–129.

Littleton, D. (2015). *When music goes to school.* Rowman & Littlefield Education. Published in partnership with National Association for Music Education.

Kratus, J. (1995). A developmental approach to teaching music improvisation. *International Journal of Music Education.* https://DOI: 10.1177/025576149502600103

Kratus, J. (2012). Nurturing the songcatchers: Philosophical issues in the teaching of music composition. In W. Bowman & A. Frega (Eds.), *The Oxford handbook of philosophy in music education* (pp. 367–385). Oxford. https://doi.org/10.1093/oxfordhb/9780195394 733.013.0020

Malloch, S., & Trevarthen, C. (2009). *Communicative musicality: Exploring the basis of human companionship.* Oxford.

Marsh, K. (1995). Children's singing games: Composition in the playground? *Research Studies in Music Education, 4,* 2–11.

Moog, H. (1976). The development of musical experience in children of pre-school age. *Psychology of Music, 4*(2), 38–45. doi:1177/030573567642005

Moorhead, G., & Pond, D. (1978). *Music of young children* [Reprinted from the 1941–1951 editions]. Pillsbury Foundation for the Advancement of Music Education.

Niland, A. (2009). The power of musical play: The value of play-based, child-centered curriculum in early childhood music education. *General Music Today, 23*(1), 17–21. https://DOI: 10.1177/1048371309335625

Pond, D. (1981). A composer's study of young children's innate musicality. *Bulletin of the Council for Research in Music Education, 68,* 1–12.

Reynolds, A. M., & Burton, S. L. (2017). Serve and return: Communication foundations for early childhood music policy stakeholders, *Arts Education Policy Review, 18*(3), 140–153. https://dx.doi.org/10.1080/10632913.2016.1244779

Reynolds, A. M., Long, S., & Valerio, W. H. (2007). Language acquisition and music acquisition: Possible parallels. In L. R. Bartel (Series Ed.), K. Smithrim, & R. Upitis (Vol. Eds.), *Listen to their voices: Research to practice: A biennial series* (Vol. 3) (pp. 211–227). Canadian Music Educators Association.

Richmond, J. W. (2013). "All in" for composition education: Opportunities and challenges for pre-service music teacher curricula. In M. Kaschub & J. P. Smith (Eds.), *Composing our future. Preparing music educators to teach music composition.*(pp. 289–304). Oxford.

Shouldice, H. (2018). Audiation-based improvisation and composition in elementary general music. In S. L. Burton and A. M. Reynolds (Eds.), *Engaging musical practices: A sourcebook for elementary general music* (pp. 113–144). Rowman & Littlefield in partnership with the National Association for Music Education.

Smith, J. (2017). Composing in early childhood. In F. Abrahams & R. John (Eds.), *Becoming musical* (pp. 281–299). Chicago: GIA.

Steever, E. (2015). *A case study on parent participation in their child's musical development.* [Unpublished master's thesis]. University of Delaware.

Thompson, K. P. (1980). Vocal improvisation for elementary students. *Music Educators Journal 66*(5), 69–71.

Wadler, H. (2019). *Facilitating songwriting with second-, third-, and fourth-grade students.* [Unpublished master's thesis]. University of Delaware.

Webster, P. (2002) Creative thinking in music: Advancing a model. In T. Sullivan & L. Willingham (Eds.), *Creativity and music education* (pp. 16–33). Canadian Music Educators Association.

Webster, P. R. (2014). 2014 senior researcher award acceptance address: Cautious optimism for the future of research in music teaching and learning. *Journal of Research in Music Education, 62*(3), 203–214.

Wiggins, J. (1999). Teacher control and creativity. *Music Educators Journal, 85*(6), 30–35.

Wiggins, J. (2015). *Teaching for musical understanding.* Oxford.

Williams, D. (2014). Music education, meaningful and relevant. In J. R. Barrett & P. R. Webster (Eds.), *The musical experience: Rethinking music teaching and learning* (pp. 284–293). Oxford.

Woodward, S. C. (n. d.). Womb sounds. ERD 001 Authentic Womb Recordings. Mastered at Mac'sound.

Young, S. (2002). Young children's spontaneous vocalizations in free play: Observations of two- to three-year-olds in a day care setting. *Bulletin of the Council for Research in Music Education, 152,* 43–53.

Young, S. (2006). Seen but not heard: Young children, improvised singing and educational practice. *Contemporary Issues in Early Childhood 7*(3), 270–280.

Young S., & Illari, B. (2012). Musical participation from zero to three: Toward a global perspective. In G. McPherson & G. Welch (Eds.), *Oxford handbook of music education* (pp. 279–295). Oxford.

....

CHAPTER 27

CULTIVATING A PURPOSE-DRIVEN COMPOSITION PEDAGOGY IN GENERAL MUSIC

....

KELLY BYLICA

THROUGH creating, manipulating, organizing, mixing, and remixing sounds, students engage in artistic endeavors that can support their development of musical skills, social awareness, and creative practice. When students compose, they are involved in the creative process from the inside out, generating ideas and moving through cycles of revision as they explore ways of sharing a musical message with the world. There are many ways music educators can and do incorporate composition into the general music classroom, including songwriting, digital creation, short notation-based prompts, and long project-based engagements, among others. Each of these pathways implies a belief about the purpose of composition in the larger ecology of students' musical experiences in school.

The performance-driven curricular structure of K–12 music education in the United States has often resulted in the use of composition as a tool for students to improve or demonstrate a functional understanding of Western classical notational literacy, particularly around note values, pitches, and scales (Burnard, 2012; Hess, 2015). In these cases, composition may be an exercise in music theory, a tool to assess student understanding of skills such as rhythm reading, dynamic markings, and notation with little acknowledgment of student knowledge, experience, and exploration beyond the confines of the music classroom. Composition in this context can become a precursor in a linear progression toward predetermined goals of functional literacy in the Western classical domain, with contextualized musical creation saved for those who may be perceived to hold an advanced level of musicianship (Viig, 2015). Composition can thus become viewed by students as a school activity disconnected from personal experience rather than an opportunity to create and explore in and through music (Crow, 2008). Such experiences have the potential to not only send a message of *what* matters, but inevitably *who* matters in the music classroom.

Composition, however, can also be a space for the development of critical literacy, where students explore social relations and personal inquiry through their creative work. When the purpose of composition converges to include discipline-specific functional skills (or what I refer to throughout this chapter as musical craftsmanship) alongside criticality and creativity, these endeavors can be opportunities for students to build musical skills while challenging narratives, considering multiple perspectives, and exploring their conceptions and understandings of themselves and others. As they share their work, students' compositions can provoke, invite, and render new meanings, helping them develop their own voice alongside and in community with others.

In an educational environment predicated on high-stakes testing, "teacher-proof" curricula, and a fragmentation of disciplines, music educators often find engaging with this type of criticality to be challenging (Benedict, 2012). This challenge is often amplified in the environ of general music; a context that, while broad, often lacks cohesion and clarity (Abril, 2016). Teaching and learning within general music education can be designed, however, to help students engage in a critical manner, encouraging them to build upon their own inquiries as they embrace opportunities to develop discipline-specific skills in tandem with broader critical understandings.

In this chapter, I consider what critical and creative compositional practices might look like when operationalized in the music classroom. Drawing from scholars who speak to critical literacy in the music classroom (Benedict, 2012; Gould, 2009), creative practices in composition (Hickey, 2012; Kaschub & Smith, 2009; Upitis, 2019), and connections between music creation and social consciousness (Bylica, 2020; Kaschub, 2009), I present a purpose-driven pedagogy of classroom composition. Within this pedagogy, I explore how criticality can strike a balance with musical craftsmanship as students enter compositional processes with the aim of simultaneously exploring musical skills while also engaging in musical creation as a form of social response. I then place these ideas within the realm of general music at multiple levels, offering ideas that argue for a notion of these classes as spaces where dispositions that are critical, creative, and artistic can be cultivated.

Defining Purpose: The Who, What, How, Where, and Why of Composition Pedagogy

What is composition?
Who composes?
How and *where* does one compose?
Why does one compose?

Some see music composition as an independent endeavor, reserved for the elite few, "advanced" or "musically gifted" students. For others, composition may be defined by an ability to notate one's musical ideas in a particular form or fashion, or perhaps more broadly as any organization of sounds and silences. It might be an opportunity for collaboration or creative practice, a tool for the assessment of musical skills, a pathway toward cognitive development, an embodied emotional experience, or even a vehicle through which one can create an artistic statement. Composition can be synonymous with songwriting or it might take place through a digital modality. It can be a career path, a hobby, a creative exercise, or a lifelong passion. There is not a single, unified definition for *who*, *what*, *how*, *where*, and *why* when discussing composition. How one responds to these questions is determined by ideological beliefs and directly impacts the ways in which one explores, teaches, and engages in and through musical creation.

These definitions are further complicated by music education's complex history with composition pedagogy. Since the Tanglewood Symposium of 1967 (Choate, 1968), music educators and scholars in North America have called for an expansion beyond the traditional Western performance-based paradigm so heavily present in music education. This includes, among other ideas, the fusion of composition and creative projects into curricula. Studies on compositional processes as well as guidance for music educators and music teacher-educators wishing to engage in compositional practices with students has thus increased over the last two decades, leading to the breadth of definitions, contexts, and rationales listed (e.g., Burnard & Younker, 2002; Hickey, 2003 and 2012; Kaschub, 2009; Kaschub & Smith, 2009 and 2013; Ruthmann, 2007 and 2008; Stauffer, 2002; Upitis, 2019; Webster, 2011, among others).

When composition is incorporated into the music curriculum, its use varies significantly in terms of how and where. For example, in the United States, opportunities for composition often occur in general music classes. One might find it unsurprising that composition might more readily find a home in these classes, where the flexibility and fluidity of a non-performance-based setting can lead to curricula designed to meet more diverse musical learning goals. Stephanie Cronenberg (2016) noted that general music is "simultaneously one of the most often used and least well-defined terms within music education" (p. 9). Frequently described by what it excludes, rather than what it includes, general music is often positioned in contrast to performance-based courses such as band, choir, and orchestra and is generally defined as being inclusive of all students and comprehensive in nature (Abril & Gault, 2016). Beyond these characteristics, however, there is little consensus as to how these classes, varying in length, focus, function, and character, are conceptualized. Though such variability can lead to opportunities to explore a wide array of experiences, such openness can also lead to "rudderless" trajectories (Reimer, 2003, p. 246) and ambiguous, amorphous goals (Regelski, 2004). In these cases, compositional engagements may focus on the *how* and *what* of music-making without necessarily thinking through the *why* and *with whom*.

Conversely, the openness presented by general music can also result in curricula that is co-designed with students based on their interests and ideas. When co-created, this type of music curricula is often responsive and possibility-oriented, rather than pre-defined and prescriptive. Compositional practices may be driven by students' musical inquiries or serve as an opportunity to respond to and engage with the world. Here the *how* and *what* are driven by the *why*. Developing a purpose-driven compositional pedagogy that begins with the students and their wonderments and curiosities can help encourage the development of dispositions and literacies that are both critical and functional.

The Limitations of Functional Literacy

There are a number of reasons why educators may prioritize functional literacy. This prioritization may mirror their own experiences in music education, they may be responding to school-based directives, or they may understand functional literacy as essential in helping students develop the technical mastery of competencies needed to function within a particular context or society (Gutstein, 2006; McLaren, 1989). Within music education, this can translate to "curricula . . . based on pre-packaged materials, such as music series books, beginning band, orchestra, and choral method books, and the U.S. National Standards" (Gould, 2009, p. 47). Practices in functional literacy are often individualistic and emphasize "efficiency and time on task," leading to singular pathways of learning and a focus on "right answers" (p. 48). Such a focus highlights a singular narrative, placing the acquisition of a predetermined set of skills as a non-negotiable hurdle necessary for future participation in music education.

Functional literacy is, at its core, about utility. In music education, it is, in part, the prioritization of the mastery of skills and concepts. These pre-determined understandings are part of a longstanding culture that is widely and deeply in place among many school music classes. Educators often acknowledge that education can and should be about the development of multiple literacies (Freire, 1970; Giroux, 2005 McLaren, 1989), including those that students bring to class from their lives and experiences outside of school, but too often functional literacy is still exalted as primary in music education. Surrounded by this narrative, functional literacy too often becomes an "endpoint in the formal process of learning," creating an ideological hierarchy that insists upon the need for (Western classical) functional skills as a baseline for musical engagement (Benedict, 2012, p. 152). Cathy Benedict noted that "for those who believe that functional literacy prepares people for the real world . . . there is a blind kind of hopeful-hope, in which the present is sacrificed for a future that desires to protect the past" (p. 157). It is of little surprise, then, that music educators often utilize composition primarily as a tool to measure and assess functional skills, thus resulting in a diluted understanding of what creating in and through music might mean and maintaining a particular historical construction of the purpose, place, and possibility of music education.

While functional literacy is important in that it helps students develop competencies that can help them engage with music, this narrative can also lead to privileging certain ways of knowing and devaluing others. Left unchecked, the "sequentialism" and methods and models of functional literacy can prioritize a culture of conformity over "moments of interaction with students' query, identity, and desire" (Schmidt, 2012, p. 6). An education that is established solely on functional literacy can serve to maintain the status quo, thus preserving, or even reinforcing and exacerbating, inequities. Concentrating solely on standardization can reduce educators' capabilities to respond to and encourage engagements with different beliefs, opinions, and ideas in the classroom (Fautley, 2015; Kannellopolous, 2015; Kratus, 2007). In such cases, music class can become predicated on a singular narrative that prioritizes predetermined outcomes, potentially leaving diverse voices, multiple ways of knowing, and divergent ideas unnoticed. Students who operate outside dominant narratives may feel silenced, believing their stories, opinions, and creative practices to be inferior (Kumashiro, 2000). Each of these consequences can lead to the creation of curricula where students do not engage with the understandings and experiences of their peers, resulting in missed opportunities for relational experiences that can add complexity and nuance to how students understand themselves, others, and the world. Consequently, criticality and opportunities for students to challenge assumptions can disappear in a culture of taken-for-granted norms where valued knowledge is narrowly understood.

Functional tasks can be beneficial. They often have a clear end goal, frequently align with national standards, and connect with performance-based practices. The concern presented lies in the idea that when functionality is the *only* purpose, music educators can be boxed into a "limited understanding of what is available in the wider world of music" and robbed of opportunities to help students engage with the multiple, complex, and dynamic ways music is explored and created (Reimer, 2012, p. 27). It is important, then, as music educators to create environments with students where they see composing as part of a larger narrative of being a musical creator in the world. In such environments, the music they create can have purpose beyond the general music classroom, cultivating encounters that demonstrate how musical work can matter in the larger world.

The Possibilities of Critical Literacy

There are multiple literacies one can develop, and a purpose-driven compositional pedagogy can also highlight critical literacy. Critical literacy is "the development of human capacity to use texts to analyze social fields and their systems of exchange—with an eye to transforming social relations and material conditions" (Luke, 2012, p. 9). They expand upon functional understandings in order to "approach knowledge critically and skeptically, see relationships between ideas, look for underlying explanations of phenomena, and question whose interests are served and who benefits" (Gutstein, 2006, p. 5). Within music curricula, then, critical literacies require an inquisitive approach to contexts, norms, and "everyday (musical) world[s]," particularly those that may be "taken-for-granted" in everyday experience (Gould, 2009, p. 48).

As Allan Luke (2012) noted, critical literacy, practically applied, "melds social, political, and cultural debate and discussion with the analysis of how texts and discourses work, where, with what consequences, and in whose interests" (p. 5). Texts, in this case, are understood in the postmodern sense as being cultural forms upon and through which meaning is constructed, such as student compositions. Here, compositions might be thought of not as objects or closed forms, but as the development of something musical that did not exist previously. Through critical literacy, there is an invitation to consider what is included in such texts as well as what is absent, negotiating various viewpoints and developing multiple counter and hybridized discourses that encourage students and educators alike to recognize the inherent partiality of individual understandings. Composition is unique in that it is the learners themselves who develop these very texts. Rather than consider the work of others, they are invited to view their own work, not only as a theoretical exercise, but as a key move in cultivating a disposition through which creative artistic practice is a means to engage critically with their worlds.

Critical literacy is not, however, solely about "unpacking myths and distortions" about individual learner experiences but about "building new ways of knowing and acting upon the world" (Luke, 2012, p. 5). Within the music classroom, this might mean redefining the *why* behind curricular musical endeavors. Composition might be framed as an opportunity to question norms and draw connections to the lived realities of everyday experience within and beyond the music classroom. Such experiences not only invite students to develop musical skills, but also to engage in dissensus, dialogue, and problem-posing, helping them cultivate multiliterate dispositions as they musically articulate their own experiences, ideas, and positionings. These shifts in educational purpose might then support the development of critical literacy over time through "everyday imagined and enacted praxis" (Martin & Brown, 2013, p. 387).

Critical literacy through composition is not a new idea. Musical endeavors that connect creative practice and social consciousness have been explored in various creative contexts (Bylica, 2020; Gaztambide-Fernández, 2011; Kaschub, 2009; Mantie, 2008). For example, Michele Kaschub's (2009) "Critical Pedagogy for Creative Artists" offered a model of a secondary general music unit that involved "establishing a framework for using tools of critical inquiry to gain a thorough understanding of complex social, political, and cultural issues" (p. 280). Together with Kaschub as researcher/educator, students spent a term listening to and composing socially conscious music about child abuse, immigration, violence, and war. Through the process, they grappled with both social and musical challenges as they sought to create artistic responses to multifaceted realities. In this example, the act of creating music was itself a social response. Composition helped students build connections between learning practice and in-the-world experience and "make an artistic statement in sound" (p. 281).

Educators may find it challenging to engage in pedagogical practice with the intention of cultivating critical literacies. Though music educators often fully recognize that children enter the classroom with their own musical experiences and understanding about the world, Kaschub (2009) noted that "trying something new, or even something familiar in a new way, is not an easy commitment within the confines of the educational enterprise" (p. 274). This is especially true when one considers structural forces, administrative priorities, and community expectations that may be perceived as being misaligned with criticality. Further, an educational climate that prioritizes "data-driven instruction, scripted lessons, and top-down decision making" as well as "increased surveillance and de-professionalization, corporatization and standardization and the fragmentation of knowledge and skills" can make criticality feel secondary (Tobias et al., 2015, p. 40).

As educators know, however, the moments of uncertainty and disruption caused by critical musical endeavors can create opportunities for students to musically grapple with the complex worlds in which they live. In recent years, there have been a number of exemplars that can help music educators reimagine what is possible within composition-based music education (e.g., Finney et al., 2021; Kaschub, 2009; Kaschub & Smith, 2009 and 2013). In these examples, music educators offer doorways-in to critical compositional practices, providing models that deliberately outline both small and large-scale projects that can be implemented in a variety of settings. Choosing to pursue projects that encourage students to work with community members (see Vignette 3) or align with larger school goals and vision (see Vignette 1) can also help alleviate potential tension between administrative and community expectations and critically driven compositional projects.

Scholars including Patrick Schmidt (2020), Cara Bernard and Joseph Abramo (2019), and Eric Shieh (2020) offer practical steps to help music educators work with administrators to reimagine the possibilities for music education to encourage educator and student autonomy. These include building one's policy knowhow and envisioning possibility-oriented futures (Schmidt, 2020), engaging in productive dialogue with administrators (Bernard & Abramo, 2019), and building bridges to policies that support critical work (Shieh, 2020). Through such practices, music educators can work with school and community members to navigate the complex tensions lived daily in educational environments.

REINVENTING PEDAGOGY: CRITICALITY AND CRAFTSMANSHIP IN TANDEM

Thus far it may seem as though I am advocating for a prioritization of criticality over functionality in the classroom and, indeed I do believe that critical literacy can and should be a central focus. Criticality, however, does not preclude functionality. Music is both an art form and a craft, and the pursuance of craftsmanship requires the development of skills. Therefore, rather than consider functionality and criticality as an either/or dichotomy, music educators might consider how both can be held in tandem in a both/and relationship.

A purpose-driven approach to composition pedagogy through a both/and relationship of criticality and craftsmanship is not linear. It is interwoven and entangled, with each building upon, challenging, and amplifying the other. It requires a dispositional shift in how composition is conceptualized in the music classroom. Criticality is not an "add-on" nor is it utilized as a "pedagogical sleight of hand" to lead back to functional skills (Benedict, 2012, p. 156). There is not a pre-determined hierarchy of knowledge one must possess before engaging with one's musical world in a critical manner. Educators need not wait until students have mastered a skill before connecting to broader critical questions, nor should criticality be reserved for students who are deemed to be advanced in a particular subject. Rather, musical skills can be developed through a process of investigating and problematizing the sociopolitical and cultural-historic conditions of students' local and global communities.

Critical approaches can create curricula where compositional endeavors not only support multiple ways of creatively doing music, but, more importantly, with multiple reasons for doing music. Bringing critical literacy to the forefront can create opportunities for relationality in the classroom where musical selves are called upon to navigate complex relationships and develop dispositions of artistic inquiry. These dispositions do not, and cannot, come about as a result of musical practices that follow a step-by-step linear process or prioritize easily assessable skills and accountability. There is, however, the possibility of their cultivation through the ways in which musical endeavors that act as catalysts for relational experiences, critical inquiry, and collaborative action are encouraged.

Critical literacy can emerge when composition is conceptualized as a multifaceted, ongoing process. Rather than presenting compositions as finished projects to be displayed or judged, spaces of sharing might help students critically interact with their classmates' creative work. By prioritizing musicality and criticality over form and function, music educators help students move from conversations that attempt to determine what a composition is supposed to be about toward what a composition might make possible. This is not an easy task. Finding productive ways to help students problematize what they are hearing without being judgmental is challenging. Music educators may not feel prepared to facilitate conversations that actively engage with topics of cultural, social, historical, and/or political natures (Robinson, 2017).

Researchers have demonstrated, however, that, when continually cultivated over time, pedagogies that deliberately engage with the social and cultural lives of communities can be encouraged through care-filled practices that invite open questioning, radical listening, and relational moments (Benedict, 2021; Stauffer, 2017). In these moments, hearing and exploring multiple responses to a composition might help students see knowledge and understanding as "partial, polyphonic, and vibrant" (Giroux, 2005, p. 104). As narratives and counternarratives are juxtaposed with one another, divergent interpretations can help extend students' abilities to re-examine their own views and critically consider the experiences that shaped them.

Critical Dispositions in Practice

Educators in various fields have found ways to use content-specific skills to investigate, interrogate, and act upon the realities of their world. Eric Gutstein's (2006) work in mathematics provides an example of functional and critical literacies working in concert with one another. His experiences with middle schoolers in Chicago highlight the need for curricula to be viewed as complex engagements bound by socio-political realities. Rather than placing functional literacy as the primary purpose of the curriculum, with criticality relegated to a distant second, critical literacies are at the heart of his educational interactions with students. In his class, students use their personal experiences to "investigate and critique injustice" through mathematics (p. 4). Mathematics is seen not as a discrete subject, but as an opportunity to understand the world in order to "become active participants in changing society" (p. 4). The work of educators Eli Tucker-Raymond and Maria Rosario (2017) with middle school students is similarly structured. They developed a curriculum that is grounded in community experience. In this class, students drew upon personal experiences, political realities, and the complexities of living in a diverse environment in their dialogical and written work. As a result, they developed skills in language arts, mathematics, social studies, and science through curricular activities that directly connected to their everyday experiences. In both of these examples, educators provided curricular engagements that encouraged students to develop content-specific skills through a critical analysis of their local realities, thus sending a message that functional skills can be developed alongside critical thought.

There are various possibilities for the actualization of a framework that prioritizes critical artistic dispositions through composition in a general music classroom. I offer here three vignettes as examples of how such ideas might be applied in a manner that aligns with the work presented in both Gutstein (2006) and Tucker-Raymond and Rosario's (2017) studies. Though each vignette is imagined, elements of these stories are based on real interactions with music educators and demonstrate practical examples of criticality through composition. In each vignette, students employ both critical and functional skills simultaneously as they artistically and musically actualize ideas drawn from the cultural, civic/political, social, economic, racial, and interpersonal structures in their worlds. These examples are not meant to be reproducible lesson plans, but they are meant to be entry points for thinking and discussion.

Vignette 1

Inspired by a district-wide initiative for increased awareness and action toward climate change, Terrell, an elementary school music educator, has decided to use this topic as a theme for fifth grade music class. He elects to begin with listening and curates a playlist of songs to spark conversation about musicians and artists engaging in activist work. The playlist includes songs that speak to environmental concerns, such as Joni Mitchell's "Big Yellow Taxi," as well as songs which engage in activism on a broader scale. The playlist prompts reactions from students, and Terrell invites them to make a list of the topics and ideas that are generated as they listen. The fifth-graders are inspired to explore further and begin an online search for other activism-driven musical movements. In the process, they begin drawing connections to the recent increase in flooding in their own community and they consider the possible human and non-human causes of these environmental changes. The students express a desire to create their own song that speaks to their community about the environment. Recognizing that this could be an opportunity for district-wide partnership, Terrell reaches out to the high school music teacher, asking if the students in her songwriting class would consider collaborating with the fifth graders in Terrell's music class on a songwriting project. The result is a series of collaborative interactions (both in person and online) wherein students from both classes make music and dialogue together. They approach the flooding in their community with a critical eye, utilizing their composition not as a memorization tool but as a way to think through an underlying phenomenon together from multiple vantage points. The high schoolers bring their experience to help the fifth graders choose and learn chords, a melody line, and a strum pattern for guitar and ukulele. The fifth graders share what they have learned to help the high schoolers write lyrics that create an artistic statement. They are excited by their final product and decide to record their song and post it to the school's website where it can be viewed by classmates, teachers, families, and community members.

Vignette 2

Elizabeth, a middle school music educator, wants to help the students in her general music class think critically about diversity, difference, and living in a plural society. Rather than use "traditional" musical instruments, Elizabeth asks students to work independently to develop a list of sounds that represent their unique experiences in the world. They then gather or create recordings that mimic each of these sounds as they develop sound compositions that represent their experiences using Soundtrap, a collaborative music and recording studio where they will use their sounds to mix a track that represents their unique experiences. The students immediately begin experimenting with editing and layering, and Elizabeth works with students independently and in small groups, occasionally interjecting for a full class lesson on concepts such as timing and foregrounding/backgrounding. Once students feel as though their compositions are ready, they share them anonymously with the class through their online learning classroom. As students listen to each other's songs, they hear compositions that represent experiences with bullying, immigration, searching for one's identity, friendship, and a host of other topics. Elizabeth asks questions as they listen, such as "What do you notice?" and "What is this composition prompting you to think about? And why?" They then utilize the compositions as catalysts for thoughtfully discussing and debating issues of structural inequity, displacement, and taken-for-granted assumptions. As conversations continue, students begin to discuss the role of artists who use their music to illuminate issues and ideas, provoking dialogue and, eventually, action. Several students from the class decide to revisit their sound compositions, making changes and edits to their work so that they can share it with community members at a local Fine Arts Night at their school. The students, now adept at leading conversation and engaging in dialogue, host a listening session with their families, friends, and community members, encouraging a community-wide discussion about some of the issues that arose from their compositions.

Vignette 3

Nia, a high school music educator, wants to develop a project that utilizes the community in which their school is located as a compositional prompt to help students analyze the ways in which urban spaces change over time. Nia hopes that engaging through music will help students develop a critical eye that considers how and why these neighborhoods have changed, encouraging them to approach ideas skeptically, consider who has benefited from these changes, and find relationships between ideas. Nia invites the students to work in small groups to choose a neighborhood in their community. Over the course of a term, students work on their projects once a week. Nia encourages them to visit these neighborhoods, research their histories, and utilize the changing landscape as inspiration for a musical composition. The students interview residents, community musicians, and city historians, inquiring about the political, cultural, musical, and economic shifts that have resulted in neighborhood change. One group in Nia's class chooses to focus on the changing architecture, developing a composition that juxtaposes two ideas: one that uses the strong, harsh lines of newly built skyscrapers as inspiration and a second that is modeled after the smaller, older neighborhood homes and apartment buildings that they find in old photos. As they work, this group uses changes in rhythm and tempo to create these two contrasting musical themes that chase one another through the piece. Another group focuses on shifts in culture, tracing the musical history of one particular neighborhood through the music of the Irish, Polish, and eventually Venezuelan communities that have called this place home. The students link these cultures together in a composition that draws upon unique characteristics and timbres of musical works from each community, developing a piece that demonstrates change over time. The students share their work in a performance in which they invite the community musicians, historians, and neighborhood residents to participate, utilizing music to make an artistic statement about the spaces and places in which they live.

In these examples, Terrell, Elizabeth, and Nia frame compositional endeavors as part of a larger purpose in which students develop musical skills through critical practice. Students create artistic works through which they approach ideas and understandings with skepticism and ask critical questions through music. In order to do so, they develop skills in songwriting, chord progression, and digital editing and composition by navigating rhythmic and melodic patterns, timbre, and musical structures. In each case, the educator helps establish a frame for critical compositional engagement and supports student inquiry, but students maintain control over the musical pathway they choose to pursue. These educators are seizing moments that already exist, drawing from current social realities, while also deliberately creating opportunities for critical dialogue, listening, problematizing, and relational development. Students' worlds have become more than an inspiration for a musical work, they have a become fully embedded part of the compositional process.

In the elementary/high school collaboration in Vignette 1, Terrell sets out a plan for connecting the lessons in fifth-grade general music to an overarching district-wide theme of climate change, but he also leaves space for flexibility and exploration. This approach invites students to reflect on an issue through historical (through the listening playlist), global (through the online exploration), and local (through the composition) lenses. Listening, performing, and composing are then pathways to critically consider an idea. Terrell's invitation to the high school students serves at least two goals: students engage in a collaborative, relational music-making experience and they learn from one another, building upon their various skills. Composition, therefore, is not utilized as a tool for assessing a functional skill, but as a way of exploring and expressing ideas related to an underlying phenomenon.

Similarly, in the middle school vignette, composition is again a catalyst to engage with local and global realities. In this example, problematization and inquiry around student experience is central to the compositional experience, creating opportunities for students to make artistic statements that demonstrate their own personal reflection. The decision to use digital audio workstations and other modalities of electronic composition is not inherently critical, as engagements with technology can fall prey to a primary focus on functionality. Here, however, the digital audio workstation is utilized to invite students to embed audio files and remix recordings for the purpose of grappling with knowledge and experience through musical creation.

Nia deliberately plans an engagement with local neighborhoods in the third vignette. Students are invited to not only recognize shifts in the community but to critically investigate the changing cityscape through music. By inviting students to meet with stakeholders beyond the school setting, Nia helps students draw a tangible connection between in-school and out-of-school experience. In spreading the project out over the term, curricular opportunities are created for students to utilize and embed the compositional and musical skills they learn in class over time. In this way, functional skills are still a necessary element of the musical experience, but they are not the only purpose or goal. Students are thinking critically and gaining skills simultaneously, potentially disrupting a linear hierarchy in favor of a more open understanding of the purpose of composition and music education more broadly.

The role of presentation and performance is foundational in these vignettes. In each example, students are developing a composition for a purpose that incorporates but also extends beyond classroom presentation. In Vignette 2, for example, students' sound compositions are presented and performed both in class and at the school's Fine Arts Night. In both cases they are not only seen as artistic works to be shared but as musical catalysts that spark dialogue and conversation about issues of community concern. Similarly, in Vignette 1, the process of creating cultivates dialogue and relationships between elementary and high school students, inviting them to think and make music together. Teachers and students require practice in a form of listening that prioritizes hearing one another through musical and dialogical experience. Each vignette highlights an opportunity for the dialogue to move beyond a functional determination of what a composition is about or how it is formed and toward composition as an opportunity to both affirm and interrogate experience and to engage with unpredictability and moments of meeting where music is felt as something more than an exercise.

These vignettes also require the inclusion of planned, deliberate, purposefully designed reflection. Rather than designing reflective practices that ask students to think about what they have learned or how they might do differently next time, critically reflective practices can help students draw connections between their compositional processes and larger socio-political and cultural-historic issues. Reflections can ground such endeavors in the realities of the worlds in which students live and learn, potentially inspiring them to engage in civic action beyond the confines of the project itself.

The examples offered in these vignettes are extended projects, but the dispositional shifts that may manifest as a result can also be supported on an everyday level. Such practice requires a constant return to questions of *why* and *for whom* as compositional experiences within (and beyond) the general music classroom are planned. Utilizing these questions as a guide for thinking and planning not only determines the *what* and *how* of composition, but also helps cultivate relational experiences and critical thought in and through musical practice.

Concluding Thoughts

Music education is inextricably connected to the socio-political and cultural-historic realities of our world (Gould, 2009; Woodford, 2019). Finding ways to embrace, navigate, challenge, and critically reflect on these connections through music may help students build critical and functional literacies in tandem. Through creative work that sees criticality not as an "add-on" or a "box to check" but a shift in thinking and understanding, students may expand upon their diverse knowledges, challenge taken-for-granted norms, and connect learning practice with structures beyond the music classroom.

Composition projects and endeavors are not transformational on their own. No part of the vignettes detailed guarantees or explicitly incites change. Indeed, there is no final achievement wherein one has become critically literate. Further, it is quite possible that without interdisciplinary support such dispositional shifts may not resonate in a manner that encourages students to view the world with a critical eye. It is possible, however, that shifts in pedagogical practices, including those in composition, create the possibility for moments that help educators and students see musical endeavors as complex, multifaceted, and, often, inextricably bound up in the world. Such experiences can help educators and students recognize privilege and the complex nature of experiences, impact how human experience is framed, and support meaningful social relationships. Through pedagogical practices that see critical and functional literacies as operating in tandem, curriculum can become a commitment to "supporting students' examination of the social, political and historical contexts that impact their developing identities, roles and responsibilities as citizens [and] artists" (Chappell & Chappell, 2016, p. 292). A purpose-driven pedagogy for composition becomes a catalyst for students to engage in critical artistic creation, helping them develop their own voice alongside and in community with others.

References

Abril, C. R. (2016). Untangling general music education: Concept, aims, and practice. In C. R. Abril & B. M. Gault (Eds.), *Teaching general music: Approaches, issues, and viewpoints* (pp. 5–22). Oxford University Press.

Abril, C. R., & Gault, B. M. (2016). *Teaching general music: Approaches, issues, and viewpoints.* Oxford University Press.

Benedict, C. (2012). Critical and transformative literacies: Music and general education. *Theory into Practice, 51*(3), 152–158. https://doi.org/10.1080/00405841.2012.690293

Benedict, C. (2021). *Music and social justice: A guide for elementary educators.* Oxford University Press.

Bernard, C. F., & Abramo, J. M. (2019). *Teacher evaluation in music: A guide for music teachers in the US.* Oxford University Press.

Burnard, P. (2012). *Musical creativities in practice.* Oxford University Press.

Burnard, P., & Younker, B. A. (2002). Mapping pathways: Fostering creativity in composition. *Music Education Research, 4*(2), 245–261. https://doi.org/10.1080/1461380022000011948

Bylica, K. (2020). *Critical border crossing: Exploring positionalities through soundscape composition and critical reflection* [Doctoral Dissertation, University of Western Ontario]. *Electronic Thesis and Dissertation Repository.* https://ir.lib.uwo.ca/etd/7000

Chappell, S. V., & Chappell, D. (2016). Building social inclusion through critical arts-based pedagogies in university classroom communities. *International Journal of Inclusive Education, 20*(3), 292–308. https://doi.org/10.1080/13603116.2015.1047658

Choate, R. (1968). *Documentary report of the Tanglewood Symposium.* Washington, DC: Music Educators National Conference.

Cronenberg, S. (2016). *Music at the middle: Principles that guide middle level general music teachers* (Publication No. 10301831) [Doctoral dissertation, University of Illinois, Urbana-Champaign). ProQuest Dissertation and Theses Global.

Crow, B. (2008). Changing conceptions of educational creativity: A study of student teachers' experience of musical creativity. *Music Education Research, 10*(3), 378–388. https://doi.org/10.1080/14613800802280126

Fautley, M. (2015). Music education assessment and social justice. In C. Benedict, P. Schmidt, G. Spruce & P. Woodford (Eds.), *The Oxford Handbook of Social Justice in Music Education* (pp. 513–524). Oxford.

Finney, J., Philpott, C., & Spruce, G. (Eds.). (2021). *Creative and critical projects in classroom music: Fifty years of sound and silence.* Routledge.

Freire, P. (1970). *Pedagogy of the oppressed.* Continuum.

Gaztambide-Fernández, R. A. (2011). Musicking in the city: Reconceptualizing urban music education as cultural practice. *Action, Criticism, and Theory for Music Education, 10*(1), 15–46.

Giroux, H. (2005). *Border crossings: Cultural workers and the politics of education* (2nd ed.). Routledge.

Gould, E. (2009). Music education desire(ing): Language, literacy, and lieder. *Philosophy of Music Education Review, 17*(1), 41–55.

Gutstein, E. (2006). *Reading and writing the world with mathematics: Toward a pedagogy for social justice.* Taylor & Francis.

Hess, J. (2015). Upping the "anti-": The value of an anti-racist theoretical framework in music education. *Action, Criticism & Theory for Music Education, 14*(1), 66–92. Act.maydaygroup.org/articles/Hess14_1.pdf

Hickey, M. (2003). *How and why to teach music composition: New horizons for music education*. MENC.

Hickey, M. (2012). *Music outside the lines: Ideas for composing in K–12 music classrooms*. Oxford University Press.

Kanellopoulos, P. (2015). Musical creativity and "the police": Troubling core music education certainties. In C. Benedict, P. Schmidt, G. Spruce, & P. Woodford (Eds.), *The Oxford Handbook of Social Justice in Music Education* (pp. 318–339). Oxford.

Kaschub, M. (2009). Critical pedagogy for creative artists: Inviting young composers to engage in artistic social action. In E. Gould, J. Countryman, C. Morton & L. S. Rose (Eds.), *Exploring social justice: How music education might matter* (pp. 274–291). CMEA/ACME Books.

Kaschub, M., & Smith, J. (2009). *Minds on music: Composition for creative and critical thinking*. Rowman & Littlefield.

Kaschub, M., & Smith, J. (Eds.). (2013). *Composing our future: Preparing music educators to teach composition*. Oxford University Press.

Kratus, J. (2007). Music education at the tipping point. *Music Educators Journal, 94*(2), 42–48. https://doi.org/10.1177/002743210709400209

Kumashiro, K. K. (2000). Toward a theory of anti-oppressive education. *Review of Educational Research, 70*, 25–53. https://doi.org/10.3102/00346543070001025

Luke, A. (2012). Critical literacy: Foundational notes. *Theory into Practice, 51*(4), 4–11. https://doi.org/10.1080/00405841.2012.636324

Mantie, R. (2008). Getting unstuck: The One World Youth Arts Project, the music education paradigm, and youth without advantage. *Music Education Research, 10*(4), 473–483. https://doi.org/10.1080/14613800802547706

Martin, G., & Brown, T. (2013). Out of the box: Making space for everyday critical pedagogies. *The Canadian Geographer/Le Géographe canadien, 57*(3), 381–388. https://doi.org/10.1111/cag.12015

McLaren, P. (1989). *Life in schools: An introduction to critical pedagogy in the foundations of education*. Longman.

Regelski, T. A. (2004). *Teaching general music in grades 4–8*. Oxford University Press.

Reimer, B. (2003). *A philosophy of music education: Advancing the vision*. Prentice Hall.

Reimer, B. (2012). Another perspective: Struggling toward wholeness in music education. *Music Educators Journal, 99*(2), 25–29. https://doi.org/10.1177/0027432112463856

Robinson, N. R. (2017). Developing a critical consciousness for diversity and equity among preservice music teachers. *Journal of Music Teacher Education, 26*(3), 11–26. https://doi.org/10.1177/1057083716643349

Ruthmann, S. A. (2007). The composers' workshop: An approach to composing in the classroom. *Music Educators Journal, 93*(4), 38–43. https://doi.org/10.1177/002743210709300416

Ruthmann, S. A. (2008). Whose agency matters? Negotiating pedagogical and creative intent during composing experiences. *Research Studies in Music Education, 30*(1), 43–58. https://doi.org/10.1177/1321103X08089889

Schmidt, P. (2012). What we hear is meaning too: Deconstruction, dialogue, and music. *Philosophy of Music Education Review, 20*(1), 3–24.

Schmidt, P. (2020). *Policy as concept and practice: A guide for music educators*. Oxford University Press.

Shieh, E. (2020). Making practice into policy: Bridging, buffering, and building in our schools. *Music Educators Journal, 107*(1), 31–36. https://doi.org/10.1177/0027432120946817

Stauffer, S. L. (2002). Connections between the musical and life experiences of young composers and their compositions. *Journal of Research in Music Education, 50*(4), 301–322. https://doi.org/10.2307/3345357

Stauffer, S. (2017, September). *Whose imaginings? Whose futures?* [Closing Keynote Address]. Society for Music Teacher Education Symposium. Minneapolis, Minnesota, USA. https://smte.us/wp-content/uploads/2020/04/SMTE2017StaufferKeynote.pdf

Tobias, E. S., Campbell, M. R., & Greco, P. (2015). Bringing curriculum to life: Enacting project-based learning in music programs. *Music Educators Journal, 102*(2), 39–47. https://doi.org/10.1177/0027432115607602

Tucker-Raymond, E., & Rosario, M. L. (2017). Imagining identities: Young people constructing discourses of race, ethnicity, and community in a contentious context of rapid urban development. *Urban Education, 52*(1), 32–60. https://doi.org/10.1177/0042085914550412

Upitis, R. (2019). *This too is music.* Oxford University Press.

Viig, T. G. (2015). Composition in music education: A literature review of 10 years of research articles published in music education journals. *Nordic Research in Music Education Yearbook, 16,* 227–257.

Webster, P. (2011). Towards pedagogies of revision: Guiding a student's music composition. In O. Odena (Ed.), *Musical creativity: Insights from music education research* (pp. 93–112). Ashgate.

Woodford, P. (2019). *Music education in an age of virtuality and post-truth.* Routledge.

CHAPTER 28

....

DEVELOPING
SOUNDCRAFTERS

Facilitating a Holistic Approach to Music Production

....

SARAH GENEVIEVE BURGHART RICE
AND ANN CLEMENTS

THERE are many names for those who create and master audio recordings. The names for the practitioners of this audio artifice have shifted over time, with former titles littered across the history of recording sound data. Still, two names that have had some staying power are *producer*, the English-speaking world's name for a recording studio manager, and *Tonmeister*, a German-speaking world's equivalent, which hearkens back to guild crafts. One way of expressing the *Tonmeister* idea's kernel is with the neologism *soundcrafter*, which we will use in this paper.

The term *soundcrafter* is particularly appropriate for use in early childhood through high school settings due to the playful and creative nature which is at its heart. Soundcrafting spans both art and technology: it is working with musicians on a musical level to help them achieve the best performances and interpretation and employing or directing the use of appropriate technology to create the best experience for listeners, including proper editing, sound balance, and other post-production skills (Colquhoun, 2018). This role balances the techniques grounded in scientific and mathematical knowledge (including microphone use, digital recording, skillful amplification, etc.) with the creative imagination to audiate possibilities that may result in unique approaches to what the finished recording might be like before the process begins. The integration of these skills fosters wonderful experiences and illusions for performers and listeners alike.

A soundcrafter is the project's creative and technical leader. Like a film director, the soundcrafter's role may include gathering ideas, collecting musicians, proposing changes to song arrangements, coaching performers, scripting sessions, supervising the recording session set up, mixing of the recording, and supervision audio mastering. Frequently in school settings, the roles of executive producer, which in commercial settings is the person who oversees business partnerships, the record or recording producer who makes creative decisions, and the sound engineer who does the technical aspects of making the recording and mixing the products overlap with one another and it common to have one student or a small group of students working collaboratively to ensure each aspect of all of these positions are covered. The key to the term soundcrafter is that it semantically breaks down the division between an audio engineer, a doer, and a producer, a director. Within this role, students are actively doing both.

Constructing Recordings

Even aficionados of live music, such as the authors of this chapter, experience most of their music mediated through recordings. It is so ubiquitous that we may be unconscious of the clever artifice employed to create a listening experience akin to live performance. Thus, one might close their eyes and imagine being in a concert. Yet recordings are far from a passive document of the sounds created by instruments and voices; elements such as intonation and timbre are co-constructed by the musicians who are recorded and by the soundcrafters. The craft involved in creating music recordings rests best upon a foundation of knowledge about how musical instruments and voices vibrate, how rooms resonate, and how loudspeakers operate.

Music recordings are stored sound data that describe air vibrations. The stored sound data is converted into electricity that causes the cones called woofers in a loudspeaker to vibrate, thereby reproducing vibrations in the air locally. Most audio recordings today store air pressure data digitally over time, meaning that a given number of measurements called *samples* are recorded over equal intervals of time, described with a *sampling rate* such as 44,100, 48,000, or 96,000 samples per second. Samples have a *bit depth*, which identifies the precision with which the samples are recorded, with a higher bit depth providing greater accuracy. Voices and instruments produce air vibrations just as loudspeakers do. Influencing the data collection through types of microphone placement is part of a soundcrafter's interpretive decision-making.

An ever-present companion as we listen to music is space, such as a concert hall, the cafeteria, an athletic stadium, or any other venue. Our ears are highly attentive to space, and our sense of localization of sound is primarily achieved through the short time interval (usually less than 50 milliseconds) that it takes for the sound wave to reach one ear and then the other. Unlike live performances that occur in specific spaces, musical recordings have the potential to distort time-related sound data related to spaces. The most common way to represent space on a recording is a *stereo image*, wherein the intent is for discrete vibration patterns to reach each ear and thereby create the time-delay cues our brains interpret as localization. Short-time periods of sound-objects/musical-events (circa 50 milliseconds or less) are processed differently by human auditory systems than more extended timer periods (circa 100 milliseconds up to circa 16 seconds).

A soundcraft curriculum should foster an understanding of what short time periods of sound objects sound like and feel like.

SOUNDCRAFTING AS MUSIC PRODUCTION AND THE MUSICAL PRODUCER

Every recording provides an interpretation from the stereo image's control and design, which gives a sense of depth or space to a recording to the intimacy, warmth, or muffled quality of a recording on an individual track. A collaborator best serves the recording of a musical group with a shared vision for what the recording would sound like from when a project begins. The production process in school settings often requires students to play multiple roles and become what Tobias (2012) has called "hyphenated musician[s]" who must be able to think and act as songwriters, performers, sound engineers, recordists, mix engineers, and producers in ways that are recursive and often overlapping.

The key to this approach is the music teacher's ability to establish an environment in which they become the facilitator of student learning, instilling a creative identity in their music students (Randles, 2012). The teacher's knowledge and understanding of the techniques and tools needed to produce quality recordings affect the students' ability to make recordings of their highest quality. Today's music students live in a digital world surrounded by recorded music. If they wish to make a career out of doing what they love, they need to know how to use the technological tools available (Crishwell & Menashe, 2009). Thus, recording is no longer an additional skill that might be included within a holistic music education, but a foundational one.

Music production is a holistic process (Hunter, Broad, and Jeanneret, 2018) where students learn comprehensive musical skills that can develop skill-building (theoretical knowledge), planning and decision-making (self-organization), communication and collaboration (running a session), and refinement of ideas and products (post-production). What defines a music producer and their involvement varies from project to project and is reliant on the musical goals and objectives of the project and capabilities of the students engaged in the process. To a lesser degree, it may also be dependent on availability and access to instruments and equipment. The music producer has to make split-second decisions and help guide the recording process toward a shared vision of the final song. This requires the ability to give verbal feedback, and musical insights to the musicians in an informed manner that explains how the technology involved will shape their sound. This is often done when it may be difficult for those who are being recorded to hear potential outcomes that far ahead in the process.

The building of sound production skills may be best suited for older students in middle or high school who can oversee the technical, creative, and social processes simultaneously. That being said, there are many opportunities for younger students to begin learning these skills to lay a foundation for soundcrafting skills that increase in complexity as they mature. For example, while early elementary students may be overly challenged by a task that requires them to place microphones appropriately to record various instruments, they can, with the teacher's careful planning and assistance, be led through a process of learning how microphone placement affects recording quality. Additionally, early elementary students typically encounter microphones only as a novelty available in a crowded auditorium when they are used to grab everyone's attention or a source of piercing feedback. Allowing early elementary students the time and permission to play with and problem-solve with audio equipment can be crucial for future musical engagement.

Production Process

Soundcrafting comes to life through a multi-stage process. Not every music production process is the same, but it is rarely completed all at once. Thus, it is helpful to categorize the work involved. We present a six-step approach that includes: (1) songwriting or composition, (2) arranging; (3) tracking; (4) mixing; (5) editing, and (6) mastering. As other chapters within this book focus intensively on songwriting and arranging, we will focus solely on the aspects of tracking, editing, mixing, and mastering within recording production.

Tracking

Tracking is the process of recording the various instruments or voices that are used to perform a song. A tracking session can be divided into those that attempt to minimize the presence of the room(s) in which instrumentalists or vocalists perform, which we will call *studio sessions*, and those that record the room's response as the instrumentalists or vocalists perform, which we will call *venue sessions*.

Studio sessions can be recorded one track at a time or simultaneously. If simultaneously, it is ideal to isolate the performers' sounds from one another as much as possible, perhaps with each performer in a separate room or with some sort of partition between them. If the tracks are recorded sequentially, the isolation takes care of itself. Headphones are required for isolation. If you lay down tracks sequentially, you listen through headphones to all previously-recorded tracks while you record the new track. Alternatively, all of the musicians being recorded at the same time listen to one another through headphones while being recorded in an isolated environment. The resulting isolated tracks provide a lot of flexibility with everything that follows.

For venue sessions, the instrumentalists and vocalists' overall sound is primarily captured by microphones arranged in *stereo configuration*. Stereophonic techniques will be described in more detail below; suffice it to say that two or more microphones have a fixed stereo pattern. Any other microphones used are designated as *spot mics*. Spot mics are supplemental tracks that can give limited post-processing options to the resulting recording, such as bringing out an instrumental solo at an opportune moment but must never overwhelm the stereo configuration's microphones or the stereo image will be destroyed.

To record tracks well, a soundcrafter needs to develop a strong understanding of best practices for how to record each instrument they are working with. This understanding involves a theoretical or intuitive understanding of the physics of vibrating bodies and the methods by which the particular microphones record vibrations. This knowledge provides the options for best placements of recording equipment and microphones for each instrument or ensemble. Admittedly, this topic is vast and it is easy to become discouraged; where should one start? Classic resources to develop knowledge about recording include Rayburn (2012) and Roads & Strawn (1996). Keep in mind, though, that there is not a single best placement for any instrument. The most important skills to develop are avoiding distortion, getting a hot signal, and correct stereophony techniques. The easiest stereo patterns to master are staples of the repertory: XY pattern and Blumlein pattern. Numerous quick tutorials on these patterns are available online.

While STEM knowledge plays a role, students should also experiment, using their ear and weighing the results of a recording session with a particular method. In addition, the producer must know how to structure a recording session to benefit the musicians, maximize the use of studio time, and to ensure the highest quality recordings are made. Thus, it also requires strong social skills and the ability to speak in musical terms to the musicians who are recording.

Editing

Editing is the process through which recording sounds are manipulated to improve overall sound quality. While advances in the ease and capabilities of capturing a great performance through tracking is easier, it is best to use these tools as a fallback, not a go-to. The amount of work a producer does editing is dependent on the quality of the recordings captured. Learning the skills of how to edit recordings ensures that the producer and the musician's vision for the recording can be met without being dependent on just the tools of tracking. Common elements that may be edited include removing breaths, cough, ringing of the phone, or any other unwanted interference; adding music intros and outro, stretching or shortening audio and sound effects, splicing together various tracks or elements of the music recorded separately or at different sittings, syncing up different musical instruments so that they all sound on the beat, pitch processing, and looping, slicing, and editing beats. There is not one single method of editing music that will work with every artist and every situation. There are many factors that lead down the trail of making the best decisions, but almost always involves the application of filters, dynamic compression, and gain. There are a variety of secondary techniques that are sometimes included, such as noise gating, panning, and reverberation.

Mixing

Mixing is the process of combining multiple tracks into another single sound file. Software devoted to mixing are often called *sound montage* or *digital audio workstations* (DAWs). It is computationally simple to mix sound files[1] but it is a mathematically difficult problem to decompose them into the state that they were before mixing. Thus, we have a *mixdown* or *bounce* that combines the files but there is no *mixing up* to take them apart. Therefore, DAWs hold a session with information such as the temporal relationships of the various component tracks and processing of these tracks in a so-called *non-destructive* fashion, meaning that the sound files have not been saved after they have been mixed. *Destructive* editing yields a single sound file result (it has been mixed). Software that traffics in destructive editing tend to be called *sound file editors*. There is significant overlap between montage/DAW programs and sound file editors, but DAWs tend to refer to computationally-intensive non-destructive sound file alterations, whereas sound file editors tend to deal with computationally-light destructive changes. This means that montage/DAW programs contain greater flexibility.

Mixing can be broken down into three categories: general mixing, moderate mixing, and fine mixing. Each category continues the refinement process. *General mixing* includes determining which recorded track on a particular instrument is the best overall then determining if there are better performances of certain sections of the songs that can be mixed into the preferred track. For example, it may be that the second recording is the overall better recording, but that the bridge section of recording three was the best for that position of the song. General mixing requires decision-making that the general editing of the best portions of each recording track be edited together. As individual perfected tracks are made, they need to be considered in relationship to other tracks that are also being perfected. This analysis between tracks and how well they fit together continues until the producer feels they have the best possible edited mix of all recordings.

Moderate mixing is completed after general editing, when the producer finds particular phrases, notes, or words that need a bit more attention. *Fine mixing* happens after you have a complete track that is working to a large degree. The purpose of fine mixing is to select a portion of the song and listen to it at the "big picture" level, meaning listen not to individual tracks but, instead, to the ways the tracks work or don't work together. Moving through chunks of the song and fine mixing can help producers avoid the trap of becoming stuck in the minutiae of general and moderate mixing.

Mastering

Mastering is the process of taking an audio mix and preparing it for distribution or performance. Mastering involves taking a collection of nearly complete mix sessions and optimizing the resulting destructive mix for listening to these sound files together (e.g., as an album), listening in relationship to other similar albums (e.g., what is the mean amplitude of my drum and bass album in relationship to Aphex Twin *Hangable Auto Bulb*?). The process of mastering requires listening to the final mix on various speakers, from fine studio monitors to the car stereo with blown-out woofers and considering whether the mix still sounds good. Each set of speakers applies a distinctive *coloration* or *filtration* to the mix. There are various methods available; one can have multiple sets of speakers available at the computer where mixing takes place, one can carry on some medium to be played in various locations, or one can attempt to simulate the result of filtration electronically.

While the ideal situation is to have multiple speakers available (with at least one set being accurate), simulating speaker coloration can be achieved with software. An advantage to this curricular path is that filters are an excellent didactic topic; these are the building blocks of what is popularly known as equalization or EQ. Filters are achieved through delaying copies of the signal. The mechanism involved may not immediately be obvious: vibrations in air involve areas where air molecules are bunched up, called compressions, areas in which air molecules are less numerous, called rarefactions, areas in which air molecules are equally spaced, where they are said to be in equilibrium, as well as situations that mediate between these states. When sound waves, alternating between compression and rarefaction, meet, they are superposed, meaning that their states are combined or added together. Thus, a period of maximal compression and maximal rarefaction that meet create a state of equilibrium—a phenomenon called phase cancellation. Such cancellations or interferences arise in a predictable and quantifiable fashion; the name of this predictive model is a *linear time-invariant system*. Their uses are at least as numerous as the lauded sinusoid tone. As computer-music master Julius Smith said: "When you think about it, everything is a filter" (Smith, 1985, 13).

Equipment Basics

For pedagogical purposes, it is helpful to have a set of equipment devoted to soundcrafting. In environments that do not have specific sound recording booths, it is logical to purchase recording equipment that can be easily stored out of the way and brought into the classroom, or other venues, as needed for various recording projects. This equipment should be of the sort that is based on individual components. The repetition of getting all of the equipment out and connecting it yet again is a learning experience for the students. Mistakes made along the way offer ample experiences for learning the intricacies of the equipment and they will gain confidence and understanding with how audio technology works by putting a recording system together. As students learn, it may be helpful if the teacher can provide an overall list of available equipment with brief descriptions of what each piece of equipment is used for and how elements can be connected together.

System components can be improved with the addition of studio monitors (a type of speakers), which are safer options for the ears of students than mixing with headphones. If single-patterned, the two microphones should be cardioid. If the microphones allow a user to switch their pattern, cardioid with the option of a bidirectional (figure 8) pattern will be useful. Condenser microphones will be a versatile and durable choice, rather than dynamic or ribbon microphones.

A range of software options can be employed in soundcrafting. As we write this chapter, there are free audio editors such as Audacity or Ardour, as well low cost but high-quality DAWs such as Reaper and AmadeusPro (approximately $50 per copy). The best-known DAWs, such as Logic, ProTools, Cubase, or Ableton (circa $350 per copy) are often an expensive proposition, although certain types of processing or

A system should ideally consist of at least the following items:

- ☐ 2 microphones (exactly the same mics)
- ☐ A stereo bar
- ☐ 2 microphone stands
- ☐ An analog mixing board
- ☐ An audio interface
- ☐ A computer
- ☐ 2 XLR cables to connect the microphones to the mixer
- ☐ 2 XLR or TRS cables to connect the mixer to the audio interface
- ☐ High-quality headphones

FIGURE 28.1. System components

Setting up and working with DAWs	The Essential Guide to DAWs – The Basics (MiscTech.net) DAWs: The Complete Guide for Beginners (edmprod.com)
Basic and More Advanced Recording and Mixing Software and Apps	The Best Audio Editing Software (pcmag.com)
Microphones	Understanding Microphones (sterlingaudio.net) Studio Microphone Buying Guide (sweetwater.com)
Analog Mixing Boards	The Best Home Studio Mixers (musicradar.com) Best Consoles for Live Mixing (musicradar.com)
Audio Interface	Best Audio Interfaces (musicradar.com) Best Audio Interfaces for Home and Studio Recording (ledgernote.com)
Computer Specifications for Music Production	Computer Specs for Music Production (homestudiorecordings.com) The Perfect Computer for Music Production (sweetwater.com) Best PCs for Music Production (musicradar.com)

FIGURE 28.2. Teacher fundamental skills for sound recording

recording require them. A good rule of thumb is that if you do not have more equipment available than what is listed in Figure 28.1, Reaper or AmadeusPro will probably be more than sufficient for your soundcrafting activities. Figure 28.2 offers a list of some of the fundamental skills that teachers should become familiar with and websites that can assist in gaining the basic knowledge needed to work with these tools.

SOUNDCRAFT SAMPLE LESSONS

This section contains practical information for teachers on lesson approaches that foster producer skills and establish music production in various music classes. Organized

The Loud One and the Soft One	
Grades PK–2	
Lesson Goal	The overarching goal of this lesson is to use a story or play to allow students to explore aspects of dynamics through amplification and to practice the roles of audio engineer and director. Areas included in this lesson idea are: 1) skill building, and 2) planning and decision making.
Preparation	Before class, the teacher sets up and secures two speakers out of reach of the students. These should be plugged into electrical power, and XLR audio cable is run from the back of the speakers to a small mixer. The XLRs closer to the mixer are disconnected. The teacher also sets up a microphone in a location obscured from view and separate from the mixer, running XLR cable from it to the mixer, but leaving it disconnected. The teacher should choose a children's story book with at least two characters or create a *short* play.
Implementation	■ When students arrive, the teacher and students decide on people to engage in the following roles: 1) Director (manages the action of the other roles) 2) Audio engineer (operates the mixer) 3) [Voice of character 1] (with a soft voice) 4) [Voice of character 2] (with a very loud voice) 5) [Actions of character 1] 6) [Actions of character 2] Depending on the reading level of the students, the teacher may perform the voices of the characters to demonstrate the play or prepare text for the students to read.
Tasks	■ The *audio engineer* first connects the microphone and the 3 speakers to the mixer with the assistance of the teacher. Mistakes and loud noises are part of the process; take this in stride, the speakers probably are not sustaining permanent damage. The routing and gain should be such that one of the speakers is the soft speaker and the other is the loudspeaker. After connecting these, the engineer must manipulate the sliders for the single microphone to route the voice actors to the speaker of correct loudness. ■ *Voice actors 1 and 2* will take turns speaking their lines into the microphone while *action actors 1 and 2* perform movements within view. While the *audio engineer* is connecting the cables, these students should rehearse their play in coordination with the *director*. After the *audio engineer* is ready, the play can commence. ■ The director may stop the action to ask that sections be performed again, as well as work through connection problems with the *audio engineer*. Once the play is complete, disconnect the audio, new students can take the roles and the process can begin again.

FIGURE 28.3. Grades PK–2 sample lesson: *The Loud One and the Soft One*

Skill and Theory Building	Students will come to understand how signal flow works by diagnosing problems with connections between the microphone, speakers, and mixer. If a cable is disconnected or is mis-routed, amplification will not occur. Through experimentation, students can also come to understand distortion, especially if they attempt to perform loud sounds when in the soft speaker role. The teacher may stop the action to point out distortion when it occurs to encourage such recognition. Feedback or boominess will probably also occur, which will provide a forum for students to experientially begin to understand the situations that give rise to these phenomena.
Planning and Decision Making	Within the lesson plan idea each character and direction role suggests a set of interpretative decisions for a student. The voice actors and director decide the dramaturgy at the global or particular level, while the audio engineer must keep track of fine-grained details and successfully execute the vision created by the director. When students spend time in the various roles, what they experience will inform their work in other roles. For example, "Did I like it when the other student gave directions harshly? No. I will take care to give my directions kindly."

FIGURE 28.3. Continued

by age ranges, these examples will cover multiple aspects of recorded sound production. These lessons ideas are organized around four components necessary to develop soundcraftings skills: (1) skill-building (theoretical knowledge), (2) planning and decision-making (self-organization), (3) communication and collaboration (running a session), and (4) the refinement of ideas and products (post-production). Not all lesson ideas will include all four components. For example, the younger grades' lesson ideas may focus more comprehensively on one or two. Figures 28.3 through 28.6 offer model lessons to highlight the development of these skills.

CONCLUSION

Soundcrafting is an important yet often overlooked aspect in the music classroom, yet an essential part of recording music. The ability to soundcraft well requires

Speed Tapas
Grades 3–5

Lesson Goal	The overarching goal of this lesson is to break down recorded music into small sections to allow students to explore the musical properties hidden within the context of larger recordings. Particularly important is practice listening to very short moments that form cues for space and timbre. Areas included in this lesson idea are: 1) skill building, 2) planning and decision making, and 3) collaboration.
Preparation	■ In advance, ask students to bring in or upload favorite recordings for your *Speed Tapas* game. Explain the tapas style of dining or show examples in preparation and mention that the recordings will be given in small portions during Speed Tapas. Engage the students in a decision-making process involving the order in which the plates (the soundfiles) should be eaten (listened to). Perhaps one of the students is the chef, with strict and specific ideas for the dining experience. Or perhaps the dining party (the class) is going out to a more relaxed experience, in which everyone at the table has a say on how to order the plates. Give a time-limit for this decision-making process. ■ When you have all the students' submissions, prepare them outside of class time. Various software can be used for this lesson but we will explain with reference to the free audio software PureData (http://puredata.info.), originally written by Miller Puckette. Place all recordings in the same folder of the computer you will play back from. You may create an image of a PureData patch or program by downloading it from http://riceklang.com/soundcrafters/ ■ It is possible to use the patch without understanding all the technical details of what the patch does. You will need to replace the filename "victory1.aiff" with the file name you wish to load and then right click the text box. You should see the windows "the_tunes" and "the_tunes2" change from being blank in appearance to showing variations.
Implementation	■ Before each plate of food is eaten (i.e., each track being listened to), you can invite the student that submitted it to say something short about why they like it. Then you can demonstrate ordinary playback by clicking on the box containing a 0 (zero) underneath "play as an entreé." If you would like to skip a certain number of seconds into the track for entreé play, you can enter that number of seconds instead of zero and click it. Click the "stop" button to stop playing the track. Next, the class can "eat" the track as tapas—in small portions. As given, the patch gives the option to play arbitrarily-selected "bites" from the track of 333 milliseconds in length (about ⅓ of a second), 25 milliseconds (1/40th of a second), 15 milliseconds (about 1/67th of a second), 5 milliseconds (1/200th of a second), or bites of 1 millisecond (1/1000th of a second). ■ Move through the bite sizes, getting progressively smaller (uncheck the toggle above the respective bize size to stop listening). After each step, ask the students how the taste has changed. How does the music sound different? Importantly, can you recognize the voice and instruments at that bite size? When the meal concludes, leave a little time for collective reflection on whether the meal overall turned out as expected. What was the experience like listening to all of the sound files as tapas? If certain students took a more authoritative role in ordering the plates, ask them to reflect on the result and discuss their leadership with those in non-leadership roles.

FIGURE 28.4. Grade 3–5 sample lesson: *Speed Tapas*

Skill and Theory Building	An important aspect of audio engineering is timbre, the details of which can sometimes be difficult to hear. The psychoacoustic experience of timbre is tied to quickly changing vibrations, especially in durations shorter than 50 or 60 milliseconds. This is the realm of phenomena such as the *transients*, which occur in the moment a musical instrument that is at rest or in a different state of activity and then is shocked into motion by an exciting force such as a bow, a finger, or a drumstick. The *Speed Tapas* lesson gets students listening to those very short sounds and hopefully activates interest in how time affects our experience of sound. As the sounds get shorter and shorter, the timbres cannot be heard as the instruments or voices that we hear at larger bite sizes.
Planning and Decision Making	*Speed Tapas* demonstrates the experience of planning for a situation in which there are unknowns. Is it okay to leave certain details undecided or unpredictable? If one desires greater control of the experience, what steps must be taken to ensure a predictable result? This exercise shows the importance of practices such as tech rehearsals for live events. It also demonstrates a practice important for mastering, which is to consider the unfolding of musical parameters such as amplitude overall in addition to at the track-to-track level.
Collaboration	As given, Speed Tapas gives experience with deciding on roles and then moving through the overall artistic experience in a particular role. At the teacher's discretion, this lesson can be expanded by involving the students in the data entry and bug-checking of the PureData software. There are often hiccups such as a file not being in a format that PureData easily accepts (e.g., a file may be submitted in an .m4a format that PureData cannot read and must be opened by a soundfile-editing or DAW program.

FIGURE 28.4. Continued

musical, social, and higher order creative skills. Musically, students need to understand the concepts of space, acoustics, amplification, instrument properties, and elements such as timber, beat and meter, key signatures, and strong structures. Socially they need to be able to communicate the recording process to the musicians being recorded and to be able to ask for repetition or changes in what can sometimes be high stress environments, where everyone is trying to do their best work. It takes creativity and organization to plan for and prepare recording spaces and how the recording season will be structured, as well as how to edit, mix, and master recorded tracks.

Learning the foundational elements of soundcrafting can occur at any age and may be best explored when the teacher becomes a facilitator of the students' learning by creating lessons that promote independence and free thinking by the students as they solve recording challenges. Comprehensive and complex tasks are made more

Live in Concert	
Grades 6–8	
Lesson Goal	The overarching goal of this lesson is to record a live performance or rehearsal and to use a DAW to complete post-production phases of the process. Areas included in this lesson idea are: 1) skill building, 2) planning and decision making, 3) collaboration, and 4) refinement.
Preparation	■ This lesson can work in the context of a concert or a rehearsal. The student recording may be the official recording of the event, or it may be a second recording of the event that happens in parallel with some more consistent recording process. ■ The students involved need to prepare with the teacher well ahead of the event, whether they are students assembled specifically to do soundcrafting or they are an entire music class or ensemble undertaking a soundcrafting task in a shorter series of lessons.
Implementation	■ Planning should begin by creating a list of the necessary equipment. Students should begin with a guided consideration of the room and the musicians that will be recorded. Certain rooms are designed to work well without amplification and others almost require amplifications. For example, a resonant old chamber with stone walls might sound great without electronic reinforcement, whereas a room with black-painted plywood walls is designed for amplification. The ensemble also makes a difference. Certain instruments, such as electric guitar or bass, will lend themselves to being recorded with an array of monophonic microphones, as they would be in a studio session. On the other hand, a string quartet will probably sound best with a stereo configuration. ■ Once the microphones are chosen, students should prepare a setup diagram and equipment list. The setup for the recording session, rehearsal, or live event should take place well ahead of time. If this is not possible (for example, because you cannot gain access to the space), then a technology rehearsal should be employed, wherein the system is setup, tested, and then torn down again. Students should also decide on a leader for the event—a student that can quickly give directives for the other students should follow. Ideally students should switch roles from event to event; one student that was the leader during the previous rehearsal accepts directives from a different leader the next. ■ The microphone setup will largely dictate the tracking for the event, which will be recorded continuously. After the event, the tracks should be saved as a session in the DAW and all equipment should be returned to the area of school that it ordinarily lives. Following the concert, the students should enter a post-production phase.
Skill and Theory Building	During tech rehearsals, students ideally should ask to explore the loudest and softest moments of the performance and adjust their recording amplitude levels to take advantage of the available bit depth as well as to avoid clipping. Clipping is a form of waveform distortion that occurs when an amplifier is overdriven and attempts to deliver and output voltage or current beyond in maximum capacity. For wind instruments and voices, students may wish to explore high-pitched sections, as overblown registers will result in higher-amplitude situations for the microphones that may not be psychoacoustically apparent for listeners.

FIGURE 28.5. Grades 6–8 sample lesson: *Live in Concert*

Planning and Decision Making	The explicit preparations listed above can be taught with templates for activity. One such template might list who the leader for the live recording session will be, along with who the assisting soundcrafters will be. Estimating the time required for each activity in a setup may be a part of templates.
Collaboration	■ Repeating this activity provides rich opportunities for students to switch between leadership and supporting roles. As one student reflects on their time in a supporting role, it will inform the sort of leadership that they undertake and *vice versa*. As students work together, they will often refine their social relationships for their group temperament and goals, while refining their group methods to achieve a shared vision for their music. ■ It is likely beneficial to allow students the freedom to create their own policies and procedures with one another, with students with higher skills or more experience working with those who have less skills or experience currently. However, the teacher has a larger task in establishing initial policies as the first students come into a social context for recording. ■ This portion of the project allows for students to explore and utilize skills of self- and community-organization. While it may be tempting for teaches to take control with things become challenging, the most authentic learning may come from moments when the student must find their own solutions. Once the student soundcrafters have established working patterns that are functional and fair, the teacher can intervene only when the social structure becomes unbalanced by a particularly autocratic student leader.
Refinement	Post-production will provide ample learning opportunities; if events such as this are not commonly available to students, then the session can be copied for various interested students to try their hand at completing it in their own way. If a stereo configuration was employed, care must be taken during editing to preserve the stereo image. Most recordings will require some filtration (equalization), dynamic compression, and gain/amplification to achieve a recording similar to what students are expecting. Teachers can guide the students to self-asses by listening to and discussing the recording and asking questions about the balance of loud and shot sections, the ability to capture a realistic sound to what was experienced live and overall balance of the sound throughout the recording.

FIGURE 28.5. Continued

Get Set – A Drum Kit Studio Session	
Grades 9–12	
Lesson Goal	The overarching goal of this lesson is to record a drum set and use the processes of production to refine the recording. Areas included in this lesson are: 1) skill building, 2) planning and decision making, 3) collaboration, and 4) refinement.
Background	As drumset is typically recorded with an array of microphones, it provides an opportunity to teach how microphones can work together. While there are a variety of possible approaches, we will suggest paths that sets the students up for success while also providing challenging opportunities. A drumset is a collection of instruments that a recording engineer may desire to isolate in a mix. For example, it includes a kick drum, a high hat, a snare drum, and a variety of cymbals. Each of the components that we mention is recorded in an idiomatic way and the developing a cohesive mix for the total drum set is similar to developing a mix for a larger ensemble of musicians.
Skill and Theory Building	<ul><li>It is important to have a basic understanding of the roles each microphone plays within the recording process. For example, the kick drum may be recorded with one microphone inside the drum and another microphone outside. If only one microphone is used, the one placed inside the drum typically provides a better-isolated sound. Inside the drum, the microphone should not directly face the kick, but rather one edge of the drumhead closest to the drummer. A good inside-the-kick microphone choice is a Shure Beta 52A. If not this, another relatively insensitive cardioid or supercardioid dynamic microphone will be a good choice. If used, the outside-the-drum microphone should be shielded with padding or pillows from vibrations traveling through the floor.</li><li>The cymbals often cannot be isolated from one another; this situation provides an opportunity to incorporate a stereo pattern into the mix. It can yield good results to record the cymbal array with a blumlein configuration, an XY, or an ORTF-like configuration in which the students can experiment with different placements for the microphone widths. Unlike a venue-session used for a stereo configuration, in which the stereo configuration must remain in the prominent foreground of the mix, the cymbals can be prominent in the mix or backgrounded, depending on the choices of the students. The stereo configuration should be directed towards the cymbals but can be placed above, in front of, or even behind the drummer. If possible, a blumlein or XY is best achieved with a stereo bar on a boom stand, while the ORTF-like configurations may be achieved with two boom stands on either side of the drumset.</li><li>Phase issues are common when setting up for this kind of session; students must learn what these sound like and how to correct them (change the offending microphone positions). A more extensive array might have a microphone or two on each drum (one for each tom, one for each head of a snare drum, & cymbal.), but a spectrum of options in between this and a stereo pair exist. One way to think of the problem is that you may want to pay special attention to instruments that are featured in the session: if it is a snare drum heavy session and you only have 3 microphones, that is where to put the third mic.</li></ul>

FIGURE 28.6. Grades 9–12 sample lesson: *Get Set—A Drum Kit Studio Session*

Planning and Decision Making	■ Planning involves detailed preparation in coordination with the drummer. A room must be secured where the session will not be disturbed, the drumset must be set up by the drummer, the microphones must be assembled and tested. ■ Recording the drum set can happen with a minimalist approach, which would include the use of 2 microphones in a stereo configuration but you more likely will want the flexibility of a multi-mic setup. It's important for student producers to draw a plan indicating where microphones will be set and what their specific purpose is in the recording process. It should be noted that plans are only what you think may happen when you begin recording and that they need to be flexible enough to change should the sound not be what was intended.
Collaboration	■ A more prepared drummer will allow everyone to record fewer takes. It is always helpful to avoid splicing takes. However, the soundcrafters need to be listening attentively enough to understand what errors or undesired events are occurring in each take, as well as making accurate decisions about whether they can be corrected in post-production. The drummer will often look to the soundcrafter to determine if a take was good (a quality and useable recording): therefore the soundcrafter must make an accurate decision about whether there is enough material to make a good recording, while also not exhausting everyone with unnecessary takes. ■ The producer should have a plan of action for communication with the drummer when the recording is taking place. They need to understand social interaction like a conductor who, which working with musicians, needed tact and professionalism to inspire the musicians with whom they are working.
Refinement	■ Especially at first, this sort of session can feel like a mammoth undertaking, yet the post-production that follows is even more gargantuan. Each track should be isolated in the mix and listened to alone, adding filters, dynamic compression, and gain, as well as some other assorted techniques such as a noise gate (removing bleed from other areas of the drumset). If computation power is strained in the DAW, each individual track may be bounced (saved destructively) to preserve computation power. Then the individual instruments can be mixed. Where certain collections of microphones may receive exactly the same processing, they may be collected into a buss to simplify the mixing process. ■ Once a satisfactory mix is achieved, studio sessions almost always benefit from the creation of an imaginary room for the mix to live in through *reverb*. Reverberation or convolution can be used to simulate the recorded drums being played in a room. With reverb, a little goes a long way; we do not mean for the drumset to be placed in a resonant imaginary cathedral. However, when the drumset is well isolated, it can deprive our ears of psychoacoustic cues that they are accustomed to processing. Thus, adding just a touch of reverb can take a dry drum set recording and add the magic dust of making it appear that it was recorded in a larger space.

FIGURE 28.6. Continued

digestible by a curriculum that spans grade ranges with younger students focusing on musical skills and foundational technical skills, middle level students working on recording and the refinement of those recordings, and high school students taking greater responsibility in the planning, set up, recording, and mastering of those recordings. Application of the skills of souncrafting to personally meaningful projects may encourage extended interest in recording and provide students foundational skills to take their interests into future levels of musical engagement.

NOTE

1. A property of sound waves is that their amplitude patterns over time can be *superposed*. In digital audio, this involves adding together their amplitude samples. From a musical perspective, such superposition may have a simple result, such as that we can super-pose a recording of a shakuhachi and a saxophone to yield a sound file in which we can hear both.

REFERENCES

Colquhoun, S. (2018). Popular music genres, music producers, and song creation in the general music classroom. *General Music Today*, 31(2), 17–20. http://dx.doi.org.ezaccess.libraries.psu.edu/10.1177/1048371317710311

Criswell, C., & Menasche, E. (2009). Redefining music technology: A rough guide to a universe of possibilities. *Teaching Music*, 16(5), 7–30. http://ezaccess.libraries.psu.edu/login?url=https://www-proquest-com.ezaccess.libraries.psu.edu/docview/61887057?accountid=13158

Hunter, M. A., Broad, T., & Jeanneret, N. (2018). SongMakers: An industry-led approach to arts partnerships in education. *Arts Education Policy Review*, 119(1), 1–11. http://dx.doi.org.ezaccess.libraries.psu.edu/10.1080/10632913.2016.1163308

Randles, C. (2012). Music teacher as writer and producer. *Journal of Aesthetic Education*, 46(3), 36–52. http://ezaccess.libraries.psu.edu/login?url=https://www-proquest-com.ezaccess.libraries.psu.edu/docview/1373090838?accountid=13158

Rayburn, R. A. (2012). *Eargle's the microphone book: From mono to stereo to surround-a guide to microphone design and application*. Taylor and Francis.

Roads, C., & Strawn, J. (1996). *The computer music tutorial*. MIT press.

Smith, J. O. (1985). Fundamentals of digital filter theory. *Computer Music Journal*, 9(3), 13.

Tobias, E. S. (2012). Hybrid spaces and hyphenated musicians: Secondary students' musical engagement in a songwriting and technology course. *Music Education Research*, 14(3), 329–346. http://dx.doi.org.ezaccess.libraries.psu.edu/10.1080/14613808.2012.685459

CHAPTER 29

....

CULTURE, CREATION, AND COMMUNITY IN HIP-HOP CLASSROOMS

....

LAMONT HOLDEN AND ADAM J. KRUSE

THIS chapter explores Hip Hop composition in school music settings. We provide an opening framing of the growing need for Hip Hop in music education and a brief intro-duction of ourselves as authors. Due to the range of possibilities with a musical practice whose foundations can be seen in stark contrast to the backgrounds and experiences of many music teachers, venturing into engagements with Hip Hop ought to be done thoughtfully and critically. For every intention a music educator may have regarding rel-evance, student engagement, or any sort of "cool factor," there exist the opportunities for cultural appropriation, stereotype perpetuation, and student alienation. To assist in the efforts of thoughtful and critical music educators interested in engaging with Hip Hop composition in their classroom, we offer cultural, musical, and pedagogical concerns for their consideration.

THE GROWING NEED FOR HIP HOP IN MUSIC EDUCATION

There are many reasons that music educators might have for wanting to include Hip Hop in their teaching. These might include more surface-level approaches like in-cluding Hip Hop songs in the repertoire of a school ensemble or analyzing the rhythm of a rap cadence using Western notation. Deeper explorations might seek to engage in culturally responsive pedagogy, create curricular offerings that reflect the reality of con-temporary musical practices and interests, or even disrupt school music's Eurocentric traditions and assumptions. There is undoubtedly growing interest around Hip Hop in the field of music education, and it is worth pausing to consider the various intentions and possibilities surrounding this interest.

Perhaps the first reason that some in music education are motivated to engage with Hip Hop culture is its undeniable popularity. Hip Hop is the most popular music in the United States (Nielsen Music, 2020) and has become a culturally dominant force in nearly every corner of the world. This may be reason enough for music educators to pay attention to Hip Hop, but its potential in school spaces may go well beyond broad student interest. From its origins in the South Bronx neighborhood of New York City in the 1970s to its global influence decades later, Hip Hop's foundations and essence have centered on Black American experiences and perspectives (Chang, 2005; Rose, 1994). That is not to say that Hip Hop is singularly Black, nor singularly American (Abe, 2009; Fraley, 2009; Love, 2016; Rodriquez, 2006), but American Blackness is and has been the centerpiece of Hip Hop culture. For music educators seeking greater representation of Black American musicians and aiming to acknowledge the indisputable global influence of Black American music, Hip Hop offers powerful examples of both.

In conjunction with who is speaking and creating in Hip Hop culture, what is being said—the message in the music—provides plentiful opportunities for exploring complex social, cultural, and political issues; understanding historical and contemporary oppression; and developing a critical consciousness. As the culture has moved and evolved for almost half a century, oppressed groups in countless contexts have adapted Hip Hop's spirit of resistance to tell their stories and speak back to their surroundings. Chaney (2018) described this as offering "resilience through resistance" (p. 81) and added that

> as social commentators, Hip Hop artists simultaneously acknowledge their historical and contemporary struggle and motivate members of a socially marginalized group to use effective coping strategies to face adversity . . . Hip Hop artists encourage their listeners to draw strength from themselves and one another, while at the same time striving to eradicate racism by advocating and taking action for social justice and equality. (p. 94)

Examining existing Hip Hop examples as well as creating original Hip Hop music can offer music students opportunities for greater understanding of the world, often with an emphasis on seeing and hearing society's most underprivileged. Hip Hop creation and performance might also provide avenues for student self-expression (Hein, 2020) and navigating social identities (Evans, 2020; Millares, 2019).

While the relationship cannot be assumed, Hip Hop pedagogies also have strong potential for connections with culturally relevant pedagogy (Ladson-Billings, 2018). Recent empirical studies published in music education venues have provided examples of Hip Hop music engagement yielding results in line with tenets of culturally relevant pedagogy such as success in traditional academic learning (Crooke & Almeida, 2017; Evans 2020), development of cross cultural understandings (Crooke & Almeida, 2017; Kruse, 2020a), and Hip Hop serving as a critical lens to see and respond to the world

(Evans, 2020; Hess 2018a). I (Adam) (Kruse, 2020b) also published a recent study considering the possibility of Hip Hop engagement contributing to decentering Whiteness in music education. In this study, I examined how three different White music teachers engaged with Hip Hop in their teaching. Results showed that commitments to considering race and decentering Whiteness were not at all inherent in engaging with Hip Hop. Treating Hip Hop as just another music genre appeared insufficient toward these ends and connecting more deeply with Hip Hop as a culture emerged as perhaps a necessary disposition for music educators interested in decentering Whiteness.

All of the positive potential of engaging with Hip Hop in music education notwithstanding, none of the elements of affirmative representation, resistance to oppression, cultural relevance, or racial justice can be assumed just because students sample a breakbeat, a Hip Hop classic spins on a turntable, or a Tupac poster hangs in the classroom. Just like Hip Hop itself, Hip Hop pedagogies are laced with contradictions and assumptions. As the authors of this chapter, we share an enthusiasm for Hip Hop and the power it brings to school music spaces. However, that enthusiasm is tempered by trepidation over opportunities to alienate young people; perpetuate racist, classist, and gendered stereotypes; and reduce a culture of resistance, ingenuity, and contextual meanings into discrete musical concepts and a standard method book style approach to creation and performance. This is the line we walk writing a chapter such as this. We hope that as a reader, you will consider the same balancing act in your application of the ideas herein.

Introducing the Authors

I (Adam) am a music education faculty member at the University of Illinois at Urbana-Champaign where I teach primarily music education students in areas of popular music and music technology. As a White, middle-class, cisgender, heterosexual male currently living without a disability, I attempt—though often fail spectacularly—to acknowledge and account for the incredible unearned privileges that accompany my employment status and identities. I have been teaching, conducting research, facilitating community partnerships, and engaging as a musician with Hip Hop for about a decade, but I come to this work as a cultural outsider. I grew up in an eclectic musical household, but Hip Hop was not a major influence for me growing up. In the 11 years I spent as a music education undergraduate and K–12 music teacher, Hip Hop was one of many musics I explored casually, but I did not begin to engage the culture seriously until life as a doctoral student and assistant professor in music education. Navigating into Hip Hop musicianship and scholarship has been eased by at least two factors: 1) I have the advantage of tremendous identity-related privilege in which I am often given the benefit of the doubt in terms of knowledge, experience, intent, access, and anything else that might create tension as I negotiate my space in the world. 2) Almost without exception, the artists, activists, educators, and scholars I have encountered in my personal and professional life who come from Hip Hop culture have been unrelentingly welcoming, curious, generous, patient and forgiving. Lamont Holden is a prime example as one of these most important and influential individuals in my life.

I (Lamont) am a School of Music faculty member at the University of Illinois at Urbana-Champaign and a professional music producer known as TheLetterLBeats. As a Black man, I feel I've lived a double life in that I've had to separate my love of rap, Black culture, and Hip Hop from all of my professional pursuits because they almost always required crossing over into White culture. This includes the field of education, where I excelled at reaching students and creating strong relationships with them because of my internalization of the culture, yet struggled to connect with my mostly White colleagues. I started making beats about four years before I finished my M.A. in education. After getting a literacy specialization certification, I started teaching myself how to make beats like I taught my students how to read. It made me a better producer but it also made me a better teacher of producing. During this journey I met Dr. Adam Kruse and participated in some of his classes. Somewhere along the line we developed the idea of "pedagogizing" Hip Hop music production and showing people how to interact authentically with the culture. I think this chapter is our most comprehensive step in that effort.

The content that follows is drawn largely from our work in classroom and community settings including years as K–12 educators, university instructors, summer camp directors, and workshop leaders. We do not pretend to offer a definitive account for all there is to know about Hip Hop and composition, but we have learned some valuable lessons through our teaching and our own musicianship that we expect might be useful to other music educators. Most of the remaining chapter is co-written, as we have shared writing duties and also because we have worked together long enough and closely enough that it is difficult sometimes for us to determine or remember where one of our ideas ended and the influence of the other begins. That said, the sections titled, "Inside Perspective" are written by Lamont. These sections are in Lamont's voice to prioritize a life lived more deeply connected to Hip Hop culture with less institutional musical influence. These are "gems" that Lamont drops and the best thing I (Adam) can do is let them shine.

CULTURAL CONSIDERATIONS

In this section of the chapter, we hope to offer considerations for music educators to understand and engage with Hip Hop as a culture. As mentioned earlier, treating Hip Hop as if it is just another musical genre, whose elements can be dropped into a music classroom without critical interrogation of the assumptions, beliefs, and values of that space, will limit Hip Hop's critical and transformative potential at best (Hein, 2020; Kruse, 2020b; Tobias, 2014). At worst, this type of approach can reify existing power structures, promote cultural appropriation, and perpetuate stereotypes. Understanding Hip Hop as a culture centers Hip Hop's Black American roots while engaging with cultural values that run deeper than any particular musical element.

Engaging with Hip Hop culture prioritizes its complex socio-political factors. That means that exploring Hip Hop's racial politics is not optional or extra (Hein, 2020; Hess, 2018b). The same is true for issues surrounding gender (Tobias, 2014), or any other seemingly political matter. Evans (2020) argued that "hip hop cultural practices are best taught when culture is introduced through a political lens that does not censor critiques of dominant power structures influencing the students' everyday lives" (p. 9). A cultural approach to Hip Hop in music education will place socio-political concepts as central—not ancillary—to music creation, performance, analysis, or appreciation.

Understanding Hip Hop as a culture also acknowledges that Hip Hop music is not a monolith. Hip Hop is teeming with endless subgenres, geographic variations, and arbitrary boundaries between traditions that have been blended, bent, and broken. Any music educator hoping to contain Hip Hop into a list of musical characteristics, a canon of repertoire, or a pantheon of musicians is truly facing a fool's errand. We believe that music educators will be much better served by understanding and embracing Hip Hop as culture with "a distinct worldview with related sensibilities and epistemologies" (Petchauer, 2011, p. 1412). Considering Hip Hop in this deeper, and more meaningful way may very well contribute to music educators not just doing Hip Hop, but being Hip Hop (Ladson-Billings, 2015; Kruse, 2016).

Inside Perspective (from Lamont)

From the perspective of a person who has lived and sought to engage themselves in authentic Hip Hop experiences since the age of five, any educator seeking to teach in this space must acknowledge lived experiences. Developing essential questions around understanding Hip Hop culture and one's relationship to the culture will help educators with this acknowledgment. Educators love to ask and answer essential questions. It's an addictive practice because it's a tool that constantly challenges you to understand everything around you. Some suggested questions:

- *Am I a cultural native or a cultural immigrant?* Asking this simple question can guide you in so many ways that have great implications regardless of context.
- *What is attracting me to this culture?* This helps you ground your practice in something that you have love and respect for. If you understand what is attracting you to the music and culture, that becomes sacred. When something is sacred to us, we treat it as such.
- *Whether a native or immigrant of the culture, am I upholding its principles?* Do you even understand what the principles of the culture are?
- *What are the values and tenets of this culture that can be understood across other cultures?* For example, remixing is building something new out of something old. Where else does this practice exist? How do other cultural practices make space

for all perspectives—big, small, popular, unpopular—while still prioritizing certain ideas and voices that keep the culture cohesive? Competition is important in Hip Hop, but while "winning" and "losing" are sometimes concrete, they are often abstract concepts. What role does competition play in artistic development in other cultures? What are the cultural experiences and values you hold, and how do they align or conflict with those in Hip Hop?

What I really love about these questions and asking them continually as the context changes—particularly important in Hip Hop because it often changes faster than other cultures—is that they deal with all types of potentially problematic issues. They reduce the opportunity to offend or encroach and leave room for the inclusion of all. Hopefully everyone in music education feels welcome to explore Hip Hop, but everyone also feels a sense of responsibility to check themselves, acknowledge their positions, and appreciate the lived experiences of those in the culture.

Hip Hop Cultural Values

We cannot possibly provide an exhaustive description of all of Hip Hop's cultural values, but some worth considering for music educators, include realness, originality, limitless influence, truth-telling, and freshness. Our descriptions of these concepts are informed by both academic and "real world" influences, and our understandings are ever evolving. Therefore, we encourage dedicated music educators to take the following as starting points for exploration, rather than codified definitions.

Realness

There is perhaps no more important, no more contested, and no more misunderstood concept in Hip Hop culture than realness (Kruse, 2018a). If music educators conceive of realness as a fixed definition (perhaps limited by demographic identities), they may think there is no way for some teachers and students to meaningfully engage with Hip Hop. As we have argued previously, acknowledging Hip Hop's foundations and our relationships to the culture is vital. However, this presents a conundrum for a field that is disproportionately White and female (Elpus, 2015), and presumably middle-class. To say that only Black individuals from the South Bronx who perform a particular type of "hard" heterosexual masculinity can participate in Hip Hop culture is simply inaccurate but glossing over the demographic foundations of the culture opens some incredibly problematic cans of worms. What then are music educators to do about realness?

Instead of seeing realness as a condition that one has or does not have, consider realness as McLeod (2012) suggested, as a "floating signifier" that moves and changes over time and in various spaces. This is not to eschew the importance of demographic identities, but rather to highlight the importance of realness as sincerity, honesty, and transparency. Speaking to and about one's local context and lived experiences, acknowledging one's identities and privilege, and drawing inspiration from personally meaningful cultural touchstones are strategies of invoking realness in Hip Hop in which all music educators and students can participate. Employing affected Black American vernacular and mannerisms, evoking stereotypical imagery of a Black urban life that is not yours, and otherwise wearing Hip Hop as a costume would be egregious examples of being insincere, dishonest, and ultimately fake. For some in music education, walking this line might be challenging, but it is perhaps the most important consideration we face.

Originality

Whether we refer to sampling already existing music for original compositions, reimagining current spaces as performance and presentation venues, rethinking music curricula to suit the needs of a new classroom context, or any form of repurposing extant material into new works, the notion that Hip Hop is built on practices of "taking things and transforming things" (Petchauer, 2012, p. 77) rings true for us. Hip Hop culture was born in spaces of limited material resources, and ingenuity in the face of these limitations is a vital part of its history (Chang, 2005). Many music educators in public school settings can likely identify with the importance of working with what you have, but this creative resourcefulness in Hip Hop goes beyond making due in less-than-ideal situations. Hip Hop culture has an imperative that artists each develop an original style that simultaneously honors predecessors while paving new paths of innovative work.

Exploring the style and identity development of Hip Hop artists, Millares (2019) offered that "the creative processes through which they [Hip Hop artists] learn and practice their art forms encourage an originality rooted in what each person brings to their point of entry into, and to their interactions with, hip-hop culture" (p. 437). Millares also suggested that "Those who wish to express artistically through Hip-hop must take the bits of technique, knowledge and advice they have gathered and put it all together in a way that no one else has" (p. 442). These positions on originality invite everyone to the Hip Hop table regardless of their background, but also lay forth an expectation to innovate. Music educators and their students can answer these calls by embracing their own influences—Hip Hop or otherwise—and generating original material outside the limitations of any perceived mold. On this point, we concur with Hein (2020), who argued that "When we teach hip-hop, let us make it our goal to use it as a tool for fostering authentic student self- expression" (p. 23).

Limitless Influence

Holding hands with the values of realness and originality, Hip Hop draws on and provides limitless influences. In contrast to some music education traditions that are built on the preservation of styles and practices, Hip Hop culture encourages continuously drawing influence from new sources. Whether it is the venerated DJing practice of "crate digging" for unheard musical examples or the celebrated obscurity and obfuscation of rare samples in beat production, Hip Hop values novel ideas. The culture's originators drew influence from material from disco, funk, soul, and R&B—and current artists still do the same—but the world of inspirational and influential material is now much wider for Hip Hop artists. At this point, there is no tradition too far removed, or genre boundary too solid, that Hip Hop artists cannot traverse (Schloss, 2014). Likewise, the influence of Hip Hop on the rest of popular culture is as widespread as any other contemporary tradition. All of this provides an endless field of exploration and discovery for music educators and their students. There is a universe of educational possibilities involved in tracing the lines of influence to and from Hip Hop culture through listening and analysis, as well as drawing new lines through original creation and performance.

Truth-Telling

As mentioned earlier, Hip Hop's foundations in resistance to oppression are incredibly important. If nothing else, Hip Hop tells the truth. This truth is not always easy to hear from privileged or uninformed points of view. However, these truths matter and often privilege marginalized voices (Alim, 2007). It is imperative for music educators to understand this if they have any hope of exploring meanings in existing examples from Hip Hop culture. There is an understandable and sometimes practical discomfort from many music educators we have encountered in workshop and conference spaces where individuals raise concerns over what they perceive as inappropriate language or themes in Hip Hop music. We cannot provide a one-size-fits-all solution for music educators to deal with the language in Hip Hop music, but we do hope that teachers will recognize at least these two points:

1. The perception of appropriateness is context-dependent and always a reflection of who holds power in a space. It is worth considering and reconsidering why certain language is deemed inappropriate, who is making that decision, and who any attempt to censor language is serving.
2. Hip Hop tells hard truths, often from marginalized perspectives. If Hip Hop's penchant for truth telling makes us uncomfortable, are we willing to critically interrogate why? What does this discomfort say about us and our experiences compared to those we encounter in Hip Hop? Who might benefit from a realistic dialogue about the truths told in Hip Hop, and who benefits from avoiding these topics?

Freshness

Part of why Hip Hop culture has remained popular and relevant for so long is that the culture is constantly shifting and changing. This value of freshness functions almost as the outcome of the previous values we have discussed. If artists are asked to reflect their own experiences and contexts, if they are expected to provide original and innovative contributions, if they can draw influence from anywhere and everywhere, and if they consistently tell challenging truths, how can Hip Hop not stay compelling and fresh? It is arguably the adaptation—and *not* the adoption—of Hip Hop around the world that has led to the culture's rapid evolution and persistent popularity. Artists everywhere are invited to take part in the culture, but they are expected to constantly bring something new to the table.

The simultaneously invigorating and overwhelming result of this rapid growth and change is that music educators will never catch up nor keep up with all there is to know in Hip Hop. Luckily, the most important arbiters of what is fresh in Hip Hop are young people. Music educators might attend professional development opportunities and helpful workshops (we might even be leading them ourselves), but it is their own students who can likely teach them what is most important to know about what is fresh in Hip Hop right now. Centering youth knowledge should be high on music educators' priority lists along with the reminder that we have both had to tell each other on countless occasions: Their Hip Hop is not your Hip Hop. Even if a music educator grew up as a Hip Hop musician, is a Hip Hop head from way back, or (claims to have) attended Kool Herc's Back to School Jam at 1520 Sedgwick Ave. in 1973, the Hip Hop that *students* enjoy will inevitably be different and should remain central in music curricula.

MUSICAL CONSIDERATIONS

Hip Hop music has important connections to Afrodiasporic traditions (Rose, 1994; Schloss, 2014) and therefore operates by different rules and with different values than those instilled in many music educators. For example, a much greater emphasis is placed on elements such as groove, feeling, flow, and rupture in Hip Hop as opposed to harmonic and melodic progressions that move away from and return to tonic. Even compared to many other practices common in other forms of popular music, Hip Hop does not always play by the same rules. In this chapter, we will introduce some of the fundamental elements of both instrumental backing tracks and lyric writing—or more colloquially, beats and rhymes. We do not include DJing and/or turntablism as part of these considerations. This incredibly valuable practice has many connections to beat production, but has so many of its own idiosyncrasies and variations that we considered this beyond the scope of the current chapter and worthy of its own chapters and articles separately.

Inside Perspective (from Lamont)

Hip Hop is about finding that place that feels good and then making a home there and then only leaving that place when the new place we are going to feels like home or we can dress it up to make it feel like home and there is a clear path back home. A great example of this is producer Just Blaze who is as Hip Hop as it gets but has told stories of a suburban upbringing. Now a multimillionaire, he regularly shows his home decor that feels like a museum of Hip Hop culture. No matter how big, small, inexpensive or expensive a home is, it can still be Hip Hop. So it stands that when considering the music itself, how it's listened to, how and when it's played and how it's made, everyone participating is trying to make it home. That's a double meaning.

One of Hip Hop's primary musical elements is the concept of a loop. The history of DJs looping drum breaks have been described much better elsewhere (Chang, 2005), but the implications of looping are ingrained in other Hip Hop compositional tools as well. For example, every digital audio workstation (DAW) has a loop function. This speaks to home because a loop always comes back to where it started. Because of that, the end and the beginning of the loop have to work in a relationship together. As a beat maker, I always start with the "home" of a song, which is the hook. When composing an intro, pre-hook or bridge, all of those parts are then derived from the hook. Every other section of the beat will contain some elements of the hook and will therefore loop as well. Everything cycles back on itself. Everything feels like home.

Sonically, Hip Hop is about textures, rhythms, pitches, and frequencies. What gets included or excluded in the various sections of a song (as just mentioned regarding looping) creates different textures, which provides vitality and difference and keeps the listener interested. The rhythm of the instrumental generally dictates how the words will be delivered by an emcee. But how the words get delivered depends on the interpretation of the person delivering them. There is no "correct" rapping cadence for a beat. Instead, every rhythm speaks to different people differently. As well, moods, seasons, lighting, and substances can all affect how the person hears and feels the rhythm. For that matter, the same goes for people who create the rhythm. The pitches—or lack thereof—generally dictate the moods that are delivered and received. For example, Lil Wayne's "Dark Side of the Moon" makes me cry because the chords are the same chords they played at my grandmother's Baptist church during the time when everyone confessed their sins and went to get baptized. Rhythms and pitches are translated as a series of frequencies for engineers of the music. Learning to adjust frequencies in a DAW with different equalizers, filters, and effects is just as important a part of Hip Hop composition as creating rhythms or pitches. These audio engineering skills are definitely an essential part of the composition process.

With all of this in mind, it's important for teachers to understand the following basic DAW functions in order to help their students. This is not necessarily an exhaustive list, but gives an idea of some of the necessary tools for Hip Hop composition in a DAW. Whatever software teachers and students might be using, there are likely plentiful online tutorials explaining these tools in detail:

- Preferences menu: Sound input/output, connections for audio interfaces and MIDI controllers
- Setting project tempo and identifying bar numbers
- Set and toggle loop/cycle feature
- Stop, play, record
- Arming tracks for recording and monitoring
- Volume, solo, mute, and pan for each track
- Create/open VST/AU/Rack *instrument* device
- Create/open VST/AU/Rack *effect* device
- MIDI entry and editing on the piano roll, including quantization and velocity

- Audio editing with waveforms, including splitting, cutting, copying, and pasting regions
- Automation
- Basic mixing plugins and effects like compression, reverb, and equalization
- Exporting a DAW project as a single audio file

Understanding Beats

Given the scope of this chapter, we can provide some basic considerations around elements of Hip Hop beat production that should be useful for music educators. I (Adam) have attempted to translate here what I have come to understand (through working with Lamont and others over the years) into language that I believe most music educators would know. Some details of these concepts will inevitably be lost in translation, but these should at least provide a starting ground for further exploration. I have included three basic areas, which I present in the order of a common compositional approach: 1) Sound Selection: Balancing Innovation and Convention, 2) Feel: Constructing a Loop, and 3) Sequence: Developing Form and Structure.

Sound Selection: Balancing Innovation and Convention

What many music educators might call "timbre" is easily one of the primary initial concerns of a Hip Hop producer. Beat makers spend a lot of time considering—and reconsidering—the qualities and details of the sounds that they use. In fact, there is an entire cottage industry where folks create "sound packs" that contain particular instrument sounds worth purchasing. While most DAWs come with a set of stock virtual instrument sounds, many producers will either avoid the stock sounds altogether or at the very least invest time editing the stock sounds in order to make them unique. Some producers will also create custom instruments out of audio samples. These might be originally recorded sounds (from conventional instruments or "found sounds"), or they might be short sounds sampled from already existing recordings. Sounds are often then turned into instruments by "mapping" them across a keyboard or drum machine. Further pitch shifting and other editing gives a producer seemingly endless possibilities to create bespoke instruments for each of their compositions.

I (Adam) recall some of my earliest hours in amateur Hip Hop studios being amazed at the amount of time producers put into browsing through folders of audio files searching for the exact right hi-hat sound, and then being further amazed as the selected sound often went under further scrutiny and evolution with the application of software plugins and effects. While producers will often spend a great deal of time fine tuning instrument sounds and seeking their own signature sound, they are also in constant dialogue with stylistic conventions. For example, if a producer is making a trap beat, there are certain 808s and hi-hat sounds that are arguably more "correct" than others. Overall, producers are often in a balancing act of strategic moves to both fit into and reject aesthetic trends. Whether trying to replicate an example or achieve an original sound, the sound selection process is incredibly important and involves high levels of listening and audio engineering skills.

Feel: Constructing a Loop

As producers develop their sounds, they often begin creating a beat by focusing on stacking instrument voices in a loop (often four or eight bars). The starting voice could be almost anything. Some producers always start with drums, others may start with samples, and others may vary how they begin on each new project. Regardless, the initial aim for many is to develop a loop that will serve as the main material for the instrumental. Loops might be premade and available within a DAW, or producers might compose them out of samples, software instruments, or original recordings. If premade or samples, producers often spend time "chopping" the samples into pieces and rearranging them, editing them with effects, pitch shifting them, changing their tempo, reversing them, or any other manner of customization.

With so many different personal approaches and so many musical traditions continually blended into contemporary beat production, it is impossible to describe a singular musical set of values during the loop construction process. However, it is somewhat safe to say that feel is an incredibly common priority. The concept of feel overlaps with what music educators would probably think of as rhythm, but the premium on how the rhythm *feels* cannot be overstated. The producer is often chasing a particular feel, and the reaction that the music elicits in the body during this process is paramount. It's not just that the music makes your head bob, but the way in which the head bobs that matters. Watching producers and onlookers in a studio space will reveal a complex language of shoulder movements, facial expressions, head movements, and more. As the loop develops into patterns that groove, it then becomes important to establish moments of rupture (Rose, 1994). These are interruptions to the groove of the pattern in the loop. Ruptures may occur via a dropped or added instrument, an added or removed beat, or any other element that breaks the flow and expectation of the established loop. They may occur regularly as part of the main loop, or they may happen less frequently in transitions between sections in the larger form, at halfway points during a long verse section, or in any unexpected moment.

Sequence: Developing Form and Structure

Like most Hip Hop composition, there are no real rules regarding form and structure, but there are some typical conventions. These are worth considering in terms of adhering to or rejecting them depending on a producer's goals. For example, it is common that verse sections of Hip Hop songs are 16 measures long and hooks are eight measures, but one would not be hard pressed to find exceptions to that formula. For many, after an initial loop is created, the producer will turn to sequencing or arranging the project into sections (e.g., intro, verse, hook). This is what most music educators would think of as the compositional element of form. Because the main loop (which often becomes the hook) typically shares so much material with other sections, it is the element that many music educators would call texture that usually distinguishes between sections in the form. The introduction of a beat may have only one or two of the voices from the originally composed loop, the verse sections typically have a thinner texture (often with a change in texture halfway through), and the hook typically has the thickest texture. Of course, there are endless variations and exceptions, but these are common practices in terms of form and structure. There are plenty of beats with different harmonic progressions and/or different material entirely in sections, some beats have pre-hooks, some have bridges, and some use complex transitions while others are the same eight bars looped for three minutes.

Understanding Rhymes

Someone writing lyrics for vocal performance in Hip Hop might consider themselves a lyricist, rapper, emcee, and/or multiple other labels. We will use these terms interchangeably for the purpose of this chapter, but for some, there are important distinctions between them and definitions are not entirely consistent across the culture. Regardless, an emcee might write lyrics without an instrumental and find a beat later, or they may write to an already chosen beat. They might have composed the beat themselves, they might have purchased or leased it from a producer, or they might have found a free beat available online. For music educators, it is worth knowing that not all producers rap, and not all rappers make beats. The possibility for students choosing roles in a music classroom setting might be worth considering.

Just like our previous section on beats, our description of the lyrical elements of Hip Hop will be necessarily reductionist. The art form is complex, it is full of individual approaches and exceptions to rules, and it continues to rapidly evolve faster than we can even write this chapter. What we offer next is simply a set of concepts that will hopefully help music educators better understand rapping and lyrical content in Hip Hop.

Rap Flow

As lyricists establish personal styles as artists, the development of a rap flow is key. We describe flow as consisting of three elements: rhyme, rhythm, and delivery. In terms of rhyming, there are many different types of rhymes, including perfect rhymes, near rhymes, slant rhymes, forced rhymes, semi-rhymes, multi syllable rhymes, and more. It is common for an emcee to employ many types of rhymes throughout a verse or song. The more creative the rhyming is, the larger the available vocabulary becomes for the songwriter. Just as important as the types of rhymes, the location of these rhymes also makes a big difference in a rapper's flow. Many beginners may focus on end rhymes (where the last syllable of one-line rhymes with another), complex combinations of internal rhymes, split rhymes that run over the bar, or holorhyme that rhymes every syllable of one line with every syllable of another provides a world of possibilities for lyricists.

In addition to the types and locations of rhymes, flow is also affected by the rhythmic cadence a rapper uses. This is largely informed by their particular feeling of subdivision on a given instrumental. For example, given the same instrumental, different rappers might rap 16th note patterns, eighth note patterns, or triplet patterns. Some rappers might do all three in the same verse. The rhythmic element of rap flow will also be affected by an emcee's relationship to the beat—whether they rap on the beat, rush ahead, or drag behind. Finally, a rapper's delivery is the last ingredient of their flow and again can include endless variation and opportunities for individuality. When we say delivery, we refer to the tone, dialect, phrasing, pronunciation of words, and other verbal characteristics that make an artist's voice distinct. Ultimately, it is the combination of an emcee's approach to rhyming, their rhythmic cadence, and their particular vocal delivery that constitutes their individual rap flow.

Lyrical Content

While rap flow refers to *how* an artist delivers their lyrics, *what* they are saying—their lyrical content—is arguably even more important. For music educators, we suggest considering three areas to better understand how lyrical content works in Hip Hop: 1. Employing metaphors, wordplay, and intertextual references; 2. Responding to context; and 3. Speaking truth to power. Many Hip Hop scholars refer to Gates's (2014) description of the African American practice of signifyin(g) when speaking about the layers of meaning found in Hip Hop lyrics. It is indeed common for rappers to use complex metaphors and creative wordplay to provide multiple meanings in their lyrics. For example, when Jay-Z raps that he "ain't one of these house niggas you bought" on Meek Mill's "What's Free" track, he is referring to President Donald Trump appointing African American Ben Carson as the US Secretary of Housing and Urban Development. The use of "house nigga" has multiple meanings as both an insult to Carson and his proximity and loyalty to Trump and a reference to the government position to which Carson was appointed. From Jay-Z's perspective, Ben Carson is a "house nigga" on multiple levels.

This practice of signifyin(g), plus the use of intertextual references (Söderman & Folkestad, 2004)—including making reference to other songs, movies, video games, and other media—often rewards listeners for their understanding or confounds listeners who do not grasp the reference or meaning. In this way, lyrical content can position listeners as insiders or outsiders. Music educators should expect to be on the outside fairly often. Engaging in discussions with students and making use of resources like Genius (http://www.genius.com) should help with unpacking the layers of meanings in existing lyrics, and better understanding how rappers employ these practices might inspire students to engage in more complex and meaningful lyric-writing themselves.

Connected to our previous section about the cultural considerations of engaging with Hip Hop, music educators should also consider the importance of lyricists responding to their own contexts. As we have described earlier, Hip Hop artists are expected to be genuine, innovate, and develop their own style. The same is true regarding their lyrical content. Part of being genuine means speaking to your own life experiences and representing your own neighborhood. While students may take inspiration from a Compton rapper, their own lyrical compositions should speak to issues in their own surroundings. This practice has shown powerful possibilities for young people in recent research studies (Evans, 2020; Hess, 2018a). Finally, it is always worth remembering Hip Hop's imperative to speak truth to power. As Hodge (2018) argued, "Hip Hop was, and still is, a way to construct thought, question authority and express anger, frustration, hate, revolutionary world-views and rebellious spirits" (p. 15). Keeping this ethic in mind during lyric writing in classroom activities is likely key to unlocking some of the more transformative possibilities of Hip Hop in music education.

Pedagogical Considerations

Alongside the cultural and musical considerations we have provided for music educators, we have some pedagogical approaches that might also assist teachers and students engaging Hip Hop in the classroom. Research studies exploring how Hip Hop musicians learn have suggested that Hip Hop musicians learning experiences do not entirely mirror those of the guitar-based rock musicians whose experiences have dominated popular music education research in recent decades (Kruse, 2018b; Martignetti & Brewster, 2020; Millares, 2019; Snell & Söderman, 2014). Therefore, pedagogical approaches informed by Hip Hop reflect some of these differences (e.g., more solitary work, more focus on original creation as opposed to listening and copying).

Inside Perspective (from Lamont)

I feel like Hip Hop is the ultimate application of project based learning and scientific process internalized. Learning by doing is in the DNA of Hip Hop's expression as art and technique. In my experience teaching new beat makers of all ages, the younger the learner, the more likely they are to just want to start doing the thing. I set up MIDI controllers with interesting sounds that can be automatically triggered without much thought to recording, mixing, or sequencing. Creating rhythmic patterns by playing a MIDI controller is an easy entry point into the craft. It's weird how graduate students are afraid to just try things and want to know so many details before they start, but I get it. Sixth graders, for example, will just come in and start. If they want to record something, they let me know and I show them how. If they want something to sound better—they really want it mixed but they don't know that yet, so we won't hinder their zone of proximal development with that—I show them the easiest and fastest way to do it.

My style of scaffolding provides corridors taking students deeper into the craft. Hopefully, it's done without encumbering students with information that takes up too much mental bandwidth and dims their curiosity. What educators might think of as a "learning curve" is often represented in the pedagogy of beat-making as a gap between a student's current skill level and their artistic tastes. My responsibility as an educator is to help bridge that gap. There is almost always some song, artist, or producer that an aspiring beat maker has heard who inspired them to start or whose sonic aesthetic they want to emulate. In the very beginning, that represents a student's target sound. This target will define their entry point and early trajectory. For example, if a student likes Dua Lipa's music, their point of entry into beat-making might be a deconstruction and classification of the elements and techniques used in Dua Lipa's records. The student's own creative work might then center around the application of similar elements and techniques.

Understanding your students' personalities, passions, and preferences is best practice. Best practice in creating Hip Hop, R&B, and other Black musical art forms is groups of people perfecting and executing roles that they're passionate about. Not every student wants to rap or sing, some want to make beats or write. Some want to engineer. Part of your job in the classroom in teaching this music and art form is to help students discover what roles may fit them best. The deeper you're willing to take your class into the culture, the more roles will become available to your students. Don't focus only on creating and performing practices, but also make time for detailed listening. As students grow as creators, they will feel like they have a new set of ears as they listen to their favorite songs with an emerging new skill set. Just like the importance of the loop in Hip Hop composition, there is a skill development loop between listening and creating. Composing will lead to improved listening, and improved listening will lead back to improved composing.

Approaches to Facilitating Hip Hop Creation

The following are suggestions, not any kind of prescribed method for teaching Hip Hop. Just like Hip Hop artists are responsible for taking inspiration and then innovating their own style, Hip Hop educators might adapt ideas from other teachers to their own context. In this way, we hope to see teaching approaches in Hip Hop that look different in different places and continually evolve and adapt—just like Hip Hop art forms do.

Acknowledging Positions

It is imperative for educators and students to acknowledge and critically question their relationship to Hip Hop culture. Using the previous information in this chapter—particularly the essential questions Lamont posed—might serve as a starting place for this work, but it should be a continuous activity. Ultimately, if music educators want to realize any of the transformational potential of engaging with Hip Hop culture, everyone involved should be thinking about their motivations, their backgrounds, and their actions. Folks who are distant from the culture, inexperienced, or uninformed are still welcome to participate, but they should be aware of the potential baggage they carry. Even those who feel well-versed may have their own baggage. Students and teachers alike may hold stereotypical views based in racism and classism or assumptions about musical values steeped in Eurocentrism. Regardless of intention, they may perform acts perceived as appropriative or culturally insensitive. In addition to understanding Hip

Hop at a culture level to inform this reflective dispositional work, we also strongly encourage engaging with Hip Hop artists in your community as consultants, guest artists, and collaborators. Their insights and skills will likely be invaluable—particularly for music educators with less experience in Hip Hop.

Building Community

At the summer youth Hip Hop Camp that we co-direct at the University of Illinois, we spend our first afternoon with the artist instructors and the youth campers getting to know one another, building trust, and developing a sense of community. That work continues all week for us and has shown to be a vital ingredient for the creative work that happens. We have two expectations for all campers: 1) Everyone has to be themselves entirely and unapologetically, and 2) Everyone is everyone else's number one fan. We encourage—and model—geeking out about niche interests, embracing idiosyncrasies, and anything else that might set artists apart as individuals. Sometimes people bond over shared interests, but especially when they don't, we celebrate these differences and honor the unique perspectives that come forth.

We also expect—and model—emphatic support of any creative work that campers share. Everyone present has an active role as audience member for one another and we practice showing and giving support to one another. There is ultimately more pressure on the listeners than the performers when we repeatedly share during the week. By the time we have our public performance at the end of this week, campers and instructors alike know one another's creations and sing and dance along as if they are attending a show by their favorite artist on an international tour. In turn, this demonstrates expected audience behavior for the rest of the performance attendees and the community vibe in the venue is simply electric. These expectations—of unapologetically being yourself and giving exuberant support to your peers—are prerequisites for our creative work. We often put as much or more effort into the community vibe with our campers as we do their musical creations and performances because we trust that youth are brilliant and given a supportive environment, they will shine.

Listening and Creating

As Lamont mentioned above, listening, and creating work together reciprocally is central to Hip Hop composition. There is a rich history in Hip Hop of drawing inspiration from obscure sources in order to bring something new to the party. Classroom work might embrace this concept. Instead of listening with the sole goal of copying, perhaps music educators and their students might learn to listen for ideas that inform creation. Understanding the loop of creating and listening might encourage deeper appreciation and skill-building while exploring endless source material for inspiration. In this way, Hip Hop creative activity in a classroom setting need not be limited to only engaging with Hip Hop recordings. Students might sample or remix existing material from anywhere, they might blend seemingly disparate musical styles into new hybrids, or they might create a brand-new aesthetic that reflects their own interests and experiences. At the end of the day, an innovative creation that flips source material into something contextually meaningful is perhaps more culturally Hip Hop than students performing a note-for-note cover of a Missy Elliott song.

Considering Representation

Participation in Hip Hop culture is rich and always growing in diversity. Examples of songs, the inclusion of guest artists, the use of instructional videos, or any other moments of representation in a music classroom should reflect this diversity. Hip Hop production—like many corners of fields related to music technology—is incredibly male-dominated. Seeing examples of female and gender diverse producers is important for everyone. It is also incredibly important to honor and include the Black American roots of Hip Hop, and its current Black American practitioners as well. However, considering representation from other angles is also incredibly meaningful for students to see themselves and others in Hip Hop culture. YouTube alone gives teachers and students access to examples of Hip Hop in countless languages, from artists of any age, from artists with disabilities, from a universe of gender expressions, and from seemingly any other perspective imaginable. Exploring how a world of individuals have connected to the culture while making a style all their own could help in developing an appreciation of Hip Hop's evolution as well as inspiring original student creation. Of course, not every example in the world will be respectful and cognizant of Hip Hop's foundations, its indelible mark of Black genius, or its connection to oppression and resilience, but these moments may also provide important opportunities for classroom discussion and critique.

Prioritizing Access and Scaffolding Success

When considering technologies to employ in a Hip Hop classroom, we recommend prioritizing those that will be most accessible and easy to use for students. This might even mean eschewing digital technologies altogether when necessary. Promoting success, instilling confidence, and building trust are far more important than preparing students for a potential career in the music industry. So many of the relevant DAW skills transfer between the cheapest and the most expensive software, that we suggest starting students on software they can also access at home. After all, engaging Hip Hop in music education should break down traditional barriers to participation, not create new ones. Also, focusing on tools that get students to making music and expressing themselves artistically right away should take a front seat compared to software with steep learning curves that require hours of experience and endless menus and settings.

In general, the practice of scaffolding smaller and simpler experiences into larger ones is worthwhile. As students grow in experience and curiosity, they may need to move to new, more powerful programs. Start with composing a four-measure loop, and then move to creating an entire beat. Write two lines that rhyme and celebrate those before trying to write an entire original song. Improvise single rhyming words before trying to freestyle an entire 16-measure verse. Whether we are teaching Hip Hop in a one-hour workshop or a semester-long course, with elementary students or adults, we generally follow these processes: Start small, then grow. Share often, celebrate enthusiastically.

The confidence that comes from these processes fuels a lot of artistic development in ways that avoid prescription or too much direction.

Supporting Youth Music

In order to keep Hip Hop pedagogies in music classrooms sustainable and fresh for the future, we highly recommend that music educators avoid dictating taste or limiting student choices. Acknowledge that Hip Hop takes inspiration from virtually everywhere and that innovation and change are expected in the culture. Even if the music educator has a favorite artist or style, it is likely not always going to match the taste of young people. Again, their Hip Hop is not your Hip Hop. Exploring Hip Hop of past eras can be educational but limiting Hip Hop to a music appreciation course centered on someone's perception of the "greats" will be missing out on so much. We encourage music educators to keep an open mind and even though they may not love every new trend, they might embrace and appreciate the constant shift in aesthetics and a priority for artists innovating new styles.

Dismissing youth's preferences for some bygone days of when people made "real" Hip Hop is arguably no better or different than ignoring popular music in favor of centuries' old orchestral music from Europe. By focusing on youth culture and encouraging students to pursue their own styles, music educators might avoid limiting Hip Hop into a schoolified institutional version that few young people will actually want to experience. Thinking back to our summer Hip Hop Camp, one of the young campers whose work has been most inspirational, engaging, and popular has sounded very little like what most would consider Hip Hop. Describing this camper's style is actually really difficult as it blends elements of indie rock, singer-songwriter vibes, pop anthems, rapping, string instruments, and general eclecticism into something entirely new. In this way, we often argue that this camper is just as Hip Hop in their core as some of the other folks who can fine tune an 808 or spit an amazing freestyle. We see no productive purpose in limiting their choices or dictating a style when they are clearly capable of developing their own.

CONCLUSION

We hope that by considering these cultural, musical, and pedagogical elements music educators are able to engage thoughtfully with Hip Hop. As opposed to following any of what we've said as a form of ultimate truth, we encourage readers to use this chapter as a launch point for further exploration and innovation. Ideally, teachers might use this chapter like an old record worth sampling. By taking bits and pieces of what is here and reimagining it for their own context in order to develop new approaches and practices, music educators would be tapped into some of the more important cultural values of Hip Hop. Remaining aware of positionality and privilege throughout and keeping the culture's foundations of resistance central will hopefully help teachers realize more of Hip Hop's liberatory and transformational possibilities in music education.

REFERENCES

Abe, D. (2009). Hip-hop and the academic canon. *Education, Citizenship and Social Justice,* 4(3), 263–272. https://doi.org/10.1177/1746197909340872

Alim, S. H. (2007). Critical hip-hop language pedagogies: Combat, consciousness, and the cultural politics of communication. *Journal of Language, Identity, and Education,* 6(2), 161–176. https://doi.org/10.1080/15348450701341378

Chaney, C. (2018). "You can never kill me": Racism and resilience in Hip Hop. *Journal of Popular Music Education,* 2(1), 81–100. https://doi.org/10.1386/jpme.2.1-2.81_1

Chang, J. (2005). *Can't stop, won't stop: A history of the hip-hop generation.* Picador.

Crooke, A. H. D., & Almeida, C. M. (2017). "It's good to know something real and all that": Exploring the benefits of a school-based Hip Hop program. *Australian Journal of Music Education,* 50(1), 13–28. https://search.informit.com.au/documentSummary;dn= 967435258266803;res=IELHSS;subject=media

Elpus, K. (2015). Music teacher licensure candidates in the United States: A demographic profile and analysis of licensure examination scores. *Journal of Research in Music Education,* 63(3), 314–335. https://doi.org/10.1177/0022429415602470

Evans, J. (2020). Connecting Black youth to critical media literacy through hip hop making in the music classroom. *Journal of Popular Music Education,* 4(3), 277–293. https://doi.org/ 10.1386/jpme_00020_1

Fraley, T. (2009). I got a natural skill . . . : Hip-hop, authenticity, and whiteness. *Howard Journal of Communications,* 20(1), 37–54. https://doi.org/10.1080/10646170802664979

Gates, H. L. (2014). *The signifying monkey: A theory of African American literary criticism* (2nd ed.). Oxford University Press.

Hein, E. (2020). Chris Thile, Kendrick Lamar, and the problem of the white rap cover. *Visions of Research in Music Education,* 35, 1–27. http://www-usr.rider.edu/~vrme/v35n1/visions/ Hein_Chris%20Thile,%20Kendrick%20Lamar,%20and%20the%20problem%20of%20 the%20white%20rap%20cover.pdf

Hess, J. (2018a). Detroit youth speak back: Rewriting deficit perspectives through songwriting. *Bulletin of the Council for Research in Music Education,* 216, 7–30. https://doi.org/10.5406/ bulcouresmusedu.216.0007

Hess, J. (2018b). Hip-hop and music education: Where is race? *Journal of Popular Music Education,* 2(1–2), 7–12. https://doi.org/10.1386/jpme.2.1-2.7_1

Hodge, D. W. (2018). AmeriKKKa's most wanted: Hip Hop culture and Hip Hop theology as challenges to oppression. *Journal of Popular Music Education,* 2(1), 13–28. https://doi.org/ 10.1386/jpme.2.1-2.13_1

Kruse, A. J. (2016). Being hip-hop: Beyond skills and songs. *General Music Today,* 30(1), 53–58. https://doi.org/10.1177/1048371316658931

Kruse, A. J. (2018a). Hip-hop authenticity and music education: Confronting the concept of keeping it real. *Journal of Popular Music Education,* 2(1–2), 149–164. https://doi.org/10.1386/ jpme.2.1-2.149_1

Kruse, A. J. (2018b). "Hip-hop wasn't something a teacher ever gave me": Exploring hip-hop musical learning. *Music Education Research*, 20(3), 317–329. https://doi.org/10.1080/14613 808.2018.1445210

Kruse, A. J. (2020a). "He didn't know what he was doin'": Student perspectives of a white teacher's hip-hop class. *International Journal of Music Education*. Advanced online publication. https://doi.org/10.1177/0255761420924316

Kruse, A. J. (2020b). "Take a back seat": White music teachers engaging hip-hop in the classroom. *Research Studies in Music Education*, 42(2), 143–159. https://doi.org/10.1177/1321103X1 9899174

Ladson-Billings, G. (2015). You gotta fight the power: The place of music in social justice education. In C. Benedict, P. Schmidt, G. Spruce, & P. Woodford (Eds.), *The Oxford handbook of social justice in music education* (1st ed., pp. 406–422). Oxford University Press.

Ladson-Billings, G. (2018). From big homie the O.G., to GLB: Hip-hop and the reinvention of a pedagogue. In C. Emdin & E. Adjapong (Eds.), *#HipHopEd: The compilation on hip-hop education* (pp. 21–26). Brill Sense.

Love, B. L. (2016). Complex personhood of hip hop and the sensibilities of the culture that fosters knowledge of self and self-determination. *Equity & Excellence in Education*, 49(4), 414–427. https://doi.org/10.1080/10665684.2016.1227223

Martignetti, F., & Brewster, J. M. (2020). Finding our way: The experiences of a rapper and his advisor in a bachelor of music programme. *Journal of Popular Music Education*, 4(1), 61–79. https://doi.org/10.1386/jpme_00014_1

McLeod, K. (2012). Authenticity within hip-hop and other cultures threatened with assimilation. In M. Forman & M. Anthony (Eds.), *That's the joint! The hip-hop studies reader* (2nd ed., pp. 164–178). Routledge.

Millares, M. D. (2019). Towards a pedagogy of deviance. *Journal of Popular Music Education*, 3(3), 435–449. https://doi.org/10.1386/jpme_00005_1

Nielsen Music. (2020). *2020 mid-year U.S. report*. https://static.billboard.com/files/ 2020/07/ NielsenMID-YEAR-2020-us-1594300786.pdf

Petchauer, E. (2011). "I feel what he was doin'": Responding to justice-oriented teaching through hip-hop aesthetics. *Urban Education*, 46(6), 1411–1432. https://doi.org/10.1177/ 0042085911400335

Petchauer, E. (2012). *Hip-hop culture in college students' lives: Elements, embodiment, and higher edutainment*. Routledge.

Rodriquez, J. (2006). Color-blind ideology and the cultural appropriation of hip-hop. *Journal of Contemporary Ethnography*, 35(6), 645–668. https://doi.org/10.1177/0891241606286997

Rose, T. (1994). *Black noise: Rap music and black culture in contemporary America*. Wesleyan University Press.

Schloss, J. G. (2014). *Making beats: The art of sample-based hip-hop*. Wesleyan University Press.

Snell, K., & Söderman, J. (2014). *Hip-hop within and without the academy*. Lexington Books.

Söderman, J., & Folkestad, G. (2004). How hip-hop musicians learn: Strategies in informal creative music making. *Music Education Research*, 6, 313–326. https://doi.org/10.1080/14613800 42000281758

Tobias, E. S. (2014). Flipping the misogynist script: Gender, agency, hip hop and music education. *Action, Criticism, and Theory for Music Education*, 13(2), 48–83. http://act.maydaygr oup.org/volume-13-issue-2/

SECTION VII

COMPOSING IN SCHOOL ENSEMBLE SETTINGS

CHAPTER 30

COMPOSITION IN BAND CLASSES

MATTHEW R. DOIRON

CREATIVITY is a vital part of music. Whether in the well-crafted solo of a professional jazz musician, the clever development of a motif in a work for chamber ensemble, or the stream-of-consciousness vocal improvisations of a two-year-old, musical creativity is apparent all around us. Create is one of the four artistic processes identified in the National Core Arts Standards (State Education Agency Directors of Arts Education, 2014). Elliott (1995) considers composition important to students' creative growth and Reimer (2003) describes composition as equally important to other areas of musical instruction.

Researchers have demonstrated numerous musical benefits to instruction in creative music-making, including increased musical understanding (Doiron, 2019; Stringham, 2010), increased motivation to practice and make music (Alexander, 2015), and, perhaps most important to ensemble directors, increased performance skills (Azzara, 1993; Stoltzfus, 2005). While composition has traditionally been viewed in the realm of musicians with an innate gift, music teachers must strive to re-brand it as an integral part of a well-rounded music education. Creating an original composition provides a platform for students to develop a deeper understanding of rhythm, melody, harmony, form, and style in a more authentic manner. Through the creative process, a student doesn't simply notice a given concept in another's music, but must understand this concept well enough to, at minimum, re-create it in their own composition.

Young children demonstrate musical creativity and movement regularly as a natural part of their physical and cognitive development. Singing and dancing allow a child to explore their own vocal and physical abilities. The musical influences children experience, songs they hear from family and friends, songs they learn from television, radio, movies, or from early-childhood music instruction all contribute to their musical understanding. Creative musical play is an important part of human development. As music teachers, we must remember that the urge to create should be nurtured and balanced with instruction that helps students develop performance skills that allow for meaningful and exciting re-creation of other's musical creations.

CHALLENGES: WHAT GETS IN THE WAY?

Since 1994, the National Standards have called for the teaching of creative musical practices (National Association for Music Education, n.d.). Leaders in the field of music education have stressed the importance of teaching the creative processes. In spite of this, common pedagogy in performing ensembles, which represent a large portion of current public-school music education, is focused primarily on performance. Several factors including lack of time, lack of pedagogy and resources, and a fundamental shift in the focus of instruction all contribute to the exclusion of composition activities from instrumental music curriculum. Paradoxically, while teachers may be hesitant to take time from performance preparation, the process of composing develops musicianship, aids music literacy, provides a means for creative expression, enhances music reading, and improves performance skills.

Time Allocation

The most commonly cited reason for not teaching composition in performing ensembles is the lack of time. Most instrumental music teachers structure their year around performance expectations. For many music teachers, outstanding public performances are the ultimate goal as they reflect well upon the teacher, the students, the program, and the school. Strong performing programs garner administrative and community support and provide some protection from budgetary woes. Consequently, many teachers are cautious about any changes that could affect the quality of performance.

Feldman and Contzius (2020) provide suggestions for finding the time to include composition into rehearsal pedagogy. These include (1) programming one fewer piece per concert or one piece at an easier grade level, (2) scheduling activities after a concert when pressure to prepare is at a minimum, (3) scheduling weekly or bi-weekly rehearsal time for composition, and (4) structuring warm-up time for composition or improvisation activities. Several researchers (Doiron, 2019; Schopp, 2006; Shewan, 2002) all noted that performing student compositions was crucial to the success of composition in performing ensemble settings. Feldman and Contzius suggested that the programming of student compositions could help encourage teachers to focus more time and energy to the process.

Composing also provides teachers a means for assessing student learning. The ability to compose demonstrates understanding and higher-order thinking skills as students are expressing and interacting meaningfully with musical content. Providing students with feedback on their composition helps them "become sensitive and informed critics of their own work" (Hickey, 1999, p. 30). The musical understanding a student develops while composing positively affects their performance. A student who has spent time adjusting articulation and adding dynamics and phrase markings in their own music is much more likely to pay attention to those markings when they see them in a rehearsal. They begin to recognize harmonic progressions, or form, or modes. They develop a deeper understanding of how music works. In short, they become a better all-around musician.

Access to Resources

The last quarter century has seen a significant effort to provide resources for music teachers interested in teaching composition. A number of books about teaching composition have been published by researchers and pedagogues (e.g., Hickey, 2003, 2012; Kaschub & Smith, 2009, 2013; Koops & Whitener, 2020; Randles & Stringham, 2013) and *Music Educators' Journal* published special issues focused on composition (March, 2016) and creativity (March, 2017). Other books used in music educator preparation programs added information on including composition in instrumental music instruction (e.g., Burton & Snell, 2015; Feldman and Contzius, 2020; Schleuter, 1997). Additionally, the National Association for Music Education (NAfME) provides several opportunities for students to submit their own compositions for evaluation and recognition (e.g., Student Composers Competition, Electronic Music Composition Competition, and Student Songwriters Competition). A number of state music education organizations have also developed similar opportunities (e.g., Music-COMP, the Illinois Music Education Association (ILMEA) Composition Contest, and the New York State School Music Association (NYSSMA) Call for Compositions). While most of these programs are structured as competitions with recognition for outstanding achievement, they all offer constructive feedback for students who participate. While composition instruction may not be widespread in instrumental music education yet, materials are more readily available now than ever before.

Pedagogical Knowledge

Many public-school music teachers have little or no formal instruction in composition nor any background in composition pedagogy (Abrahams, 2000; Stringham et al., 2015; Piazza & Talbot, 2021). Musical rehearsals focus almost exclusively on the accurate re-creation of music composed by others. This process, an accurate decoding or reading of a visual representation of music, is developed through regular practice that doesn't necessarily engage students' creative abilities. For this reason, many accomplished student musicians are intimidated by the creative process as they have not developed their creative musical skills. To address this underdeveloped area, it is important to have an understanding of the sequence and scope of how we learn music.

A practical analogy for musical learning is the sequence of events in language acquisition. The ability to acquire verbal skills is primarily dependent on the capacity to hear and discriminate sounds and then affix meaning to those sounds. The ability to meaningfully interact with musical vocabulary in both generative and re-creative settings is also dependent upon the same aural differentiation and identification.

A young child spends several years listening to and then babbling in her native language. She imitates what she hears and eventually begins to attach meaning to sounds for familiar actions (e.g., walk, eat, play, etc.) and familiar objects (e.g., ball, face, dish, etc.). She develops her understanding of meaning and syntax by chaining the words she knows into phrases (e.g., play ball!). In the first six years of life, a child will develop an expressive vocabulary of more than 2,000 words and a receptive vocabulary of 20,000 words (Stahl, 1999). During this time, many children will also be exposed to written language, first by looking at language with pictures while someone reads to them and then learning to say and draw (write) the letters that form the basis of written language. Children learn to write meaningful things like their name, or words for objects in their everyday life or favorite stories. Gradually, they gain reading independence and then begin to develop the ability to generalize the unfamiliar. Initially, conversational vocabulary is larger than reading or writing vocabulary but in later years, the reading vocabulary will surpass the spoken vocabulary. Finally, children learn specifics of sentence structure and grammar. Second language acquisition, while differing in a few particulars, largely follows the same pathway. While it may be easier for young children to learn a language due to brain development and plasticity, the process does not change significantly based on chronological age.

Music learning follows a similar sequence to language learning. A child spends months listening to and babbling in her native musical language (the musical sounds in her environment.) As familiarity with music develops, she begins to imitate the tunes that she hears. If she is fortunate, she has people in her life who interact with her musically, singing, moving, and chanting. Even if most of the people in her physical location do not usually make music, she will hear songs on the radio, on children's television shows, or streamed audio and video. Rhythmic and tonal patterns function as the words of music that she will reuse and combine in her stream-of-consciousness improvisations while she plays with music. Without formalized instruction in music, many people will never learn to read musical notation, although that doesn't necessarily inhibit musical growth (think of the number of musicians who play very well "by ear").

Based on the parallel between language and music, students who learn to read music notation should begin with familiar tunes. The recognition of rhythmic, tonal, and melodic patterns, rather than individual notes, allows the advancing reader to recognize larger patterns such as tonal patterns that imply the underlying harmonies of the music or recurring rhythmic and melodic motifs that allow us to recognize simple musical form. As with advancing language readers, the students will begin to read unfamiliar music when they have had enough familiar music from which to generalize. Finally, students may be taught music theory by naming and describing musical elements that they already know aurally. If a theoretical concept cannot be audiated, that is, if it does not cause a student to correctly recall or imagine a specific musical sound, it isn't useful to that student's ability to improvise or compose.

Change in Focus

Musical ensemble rehearsals require large amounts of preparation and structure to be productive. Equipment must be gathered and arranged, seating is typically pre-arranged so like instruments can be grouped in a particular configuration (clarinets on the left, flutes on the right, etc.) Warm-up routines are often developed to help instrumental music students to focus their attention on the given tasks of the day. In rehearsal mode, the ensemble performs a given passage and the director stops, corrects problems, and then continues. Once most of the technical demands are addressed, the director will work with the group to shape a phrase or to refine a crescendo. Some teachers are remarkably efficient and have refined their ability to polish a musical performance with breathtaking results. Rehearsals such as these are examples of a convergent musical process. All of the activities are focused on finding the *correct* musical answer.

By contrast, Reimer (2003) suggests that teaching composition more closely follows the process from the art studio, not the rehearsal room. Creative musical activities are often more divergent in nature. When creativity is the goal, teachers could encourage a student to find several (or many) right answers and then help them decide which idea works best. Teachers may also model simple examples of creativity by ornamenting a familiar passage in a piece, improvising a new ending to a musical phrase, or composing simple variations on a given rhythm or melody. Modeling the process aurally is of vital importance. Music is, first and foremost, an aural art form and helping students develop aural skills that allow them to feel comfortable creating and understanding music without notation provides numerous benefits. It gives students a basis for interactive music-making. It helps them understand basic music theory concepts in a non-theoretical manner. Perhaps most important to ensemble directors, it facilitates deeper understanding in performance settings where students only have access to a limited amount of visual information (i.e., their individual part) with which to understand a whole piece of music.

CREATING THE ENVIRONMENT

Mistake-Safe Zone

Several factors are crucial in building an environment that is conducive to teaching composition. First and foremost, students must feel safe and comfortable while making music. If students regularly sing, chant, play, and move in their general music classes, they will have little problem doing the same things in an instrumental setting. This is by no means a new concept. Almost a century ago, music educators understood the importance of connecting new skills to the student's established knowledge. Maddy and Giddings (1928) wrote:

> Pupils learn to read vocal music by using the Do, Re, Mi syllables. Since they learn their songs by this method, does it not seem logical that they also use these syllables when they first enter the new realm of music represented by the instrument they wish to learn? There are enough necessary new details to bother them when changing from vocal to instrumental music, without having to learn a whole new vocabulary at the same time. (pp. 4–5)

If, however, students did not sing, chant, and move in classroom music, or if they are already developing or accomplished performers on their instrument, they may already have developed an assumption that band rehearsals do not include singing and chanting. In this case, as their teacher, we have another task to add to our "to do" list. Asking a student to sing musical ideas before performing them allows a teacher to understand whether the problem is conceptual (e.g., the student does not have an appropriate musical response) rather than technical (e.g., the student has a musical response but can't yet perform that idea on their instrument). The former requires further teaching of the concept. The latter provides great intrinsic motivation for students to further develop their performance skills.

Developing Rhythmic Understanding and Readiness

Using the music learning/language learning analogy, our conversational vocabulary is more advanced than our written vocabulary. That is, students should be able to say (or sing/play) things that they cannot yet read or write (read/compose). A language teacher helps students learn proper usage and spelling to build vocabulary and written composition skills. Music teachers should simply do the same thing in music lesson and ensemble settings. The key is to teach what most people would call music theory in a non-theoretical manner. That is, we should name and explain things after a student develops an aural understanding. This requires us to regularly spiral back to help students connect concepts and deepen their understanding of music they can audiate and perform.

Rhythm and movement are inextricably linked. Encouraging students who struggle with rhythm to move and chant will help them feel pulse and subdivision. When chanting rhythms with students, I ask them to pulse macrobeats (i.e., the beat) in their heels, and microbeats (i.e., the subdivision) on their leg with fingertips. While some elementary students will manage this task with relative ease, I find that that some university music majors struggle with this task at first. This situation is actually quite normal. Gordon (1995) theorized that music aptitude, or potential to achieve in music, is normally distributed. Just like everyone has potential to achieve in language, all students

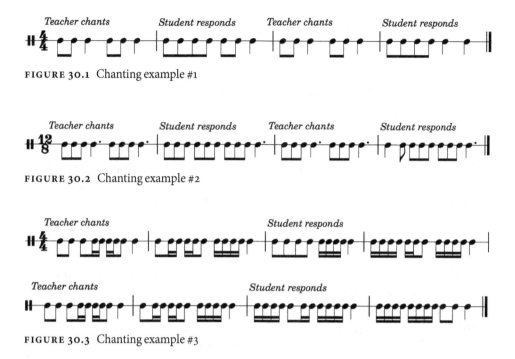

FIGURE 30.1 Chanting example #1

FIGURE 30.2 Chanting example #2

FIGURE 30.3 Chanting example #3

have potential to achieve in music. Students with lower aptitude may simply require more support. Creative musical tasks allow students to work at an appropriate level of challenge.

The goal of rhythmic readiness activities is to help students aurally create their own rhythms in a variety of meters and then to bring contextual meaning to them via use of a rhythmic system (e.g., 1-e-+-a, *du-ta-de-ta*, *ta-ka-di-mi*, etc.). Begin by chanting a one- or two-measure rhythm (see Figure 30.1) to the students and invite students to chant a response, in time, over the next measure(s). At this point, students should use a neutral syllable when chanting. After repeating the process several times, ask several students to share their responses.

The rhythmic context should reflect the literature they are currently learning to perform. Difficulty should be based on students' musical abilities. If they have greater rhythmic facility, you could use more challenging antecedent phrases. For example, Figure 30.2 may be appropriate for beginner level student musicians while Figure 30.3 would likely be more appropriate for more advanced students as the rhythms are more complex and the phrases are two measures long.

After the students have improvised consequent phrases, the teacher may need to help them write the phrases they improvised. This is done by bringing rhythmic context to the improvised rhythm using syllables from the chosen rhythm system. It is important that the musical sound comes before the process of writing. We would not admonish a four-year-old not to say words that he cannot spell. Likewise, we should not constrain his musical development to rhythms that he can write. The drive to read and write what one can speak is an important factor in the intrinsic motivation to improve reading and writing skills.

Developing Melodic and Harmonic Understanding and Readiness

Melodic readiness activities allow students an opportunity to develop an understanding of how melodies are constructed. Harmonic readiness activities help students understand harmony in both a vertical and linear manner. This understanding will inform the construction of their own melodies as well as the harmonization of pre-existing melodies.

As with the rhythmic readiness activities, the goal is to bring contextual understanding to familiar materials that have been learned aurally. Context is brought to melodic material via a tonal system. I use moveable-*do* solfège with *la*-based minor to discuss and analyze all tonal examples and rhythm syllables developed by James Froseth (sometimes referred to as "the Gordon System") to discuss and analyze all rhythmic examples. I have colleagues who prefer various tonal and rhythm systems including *do*-based minor or numbers for tonal analysis and performance, and "Takadimi" or "*1-e-and-a*" for rhythm. I don't mean to diminish the efficacy of other systems. Each teacher should feel free to choose the tools they find most effective for bringing contextual meaning to music.

Jazz musicians learn standard tunes to develop their skills. Kodàly suggested that students begin music learning with folk songs from their native land. Band music also has standard tunes (see Figure 30.4) for a list of tunes produced by a brief search of five different beginning band books).

Every one of these songs is worthy of study for melodic and harmonic structure. They are gems that have each stood the test of time—at least 75 years. Similar literature lists can be compiled for more advanced ensembles based on the most common and familiar literature.

Azzara (2015) lists four skills essential to developing comprehension. Students must learn to (a) group pitches into meaningful patterns and phrases, (b) compare patterns,

	Beginning Band Standard Tunes	
Au Clair de la Lune (Pierrot)	Frere Jacques	Long, Long Ago
Aura Lee	Go Tell Aunt Rhody	Mary Ann
Bingo	Good King Wenceslas	Mary Had a Little Lamb
Down by the Station	Hot Cross Buns	Ode to Joy
Down in the Valley	Jolly Old St. Nicholas	Skip to My Lou
Dreidel Song	Lightly Row	Twinkle, Twinkle Little Star
Erie Canal	London Bridge	The Saints Go Marching In

FIGURE 30.4 Beginning band standard tunes

FIGURE 30.5 Three example tunes

phrases, and tunes, (c) interact when performing, and (d) anticipate and predict patterns and phrases. To exemplify these skills we will examine three of the tunes from Figure 30.4 (see Figure 30.5).

Sing through the tunes, one at a time. Focus on the rhythmic aspect of each tune. Are there meaningful patterns that are repeated? Do the phrases have similarities? Does the tune have a sense of unity? Does it have a sense of variety? After performing the first and second tunes, did you notice any similarities between "Mary Had a Little Lamb" and "London Bridge?" After singing and thinking about the first two tunes, were you making any predictions about "Go Tell Aunt Rhody?" Did you find more similarities? Did you find any differences? Take a few moments and repeat this process, focusing on the melodies, and answering the same questions. Finally, repeat the process a third time, focusing on the harmonic structure of each.

Now that you have had an opportunity to sing the songs several times and ask yourself those questions, let's see if we noticed the same things. There is considerable reuse of rhythmic material in "Mary Had a Little Lamb." Measure 5 is an exact rhythmic repeat of measure 1. Measures 2, 3, and 4 are rhythmically the same, as are measures 6 and 7. As we look at "London Bridge," measures 1 and 5 are the same as are measures 2, 3, 4, and 6. In fact, the first six measures of both songs are rhythmically identical. "Go Tell Aunt Rhody," while not using the same rhythms, does have significant reuse of rhythmic material. Measures 1, 3, 5, and 6 are all the same rhythm and measure four is a mirror image of that rhythm. Zooming out from patterns to phrases, each tune repeats the first half of the antecedent rhythmic phrase, varying only the last two measures. Generalizing from our answers to these questions helps us to understand that at least some well-written songs reuse rhythmic material but not in strict imitation. This is one way that a composer balances unity and variety in a composition.

When examining the pieces tonally, we find that melodic material is reused in much the same fashion as rhythmic material. Each melody moves primarily by step with occasional skips. Each melody is entirely diatonic. Harmonically, all three pieces use the same two chords, tonic and dominant. In fact, they all follow the same harmonic progression. With only one exception, each melody features a chord tone on every beat of every measure.

Now that you have taken a more in-depth look into the construction of these three well-worn tunes, do you have some new ideas you could use when composing your own tunes? Have you ever thought about the construction of a simple song in this manner? I certainly hadn't when I was a young teacher. My experience had exclusively been unidirectional. Someone presented me with notation, and I tried to re-create that notation correctly, use correct fingerings, play the right rhythms. My performance lacked comprehension because I was too focused on musical minutiae to look for patterns. To draw further parallels with our language/music analogy, individual notes are like individual letters. We don't spell when we read or speak, we group letters into meaningful chunks.

With practice, our ability to decode notation and re-create notated music improves. Sadly, many wind players rarely develop an understanding of functional harmony because they play instruments that can produce only one note at a time. To develop harmonic understanding, Grunow, Azzara, and Gordon (2020) use tonal patterns (see Figure 30.6) that outline harmony for a given piece of music.

The examples above are all based on tonic and dominant harmony. This is a good place to begin as it presents students with an either/or choice. All the patterns are either tonic patterns (any combination of *do*, *mi*, and *so*), or dominant patterns (any combination of *so*, *ti*, *re*, and *fa*). Like the rhythmic readiness activities, these are sung by the teacher and imitated by the students using a neutral syllable first. Initially, the patterns are presented in the same order, so they become predictable. Gradually the teacher introduces solfège to the patterns. As students learn to identify the patterns as tonic or dominant, the order is changed. As harmonic understanding deepens, students may improvise their own tonic and dominant patterns.

The second step to building harmonic readiness is helping students apply their developing understanding of chords to the harmonic structure of a given piece of music.

FIGURE 30.6 Tonal patterns

FIGURE 30.7 "Mary Had a Little Lamb," melody and bass line

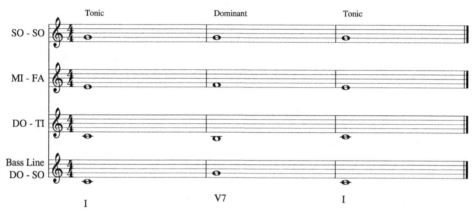

FIGURE 30.8 Simple linear harmony

Azzara and Grunow (2006) developed a process for students to sing, play, and understand harmony in a linear manner. After learning the melody of a song, students are
taught to sing and play a bass line by improvising rhythms on the roots of the chords (see
Figure 30.7).

Once the student learns the bass line, inner voice lines may be added using the following voicings (see Figure 30.8).

These harmony parts are similar to guide tone lines used by jazz musicians. That is,
they provide a linear pathway that helps the performer move as little as possible while
navigating the harmony of the piece. As with all the prior steps, this task should be
learned aurally.

As students become more comfortable with tonic and dominant chords, the same process can be repeated with new tunes to expand students' knowledge and skills. Choices
in literature should include tunes in major and minor keys, with tonic, dominant, and
subdominant harmony. Modal tunes also work well as students will find connections to
contemporary band literature and classic rock songs, many of which are in Mixolydian
and Dorian modes. There are a number of online resources and crowdsourced lists of
popular music written in various modes. This process is a powerful teaching tool as it is
adaptable to any piece of music.

Improvisation as an Instructional Tool

Improvised endings are a beneficial activity for students to grow their creative skills and a gateway to composition. While this section is focused primarily on readiness activities, invented endings are great beginning composition exercises. Sarath (1996) delineated between composition and improvisation, stating improvisation is the "spontaneous creation and performance of musical materials" (p. 3) while composition is a process that allows for reflection and revision. In a study involving non-notated composition, Kratus (1989) differentiated between improvisation and composition by asking a student to repeat their musical creation, defining composition as "a unique, replicable sequence of pitches and durations" (p. 8). If a student "finalizes" a response in an invented endings activity, even if it only an aural response, it should be considered a composition.

As you can see from the relative lengths of the descriptions in the previous section, developing melodic and harmonic understanding is much more time consuming than developing basic rhythmic understanding. This should not preclude you from asking students to sing invented endings to melodies before you have "thoroughly covered the topic." Remember that musical abilities vary widely. Some students will show great success with relatively little input from their music teacher while others may struggle even after several years of music class. Student responses to creative tasks help us to understand individual differences and adapt our instruction to help each student to more meaningful levels of creativity.

Whole-class improvised ending activities are useful for giving each student a mistake-safe zone to explore musical possibilities. I would encourage you, however, to listen to some individual responses, even if you only ask for volunteers at first. You may continuously sing the antecedent phrase for any students who indicate that they have an ending they want to share. Perhaps you could have the whole class repeat student responses. Success at simple tasks will build confidence and a greater willingness to take musical chances. As students become more comfortable with this process, feel free to add constraints to the challenge (e.g., you must end on *do*, you can't begin on *mi*, reuse a rhythm from the first phrase). The goal is to grow students' audiation and instinctual response to musical settings. Just keep the challenge appropriate to students' skill levels. Something as simple as an improvised two- or four-measure response may provide insight into a student's depth of understanding. Consider the examples in Figure 30.9.

This antecedent phrase was written to be used with "Mary Had a Little Lamb," "London Bridge Is Falling Down," and "Go Tell Aunt Rhody." It consists of simple rhythms and uses the same harmonic pattern. All four student responses demonstrate rhythmic understanding. They are eight beats long and use similar rhythmic patterns. Student One sings a response that does not reuse the harmony from the model songs or the antecedent phrase. The other three responses all fit the harmonic structure of the given melodies. Student Two uses greater rhythmic variety but a more limited palette of pitches while Student Three uses only macrobeats but a wider range of pitches. Student Four sings a melody that reuses the first half of the antecedent phrase and then

FIGURE 30.9. Examples of student-invented endings

outlines the dominant chord to end on *do*. While Response One doesn't fit the harmonic structure, it is not incorrect. It simply indicates that the student may not infer the same harmony or that they need more time and experience to develop their harmonic understanding. Responses Two and Three may indicate greater harmonic understanding. Response Four is least likely to be an accidental indicator as it demonstrates both a reuse of the source material and a more thorough harmonic understanding. I would encourage you, as the teacher, to take a moment to highlight the techniques that make Response Four exemplary, or, better yet, ask the students to point out these things.

STRUCTURING REHEARSALS FOR CREATING AND PERFORMING

Thomas (2013) described singing as "the first and most important step to encouraging creative musicianship" (p. 48). He believes students who are afraid of singing overcome that fear when it becomes part of their daily routine. In warm-ups, the students sing a tuning note before matching that pitch on their instrument. As students gain familiarity with solfège, Thomas suggests simple call-and-response activities, where the students sing the solfège and then play the melody or pattern they sang. The process expands to singing scales and simple songs and melodies from method books and band literature. Eventually, they move to two-, three-, and four-part singing and playing, transposing the given lines for their particular instruments in the moment.

Hartz (2015) described an award-winning Texas band program that begins each year learning children's tunes by singing and using Curwen hand signs. Every day the band uses warm-up time to hone aural skills, build simple arrangements by ear, and chant and clap rhythms using function-based rhythm syllables. The students' progress from studying and performing children's songs to melodic source material from the literature they are performing in band.

The teachers use improvisation as an educational tool, and improvisation and composition as a means of assessing student understanding.

Shewan (2009) describes singing as "paramount to becoming a fine musician." He suggests a warm-up procedure whereby students learn to sing and then play melodies from their band literature by ear. The objective is to develop deeper understanding by "connecting the brain and the ear via the voice." This aural understanding forms a basis not only for composing but also everyday rehearsal skills. Shewan summarizes the importance of aural skills:

> All the student has in front of them is their own part, so [they] can't look at a score. . . . [or] line up all the chords and figure it all out visually. They have to figure it out aurally. So, they're listening to the other parts and making their comments and their observations based on what they hear, rather than what they see.

Each of these teachers spend considerable time building aural, analytical, and creative skills that are fundamental to the pedagogical approach that each teacher uses when teaching composition. While much of this work begins in warm-up activities, the concepts are made more concrete by connecting them to the literature being performed. This is not a "one off" task. Concepts such as melodic development, harmonization, and form are reinforced at every opportunity. Intonation problems are corrected by singing passages, adjusting intonation vocally, and then matching that procedure with instruments. These teachers and the processes they use are compelling because in addition to prioritizing musical creativity, all three programs have received national recognition for outstanding performance. When done well, teaching the necessary skills to create, to improvise, and to compose, enhances music curricula with deeper student understanding, higher-quality performances, and meaningful opportunities for students to develop their own independent musical voice.

Composition Activities and Assignments

The following activities are examples of composition assignments I have used or observed other teachers using with students at all levels of instruction. The literature that students are learning and performing, whether that be tunes from a method book or published literature for their ensembles, represent the best source materials for these activities. The goal is to help the students be creative with the knowledge and skills that they have mastered. Some of these activities will be easy to use immediately, others will require time for students to build greater content knowledge and skills. The five activities presented below begin with basic rhythm composition before adding harmonic and melodic elements. They are generally presented in increasing level of difficulty although each activity can be adapted to make it easier or more challenging. Student work is included for most activities to provide insight into what may be possible if we help our students find and develop their creative musical voice.

Composing Rhythmic Warm-Up Activities

An excellent first step for beginning composers is creating rhythmic warm-up activities for their ensemble. There is no time constraint or concern over whether a piece can be effectively programmed. Furthermore, students can be creative rhythmically regardless of their level of tonal understanding. They can be encouraged to find challenging rhythms from their performance literature and write exercises that will help the ensemble read, understand, and perform those rhythms (and others that may be similar). Students with more developed rhythmic skills may compose longer rhythmic phrases or rhythm duets, focusing on reuse and interaction of rhythmic material.

Assembling a Rhythmic Trio

Merriam-Webster (n.d.) defines composition as "arrangement into specific proportion or relation and especially into artistic form." Here is a simple composition activity based on Holst's *First Suite in E*(1984) that can be easily scaled up from a handful of two-measure rhythms to a much larger rhythm ensemble piece. To provide greater connection to the literature they are performing, students extracted rhythms from the third movement. Four rhythms that students extracted are in Figure 30.10.

The teacher helped students assemble their patterns into a question/answer format which, when repeated formed an eight-measure phrase. Two phrases were assembled into a larger ABA rhythm composition. Figure 30.11 is the assembled 24-measure ABA composition.

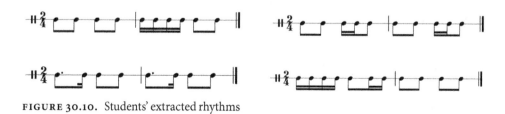

FIGURE 30.10. Students' extracted rhythms

FIGURE 30.11. Assembled ABA composition

FIGURE 30.12. Assembled ABA rhythm trio

After assembling the rhythmic composition, students then completed a group analysis of rhythms Holst used to help them plan a "motor" to accompany their composition. An example of a student group's ABA rhythm composition is in Figure 30.12.

Harmonizing a Scale/Warm-up Chorale

As students develop their harmonic understanding, harmonizing a scale with limited choices for what harmonies to include can help them to understand the process

FIGURE 30.13. Harmonized scale I, IV, V^7

of harmonizing pre-composed melodies. Students can harmonize a scale using only primary (I, IV, V7) chords (See Figure 30.13 for an example). Familiarity with primary chords can be developed by having students sing and identify tonal patterns that include pitches from tonic, subdominant, and dominant chords (see Figure 30.7). Using the scale as a melody, students can choose appropriate I, IV, and V7 chords that fit with the given scale pitches and write harmony lines that will outline the primary chords of the given key.

After students develop some facility with the process, they can harmonize simple melodies as warm-up chorales. Begin with short phrases and make sure that the source material is appropriate for the harmony they can use (e.g., do not give the students a phrase that has accidentals or modulates to a new key.) This process will be more effective if you provide the students with examples of four-part chorales they can read and perform. After they can sing, play, and aurally recognize how phrases end, you can name those given cadences (e.g., authentic cadence or plagal cadence.) As your students' understanding of harmony grows, so can their palate for harmonizing scales and melodies. Just remember to always start with an aural idea, help the students to understand it contextually, and then name it and discuss music theory.

Composing Variations on a Theme

When students compose variations on a theme, they are demonstrating higher order musical thought. Playing a melody is a relatively simple task. Changing the melody from one meter to another or one key or mode to another demonstrates the ability to conceive of source material through various musical lenses. Composing variations also allows for greater differentiation as students can engage with the musical material at whatever level their skills will allow. For students who haven't written variations before, teachers may introduce the concept by playing a recording of variations on simple themes such as Mozart's *Variations on "Ah vous dirais-je maman"* for piano or Alfred Reed's *Variations on LBIFD* ("London Bridge is Falling Down") for brass quintet. These are particularly useful because the source material is so familiar. More advanced examples might include John Barnes Chance's *Variations on a Korean Folk Song* or James Barnes' *Fantasy Variations on a Theme by Niccolo Paganini*, as the theme is plainly apparent through most of the variations in both pieces.

This kind of activity works well in warm-up routines. After playing a scale and a tune in the same key, the teacher, or a chosen student, plays a variation on the tune. After each variation, a member of the class describes the variation ("He changed the meter to $\frac{6}{8}$" or "She played the tune in Lydian"). In addition to allowing each student the opportunity to compose, adding descriptions provides a platform for students to build contextual knowledge. The activity can culminate with everyone attempting to play the variation by ear.

One of the keys to engaging students in composition is performing student work (Doiron, 2019). Using student composed variations in a "Theme and Variations on _____" is an excellent way to include many student compositions in a concert. Initially, the teacher may need to arrange the theme and assemble the variations although the students will undertake this task as well once they have a good model for doing so. Figures 30.14 has examples collected from students who were writing variations on "Twinkle, Twinkle Little Star" using Charles Ives *Variations on America* (1949) as a model. The first variation set the melody in $\frac{6}{8}$ time and ornamented it with large skips while the second featured the melody set as a dance in a minor key. Figure 30.15 is an interlude written in two keys (B♭ major and G major) and separated by two beats that eventually resolves into G minor. The student who wrote this was exceptionally proud of it as the Ives example also featured an interlude with the melody in canon written in F major and D♭ major at the same time.

Composing a Basic Contrafact

A contrafact is a musical composition based on the harmonic structure of an existing piece of music. Many jazz greats have written new melodies based on the chord progression of a tune from their standard repertoire. As we discussed above, elementary musicians also have a standard repertoire, one that provides the same opportunity to improvise and compose upon. I break this task into several parts to enable feedback and revision. The three composition tasks are provided in Figure 30.16. Figure 30.17 shows one fifth-grade student's composition as it evolves through the various stages.

The first assignment only allows chord tones so the teacher can check for harmonic understanding (i.e., does the student know what notes fit the given chord?). The second assignment allows the student to add non-harmonic tones to the melody. Assignments

FIGURE 30.14. "Twinkle, Twinkle Little Star" variations

FIGURE 30.15. "Twinkle, Twinkle Little Star" interlude

Contrafact Assignment #1

Using the chord progression from the model song, write the bass line on the bottom staff and your own melody on the top staff.

- Use one rhythm with a little variation at the end.
- Use only chord tones.
- End on *do*.

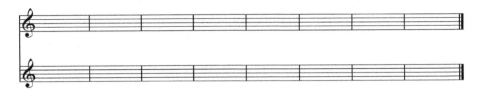

Contrafact Assignment #2

Using the chord progression from the model song, write the bass line on the bottom staff and your own melody on the top staff.

- You may use chord tones, passing tones, and neighboring tones.
- Use one rhythm with a little variation at the end.
- End on *do*.

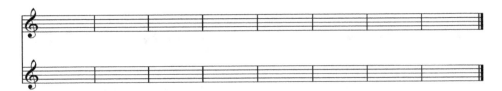

Contrafact Assignment #3

On a new piece of staff paper, use your composition from assignment two and compose a quartet by writing two inner voices.

- Be as lazy as you can with the inner voices. (*do-ti-do*) (*mi-fa-mi*)
- Choose a rhythm pattern that complements your melody and use that for BOTH inner voices.

FIGURE 30.16. Three-part contrafact composition assignment

One and Two may be combined if a student already has a melody that includes passing or neighboring tones. They have been separated in this case to help students who may need a more step-by-step process. The third assignment uses the linear harmony from Azzara and Grunow (2006).

The completed four-part arrangement above would be a great addition to a performance. Having students compose and arrange duets, trios, and quartets allows them the added responsibility of chamber playing. Parts can easily be adjusted or transposed for other instruments. If the bass line is too easy, encourage the students

Assignment One

Assignment Two

Assignment Three

FIGURE 30.17. Fifth-grade student composition

to alternate between the root and fifth of each chord. If the inner voice parts seem boring, add the rhythm from the horn part of a march. A student could write a similar melodic part (a harmony line) or a second part that was rhythmically and melodically simpler and the two melodies could work as a partner song. These tasks provide an opportunity to discuss harmony, parallel motion, complete voicing of triads, or any number of other pertinent topics because they are no longer theoretical. That is, the students are using all this information to adapt their own musical creation. The possibilities are only limited by the boundaries of the songs that the students know and can audiate.

Composing a More Advanced Contrafact

As students musical understanding grows, composition tasks can be adapted to meet individual student's skills and knowledge. As with all the composition activities listed in this chapter, beginning with basic understanding of appropriate source material is crucial.

FIGURE 30.18. Fifth-grade student 12-bar blues composition

FIGURE 30.19. "St. Louis Blues"

When choosing that material, it is important to make sure your choices represent the music you want your students to emulate. Young composers will often produce compositions that are quite similar to the source material you provide. As with language, we begin by imitation and slowly find our voice. Figure 30.18 is an outstanding example of how a student begins by imitating source material and morphs that material into an original composition. The piece was composed by a fifth-grade student who was in his second year of playing a band instrument.

The student was a member of the school jazz band. They had been learning to play *St. Louis Blues* (notated in Figure 30.19) in rehearsals as a vehicle for learning to improvise. *St. Louis Blues* is a great exemplar piece as it is easy to learn by ear, it follows a very common 12-bar blues progression, it has both melody and lyrics that follow an AAB pattern and there are hundreds of recordings of jazz greats who have played it.

When we compare the student composition to *St. Louis Blues*, we notice that the first measure shares all the same pitches with a varied order. The second, third, and fourth measures of the student composition use the same pitches as measures two and three of *St. Louis Blues*. The fifth and sixth measures arpeggiate up beginning on the same notes but the student has extended each arpeggio a third higher. Measures 9 and 10 use the same rhythm as measure 9 of St. Louis Blues while arpeggiating the triads in root position. The student provides a sense of unity for the composition by reusing rhythmic motives throughout and ending each line with the same lick. Perhaps the connection to *St. Louis Blues* was not apparent on the first reading the student composition. After learning what the students were using for source material, the connections become more obvious.

While this example deals with the blues, the process could be easily adapted for composing in any musical form or style. Simply find great exemplars, help the students construct the requisite rhythmic, melodic, harmonic, and stylistic knowledge and then let them adapt and compose. Help the students solve problems by suggesting several solutions and allow them to choose the one they find most appealing or appropriate. As composition becomes a more regular part of their musical routine, they will become more self-sufficient musicians, nurturing their own musical growth.

ASSESSING STUDENT COMPOSITIONS

Assessment is an essential part of the educational process. For a music teacher however, the word assessment may conjure multiple images. It could pertain to state or federal testing that occurs annually in all public schools (e.g., "The state education assessments are going on this week"). It could describe the state solo and ensemble or large group music festival (e.g., "We are playing at the VBODA District Concert Assessment this weekend"). Additionally, it may mean the procedure we use to evaluate how successful a lesson was or the process by which we provide feedback or assign grades. In this section, I will use the term assessment to generally describe the process of providing feedback and evaluating the quality of student work.

Consensual Assessment Technique, Rating Scales, and Rubrics

Amabile (1982, 1996) developed Consensual Assessment Technique (CAT) to overcome the lack of a clear definition of creativity. Amabile (1982) theorized "A product or response is creative to the extent that appropriate observers independently agree it is creative" (p. 1001). She further clarified that "appropriate observers" were experts in the domain in which the product was created. Several studies of student music composition used measures based on CAT (Hickey, 2001; Menard, 2015; Priest, 2001). Furthermore, student compositions submitted for consideration in many local, state, and national level competitions are evaluated using some form of Consensual Assessment Technique.

Rating scales and rubrics are evaluation tools that delineate the criteria for student work across various levels of success. Azzara and Grunow (2006) developed rating scales to measure a variety of musical content including rhythm, expressive elements, harmonic progression, and improvisation skills. Stringham (2010) adapted those rating scales as part of a study involving high school student composers. Hickey (1999, 2013) advocated using rubrics to provide students with a clear understanding of how their compositions will be assessed. The article detailed the process of constructing and adapting rubrics and included several examples of rubrics designed for evaluating various student compositions. Beginning composers may benefit from rubrics that help to support their creative efforts through the early stages. Deutsch (2016) agrees that rubrics can be helpful with some tasks but cautions that no rubric will be applicable to all tasks or compositions. While a well-constructed rubric or rating scale, designed for a particular assignment, may provide a basis for meaningful discussion, a poorly constructed or generic one is likely to be interpreted as a checklist that could cause students to focus on the stated criteria to the exclusion of other creative possibilities.

Formative and Summative Assessment

Formative assessment focuses on monitoring learning to providing students with ongoing feedback to improve skills and knowledge. Formative feedback is given frequently, and the assignments are often not graded. Deutsch (2016) provided a direct and thorough statement on formative assessment.

> The purpose of assessment in composition is to enable students to better achieve their aesthetic goals. Composition teachers must continually seek to understand their students' expressive intentions in order to provide instruction and feedback that makes this possible. Therefore, assessment should be embedded throughout the teaching and creative process—a procedure commonly referred to as formative assessment. (pp. 53–54)

Initially, all feedback will be teacher-driven. As students become more comfortable with the process, they should be encouraged to begin exchanging peer feedback. Teachers may need to help the students provide feedback appropriately, encouraging a balance between positive comments and constructive criticisms. Stringham (2016) provides a number of suggestions to help students provide peer feedback including (a) critiquing a piece of music the students are performing to model appropriate music criticism, (b) focusing on a range of attributes in each piece, and (c) providing alternative ideas when making a critical comment. As students become more adept, each discussion will help students deepen their understanding of the process whether they are receiving or providing feedback.

By contrast, summative assessment is focused on evaluating student learning, usually at the conclusion of a unit of study, by comparing it to a standard or benchmark. In a study of two high school band directors with award-winning programs who prioritize composition for all their students, Doiron (2019) described visceral reactions to summative assessment from both participants. When asked about how student compositions are assessed, both immediately discussed summative assessment. The first participant responded:

> Assessment is dangerous. . . . With fledgling composers, everybody writes, everybody creates something, and they often love that piece that isn't good. It often means something to them. And what are you going to do? Are you going to give it an 84? Really? Do you think that kid's ever going to write again? No. You give him a 77. "Oh, I stink at that." (p. 74)

The other stated:

> We all get fed the line that if you don't assess, kids won't think it's important, so they won't be motivated to do a good job but that's a total lie. The hyperfocus on assessment kills the joy in almost everything you do in school. (p. 102)

When asked a follow-up question on formative assessment, each responded that the formative feedback process was never-ending, integrated into the teaching and learning process at every step. When asked how they assign grades, the first said that all student compositions that were completed with reasonable effort from the student received an A because he didn't want students to base their creative ability on a grade. The second said he does not grade creative work because he feels that it undermines a student's intrinsic motivation to create. Ultimately, neither of these teachers are opposed to assessment. They are opposed to the misuse of summative assessment in an educational environment that has become increasingly driven by high-stakes testing. As expert teachers in that environment, they work to protect their students' emerging sense of musical creativity while providing ongoing, quality, meaningful feedback that facilitates students' musical growth.

Deutsch (2016) proposed "Summative assessment is actually formative assessment, but on a larger temporal level. Each project, each year of growth, each stage of development is part of the formative trajectory of students' growing mastery" (p. 58). The ideal situation occurs when a student's intrinsic drive to create is nurtured. That student writes, revises, and polishes an original composition. With some help from their peers and music teacher, they hear their piece performed. Constructively critical commentary and positive reinforcement are the necessary steps to make this process work. As teachers we should strive to frame that feedback in a manner that is both informative and inspirational.

CONCLUSION

In his book *The Natural Way to Draw*, Kimon Nicolaides (1941) defines drawing as a perceptual challenge, not a technical one, telling his readers that "(l)earning to draw is really a matter of learning to see" (p. 5). I would suggest that learning to compose is also a perceptual challenge, one that involves learning to hear with greater depth and recognition. Re-focusing my teaching in this direction has not only had a profound effect on my students, it has reinvigorated my passion to be more musically creative. It has caused me to deepen my understanding of musical pedagogy as a teacher and helped me find greater depth and meaning in music-making as both a performer and a conductor. I hope you find it has the same impact on your students (and on you, too!).

REFERENCES

Abrahams, F. E. (2000). *Implementing the national standards for music education in pre-service teacher education programs: A qualitative study of two schools* (9965947.) [Doctoral dissertation, Temple University]. ProQuest Dissertations and Theses Global.

Alexander, D. L. (2015). *Intrinsic motivation in a collegiate secondary music instrument class* (1667772264.) [Doctoral dissertation, University of Rochester]. ProQuest Dissertations and Theses Global.

Amabile, T. M. (1982). Social psychology of creativity: A consensual assessment technique. *Journal of Personality and Social Psychology, 43*(5), 37–63.

Amabile, T. M. (1996). *Creativity in context: Update to the social psychology of creativity.* Westview.

Azzara, C. D. (1993). Audiation-based improvisation techniques and elementary instrumental students' music achievement. *Journal of Research in Music Education, 18*(4), 328–342.

Azzara, C. D. (2015). Improvisation and composition: Developing musicianship in instrumental music. In S. L. Burton & A. H. Snell II (Eds.), *Engaging musical practices: A sourcebook for instrumental music* (pp. 181–198). Rowman & Littlefield.

Azzara, C. D., & Grunow, R. F. (2006). *Developing musicianship through improvisation.* GIA Publications, Inc.

Burton, S. L., & Snell II, A. H. (Eds.). (2015). *Engaging musical practices: A sourcebook for instrumental music.* Rowman and Littlefield.

Deutsch, D. (2016). Authentic assessment in music composition: Feedback that facilitates creativity. *Music Educators Journal, 102*(3), 53–59.

Doiron, M. R. (2019). *Composition in secondary instrumental music education: Two case studies* (2229482402). [Doctoral dissertation, University of Rochester]. ProQuest Dissertations and Theses Global.

Elliott, D. J. (1995). *Music matters: A new philosophy of music education.* Oxford University Press.

Feldman, E., & Contzius, A. (2020). *Instrumental music education: Teaching with the musical and practical in harmony.* Routledge.

Gordon, E. E. (1995). *Musical aptitude profile* (2nd ed.). GIA Publications, Inc.

Grunow, R. F., Azzara, C. D., & Gordon, E. E. (2020). *Jump right in: Recorder book with MP3*. GIA Publications, Inc.

Hartz, B. (2015). *Cultivating individual musicianship and ensemble performance through notation-free learning in three high school band programs*. (Electronic Thesis or Dissertation).

Hickey, M. (1999). Assessment rubrics for music composition. *Music Educators Journal*, 85(4), 26–33.

Hickey, M. (2001). An application of Amabile's consensual assessment technique for rating the creativity of children's musical compositions. *Journal of Research in Music Education*, 49(3), 234–244.

Hickey, M. (Ed.). (2003). *Why and how to teach music composition: A new horizon for music education*. National Association for Music Education.

Hickey, M. (2012). *Music outside the lines: Ideas for composing in a K–12 music classroom*. Oxford University Press.

Hickey, M. (2013). What to do about assessment. In C. Randles & D. A. Stringham (Eds.), *Musicianship: Composing in band and orchestra* (pp. 39–50). GIA Publications, Inc.

Holst, G. T. (1984). *First suite in E-flat for military band*. Boosey and Hawkes.

Ives, C. E. (1949). *Variations on America*. Theodore Presser Company.

Kaschub, M. & Smith, J. (2009). *Minds on music: Composition for creative and critical thinking*. Rowman and Littlefield.

Kaschub, M., & Smith, J. (Eds.). (2013). *Composing our future: Preparing music educators to teach composition*. Oxford University Press.

Koops, A., & Whitener, J.L. (2020). *Composition concepts for band and orchestra: Incorporating creativity in ensemble settings*. Rowman and Littlefield.

Kratus, J. (1989). A time analysis of the compositional process used by children ages 7–11. *Journal of Research in Music Education*, 37(1), 5–21.

Maddy, J. E., & Giddings, T. P. (1928). *Instrumental class teaching: A practical teacher's guide in instrumental music classes for use with "The Universal Teacher."* Willis Music Company.

Menard, E. A. (2015). Music composition in the high school curriculum: A multiple case study. *Journal of Research in Music Education*, 63(1), 114–136.

Merriam Webster. (n.d.). Composition. In *Merriam Webster's dictionary*. Retrieved May 15, 2021, from https://www.merriam-webster.com/dictionary/composition

National Association for Music Education. (n.d.). National standards archives. https://nafme.org/my-classroom/standards/national-standards-archives/

Nicolaides, K. (1941). *The natural way to draw*. Houghton Mifflin.

Piazza, E. S., & Talbot, B. C. (2021) Creative musical activities in undergraduate music education curricula. *Journal of Music Teacher Education*, 30(2), 37–50. https://doi.org/10.1177/1057083720948463

Priest, T. L. (2001). Creativity assessment as a predictor of creativity in performance and composition. Contributions to *Music Education*, 28(1), 61–79.

Randles, C., & Stringham, D. A. (Eds.). (2013). *Musicianship: Composing in band and orchestra*. GIA Publications, Inc.

Reimer, B. (2003). *A philosophy of music education advancing the vision* (3rd ed.). Prentice Hall.

Sarath, E. W. (1996). A new look at improvisation. *Journal of Music Theory*, 40(1), 1–38. https://doi.org/10.2307/843921

Schleuter, S. L. (1997). *A sound approach to teaching instrumentalists* (2nd ed.). Schirmer Books.

Schopp, S. E. (2006). *A study of the effects of national standards for music education, number 3, improvisation and number 4, composition on high school band instruction in New York state* (3225193) [Doctoral dissertation, Columbia University]. ProQuest Dissertations and Theses Global.

Shewan, S. C. (2002). *The Williamsville East composition project* (3057603) [Doctoral dissertation, University of Rochester]. ProQuest Dissertations and Theses Global.

Shewan, S. C. (2009). Through the eyes of a composer. From *NYSSMA Music Views: Standards-based teaching and learning across the state* [video recording]. United States: New York State School Music Association.

Stahl, S. A. (1999). *Vocabulary development*. Brookline Books.

State Education Agency Directors of Arts Education. (2014). *National Standards for Music Education*. Retrieved from http://nationalartsstandards.org/

Stoltzfus, J. L. (2005). *The effects of audiation-based composition on the music achievement of elementary wind and percussion students*. [Doctoral dissertation, University of Rochester]. ProQuest Dissertations and Theses Global.

Stringham, D. A. (2010). *Improvisation and composition in a high school instrumental music curriculum* (3445843) [Doctoral dissertation, University of Rochester]. ProQuest Dissertations and Theses Global.

Stringham, D. A. (2016) Creating compositional community in your classroom. *Music Educators Journal, 102*(3), 46–52.

Stringham, D. A., Thornton, L. C., & Shevock, D. J. (2015). Composition and improvisation in instrumental methods courses: Instrumental music teacher educators' perspectives. *Bulletin of the Council for Research in Music Education, 205*, 7–25.

Thomas, G. (2013) Creating momentum for improvisation in instrumental music. *VMEA Notes, 67*, 47–49.

CHAPTER 31

....

COMPOSITION IN
CHORAL SETTINGS

....

KATHERINE STRAND

THIS is a chapter about providing students with an entrée into composing choral music through exercises and projects that will help them to think deeply about what they have to say to the world as creative choral musicians. These projects are informed by the creative processes described by current choral composers and by my pedagogical explorations into teaching composition with my choirs.

I frame this chapter through the lens of social and emotional learning (SEL), which has become a focus during the past few years. It is common for experienced teachers to pay little attention to new educational trends, amending the language we present to administrators for show, or to "tack on" the new trend as an addendum (whole language learning, reading across the curriculum come to mind) to our core curricula. There are research studies demonstrating that simply singing in a choir can have positive social and emotional benefits (Dingle et al., 2012; Ros-Morente et al., 2019). We also help students to manage stage fright, cope with disappointment, learn repertoire from diverse social and cultural groups, learn to communicate through music and gesture, and develop leadership skills in choir.

However, as music education pedagogues Scott Edgar (2019) and Wendy Hart Higdon (2017) wrote, music teachers should consider SEL pedagogical ideas more deeply because social and emotional learning is fundamental to our curricular goals. Scott Edgar (2019) wrote that SEL is not "one more thing" we should add to our teaching but that teaching for SEL is "the" thing central to learning to make music. We in choral music often claim to teach creativity and enable students' personal expression in school. The American Choral Directors Association advocacy statements (ACDA, 2020) include statements like "The arts, with their strong emphasis on team-building and self-reflection are supremely suited to re-ignite students' interest in learning through collaboration, while simultaneously fostering creativity, critical thinking, and communication." Michele Kaschub (2015) wrote that we must teach musical intelligence (the ability to interpret composer intentions and personal interpretations or choral scores) because, as she wrote, "empathy, creativity and artistry are key components in the work of choral musicians" (p. 16–17). I argue further that teaching choral composing processes can provide yet deeper and more meaningful self- and social-awareness skills, self-management, relationship skills, and responsible decision-making skills (CASEL, n.d.) as well as creative musical intelligence. Here are some ways that teaching students some composing skills may help students:

- *Self-awareness* includes the ability to recognize one's emotions and express them in a positive way, recognizing and expressing one's thoughts and values, and then understanding how one's emotions, thoughts, and values can influence one's behavior. Students who learn to express a text through music think deeply about the text and reflect on their own response to it, discussing ideas with classmates.
- *Self-management* involves the ability to regulate one's emotions, thoughts, and behaviors to work toward goals. Composing exercises help students to interpret the ideas and emotions that arise from engaging with texts into musical gestures, gaining a positive outlet for those ideas and emotions. Composing also involves setting independent goals for conveying one's intent for a text, then working toward those goals.
- *Social awareness* involves the ability to notice and understand other people's emotions, taking others' perspectives, and empathizing with others. Students will find that their interpretations and creative ideas will differ from their classmates and so learn about their classmates' perspectives. Their discussions and work to learn to sing each other's work can lead to greater empathy.
- *Relationship skills* involve the ability to communicate, listen, cooperate, resist inappropriate social pressures, negotiate conflict, and seek and offer help to others. Composing conversations engage students in collaboration.
- *Responsible decision-making* involves making constructive choices about personal behavior and social interactions. While composing activities might not involve students in direct discussions about ethical decision-making, choosing and interpreting texts may involve them in those conversations. Composing also gives students a constructive outlet for their ideas and emotions.

Curricular change is difficult. It means rethinking what we do well in light of what we might achieve with adaptation. Estelle Jorgensen (2010) wrote that we should not change our music curricula for change's sake alone. Instead, we should critically reflect on our past and ways that our field can improve. She believes we can have an important impact on students' lives, writing: "We are in a position to imbue lived life with imaginative thought and practice and nourish the hearts, minds, souls, and bodies of young and old alike" (p. 23).

Dominick DiOrio (2016) wrote that "Composition can and should be taught to all students in K–12 schools, and it can and should be taught by you to your young singers through their experience in the school chorus" (p. 15). He argued that all choral students should experience composing to help them see that composers are not special individuals gifted by higher powers and that composing is valuable for helping students to develop their minds, writing "Our brains are formed and molded by our imaginations. Composing is crucial to this development, to say nothing of the power of music to provide meaning, depth, and enrichment to one's life" (p. 16).

Choral composers like Libby Larsen (2007), David Childs (2007), James Mulholland (2007), Kirk Mecham (2007), and Randall Stroope (2007) believe that students should learn harmony, counterpoint, and musical forms in order to learn to compose. Libby Larsen (2007) wrote that she recommends young composers should practice ear training and rhythmic dictation to be able to hear intervals and rhythms, advocating that they practice taking dictation with everyday sounds, like birdsong, car engines, speeches, and appliances (p. 54). René Clausen (2007) and James Mulholland (2007), additionally, recommend that novice composers learn about the voice and its capabilities, including vocal ranges and timbre on vowels and consonants. Teaching composition as part of the choral curriculum can help teachers to create a comprehensive music curriculum to involving music theory and vocal pedagogy as well as choral and performance skills.

CHORAL COMPOSERS GIVE ADVICE

Many contemporary choral composers have provided us with ideas to use when teaching our students to compose. Teachers can use these ideas down to create warm-up exercises, explorations to help students analyze repertoire, and long-term projects that take place inside and outside the choral classroom. A portion of a class period once a week, or even just a few minutes each day, might be devoted to composing exercises that build students' knowledge, vocal skill, and love for choral music.

Finding Inspiration

For James Mulholland (2007), creative inspiration comes from experimenting at a piano. Eric Whitacre (2019), on the other hand, finds that the evocative quality of chords sung by people inspires him, experimenting with a great variety of chords and ancillary tones to find different emotive qualities. He practices these chords with his choral group, building and recording each separately to create a library of sonic moments for future use. Gwyneth Walker (2007) wrote that she begins her compositions by mapping out the chord progressions and form, so practice mapping these can be valuable experiences for learners. André Thomas (2007) wrote that he can be inspired to compose by a series of chords, a particular rhythm, or the musical form of a piece that he enjoys. He recommends that composers keep an idea journal of just such musical ideas.

Like Larsen, Childs, and Mulholland, the many composers who wrote chapters for *Composers on Composing for Choir* (Wine, 2007) suggest that we think about introducing students to choral music through listening experiences. Many of these composers recommend that inspiration should come listening to specific pieces by Bach, Mozart, Palestrina, Haydn, Handel, and also Dawson, Nystedt, Ligeti, Barber, Howell, and Walton. John Rutter (2007) recommends that students listen to Bernstein's *Chichester Psalms*, but wrote that "life wouldn't be the same without Igor Stravinsky's *Symphony of Psalms* and the Maurice Durufle *Requiem*" (p. 174). Choral music, solo vocal, opera and musical theater, popular and folk genre repertoire can all help them to love all the ways that the voice can impact and inspire us. I believe that we should find composers and choirs from non-European traditions including Fabian Obispo, the Senegalese Julien Jouga Chorale, the Creole Choir of Cuba, the Peiyang Chorus of Tianjin University, and the Zamir Choir of Boston. These choral ensembles can offer the choir teacher and student composers many innovative ideas.

Working with Text

For several composers, inspiration must come from meaningful poetry and prose. Morten Lauridsen (2007) recommends that students "read poetry and build a vast personal poetry library" (p. 77). David Childs (2007) wrote that everything comes from the text which, in turn, must be individually meaningful to the composer. He recommends spending time to discuss the meaning of the words to uncover all of the meanings, implications, important moments, and the words that suggest movement and stasis (p. 7). Gwyneth Walker (2007) also believes that the most important thing a choral composer can do is to illuminate the text. Her composing process is inspired by the central images or metaphors. She wrote, "It is important that these poetic images translate clearly into musical expression. Often, the accompaniment is the central means of creating imagery. The tenor of the poem may be established within the opening measures of accompaniment."

James Mulholland (2007) recommended that composers explore speaking the text over and over, experimenting with emphasizing different words in each repetition, to find various meanings in the text. He wrote that "the music should not distract from the poem but act as a thesaurus for appreciation and understanding" (p. 130). The text can dictate the meter, overall tempo, and the speed of the rhythm to the composer, but he advised that the most emotional moments in a text must be examined carefully to avoid cliché musical gestures. Mulholland recommended that students should practice finding the natural scansion of the text (p. 131), then create a graphic representation of the metrical pattern. Students learn the "slash and x" style to represent the ictus (stressed) and nonictus (nonstressed) syllables, in which stressed words should be marked with a "/" slash. The stressed words that are "demoted" from the most important stressed words receive a "^" sign while unstressed receive an "x."[1]

On the other hand, Ola Gjeilo (Schmidt, 2012) finds inspiration from texts but uses their sonic elements, the vowel and consonant sounds, to create expressive meaning in his music. Schmidt wrote of Gjeilo's composing process of working with texts: "(1) breaking apart the text, (2) diverting from setting words with traditional descriptive phrase shape and word stress, and (3) working to create a musical atmosphere" (p. 12). The text serves as a vehicle for conveying whatever meaning that Gjeilo wishes to convey. Schmidt quoted Gjeilo saying, "The words, for me, are more of a servant to the music . . . rather than the other way around" (p. 12).

Reflecting on the Process and Product

Gwyneth Walker (2007) wrote that "Writing music is never easy, even for accomplished composers with professional careers. Time is needed for reflection, criticism, and experimentation, which allows the imagination to 'play' " (p. 231). Reflection should take place during the composing process and after a piece of music has been performed live (which can, of course, happen in the choral rehearsal room). David Childs (2007) recommends that students take time for musical ideas to "ferment" in the mind as they create. Randall Stroope (2007), similarly, wrote that students should take the time to think about their compositions after a performance, letting the piece "cook" in their minds, and then think how and if to revise the work (p. 196).

Structuring Composing Exercises and Projects

Like learning to sing, composing is a set of skills that must be developed with practice and patience. Early composing exercises can serve as ways to help students learn music theory and the human voice by developing a sense of vocal ranges, melodic and rhythmic phrasing, chord functions, musical form, voice-leading, reading, and aural skills. Exercises can help them develop text ideas, such as discussing the meaning of a poem, practicing scansion, or musical ideas such as choosing a cadence for the end of two phrases, improvising a melody over a simple chord progression.

For each exercise, teachers should help students to develop intentions to articulate what the text or musical gesture means to them. No exercise should be given simply for technical purposes but should always seek convey a physical sensation, idea, or emotion. This means that teachers should always ask, "Why did you make that choice?" or "To what end did you choose to . . .?" until thinking *why* and *to what end* becomes second nature. Each of these exercises is also designed to help students learn or practice at least one of the topics of social and emotional learning. An introduction to the exercise will be followed by a brief description of the SEL benefit that a teacher should focus upon.

Holistic qualities of performing and visual arts can help students to link "What I want to convey" with "How I want to convey it." One way to communicate an expressive intention is through the choreographer Rudolf von Laban's four categories of *speed*, *weight*, *direction*, and *flow* to help them uncover aspects of choral works (Brooks, 1993). As

Libby Larsen (2007) describes, *speed* refers to the rapidity of movement with opposites of "quick" versus "sustained." Larsen wrote that composing should mean finding a balance between types of movement and stillness. *Weight* refers to the quality of heaviness or buoyancy, *direction* refers to whether the movement is in a direct path or follows an oblique/indirect path, and *flow* refers to the relative freedom or quality of being bound in movement.

In order to complete exercises, teachers should help students create a lexicon of descriptive holistic terms and lists of these terms should be visible for them to use in analysis and composition. The teacher may have students brainstorm words describing different qualities of flow, for example, like "dragging," "lugubrious," "spritely," "flowing," and "erratic." They can then use the terms to decide upon the intent for flow in repertoire they are singing. If learning Morten Lauridsen's "Dirait-on" (1994), for example, they might decide that the melody and accompaniment of the opening verse are hesitant, restrained, and wave-like in comparison to the chorus that floats freely. Considering the holistic qualities helps students to question why and how a composer makes artistic choices. Further, greater vocabulary will help students to articulate their own creative intent and support self-awareness.

Exercises and projects can take place in a number of contexts. Novice composers can benefit from teacher-led practice with the full ensemble, followed by homework exercises for guided practice. Students can be organized into pairs or small groups to reflect on how they made creative choices, listen to each other's homework, and provide feedback to each other. They can be grouped to practice improvisations or complete longer projects, to discuss meaningful texts and reflect on compositional products. There will be students who prefer not to talk about their emotions and interpretations with peers. Deeply meaningful texts can hit students close to the heart and their emotional/social growth might be best supported by speaking to a trusted individual. These students would benefit from sharing with the teacher or a single friend through voice memos, a journal, or an in-person conversation. Whenever discussing texts, it is a good idea to provide options.

Longer composition tasks should be given as individual projects. Aspects of the process may be completed in groups or paired discussion, but the creative work of a young composer should involve sitting with their own ideas, testing out musical gestures, and arriving at their own musical decisions. Their individual work is part of developing responsible decision-making skills.

There are many composition tools available to students. They can compose with paper and pencil at the keyboard, guitar, or a melody instrument or work with friends to develop a live performance. They can use score notation programs with record features to help with transcriptions or DAW[2] track notation and video programs to create layers of sound. Any tool that a composer uses provides affordances, things that it can help the composer do, and also limitations, things that are difficult or impossible. For example, writing on staff notation at the keyboard allows for students to play chords and melody as well as sing to hear themselves, as well as seeing how melodies, harmonies, and accompaniment fit vertically. However, they may find this form of transcription inordinately time-consuming or may not have keyboard skills to play what they can hear with their inner ears. Conversely, the loops in track programs make beats and chord progressions easy to create but students may not have the knowledge to name the chord progressions they hear in packaged form nor the skill to build more complex musical forms. The teacher should think carefully about the tools to teach and provide for each composing exercise for the affordances and limitations that it brings.

The teacher should always add an element of reflection for students to consider how they make creative decisions, the criteria they bring to bear in determining more or less successful explorations, and the relative success of compositional products toward their artistic intent. Paper and electronic journals can be as useful as in-person discussions and allow students to share their reflections during the creative process with the teacher. Students can also use journals to write down ideas about their interpretations and intent for texts, and to map out creative musical ideas involving scansion, melody, form, chord progressions, and voicing.

Students must hear what they create, and preferably with live voices, in order to be able to evaluate their creative efforts. Teachers should record and store student performances of compositions for reflection and feedback. Young composers should be encouraged to revise and rework creations after teacher, peer, and self-feedback, allowing for the mental "cooking" thought processes to bear fruit (Stroope, 2007).

Performance and recording can become cumbersome; a single composition project with a choir of 75 students could take a year to read and record! Instead of full-choir performances of individual works, teachers can assign chamber groups to rehearse and perform each other's creations, giving projects for specific voice groupings so everyone can create and perform. Project groups will allow post-performance reflection so individuals can learn how their creation works for the voices in their chamber group and how the arrangement of consonants and vowels supports or deters from their artistic intent because of either rhythm or vocal range. It will be best for project groups to work together for several projects so students can develop a supportive community for each other.

EXERCISES FOR NOVICE COMPOSERS

Choral teachers become experts at extracting exercises from repertoire for warm-up exercises to make learning the repertoire easier. There is also a treasure trove of composition exercises to benefit students, from developing the voice to learning about chords and counterpoint.

Exercises with Counterpoint

Starting with a simple cantus firmus (c.f.), the teacher can provide simple rules to first species counterpoint and have students experiment in sections (or as

FIGURE 31.1. Example of a species counterpoint cantus firmus (Chase, 2020). Accessed https:// hellomusictheory.com/learn/species-counterpoint/.

individuals over a section) to produce a vocal line over the c.f. (Figure 31.1). Some basic rules are to (1) begin and end on unison, octave, or fifth, (2) notes can only move with the cantus firmus (in whole notes), (3) avoiding parallel fourths and fifths, (4) avoid singing the same intervals more than three times in a row, (5) attempt to sing in contrary motion to the c.f., particularly when the c.f. skips (Mann, 1965).

A teacher can record the c.f. on piano in a DAW program and provide written notation. Students should notate a countermelody and then perform on a second track, then listen and reflect on what they heard. Alternately, the teacher can teach students to sing the c.f. and some students then take turns singing the c.f. while other students improvise a countermelody line individually. For improvisations, teachers can tell students to follow rules 1 and 2. In hearing each other, students will discover that it sounds different when one avoids singing parallel to the c.f., especially parallel fourths and fifths. They will also notice that contrary motion is more interesting than parallel motion. Once they have completed this exercise, they will be able to search through familiar repertoire to find which counterpoint rules the composer followed and discuss reasons for deviating from traditional counterpoint rules. An exercise like this gives students practice in self-awareness by developing their musical listening and practicing their skills at describing what they hear with nonjudgmental language.

For another exercise, students should learn to sing a simple folk song like "Tideo" (Figure 31.2).[3] Once learned, the song should be analyzed for the interval size and directions, tonal center, and key. Next, students should discuss ideas about some emotional or sensual quality they might want to convey about the lyrics and melody through a countermelody or descant. They should then explore a variety of ways to translate their intent. This exercise might be completed in sections, with each section working together to notate and record themselves singing the descant while other sections sing the melody. It will benefit everyone to hear each other's descants because they will have the chance to hear a variety of approaches and make their own decisions about what conveys a specific intent. An exercise like this will engage students in self-management skills because they begin to think about what they want to communicate and how to communicate effectively through music. For a first exploration into this exercise, it may be best to avoid assessing for success or failure but allow students, instead, to enjoy creating and sharing their reflections on the process of decision-making.

FIGURE 31.2. The folk song, "Tideo"

Exercises with Chord Progressions

In planning chord progressions, the teacher can provide some simple tools to work with. Students should learn to name key signatures and have a chart of chords with Roman numerals to reference as they work. They should also have access to letter names and notation for major and minor chords so they can easily see, for example, that the notes of any type of C chord are C, E, and G. The chart can include examples of adding a seventh scale degree to a chord and names of first and second inversions. The example below will provide steps for this exercise.

For a first exercise, the teacher can have students analyze chords that accompany an arrangement of a folk song. The students would first listen to a recording of an arranged folk song, like the SATB arrangement of "Now Is the Cool of the Day," written by Jean Ritchie, arranged by Peter and Jon Pickow, and adapted by James Erb (1971), taking notes about the sense of flow, weight, direction, and speed as the piece progresses (teacher may have each section tracking one holistic element) on scrap paper. Following a whole-class discussion of what students heard and reasons they posit for the composer's decisions, the teacher should provide the chord progression and melody for a section of the piece for analysis. Figure 31.3 shows a condensed score for the opening voices of the chorus. Here, the teacher should have the students name the notes for each measure vertically to arrive at the chords by letter name. They should then review key signatures so they can name the chord functions. They can then discuss the reason that James Erb would include the dissonances in each measure and how the choice to leave the thirds out of most chords impacts the way they sound. Ten minutes of analysis can yield a treasure-trove of musical ideas for students, including how to use iii and vi chords, how to achieve a sense of flow or stasis with the rhythmic choices and long non-chordal tones in accompaniment voices. Analysis exercises that include "why" as part of the analysis help students to practice social awareness, interpreting the intentions of the composer to convey some quality of emotion or sensation.

FIGURE 31.3. Notes and chords used in the opening of chorus of "Now Is the Cool of the Day," written by Jean Ritchie, arranged by Peter and Jon Pickow, and adapted by James Erb (1971). Lawson Gould Publishers.

FIGURE 31.4. An experiment with a chord progression

For another exercise, students can experiment with chord progressions with chordal instruments, notation programs, or online music tools like Chrome Music Lab Arpeggios[4] to find a short chord progression (e.g., four bars of half notes) that they like as a homework exercise. Once they have arrived at a chord progression, they should write the letter names out and, if appropriate, the chord functions within a key signature (however, their chosen progressions may or may not fit common chord functions within a key). Next, students should notate the chord progression in root form and, even if it looks quite strange, explain why they like the chords in the order they chose. Figure 31.4 provides an example of a progression that a student might find.[5]

Students should play the progressions for each other in small groups and group members provide feedback on the emotional and holistic qualities that they hear. These shares with discussion help students to practice social awareness and self-management, negotiating how to describe their interests and respond to others' creative works in positive ways.

Students can learn more about part writing and the best ways to set individual voice parts by setting the progression to two treble clefs for SSAA or a grand staff and bringing the root down to the lowest voice (for example, the tenor voice could be voiced in the bass or treble clef) They will also hear differences in the expressive qualities between piano/program and the human voice. Based on what they hear, students may revise the progression (for example, the second and third chords in Figure 31.5) to provide a smoother bass voice. Further rearranging the chord tones to create smoother vocal lines

FIGURE 31.5. Voiced chord experiment with Chords 2 and 3 changed

FIGURE 31.6. Revised voicing with a remaining tenor challenge

may also reveals that the tessitura is uncomfortable for one or more voices (for example, the soprano in Figure 31.5), so the novice composer can be guided to rearrange pitches once more (Figure 31.6).

Students should continue to experiment with voice placement to address difficulties that individual voices have (e.g., the tenor in Figure 31.6). They quickly discover voice-leading, range and tessitura, and evocative qualities that individual lines can sing as they experiment with voicing chord progressions and can also learn how passing and neighbor tones can help voices to transition between chords or can bring movement to the progression. They are likely to discover challenges such as the sound of parallel motion and difficult voice leadings in these exercises. These problems will help them to seek solutions that will, in turn, allow the teacher to provide instruction on common chord tones, common chord progressions, and cadences. Experimenting with voicing and re-voicing the vocal lines will help students to learn more about social awareness (how other's will experience their music) and responsible (responsive, in this case) decision-making.

For a third exercise, the teacher can lead the choir in building chords. Starting with a pitch in the lowest voice, the teacher can have students stagger breath while holding the pitch, then add more voices to build a chord (open or closed) that includes sevenths, ninths, elevenths, and thirteenths tones. The notation should be with provided and the chord labeled for students. The teacher can then stop voices or bring the chord back to a simple root position, move the fifth to another voice and add a non-chord tone. The whole exercise should be recorded, and the file named. Students can listen to the chords they created and then discuss the expressive qualities of the chords they have sung and keep them in a chord library. Such exploration and discussion can help students to build their self-management skills because they will collect a library of musical chords, complete with the qualitative impact of each chord, to be able to express themselves through music.

Exercises Creating Layered Ostinatos

Layered ostinatos form the basis for circle singing, in which students form a circle and sing two to four layers of ostinatos while they take turns stepping into the center to improvise. Stephen Paparo (2016) provided guidance for chorus teachers to incorporate circle singing as a creative activity in choirs. A student leader should stand in the center of the circle and improvise a short melodic or rhythmic pattern, repeating the phrase and "giving it" to one part of the circle. A first layer of sound could also come from a song that the choir is already learning (bass line phrases often make good first ostinato layers because they outline or imply chord progressions). From there, the leader adds a second ostinato layer, inventing what they think will go along with and support the first ostinato, up to four ostinato layers. While the circle repeats their parts, individuals go into the center and have the opportunity to improvise freely, until they feel they've finished and trade places with a different student. A teacher often finds that students, once circle singing is introduced, will practice creating and layering ostinatos outside as well as inside of choir class. To move beyond layering ostinatos, the teacher should record students and play the music back for them. Each layer should be extracted and notated, giving students a chance to practice dictation and analyze the music they have created. They are often surprised to find chord progressions they have created through the layered ostinatos. Circle singing builds relationship skills and responsible decision-making about how to act in the different roles.

Alternately, a program like Kandinsky in the Chrome Music Lab[6] or an online DAW with loops will create an ostinato for students to improvise over. Short loops can be found or built, and then students sing over the repeated ostinatos. These explorations should be recorded and students journal about what they discovered about complementary rhythm, contrary motion, imitation, and the other musical gestures they work with. As before, this exercise can help students practice their relationship skills and responsible decision-making.

For another exercise, students can practice adding an ostinato to accompany this song (see "Tideo," Figure 31.2). Students should determine or find the underlying chords for the song (a I chord, or a I–I–V–I progression in each measure). The teacher should direct students to experiment with different spoken and sung ostinatos with the intent to convey different emotional and holistic qualities. If students have difficulty thinking of different types of ostinatos, the teacher should play recordings of some folk or children's songs set with ostinatos to great effect, like Fabian Obispo's (2011) *Mamayog Akun.* The opening of this popular and challenging choral work sets the bouncy and light children's song to strongly rhythmic, swinging ostinatos to produce a dance-like effect.[7] Since different ostinatos will impact the effect of the song, students will practice their self-awareness in discussing what each type of ostinato adds to the expression of the song.

Exercises Practice Painting Emotional Qualities with Vowel Sounds

Exercises to practice composing with consideration for the sounds of words should begin with conversations about poetry and prose and reflections on the impact that different vowel sounds can have. Edgar Allen Poe's poetry can be effective for inspiring discussions. Students can read, for example, the first verse of *The Bells*,[8] with its playful "ih" and "in" and "ah" sounds that express joy, compared with the fourth verse that moves from "ah" to "oh" to "oo" to express foreboding and sorrow.

> While the stars that oversprinkle, all the heavens, seem to twinkle
> With a crystalline delight;
> Keeping time, time, time, in a sort of Runic rhyme,
> To the tintinabulation that so musically wells
> From the bells, bells, bells, bells,
> Bells, bells, bells—
> From the jingling and the tinkling of the bells.

And from the fourth verse:

> For every sound that floats from the rust within their throats
> Is a groan.
>   And the people—ah, the people—
> They that dwell up in the steeple,
>   All alone,
> And who tolling, tolling, tolling,
> In that muffled monotone,
> Feel a glory in so rolling
> On the human heart a stone—

Hip-hop artists and modern poets provide a wealth of powerful text to unpack and explore. Troy Osaki (2016), for example, speaking as Bruce Lee in his poem "Year of the Dragon" says: "I knew the reason why they sidestepped my fight scenes was to avoid staining their screens with slanted eyes." The impact of this line lies not only in words like "fight scenes" and "staining . . . screens" and "slanted eyes" but in the long "a," long "e," and the "ah" that give a brilliance to the words. Students might compare the way Poe used those same vowels to convey happiness while Osaki uses them to convey anger, exploring together why these two emotions relate to the same vowel sounds.

For another exercise, students should work in groups to sing a simple chord progression on one vowel sound, then explore changing vowels in single voices or through the progression. Recording themselves, they will discover that closed "oh" and "oo" and "eh" vowels sound quieter than the more open vowels as well as the impact of different vowel sounds. We can all sometimes take for granted how different vowel sounds can produce an emotional impact, so analysis and discussion here will help bring social awareness to students by highlighting this important aspect of language. These exercises can also help students as novice composers to practice their self-management, learning to make decisions about how to express an emotion through the text of a poem they set to music.

Project 1: Arranging a Folk Song

It can be a challenge to find folk song that can serve as the basis for an arranging exercise. Many great folk songs have already been used in choral arrangements and the students will know these from their years of singing in choirs. Additionally, some folk songs have been found to be fairly problematic; songs like "Jim Along Josie" (Waller-Pace, 2019) and "I've Been Working on the Railroad" (Ermolaeva, 2019), with racist backgrounds, while songs like "The Lion Sleeps Tonight" and "My Lord, What a Morning" involve appropriation, should be researched and their historical as well as textual meanings discussed. Many of the songs can serve to help students to develop more interest in seeking social justice for themselves and their peers. Students should learn how to be sensitive to the ways that songs can express cruelty and unkindness, developing their social awareness and responsible decision-making abilities.

Public domain music is useful for finding songs, both because there would be no licensure issue if an arrangement is performed in public and because it is worthwhile to teach students about copyright. There are indexes of public domain folk songs that can be perused for ideas.[9] Many songs from early pop and rock traditions are also now in the public domain, such as "Rockin' Robin," "House of the Rising Sun," and even "Love Me Do" (Mersereau, 2015). As David Childs (2007) and Gwyneth Walker wrote, it will be important for students to connect to the song selected, so it will be a good idea to give the students a list of folk songs to choose from.

Determine the Word Stresses and General Rhythm of the Text in Melody

In the case of "Rockin' Robin" by Leon René (1958) it may seem unnecessary to write out the scansion but such well-known songs can provide novice composers with good practice. Even pop songs can be interpreted in a host of ways, so discussion around syllables may give students creative insights. For example, the song "Rockin' Robin," there are some places where there could be different interpretations of the level of stress. I landed on the following scansion for the introduction and first verse:

```
  /    x  x  ^ x  x  x   x   ^ x   /   x  x ^ x  x  x
Tweedle-lee-deedle-lee-dee (doo-doo-doo), tweedle-lee-deedle-lee-dee (3x)
```

/   /   ^   /
Tweet Tweet . . .Tweet Tweet.
x /   x x ^ x ^ x   x   /   x x   x ^   x   x x /   x   ^ /
He rocks in the treetop all day long, Hoppin' and a-boppin' and a-singing his song
^ x x x ^   x / ^ /   /   x x   x ^ x x /   ^   ^
All the little birds on Jay Bird Street Love to hear the robin go tweet tweet tweet

Discuss the Meaning of the Text

Not all folk songs convey a deep sense of meaning but the holistic qualities can give students a lot to work with. The history of the song may also provide creative ideas. For example, comparing the two recordings of "Rockin' Robin" would allow the students to think about the ways that these two artists created different musical journeys for listeners. Michael Jackson's 1972 version (Galaxy Music Notes, 2020) is arranged for the boy soprano voice in C major and is in a much higher key than the original version, recorded by Bobby Day and the Hollywood Flames in 1958 (Galaxy Music Notes, 2020). The 1958 version provides stronger rhythmic gestures and a backbeat (verses using a rhythmic accompaniment on beats 2, 2+ and 4), and is in G major for the tenor lead. The verses are a cappella with brass echo, then vocal echo "tweets" in harmony under the chorus. Jackson's recording has a strong downbeat until the chorus, when the backbeat starts in the accompaniment instruments. The two versions of this song could be presented for students to discuss reasons for the changes made to the key, rhythmic structure, and accompaniment.

Students should next decide upon the emotional and holistic qualities they intend to convey to the audience in their own arrangement. it may be beneficial for them to write their ideas in a composing project journal and hold a partner discussion to brainstorm the ideas with a peer, which would allow them to practice self-awareness and relationship skills. Students may, for example, decide that "Rockin' Robin" should have a feeling of joy, swiftness, bounce, direct movement (rather than stopping the flow of the song to add atmosphere or development), and to flow freely, all of which might inspire listeners to dance.

Determine Voice(s) for the Melody Line and the Chord Structure that Brings out the Melody

If using the 1958 version for inspiration, students might want to perform the song in G major, suggesting the tenor or alto sing the melody. Students can easily find the chords for most public domain songs by searching online. The chords for "Rockin' Robin" are I7 throughout the verses, then IV–I–IV–V–I progression in the chorus. The tenor or alto voice can hold the melody throughout (the top voice in Figure 31.7) or students may decide to give the melody to a different voice in the chorus, allowing the other voices to

FIGURE 31.7. "Rockin' Robin," homophonic chorus ending

echo "tweets" or lyrics. Or, they might decide that all voices joining together to end the chorus would express joy through the homophony (Figure 31.7).

As they begin to write parts, students should learn that voicing a chord progression can easily lead to static accompaniment voices. Alternatives to homophony can include arpeggiations, passing or neighbor tones, solo singing with rhythmic accompaniment, imitation in voices, or vocables like "oo" and "ahh." These alternatives can enliven the energy and emotional quality of an arrangement.

Experiment with Imitation

Once students have learned the chords to accompany their melody, they can begin to experiment with imitation and descants. Gwyneth Walker (2007) wrote that she prefers to adapt songs in innovative ways rather than reproducing the song as it would originally be heard. The original version of this song uses a call-and-response style in the chorus, which can sound similar to imitation. However, students should be encouraged to explore different ways that imitation could be used. For example, singers could decide they want to use words rather than the original "tweets" (Figure 31.8) or add imitation to the verses for greater movement (Figure 31.9).

Arranging Musical Ideas into a Completed Piece

Once students have decided on musical ideas, they should arrange those ideas into a whole. Simple folk and pop songs are the quickest to put together because of the pre-existing AB form but students should think of any form as an emotional journey, taking the audience from whatever mood they experience at the start to the desired

FIGURE 31.8. Experimenting with imitation in chorus

outcome. Students should listen to examples of effective folk song arrangements to begin this step.

PROJECT 2: CREATING A MELODY FOR A SELECTED TEXT

Students may enter this project with little understanding of prosody or melodic phrasing. It is common for novices to create simplistic, stepwise melodies rather than complex contours, so they will need help to express their artistic intentions, encouraging them to revise initial attempts with leaps, rests and held notes. However, early novice experiments with accompaniment chords can result in strange progressions and unplanned dissonances. The teacher may need to withhold criticism while students

FIGURE 31.9. Experimenting with imitation in verse

listen to their results to allow them the chance to reflect on more and less successful moments, guiding rather than steering students (Childs, 2007).

Students should begin this composing project by collecting personally meaningful texts. It is a good idea for the teacher to create a folder for students to place texts they like, a library for students to choose from. Texts can be found anywhere for a project that will not be performed or recorded for the public but, if the teacher plans to perform any resulting composition, they will need to seek licensure for any text that is not in public domain.

Analyze the Prosody and Interpret the Meaning of the Text

Once students decide upon the texts, they should spend some time thinking and journaling about the overall meaning of the text and then how meaning is fashioned by the meaning, sound qualities, and inflection of the words. They should mark places where they sense movement or stasis and where the text suggests musical form. Students should then share their texts in pairs or small groups to discuss their interpretations and uncover more ideas through peer reflections. Sharing in a non-judgmental environment will help students to expand upon their knowledge of their own and other's values, beliefs, and ideas, helping them to develop self-awareness, social awareness, and relationship skills.

In this example, a poem called by Theodosia Garrison and called "The Burden" (Public Domain Poetry), I added bold to words and phrases that appeared to me to have greater emotional weight. Words that suggest stasis are underlined.

> The **burden that I bear** would be no less
> Should I **cry out** against it; though I fill
> The <u>**weary day**</u> with sound of my distress,
> It were **my burden** still.
> The burden that I bear may be **no more**
> For all I bear it **<u>silently</u>** and stay
> Sometimes to **laugh** and <u>listen</u> at a door
> Where **joy keeps holiday.**
> I ask no more **save only this** may be—
> On **life's long road**, where many comrades fare,
> One <u>shall not guess</u>, though he keep step with me,
> The burden **that I bear.**

This poem expresses a hope to carry our own troubles without troubling our comrades, even while thinking about times when we might be tempted otherwise. Thinking of the holistic qualities, the first verse feels sluggish and heavy, the second showing forward momentum but slowing on the last line. The third section feels gentler and lighter, but with steady forward momentum. The emotional journey might be to start with sorrow and move to a sense of peace.

Students should next add scansion to their texts to think about word rhythms. The example below might convey the heaviness of this burden rather than the person who is carrying it.

x /   x   x ^ /   x   x ^ / x   x / ^ x ^   x
The bur-den that I bear would be no less should I cry out against it;

Students should experiment, one section at a time, how to write and/or speak the scansion with rhythm. Students should record and share different interpretations, learning how rhythm can bring out different meanings in the text. Transcribing the rhythm may be a challenge for novice composers so the teacher may have them record themselves speaking in rhythm or employ the record function of a notation program to assist students. As with all creative activity, this first chosen rhythm should be considered a draft (Figure 31.10).

FIGURE 31.10. "The Burden," first phrase rhythm idea

Use Inflection to Create a Melodic Line

Spoken inflection should serve as an initial map for a melodic line, in which words with heightened meaning or emotion tend to inflect upward with a held pitch or use larger upward or downward leaps. Students should practice inflecting the text in different ways and record their experimentations to find one interpretation that conveys the meaning they intend. Once a student has decided upon a spoken inflection, they should experiment with translating the contour into a pitched melodic line, considering vocal placement and range. For example, in Figure 31.11 the word "bear" and "cry," rising in pitch to the head voice of a treble singer lightens the sound quality while expressing emotion. André Thomas (2007) suggested that the composer should not be impatient with the text but, rather, allow the melody to evolve with that exploration and revision process.

FIGURE 31.11. "The Burden," first transcription

The record function of a notation program will help students to move quickly through the process of transcribing their melodies. The teacher can either provide a key signature at the start of a melody-composing project, or the teacher can set a notation program to the key to C major and $\frac{4}{4}$ time for students to record, then help each student to adjust the key and time signature as altered pitches and word rhythms suggest.

Determine the Accompanying Chords

There are many ways to make chords available for student exploration, from keyboards and chord instruments to recorded individual chords from online programs like the Chrome Music Lab Arpeggios, or loops in online DAWs. Students should begin by identifying the major and minor chords (by letter name) in the key of their melody, then identify possible chords for the first note of each measure by looking at the pitch on the first beat. They should try singing each measure with possible chords to determine the best fit for their intention, notating the block chord under the melody. Next, students

FIGURE 31.12. "The Burden," revised melody with chord accompaniment

should review the rest of the notes in each measure to determine whether chords should be changed for rhythmic effect, to stress important words, or to provide a sense of movement in the line. In Figure 31.12, for example, the i–V in the first measure worked but the words "no less" felt like they needed emotional weight. I placed chords in contrary motion, III–iv–I, under those words. The third measure suggested a iv–I plagal cadence for an "amen" spiritual reference. After exploring the chords, I found that the original ⁴⁄₄ time did not fit the word stresses as well as ⁵⁄₄ time. Further, changing the last note of the phrase from a middle C to a repeated G helped to de-emphasize that unimportant syllable.

Students should record themselves and/or classmates singing and playing accompaniment chords and use the recording to reflect on more and less successful moments. They can also consider their composition processes and difficulties in class discussions, so everyone can hear each other and brainstorm possible solutions.

PROJECT 3: MAPPING OUT A FULL CHORAL WORK

Both students and the teacher should practice many exercises and each many times before working on a complete choral composition project. The students should complete this project in a series of scaffolded steps, checking in for reflection and feedback from peers and the teacher at each step.

As before, the process of composing a longer work should begin with each student selecting a personally meaningful text, interpreting and discussing the meanings of this text with peers and in journal entries. Text analysis, speaking the text over and over, finding places of movement and stasis, writing out ideas for scansion, all follow this selection. Students should then determine what emotional journey they wish to take with the text. They may find that a melody springs to mind at this stage.

From here, students should map out the musical form that will support the overall intent for the emotional journey and the holistic qualities. The mapping process should be described in journals and discussed with peers or the teacher. Students may create a work that includes piano, guitar, or DAW tracks, or may choose an a cappella work. The artistic intent for the text should guide this choice, although skill with those tools will certainly play a part in the selection. Students should keep the emotional journey and intent in the map as they write and make first attempts to map chords. For example, a student may begin their map with the key and time signatures and explanations for their choice and then label ideas for each part of the form:

- *Key D major, $\frac{3}{4}$ time: Flowing, light and dance-like*
- *Introduction: Begin gently, "oo" vowel–I7–vi9–ii–II7–V7*
- *Verse 1: Use half-quarter rhythmic patterns to support the dance-like quality, along with chord changes on beat 1 of each measure (end in ii–V–I dominant cadence)*
- *Bridge: Same as introduction, bringing energy back to "zero"*
- *Verse 2: As verse 1 but add some held notes, repeated text, and change chord accompaniment to every two beats to build emotional energy. Include a descant in imitation with the melody, ending the verse on modulation up a full step to E major: change ii–V–I to ii–V–VI–VI7 (V7 in new key—new I)*
- *Verse 3: straight in, homophonic, and chords on downbeat of each measure to build energy*

Students should then begin exploring how to express the prosody of each part of the text in a melody and decide what voice would express the melody best. For each section, they should decide on texture and create accompaniment voices (and instruments) as appropriate. Introductions, bridges, and codas should be added to create mood and the chosen holistic qualities that will move the piece forward in its journey. Finally, students should perform their works for and with each other, reflecting afterward on what they might adapt or revise to better achieve their intent.

In conclusion, adding composition to a choral classroom should involve students in analysis, experiments with vocal capabilities and music theory concepts, deep reading of texts, and conversations with each other. The many ways we engage students in composing will support their social and emotional learning needs. Composition projects can help them to articulate their emotions, beliefs, and values, develop goals for communicating intentions, and express themselves in positive ways. Even a few exercises in a whole year of choral rehearsals can be enough to inspire them toward a rich, creative, musical life.

Notes

1. Novice composers should learn that English is a stressed-syllable rather than a stressed-pulse rhythmic language, so several words may fall as function, or non-ictus, words. For example, the words "Cats chase rats" takes three beats to say, each word stressed. Add "The cats chase the rats" and there are still three beats with a pickup to the first beat. Add more words "The cats will chase all the rats" and the sentence still takes only three beats.
2. Digital audio workstation programs may include GarageBand, Audacity, Soundtrap, or BandLab. Some are downloadable programs or apps and some are cloud-based.
3. A history of this song, often called "Jingle at the Window" can be found in the Library of Congress or fiddler texts such as the *Traditional Tune Archive*: https://tunearch.org/wiki/Annotation:Jingle_at_the_Window
4. This program can be found at https://musiclab.chromeexperiments.com/Arpeggios/
5. I experimented with Chrome Music Lab Arpeggios (https://musiclab.chromeexperiments.com/Arpeggios/) to find this, and notated the chords on the free notation program MuseScore.
6. Kandinsky allows anyone to create a simple ostinato with percussion, vocal, and melody sounds. It can be found at https://musiclab.chromeexperiments.com/Kandinsky/
7. A fine recording of Mamayok Akun can be found as sung by the Philippine Madrigal Singers at https://www.youtube.com/watch?v=XXv6w1LNjmI
8. I found this poem and many other poets whose work is in the public domain at poets.org
9. I have found "SongScouting" to be a useful resource. This website has a long list of public domain songs from a number of cultures. https://songscouting.wordpress.com/what-about-these/these-are-public-domain/. IMSLP has a list of folk song collections, books in which folk songs can be found. https://imslp.org/wiki/Category:Folk_Songs,_American/Collections Some of these texts are very old and use language considered inappropriate now but the collections are nevertheless useful and would provide an opportunity for a conversation with students about the ways that language has changed over the last 200 years.

References

ACDA. (2020). Arts education is essential. Accessed https://acda.org/wp-content/uploads/2020/06/Arts_Education_Is_Essential-unified-statement.pdf

Brooks, L. M. (1993). Harmony in space: A perspective on the work of Rudolf Laban. *Journal of Aesthetic Education*, 27(2), 29–41. Stable URL: https://www.jstor.org/stable/3333410

Chase, S. (2020). A quick guide to species counterpoint. Accessed https://hellomusictheory.com/learn/species-counterpoint/. Surrey, UK: Hello Music Theory

Childs, D. N. (2007) David N. Childs. In T. Wine (Ed.), *Composers on composing for choir* (pp. 1–24). GIA Publications, Inc.

Clausen, R. (2007). René Clausen. In T. Wine (Ed.), *Composers on composing for choir* (pp. 25–38). GIA Publications, Inc.

Collaborative for Academic, Social, and Emotional Learning (CASEL). (n.d.) *SEL is . . .* Accessed https://casel.org/what-is-sel/

Dingle, G. A., Brander, C., Ballantyne, J., & Baker, F. A. (2012). "To be heard": The social and mental health benefits of choir singing for disadvantaged adults. *Psychology of Music*, 41(4), 405–421. https://doi.org/10.1177/0305735611430081

DiOrio, D. (2016). Foreword. In K. Strand & J. Kerchner (Eds.)., *Musicianship: Composing in choir* (pp. 15–17). GIA Publications.

Edgar, S. (2019). Music education and social-emotional learning: The heart of teaching music. Accessed https://nafme.org/music-education-social-emotional-learning/. Reston, VA: National Association for Music Education.

Erb, J. (arr.) (1971). *Now is the cool of the day*. Lawson-Goud Publishers.

Ermolaeva, K. (2019). *Dinah, put down your horn: Blackface minstrel songs don't belong in music class.* Accessed https://gen.medium.com/dinah-put-down-your-horn-154b8d8db12a. San Francisco, CA: A Medium Corp.

Galaxy Music Notes. (2020). How this public domain song "Rockin' Robin" became so popular. Accessed https://galaxymusicnotes.com/pages/how-this-public-domain-song-rockin-robin-got-so-popular.

Garrison, T. (n.d.) The burden. Accessed https://www.public-domain-poetry.com/theodosia-garrison/burden-16109

Higdon, W. H. (2017). Social and emotional learning in the performing arts classroom. Accessed at https://nafme.org/social-emotional-learning-performing-arts-classroom/.Res ton, VA: National Association for Music Education

Jorgensen, E. R. (2010). School music education and change. *Music Educators Journal, 96*(4), 21–27. doi:10.1177/0027432110369779

Kaschub, M. (2016) Comprehensive choral artistry: Developing musical intelligence through empathetic, creative and artistic practice. Accessed at https://www.researchgate.net/profile/ Michele-Kaschub/publication/315378946_Comprehensive_Choral_Artistry_Developing_ Musical_Intelligence_Through_Empathetic_Creative_And_Artistic_Practice/links/58cdb 21ea6fdcc5cccbbe768/Comprehensive-Choral-Artistry-Developing-Musical-Intelligence-Through-Empathetic-Creative-And-Artistic-Practice.pdf. ResearchGate GmbH

Larsen, L. (2007). Libby Larsen. In T. Wine (Ed.), *Composers on composing for choir* (pp. 39–68). GIA Publications, Inc.

Lauridsen, M. (1994). *Dirait-on*. Southern Music Publishing Company, Inc.

Lauridsen, M. (2007). Morten Lauridsen. In T. Wine (Ed.), *Composers on composing for choir* (pp. 69–82). GIA Publications, Inc.

Mann, A. (1965). *The study of counterpoint from Johann Joseph Fux's Gradus ad parnassum* (Rev. ed.). W. W. Norton.

Mecham, K. (2007). Kirke Mecham. In T. Wine (Ed.), *Composers on composing for choir.* (pp. 83–120). GIA Publications, Inc.

Mersereau, J. (2015). Six songs surprisingly in the public domain. Accessed https://ontheaside. com/music/6-songs-surprisingly-in-the-public-domain/

Mulholland, J. (2007). James Mulholland. In T. Wine (Ed.), *Composers on composing for choir* (pp. 121–150). GIA Publications, Inc.

Obispo, F. (2011). *Mamayog Akun*. Earthsongs.

Osaki, T. (2016). Year of the dragon. Directed by Quinn Brown & Troy Osaki. Accessed: http:// seattleaaff.org/2017/films/year-of-the-dragon/

Paparo, S. (2016). Circle singing: Composing improvisation and improvising composition. In K. Strand & J. Kerchner (Eds.), *Musicianship: Composing in choir* (pp.131–149) GIA Publications, Inc.

René, L. (1958). Rockin' Robin. *Class Records*. Accessed https://galaxymusicnotes.com/pages/ how-this-public-domain-song-rockin-robin-got-so-popular.

Ros-Morente, A., Oriola-Requena, S., Gustems-Carnicer, J., & Filella Guiu, G. (2019). Beyond music: Emotional skills and its development in young adults in choirs and bands. *International Journal of Music Education, 37*(4), 536–546. https://doi.org/10.1177/025576141 9853634

Rutter, J. (2007). John Rutter. In T. Wine (Ed.), *Composers on composing for choir* (pp. 151–188). GIA Publications, Inc.

Schmidt, B. A. (2012). The choral music of Ola Gjeilo: A new vision of the choral instrument in the 21st century. Unpublished doctoral dissertation, University of North Texas. Accessed http://citeseerx.ist.psu.edu/viewdoc/download?doi=10.1.1.901.7302&rep=rep1&type=pdf

Stroop, R. (2007). Randall Stroop. In T. Wine (Ed.) Composers on composing in choir (pp 189–206). GIA Publications, Inc.

Thomas, A. (2007). André Thomas. In T. Wine (Ed.), *Composers on composing for choir* (pp. 207–224). GIA Publications, Inc.

Walker, G. (2007). Gwyneth Walker. In T. Wine (Ed.), *Composers on composing for choir* (pp. 225–251). GIA Publications, Inc.

Waller-Pace, B. (2019). Jim Along Josie. Accessed https://decolonizingthemusicroom.com/songs-%26-stories/f/jim-along-josie. Fort Worth, TX: Decolonizing the Music Room.

Whitacre, E. (2019). *Composing for choir with Eric Whitacre*. Accessed https://www.youtube.com/watch?v=s5jfyt5Tazw. London: Spitfire Audio.

Wine, T. (Ed.) (2007). *Composers on composing for choir*. GIA Publications, Inc.

CHAPTER 32

....

COMPOSING IN ORCHESTRA

....

MICHAEL HOPKINS

THIS chapter will review the literature on composing in orchestra classes and provide examples of composing projects for orchestra directors who teach at different levels. In this chapter the term "orchestra" refers to ensembles consisting primarily or exclusively of bowed stringed instruments—violin, viola, violoncello, and double bass. Orchestra programs are less common in schools than band and choir programs. Elpus and Abril (2019) estimated that only 2% of 2013 high school graduates in the United States were enrolled in orchestra, compared with 13% for choir and 11% for band. The literature on composing in orchestra classes is also relatively small compared with other areas of the music curriculum, and I will therefore be drawing extensively upon research and practitioner articles that come from outside the string education literature. The chapter will begin by providing brief background on orchestra teachers' attitudes toward composing. I will then describe the benefits of composing projects in orchestra classes and the challenges teachers face when implementing composing projects. An emphasis will be placed on challenges that arise during collaborative composing projects, and recommendations for mediating those challenges. The chapter will conclude with a review of composing projects from the literature that can be implemented in orchestra classes for students at different ages and levels of playing experience. My goal is to provide the reader with answers to four common questions teachers have: (a) What is the role of the teacher in a composing project? (b) How do I plan and implement an effective composing project? (c) How much time will this take? and (d) How will a composing project impact our performance preparation?

PERSONAL BACKGROUND

Over the past 25 years I have tried numerous composing projects with orchestra students and collaborated with many colleagues to implement new approaches. My interest in student composing projects began when the Music Educators National Conference (MENC) released the first set of National Standards for Arts Education in 1994. Standard 4 stated that all students should have experiences "composing and arranging music within specified guidelines" (Consortium of National Arts Education Associations, 1994). Over the next decade many states developed standards based on the skills and knowledge called for in the 1994 National Standards (Lehman, 2008).

I had been teaching band and orchestra for several years and had just begun my graduate studies at the University of Michigan at the time the Standards were released. The lead author, Paul Lehman, was an associate dean at Michigan, so there was discussion of the Standards in our coursework. I had been composing music for my orchestra students to play, so I was particularly struck by Standard 4, which stated all students should have experiences composing and arranging music within specified guidelines. My first reaction was, "How in the world are we supposed to do that in band and orchestra ensemble classrooms?" But my professors gave me some persuasive rationales for why creative music-making is important for all students. As I started exploring the literature, I realized that leaders in music education had been calling on the profession to include more creative activities like composing for several decades.

I learned that leaders in music education had been advocating for the inclusion of creative experiences within music curricula since the 1950s and 60s (Davies, 1963; Madison, 1958; McMurray, 1958; Mursell, 1953). There were many initiatives within music education in the 1960s and 70s to promote student composing in schools, including the 1963 Yale Seminar (Mark, 1996), the Contemporary Music Project for Creativity in Music Education (CMP, 1973), the Teaching of Comprehensive Musicianship Program (Mark, 1996), and the Manhattanville Music Curriculum Program (Biasini, 1971). Despite these efforts aimed at promoting the inclusion of composing activities for students, composing remained largely absent from school music programs during the 1970s and 80s (Eisner, 1982; Leonhard, 1988; Ling, 1974).

I was hired in 1995 as the music director for the Michigan American String Teachers Association (ASTA) Junior High String Camp, a position I held for the next eight years. I started including composing projects in the large ensemble as part of the camp experience. Every student composed some rhythmic patterns, motives, and short melodies over a background chord progression, and then I would collect the worksheets and a few students would help me enter the fragments into Finale software and organize it, and by the end of the week we would have an "Ubercomposition" that we could perform. These projects were enormously successful. I was taken aback by how motivated students were to do the projects and perform the pieces for their parents.

Orchestra Teachers' Attitudes toward Composing

Composition received significant attention from music educators in the United States after the release of the National Standards for Arts Education in 1994 (Strand,

2006). In the first decade of the 21st century there were many pedagogical articles and books published to give teachers composing ideas and inspiration (Bolden, 2007; Bush, 2007; Fehr, 2011; Kaschub & Smith, 2009; Moore, 2010; Newberry & Strand, 2007; Ruthmann, 2007; Stambaugh, 2003), yet far fewer publications were specifically targeted toward orchestra teachers (Norgaard, 2005; Turner, 2006). The ASTA National Curriculum (Benham et al., 2011) included Creative Musicianship as a specific content area of study. Most of the learning tasks described in the curriculum were focused on improvisation, however, four of the tasks described specifically involved composing.

Researchers reported that music teachers in all areas rarely included composing experiences in their classes (Orman, 2002; Phelps, 2008; Schopp, 2006; Strand, 2006). The most commonly cited reasons for not including composing were a perceived lack of time, too many other learning activities to cover, uncertainty or fear about teaching composing, and a lack of professional training.

To better understand how composing was being implemented in orchestra classrooms, I surveyed orchestra teachers (Hopkins, 2013a) with items that examined (a) beliefs of composing as an appropriate and valuable activity for an orchestra class, (b) perceptions of composing as difficult to include because of music performance pressures and availability of instructional time, (c) educational preparation to teach composing (college training, professional development, access to materials, self-confidence in ability to plan for composing instruction, self-confidence teaching composing, self-confidence in music technology skills), (d) concerns about maintaining a teacher-centered versus learner-centered classroom environment.

My findings indicated that implementation of Standard 4, "Composing and arranging music within specified guidelines," was uneven throughout the string education profession, with teachers almost evenly divided over the inclusion of composing experiences within school orchestra curricula. Approximately half of the respondents included composing experiences at least once a year, and half rarely or never included composing in their curricula. However, the vast majority of respondents believed composing can be an appropriate and valuable activity for an orchestra class.

My findings also suggested that since the release of the National Standards in 1994, Standard 4 had made an important impact on string education. Orchestra teachers born in 1975 or later reported higher levels of pre-service composing experiences and more positive beliefs toward including composing in the school orchestra curriculum. The teachers who had more pre-service composing experiences were found to have more positive beliefs toward including composing in the school orchestra curriculum, but very few of the respondents had received training in teaching composing within their music education coursework. Other researchers have recently found that orchestra teachers often still feel insecure about leading composing activities and may pass this insecurity on to their students (Pellegrino, Beavers, & Dill, 2019). Orchestra teachers are often looking for ideas about how to design composing projects. As Lehman (2008) observed, teachers with no training in how to teach composing are unlikely to feel comfortable including composing in their classes. Many orchestra teachers who exclude composing from their curriculum may do so simply because they do not feel comfortable leading a composing activity.

My research findings suggested that many orchestra teachers who believe composing is valuable for students do not include it due to performance pressures. For example, 94% of respondents agreed they were always busy preparing for the next performance, 91% agreed that it was difficult to find the time to teach composing in their orchestra classes, and 59% reported they value composing but are unsure where to fit it into the curriculum (Hopkins, 2013a). Several other researchers have also found that ensemble directors do not include composing because they believe there is not enough instructional time to accomplish their other curricular goals (Menard, 2015; Schopp, 2006; Strand, 2006).

The respondents who included composing in their classes structured the projects in different ways. The most common approach was a concurrent approach (33%), with students composing individually in the classroom setting. Thirty percent of respondents gave composing assignments for students to complete individually outside of class. Twenty-three percent of respondents used collaborative composing in small groups (e.g., duets, trios, quartets), while 15% used collaborative composing with the entire large ensemble.

One of my research findings was that teachers who work at the middle school level were more likely to include composing in the curriculum than teachers who work exclusively at the high school or elementary level (Hopkins, 2013a). Middle school seems ideally suited for orchestra composing projects. Middle school students have developed their performance skills and knowledge of the notation system, but do not have the demanding concert and festival performance pressures characteristic of so many high school programs.

Taken collectively, the research findings indicate an ongoing need for improved teacher training in composing pedagogy. For pre-service teachers, composing projects can be included within string techniques classes, orchestra methods classes, and fieldwork. For in-service teachers, conference and workshop presentations emphasizing strategies for including composing while still maintaining quality music performances remain important and need to have a continued presence at state and national teacher conferences. Continued development of print and online pedagogical materials for including composing in orchestra classes is important for the string education profession. Professional development providers need to offer teachers examples of how they can include composing projects while also preparing for their performances. The next section will include suggestions for addressing that ongoing issue.

BENEFITS OF COMPOSING IN ORCHESTRA

There are many musical and non-musical benefits for students who participate in composing projects. Researchers have learned that students find good composition instruction and activities to be exciting, engaging, enjoyable, and interesting (Menard, 2015; Taft, 2019). The self-determination theory of motivation may help explain why this is so. Ryan and Deci (2000) identified three needs that are essential for growth, social development, and personal well-being: (a) competence, (b) relatedness (i.e., connections and associations with others), and (c) autonomy. I will describe how composing addresses each of these three needs.

Competence

Deci and Ryan (2000) explain that intrinsic motivation is maintained when our students feel stimulated and challenged. Composing stimulates students by helping them understand music from a different perspective than as a performer. Composing provides insights into form, theory, harmony, and the creative process (Koops, 2013; Menard, 2015). When students are composing they learn that achievement in performance isn't the only valid expression of musicianship. Some of our students may musically thrive as composers, enhancing their sense of musical competence.

Composing also gives students an opportunity to showcase their performance competence (Chartier, 2009; Hopkins, 2013b; Riley, 2006). I have found that students' performance skills are often enhanced through participation in composing projects. When students write music to play they challenge themselves, but they never write music they are incapable of playing. Therefore, composing projects lead to an enhancement of students' performance skills in a way that they find manageable. A common reason ensemble directors state for not doing composing projects is that it will take time away from preparing for a performance. My experience suggests that composing projects not only enhance performance skills, but they also increase feelings of competence by allowing students to think at a much deeper level about the connections between music composition and performance.

Relatedness

In self-determination theory, relatedness refers to the human need to feel socially connected. Collaborative composing has great potential for enhancing feelings of relatedness to others, especially when students are asked to compose collaboratively. Research on collaborative learning has revealed that students working in small groups promote each other's success by: (a) giving and receiving help and assistance, (b) exchanging resources and information, (c) providing feedback on taskwork and teamwork behaviors, (d) challenging each other's reasoning, (e) advocating increased efforts to achieve, (f) processing how effectively group members are working together, and how the group's effectiveness can be continuously improved (Johnson & Johnson, 1998). Students collaborating in small groups engage with each other's ideas and establish shared meaning. They negotiate, compromise, and reach consensus to achieve a goal. These skills are fundamental for entering the professional work force and the world community. My own research has revealed that there is a relationship between the balance of a group's collaboration and the quality of the resulting music composition (Hopkins, 2015). Chamber music participation has been promoted by string educators for improving attitudes toward music and music participation, promoting leadership ability, and developing communication, time management, empathy, and awareness (Leshnower, 2001; Trapkus, 2018; Zorn, 1973). When students are asked to compose collaboratively in small groups they have the opportunity to engage their musical imagination, creativity, and problem-solving skills in ways that are quite different from the skills used to interpret canonical repertoire.

Another aspect of relatedness promoted by composing is the potential for student compositions to enhance cultural understanding between students from diverse backgrounds. Orchestra directors have been interested for many years in diversifying the repertoire performed by school orchestras (Rotjan, 2018). What better way to diversify repertoire than to ask students to create an original composition? It is difficult to imagine any music that is more culturally relevant to students than music they composed themselves.

Autonomy

Autonomy refers to our students' need to self-regulate their experiences and actions (Ryan & Deci, 2017). Composing projects that take place in ensemble settings foster student-centered classroom environments (Webb, 2013), which lead to stronger feelings of autonomy.

Doing a composing project changes your role from ensemble director to a facilitator. This is often referred to as a "flipped classroom" or learner-centered versus teacher-centered instruction (Scruggs, 2009). This model of learning is prevalent in many subject areas within school, but used less often in large ensembles. When students compose, their musical autonomy is revealed. They show the teacher what they understand about how music is structured and organized. Through composing projects, I have learned that my students intuitively understand a great deal about musical structure and form that would not likely be revealed in a typical orchestra rehearsal. Feelings of autonomy also develop from composing because students have control over many aspects of their composition. This lies in stark contrast to the performance of large ensemble repertoire, where students must follow a set of elaborate instructions provided by the composer and conductor.

Showcasing Your Orchestra Program

There has been a very clear trend over the past two decades toward an emphasis on creativity, innovation, problem-solving, and collaboration in education. The P21

Framework for 21st Century Learning (2007) states that "Learning and innovation skills are what separate students who are prepared for increasingly complex life and work environments in today's world and those who are not. They include: creativity and innovation, critical thinking and problem solving, communication and collaboration." In 2014 the National Coalition for Core Arts Standards released a new set of voluntary standards for music with a framework that includes Creating, Performing, Responding, and Connecting (NCCAS, 2014). Project-Based Learning is a current movement in education that includes five components. The project is: a) central to the curriculum, b) arranged around "driving questions" that guide students to the main principles or concepts, c) focused on a constructivist investigation that involves inquiry and knowledge building, d) student-driven (students are responsible for designing and managing their work) and e) authentic (focusing on real-world applications) (Thomas, 2000, pp. 3–4). Composing projects provide string educators with opportunities to showcase their music programs in ways that connect with schools' overall mission and vision for student learning, thereby strengthening the importance of the orchestra program within the overall curriculum.

CHALLENGES OF COMPOSING PROJECTS

There are challenges for teachers to be aware of before starting a composing project, particularly one that will require student collaboration. Anyone who has ever been involved with a group project is aware of some or all of these pitfalls. Obstacles to effective group interaction include (a) off-task talk; (b) social loafing, in which some students allow other students to do all of the work; (c) unequal interaction; (d) negative interactions such as anger, ridicule, and racist or sexist remarks; (e) working independently instead of together, or splitting up work instead of collaborating; (f) low-quality interactions that do not involve much thinking; and (g) reinforcement of students' beliefs that some students are not capable of contributing (Chinn, 2010). In addition to these obstacles, I will briefly describe other variables that may influence collaborative composing projects.

Time

In my own research, I found that when groups had less time to compose their pieces, the amount of off-task talking and playing was reduced, with little impact on compositional quality (Hopkins, 2015). As Parkinson's Law states, "Work expands so as to fill the time available for its completion" (Editorial, 1955). I recommend adding time to the project as needed rather than providing students with more time than they need from the outset. In my research I noted that productivity increased as the deadline neared.

Friendship and Gender

A number of researchers have found friendship to have a positive influence on student interactions and the resulting composition (c.f. MacDonald, Miell, & Mitchell, 2002). Many of these research findings occurred with elementary or middle school students. In my research with high school students (Hopkins, 2015) I found that some groups of close friends were prone to high levels of off-task talk and social loafing, in which some students were allowed (or expected) to do all the work.

Some researchers have found that in mixed gender groups of students who are nine to 11 years old, girls take control of musical tasks and, in general, that these groups cooperate less well than single-gender groups (Burland & Davidson, 2001; Morgan, Hargreaves, & Joiner, 1997). However, in my research of high school students (Hopkins, 2015) the mixed gender groups had high levels of collaboration. The two weakest collaboration scores were in the all-female groups. One possibility for this contradictory finding is that gender groupings may vary in their effectiveness at differing levels of maturity and development. Teachers should definitely take into consideration the age, gender, and friendships among students when forming collaborative composing teams. As Berg (1997) noted, gender influences the status of individuals within chamber groups, and gender can influence the linguistic forms used and the quality of interactions.

Coaching Teams

Ensemble directors often provide direct instruction and may struggle to adapt to their new role as a facilitator. You do not want to hover over students as they engage in the creative process, so take a few minutes before the composing begins to provide suggestions about how to help and support each other as a team. Explain to your students the importance of balanced collaboration and participation to help reduce the amount of time spent off-task. Advise students to seek you out if their group is experiencing a decline in productivity. As students compose, be prepared to differentiate instruction by providing higher levels of guidance to groups with less experience, and greater levels of independence to groups with more experience. If you check in on a group and they appear to be distracted, remember that sometimes students need to take a creativity pause by talking about something unrelated to the task. Sometimes the best musical ideas are generated after a brief period of being "off-task." When students give a "work-in-progress performance" for you they may make negative comments about their compositions (e.g., "It's not very good"). Remind them that they can always make changes. Ask them to brainstorm how they might further develop their musical ideas to make the piece more exciting. Resist the urge to propose your own solutions! Some slight changes in pitches or rhythm or dynamics often make an enormous difference in how music is perceived.

Notation

A composition needs to be preserved in some type of medium. It can be an audio recording, or a score of some type. The creative process works best if students are encouraged to develop well-formed musical ideas before they are required to record or write the ideas on paper in standard notation. I think that preserving compositions using standard notation is extremely valuable for students, however, if students are notating as they compose, rather than after they have a well-formed idea, the process of notating will slow down and may interfere with the creative process. Many students will need help translating their musical ideas into correct notation. They may also write notes on paper first and then discover how those notes sound by playing on their instrument, which is in some sense the opposite of composing. In the early stages of the creative process, it may be helpful to make audio recordings or notational sketches of preliminary ideas and translate the finished product into a score using standard notation.

Figure 32.1 provides a succinct summary of the benefits and challenges that orchestra teachers should prepare for when planning composing projects.

Benefits to Students and Teachers
■ Composing engages students' musical imagination, creativity, and problem-solving skills.
■ Composition activities can help students better understand musical structure and theory.
■ The act of composing and the performance of student compositions can be highly motivational.
■ Students take pride and ownership in their work.
■ Composing allows students to reveal to their teacher what they know and understand about music.
■ The teacher takes on the role of facilitator rather than director.
■ Collaborative composing in small groups allows students to promote each other's success.
■ Composing provides students with an opportunity to showcase their performance competence.
■ Composing projects can enhance cultural understanding between students from diverse backgrounds.
■ Composing projects allow the teacher to showcase their creative, project-based curriculum.
Challenges to prepare for:
■ Size of composing groups impact potential for collaborative learning
■ Students may need coaching on how to help and support each other
■ Time allotted for completion of the project needs to be managed carefully
■ Friendships, gender, musical experience, and leadership characteristics impact student collaborations
■ Notation requirements may impact the composing process and time required for completion

FIGURE 32.1. Considerations for composing in orchestra

SAMPLE COMPOSING PROJECTS

My own research (Hopkins, 2013a) revealed that orchestra teachers use a diverse array of composing activities in their classrooms. The most frequently described project was composing melodies to specified guidelines (48%). Composing variations on a theme (11%) was the next most common type of project. Other types of projects included: arranging folk, classical, or pop material (8%); using non-traditional notation or special effects or techniques (4%); composing chamber music (7%); and composing chorales (2%). All of these different approaches can be found in the literature. Many composing projects presented in the literature are adaptable for both band and orchestra. In this section I will limit the composing projects I review to those that have been published specifically for use in the string orchestra classroom. In the United States, string instruction commonly begins in fourth, fifth, or sixth grade (Smith, Mick, & Alexander, 2018). I will describe beginning level composing projects that will be appropriate for students in grades four, five, and six, intermediate composing projects appropriate for students in grades seven and eight, and advanced composing projects for high school students in grades nine through 12.

Beginning Level Composing Projects

Turner (2006) advocated for beginners to start learning compositional processes as soon as they can play three or four pitches. Many of the simple tasks she described involve writing in standard notation, once students have learned to write clefs, bar lines, notes, and rests, and can take simple dictation. Turner's sequence began with writing rhythmic patterns on a single pitch, moving to melodic patterns that gradually increase in length and range, creating accompaniments, ostinato patterns, and harmonizing melodies. While none of the composing project ideas are described in detail, Turner's article is one of the few places in the string education literature that present several simple ideas that can be used in beginning string classes.

Composition is an ideal way to combine creativity and music theory for beginning students. Norgaard (2005) presented three projects that he used in both string classes and private lessons. Norgaard's simplest project, which could be used in beginning string classes, involved taking simple melodies from beginning method books that include only quarter and half notes (e.g., "Lightly Row") and converting them into fiddle tunes consisting entirely of eighth notes by adding passing tones, neighbor tones, and appoggiaturas on the weak beats, maintaining the notes of the original melody on the strong beats. A slightly more advanced project involved creating variations on a traditional fiddle tune consisting entirely of eighth notes (e.g., Bill Cheatham). Students were asked to alter the pitches of the melody that are on the offbeats for Variation 1 by using other neighbor tones, which preserved the nature of the original tune. In the second

variation, students were asked to alter the last measure of each phrase. The only stip-
ulation was that the last note should be the root. The third variation involved altering
the tune by changing the pitches on the strong beats to other chord tones. Norgaard
provided suggestions for how teachers can use the project for theory instruction on
harmony and chord progressions. He advocated for students to write their variations
in standard notation so they can receive instruction on stem direction, beaming, and
note spacing. Norgaard's third composition project involved students creating original melodies. He suggested beginning the activity by giving students a piece of staff
paper, asking them to compose a tune without giving any guidelines, followed by giving
them a blank piece of paper and asking them to draw a picture without any guidelines.
Norgaard suggested most students will find drawing a picture easier because they develop a mental image or model during the drawing activity. The teacher can then explain
how composers use models of form that guide the compositional process, and provide
examples of structural models that can guide the creation of a melody. Norgaard related the form of a melody to sentence structure, and recommended students analyze
melodies by a diverse selection of composers for uses of repetition, fragmentation, and
cadence points to help guide them as they compose melodies.

Some projects combine individual composing with collaborative elements. For example, Webb (2013) described a warm-up chorale project designed for orchestra
students in their second year of study. The teacher wrote a diatonic chord chart on the
board that indicated the Roman numeral for each chord and the names of all pitches
in each chord. Students began by selecting a melody and then copying it to manuscript
paper. Webb suggested using a line from a method book. The students then chose a
suitable Roman numeral for each pitch of the melody by referring to the chord chart
on the board and writing the numbers down on their manuscript paper. Students
then harmonized the melody with pitches from those chords, and then added passing
tones, dynamics, slurs, and bowings. Webb described the flexibility of this project and
that there are many possibilities for varying the project. The project could be done individually or collaboratively, and the harmonization could be done using aural-based
approaches, a notation-based approach, or a combination.

Straub, Bergonzi, and Witt (1996) described three composition projects. The first
was a small group project for beginners to create a programmatic piece (e.g., jumping
music, or a piece about a cat) by exploring sounds they can make with their instruments
including pizzicato, col legno, ponticello, glissando, and non-pitched sounds like
knocking on the instrument.

The second project involved students watching a horror film scene and providing a
soundtrack using harmonics, bowing behind the bridge, snap pizzicato, trills, fingered
tremolo, and the other techniques listed above.

The focus of the third project, "flight of the mosquito," was for students to brainstorm
sounds they could make with their instruments to depict a mosquito flying through
a line drawn on a chalkboard. Again, the authors suggested using special techniques
and effects like tremolo, rubbing strings, pizzicato, and bending pitches to depict the
mosquito's flight.

Their project descriptions do not contain detailed procedures, but they do suggest students notate the compositions using either standard notation or alternative notation systems that they choose. The emphasis in these projects is about creating tension and release using elements like repetition, variation, and dynamics. They do not require students to have well-established technique or background knowledge of chords or scales to complete, and help students learn about the variety of timbres that can be produced on stringed instruments.

Intermediate Level Composing Projects

Giebelhausen (2013) described a multi-movement project inspired by Vivaldi's *Four Seasons*. After spending a class listening to and describing the compositional characteristics of Vivaldi's concertos, students form groups of three to five and plan for a multi-movement work based on weather, with each member of the group responsible for composing one of the movements for the instrumentation of their group. The project is designed to take place over six or seven class periods using approximately 15 minutes per class, with groups performing their compositions at the end of the project.

Theme and Variations (TAV) is a useful technique for developing composers because it provides a secure structural framework, while also providing many opportunities for distinctive musical choices to be made by students. As part of a research project, Chartier (2009) developed a TAV composing project for an eighth-grade orchestra class. Students listened to the TAV in the second movement of Haydn's Symphony no. 94 and then composed an eight-measure theme in small groups of two or three. Once the theme was composed the groups each composed one or two variations on their themes. Students were required to notate the theme and the variations, and Chartier required that students perform their pieces in higher left-hand positions on their instruments (i.e., not in first position) to align with performance goals.

I have also utilized TAV extensively in composing projects with middle school students (Hopkins, 2013b, 2013c, and 2019). I find that when we ask seventh graders to generate ideas about how a theme can be varied they will generate enough ideas to fill a large chalkboard. I have done projects where students compose individually and others where students compose collaboratively. Both types of projects can be beneficial, but my preference is for the collaborative projects in chamber groups of three to five students. We provide students with an existing theme that they are very familiar with and ask them compose a variation or two. Notation is not required. I have asked many groups of students (and teachers!) to compose Variations on "America" ("God Save the Queen") and I am always amazed at the incredible variety of variations that emerge. If we have enough time available, I like to ask each group to compose a pair of contrasting variations. For closure, the simplest option is to have each chamber group perform their variation. A second more complex (but beneficial) option is to help the students write the variation down in music notation and pass out each group's variation score to everyone and perform the TAV as an orchestra.

Another type of project I have seen in middle school orchestra is composing in chamber music groups to create programmatic music inspired by a story. My colleague, Abigail Alwin, asked her students to create incidental music to be played while the story of *The Lorax* by Dr. Seuss was read aloud by a narrator. She began the project on Dr. Seuss's birthday (March 2) and performed the music on Earth Day (April 21). I have described this project in detail elsewhere (Hopkins, 2019) so won't describe all the procedures here, but I do want to highlight the compositional technique we promoted with the students.

We wanted the seventh-grade students who had been playing their instruments for two years to have a simple composing system for quickly generating interesting sounding ideas. We demonstrated an "additive ostinato" (i.e., looping) approach by layering ostinato patterns on top of each other. I played a very simple 1 measure bass line—a simple rhythmic pattern on the open D string. Abby added a two-measure cello pattern on top of my bass line. These types of patterns are often referred to as "riffs" or "licks" among rock and jazz musicians. We asked a student to add a simple violin pattern on top of that, and we had something that sounded pretty cool! We had the entire orchestra split into three groups and created more loops together. Abby referred to these loops as "motors." These motors became the engines that drove the compositional process. The students realized how straightforward and easy it is to generate ideas this way. When we split them into chamber groups to write music for their part of the story, all of the groups spontaneously created really great ideas. This type of project is really wonderful because there is so much that can be learned in terms of musicianship, literacy, dramatic import when narrating, and timing in performance.

Advanced Level Composing Projects

Hamilton (2013) developed a project for students to learn how to create simple accompaniments when presented with a lead sheet containing only melody and chord symbols. Over the course of three 45-minute sessions, students learned how to read and interpret chord symbols and then created their own harmonized arrangement for a familiar melody. As the sessions progressed, the students were introduced to rhythmic, voicing, and embellishment concepts for enhancing the arrangement.

I observed a high school orchestra chamber group composing project that became the basis for one of my research studies (Hopkins, 2015). The teacher would do the project in May, after the final orchestra concert of the year, but before he had to prepare his orchestra to perform at graduation. He asked students to select themselves into groups of three, four, or five, and create a two to four-minute chamber piece for their group to perform. Students were required to perform on their orchestra instrument. The composition did not need to be scored in traditional notation but had to be documented in some form. The teacher gave the students considerable flexibility in their approach, but he requested that the piece have a harmonic structure, have a conceptual idea, or a programmatic idea. Each group was required to make a video-recorded performance of their composition, and the musical quality of a group's performance (e.g., rhythmic precision, intonation, tone quality) was part of the rubric assessment criteria. The range of compositional approaches and resulting pieces was very impressive.

Conclusion

There has been an explosion of interest among orchestra teachers in eclectic string styles (e.g., folk fiddling, jazz, rock, mariachi) since the beginning of the 21st century (Benham et al., 2011). While interest in composing activities has increased in orchestra classes over the past 25 years, currently there appears to be much more interest in eclectic styles and improvisation than in composing. For example, at the 2020 national ASTA conference, there were 17 sessions whose title or target focus was on eclectic styles, but only two sessions specifically targeted toward teaching composing (one of which was specifically focused on composing cadenzas). I know from personal experience that sessions on composing tend to be less well attended than sessions focusing on performance topics. Still, the research data clearly indicates that creative musicianship is of increasing importance to string educators and composing projects are valued as an important part of the curriculum. Professional development that combines eclectic styles with a composing curriculum may be a useful path forward. Composing projects appear to be implemented on an occasional basis by many orchestra teachers rather than as an ongoing regular part of a sequential performance-based curriculum. A close friend and mentor once suggested to me that when the state organizations responsible for running the large group or solo and ensemble festivals decide to require all groups to perform an original collaboratively composed student composition at festival, that is when we will see teachers begin to show a stronger interest in conference and workshop sessions on teaching composing.

I will end with my research "wish list." We have a very small body of research that describes what orchestra teachers are doing with composing in their classrooms. Future research should continue to examine in greater depth the varied approaches to teaching music composition used by orchestra teachers and the way teachers define composition. It is likely different types of composing activities result in varied musical and cognitive development. Further research is needed to demonstrate the variety of benefits composing in an orchestra class may have on the development of musical skills. There is truly nothing more thrilling for me than to witness a group of students create something that is new and beautiful and belongs completely to them. I hope that teachers will continue to publish pedagogical articles and present sessions at conferences about the exciting things they do with composing in their orchestra classrooms. Enthusiasm is contagious, and perhaps someday we will reach a tipping point where composing projects are viewed as something that is essential, rather than an add-on for teachers who have some extra time available between preparing for performances.

References

Benham, S. J., et al. (2011). *ASTA string curriculum: Standards, goals and learning sequences for essential skills and knowledge in K–12 string programs.* American String Teachers Association.

Berg, M. H. (1997). *Social construction of musical experience in two high school chamber music ensembles.* Unpublished doctoral dissertation, Northwestern University.

Biasini, A. (1971). *MMCP interaction* (2nd ed.). Media Materials.

Bolden, B. (2007). Collaborative class composing. *Canadian Music Educator, 49*(1), 44.

Burland, K., & Davidson, J. W. (2001). Investigating social processes in group musical composition. *Research Studies in Music Education, 16,* 46–56. https://doi.org/10.1177/1321103X010160010901

Bush, J. E. (2007). Composing and arranging in middle school general music. *General Music Today, 21*(1), 6–10. https://doi.org/10.1177/10483713070200040501

Chartier, K. (2009). Integrating composition into one eighth-grade orchestra classroom. (University of Massachusetts Lowell).

Chinn, C. (2010). Collaborative and cooperative learning. In C. S. Clauss-Ehlers (Ed.), *Encyclopedia of cross-cultural school psychology* (pp. 229–232). Springer Science+Business Media. https://doi.org/10.1007/978-0-387-71799-976

CMP. (1973). Contemporary Music Project. *Music Educators Journal, 59*(9), 33–48. https://doi.org/10.2307/3394301

Consortium of National Arts Education Associations. (1994). *Dance, music, theatre, visual arts: What every young American should know and be able to do in the arts: National standards for arts education.* Reston, VA: MENC.

Davies, P. M. (1963). Music composition by children. In W. Grant (Ed.), *Music in education* (pp. 108–115). Butterworths.

Deci, E. L., & Ryan, R. M. (2000). Human needs and the self-determination of behavior. *Psychological Inquiry, 11*(4), 227–268. https://doi.org/10.1207/s15327965pli1104_01.

Editorial: Parkinson's Law. [Editorial]. (1955). *Economist* (November 19), 635.

Eisner, E. (1982). *Cognition and curriculum.* Longman.

Elpus, K., & Abril, C. R. (2019). Who enrolls in high school music? A national profile of US students, 2009–2013. *Journal of Research in Music Education, 67*(3), 323–338. https://doi.org/10.1177/0022429419862837

Fehr, R. C. (2011). A creative experience for music teachers: Introduce young students to composition. *Teaching Music, 18*(6), 11.

Framework for 21st century learning. (2007). Retrieved from: http://www.p21.org/our-work/p21-framework.

Giebelhausen, R. (2013). Seasonal suites. In C. Randles & D. Stringham (Eds.), *Musicianship: composing in band and orchestra* (pp. 233–242). GIA Publications.

Hamilton, M. (2013). Creating accompaniments in high school orchestra. In C. Randles & D. Stringham (Eds.), *Musicianship: Composing in band and orchestra* (pp. 243–253). GIA Publications.

Hopkins, M. (2013a). Factors contributing to orchestra teachers' inclusion of composing activities in their curricula. *String Research Journal, 4,* 15–36. https://doi.org/10.1177/19484992130100402

Hopkins, M. (2013b). A descriptive case study of two veteran string teachers' perceptions of including composing in middle school orchestra. *Bulletin of the Council for Research in Music Education, 196,* 25–44. https://doi.org/10.5406/bulcouresmusedu.196.0025

Hopkins, M. (2013c). March from the Nutcracker theme and variations. In C. Randles & D. Stringham (Eds.), *Musicianship:Composing in band and orchestra* (pp. 223–232). GIA Publications.

Hopkins, M. (2015). Collaborative composing in high school string chamber music ensembles. *Journal of Research in Music Education, 62*(4), 405–424. https://doi.org/10.1177/002242941 4555135

Hopkins, M. (2019). Collaborative composing in middle and high school chamber music ensembles. *American String Teacher.* https://doi.org/10.1177/0003131318816084

Johnson, D. W., & Johnson, R. T. (1998). Cooperative learning and social interdependence theory. In R. S. Tindale, L. Heath, J. Edwards, E. J. Posavac, F. B. Bryant, Y. Suarez-Balcazar, E. Henderson-King, & J. Myers, (Eds.), *Theory and research on small groups* (pp. 9–36). Plenum Press.

Kaschub, M., & Smith, J. (2009). *Minds on music: Composition for creative and critical thinking.* Rowman & Littlefield Education.

Koops, A. P. (2013). Facilitating composition in instrumental settings. In M. Kaschub & J. P. Smith (Eds.), *Composing our future: Preparing music educators to teach composition* (pp. 149–166). Oxford University Press. https://doi.org/10.1093/acprof:oso/9780199832286.003.0008

Lehman, P. (2008). A vision for the future: Looking at the standards. *Music Educators Journal, 94*(4), 28–32. https://doi.org/10.1177/00274321080940040103

Leonhard, C. (1988). The human values of music education. In J. T. Gates (Ed.), *Music education in the United States: Contemporary issues* (pp. 185–192). University of Alabama Press.

Leshnower, S. (2001). Member2Member: Coaching ideas—teaching leadership through chamber music. *American String Teacher, 51*(4), 47–48. https://doi.org/10.1177/00031313010 5100407

Ling, S. J. (1974). Missing: Some of the most exciting creative moments of life. *Music Educators Journal, 61*(3), 40; 93–95. https://doi.org/10.2307/3394616

MacDonald, R. A. R., Miell, D., & Mitchell, L. (2002). An investigation of children's musical collaborations: The effect of friendship and age. *Psychology of Music, 30,* 148–163. https://doi.org/10.1177/0305735602302002

Madison, T. H. (1958). The need for new concepts in music education. In N. B. Henry (Ed.), *Basic concepts in music education, the fifty-seventh yearbook of the national society for the study of education, part 1* (pp. 24–25). National Society for the Study of Education.

Mark, M. L. (1996). *Contemporary music education* (3rd ed.). New York: Schirmer Books.

McMurray, F. (1958). Pragmatism in music education. In N. B. Henry (Ed.), *Basic concepts in music education, the fifty-seventh yearbook of the national society for the study of education, part 1* (pp. 46–47). National Society for the Study of Education.

Menard, E. A. (2015). Music composition in the high school curriculum: A multiple case study. *Journal of Research in Music Education, 63,* 114–136. https://doi.org/10.1177/002242941 5574310

Moore, P. (2010). Getting an early start in music composition. *Teaching Music, 18*(3), 57.

Morgan, L., Hargreaves, D. J., & Joiner, R. W. (1997). How do children make music? Composition in small groups. *Early Childhood Connections, 5,* 15–21.

Mursell, J. L. (1953). *Music in American schools* (2nd ed.). Silver Burdett.

NCCAS. (2014). National Core Arts Standards: A conceptual framework for arts learning. Retrieved from http://www.nationalartsstandards.org/.

Newberry, E., & Strand, K. (2007). Teachers share practical advice on classroom composing. *General Music Today, 20*(2), 14. https://doi.org/10.1177/10483713070200020104

Norgaard, M. (2005). Integrating music theory and composition into the string curriculum. *American String Teacher*, 55(2), 58–62. https://doi.org/10.1177/000313130505500208

Orman, E. K. (2002). Comparison of the national standards for music education and elementary music specialists' use of class time. *Journal of Research in Music Education*, 50(2), 155–164. https://doi.org/10.2307/3345819

Pellegrino, K., Beavers, J. P., & Dill, S. (2019). Working with college students to improve their improvisation and composition skills: A self-study with music teacher educators and a music theorist. *Journal of Music Teacher Education*, 28(2), 28–42. https://doi.org/10.1177/1057083718787825

Phelps, K. B. (2008). *The status of instruction in composition in elementary general music classrooms of MENC members in the state of Maryland*. Unpublished master's thesis, University of Maryland–College Park.

Riley, P. E. (2006). Including composition in middle school band: Effects on achievement, performance, and attitude. *Update: Applications of Research in Music Education*, 25(1), 28–38. https://doi.org/10.1177/87551233060250010104

Rotjan, M. (2018). What's your rep? Integrative approaches and perspectives to repertoire selection. *American String Teacher*, 68(1), 38–42. https://doi.org/10.1177/0003131317743170

Ruthmann, A. (2007). The composers' workshop: An approach to composing in the classroom. *Music Educators Journal*, 93(4), 38. https://doi.org/10.1177/002743210709300416

Ryan, R. M., & Deci, E. L. (2000). Self-determination theory and the facilitation of intrinsic motivation, social development, and well-being. *American Psychologist*, 55(1), 68–78.

Ryan, R. M., & Deci, E. L. (2017). *Self-determination theory: Basic psychological needs in motivation, development, and wellness*. Guilford Publications.

Schopp, S. E. (2006). *A study of the effects of national standards for music education, number 3, improvisation and number 4, composition on high school band instruction in New York state*. (Teachers College, Columbia University). Retrieved from: http://search.proquest.com/docview/305361987?accountid=14667

Scruggs, B. B. (2009). *Learning outcomes in two divergent middle school string orchestra classroom environments: a comparison of a learner-centered and a teacher-centered approach*. (Georgia State University). Retrieved from: http://digitalarchive.gsu.edu/music_diss/1

Smith, B. P., Mick, J. P., & Alexander, M. L. (2018). The status of strings and orchestra programs in U.S. schools. *String Research Journal*, 8(1), 15–31. https://doi.org/10.1177/1948499218769607

Stambaugh, L. (2003). Take a chance with aleatory composing. *Teaching Music*, 10(5), 26.

Strand, K. (2006). Survey of Indiana music teachers on using composition in the classroom. *Journal of Research in Music Education*, 54, 154–167. doi: https://doi.org/10.1177/002242940605400206

Straub, D. A., Bergonzi, L. S., & Witt, A. C. (1996). *Strategies for teaching; strings and orchestra*. Music Educators National Conference.

Taft, S. A. (2019). Composition in the ensemble classroom: Ideas from eight researcher-designed methods. *Update: Applications of Research in Music Education*, 38(1), 25–33. https://doi.org/10.1177/8755123319846542

Thomas, J. W. (2000). A review of research on project-based learning. San Rafael, CA: Autodesk Foundation. Retrieved from: https://www.asec.purdue.edu/lct/HBCU/documents/AReviewofResearchofProject-BasedLearning.pdf

Trapkus, P. (2018). Structuring an effective chamber music class. *American String Teacher*, 68(3), 26–30. https://doi.org/10.1177/0003131318777466

Turner, K. (2006). Composition in orchestra class. *Teaching Music, 14*(2), 32.

Webb, R. S. (2013). Constructing a warm-up chorale in the string orchestra. In C. Randles & D. Stringham (Eds.), *Musicianship: Composing in band and orchestra* (pp. 215–221). GIA Publications. MK: This works for me.

Zorn, J. D. (1973). Effectiveness of chamber music ensemble experience. *Journal of Research in Music Education, 21*(1), 40–47. https://doi.org/10.2307/3343977

CHAPTER 33

....

INTERACTIVE COMPOSING IN SCHOOL JAZZ ENSEMBLES

....

DOUGLAS T. OWENS

THE instrumental jazz ensemble has long been a music performance offering in the schools. The existence of the ensemble has traditionally presented students an opportunity to study and perform a range of music from various jazz traditions, Afro-Cuban and Brazilian styles, rock, funk, and contemporary styles. Improvisation is central to the music; while many students have participated in the creative activity of improvisation, opportunities should be created for students to compose music for the jazz ensemble.

The existence of composition activities in the jazz ensemble is extremely rare. The performance-based approach has remained prevalent, although the importance of composition in school music instruction is well-developed in music education pedagogy. However, composition in ensemble instruction has been included in the National Core Arts Standards (NCCAS, 2014), and frequently discussed in literature (Koops, in Kaschub and Smith, 2013; Koops, 2009; Hickey, 1997). Composition in the school jazz ensemble is discussed, but minimally (Knaster, 2016; Koops, 2009). McCurdy, in Miles and Carter (2008), discusses ideas for jazz solo transcription, and the creation of "Instant Arrangements" (pp. 38–40).

The listening skills used by jazz musicians in rehearsal and performance, especially when improvising, are unique and essential. Jazz musicians should have multiple experiences listening, interpreting, and performing jazz, along with the ability to transpose music in any key signature, and utilizing their interpretive abilities to arrange and improvise music in performance. Reimer (2003) emphasized the importance of listening "as the basic source from which ideas and possibilities spring" (p. 260). As such, students in the jazz ensemble must be exposed to jazz and additional musical genres via listening, which ultimately informs performance and composition practice.

The jazz ensemble is one possible component of a comprehensive instrumental music program. For those planning to add composition into their jazz curriculum, the assessment of prior student musical knowledge and experience is important in order to focus on learning the genre. Students in the jazz ensemble should have prior instrumental experience, as the ensemble experience enhances their existing musicianship. The ensemble instrumentation can be traditional (saxophones, trumpets, trombones, guitar, piano, bass, drums) or can include additional instruments to create a more inclusive jazz experience.

Listening to jazz styles is an essential approach to performance and composition. Gaining familiarity with the multiple styles within the jazz genre is necessary. This chapter will introduce listening and compositional approaches that can be readily applied within the jazz ensemble rehearsal, at the middle and high school levels.

BALANCING PERFORMANCE AND COMPOSITION IN THE JAZZ ENSEMBLE

Performance is a major aspect of instruction in any school ensemble. In the jazz ensemble, rehearsal time may be limited, and an understandable concern may be the added time required to incorporate composition activities into the curriculum. When incorporating composition lessons into the jazz ensemble rehearsal, initial start-up challenges will exist. However, the time invested in any creative musicianship during the jazz ensemble rehearsal, including composition and improvisation, will benefit the student comprehension and musicianship levels while preparing for any performance. Additional organizational time may be needed at first, but by mapping the composition activities to an existing jazz ensemble curriculum or method book, the bulk of the work can be very accessible to all students.

THE IMPORTANCE OF LISTENING IN THE JAZZ ENSEMBLE

Jazz studies in schools at all levels should have integrated listening and score study activities that can support performing, improvising, and composing. Various professional jazz musicians and their ensembles have created the history and foundational style of jazz through composition, performance, and improvisation. Several musicians have built upon that history to date, updating the compositional and performance styles over time. The music of the jazz big bands/jazz orchestras including Duke Ellington, Chick Webb, Count Basie, Benny Goodman, Glenn Miller, The International Sweethearts of Rhythm, Woody Herman, Stan Kenton, and many others should be explored. Also, the music of contemporary ensembles including the Maria Schneider Orchestra, the Jazz at Lincoln Center Orchestra, the Christian McBride Big Band, the Vanguard Jazz Orchestra, the Clayton-Hamilton Jazz Orchestra, the Bob Mintzer Big Band, the DIVA Jazz Orchestra and many others should be considered when composing music in the jazz style.

To introduce the listening process with your students, consider selecting a "band of the week" or other activity, and assign students listening activities featuring specific composers or ensembles. YouTube or other sources provide good access to the music. In jazz ensemble rehearsals, the director can facilitate discussion while sharing the various techniques used by the composers and instrumentalists. Provide weekly topics and discussion points that will enhance the composition and performance of jazz. This process is an outstanding way to build a jazz listening library for schools. The sources are limitless, and can extend to the music of jazz combos, individual musicians, and other jazz-related approaches.

Use Jazz Ensemble Method Books to Organize Composition Study

The teaching and rehearsal of jazz style, articulation, rhythm, syncopation, harmony, chord progressions, improvisation, etc. is organized effectively by the various jazz ensemble performance method books designed for beginning and intermediate jazz students. Several jazz ensemble method books offer a measured, sequential approach to building experience and musicianship in jazz (See Figure 33.1).

The introduction of jazz, Afro-Cuban, Brazilian, rock and funk styles via reading, listening, and interpretation of the music creates an essential foundation and should be an ongoing process. Students should have frequent opportunities to rehearse in an ensemble setting to focus on multiple musical elements and styles, and to gain a sense of the full jazz ensemble sound. While practicing on their own, the recorded accompaniment tracks that align with the selected jazz ensemble method books provide the students with a stylistic reference and the potential motivation to practice. The school jazz ensemble provides a natural access point for compositional ideas. Enhancing the existing performance-based jazz method book material with content-aligned composition lessons is ideal. Multiple opportunities for teacher-led group composition, student-centered small group composition, and individual composition can occur. An approach featuring the "layering" of techniques will be discussed, beginning with rhythm exercises, continuing with melodic and harmonic ideas, and adding the rhythm section.

Beginning with a Rhythm-Focused Approach

Once the students exhibit confidence and good levels of success in rehearsal while echoing rhythms and music presented by the teacher, reading music from a jazz method book, and incorporating the aforementioned concepts, the addition of exercises to encourage compositional ideas should be included. As a main focus of the jazz method books is on rhythm and style, the creation of short rhythmic compositions that

Title and publication year	Author	Publisher
The Articulate Jazz Musician: Mastering The Language of Jazz (2013)	Caleb Chapman, Jeff Coffman	Alfred Music Publishing
Essential Elements for Jazz Ensemble: A Comprehensive Method for Jazz Style and Improvisation Book 1 (2000)	Mike Steinel	Hal Leonard
Essential Elements for Jazz Ensemble: A Comprehensive Method for Jazz Style and Improvisation Book 2 (2019)	Mike Steinel	Hal Leonard
First Place for Jazz: Introductory Method for Jazz Ensemble (2011)	Dean Sorenson	Kjos Music Press
Jazz Zone . . . The Beginning (2019)	J. Richard Dunscomb, ed. Peter BarenBregge	Print Music Source
Standard of Excellence Jazz Ensemble Method (1998)	Dean Sorenson	Kjos Music Press
Standard of Excellence Advanced Jazz Ensemble Method (2004)	Dean Sorenson	Kjos Music Press

FIGURE 33.1. Selected jazz ensemble method books

incorporate rhythmic and style ideas is an effective approach. Such compositions should initially be teacher-facilitated, with students contributing various rhythms and articulations to be displayed on a white board or via technology.

For a first effort, consider basing the first rhythmic composition exercise on a style and short piece from a method book or other source provided to the students. Determine the composition length, use the same time signature, and set some initial guidelines such as rhythm usage (half, quarter, and eighth note rhythms and rests are suggested, although various creative approaches can certainly be utilized). The director can create the first measure, and the students can contribute their ideas at that point. All details can vary based on student comprehension and lesson pacing. Once completed, have the students clap and sing the rhythms on one pitch, following which they can play the composed rhythms on their instruments (See Figure 33.2).

The process can be repeated with increasingly challenging rhythms, including eighth notes in a swing style, which should be incorporated early in the process. Emphasize the importance of swing eighth notes; model the style for the students, and play the related exercises/pieces in a selected method book or jazz ensemble music. Using the same composition, articulation, accents, and syncopation in a jazz context can easily be added, as multiple examples exist in the jazz lesson books and beginning and intermediate level jazz ensemble music.

Director composition   Sample student response compositions

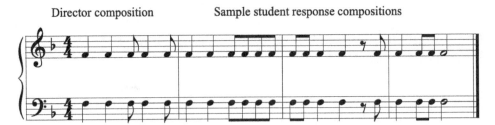

FIGURE 33.2. Shared composition

For each rhythm-focused composition lesson, find recorded examples of music that presents swing style, with articulation, accents, and syncopation in a jazz context with a focus on rhythm. The eight-measure introduction to the Wild Bill Davis arrangement of Vernon Duke's "April in Paris" (1955) as performed by the Count Basie Orchestra provides one example. The introduction features the trumpet section and lead alto saxophone playing swing eighth notes, with limited note changes and harmony. Consider creating listening guides to align with discussions and some essential questions. Select your own music for listening as appropriate. Have the ensemble members listen to the example, and then ask them essential questions to extend the experience. Sample essential questions and rhythmic analysis activities could be as follows:

- What instrument sections are heard the most in the introduction of "April in Paris?"
- What rhythms are heard the most in the introduction of "April in Paris?" Clap or sing the rhythms.
- How should the rhythm that is heard the most in the introduction of "April in Paris" be notated? (The director can write the answers on the white board or via a notation program projected in the room).
- Are any other rhythms heard in the introduction of "April in Paris?" If so, what rhythms are played by what instruments? Clap the additional rhythms that you hear in the recording.
- Is syncopation heard in the introduction of "April in Paris?"
- Do you hear any other elements that contribute to the introduction of "April in Paris?"

The short introduction to "April in Paris" illustrates the importance of rhythm, but also demonstrates that the repeated swing eighth note rhythms and the entire motive as rhythmically important elements used to introduce the piece. In a sense, the entire band is setting up the swing feel, before it may be apparent. Also, the multiple instrumental parts present illustrate some of the layers of rhythmic parts possible in a jazz ensemble. Possible corresponding composition activities could be as follows:

- Have the students suggest changes to the existing notated rhythms on the board. Limit the length to two measure phrases, similar to the introduction to "April in

Paris." Set a tempo, and have the students clap the rhythms, then sing and play the new rhythms on one note.

- Create a new rhythm pattern that emphasizes the swing style. Set a tempo, and have the students clap the rhythms, then sing and play the new rhythms on one note.

As an extension to this lesson, have the students listen to the next 16 measures of "April in Paris." Additional sample questions and rhythmic analysis activities include:

- What additional rhythmic elements do you hear?
- Do some rhythms repeat?
- What rhythms are being played by the saxophones?
- Listen closely for the guitar part. What rhythms are played by the guitarist?
- What rhythms are played by double bass?
- What rhythms are played by the drummer?

Another suggested rhythm lesson can be focused on the introduction section in the Bob Mintzer composition "Computer" (1984). "Computer" is a funk style piece that features a repeated quarter note/eighth note melodic part in the trombone section during the 16-measure introduction. Three melodic parts with distinct rhythms are layered during the introduction. The conga drums provide a fourth layer, introducing a rhythmic groove that continues into the A section of the piece. The main melody of the A section is built on the introductory rhythmic idea. In addition to the previous approach and questions, examples of essential questions and analysis of "Computer" could be as follows:

- What instrument sections are the heard the on the introduction of "Computer?"
- How should the melody and rhythm that is heard the most on the introduction of "Computer" be notated? Clap or sing the rhythms.
- Does a secondary melodic part exist? If so, in what instruments is the secondary part played?
- Clap or sing the rhythms from the secondary part.
- After the first eight measures, does a third melodic part exist?
- Do additional rhythmic parts appear? If so, in what instrument(s)?

By connecting with existing music examples, the students can begin to visualize their own approaches to the composition process. The short rhythmic composition process can be continued with small groups of students working together. The groups can be based on their instrumental sections, and compositions can be built on increasingly challenging rhythms. The director can suggest added elements as appropriate to the level of the students, such as including specific articulation to enhance rhythmic accuracy, the use of uniform phrase releases to emphasize section accuracy as needed, etc. Multiple elements can be included to extend the compositional experience. The focus should continue to be on creativity, embracing the new process and the ensuing ideas.

The jazz ensemble director should determine the overall pacing of the composition lessons. Alternating the rehearsal of method book exercises with compositional activities provides variety and new musical contexts for the students.

The Addition of Melodic Ideas

Beginning level jazz ensemble method books often initially feature unison compositions in jazz swing style. The teaching and learning of such music affords an opportunity to add more approaches to the in-rehearsal composition activities. Continue to reinforce the lesson book techniques and music by clapping rhythms in context, singing the music, and playing the music. A teacher-led arranging session of a short piece from a jazz method book or other source may spur creativity among the students. The addition of melodic ideas can be encouraged to happen organically, or structure can be added more quickly, based on the level of student experience. Initially, the use of one, two or three different notes, and scales can be applied to the existing rhythms, as illustrated in Figure 33.3.

Figure 33.4 is a 16-measure example of melodic composing from my jazz ensemble composition "A New You" (Owens, 2003), and illustrates how a short melodic idea can be developed. The entire composition is based on the 32-measure song form chord progression from "There Will Never Be Another You" (1942), by Harry Warren with lyrics by Mack Gordon. The first three-measure idea is presented, followed by a melodic answer that is somewhat sequenced, and rhythmically lengthened. A new idea is presented at letter B, while maintaining the same phrase length, is followed by another melodic answer and a transition to the next 16 measures, which begin with a restatement of the melody in measures 1–7. All notes work well with the original chord progression (See Figure 33.4).

Once the melodic composition process is familiar to the students, provide additional time for the students to create their own notated arrangement of a few measures, over limited chord progressions. When this is completed, have the students share their work, and have them reflect on the composition and process.

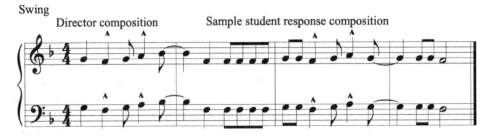

FIGURE 33.3. Prompted composition

FIGURE 33.4. Excerpt from "A New You," Owens, D. T. (2003)

Experimenting with Harmonic Approaches

The inclusion of harmony, extended chords, and chord progressions is an important step in the progress of the student jazz composer. Continuing with the alignment with the jazz ensemble method book, blues chord progressions are typically featured initially.

The 12-bar blues form is generally introduced early in jazz ensemble method books. In its basic form, the 12-bar blues features 12 measures total, with the following harmonic structure:

- four measures of the I chord;
- two measures of the IV chord and two measures of the I chord;
- two measures of the V chord and two measures of the I chord.

Multiple listening examples from jazz method books and from jazz history (and other styles) can be shared to provide examples of harmonic context for the students. It is important to consider and listen to small group/combo jazz as well. Suggested examples include:

- "Dippermouth Blues" (1923), King Oliver, composer; recorded by King Oliver's Creole Jazz Band. This early jazz piece features collective improvisation.
- "The St. Louis Blues" (1925), W. C. Handy, composer; Bessie Smith, vocalist. Bessie Smith sings the melody and Louis Armstrong plays the muted cornet solo and responses. This blues includes a six-measure bridge.
- "West End Blues" (1928), King Oliver, composer. This early jazz piece features Louis Armstrong and His Hot Five. The featured solos include Armstrong's famous trumpet introduction, trombone, clarinet, scat singing, piano, and trumpet.
- The form and chord progressions heard in each piece should be discussed in detail and reinforced via performance-based listening exercises. Some essential questions and analysis of "West End Blues" could be as follows . . .
- In what key is this piece performed?
- How many measures are included in the overall form of this piece?
- What instruments are performed in this recording?
- In which instruments is the harmonic progression represented?
- In what ways is the harmonic progression presented differently on each repeat of the form?
- Do the notes in the 12-bar blues harmonic progression differ from the basic progression at any time in the piece?
- In what other ways can this piece be ended?

Such 12-bar blues listening exercises can easily flow into melodic-based composition exercises. For example, call-and-response exercises can build performance confidence in the 12-bar blues form and can also add to the level of creativity of compositional ideas. A director-led 12-bar call and response exercise can return to a rhythm-only focus, developing one measure at a time. Then notes can be added, with the response happening as desired (one, two, or more measures). The echoed imitation of ideas is appropriate at first, while changing the rhythms, notes, accents, etc. within the provided structure should be encouraged for added opportunities for creativity.

Using 12-bar blues chord progressions, the call-and-response focus can happen over the entire form. This process can be repeated with a student leader, with the entire band or individual sections. Create an audio recording of these lessons for reflection and the noting of compositional reference points (style, rhythm, form, range, and other musical ideas to be referenced in the future). An audio resource library could be created for students to access individually or in small groups as they compose. This type of activity can take multiple forms, based on the lesson outcomes.

Returning to the director-led, small group, or section composition approach, students should compose their ideas over the 12-bar blues progression in the same keys that have been learned previously. A section-based approach reduces the need to transpose parts; the students can more easily compose for their familiar instruments first, then add instruments as their skills improve. Any initial ideas can be based on specific melodic lines from a jazz ensemble method book or other melodic material.

For another approach, have the students compose in four measure sections, then move to the next four measures, until everyone has had a chance to compose over the entire form. When regrouping as an ensemble, the students can choose which four-measure composition they will share. The shared composition will be combined with two other four-measure compositions to create the whole piece. In this manner, the compositions can then be played with the rhythm section, providing good practice for all students.

Addressing the Rhythm Section

Young composers need make decisions about the overall style and groove of their compositions. This includes learning about the roles of rhythm section instruments in a jazz ensemble. Various concepts can be introduced via jazz method books, jazz ensemble music, and by individual and guided listening to jazz music. For example, comping (accompanying) is typically introduced fairly early in the piano and guitar jazz ensemble method books. Chord voicings may be included as well. As an alternative, the guitarist and pianist may continue playing in a melodic role. The bassist should continue to provide the foundation to the chords, while expanding their harmonic and rhythmic knowledge (with guidance as needed), based on the style of the composition. For a jazz swing piece, this will initially be illustrated in music notation, but will later progress to chord symbols that must be creatively interpreted and realized. The drummer needs to incorporate style and time-keeping ideas from method book examples, then apply the ideas to the new compositions. Also, the drummer needs to interact with the ensemble parts, supporting them as needed.

All jazz method books, including drum set books, typically present sample rhythms within, based on specific styles. This will have been developed in discussion with the director, who observes and assists as needed. The listening sessions contribute greatly to the groove determination process. At some point, all instrumentalists should participate in this process, so they are aware of the rhythmic impact with their own pieces.

The compositions can be shared via in-rehearsal performance by each section. Knowing that the length and frequency of school jazz rehearsals are limited, provide added materials to encourage the students to practice composition ideas at home in addition to their individual instrumental practicing. The students can write their ideas on paper, sing or play them into a cell phone recording app, or use a free web-based notation program to do so.

THE IMPACT OF IMPROVISATION

Jazz ensemble teachers at all levels can use melodies in their ensemble repertoire to highlight good ideas for composing melodies. For those using jazz ensemble method books, there are regular opportunities for improvisation built in, alongside the introduction of new exercises and music. Within the method books, new melodic ideas are introduced, and the length of exercises and pieces increase. Also, the director may choose to have the ensemble read sheet music at an appropriate level. The new melodic ideas provide a good setting for improvisation and composition ideas. The increased length of the method book pieces facilitates an introduction to musical form and chord progressions, as discussed and presented in the method books. Students will begin to realize possible connections to their own compositions.

Student improvisation could include small group or collective improvisation to establish student confidence. Those students that are additionally proficient may want to improvise on their own. The same approach can be applied to the connected composition activity, with the added benefit of using some melodic and rhythmic ideas from the group improvisation, or from the soloists. This is an opportunity for the director to audio record the class session to later notate and share the ideas shared by the students. Alternatively, the students could listen to the prior ideas and create their own group composition sessions. The connections between composing and improvising should become apparent with each exercise.

While the previous blues-based exercises offer a good introduction to the call-and-response approach and overall form, it is important for the director to model improvisation and continue to provide sample melodic and rhythmic ideas for students at this level. Of great importance is taking the time needed for improvisation. The modern jazz ensemble method books provide online access to recorded practice tracks, complete with rhythm section. With guidance, and creative encouragement and motivation from the jazz ensemble director, students can practice improvisation on their own and arrive at rehearsals with new ideas and confidence for improvisation.

Improvised solo ideas can contribute to compositions. If a cell phone or other recording device is available, students can record their improvised solos in rehearsal, or during their own practice time. The music practice app SmartMusic includes some jazz music, and can be used for improvisation as well. The solos could then be transcribed for use in future compositions. Also, the transcription of solos from jazz recordings is an excellent and frequently used method to develop improvisational and compositional ideas.

Expanding on Melodies

Melodic development is important to the composition process. One next step in melodic writing is to create riffs. Riffs are melodic patterns comprised of a limited number of notes, then repeated (Pick & Cullum, 2010). In the late 1920s jazz ensemble, this practice was heard in the solos of Louis Armstrong (Pick & Cullum, 2010), in the music of Walter Page's Blue Devils, and notably in the 1930s with the Bennie Moten Orchestra, with his riff-based piece "Moten Swing" (1932) (Tucker, 1985), among others. William "Count" Basie played piano on the recording, and following Moten's death in 1935, the orchestra ultimately became the Count Basie Orchestra (Pick & Cullum, 2010; Tucker, 1985).

Time	Details
0:00	Key: F major. Count Basie plays eight-measure introduction on piano accompanied by bass, guitar, and drums in a jazz swing style.
0:11	Count Basie plays the first chorus of 12-bar blues piano solo
0:28	Count Basie plays the second chorus of 12-bar blues piano solo.
0:46	Key change to D flat major. Herschel Evans tenor saxophone solo, supported by muted and harmonized trumpet riff number 1 played in the background
1:03	The George Hunt trombone solo is supported by harmonized saxophone riff number 2 played in the background.
1:19	The Lester Young tenor saxophone solo is supported by muted and harmonized trumpet riff number 3 played in the background
1:36	The Buck Clayton trumpet solo starts with a riff, then expands. Harmonized saxophone riff number 4 is played in the background.
1:53	Count Basie plays a sparse piano solo, with rhythm section supporting.
2:10	The saxophones and trumpets play riff number 5 and riff number 6, each different, simultaneously. Trombones play a harmonized note on beat four, tied to a half note of every other measure. This could be considered riff number 7.
2:27	The saxophones play riff number 8 that is the famous melody of the piece. trumpets continue to play riff number 6. The trombones continue to play riff number 7.
2:44	The saxophones play riff number 9. Trumpets continue to play riff number 6. The trombones continue to play riff number 7, this time along with the snare drum.

FIGURE 33.5. Listening Guide: Riff figures and improvisation in "One O'Clock Jump"

The director can create a guided listening exercise based on various riff-based jazz pieces. The Count Basie piece "One O'Clock Jump" (1937), performed by the Count Basie Orchestra, is a suggested starting point. The piece is a 12-bar blues, the majority of which is built on riffs and improvisation until the familiar melody near the end. A sample listening guide based on the riff figures and improvisation in "One O'Clock Jump" is shown in Figure 33.5.

Students can identify various elements found in "One O'Clock Jump" including style, form, articulation, dynamics, timbre, etc. Class discussions can be initiated around specific questions, such as of how many different riffs exist, which instrumental sections play the riffs, how the riffs align with the improvised solos, how the rhythm section interacts with the riffs, etc. Open discussion and re-listening to the music can spark compositional ideas. Additional riff-based pieces recommended for listening can include:

- "Moten Swing" (1932), composed by Benny Moten and recorded by Count Basie and His Orchestra
- "Sing, Sing, Sing" (1937), composed by Louis Prima and recorded by Benny Goodman and His Orchestra
- "Jumpin' at the Woodside" (1938), composed by Count Basie and recorded by and Count Basie His Orchestra

- "In a Mellotone" (1940), composed by Duke Ellington and recorded by Duke Ellington and His Famous Orchestra
- "C Jam Blues" (1942), composed by Duke Ellington and His Famous Orchestra

As a composition activity, the director can select a key signature and time signature for the group, and students can divide into sections to compose their own two-measure riffs. The process can be reinforced by singing their riff ideas, playing them on instruments, then committing the ideas to the composition.

At this point, beginning jazz composers should be able to contribute to large group or small group 12-bar blues compositions. Once notated on paper and completed, the students should play the pieces in rehearsal. More important than performance at this point is providing opportunities for the students to make informed musical decisions that contribute to the entire compositional process, and to have decision-making authority with the process. The rehearsal should be audio-recorded and will provide an opportunity for the students to read and hear the new melodic riffs alongside their peers' compositions and to have a first-hand view of what is effective for their instruments. After the rehearsal/recording of the music, allow the students to ask questions, offer suggestions, make edits/changes, etc., while providing their justification for such changes. A list of the larger edits should be made for a final rehearsal. This could be a transformational experience for the young composer.

Instrumental Workshops

Instrumental workshops are an opportunity for student composers to additionally understand the various instruments and timbres available to them. In this context, an instrumental workshop can build upon guided listening lessons. Specific topics can be presented in the context of the music played and/or by instrumental section, to include the range and timbre of all traditional jazz instruments, an introduction to brass mutes, articulation styles, and a discussion of any jazz-related notation used by composers. Added information should be provided about the rhythm section instruments piano, guitar, bass guitar/double bass, drum set, and auxiliary percussion. The director can facilitate these discussions by presenting the music being discussed via the available online performances of jazz ensemble originals and arrangements, presented along with the musical scores at various publisher YouTube channels. The visual aspect of seeing the score, and isolating examples common to jazz is a valuable practice. The examples can be selected via the various music grade levels at and beyond their current performance levels.

Another possibility is inviting a guest jazz ensemble that is more experienced than your own group, or individual musicians to demonstrate the instruments via their music. This experience could provide musical perspective and may be good motivation for the student composer to see advanced possibilities. The workshops can provide ongoing discussions as the middle school jazz ensemble develops musically. Future areas can be style-based, or composer based. Also, this process reinforces the importance of purposeful listening to music with the compositional process in mind.

Moving on to Bebop

In this section, melodic and rhythmic composing in the bebop style will be presented. Intermediate composers in the jazz ensemble can quickly build upon their past experiences. Guided and independent listening experiences should continue. Teacher-led class composition can continue; however, additional student-centered small group and individual composition projects of varying lengths should be created at this level.

Additional melodic and rhythmic interpretation and composition activities should be presented via multiple styles. The bebop style is commonly included in jazz ensemble method books. When learning bebop style, extended harmonies, chromatic passages featuring added eighth note and triplet rhythms, and added articulation present new challenges for the intermediate level jazz composer. Listening to the pioneering bebop era musicians Charlie Parker (alto saxophone) and Dizzy Gillespie (trumpet) is essential. Many other musicians followed their lead with this landmark musical style change.

As will be discovered by listening to many small groups/combos and bebop era musicians, the melodic parts were doubled or harmonized by one or two instruments. Similar to early small group jazz music, jazz combo pieces in the bebop style typically feature a statement of the melody, called the "head," which is often repeated. Following the statement of melody, the musicians individually improvise over the chord progressions. Following the solos, the head is repeated, sometimes ending with a tag or extension to close the piece. The music was sometimes composed over the familiar blues chord progressions, an existing 32-bar song form popular with Tin Pan Alley composers of Broadway musicals and/or show tunes, or other chord progressions.

The selection of medium groove (medium tempo) pieces such as Charlie Parker's "Now's the Time" (1945) and "Billie's Bounce" (1945) provide a good introduction to the bebop style. The musicians on these pieces are Charlie Parker, alto saxophone; Miles Davis, trumpet; Bud Powell, piano; Curley Russell, bass, and Max Roach, drums (Burlingame, n.d.). Now's the Time and "Billie's Bounce" have similar chord progressions, which provides familiarity to the listener and to the developing composer. In this way, perhaps the creative focus can be dedicated to melodic and rhythmic ideas.

"Now's the Time" features a 12-bar blues form that should now be familiar to the students. The director should play a 12-bar blues progression in F major, or have the rhythm section play the 12-bar blues progression in F major from an existing piece to remind the students of the progression. The piece is very accessible and does not feature the potentially intimidating fast tempo of many other bebop pieces. The students will immediately notice the smaller combo instrumentation, as compared to the jazz ensemble. Upon listening to the recording, the following sample essential questions can be asked and discussed:

- Following the eight-measure introduction, does the 12-bar blues chord progression in "Now's the Time" sound the same, or different than previous examples? If it sounds different, how? Some differences include the addition of the IV^7 chord in measure two, the use of dominant seventh chords throughout rather than triads, as such:

F: ||: F^7 | B♭^{7} | F^7 | F^7 | B♭^{7} | B♭^{7} | F^7 | F^7 | Gm^7 | C^7 | F^7 | C^7:||

- In what way does the piano comping style interact with the melody?
- In what way does the piano comping style interact with the soloists?
- How does the walking bass style impact the first statement of the melody?
- How does the walking bass style impact the solo sections? Does the bass playing differ during the piano solo?
- In what ways does the drum set interact with the melody?
- In what ways does the drum set interact with the soloists?

"Billie's Bounce" features the same key and similar 12-bar blues form with a slightly faster tempo but is still technically approachable. Essential questions for the students can include:

- What are the similarities between "Now's the Time" and "Billie's Bounce"?
- What are the differences between "Now's the Time" and "Billie's Bounce"?
- How is the 12-bar blues chord progression different in "Billie's Bounce"?
- Did you notice different chords in measure eight? If so, what are they? (director guidance may be needed to explain the ii–V^7–I turnaround in measure eight to measure nine)
- How does the piano comping differ from the comping in "Now's the Time?" How does the different comping style impact the music?
- What are the differences in the drum set playing?

During Charlie Parker's and Miles Davis' solos on both pieces, the interaction between the soloist and the rhythm section should be emphasized. Sample essential questions specific to the solos can include:

- On "Billie's Bounce," how would you describe the development of Charlie Parker's alto saxophone solo?
- What types of rhythmic and melodic ideas did Charlie Parker use on his alto saxophone solo?
- Is the first chorus of Charlie Parker's solo rhythmically challenging? If so, why?
- In what ways does Charlie Parker change the musical activity in subsequent choruses of his solo?
- What rhythm section instrument(s) interact the most with Charlie Parker during his solo? Why do you think so?

- How would you describe the development of Miles Davis's trumpet solo?
- What types of rhythmic and melodic ideas did Miles Davis use on his trumpet solo?
- In what ways does Miles Davis change the musical activity in the two choruses of his solo?
- What rhythm section instrument(s) interact the most with Charlie Parker during his solo? Why do you think so?

"Groovin' High" (1944), composed by Dizzy Gillespie, was composed using the same chord progression and 32-bar song form of "Whispering" (1920), composed by Paul Whiteman (Burlingame, n.d.). The eighth-note rhythms emphasize the importance of jazz articulation throughout. The 1947 Carnegie Hall performance of "Groovin' High" featured Dizzy Gillespie, trumpet; Charlie Parker, alto saxophone; John Lewis, piano; Al McKibbon, bass; and Joe Harris, drums. The "Groovin' High" chord progression, after the recorded introduction (and with a ii–V turnaround at the end) is as follows:

$E\flat$: $\|$: $E\flat^{maj7}$ | $E\flat^{maj7}$ | Am^7 | D^7 | $E\flat^{maj7}$ | $E\flat^{maj7}$ | Gm^7 | C^7 | F^7 | F^7 | Fm^7 | $B\flat^7$ |

$[^{1.}$ | Gm^7 | $F\sharp m^7$ | Fm^7 | $B\flat^7$:$\|$ $[^{2.}$ | Fm^7 | $A\flat m^7$ $D\flat^7$ | $E\flat^6$ | Fm^7 $B\flat^7$ $\|$

The sample essential questions for the students can include many of the same used for "Now's the Time" and "Billie's Bounce," in addition to the following:

- How is "Groovin' High" similar to "Now's the Time" and "Billie's Bounce?"
- How is "Groovin' High" different than "Now's the Time" and "Billie's Bounce?"
- How does the form differ from "Now's the Time" and "Billie's Bounce?"
- How does the chord progression differ from "Now's the Time" and "Billie's Bounce?"

The listening activity can greatly inform the student composition experience, and the music selections are certainly the decisions of the jazz ensemble director. After listening to examples of the bebop style, the intermediate level jazz composer can begin to incorporate added ideas and approaches. The application of specific musical parameters is suggested, such as increased or varied tempi, inclusion of eighth and sixteenth notes, use of riffs, use of contemporary harmonies and chord progressions, etc. Students can continue to write their melodic ideas, with close attention to the form and the space needed for improvisation. The bebop style presents an opportunity to compose for the smaller combo instrumentation, however, the concepts can be set to the full jazz ensemble as well.

Learning Afro-Cuban and Brazilian Styles

The intermediate level composer should become familiar with Afro-Cuban and Brazilian music and its influence on the music for jazz ensemble and jazz combo. Cuban trumpeter Mario Bauzá, trumpeter/composer Dizzy Gillespie, Cuban percussionist Chano Pozo, and many others highly influenced Afro-Cuban music that is very common today. An exploration of *son clave* and *rumba clave* styles, and their importance to the mambo, cha-cha-cha, bolero, rumba, and Afro-Cuban $\frac{6}{8}$ dance styles must be studied to incorporate the many elements into compositions (Dunscomb and Hill, 2002).

"Manteca" (1947), composed by Dizzy Gillespie, Luciano "Chano" Pozo, and Walter "Gil" Fuller, is a long-standing and often arranged composition for the jazz ensemble. The original features the conga drums and bass in the introduction, followed by a layering of riffs. Gillespie completes the layering of instruments by adding a short bebop-style solo. The piece is a good example to include in composition instruction due to the inclusion of jazz, bebop, and Afro-Cuban styles. The piece features multiple call-and-response riffs, shout choruses, and a bebop-infused solo section that is combined with the continued playing of the patterns on the conga drums. After listening to "Manteca," essential questions could be as follows:

- What is unique about the introduction of "Manteca?"
- What is the role of the conga drums and the double bass in the introduction of "Manteca?"
- What composition techniques are used in the introduction of "Manteca"?
- In what way does Gillespie alternate the riffs in the introduction of "Manteca"?
- What composition techniques exist at the start of the A section of "Manteca"?
- What musical style changes happen in the bridge of "Manteca"? (The melody is played without syncopation, yet the double bass is playing a walking part as in jazz swing style; the trumpets answer the saxophone melody with a part featuring swing rhythms and articulation; Gillespie solos in a ballad-like style, etc.)

Such questions can inform future compositional approaches. To enhance the study of Afro-Cuban music, the music of Mario Bauzá, Cachao, Paquito D'Rivera, Tito Puente, Poncho Sanchez, Arturo Sandoval, and many more can provide foundational concepts relating to composition for the jazz ensemble (Dunscomb and Hill, 2002).

The young composer needs to learn a variety of styles to gain familiarity and for potential future use in their compositions. The Brazilian bossa nova style is a combination of the samba style, with jazz harmony and often 32-bar song form (Spitzer, n.d.). Antonio Carlos Jobim composed over 300 bossa nova songs; Jobim and João Gilberto popularized the style (Dunscomb and Hill, 2002). Gilberto's album *Chega de Saudade* (1959) featured the bossa nova style throughout. His 1963 collaboration with tenor saxophonist Stan Getz, *Getz/Gilberto*, provides multiple stylistic models throughout.

Although syncopation does exist in Brazilian styles, swing articulation and style are not typically applied. The bossa nova rhythm section will feature a rhythmic comping style in the guitar, a piano style that is fairly sparse yet could compliment and alternate playing with the guitar when possible, a bass guitar/double bass rhythmic style featuring half notes that align with the bass drum at times, or other rhythms that employ a harmonic style featuring chord roots, fifths, and passing tones. The drum set should not be overplayed but should emulate the percussion styles of the samba orchestra.

Additional Brazilian styles include samba, samba modern, and Baião. Additional Brazilian composers include Gilberto Gil, Milton Nascimento, Airto Moreira, and Flora Purim (Dunscomb & Hill, 2002). Additional concepts for the intermediate jazz composer include the discussion of expanded harmonic and melodic ideas including motivic development, modes, extended forms, chord progressions etc. An added focus on the role of the rhythm section instruments is needed, discussing piano and guitar comping styles, bass line construction, drum set fills, rhythmic set-ups, and the importance of the rhythm section as a foundational section of the jazz ensemble.

Advanced Student Composers in the Jazz Ensemble

Advanced student composers at the high school level should continue to expand their experiences and work toward larger individual projects. While selected beginning and intermediate jazz ensemble method books are no longer an essential guide at this level, the music being studied and rehearsed in the jazz ensemble can inform the compositional process.

Listening experiences should expand beyond the current performance level of the jazz ensemble. Contemporary music from composers such as Maria Schneider, Carla Bley, Terence Blanchard, Christian McBride, and many others should be studied. For instance, a review of the Maria Schneider Jazz Orchestra recordings will initially reveal the traditional jazz ensemble instrumentation. However, Schneider adeptly expands the instrumentation to the full range of woodwinds, a full flugelhorn section, accordion, and auxiliary percussion on select compositions.

Multiple opportunities for score study should exist, and the in-depth study of music currently being prepared for performance is suggested. The continued importance of listening, learning of additional musical styles, and experimentation with contemporary techniques and instrumentation should be emphasized. Student composers at all levels should have opportunities to perform their compositions at every level. In addition, they should interact with a diverse group of professional jazz composers at all levels of the learning process.

Composition Project Ideas for Intermediate and Advanced Student Composers

Intermediate and advanced student composers should be able to work independently, be familiar with a variety of jazz and jazz-related styles, identify and compose in swing and other styles, use 12-bar blues, 32-bar song form, and other forms as a basis for their compositions, etc. For a major composition project, have the students compose a section of a piece, or a full piece based on the chord progression and form of an existing piece in a selected style. A jazz or bossa nova standard is suggested. It is hoped that the many listening activities help to inspire stylistic choices for the student composers. The director may need to guide the students in this area. This is an additive project that can lead to a completed section of a composition or an entire composition.

Multiple approaches can be taken for such a project, however, at an advanced level, the potential for being overly prescriptive does exist. The director should primarily guide from a distance, perhaps setting specific timelines or deadlines for the completion and review of sections of the composition. For those composers that require more direction, starting the composing project with the saxophone section and its SATB voicing, along with the desired form and style, can help to organize an entire composition. This can lead to decisions regarding the creation of new musical ideas, or the doubling of certain saxophone parts or melodic lines in the trumpet section, or lower saxophone parts in the trombone section, among other approaches. Each jazz ensemble section can sight read and record major sections of the composition as the project is in progress so the composers can hear their work played by actual instruments, and not just the reproduction from the notation software.

The use of style-appropriate articulation is highly suggested at this level. Also, clear markings indicating phrasing, releases, and dynamics, must be included. The piano, guitar, and bass parts should include chord progressions and notation as necessary. The drum set parts should indicate style, the overall feel, rhythmic figures that need support from the drums, melodic figures that require rhythmic set-ups, the intended articulation, anticipation of dynamics, the suggested variation of cymbal patterns, etc.

The final projects should be rehearsed and recorded along with the other rehearsal repertoire. Consider having the advanced composer run the music rehearsal, or at least provide an introduction to the music prior to the rehearsal. The composer needs to understand all phases of the rehearsal and performance in order to have the complete concept in mind, from the initial compositional ideas to the actual performances of the music. A jazz ensemble concert including or featuring student compositions would be an added extension to the existing jazz program.

Additional Activities

Consider composing with lead sheets only and having the ensemble members help develop the flow, fill out harmonies, etc. This could develop as a group composition after the individual shares a lead sheet of their composition ideas. Consider creating time for "composition workshops" outside of the jazz ensemble rehearsal to encourage students to compose and collaborate with their peers as needed. The intermediate and advanced high school composers need sections and full ensembles to read their work in progress, as played by live musicians. The school jazz ensemble can read new student compositions during the jazz ensemble rehearsal, at a pace and frequency that is appropriate. In order to save time, the score and parts to each composition should be made available to the director in advance. The director can audio record the reading sessions for future review by the composers. A peer-review process can be utilized, and individual jazz ensemble members can provide feedback during or after the reading session. The process benefits all musicians, as the frequent reflection and discussion of the compositional process should occur at every level. Composers need time to reflect and try new ideas. While digital notation and playback works well, the live reading sessions provide excellent experience for the composer and band members.

University jazz ensembles sight-read music regularly. To extend the reading session experience, the high school director should consider inviting an area university jazz ensemble to read student compositions. If this is not possible to do in person, perhaps the university ensemble director would consider reading and recording the music. A professional jazz ensemble may be available as well. This activity could be combined with a clinic or shared rehearsal situation.

University music education students need to observe this composition process in school jazz ensemble rehearsals. At times, students assume that the performance ensemble is the only area of teaching and learning music, as they may have been previously instructed in that manner. Although composition is included in various music standards, the "performance only" approach must be modified to include more diverse student musical experiences.

The student jazz composer can greatly benefit from having a professional jazz composer share their techniques, processes, and ideas with the students, and perhaps share a work in progress. Consider hosting an in-person clinic for this purpose. The composer may be willing to have the school ensemble read their music, which could provide specific insight.

Conclusion

The jazz ensemble director can use a variety of approaches to incorporate composition into the middle and high school jazz ensemble rehearsal settings. Figure 33.6 offers a list of resources and/or organizations where teachers may find a wealth of information regarding jazz education, history, and performance. Figure 33.7 provides a discography that may be used to develop young musician's knowledge of jazz styles and practices.

- *The Articulate Jazz Musician: Mastering the Language of Jazz*, (jazz ensemble method book) Caleb Chapman, Jeff Coffman.
- DownBeat Magazine: https://www.downbeat.com
- *Essential Elements for Jazz Ensemble*, (jazz ensemble method books), Book 1 and Book 2, Mike Steinel.
- *First Place for Jazz Introductory Method for Jazz Ensemble*, (jazz ensemble method book), Dean Sorenson
- Jazz Education Network: Organization with a focus on jazz education, performance, and research. https://jazzednet.org
- Jazz at Lincoln Center: Live and streaming performances, education and more. https://www.jazz.org/
- Jazz Academy, part of Jazz at Lincoln Center: Education and resources regarding jazz technique, history, and performance: https://academy.jazz.org/media-library/
- Jazz Pedagogy: The Jazz Educator's Handbook and Resource Guide. Comprehensive guide to jazz, Afro-Cuban, Brazilian music performance for the school jazz ensemble.
- JazzStandards.com: Information and research about jazz standards, including history, theory, etc. http://www.jazzstandards.com
- *Jazz Zone . . . The Beginning.* (jazz ensemble method book), J. Richard Dunscomb.
- Library of Congress Jazz Collections: https://blogs.loc.gov/music/category/jazz/
- Smithsonian Jazz: Concerts, education, historical archives, exhibitions. https://americanhistory.si.edu/smithsonian-jazz
- *Standard of Excellence Jazz Ensemble Method*, (jazz ensemble method book), Dean Sorenson and Bruce Pearson.
- *Standard of Excellence Advanced Jazz Ensemble Method*, (jazz ensemble method book), Dean Sorenson and Bruce Pearson.
- *Teaching Music through Performance in Jazz*: Edited book series focused on performance pedagogy, listening, and teaching resources. https://www.giamusic.com/store/teaching-music-through-performance-jazz

FIGURE 33.6. Material and organizational resources

Benny Goodman and His Orchestra. (1937). Sing, sing, sing [Song]. Victor.

Benny Moten's Kansas City Orchestra (1932). Moten swing [Song]. Victor.

Christian McBride Big Band (2011). *The Good Feeling* [Album]. Mack Avenue.

Count Basie and his Orchestra (1955). "April in Paris" [Song]. On *April in Paris* [Album]. Verve.

Count Basie and his Orchestra (1938). Jumpin' at the Woodside [Song]. Decca.

Count Basie and his Orchestra (1937). One o'clock jump [Song]. Decca.

Duke Ellington and his Famous Orchestra (1942). C jam blues [Song]. Victor

Duke Ellington and his Famous Orchestra (1940). In a mellotone [Song]. Victor.

Dizzy Gillespie and his Orchestra (1947). Manteca [Song]. RCA Victor.

Gilberto, J. (1959). Chega de saudade [Song]. On *Chega de saudade* [Album]. Odeon.

Gillespie, D., Parker, C. Lewis, J., McKibbon, A., Harris, J. (1947). Groovin' high [Song]. On *The complete live performances on* Savoy [Album]. Savoy.

King Oliver's Creole Jazz Band (1923). Dippermouth blues [Song]. Okeh.

Louis Armstrong and His Hot Five (1928). West end blues [Song]. Okeh.

Mintzer, B. (1984). Computer [Song]. On *Incredible journey* [Album]. DMP.

Parker, C., Davis, M., Powell, B., Roach, M. (1945). Billie's bounce [Song]. On *The complete original master takes: The savoy recordings* [Album]. Savoy Jazz.

Parker, C. Davis, M., Powell, B., Roach, M. (1945). Now's the time [Song]. On *The complete original master takes: The savoy recordings* [Album]. Savoy Jazz.

Schneider, M. (2000). *Allégresse.* [Album]. Enja Records.

Schneider, M. (1996). *Coming About* [Album]. Enja Records.

Smith, B. (1925). The St. Louis blues. [Song]. Columbia.

The Very Big Carla Bley Band (1991). *The Very Big Carla Bley Band* [Album]. Watt.

Toshiko Akiyoshi – Lew Tabackin Big Band (1976). *Road Time Shuffle* [Album]. BMG.

FIGURE 33.7. Selected discography

The methods and models shared in this chapter can be used to introduce and develop young jazz composers' skills and interests. Most importantly, the use of creative approaches by supportive directors will help students find their compositional voices—and perhaps their place in history—within the evolving sounds and practices of jazz musicians.

REFERENCES

Burlingame, S. (n.d.). *Billie's bounce* (1945). Jazzstandards.com. https://www.jazzstandards. com/compositions-1/billiesbounce.htm

Burlingame, S. (n.d.). *Groovin' high* (1944). Jazzstandards.com. http://www.jazzstandards. com/compositions-1/groovinhigh.htm

Count Basie and his Orchestra. (1937). One o'clock jump [Song]. Decca.

Dunscomb, J. R. & Hill Jr., W. L. (2002). *Jazz pedagogy: The jazz educator's handbook and resource guide.* Warner Brothers Publications.

Hickey, M. (1997). Teaching ensembles to compose and improvise. *Music Educators Journal,* *83*(6), 17–21. https://www.jstor.org/stable/3399019

Jazz at Lincoln Center. (n.d.). *Jazz academy.* https://academy.jazz.org/

Knaster, J. M. (2016). *Middle school jazz band students' experiences composing and improvising.* (Publication No. 10157396) [Master's thesis, University of Delaware]. ProQuest Dissertations Publishing.

Koops, A. P. (2013). Facilitating composition in instrumental settings. In M. Kaschub & J. P. Smith (Eds.), *Composing our future: Preparing music educators to teach composition* (pp. 149–166). New York: Oxford University Press.

Koops, A. P. (2009). *Incorporating music composition in middle school band rehearsals* (Publication No. 3389504) [Doctoral dissertation, University of Southern California]. ProQuest Dissertations Publishing.

McCurdy, R. C. (2008). Rehearsal techniques: A holistic approach integrating composition, improvisation, theory, and cultural considerations in the rehearsal. In R. Miles & R. Carter (Eds.), *Teaching music through performance in jazz* (pp. 27–46). Chicago: GIA Publications, Inc.

Owens, D. T. (2003). *A new you: Composition for jazz ensemble.* Self-published.

Pick, M. M. & Cullum, J. (2010). *Riffs and shouts: The building blocks of jazz.* Riverwalk Jazz. https://riverwalkjazz.stanford.edu/?q=program/riffs-and-shouts-building-blocks-jazz

Reimer, B. (2003). *A philosophy of music education: Advancing the vision* (3rd ed). Pearson Education, Inc.

National Coalition for Core Arts Standards (2014). *National core arts standards: Music: Composition and theory strand.* https://www.nationalartsstandards.org/ sites/default/files/2021-11/Music%20Composition%20and%20Theory%20at%20a% 20Glance%203-4-15.pdf

Spitzer, P. (n.d.). *Jazz theory: Bossa nova.* Jazzstandards.com. http://www.jazzstandards.com/ theory/bossa-nova.htm

Tucker, M. (1985). Count Basie and the piano that swings the band. *Popular Music, 5,* 45–79. https://www.jstor.org/stable/853283

SECTION VIII

INTERNATIONAL PERSPECTIVES ON COMPOSITION PEDAGOGY

CHAPTER 34

··

COMPOSITION PEDAGOGY IN AUSTRALIA

Rethinking Teaching and Learning in Music Education through Composition and Creativity

··

RENÉE CRAWFORD

Prelude

Music education in the hands of an appropriately trained educator, who intimately understands the artistry of the discipline, has the power to develop crucial intrinsic and extrinsic attributes in students. Despite strong international empirical research, indicating that engaging with music learning has the potential to develop student's academic, social, and personal development, the arts are often one of the first learning areas to be omitted from school programs and curriculum. Given the diminishing status of music and arts education in Australia, it is timely to use further research-based evidence to continue this conversation: Demonstrating the value of music education in rethinking teaching and learning. Reconsidering what might be important in the educational landscape in developing key 21st century skills and knowledge. A focus on composition pedagogy and creativity in music education is intended to challenge the current rhetoric about what should be considered essential and non-essential learning, so that education authorities and policy-makers are compelled to make considered and informed decisions that include providing children and young people the opportunity to engage with a quality music education and experience a holistic learning approach.

This chapter will provide an outline of the current music education context in Australia and the curriculum that is used as a framework across the states and territories. This discussion will include a consideration of how composition is situated within music education, the expectations and types of experiences that children and young people may have as composers and the tools and techniques teachers may use when engaging students in composition. The theoretical underpinning of the approach discussed will be drawn from Crawford's (2008 and 2014) multidimensional/non-linear teaching and learning model. This will be followed by three case studies that exemplify the impact of the composition pedagogy used across different educational contexts in Australia and how teachers might apply the ideas explored within their instructional practice. The chapter will conclude with a summary of key lessons learned from these cases that provide a set of recommendations for practice.

The Value of Music Education: An Australian Context

Music education can develop critical intrinsic and extrinsic attributes in students if taught in an authentic, innovative, and experiential way that challenges learners to think creatively and critically. Research studies, in Australia and internationally, provide compelling evidence that supports that engaging with music learning and school-based arts education has the potential to develop not only important aesthetic values, but students' academic, personal, and social development skills and knowledge (Bryce et al., 2004; Burnard, 2008; Crawford, 2017a, 2020a, 2020b; Deasy, 2002; Guhn et al., 2020; Karkou & Glasman, 2004; Karlsen, 2013; Marsh, 2015; McFerran et al., 2017; Ojukwu, 2017). Despite this strong empirical research, music and the arts are often considered one of the first subject disciplines to be omitted from school programs and curriculum.

In the Australian context, it has been a considerable number of years since the 2005 national review of school music education recommended that improving and sustaining the quality and status of music education in schools should become a priority and sufficient funding to support effective music education should be provided (Pascoe et al.). Also patently neglected is the 2013 Parliamentary inquiry into the extent, benefits, and potential of music education in Victorian schools, which made 17 recommendations to improve music education, including a call for the development of a music education strategy to ensure that all students have the opportunity to experience a quality school music education program (Education and Training Committee, 2013). More recently, the federal government announced a university fee restructure, which will see an increase of 113% in the cost for arts and humanities degrees in Australia (Tehan, 2020). This may have dire consequences for discipline areas such as music education at all levels including pathways to further study (Crawford, 2020c). This sends confusing messages about the relative value and import of some disciplines over others. Discounting the value of music and arts education disregards vital intrinsic and extrinsic values that are embedded in such disciplines.

Curriculum and policy documents in Australia and internationally are littered with the importance of developing 21st century skills and knowledge, such as creative and critical thinking, intercultural competence, and socially inclusive behaviors. A holistic education that develops such skills and knowledge cannot be achieved without the inclusion of music education. Governments cannot understate that the arts and humanities contribute to critical jobs for the future. Reducing learning to non-essential and essential skills and compliance requirements, will have a lasting impact on society and catastrophic consequences for highly multicultural countries like Australia.

Although music is often referred to as being part of the arts domain, music itself has always been a discrete discipline with a lengthy and valued academic history that can be traced to Plato, Aristotle, and Socrates. When universities were established in the Middle Ages, music was one of the liberal arts and taught in conjunction with arithmetic, geometry, astronomy, grammar, logic, and rhetoric. While 264 music courses are offered by 45 tertiary and higher institutions in Australia, there has been increasing pressure to justify the value of music in education and schools. This has led to two distinctive ways of thinking about music: extrinsic benefits of music as related to academic and/or cognitive development and psychosocial well-being, as opposed to intrinsic benefits that relate to direct musical and aesthetic values (Crawford, 2020b). While this distinction can be useful for targeted advocacy, it can present numerous challenges in defining what might be considered musical or non-musical and has the potential to devalue the musical intrinsic elements completely. It was therefore encouraging to observe that in the case studies explored in this chapter that music programs are designed on the premise that musical participation affords opportunities to enrich human experience in holistic and integrated ways, valuing a balance of intrinsic and extrinsic benefits and formal and informal learning.

In order to educate toward holistic learning and recognize that students have different interests and learn in diverse ways, then there needs to be a reconsideration of what is considered essential or non-essential learning. Fostering student differences through musical experiences will not only motivate and stimulate learning but provide avenues for all students to achieve and experience success in their education. Thinking seriously about *what* we teach, *how*, and *why*, will contribute positively to a society that educates for a future that values diverse thinking and skill sets. The case studies presented in this chapter represent different educational contexts that will challenge the current rhetoric about the devaluing of the arts. Ideas explored will illuminate how engagement with music and the arts through composition pedagogy can develop creative and critical thinking, build social inclusive skills and intercultural competence, and use technology to enhance music learning opportunities. Firstly, a consideration of how music and composition is situated in the Australian curriculum will provide further context.

MUSIC AND COMPOSITION IN THE AUSTRALIAN CURRICULUM

In 2009, the council of commonwealth and state and territory education ministers approved "The shape of the Australian curriculum," which guided the development of the national curriculum framework (ACARA, 2016). The working paper reflected the position adopted by ministers collectively in the 2008 Melbourne declaration on educational goals for young Australians. In December 2012, Version 4 of "The shape of the Australian curriculum" was approved by the Australian Curriculum, Assessment and Reporting Authority (ACARA), who later produced the finalized national curriculum framework for years Foundation-10 in 2015. This was adopted by most state and territories, with the exception of Victoria and New South Wales, who currently use their own state-based curriculum while incorporating elements of the national framework and priorities. For example, the Victorian curriculum Foundation-10 outlines what every student should learn during their first 11 years of schooling: "The curriculum is the common set of knowledge and skills required by students for life-long learning, social development and active and informed citizenship. . . . [It] incorporates the Australian curriculum and reflects Victorian priorities and standards" (VCAA, 2020). School authorities are ultimately responsible for the implementation of the national framework in their schools, making decisions about the extent to which the Australian curriculum is implemented, ensuring alignment with system and jurisdictional policies and requirements. A national senior secondary curriculum is being developed for many subject disciplines and as such, most continue to use state and territory-based curriculum. In Victoria, this is the Victorian Certificate of Education (VCE) and in New South Wales the High School Certificate (HSC). In addition, there are the industry-based Vocational Education and Training (VET) courses that are offered across Australia.

Music is found within the arts learning area of the Australian curriculum and the content descriptions in each arts subject reflect the interrelated strands of "making and responding." "Making" includes "learning about and using knowledge, skills, techniques, processes, materials and technologies to explore arts practices and make artworks that communicate ideas and intentions," and "Responding" entails "exploring, responding to, analysing and interpreting artworks" (ACARA, 2018a). The learning area encompasses five arts subjects—Dance, Drama, Media Arts, Music, and Visual Arts—across five bands of year levels: Foundation to Year 2, Years 3 and 4, Years 5 and 6, Years 7 and 8, Years 9 and 10. In music, the three pillars of listening, performing, and composing are used to engage with the two strands making and responding:

> Making in Music involves active listening, imitating, improvising, composing, arranging, conducting, singing, playing, comparing, and contrasting, refining, interpreting, recording and notating, practising, rehearsing, presenting and performing. Responding in Music involves students being audience members listening to, enjoying, reflecting on, analysing, appreciating, and evaluating their own and others' musical works." (ACARA, 2018b)

Making and responding involve developing aural understanding of the elements of music through experiences in listening, performing, and composing, which underpin all musical activity. Students use their voice, body, instruments, found sound sources, and technology to make music, which is recorded and communicated as musical notation, symbols, and audio recordings. Students develop analytical skills and aesthetic understanding with increasing experience of the elements of music.

Sequential learning is implied in the curriculum as the expectation is that students' exploration and understanding of the elements of music, musical conventions, styles, and forms will expand with their continued active engagement with music. Students are expected to recognize their subjective musical preferences and consider diverse perspectives through listening, performing, and composing music from a broad range of styles, practices, traditions, and contexts, which will inform the way that they interpret music as performers and respond to the music they listen to. This is intended to culminate in the development of their own musical voice as composers and their own style as musicians.

In the Australian curriculum, music is learned through developing skills and knowledge associated with the elements of music. Therefore, musical ideas are developed through exploring rhythm, pitch, dynamics and expression, form and structure, timbre, and texture. In each of the five bands, students learn about increasingly complex forms of music as they make and respond to different musical styles and genres, from a range of historical and cultural contexts. These may include music in film and media, instrumental genres and songs, new music trends, and folk and art music from varied cultures, traditions, and times. To develop deeper connections and understanding of the purpose of music, teachers should begin with music students have experienced in their own lives and community. This authentic and realistic link to personal experience may then provide a platform to develop understanding of and the ability to draw from the "histories, traditions and conventions of music from other places and times including Australia, Aboriginal and Torres Strait Islander cultures, Asia and other world cultures" (ACARA, 2018b).

Consistent with the approach and principles of Crawford's (2008 and 2014) multidimensional/non-linear teaching and learning model discussed later in the chapter, curriculum advice indicates that students' musical skills are best developed through activities that integrate the techniques and processes of music that combine listening, composing, and performing. Figure 34.1 summarizes ACARA's suggested application of listening, composing, and performing in the two strands of the curriculum (2018b):

In the process of developing musical skills and knowledge, students learn that meanings can be generated from different perspectives and that these viewpoints may shift according to different authentic contexts or world encounters. As students make, investigate, or critique music from various perspectives, as composers, performers, and audience members, they interrogate, explore, and investigate meanings and interpretations in multidimensional ways. Meanings and interpretations are informed by societal, cultural, and historical contexts, and an understanding of how elements, materials, skills, and processes are used. Challenging thinking and meaning construction provide the basis for making informed critical judgements about the music students create and the music they interpret as musicians and listen to as audiences. The complexity and sophistication of such thinking will change across the curriculum continuum from Foundation to Year 10,

Making & Responding through:	Curriculum – Definition	Curriculum – Learning experiences
Listening	The process through which music is experienced and learnt.	Listening to, analysing, and comparing a range of repertoire. Developing aural skills (ear training) as the technique for discriminating, identifying, interpreting, and applying musical concepts is essential for all listening, composition and performing activities.
Composing	A broad term for creating original music.	Improvising, organising musical ideas, creating accompaniment patterns, and arranging and writing original works, either individually or collaboratively.
Performing	Playing instruments, singing or manipulating sound using technology, either as an individual or ensemble member.	Learning songs, instrumental pieces, accompaniments, and works composed by self and others. Audiences can include the teacher, peers in class, the wider school community, and public audiences.
Additional activities	To support the above learning experiences	Learning and creating notation to record and communicate musical ideas. Reading, writing, and interpreting a range of terminology, notation and scores. Making audio recordings of compositions and performances using technology. Developing skills and techniques to discuss their own music and the music of others.

FIGURE 34.1. Making and responding through listening, composing, and performing

and in the later years will incorporate consideration of philosophies and ideologies, critical theories, institutions, and psychology.

General capabilities play a significant role in the Australian curriculum, encompassing knowledge, skills, behaviors, and dispositions intended to equip young Australians with the ability to live and work successfully in the 21st century. Students demonstrate development of a capability "when they apply knowledge and skills confidently, effectively and appropriately in complex and changing circumstances, in their learning at school and in their lives outside school" (ACARA, 2018c). Three of the general capabilities will be briefly discussed due to their relevancy to the arts and music curriculum and link to the case studies later presented. These are: "critical and creative thinking," "personal and social," and "intercultural competency capabilities."

"Critical and creative thinking" is integral to making and responding to artworks within the arts learning area of the curriculum.

> Students draw on their curiosity, imagination and thinking skills to pose questions and explore ideas, spaces, materials and technologies. They consider and analyse the

motivations, intentions and possible influencing factors and biases that may be evident in artworks they make to which they respond. (ACARA, 2018c)

In the cases described, students experiment, take risks, make choices, and consider possibilities when expressing their ideas, concepts, thoughts, and feelings creatively. Students are provided with opportunities to reflect and receive and offer constructive feedback about past and present artworks and performances. Communicating and sharing their thinking and innovations as well as challenging interpretations and artistic expression to a variety of audiences is an important part of developing both critical and creative thinking.

The "personal and social" capability is relevant to music and the arts as students identify and assess personal strengths, interests, and challenges. In the cases described, students are composers/art makers, performers, and audience. Students develop and apply personal skills and dispositions, such as self-discipline, goal-setting and working independently, initiative, confidence, resilience, and adaptability. Students develop emotional intelligence through learning to "empathise with the emotions, needs and situations of others, to appreciate diverse perspectives, and to understand and negotiate different types of relationships" (ACARA, 2018c). Students should be provided with opportunities to work with others and in these contexts develop and practice social skills to communicate effectively, work collaboratively, make considered group decisions, and demonstrate leadership.

The "intercultural understanding" capability enables students to explore the influence and impact of cultural identities and traditions on the practices and thinking of artists and audiences:

> Students develop and act with intercultural understanding in making artworks that explore their own cultural identities and those of others, interpreting and comparing their experiences and worlds, and seeking to represent increasingly complex relationships. Students are encouraged to demonstrate empathy for others and open-mindedness to perspectives that differ from their own and to appreciate the diversity of cultures and contexts in which artists and audiences live. (ACARA, 2018c)

Through engaging with music and artworks from diverse cultural sources and contexts, students are challenged in the cases studies to consider accepted roles, ideas, sounds, beliefs, and practices in new and different ways.

On June 12, 2020, the education ministers agreed that it was timely to review the current Foundation-Year 10 Australian curriculum, ready for implementation in 2022 (ACARA, 2020). This has come at a time of much controversy in Australia about what should be included in the curriculum and what should be considered essential and non-essential learning. Music and arts educators wait in anticipation to prepare for yet another battle that will no doubt resemble one from the not too distant past where strong advocation was required to have the arts included as part of the Australian curriculum (Ewing, 2010). Despite the current curriculum encouraging a sequential music learning experience, this is rarely achieved in reality, with the ongoing marginalization of music and arts education. This includes reduced time in school programs, a paucity of available resources and funding that is being prioritized to other subjects, a diminishing investment of pre-service teacher education, a reduction of music specialist teachers overall and a lack of ongoing teacher professional learning to provide appropriate development to ensure that curriculum is interpreted and enacted with rigor and integrity. A critical conversation about music and arts being considered essential learning is required if we are to develop creative and critical thinkers with high levels of emotional intelligence and intercultural competence.

Theoretical Underpinning: Approach to Music Education and Composition Pedagogy

The approach to music education and composition pedagogy in the cases discussed use Crawford's (2008) multidimensional/non-linear teaching and learning model. Using a constructivist framework, this model relies on the tenets of authentic learning/experiential learning, student centered learning/valued knowledge and holistic learning/whole-person phenomenon (Crawford, 2008, 2014). The theoretical underpinning for this model and its intersection with composition pedagogy is described in this section and later articulated in Figure 34.2.

The model prescribes students be provided with opportunities to connect new knowledge with prior understanding, aligning with Piaget's (1954 and 1968) beliefs that the learner must be active to be engaged in real learning. Constructivists take this notion further: the learning environment should contain a meaningful context to construct knowledge, one that brings the real world into the classroom (Brown et al., 1989). Traditional learning situations in which students are passive recipients of knowledge are inconsistent with the learning situations that occur in real life (Lave, 1988). If learning is to be authentic, students should be engaged in genuine learning problems or tasks that foster the opportunity for them to make connections between new material and prior knowledge. When engaged in authentic learning activities, students recognize the significance of what they are learning because the activities and tasks emulate real-life experiences related to the students and their world (Crawford, 2014). A current definition of authenticity states that knowledge, whether it is moral or informational, is based on consciousness, experience, and reflection (Marra, 2004).

With appropriate teacher facilitation and scaffolding, composition can be an authentic activity where students can learn to think critically, creatively and in multidimensional ways. They can communicate ideas multimodally, challenge their thinking, collaborate with peers, self-direct their learning, experiment with sound and musical elements, and create multiple possibilities/solutions that lead to informed

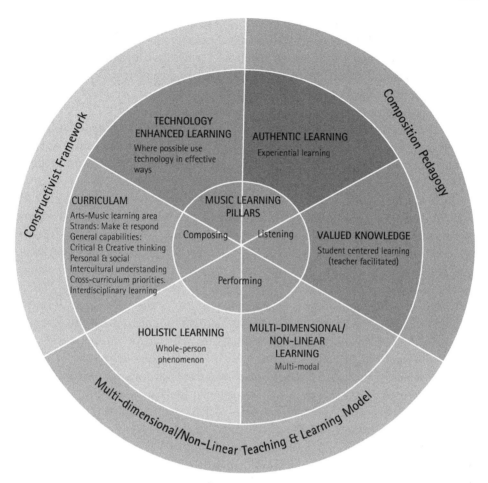

FIGURE 34.2. Framework for using Crawford's (2008 & 2014) multi-dimensional/non-linear teaching and learning model with composition pedagogy

decision-making. The learning process allows students to explore, discuss, and meaningfully construct concepts and relationships in defined contexts that involve real-world problems and issues.

Compositional activities involving increasingly complex forms of music, and different musical styles and genres, from a range of historical and cultural contexts and traditions, allow students to develop their own authentic musical voice and an appreciation of diverse musics. Socially inclusive practices and building intercultural competence are not only embedded in the learning opportunities students have to collaborate in creative endeavors, but the ways that thinking and meanings can be generated from different perspectives about music and its purpose that shift according to different authentic contexts or world encounters. Burnard (2012) conceptualizes distinctive forms of musical creativity that are rendered differently in response to experiencing music in different practice-based socio-cultural contexts. This contextually situated view of musical creativity allows learners to make and respond to music based on their socio-cultural background and experiences (Kokotsaki, 2012).

Meaningful connections to personal experiences with music in their own lives and society are then considered a form of valued knowledge and consistent with the constructivist framework (Crawford, 2014). In the case studies presented, composition is situated at the center of learning and real-world experiences that align with (and stem from) students' own interests and motivations are used as a springboard to deepen knowledge and broaden students' musical experiences. Katz and Raths (1982) and Paul et al. (2001) explain that authentic learning activities should be context specific and involve authentic problems or issues that need to be solved within an environment that resembles and emulates actual professional practice, providing a "need to know." Research indicates that students tend to be highly motivated when working directly within an authentic context (Barrows, 1986; Kinsley & McPherson, 1995; Paul et al., 2001) and engaging in experiential learning (Elliott, 1995; Kolb, 1984) with content that is interesting to them and in turn considered valued knowledge (Crawford, 2014, 2017b). In this regard, engaging with the process of composition is purposeful, experiential, and reflective.

Holistic learning/whole-person phenomenon encompasses the collective ideas of valued knowledge, authentic/real-life learning, and multidimensionality/non-linearity (Crawford, 2008). It relies on the balance of intrinsic and extrinsic attributes and values inherent within learning music. Learning in such a context, although teacher facilitated, is student centered and self-directed, resembling the natural processes of real life, where students experience working as composers and artists. While the whole-person phenomenon has been used in other disciplines such as the medical field, in the educational context it is grounded by Dewey's theory of experience (1958) as a way to think of learning as related to natural processes that contribute to the development of the whole person. In this context, the educational outcomes are holistic and consider the academic, personal, and social development of students. Learning is inspiring and highly motivational, often characterized as recursive and non-linear, engaging, self-directed, and meaningful from the learner's perspective (Crawford, 2008; McCombs, 2000 and 2012).

A current definition of composition learning in music education refers to "the result of creative thinking in music that takes shape in a process of bringing a musical product into existence by an individual or group of composers" (Randles et al., 2012). While this is true in one sense, the multidimensional teaching and learning model delineates the type of process described, suggesting that engagement with compositional activity has the capacity to develop students' critical and creative thinking. This slightly more complex view of composition learning aligns with the ideas about composition teaching and learning found in the seminal works *Minds on music: Composition for creative and critical thinking* and *Composing our future: Preparing music educators to teach composition* (Kaschub & Smith, 2009 and 2013). Paynter's (1982 and 1992) principles for music learning identify composition as the superior musical activity and locates it at the heart of the music curriculum. This is consistent with the cases presented in this chapter and the ideas suggesting rethinking teaching and learning in music education through composition and creativity.

Demonstration of Composition Pedagogy in Practice

The 21st century has seen a distinct shift away from the skills associated with a knowledge economy toward the skills needed for a creative economy. The growing relationship between creative capability, the need for ongoing innovation, and the globalization of economic activity has bought about increasing political and economic influences on education (Craft & Jeffrey, 2008; Sahlberg, 2006). There is a persistent and pervasive educational and social demand to develop 21st century students who are creative thinkers (Craft, 2008). Despite this, in a recent study conducted by Crawford (2019) it was clear that students and teachers often perceive engaging in creative endeavors as risky business and tend to avoid it focusing attention primarily on critical thinking. The study also found clear evidence to suggest that teachers struggled with understanding how to enact the creative elements of the critical and creative curriculum (Crawford, 2019). Key barriers to nurturing experimental dispositions in students such as creativity, can be attributed to the narrowing of the curriculum due to national high-stakes standardized testing, influencing the ways that schools situate learning that in turn have potentially negative ongoing impacts on teachers' pedagogy. Berliner (2011) argues that schools are narrowing the curriculum by increasing the lesson time focused on high stakes test content and skills, reporting that up to 35% of time previously devoted to subjects such as social studies, physical education, art, and music had been redirected to test preparation. Darling-Hammond (2006) has also expressed concern about how low-quality testing regimes and test preparation have led to a narrow curriculum, increasingly disconnected from the higher-order skills required for success in today's world. An acknowledgment of important curriculum threads, such as the critical and creative thinking general capability, indicates an appreciation of these skills in Australia. However, how they are enacted and within which disciplines, tells a different story about the perceived value of certain subjects over others, for example, science, technology, engineering, and mathematics (STEM) over the arts. The critical and creative thinking curriculum should not detract from discipline-based learning, as it can support the development of effective and innovative thinking that will enhance student learning outcomes within and across disciplines.

Case 1: High Performing Primary Government School Exploring the Critical and Creative Thinking Curriculum through Composition and Literacy

This case (Crawford, 2020d) uses a concept-based curriculum and interdisciplinary approach that situates composition at the center of learning. Developing interdisciplinary learning spaces can enable practitioners to teach integrated content that develops creative and metacognitive thinking and covers content effectively, while halting preoccupations with standardized testing. Focusing on higher order thinking skills may develop students who are creative, curious, resilient, and resourceful, preparing them for lifelong learning so that they can thrive in a fast-changing world. However, developing practice requires time, in-depth understanding, and experimentation. Collaborative practitioner research was used to identify and develop the teaching and learning strategies and classroom practices used by three key learning specialists in a primary school setting when enacting the critical and creative thinking curriculum (Crawford, 2020d).

One of the key aims was to work with these teachers to increase professional efficacy in the explicit teaching of thinking skills, including creativity, metacognitive processes, and collaborative learning in the curriculum. Three collaborative professional development workshops were provided to develop teachers' understanding of how creativity can be fostered as well as used to enhance critical thinking. As the school in this case has a one-to-one iPad program, the use of creative applications and technology were utilized. Classroom observations and student work samples were used to assess student learning outcomes and provide an evidence-base for this practice. The content and learning tasks in the sequence of lessons used were varied in the degree of complexity and guided instruction provided, according to student year level and ability.

Lesson Sequence Outline

Stage 1—Engagement Exploration: Students explore sound and conduct a series of creative musical experiments through Chrome Music Lab (CML). The platform provides interactive music experiences, which are built with freely accessible web technology such as Web Audio API, WebMIDI, Tone.js and is designed to work across a range of devices simply by opening the site on a web browser such as Chrome. Students went through each element of the music lab discussing the different ways sounds could be made, what sounds "looked like" using different aspects of the site. Students completed a musical scavenger hunt to explore the elements of music within the context of the different interactive aspects within CML. Some examples include: Song Maker—Compose a melody using the pentatonic scale (you can change the scale in the Settings area); Spectrogram—Choose two sound sources (from the icons at the bottom) and write down three differences between each of the spectrograms for those sounds; Kandinsky—Draw some horizontal lines on the screen at different heights. What is the difference between the lines drawn at the bottom of the screen and those drawn in the middle or the top of the screen? Explore differences in sound qualities as determined by the colors, lines, and shapes.

Stage 2—Exploration of music and emotion through different music pieces: Students were asked to listen to a range of different pieces of music and to identify how these pieces made them feel and why. This activity would directly lead to creating their own music piece to accompany and match a spoken word poem. Once students had listened to the music piece, they were asked to identify which specific instruments created the sounds that influenced their emotions, and through guided critical listening and analysis develop an understanding of how the instrumentation and musical elements were used to create these emotional responses. Peer discussion and feedback were encouraged and the suggestions were highly constructive as new knowledge was constructed using authentic context-specific examples and prior knowledge. Pre-established mutually agreed-upon behavioral expectations meant that students understood that all perspectives and opinions were valued.

Stage 3—Creation of music: Students were instructed to compose a piece of music using a music composition program of choice. Students already had some knowledge of the technology applications available to them and made choices based on their prior use and understanding of the tools available, such as GarageBand and Song Maker in CML. They also expressed preference to compositional platforms that provided a diverse suite of sound samples, sound combinations, effects, and instruments available to them. Criteria for this piece of music was that it had a clear structure, elicited purposeful emotional responses from the listener, and provided an appropriate background soundtrack to the emotive poem students had written to accompany this. Students used the knowledge constructed from classroom discussions and sound experiments from previous lessons to create a range of emotional responses and were able to articulate with clarity why they made certain choices. Students clearly appreciated the creative freedom and independently worked on pieces that presented a range of complex sound development and layering. An important part of this stage was to engage in collaborative learning by testing emotional responsivity and interpretations of the music created through seeking peer feedback. An opportunity was also provided for a larger classroom discussion where further feedback could be received. Students were excited to play their music for each other, eagerly awaiting peer reactions and opportunities to discuss their decisions and compositional intentions. It was clear that the supportive learning environment dispelled any issues related to reluctance in sharing music created. Students had an opportunity to apply any feedback received that they thought would enhance their musical pieces.

Stage 4—Live performances: Students performed the poems with their soundtrack backings. The audience provided feedback on the soundtrack and the performance, drawing links to program music and popular motives and rhythms in films. Each student reflected on the learning process and on their experiences as both a composer and audience member.

Stage 5—Artwork: Students reviewed an artist that they felt exhibited emotion in their work. Students were then asked to create an album cover for their spoken word poem and soundtrack inspired by this artist—emulating and interpreting their artist's ideas and the emotion they hoped to convey.

A number of elements from the critical and creative thinking curriculum were explored that align with the multidimensional/non-linear teaching and learning model, such as authentic learning that is student-centered and considered valued knowledge. Higher order thinking skills, such as analytical and critical thinking skill development, were balanced with creative endeavors to explore aesthetic perspectives and emotional responsivity (Crawford, 2020d). Curriculum threads include music and general capabilities as well as interdisciplinary links to literacy, visual arts, and technology to enhance learning outcomes. Due to the positive outcomes of the approach used to enacting the critical and creative thinking curriculum, school-wide implementation was endorsed by the School Improvement Team (Crawford, 2020d).

Case 2—Composition and Practical Music-Making for the Development of Socially Inclusive Practices and Intercultural Competence in an F–12 School

This case (Crawford, 2020a) responds to the fact that Australia is one of the most multicultural countries in the world. As a result, schools are become increasingly culturally diverse and cross-cultural exchange challenges traditional pedagogies and learning environments. The primary aim of this research was to investigate the impact of music and the arts on the learning, social, and personal development of students with refugee backgrounds in an Australian Foundation–Year 12 (F–12) school (Crawford, 2020a). Socially inclusive practices and the development of intercultural competence were a focus, given the emphasis of these general capabilities in the Australian curriculum, which acknowledges the country's culturally rich and diverse student cohorts. A number of school-based musical experiences through collaborative composition and ensemble performance provided the development of important intrinsic and extrinsic attributes, but also, opportunities for cross-cultural exchange and negotiation. Music education was used as a vehicle to engage young refugee background students, which was indicative of three primary themes: personal well-being, social inclusion (a sense of belonging), and an enhanced engagement with learning.

Key findings from this case study research indicated that a music classroom that fostered socially inclusive practices resulted in a positive transcultural learning space (Crawford, 2020a). This research raises critical awareness of the important role of music education and the arts in contemporary and culturally diverse school contexts at a time when Australian government and education authorities are making drastic decisions about what should be considered essential and non-essential learning (Tehan, 2020). Decisions to exclude the arts will deny students holistic learning opportunities and a quality education that consider the whole person (Crawford, 2020c). Given that this case study highlighted the benefits of interdisciplinary learning through musical activity (confirmed to be more effective than the actual discipline itself, e.g., English), then removing music and the arts from the curriculum and school programs will have additional consequences on the learning development of the refugee and migrant student population.

The music program in this case is driven by a constructivist framework that uses experiential learning. Students have clear, mutually agreed-upon learning goals and performances to aim for throughout each of the four terms of the school year. The music teacher explained that music provides an opportunity for all students to experience success with their learning and develop positive attitudes toward schooling. There were many instances of students who were not progressing in literacy and numeracy who were able to develop important associated skills and knowledge through musical activities such as composition. Using critical listening and analytical thinking processes, students would lead in the deconstruction of lyrics and music of songs from Australia and around the world, developing skills and knowledge of how the elements of music intersected and worked in combination. They developed interpretations and understanding of different perspectives and purposes for music. This scaffold provided fundamental skills and knowledge for students to engage with creative endeavors and compose their own collaborative compositions. Working in groups of four, students used various compositional devices and negotiated choices about musical style, genre, and lyrics as well as the tools to compose and instruments to perform the piece. The activity was completed with classes in Years 5–10 and was varied in complexity across the curriculum continuum, providing more creative freedom and less guided instruction for students in the higher year levels. Compositions were performed in classes, which was established as a safe and supportive space for creative expression, experimentation, and risk-taking. Opportunities were provided for positive and constructive peer feedback to validate the effort students had committed to this work, while building resilience through the feedback and suggestions received that could be applied to improve compositions and performances. Students would keep a composition journal throughout the project, which would help develop collaborative and individual learning goals, metacognition and critically reflective practices. After students applied the peer feedback to their compositions and performances, they would have an opportunity to perform these to the school at a term concert. Although the compositional journey was as important as the end-product, it was crucial to provide an opportunity for students to showcase their work to the school and wider community. For the students in this case, this project and music education validated their learning achievements and played a critical role in consolidating friendships and providing a sense of belonging in the school community.

The analysis of student interview data from this case revealed that engagement in music education was experienced as a form of enjoyment. Learning tasks related to the compositional and performance projects were perceived by students as meaningful and valued knowledge and skills (Crawford, 2020a). The findings suggest that engagement with learning was fostered because students enjoyed the classes that occurred in a supportive space in which they could express themselves, take risks, and experiment, without the stress or pressure to achieve that they often associated to subjects such as English or mathematics. Acquiring new music skills that students could then share with others was important to them. Students also referred to self-expression as not only a creative or artistic endeavor, but one directly related to language acquisition and communication development. Although music was connected to skills and knowledge in the literal sense, the experiential and practical teaching and learning approach through composition and performance opportunities were regarded as something very different to what other subjects offered. Students did not feel the same pressure as in other subjects, yet they demonstrated improvement in personal, social, and learning outcomes in curriculum areas related to music, general capabilities, and interdisciplinary aspects. The students themselves indicated knowledge of the opportunities that learning English and communication could provide and had expectations of this, but students expressed that this was easier for them to achieve in music. Further research would be required to identify where such expectations and pressures related to academic achievement and the emphasis of English skills and knowledge development may be derived.

Through cooperative teamwork within composition groups and musical ensembles, students also generated an appreciation of creativity, a sense of personal achievement, learning to work together, mutual respect, compromise and valuing the skills, knowledge, and perspectives of peers. Socially inclusive practices are engendered within the process of music-making, and students expressed

> the reliance of peers within the context of ensembles, which is inherently social, requiring collaboration and turn taking, [resulting] in opportunities for a group performance. The formation of respectful behaviors, roles, and identities have manifested through the social interactions which are central to ensemble work and embedded within this community of musical practice (Kenny, 2014 and 2016; Parker, 2010; Pitts, 2005). (Crawford, 2020a, p. 263)

The socially inclusive pedagogic practices democratize music learning as a social practice and foreground high-status creative projects and performances in the school and community, as a central outcome that students are proud to share (Burnard, 2008; Crawford, 2020a). In addition to the socially inclusive practices used in this case, the composition pedagogy encompassed a constructivist approach that used flexible and experiential learning that

- developed rapport with students through a genuine interest in their learning and well-being;
- allowed time to carefully listen to students in class, which included establishing and understanding of the visual cues and body language;
- the learning experiences designed were meaningful and engaging, generating intrinsic motivation through musical teamwork and agency;
- fostered cultural exchange-negotiation-transculturation through the valuing of music from diverse cultures and traditions;
- established clear and consistent classroom expectations and management, which over time resulted in students facilitating their own self-regulation of behaviour. (Crawford, 2020a, pp. 263–264)

Socially inclusive behaviors and intercultural competencies were developed through the process of cultural exchange and sharing; "Students' existing competencies and knowledge were validated, and they had the opportunity to articulate those competencies and knowledge into the new context" (Crawford, 2020a, p. 265). It is timely to consider the impact of music and in particular composition and the creative arts on students' personal well-being, social development, and engagement with learning, given the current narrative about what should be considered essential learning. It is imperative to question how education is approached and the pedagogies used if music and arts educators are to continue reaffirming its important place in the curriculum and school programs. This case highlights the significant role that music and the creative arts might play in addressing the complexities of globalization and suggest its criticality in highly multicultural countries, such as Australia.

Case 3—Technology used to Enhance Composition and Music-Making in Rural and Remote Secondary School Settings (Online Music Education Project)

This case (Crawford, 2017b) discusses an online music education project, designed to address the disparity in the provision of music education programs in regional and remote schools in Australia and proposed that using a range of Web 2.0 technologies to teach and learn music may in part resolve this issue. Project aims included:

- Providing students and teachers within rural and remote schools access to high-quality music learning materials and resources.
- Facilitating the use of online music technology in a blended learning context through engaging students in the development of online music compositions and soundscapes.

Disadvantaged student populations in low socio-economic areas were restricted by factors such as location and cost, hindering opportunities for students to engage with appropriately trained instrumental music teachers, musicians, and access to professional music concerts. Technologies and Web 2.0 platforms were used to find sustainable and equitable ways to enhance learning experiences that are relevant to real-life, which many of these students would otherwise not have had access to. Music specialist teachers incorporated the Interact Music Project into their curriculum, providing a range of interactive and visual music learning resources such as instrumental lessons on a range of instruments and practice techniques, composition tasks to scaffold concrete knowledge and skills while encouraging creative and critical thinking, performance skills, and critical listening activities.

Students were guided in developing music composition skills and knowledge using the open-sourced audio software Audacity. This fast-multi-track audio editor and recorder has features that include envelope editing, mixing, built-in effects, and plug-ins. Depending on the types of computers and digital devices available, students could also utilize open-sourced software FL Studio, GarageBand, Noteflight and Music Maker. Students created their own compositions and shared their work on the Interact Music Project website. A key element of the project was the use of peer feedback via a blog, allowing students and teachers across schools to share, collaborate, and comment on their compositions and soundscapes. At the time, blogs and social media had been used in informal music learning for a number of years (Salavuo, 2006 and 2008; Waldron, 2013). This project sought to formalize this practice. New communication technologies provided remote access to city-based instrumental teachers and musicians as a supplement to the work achieved in class. Online video conferencing workshops were run with expert musicians from various professional orchestras and bands and webcast from the studios in the main city. Through the use of virtual online classroom software Elluminate, the students were able to listen and watch musicians performing and practicing and composers working through compositional ideas and techniques in practice. A range of musical genres, styles, and instrumentation were explored and experimented with. Students had opportunities to develop their own music learning through creating compositions and/or playing an instrument. They could ask questions and make comments of these musicians and composers by typing into the chat window. The primary content to be used in the classroom was designed as 10 learning modules to be set during the course of the year and the sequence expected that by the middle of the year students will have progressed to the end of module 5 and subsequently module 10 by the end of the year. This was a self-directed student learning approach so that students could work through at their own pace and the teacher would facilitate introductions to each module including providing detailed guidance to key musical ideas, skills, concepts, and knowledge, as well as assistance on individual project work. This blended learning context was found to be highly effective. Although each module includes consideration of differentiated learning in terms of styles and ability levels, extension activities were provided in each module for advanced students.

A mixed method research design using a sample size of 20 Year 7 and 8 (ages 12–14) general music classes in secondary schools consisting of 20 teachers and 440 students was used to investigate the impact of the online music project. Results were significant, indicating that 98% of participating students completed all self-directed learning modules by the end of the year and a major factor in this was changing student expectations about music being not interesting, engaging, authentic, or valued knowledge (Crawford, 2017b). There was a notable increase from the data captured at the beginning of the year when only 140 students or 32% said they think they would use the music project outside of school time, to halfway through the year when the figures indicated that 300 students or 68% were actively using it outside of school time, which increased to 410 students or 93% by the conclusion of the year (Crawford, 2017b). This was correlated with the music teachers who expressed benefits of using technology in an innovative and multidimensional way as they could see the immediate value for their students' learning and the clear progress that was made across the year. The music project enabled students to build skills in using technology to support the development of music compositions and soundscapes, learning an instrument, and participating in music skill development and knowledge workshops.

The success of the project was largely attributed to the multi-dimensional learning environment that fostered metacognitive processes and multi-modal ways of creating and reflecting. The online platform was designed to be student centered and self-directed, providing a supportive space for creating, sharing, collaborating, and receiving feedback synchronously and asynchronously. The opportunity for students to work with musicians and composers, and to experience high quality music performances through partnerships with professional orchestras and bands developed students' understanding of musical expression and inspired creativity in ways that would not have otherwise been afforded to these rural and remote located students. The benefits of such technology creating opportunities for quality music education experiences within authentic and real-life contexts supports current curricula objectives and the thinking and requirements of contemporary society.

RECOMMENDATIONS FOR PRACTICE AND CONCLUDING THOUGHTS

There is indisputable research evidence that indicates that quality music and arts education can develop critical intrinsic and extrinsic attributes in students if taught in an authentic, innovative, and experiential way that challenges learners to think creatively and critically. Engaging with music learning and in particular tasks such as those afforded through composition and performance opportunities, provide processes and experiences that engender a distinctive and critical set of understandings, knowledge, and skills that are required to navigate an unpredictable and ever-changing world. Despite this compelling argument and the statements in the Australian curriculum continuum supporting a sequential learning progression and quality arts education, this is rarely seen in reality:

> Realising this aspiration continues to be threatened by a number of issues including the ongoing marginalisation of education in and through the arts, a dearth of teacher professional learning in the arts and an emphasis on reductive definitions of what it means to be literate. (Ewing, 2020, p. 75)

This has recently been amplified in Australia by debates about what should be considered essential and non-essential learning in the curriculum and school programs, sending confusing messages about the perceived value of some disciplines over others (Crawford, 2020c). Cultivating important 21st century skills and knowledge in truly authentic ways that provide students with a holistic learning experience can only be achieved if the thinking by governments, policy-makers, and education authorities change. For example, pretending that the same complex level of creativity explored in music and arts education can be achieved through disciplines such as science, is naive and short sighted. Students need to be provided with opportunities to pursue a range of interests that cater to different learning abilities and modes. This requires a consideration of the important key skills, knowledge, and perspectives that different disciplines can provide young people, particularly if educating toward a society that values diverse thinking and skill sets.

The case studies presented in this chapter represent different educational contexts in Australia that challenge the current rhetoric about the devaluing of the arts, highlighting how engagement with music through composition pedagogy can develop creative and critical thinking, build social inclusive skills and intercultural competence, and use technology to enhance music learning opportunities. Crawford's (2008 and 2014) multi-dimensional/non-linear teaching and learning model was used as the theoretical underpinning for the approach applied in the cases. A framework exploring the intersections between the model and the composition pedagogy used in the cases is presented in Figure 34.2, and to provide a platform for how teachers might apply the ideas and recommendations within their practice.

The middle circle in the framework is representative of the three pillars of music learning identified in the Australian curriculum as listening, performing, and composing. These principal activities should be approached with consideration to the key tenets of the multi-dimensional/non-linear teaching and learning model: authentic and experiential learning; valued knowledge, multi-dimensional learning, and the holistic learning/whole person phenomenon. Also found in this middle section are the curriculum threads (music learning strands make and respond), general capabilities (critical and creative thinking, personal and social development, and intercultural understanding), cross-curriculum priorities and interdisciplinary learning, and where possible, technology-enhanced learning. This is encapsulated in a constructivist framework that supports both composition pedagogy and the multi-dimensional/non-linear teaching and learning model. Students' engagement with music learning in the three cases described provided visible intrinsic and extrinsic benefits. In all cases composition was placed as the central learning activity that provided behavioral, emotional, and cognitive dimensions. Learning experiences are considered relevant and knowledge is valued by the students as tasks are authentic, contextual, and purposeful and respect different cultural traditions and diverse perspectives. Creative endeavors are encouraged and risk-taking and experimentation are normalized as part of the learning process, which students take responsibility for. A supportive and constructive learning space is established that enhances peer collaborative learning, socially inclusive practices, and intercultural competence. In addition to social development, making and responding to music through composition can enhance personal development and interdisciplinary learning opportunities, such as building English and literacy skills and knowledge. Recognition of these outcomes is not intended to undermine the fact that music is a discipline in its own right, and the intrinsic attributes and aesthetic values that are developed through engagement with learning music and the arts are part of the very fabric of humanity. This makes an important contribution to lifelong learning and our historical and cultural identity. If thinking about music learning as an experience whichis fundamental to providing holistic learning, then valuing a balance of both intrinsic and extrinsic benefits is required. This was certainly identified as an important aspect to the success of the pedagogical approach used in the cases presented.

Composition pedagogy and creativity in music education as discussed in this chapter is intended to challenge the current rhetoric about what should be considered essential learning in schools and how the Australian curriculum may be enacted. Unequivocal research evidence implores governments, policy-makers, and education authorities to make considered and informed decisions that include providing young people the opportunity to engage with a quality music education and experience holistic learning. Only then will young people in Australia and around the world be able to contribute positively to society and be truly prepared for the unpredictable and uncertain nature of life itself.

References

Australian Curriculum, Assessment & Reporting Authority (ACARA). (2012). *The shape of the Australian curriculum, Version 4.0*. https://acaraweb.blob.core.windows.net/resources/The_Shape_of_the_Australian_Curriculum_v4.pdf

ACARA. (2016). *Development of the Australian curriculum*. https://www.acara.edu.au/curriculum/history-of-the-australian-curriculum/development -of- australian-curriculum

ACARA. (2018a). *Key ideas: The arts Australian curriculum, Version 8.4*. https://www.australiancurriculum.edu.au/f-10-curriculum/the-arts/key-ideas/

ACARA. (2018b). *Structure: Learning in music; The arts Australian curriculum, Version 8.4*. https://www.australiancurriculum.edu.au/f-10-curriculum/the-arts/music/structure/

ACARA. (2018c). *General capabilities: The Australian curriculum, Version 8.4*. https://www.australiancurriculum.edu.au/f-10-curriculum/general-capabilities/

ACARA. (2020). *Review of the Australian curriculum*. https://www.acara.edu.au/curriculum/curriculum-review

Barrows, H. S. (1986). A taxonomy of problem-based learning methods. *Medical Education*, 20(6), 481–486. https://doi.org/10.1111/j.1365–2923.1986.tb01386.x.

Berliner, D. (2011). Rational responses to high stakes testing: The case of curriculum narrowing and the harm that follows. *Cambridge Journal of Education*, 41(3), 287–302. https//doi.org/10.1080/0305764x.2011.607151

Brown, J. S., Collins, A., & Duguid. P. (1989). Situated cognition and the culture of learning. *Educational Researcher, 18*(1), 32–42. https//doi.org/10.3102/0013189X018001032.

Bryce, J., Mendelovits, J., Beavis, A., McQueen, J., & Adams, I. (2004). *Evaluation of school based arts programs*. Australian Council for Educational Research.

Burnard, P. (2008). A phenomenological study of music teachers' approaches to inclusive education practices among disaffected youth. *Research Studies in Music Education, 30*(1), 59–75. https//doi.org/10.1177/1321103X08089890

Burnard, P. (2012). *Musical creativities in practice*. Oxford University Press.

Craft, A. (2008). Tensions in creativity and education: Enter wisdom and trusteeship? In A. Craft, H. Gardner, & G. Claxton (Eds.), *Creativity, wisdom, and trusteeship: Exploring the role of education* (pp. 16–34). Corwin Press.

Craft, A. & Jeffrey, B. (2008). Creativity and performativity in teaching and learning: Tensions, dilemmas, constraints, accommodations, and synthesis. *British Educational Research Journal*, 34(5), 577–584. https//doi.org/10.080/01411920802223842

Crawford, R. (2008). *Authentic learning and digital technology in the music classroom*: PhD thesis. Australia, Victoria: Monash University.

Crawford, R. (2014). A multidimensional/non-linear teaching and learning model: teaching and learning music in an authentic and holistic context. *Music Education Research*, 16(1), 50–69. https//doi.org/10.1080/14613808.2013.812627

Crawford, R. (2017a). Creating unity through celebrating diversity: A case study that explores the impact of music education on refugee background students. *International Journal of Music Education*, 35(3), 343–356. https//doi.org/10.1177/0255761416659511

Crawford, R. (2017b). Rethinking teaching and learning pedagogy for education in the twenty-first century: Blended learning in music education. *Music Education Research*, 19(2), 195–213. https//doi.org/10.1080/14613808.2016.1202223

Crawford, R. (2019). *Connected2Learning: Thinking outside the square—Final project report: Curious about learning? Why?* Monash University.

Crawford, R. (2020a). Socially inclusive practices in the music classroom: The impact of music education used as a vehicle to engage refugee background students. *Research Studies in Music Education*, 42(2), 248–269. https//doi.org/10.1177/1321103X19843001

Crawford, R. (2020b). Beyond the dots on the page: Harnessing transculturation and music education to address intercultural competence and social inclusion. *International Journal of Music Education*, 38(4), 537–562. https//doi.org/10.1177/0255761420921585

Crawford, R. (2020c, July 26). Cost of music degrees likely to increase in line with arts degrees. *National Tribune*. https://www.nationaltribune.com.au/cost-of-music-degrees-likely-to-increase-in-line-with-arts-degrees/

Crawford, R. (2020d). *Critical and creative thinking: Developing metacognition and collaborative learning in the curriculum: Critical and creative thinking curriculum—Final project report*. Monash University.

Darling-Hammond, L. (2006). Constructing 21st-century teacher education. *Journal of Teacher Education*, 57(3), 300–314. https//doi.org/10.1177/0022487105285962

Deasy, R. (2002). *Critical links: Learning in the arts and student academic and social development*. Arts and Education Partnership.

Dewey, J. (1958). *Experience and Nature*. (2nd ed.). Dover.

Education and Training Committee. (2013). *Inquiry into the extent, benefits and potential of music education in Victorian schools*. Parliament of Victoria, Australia. Retrieved from https://www.parliament.vic.gov.au/file_uploads/Music_Education_Final_041113_FJWsJhBy.pdf

Elliott, D. (1995). *Music matters: A new philosophy of music education*. Oxford University Press.

Ewing, R. (2010). *The Arts and Australian education: Realising potential*. AER58. Australian Council for Educational Research. https://research.acer.edu.au/cgi/viewcontent.cgi?article=1020&context=aer

Ewing, R. (2020). The Australian curriculum: The arts; A critical opportunity. *Curriculum Perspectives*, 40(1), 75–81. https//doi.org/10.1007/s41297-019-00098-w

Guhn, M., Emerson, S. D., & Gouzouasis, P. (2020). A population-level analysis of associations between school music participation and academic achievement. *Journal of Educational Psychology, 112*(2), 308–328. https//doi.org/10.1037/edu0000376

Karkou, V., & Glasman, J. (2004). Arts, education and society: The role of the arts in promoting the emotional wellbeing and social inclusion of young people. *Support for Learning, 19*(2), 57–65. https//doi.org/10.1111/j.0268-2141.2004.00321.x

Karlsen, S. (2013). Immigrant students and the "homeland music": Meanings, negotiations and implications. *Research Studies in Music Education, 35*(2), 161–177. https//doi.org/10.1177/13211 03x13508057

Kaschub, M., & Smith, J. (2009). *Minds on music: Composition for creative and critical thinking.* Rowman & Littlefield Education.

Kaschub, M., & Smith, J. (Eds.). (2013). *Composing our future: Preparing music educators to teach composition.* Oxford University Press. https//doi.org/10.1093/acprof:oso/9780199832 286.001.0001

Katz, L., & Raths. J. L. (1982). The best of intentions for the education of teachers. *Action in Teacher Education, 4*(1), 8–16. https//doi.org/10.1080/01626620.1982.10519084.

Kenny, A. (2014). Practice through partnership: Examining the theoretical framework and development of a "community of musical practice". *International Journal of Music Education, 32*(4), 396–408. doi:10.1177/0255761413515802

Kenny, A. (2016). *Communities of musical practice.* Routledge

Kinsley, C. W., & McPherson. K. (1995). *Enriching the curriculum through service learning.* Association for Supervision and Curriculum Development.

Kokotsaki, D. (2012). Pre-service student-teachers' conceptions of creativity in the primary music classroom. *Research Studies in Music Education, 34*(2), 129–156. https//doi.org/10.1177/1321103X12466770

Kolb, D. A. (1984). *Experiential learning: Experience as the source of learning and development.* Prentice Hall.

Lave, J. (1988). *Cognition in practice: Mind, mathematics and culture in everyday life.* Cambridge University Press.

Marra, T. (2004). *Authentic learning.* University of Michigan. http://www-personal.umich.edu/_tmarra/authenticity/authen.html

Marsh, K. (2015). Music, social justice, and social inclusion: The role of collaborative music activities in supporting young refugees and newly arrived immigrants in Australia. In C. Benedict, P. Schmidt, G. Spruce, & P. Woodford (Eds.), *The Oxford handbook of social justice in music education* (pp. 173–189). Oxford University Press.

McCombs, B. L. (2000). Assessing the role of education technology in the teaching and learning process: A learner-centred perspective. Secretary's Conference on Educational Technology. http://www.ed.gov/print/rschstat/eval/tech/techconfoo/mccombs_papers.html.

McCombs, B. L. (2012). *Developing responsible and autonomous learners: A key to motivating students.* American Psychological Association. http://www.apa.org/education/k12/learners.aspx.

McFerran, K. S., Crooke, A. H. D., & Bolger, L. (2017). Promoting engagement in school through tailored music programs. *International Journal of Education & the Arts, 18*(3), 1–28. http://www.ijea.org/v18n3/

Ministerial Council on Education Employment, Training & Youth Affairs (MCEETYA). (2008). *Melbourne declaration on education gaols for young Australians.* https://docs.acara.

edu.au/resources/national_declaration_on_the_educational_goals_for_young_australi
ans.pdf

Ojukwu, E. V. (2017). Music education: A vehicle for fostering positive youth development. *Journal of Arts and Humanities, 18*(2), 489–506. https//doi.org/10.4314/ujah.v18i2.28

Parker, E. C. (2010). Exploring student experiences of belonging within an urban high school choral ensemble: An action research study. *Music Education Research, 12*(4), 339–352. doi:10.1080/14613808.2010.519379

Pascoe, R., Leong, S., MacCallum, J., Mackinlay, E., Marsh, K., Smith, B., Church, T., & Winterton, A. (2005). *National review of school music education: Augmenting the diminished.* Department of Education, Science and Training, Australia. Retrieved from http://www.cur riculum.edu.au/leader/school_music_review_report,12505.html?issueID=9802

Paul, S. J., Teachout, D. J., Sullivan, J.M., Kelly, S. N., Bauer, W. I., & Raiber, M. A. (2001). Authentic-context learning activities in instrumental music teacher education. *Journal of Research in Music Education, 49*(2), 136–145. https//doi.org/10.2307/3345865.

Paynter, J. (1982). *Music in the secondary school curriculum: Trends and developments in class music teaching.* Cambridge University Press.

Paynter, J. (1992). *Sound and Structure.* Cambridge University Press.

Piaget, J. (1954). *Construction of reality in the child.* Basic Books.

Piaget, J. (1968). *On the development of memory and identity.* Clark University.

Pitts, S. E. (2005). *Valuing musical participation.* Ashgate.

Randles, C., Kratus, J., & Burnard, P. (2012). Composition learning in music education. In: Seel, N.M. (Eds.), *Encyclopedia of the sciences of learning* (pp. 686–688). Springer. https//doi.org/ 10.1007/978-1-4419-1428-6_1676

Sahlberg, P. (2006). Education reform for raising economic competitiveness. *Journal of Educational Change, 7*(4), 259–287. https//doi.org/10.1007/s10833-005-4884-6

Salavuo, M. (2006). Open and informal online communities as forums of collaborative musical activities and learning. *British Journal of Music Education, 23*(3), 253–271. https//doi. org/10.1017/S0265051706007042

Salavuo, M. (2008). Social media as an opportunity for pedagogical change in music education. *Journal of Music, Technology and Education, 1*(2), 121–136. https//doi.org/10.1386/jmte.1.2

Tehan, D. (2020, June 19). *Minister for education Dan Tehan National Press Club address.* Ministers' Media Centre, Department of Education, Skills and Employment, Australia. https://ministers.dese.gov.au/tehan/minister-education-dan-tehan-national-press-club-address?utm_source=miragenews&utm_medium=miragenews&utm_campaign=news

Victorian Curriculum & Assessment Authority (VCAA). (2020). *The Victorian curriculum Foundation-10.* https://victoriancurriculum.vcaa.vic.edu.au/

Waldron, J. (2013). User-generated content, YouTube, and participatory culture on the Web: music learning and teaching in two contrasting online communities. *Music Education Research, 15*(3), 257–274. https//doi.org/10.1080/14613808.2013.772131

....

CHAPTER 35

COMPOSITION PEDAGOGY IN THE CZECH REPUBLIC

....

VÍT ZOUHAR

MANY pupils, students, and music education teachers in the Czech Republic have gained experience in composing over the past 20 years. Most of them are not composition students at conservatoires, or music universities, but pupils and students at primary or secondary schools (Zouhar & Medek, 2010; Medek et al., 2014). Some teachers assign classroom composing in music education classes in primary, secondary, and grammar schools, in general music lessons and in some instrumental classes at primary art and music schools (Všetičková, 2014). Music education students at some universities learn didactic techniques on how to incorporate and develop compositional activities in music education lessons (Synek, 2008; Synek, 2012; Všetičková, 2011; Zouhar, 2004). In recent years, some composition students at art and music universities have developed procedures for teaching primary and secondary students how to compose their own pieces (Dvořáková, 2005; Medek et al., 2014; Vítková, 2011). Leading orchestras and music institutions such as the Czech Philharmonic Orchestra, Brno Philharmonic, Hradec Králové Philharmonic Orchestra, National Theatre Brno, Berg Orchestra, and many others have introduced children and parents to composing within their educational programs (Hořínka, 2019; Synek, 2012). During the past 20 years, group composing was gradually incorporated into non-artistic music education and leisure educational programs. The starting point for many activities was *Different Hearing* (*Slyšet jinak*) *Program* founded in 2001 (Medek et al., 2014; Synek, 2008; Zouhar, 2004). However, in Czech national curricular materials for general music education, composing is not mentioned as one of the separate activities (Ministry of Education, Youth and Sports, 2005, 2007, 2010a, 2010b, and 2021).

This chapter is focused on the current state of composition pedagogy in the Czech Republic aimed at young people aged six–19, respectively 19+. It is distinguished between individual artistic education and general group music education as well as non-formal educational projects.

Composing in the Classroom and Concepts of Music Education

Composition pedagogy has traditionally been associated with artistic music education in the Czech Republic (Boleška, 1905; Fukač, 1997; Knittl, 1896). In recent years,
however, it has become a strong topic of general music pedagogy and music education
(Drkula, 2006; Synek, 2005, and 2011; Všetičková, 2010, and 2015; Medek et al. 2014;
Zouhar & Medek, 2010). Since the 1970s, three generations of pupils and students in
former Czechoslovakia have been able to compose and improvise in music education in primary and secondary schools. They could become familiar with elementary
composing and experience the creation of music. In 1969, the two volumes of Carl Orff's
Schulwerk, in a Czech adaptation by composers Hurník & Eben (1969), were published
with concrete compositional stimuli. During the 1960s, composing was also one of the
new topics of music pedagogy (Melkus, 1969; Synek, 2011). And in the 1970s, the *Czech
Schulwerk* (*Česká Orffova škola*), became a part of the curriculum for general music education in primary at secondary education. Future music education teachers were methodically prepared for its use at universities. But the concept of music education in
former Czechoslovakia continued to emphasize mostly vocal, instrumental, dance, and
listening activities. Teachers have therefore rarely exceeded the performative framework of music education (Knopová, 2011; Všetičková, 2014).

There were several reasons for this. Doubts about the aesthetic value of children's
compositions and their effectiveness for the development of musical skills date back to
the 1930s. Helfert (1930) wrote:

> Therefore, I am always skeptical about efforts to include in music education also
> exhortations to children's melodic creativity. However, it is certain that such active
> synergy of children can increase children's interest in music. But the question is
> whether this leads children to the unhealthy view that music can be created as easily
> and mechanically as they have invented "their" melodies, and whether the time thus
> spent could not be used for more beneficial and fruitful synergy. (p. 27)

A similar opinion can be found later in the Poš's foreword for the first volume of the
Czech Schulwerk (Hurník & Eben, 1969). In contrary to Orff (1969) he was skeptical
about aesthetic values of children works: "The compositions created by children are valuable in that they provoke musical creativity in the child (children are always impressed
by "their" song), but on the other hand, it should be critically said that a folk song almost always has more aesthetic value than the most musical piece of novice composers."
(Hurník & Eben, 1969, p. 7). This belief prevailed in music pedagogy in Czechoslovakia
until the end of the 1980s (Váňová, 1989) and continued at the beginning of the new
millennium. *The Framework Education Program for Primary Education* (Ministry of
Education Youth and Sports, 2005, 2017, 2021) and the *Framework Educational Program*

for Secondary General Education (Grammar School) (Ministry of Education Youth and Sports, 2007), the Czech national curriculum, were also influenced by this skepticism.

Another argument that spoke against the composing activities in primary general music education were challenging prerequisites such as talent, musical instruments skills, and knowledge of music theory. Some music educators and composers believe it is not possible to compose, without knowledge of notation, music grammar, syntax, and performing skills. The Western concept of the term "composition" moved away from traditional principles during the 20th century, when composers emphasized new processes, principles, methods and poetics. But key fundamentals of the teaching composition are still harmony, counterpoint and forms for many music teachers and composers. The emphasis on talent and many years of individual study of composition techniques and music theory was therefore a generally perceived prerequisite for composing. These demands and image of exceptionality prevented incorporation of composition pedagogy into general music education. Although the objectives, methods, and means of elementary composition in the context of general music education are different from composition programs within artistic education.

Concepts of Composition

The focus on the artwork, its aesthetic values, and the theory of composition, corresponds to earlier meanings of the term "composition" in Czech general and music dictionaries during the 20th century. They are similar to other dictionaries across the globe. Boleška (1905) defined the term "composition" in the general *Otto's Dictionary* (*Ottův slovník naučný*) as combining of sounds: "A composition in music is an activity based on elements of sound new combinations" (p. 265). He placed emphasis on the exceptional talent of the composer and on his knowledge of music grammar, stating, "The ability to compose music is based on innate talent, which is much more special than the gift for music in a broader sense, but like this, it must be put on the rails of regular practice in an orderly way" (p. 265).

Boleška was a graduate of the Prague Organ School and at one time a private composition student of Antonín Dvořák. In his conception, the grammatical part of the composition theory (harmony, counterpoint) is connected with the aesthetical. Boleška accentuated knowledge of all disciplines: "The true creative freedom is opened up by scholars, skilled in harmony, in the study of counterpoint and the style of imitation, i.e., imitation, cannon, and fugue" (p. 265).

This definition grows from that time, when Dvořák lectured composition at the Prague Conservatoire and led the institution until 1904 (Branberger, 1911).

More than ninety years later, Fukač (1997) defined composition more openly in the *Dictionary of Czech Music Culture* (*Slovník české hudební kultury*). Notation is no longer necessary condition there, but a closed, complex artwork still is. The composition is a musical structure ("most often notated") which is achieved by "composition-ally technical, usually theoretically justified" procedures (p. 833). Fukač's definition is complemented by composition theory: "a didactic discipline, whose sub-disciplines are considered to be diverse theories (about melody, harmony, counterpoint, etc.)" (p. 833). The emphasis on musical grammar and syntax is obvious. This meaning of the term "composition" determined both composition pedagogy and teaching composition programs at conservatoires and music universities, and general music education.

In 2001 the *Different Hearing Program* was founded in Olomouc, Czech Republic (Synek, 2008; Zouhar, 2004). The program is focused on music creativity and elementary composing within general music education. The term composition was defined as very open cluster of possibilities: "Every sound is understood as musical. Every object as a musical instrument. Spontaneous interaction between sounds as improvisation. Their graphic or verbal fixation as a musical composition" (Zouhar, 2004, p. 11). Such a broad meaning resonates with Cage's earlier definition of composition (1973, p. 62). It opened a new space for elementary composing in general music education. Not the artwork but the artistic process, not the aesthetic value of the composition, but the experience with creating and experimenting with sounds are moved forward and changed the traditional meaning of the term "composition" in the educational context.

Artistic, General Music and Non-formal Music Education: Different Roles of Composition Pedagogy

Music education in the Czech Republic is based on three pillars: artistic education, general education, and non-formal education. Composing and composition pedagogy are embodied in different ways in all of them. In each pillar, however, composing has a different role and status; it is aimed at different groups of pupils, students, and clients. It has other objectives, goals, and outcomes and it is otherwise designed and organized.

Artistic Education

Artistic education in music is focused on talented students and on the development of future music professionals. They are selected by admission tests and the teaching process is based on teacher-student one-to-one interaction over years. Composition programs and individual composition pedagogy are focused on the all-round sharpening and deepening composition skills and knowledge. Talented students strengthen their competences to create their compositions in written, audio or multimedia forms. Composition programs are provided at all levels of the artistic educational system from aged six to 21+ at some basic art and music schools, conservatoires and art and music universities.

Art and music basic schools are designed for talented pupils aged 6 to 19 who want to develop their instrumental, singing, or composition skills, and dance, and art talents too. It is a formal leisure education. More than 160 basic art schools supported by municipalities or private entities are providing programs in music, art, dance, and drama. The basic arts and music education is divided in two levels. The majority of all pupils (aged 6 to 14) are educated at the first level. Some pupils aged 15 to 19 are joining the second level. Basic art and music schools are also open to pre-school education for children from 4 to 6 as well as to adults in lifelong learning. Composition and Electroacoustic Music programs are provided only by a few schools. These programs are regulated by the *Framework Education Program for Basic Art and Music Schools* (Ministry of Education, Youth and Sports, 2010b). It is implemented by school educational plans in every institution.

Only five of the nineteen conservatories in the Czech Republic provide composition programs, two in Prague, others in Brno, Ostrava, and Plzeň. They train talented students from ages 14 to 19, sometimes 21. The composition programs are designed as individual and they are aimed to develop abilities of future composers. The basic prerequisites are composition portfolio, basic knowledge of music theory and instrumental skills, which the candidates demonstrate in the entrance talent tests. The study is based on one-to-one teacher-student interaction and takes mostly four or six years. Composition programs are regulated by the National *Framework Education Program for Education in Music* (Ministry of Education, Youth and Sports, 2010a). At the institutional level they are followed by School Education Plans.

Only two Czech universities provide composition programs: The Academy of Performing Arts in Prague and the Janáček Academy of Music and Performing Arts in Brno. They offer composition programs and specializations including electroacoustic music and film music in the undergraduate (BA and MA) and postgraduate (PhD) levels. The study of composition at both universities is focused only on teaching future music professionals. Here, too, the teaching is designed as individual (one-to-one) and necessary prerequisites are knowledge in music theory and composition skills including a composition portfolio. The undergraduate curriculum of the composition program also includes courses of pedagogical propaedeutic and methodology of teaching composition. These courses are primarily focused on teaching music theory and individual composing pedagogy. However, students are also familiar with the principles and methods of composing in the classroom and the use of music technologies for composing within general music education.

General Music Education

General music education focuses on education of all children. They are educated without any selections or distinctions. Music education courses are mandatory for the compulsory general education at basic (6–10) and lower secondary (11–15) level. Some grammar schools (16–19) are providing elective music courses. Lessons are based on teacher-class interaction. Music education courses deepen mostly vocal and listening skills and know-ledge in elementary music theory and history. Pupils and students are motivated to ac-tively participate in group vocal, instrumental, and listening activities. All courses are regulated by the national curriculum in music education, the *Framework Education Program for Primary Education* (Ministry of Education, Youth and Sports, 2005, 2017, 2021) and the *Framework Education Program for Secondary General Education (Grammar Schools)* (Ministry of Education, Youth and Sports, 2007). These are followed by school education plans implementing national regulations at institutional level.

Composing is not defined as a separate activity in these frameworks. Some vocal and instrumental sub-activities, focused on the general development of musical creativity, are defined there (Medek et al., 2014; Synek, 2008). But composing is not systematically developed in general music. It is up to teachers, as to how far they use the methodology and didactic principles of group composition pedagogy in their classes.

General music group composition pedagogy is based mostly on principles of experiential pedagogy (Kaschub & Smith, 2009; Mills & Paynter, 2008; Paynter & Aston, 1970; Synek, 2008) and post-indeterminacy composition approaches (Schafer, 1986; Zouhar, 2005; Zouhar & Medek, 2010) in the Czech Republic. Composition activities are focused on the pupils' and students' experience with creating sounds, with the process of group composing and performing (Synek, 2008). The education is focused on stimulation and development of wide range of musicality and creating experiences for group composing and performance. In this concept of general music education, composition is a tool to acquire new competencies and to develop musicality in a broadest sense. It is therefore not a systematized training for the acquisition of composing skills and knowledge, but to sharpen creative skills through music games and sound experiments. (Medek et al., 2014). Most of these activities are in-spired, triggered, and based on the *Different Hearing Program* and its methodology and the context of the "barrier-free music education" (Medek et al., 2014, p. 67).

Future general music education teachers of primary and secondary schools are studying in bachelor's and follow-up master's degree programs at the pedagog-ical faculties of eight universities. Curricular materials mostly do not include regular courses on composition pedagogy. Only Palacký University Olomouc and the Faculty of Education offer creativity courses in which students become familiar with composition pedagogy, following the compositional educational program *Different Hearing* (Medek et al., 2014; Synek, 2008, 2012).

Non-Formal Music Education

Parallel to artistic and general music education some institutions provide non-formal music workshops and courses for young people and adults, using group composition pedagogy. These courses play a key role as motivation for young people to create their musical ideas and perform their own compositions, when formal general music edu-cation does not offer composing activities in the classroom. They build conditions for the development of creativity and diverse skills for adults, and they get an experience that they did not have in music education in their youth. For teachers, these courses and workshops were and are also an inspiration and methodological support for how to use composition pedagogy in classrooms and inspire their own pupils to compose and to be creative. And how to use compositional pedagogy to meet the goals of general music education set out in the framework education programs. In addition, courses offer educational tools how to introduce clients to existing music, using composition activities.

Non-formal music education is provided by music institutions and festivals (Czech Philharmonic Orchestra, Brno Philharmonic, National Theatre in Prague, National Theatre in Brno, Berg Orchestra, Exposition of New Music Festival, Brno, The Leoš Janáček International Music Festival etc.), educational institutions (Palacký University Olomouc, Janáček Academy of Music and Performing Arts Brno, Jan Neruda Grammar School, Prague, etc.), societies, and non-profit organizations (Society for Music Education, Orff Society, Association Q, etc.).

Educators and composers apply group composing methodology mentioned in the context of general music education. They use it for free composing activities and for workshops introducing and accessing existing compositions (Bakla, 2005; Flašar & Kyas, 2005; Synek, 2012). 2011 Hradec Králové Philharmonic Orchestra realized eight weeks *Different Hearing* course for primary and secondary schools focused on introduction for existing compositions. Students composed their own group compositions based on principles of existing works. They learned to know these pieces only by their own composing and performing activities. At the closing concert students' compositions and these original works were performed together. From 2015 to 2019, the Czech Philharmonic Orchestra provided composition workshops as part of a large educational program. Hořínka and Kyjovský led 90-minute workshops for children *Composing on Demand* (Hořínka, 2019). During 2016–2019, the *Different Hearing* team of Synek, Coufalová, Všetičková, and the author of this chapter realized workshops for teachers and their pupils entitled: *Do you want to hear differently?* Within a few weeks, the pupils composed their compositions during their music education lessons under the guidance of their teachers as well as members of the Czech Philharmonic Orchestra. Together they performed their compositions as part of the Czech Phil educational concerts. In 2015, the Brno Philharmonic held a four-week workshop led by Všetičková, Medek, Medková, Páchová and the author of this text. The workshop focused on animations of existing compositions. Other institutions such the National Theatre Brno, Exposition of New Music Festival, Janáček Brno Festival, The Leoš Janáček International Music Festival and others organized composition workshops for schools too.

COMPOSITION PEDAGOGY

Individual composition pedagogy

The term "composition pedagogy" is not included in any Czech music dictionary, similar to *The New Grove Dictionary* (Tyrrell, 2001) or the *Die Musik in Geschichte und*

Gegenwart (Finscher, 2008) dictionary. But several of the articles about composer's schools are given by the *Dictionary of Czech Music Culture* (Fukač et al., 1997), including Dvořák's, Suk's, Novák's, Janáček's, Hába's, and other schools. The term "school" is clarified in several meanings there, none of which emphasizes the methodology of teaching composition. It often means a "class" led by the teacher-composer, or suggests common aesthetic priorities between teacher and students. But it does not focus on the teaching itself and methodological and didactical approaches. This is because individual composition lessons were guided and are still guided at art and music schools, conservatoires, and music universities by the framework curriculum, not by detailed methodology and didactical teaching texts. Due to the traditionally small number of composition students and individual lessons, there were no reasons to systematically develop composition pedagogy for individual artistic education. The methodology of individual teaching composition has been passed down from teacher to student since the late 19th century at music institutions in the countries of today's Czech Republic.

Before a separate composition program was established at the Prague Conservatoire in 1889, the training in composition was provided at the Organ School in Prague and also privately (Branberger, 1911; Freemanová, 2011). Although the composition was not one of the main focuses of the Organ School, unlike organ and later choirmaster, its teachers, pupils, and alumni played a key role in the formation of composition schools in Bohemia and Moravia. Dvořák, Foerster and Janáček were among the most important students of the Organ School, who later influenced generations of composers. Since its foundation in 1811, the Prague Conservatoire has been focused on teaching instrumentalists and later singers. In 1889, a separate organ, composition, and piano "school" was established at the Prague Conservatoire by merging with the Organ School in Prague. Knittl noted in 1896:

> Is the school closed to pupils of less talent for the composition? Not. Every student of an instrumental school has the right to attend it, and perhaps he could not keep up with the gifted, after all—if he has enough diligence and will, he can learn much about what is useful for his future life. (p. 207)

The basis of the teaching composition at art and music universities is the modified oral method of the master school, where an experienced composer-teacher guides his student from simpler compositional tasks and structures to more complex, from solo compositions to orchestral ones. Some composers-teachers in one person have published didactic texts about harmony, musical forms, etc. (Knittl, Janáček, Hába, and others), but not about teaching composition. Collective courses like harmony required this methodological and didactic approach. But individual composition courses designed on students' abilities do not need didactic texts as much as collective courses. In the composition lessons, the composer-teacher was, and still is, able to pass on to the students' needs and the current state of the composition on which the student is working. Neither the textbook nor the detailed methodology is necessary in such situation. It couldn't be detailed or flexible enough. It couldn't solve every problem. Methodological and didactic procedures in teaching composition at the Prague Conservatoire by Dvořák, Suk, Novák, Foerster, or Hába are therefore only marginally mentioned in their correspondence and in memoirs of their students. None of them wrote a treatise about teaching composition. A similar situation was also in the second half of the 20th century and prevails to these days both in conservatories, universities, and elementary art schools. Some Czech composers-teachers have published their texts on poetics and methods since the 1960s (Kapr, 1967; Kohoutek, 1970; Piňos, 1971; Ištvan, 1973; Medek, 1998), but they are not authors of didactic textbooks for individual composition pedagogy. They pass on their pedagogical experience orally during composition lessons. However, the practically oriented individual composition lessons were and still are very effective. This is due to three factors: highly experienced mentors with flexible response to student needs, highly motivated students and large number of one-to-one teaching hours.

Only a few Czech texts on individual composition pedagogy have been published during last decades. Janeček, (1969) described two methods of teaching and studying composition: compositional and analytical. He recalled that the teacher should combine the two methods according to the needs of the students and learning objectives. The first one is challenging and Janeček recommends applying it only if the aim of the study is composition (p. 105). The second he prefers in the case of theoretically oriented study programs (p. 107).

Kohoutek (1989) deals only with the general problems of teaching composition as one of the components of Marxist education. He briefly mentions entry and outcome profiles of the graduate student and notes the key role of the composition course for college level education. But he described neither the structure nor methodology of this course. The temporary context of the 1980s is completed by Kohoutek's defense of experimental work: "I do not consider the opinion that the university music school does not belong to an experiment: understandably not *per se*, but in the sense of creative research; it is not correct" (p. 36).

Kvěch's (2013) *Fundamentals of Classical Music Composition: Notes for Future Composers* is linked with standards and methodology of teaching composition, in his case at the Prague Conservatoire. This book is not a composition textbook for secondary education or a guide on how to compose, rather a sequence of partial problems. It connects the treatise on forms, harmony, orchestration, and others in a holistic treatise on composition, which contains everything necessary the composer needs to know. The phrase "classical composition" relates to the Kvěch's own aesthetic, who was an advocate of the artwork, masterpiece, and craftsmanship and a composer, who was skeptical of much that brought Western music after 1945.

In recent years, two publications are inspiring for individual composition pedagogy at basic art and music school level. Hanousek & Ščerba (2013) point out some general principles. They recommend to start teaching composition with structure and to move the music theory training (harmony, counterpoint) to the second level of education (i.e., over 14 years). Performing skills are an important prerequisite for studying composition:

> The teacher should not follow the template when teaching the composition; the lessons should be set entirely individually according to the pupil's profile. At first, the teacher should not significantly influence the novice composer with his preferred practices. They must find out what genre or style the pupil prefers and set the next steps accordingly. (Hanousek & Ščerba, 2013, p. 3)

The output skills of the composition graduates are ranged from "motivic development (rhythmic, melodic, harmonic and combined)" until "a sonata cycle, [a pupil] composes compositions in Baroque forms (invention, passacaglia, fugue), composes a composition for a small chamber orchestra, composes composition for a symphony orchestra" (Hanousek & Ščerba, 2013, p. 4). And two most common mistakes are noted there: "The teacher does not give the pupil enough space to improvise . . . [and] when teaching the composition, the teacher forces his own musical tastes" (p. 4).

Mimra et al. (2020) presented best practice impulses for individual composing pedagogy at basic art and music schools. His publication includes didactic descriptions of 17 teaching hours focused on diverse topics: improvisation, compositional structural work with tones, folk songs, and lyrics, to orchestration for chamber orchestra and compositions for large orchestra.

Group composition pedagogy

The first remarks on composing in general music education appeared in Czech music journals during the 1950s and 1960s. Reflections of foreign projects (*The Contemporary Music Project for Creativity in Music Education, Schulwerk*) were accompanied by calls for cooperation between composers and educators in music education (Melkus, 1969; Poledňák, 1963–64, Poledňák & Budík, 1969; Synek, 2011). Composer and educator Kaňák (1963 and 1966) described his experiments with composing in music education in the ninth grade. In 1970, Orff's Schulwerk was introduced into the music education curriculum. However, this provoked negative feedback, which postponed the compositional activities in music education for several more years (Synek, 2011).

During the 1970s and 1980s, Czechoslovak music pedagogy was isolated from foreign impulses, and the aesthetic canon of contemporary music in music education was socialist realism. The emigration of some Czech educators (Jurkovič, Poš) and limited foreign contacts meant the preserved concepts of music education. The political changes after 1989 brought pluralism and new impulses for music education and composition pedagogy.

In the 1990s, teachers and composers in the Czech Republic gained new experience in composition in general music education. Popovič (1994–1995) experimented with music education students at Charles University with the *Manhattanville Music Curriculum Program*. And some other educators reflected new impulses for their work

(Synek, 2011c). Wider interest in group composition pedagogy came after 2001, when the author of this chapter founded the *Different Hearing Program* at the Palacký University Olomouc (Synek, 2008a; Zouhar, 2004). The program forced new methodology, didactic tools, and classroom composing workshops for students, teachers, and educators (Synek, 2008; Medek et al., 2014; Zouhar & Medek, 2010). The inspiration for this program were projects *Klangnetze*, by Schneider, Bösze, and Stangl (2000), and Gründler, and *Response*.

Different Hearing

The focus of the *Different Hearing Program* is elementary composing in the classroom. Through group composing activities and sound games, students at all levels of education from ages 6 to 19+ develop and improve their creative competencies and strengthen their communication and concentration abilities. Teachers encourage an active access to all musical activities on principles of experiential pedagogy. They are students' partners, who encourage, motivate, and stimulate their creativity. Anyone can participate in this "barrier-free music education" regardless of their abilities, skills, age, and previous musical experience (Medek et al., 2014, p. 67). Anyone has equal access to music, sound material, development of musical instruments, performance, and composing. The students' own experience with group composing precedes their theoretical knowledge.

A child in art education was the inspiration for this program (Zouhar, 2004). For the first stroke with a pencil or brush or for modeling, it is enough to hold the tool in its hand and start creating. The child does not need to know the techniques of drawing, working with colors, or principles of composition. All this will or may follow. And the same is enough for young people creating first sound objects.

The starting point of the *Different Hearing* methodology are games with sounds, voices, and objects of daily use. Students are playing these objects like musical instruments, and they are observing, discovering, creating, and interacting with voice and sounds at all phases of the process. For their fixation, they create instructional or graphical symbols. They use them for group composing and for creating graphic or instruction scores. The teaching and learning process is based not on knowledge of notation, composing principles, or musical syntax and grammar, but on a play with sounds. By joining (composing) sounds, students create new sound surfaces and compositions. They perform these pieces by themselves, or together with teachers or other performers. The methodology is designed as a free educational system, modified and extended according to students' needs and learning objectives. It's an open source, not developed in detail for pre-primary, primary, and secondary education. Teachers can complete it themselves according to their needs (Coufalová et al., 2013; Medek et al., 2014).

The methodology is divided into four stages: initiation, material (sound), structure (composing), and performance. The first stage (initiation) consists of three types of sound games focusing on stimulation, concentration, and communication. In the second stage (material) students are attracted to search for and create their own sounds, to perform them and to produce simple musical instruments. The third stage (structure) is aimed at group composing in classrooms. Students are motivated to improvise with their own sounds and to compose graphic or instruction scores. And the last stage (performance) is focused on the performance of the group compositions, new orchestrations, and next performances by other group of students (Coufalová & Synek, 2014; Synek, 2008; Všetičková, 2010).

The *Different Hearing* methodology does not test students' musical talent, or knowledge. Lessons don't start with composition techniques, musical forms, or methods, but with sound games. Without any training, students play with sounds, and create graphic scores and group compositions under teachers' guidance. They compose first and later they could be familiar with music grammar and syntax. Only then theoretical anchoring can follow, depending on students' knowledge and abilities and concrete learning objectives. But this is just a possibility, not a necessity.

This procedure may seem opposite to the process of teaching composition. But this sequence is a similar way of a composer's work, who experiments with material first. And on that basis, he determines the shape and structure of his composition. This experience of creation, discovering, and joining sounds, is crucial for the initial phase of classroom composing and for students. This may be followed by other procedures that enhance the compositional experience. The experience with producing sounds and playing sound games is fundamental for the initiation of students to compose.

Different Hearing Program is based on co-teaching and supports cooperation between teachers, composers, and musicians on teaching (Synek, 2011). Its methodology alternates and extends the curriculum of general music education for primary and secondary schools with group composition activities (Medek et al., 2014; Synek, 2008). It connects and stimulate the composition, vocal, instrumental, and listening activities and can be used for many objectives of the Czech *Framework Education Programmes* for primary and secondary education (Synek, 2008). Teachers, educators, and composers are using the complete four phases learning process or its individual phases only, according to specific learning objectives.

Both educators and composers are members of the *Different Hearing* team since 2003, when teachers and students of the Janáček Academy of Music joined this program and complemented the Palacký University team. They are working together and changing their roles. Educators are composing, composers are educating, and together they are co-teaching, lecturing at universities, leading workshops, and publishing texts. Numerous studies, methodological publications, conference papers, and three books focused on *Different Hearing* methodology were published (Coufalová at al., 2013; Medek et al., 2014; Kopecký et al., 2014). They influenced many teachers, educators, and parents.

Composing Educators

Among the most active authors focusing on group composition pedagogy are members of *Different Hearing* team with rich pedagogical experience: Synek (2004,

2005, 2008a, 2008c, 2011a, 2011b, 2011c, and 2012a), Coufalová & et al.,2013, Coufalová & Synek, 2014, Všetičková (2010, 2012, 2015), and the author of this chapter. We all are experienced lecturers and mentors of the *Different Hearing Program* at the Palacký University Olomouc Department of Music Education, where the program was founded 2001.

Synek is focusing on music-pedagogy tasks (2004, 2005, 2012b). His dissertation was dedicated to elementary composing and the methodology of the *Different Hearing Program* (2008). He also led and described workshops, where students are introduced to existing compositions only through their compositional activities (Synek, 2008a and 2012). Recently Synek dedicated his publications to experiential pedagogy and methodology of DIY musical instruments and their use in group compositions (Coufalová et al., 2013; Coufalová & Synek 2014; Synek, 2008b;). He is the coauthor of all three Different Hearing books.

Coufalová focuses on strengthening performing competencies when composing in classrooms. Together with Synek and Medek they published a book about the production of DIY instruments (Coufalová et al., 2013; Coufalová & Synek, 2014). Coufalová and Synek described possibilities of further use of the methodology of *Different Hearing* in project activities, from free composition, through animation programs and multimedia projects (VJ and multimedia) (Coufalová & Synek, 2014).

Všetičková (2015) has developed the *Different Hearing* methodology for listening activities. She dealt in detail with compositional activities using principles of minimal music in her dissertation (Všetičková, 2011) and other studies. She also clarified the importance of graphic scores in the compositional activities of the *Different Hearing* methodology (Všetičková, 2014a).

Together with the author of this chapter, this trio made a significant contribution to strengthening the composition motivation in general music education and teachers' composing competencies. We carried out dozens of courses and methodically led hundreds of teachers under lifelong programs supported by the European Commission (IVOK, 2017–2019) and carried out workshops for music institutions (Czech Philharmonic Orchestra, Brno Philharmonic Hradec Králové Philharmonic, Exhibition of New Music) (Bakla, 2005; Flašar & Kyas, 2005, Synek, 2012).

The *Different Hearing Program* is currently the most active program in the Czech Republic for the composing in the classroom and group composition pedagogy in general music education. The numerous studies focused on experiences from workshops (Synek, 2004; Dvořáková, 2004; Medek, 2004), compared compositional activities in music education abroad and in Czech schools (Všetičková, 2014b; Zouhar, 2008), curricular materials, and theoretical reflections (Synek, 2011a, 2011b, and 2011c), and brought new methodological procedures. The topic of classroom composing has also become the subject of master theses and dissertations (Drkula, 2006; Jandová, 2012; Skřebská, 2017 and 2019; Stecová, 2015 and 2017; etc.). The *Different Hearing Program* was also mentioned as one of the starting points for the amendment of the general music education curriculum (Grobár et al., 2019).

Composers in the Classroom

Several composers are engaged in composition pedagogy in formal or non-formal music education in the Czech Republic. Melkus (1969) proposed the cooperation between teachers and composers in music education in the late 1960s. But it didn't happen for several years. In 2003 educators and composers were teaching together for the first time. Teachers and students of the Department of Composition at the Janáček Academy of Music (JAMU) entered the Different Hearing program and worked together with teachers and educators (Zouhar, 2004; Synek, 2008; Medek et al., 2014).

Medek (2004; Medek et al, 2010; Zouhar & Medek, 2010, and 2014) is the most active composer in the context of classroom composing as educator, innovator, and author. He serves as professor of composition and has been a member of the *Different Hearing* team since 2003. Together with the author of this chapter he has published several studies and is the co-author of the books *Different Musical Instruments* (Coufalová et al., 2013) and *Composing in the Classroom: Different Hearing: Experiences in Czech Music Education* (Medek et al., 2014). During the years he led and co-led many workshops for music festivals (Exhibition of New Music Brno, 2005; Ad Libitum Festival Warszawa, 2006), orchestras (Brno Philharmonic, 2015), and young composers (since 2005). He motivated his former students Dvořáková, Medková, Kavan, and other young composers for classroom composing.

Dvořáková and Medková are active composers, teachers, and *Different Hearing* team members since 2003. Dvořáková described compositional processes in the *Different Hearing Program* (2004, 2005) and differences between individual and group composition pedagogy within Workshops for the Youngest Composers (2006). Medková (née Žalčíková) focused her studies to teamwork and parallels between group elementary composing and composing in a team by professional composers (Gojowy, 1971; Medek et al., 2014). Both of them have led many workshops and teach individual composition courses and piano class at basic art and music schools. Dvořáková has also been leading the Workshop for the Youngest Composers since 2005. It is the only educational venue in the Czech Republic that combines individual and group composition lessons.

Over the past 20 years, many composers have expressed their belief that everyone can compose. Dlouhý, professor of composition and head of the Department of Composition at JAMU in Brno, noted already in 2002:

> Mostly at the school, the teaching of composition start[ed] from harmony, from traditional forms. However, the [current] time is completely different; harmony [has not been] used for fifty years. I miss moving to the experimental plane, because the contemporary composition is based on sound, for example. [Children] should be able to get acquainted with specific sounds and create sound ètudes from them in musical teaching and in the teaching of composition; [they should] try different rhythmic structures: not specific rhythms, but, e.g., different rhythm densities. (Adámková & Dlouhý, 2002, p. 17)

Rataj (2019) came to the same conclusion. In the essay "Can anyone be a composer today?" this composer, performer, and professor of composition at the Academy of Performing Arts in Prague replies:

> I declare that everyone can be a composer at the moment. It seems to me that this thesis is fundamentally related to the discussion of the future development of the teaching of creative artistic disciplines, and musical composition in particular." (Rataj, 2019)

The next composer with the same meaning on everyone's creativity is Hořínka (2019), professor of composition and the head of the Department of Composition at the Prague AMU. He notes: "The creation of music can then be a unique form of acquiring otherwise unattainable knowledge. I firmly believe that anyone can do so, whether they feel like a musician or not" (Hořínka, 2019, p. 14). In 2005, the author of this chapter led a controversy when he published his study *Everyone Can Be a Composer* (Zouhar, 2004). Fifteen years later, the fact that everyone can compose no longer causes heated discussions.

Hořínka is one of those composers-educators who has led workshops for children focused on classroom composing. He presents his workshops within the educational programs of the Czech Philharmonic Orchestra and formerly the Berg Orchestra. He initiates his didactic procedures for group composing by listening activities and partly follows the *Different Hearing* methodology. In his workshops, listening activities are the starting point for the reproduction and fixation of the sounds and inspiration for creating others: "We warm our ears by briefly listening to the silence, fixing the sounds into the graphic score, and then reinterpreting, [and] stylizing, whether through the sounds of the body or on DIY instruments" (Hořínka, 2019, p. 12). He thematizes the listening activities on the basis of his own experience: "From the point of view of an ant; inside my body; or what I am most afraid of" (p. 12). Currently, he is focusing on experiential pedagogy and workshops for adults using sound interventions. Some other composers contribute their experiences, participate in workshops, and publish about methods of composing in the classroom, especially Graham (Šťastný, 2005 and 2008); Adámková & Dlouhý, 2002; Vítková (2011); Vörösová, and others.

CONCLUSION

Composition pedagogy has gained many impulses in artistic and general music education in the Czech Republic over the past 20 years. Music education teachers and composers have adopted didactic tools on how to incorporate composing into general music education and leisure activities. Music educators and composer-educators have confirmed based on empirical knowledge an earlier assumption that compositional activities can be developed by every child and every person and creative activities contribute not only to its development, but also to overall knowledge, skills, and abilities.

In 2021, composing is not included in primary and secondary general music curriculum. But based on innovations of music education teacher study programs and intensive courses for adults, more and more teachers are already prepared to use composition activities to develop the musical abilities of young people. And based on innovations of composition programs, more and more young composers can motivate pupils and students to compose in formal and non-formal music education. Composing has gradually become a natural activity for young people just like drawing or painting in the Czech Republic.

References

Adámková, J., & Dlouhý, D. (2002). Od kaňonu ke hvězdám [From the Canyon to the Stars]. *Talent, 4*(3), 16–20.

Bakla, P. (2005). Radost Slyšet jinak [The Joy of Different Hearing]. *His Voice, 5*(4), 26–27.

Balada, J., Jeřábek, J., & Tupý, J. (2006). *Rámcový vzdělávací program pro základní vzdělávání* [Framework Education Program for Primary Education]. Research Institute of Education.

Boleška, J. (1905). Skladba. [Composition]. In *Ottův slovník naučný: Dvacátýtřetí díl* [Otto's Dictionary: Part 23] (p. 265). Publisher J. Otto.

Branberger, J. (1911). *Das Konservatorium für Musik in Prag zur 100-Jahrfeier der Gründung im Auftrage des Vereines zur Beförderung der Tonkunst in Böhmen*. Verein zur Beförderung der Tonkunst in Böhmen.

Cage, J. (1973). *Silence: Lectures and writings*. Wesleyan University Press

Coufalová, G., & Synek, J. (2014). Composing in the classroom: The Different Hearing programme: Experiences in Czech music education. In *SGEM Conference on Psychology & Psychiatry, Sociology & Healthcare, Education. Conference Proceedings. Volume III* (pp. 169–175). doi: 10.5593/sgemsocial2014/B13/S3.023

Coufalová, G., Medek, I., & Synek, J. (2013). *Hudební nástroje jinak: Netradiční využití tradičních hudebních nástrojů a vytváření jednoduchých hudebních nástrojů* [Musical Instruments Differently: Non-traditional use of traditional musical instruments and creation of simple musical instruments]. Janáček Academy of Music and Performing Arts.

Drkula, P. (2006). *Hudební tvořivost v aktuálních proměnách obecného a pedagogického anglofonního diskurzu* [Musical creativity in the current transformations of general and pedagogical Anglophone discourse. Dissertation. Palacký University Olomouc].

Dvořáková, M. (2005). Kompoziční aspekty projektu Slyšet jinak [Compositional Aspects of the Different Hearing Project]. In L. Dohnalová (Ed.). *Hudební improvizace.* [Musical Improvisation.] *Proceedings from a national conference* (pp. 7–9). Czech Music Council, Theatre Institute.

Dvořáková, M. (2004). Stručná zpráva o projektu Slyšet jinak [A Short Report on Different Hearing Project]. In V. Zouhar, I. Medek, & J. Synek (Eds.), *Slyšet jinak 03: tvořivost a improvizace v hudební výchově na zvláštních školách* [Different Hearing 03: Creativity and Improvisation in Music Education at Special Schools] (p. 48). Janáček Academy of Music and Performing Arts in Brno.

Dvořáková, M. (2006). 2. ročník dílny pro nejmladší skladatele [Second Year of The Workshop for the Youngest Composers]. *Talent, 8*(3), 27.

Finscher, L. (Ed.). (2008). *Die Musik in Geschichte und Gegenwart*. Bärenreiter-Verlag. https://www.mgg-online.com/

Flašar, M., & Kyas, O. (2005). Radost Slyšet jinak [The Joy of Different Hearing]. *Opus musicum, 37*(4), 18–20.

Fukač, J. (1997). Skladba [Composition]. In J. Fukač, J. Vysloužil, & P. Macek (Eds.), *Slovník české hudební kultury* [Dictionary of Czech Music Culture] (p. 833). Editio Supraphon.

Freemanová, M. (2011). In the shadow of the conservatoire: The Prague Organists College (1830–1889/1890). *Hudební věda* [Music Science], *48*(4), 369–392.

Gojowy, D. (1971). Komponieren im Kollektiv: Zur Arbeit des Brünner Komponistenteams. *Musik und Bildung, 3*(6), 302–303.

Grobár, M., Holubec, J., Charalambidis, A., Kodejška, M., Lišková, M., Prchal, J., Synek, J., & Šobáňová, P. (2019). *Umění a kultura: Hudební výchova; Podkladová studie* [Art and Culture: Music Education; Background Study]. NÚV.

Hanousek, P., & Ščerba, L. (2013). *Skladba: Základní přehled pedagogických témat* [Composition: Basic overview of pedagogical topics]. MŠMT.

Helfert, V. (1930). *Základy hudební výchovy na nehudebních školách* [Fundamentals of Music Education at Non-Music Schools]. Státní nakladatelství.

Hořínka, S. (2019). Naslouchat světu, žít hudbu [Listen to the World, Live Music]. *Gymnasion, 13*(2), 11–14.

Hurník, I., & Eben, P. (1969). *Česká Orffova škola: Díl 1*. [Czech Orff's School: Part 1]. Supraphon.

Hurnik, I., & Eben, P. (1969). *Česká Orffova škola: Díl 2*. [Czech Orff's School: Part 2]. Supraphon.

Ištvan, M. (1973). Metoda montáže izolovaných prvků v hudbě. [Method of Assembly of Isolated Elements in Music]. Panton.

Jandová, M. (2012). Aplikace a reflexe principů projektu Slyšet jinak: Modelová výuka pro Cyrilometodějské gymnázium Brno. [Application and reflection of the principles of the Different Hearing Project: Model lessons for Cyril and Methodius Grammar School in Brno. Master's thesis, Masaryk University]. https://is.muni.cz/th/p8zu4/Aplikace_a_reflexe_pri ncipu_projektu_Slyset_jinak._Modelova_vyuka_pro_Cyrilometodejske_gymnazium_B rno.pdf

Janeček, K. (1969). Skladatelské studium [Composition Studies]. *Hudební rozhledy, 22*(1), 8–9; (4), 105–107.

Kaňák, Z. (1965–1966). Tvůrčí principy v hudební výchově v 9. ročníku [Creative Principles in Music Education in the 9th Grade]. *Estetická výchova, 7*, 284–287.

Kaňák, Z., & Pavlíková, V., & Vošlajerová, M. (1963). *Hudební výchova pro 9: ročník ZDŠ* [Music education for the 9th grade at primary and secondary schools]. Státní pedagogické nakladatelství.

Kapr, J. (1967). *Konstanty* [Constants]. Panton.

Kaschub, M., & Smith, J. (2009). *Minds on music: Composition for creative and critical thinking*. Rowman & Littelfield Education.

Knittl, K. (1896). Jak upraveno je vyučování theoretické v prvém ročníku komposiční školy na pražské konservatoři [How the Theoretic Teaching is in the First Year of the Composition school at the Prague Conservatoire]. *Dalibor, 18*(27–28), 205–213.

Knopová, B. (2011). Hudební výchova na gymnáziích a její realizace v praxi, [Music Education in Grammar Schools and its Implementation in Practice]. *Teoretické reflexe hudební výchovy, 7*(2), 3–4. https://www.ped.muni.cz/wmus/studium/doktor/teoreticke_reflexe_7_2/knopova.pdf

Kohoutek, C. (1989). *Hudební kompozice: Stručný pohled z hlediska skladatele* [Musical Composition: A brief look from the composer's point of view]. Editio Supraphon.

Kohoutek, C. (1970). *Projektová hudební kompozice.* [Project Musical Composition]. Janáček Academy of Music and Performing Arts.

Kopecký, J., Synek, J., & Zouhar, V. (2014). *Hudební hry jinak: Tvořivé hry a modelové projekty elementárního komponování* [Different music games: Creative games and model elementary composing projects]. Janáček Academy of Music and Performing Arts in Brno.

Kvěch, O. (2013). *Základy klasické hudební kompozice: Poznámky pro budoucí skladatele* [Fundamentals of classical music composition: Notes for future composers]. Togga.

Medek, I. (2004). Několik poznámek k hudební kreativitě. [A few comments on musical creativity]. In V. Zouhar & I. Medek, & J. Synek (Eds.), *Slyšet jinak '03: Tvořivost a improvizace v hudební výchově na zvláštních školách* [Different Hearing '03: Creativity and improvisation in music education at special schools] (pp. 24–27). Janáček Academy of Music and Performing Arts.

Medek, I. (1998). *Úvod do procesuality jako komplexní kompoziční metody* [An Introduction to processality as a complex composition method]. Janáček Academy of Music and Performing Arts.

Medek, I., Synek, J., & Zouhar, V. (2014). *Composing in the classroom: Different Hearing; Experiences in Czech music education.* Janáček Academy of Music and Performing Arts in Brno.

Medek, I., Zouhar, V., & Žalčíková, L. (2010). To the Teamwork Creativity. In *Filosofické koncepcie v hudbe a umení 6., sborník mezinárodní conference. Akadémia umení v Banskej Bystrici a HUAJA Banská Štiavnica* [Philosophical concepts in music and art 6, Proceedings. Academy of Arts Banská Bystrica and HUAJA Banská Štiavnica] (pp. 31–33). Akadémia umení Banská Štiavnica.

Melkus, L. (1969). Problematika hudební výchovy na všeobecně vzdělávacích školách a příprava hudebních pedagogů [Music education at comprehensive schools and training of future teachers]. In V. Holzknecht & V. Poš (Eds.), *Člověk potřebuje hudbu* [People Need Music] (pp. 75–76). Panton.

Mills, J., & Paynter, J. (Eds.). (2008). *Thinking and making: Selections from the writings of John Paynter on music in education.* Oxford University Press.

Mimra, R., et al. (Eds.). (2020). *Podněty k didaktikám pro práci s žáky se SVP v uměleckém vzdělávání: Hudební obor* [Suggestions for didactics for working with pupils with SEP in art education: Music]. University of West Bohemia, Pilsen.

Ministry of Education, Youth and Sports. (2007). *Rámcový vzdělávací program pro gymnázia* [Framework education program for secondary general education (grammar schools)]. VÚP. https://www.edu.cz/wp-content/uploads/2020/08/RVPG-2007-07_final.pdf

Ministry of Education, Youth and Sports. (2010a). *Rámcový vzdělávací program pro obor vzdělávání. Hudba 82-44-M/01.* [Framework Education Program for Education: Music 82-44-M/01]. Národní ústav odborného vzdělávání. https://www.edu.cz/rvp-ramcove-vzdelavaci-programy/ramcove-vzdelavaci-programy-stredniho-odborneho-vzdelavani-rvp-sov/konzervatore/82-umeni-a-uzite-umeni/

Ministry of Education, Youth and Sports. (2010b). *Rámcový vzdělávací program pro umělecké školství* [Framework Education Program for Primary Art and Music Schools]. VÚP. https://www.msmt.cz/file/31244/

Ministry of Education, Youth and Sports. (2005, 2017, 2021). *Rámcový vzdělávací program pro základní vzdělávání* [Framework Education Program for Primary Education]. MŠMT. https://www.edu.cz/rvp-ramcove-vzdelavaci-programy/ramcovy-vzdelavacici-program-pro-zakladni-vzdelavani-rvp-zv/

Orff, C. (1969). *Schulwerk: pohled do minulosti a do budoucnosti* [Schulwerk: A View of the Past and the Future]. In V. Poš (Ed.), *Comenium Musicum 7: Perspektivy Orffovy školy v hudební výchově* [Perspectives of the Orff's School in Music Education] (p. 25–31). Supraphon.

Paynter, J., & Aston, J. (1970). *Sound and silence: Classroom projects in creative music.* Cambridge University Press.

Piňos, A. (1971). *Tonové skupiny* [Tone Groups]. Panton.

Poledňák, I., & Budík, J. (1969). *Hudba–škola–zítřek: Projekt modernizace pojetí a osnov hudební výchovy na ZDŠ* [Music–School–Tomorrow: Project of Modernising the Music Education Conception and Curriculum at Primary and Secondary Schools]. Supraphon.

Poledňák , I. (1963–64). Tokijské sněmování o hudební výchově [Tokyo Congress on Music Education]. *Estetická výchova* [Aesthetics Education], *5*(5), Supplement, 15–16.

Popovič, M. (1994–95). Manhattanvillský program [The Manhattanville Program]. *Hudební výchova* [Music Education], *3*(1), 12–13.

Rataj, M. (2019). Může dnes být hudebním skladatelem každý? [Can Anyone Be a Composer Today?] [online]. *operaplus.cz.* https://operaplus.cz/michal-rataj-muze-dnesbyt-hudeb nim-skladatelem-kazdy

Schafer, R. M. (1986). *The thinking ear.* Arcana Editions.

Schneider, H., Bösze, C., & Stangl, B. (Eds.). (2000). *"Klangnetze" Ein Versuch, die Wirklichkeit mit den Ohren zu erfinden.* Pfau-Verlag.

Skřebská, K. (2017). *Komparace projektů Slyšet jinak na základní škole a na základní škole speciální* [The comparison of Projects "Slyšet jinak" in elementary school and in special elementary school. Bachelor's thesis, Palacký University Olomouc]. Palacký University Olomouc. https://theses.cz/id/fw66l1/Bakal_k_prce_Kate_ina_Sk_ebsk.pdf

Skřebská, K. (2019). *Program Slyšet jinak a Montessori pedagogika* [Program "Different Hearing" and Montessori pedagogy. Master's thesis, Palacký University Olomouc]. Palacký University Olomouc. https://theses.cz/id/31akw7/Program_Slyet_jinak_a_Montessori_ped agogika.pdf?zpet=%2Fvyhledavani%2F%3Fsearch%3Dpedagogika%26start%3D1

Stecová, A. (2015). *Metody komponování populární hudby v hudební výchově s užitím artificiálních prvků.* [Methods of popular music composition in general music education using classical music elements. Bachelor's thesis, Palacký University Olomouc]. Palacký University Olomouc. https://theses.cz/id/muojht/BP_Stecov_Aneka.pdf

Stecová, A. (2017). *Populární hudba a informální učení: reflexe britského přístupu v hudební výchově a možná aplikace v kontextu českého školství* [Popular music and informal learning: Reflection of the British Approach in music education and possible application in the context of Czech education. Master's thesis, Palacký University Olomouc]. Palacký University Olomouc. https://theses.cz/id/jypnfh/Stecov_Ane_ka_DP.pdf

Synek, J. (2011a). Composing in the Classroom: cíle programu Slyšet jinak [Goals of the Different Hearing Program]. In *ACTA FACULTATIS PHILOSOPHICAE UNIVERSITATIS PREŠOVIENSIS, Zborník katedry hudby Inštitútu hudobného a výtvarného umenia*

Filozofickej fakulty Prešovskej univerzity v Prešove, De Musica II [Compendium of the Music Department of the Institute of Musical and Visual Art of the Faculty of Arts of Prešov University in Prešov, De Musica II] (pp. 161–172). Prešovská univerzita v Prešove.

Synek, J. (2012a). Děti se těšily na koncert filharmonie aneb výchovný koncert jinak [The children were looking forward to the philharmonic concert or educational concert differently]. *Hudební výchova, 20*(4), 68–69.

Synek, J. (2008a). *Elementární komponování a jeho význam v edukaci* [Elementary composing and its significance in education. Dissertation. Palacký University Olomouc]. Palacký University Olomouc http://slysetjinak.upol.cz/files/Synek_Elementarni_komponovani_a_jeho_vyznam_v_edukaci.pdf

Synek, J. (2012b). Inovace předmětu Didaktika hudební výchovy na Univerzitě Palackého v Olomouci [Innovation of music education teaching preparation at Palacký University in Olomouc]. In A. Prídavková & M. Klimovič (Eds.), *Komplexnosť a integrita v predprimárnej, primárnej a špeciálnej edukácii* [Complexity and integrity in pre-school, primary, and special education] (pp. 495–497). Vydavateľstvo Prešovskej univerzity v Prešove.

Synek, J. (2011b). Komponování ve třídách: reflexe projektů zaměřených na komponování dětí v české hudební publicistice od 50. let 20. století: 1. díl [Composing in the classroom: Reflection of projects for children's composition in Czech music journalism from the 1950s: Part I]. *Opus musicum, 43*(3), 46–57.

Synek, J. (2011c). Komponování ve třídách: reflexe projektů zaměřených na komponování dětí v české hudební publicistice od 50. let 20. století: 2. díl. *Opus musicum, 43*(4), 44–53.

Synek, J. (2005). Pedagogické aspekty projektu Slyšet jinak [Pedagogic Aspects of the Different Hearing Programme]. In L. Dohnalová (Ed.). *Hudební improvizace* [Musical Improvisation]. *Proceedings from a nationwide conference* (pp. 9–12). Czech Music Council, Theatre Institute.

Synek, J. (2004). Slyšet jinak: třikrát jinak. [Different Hearing: Three Times Different]. In V. Zouhar, I. Medek, & J. Synek (Eds.), *Slyšet jinak '03: Tvořivost a improvizace v hudební výchově na zvláštních školách* [Different Hearing '03: Creativity and improvisation in music education at special schools] (pp. 28–34). Janáček Academy of Music and Performing Arts.

Synek, J. (2008b). Výroba dětských hudebních nástrojů ve škole [Crafting Children's Musical Instruments at School]. In J. Říha & I. Ašenbrenerová (Eds.), *Aktuální otázky současné hudebně výchovné teorie a praxe III* [Current issues in contemporary music education theory and practice III] (pp. 41–49). UJEP.

Synek, J. (2008c). Zpřístupňování soudobé hudby v rámci programu Slyšet jinak [Making Contemporary Music Accessible within the Different Hearing Programme]. In K. Steinmetz & J. Černohorská (Eds.). *Inovace v hudební pedagogice a výchově k poctě Lea Kestenberga (1882–1962). Sborník z mezinárodní muzikologické konference konané 29. listopadu-1. prosince 2007 v Uměleckém centru Univerzity Palackého v Olomouci* [Innovation in music education and lessons in honor of Leo Kestenberg (1882–1962). Proceedings of the International Musicological Conference at the Art Center of Palacký University Olomouc on 29 November to 1 December 2007] (pp. 191–196). Palacký University Olomouc.

Šťastný, J. (2005). Problémy výuky improvizace na vysoké hudební škole [Issues with Teaching Improvisation at Music Universities]. In L. Dohnalová (Ed.). *Hudební improvizace* [Musical Improvisation]. *Proceedings from a nationwide conference.* (pp. 24–26). Czech Music Council, Theatre Institute.

Šťastný, J. (2008). Slyšet jinak [Different Hearing], A2, 1(37). http://www.advojka.cz/archiv/2008/37/slyset-jinak.

Tyrrell, J. (Ed.). (2001). *The New Grove dictionary of music and musicians*. Oxford University Press. https://www.oxfordmusiconline.com/grovemusic

Váňová, H. (1989). *Hudební tvořivost žáků mladšího školního věku* [Musical creativity of the younger schoolchildren]. Editio Supraphon.

Vítková, L. (2011). Ještě jednou o projektu Slyšet jinak [Once more on Different Hearing]. *Talent, 13*(8), 14–15.

Všetičková, G. (2012). Classroom Composing in Music Education with Regard to Minimal Music. In J. Luska (Ed.), *Interdisciplinary research on the music culture: Anthology of PhD thesis competition* (pp. 111–150). Palacký University Olomouc.

Všetičková, G. (2014a). Graphic Scores and Visualisation of Music: Experience from the Czech Different Hearing Creative Programme. In *SGEM Conference on Arts, Performing Arts, Architecture and Design: Conference Proceedings* (pp. 321–328). doi: 10.5593/sgemsocial2014/B13/S3.023.

Všetičková, G. (2014b). Komponování dětí jako součást hudební výchovy v Anglii a České republice: minulost, současnost (a budoucnost?) [Composing children as part of music education in England and the Czech Republic: Past, present (and future?)]. In P. Hala (Ed.). *Musica viva in schola XXIV* (pp. 117–131). Masaryk University Brno. http://www.ped.muni.cz/wmus/studium/sborniky/musica_viva_in_schola_xxiv.pdf.

Všetičková, G. (2011). Komponování dětí v hudební výchově s přihlédnutím k hudebnímu minimalismu [Children's composition in music education with regard to musical minimalism. Dissertation. Palacký University Olomouc]. Palacký University Olomouc. https://theses.cz/id/g7errl/G_Vetikov_-_Komponovn_dt_v_hudebn_vchov_s_pihldnutm_k_hud.pdf

Všetičková, G. (2010). Komponování jako součást hudební výchovy [Composing as a part of music education]. *Talent, 13*(6), 2010, 6–11.

Všetičková, G. (2015). Poslech a vnímání jako východisko pro tvořivé aktivity v hudební výchově: Zkušenosti z programu Slyšet jinak. [Listening and perception as a starting point for creative activities in music education: Experience of the program Different Hearing]. *Musicologica Olomucensia, 21*, 113–128.

Zouhar, V. (2005). Ke genezi programu Slyšet jinak [Genesis of the Different Hearing Programme]. In L. Dohnalová (Ed.). *Hudební improvizace* [Musical improvisation]. *Proceedings from a National Conference* (pp. 3–6). Czech Music Council, Theatre Institute.

Zouhar, V. (2008). Komponování ve třídách. Poznámky k prvním americkým a britským projektům [Composing in the classroom. Notes on the First American and British Projects]. In K. Steinmetz & J. Černohorská (Eds.). *Inovace v hudební pedagogice a výchově k poctě Lea Kestenberga (1882–1962). Sborník z mezinárodní muzikologické konference konané 29. listopadu-1. prosince 2007 v Uměleckém centru Univerzity Palackého v Olomouci* [Innovation in music education and lessons in honor of Leo Kestenberg (1882–1962). Proceedings of the International Musicological Conference at the Art Center of Palacký University Olomouc on 29 November to 1 December 2007] (pp. 186–190). Palacký University Olomouc.

Zouhar, V. (2004). Slyšet jinak: Každý může být skladatelem [Different Hearing: Everyone Can Be a Composer]. In V. Zouhar, I. Medek & J. Synek (Eds.), *Slyšet jinak '03: Tvořivost a improvizace v hudební výchově na zvláštních školách* [Different Hearing '03: Creativity and improvisation in music education at special schools] (pp. 11–23). Janáček Academy of Music and Performing Arts.

Zouhar, V. (2007). Slyšet jinak: Komponování jako výuková metoda i nástroj k poznávání hudebních skladeb [Different Hearing: Composing as a Teaching Method and Tool for Learning Music Compositions]. In *Aeduca 2006* (pp. 1–5). Palacký University Olomouc.

Zouhar, V., & Medek, I. (2010). Music making in the classroom: possibilities for Czech music education. In The 2nd World Conference on Arts Education, May 25–28, 2010, Seoul. (pp. 1–3). UNESCO. https://www.researchgate.net/publication/228691574_Music_making_in_the_classroom_possibilities_for_Czech_music_education

CHAPTER 36

COMPOSITION PEDAGOGY IN FINLAND

From the Margins to the Center of Music Education

HEIDI PARTTI

A central aim of Finland's current music education system is providing every student with opportunities to explore the potential of sounds and music through composition and improvisation. Although in previous decades creative music-making activities were already acknowledged in Finnish music education, the role of musical composition has become more central than ever before in the recently reformed national core curriculum documents—including those for basic education, general upper secondary education, and extracurricular music education. As a result of these reforms, every child in Finland is now expected to be regularly offered possibilities not only for playing, singing, listening, and moving to music but also creating their own music through composing in school. Musical composition also has an increasingly central role in the music instruction provided by extracurricular music education institutes. This makes it possible, at least in principle, for one to receive teaching in composition throughout the whole system of formal music education in Finland. In addition to the prominence of musical creativity in curricular documents an increasing interest in music education research toward questions revolving around composition pedagogy has also arisen. During the past few years, multiple Finnish researchers have published empirical case study reports and conducted practical research projects on (classroom) composition (e.g., Muhonen 2016; Huttunen 2017; Ojala 2017). The first Finnish anthology of composition pedagogy, *Säveltäjäksi kasvattaminen* [Educating toward composing] (Ojala & Väkevä, 2013a), includes several study reports along with more theoretical explorations into composition pedagogy by Finnish scholars and practitioners in music education; while the book *Säveltäjyyden jäljillä* [On the trail of creative music-making] (Partti & Ahola, 2016) discusses the role of composition in schools and aims to provide music educators with practical ideas on how to facilitate musical composition activities in their classrooms. Despite the growing interest toward and emphasis on composition, creative music-making activities are, however, yet to be systematically established in music classrooms and music teacher education institutions.

In this chapter, I will discuss the aims and practices of composing in the Finnish formal music education system. I will first provide an overview of how composition is situated within the system by introducing and exploring the role of composition in basic education and extracurricular music education. After this, I will examine more closely how music educators are equipped to facilitate musical composition. Finally, I will turn to the wider question of possibilities opened up through musical composition in educational contexts. I will put forward a suggestion that viewing composing as a creative activity available to everyone holds great potential for not only musical meaning-making, but also for cultural participation and the building of a shared future between people from diverse backgrounds and with different starting points—not only in Finland, but also elsewhere in the world.

MUSICAL COMPOSITION IN FINNISH MUSIC EDUCATION

Since the mid-20th century, Finnish music education has journeyed from (mostly) singing hymns and patriotic songs in post-war era schools to the active and diverse music education of today. Music is a compulsory subject in comprehensive schools (students aged seven to 16 years old) and all children receive (a minimum of) one 45-minute lesson a week in grades one through seven. In grades eight and nine students may choose music as an optional subject. In addition to this minimum amount of music instruction, primary schools may offer additional lessons weekly. In primary schools (grades one through six), music is most often taught by the classroom teacher (who holds a master's degree in general education), while in the lower secondary school (grades seven through nine) and upper secondary school (students aged 16 to 19 years old) music is taught by a specialized music subject teacher (who holds a master's degree in music education).

In Finland, the *Finnish National Core Curriculum for Basic Education* provides a common basis for school teaching in grades one through nine, although the core curriculum leaves plenty of autonomy for teachers to decide upon the contents and pedagogical approaches used in their teaching practice. According to the core curriculum, the aim of music as a school subject is "to create opportunities for versatile musical activities and active cultural participation" (FNAE, 2016a, p. 453). Teachers are therefore encouraged to provide rich and relevant activities for heterogeneous groups of students with various needs. Although the core curriculum does not require any particular musical style or genre to be included in general music education, the significance of popular music in education has already been apparent for quite some time (see, e.g., Westerlund, 2006; Väkevä, 2006). A typical music classroom in Finland is equipped with a drum kit, electric bass, guitars, keyboards, microphones, and other music technology, and music teachers are educated to offer students opportunities to explore diverse musical landscapes without drawing strict lines between classical, folk, or popular musics.[1]

The teaching methods and classroom activities also vary from one situation to another. As highlighted in a study conducted with experienced music teachers working in primary and lower secondary schools in Finland, both the curricula and the music educators' own articulations of their pedagogical practices are very much characterized by a higher *ethos of versatility* (Muukkonen, 2010). This ethos manifests in the multiplicity of educational approaches as well as musical styles and activities used in school music instruction. Musical skills, knowledge, and concepts are typically learned through numerous activities, such as singing, playing instruments, moving and listening to music, composing and improvising, interacting exercises, building one's own musical instruments, and attending concerts and other arts events (Partti, 2016).

Musical Composition in Primary and Lower Secondary Schools

In the national core curriculum, musical composition and other creative activities are expected to be taught to all students in all grades (FNAE, 2016a). This objective is linked to the wider aspiration of encouraging children to develop "a *creative relationship* with music" (FNAE, 2016a, p. 488, my emphasis) during their years in comprehensive schools. Offering children opportunities to compose their own music individually and/or in collaboration with others is also considered beneficial for their overall growth and cognitive development as well as their intuitive and aesthetic thinking. Musical composition is for everyone as it supports the development of children's creative thinking:

> The pupils are guided in developing their thinking skills and perception by regularly providing them with opportunities for working with sound and music as well as for composing and other creative production. (FNAE, 2016a, p. 454)

Both in the core curricula for basic education and for upper secondary education, musical composition is conceptualized in the broadest sense of the word without limiting it to any specific method, technique, form, style, or genre. In other words, composition in Finnish education may refer to any creative music-making activity from writing songs or creating score-based music to arranging or improvising music; and from forming soundscapes or sound collages to building loops, riffs, and remixes. Composition activities can also take place within any musical style or genre, with or without the use of music education technology, such as digital audio workstations, digital instruments, modular platforms, or multi-track audio editors.

Understanding musical composition in this broad sense facilitates its practice in various pedagogical situations and contexts. Indeed, a primary school music teacher has multiple opportunities to incorporate musical composition and creative production as part of almost any classroom activity from learning the alphabet to celebrating special occasions throughout the academic year. Finnish teacher-educator and researcher Sari Muhonen (2013a) encourages teachers in primary classrooms to nurture students' "everyday creativity, creativity with a small c" (ibid., p. 13), as a key ingredient of daily life. In her study on *songcrafting*, Muhonen (2016) shows how collaborative composition can open opportunities to support children's musical agency and creative capabilities in the classroom. By incorporating songcrafting into other school practices, composition and creative collaborations are viewed not as a separate task, but as an inherent part of all teaching and learning. This kind of creative music-making highlights the nature of composition as a musical exploration and a form of playing that does not necessarily always require dedicated time and space. Rather, as suggested by the Finnish teacher-educator Marja Ervasti (2013), composition can be adopted as a pedagogical practice that penetrates learning processes and takes place in a "surreptitious manner" (p. 113, my translation) and as brief experiments among other educational activities.

Another concrete and exciting example of the possibilities of composition in primary school education is provided by the Finnish music educator and researcher Hanna Nikkanen in her case study on composition activities within music ensemble[2] classes (Karjalainen-Väkevä & Nikkanen, 2013). The classes took place after school hours as an extracurricular activity, but were facilitated by the music teacher in the school premises. The children were instructed in playing the instruments (such as guitar, bass, ukuleles, and drums) and their ensembles were given opportunities to publicly perform in school events. The repertoire choices were made by the children themselves and many decided already from the outset to compose their own songs. A crucial factor impacting their eagerness to compose was the model set by previous ensembles: after witnessing groups performing their own material in a concert, the majority of the ensembles set up the following year not only took composing for granted, but were motivated by the possibility to compose their own repertoire. The role of the teacher was to help the children identify and develop their creative ideas into complete songs by, for instance, introducing different ways to continue the melody line or chord progression. According to Nikkanen (ibid.), the annual concert offered extra motivation for the ensembles to finalize their compositions and provided the children with valuable opportunities to express something about themselves and hear each other's stories in the form of musical compositions.

Muhonen (2013b) reminds us that an essential task of the music teacher is to create opportunities for creative music-making and not only notice, but seize the musical ideas coming from the students. Although opportunities to facilitate extensive composition projects may be limited, creative music-making and collective creative inquiries can have a central role in school instruction. In the Finnish school, this is enabled by the flexibility of the curriculum and the inclusion of integrated instruction and multidisciplinary learning modules as part of the school culture. In the core curriculum for basic education (FNAE, 2016a), the aim of integrated instruction is understood in terms of safeguarding "every pupil's possibilities of examining wholes and engaging in exploratory work that is of interest to the pupils" (p. 33). In other words, students are helped to "see the relationships and interdependencies between the phenomena to be studied" (p. 32) by systematically including multidisciplinary learning modules as part of school instruction. This multidisciplinary pedagogical approach provides a teacher with various opportunities for holistic instruction where music and musical composition can be integrated with other subjects and activities in pursuit of helping students to combine knowledge and skills in various fields in the communal building of knowledge. In this way musical composition in primary school education can also become a natural part of self-expression, learning, and communication in the form of creative explorations that are accessible to everyone. Importantly, however, in order to facilitate these processes, classroom teachers need to be equipped with adequate skills in composition pedagogy. I will return to this theme later in the chapter.

The Finnish music educator Mirja Karjalainen-Väkevä provides a detailed narrative on teaching composition in a lower secondary school as part of the eighth-grade optional music classes (Karjalainen-Väkevä & Nikkanen, 2013). The composition period conducted by Karjalainen-Väkevä was preceded by a student survey that provided the teacher with important information on students' expectations, needs, musical tastes, experiences, and concerns regarding composing. By utilizing this information, Karjalainen-Väkevä was able to customize her teaching to the students' needs and form the student-groups in ways that would best support the creative work. In her strategies for teaching composition Karjalainen-Väkevä drew heavily on principles and activities from drama pedagogy. She reports to have used, for example, the concept of the contract, a mutual agreement negotiated as a group before embarking on the creative activities regarding the aims and conditions for working. The students were taught, and regularly reminded of, the principle of accepting (see, Johnstone 1999), and its role in establishing the fruitful conditions required for creative work, as well as the importance of listening and responding as cornerstones of positive interaction. The composition process began with small group musical improvisation activities during which the teacher circulated to assist the student groups with seizing and developing the impulses and initial ideas that arose from the group improvisation. Like Nikkanen, Karjalainen-Väkevä (Karjalainen-Väkevä & Nikkanen 2013) highlights the importance of the public performance as part of the composition process. She points out, however, that the aim of the performance is to support students' learning processes and should therefore be pedagogically planned by the teacher to give students an opportunity to "safely stretch the boundaries of their comfort zones" (ibid., p. 73, my translation).

Musical Composition in Upper Secondary Schools

The *General Upper Secondary Education Syllabus* highlights the importance of providing students with opportunities to "experiment bravely with new and even uncommon musical ideas, also together with others" (FNAE, 2019, p. 350, my translation). In this recently reformed curriculum (implemented in August 2021) the development of active musical agency and creative thinking are among the general aims of music instruction in upper secondary education (students aged 16 to 19 years old). Creative music-making is understood in terms of exploratory processes that require time and peace for thinking, with music education offering students possibilities to find novel solutions and use their imaginations (FNAE, 2019).

Music educator Sakari Antila (2013) writes about his experience facilitating the process of writing a musical. The initiative for the project had come from the students and Antila, who at that point of his career as a music educator felt keen to challenge himself, decided to give it a go. The project provided opportunities for multifaceted creativity, as it integrated music into various other areas of expression, such as writing, acting, and visual arts. It also required courage from both the teacher and students. Antila was not particularly experienced in facilitating composition and had been, in fact, somewhat reluctant toward the idea of teaching composition in schools. His experiences of composing were personal and did not seem to fit with group-based school activities. Nevertheless, he challenged himself and his students to explore something new with the desire to witness risk-taking and "leaps into the unknown" (Antila, 2013, p. 101, my translation). Students composed in small groups formed according to their interests. At the end of each composition session, students had the chance to share their ideas with other groups and "together agonize over the unbearable difficulty of composing," as described by Antila (2013, p. 103, my translation). After finishing the composition phase, songs were arranged for the instruments available, and practiced together for the performance. The role of the teacher was to offer guidance, advice, and instruction, but also (often above all) to inspire and keep everyone on board. Reflecting on the experience from his own perspective, Antila does not try to hide the difficulties he faced as a teacher facilitating the large-scale project that took him firmly outside his core areas of experience and expertise as a music educator. Yet, the benefits of the experience clearly exceeded the hardships, as it helped him find a new angle to musical composition, to view it as a form of playing, venturing, "and even messing around" (ibid., p. 99, my translation)—indeed, as a creative practice available for everyone.

Musical Composition in Extracurricular Music Education

In addition to general music education in schools there are various opportunities for extracurricular music education in Finland (see, Korpela et al., 2010). While instruction in schools is offered free of charge, one can receive affordable instruction in multiple arts, such as dance, music, theater, and visual arts, in the institutes of basic education in the arts. An extensive network of music institutes provides music education for children, young people, and adults. A network of music institutes is spread across the country and the majority receive substantial funding from the government, which makes studying in music institutes more accessible.

Instruction in music institutes follows the objectives and key contents as stated in the *National Core Curriculum for the General and Advanced Syllabi for Basic Education in the Arts* (FNAE 2018). Instruction in music institutes is goal-oriented, advancing from one level to another, and aims to provide the students with opportunities for self-expression as well as a basis for vocational studies in higher music education, if they so wish. According to this curricular document, the task of music instruction in extra-curricular music education "is to create the preconditions for a good relationship with music and for a lifelong interest in music" (ibid., p. 48). Students are supported in the development of their aesthetic, creative thinking, and social skills. Alongside performing and listening skills, such as singing or playing an instrument, as well as aural and structural awareness, the instruction aims to "guide pupils to musical expression [and] to encourage pupils to produce their own musical ideas and solutions" (ibid., p. 49). Composition, arranging, and improvisation are included among the main objectives of tuition of the advanced syllabus. Moreover, in many music institutes in Finland, it is now (or in the near future) possible to have composition as one's main subject of study instead of a musical instrument.

Although composition has a more central role in the recently introduced curriculum, many music institutes have already offered composition classes for some time. As described by the Finnish composer and music educator Sanna Ahvenjärvi (2013), the composition classes may take place individually or in small groups, depending on the needs and interests of the students. The starting point for composition can be almost anything: an improvisation that the student hopes to learn to notate or a melody that the student has composed for their own instrument and wishes to extend into a piece for an ensemble, for instance. Together with the teacher it is possible to continue to further explore the aesthetic possibilities and acquire new skills in composition. Although music institutes have traditionally specialized in teaching (mostly) Western classical music, there are now an increasing number of opportunities to receive instruction in pop/jazz and folk musics. This can also be seen in composition pedagogy. As expressed by Ahvenjärvi (2013), when initiating a new composition, it is the student who sets the stylistic framework: "My task as a teacher is to help the student keep the composition as stylistically coherent as possible—uniform, as it were" (p. 142, my translation). The Finnish composer Pasi Lyytikäinen (2020) also emphasizes the importance of respecting students' musical inventions and decisions. Although the role of the teacher is to teach the student how to edit, improve on, and proceed with their musical ideas, this should always follow the principle of appreciation and openness, viewing all of the student's musical inventions as "potentially contain[ing] elements of artistic value" (ibid., n.p.).

Ahvenjärvi (2013) reports her journey as a composition teacher who initially only taught the students taking composition classes to her recent practice of integrating composition, arrangement, and improvisation into all her teaching, including piano, music theory, and solfége. Like Ahvenjärvi, many other Finnish music educators have noticed the opportunities composition offers particularly in the teaching of theoretical subjects in music institutes (see, e.g., Ilomäki, 2013; Kuoppamäki, 2015; Klami, 2020). In Finland, music theory and solfège are taught as a separate subject, most often in a course called Basics of Music, (BoM, *Musiikin perusteet*). According to the music educator and researcher Anna Kuoppamäki (2015), recent years have been marked by efforts to reform the BoM course to better correspond to the overarching curricular aims of "nurturing students' lifelong relationship with music, and the possibilities for self-expression in and through music" (ibid., p. 29). Integrating composition and improvisation in the BoM course offers indispensable opportunities for music educators looking for more creative and hands-on approaches to their teaching of music theory. Ahvenjärvi (2013) illustrates how utilizing atonal harmonies and novel instrument playing techniques in improvisation has offered an easy access point for students to contemporary art music and new aesthetic landscapes. Composition and improvisation have also significantly contributed to the development of students' interaction skills and group coherence (ibid.). Inventing one's own rhythmic patterns or compositions helps in building bridges between theory and practice and brings the elements of play and creativity into the BoM lessons, as pointed out by Kuoppamäki (2015).

Although the central role of composition in the recently reformed core curriculum for basic education in the arts has received an excited response, it has also brought up a number of questions in many music institutes. One of the questions has to do with the challenge of recruiting music educators with the competence of providing goal-oriented composition instruction. As pointed out by the Finnish composer and composition teacher Markku Klami (2020), it may be feasible to divide introductory composition education into two portions: composition coaching and composition teaching. He suggests that the former with its aim of creative activities and musical explorations could be facilitated by competent music educators and take place mostly in group tuition situations; whereas the latter, which refers to broader and more systematic composition studies, would ideally be taught by a professional composer in one-on-one tuition situations. Time will tell what kind of solutions the Finnish music institutes will come up with and what implications their choices might have for the higher education of music teachers and composers.

Music Education Technology Enabling Composition Processes in Schools

Many of the recently published research reports on composition pedagogy in Finland also address the role of technology in opening ever-new possibilities for creative music-making activities in school. As witnessed in out-of-school contexts, such as online music communities, technological innovations have transformed the ways people can participate in music-making by creating new works from scratch, engaging in digital sound explorations, and playing along with commercially produced content (Partti & Westerlund, 2012; Michielse & Partti, 2015). The rapid development of music education technology can be viewed as a welcome addition to the opportunities to facilitate musical composition also in the school context. It is therefore not insignificant that in the Finnish core curriculum for basic education (FNAE, 2016a) ICT skills are understood both as a goal *and* a tool for learning, and the use of technology in music instruction is viewed as one way to promote the development of students' creative and expressive skills. Music education technology may offer major possibilities for musical expeditions in the classroom, especially when teaching large and heterogeneous groups of students from diverse backgrounds and with varied competencies in music (e.g., Juntunen 2018). Furthermore, the creative and versatile use of educational technology can also be integrated into other important aims of education, such as teaching media literacy and critical thinking.

Finnish music educator and researcher Aleksi Ojala (2017) developed practical e-learning materials and theoretical principles for a pedagogical approach named Learning Through Producing (LTP) that aimed to open one possible way of advancing collaborative and technologically aided creative music-making activities in upper secondary school. Ojala's research shows how digital technology can be harnessed for musical learning and sustained interaction with shareable musical artifacts such as tracks and music videos. The LTP approach enabled students to construct their musical knowledge and skills as well as negotiate their musical identities through creative music-making practices, such as arranging, songwriting, sound engineering, recording, and mixing. Importantly, however, Ojala considers the role of technology not as a replacement, but as an augmentation to the use of (electro) acoustic instruments and face-to-face interactions in the music classroom. While the use of e-learning materials and mobile devices can provide significant opportunities for personalized learning, for instance, the importance of hands-on music making with peers and teachers provides vital opportunities to build a collective knowledge and skill base in music.

The potentials of technology for supporting classroom composition projects has also been investigated by Marja-Leena Juntunen (2018 and 2020), through the case of a Finnish lower secondary school music teacher using tablet computers in a seventh grade music classroom. In this case, the music teacher designed a project that aimed to use music education technology in creative activities in ways that would support the active, bodily, and creative engagement of students. Reporting on the case, Juntunen (2018) shows how the integration of multiple forms of creative expression (such as movement and music exercises, improvisation, and composition, as well as recording and editing a video) enabled a space that developed students' musical skills and understanding. The use of tablet computers was also seen to increase students' motivation. Perhaps even more importantly, the project succeeded in offering possibilities for students' multimodal experiences and expression, exemplifying how the integration of technology in creative processes can make students' agency visible to the teacher and to the students themselves. The study also offers a significant example of possible ways to advance creative engagement and a pedagogically safe environment for approaching composing from various angles.

Finnish researcher Sara Sintonen (2013) points out the significant opportunities technology-enabled creative music-making opens for advancing students' digital empowerment and cultural participation. Sintonen examines the use of digitized sound as part of multimodal digital storytelling and as a tool for self-directed and creative expression. By utilizing digital recording and editing techniques in the processes of examining sounds it is possible to introduce students to the worlds of music and sounds and guide students to trust their own ears when making decisions. In this way digital technologies can also be understood to broaden the focus of composition pedagogy from the end product (i.e., songs, compositions) to the process of exploring the potential of sounds and music by enabling alternative approaches and musical practices, such as instant composition or sound painting (Sintonen, 2013). Such activities may or may not result in musical products, but this is neither required nor an end in itself. Indeed, as I have suggested elsewhere (Partti, 2020, n.p.), it would often be more appropriate to talk about the *pedagogy of composing* rather than composition pedagogy in school, as "the latter brings to mind the end product—a composition—while 'pedagogy of composing,' or 'composing education' puts the focus on doing, the activity of composing."

Equipping Teachers to Facilitate Composition

From the perspective of an individual music teacher, a curriculum that emphasizes versatility and creative production may not only be an inspiring opportunity, but also an entity that raises puzzling questions. In addition to the musical skills and pedagogical competencies it requires from teachers, it also calls for them to weigh their choices against the available resources and tools. In this section, I will examine more closely how music educators are equipped to facilitate musical composition.

The Double-Edged Sword of Pedagogical Freedom

As mentioned above, Finnish teachers have plenty of pedagogical freedom to make decisions about their teaching practices including, for instance, the amount of curricular time allocated for composition or the methods and tools used when teaching music. The role of the national core curriculum is to outline the regulations and offer guidance to education providers who then create a local curriculum, which more precisely considers the local specificities and needs of students (FNAE, 2016b). As this curriculum creation is led and conducted by teachers, schools, and municipalities (instead of the state), teachers hold a key role in pedagogical decision-making and curriculum development (Sahlberg, 2015, p. 122). Furthermore, there are no standardized tests or other external control mechanisms in place. This gives teachers a lot of autonomy and responsibility in curriculum implementation and student assessment.

This autonomy is greatly valued and widely accepted by the education community in Finland. Teachers are highly educated and therefore respected and trusted as professionals who are able to teach creatively, provide personalised learning opportunities for their students, and assess students' progress "against their respective characteristics and abilities, rather than by a reliance on uniform standards and statistical indicators" (Sahlberg, 2015, p. 123). Schools are expected to learn from rather than to compete against each other, and teachers are encouraged to meet the needs of their students instead of teach to the test. In an ideal situation, pedagogical freedom allows the teacher to follow their innovative ideas without being restricted by ready-made instructional methods or formulas. As noted by Randles and Muhonen (2014), there are a number of opportunities for a music teacher with skills and professional flexibility to incorporate composition activities as part of music instruction in Finnish schools. The option for combining the creative production of music with other school subjects, especially in primary school, is also rather exceptional, even on a global scale. This potential for integrating musical composition into other subjects, in turn, opens up multiple "possibilities for creative activities without subject boundaries and tight schedules" (ibid., p. 14).

The pedagogical freedom enjoyed by teachers, however, can bring about shortcomings in comparability and consistency as well as in learning outcomes (Juntunen 2017). Due to the considerable amount of professional autonomy, including decisions on how and how much to teach composition, the implementation of the objectives differs from one classroom to another. Furthermore, the responsibilities of expanding one's teaching repertoire and determining students' personal progress can weigh heavily on the shoulders of an individual teacher. This may be particularly burdensome for music teachers, who often experience isolation and suffer from a lack of collegiality when working as the only music teacher in their school (Muukkonen, 2010; Burnard, 2013). Also, teachers' competencies to teach music and musical composition vary significantly, particularly among general classroom teachers (Suomi, 2019). As pointed out by Huttunen (2017), classroom teachers are in urgent need for "tangible support, models, tools, and help" (ibid., p. 12, my translation) in order to offer their students with opportunities to learn music through "singing, playing instruments, listening, moving, improvising, and composing as well as through cross-disciplinary work in artistic subjects," as guided to do in the core curriculum (FNAE, 2016a, p. 152). According to a survey conducted with music teachers and classroom teachers (Partti, 2016), as many as 75% of teachers felt that they had not been equipped with adequate tools and skills for teaching composition during their studies, and 80% of teachers voiced their hope for professional development in composition pedagogy. Thus, although composition pedagogy has received much more attention in recent years, one could argue that the aim of "regularly providing [students] with opportunities for working with sound and music as well as for composing" (FNAE, 2016a, p. 454) is yet to be systematically established in and across the system.

Mind the Gap! Increasing Opportunities for Professional Development in Composition Pedagogy

The past years have brought about various composition initiatives in Finland. Many of the recent initiatives have sought not only to inspire children and young people to make their own music, but also to equip teachers with the skills and tools needed to facilitate composition in various music educational contexts. Such projects include, for instance, *BiisiPumppu* (2013–2014), a classroom composition initiative organized by the Finnish Composers' Copyright Society Teosto (see, Partti & Väkevä, 2018); the multidisciplinary arts project ITU (2013–2015); and the *Ääneni äärelle* project initiated by the Society of Finnish Composers in 2017 with the particular aim of responding to the pedagogical needs arising from the reform of the curriculum regarding the teaching of composition in extracurricular music institutes.

So far, one of the largest professional development projects was *SÄPE—Composition Pedagogy Training* (Metropolia, 2020). This joint project (2016–2020) organized by multiple institutions aimed to provide practical tools for guiding composition in schools and music institutes. Hundreds of classroom teachers, music subject teachers, and music pedagogues were trained to creatively make music and facilitate musical composition at different educational levels. A guiding principle in the project was the nurturing of shared expertise of the participating teachers. By contributing their expertise, ideas, and knowledge of local contexts, the participating teachers were able to develop new ideas and tools for their own work. Importantly, the training weekends and networking of colleagues provided during the project offered the participants with collegial support and the courage to extend their teaching into the area of composition pedagogy. A tangible result of the SÄPE training is the "recipe book" (Hartikainen, 2017), which includes best practices and ideas for composition pedagogy developed by the trainers and participants. By following the step-by-step instructions, it is possible for teachers to begin facilitating creative music-making with their own students. The e-book *Reseptejä säveltämisen ohjaukseen* [Recipes for facilitating composition] (ibid.) is available for free (in Finnish).

Another recently launched resource for composition pedagogy is the *Opus 1: Composition pedagogy materials databank* (Opus 1, 2020). Published in Finnish in 2018, it now also includes a partial version in English and Swedish. The Opus 1 website offers introductory insights into the teaching of composition along with a diverse range of composition assignments particularly suitable for group tuition, small group tuition, and individual tuition in music institutes. These and other online resources (e.g., Partti & Ahola, 2016) are expected to help and inspire music educators in fostering the culture of composing and exploring the world of creative music-making with their own students.

Another example of the recent initiatives aiming to support teachers in their development of composition pedagogy is the European cooperation *Future Songwriting* (2018–2020). The project was initiated and coordinated by the Finnish Composers' Copyright Society (Teosto) and co-funded by the European Commission under the Creative Europe program along with seven consortium partners. Future Songwriting took place in 15 schools in Finland, France, and Germany with a particular emphasis on the professional development of teachers' competencies facilitating technology-enabled composing practices in music education. During the project, the training group—comprised by three professional songwriters/music producers—visited the participating schools to advise teachers on the use of a digital audio workstation (DAW) and to provide students with opportunities for technology-based musical composition. According to the research data, the majority of participating teachers considered the project to be very helpful and relevant (Partti, Weber, & Rolle, 2022[2021]). Teachers pointed out various aspects of *Future Songwriting* that can be understood to have supported the development of their competence in digital technology-enabled composing. In particular, a heightened sense of confidence and courage, kindled by the project, can clearly be seen throughout the teacher interviews and surveys (ibid.). This is significant, as teachers' personal attitudes and beliefs can have a significant impact especially on the development of their technological, pedagogical, and content knowledge (Gall, 2016). Based on these results, it can be expected that by helping teachers overcome their uncertainties and immerse themselves in activities, teachers can gain confidence and competence in teaching composition.

Initiatives such as the ones introduced above can have an important role in bridging the gap between curricular aims and classroom activities by supporting the professional development of teachers already working in the field. In addition to equipping teachers with current know-how, skills, and ideas for teaching composition, these initiatives can also offer important opportunities for collegial support and encourage teachers to try new practices in their teaching. As I have stated elsewhere (Partti, forthcoming), such initiatives have potential for facilitating professional learning communities for teachers to continue to develop their competencies in composition pedagogy in collaboration with their colleagues, long after the project ends.

BACK TO THE FUTURE OF COMPOSITION PEDAGOGY IN FINNISH MUSIC EDUCATION

In this chapter, I have introduced the role of musical composition in today's Finnish educational system. I have demonstrated how the earlier tendency of including composition as an add-on to (what have been perceived as) more essential activities—especially singing and playing instruments—is now being replaced by a new way of viewing composition as an autonomous and fundamental part of music education. I have also discussed the opportunities and challenges this centrality of composition presents to music educators and classroom teachers and, ultimately, to music teacher education, which is now called upon to take a more active role in equipping current and future teachers with the skills and knowledge needed to foster experimental attitudes and musical creativity in schools. While envisioning an increasingly strong emphasis on creative music-making practices in the future of Finnish music education, it is also helpful to understand the path that has led to this point in history.

Returning to the Earlier Vision of Composing

Although composition and other creative activities have a central role in the current curricular documents in Finland, the aim of guiding students in musical expression is by no means completely unprecedented. As shown by Muukkonen (2010) and Suomi (2019), among others, the goals and contents of music instruction in Finnish schools have aligned themselves with international movements and methods (such as Orff or Dalcroze) as well as educational research. An early milestone in the journey of Finnish music education was the establishment of the International Society for Music Education (ISME) in the 1950s, which allowed a small and geographically remote country to access the wealth of modern music educational thinking and global ideas that were quickly adopted in Finnish music education (Louhivuori, 2005). Kankkunen (2010) discusses the impact of wider international trends in Finnish music education and points out the rise of the increasing awareness "of the concept of sound as material for musical expression" (p. 120) in the late 1960s. Inspired by the contemporary music of the time as well as the sonic aesthetics practices in British schools in particular, the Finnish music educator Liisa Tenkku put forward a proposition for the inclusion of sonic environment education in the very first Finnish comprehensive school music curriculum in 1970 (Kankkunen, 2009; 2010). It is no coincidence that the increasing interest of music educators in sound and the sonic environment took place in the mid-20th century. The wealth of new and unorthodox musical styles, experimental techniques, and electronic music inspired Tenkku and others to introduce avant-garde aesthetics also to children—and what better way to do it than by giving them a chance to experiment and play with sound materials. By the 1970s the understanding of the significance of offering students opportunities to create and express their own musical ideas in school—opportunities for "musical invention" (*musiikillinen keksintä*) as the activity was referred to for decades—was already established, albeit the term "composing" did not occur among the key content areas of music instruction in the national core curriculum until 2014. One can only speculate the reasons for this slow arrival. Perhaps the term was attached to too much historical significance, including the great legacy of Jean Sibelius, Finland's best-known composer whose music also played an important role in the struggle for Finnish independence. Or, maybe the term composing had for too long been narrowly defined as an undertaking requiring extensive professional skill and thus making it somehow inappropriate to be used in the school context. Regardless of the reasons, the *ethos* of composing can be seen in music curricula throughout the years, although its role has not been particularly central until very recently. Following the early excitement of musical inventions, the fate of classroom composition was to remain in the margins while other activities, particularly singing and playing music made by *professional composers*, were considered more essential.

One could argue that the first decades of the new millenium have marked a return to the late 1960s ideas of Tenkku and others, at least in terms of the emphasis on musical inventions and creative interactions with the sonic environment and musical artefacts. Since then, there have been two significant developments, namely in music teacher education and in understandings related to the meanings of musical composition. To conclude, I will briefly discuss these two areas in regards to composition pedagogy in Finland.

Educating Teachers to Drive Change

Reading the propositions of Liisa Tenkku, Ellen Urho, and other visionaries of Finnish music education approximately half a century ago, I am struck by the boldness and innovativeness of their thinking. Why did it take such a long time for their visions to become rooted in and across the whole educational system? One answer likely has to do with teacher education, as it is not the innovative curricular documents nor even a few visionaries, but *teachers*, who are (or are not) driving change in educational systems. As is often the case of visionaries, perhaps during their lifetimes the time simply was not ripe for their inventive ideas and approaches. What Tenkku and others were envisioning required music teacher education institutions to take a role in preparing teachers to put that vision into practice. This work is only now well on its way, although we still have miles to go.

An example of recent efforts to support the development of future music teachers' creative musicianship and composition pedagogy is the introduction of *Creativity and composition (pedagogy)* as one of the cross-curricular competencies in the Music Education Degree Programme at the Sibelius Academy of the University of the Arts Helsinki. The aim of this cross-curricular approach is to offer student-teachers with multiple and frequent opportunities for creative explorations throughout their studies and to view creativity and composition as a competence that crosses the boundaries of various fields of skills and knowledge rather than a separate "composition course" taking place in isolation from other studies. Centering the advancement of student-teachers' creative agency also marks a shift in focus in music teacher education: a step away from enculturation (only) into existing musical traditions toward a culture that develops practices out of the students' *own* creative ideas.

Challenges in the coming years include, for instance, the meaningful and versatile integration of digital technology to serve composition pedagogy (Partti et al., 2022[2021]). Opportunities for collaborative creativity and group-composition activities are also yet to be fully realized in music teacher education. The advancement of collaborative approaches also challenges the limited and individualistic—as well as often highly gendered—view of musical creativity as the prerogative of those with special talent and skills. Educating future music teachers in Finland and elsewhere to embrace an attitude of openness and pedagogical flexibility in the area of composition pedagogy is, indeed, a key to fostering music education where everyone has the right to freely explore and discover the landscapes of music.

Beyond Creativity: Composing as a Way to Build a Shared Future

Understandings of the meanings and justifications of musical composition have become broader and more diverse. Such multiple meanings of composing can clearly be seen in Finnish research and the case studies I have referred to in this chapter. As already understood by Tenkku and colleagues in the early days of Finnish composition pedagogy, creative music-making can usher children into new musical landscapes and lower the threshold for stepping into and appreciating previously unfamiliar sonic environments. Musical composition can also be used as an effective and inspiring approach for learning about music. Integrating composition with the teaching of musical structures and stylistic features, for instance, may significantly help the student in understanding the theories and practices of music (e.g., Ahvenjärvi, 2013).

Importantly however, the process of musical composition is not only about getting acquainted with music and inventing musical ideas, but also about exploring, scrutinizing, and playing with sounds and music—indeed, about finding one's own voice among other voices and taking one's place as an author, reformer, and innovator of (musical) culture (Ojala & Väkevä, 2013b; Partti, forthcoming). For a growing child or young person, musical composition can therefore offer a significant means of self-expression and identity construction (Partti & Westerlund, 2013; Ojala, 2017), aesthetic decision-making (Sintonen, 2013), and the development of creative agency (Muhonen, 2016; Juntunen, 2018). For groups of people, collaborative creative processes may offer a means of communication and constructive interaction (Karjalainen-Väkevä & Nikkanen, 2013) and in this way support a sense of community while preventing social exclusion (Antila 2013). Furthermore, as indicated by an analysis of the pedagogical thinking of several esteemed composer-teachers (Puukka, 2020), musical composition can even contribute to the processes of ethical subjectification, understood here as the effort to exist in and with the world in a responsible, "grown-up" way, to use the terminology of educational theorist Gert Biesta (2017b, p. 17). Similarly, Ojala and Väkevä (2013b) refer to composing as a "practical research process" (p. 10, my translation) and discuss the possibilities that creating music offers for students to "come to terms with the world and with other people" (p. 17, my translation).

These and many other possible meanings of composing are of importance and should not be viewed as mutually exclusive, but rather, situational, interactive, and overlapping. The diverse meanings of composing for both individuals and groups highlight the pedagogical possibilities of composing to promote active cultural participation and spark the desire in students for wanting to come into and remain in dialogue with each other and to explore different ways of being in the world (see, Biesta, 2017a). The existential opportunities that can be opened up by composing can be regarded as specifically central in a time of growing inequalities, social divisions, and conflicts. A deepening understanding of the various opportunities that composing can offer to students with different starting points and diverse backgrounds also challenges the narrow conceptualizations of musical composition as a way of merely advancing individual creativity or students' "innovation skills." Instead, musical composition practices can be understood to provide a space for encountering the self *and* the world and in this way create shared musical spaces where intersubjective responsibility and the building of a shared future are made possible.

NOTES

1. During the Music Education Degree Programme at the Sibelius Academy of the University of the Arts Helsinki, student-teachers are expected, among other goals, to learn to master different musical styles on several instruments, lead choirs and bands, and arrange material for various kinds of ensembles.
2. In the Finnish school context music ensembles most often refer to music groups that include instruments typical of a rock band (e.g., electric and acoustic guitars, bass, drums, keyboards) as well as so-called classroom instruments, such as ukuleles and percussion instruments. Music ensembles may also include other instruments played by students.

REFERENCES

Ahvenjärvi, S. (2013). Kokemuksia sävellystunneista sekä improvisoinnista yleisen musiikkitiedon tunneilla. In J. Ojala & L. Väkevä (Eds.), *Säveltäjäksi kasvattaminen. Pedagogisia näkökulmia musiikin luovaan tekijyyteen* (pp. 141–147). Opetushallitus.

Antila, S. 2013. Kertomus lukiomusikaalin säveltämisestä ryhmätyöskentelynä. In J. Ojala & L. Väkevä (Eds.), *Säveltäjäksi kasvattaminen. Pedagogisia näkökulmia musiikin luovaan tekijyyteen* (pp. 99–112). Opetushallitus.

Biesta, G. (2017a). *Letting art teach: Art education 'after' Joseph Beuys.* Artez Press.

Biesta, G. (2017b). *The rediscovery of teaching.* Routledge.

Burnard, P. (2013). Introduction. In E. Georgii-Hemming, P. Burnard, & S. Holgerson (Eds.), *Professional knowledge in music teacher education* (pp. 1–15). Routledge.

Ervasti, M. (2013). Musiikillisia sormenjälkiä. In J. Ojala & L. Väkevä (Eds.), *Säveltäjäksi kasvattaminen. Pedagogisia näkökulmia musiikin luovaan tekijyyteen* (pp. 113–125). Opetushallitus.

FNAE. (2016a) = Finnish National Agency for Education. (2016). *National core curriculum for basic education 2014.* Finnish National Agency for Education.

FNAE. (2016b) = Finnish National Agency for Education (2016). *New national core curriculum for basic education: focus on school culture and integrative approach.* https://www.oph.fi/sites/default/files/documents/new-national-core-curriculum-for-basic-education.pdf

FNAE. (2018) = Finnish National Agency for Education. (2018). *National core curriculum for the general and advanced syllabi for basic education in the arts 2017.* Finnish National Agency for Education.

FNAE. (2019) = Finnish National Agency of Education. (2019). *Lukion opetussuunnitelman perusteet.* Finnish National Agency for Education.

Gall, M. (2016). TPACK and music teacher education. In A. King, E. Himonides, & A. Ruthmann (Eds.), *The Routledge companion to music, technology, and education* (pp. 305–318). Routledge.

Hartikainen S. (Ed). (2017). Reseptejä säveltämisen ohjaukseen. *Metropolia Ammattikorkeakoulu.* URN:ISBN:978-952-328-051-9

Huttunen, T. (2017). *Osallistava sävellytysmenetelmä musiikinopetukseen Peruskoulun opetussuunnitelman 2014 tavoitteita ja oppimisen ydinmetaforia toteuttamassa* [Doctoral dissertation, University of Jyväskylä].

Ilomäki, L. (2013). Säveltäminen musiikkioppilaitospedagogiikan haastajana. In J. Ojala & L. Väkevä (Eds.), *Säveltäjäksi kasvattaminen. Pedagogisia näkökulmia musiikin luovaan tekijyyteen* (pp. 126–140). Opetushallitus.

Johnstone, K. (1999). *Impro for storytellers.* Routledge.

Juntunen, M.-L. (2017). National assessment meets teacher autonomy: A case study of national assessment of learning outcomes in music in Finnish basic education. *Music Education Research, 19*(1), 1–16. http://doi.org/10.1080/14613808.2015.1077799

Juntunen, M.-L. (2018). Using socio-digital technology to enhance participation and creative engagement in a lower secondary music classroom. *Nordic Research in Music Education Yearbook, 18*, 47–74.

Juntunen, M.-L. (2020). Embodied learning through and for collaborative multimodal composing: A case in a Finnish lower secondary music classroom. *International Journal of Education & the Arts, 21*(29). http://doi.org/10.26209/ijea21n29

Kankkunen, O.-T. (2009). Vihreä viserryskone: uusi ääni 1970-luvun suomalaisessa musiikkikasvatuksessa. *Finnish Journal of Music Education, 12*(1), 36–59. https://sites.unia rts.fi/documents/166984/205664/FJME_VOL12nro1_nettiversio.pdf/01ab2487-585c-480b-b9e0-3fd9ce6ba29b

Kankkunen, O-T. (2010). Listening to sounds in sonic praxis. In: I. Rikandi (Ed), *Mapping the common ground: Philosophical perspectives on Finnish music education* (pp. 114–145). BTJ Finland Oy & Sibelius-Akatemia.

Karjalainen-Väkevä, M., & Nikkanen, H. (2013). Opettajan roolit säveltämisen ohjaajana ala- ja yläkoulussa. In J. Ojala & L. Väkevä (Eds.), *Säveltäjäksi kasvattaminen. Pedagogisia näkökulmia musiikin luovaan tekijyyteen* (pp. 64–82). Opetushallitus.

Klami, M. (2020). *Stories, improv and continuous motion: Thoughts about teaching composition.* Opus 1: Composition pedagogy materials databank [website]. Finnish Composers. https://www.opus1.fi/en/stories-improv-and-continuous-motion-thoughts-about-teaching-comp osition/

Korpela, P., Kuoppamäki, A., Laes, T. Miettinen, L., Muhonen, S., Muukkonen, M., Nikkanen, H., Ojala, A., Partti, H., Pihkanen T., & Rikandi, I. (2010). Music Education in Finland. In I. Rikandi (Ed.), *Mapping the common ground: Philosophical perspectives on Finnish music education* (pp. 16–31). BTJ Finland Oy & Sibelius-Akatemia.

Kuoppamäki, A. (2015). *Gender lessons: Girls and boys negotiating learning community in basics of music* [Doctoral Dissertation, University of the Arts Helsinki]. http://urn.fi/URN:ISBN:978-952-5959-89-5

Louhivuori, J. 2005. *Musiikkikasvatuksen vuosikirja 2002–2004.* Gummerus

Lyytikäinen, P. (2020). *Student-oriented composition teaching.* Opus 1: Composition pedagogy materials databank [website]. Finnish Composers. https://www.opus1.fi/en/oppilaslahtois yys-savelluksen-opetuksessa/

Metropolia. (2020). *SÄPE: Säveltämisen pedagogiikkaa koulutus* [project website]. https://www.metropolia.fi/fi/opiskelu-metropoliassa/osaamisen-taydentaminen/opetustoimen-henkilostokoulutus/saveltamisen-pedagogiikkaa

Michielse, M., & Partti, H. (2015). Producing a meaningful difference: The significance of small creative acts in composing within online participatory remix practices. *International Journal of Community Music, 8*(1), 27–40. http://doi.org/10.1386/ijcm.8.1.27_1

Muhonen, S. (2013a). Songcrafting: A teacher's perspective of collaborative inquiry and creation of classroom practice. *International Journal of Music Education, 32*(2), 185–202. https://doi.org/10.1177/02557614135066

Muhonen, S. (2013b). Lasten musiikillisen luomisprosessin tukeminen alakoulussa— esimerkkinä sävellyttäminen. In J. Ojala & L. Väkevä (Eds.), *Säveltäjäksi kasvattaminen. Pedagogisia näkökulmia musiikin luovaan tekijyyteen* (pp. 83–98). Opetushallitus.

Muhonen, S. (2016). *Songcrafting practice: A teacher inquiry into the potential to support collaborative creation and creative agency within school music education* [Doctoral Dissertation, University of the Arts Helsinki]. http://urn.fi/URN:ISBN:978-952-329-024-2

Muukkonen, M. (2010). *Monipuolisuuden eetos. Musiikin aineenopettajat artikuloimassa työnsä käytäntöjä.* [Doctoral Dissertation, Sibelius Academy]. http://urn.fi/URN:ISBN:978-952-5531-82-4

Ojala, A. (2017). *Learning through producing: The pedagogical and technological redesign of a compulsory music course for Finnish general upper secondary schools* [Doctoral Dissertation, University of the Arts Helsinki]. http://urn.fi/URN:ISBN:978-952-329-088-4

Ojala, J., & Väkevä, L. (2013a). *Säveltäjäksi kasvattaminen: Pedagogisia näkökulmia musiikin luovaan tekijyyteen.* Opetushallitus.

Ojala, J. & Väkevä, L. (2013b). Säveltäminen luovana ja merkityksellisenä toimintana. In J. Ojala & L. Väkevä (Eds.), *Säveltäjäksi kasvattaminen. Pedagogisia näkökulmia musiikin luovaan tekijyyteen* (pp. 10–22). Opetushallitus.

Opus 1. (2020). *Opus 1: Composition pedagogy materials databank.* https://www.opus1.fi/en/

Partti, H. 2016. Muuttuva muusikkous koulun musiikinopetuksessa. *Finnish Journal of Music Education, 19*(1), 8–28.

Partti, H. (2020). Access all areas! Everyone is a composer. *Opus 1: Composition pedagogy materials databank* [website]. Finnish Composers. https://www.opus1.fi/en/access-all-areas-everyone-is-a-composer/

Partti, H. (in press). Mapping the Field of Composing Pedagogy in Finland: From Musical Inventions to Cultural Participation. In K. Devaney, M. Faultley, J. Grow & A. Ziewenmayer (Eds.), *The Routledge Companion To Teaching Music Composition in Schools: International Perspectives.* Routledge. [Accepted for publication in January 2021].

Partti, H., & Ahola, A. (2016). *Säveltäjyyden jäljillä: musiikintekijät tulevaisuuden koulussa.* Sibelius-Akatemia. https://helda.helsinki.fi/bitstream/handle/10138/169020/Saveltajyyden_jaljilla_Partti_Ahola.pdf?sequence=1

Partti, H., Weber, J & Rolle, C. (2022 [2021]). Learning a skill, or lerning to learn? Supporting teachers' professional development in music education technology. *Journal of Music, Technology & Education, 14*(2&3), 123–139. https://doi.org/10.1386/jmte_00037_1

Partti, H. & Westerlund, H. (2012). Democratic musical learning: how the participatory revolution in new media challenges the culture of music education. In A. Brown (Ed.), *Sound musicianship: Understanding the crafts of music* (pp. 300–312). Cambridge Scholars Publishing.

Partti, H. & Westerlund, H. (2013). Säveltäjyyden merkitykset osallistumisen kulttuurissa ja tulevaisuuden musiikkikasvatuksessa. In J. Ojala & L. Väkevä (Eds.), *Säveltäjäksi kasvattaminen. Pedagogisia näkökulmia musiikin luovaan tekijyyteen* (pp. 23–32). Opetushallitus.

Partti, H. & Väkevä, L. (2018). SongPump: Developing a composing pedagogy in Finnish schools through collaboration between professional songwriters and music teachers. In C. Christophersen & A. Kenny (Eds.), *Musician-teacher collaborations: Altering the chord* (pp. 73–84). Routledge.

Puukka, J. (2020). *Mistä puhumme kun puhumme säveltämiskasvatuksesta.* [Master's thesis, University of the Arts Helsinki].

Randles, C., & Muhonen, S. (2015). Validation and further validation of a measure of creative identity among USA and Finland pre-service music teachers. *British Journal of Music Education*, 32(1), 51–70.

Sahlberg, P. (2015). *Finnish lessons 2.0. What can the world learn from educational change in Finland?* Teachers College Press.

Sintonen, S. 2013. Tunnarikin on sävellys: mediapedagoginen näkökulma digitaaliseen ääneen. In J. Ojala & L. Väkevä (Eds.), *Säveltäjäksi kasvattaminen. Pedagogisia näkökulmia musiikin luovaan tekijyyteen* (pp. 193–202). Opetushallitus.

Suomi, H. 2019. *Pätevä musiikin opettamiseen? Luokanopettajaksi valmistuvan musiikillinen kompetenssi perusopetuksen opetussuunnitelman perusteiden toteuttamisen näkökulmasta* [Doctoral dissertation, University of Jyväskylä].

Väkevä, L. (2006). Teaching popular music in Finland: What's up? What's ahead? *International Journal of Music Education*, 24(2), 129–134.

Westerlund, H. (2006). Garage rock bands: A future model for developing musical expertise? *International Journal of Music Education*, 24(2), 119–125. https://doi.org/10.1177/0255761406065472

CHAPTER 37

....

COMPOSITION PEDAGOGY
IN GERMANY

....

CHRISTIAN ROLLE AND JULIA WEBER

In German, the term "composition" is closely associated with art music, more precisely with the Romantic idea of the composer. That is one reason why the verb "to compose" is hardly used in music education. Composing is generally understood to be a talent and not a skill that can be taught, which leaves the public believing that only geniuses can compose. As a result, the term "composing" has been avoided in the context of school and music education and students are said to be able only to "create" or "invent" a piece of music (Musik erfinden) or to craft sounds (Klänge gestalten). Exceptions exist, and sometimes the term "compose" is explicitly used as a criticism of a narrow concept bound to the Romantic tradition. Over the last decade, teaching of songwriting is more and more common in the music classroom, but it is rarely rooted in the curriculum. Thus, music composition pedagogy often means experimenting with unusual sounds in the tradition of contemporary art music. In this chapter, we will mostly use the term "New Music" with capital letters to refer to art music practices, which has also been called post-serial or postmodern classical music and have developed since the middle of the 20th century. We will present an overview of the history and common practices of contemporary composition pedagogy in Germany and the related educational discourses.

The focus of this chapter is on Germany but large parts of it apply to composition pedagogy in other German-speaking countries as well and some examples in this article are from Austria. Though the focus is on composition pedagogy in general schooling, the text also hints at other areas of music education. In many places primary and secondary schools collaborate with communal music schools or concert halls, or they invite composers to get involved in projects. Ideas and concepts of composition pedagogy often relate to different institutional contexts even if the conditions and implementation challenges differ. Although this chapter is about composition pedagogy, it also includes music improvisation. They are difficult to separate. Composition in the music classroom often begins with exploration and improvisation and that does not necessarily lead to notated music. Composition pedagogy in schools is dominated by collaborative composition and in most cases composers and performers are the same persons.

INSTITUTIONAL BACKGROUND

In Germany, the school system is governed by the 16 federal states (Bundesländer). Music education is understood as an essential part of general education, which means that all children have to visit music classes at least up to grade seven (Kertz-Welzel, 2005). There are choir classes or string classes here and there, but the curriculum for music generally covers many different contents and activities like singing, playing instruments, listening to music, and music history or music theory. Beyond that, students have the opportunity to participate in music ensembles offered by many primary and high schools. Community music schools provide even more specialized music education like instrumental lessons. In the following, we will focus on general music classes. The curricula vary from state to state. Although there are some agreements concerning the core subjects between the federal states, there is no national curriculum. The situation is similar in Austria.

In Germany, preschool education is not part of the public educational system. Primary school starts at the age of six and usually lasts for four years. In primary school music is often taught by generalists without formal higher music education (Lehmann-Wermser et al., 2020). In all federal states, composition is required in the curriculum in one way or another even if it is not called composition. Instead we can find paraphrases like "creating music" or "sound design" (Grow, 2018). Curricula call for improvising and experimenting with musical instruments, students performing their invented songs, or using graphic notation for the music created. Musical creativity is considered important. Despite the music education courses offered by various institutions, many primary school teachers still lack the expertise to teach composition or at least lack the confidence. Nevertheless, many still try to give easy tasks for improvisation or encourage the students, for example, to set stories to sound (see section in this chapter, "Typical Composition Assignments and the Tradition of New Music"). In some places, particularly in urban areas, music education is supported by local concert halls or opera houses. Composing can be part of music promotion and education programs of such institutions. Composition projects may also be part of collaborations with local artists.

After primary school there are several ways to continue with secondary schooling. In most German federal states, the division of children into different types of schools begins very early, usually at the age of 10. Parents have to choose the appropriate kind of secondary school, depending on their children's performance in primary school. There is the Gymnasium (eight to nine years) that grants access to universities and there are other secondary schools that have different names in different states (e.g., Gemeinschaftsschule). The latter grant access to vocational training after five to six years. Music education is well developed at the Gymnasium, firmly embedded as a compulsory subject up to the ninth or 10th grade and still part of the curriculum in the final school years (11–13). However, there are difficulties in staffing the other types of secondary schools with well-educated music teachers. Music is not considered one of the core subjects. As already explained on the curricula for primary school, the term "composing" is also avoided in the curricula for secondary schools. Different types of secondary schools may emphasize different content and activities and this emphasis has shifted over time.

Historical Perspective on Composing in Schools in Germany

For a long time, singing was the only activity intended for general music classes in Germany. This was still true in the 1920s when Fritz Jöde (1928) wrote his book *Das schaffende Kind in der Musik* (*The creative child in music*). By promoting the idea to develop creativity in music education he did not commit to music composition, but instead used the argument to justify music in schools. He argued that singing was a creative activity and creative powers were needed to sustain life. This thought is typical of the progressive education movement (Reformpädagogik) that was influential in music education at that time. It facilitated later attempts to establish composition pedagogy.

Carl Orff's *Schulwerk* can be considered another precursor. Based on his work at the Guntherschule in Munich in the 1920s Orff developed his well-known approach. Creating music is crucial here. "Improvisation is the starting point of elemental music making" (Orff, 1978, p. 22). What is most important is that he provided a strong argument for considering student compositions as valuable. However, even though Orff instruments can still be found in almost every music classroom in Germany and Austria, Orff's music for children is hardly used; his *Schulwerk* largely fell into oblivion. During the 1960s, music education in German schools underwent changes. Music appreciation replaced making music as a key part of music lessons. Singing traditional songs was no longer the main activity. In his influential book *Unterweisung im Musikhören* (*Teaching music listening*) Dankmar Venus (1969) argued that in music education the content of teaching must be perceived as music practices. Determining the music curriculum, he suggested, should be based on the distinction between production of music (improvising and composing), reproduction (performing), reception of music, transposition (transforming music into other forms of medial expression like dancing) and reflecting on music (e.g., by addressing historical and cultural contexts). However, it is not by accident that the title of his book emphasizes listening to music. Even though Venus claims that all music practices are equal and independent, they all seem to serve music listening pedagogy in the end.

There were counter movements to an art-oriented approach to music education. Since the beginning of the 1970s, new ideas emerged that were inspired by philosophies and practices of post-serial music and composers like John Cage. In these views, improvising and composing was crucial, strongly linked together, and difficult to separate. Gertrud Meyer-Denkmann (1972, 1977) was a music educator, composer, and musicologist who developed a concept of music education and methods that were based on structures and practices of New Music. It focused on experiments in sound, sought to understand the process of musical experience, and rejected the idea of the autonomous artwork. Aleatoric music, performance art, and sound collage provided the model for composing in the classroom instead. In accordance with the political zeitgeist of that time this was justified by the desire to change social conditions. Avant-garde aesthetics and social criticism were the basis for developing a concept that encouraged students to work as many composers of New Music do. Together with several co-authors Rudolf Frisius published the textbook *Sequenzen* in 1972 with similar intentions and comparable content. What students do, the authors wrote, is "analyze given sounds beyond tonality and measure. In the process, they discover elemental sound qualities and structures" (Frisius & Arbeitsgemeinschaft Curriculum Musik, 1972, p. 12).

Composers play an important role in the history of composition pedagogy in Germany and Austria. Dieter Schnebel, who composed many pieces for children, wrote the preface for Gertrud Meyer-Denkmann's book *Struktur und Praxis Neuer Musik im Unterricht* (*Structure and practice of New Music in the classroom*). The few publications of the composer Paul Dessau about music education in schools (Dessau, 1968) are also interesting to note even though his ideas received little attention. Based on his experience as a music teacher he called for a production approach to music education, emphasizing that inventing music is essential for children's musical development. Of particular importance are the community operas Hans Werner Henze produced at the festival Cantiere Internazionale d'Arte in Montepulciano/Italy and in Deutschlandsberg/Austria (Henze, 1984 and 1986). He took a unique approach to music education by allowing the participation of many people in composing music theater pieces. This effort was a type of cultural education motivated by a desire to link lay music and amateur art to professional music and art. As a Marxist, Henze was driven by the wish to contribute to social development. He considered it his duty to engage actively in the process of developing social awareness and critical faculties toward a humane society. These were not school-based projects but there was great interest in Henze's work, and his community operas served as a model for similar projects within or in cooperation with schools intending to promote cultural participation.

Since the 1980s popular music has increasingly found its way into the curriculum. This was associated with changes in classroom activities. On the one hand, pop and rock music became increasingly accepted as teaching content. On the other hand, more emphasis was placed on making music in the classroom. In addition to singing, music listening, analyzing music, and learning about music history, students were playing music on different instruments. Simple arrangements were written suitable for students without any prior experience. Volker Schütz (1981 and 1982), one of the pioneers of popular music education in the general classroom in Germany, stressed that teaching popular music must be guided by the everyday life experiences and musical activities of the students. He was convinced that understanding music is only possible if students have the opportunity to perform and, furthermore, to invent music. Composition, in his view, is key to understanding music. Based on this popular music pedagogy Schütz suggested courses that lead to students' working out their own songs. He was fully aware that this was a challenging goal. As then, songwriting remains a rare part of the music teacher education curriculum that is dominated by performance and musicology. The shortcomings in music teacher education still concern composition pedagogy regardless of the music genre. Because of these obstacles in implementing teaching methods for composition, it can be assumed that many innovative concepts remained on paper. At the least, it takes a long time from developing models of composition pedagogy, developing the curricula in different states, and creating the prerequisites in teacher education to get to the actual implementation in the classroom. This is one reason why collaborations with artists are popular. Since the late 1980s many cooperative school projects with visiting composers have been initiated, often supported by concert halls or similar institutions. *Response* served as a model, imported from the UK and for the first time realized in 1988 with musicians of the London Sinfonietta and the Ensemble Modern (Voit, 2018a). Since then, different series of comparable projects have been launched: *Querklang*, located in Berlin, or *Klangradar 3000* in Hamburg. In many cases, however, these programs also have other objectives. The students' compositions refer to a specific musical work, almost always from the field of New Music. The aim of encouraging students to compose and the desire to break down barriers and to provide access to contemporary art music are often blurred. Music education and music promotion may overlap, particularly if the concert hall involved is mainly interested in audience development. Additionally, the artists involved might not be familiar with the classroom situation and might not be well prepared to act as educators. In these circumstances, conflicts and misunderstandings may arise (Rolle et al., 2018). However, that does not change the fact that the large majority of these projects are carried out with high commitment by the visiting composers and the teachers involved, and that they can open up spaces for creativity.

Parallel to the growing number of collaborative composition projects, renewed impetus for composition pedagogy was provided by several publications during the 1990s. Ortwin Nimczik (1991) wrote a book called *Spielräume im Musikunterricht* (*On margins in the music classroom*), discussing pedagogical aspects of creative work in music. He also based his ideas on composition practices from the area of New Music, but in addition he referred to concepts of education. Building on this theoretical framework, Ortwin Nimczik published assorted teaching materials during the following years and was also involved in launching the composition competition called *Teamwork* for music classes and ensembles in schools inventing pieces of New Music, which is organized by the German music teacher association BMU.

The lively discussions on aesthetic education held in several educational disciplines during the 1990s in Germany provided important ideas for developing composition pedagogy. At stake was the meaning of arts education in the school curriculum as well as the question of how teaching music could contribute to education (in German

"Bildung"). In retrospect, this debate might have been a reaction to emerging neoliberal ideas that were feared to affect education by focusing on measurable goals, efficiency, and usefulness. Insisting on the intrinsic value of the arts and on the meaning of aesthetic experience for education can be seen—and in fact was seen—as acts of resistance. This has consequences for how music education views itself. Thus, the philosophical discussion affected concepts of good teaching in the arts. Against this backdrop, music education should be more than teaching and learning facts about music; it is not only about acquiring musical skills. The discussion draws attention to the aesthetic dimension of music and the importance of creative processes offering opportunities for musical experience (Rolle, 1999). Based on this theoretical framework Christopher Wallbaum (2000) developed a model of teaching composition—he speaks of "producing music"— using an approach that is oriented both toward the process of composing and the created product. Aesthetic experience and music as aesthetic practice are core concepts of his philosophy of music education. The model suggests providing spaces where the students could discuss the quality of their work. If composition is collaborative in nature, there must be opportunities to exchange ideas and to discuss intermediate results in order to come to joint decisions. There must be room for what Rolle and Wallbaum (2011, see also Rolle, 2014) call "aesthetic argument." Teaching composition raises issues of evaluating music, and teachers ought to find ways to give students the responsibility for negotiations on the artistic quality of their music.

Typical Composition Assignments and the Tradition of "New Music"

In German music textbooks and other materials for teachers one can find numerous composition tasks that are oriented toward popular music. Many of these focus on composing a class song or a rap. There also are suggestions for lessons on electronic music production. Nevertheless, assignments that refer to the tradition of New Music still dominate.

As mentioned before the term "composition" is strongly connected to art music and was not used in educational contexts for a long time. Matthias Schlothfeldt (2009) even distinguishes between composition assignments and creational tasks (in German "Gestaltungsaufgaben"). The latter are provided to the students by the teachers and are embedded in a larger teaching context. Solving a creational task serves as a means to the end of teaching other musical skills or competencies. Creational tasks serve to apply or secure learning outcomes, for example, securing knowledge of the rondo form by inventing a rondo. In a composition task, composing is an end in itself and the students can only set their own composition assignment. Here the students themselves determine the means and the approach, and are responsible for their own decisions. They are less guided by external guidelines. To continue the example, the students only compose a rondo if this is the form they need to express themselves musically in the way they want.

The need to conceptually differentiate tasks, to the extent of using different names, demonstrates the cultural depth of the term "composition." This is closely connected to the idea that in composing, an autonomous artist goes through a self-determined process that serves no other purpose than to create a composition. Helmut Schmidinger (2020, p. 192), however, points out that the term "composition" should also be used for putting together known elements in order to relax the pedagogical approach to composing. We agree with this view and therefore, we identify all assignments that ask students to invent music as "composition assignments" in the following.

There are different models suggesting how the composition process can be structured in pedagogical contexts. Listening and reflection are essential elements in these models. We will present one of those. Renate Reitinger (2008) distinguishes 10 phases in the composition process (see Figure 37.1).

Many assignments are structured accordingly. We will present a couple of these assignments that are descriptions of lessons as they are found in textbooks for the general music classroom.

Composing with Everyday Objects and Sounds

The first cluster of tasks that we present is comparable in the choice of material that is used for the composition. The tasks have in common that either everyday objects are used as instruments or everyday sounds are the basis for the composition.

Assignment 1: Sounds Becoming Music

The assignment is suggested in a textbook for music lessons at the beginning of secondary school (grades five through seven, ages 10 to 13). It is proposed as the final project of a unit plan on the theme "Soundtrack of my everyday life" (Brassel, 2012, pp. 201–213). In this series of lessons, the students have to reflect on how music structures their day. Thus, they reflect on background music in different situations (e.g., shopping or sports), they learn about the ear, and there is a lesson about mobile phones and ringtones.

The assignment of the final project (Brassel, 2012, p. 213) is structured into three different tasks. First, the students see a graphic notation and are asked to describe what sounds they would expect if this piece of music was played with cell phones.

In the second task they are required to compose a one-minute piece of music using the ringtones of their cell phones only. They need to choose a suitable title for their piece. Finally, they are asked to notate the composition using a graphic notation.

The third task is to first show their graphic notations to their classmates and the classmates are asked to describe what they expect to hear. Then each group has to present their composition and their classmates are asked to describe what the composition expresses and what the title could be.

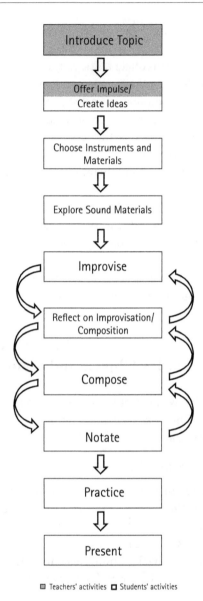

FIGURE 37.1 Structure of the composition process (Reitinger, 2008)

It is not specified whether the composition ought to be put together on the computer or with an app, or played live using the phones as instruments.

The composition uses sounds of everyday lives and cell phones are used as an instrument. Similar assignments often use cell phones as a recording device and the pupils walk around in their schools or in town to collect sounds. This clearly picks up a compositional technique that was used in the tradition of *musique concrète*. Examples for this can be found internationally, for example in Maud Hickey's (2012, p. 78) book *Music outside the lines*. When sounds are recorded with cell phones or other mobile devices the sounds are often manipulated with a software afterward.

Assignment 2: Cold

This assignment is taken from a book in which the author published different composition tasks that are all inspired by his love for contemporary art music (Schneider, 2017, pp. 69–71). The room has to be prepared before the students enter. The chairs ought to be put in a circle and a pair of stones and a piece of aluminum foil are placed under each chair.

Schneider suggests different actions for a warm-up. In the first warm-up the sounds "s" and "sh" are used and the students are asked to change the sound from a sharp s-sound to a more sonoric one, to "sh" and back without using a conductor, just by listening to each other. In the second warm-up the students have to create sounds to the topic "cold" by using their body and voice to create sounds. Afterward they are asked to pick up the aluminum foil without making any noise. One person starts by shaking the foil softly and this sound travels through the circle and increases in the process until it is "stormy" and goes back to complete silence. After that exercise, the students are asked to try different ways to create sounds with the stones. Everyone invents a short motive, which is presented in the circle.

After these warm-ups the students form groups. The task is to create a piece three to five minutes long on the topic "cold" and the students should be able to repeat the piece. They are asked to choose other instruments (e.g., piano, flute, guitars, strings, mouthpieces of brass instruments) in addition to the foil and the stones. The pieces are afterward presented in a way in which no interruption is necessary between pieces. The teacher decides the order of the presentations. In between the groups the teacher presents recordings of pieces that also have "cold" as a theme (e.g., Antonio Vivaldi, "Winter" from *The Four Seasons*, Hans Abrahamsen, "Schnee [Snow]"). The presentation is followed by a reflection and the students have the opportunity to change their composition before their final presentation.

There are many other examples for tasks in which everyday objects can be used along with music instruments or the voice. In a textbook for primary schools, for example, we can find a task where the students are asked to find scary sounds using all kinds of material (Küntzel, 2012, p. 83) or they are asked to create a certain atmosphere by using their voice, their body, instruments, or other objects (Küntzel, 2012, p. 43). Through the use of the experimental sounds, these tasks are informed by New Music practices (see Reflection 1).

Assignment 3: An Exercise

This assignment was published on a website for composition pedagogy in Germany (www.kompaed.de). The assignment can be adapted to different learning levels and can be performed with different age groups (Schlothfeldt, 2018).

The assignment is structured in six steps. In the first step the students are asked to listen to one minute of silence. The task is to notate the sounds they hear during this minute either while listening or afterward from memory. How detailed the sound events are notated can vary depending on the students' level of knowledge. It can range from graphic notations to precise rhythmic and melodic notations. All of them use a simple coordinate system as a score. The y-axis shows the different sounds that are heard, and the x-axis shows the progression over time. This score is the starting point for the piece to be created.

In the second step the elements on the score are realized on musical instruments, with the voice or imitated with other objects that are available. The students are asked to try to imitate the sounds they have heard. If necessary, the notation should be changed or modified in a way that it represents the slightly new sounds. In a third step the students can create new sounds with the instruments/objects they have chosen and notate them, so they can be used as further composition material.

Afterward, in the fourth step, they take all the elements they have notated so far and put them together in a new form. The piece can still be limited to one minute but it doesn't have to be. However, the original sequence is discarded in this step and the events are rearranged.

In the fifth step the students shall reflect on their piece by analyzing it. They shall answer questions like: How many parts does the composition have? How are the different elements connected? Are there variations? After this reflection they can change the piece, if necessary.

In the final sixth step they have to present their piece, initially in the classroom, but a public presentation may follow.

This assignment uses everyday sounds but only as the basis for the composition, not as its material. The kind of notation is typical of similar tasks. In a book for primary school the same way of notating a piece is used in a composition assignment with the title "An interesting soup" in which the students are asked to find interesting spices for their musical soup (Küntzel, 2012, p. 55). Hans Schneider (2017, p. 120) suggests putting the organized system in a long paper roll on the floor, so that the students can note the single elements on cards that they can rearrange easily.

Reflection 1

There are differences but also some interesting commonalities between the three assignments that were presented so far. In the first example everyday sounds were used and put together to a composition. The students choose what they want to express with the given material. In the second assignment everyday objects are used as instruments to compose music for a certain given atmosphere (the cold). In the third assignment, the random everyday sounds heard in one minute of silence are used as a starting point for a composition with musical instruments.

The idea to use everyday sounds and soundscaping as shown in Assignments 1 and 2 is connected to the tradition of musique concrète (e.g., Karlheinz Stockhausen). As mentioned in Section 3, this idea of using experimental sounds in the classroom was introduced by authors like Gertrud Meyer-Denkmann (1972 and 1977) in the 1970s. In the tradition of John Cage (and others) one of the goals is to make the students understand that every sound can be turned into music and that the listeners' perspective is important. This is especially important in Assignment 3.

Another typical task that is closely connected to the mentioned ones is building new instruments out of everyday objects and composing with those instruments. Roszak (2014) and Schneider (2017, p. 43) offer a lot of good ideas for building experimental instruments. Building instruments is often practiced in schools because it is an interdisciplinary task; in addition, some schools have a lack of instruments, thus, they can use the created instruments as a resource. Furthermore, if these instruments are used in composition assignments, it leads to more experimental compositions, which is considered useful to avoid clichés.

This practice, inspired by the music avant-garde of the 1950s and 1960s, is widespread in Germany and Austria even today. Music composition in the sense of sound experiments is still alive in music pedagogies, teaching methods, and school projects even if the aesthetic superstructure might be missing. In many cases, this is done without any theoretical foundation in a kind of pragmatic way. The orientation toward art-music practices seems not to be decisive but instead the success of an experimental approach to music composition lies in the fact that it does not need particular prerequisites like notation skills or skills in playing an instrument. Not much more is required than the willingness to participate. This is why these teaching methods appear to be suitable for music education in general schools. They are inclusive, one might say, however, the question arises as to whether this approach ensures the advanced development of musicianship.

Composing Music to Stories or Poems

The first three assignments focused on the use of everyday sounds or objects as material for the composition. In the following group of assignments, the starting points for a composition are stories or poems.

Assignment 1: Sound Scene with the Voice

In this assignment the students compose a piece on the basis of a comic or a picture story (Brassel, 2012, p. 105), which has a storyline but less text than fairy tales for example, which are also used in assignments especially for primary school.

The first assignment that is presented here is based on a *Peanuts* comic with Snoopy, which can be found online (https://images.app.goo.gl/hC98AWBBq8zihj996). The project is included in a textbook for secondary school (grade five to seven) and is part of a unit plan which is called: "Discover your voice." The assignment follows a lesson about Cathy Berberian's famous piece *Stripsody*. The assignment is to transfer the *Peanuts* comic to a choral piece. The students are asked to use the various expressive possibilities of the voice for this purpose. The process is divided into three tasks. In the first one, the students are required to get familiar with the comic. Then, they are asked to decide for which parts of the story they want to use words, and which parts they want to represent without words. As a tool they get a collection of ideas like: repeat syllables, words or group of words; speak rhythmically; sing without text. The third task is to decide on the final arrangement and form and to record the result.

A similar task is given to smaller children in a different book and is called "Sound puzzle" (Kotzian, 2014, pp. 12–15). Instead of a comic, Kotzian offers short picture stories about funny incidents (e.g., falling over a dog carrying a birthday cake). Because the assignment is meant for children at the beginning of primary school the task is first led by the teacher and the children choose a second story to compose the music themselves. They can also use their voice or instruments.

Assignment 2: In the Fog

Another text form that is often used for composition assignments is poems. This assignment is taken from a book about composing with small children in preschool or primary school (Reitinger, 2008, pp. 256–258).

The text was written based on a poem by the German poet Eduard Möricke. The poem consists of only four lines and the content is the following: the world is still sleeping in the fog and all the sounds are still dreaming. As soon as the fog lifts you can hear a lot. First of all, the text is presented in single verses and the task is to put it together in the right order. The group is asked to talk about the meaning of the poem and to collect associations, thoughts and ideas about the content. The teacher hides the instruments under a big cloth, which symbolizes the fog. It is taken away and each child has to choose an instrument and to experiment with it. The task is to produce "foggy sounds" or sounds connected to the associations that were collected before.

After exploring the sounds, the children are asked to create a "chain of sounds" in a group improvisation. One child has to conduct the improvisation by moving the white cloth, which symbolizes the fog. The other children have to react to the movement. They can discuss the meaning of certain movements and connect certain parameters with certain movements.

In the next task the children are asked to invent music which symbolizes things, animals, or people that could appear when the fog disappears. They are asked to present their results and the other children are asked to guess what appears out of the fog. In the next step, the children are asked to invent music that matches the form of the poem. The task is to make clear when the fog starts to disappear. After the presentation the children have to discuss how the others made the change clear.

The next task is to speak the poem and to find a rhythm. Afterward, this rhythm has to be transferred into a melody, using mallets or piano. The children can experiment with different scales like pentatonic, diatonic, or chromatic scales. For the presentation, one half of the group is asked to play the "chain of sounds" while the other children are asked to play their melodies as solos one after the other. The last task is to agree on an arrangement and to put all invented elements together.

Hans Schneider (2017, pp. 93–99) also suggests different poems to put them into music. He uses Dadaist poems, which are more suitable for an older age group, because the text and the form is more experimental and abstract than the poem in Reitinger's assignment.

Reflection 2

Setting texts and poems to music is a popular way to introduce students to composing at all ages. It is used both for finding adequate sounds to atmospheres and contents and for finding a form. Since a text has already a certain progression, the students do not have to invent a form and so they are given the possibility to focus on how such a progression can be represented musically. Depending on the text, these assignments can be used in all age groups. In setting Dadaist poems to music, a higher level of abstraction is required, and thus it is adequate for older age groups. The texts used for younger children are easier to grasp. In addition to narrations and poems, picture stories, comics, or illustrations to the text are often used. A picture story or a comic has another advantage, because the course of the story is still clear, but there are no words that can influence the composition.

Even though this type of assignment is less obviously linked to means of New Music, the results are still experimental, because the instructions often lead to results that are tonally and metrically free and can be described as a series of sound events.

Some question to what extent the result has an artistic quality, especially if the task neither attends to the text nor can stand on its own, detached from the text. Rather, the presented assignments try to ensure that the result is a piece of music that can stand on its own even without knowledge of the underlying story. Overall, it makes sense to orient the composition process to a text in educational contexts. In addition to texts, paintings or graphics are often chosen as starting points for compositions. This approach is helpful because students can orient on what they see as they select and organize sounds. The interpretation of graphic scores also is used as a starting point, since these offer creative freedom to the performers (Schneider, 2017, pp. 113–135). The advantage of images and scores over texts is that it is easier to detach from the template, because a painting may be less concrete than a storyline. Mostly, pictures from the 20th or 21st century are used, because they are already characterized by a high abstraction (Voit, 2018b).

Compositions as Models for Students' Creations

Assignment 1: El Cimarron—Hans Werner Henze

The assignment is based on the composition *El Cimarrón* by the German composer Hans Werner Henze (1926–2012), which is a piece for voice, guitar, flute, and percussion (Oberschmidt & Schläbitz, 2014, pp. 48–54). The setting of the piece is the Cuban War of Independence told from the perspective of a veteran, telling the story of his life. As students engage with a modern tonal language, they are encouraged to break free from their own normalized notions about music and expand their experiential space.

The first task is to read a part of the text that is called *Slavery*. The pupils read a comment about the composition that says that the content and the music merge to a unity. They are asked to discuss what kind of music they expect, based on this comment. After that they listen to Henze's composition and compare it with their expectations.

In the next task the pupils are confronted with the text that they are asked to set into music. The text has the title *The Escape*. In the first step they are asked to work with the text and to read it carefully, divide it into sections, collect ideas and associations to these sections.

The author identifies potential problems and gives advice on what teacher interventions might be needed. One hint is to advise the students to compose an introduction, interludes, and an outro to avoid only illustrating the words in the text.

After the students presented their own pieces, Jürgen Oberschmidt suggests they compare these with Henze's solution by writing reviews of their classmates' pieces. Even though this task centers on a political piece by Henze, it is not connected with Henze's visions of cultural education and community music (see the section in this chapter, "Historical Perspective on Composing in Schools in Germany").

Assignment 2: Les Quatre Coins—Erik Satie

This assignment is the end of a unit plan about Erik Satie's *Les quatre coins* (Brassel, 2012, p. 18). In this piece for piano Satie sets a movement game to music, which is based on a cat, chasing four mice that are in four corners. Every mouse is symbolized by one tone. The children analyze the composition and try to understand what happens in the game. Therefore, they learn the names of different tones and how these tones in different octaves are notated in a piano score. This shows how the tasks are often closely interwoven with teaching various other competencies, therefore composing for the sake of composing is not the only goal.

The children get the task to change Satie's composition (see Opportunity 1) or to compose a different story by using only five tones (see Opportunity 2). So, the results can't be compared with Satie's original composition, although they are based on his piece.

Opportunity 1

The students are asked to change Satie's storyline. First, they are asked to expand the section where the cat is teased by the mice, which is very short in the original composition. Afterward, they can expand the end of the composition by telling what happened to the other mice or they can change the end and are given three possibilities. But they can also think about their own ideas for a different end and realize them. The three possible ends that are suggested are the following: 1) The cat tries to catch a mouse again and again without succeeding. 2) The mice free their friend that was caught by the cat. 3) The mice put the cat to flight.

Opportunity 2

The pupils are asked to compose a piece for piano or another instrument by using only five different notes that are given (E, F, B, C, D). First, they are asked to invent a story that includes five roles, for example a policeman who hunts four bank robbers or a tamer in a circus who tames four tigers. They are asked to construct the different steps of the story. Afterward, the task is to invent adequate musical movements that match the actions and to arrange them in a musical form. In the last task the students are asked to notate the score and to present their piece.

Reflection 3

In this group of tasks, the connection to the Response tradition (see section in this chapter, "Historical Perspective on Composing in Schools in Germany") becomes obvious. The biggest difference is that it is not the composer of the reference work who works with the students, but the composer is, in a sense, represented by the teacher. The students are asked to create their own music inspired by music of other composers. The role of the reference composition is very different. In Assignment 1 the students set a part of the text in music which was also used by the composer. They listen to the original composition afterward. In the second assignment the children use the same material and they continue the composition or compose an extension after having analyzed the composition.

One aspect that may need to be critically considered is the comparison of the student compositions with the original composition, as suggested in the first assignment. This could give the impression that the original composition is the sample solution that the students can reach more or less. It creates a competition with the composer of the reference music. As a result, there is a danger that the students' compositions will be taken less seriously and be devalued.

The tasks presented in this section are certainly only a very small and exemplary selection. However, they served to illustrate how either traces of New Music are directly reflected in them or how single elements of New Music are being used (e.g., being metrically free; using experimental sounds). The reduction, which is necessary in pedagogical contexts, can easily result in rather embarrassing compositions, which can neither meet the demands of the students nor the demands of the teachers. However, some tasks could be presented in which this balancing act between artistic demand and simultaneous reduction succeeded very well.

RESEARCH ON COMPOSITION PEDAGOGY IN GERMANY

In this section, we want to provide an overview of current research in the field of composition pedagogy in Germany. We do not claim to offer a complete list, but rather to present some significant research foci.

There is much research that focuses on the theoretical and didactic examination of the field of composition pedagogy. Researchers have developed concepts and discuss issues of philosophy of music education (e.g., Handschick, 2015; Nimczik, 1991; Sachsse, 2020; Wallbaum, 2000; Ziegenmeyer, 2016). In this area, there are numerous publications by composers who structure the composition process based on their experience, offer reflections on different approaches and provide orientation for composers and teachers (e.g., Beck, 2020; Friedrich, 2016; Roszak, 2014; Schlothfeldt, 2009; Voit, 2018c). An initiative of the Musikakademie Schloss Weikersheim has been stimulating the discourse on composition pedagogy for secondary and community schools for several years through regular symposia and discussion groups (Jeunesses Musicales Deutschland [JMD], 2016; Schlothfeldt & Vandré, 2018; Vandré & Lang, 2011). In addition, Joana Grow (2018) published an overview of composing in primary schools in Germany.

There have been more and more empirical studies examining the field of composition pedagogy in recent years. Numerous funding lines were offered by the German federal ministry of education and research, the main aim of which is to promote teacher training and continuing education. From 2014 to 2017 the federal ministry funded the development and the testing of a program for further education. The training was offered to composers who were already working in the field of composition pedagogy or planning to work pedagogically. This training was accompanied by research analyzing the challenges the composers face in these projects (Rolle et al., 2018; Weidner et al., 2019). Furthermore, based on the data which were collected during the project, Julia Weber (2021) analyzed the influence of beliefs on the composer's actions and she describes how intervening in the compositional process of the students is a kind of taboo for the teaching composers.

ModusM is another research that is a cooperation between the Universities Bielefeld and Dortmund and the Universities of Musik in Freiburg and Luebeck. The long-term goal of ModusM is to develop concepts for music teacher education. Therefore, the researchers investigate the interactions and the decision-making in the processes of composition and improvisation (Buchborn et al., 2019; Kranefeld & Voit, 2020; Meisterernst, 2020; Theisohn & Buchborn, 2020). The choice of instruments (Langner, 2020) and the role of objects and things is researched as well within this project with a special focus on the use of digital media (Duve, 2020; Kranefeld et al., 2019). In addition, the role of portfolios in guiding and reflecting on compositional processes is explored (Ehring & Thienenkamp, 2020; Janczik & Voit, 2020).

In the project LINKO, which was funded by the German Federal Ministry of Education and Research from 2016 to 2019, the researchers analyzed teachers' interventions in composition processes using videos as observation data (Kranefeld et al., 2018). They distinguish between different patterns of interventions. Among other results, they describe a pattern of ambiguity that is typical for teachers' interventions (Kranefeld & Mause, 2020; Mause, 2020).

The project Future Songwriting (2018–2020) is an international project that was co-funded by the Creative Europe program of the European Union. The goal was to test a program for further education for teachers in Finland, Germany, and France, which was developed by three Finish artists (INTO School). The teachers were trained in the use of the GarageBand app for songwriting in the classroom. The project was accompanied by an evaluation and research focusing on the teachers' perspectives on composing with digital tools (Partti et al., 2021; Weber & Rolle, 2020).

Many research projects on music technology and digital media have been funded in recent years, some of them investigating issues of music production and music composition. The cooperative research project MuBiTec (Jörissen et al., 2019) focuses on music-making with apps on tablets and smartphones. One of the sub-studies (AppKOM) examines the effects of using such digital media technologies for composition in non-formal music education services on the development of musical competencies and related constructs. Based on a quasi-experimental research design songwriting with band instruments is compared to songwriting with apps on tablets. Research on digital media is often connected with research on music producing and songwriting (Ahner, 2020; Godau & Haenisch, 2019).

In Austria, Wilfried Aigner (2017) examined a project in electronic music production (*eCompose Austria*). He chose a design-based-research approach that aimed at the development of a teaching-learning environment based on research in the classroom. The results are, on the one hand, an intervention (concept and methods for teaching electronic music production) and, on the other hand, insights into students' compositional processes and the role of teachers. Thomas Gottschalk also chose a design-based research approach that focuses on how the students' abilities to reflect on what they compose is linked to the composition process itself (Gottschalk & Lehmann-Wermser, 2013; Gottschalk & Rolle, 2021). Thus, on the one hand, Gottschalk investigated how students discuss their collaborative compositions (see section in this chapter, "Historical Perspective on Composing in Schools in Germany" about initiating an "aesthetic argument" in the classroom) and how they can develop the needed music-related argumentative competence. On the other hand, the research contributes to composition pedagogy by developing an intervention that promotes the students' ability to compose. How composition provides opportunities for aesthetic experience and thereby contributing to music education was empirically examined by Elias Zill (2016).

Evaluation is part of many collaborative projects with composers visiting schools. Some results are of interest not only for the project evaluated. The project documentation and reflection on a response project in Essen is an example for this kind of research. It contributes to the development of composition projects that involve many different participants from different institutions (Schatt, 2009). Julia Wieneke (2016) interviewed experts on composition pedagogy in the field of New Music. From the analysis of the interviews, she developed quality criteria for such composition projects in New Music.

Conclusion

Things change quickly, and this chapter will soon need to be revised. It is only a snapshot. Composing is not yet firmly anchored in the German curricula, neither at the school level nor in music teacher education, and many teachers do not feel able to compose with the students. This is particularly true when the teachers are generalists who have not studied music. Furthermore, there is neither an agreement as to how to teach nor how to assess composition or, more fundamentally, if it is possible at all. This is a hindrance to strengthening the role of composition at least in German secondary school, where assessment as grading is seen to have an important function (Lehmann-Wermser, 2019). As a result, composing mainly exists in the form of projects and is rarely a natural part of music lessons. Curricula change gradually, however, and in recent years composing has been increasingly included. The current development is strongly driven by the process of digitization. Electronic music production and hip-hop are more and more integrated even though compositional techniques of New Music are still key for teaching composition. This results from the historical developments in German composition pedagogy (see section in this chapter, "Historical Perspective on Composing in Schools in Germany") and is visible in many assignments for music lessons (see section "Typical Composition Assignments and the Tradition of New Music"). However, this changes as students' and teachers' listening practices change and as digital media provide desirable opportunities for inclusive education, sound variety, easy access to recording, and distribution of compositions.

These developments are reflected in numerous research initiatives (see section in this chapter, "Research on Composition Pedagogy in Germany") even though it must be noted that research on composition pedagogy in Germany is only at the beginning and that there is a need for more international collaboration. So far, we know little about quality criteria for composition assignments and there are only a few suggestions and hints for teachers on how to accompany processes of composition. Issues of giving feedback and of evaluating composition should be the object of research. Although there is general agreement that composition ought to be linked to other teaching content, adequate methods and assignments are missing, such as how improvisation and composition can become part of ensemble classes or can be combined with music appreciation. Issues of cultural participation are discussed and there is no doubt that teaching composition should cover a variety of music cultures and promote cultural interchange but uncertainty exists as to how to find a sensitive approach to cultural encounters resulting in music that is worth listening to because it is, at least to some extent, based on understanding. Composition pedagogy in Germany needs to address these issues.

REFERENCES

Ahner, P. (2020). Learning environments and learning tasks with synthesizer apps in secondary schools. In A. Houmann & E. Sæther (Eds.), *EAS publications: Vol. 9. Make music matter: Music education meeting the needs of young learners* (pp. 225–240). Helbling.

Aigner, W. (2017). Komponieren zwischen Schule und Social Web. (1. Auflage). In *Augsburger Schriften: Vol. 144*. Wißner-Verlag.

Beck, T. T. (2020). *Ein Dreiklang ist kein Wald oder: Praxisschock Kompositionspädagogik? Sachdienliche Hinweise für Schule und Musikschule*. ConBrio.

Brassel, U. (Ed.). (2012). *Musikbuch* (1. Aufl., 1. Dr). Cornelsen.

Buchborn, T., Theisohn, E., & Treß, J. (2019). Kreative musikalische Handlungsprozesse erforschen. In V. Weidner & C. Rolle (Eds.), *Musikpädagogische Forschung: Praxen und Diskurse aus Sicht musikpädagogischer Forschung* (1st ed., pp. 69–85). Waxmann.

Dessau, P. (1968). *Musikarbeit in der Schule*. Verl. Neue Musik.

Duve, J. (2020). Komponieren am Raster: Fallanalytische Perspektiven auf Prozesse des Musik-Erfindens mit digitalen Medien. In U. Kranefeld & J. Voit (Eds.), *Musikunterricht im Modus des Musik-Erfindens* (pp. 97–110). Waxmann Verlag GmbH.

Ehring, C., & Thienenkamp, H. (2020). Gestalterische Begleitung von Kompositionsprozessen mittels Portfolioarbeit. In U. Kranefeld & J. Voit (Eds.), *Musikunterricht im Modus des Musik-Erfindens* (pp. 153–168). Waxmann Verlag GmbH.

Friedrich, B. (2016). *Klangwelten des 21. Jahrhunderts in der musikalischen Bildung: Kompositionspädagogik in Theorie und Praxis. Schriftenreihe Didaktik in Forschung und Praxis: Band 86*. Verlag Dr. Kovač.

Frisius, R., & Arbeitsgemeinschaft Curriculum Musik. (1972). *Sequenzen—Musik Sekundarstufe 1: Elemente zur Unterrichtsplanung. Musik Sekundarstufe I*. Klett.

Godau, M., & Haenisch, M. (2019). How popular musicians learn in the postdigital age: Ergebnisse einer Studie zur Soziomaterialität des Songwritings von Bands in informellen Kontexten. In V. Weidner & C. Rolle (Eds.), *Musikpädagogische Forschung: Praxen und Diskurse aus Sicht musikpädagogischer Forschung* (pp. 51–67). Waxmann.

Gottschalk, T., & Lehmann-Wermser, A. (2013). Iteratives Forschen am Beispiel der Förderung musikalisch-ästhetischer Diskursfähigkeit. In M. Komorek & S. Prediger (Eds.), *Fachdidaktische Forschungen: Bd. 5. Der lange Weg zum Unterrichtsdesign.* (pp. 63–78). Waxmann.

Gottschalk, T., & Rolle, C. (2021). Reflexionsfähigkeit als Dimension musikalischer Kompetenz? In K. Schilling-Sandvoß & M. Spychiger (Eds.), *Festschrift für Werner Jank.* (pp. 139–153). Helbling.

Grow, J. (2018). *Komponieren im Musikunterricht der Grundschule. Empirische Forschung zur Musikpädagogik*. Lit.

Handschick, M. (2015). *Musik als „Medium der sich selbst erfahrenden Wahrnehmung". (1., 2015). Schriften der Hochschule für Musik Freiburg: Vol. 3*. Olms, Georg.

Henze, H. W. (1984). *Musik und Politik: Schriften u. Gespräche 1955–1984* (edited by Jens Brockmeier, 2nd edition). Dt. Taschenbuch-Verl.

Henze, H.-W. (Ed.). (1986). *Lehrgänge Erziehung in Musik: Neue Aspekte der musikalischen Ästhetik III*. Fischer.

Hickey, M. (2012). *Music outside the lines: Ideas for composing in K–12 music classrooms*. Oxford University Press.

Janczik, L., & Voit, J. (2020). Das Portfolio als Instrument musikpädagogischer Unterrichtsforschung. In U. Kranefeld & J. Voit (Eds.), *Musikunterricht im Modus des Musik-Erfindens* (pp. 127–152). Waxmann Verlag GmbH.

Jeunesses Musicales Deutschland (Ed.). (2016). *Musik erfinden: Symposion zur Kompositionspädagogik*. JMD

Jöde, F. (1928). *Das schaffende Kind: Eine Anweisung für Lehrer und Freunde der Jugend: 1. Teil: Zur Theorie des Schaffens 2. Teil: Aus der Praxis des Schaffens*. Kallmeyer.

Jörissen, B., Schmiedl, F., Möller, E., Research Group DiKuBi-Meta, Subproject 1, Godau, M., Eusterbrock, L., Fiedler, D., Haenisch, M., Hasselhorn, J., Knigge, J., Krebs, M., Nagel, M., Rolle, C., Stenzel, M., & Research Group MuBiTec. (2019) Digitalization and arts education: New empirical approaches. In B. Münzberger, S. Konietzko & Goudis, Julia (Eds.),

Contemporary Research Topics in Arts Education: German-Dutch Perspectives (pp. 22–29). Rat für kulturelle Bildung e.V. https://www.flipsnack.com/RatKulturelleBildung/contempor ary-research-topics-in-arts-education/full-view.html

Kertz-Welzel, A. (2005). General music education in Germany today: A look at how popular music is engaging students. *General Music Today, 18*(2), 14–16.

Kotzian, R. (2014). *Musik erfinden mit Kindern: Elementares Improvisieren, Arrangieren und Komponieren. Ausgabe mit DVD*. Schott Music.

Kranefeld, U., & Mause, A.-L. (2020). Anleitung zum Eigen-Sinn? Ergebnisse einer videobasierten Studie zur Begleitung von Gruppenprozessen des Musik-Erfindens. In S. Timm, J. Costa, C. Kühn, & A. Scheunpflug (Eds.), *Kulturelle Bildung* (pp. 113–128). Waxmann Verlag GmbH.

Kranefeld, U., Mause, A.-L., & Duve, J. (2019). Zur Materialität von Prozessen des Musik-Erfindens. In V. Weidner & C. Rolle (Eds.), *Musikpädagogische Forschung. Praxen und Diskurse aus Sicht musikpädagogischer Forschung* (1st ed., pp. 35–50). Waxmann.

Kranefeld, U., Mause, A.-L., & Meisterernst, M. (2018). *Zur Erforschung von Lernbegleitung in Gruppenkompositionsprozessen*. JMD. https://www.kompaed.de/artikel/handlungsfelder/ ulrike-kranefeld-anna-lisa-mause-miriam-meisterernst-zur-erforschung-von-lernbegleit ung-in-gruppenkompositionsprozessen/

Kranefeld, U., & Voit, J. (Eds.). (2020). *Musikunterricht im Modus des Musik-Erfindens*. Waxmann Verlag GmbH. https://doi.org/10.31244/9783830991700

Küntzel, B. (2012). *Kolibri: Musikbuch ¾ (Serie A)*. Schroedel.

Langner, J. (2020). „Wenn ihr da 'n Keyboard wollt": Bedeutungszuschreibungen bei der Auswahl von Instrumenten im Kontext des Musik-Erfindens. In U. Kranefeld & J. Voit (Eds.), *Musikunterricht im Modus des Musik-Erfindens* (pp. 81–96). Waxmann Verlag GmbH.

Lehmann-Wermser, A. (2019). Assessment in German Music Education. In T. S. Brophy & A. Lehmann-Wermser (Eds.), *The Oxford handbook of assessment policy and practice in music education, Volume 1* (pp. 233–252). Oxford University Press.

Lehmann-Wermser, A., Weishaupt, H., Konrad, U., & Bertelsmann Stiftung. (2020). *Musikunterricht in der Grundschule*. Bertelsmann Stiftung. https://doi.org/10.11586/2020007

Mause, A.-L. (2020). „Du könntest das einbauen, wenn du die Katze mitbringst": Das Ringen um Vorgaben innerhalb von Prozessen des Musik-Erfindens. In U. Kranefeld & J. Voit (Eds.), *Musikunterricht im Modus des Musik-Erfindens* (pp. 55–65). Waxmann Verlag GmbH.

Meisterernst, M. (2020). „Dann spiele ich lieber, was es schon gibt": Fallanalytische Betrachtungen von Schülervorstellungen zum Komponieren. In U. Kranefeld & J. Voit (Eds.), *Musikunterricht im Modus des Musik-Erfindens* (pp. 111–126). Waxmann Verlag GmbH.

Meyer-Denkmann, G. (1972). *Struktur und Praxis neuer Musik im Unterricht: Experiment und Methode* (1.–5. Tsd.). Rote Reihe: Vol. 43. Universal Edition.

Meyer-Denkmann, G. (1977). *Experiments in sound: New directions in musical education for young children*. Universal Edition.

Nimczik, O. (1991). *Spielräume im Musikunterricht: Pädagogische Aspekte musikalischer Gestaltungsarbeit*. Peter Lang.

Oberschmidt, J., & Schläbitz, N. (Eds.). (2014). *EinFach Musik: Komponieren und improvisieren im Musikunterricht*. Schöningh.

Orff, C. (1978). *The Schulwerk* (M. Murray, Trans.) [Schulwerk. Elementare Musik. Tutzing 1976]. *Dokumentation Carl Orff und sein Werk: Vol. 3*. Schott Music Corporation.

Partti, H., Weber, J., & Rolle, C. (2021). Learning a skill, or learning to learn? Supporting teachers' professional development in music education technology. *Journal of Music, Technology & Education, 14*(2), 123–139. https://doi.org/10.1386/jmte_00037_1

Reitinger, R. (Ed.). (2008). *Musik erfinden: Komposition von Kindern als Ausdruck ihres musikalischen Vorstellungsvermögens.* ConBrio.

Rolle, C. (1999). *Musikalisch-ästhetische Bildung: Über die Bedeutung ästhetischer Erfahrung für musikalische Bildungsprozesse. Perspektiven zur Musikpädagogik und Musikwissenschaft* Bosse.

Rolle, C. (2014). Ästhetischer Streit als Medium des Musikunterrichts: Zur Bedeutung des argumentierenden Sprechens über Musik für ästhetische Bildung. *Art Education Research 5*(9). (pp. 1–8). https://blog.zhdk.ch/iaejournal/files/2014/12/AER9_rolle.pdf

Rolle, C., & Wallbaum, C. (2011). Ästhetischer Streit im Musikunterricht. In J. Kirschenmann, C. Richter, & K. Spinner (Eds.), *Reden über Kunst: Projekte und Ergebnisse aus der fachdidaktischen Forschung zu Musik, Kunst, Literatur* (pp. 507–535). Kopaed.

Rolle, C., Weidner, V., Weber, J., & Schlothfeldt, M. (2018). Role expectations and role conflicts within collaborative composing projects. In C. Christophersen & A. Kenny (Eds.), *Musician-teacher collaborations: Altering the chord* (pp. 50–61). Routledge.

Roszak, S. (2014). Elementares Komponieren: Ein kompositionsdidaktisches Modell zum Erfinden experimenteller Musik. *Zeitschrift Ästhetische Bildung, 6*(2). (pp. 1–23). http://zaeb.net/wordpress/wp-content/uploads/2020/12/86-345-1-PB.pdf

Sachsse, M. (2020). Musik-Erfinden im Zeichen des Kreativitätsdispositivs. In U. Kranefeld & J. Voit (Eds.), *Musikunterricht im Modus des Musik-Erfindens* (pp. 11–42). Waxmann Verlag GmbH.

Schatt, P. W. (Ed.). (2009). *Unser Faust: Meet the composer.* (1. Aufl.). ConBrio.

Schlothfeldt, M. (2009). *Komponieren im Unterricht. Folkwang-Studien: Vol. 9.* Olms.

Schlothfeldt, M. (2018). *Eine Übung.* JMD https://www.kompaed.de/artikel/materialien/matthias-schlothfeldt-eine-uebung/

Schlothfeldt, M., & Vandré, P. (Eds.). (2018). *Weikersheimer Gespräche zur Kompositionspädagogik.* ConBrio.

Schmidinger, H. (2020). *Kompositionspädagogik: Theoretische Grundlegung als Fachrichtung der Musikpädagogik.* Wißner-Verlag.

Schneider, H. (2017). *Musizieraktionen: Frei, streng, lose: Anregungen zur V/Ermittlung experimenteller Musizier; Und Komponierweisen.* Pfau.

Schütz, V. (1981). Zur Methodik rockmusikalischen Musizierens im Klassenverband: Teil 1. *Musik & Bildung* (7/8), 464–469.

Schütz, V. (1982). *Rockmusik-eine Herausforderung für Schüler und Lehrer.* Isensee.

Theisohn, E., & Buchborn, T. (2020). Moldau oder Waschmaschine? Von kontroversen Aushandlungen zu einer konstruktiven kompositorischen Gruppenarbeit. In U. Kranefeld & J. Voit (Eds.), *Musikunterricht im Modus des Musik-Erfindens* (pp. 67–80). Waxmann Verlag GmbH.

Vandré, P., & Lang, B. (Eds.). (2011). *Komponieren mit Schülern: Konzepte–Förderung–Ausbildung.* ConBrio.

Venus, D. (1969). *Unterweisung im Musikhören.* Noetzel.

Voit, J. (2018a). *30 Jahre Response: Historischer Rückblick und Typologie aktueller Erscheinungsformen.* JMD https://www.kompaed.de/artikel/praxisbeispiele/johannes-voit-30-jahre-response/

Voit, J. (2018b). *Die rätselhaften Landschaften des Monsieur Tanguy: Ein Kompositionsprojekt zu Bildern des französischen Surrealismus.* JMD https://www.kompaed.de/artikel/materialien/johannes-voit-die-raetselhaften-landschaften-des-monsieur-tanguy/

Voit, J. (2018c). *Komponieren zu Bildern: Kompositionspädagogische Überlegungen zu Bildender Kunst als Auslöser für Gruppenkompositionsprozesse.* JMD https://www.kompaed.de/artikel/praxisbeispiele/johannes-voit-komponieren-zu-bildern/

Wallbaum, C. (2000). *Produktionsdidaktik im Musikunterricht: Perspektiven zur Gestaltung ästhetischer Erfahrungssituationen. Perspektiven zur Musikpädagogik und Musikwissenschaft: Vol. 27.* Bosse.

Weber, J. (2021). *Stimmigkeit und Dissonanz: Zum Zusammenhang zwischen Überzeugungen von Komponist*innen und ihrem musikpädagogischen Handeln.* Waxmann.

Weber, J., & Rolle, C. (2020). Überzeugungen von Lehrkräften zu Musik und Technologie. In K. Kaspar, M. Becker-Mrotzek, S. Hofhues, J. König, & D. Schmeinck (Eds.), *Bildung, Schule, Digitalisierung* (1st ed., pp. 109–114). Waxmann.

Weidner, V., Weber, J., & Rolle, C. (2019). Kompositionsprozesse in pädagogischer Praxis oder Der „Spagat zwischen Freiheit, Laufenlassen und die Zügel in die Hand nehmen". In J. Ludwig & H. Ittner (Eds.), *Research. Künstlerisch-pädagogische Weiterbildungen für Kunst- und Kulturschaffende: Innovative Ansätze und Erkenntnisse* (pp. 73–96). Springer VS.

Wieneke, J. (2016). *Zeitgenössische Musik vermitteln in Kompositionsprojekten an Schulen. Studien und Materialien zur Musikwissenschaft: Band 88.* Georg Olms Verlag.

Ziegenmeyer, A. (2016). Komponieren: Eine Chance für den inklusiven Musikunterricht? *Diskussion Musikpädagogik (70),* 36–42.

Zill, E. (2016). *Den eigenen Ohren folgen: Musikalisch-ästhetische Erfahrungen im Kontext produktionsorientierter Schulprojekte. Empirische Forschung zur Musikpädagogik: Band 7.* Lit.

CHAPTER 38

EVERYONE CAN MAKE MUSIC CREATIVELY

The Process of Implementing Ongakudukuri in Japanese Music Education

TAICHI AKUTSU

IN Japan, music is considered a universal phenomenon. Music does not exist to be isolated in concert halls, specialized venues, or music classrooms. Rather, it is found throughout the culture as is revealed through formal and informal traditions within families and communities. While some people find music in the simple sound of wind—from a soft summer breeze to a strong, howling blow, others prefer their music to be more conceptual in nature. Works such as *4'33"* by American composer John Cage (1912–1992) have been widely accepted in Japan and have been considered models of progressive composition since the 1980s.

MUSIC IN THE DAILY LIFE OF JAPANESE PEOPLE

Music is embedded in Japanese child-adult communication as a part of their daily lives. Babies are sung lullabies and occasionally caregivers create songs and chants for children in an improvisational manner. Children are also surrounded by various nursery rhymes and traditional folk songs called *warabeuta*. Many *warabeuta* contain very simple imitation and/or call-and-response sections in a narrow range of pitches. Similar to *warabeuta*, in Japan, for example, kindergarten teachers often call a child's name with a musical chant daily. For example, "Nene-chan" (*la-so-la*) is used to call a female child's name, so that the child will answer "Ha-a-i" (*la-so-la*) which means "Yes." Another example is found in *kakurendbo*, a popular version of hide-and-seek. During the game, the seeker asks the one who is hiding, "Mo-ii-kai" (*fa-la-so*), so that the person who is already hiding answers "Mo-ii-yo" (*fa-la-so*) to indicate that they are ready to play. The pattern is very popular among Japanese people and is often played through the hand clapping of all attendees at various sorts of events. It is usually called *sansannanabyoshi*, meaning three-three-seven rhythmic pattern. It is especially popular for school children because it is always used to cheer sports activities at schools and in communities (Ishigami, 2018). The pattern is often performed independently by a team's cheering section, again, through hand clapping (Ishigami, 2016).

Japanese youths are drawn to a variety of popular musics. Most listen to Japanese popular music, "J-pop," which is created by young artists and amateur musicians. Recently, many young people have begun to enthusiastically embrace the Korean popular music known as "K-pop." Moreover, many Japanese young people listen to anime songs that use *vocaloid* (a modern singing synthesizer) partnered with visual images. Nearly all populations of Japan listen to music, a large number perform music, and some even compose.

The Japanese calendar is full of celebrations marked by *matsuri*, the carnivals of Japan. These events are an expression of culture and always feature music consisting of the use of voices or singing, playing instruments, and dancing. For example, there is a famous carnival called *Awaordori* in Tokushima in Shikoku Island. *Awa* is the former name for Tokushima Prefecture, and *odori* simply means dance. In early August every year, in Tokushima, dancers and audiences come to gather in the thousands to participate and watch this dance, which dates back 400 years in the area. The nickname comes from the lyrics to a common dance song, which translates as follows: "Fools dance and fools watch; if both are fools, you might as well dance." The groups dance through designated spectator areas in a procession, playing traditional musical instruments called *narimono*. In the Taisho period, even the violin was considered a part of *narimono* along with Japanese traditional instruments.

The Asian Concept of Creativity as a Foundation of Japanese Music Education

Surprisingly, the Asian view of creativity has an explicit connection to Japanese music education, especially creative music-making. From an Asian perspective, creativity is more about the process than the result. The process includes connecting to a larger reality by reconfiguring existing elements from the past. Thus, the Asian view is that tradition is not the opposite of creating (Lubart, 2010), but part of the process. Confucian philosophy describes learning as an ultimate human pleasure. People are meant to learn from the past reflectively so to discover a new meaning or personal understanding (Koyasu, 2010). Similarly, in India, creativity is considered as a natural desire of human beings "to renew and transform pre-existing knowledge to adjust their environment suit to them" (Misra, Srivastava & Misra, 2006, p. 424). Koyasu (2010) suggests that invention will only occur by reviewing the past, not just to acquire knowledge or skills, but to construct and develop a future with creative insight.

Yamada (2002) explains that imitation or analogy is considered central to the re-creating process. In the Edo era (1603–1868), a type of woodblock painting called *Ukiyo-e* became very popular among ordinary people. In fact, the way to learn how to draw the *Ukiyo-e* was exclusively through imitation. Evidence of how people in Edo learned the *Ukiyo-e* by imitation is drawn from the fact that there were many *Ukiyo-e* of beautiful women drawn by different artists, but these paintings share similar structure. Although there is some uniqueness in the paintings, artists imitated each other's work and original insights are based on the similar framework. This process was common, though there was no obligation or restriction requiring imitation at the time. Consequently, Runco (2007) argues that Katsushika Hokusai (1760–1849), an *Ukiyo-e* painter in the Edo era, exemplifies various aspects of creativity in traditional Japan, and suggests that those very similar paintings were accepted by the Japanese culture because of their common structures. In fact, Hokusai's exceptional ability to draw with great accuracy was learned by this same type of imitation. He drew *Fuji* in the traditional style of *Ukiyo-e*, yet his paintings are conceived to be truly creative. These views of creating by imitation are deeply rooted in the learning process of Japanese traditional art. Imitating first, adding new ideas, elaborating details, and finally finding one's own manner of expression comprise the traditional conception of Japanese creativity. These processes are quite like the use of imitation and call-and-response to elaborate and to expand on pre-existing musical fragments.

The Processes of Re-Creating in Learning and Teaching

The traditional Japanese approach to learning and teaching emphasizes children's free and structured play. Wilson (2006), describing the work of Zeami, notes that in approaching art, the Japanese avoid feeding any specific instructions to young beginner students. Back in the 500s, the first pedagogy book of Japanese *noh*, a dramatic art form comprised essentially of mime or role playing and poetic chanting, was written by Zeami, a *noh* actor, teacher, and aesthetician. Zeami described *noh* teaching and learning in terms of developmental stages ranging from early childhood to adult. Although Zeami suggested age seven as "the time to begin this art," children younger than 12 or 13 years of age should not be criticized or given specific instructions on how to sing or dance in the lessons (Wilson, 2006). Zeami described how children could mimic, dance, and sing spontaneously as they wished, but "should be left to perform" as they will or the children lose heart and the natural flow of the performance (Wilson, 2006, p. 63). The book continues to draw the developmental stage of *noh* learning as a lifelong process though the sixth decade and described the importance of understanding *noh* as a total art form. Indeed, the emphasis of the book was on acquiring flowering spirit of the *noh* with a subtle nuance, "with a kind of grace with its unique quality of the performance" (Wilson, p. 147).

According to Ikuta (2007), there is almost no "how to" or "step-by-step" instruction available for students learning Japanese traditional art, dance, music, or martial arts. Instead, students experience the art by being with a teacher and imitating the teacher's performance, as well as the attitude toward the art-making. Ikuta (2011) defines *Kata*, a basic form of learning in Japanese traditional art, as an ability to adapt teachers' art as the total idea. The element of imitation differs from simple mimicry because the adaptation process requires students to possess intrinsic motivation, passion, commitment, and critical thinking skills (Ikuta, 2011). Yamada (2002) describes this learning process as "mindful imitation," and interprets it as a Japanese perspective of creative learning. Consequently, in traditional Japan, creativity is seen as an adapting process and as a way of learning from each other. As will be shown later in this chapter, the approach is closely related to Japanese composition pedagogy, *ongakudukuri*. In music education, children are introduced to composition through a play-oriented introduction followed by listening to various musical genres, and then students create music based on what they have learned.

Finally, there is a connection between Asian notions of creativity and the Western perspectives that recognize children's creativity in a social context rather than as an individual trait. Although many creativity scholars have agreed to define creativity as novel and useful (Amabile, 1996) or novel, appropriate, and high quality (Matlin, 2009), there have been controversies and differing opinions on the definition of creativity in the everyday sense. Some creativity researchers suggest that there are certain cognitive universals to support the view that everyone is creative, including children (Runco, 2007; Richard, 2009). Csikszentmihalyi (1990) reserves the larger-C creativity for geniuses or especially talented people, while "the neat things children often say, or the creativity we all share just because we have a mind and we can think" is described as a smaller-c creativity. From the standpoint of social psychology, Amabile (1996) points out the importance of conducting research on a non-eminent level of creativity as a normal cognitive ability in our everyday lives. Many subcategories have been added to describe the subjective and personal creativity of our daily lives as mini-c creativity or everyday creativity (Kozbelt, Beghetto, and Runco, 2010). "Mini-c creativity captures the idea that even very young individuals and those without a large amount of knowledge construct personal understanding of the world" (Ward and Kolomyts, 2010, p. 96). In addition, Richard (2009) explains everyday creativity as a universal capability both for adults and children, noting: "We humans are often 'everyday creative,' or we would not even be alive. To cope with changing environments, we improvise, we flexibly adapt. . . . and change the environment to suit us" (p. 3).

Everyday creativity is a way of life and learners generate new perspectives by using their own observations and experiences to creatively adapt.

CREATIVITY, THE JAPANESE CURRICULUM, AND INSTRUCTIONAL CHALLENGES

The Japanese Ministry of Education, Culture, Sports, Science and Technology (MEXT, 2007) emphasizes the enhancement of children's creativity and describes that developing rich feelings and the ability to express oneself by expressing experiences and thoughts is crucial to the education of children. Specifically, the Japanese Course of Kindergarten (MEXT, 2007) addresses the influence of creativity as follows:

> As children often express themselves in a simple manner, teachers should encourage them to enjoy expressing themselves in various childlike ways by being receptive to this kind of expression and by acknowledging the willingness of the children to express themselves.

The intent of this guidance is supported by Young's (2003) research in early childhood education, in which young children's spontaneous voice play revealed original verbal phrases that might be considered chants on simple rhythmic and melodic ideas. Unfortunately, the training of Japanese music education specialists tends to overlook the creative aspects of music learning. Rather, institutions follow a Western-conservatory model which tends to favor piano technique, playing, and skill-building (Shinkai, 2012) in response to the high demand for piano performance by child care workers (Yasuda and Nagao, 2010). This process prepares teachers to engage children in singing performance accompanied by the teacher "but not to compose" (Burnard, 2012, p. 1). Therefore, while Japanese curriculum documents[1] emphasize the importance of creativity, teacher training courses leave little room for "variety, independence, creativity and sense of identity" (Burnard, 2012, p. 1).

THE EVOLVING JAPANESE "COURSE OF STUDY"

Professor Hajime Takasu served as the Senior Curriculum Specialist at the Japanese Ministry of Education, Culture, Sports, Science and Technology (MEXT) from 2003–2010. In 2005, he was charged with the task of revising the "Course of Study" and overseeing the creation of a new "Course of Study for Music." Takasu described the change in focus from the existing curriculum to the new version to be about creativity. This section overviews Takasu's 2016 description of how the Japanese government nurtures children's creativity and what kind of creativity it targets.

Historical Overview of the "Course of Study"

Since 1958, the Course of Study has been revised in every decade. Although early versions of the curriculum gave some attention to children's creativity, there has been an ongoing process to push creativity into the school music curriculum in Japan. In 1989 the Course of Study for Music specifically introduced creative music-making activity. Content was drawn from John Paynter's *Sound and Silence*. In addition to its focus on creativity, the Courses of Study developed in 1989 and 1998 tried to change from teacher-centered teaching to student-centered learning though the inclusion of creative musical activity (Takasu, 2016). Takasu recalled his experience as follows:

> Most school teachers from elementary to high school level could not understand the intention of the Course of Study. Indeed, school teachers persisted in singing, in which if teachers really understood music itself and could draw forth students' interpretation, singing should have been beneficial musical learning, but most singing activities were carried out through teachers' instruction such as encouraging precise pitch, rhythm, pronunciation, and articulation before nurturing students' motivations to sing positively. As a result, school music fell into just a reproduction of written notation. Other musical activities such as playing instruments, composing, and appraising have been implemented slightly or not at all, although the conditions were contrary to the Course of Study. (Takasu, 2016, p. 3)

The Minister of MEXT submitted a request to the Central Council for Education in February 2005 seeking a revision of the Course of Study. At the same time, a swift review of laws related to the Course of Study were undertaken. The legal foundations of the Course of Study are endowed by three hierarchical acts under the constitution: the Basic Act of Education; the School Education Law; and the Regulation of School Education Law, which regulates the number of lessons of each subject (Takasu, 2016). Takasu describes the influence of 21st Century Skills on the Basic Act of Education and the School Education Law in Japan:

> We need to look at 21st Century Skills, before glancing over the influence on they have had on Japanese education laws. 21st Century Skills are, as you may well know, very famous among educators and are a predominant idea at a worldwide level. Therefore, I would like to very briefly mention the outline of the skills. . . . Keywords should be "knowledge-based society," "globalization," "society for sustainable development" and "diversification of vocation." These keywords come from social problems, which each country faces, such as energy affairs, population expansion, declining birth rates, and aging populations. These social problems are pressing matters. Every country needs to collaborate to resolve these matters by using ICT as a tool and the basic skills for problem-solving, judging, and expressing of one's thinking will be required of children. From the viewpoint of creativity, which is the first skill of 21st Century Skills, the nest society does not need homogeneous human resources but rather creative workers who create new ideas or develop new connections of which

others have never thought, and who become those who restructure the social status quo. The ideas of 21st Century Skills exerted influence on the reform of the Basic Act of Education in 2006, which had never been executed before in the postwar period. As far as "creativity," the preceding sentences of the Basic Act of Education refers to creativity twice in the limited three paragraphs. In terms of the School Education Law, which was reformed to a large degree and first executed after World War II, set up as a new article which regulates children's abilities and achievements acquire through school education. This article says that teachers are to make children acquire basic knowledge and skills, and nurture children's thinking, judging, expressing and other abilities needed for problem-solving using such knowledge and skills. We can find out the similarities between 21st Century Skills and the School Education Law. As the School Education Law was reformed in 2007, we can see [that] the influences of 21st Century Skills appeared around 2000." (Takasu, 2016, pp. 4–5)

To reflect the language of education law, the areas of Expression and Appreciation were renamed as Music-Making. This new area included singing, instrument playing, creative music-making, and appraising (Takasu, 2016).

Further, MEXT strongly recommended that teachers implement the creative music-making entitled *ongakudukuri*. This consisted of improvising, including sound playing or music playing adhering to specific rules, and composing based on musical structures to develop sounds into music (Takasu, 2016). At the same time, MEXT also recommended teachers implement appraising, as students can gain many ideas and come to understand the structures of music, which will become the basis of music that students will make (Takasu, 2016). Takasu recalled the process and described the rationale:

> Students cannot create music [in a] vacuum. Through creative music-making, students will understand how sounds lead to music. As a result, students can realize what music is, and how to create music. In realizing and processing, students encourage themselves through thinking, decision-making, and self-expression skills, so they can be creators who create the next music culture. Furthermore, as students understand what music is and the processing sounds become music, they can re-create existent music through their new interpretation with an affirmative attitude. Also, traditional music must be important not only as a basis for thinking new ideas but also identities as Japanese. Teachers need to teach traditional music not to bring students up as the inheritors but creators. We need to teach students how to develop their new music based on traditional music. Such a viewpoint has been forgotten in school music education. The current Course of Study, therefore, reinforces the content of traditional music. (Takasu, 2016, p. 6)

Since 1998, MEXT has not prescribed instructional methods. MEXT concentrates on the development of subject matter by local committees of education and allows local committees of education to identify the appropriate methods for their own students according to the character of their locality. Nevertheless, in terms of creative music-making, those activities have been done in groups in general. Therefore, it is difficult to pursue individual improvising and composing activities in Japan. As Takasu (2016) notes, students working in groups can share ideas with each other and discover new things which they might not learn on their own. Teachers appreciate the efficiency of group activities for music learning as group work is common in Japanese education.

IMPLEMENTING ONGAKUDUKURI: AN INTERVIEW WITH PROFESSOR YUKIKO TSUBONOU

Professor Yukiko Tsubonou has advocated for the importance of enhancing musical creativity in children since the beginning of her career and has taken part in spreading "Creative Music-Making" through music lessons at the kindergarten, school, and university levels in Japan. Through her activities based on Creative Music-Making, she made several observations, including the idea that people need some rules, such as repetition or Q&A, to create music. It is difficult to work with musical elements, such as timbre or rhythm, without some form of guidance, as the rules that bind music are the foundations of musical traditions in various cultures (Tsubonou, 2019). Other observations are revealed in Professor Tsubonou's interview responses.[2]

> Q: *Why do we call creative music-making Ongakudukuri instead of calling it as composition or improvisation?*
> A: Originally, there used to be a direction naming music-making as composition, but I insisted that it should be creative music-making. I especially emphasized the word "creative" in the process and in the sentence. When it came to translate the sentence into Japanese, we first named them as *sozotekiongakugakushu* or *sozoteki ongakudukuri*. But the name was too long and too formal, so we decided to simply call it *ongakudukuri*. We made the word shorter!
> Q: *What did you most emphasize in the process of designing the curriculum of ongakudukuri?*
> A: Very important point! First, we put emphasis on including all musical genres such as contemporary music, classical music, popular music, Japanese traditional music, and world music. By broadening horizons, learners can use all different musical ideas to make music in *ongakudukuri*. Second, as for musical materials, *ongakudukuri* can include any sounds found in our environment. Third, we also emphasize the element of improvisation. Lastly, and most importantly, we consider creativity as a foundation and an essential element in *ongakudukuri*, and in music education in general. I want students to consider *ongakudukuri*, not only for acquiring specific skills or knowledge, but I want them to understand *ongakudukuri* to create their own music for their own expression. For example,

in *ongakudukuri*, we would not ask them to master music theory or knowledge of harmony and such, but I want them to create music even though the work is very simple and a construct of their own musical world. To do so, creativity becomes the most important key, I think. Therefore, when we are asked what to teach in and through *ongakudukuri*, the underlying answer is to nurture creativity.

Q: *What was the root and when did an original thought come to your mind to develop the idea of ongakudukuri? How did you feel the necessity of creative music-making in Japanese music education?*

A: Well, if I should think about the roots in my experience, that would go back to my university years. In my years at Geidai, one of the most historical conservatories in Japan, I pursued improvisational music-making with my fellows. For me, my life at the university was not that exciting. I wanted to try much more exciting things. At the art festival at the university, I wanted to try something like the avant-garde. It was back in the year of 1968.

Q: *Wow. What kinds of experimentation did you try back then?*

A: Well, we performed John Cage, Steve Reich, Moroi's *Shakuhachi* and *Viwa*, Toru Takemitsu, Shuko Mizuno of Chiba University, Takehisa Kosugi, Yuji Takahashi, and Toshi Ichiyanagi. Mizuno and Kosugi were my fellow learners, and their music was in the direction of avant-garde. Kosugi even used an electric fan and several microphones hanging from the ceiling, made the sound of howling and considered this music. The program of the concert included *Five Pieces for Shakuhachi Chikurai* and *Five Dialogues*, Makoto Moroi; *Music for Amplified Toy Piano*, John Cage; *Piano Phase for Two Pianos*, Steve Reich; *Cross-Talk for Two Bandneons & Tape Music*, Toru Takemitsu; *Chromamorphe II*, Yuji Takahashi; *Autonomy for voice*, Shuko Mizuno; *Mano-Daruma*, electronic (first performance in Japan), Takehisa Kosugi; and the opera *Singing about Tadanori Yokoo*, Toshi Ichiyanagi.

Q: *This sounds very exciting. Were there any professors who supported the avant-garde direction or who taught contemporary music as a regular curriculum of the conservatory?*

A: Not at all. I was one of the producers to create such a movement and sensation. I also performed by singing.

Q: *Was there written music with notation?*

A: It was mostly not like regular notation. It was popular in the music world. Do you know Steve Reich? The second premiere of his piano concerto, entitled *Piano Phase*, was in my concert in Japan!

Q: *Are there other beginnings of your involvement with composition or contemporary music?*

A: I composed in my childhood in my elementary years. I was age 10 in . . . fourth grade back in 1958. Back then, my parents built a new house in the suburbs, and I transferred to an elementary school from the fourth grade. The new house had the piano. In fact, I had been learning the piano, but my old house just had an organ, and I didn't practice much. My new environment at home pushed me to practice piano and to compose. I made a piece for solo piano at this time. I remembered that I borrowed the chords from the pieces I had learned in my piano lessons, and I composed by using the chords.

Q: *Did anyone teach you how to compose?*

A: No. It was a very natural process. I remember in my childhood I told my mother "I made a piece," when I was a student at a local music school for children. The name of the school was *Kodomo-no Ongakukyoshitsu*, meaning Kyoto Music School for Children, which belonged to Kyoto Geidai. Kyoto Geidai was back then called *Kyoto Tankidaigaku*. I played my own composition for my mother. My mother told me to bring the piece to the music school for the teachers to hear. My teacher brought the piece to a professor of composition at Kyoto Geidai. Then, the processor decided to create a composition class at the *Kyoto Kodomono Ongakukyoshitsu*. Ever since, I composed many pieces. In my middle school years, I wrote a piece for the class and the class sang the song in a concert. I recently found a picture of everyone singing this piece and I was playing the piano accompaniment. The lyrics were written by the teacher. I also made a school song for this junior high school because the school didn't have any songs. Some of the piano music I wrote when I was in and around junior high school years were performed at the Yasaka Kaikan in Kyoto, the only concert hall in Kyoto at that time.

Q: *When did you decide to pursue a musical career professionally?*

A: I decided to go to a music high school called Horikawa High School. I was already influenced by contemporary music. There were very few fellows who were into contemporary music. Although my intention was becoming a composer, I decided to go to Gakuri-ka at Tokyo Geidai as my mother suggested. Back then there were almost no female composers in Japan. I think that is related to the situation surrounding Japanese women at that time. When a woman got married, she became a full-time housewife, and the only people who had a job were school teachers. Under such circumstances, the piano teacher was a possible job for women who got married and could still work by staying at home. Therefore, instead of pursuing the composers' career, I entered the school as a piano major, even though I disliked practicing the piano. I went to the music science department at Tokyo University of the Arts, Geidai, where I held a contemporary music festival, and I fell in love with a composer and got married. I was not able to stifle my creativity to deal with contemporary music and being creative unlike regular conservatory students. As my mother predicted, I was forced to live in poverty with my husband for few years after I graduated.

Q: *As for creativity, do you think that every child could become creative? I think it is rare that Japan implemented ongakudukuri as a course and all children in all areas of Japan create music in school.*

A: The Japanese Course of Study requires all the elementary schools to teach *ongakudukuri*; however, I think it still depends on the teacher. Some teachers I know put less emphasis on music-making or creative directions, but I rarely see elementary children who dislike music because of the creative music-making in school. But in middle schools, it is somewhat difficult to implement the *ongakudukuri* at this moment. I was thinking about the reasons. I think that in middle schools in Japan, all schools have a specialist in teaching a general music curriculum. They are mostly trained in a music performance area professionally from the early stages. When they hear music-making, they immediately think how to put the pitch and rhythm together by following basic music theory, typically what they learned in their teacher training or conservatory training. Their training was mostly based on classical music, so they never experienced using different musical genres, materials, or improvisation to create music. They simply never improvised and composed music. When I learn about their music learning experiences, I find that many of their pure intentions in early stages were to win higher prizes in the chorus or brass band in high school, or to compete in solo performance.

Q: *I know in Japan, although all music classes are considered as general music, in many elementary schools, especially upper grades, they have a music specialist, and in lower grades, the classroom teachers teach music. Are there similar situations with elementary school music specialists?*

A: Yes. Some specialist teachers teach excellent classes, but there are many obstacles to implement *ongakudukuri* for music specialists. I saw a class just lining up *do-mi-so*, *do-fa-la*, and such in written musical notation to create melodies and to combine with dissonant notation following traditional musical theory. It looked very boring to use primary triads. I am still trying to implement a creative direction better suited to middle and high school students.

Q: *Are there any practices that you recommend?*

A: In my journal, the *International Journal of Creativity in Music Education*, there are various practices, for example, to use chords, but blue notes in the chords. There are practice examples in my journal. I also use koto or gagaku to create music. There is also a lesson that uses Japanese Haiku. Professor Suga recently pursued an innovative practice called prepared koto, by adapting John Cage's idea [of] prepared piano to Japanese traditional instruments.

Q: *Do you also have an experience to observe and/or participate in creative activities of younger children in early childhood education settings?*

A: When I visited a local public kindergarten class, one of the children started talking to me. Actually, she asked me to create music together. The student had a lyric already prepared and the child and I composed a melody together. Although I mostly sang the tune and composed it with her, the child said, "I made a song," and told everyone in the room. Some even played the tune on the piano and instruments in the room even though they could not play the exact notes. This is a very impressive moment. Unfortunately, this is rare because many teachers do not notice children's spontaneous musical expressions.

Many kindergartens and nurseries handle instruments too carefully and children are not able to access the musical instruments, including pianos, freely even in the free play period. Many Japanese public kindergartens and nurseries pursue a lot of free play and free play–based childcare; however, the realm of creative music-making and free musical play are restricted. Instead of teaching music, their music-making must be embedded in their daily lives and free play.

I also tried implementing creative music-making with my former doctoral students by using the African drum. In other occasions, we asked children to create the loudest hand clap in the room. Some children stood on the chair or tried his clapping very fast to achieve creating the sound as loud as possible. It was fun and amazing! I also thought scaffolding was also important . . . [I had] principals get into the children's circle and try something unique and creative so that many children laugh at the principal but still they really enjoyed the sound. On the next day, many children would imitate the principal and then expand the ideas, and many children would start following them. In contrast, when we tried a very soft sound by clapping, one of the boys was touching his hair. Although he did not follow the instruction of teacher, for him, touching his hair was creating a very soft sound. I thought this was very creative. My doctoral student, as a facilitator, first asked the boy, "What happened?" as she did not notice that he was creating the soft sound. Soon after, she discovered that the act of touching his hair was his musical expression. Again, in creative music-making, leaders' scaffolding, facilitating, and creative stance are the most important factors to encourage children to create music. Later that boy became an education major. I was very happy to know!

Q: *Are there any challenges implementing such a creative practice in the kindergarten?*

A: Very important point. First, the principal told us that children would not understand the terminology of loud and soft sounds. She thought children could not understand the concept concretely. The principal suggested that we use examples such as the sound of elephants or the sound of small insects. I totally rejected the suggestion. Unfortunately, even some Japanese music textbooks for elementary children still introduce the concept of loud and soft in words, instead of letting children experience the difference.

Q: *How do you view music textbooks for schools?*

A: Well, when I taught a course for elementary teachers, one of the teachers simply used music textbooks to mock teach *ongakudukuri*; the musical product was 100% sound effect and not creative music-making. I was disappointed that creative music-making was not taught clearly to them.

Q: *Do you think textbooks could still contribute to spread of the idea of ongakudukuri nationwide?*

A: Ever since the Japanese Course of Study in Music first mentioned expression through music-making, a great many lessons on music-making have become available; however, most of the lessons focus on adding sound effect to stories. I regret that the meaning of music-making was not understood clearly. I began thinking about how to change the direction from the sound effect to actual music-making. Japanese textbooks influence each other. For example, when I make a textbook, and write a section of *ongakudukuri*, another publisher can imitate the idea or elements. It is more important for me and my colleagues to visit all areas of Japan and demonstrate the practice and construct the practice with the local teachers. In Japan, the lesson study called *jugyo kenkyu*[3] is popular and many teachers participate in the learning opportunities to gather new information and construct the innovative practice. Textbooks are not everything and are somewhat limited as a way to share the practice. For my understanding, the *jugyo kenkyu* was much more effective than writing textbooks to share the practice and learning from each other.

Q: *Did you visit many locations to share the direction of creativity in Japanese music education?*

A: Yes. Since 1984, I traveled all around Japan to share the idea and direction of *ongakudukuri*. Some years, I traveled 30 or more times a year offering workshops, demonstrations, and lectures. I covered most of the areas of Japan.

The Japanese Course of Study

The Japanese Course of Study consists of two areas: Music-Making and Appraising. *Ongakudukuri*, creative music-making, is considered as a part of Music-Making along with singing and instrumental playing; however, it is often combined with the area Appraising and music performance. In Japan, *ongakudukuri* encourages every student to participate in musical activities no matter their previous musical experience or skills on instrumental playing or note reading. In addition, *ongakudukuri* covers all genres of music exist in the world.

Although *ongakudukuri* is open to integrate any genres of music, the pedagogy based on the Course of Study places emphasis on teaching musical structure including repeating patterns, repetition, call and response, changes of music, relationships among phrases, and overlapping of more than two tunes. For example, Ravel's *Boléro* is an excellent example of repetition in that it contains a rhythm repeated for 169 times (Tsubonou, 2017). Surprisingly, the piece consists of just two melody lines built atop the rhythm. Students first listen to the music to discover how the music expands, and to identify the dynamic changes and orchestration that makes the piece interesting. Next, students would use the idea that music was constructed by repeated patterns, and they would create music that has repetition. In *ongakudukuri*, the structural understanding of music is very important, and there should be always a strong tie between music listening and creative music-making (Tsubonou, 2019). Consequently, in *ongakudukuri*, elaborating on a pre-existing musical idea would become a model for students to use as they create music.

The overall objective of Japanese music education is "To encourage pupils to cultivate their sentiments, fundamental abilities for musical activities, a love for music as well as a sensitivity toward it, through music-making and appraising" (MEXT, 2007). Figure 38.1 shows MEXT in grade levels 1 and 2.

Grades 1 and 2

1. Objectives

    (1) To encourage pupils to enjoy music and take an interest in it, and to educate them to increase their life satisfaction by enjoying music.

    (2) To encourage pupils to cultivate their basic abilities for music-making.

    (3) To encourage pupil's familiarity with a variety of music and to cultivate their basic abilities for listening to music overall.

2. Content Areas

    A. Music-Making

    (1) Singing: The following should be taught through singing.

        a. Singing after listening to the models and singing from memory in solmization.

        b. Singing with emotion and imagination suitable for lyrics.

        c. Singing with attention to one's own voice and pronunciation.

        d. Singing in unison while listening to others and the accompaniment.

    (2) Playing Instruments: The following should be taught through playing instrument.

        a. Playing instruments after listening to the models and playing by rhythm notations.

        b. Playing instruments with emotion and imagination.

        c. Playing simple rhythmic patterns and tunes with attention to timbre.

        d. Playing instruments in unison while listening to others and the accompaniment.

    (3) Creative Music Making: The following should be taught through creative music making.

        a. Enjoying musical games with various sound sources, including human voices.

        b. Creating simple musical pieces from various sound sources based on musical structures.

    (4) The teaching materials for music-making should contain the following.

        a. Unison songs and rounds including those in the list-c below, allocated to each grade.

        b. Instrumental pieces with simple rhythmic accompaniment or with the lower part, based on the songs that have already been learned.

    B. Appraising

    (1) The following should be taught through appraising.

        a. Listening to musical tastes that make each piece of music expressive.

        b. Listening to combined musical elements.

        c. Listening to pieces with emotion and imagination, responding to them imaginatively either through verbal or some other means, and enjoying performance as well as the music itself.

    (2) Teaching materials for appraising should contain the following.

        a. Traditional children's songs and play songs from Japan and abroad that will exhilarate pupils and prompt physical movements such as marching and dancing, and pieces that evoke scenes from everyday life.

        b. Amiable pieces to recognize musical elements easily.

        c. Amiable pieces with various performance styles, to recognize the characteristics of the timbre of instruments and human voices easily.

There was also a list of Common Items for each activity as follows:

(1) The following should be taught through Music-Making and Appraising.

    a. To perceive (a) and (b) among the musical elements, and to be sensitive toward their goodness, enjoyment, and beauty.

        (1) Elements characterizing music, such as timbre, rhythm, tempo, melody, dynamics, beat and phrase.

        (2) Musical structures, such as repetition, and Q&A.

    b. To become familiar with notes, rests, and other notational symbols as well as with musical terms, through musical activities.

FIGURE 38.1. MEXT Guidance for Creative Music-Making

Grades 3 and 4
1. Objectives
    (1) To encourage pupils to develop an interest in music, and to educate them to increase their life satisfaction with music.
    (2) To encourage pupils to cultivate their basic abilities for music-making.
    (3) To encourage pupils to become familiar with a variety of music and to cultivate their basic abilities for listening to music overall.
2. Content of Creative Music Making
The followings should be taught through creative music making.
    a. Improvising with various musical ideas, based on diverse sound sources and their combinations.
    b. Creating simple musical pieces based on musical structures as well as one's own intention, using various sound sources.

Grades 5 and 6
1. Objectives
    (1) To encourage pupils to enjoy music creatively and take an interest in it, and to educate them to increase their life satisfaction through music.
    (2) To encourage pupils to cultivate their basic abilities for music-making.
    (3) To encourage pupils to become familiar with a variety of music and to cultivate their basic abilities for listening to music overall.
2. Content of Creative Music Making
The following should be taught through creative music making.
    a. Improvising with various musical ideas, based on previous musical experiences.
    b. Creating simple musical pieces based on musical structures as well as the perspective for music as a whole, using various sound sources.

MEXT guidance for syllabus design:
The following should be handled with respect to creative music making.
    a. Advice should be given so that pupils acquire various creative musical ideas through musical games and improvisation, such as imitating rhythms and melodies, or finding various sounds from something familiar.
    b. When necessary, advising pupils on how to record the music created.
    c. Using non-metrical rhythms, scales used in Japanese music and scales that are atonal, according to the ability of pupils.

FIGURE 38.1. Continued

The Course of Study in Practice

Since 2007, Japanese Course of Study in Music has indicated creative music-making with detailed description of musical structure; however, the Course encourages teachers to select music locally from a wide range of musical repertoire and genres. The following three demonstrate connections between the Japanese curriculum the teaching of *ongakudukuri*. Each case was selected by Professor Tsubonou. For the first two cases, the teachers contributed their lesson plans and detailed notes for use in this chapter.

For the final case, Professor Tsubonou shared her lesson and video excerpts to highlight practice.

Case 1

This lesson was created for fifth graders at a public elementary school in Tokyo. The lesson focused on appreciating Japanese traditional music with a special emphasis on understanding the technique of koto playing. Although the lesson focused on music appreciation, the lesson also included creative music-making. The koto (箏), a Japanese plucked string instrument, was central to the lesson.

The students experienced koto playing when they were in the fourth grade. In an ensemble setting they performed "Sakura Sakura," which is a song depicting spring and cherry blossoms. As fifth graders, the students learned various performance techniques for koto playing including staccato, scratching, and glissando. Specifically, the students played the main melody, drone, and *a-i-no-te*, an interjected chant. The drone part consisted of a repeated pattern called *su-go-mo-ri-ji* and the lesson aimed to help students understand the pattern and to let students to create a melody to fit with the drone. The lesson was conducted using the TAS model which consists of a teacher, advisor, and supporter. In this case, aside from the teacher, there was an advisor to help the teacher incorporate the pattern of accompaniment and to expand the lesson, and a supporter who performed a koto demonstration and assisted with the technical issues of playing the instrument.

The lesson of the day began by letting the children perform "Sakura" on the koto. Next, they listened to "Sakura" variations and students discovered different ways of playing the piece through the use of variation. The supporter gave some technical advice on *koto* playing by modeling different techniques, which the students then practiced. Students then joined groups of three to four and used the techniques they had learned from listening and form the supporter's performance to create a melody which, per the assignment, consisted of eight notes.

The goal of the lesson was to embed creative music-making in musical appreciation. By listening to several different versions of "Sakura" and learning koto playing along with studying how the musical structure of the drone related to the melody, students were prepared to create their own variations. As an example, the teacher and supporter performed koto as a duet, with the teacher playing the drone and the supporter playing the main melody. This model helped students understand how the melody was constructed along with the accompaniment.

Students were not given specific instructions as to how they should compose; however, the teacher suggested that students focus on how to connect phrases and overlap two or more lines like the main melody and accompaniment. Students were encouraged to discuss these ideas with the members of their group and listened to other groups' products during the last minutes of the lesson. Moreover, the students connected their group compositions and made them into a larger work.

Case 2

The next lesson aims for students to appreciate music of Japan and the world by focusing on gamelan and Debussy. In this lesson, creative music-making is found in listening and appreciation. The lesson was implemented in a public elementary school in Saitama Prefecture.

The objectives of the lesson were two-fold. First, students would experience and understand the relationship among timbre, melody, and musical expression. Second, students would gain knowledge of both Japanese and world music perspectives as a foundation for the creation of their own percussion pieces. Students were asked to listen to, perform, and discuss the traits of the music they studied in class before they worked in small groups to compose their own music.

The activities of the lesson took place in two phases. First, the teacher invited a gamelan player as a guest, along with nine university students from Kaichi International University and Tokyo Seitoku University, to support teaching gamelan to the students. The guests performed a piece called *Qubogiro* at the beginning of the lesson and then the students selected instruments and learned to perform the same piece. In the second phase of the lesson, the students were asked to create music featuring the characteristics of gamelan. Each group composed, rehearsed, and presented their music in class. During the latter half of the second lesson, the students listened to Debussy's *Estampes*, "Pagodes." Students discovered that there was a connection between gamelan music and Debussy. Each group then improvised music and performed for each other.

Following the lesson, students offered the following reflections:

Student A (Female)

I found that each country owns a unique musical culture and each had a different trait of music-making. For example, gamelan had a lot of repeated notes and patterns, and between those patterns, they inserted various instruments to design the music. They also added a great many changes of the tempo.

Student B (Male)

I composed the music based on what we heard. I discovered that music has no single answer by doing *ongakudukuri*. In our group, we set a melody and arranged by discussion in the group. I also discovered my favorite musical style . . . gamelan.

Student C (Female)

I enjoyed listening, playing, and creating various different rhythms. [My group mate] was particularly interested in the rhythmic misalignment and overlapping. Our group purposefully added both misalignment and overlapping and added change of the speed like gamelan style.

As is illustrated by the students' reflections, they enjoyed listening to and creating gamelan-like sound in small groups. Video of the students' gamelan inspired pieces can be found at https://www.icme.jp/jd/en07/kodomono_sakuhin.mp4 (Tsubonou, 2020).

Case 3

The final case features a concert designed by Professor Yukiko Tsubonou. The concert was held at Tokyo University and the participants created all of the music by working in small groups. Musical styles included gamelan, the folk music of Nepal, Japanese traditional folk tunes, and many other musical genres and styles. Some composers participated by using musical instruments of East and West, and some even used less formal instruments such as a whistle. The concert was held on January 6, 2020, at Tokyo University, and it was designed with the following theme: Everyone Can Create Music. The following is an excerpt of Professor Tsubonou's remarks:

> In Japan, creative music making has been incorporated into the Course of Study, revised in 2008, and is now being implemented in schools as an activity that allows anyone to be creatively involved in music even if they do not have the skills to read music or play musical instruments. I believe that the aims of creative music-making are to foster creativity, to develop communication skills—because the focus is on making music in groups—and to acquire a broad musical perspective.
>
> This lesson targets not only students who have various musical backgrounds and those who have been engaged in musical activities in various ways but also students who have been looking for something new and have never been involved in musical activities until now. Therefore, I designed and conducted every workshop keeping in mind that all of them could participate using their feelings and creativity. Taking up classical, jazz, pop, ethnic music from around the world, and contemporary music as materials, each student made their own music, especially focusing on the rhythm and scale of the genre of music selected for them while experiencing the commonality and uniqueness of them.
>
> We performed an improvisational activity called "Musical Game" almost every session using clapping and other sounds produced around us. The creativity of the students was first reflected in this musical game and led to the next music-making experience. Many students slightly deviated from the set of rules of the musical games and quickly created their own "world."
>
> The design of this open studio differs from that of a normal music or lecture room: it has a big partition and thick pillars; some desks and chairs are arranged irregularly; and the seats are facing different directions. At first, I thought it would be difficult for everyone to make music in this studio while participating with each other, but each person was actually able to participate in making music after choosing a preferred location, facing a desired direction, and measuring an appropriate distance from me. It seems that the freedom given to choose their position shaped the unconstrained atmosphere of the whole workshop.
>
> The last lesson included holding a concert involving all participants while gradually expanding their "musical worlds" through these workshops. I think they enjoyed making music together to the fullest and that their seriousness and passion, as well as their creativity, gave rise to a power that overwhelmed me.

CONCLUSION

The Asian view of creativity, holding that people are meant to learn from the past reflectively to discover new meanings and develop new personal understandings, has been applied not only in the consideration of children's creativity through *ongakudukuri*, but also in the re-creation of the Course of Study, particularly in music. While the process of evolving educational practice is ongoing, considerable advances have been made in engaging children with music through activities that allow them to explore their creativity and musicality. An important aspect in the evolution of practice is to reframe teacher education so that the creative music-making is not limited to the practices of childhood music-making, but also to those preparing to teach. As these two worlds grow and inform each other, creative music-making in education will further evolve and set the stage for a new cycle of reflection and development.

NOTES

1. The Japanese Course of Study, revised in 2008, places creative music-making as a part of the expression section of the curriculum for both primary and secondary school music. In Japan, the primary level covers first to sixth grade, and the secondary applies to seventh to ninth grade.
2. The interview with Professor Yukiko Tsubonou was co-constructed by a team of researchers who corroborated details using documental research from Japanese sources in the form of school music curriculums, related textbooks, and other documents.
3. A form of professional development.

REFERENCES

Amabile, T. (1996). *Creativity in context: Social psychology of creativity*. Westview Press.

Ames. R. T., & Rosemont, Jr. H. (1998). *The analects of Confucius: A philosophical translation*. Random House.

Burnard, P. (2012). *Musical creativities in practice*. Oxford University Press.

Csikszentmihalyi, M. (1990). *Flow: The psychology of optimal experience*. Harper and Row.

Ikuta, K. (2007). *Waza kara shiru*. Tokyo University Press.

Ikuta, K. (2011). *Waza gengo*. Keio University Press.

Ishigami, N. (2018). Fostering children's musical creativity based on a simple rhythm pattern. *International Journal of Creativity in Music Education*, 6, 11–23. Institute of Creativity in Music Education.

Jackson, S. A. & Marsh, H. W. (1996). Development and validation of a scale to measure optimal experience: The flow state scale. *Journal of Sport and Exercise Psychology*, 18, 17–35.

Koyasu, N. (2010). *Shisōshika-ga yomu rongo*. Iwanami.

Kozbelt, A., Beghetto, R., & Runco, M. A. (2010) Theories of creativity. In J. C. Kaufman & R. J. Sternberg (Eds.), *The Cambridge handbook of creativity*. 20–47. Cambridge University Press.

Lubart, T. (2010). *Cross-cultural perspectives on creativity*. In J.C. Kaufman & R.J. Sternberg (Eds.) *The Cambridge handbook of creativity*. 265–278. Cambridge University Press.

Matlin, M. W. (2009). *Cognition*, 7th edition. Willey.

MEXT (2007). *Japanese Course of Study*. Ministry of Education, Culture, Sports, Science and Technology.

MEXT (2007). *Japanese Course of Kindergarten*. Ministry of Education, Culture, Sports, Science and Technology.

Misra, G. Srivastava, G. M., and Misra, I. (2006). Culture and facets of creativity: The Indian experience. In J. C. Kaufman & R. J. Sternberg (Ed.), *The international handbook of creativity* (pp. 421–455). Cambridge University Press.

Richard, R. (2009). *Everyday creativity and new views of human nature: Psychological, social and spiritual perspectives*. American Psychological Association.

Runco, M. A. (2007). *Creativity theories and themes: Research, development and practice*. Elsevier Academic Press.

Saito, T. (2004). *Kodomo-no shūchūryoku-wo takameru*. Bunshun.

Shinkai, S. (2012). Piano education at nursery school. *Bulletin, Fuji Women's University*, 49(2), 147–153.

Takasu, H. (2016). Creativity in Japanese course of study (statutory) for music. *International Journal of Creativity in Music Education*, 4(0), 2–7. Institute of Creativity in Music Education.

Tsubonou, Y. (2021). *Everyone can create music*. Open Studio iii, University of Tokyo. Retrieved on May 27, 2021, from https://openstudio-utokyo.com/archive/20200106-1359/

Tsubonou, Y. (2020), Establishment of TAS model and its meaning in music education: Seeking new partnerships in school education. *International Journal of Creativity in Music Education*, (7), 2–13.

Tsubonou, Y. (2019). Significant points to keep in mind when making music. *Elementary Music Education Law*, 83–84. Ongaku no tomo sha Corp.

Tsubonou, Y. (2018). Preface: Special issue: Musical creativity through breaking the rules and traditions. *International Journal of Creativity in Music Education*, 6, 2. Institute of Creativity in Music Education.

Tsubonou, Y. (2017). Establishment of TAS model and its meaning in music education: Seeking new partnership in school education. *International Journal of Creativity in Music Education*, 7, 2–14. Institute of Creativity in Music Education.

Tsujimoto, M. (2010). *Edo-no manabi*. In Y. Saeki (Ed.), *A companion to the cognitive science of learning*, 62–80. Taisyūkan.

Ueno, M. (2012). The diffusion of Japanese traditional music caused by sheet music: Playing Japanese traditional music with Western musical instruments from the middle *Meiji* period to the *Taisho* period. *Nihon Dentō Ongaku Kenkyū*, 9(3), 21–42.

Ward, T. B., & Kokomyts, Y. (2010). Cognition and creativity. In J. C. Kaufman & R. J. Sternberg (Eds.), *The Cambridge handbook of creativity*. 93–112. Cambridge University Press.

Wilson, W. S. (2006). On Zeami. *The flowering spirit: Classic teachings on the art of no*. Kodansha International.

Yamada, S. (2002). *Nihon Bunka-no Moho-to Souzou*. Tokyo: Kadokawa.

Yasuda, H., & Nagao, C. (2010). The relationship between the popularity of piano in kindergartens and day nurseries and the piano teacher's interest in early childhood education training. *Bulletin, Nara Education University*, 59(1), 159–174.

Young, S. (2003). *Music with the under-fours*. Routledge.

CHAPTER 39

MUSIC COMPOSITION IN MUSIC EDUCATION

The Case of Uganda

BENON KIGOZI

MANY beliefs and principles underlie Uganda's music education through which music composition is achieved. The process of music education begins right from birth through the non-formal, informal, and formal realms of knowledge transmission and perception. Non-formal education is community-based and occurs outside the school system. It has no age limit and is a lifelong education that offers community members with many opportunities for music-making. Informal education is natural and spontaneous, with no structure or levels of hierarchy. Knowledge is acquired through experiences based on observations that allow learners to acquire crucial information. Lastly, formal education happens at school with a prescribed academic curriculum. Each of these realms represent knowledge transfer in Uganda.

Music composition mainly takes place within the oral tradition where cultural knowledge, tradition, and material are transmitted from one generation to another verbally in speech, folk tales, or even songs. An oral composition exhibits high levels of knowledge and engagement with the musical traditions of the culture. These compositions require high levels of perception and the recognition of specific norms and practices that govern the creative principles, elements, and approaches through which it is realized and transferred. If created with an authentic knowledge of the musical culture and with an understanding of the music's intended use, a composition will not be notated. In fact, until just a few years ago, music was not notated in Uganda.

Senghor (1958) affirms that "Black Africa has had the good fortune to ignore writing, even when it was not aware of its existence . . . for writing impoverishes reality. It crystallizes it into fixed categories and freezes it, when reality is properly alive, fluid and shapeless" (pp. 238–239). Music composition as a dynamic activity, requiring the interplay of different roles within the culture, and calls for attention to understanding the context in which music is being made, such that the work portrays the full intention and contextual significance within the community. There is no doubt that the culture is the first composer as it is the one that sets the tone regarding the raw materials, including elements and concepts that are assembled into what then becomes *a music composition*.

THE AFRICAN PHILOSOPHY OF INDIGENOUS MUSIC EDUCATION

The African perspective of music education in general addresses the holistic, integrated cultural approach of music education as opposed to that based on the individual elements and concepts as is more common in the West. Africans base music creativity and practice on a series of concepts that bear specific indigenous methods of execution. African education is practical, aural-oral, and informal. It demonstrates logic and a systematic philosophy in music creativity and performance that is based on listening and observation as pivotal elements of acquiring the basic skills.

Written composition, oral composition, and improvisation inspire expression and creativity. Ugandans, however, feel that music education within schools should transmit the cultural contexts and music methods specific to Africa. According to Flolu (2000), "Africa-sensitive education denotes the natural, political, social, and cultural growth arising from acting and interacting with the environment which consists of groups and individuals within the community" (pp. 25–29).

In rural Uganda, where much of music composition happens, knowledge is perceived to be in one's head rather than residing in books. Instruction is therefore achieved through immersive participation rather than through the presentation of abstract concepts. Transmission, and ultimately perception, is achieved by doing rather than by reading about an idea or experience. Flolu (2005) asserts that "African education referred to here is aural-oral and mostly informal . . . listening and observation interwoven by memory remain the key elements of acquiring the basic skills of social adjustment" (in Herbst, pp. 109).

According to Kigozi (2008), the African perspective "refers to philosophical models that are based on African concepts and aesthetics other than those that are practiced in Europe and America. The philosophy addresses the integrated and holistic approach of the musical arts in education as opposed to individual music elements and concepts out of context" (pp. 26). Conversely, Nzewi (2003) asserts that the "arts discipline of music, drama, poetry and costume arts are seldom separated in creative thinking and performance practice . . . in the African indigenous musical arts milieu" (p. 13). Music, dance, poetry, drama should not be separated in education, but integrated with composition and performance.

As performances happen during social events, what is music and what is not music is usually unclear as the musical elements are experienced and heard together in daily life (Mbabi-Katana, 1972 in Kigozi, 2008). Musical engagements involve genealogies, mythologies, proverbs, legends, oral history, dance, drama, and speech; all are embodied in a composition and its subsequent performance. Given the complex intertwining of culture and music-making, teaching practices in Uganda are yet to effectively incorporate indigenous music composition into general instruction. To offer a composition pedagogy that is authentic to oral traditions, music composition must be transmitted in context, with a proper frame of reference, and must apply the approaches specific to Uganda—and by extension, African practice (Kigozi, 2008).

CONSIDERING MUSIC COMPOSITION IN CONTEXT

It is odd to think of music composition as a process of creating a piece by combining elements of music, as is the more common notion in the West. From an African perspective, creativity always results in something original and new. Fontana (1988) asserts that creative thinking involves originality and fluency that breaks away from existing patterns and introduces something new. Stein (1974) agrees, suggesting that creativity is more than just combining elements of music but encompasses bringing forth a novel product. While Onyeji (2019) points out that the process of composition involves creating, assessing, appreciating, and approving music or discarding musical idea, Rogers (1959) notes the importance of context stating that any novel product stems from amalgamation of the task of an individual on one hand, and the influence of people, events, materials, and life circumstances, on the other. These observations highlight the inter-relationship between the creator and their surrounding contexts.

The circumstances that form the setting for music-making, as well as the situation in which the music is made, are critical contexts in African music-making. In Uganda these contexts are categorized as cultural and social. The cultural context impacts the composed music and its performance as it requires an understanding of the specific norms and cultures of the communities that govern creative principles, elements, and approaches. Therefore, music as a means of cultural expression stresses communal over individual music-making. The processes reflect the ethos of community and are evidenced in the music that arises from social interaction. Further, the social context denotes a particular classification of people in whose locality the music composition is happening. This might be a school, place of worship, or other location. The social context also shapes the musical composition; the more formal the context of creation, the more structured the music created.

Though music composition arises from varied social and cultural contexts and experiences, participation aims to address the cognitive domain through the acquisition of knowledge, the psychomotor domain through the acquisition of skills, and the affective domain through activities that require responding to and in creative acts. For these aims to be fulfilled, music educators need appropriate resources and equipment coupled with effective pedagogical skills (Blaak, Openjuru, and Zeelen, 2013). Borko and Putman (1996) state that in order to maintain authenticity of the activity in the classroom teaching, the teacher must use the kind of thinking and problem-solving skills that are fostered by the activity, which are important beyond school settings, in the wider community. In Uganda, this remains a challenge.

Composition in Uganda has typically been learned through oral traditions, musical festivals, and spontaneous creativity. Presently, Uganda finds itself with multiple approaches to music education. Music is taught formally in schools and non-formally/informally based on the oral tradition known as *Okugunjula*. This approach seeks to preserve the musical past and traditional indigenous education. Music education is also taught formally based on Western traditions and administered by the Department of Education.

Schooling in Uganda

Figure 39.1 represents the structure of Uganda's education system for learners between the ages of 3 and 18. In the urban centers, students learn music within the formal school

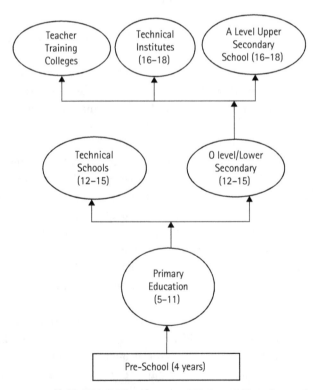

FIGURE 39.1. Structure of Uganda's education system for learners aged 3–18

context. Children in formal school settings often struggle with concentration. As they are naturally inclined to explore and practice mimicry, they learn best through play. Thus, approaches and methods that favor play are common in Ugandan formal school contexts.

The main challenge in these schools has been the use of tribal languages for instruction. The choice of language used in facilitating activities, as well as in the general teaching and learning, should ensure a commonality between learners. Yet, rural music teachers often use their tribal language to lead instruction in a formal class setting comprised of many tribes. As Borko and Putman (1997) have noted, instructional language must be considered within the context of teaching and learning if education is to be successful.

In the lower levels of schooling, music teaching is led by the classroom teacher rather than a music specialist. This is different from the high school where specialists are charged with the role of teaching and developing the music program. The curriculum established for all levels of music education is composed of generalized statements which educators are free to interpret. As such, there are many different views and opinions on how music composition should be taught in schools.

With a scarcity of well-prepared music teachers, opportunities to compose music often focus on lyrical composition. Learners at primary level schools are encouraged to communicate messages through singing "own-composed" songs. These often include repeated patterns, short phrases, or even rhymes. As time goes on, students interact with forms of notation. Music is not considered a core subject, thus there are limited resources for learners at institutions where music is treated as an extracurricular activity.

Music as a Compulsory Subject

In 2000, the government of Uganda, through its Ministry of Education and Sports, declared music a compulsory subject to be taught by all primary schools (Uganda, 2000). The resulting music curriculum stresses examinations of the final product rather than the practical processes through which learners derive the product. Classroom teachers at lower levels of schooling are not enthusiastic about teaching music, and those that are keen use varying and uncoordinated methods and approaches of inculcating music creativity. As a result, music creativity and indeed music composition are yet to take root in schools across the country.

One would think that music composition might be enriched through the variety of ideas, methods, and approaches teachers employ, yet instruction remains a significant challenge. The divergent opinions and ideas pursued by educators detract from the goal of well synchronized and standardized modes of assessment and evaluation as are needed for the ordinary and advanced levels of examination administered by the Uganda National Examinations Board (UNEB). As teachers train students to pass examinations rather than acquire sustainable creative skills, it is fair to say that the educational and creative skills that learners out to gain through school education are not prioritized in practice.

Though the current curriculum is a tremendous improvement over its previous iteration, it needs to be executed with caution to realize its intended outputs. Much of the formal music education presented in the school curriculum is Western in nature, structure, content, and design. The propagation of this Western-based curricula and traditions, in Uganda and indeed the whole of Africa, has been advanced for years while various scholars on the African continent have noted with concern the need to develop a pedagogical approach that reflects the compositional realities of African cultural practices. As Idolor (2005) points out, "The music curricula must be based on Africa sensitive music theory and practice" (pp. 87). Similarly, Masoga (2003) asserts that "it is wise to start with knowledge about the local area which students are familiar with and then gradually move to the knowledge about regional, national and global environments" (pp. 48).

An Evolving Mission

With the guidance and facilitation of the Ministry of Education and Sports, music educators across Uganda have worked through a series of mission, vision, and guiding statements concerning what music education, including music composition, should look like in schools. They have proposed and withdrawn multitudes of ways of teaching music composition in an effort to equip learners with skills for the challenges ahead. Despite all the time and effort put into the search for an appropriate pedagogy, the combination of the formal school environment, methods, and instructional strategies isolates learners from their musical cultures, traditions, and norms.

The frustration and feeling of inadequacy experienced by music teachers is balanced by learners who are naturally and inherently musical. This makes teaching somewhat easier for music educators who are continuously searching for ways to tap into learners' inherent reservoirs of enthusiasm. However, teaching which leans strongly toward Western strategies has led to reliance on staff notation as the sole method of documenting music composition. According to Kigozi (2016), "The rationale for the music syllabus focuses on Western strategies rather than a true African context that reflects appropriate philosophical models that fit in an African context" (p. 12). Music composition sessions are seen as avenues for students to experiment with Western musical instruments, especially recorders in schools that can afford them, creating a sense of cultural isolation in learners experiencing and absorbing an explicit bias.

Curricular Reform

In 1999 the Ministry of Education and Sports, working through the National Curriculum Development Centre, reviewed the curriculum of Uganda. The work was guided and inspired by 1) the report of the education policy review commission entitled *Education for National Integration and Reform* (Uganda, 1989); 2) the government's *White Paper on Education* (Uganda, 1992) addressing the recommendations in the report, and 3) the report of the curriculum review task force issued by the Ministry of Education and Sports (Uganda, 1993). The resulting curriculum became effective in January 2000 in all schools operating under the Uganda formal education system.

Unlike the previous curriculum, the new school curriculum of performing arts and physical education was designed to address the broader aims and objectives of education as stated in Article 13 of the Education Policy Review Commission's 1989 report and in the 1992 *White Paper on Education*. Specifically, the following goals were identified:

a) to develop cultural, moral and spiritual values of life, (Uganda, 2000).
b) to promote understanding and appreciation of the value of national unity, patriotism and cultural heritage, with due consideration of international relations and beneficial interdependence, and
c) to inculcate moral, ethical and spiritual values in the individual to develop self-discipline, integrity, tolerance, and human fellowship.

The new curriculum merges the performing arts, including music under which music composition, dance, and drama, are taught, with physical education. By merging the performing arts and physical education, it was hoped that greater integration would occur. This merger however falls short of attaining the African philosophy that fits Uganda as a nation. The disadvantages of merging the performing arts with physical education are echoed by Reimer who asserts that policy-makers should avoid:

- Submerging the character of each individual art by focusing exclusively on family likeness rather than compatibility,
- Assuming that surface similarities among the arts show up underlying unities when in fact they usually do not,
- Neglecting specific perception reaction experiences in favor of a generalized, disembodied "appreciation of the arts," and
- Using non-artistic principles to organize the program to give an impression of unity. (Reimer, 1989, p. 230)

Some music teachers have advocated for the inclusion of both the African/oral and Western approaches in the same curricula. However, it does seem academically futile to subject both approaches to the same system of education, as the two are difficult to combine. While formal music education is easily standardized,

oral traditions and expressions are typically passed on by word of mouth which usually entails variation, in lesser or greater degree. The enactment involves a combination differing from genre to genre, from context to context and from performer to performer; of reproduction, improvisation and creation. This combination renders oral traditions and expressions particularly vibrant and attractive. (UNESCO, 2006)

OKUGUNJULA: THE ORAL TRADITION

The *Baganda* people of Uganda have a concept of educating the young that involves almost every member of the clan, including friends and all family members. This type of education uses *Luganda*, the local language of the Baganda people, and is known as *Okugunjula*, which is translated as "upbringing." According to Kigozi (2008),

> *Okugunjula* is an indigenous concept of educating the young involves every member of the clan, friends and family. Inherent in this oral tradition is the act of preparing, training, and transforming a learner into a mature and responsible citizen. Therefore, the act of preparing, training, and transforming a young child into a responsible member of society was always of utmost importance to the community. A child had to be inducted into the heritage of his predecessors which is manifested in the music, poetry, art, drama, dance and stories including mythologies, legends, genealogies, proverbs and oral history of the land. (p. 18)

Within *Okugunjula* informal environments happen mainly during community events and gatherings outside school. This provides many opportunities for learners' to directly engage with musical activities. Learners compose as well as perform music through oral processes as part of indigenous education from the very onset. While learners are normally in position to make music at all times, strategies for imparting creativity and knowledge are dependent on how music is accessed.

In the rural areas, learners are brought up immersed in the oral tradition of creating music by through listening and observation. While composing in these contexts is based in oral traditions, high levels of creativity, knowledge, and engagement of the traditions of the culture are demonstrated. Creativity is not simply about creating a piece, but rather a dynamic activity involving interplay between several role players within the culture. It calls for composers to understand the context in which music-making is happening, thus allowing the composition to portray the full intentions and contextual significance of the community. Consequently, culture should be considered as the first composer; it sets the tone regarding the raw materials, including the elements and concepts that are assembled into what then becomes a music composition representing the process and final product of musical creativity.

Under the oral processes, learners become active listeners. Listening is the main conduit through which creativity is perceived by the very young. There is evidence of creative norms and practices supporting the idea that music composition and performance in traditional cultures has a conceptual basis. The ability to perceive the manipulation of sound is largely dependent on active listening rather than on aural skills and general music literacy. For every sound made by learners in the oral, non-formal, and informal environments, whether controlled on not, there is a degree of learning that happens ranging from awareness of the feelings arising from the sound produced to emotional feelings produced from hearing the created sound. Learners organize their sounds for personal pleasure and effect on their peers whenever they meet to play. As they grow and develop, they become more familiar with their environments, often using their own bodies as immediate source material.

The oral tradition of *Okugunjula* defines how people live within the same culture. They are bound together in harmony defined by how they transact lives based on music-making on a regular basis. Music is not only experienced but lived without restrictions and undue interference regarding rules and procedures. Everyone participates without worrying of conventions and regulations as it is in the West, which is one of the main attributes of the music-making process of *Okugunjula*. What might be considered in the West as rude behavior—people interrupting performances by adding in with clapping, singing, dancing, shouting, and stamping—is what makes the oral tradition correct and effective in imparting creative skills.

The *Okugunjula* uses high levels of narrating, listening, and memory, all of which are core pillars of a comprehensive education. It is also a vehicle of intergenerational transfer of social philosophy, values, and crucial information. The government of Uganda has yet to prioritize the development and safeguarding of the oral tradition just as it has prioritized health, agriculture, wealth creation, and human rights, among others. Even though the oral tradition has good cultural and educational intentions in terms of preserving as well as enriching development interventions, it has been a challenge to reclaim it and effectively integrating it into the structured school system.

Music Education and National Unity

To repair the social effects brought about through years of ethnic conflict and civil wars, the government of Uganda decided to introduce a music education program to promote national unity and pride. The government sponsors music competitions amongst schools based on music creativity and performance. The main objective for the music festivals is defined by the mutual process of socialization and educating the masses about children rights and the country's constitution. As part of the reforms aimed at the education sector, these programs feature primary and secondary school music festivals. Learners at all levels experience the processes of music composition during the annual district and national level music festivals.

The integrated art forms of the festivals include music, poetry, dance, drama, and costume. The festivals present opportunities for learners to engage music creativity based on folk songs, plays, skits, poems, and music pieces based in the Western classical style. Each year a different theme is identified. As a result of the national festivals, schools began to offer similar internal music programs. Each year, schools organize inter-house and inter-class music competitions that require students to create original compositions through processes guided by festival directors, demonstrators, and trainers. These low-pressure experiences create more platforms for creative collaboration amongst learners. They learn to work toward a common goal, share ideas, and respect each other's contributions. The timeline for presenting compositions drives students to quickly develop these skills as they work.

Within the prescribed festival criteria, space is provided for performance composition, a type of creative performance inherent in indigenous African musical practices involving the re-composing of familiar indigenous songs during musical performances. Performance composition involves the use of compositional techniques in the creative processes that include preparation, incubation, illumination, and verification. Performance composition varies from improvisation with regard to the way compositional techniques are used in the composition processes.

Spontaneous Creativity

Adedeji (2005) states that each African country uses relevant and workable methods, even those that are yet to be systemized into theories. He further points out features of African music such as repetition, oral, improvisation, extemporization, spontaneity, creation and recreation, percussiveness, sacredness, boisterousness and expression of exuberance and high spirits, integration of other arts, audience participation, and an unlimited world of sounds. These features are also situated within approaches to teaching and learning that include apprenticeship, parenting, imitation, lifelong development, and metaphysical dimensions. Dramatic movements and dance are also spontaneously introduced by the audience and, even though it may seem incompatible, that is how spontaneous improvisations and compositions are made. It is the process rather than the product that matters here, and learners benefit from these positive experiences.

Performances of indigenous traditional folk songs are another way in which learners directly experience music. The value and entertainment aspect of the indigenous traditional folk songs is inherent in the extent to which the audience interacts with the performers and narrator through music and dance and through dialogue and comments. Because all songs begin, accompany, and conclude with a story, the musical arts form part of the performance, creating a spontaneous composition in which both the performers and the audience—including parents of learners—have equal opportunities to express creativity through music and dramatic ideas. In these settings, learners are exposed to a complex array of improvisation and spontaneous creativity activity as well as other forms of music creativity. This level of creativity and expression flows naturally from every learner and should merely be unlocked (Slade, 1966). Music educators across secondary schools talk of notable development in their instructional skills resulting from teaching composition in a manner that embraces creative immersions rather than one that follows a prescribed, book-oriented, music education curriculum. Teachers, together with students, gain confidence in their skills and abilities as they learn together. This process empowers teachers to better ascertain students' compositional needs and capabilities. It also reinforces the value of teachers stepping out of their comfort zone to stretch beyond their training as they challenge their students, as well as themselves, to take musical risks.

Educators' Preparedness and Teaching Strategies

The low priority accorded to music education is not restricted to time allocation, but also includes how music educators are trained and certified across the country. Music educators in Uganda fall into three categories: (1) certified music educators with general music instruction methods, but inadequate content. These include teachers with knowledge about teaching, learning, and learners, rather than knowledge specific and attuned to the teaching of music as a subject and the subject matter content, (2) music teachers with non-formal and informal music training and experience who decide to acquire knowledge and experience on their own through experience outside any organized institution, and (3) non-certified music educators with a degree in music and a firm grip on to the content knowledge but who are short on the requirements for advanced degrees, such as educational theory and teaching practice.

Each of these three groups approaches the teaching of music creativity in different ways. As a result of inadequate training of music educators on the ground and a lack of policies that support music composition within an oral tradition, the greatest resource aiding learner's creativity is listening and observation. Having music training experiences rooted in the Western approaches where the content and methods of teaching are focused on Western classical music as the highest form of musical experience an improper match for a classroom full of local indigenous learners. Unlike in other academic areas where observation and analysis form major concerns of the learning experience, in music composition the elements of imagination, creativity, and self-expression require a competent music instructor to extract musical ideas from learners.

With teachers under-prepared to execute their role as guides and music composition framed as a time consuming and complex activity, many teachers decide to use their allotted instructional time to play music games. A secondary school music teacher in Kampala District admitted that he does not offer a music composition experience to his students since there is little time for music, arguing that music history seems more fitting and quite sufficient for a music lesson. Another teacher, at the Makerere College School, blamed the absence of music composition in his classroom on his temperament, saying that "if learners failed to compose after several trials, I surrender because I do not possess the motivation to continue." Such positions leave students underserved. As Lave and Wenger (1991) have noted, it is the characters and the behaviors of educators that has the greatest impact on teaching and learning because educators have the power and status to structure the experienced curriculum.

The Music Teacher's Role

Music teachers can be important facilitators of music composition activities. Yet, the most common teaching methods used by Ugandan teachers—assuming an author-itarian role and lecturing—contravene the very behaviors needed for composition to be rewarding and successful. Although the choice of teaching strategies is left to the discretion of the classroom teacher, only a handful of music educators across the country apply methods conducive to learners' active participation in practical learning experiences. The majority of teachers prefer to talk, taking time explain to learners concepts for which learners have no knowledge base or relevant experience. Muzumara (2011) asserts that the choice of method is determined by factors that include, among other things, available amount of time and teaching resources. Ugandan teachers are not fully prepared to understand their students or to use instructional strategies that can best enhance the learning process. Significant change is needed.

Ugandan teachers often confess that they are uncomfortable teaching music compo-sition and physical education together. They acknowledge that in inadequate training, limited prior experience, and lack of content knowledge as important challenges in their practice. According to Killian and Dye (2009), teachers believe that their teaching improves when they use a student-led approach. As teachers move toward more student-centered approaches in which they facilitate and encourage learners to express their creativity, more meaningful creative processes and learning are taking place.

Indeed, the learner-centered approach is one that education returns to time and time again. Finlay-Johnson in 1911 and Slade in 1958 both stress that learners should be given the opportunities to absorb big stories and joyously explore and examine the world and its multitude of mysteries. More recently, Sekalega (2018) has noted that the learner-centered approach can be used to develop students' natural behaviors of play, improvising, and experimenting as means of accessing their innate musicality. The student-led approach is increasingly common in schools where music educators are standard classroom teachers. It is successful in these settings because it relies on devel-oping learners' emotional and creative skills through experimenting with a variety of options. As music educators facilitate student-led creativity sessions, they grow more confident in their teaching as they observe students exhibiting new skills and abilities. These approaches help students and teachers alike increase their interest in music ed-ucation, which in turn leads to improved skills of musical perception, expression, and enjoyment.

Community Musicians as Demonstrators and Teachers

Drawing on the expertise and experience of community musicians as demonstrators and "teachers" has been of great importance in imparting music creativity skills to learners. Shizha (2005) has noted that local people are a vital source of indigenous knowledge that can contribute to the learning in schools. Community musicians in Uganda who are semi-retired, talented, and musically competent, are willing to contribute toward the development, growth, preservation, and conservation of music traditions. They are regularly invited into schools to demonstrate and share skills with learners through well-structured, researched, and highly organized processes of music composition.

Collaborations with community musicians allow both the school and the community to engage in constant dialogue that promotes indigenous ways of explaining local solutions for local challenges. Therefore, community participation in school life transforms and challenges dominant power relations and offers the possibility of producing constructive knowledge appropriate to African modes of thinking. As African music education relies on visual and memory preservation as part of the oral process, the absence of reading and writing does not negate the value of the teaching and learning facilitated by local community musicians. Rather, musical activities relating to music composition are refined through various oral-aural processes that occur informally and naturally in direct, participatory experiences involving thematic examination, sound mediums, and the coherent whole.

Composing in the African Philosophy

Music educators in Uganda debate whether learners should be taught composition, through composition, or about composition. They also question whether the focus of music composition should be on the process or the product. With multiple systems in play, creating a unified composition pedagogy that accounts for different perspectives is complex.

On paper, learners are exposed to three approaches to music composition training in the formal school system. Formally trained teachers use the teacher-centered or skill-based approaches wherein learners study Western classical music theory and staff notation. With this approach, the methods, theory, and practices are mostly unrelated to learners and their cultural orientation. Euba (1989) points out that an intimate practice of the traditional music is key to the discovery of new creative and performance techniques based on African models. Teachers that emphasize learning about composition through theory rather than teaching music composition in the more practical sense focus on "about" composition in examination-packed and non-interactive sessions. They also constantly compromise the expected learning outcomes of composition study. While many music teachers consider the learner-centered approach most successful as a method of teaching music composition, others have a passive attitude and feel that there is no one "right" or "wrong" method for achieving the desired outcomes. They argue that combining the learner-centered and skills-based approaches promotes effective teaching and learning of music creativity.

Music in Uganda's Geographic Regions

The type of music learners are exposed to in non-formal and informal environments is purely traditional indigenous folk music taught orally. This music is divided into four subgenres matching the four main regions of the country. The central and eastern, the south western, the northern, and the eastern region. The central and eastern region of the country is the largest. Music from this region is very melodic and very rhythmic. It is based on an equidistant pentatonic scale with a strong simple compound meter. Songs and dances are accompanied using drums, xylophones, rattles, flutes, and tube fiddles. Western Uganda breeds Nilotic music which encompasses duple meter with two units of length and tonal characteristics. It is mainly accompanied by leg rattles, flutes, and hand-drums. The southwestern region offers delicate and slow music accompanied by pots hit with banana fibers, rattles, flutes, and drums. The northern region mainly practices group instrumental music accompanied by singing. The males play the *agwara*, an indigenous horn, blown sideways, and the females clap while providing subtle vocal accompaniments. Learners are exposed to all the above subgenres. Music composed in this process is integrated with dance, drama, costume, and singing. Practices are rooted in the indigenous African concept and philosophy of music as "sonic dance" and "dance as visual music," partnered with indigenous traditional costume, and not written down.

Direct experiences of music composition are built on a foundation of listening, observation, and imitation. The informal oral environment allows learners to experience the possibilities and limitations of sound production including body percussion and the range and quality of their voices before they begin to use instruments. Learners shake seeds, splash water, and hit sticks, expanding their scope of creativity in the "indigenous music creativity class" before they experiment putting these sounds and practices together to compose songs. As they explore the indigenous processes, learners gain an understanding of the expectations of society while they become part of the musical culture in which they live.

With experience, learners come to understand the cultural constraints that shape music-making and learn to manipulate various sounds in more mature and organized ways. Through work with their peers, parents, and the wider community, they develop the skills necessary to refine music compositions with regard to rhythmic structures, melodic structures, and music form. For, as Flolu (1998) notes, "the child's ability to learn music-making and composing relies largely on the degree of exposure the child has to music" (108).

Instrumental sessions have principals that govern the induction of new learners into the composition and performance ensembles. New learners are normally allocated the easiest instrumental parts, and through listening and observation they learn to play the underlying thematic and melodic layers that are the reference for the experienced performers to exercise their creativity. Vocal music experiences find root in the tonality of Ugandan languages where rhythm and melody grow out of the accents and tones of speech. Learners experience the processes of going from speech to song, reciting together, and then discovering rhythm and melody through tones and accents of speech is most common.

Everyone in the community understands that the oral tradition is intertwined with other spheres of life, and they adhere to the concept of space and sharing that are crucial attributes of musical creativity. Space and sharing are inculcated musically through encouraging learners to create melodic and rhythmic structures and providing the space for a second line to be added later. This shared experience ensures that the rhythmic and melodic structures of the composition are built together by many people rather than just one person. The experience of focused listening to the contributions of others during ensemble performance helps learners develop good listening skills. In spending time establishing a sense of inter-dependence, learners develop a greater understanding of their traditional norms and cultural beliefs. These processes and communal actions enable learners to develop a sense of self-discovery as the creative abilities imperative for comprehensive oral performance and composition blossom.

The community-building aspect of the indigenous oral tradition helps learners balance the intense individualism reflected in Western music as represented by the idea of great composers, solo performances, and the competition and trauma of music examinations. While Western music genres portray one set of ideas about how humans treat other humans, entertainment, money, and fame, the traditional indigenous music compositions offer a different view emphasizing how to address societal issues in ways that benefit humanity and the environment. Through indigenous practices, learners sense the value of community. They learn that every member of the community is required to participate in events that anchor the spheres of life including harvest and farming, coronation ceremonies, funerals, circumcisions, marriages, births, and initiation ceremonies. Further, they learn that music should reflect the traditions, norms, and cultures of their communities. Music composed and re-composed in this way reflects the real-life events as its content and development is determined by the context and audience.

There is great benefit in accessing music-making opportunities together. As learners interact with each other, they create platforms for somatic relationships where they may air out grievances, reconcile with each other, mend bridges, and share the spirituality offered through oral traditions. Learners bond as one entity. It is at such ceremonies that raw and young musical talent is discovered. Through the process of apprenticeship, young people may develop the full potential of their innate creative abilities and become cultural referents responsible for preserving as well as extending the repertory.

MOVING FORWARD: CHALLENGES TO BE ADDRESSED

If there is to be any change in the delivery of composition instruction in music education, several key concerns must be carefully considered and systematically addressed.

First, the oral tradition must be re-contextualized into the formal education system. Its practices must be re-introduced through the combination of face-to-face transmission emphasizing learning-by-ear as well as use of field recordings. The use of all forms of recording equipment, from tapes to cell phones, should be embraced in the classroom setting for learners to record performances of peers and teachers for educational purposes. As outlined earlier in this chapter, the relationship between formal, non-formal, and informal music education has not been effectively explored by music educators. Closer links should be forged between all music education platforms for a well-balanced program that fosters an equal redistribution of music educators amongst schools.

Second, a choice must be made about the relationship between Western and African philosophical perspectives as they apply to music education. The current rationale for music education in Uganda is based on Western models and approaches. This frame does not reflect the needs and interests of a population who hold very different cultural values and who practice a uniquely African form of music-making. The Ministry of Education and Sports must address how music composition can be effectively presented within the curricula. A true African rationale for composition within music education must reflect the appropriate philosophical model within Ugandan contexts (Nzewi, 2001). A modern system that values indigenous African models and which provides appropriate resources should be made available for generating such content and developing its pedagogy. This will bring about a method that reflects the pragmatic approach and which helps young people to understand their immediate environment with a deeper grasp of their social-cultural base.

Third, the availability of appropriate resources presents an ongoing challenge. With the introduction of Universal Primary Education, the government's strategic investment plan proposed a 50% increase in expenditure on primary schools (Ndeezi, 2001). The intent was to subsidize school fees at 50% for primary education. With persistent high levels of inflation, the stipulated funds have long ceased to be adequate (Elwana, 2000). Further, the overwhelming response to free Universal Primary Education and Secondary Education initiatives, the numbers in schools across the country has more than doubled. While increased access to education is critical, inadequacies in facilities and resources have also risen. Class sizes will need be addressed to ensure adequate and favorable environments for learning. Similarly, additional infrastructure is needed to adequately supply facilities and resources.

> This overwhelming response nationwide posed challenges concerning staffing, teaching and educational materials. In various parts of the country, the response was so high that some classes were conducted under trees. In urban centers, government-aided schools had equally overwhelming enrollment figures, which have raised questions about the quality of arts education. (Kigozi, 2008)

Fourth, the importance of music education must be made clear. Nzewi (1999) recounts "the reality [that] in many cases . . . music is not regarded by Africans to be a subject worthy of study, yet its value in the social, emotional, physical and in-tellectual growth is undisputed by music educators" (pp. 79). Music, as part of the broader arts, should positioned as equal to other arts subjects. For music education to attain the goals it has been challenged to achieve, it must be designed to enable learners to demonstrate individual as well as group creativity in meeting authentic challenges within diverse music practices. The current nature and structure of music education is largely determined by the general education system, with music teachers and administers playing a generic role in its implementation. If music teachers had a greater voice in determining how music education would be offered, change might be more forthcoming.

Fifth, the type of music education learners receive is largely dependent upon their locality. Music education should not be left to whim of individual schools but made compulsory from the start to the conclusion of schooling. This will guarantee teachers a platform to advocate for sufficient allocations of class time. Further, no matter how good and relevant the new music education curriculum may be, it can only be properly implemented when resources at underprivileged schools match what is offered to those in more privileged schools.

Sixth, the Ministry of Education and Sports should recognize that the future of the music education discipline lies in the development of music educators. They should en-sure financial assistance toward the effective development of practicing music educators so that teachers are competent and feel confident in handling all aspects of music com-position within music education.

Finally, the government should foster studies investigating areas related to music education. Such studies should involve music educators and explore topics that hold promise for improving instruction related to music creativity. The findings from such studies could serve to inform the creation of an articulated national agenda for research in the field of music with a focus on significant problems and issues of music education. Involving teachers and teacher-educators in such studies will em-power them to become agents in the improvement of their own practice and as well as enhance the effectiveness, usefulness, and relevance of the teaching and learning of music and music creativity.

CONCLUSION

While the skill-based and the child-based approaches are indeed suitable for the formal school setting for secondary and high school students, the non-formal, informal, and oral processes are equally important in laying a firm and culturally authentic foundation for learners of all ages. The culture will usually access forms of intelligence apart from those intelligences traditionally and customarily treasured in educational structures and systems. Therefore, music composition curricula should be all-inclusive, encompassing prescribed curricula at all levels of education. The *oral tradition* ought to be linked with the mainstream curricula as it empowers learners with the knowledge and skills of their cultural heritage in addition to imparting creativity and performance skills in accordance with learners' cultures, norms, and traditions. Ugandan music must therefore be taught in context and through methods that are specific to its respective communities, rather than simply adopting a Western approach that fails to offer a culturally relevant education for Africans. Nzewi (1999) warns that

> to introduce Africans to modern music learning and appreciation of European music thoughts, contents, practices and pedagogy is a radical, de-acculturating process. It continues to produce the crises of cultural inferiority, mental inadequacy, and pervasive, cultural-human identity characterizing the modern African person in modern social, political, educational and cultural pursuits. (p. 72)

It is important to note that learners naturally integrate creative and performance behaviors in their daily lives with the ultimate aim of encountering music creativity to gain knowledge as well as experience it within the norms, traditions and cultures of the land. As Masoga (2003) asserts,

> We cannot talk of the African Philosophy and not address the issue of content that is being delivered as music education across the continent of Africa. Africa-sensitive music education must breed curricula of music that are relevant and focus on teaching about Africa in Africa. The absence of a comprehensive African relevance in the curricula which is taught in Africa for African students as recipients of such content is detrimental to African scientists and the leaders of tomorrow. (p. 5)

The challenges faced by music education in terms of composition remain many. It is hoped that through ongoing discussions and exploration of practice, an African philosophy of music composition pedagogy that honors African oral traditions will emerge as a central tenet of Ugandan national curriculum.

REFERENCES

Adedeji. (2005). Hymns sacred and secular: use of poetry in religious literature and in the religious education system of Judaeo, Christians, and the traditional Yoruba of Africa. *Religion and Society, 50*(2), 62–78.

Blaak, M. Openjuru, G. L., & Zeelen, J. (2013). Non-formal vocational education in Uganda: Practical empowerment through a workable alternative. *International Journal of Educational Development, 33*(1), 88–97.

Borko, H., & Putman, R. (1996). Learning to teach. In D. Berliner & R. Calfee (Eds.), *Handbook of educational psychology* (pp. 673–708). New York: Macmillan.

Elwana, D. (2000). Uganda hits universal primary education target. Newsletter of the world education (WEF) forum in Dakar. Paris: UNESCO Success stories. *The UNESCO Courier, 53*(3), 22–23.

Euba, A. (1989). *Essays on music in Africa*. African Studies Center. (Two Volumes).

Flolu, E.J. (1998). In search of an African and relevance oriented music education system for Ghanaian schools. UBUNTU: Proceedings of the 23rd ISME Conference. Pretoria: UNISA, 183–190.

Flolu, J. (2000). Re-thinking arts education in Ghana. *Arts Education Policy Review*, Taylor and Francis. *101*(5), 25–29.

Flolu, E. J. (2005). *An ethnic approach to music making as a strategy for teaching African music: the need for systematic research* (pp. 180). Cape Town: African Minds.

FLOLU, J. 2005. An ethnic approach to music making as a strategy for teaching African music: the need for systematic research. In Herbst, A. (Ed.), *Emerging solutions for musical arts education in Africa* (pp. 109). Cape Town. African Minds.

Fontana, D. (1988). *Psychology for teachers*. BPS & Macmillan Publishers, Ltd.

Idolor, E. G. (2005) Music in African societies. African culture and civilization by S. Ademola Ajayi/Ibadan Cultural Studies Group. 57–70.

Kigozi, B. (2008). *Music Education in Uganda: An evaluation of music education in elementary schools in Buganda; A way forward*. Scholar's Press.

Kigozi, B. (2016). Music education in Uganda [Web blog post]. Retrieved from http://musici nafrica.net/music-education-uganda

Kigozi, B. (2017). Why say it if you can sing it? Perspectives on the significance and usage of music in Africa. *Pan African Journal of Musical Arts Education: Research and Practice, 1*(2) 17–25.

Killian, J. N., & Dye, K. G. (2009). Effects of learner-centered activities in preparation of music educators: Finding the teacher within. *Journal of Music Teacher Education, 1*(1), 9–24.

Lave, J., & Wenger, E. (1991). *Situated learning: Legitimate peripheral participation*. Cambridge University Press.

Masoga, M. A. (2003). *Establishing dialogue: Thoughts on music education in Africa*, Alternation.

Mbabi-Katana, S. (1972). *Proposed music curriculum for first eight years of schooling in Uganda*. Unpublished doctoral dissertation, Northwestern University.

Muzumara, P. (2011). *Teacher competencies for improved teaching and learning*. Bhuta Publishers.

Ndeezi, A. (2001). Focus on policy universal in Uganda: Enabling education network. *Newsletter* (4), 4–8. April 3.

Nzewi, M. (1991). *Musical practice and creativity: An African traditional perspective*. Bayrueth: Iwalewa-Haus, University of Bayreuth.

Nzewi, M. (1999). Strategies for music education in Africa. Towards a meaningful progression from tradition to modern. In C. Van Niekerk (Ed.), *Conference proceedings of 23rd International Society for Music Education World Conference* (pp. 456–486). Unisa.

Nzewi, M. (2001). Music education in Africa: Mediating the imposition of western music education with the imperative of the indigenous African practice. In C. Van Niekerk (Ed.), *PASMEC Conference Proceedings* (pp. 18–37). Lusaka, Zambia.

Nzewi, O (2013) *Embedding the traditional concept of community within contemporary, indigenous musical arts training in Africa. Collaborative learning in Higher Music Education* (pp. 23–24). Ashgate Publishers (2).

Onyeji, C (2019) Composing art music from indigenous African musical paradigms. In *Music education in Africa*. Routledge 9780429201592 (1)

O'Toole, J., Stinson, M., & Moore, T. (2009). *Drama and curriculum: A giant at the door*. Springer.

Reimer, B. (1989). *A philosophy of music education* (2nd ed.). Prentice-Hall.

Rogers, C. R. (1959). Toward a theory of creativity. In H. H. Anderson (Ed.), *Creativity and its cultivation* (pp. 69–82). New York: Harper & Brothers.

Senghor, L.S. (1958). *Liberte I: Negritude et humanisme.* Education Du Seuil.

Sekalega, L. B (2018) Examination of Effective Music Pedagogies in Ugandan Urban, Suburban, and Rural Secondary Schools: An Empirical Study. Unpublished Thesis Texas Tech University.

Shizha, E. (2005). *Reclaiming our memories: The education dilemma in postcolonial African school curricula; A Nigerian cultural perspective* (pp. 65–81). Palgrave Macmillan

Slade, P. (1958). *An introduction to child drama.* University of London Press.

Slade, P. (1966). *Child drama and its value in education.* Educational Drama Association.

Stein, M. I. (1974). *Stimulating creativity* (Volume 1). Academic Press.

Uganda. (1997). *Universal Primary Education.*

Uganda. (1999). *Education Strategic Investment Plan.* Ministry of Education and Sports.

Uganda. (1989). *Education for National Integration and Reform.* UPPC, Entebbe.

Uganda. (1992). *Government White Paper on Education.*

Uganda. (1993). *Curriculum Review Task Force.*

Uganda. (2000). *Performing Arts and Physical Education Syllabus.* Kampala: Ministry of Education and Sports:

Uganda. (2001). *The Uganda Primary Schools Curriculum.* National Curriculum Development Centre.

UNESCO. (2006). *The Intangible Heritage Messenger.* UNESCO.

Wilson, C. B. (1986). *The Curriculum Enrichment Programme in African Music Education,* No. 5, 1987, University of Cape Coast. (12–17). ISBN 135798642.

CHAPTER 40

....

MUSIC COMPOSITION IN PORTUGUESE CLASSROOMS
Searching for Possible Routes

....

ANA LUÍSA VELOSO

PRELUDE

....

Music composition is a way of communicating with others, a way of sharing feelings and ideas, and a powerful tool for pupils to create meaning for and critically reflect on their experiences in the world (Barrett, 2003; MacDonald, Miell, & Morgan, 2000; Partti & Westerlund, 2013; Veloso, 2017). In this sense, several researchers have spoken of music composition—in the broad sense of its definition, including exploration, experimentation, and improvisation—as a powerful pathway not only for the development of musical thinking, but also, and perhaps more importantly, for children's personal and social growth (Barrett, 2003; Kaschub & Smith, 2009, Veloso, 2017; Veloso & Mota, 2021; Veloso & Carvalho, 2012). In what regards musical thinking, researchers (Faulkner, 2003; Veloso, 2017; Wiggins, 2007) have emphasized and described the diverse dialogues—musical, verbal, gestural—that pupils establish with their peers when composing, explaining how these dialogues might be a source for the expansion and/or transformation of children's' musical ideas, and for the manners through which pupils create new and expand former musical knowledge. At the same time, scholars (Barrett, 2003; Kaschub & Smith, 2009, Veloso, 2017) have also stressed that when music composition is approached through a perspective that values children's thoughts and feelings, on a joint effort to create something new together, they will most likely exceed their fears, critically reflecting on their lives and their relations with others, growing musically, personally, and socially.

I believe it is for these reasons that is so fundamental to rethink music composition in the Portuguese music classrooms. The problematic point is that in Portugal, music composition in general schools ended up becoming the least prioritized aspect of the "making music triangle"—listening, performing, and composing—and has not yet seen the full light of day as a creative and imaginative musical activity in its own right. There are many reasons why teachers may avoid composition. However, as we reach the second decade of the 21st century, and a new generation of music education teachers arises, it seems now imperative that these educational professionals embark on a journey where they might face their fears (Stringham, 2016; Hickey, 2012; Kaschub & Smith, 2013; Shouldice, 2014), engaging, together with their pupils, in truly creative activities in the classroom.

It is with these ideas in mind, and a willingness to reflect on our common past and present practices as music teachers and researchers, that I present this chapter, aiming to move toward a future where music composition has an unambiguous place, alongside with what are the more common practices of listening and performing.

A Brief Historical Overview of Music Education in Portugal

The first documents related to the development of music in the general school curriculum appeared in 1878, when the discipline of "canto coral"[1] was introduced in the early years of primary education. Until then, music in Portugal was learned only at the so-called Conservatório Real in Lisbon, currently Conservatório Nacional, founded in 1835 by the Portuguese writer Almeida Garrett. Later, with the beginning of the dictatorship in 1986, "canto coral," besides maintaining its place as a subject of the curriculum, developed also into a space to exalt the country and strengthen pupils' national sense. Anyway, and despite its political purposes, this discipline always had a small place in the curricula focusing mainly on musical theory and some singing. Besides, "canto coral" was taught by teachers with no professional training in education, and that were not prepared to significantly involve their pupils in the activities implemented in the classroom.

In the late 1960s, music education was marked by a new and vigorous stream: inspired by the international emphasis on art education and by the visit of several music educators philosophically related to the ideas of Dalcroze, Orff, or Willlems, the Portuguese music education community emphasized that pupils should be involved in several musical practices. The focus was no longer on music theory (which should be introduced later) but on the ways children could actively engage music. This was also the beginning of a period devoted to reflection about the goals, practices, and values of music education in schools. Institutions such as Associação Portuguesa de Educação Musical (APEM), or Calouste Goulbenkian Foundation, organized several seminars, conferences, and workshops, spreading a new philosophy for music education and inviting innovative and inspiring music educators and musicians such as John Paynter or Murray Schaffer (Mota, 2001).

In 1974, Portugal underwent a series of major political, social, and economic changes as a consequence of the democratic revolution that took place on April 25, signaling the end of the dictatorship and colonial regime. Since that date, and according with our constitution, Portugal is a democratic state based on the rule of law, the sovereignty of people, the pluralism of democratic expression and respect for fundamental rights and freedoms of all citizens. The revolution re-established the fundamental rights and liberties for all, which are now documented in the constitution of the Portuguese Republic. During this period, music education was not a major concern of the political agenda. However, at that time, music became a way of expressing the novel ideas of a democratic country; young people saw many of their feelings and thoughts disclosed in this "political engaged music" (Mota, 2001, p. 152), that slowly also became a part of many activities inside the music classroom. After 1974, there was also an emergence of pop/rock bands and musicians who composed their own songs without having any formal knowledge about music education. They composed and played by ear (as they do nowadays), incorporating styles and rhythms from Portugal's past African colonies in their songs. This also had an impact on music education. As stated by Mota, "Some young teachers have begun incorporating this music and its powerful rhythms in their music classrooms which is a total new direction to the Portuguese music" (Mota, 2001, pp. 152–153). Later, these pop/rock bands were also influenced by UK and American counterparts and by the lifestyle of diverse musicians living in these countries.

In 1983 took place what we might consider to be the first major reform of artistic education in Portugal, explicit in law 310/83. This law defines, among other things, universities and polytechnic institutes as the higher education institutions for the graduation of musicians and music teachers. Within this system, the training of professional musicians and teachers of specialized music education—which started to be concentrated in universities and music colleges—was differentiated from the training of music education teachers in general education, which became essentially assigned to the new colleges of education. Thus, if until then, music teachers were trained only at the conservatory, specializing in instrument, composition, or singing, from 1983 onward, the training of music teachers started to have not only the musical component but also the entire pedagogical component connected to educational sciences. This aspect was extremely important for the development of music education in our country, since, for the first time, teachers were educated to develop a critical and reflective perspective on the pedagogical and didactic issues related to music education (Mota, 2014 and 2015).

MUSIC EDUCATION AND MUSIC COMPOSITION IN THE GENERAL SCHOOL CURRICULA

Presently, compulsory education in Portugal is divided into four learning cycles. The first three cycles are part of what is named as "Basic Education," and the last cycle as

	Number of Academic Years	Pupils' Age	Music Education as a Curriculum Subject	Professional responsible for teaching music education
1st Cycle	4	6-9	Compulsory	Primary Teacher
2nd Cycle	4	10-11	Compulsory	Specialist Music Teacher
3rd Cycle	3	12-14	Optional in the two first years of the cycle. Non-existent in the third.	Specialist Music Teacher
Secondary School	3	15-18	Non-existent	Non-existent

FIGURE 40.1. Music education during compulsory schooling

"Secondary Education." As shown in Figure 40.1, music education is a compulsory subject only in the first and second cycles of education.

This was not always the case, since the first major change in school education in Portugal occurred as a result of the national reform of the educational system and the publication of the Basic Law of the Educational System, in 1986. This law not only defined the third cycle of education as the level of compulsory education,[2] as it transformed music education into a mandatory subject of the curriculum. The law also pronounced the formulation of a new curricula for teacher education, disclosing further the highly innovative idea of the possibility for primary teachers to work collaboratively with a specialized teacher in the school subjects related to the arts (Boal-Palheiros, 1993; Mota, 2007). However, the various governments that led the country following the publication of this law were somehow negligent toward art education, addressing it—even in the 21st century, as we will see later in more detail—into an isolated, remote space in the curricula, highlighting, at the same time, those areas related to logical-mathematical thinking such as mathematics, science, or languages.

This was a period of heated debates among music education teachers and scholars as they discussed different perspectives and points of view on what should be prioritized in the practice of music education and consequently, in the education of teacher-students respecting this specific knowledge area. These debates were based essentially on the ideas of innovative contemporary educators and researchers, especially Anglo-Americans (Mota, 2014), that gave a fundamental contribution to the construction of what should be an inclusive, democratic, and participatory music education.

The First Cycle of Education

During the first cycle of education, music education is a compulsory subject of the curriculum as part of a block of five hours of artistic education, and should be taught by primary teachers. However, many primary educators—as it has been documented all over the Western world—do not feel confident about teaching music (Economidou Stavrou, 2013; Hogenes, Oers, & Diesktra, 2014; Mota, 2007, 2014; Shouldice, 2014; Veloso, Ferreira, & Bessa, 2019), arguing that their teacher training didn't give them sufficient preparation in what regards music teaching and learning. Thus, feeling unprepared to develop a music education curriculum in their classes, these teachers are often afraid to move much beyond the teaching of simple songs, the development of movement activities and, sometimes, the introduction of very simple tasks that involve the use of musical instruments.

To overcome this gap, and following a philosophy based on a "full-time school" maxim, in 2006 the Ministry of Education launched a program that consisted of "10 weekly hours of extracurricular activities (English, music, sports) taught by specialist teachers, that children attended on a voluntary basis" (Boal-Palheiros & Encarnação, 2008, p. 98). A music syllabus was created with specific guidelines intended to help teachers to develop their work. The Portuguese Ministry of Education entitled these activities "Curriculum Enrichment Activities" (CEA). And although, at least in in principle, this program did not remove the mandatory teaching of music education within the curriculum, the implementation of these activities has been the cause of strong ambiguities, as there is repetition of music in both curricula (Araújo & Veloso, 2016; Mota, 2007, 2014) and some ambiguity regarding who is truly responsible to teach music education in primary schools. Moreover, in addition to the implementation of these activities, there was also a setback in terms of the professional qualifications required to teach music within this program. In fact, and although it was initially claimed that to teach music, a graduation on music education was necessary, in practice, the music classes have often been taught by young persons who have only attended a basic or secondary school degree in music at the conservatory or at a music academy. In both cases, music composition activities are almost nonexistent. Even when we talk about CEA, where teachers have at least some music training, it is rare for teachers to feel comfortable enough to develop music composition activities and projects. In fact, and similarly to what happens to music specialist throughout the several years of general school in some European countries and the United States (Boal-Palheiros & Boia, 2017; Klader & Lee, 2019; Stringham, 2016), they prefer to focus their practice on vocal and instrumental performance or on a more theoretical approach to music education.

Graça Mota (2007), outlining some concerns about the implementation of music as an enrichment activity, explained that with the new program, music education could be discarded from the elementary curriculum in some schools. Pupils not attending afterschool enrichment activities could be in danger of not receiving any music education. As a possible solution, Graça Mota (2007) advocated for a collaborative work between the primary teacher and a music specialist—that was, as we have already seen, predicted in the Basic Law of the Educational System. This collaborative work could be done through the implementation of projects that, on the one hand, would have their focus on making music, through performance, composition, or audition, and, on the other hand, would embrace a real interdisciplinary process relating music with other arts and also with other curriculum subjects. However, until now, this has not become general practice; pupils receive music education in primary schools within the voluntary "curricular enrichment activities," while provision of musical activities in school hours depends solely on the particular primary teacher. Notwithstanding, there is an exception to this generalized practice. In the Madeira Island—that has political autonomy regarding the implementation of the curriculum—the current education model in primary schools is similar to the one advocated by Graça Mota (2007). In fact, in Madeira, children attending primary school have music classes with a specialist music teacher during curricular hours. However, a recent three-year case study developed by CIPEM[3] about music education in the Madeira Island's in primary schools, shows that musical activities in these schools also focus mainly on vocal and instrumental performance and that music composition is, once again, almost absent from the activities and projects planned and implemented in the classroom (Mota & Abreu, 2014; Mota & Araújo).

The Second Cycle of Education

In the second cycle of education the curriculum that prevails nowadays was inspired in the Manhattanville Music Curriculum Project (MMCP), organized through a spiral around five main concepts: timbre, dynamics, pitch, rhythm, form. This syllabus was published in 1991 by a scientific committee that worked on the basis of an epistemological ground that highlighted the conceptual development theorized by scholars such as Jerome Bruner (1977). It was the first time that Portugal had a music education program based on a logic of musical development and that offered an innovative way to teach and learn music. This educational program intended to move away from some retrograde practices, to bring contemporary music into the classroom and to help pupils to achieve a conceptual understanding of music through exploration and experimentation. However, the Ministry of Education misunderstood the guidelines given by this committee, transforming what was a spiral in a closed grid. Thus, many music teachers began using music to exemplify the meaning of concepts, or to "test" students regarding those concepts. It also led to an emphasis on music theory, rather than on making music.

Despite this difficulty, and as mentioned before, at the end of the 20th century a rich discussion arose in Portugal, concerning what should be the priorities for a music education practice that was intended to focus on meaningful musical activities, and informed by values such as inclusion, pedagogical differentiation, and the active participation of pupils.

One of the theorists that influenced this discussion was Keith Swanwick, who proposed a model of musical development based on the analysis of children's music compositions (Swanwick & Tillman, 1986; Swanwick, 1988). This analysis stood, at the same time, for a curriculum centered on music-making, and where composition, alongside performance and music listening, could be ensured a relevant place (Swanwick,

1979). For the author, composition was central to music learning and should be understood from a global perspective:

> Under this heading is included all forms of musical invention, not merely works that are written down in any form of notation. Improvisation is, after all, a form of composition without the burden or the possibilities of notation. Composition is the act of making a musical object by assembling sound materials in an expressive way. There may or may not be experimentation with sounds as such. A composer may know what the materials will sound like from past experience in the idiom. Whatever form it may take, the prime value of composition in music education is not that we may produce more composers, but in the insight that may be gained by relating to music in this particular and very direct manner. (1979, p. 43)

This approach to music composition and its contextualization in what Keith Swanwick named as "The Comprehensive Model for Musical Experience" had strong repercussions on the panorama of music education classes regarding musical creativity and specific music composition projects. In this particular aspect, it seems fair to say that Swanwick was, therefore, a fundamental scholar in the introduction of music composition in music education classes in Portugal. In fact, with this new theoretical lens it became clear that it was of crucial importance to offer opportunities to children where they had the chance to express themselves musically through the creative manipulation of musical material.

Another essential milestone in the development of music composition in the classroom is directly related to the work developed by educators/composers such as Brian Dennis (1975), Murray Schafer (1976), and John Paynter (Paynter & Aston, 1970). These authors stood fiercely for a music education in which creativity occupied a broad and significant space in children's musical experiences. John Paynter and Peter Aston, in their book *Sound and silence* (1970), refer to making music as a response to life and the world around us. Being an art, as the authors continue to explain, this response is creative, allowing children to express thoughts and feelings through the medium of sounds, using their imagination. Paynter and Aston developed a music education philosophy based on the active exploration of sounding objects and musical instruments by the pupils, the use of techniques similar to those adopted by contemporary composers and a vision of the teacher as a guide and facilitator.

These educators/composers were part of the so-called *creative music movement* in the 1960s and 1970s. This movement included several musicians and educators who sought to introduce in the classroom a more open and comprehensive view on music composition that could go beyond the tonal paradigm and include in its practice the entire sound palette that surrounds us. At the same time, it is a perspective developed through a new epistemology based on "a plurality of knowledge forms, the recognition that there were different ways of knowing, different ways of making meaning and significance, different kinds of truth" (Finney, 2011, p. 18). Paynter visited Portugal more than once, invited by APEM. During his visits he gave seminars, workshops, sharing his philosophy and encouraging teachers to plan and implement creative projects and activities in the classroom. This had a significant influence in the development of music composition in Portuguese classrooms, as teachers that participated in these workshops responded with high levels of enthusiasm. These teachers also developed a strong sense of commitment toward the inclusion of creative practices in their classrooms, planning and implementing ideas that were either acquired in the workshops, or developed afterward, when reading these authors' books or sharing ideas with other colleagues. However, in practical terms, the *creative music movement* had no enduring influences in Portugal. Although important, the work developed though these workshops and the discussions and transformations they initiated were not systematically developed in a way that could significantly influence the education and work of most music education teachers.

21ST CENTURY MUSIC COMPOSITION AND VISIONS FOR MUSIC EDUCATION

A great part of the theoretical and practical field about music composition in the Portuguese classrooms, from the *creative music movement* to our days, is clearly connected to social constructivism (Vygotsky, 2007) and cultural psychology (Bruner, 1986, 1990, and 1996; Barrett, 2011). These perspectives advocate that mental activities, including creativity, cannot be separated from action, the materials that are being used, and the social and cultural context in which they occur. It was in this context that Margaret Barrett proposed a definition of music composition "as a meaning-making process that is fundamental to the intellectual, social, and emotional life of the child" (Barrett, 2003, p. 3) consisting in a "dialog between the child as musician and composer, the emerging musical work, the culture that has produced the composer and the emerging work, and the immediate settings in which the transaction takes place" (Barrett, 2003, p. 6). This definition, based on the ways children create meanings from their creative musical activities, is of great significance for Portuguese teachers and researchers, once that, on one side, is focused on the process, and, on the other, reminds us that any evaluation of musical products resulting from music composition activities cannot be separated from the specific context in which they emerged.

Following a theoretical axis based on these perspectives, in 2001, the Portuguese policy makers designed a curriculum model that was named as "National Curriculum for Basic Education: Essential Competencies" (NCBE) (2001). The idea of this document was not to replace the older syllabus inspired in the MMCP, but to be the ground in which this document should be approached. Music education appeared in the NCBE as a part of artistic education, that was itself organized around four building blocks: creativity, expression and communication, artistic languages, and arts in context. Within this whole, music education was then approached around a series of musical competences, highlighting music as a social practice. These competences were, in turn, also focused on four main building blocks, namely perception, performance, creation, and musical cultures in context, suggesting also different possibilities to relate music with other arts and with other subject matters. Writing about this document Graça Mota stressed that:

It should be noted that the publication, in September 2001, of the Essential Competences of the National Curriculum for Basic Education (Portugal, 2001) contributed to a clarification of the place that music "should assume in the curriculum . . . [embracing] an unequivocal epistemological status regarding its structure and development, in the set of all other disciplines" (Mota, 2014, p. 44). Music composition, included in the block "creation," was clearly considered as a practice on its own right, that should be promoted and developed by teachers in their classrooms. In fact, not only was creativity one of the building blocks of art education, to which music composition could give an obvious contribution, but the document also contained several practical suggestions to develop music composition in the classroom. These suggestions were not of the "recipe type." Rather, they worked as models to foster the imaginative skills of teachers, to enhance more creative learning contexts and to foster the development of music composition activities and projects.

The philosophy underlying this proposal was highly innovative and in line with contemporary theoretical understandings forecasting music education as a social practice and seeing pupils as active and creative practitioners. In this sense, the NCBE gave professors from universities and colleges a new tool to strengthen those teaching philosophies that emphasized the creative work of pupils. The ideas presented in the NCBE from 2001 were strongly discussed among students and professors in the music education academy, not only in the regular classes but also as part of the numerous short-term training courses and workshops that these institutions offered. As a consequence, many music education teachers began looking at their practices through a different lens, searching for literature about creativity and music composition in the classroom, reflecting on the learning situations they were creating for their pupils, and embracing, as much as possible, this new vision that emphasized creativity and composition as a crucial tenet on the development of music education.

However, in the recent past, and similarly to what happened in many other European countries, Portugal suffered from a major financial and economic crisis, which affected both individual, community, and institutional dimensions of Portuguese lives. This crisis also had a strong and negative impact on the Portuguese education system. In what concerns music education, many ambiguous and negative aspects emerged, concerning not only the place of music education in the Portuguese curriculum but also the role, status, and professional development of music teachers. In 2011, the ministry of education revoked the NCBE, arguing that education should be focused on declarative knowledge and measurable goals, and not on key competences. The minister added that it was his intention to create a curriculum based on target goals, but the truth is that these goals were never defined to music education. Instead, and at that time, the government proposed again the old syllabuses from 1991 (first and second cycles of education), that are nowadays completely out of date. Most teachers, and especially those graduated after 2001, felt an enormous frustration when the NCBE was revoked. Their education during university or college had been decisively supported by this document and by the theoretical perspectives underpinning it. Therefore, teachers felt disappointed, deceived, and very confused, as the legal documents used since 2011 were in total disagreement with what they had learned.

Essential Leanings: Reclaiming the Music-Making Paradigm

In March 2016, the minister of education invited several Portuguese personalities to join a working group whose main goal was to create a document that outlined the "profile for the 21st century student in the end of compulsory education." This profile should be based, on the one side, on a humanistic understanding of the student, and on the other, on "The Future of Education and Skills 2030" (OCDE, 2018). With these ideas in mind, a group of committed individuals sought to develop a profile centered on the development of each student as a personal and social being, an autonomous citizen with initiative, who is responsible, creative, and has the capacity and desire to learn throughout life.

The document was released for public comment in early 2017 and published by the Ministry of Education later that same year. In what regards the document "Essential Learnings" (EL), it is important to highlight that, contrary to what had previously happened, teachers had an important word to say in this process. In fact, in 2016, the secretary of state for education, João Costa, asked the Portuguese teachers' professional associations to participate in the process of defining a set of "essential learnings" in each curricular area, within a perspective of horizontal and vertical curricular articulation.

This request was justified by the need to focus on the capital contents of each subject, to give more time to deepen each topic within each subject matter, to develop an interdisciplinary approach to the curriculum, to promote greater student interaction, and to make teaching and learning processes more effective. A working group was therefore created that included APEM board of directors, and the Program of Aesthetic and Artistic Education of the ministry of education; the work was carried out jointly with other artistic areas to create "common learning organizers for artistic education," that could be the base for the definition of the essential learning experiences within each artistic discipline. In what concerns music education, when this task was completed, the document was analyzed by a group of experts invited by APEM that included not only researchers but also music education teachers and primary teachers. The final version of the document was then sent to the ministry of education, disclosed in March for public discussion and published in 2018.

Although it is too soon to fully evaluate the consequences and impact of the implementation of this new legislation, for now it is possible to say that, despite the efforts of the government and of institutions such as APEM, the EL felt short of the expectations of those that created and published it. The problem seems to lie in the fact that the

EL cohabit with the two older syllabuses from 1991(Ministério da Educação, 1991a and 1991b) that have been serving, for years now, and especially after 2011, as the foundation for the school textbooks that teachers use on a daily basis and that are at odds with the EL. Thus, these textbooks do not represent the document published in 2018, that is, as we previously saw, aligned with contemporary socio-cultural and humanistic perspectives, focused on musical competences and not on concepts. This situation is the cause of many misunderstandings and confusions, with many teachers somehow navigating between the textbooks and both legal and curricular directives, having serious difficulties to articulate them. There is, therefore, the urgent need to develop research project in schools, involving teachers, students, and policy-makers to try to understand how this issue might be exceed, and how the EL might be fully used by teachers on their daily classroom work. Only then it will be possible to comprehensively discuss the benefits and shortcomings of this document and how music composition might be comprehensively developed in the context of this new legal normative.

EXAMPLES FROM PRACTICE

In this section I briefly describe two approaches to music composition developed by myself in music classrooms and workshops with children. I do so to illustrate some of the practices that have been taking place in Portuguese music classrooms, knowing that I do not exist in isolation, and that my work reflects my entire learning journey as a music education teacher and researcher. Thus, what I report now is a mirror of my own teacher education in the university, the many conversations I had with other teachers, researchers, and musicians, all that I have learned while attending and presenting in conferences or seminars, and, of course, what I have also learned while writing and reflecting about these matters, through the lenses of the many actors that have participated in these projects.

The definition of the two approaches to music composition is a result of the analysis of some of the main creative projects I have developed with children as a teacher and researcher, from 2005 to the present moment. During this period of time, that includes my graduation in music education[4] and my PhD in music[5] (pedagogy), and that was of paramount importance in my professional life, I developed a perspective on music composition as a social practice, profoundly embedded in pupils' cultures and living contexts, much in the sense of what is presented during the first section of the chapter (Barrett, 2003 and 2011; Kaschub & Smith, 2009 and 2013; Veloso, 2017; Veloso & Mota, 2021). Thus, in my classroom, I always tried to implement activities and projects that valued children's interests and backgrounds. This was especially true when approaching music composition activities, as I always tried to encouraged pupils to develop their musical pieces and songs from their lived experiences, from their thoughts and feelings, and from their views and reflections about the world. This approach to teaching and learning music was supported not only by the literature I had studied and the practices I had observed since my graduation in music education, but also by the legal norma-tive that invigorated at that time—the NCBE (2001). The NCBE was published during my first college year and had an enormous influence in my practice as a teacher and research. In fact, I found in the NCBE the legal fundaments to develop a music educa-tion practice based on the theoretical and philosophical perspectives that were at the center of my education. This allowed me to develop, in congruence with my own ideas and beliefs, an inclusive and democratic music education practice, based on children's specific contexts of living and ways of relating to sound and music, emphasizing pupils' agency, creativity, and imaginative action.

I have picked one example from each approach, that I present now as an illustration of similar projects developed in music classes and workshops with children from six to 11 years old. This means that the examples that I outline next refer to the first and second cycle of education (primary school and first years of middle school) that are, as we have seen before, the years in which music education is a compulsory subject of the Portuguese school curriculum.

The Rhizomatic Approach

In biological terms, the rhizome is an underground root system that grows horizontally and outward, the way and ginger roots. In this sense, it is in opposition to arbor roots that give birth to trees that grow vertically and upward. Translating this into a philo-sophical field, Semetsky (2008) notes that the rhizome is a nonhierarchical system with no beginning or end, that spreads through "movements in diverse directions instead of a single path, multiplying its own lines and establishing the plurality of unpredictable connections" (p. xv).

If we think about music education and music composition from the perspective of the rhizome, we are faced with a structure that metaphorically allows pupils to grow and de-velop pathways in new and unexpected ways, through diverse "lines of flight" or "creative musical routes" that they trace while creating meaning to their lived experiences (Lines, 2013 Schmidt, 2012). Acknowledging music composition from this point of view means recognizing children's' interests and past experiences, emphasizing that there are many and diverse paths that pupils might take during their creative voyages—paths that are distinguished by their uniqueness and that are, as Margaret Barrett (2003) would put it, related to the specific relationships each child establishes with the available tools and re-sources while she is composing, the music that is being created, and those that might take an important part in this process (her peers, teachers, parents). Furthermore, it is an ap-proach that strongly depends on the specific motivations, actions, and initiatives taken by each pupil, and that needs, therefore, a classroom environment where children feel safe and encouraged to manifest and express their feelings, thoughts, ideas, or desires.

Figure 40.2 shows an excerpt taken from my field notes, written after a session of a music workshop implemented from 2015 to 2017 in a Portuguese state school (Veloso

Today Daniel showed me a musical piece on the guitar that he composed. He asked me to listen to him before the beginning of the music session, during the class break. We looked for a quiet place in the corridor and crouched together. He smiled at me, a little bit nervous, but clearly very excited for the opportunity to show me his new musical piece. The first thing he did was to put a guitar capo on the third fret of the guitar. This made me smile and wonder how he had had that idea. He took one deep breath and began to play, using his thumb to play the lower strings of the guitar and his index finger to play the remaining three stings. It was quite unusual because he used his index finger in one single movement downward, as if he was "sweeping" the strings. The chord progression, made through smooth arpeggios, was quite complex and beautiful. We immediately began talking about possibilities to expand what he had composed. When I asked him why he had used the guitar capo, he told me "I saw this on youtube several times. With several guitarists. I got curious. So I picked my dad's guitar capo and I began to experiment, and when I experimented here, it sounded really cool!" When asked about how he had composed this music, he replied that he had done it during a day in which he was feeling in a "kind of melancholic mood", thinking about "his friends and about music". He then picked the guitar, began to improvise, to "try on the guitar" until he had something that pleased him.

FIGURE 40.2. Field notes, November 2016

& Mota, 2021). This workshop was developed in a classroom context, with pupils aged between nine and eleven years old, during two academic years—encompassing pupils' last year of primary school and the first year of middle school. The workshop, which occurred once a week for an hour and a half, as another activity of the curriculum, was developed as a follow-up of a case study already documented elsewhere (Veloso, Ferreira, & Bessa, 2019). Throughout the workshop, pupils developed several interdisciplinary activities and projects through differentiated pathways, in a creative, informal, and collaborative approach to music-making. They had several musical instruments at hand, that included not only the Orff ensemble but also guitars, bass guitars, drums, keyboards and other handmade invented sounding objects and instruments. I acted both as a researcher and facilitator, guiding students in specific tasks, suggesting tools and ways for developing the work, giving cues in specific ways to approach musical instruments, always valuing pupils' specific musical backgrounds and interests. As part of the workshop, pupils gave several concerts to the school community, organizing also open rehearsals and performing at other school events such as exhibitions or seminars.

Daniel, a 10-year-old boy who loved to play the guitar, composed this particular piece of music following his ear, his intuition, what he was feeling. He was neither concerned about any specific task given to him in the classroom, nor about the "correct ways" of making music or playing guitar. He was concerned with the music, the overall sound and what he was expressing through it. His approach to music composition was one of trial and error, involving multiple attempts, and, as he explained later, multiple moments of experimentation where he tried out his ideas "once and again, playing, listening, playing again, organizing and putting the sounds together," until he finally felt he had something he enjoyed and wanted to share with other persons. After this moment, I encouraged Daniel to present his musical piece to his peers. Not only did he do that with great confidence and joy, but he also talked about other musical instruments he would like to put together with the guitar, inviting some of his colleagues to join him. Together, and for a period of three weeks (three music sessions), the group created a new musical piece that evolved from Daniel's first ideas.

During this period, they rehearsed by themselves in a different room while I was working with the rest of the class. From time to time, they invited me to join them, to share my thoughts about what they had done so far, asking questions, and exposing their views and ideas. In the end of the academic year, they proudly presented their musical piece in a concert organized to all the school community. I remember they were so proud.

Daniel was the first pupil from his class to approach music composition in this way, but many others followed him. Experimenting on guitars, percussive sounding objects, invented musical instruments, or using their own voices, many pupils began to present, on a regular basis, their own musics: Original compositions, arrangements of other songs, small ideas that they didn't know yet how to develop and expand, each child bringing a new and fresh manner of picking sounds and organizing them, each one of them designing a unique path in their journey within music composition.

Embodying the metaphor of the rhizome, pupils traced multiple and divergent routes in a horizontal and non-hierarchical process. I believe that, in this way, music composition grew into a powerful means of communication through which pupils could express their thoughts and feelings, envisaging music as a place where there are no dichotomies regarding good or bad and where each one of them could embrace her/his own individual and unique path. Thus, we might perhaps say that, when conceived "rhizomatically," music composition projects might be understood as journeys with diverse points of departure and different points of arrival, where pupils are not afraid to take risks, to experiment, to listen, to play, and to try once and again, communicating their ideas in creative and, quite often, surprising ways.

The Thematic Approach

In the thematic approach, I usually invite children to create their music departing from other media, mostly from the artistic realm. I might use a painting, a film, a story, a poem. This object/idea is what Acaso y Megias (2017) named as "detonante," a "spark" that helps children to travel along new imaginary landscapes, and through which they connect (in the specific case of music education) a set of ideas with musical material.

The "spark" is used, therefore, to stimulate children's' curiosity and, as a follow-up, emotions such as surprise or wonder. This approach to music composition is in line with recent findings on the fields on neurobiology and arts education that have shown consistently that such emotions have a decisive role in fostering our attention and our desire to think and reflect, and are, thus, essential to learning and to the development of creative activities (Damásio, 2000 and 2001; Teruel, 2013; Piersol, 2014; Veloso, 2017; Veloso, 2020). Motivated by strong feelings of surprise and wonder, pupils direct their attention and thinking processes toward what is being explored. This is the beginning of creativity and transformation. Slowly, they engage in a process led by their imagination, connecting different symbolic worlds, transforming their thoughts, ideas, and images into sounds and music. At the same time, and much in line with what I previously mention about the importance of pupils' personal and social backgrounds (Bruner, 1986, 1990, and 1996; Vygotski, 2007), in this approach, the "spark" typically emerges from ideas or themes that are significant for children's' lives. Ideas that evoke their interests and preoccupations, and that, many times, relate to sensitive issues such as difficult familiar relationships, discrimination, gender issues, or bullying. This practice is, in a sense, much aligned with the "political engaged music" (Mota, 2001, p. 152), mentioned in the "Brief Historical Overview" earlier in this chapter, as it tries to give voice to children's thoughts and feelings without censure, bringing to the fore those issues that are part of children's daily struggles when they try to cope with world.

An example of this approach is found in Project Bernardino, based on a book written by Manuela Bacelar. The project is designed for six-year-olds and was developed in a primary state school. *Bernardino* tells the story of a young lion that was quite different from all the other lions. Bernardino was vegetarian. This was the cause of great sadness and concern to his father, who could not understand his son's way of living. Sad and lonely, Bernardino ran away from home. Throughout his journey he met many friends, and one of these friends taught him how to play the flute. Bernardino was a good student, learning fast and becoming a great musician that toured around the world. One day he came back home to see his father. And although his father was still concerned about his son's choices in life, in the end Bernardino conquered his heart with the music he created. The story and the many themes that emerged from it—especially related with difficult familiar relationships—were the *detonante*, the "spark" given to pupils to begin their creative process. The idea of using *Bernardino* as a *detonante* came about because this book was part of pupils' reading list on their general class, and their primary teacher thought it could be a good idea to introduce the book by relating the words and illustrations with music. When she talked to me about this, it made perfect sense, and we both decided to develop the project together. Our intention was that pupils could have an opportunity to reflect on the ideas evoked by the life of this young lion, his relation to his father, to his friends, and to music. The project[6] was developed in four key moments, as shown in Figure 40.3.

Pupils participated in this project with great enthusiasm, connecting the book's story with their specific life experiences, and using them as a base for the development of musical ideas. They established a truly strong emotional connection with the story and were, therefore, quite motivated to engage in all the tasks involved in the project.

The final concert mentioned in last phase of the project (Figure 40.3) was organized by teachers, parents, pupils, and other school workers. Everybody participated

Key moments	Activities
Awakening	1. I presented the book to pupils reading it aloud while exhibiting a slideshow with the books' illustrations. 2. The class discussed some of the books' main topics and themes such as parenthood, friendship, and how music sometimes becomes like a magic door to peoples' hearts.

Framing	1. I asked pupils to gather into small groups, from three to five elements. I tried to intervene the least in this process, giving them total freedom to choose the colleagues they wanted to work with.
	2. Each group chose an illustration that to explore it musically, following some of the questions:
	  ■ What ideas/feeling do you want to transmit?
	  ■ How would you characterize the 'sound mood' corresponding to this illustration?
	  ■ What instruments could best contribute to the composition of such a sound mood?
	3. Groups began to discuss ideas. In this stage I moved from one group to the other, asking questions, giving suggestions, exploring their thoughts and feelings about the music they wanted to create.

Creating	1. The small groups began to explore and develop the initial ideas they had discussed in the precious sessions, using their voice, musical instruments and diver sounding objects. I assigned each group to a different space in the school, occupying places that at the time were empty. 2. Each group presented their original musical piece to the rest of the class 3. In the end of each presentation, the class reflected on what they had heard. Pupils took this task very seriously, focusing on relevant issues such as the relationship between the illustration and the music, the instrumentation chosen by the group, or the form and structure of the music composition. In the following session we started exactly at the point we had left the previous one. 4. Ideas from each small group were grouped into a larger musical piece that evolved in a process of trial and error, experimentation, improvisation and verbal dialogues
Presenting/ Evaluating	1. In the end of the academic year the class presented the final musical piece in a concert to the school community. 2. After the concert pupils saw a video of their performance and had the chance to discuss not only the presentation but also the entire compositional journey. In addition, they also wrote self-reports sharing what were the most important and special moments during the music composition project.

FIGURE 40.3. Project Bernardino—key moments

enthusiastically, working in close collaboration. In the day of the concert the pupils seemed extremely excited. However, this doesn't seem to have had a negative influence on their performance. On the contrary. When their time arrived, they stepped into the stage smiling and happy, but deeply concentrated. The performance was a very beautiful moment that the audience deeply appreciated, something that was visible in the end of the concert, in their joyful gestures and words.

Later, after watching the video of their performance, when discussing and reflecting on the process they focused specially on two issues: First, the possibility to experiment and interact with musical instruments from the very beginning. Pupils clearly stressed that this had been of paramount importance in their journey. Many stated they felt like "real musicians," when experimenting or improvising with the available musical instruments and sounding objects. The second issue that was mentioned, was the importance of working in groups. Pupils clearly looked at the group as an essential part of the venture, developing a strong emotional attachment and sense of belonging toward their peers. Moreover, they mentioned frequently how the group opened their own imagination to other musical possibilities, highlighting how the collaborative work became a means to do better, to work harder, and to develop ideas that, otherwise, would never exist.

The thematic approach is neither better nor worse than the rhizomatic approach. It is different, as, at least in the beginning, pupils' ideas depart from something that is presented and chosen by the teacher, and by the questions/suggestions that guide the transition from the *detonantes* to the music. However, this presentation is only an invitation, a platform for pupils to begin thinking creatively through sounds. Therefore, in this approach it is also of extreme importance that pupils might have the opportunity to work on their own, to express and discuss their ideas with their peers, to experiment once and again without fear of doing "the wrong thing." The job of the teacher is to guide, to ask questions and pose new challenges, listening carefully, and creating a classroom environment that might offer the conditions to a genuine and creative dialogue.

In Search of New Routes

Since 1974, many teachers, musicians, scholars, and researchers have been making strong efforts to promote and establish music composition as an integral and regular activity within music education in general schools. However, and despite the excellent composition practices that were and are developed in some of our classrooms, the truth is that it is not yet possible to say that music composition has become widespread in Portuguese general schools. From my experience working as a teacher and researcher in several schools, and also from discussing these matters with music education teachers and researchers, I still feel there is a certain anxiety when it comes to plan and implement music composition projects in the classroom. Teachers seem to fear failing in planning the adequate strategies; that their pupils—not used to this kind of activities—will not commit themselves to work seriously; that they will be unable to manage a noisy and chaotic classroom; that in the end they have nothing to present as a fruit of their work. It is in this way that I have to admit—not without some perplexity—that even now, in 2020, it is possible to find in Mota's words, written in 2001, a significant parallel in relation to what is happening today:

> Although the curriculum clearly prescribes the three areas of composing, listening and performing, composition is largely excluded. Children, instead, do a lot of notation, music reading and aural-training activities which often diminish their motivation to continue learning music. . . . This is exacerbated by the way in which some teachers who have difficulty managing the classroom environment use these activities as a means of controlling pupils: other, more interesting musical activities, such as composing and performing, are thus perceived as being of secondary importance. (Mota, 2001, p. 155)

Analyzing what has been described in the first part of this chapter, it is clear that part of the problem seems to be related to the teachers themselves and to their education in college and university (Economidou Stavrou, 2013; Kaschub & Smith, 2013; Mota, 2007; Stringham, 2016). Thus, to address this issue in Portugal, I suggest four changes be made to teacher preparation. First, initial teacher training should focus more on creativity and creative activities, both in theoretical and in practical terms, through the development of workshops, seminars, and projects involving professors, researchers in the field, and also contemporary composers and musicians. These moments should be organized in such a way that teacher-students have enough room to reflect on their perceptions, beliefs, doubts, and fears in shared, open dialogues with all those involved in their training. Learning is strictly related to the reorganization and transformation of old perspectives into new ones (O'Neill, 2012). Leading students to such moments where they might move beyond their pre-conceptions and beliefs should, therefore, be an aim of all learning institutions, including, of course, the colleges and universities that educate future music education teachers.

Second, teachers should have more time during their teacher training period to implement creative projects and activities in the classrooms, working together—and as soon as possible—with children and youth. This would give them more confidence, as they would have the opportunity to see, listen, and analyze their planned projects and activities in real contexts, critically reflecting on children's' words, actions, feelings, and ideas.

Third, these moments shouldn't be exclusive of initial teacher training. On the contrary. Teachers should have the opportunity to engage and participate in such educational initiatives throughout their professional lives, so that their practice might not stagnate in time.

Finally, it would also be necessary to give teachers new tools and materials to teach. The old classroom, equipped with a few Orff instruments and soprano recorders, and with desks and chairs distributed in rows, is no longer appropriate. Schools and teachers need autonomy to organize their classrooms in line with the projects that are being developed, modifying issues related to space and time according to the best interest of their pupils. They also need new musical instruments, related to contemporary practices of different styles and genres, and equipment related with music technology. A special note here should be made in recognizing that the digital age has enriched and transformed music-making through unique and appealing resources. Nowadays, children and youth are very familiar with electronic and digital tools in other realms of their experience (O'Neill, 2015; Seedorf & Schultz, 2017). Why shouldn't teachers enhance those skills in their music education classrooms? This would be an excellent way not only to strengthen children's expertise on electronic and digital devices and means, but also to promote the development of music projects where they might combine acoustic and digital resources, acknowledging students' diverse cultural backgrounds, and opening them to other creative possibilities.

Throughout this process that involves multiple interactions of numerous and sometimes quite different realities, it seems also important that the teacher might look at herself not as the "holder of the truth" but as another, more skilled collaborator. A musician that brings into the classroom, like the rest of her pupils, all her musical and non-musical past experiences. Someone who is open to share these experiences with her pupils—guiding them on their individual and collaborative paths, broadening their horizons while reflecting, questioning, and challenging—can create a musical community where pupils might feel safe to try, to explore, or as Rancière (1991) would put it, "to speak."

Acknowledgements

To Professor Graça Mota, for her invaluable contribution to the development of Music Education practice and research in Portugal, and for everything she taught me throughout the years.

Notes

1. "choral singing"
2. Nowadays compulsory education includes also the secondary school.
3. Research Centre for Music Psychology and Music Education, currently a pole in Porto Polytechnic of Institute of Ethnomusicology, Center of Studies in Music and Dance.
4. Porto College of Education, Porto Polytechnic.
5. Aveiro University.

6. In this school, and for this particular project, the class was divided into two groups of 12 pupils each. This was agreed between their primary teacher, the school director and me at the beginning of the project, so that these pupils could benefit the most from their music sessions, that occurred once a week, for 60 minutes. Thus, when I was working with one of the large groups (12 pupils each), the primary teacher was working with the rest of the class. After a short break we would switch the groups.

References

Acaso, M., & Megías, C. (2017). *Art thinking: Cómo el arte puede transformar la educación*. Ediciones Paidós.

Araújo, M. J., & Veloso, A. L. (2016). Música como Prática Social: Uma Reflexão Crítica sobre a Atividade de Educação Musical no 1.º Ciclo do Ensino Básico no Âmbito das Atividades de Enriquecimento Curricular. *Revista Portuguesa de Educação Artística*, 6(1), 65–78. https://doi.org/10.34639/rpea.v6i1.15

Barrett, M. (2011). Towards a cultural psychology of music education. In M. Barrett (Ed.), *A cultural psychology of music education* (pp. 1–16). Oxford University Press.

Barrett, M. S. (2003). Freedoms and constraints: Constructing musical worlds through the dialogue of composition. In M. Hickey (Ed.), *Why and how to teach music composition: A new horizon for music education* (pp. 3–27). MENC.

Boal-Palheiros, G. (1993). Educação Musical no Ensino Preparatório. *Associação Portuguesa de Educação Musical*. https://recipp.ipp.pt/handle/10400.22/11541

Boal-Palheiros, G., & Boia, P. D. S. (2020). Formação de professores de música e práticas de educação musical nas escolas (pp. 117–141). Politécnico do Porto. Escola Superior de Educação. CIPEM/INET-md. https://recipp.ipp.pt/handle/10400.22/16994

Boal Palheiros, G. & Encarnação, M. (2008). Music education as extra-curricular activity in Portuguese primary schools. In G. Mota & S. Malbrán (Eds.) *Proceedings of the XXII ISME International Seminar on Research in Music Education*. Porto, Portugal: ESE/FCT, p. 96–104.

Bruner, J. (1977). *The process of education*. Harvard University Press.

Bruner, J. (1986). *Actual minds, possible worlds*. Harvard University Press.

Bruner, J. S. (1990). *Acts of meaning*. Harvard University Press.

Bruner, J. S. (1996). *The culture of education*. Harvard University Press.

Damasio, A. (2000). *O Sentimento de Si: O Corpo, a Emoção e a Neurobiologia da Consciência*. Publicações Europa América.

Damasio, A. (2001). *O Erro de Descartes: Emoção, Razão, e Cérebro Humano*. Publicações Europa América.

Dennis, B. (1975). *Projects in sound*. Universal Edition.

Economidou Stavrou, N. (2013). Fostering musical creativity in pre-service teacher education: Challenges and possibilities. *International Journal of Music Education*, 31(1), 35–52. https://doi.org/10.1177/0255761411431391

Faulkner, R. (2003). Group Composing: pupil perceptions from a social psychological study. *Music Education Research*, 5(2), 101–124. https://doi.org/10.1080/1461380032000085504

Finney, J. (2011). *Music education in England, 1950–2010: The child-centered progressive tradition*. Ashgate.

Hickey, M. (2012). *Music outside the lines: Ideas for composing in K–12 music classrooms*. Oxford University Press.

Hogenes, M., Oers, B. V., & Diekstra, R. F. W. (2014). Music composition in the music curriculum. *US-China Education Review A, 4*(3), 149–162. https://doi.org/10.17265/2161-623X/2014.03A.002

Kaschub, M., & Smith, J. (2009). *Minds on music: Composition for creative and critical thinking.* R&L Education.

Kaschub, M., & Smith, J. P. (2013.). Embracing composition in music teacher education. In M. Kaschub & J. P. Smith (Eds.), *Composing our future: Preparing music educators to teach composition* (pp. 5–13). Oxford University Press.

Kladder, J., & Lee, W. (2019). Music teachers' perceptions of creativity: A preliminary investigation. *Creativity Research Journal, 31*(4), 395–407. https://doi.org/10.1080/10400419.2019.1651189

Lines, D. (2013). Deleuze and music education: Machines for change. In D. Masny (Ed.), *Cartographies of becoming in education* (pp. 21–33). Brill Sense.

MacDonald, R., Miell, D., & Morgan, L. (2000). Social processes and creative collaboration in children. *European Journal of Psychology of Education, 15*(4), 405–415. https://doi.org/10.1007/BF03172984

Ministério da Educação. (1991a). Organização curricular e programas ensino básico—1º Ciclo. http://curricula-depot.gei.de/handle/11163/1348

Ministério da Educação. (1991b). Programa de Educação Musical do 2º Ciclo do Ensino Básico. https://www.dge.mec.pt/sites/default/files/ficheiros/eb_em_programa_2c_i.pdf

Ministério da Educação. (2001). Currículo Nacional do Ensino Básico—Competências Essenciais. Lisboa: Ministério da Educação. http://metasdeaprendizagem.dge.mec.pt/metasdeaprendizagem.dge.mec.pt/wp-content/uploads/2010/09/Curriculo_Nacional1CEB.pdf

Mota, G. (2001). Portugal. In D. J. Hargreaves & A. C. North (Eds.), *Musical development and learning: The international perspective* (pp. 151–162). Continuum

Mota, G. (2007). A Música no 1º Ciclo do Ensino Básico: Contributo para uma reflexão acerca do conceito de enriquecimento curricular. *Revista de Educação Musical, 128–129,* 16–21.

Mota, G. (2014). A educação musical em Portugal: Uma história plena de contradições. *DEBATES: Cadernos do Programa de Pós-Graduação em Música, 0*(13), 41–50.

Mota, G. (2015). La formación de profesores de educación musical en Portugal. Aportaciones para una reflexión contextualizada. *Revista Internacional de Educación Musical, 0*(3), 41–50.

Mota, G., & Abreu, L. (2014). Thirty years of music and drama education in the Madeira Island: Facing future challenges. *International Journal of Music Education, 32*(3), 360–374. https://doi.org/10.1177/0255761413515803

Mota, G., & Araújo, M. J. (2013). Music and drama in primary schools in the Madeira Island: Narratives of ownership and leadership. *Music Education Research, 15*(3), 275–289. https://doi.org/10.1080/14613808.2013.772130

O'Neill, S. A. (2012). Becoming a music learner: Toward a theory of transformative music engagement. In G. E. McPherson & G. F. Welch (Eds.), *The Oxford handbook of music education* (Volume 1, pp. 163–186). Oxford University Press. https://doi.org/10.1093/oxfordhb/9780199730810.013.0010_update_001

O'Neill, S. A. (2015). Youth empowerment and transformative music engagement. In C. Benedict, P. Schmidt, G. Spruce, & P. Woodford (Eds.), *The Oxford handbook of social justice in music education* (pp. 338–405). Oxford University Press. https://doi.org/10.1093/oxfordhb/9780199356157.013.25

OCDE. (2018). The future of education and skills: Education 2030 | VOCEDplus, the international tertiary education and research database. https://www.voced.edu.au/content/ngv:79286

Partti, H., & Westerlund, H. (2013). Envisioning collaborative composing in music educa-tion: Learning and negotiation of meaning in operabyyou.com. *British Journal of Music Education, 30*(2), 207–222. https://doi.org/10.1017/S0265051713000119

Paynter, J., & Aston, P. (1970). *Sound and silence: Classroom projects in creative music.* Cambridge University Press.

Piersol, L. (2014). Our hearts lean up: Awakening wonder within the classroom. In K. Egan, A. Cant, & G. Judson (Eds.), *Wonder-full education: The centrality of wonder in teaching and learning across the curriculum* (pp. 3–21). Routledge.

Rancière, J. (1991). *The ignorant schoolmaster: Five lessons in intellectual emancipation.* Stanford University Press.

Schafer, R. M. (1976). *Creative music education: A handbook for the modern music teacher.* Schirmer Books.

Schmidt, P. (2012). Ethics or choosing complexity in music relations. *Action, Criticism, and Theory for Music Education, 11*(1), 149–169.

Semetsky, I. (2008). (Pre)facing Deleuze. In I. Semetsky (Ed.), *Nomadic education: Variations on a theme xby Deleuze and Guattari* (pp. vii–xi). Sense Publishers.

Seedorf, M., & Schultz, C. M. (2017). Digital media and electronic music in the classroom: The loop ensemble. In T. Bovermann, A. de Campo, H. Egermann, S.-I. Hardjowirogo, & S. Weinzierl (Eds.), *Musical instruments in the 21st century: identities, configurations, practices* (pp. 167–179). Springer.

Shouldice, H. N. (2014). Teachers' beliefs regarding composition in elementary general music: Definitions, values, and impediments. *Research Studies in Music Education, 36*(2), 215–230. https://doi.org/10.1177/1321103X14556574

Stringham, D. A. (2016). Creating compositional community in your classroom. *Music Educators Journal, 102*(3), 46–52. https://doi.org/10.1177/0027432115621953

Swanwick, K. (1979). *A basis for music education* (1st edition). New York: Routledge.

Swanwick, K. (1988). *Music, mind, and education.* Routledge.

Swanwick, K. (2002). *A basis for music education.* Routledge. https://doi.org/10.4324/978020 3422434

Swanwick, K., & Tillman, J. (1986). The sequence of musical development: A study of children's composition. *British Journal of Music Education, 3*(3), 305–339. https://doi.org/10.1017/S0265051700000814

Teruel, F. M. (2013). *Neuroeducación: Solo se puede aprender aquello que se ama.* Alianza

Veloso, A. L. (2017). Composing music, developing dialogues: An enactive perspective on children's collaborative creativity. *British Journal of Music Education, 34*(3), 259–276. https://doi.org/10.1017/S0265051717000055

Veloso, A. L. (2020). Rethinking experimental music within music education: Thoughts and feelings after a voyage through the Project INsono. *Revista Electrónica de LEEME, 0*(46), 49–67. https://doi.org/10.7203/LEEME.46.17409

Veloso, A. L., & Carvalho, S. (2012). Music composition as a way of learning: Emotions and the situated self. In O. Odena (Ed.), *Musical creativity: Insights from music education research* (pp. 73–91). Ashgate Publishing, Ltd.

Veloso, A. L., Ferreira, A. I., & Bessa, R. (2019). Adapting a music listening app to engage pupils in personal and social development: A case study. *Bulletin of the Council for Research in Music Education, 220*, 63–83.

Veloso, A. L., & Mota, G. (2021). Music learning, engagement, and personal growth: Child perspectives on a music workshop developed in a Portuguese state school. *Music Education Research, 23*(4), 416–429. https://doi.org/10.1080/14613808.2021.1929140.

Vygotski, L. (2007). *A Formação Social da Mente.* Martins Fontes.

Wiggins, J. (2007). Compositional process in music. In L. Bresler (Ed.), *International Handbook of Research in Arts Education* (pp. 453–476). Springer Netherlands.

SHAPING THE FUTURE OF COMPOSITION IN MUSIC EDUCATION

CHAPTER 41

....

ADVANCING PEDAGOGY THROUGH TEACHER ASSESSMENT AND PROGRAM EVALUATION

....

DAVID A. STRINGHAM

School music offerings are often touted as experiences wherein students can express themselves, escape the monotony of "core subject" learning, and be creative. It is curious, therefore, that students developing skill creating original music is underprioritized in music learning and teaching and rarely considered in assessing music teachers or evaluating music programs. While stakeholders would likely question a visual art curriculum in which students do not produce drawings, paintings, or sculptures— or an English curriculum with "no time" for creative writing, poetry, journaling, or playwriting—schools and communities in the United States seem satisfied with music curricula in which students become (often remarkably) adept at reproducing others' artworks without being guided in making their own.

Certainly, arguing for making music composition a central part of United States music education is beyond this chapter's scope. Music teachers' perspectives on composition's relevance and importance appear to be mixed, including benefits (e.g., student ownership, increased musical understanding) and impediments (e.g., lack of resources, culture of band performance) to engaging students in composing (Menard, 2015; Shouldice, 2014). Other researchers have documented teachers' varied incorporation of composition (Hash, 2020; Shouldice, 2014).

I present this chapter from the perspective of a music educator who has decided that it is essential for students not only to learn to perform others' music, respond to music, and make connections between music and other disciplines—but also for them to learn to create their own music. This position aligns with voluntary national standards (State Education Agency Directors of Arts Education, 2014) and ostensibly compulsory standards in many states (e.g., Arizona Department of Education, 2020; Virginia Department of Education, 2020).

Composition-related criteria grounded in these standards could be useful not only for music teacher assessment and music program evaluation, but also for enhancing pedagogy and music teachers' practice. This offers teachers opportunities to develop pedagogical, technological, and/or content knowledge lacking from their own education (e.g., Hewitt & Koner, 2013; Piazza & Talbot, 2020; Stringham, Thornton, & Shevock, 2015), leading to collaboration and interaction with colleagues outside the school building, ameliorating isolation that is common among music teachers, and positioning them to pursue music-specific professional development. And while a teacher's decision to facilitate composition experiences will benefit students as they perform with greater comprehension, analyze and respond to music more deeply, and make more informed connections between their school music experiences and the rest of their lives, it will also afford them opportunities to share their own ideas through generative creativity and expression.

Why This Chapter?

Like any teacher, a music teacher spends considerable time planning, reflecting, developing, and evaluating instruction. These practices demonstrate a teacher's investment in reflecting not only on their effectiveness, but also on how they might improve. A teacher considering giving composition greater prominence in students' learning may have little experience composing themselves and limited education related to teaching composition. While a variety of resources provide ideas for lessons and units that may encourage teachers to incorporate composition (e.g., Hickey, 2012; Kaschub & Smith, 2009; Kuhn & Hein, 2021; Randles & Stringham, 2013), there are fewer tools for helping music teachers reflect on music composition pedagogy. What are they doing well? Where might they grow? How might focusing on composition change their building- or district-level music program? This chapter is intended to assist music educators in considering these and other questions related to teacher assessment and program evaluation.

Context: Music Teacher Assessment and Program Evaluation

Informal assessment and evaluation practices are part of our everyday lives, as we make decisions about what to wear or discuss our favorite sports team's performance with colleagues. Similarly, stakeholders routinely make informal judgments about music teachers and school music programs based on a variety of inputs: a parent's email interaction with a teacher, an assistant principal's unannounced observation, or state choral festival ratings. These informal evaluations are often for private purposes, use information assembled in one's head, and combine observations with existing knowledge (Owen, 2020). Many stakeholders' informal assessments of music teachers are informed by their own prior experiences with school music. In this chapter, I will address how concepts underlying informal observations might be extrapolated to more formal frameworks and procedures.

Music Teacher Assessment

Teacher assessment provides structure to set instructional and professional goals that align with state policy and district curriculum, articulates a common framework for dialogue among stakeholders, incorporates mechanisms for professional accountability and growth, and offers some degree of objectivity to guide what are often high-stakes conversations about teachers' careers and students' education. Yet, music teacher evaluation is not without challenges. Often, it is politically contentious but mandatory, continually changing, not music specific, and conducted by evaluators without a music teacher background—creating a potentially adversarial context for music teacher evaluation (Bernard & Abramo, 2019).

Further, music educators hold varied conceptions of teaching effectiveness that may include core teaching practices, pedagogical content knowledge, and/or skills and knowledge important to successful music teaching (e.g., Haston & Leon-Guerrero, 2008; Miksza, Roeder, & Biggs, 2010; Millican & Forester, 2019). These conversations often do not include a teacher's skill and knowledge related to composition, pedagogical content knowledge related to composition, or a teacher's dispositions with respect to including composition within their curricula.

Bernard and Abramo (2019) offer a pragmatic and hopeful outlook on music teacher assessment. Although it may be used punitively, "it ultimately can be—and should be—used to help teachers to dialogue with other educators and improve their teaching" (p. 6). Ideally, music teachers proactively leverage their expertise to advocate for their decisions, engage with evaluators and evaluation systems, and grow professionally.

Program Evaluation

Stakeholders may combine existing knowledge and observations in different ways (e.g., an administrator who is an enthusiastic avocational vocalist and community theater performer, a parent who has never taken a music class, a student who listens to and produces hip-hop music and is choosing a string instrument to play in a required "exploratory" class). To navigate informally and personally constructed perspectives, a formal process of program evaluation may be useful, considering:

What is the underlying basis for selecting evaluation criteria? What evidence will be used and on what standards will it be judged? How will conclusions be made and presented (Owen, 2020)?

As with teacher assessment, program evaluation can have both positive and negative effects, including increasing awareness of student engagement, justifying increased funding, and deepening understanding among stakeholders (Moreno, 2014). While these efforts "can introduce unforeseen tensions and animosities within the personnel, curriculum, and context in the classroom, program evaluations have the ability to uncover and disclose unintended factors that constitute the success of a program" (p. 33).

Music teachers often "lack a working knowledge of program evaluation methods that can help them further refine music programs at the local level" (Ferguson, 2007, p. 4). Program evaluation may include varied data (e.g., student performance assessments, budget expenditures, stakeholder perspectives). Findings may be used summatively, as a "report card" (Ferguson, 2007, p. 4), or formatively to guide decision-making. Further, what constitutes a "program" might vary, from a unit plan to a sequence of all offerings in a school district (Ferguson, 2007). While a music administrator may wish to facilitate a more holistic curricular program evaluation, I will primarily focus this chapter toward teachers evaluating courses and students they teach.

SETTING THE STAGE: A HYPOTHETICAL CONTEXT FOR ADVANCING COMPOSITION PEDAGOGY

I provide a hypothetical scenario (Figure 41.1) informed by my own experiences as a high school instrumental music teacher. If you work in other teaching settings (e.g., elementary general music, middle school choir, secondary general music), I invite you to make transfers from my experiences to yours.

A teacher in this situation might begin with familiar and available resources, such as *Understanding By Design* (Wiggins & McTighe, 2005). Wiggins and McTighe (2011) suggest considering three stages of backward design: Stage 1 (Identify desired results), Stage 2 (Determine acceptable evidence), and Stage 3 (Plan learning experiences and instruction accordingly). These sequential stages help teachers avoid "the all-too-common 'twin sins' of planning and teaching": activity-oriented teaching and content coverage (2011, pp. 8–9). Further, this line of thinking positions composition centrally, beyond an activity that takes place in a particular class period or a topic that is "covered" through a lecture about compositional process or a particular composer's background. By conceptually avoiding these "twin sins," composition becomes part of an important artistic process (i.e., creating) that also draws on, and develops connections

I teach concert band, wind ensemble, jazz ensemble, and weekly pull-out lessons for 100 students. I also conduct the school musical pit orchestra and assist my principal (who played trombone in his university's marching band) in preparing an extracurricular marching band to perform in our Memorial Day parade each year.

Two years ago, I hosted Helene, a student teacher who studied composition as her primary instrument in her music education degree. Helene had the extensive repertoire knowledge and seemingly otherworldly aural skills that one might imagine a composer would possess, knew her secondary instruments inside and out, and believed that composition was not a pursuit only for AP Music Theory students or future music majors, but for every student. We had long conversations about standards, *Music Educators Journal* articles, music teacher education programs, and the demands on my time as a high school instrumental music teacher.

I watched Helene infuse composition pedagogy throughout her work with students. She convinced me to organize pull-out lessons into chamber groups to expose students to more repertoire, composers, and compositional techniques. Students started writing variations, improvising extensions to sequences, and talking about creating tension and releasing it at arrival points. She helped me to look at wind ensemble and concert band scores like a composer. We certainly still made sure that students played their repertoire well, but they were also understanding more about why they were attending to issues of balance, intonation, and blend. And the students were composing! Most of what they wrote wasn't thrilling (much of it sounded like exercises from a band method book) but some of it was delightful—like the woodwind quintet Raj worked on with Helene when we had hall duty. Students started bringing in music that they had never told me about making (but I guess I hadn't asked!) that ranged from original pop songs they recorded with Audacity to a live coding work a student created in Sonic Pi.

I was excited—and terrified—as we approached the end of Helene's time with us. I could see that incorporating composition would be a good thing for my students (and frankly, for me). But I also felt very uncomfortable. How could I stand in front of my wind ensemble professing to be a knowledgeable professional when I knew so little about composition? In college, I composed a few chorales in theory class, and I vaguely remember a professor's presentation on composition in elementary general music. But most of what I knew about composing, and teaching composition, I had learned from Helene over the past eight weeks. Fortunately, she could remain a resource—she was just hired for the middle school band vacancy at a neighboring middle school.

My principal dropped by a couple of days later to talk about the upcoming Memorial Day parade, and I shared some of the thoughts and experiences I'd been having over the past eight weeks. We set up a longer meeting the following week, and he enthusiastically agreed to support me in developing a two-year plan to reach two goals: (a) each student composes at least one piece of music each year and (b) any school-organized public performance of a student group includes at least one student composition. We agreed to make this the focus of my professional growth plan.

FIGURE 41.1. A hypothetical teaching scenario

with, skills and knowledge related to performing, responding, and connecting. This approach would align with four processes and 11 anchor standards in National Core Arts Standards for Music (State Education Agency Directors of Arts Education, 2014). These core arts standards also include enduring understandings and essential questions inspired by *Understanding by Design* (Wiggins & McTighe, 2005) that may be useful in planning instruction.

What might be a desired result for high school instrumental music students with respect to composition? Your state's standards for music education or your school district curriculum may offer some helpful guidance, but desired results you specify will likely be unique based on student interests and background, available resources, and your experience with composition and composition pedagogy. I suggest specifying results that engage and challenge your students, and that leave you as the teacher feeling "uncomfortable but not paralyzed" (McClurken, 2010). Since composition is a practice underemphasized in many music teachers' pre-service education, expanding and enhancing composition pedagogy provides opportunities to model a growth mindset while facilitating composing opportunities for students. After identifying desired results, you might consider acceptable forms of evidence—and then begin planning learning experiences and instruction accordingly.

In the hypothetical situation described above, I identified two desired results: (a) each student composes at least one piece of music each year and (b) any school-organized public performance of a student group includes at least one student composition. Acceptable forms of evidence for these results might include (but are not limited to) scores and recordings (result *a*) or concert programs or recordings (result *b*), alongside other performing, responding, and connecting outcomes.

As I worked toward this two-year goal, I would improve my pedagogy and student outcomes using teacher assessment and program evaluation processes. In the following sections, I will describe existing frameworks for each, and offer suggestions for expanding and modifying these models. These ideas are intended to be applicable not only for music teacher assessment and music program evaluation, but also for reflecting on and improving one's pedagogy. That is, a teacher who is intentional about setting composition-related goals will consider metrics by which students' achievement will be measured, specific skills and knowledge students should develop, and specific learning experiences in which students will engage.

ADVANCING PEDAGOGY THROUGH TEACHER ASSESSMENT

In this section, I briefly describe three music teacher assessment frameworks and offer composition-specific modifications. These may be useful self-assessment tools and promote dialogue with evaluators and administrators. While these music-specific resources may certainly assist music teachers—and other stakeholders (e.g., administrators, evaluators)—as they exist, specific to this chapter, they generally conceptualize and describe music teaching as emphasizing performance-related skills, with few examples of using these frameworks to improve composition pedagogy. While they may not describe composition pedagogy with the same level of priority or nuance given to teaching music performance, they are readily adaptable.

Danielson

The Framework for Teaching Evaluation Instrument, 2013 Edition (Danielson, 2013), presents

> aspects of a teacher's responsibilities that have been documented through empirical studies and theoretical research as promoting improved student learning . . . [that] seek to define what teachers should know and be able to do in the exercise of their profession. (p. 1)

The framework comprises four domains: planning and preparation, classroom environment, instruction, and professional responsibilities. Within these domains are nested 22 components, each with multiple elements and indicators, and four levels of performance (i.e., unsatisfactory, basic, proficient, distinguished). For example, within the domain of *planning and preparation*, one component is *demonstrating knowledge of content and pedagogy*. Two elements of that component are "knowledge of content and structure of the discipline," and "knowledge of content-related pedagogy," and two indicators of that element are "lesson and unit plans that reflect important concepts in this discipline" and "feedback to students that furthers learning."

More recently, the Danielson Group (2019) published a series of music education scenarios. Not a prescriptive document, it provides example scenarios, few of which relate to composition. Those that are included most often appear at the "distinguished" level. For instance, consider this "distinguished" example of "setting instructional outcomes": "Using poems created in language arts class, the students, working in dyads of poet/composer, will compose and record original songs using GarageBand software." An example of "proficient" in "Demonstrating Knowledge of Resources" is: "The music theory teacher is taking an online course to learn how to better use GarageBand with her students."

While I am glad that examples of composition instruction appear in this document, relatively isolated examples at "proficient" and "distinguished" levels could reinforce misperceptions that teaching composition is a pursuit for teachers with composition training, or for particularly advanced students with enough advanced theory knowledge to begin composing. A broader range of examples could help teachers and other stakeholders conceptualize what it might "look like" to describe composition-related pursuits in this framework. With that in mind, I present examples of composition-related scenarios for the component "Designing student assessments" that might be observed in a high school instrumental music classroom pursuing two hypothetical goals I created earlier in this chapter. These appear in Figure 41.2, along with descriptions of levels and their critical attributes.

	Critical Attributes	Music Composition-Specific examples
Unsatisfactory: Level 1 Assessment procedures are not congruent with instructional outcomes and lack criteria by which student performance will be assessed. The teacher has no plan to incorporate formative assessment into the lesson or unit.	**Critical Attributes:** • Assessments do not match instructional outcomes. • Assessments lack criteria. • No formative assessments have been designed. • Assessment results do not affect future plans.	**Music Composition-Specific examples:** • The teacher does not assess students' composition achievement in music class. • Students' composition achievement is assessed with a written music theory test.
Basic: Level 2 Assessment procedures are partially congruent with instructional outcomes. Assessment criteria and standards have been developed, but they are not clear. The teacher's approach to using formative assessment is rudimentary, including only some of the instructional outcomes.	**Critical Attributes:** • Only some of the instructional outcomes are addressed in the planned assessments. • Assessment criteria are vague. • Plans refer to the use of formative assessment, but they are not fully developed. • Assessment results are used to design lesson plans for the whole class, not for individual students.	**Music composition-specific examples:** • Students' in-class work on a composition assignment is assessed using a check minus/check/check plus entry in the teacher's gradebook. • Students are given a written test on key signatures, note names (including enharmonic spelling), and modes; the teacher uses results from this assessment to create parameters for a future class composition project.
Proficient: Level 3 All the instructional outcomes may be assessed by the proposed assessment plan; assessment methodologies may have been adapted for groups of students. Assessment criteria and standards are clear. The teacher has a well-developed strategy for using formative assessment and has designed specific approaches to be used.	**Critical attributes:** • All the learning outcomes have a method for assessment. • Assessment types match learning expectations. Plans indicate modified assessments when they are necessary for some students. • Assessment criteria are clearly written. Plans include formative assessments to use during instruction. • Lesson plans indicate possible adjustments based on formative assessment data.	**Music composition-specific examples:** • Students complete a listening test in which they aurally identify compositional techniques in unfamiliar repertoire; written scores are provided for a student who is hard of hearing and three students who struggle with aural processing. • Students are given a monthly assessment to track their growth as composers; the teacher uses these results to design future lessons for three groups of students who are struggling with melodic development, instrument ranges, and imitation.
Distinguished: Level 4 All the instructional outcomes may be assessed by the proposed assessment plan, with clear criteria for assessing student work. The plan contains evidence of student contribution to its development. Assessment methodologies have been adapted for individual students as the need has arisen. The approach to using formative assessment is well designed and includes student as well as teacher use of the assessment information.	**Critical attributes:** • Assessments provide opportunity for student choice. • Students participate in designing assessments for their own work. Teacher-designed assessments are authentic, with real-world application as appropriate. • Students develop rubrics according to teacher-specified learning objectives. • Students are actively involved in collecting information from formative assessments and giving input on future lessons.	**Music composition-specific examples:** • Students are given the option of developing and notating their composition using notation software, a digital audio workstation, or with a pencil and staff paper. • Students and teacher collaboratively design a rubric for self-assessment and peer assessment; this rubric will be used to decide which student pieces are played on the winter concert. • Based on those self-assessments and peer assessments, students will suggest content for composition-related instruction in the following marking period.

FIGURE 41.2. Descriptions, critical attributes, and music composition specific scenarios for designing student assessments

Doerksen

Doerksen (2006) offers a resource for evaluating music teachers who offer instruction to performing groups. While noting that this instruction "is usually limited—rightly or wrongly—to the development of individual and group performance skills," and suggests that a relevant performance indicator might be "teaches to and assesses specified [NAfME] National Standards for Music" (p. 23), the text primarily presents music teachers as large ensemble rehearsers. Still, Doersken offers useful documents, evaluation considerations, and frameworks for conversations between music teachers seeking to incorporate composition and administrators.

Doerksen provides job descriptions for ensemble-based music teachers, including responsibilities at varying degrees of specificity. While sample responsibilities include broad references to teaching to and assessing national standards, more specific references are primarily related to music performance, such as: "Conducts rehearsals and performances, demonstrating understanding of differences in style among various types of music" or "Identifies and diagnoses problems in individual and group performance skills, and prescribes appropriate and effective corrective feedback" (p. 13). While Doerksen's text is explicitly oriented toward teachers of music performance groups, a teacher whose teaching assignment includes music performance groups and who seeks to improve their composition pedagogy could negotiate that as part of their job description with their supervisor. For example, the descriptor "designs or selects and uses planned sequences of instruction so that students acquire skills in string technique and music reading" (p. 13) could be expanded to include "skills in composing music for string instruments" or "skills in creating original music."

Similarly, in conversations about goals and objectives, Doerksen suggests that a pre-observation conference might include discussion of class activities, including, "a warm-up period, a time for working on group technique, and a time for working on repertoire" or establishing "position, breathing, and tone production" with beginning students. In a pre-observation conference with their principal, a teacher might explain that the lesson being observed will also include time for skill and knowledge development related to composition. This might include not only explicit time devoted to students composing, songwriting, or producing, but also intentionally-selected activities to help students develop skills and capacities for creating music.

For example, students might develop aural skills by learning important elements of their repertoire by ear as a warm-up (e.g., Shewan, 2009; Snell, 2015). In another lesson, they might engage with cinematic or literary works and make connections to a piece they are studying (e.g., Sindberg, 2012). They might also develop interrelated capacities as performers and listeners using Kaschub and Smith's (2016) principle pairs continua of motion-stasis, unity-variety, sound-silence, tension-release, and stability-instability to discuss repertoire they are rehearsing. As Kaschub and Smith note:

> Music-making and the capacities that support it are dynamic in nature and execution. Listeners who tap their feet or drum on their steering wheels are adopting performer actions as they contribute their own sounds, performers who wonder why a composer has crafted a line in a particular way are exploring the composer's intent, and composers who imagine their work as it will be experienced by an audience assume the listener's ear. (p. 39)

Onuscheck, Marzano, and Grice

Based on Marzano (2017), Onuscheck et al. (2020) offer an art- and music-specific instructional model with three overarching categories (i.e., feedback, content, context) and ten design areas (e.g., using assessments, building relationships, communicating high expectations). Within these design areas, Onuscheck et al. articulate 43 more detailed elements (e.g., formal assessments of individual students, academic games, probing incorrect answers with reluctant learners) and offer "additional, subject-specific strategies that teachers can use to increase students' response rates" (p. 5). Similar to Danielson's performance levels, Onuscheck et al. provide five-point rating scales for teacher self-reflection.

Like Doerksen (2006), Onuscheck et al. (2020) cite four artistic processes in National Core Arts Standards as a reference point for establishing goals; however, the majority of the text is written through a lens of a performance-centric music education. For example, the authors state "celebrating success in music has two facets: (1) celebrating the ensemble and (2) celebrating the individual . . . in relation to the ensemble" (p. 20) and seem to conflate learning to perform a piece of music in an ensemble with "the process of creating music" (p. 25). (To be clear, while there are creative elements of preparing a piece of music for performance, National Core Arts Standards clearly delineate performing music from creating original music.) Similarly, while authors acknowledge that engaging students with composition *could* be part of what a teacher does (e.g., "music portfolios could consist of . . . original compositions or lyrics" [p. 27]), statements about performance-centric objectives are more frequent and more explicit (e.g., "the teacher will ask students to use a pencil to mark sections of the music that require reminders" (p. 63) or "when the teacher stands at the podium or in front of the class and raises his or her hand, this signals to the students to be quiet immediately" [p. 105]).

This framework could easily be expanded to provide teachers and evaluators with additional composition-specific strategies. Additionally, numerous visual art examples (where students creating original art seems more commonplace) in this text could be readily adapted. In Figure 41.3, I offer composition-specific strategies for four of Onuscheck et al's (2020) 43 elements.

Element	Music composition-specific strategies
Constructing Practice Sessions (pp. 43-44)	■ Warm up by playing a scale, chorale melody, or folk tune, then improvise and play it several different ways (e.g., articulations, melodic embellishment). ■ Identify a spot in your ensemble repertoire that you struggle with. Compose, then practice, a short etude that helps you work on that challenging excerpt.
Assigning Purposeful Homework (p. 72)	■ Learn repertoire by ear, then write it down. ■ Listen to repertoire and journal about selected rhythmic, melodic, harmonic, and expressive elements. ■ Find an example of a selected compositional technique in your personal library and bring it in to share with the class.
Using Academic Games (pp. 94-96)	■ Provide small groups of students with the first and last measures of a familiar melody (with the others blank). The first student fills in one measure, then passes the sheet around the circle, each student completing one measure at a time and discussing their work until there is new material filled in. ■ In the spirit of Food Network's *Chopped*, give students a compositional "ingredient basket" (e.g., triple meter, whole tone scale, no scalar motion, start and end on same pitch) and five minutes to create an interesting melody.
Motivating and Inspiring Students (pp. 98-100)	■ Share musical examples, interviews, podcasts, etc. showcasing composers engaging with current social, political, and/or economic issues. ■ Share student compositions in public forums (e.g., concerts, websites, social media). ■ Create venues for more experienced musicians to perform student work. ■ Empower student leaders who may have interest in a future teaching career to mentor less experienced composers.

FIGURE 41.3. Composition-specific strategies for four elements (Onuscheck et al., 2020)

ADVANCING PEDAGOGY THROUGH PROGRAM EVALUATION

In this section, I will describe two program evaluation frameworks that could be adapted to my hypothetical scenario. I offer adaptation suggestions that could guide data collection to help evaluate our school's instrumental music program with respect to music composition, and use findings formatively to make plans for subsequent academic years.

Then, I will describe and discuss two examples of recognitions—one from a state music education association and the other from a national professional organization—that lie somewhere between individuals' informal assessments of a school music program and a rigorous program evaluation such as those described by Pennell (2020) and Wesolowski et al. (2019). I offer ideas for how music teachers and other stakeholders might encourage organizations to adapt their criteria to consider music composition an important element of their evaluative process.

Pennell

Pennell (2020) offers a model from PK–12 literacy education that is readily transferable to evaluating a K–12 music education curriculum. As in literacy education, where students develop a variety of skills (e.g., listening, speaking, reading, writing), music educators are tasked with facilitating student learning around diverse knowledge and skills associated with processes of creating, performing, responding, and connecting. Pennell frames this process in six overarching constructs: foundational skills, comprehension (K–3), comprehension (4–12), classroom literacies and independent reading, vocabulary, and writing. Pennell's approach can evaluate an entire K–12 literary curriculum or one aspect of a curriculum.

While these overarching constructs are all relevant to music education (e.g., What are foundational skills for musicianship? What does it mean to comprehend music at K–3 and 4–12 levels? What musical vocabulary should a student develop?), I will focus here on Pennell's (2020) chapter on the foundational skill of writing. The challenge of teaching students to write (in our case, compose) is not unique. Pennell summarized recent research indicating that "after third grade, very little instructional time is devoted to writing. Moreover, expectations for academic writing, both in and out of the classroom, remain scant. Given writing's pragmatic purposes and cognitive super-power, this is an unfortunate reality" (p. 96). I will describe three elements of Pennell's structures for evaluating writing and suggest how they might be applied to teaching composition.

Writing Framework

Pennell suggests districts adopt a writing framework, a non-negotiable that outlines "how educators will approach daily writing instruction and plan that instruction throughout the year" (p. 97). This plan might include daily allotment for writing, a year-long calendar of genres to be covered, and tools for instructional design.

Whether my district chose to adopt such a framework, I could choose to audit my most recent year of teaching, keeping in mind my goals of (a) every student composing at least one piece each year, and (b) any school-organized public performance of a student group including at least one student composition. This evaluation may have revealed that in the previous year, I approached composition in my classroom through a composition unit beginning after the spring concert and state performance assessments. As I reflected, I realized that the timing of this unit made it impossible for students' works to be played until the following year, and that students were feeling like the year was "over" after those concerts—motivation and positive momentum they felt through winter culminated in those performances. Further, because students seemed to perceive this composition unit as disconnected from what happened in the rest of the school year, I found they were not making connections between concepts we worked on in preparing repertoire and their compositions. While time spent on phrasing, tonality, and tension and release while perfecting beautiful melodies in Vaughan Williams's *Folk Song Suite* led to a musically satisfying performance last April, melodies in students' compositions were awkward and felt mechanical.

Through this reflection, I realized that composition needed to be a more consistent presence in my classroom, and I decided to adopt a "composition framework" in my classroom. I might, for example, determine that: (a) I will spend 30 minutes of classroom time each week engaging students in composing; (b) I will focus on genres of imitative counterpoint, theme and variations, and electronic music (overlapping with plans for students to perform Frescobaldi's *Toccata*, Chance's *Variations on a Korean Folk Song*, and Shapiro's *Lights Out*); and (c) use three existing books related to facilitating music composition (Freedman, 2013; Hickey, 2012; Randles & Stringham, 2013) and the *Understanding by Design* framework (Wiggins & McTighe, 2005, 2011, and 2015) as tools for instructional design.

Writing to Learn

Pennell describes Writing to Learn as "quick and meaningful writing tasks that promote critical interaction with a text or concept" (2020, p. 83) and distinct from Learning to Write, a process of prewriting, drafting, revising, and editing. This language literacy practice might be employed in disciplinary classes (e.g., an engineering notebook in science, an annotated bibliography of primary sources in history).

In my classroom, there are two approaches I could take to adapting this notion of Writing to Learn. I might use it in Pennell's originally intended sense, helping students engage in developing language literacy. Students might contribute to a journal through a series of listening activities in which they respond to pieces based on Kaschub and Smith's (2016) MUSTS and apply their contributions to creating their own compositions. I could also adapt this approach to writing music by developing a series of quick and meaningful composition tasks to promote interaction with a text or concept (e.g., Hickey's (1997) SCAMPER toolbox) to develop a variation on a theme from Frescobaldi's *Toccata*.

Digital Composition

Pennell suggests that given ubiquitous social media and digital tools, it is essential that students know how to create and consume digital texts. Pennell defines these texts as multi-modal, non-linear (e.g., hyperlinks on a web page), malleable (i.e., can be continuously edited), and shareable. These tools, Pennell suggests, should contribute a sense of purpose and authenticity around the writing process.

Musicians interact with a variety of digital tools in their work, and I might provide students opportunities to engage in digital composition using these tools. As a high school instrumental music teacher, I might engage my students in sampling their acoustic instrument and using it in a digital audio workstation project, facilitate a discussion about how composers share their music using digital tools (e.g., SoundCloud, TikTok, YouTube), or assign chamber groups to collaborate on their own arrangement of "Arirang" (the folk song in Chance's *Variations on a Korean Folksong*) using Bandhub.

Wesolowski, McDaniel, and Powell

Wesolowski et al. (2019) offer an ecological approach to school music assessment as "a method for helping music teachers investigate the school, student, and community factors that affect their music programs and identifying the values associated with these factors" (p. 493). Their framework includes three spheres of influence: school (i.e., institutional values, standards and curricula), student (i.e., individual values, person-in-environment), and community (i.e., local values, community attachment). Exploring these spheres could reveal relevant information for evaluating efforts to enhance composition pedagogy.

For example, teachers might discover a mismatch surrounding institutional values (e.g., standards, curriculum). State standards may call for students to engage in composing music, a district curriculum might conflate performing with creating and not explicitly indicate students should engage in composing music, and the building principal may be calling for a schoolwide emphasis on citizenship skills. This may highlight need for stakeholder conversations to align expectations and make curricular decisions based on these values; in this situation, I might plan to study repertoire with connections to citizenship (e.g., Ronald LoPresti's *Elegy for a Young American* and Omar Thomas's *Of Our New Day Begun* are both inspired by acts of violence against United States citizens by other United States citizens) and ground that year's composition project in creating works examining United States immigration policies and citizenship.

Wesolowski et al. suggest that students' individual values might be examined through five dimensions of human development (i.e., physical, affective, cognitive, spiritual, and social). How might students value creativity generally, and composition specifically, through these lenses? How might creating music afford students a platform to explore existential issues such as identity and purpose (spiritual)? How does hearing one's original piece performed make a student feel (affective)? Do they find collaborative composition energizing or draining (social)? Better understanding how your students value composing and creating could provide valuable information to guide planning.

Community members' values and perspectives are also important when considering a comprehensive evaluation of a school music program. Wesolowski et al. suggest exploring this through a three-dimensional model of (a) interpersonal relationships, (b) participation, and (c) sentiments. How do stakeholders interact in the process of advocating for and influencing individual students and the school music program at large (interpersonal relationships)? What are community members' perceptions of ways in which they are directly and indirectly affected by the school music program (participation)? For example, a community member might be directly affected by engaging

Original Question	Composition-focused Modification
Do I consider my own potential cultural biases when making assessment and curriculum decisions (e.g., favoring Western art music)?	Do I consider my own biases when determining what types of composition will be recognized in curriculum decisions (e.g., favoring Western notation and concert band instrumentation)?
Is the reasoning that goes into curriculum and assessment decisions transparent to students?	Is the reasoning that goes into making composition a more central part of curriculum and assessment decisions transparent to students?
Has my program created partnerships with important community institutions?	Has my program created partnerships with local composers?
Do my assessments create a positive or negative classroom environment or otherwise impact my classroom culture?	Does my composition pedagogy create a positive or negative classroom environment or otherwise impact my classroom culture?
Are my assessments progressive (vis-à-vis a spiral curriculum)?	Are my expectations for composition tasks progressive (vis-à-vis a spiral curriculum)?

FIGURE 41.4. Composition-focused adaptations to the questions of Wesolowski et al. (2019)

with the school music program by attending a concert; they might indirectly be affected by that concert attendance shaping their perceptions of specific music genres or practices. How do students feel about their local musical community (within and beyond the school) and their contributions to it (sentiment)?

Wesolowski et al. suggest that understanding institutional, student, and community value spheres can provide six streams of validity evidence to construct an ecologically valid school music assessment framework: (a) standards-aligned curricula and formal knowledge, (b) classroom democracy and student perceptions, (c) student self-efficacy and autodidactic knowledge, (d) local music and traditional knowledge, (e) locally and culturally appropriate teaching and ethnographic data, and (f) community service and community perceptions. The authors provide 60 questions that may be useful in facilitating data collection. Many could be readily adapted to a program evaluation initiative focused on composition, and could be used for self-reflection or to inform data collection. Wesolowski et al.'s original questions and composition-focused adaptations are listed in Figure 41.4.

RECOGNITION AS PROGRAM EVALUATION

Somewhere between formal program evaluation strategies and informal program evaluations made by school and community stakeholders are structured recognition programs offered by state and national organizations. These initiatives, which perhaps might be considered "semi-formal," confer an endorsement from some external organization and are often perceived as evaluations of a school music program.

State Music Education Associations

For example, Virginia Music Educators Association's "Blue Ribbon Award" is "the highest award given to school music programs in the Commonwealth of Virginia." To be recognized with this designation, the "top performing groups of each ensemble course taught at the school (band, choir, and orchestra)" must perform two pieces from selected repertoire lists at a district assessment event, opt to sight-read or sight-sing as part of that assessment, and each receive a final "Superior" rating. Individuals can also view a chart showing which schools have received this designation over the previous 19 years (Virginia Music Educators Association, 2020).

While readers may problematize various elements of this protocol, specific to this chapter, it is concerning that an award including a certificate and congratulatory letter sent to a principal—conferring a sense of excellence—is based on only some elements of what that state's standards (Virginia Department of Education, 2020) suggest teachers teach and students learn. To be clear, I am not suggesting de-valuing music performance—only that a potentially-misconstrued recognition of this type should encompass the breadth of what a comprehensive music education includes if it represents "the highest award given to school music programs."

Such awards could be modified to reflect a more expansive, standards-aligned, and aspirational view of school music programs. For example, Randles (2010) suggested that as part of large ensemble festival/assessment events, groups would be expected to perform not only prepared repertoire, but also "a piece that they worked to create themselves with the assistance of the teacher" (p. 145). The submission process for this recognition could call for examples of student compositions, concert programs showing performance of student work, or documenting a number/percentage of students making a submission to the state music education association's annual composition festival.

National Organizations

A "signature program" of the National Association of Music Merchants Foundation, Best Communities for Music Education (BCME) "recognizes and celebrates school districts and schools for their support and commitment to music education and efforts to assure access to music for all students as part of a well-rounded education." To be considered for this recognition, a stakeholder completes a survey "aligned with goals for equity and access to music education for all students, and also with national standards for music education." BCME's website (NAMM Foundation, 2021) enumerates several benefits to participation: national recognition; community recognition; increased visibility of music education in your district, school, and community; program validation of your school or district's support for music education; and access to a program auditing tool for your music program. This survey includes general questions about the presence (or lack thereof) of composition in a school's music program. There are more nuanced questions that move beyond *whether* something is happening to gather information about ways in which, and the extent to which, other elements are part of the curriculum. For example, other items ask: "What percentage of your elementary school students have an opportunity to perform music before an audience each year?" and "What percentage of your high schools have adequate performance venues with appropriate properties of acoustics, lighting, secure storage, and sound?"

It is worth noting that this survey includes questions that address a number of important issues (e.g., including students with disabilities, Title I students, community music opportunities, resources to support non-traditional and/or non-Western music forms). But—again, specific to this chapter—it is concerning that for an award carrying perceived rigor and endorsement conveyed by a national organization, there is limited information collected about if or how students are composing—or creating music more broadly—in these school communities.

While it is commendable that there is some information collected with regard to creating music in this survey, a single experience in one course could "check that box." While it certainly is preferable for students to have one experience with composition each year than none, a survey that does not inquire more deeply into creative experiences generally (and composition experiences more specifically) may lead teachers, administrators, and other stakeholders toward the "twin sins" view of composition in music education mentioned earlier in this chapter—that is, that including some content and activities related to music composition is an exemplary achievement. To think about composition in higher regard, and gather more rigorous data, some adaptations of existing questions could be useful. For example: (a) What percentage of music instruction at your high school is devoted to creating music? Performing music? Responding to music? Connecting? (b) Do middle school students have access to hardware and software to compose music digitally (e.g., microphones, USB keyboards, digital audio workstations)? (c) What percentage of elementary school students have an opportunity to create original music each year?

From Hypothetical Scenarios to Real Life

As you have read this chapter, I hope that examples from this scenario have brought to mind opportunities—and challenges—from your real-life teaching settings. This material is not intended to be prescriptive, or as a one-size-fits-all solution to "fix" your curriculum by imitating goals or use of existing tools suggested in this chapter. Rather, it is intended to provoke thought about how you might reflect on your teaching and your programmatic structures to continually improve them for your students' benefit.

Making changes to your teaching and your curriculum more broadly may meet with skepticism, and even resistance, among some stakeholders. With that in mind, I conclude this chapter with some ideas for engaging with students, parents, administrators, and professional organizations as you consider broadening your instructional priorities.

Students

A wise colleague of mine once said that "students will think fourth grade band is whatever you tell them it is." Secondary and university teachers' students have spent years being socialized into a particular view of musicianship and music learning. Some may not have been invited to think about being a composer as part of being a musician, and may be hesitant to engage in composition activities. It may be helpful to share other students' perspectives. In various research studies, students have reported finding benefit and meaning in creating music. For example, Menard (2015) identified benefits general music and band students associated with composition: opportunities for personal discovery and expression, increased interest in music, increased musical understanding, increased understanding of compositional processes, and general enjoyment. They also identified challenges of self-criticism, time constraints, and understanding the composition process; more specifically, band students indicated that performance culture traditions and lack of fundamental music knowledge were impediments.

These perceptions of benefit and meaning extend beyond PK–12 school music education settings to higher education- and community-based settings. For example, university students in a songwriting course described self-expressive, therapeutic, and emotionally stabilizing benefits of writing and performing original songs in a semester-long course (Riley, 2012). Cohen and Wilson (2017) described both musical successes (e.g., improved skills using solfège to decode melodies) and social successes (e.g., overcoming inhibitions, and feeling a sense of value and accomplishment when their original works were performed) that incarcerated men experienced participating in a songwriting workshop. Music therapy and arts and health literature is also replete with examples of musically and personally beneficial composing experiences (e.g., Clark, et al., 2020; Hoover, 2021).

Parents

Just as students may have preconceived notions about what music instruction should entail, parents often lean on their own school music experiences—which may have happened 10, 20, or 30 years ago—as they make judgments about your classroom. In my experience, regardless of those preconceptions, parents get excited about their student's compositions being performed. Some parents may become more excited about composition once they experience public performance of their child's work. Similarly, *informances* (e.g., Reese, 2009) may illuminate day-to-day learning that may not be immediately visible at a concert.

Administrators

Doerksen (2006) notes that many administrators may have firmly held opinions about music instruction from their own experiences and often "hold onto their casually formed opinions with bulldog tenacity, and their faith in their own judgments is rarely shaken" (p. xi). If you encounter a resistant administrator whose conception of music education does not include composition, one strategy might be to draw on your administrator's disciplinary background. For example, a principal who previously taught foreign language will understand the importance of teaching students to listen to, speak, read, and write in this new language, and that developing those skills will be mutually beneficial to others. Explaining your desire to teach students to listen, improvise, read, and compose by drawing these comparisons may be helpful. Similarly, an administrator with background teaching history may be familiar with Stanford History Education Group's "Reading Like a Historian" initiative (Stanford History Education Group, 2021) and see parallels between that approach and a music teacher's efforts to compare and contrast multiple primary sources (e.g., recordings, scores) to help students understand how composers might solve musical problems. More broadly, knowing your administrator, their background, and professional pressures (e.g., district initiatives, state mandates) can help you be prepared to engage in these conversations. (See Bernard & Abramo, 2019, Chapter 7, for additional strategies.)

Another dimension of a music educator's work may be educating administrators about how music education is changing (and has changed since they participated as students). You may need to explain that performances administrators might expect are one dimension of music learning. Show them your state's standards and engage them in a conversation about wanting to meet them. What administrator would not be open to that conversation? You might propose to develop a one-, two-, or five-year plan to reconfigure your curriculum for balanced alignment among standards, perhaps using a framework described in this chapter as a model. And if your school or district doesn't have a music curriculum, these conversations would be a great time to suggest writing one!

Professional Organizations

While not explicitly intended as teacher and/or program evaluation, professional organizations' recognitions provide external validation and are often interpreted by stakeholders (e.g., administrators, parents) as such. Many state MEAs recognize students, teachers, schools, and/or districts; however, these accolades focus primarily on music performance. It is notable—and indeed heartening—that many state MEAs have developed composition-focused programs (e.g., New York State School Music Association, 2021; Virginia Music Educators Association, 2021). While these initiatives focus primarily on students, they could also promote a more holistic view of music teacher and/or program evaluation that considers music composition an important element.

Similarly, MEAs often recognize music teachers for performing groups, organizational service, or innovative course offerings. Related recognitions could celebrate teachers who increasingly centralize composition. Similarly, music teachers' evaluations may include the number of students who participate in solo and ensemble festivals each year. While these events typically do not welcome student compositions, there are models for more expansive repertoire selection. Maryland Music Educators Association (2021) recently offered a Solo & Ensemble Festival for which "there is no approved repertoire list, no instrument/vocal styling restrictions, and students and educators are encouraged to select repertoire that is representative of the student's personal experiences and culture." While this structure does not necessitate students performing their own composition, it allows them to do so.

Educating and engaging stakeholders can support changes that enhance your students' composition learning. Teacher assessment and program evaluation frameworks shared in this chapter can promote self-reflection, dialogues with stakeholders, and data collection to thoughtfully consider modifications. As Wesolowski et al. (2019) remind us, "it is through such honest reflection that music educators can move their programs and the profession toward a more holistic approach to music education" (p. 504).

REFERENCES

Arizona Department of Education. (2020). *Arizona arts standards.* https://www.azed.gov/standards-practices/k-12standards/arts-standards

Bernard, C. F., & Abramo, J. M. (2019). *Teacher evaluation in music: A guide for music teachers in the U.S.* Oxford University Press.

Clark, I. N., Stretton-Smith, P. A., Baker, F. A., Lee, Y. C., & Tamplin, J. (2020). "It's feasible to write a song": A feasibility study examining group therapeutic songwriting for people living with dementia and their family caregivers. *Frontiers in Psychology, 11,* 1951. https://doi.org/10.3389/fpsyg.2020.01951

Cohen, M. L., & Wilson, C. M. (2017). Inside the fences: Pedagogical practices and purposes of songwriting in an adult male U.S. state prison. *International Journal of Music Education, 35*(4), 541–553. https://doi.org/10.1177/0255761416689841

Danielson, C. (2013). *The framework for teaching: Evaluation instrument.* Danielson Group.

Danielson Group (2019). *The framework for teaching: Music education.* Danielson Group.

Doersken, D. P. (2006). *Evaluating teachers of music performance groups.* Rowman & Littlefield Education.

Ferguson, D. A. (2007). Program evaluations in music education: A review of the literature. *Update: Applications of Research in Music Education, 25*(2), 4–15. https://doi.org/10.1177/87551233070250020102

Freedman, B. (2013). *Teaching music through composition: A curriculum using technology.* Oxford University Press.

Hash, P. M. (2020). Remote learning in school bands during the COVID-19 shutdown. *Journal of Research in Music Education, 68*(4), 381–397. https://doi.org/10.1177/0022429420967008

Haston, W., & Leon-Guerrero, A. (2008). Sources of pedagogical content knowledge: Reports by preservice instrumental music teachers. *Journal of Music Teacher Education, 17*(2), 48–59. https://doi.org/10.1177/1057083708317644

Hewitt, M., & Koner, K. (2013). A comparison of instrumental music methods course content at NASM-accredited institutions. *Bulletin of the Council for Research in Music Education, 197*, 45–61. https://doi.org/10.5406/bulcouresmusedu.197.0045

Hickey, M. (1997). Teaching ensembles to compose and improvise. *Music Educators Journal, 83*(6), 17–21. https://doi.org/10.2307/3399019

Hickey, M. (2012). *Music outside the lines: Ideas for composing in K–12 music classrooms.* Oxford University Press.

Hoover, S. A. (2021). *Music as care: Artistry in the hospital environment.* Routledge.

Kaschub, M., & Smith, J. (2009). *Minds on music: Composition for creative and critical thinking.* Rowman & Littlefield Education.

Kaschub, M., & Smith, J. P. (2016). The big picture: Developing musical capacities. *Music Educators Journal, 102*(3), 33–40. https://doi.org/10.1177/0027432115622535

Kuhn, W., & Hein, E. (2021). *Electronic music school: A contemporary approach to teaching musical creativity.* Oxford University Press.

Maryland Music Educators Association. (2021). *Fall 2020 solo and ensemble festival.* https://www.mmea-maryland.org/fall-2020-solo-ensemble-festival

Marzano, R. J. (2017). *The new art and science of teaching.* Solution Tree Press.

McClurken, J. (2010). *Teaching and learning with student-generated, online, creative, and public new media* [Conference session]. Teaching and Learning with Technology Conference, Harrisonburg, VA, United States.

Menard, E. A. (2015). Music composition in the high school curriculum: A multiple case study. *Journal of Research in Music Education, 63*(1), 114–136. https://doi.org/10.1177/0022429415574310

Miksza, P., Roeder, M., & Biggs, D. (2010). Surveying Colorado band directors' opinions of skills and characteristics important to successful music teaching. *Journal of Research in Music Education, 57*(4), 364–381. https://doi.org/10.1177/0022429409351655

Millican, J. S., & Forester, S. H. (2019). Music teacher rankings of selected core teaching practices. *Journal of Music Teacher Education, 29*(1), 86–99. https://doi.org/10.1177/1057083719867682

Moreno, M. (2014). Program evaluation: A review of impact, method, and emerging trends for music education. *Canadian Music Educator, 55*(3), 32–37.

NAMM Foundation. (2021). *Best communities for music education.* https://www.nammfoundation.org/what-we-do/best-communities-music-education

New York State School Music Association. (2021). *NYSSMA composition/improvisation committee.* https://www.nyssma.org/committees/compositionimprovisation/

Onuscheck, M., Marzano, R. J., & Grice, J. (2020). *The new art and science of teaching art and music.* Solution Tree Press.

Owen, J. M. (2020). *Program evaluation: Forms and approaches* (3rd ed.). Routledge.

Pennell, C. (2020). *Evaluating the K–12 literacy curriculum.* Routledge.

Piazza, E. S., & Talbot, B. C. (2020). Creative musical activities in undergraduate music education curricula. *Journal of Music Teacher Education. Journal of Music Teacher Education, 30*(2), 37–50. https://doi.org/10.1177/1057083720948463

Randles, C. A. (2010). *Creative identity in music teaching and learning* [Doctoral dissertation, Michigan State University]. https://search.proquest.com/dissertations-theses/creative-identity-music-teaching-learning/docview/815436204/se-2?accountid=11667

Randles, C., & Stringham, D. (Eds.). (2013). *Musicianship: Composing in band and orchestra*. GIA Publications.

Reese, J. (2009). Lift the hood and get dirty!: A closer look at informances. *Music Educators Journal, 96*(2), 27–29. https://doi.org/10.1177/0027432109351405

Riley, P. E. (2012). Exploration of student development through songwriting. *Visions of Research in Music Education, 22*. Article 6. Retrieved from http://www.rider.edu/~vrme

Shewan, S. C. (2009). Through the eyes of a composer. From *NYSSMA Music Views: Standards-based teaching and learning across the state* [video recording]. New York State School Music Association.

Shouldice, H. N. (2014). Teachers' beliefs regarding composition in elementary general music: Definitions, values, and impediments. *Research Studies in Music Education, 36*(2), 215–230. https://doi.org/10.1177/1321103X14556574

Sindberg, L. K. (2012). *Just good teaching: Comprehensive Musicianship through Performance (CMP) in theory and practice*. Rowman & Littlefield Education.

Snell, A. H., II (2015). Teaching everybody everything. In S. L. Burton & A. H. Snell, II (Eds.), *Engaging practices in instrumental music* (pp. 161–178). Rowman & Littlefield Education.

Stanford History Education Group. (2021). *Reading like a historian*. https://sheg.stanford.edu/history-lessons

State Education Agency Directors of Arts Education. (2014). *National core arts standards*. http://www.nationalartsstandards.org

Stringham, D. A., Thornton, L. C., & Shevock, D. J. (2015). Composition and improvisation in instrumental methods courses: Instrumental music teacher educators' perspectives. *Bulletin of the Council for Research in Music Education, 205*, 7–25. https://doi.org/10.5406/bulcouresmusedu.205.0007

Virginia Department of Education. (2020). *Music standards of learning for Virginia public schools*. http://doe.virginia.gov/testing/sol/standards_docs/fine_arts/2020/2020fasol-music.pdf

Virginia Music Educators Association. (2020). *Blue ribbon award*. https://www.vmea.com/index.php/awards/blue-ribbon

Virginia Music Educators Association. (2021). *Composition festival*. https://www.vmea.com/index.php/events-menu/composition-festival

Wesolowski, B. C., McDaniel, B. C., & Powell, L. M. (2019). Assessing what is valued: An ecological framework for school music assessment. In T. S. Brophy & M. Haning (Eds.), *Advancing music education through assessment: Honoring culture, diversity, and practice* (pp. 493–509). GIA Publications.

Wiggins, G., & McTighe, J. (2005). *Understanding by Design* (2nd ed.). ACSD.

Wiggins, G., & McTighe, J. (2011). *The Understanding by Design guide to creating high-quality units*. ASCD.

Wiggins, G., & McTighe, J. (2015). *The Understanding by Design guide to advanced concepts in creating and reviewing units*. ASCD.

CHAPTER 42

....

COMPOSITION, POLICY, AND THE FORMATION OF AGENCY

Pathways in Teacher Education and K–16 Practice

....

PATRICK SCHMIDT AND JASHEN EDWARDS

INTRODUCTION: POLICY FRAMING AND PROFESSIONAL AGENTIC ACTION

SOCIAL pressure toward change has always been the catalyst within policy and leadership. When social pressure toward change is weak, traditionalism tends to win the day. When demand for change increases—pushed by cultural shifts, economic stresses, social anxieties, professional rethinking, or catastrophic events—leadership action follows (or is replaced) and policy lines are redrawn. In fact, several policy theories speak of this, highlighting the ways in which a confluence of events/factors are necessary for change to take place (*multiple streams theory*) or of how incremental change or periods of stability are often pushed forward by moments of substantive disruption (*punctuated equilibrium*).

In what follows, we borrow from several policy analytical concepts to explore change toward greater agency and equity in music education curricula. We use Pemberton (2003) and the notion that "peripheral actors with little obvious power can exert great policy power through the medium of a policy network" to demonstrate the importance of personal policy action and how it may intersect, and thus be amplified, by networked structures. Consequently, we highlight ways in which music teachers in North American schools and universities are challenging themselves, their students, and their school communities to think and act creatively and politically. They are doing so through composition, songwriting, beat-making, soundscapes, and other forms of creative music engagement. Here, we use their work as both anchoring stories—examples of feasible incremental local and even personal policy redirection (i.e., *policy know-how*)—as well as design challenges, or ways to develop an architecture for more widespread redirection of music teacher training and practice within the field.

Our hope is to establish an understanding of policy as the actualization of personal and collective intention, using composition as one potential "policy congruence" force, that is, a point of concerted effort that emerges when the policy "feels" right and appropriate, thus determining "the degree to which we may see joint action" (Grin & Van de Graff, 1996, p. 45). Throughout we are guided by the notion of "policy lesson drawing," embedding in the text signposts for action within PreK–16 classrooms.

Composition and the Expansion of Music Education's Convenient Knowledge

Calls for change to music education practice have been ongoing, gaining greater resonance in the last decade. Discursively, the music education profession is undoubtedly becoming more diverse and progressive, placing greater value on action toward equity and social justice (Allsup, 2016, Benedict & Schmidt, 2011; Benedict et al., 2015; Gould, 2007), decolonization and racism (Bradley, 2012, Hess, 2017; Prest & Goble, 2021), focusing on intercultural action (Karlsen & Westerlund, 2010), as well as pedagogically non-normative practice (Kallio & Länsman, 2018). One needs not to be a radical, however, to understand that disciplines (as any consensual space of practice) tend to privilege the propositions that best serve their established scopes or parameters of action. This means that disciplines look for—and straightforwardly reward—what could be called *convenient knowledge*, that is, knowledge and practice that easily maps onto and fortifies established disciplinary parameters (Foucault, 1971). Today, and for the better part of the last 80 years, the convenient knowledge of music education has been made manifest through the Western, classically oriented ensemble and the structural periphery—and at times absence—of other practices such as composition.

Many have offered critiques of this model, the challenges of the apprenticeship parameters it fosters (Allsup & Benedict, 2008; Kaschub & Smith, 2013; Mantie, 2012), and the resilience of the cultural norms upon which it is built and how it can be grafted onto other practices (Dyndahl, 2013). Music education's convenient knowledge is not empty, of course. Many still support it and have made their lives and livelihoods in and through it. We acknowledge its value even as its educational shortcomings are glaringly patent to us. It is important to clarify, then, that this convenient knowledge is not simply referent to genre, aesthetics, economic exclusion, cultural-artistic norms (and with it, whiteness). Just as significant are practices that privilege efficiency, a certain labor ethic, and managerial capacity, among others.[1] It must also be said that the issue is not simply ideological or of professional traditionalism. The ensemble has such a hold as music education's convenient knowledge because it aligns rather well with the general

demands of schooling in late-modernity: It signals middle-class values, it functions efficiently (large groups of students with reduced time and labor cost), it inculcates norm/
rule-bound behavior, and it delivers visible/assessable outcomes. Which is to say, progressive and systemic changes will require more than dispositional shifts, as structural
change demands *policy activism*.

Policy in New Terms

Efforts aimed at understanding the historical challenges toward openings, diversity, and
renewal in curricular practice require a networked approach where the ideological, pedagogical, and content intersect with the enactment of professionally driven and personally sustained policy practice. One of us (Schmidt, 2020a) has argued that this demands
a rethinking of the ways in which we understand and value the intersection between
policy practice and teacher practice, highlighting the fact that "*policy* does not just
happen. People do policy" (Schmidt, 2020b, p. 25). In these terms, we are convinced that
"reclaiming educators' identity as partners in the policy process is critical to the future
of the teaching profession" (p. 26). Music educators have a history of being "adept at the
political," and as professionals we are repeatedly compelled to find "alternative solutions
to constraints in curriculum, scheduling, or budgets" (p. 26), but as a field we have failed
to openly portrait how and systematically argue that curricular change demands policy
be seen as a form of teacher practice.

It is patent to us that composition is a needed pathway for the renewal and expansion of music education influence in learning environments. Just as apparent is that
music professionals must develop policy know-how if the challenges and possibilities
of reclaiming composition is to be enacted. Given the distance that currently exist between policy practice and educators, a first step is to reclaim it, understanding policy engagement as the work we do in creating the conditions for the practices we think matter
most—particularly when we come to see policy practice as centrally concerned with inquiry and change (Schmidt, 2009 and 2017). Following the sociologist and policy scholar
Stephen Ball (2003 and 2016), we argue that educators can and do play multiple roles
in policy practice within schooling, taking the role of, for example, policy narrators,
critics, enthusiasts, transactors, and translators, while of course also of outsiders and
receivers.[2] Erich Shieh (2020) further provides insight as to how music teachers cannot
just respond to policy but also create new spaces for it in our schools, describing policy-
practice strategies in the contexts of bridging, buffering, and building. This and other
growing scholarship places policy practice as familiar to the most significant ideas in
teaching: first, that inquiry must lead action, and second, that opportunities for change
must be constantly considered, given the shifting sets of cultural, social, ideological,
technological, psychological, and personal conditions on which learning takes place—
see Schmidt (2020a) for a detailed discussion on this.

Policy practice in this sense then mirrors core aspects of compositional practice: 1)
curiosity and inquiry, 2) imagination and play, and 3) tinkering and tweaking toward

dynamic and concrete change. Facilitating spaces for composition then can also help students and teachers develop and practice the kinds of sensibilities needed to move in the world with transformative consciousness.

Curriculum Policy at the Center and Periphery

Decentering our existing convenient knowledge requires more than establishing a managerial understanding of the status quo and taking advantage of it—what we call admin or managerial savvy. We want to make a distinction that while the latter is part of policy know-how, and policy implementation is particularly beholden to administrative savvy, policy practice, and know-how are, however, broader concepts, which involve strategic planning, framing capacity, communicative skills, collaborative partnering, stakeholder engagement, visioning, consensus building, and programmatic expertise, among others.

As we see it then, breaking with ensemble-based *convenient knowledge* will require more than representative diversity of practices—replacing one system or sets of music for another, as the field has done at times with informal practices and popular music (see Georgii-Hemming & Westvall, 2010). Partially divesting ourselves from historic efforts to bring particular *musics* from current curricular periphery to the curricular "center" or "core" is a major challenge; particularly as whiteness and privilege remain key factors in how musics are legitimized. We pinpoint and discuss two legitimizing constraints later in this chapter—notions of genius and limitations of notation—both of which are in effect elitist and exclusionary while often conceived as customary requisites for compositional engagement and evaluation. We should also not forget that traditional arguments around "quality music repertoire" perfectly map onto educational policy that over-privileges standardization, accountability, and "objective" learning outcomes. Such discourses, however, continue to place *music* (i.e., concrete cultural-specific idealized product) at the center, often distracting from curricular policy and dialogue directed toward how musical learning and creating (i.e., musical engagement and exploration as a dynamic collaborative process) can become a strong contributing factor to the challenges faced by schooling in general and curricular relevance in particular. Our point is that the rhetorical, advocacy-based efforts toward valuing *music* as a disciplinary practice that must be recognized on its own rights, have consumed significant professional oxygen. These have drained energy that could otherwise be directed toward exploring music curricular efforts prizing equity, openness and innovation, intersectionality, social relevance, and personal meaning.

Today, this may be driven by policy strategies aimed at elevating the role of the "peripheral." Central here is the notion that the periphery can and often does function according to parameters that are different from the core. *Periphery* as a concept tends to be a) outward-looking, b) inviting of collaboration, c) expansionist to boundaries, more willing to take risks, d) pedagogically adaptive, and e) less concerned with legitimate knowledge and legitimized actors. We believe that *composition* writ large can and should be seen as a signifier for reclaiming the *peripheral* in music education. This means that it can focus on creating, while making use of performing and reproducing. It can be slightly disruptive, while a well-integrated part of the field. *Composition* in these terms can amass one such "bridging" space, pushing the boundaries of curricular practice, and thus come to be understood as more than an *activity*, sub-practice, or tool, but as a compelling element in eliciting student voice and agency toward social change.

Composition and Policy Change

In policy terms, strategic action that would incentivize *composition* as a diverse pedagogical practice could place music education more visibly in the service of educative projects aiming to engage in cultural production (Gaztambide-Fernandez, 2020). This could foster a commitment to connections between learning, schooling, and the world around us. In such an integrative view, what may also become more evident to music educators in schools is that "most individuals are not merely the subjects of power but play a part in its operations" (Miller & Rose, 2008, p. 53), working not just to assert one's right of existence, and rather focusing on how their presence helps to guarantee diverse, multi-modal, creative, and relevant learning rights for students.

From this perspective, a commitment to composition embodies some key characteristics of what Ruben Gaztambide-Fernandez (2020) calls *cultural production* and may in fact help "develop a pedagogy and a practice of creative symbolic work that more effectively encapsulates the complexities of lived experience in and through creative expression and symbolic work" (p. 7). We would like to argue that a commitment to *composition* then could be the pragmatic, tangible pathway toward a cultural production framing that could also further facilitate a view of music education as "community-oriented work," placing music curricular efforts perhaps at the intersection of "geographic awareness, framing disposition, activism, and policy engagement" (Schmidt, 2018, p. 411). Such a framing could become a "leading disposition toward more diverse models of interaction with music-learning, music-making, and music-practicing that [even when functioning within schools] are 'out-in-the-world'" (Schmidt, 2018, p. 405). This could be strategically operationalized by a coalition dependent on stronger policy know-how fostered by so disposed music teacher education programs, and a professional commitment from leading music educators working in K–12 settings. It could become a powerful tool to decolonization and culturally relevant teaching and learning.

Resonant Spaces for Composing in the Classroom—De-centering Music

To place the ideas and concepts discussed above in practical terms we sought the insight of several practitioners working in the US and Canada who have nurtured the dispositions toward and experiences enacting the kind of policy practice we argue for in this chapter. Below we highlight the insight, expertise, and practices of teachers doing this work, today. We present these in the form of three cases across middle and high school and university in general, choral, and wind ensemble.

Composing as Non-negotiable

Joanna is a Canadian middle school teacher with near 10 years of experience. Her background is rather traditional, as she says, but was marked by a positive experience with a co-curricular program called *School Alliance of Student Song Writers*. At a time where her training and previous experiences were proving somewhat limited, particularly in relation to her efforts to reach more students and to engage them fully, the Alliance, a network-based, district-led, cross-school program, created both a space for professional development and curricular re-imagination. Central to her efforts, and those of the Alliance, was the idea of providing a curricular space that would "give the students the opportunity to create themselves"—the double entendre being intentional. Joanna spoke about the fact that once she became part of the program and brought it to her own school, her aims shifted from delivering content and teaching concepts, to "applying the musical concepts in the creation of new material." As she articulated, "once I saw that as possible . . . once understanding became key, it was not enough that they [students] simply reproduce, play the work of others." Following the parameters discussed here, *composition* was understood broadly by Joanna, where the aim of musical learning was a process where scaffolding was variable and where movement, singing, instrumental playing were precursors to, and found their way into, creating. This led to a "change in my teaching" with new commitments articulated thusly, "I really saw this moving forward, for me, when I made the program and what it offered as a non-negotiable."

Joanna's story speaks of a shift from big P policy to small p policy practice—policy know-how in motion. She spoke clearly about the need for catalysts to enact the program, how she benefited from the program history, the network of teachers who helped her, and the district-wide support for the program existence. Framing the relationship between wider support and personal policy commitment, she articulated the linkage between the elements, the catalysts, that together meant implementation was possible and sustainability was attainable (the program has over a decade). The circle went: *people, structures, program, practice, people*—with commitment, in all levels, being key.

Without articulating any policy theory—or really uttering the word—Joanna talked about central policy practice dispositions (see Figure 42.1) that made the program and a new curricular vision succeed.

While there are many lessons here, the articulation that this new venture led Joanna to re-think the role and place of creating within the learning process is key. This was not simply a manner of adding a potential "standard" of practice; it was not simply about "aligning with state curriculum requirements." Rather, it was a welcomed opportunity to teach differently, to create a "community of song writers" and provide a "creative

Curricular policy efficacy was linked to networked efforts;	• Teachers understood they needed to create ways to encourage others, developing new sets of curricular values, while also facilitating professional development and supporting new interest.
Sustainability depended on (new) visibility;	• The program needs to be seeing by multiple constituents (including teachers and students), but advocacy was based on learning impact, curricular alignment with school/district wide aims, and a focus on equity and social reach.
Linking opportunity for learning and strategic professional growth;	• The importance of "creating spaces for engagement and excitement" for students, while not forgetting that teachers too need curricular and pedagogical spaces for renewal— "to be labs for the teacher herself". • Programs were to be only partially replicated, prizing adaptability and taking on the character of the teacher and the students in different schools.
Policy practice at the intersection of management and leadership;	• Technical conditions for success were not dismissed: makeshift space and carts, licenses for materials, 1-to-1 Chromebooks, instruments, and class time/schedule, • Opening lines of communication, voicing a vision and knowing when to retrieve. • Making 'wins' visible and circling back to support network when things got tough.

FIGURE 42.1. Joanna's observations

connection between challenges in our [hers and students'] lives." We interpret the decision to make *composition* as a manifestation of certain educational values and a *non-negotiable*, as a moment of policy enactment (Ball, Maguire, & Braun, 2012); the leap into a new professional practice and an engagement in the politics of doing what was necessary to see the vision through. This was a moment of taking ownership as well, as Joanna articulated, establishing her personal policy practice, seeing herself critically engaged in the continuum between "other peoples' objectives and my own objectives."

"When We Gonna Change?"

Some high school choir directors may "exclude composition,"[3] thinking it antithetical to "expectations and pressures of ensemble teaching." Indeed, "external authorizing bodies" and internal and ingrained beliefs (i.e., convenient knowledge) can and often do de-legitimize student composing, especially in ensemble settings where products are practiced to perfection and then to performance. However, as this Chicago high school choral director has articulated and successfully shown, "Composing can enrich the ensemble classroom, create a stronger sense of community, [and] create more skillful musicians." For Casey, his disposition toward composing in the choral classroom began to shift during his undergraduate years, specifically in his Philosophy of Music Education course where he was asked to think about: *Who is doing the creative work? Who is the creative person in ensemble settings?* Casey's high school initiated a co-curricular program called Colloquium Day whereby students can register each semester for a variety of curricular activities, a "non-traditional space" that nevertheless functioned well "at the periphery of core subjects." This led to a songwriting course and a secured partnership with a local organization called CAPE (Chicago Arts Partnership in Education). Paired with poet Ladan Osan, Casey and the colloquium students (some choir members, others not) composed original pieces expressing their views of a city that had come under fire as the "national punching bag of Donald Trump." In these compositional activities students could sound out "how they hear and see their city" reinforcing how students are capable of being creative *and* critical, and could and should do so in the choral classroom space.

One opportunity came during the height of district budget cuts. The students at his school would be disproportionally affected as a result since "the State funding system was known to be the most inequitable in the country." He decided to invite choral students from across his choirs to compose a piece addressing this issue. His choristers had already been introduced to "protest songs and music from Apartheid South Africa" so he encouraged them to consider how their own song could express their frustrations and fears. The outcome, the song "When We Gonna Change?" garnered critical acclaim across news stations and media outlets in Chicago and was performed at a rally in front of the Chicago Board of Education. The following year, other choristers joined and composed a sequel: "Which Side Are You On?" They took this song on the road to the state capital of Springfield where they performed on the steps of the governors' headquarters to a body of legislators.

Casey said,

> Students were composing what reflected their identity, creating original work, creating for an authentic audience. . . . Not just a school choir concert, this was a performance that got media attention, [with] politicians watching the performance. . . . Composition created an opportunity for students who may have never considered themselves someone who had the talent or wasn't special enough that they have that kind of platform. . . . We [could] just totally change how a young person conceives of themselves.

Duet for Heart and Breath

For Dr. S, facilitating spaces for her students to be creative is paramount. She feels so much of musical training can "deaden" creative processes, particularly as it relates to composing where "students are told, you can't break the rules until you know what the rules are . . . [and] you have to pass through all these gates before you're allowed to be creative, by the time you get there you've internalized that you don't have any creativity."

Seeing this as "a tragedy," she encourages her students to listen and collect sounds from their environment and use these in composing original pieces. This she does not only in her mixed-majors course on social justice arts education, but equally significantly with her traditional wind ensemble students. At a recent honors festival, one of the university's major "recruitment events," she wondered how she might facilitate an activity for "students to feel connected to one another even though they are in two separate bands and create something together." Realizing that both ensembles' repertoire "dealt with the notion of 'what is home' and why is home important, and what happens when your notion of home is shaken," she asked the 100 performers (including many international students) to record sounds related to their conceptions, experiences, and memories of home. Scored for large ensemble and set against ambient melodic passages all students could play, sounds of "trains, washing machines, pets snoring, and the jingle of mother's bangle bracelets" and many others filled the auditorium. Dr. S recalls, "Students listened smiling as their sounds filled the air. . . . at the end of the performance the hall was so quiet you could hear a pin drop. . . . It was a surprisingly moving experience. . . . [There was] a sense of unity between students, audience, and conductors sharing and connecting in that moment through sound."

What Joanna, Casey, and Dr. S have in common is their commitment to providing spaces for their students to actively re-engage and share their voices through a creative medium such as composition. Whether in general music classes or traditional ensembles, student voice can lead to student agency, which in turn may lead to the kinds of inclusive, diverse, equitable, culturally relevant, responsive, sustaining, and just pedagogies many music educators today aspire. More than just an activity, however, or tool, composing showed itself as indispensable curricular aims inviting and celebrating "creative expression and symbolic work" of students. Thus, cultural production was paramount to actualizing these teachers' and students' intentions. Another significant commonality shared between these three teachers has to do with their approach to music and so-called musical elements of composition. They created resonate spaces for composing in the classroom by expanding their view of and "De-centering music"—a philosophical and pedagogical practice that troubles "the Eurocentric origins of the word 'music' [and] unseats music from its place of hegemony" (Recharte, 2019, pp. 69–70). Recharte further suggests,

> This de-centering of music has the advantage of possibly enabling music educators to transcend the hierarchy of musical styles that organizes which sounds are deemed more musical than others and avoid some of the problematic requirements of traditional music education. (p. 82)

Ordinary conceptions of composition, composing, and composers are entangled in a problematic paradigm of cultural objects propagating colonialist patriarchal dos-and-don'ts (Cox, 2017). If composition is to move beyond the periphery and into the core of curriculum policy and practice, then re-evaluating terms and concepts born from such music ideals is critical. We argue that a decentering of music is already present in the practices of these teachers, and also of many others. This current handbook is a testament to the field's commitment to reframing pedagogical sensibilities around music/sound (Rice & Clements, in this volume, "Developing Soundcrafters: Facilitating a Holistic Approach to Music Production"), aesthetics, originality, and genius (Smith, in this volume, "Vocabularies of Genius and Dilemmas of Pedagogy"), for example. Powerfully, they show that ultimately it is the combined sensibilities of teachers and their students to tune in and listen deeply to their "Sonic Commons" (Odland & Auinger, 2009). By opening their ears, hearts, and mind to sounds informing and impacting their lives, and responding by sounding out their individual and collective creative critical consciousness, these teachers and their students challenged long-held assumptions about what constitutes music and thus, composition.

TROUBLING COMPOSITION—TOWARD A RENEWED PERSPECTIVE

Similar to policy, composition can often start in private and is primarily guided by two factors: value and preservation. Before finding its way into a public sphere (in our case music education spaces), compositions, like policies, may be constructed upon presumed "truths" and are ultimately concerned with advancing, conserving, and preserving these as invaluable, inevitable or natural, and worthy of emulation and obedience. In order to move toward a renewed perspective wherein student-centered cultural production and composition are central to curricular policy and practice, it is important to locate the ways products (and processes) of composing become "institutionalized and canonized . . . fixed . . . regarded as traditional . . . valued and preserved" (Jorgensen, 1997, p. 25). For it is in private personal "belief templates" (Wallace, 2009, p. 43) about composition, composing, and composers wherein values are stenciled, etched, and preserved into policy and practice.

Composition, as has been articulated, is unarguably informed by a Eurocentric-driven narrative that has defined it, *and* the people consecrated to do it: composers. Such demarcations are abundantly acknowledged in our field as are their limitations (Hickey, 2012; Shouldice, 2014; Thompson, 2007; Woodford, 2002). So, when music teachers such as the ones presented earlier think and act counter to convenient knowledge by facilitating spaces for composing and other forms of student-centered sound and music creation it is not without significance. Their dispositions, framing, and belief templates may illuminate ways for others to think and do differently in their own music classrooms as they too practice principles of policy know-how at the micro level. Not only did these teachers de-center music, but they also adopted an attitude that acknowledged their students' "musical and compositional capacities" (Kaschub & Smith, 2021, pp. 67–68). While these may seem axiomatic, they are not, because music education policies and practices that have governed generations of music teachers and learners, especially in reference to composing, are based upon the value and preservation of two prescriptive and privatizing concepts: *genius* and *notation*. Indeed, these two factors can (and sometimes do) impede music teachers from promoting composition in their pedagogical philosophy and practice, as notions of genius and the privileged and perceived permanence of notation are engrained in the fabric of American education generally, and music education specifically.

Composing Colonialism: Implications and Limitations of Genius and Notation from Manifest Destiny to the the Mozart (neglect) Effect

As a founding and dominant figure in American public education policy professing an "ideology of democratic schooling" (Carpenter, 2013), Thomas Jefferson's framing of learning and teaching, and of musical skills, are worthy of some attention. His educational policies were built upon a hierarchical pyramid favoring white males who "demonstrated the best and most promising genius and disposition" (p. 5). Jefferson sought "twenty of the best geniuses [to] be raked from the rubbish" (p. 5) and only those persons could be selected to attend regional grammar schools paid for by the public purse. This elitism was coupled with racism. In his *Notes on the State of Virginia*, Jefferson (1982/1787) viewed US enslaved blacks' "imagination . . . dull, tasteless, and anomalous" (p. 146). He claimed: "In music they are more generally gifted than the whites, with accurate ears for tune and time, and they have been found capable of imagining a small catch. Whether they will be equal to the composition of a more extensive run of melody, or of complicated harmony, is yet to be proved" (p. 147).

One could pause to wonder whether or not, if Jefferson had lived long enough to be in attendance at New York's Aeolian Hall on February 12, 1924 for Paul Whiteman's, *An Experiment in Modern Music* concert, if he, like the "great conductor and music educator of the day Walter Damrosch" would have agreed that Gershwin had "made a lady out of jazz" (Berrett, 2004, p. 217, *fn*10)? Or what if he had lived to the year 2019 and sat and heard Terrance Blanchard's *Fire Shut Up in My Bones*—the Met's first staged opera by an African-American composer (Cooper, 2019)? Or, in the year 2020, he had listened to the complex crossover compositions of Rhiannon Giddens as she "reconstruct[ed] Black pain with the banjo" (Martin & Desoto, 2018)? Jefferson's notion of genius supplements high-held belief templates around so-called great composers, and the combination represents a small but important fraction of a history that continues to inform musical practice and value today.

In his 1991 year-end review for *Pulse!* magazine, American music critic Allan Koznin responds to the question "Is classical music dying?" Koznin discusses in his feature article, "Changing of the Guard," how classical music record companies were responding to the then-recent demise of some of its titans—Aaron Copland and Leonard Bernstein—and frantically working to reorganize labels and catalogue selections to include new blood. He notes: "The classical record business waltzed along happily for another year—some say it is concealing a bit of a limp, which may lead to a permanent disability some time down the road." Koznin cites record companies' fiscal limp as their near neglect of young talent. Is not one job of music educators to facilitate students' musical *and* compositional capacities (i.e., *new blood*)?

How can "young talent" be fostered in spaces where belief templates about genius (and even *talent*) taints conceptions of accessibility and agency to music and music-making? Resonance theorist Hartmut Rosa (2020) critiques the so-called power of art, noting "the belief that the creation of a work of art requires 'breath' of a muse, of genius, of spirit, of God" (p. 281) effectively nullifies one's relationship with their creative self, making them either a docile non-agentic conformist slave to the whims of a genie, or one who does not see that art is a product of being alive and in touch with the world around them along with the development of skill, craft, and technique. As Joanna eloquently expressed: "Give the students the opportunity to create themselves."

Notation

Similar to debilitating notions of genius, concepts around notation can also play a role in how musical and compositional capacities are understood and approached. Script (i.e., the written word) has historically served the interests of a select privileged few.[4] From Manifest Destiny to the Mozart Effect, education policies, practices, and particularly "how-to" texts or manuals have been at the forefront of civilizing and codifying an Other; a "smartening them up" for participation and "success" in a so-called field of practice within "civilized" industrialized society. Indeed, "the arts and particularly music have been central to European colonizing and evangelizing projects throughout history" (Recharte, 2019, p. 71). In his controversial book, *The Alphabet Versus the Goddess: The Conflict Between Word and Image*, Leonard Shlain (1999) contends, "One pernicious effect of literacy has gone largely unnoticed: writing subliminally fosters a patriarchal outlook" (p. 25) as it promotes a *linear, sequential, reductionist*, and *abstract* view of the world. Shlain argues that, when script entered into early societies it did so as a means of mass communication and also asserted (author)itarian control. As a result, power imbalances became more prevalent as ways of knowing and being in the world guided by *holistic, simultaneous, synthetic*, and *concrete* perspectives were diminished and dismissed.

Considering composition from this perspective a few limitations come to light. Take, for example, AP and undergraduate music theory courses. These are typically the first places where students are formally introduced to "the great composers" and offered opportunities to abstract, dissect, analyze, and revere the "great works" of the canon. Typically, music students are not encouraged to compose their own pieces in these courses. Unfortunately, music theory courses can also be one of the first places where students are informally, indirectly introduced to a belief template that distances them from composing, as they are led to understand that until they know and follow the rules of "the great composers," composing original music should wait. Recall Dr. S's remark about "breaking the rules": *"By the time you get there you've internalized that you don't have any creativity"*—"there," being after such courses. This entangled estrangement is evident in music theory professor Steven Laitz's (2012) preface to *The Complete Musician*,

> Music students often suffer through their theory and aural skills courses, viewing them as not particularly relevant—perhaps even painful—sidelines of their musical studies. This is a shame since an unsatisfying experience early on usually has an adverse effect on students' attitudes. (Laitz, 2012, p. xii)

What often goes unrecognized in specialized discourse of musical training is what Walter Piston prefaces in his classic harmony text:

> We must realize that musical theory is not a set of directions for composing music. It is rather the collected and systematized deductions gathered by observing the practice of composers over a long time, and it attempts to set forth what is or has been *their* common practice. It tells not how music will be written in the future, but how music has been written in the past. (Piston, 1978/1941, p. xix, italics added)

That Piston acknowledged this well over five decades ago, and still students "often suffer," speaks to the convenient knowledge strongholds abundant in fallacies like genius, notation, and other "terms and concepts, like talent, musical, musicianship, and appreciation" (Recharte, 2019, p. 69). Recognizing that said "fundamentals" are nothing other than codes, "collected and systematized deductions" designed to manipulate sonic material within a very specific set of tones and within a culturally contrived temperament system, could help ward off students' and teachers' feelings of alienation from their composer/creative selves, while also dissuading them from measuring their creative ideas toward an Idealized perfection of harmony. Much of the talk in composer-speak is about finding one's "own voice." One struggle with finding one's own compositional voice could stem from a constant comparison of that voice to voices of the dead past "great composers" that have been deemed perfect. Curtailing unhealthy comparisons and unrealistic expectations could offer relief and help students attune their ears to hear and listen and be more present in *their* lived and un-idealized soundworlds.

We do well, like the music teachers highlighted in this chapter, to actively confront our belief templates by grappling with questions such as: What do such views around genius and notation preserve? Could it be that such thinking reifies, even glorifies hegemonic and patriarchal Eurocentric ideologies? Who gets underserved or not served at all if one thinks composing is meant for a genius few? Or, that other forms of music creation (e.g., songwriting, beat-boxing, DJing, rapping, soundscaping, etc.) do not denote "real" composing? Could it be that some music education policies and classroom/studio practices are inadvertently seeking out the "best geniusses," perhaps "raking" over those not showing "promise"?

It is without question that neoliberal notions of "promise" or "potential" are propelled by a Western ideal of "success," which today madly manifests itself via cut-throat competitiveness and high-stakes assessment and standardization that values an "acceleration" (Rosa, 2013/2005) toward a consumeristic-driven sellable "creative" product over deeply reflective imaginative creative critical processes (Haiven & Khasnabish, 2014). For music educators who have inherited and work within this faulty system, it is worth never forgetting that curricular policies and pedagogical practices of yesterday can (and do) still haunt, rearing their ugly head. Segregation and siloing may be seen today in K–16 music programs and departments across North America. While these boundaries and bunching of music students may not be directly drawn along color, class, or gender lines completely, they are often drafted via conceptions of "genius" or "natural talent" as evinced through the conservatory model's auditioning processes, ensemble seating arrangements, or choice of student soloists—thus, still buying into a traditionalist or conservationist view of music teaching and learning. As music educators work to "take account of issues of oppression" so as to disrupt "the status quo" (Wright, 2016/2010, p. 276), it is all the more important to recognize where we may implement changes in perception, policy, and practice.

HIGHER MUSIC EDUCATION AND THE ESTABLISHMENT OF NEW CONGRUENCES

Any kind of engagement in policy practice change requires serious consideration of the relationship between adoption, enactment, and legitimization. This is to say that potential *systemic openings* for music education curricula expanding the ensemble-performance nexus would require: 1) a clear rationale, 2) social and cultural impetus or pressure, 3) models of practice and action, 4) the experiences of policy practitioner enthusiasts, and 5) ongoing support and networking.

As we articulated above and as proposed elsewhere (see Kaschub and Smith, 2014) rationales for action are as multiple as convincing. Here, we argued that placing *composition-as-music/sound-creation-and-manipulation* functioning as an *umbrella concept* that is capable of opening up curricular space that is exploratory, socially engaged, and personally meaningful and that more easily intersects with general educational curricular concerns, is a policy practice that deserves attention. *Composition* as a space where creation or a form of *cultural production* can complement learning about, listening to, and performing/interpreting music is also central. We argue this is critical particularly if we are to consider musical practices as opportune ways to foster equity, diversity, and a decolonizing curriculum that goes beyond awareness (Bylica, 2020; Gaudry & Lorenz, 2018). To see this actualized, work toward policy priorities that would de-center music and establish curricular and programmatic spaces where composing can claim space into the ensemble-performance nexus is necessary.

It is also clear to us that in 2021 social and cultural demand for changes in music education were, to use a policy theory image, finding a moment of convergence where traditional equilibrium is being punctuated, It is doubtless that multiple efforts to adapt choral and instrumental practices are well intentioned and responsive to calls for equity, decolonization, culturally relevant pedagogies and directive-hierarchical pedagogy (Marcho, 2020; Palkki & Caldwell, 2018; Shaw, 2015; Costa-Giomi & Chappell, 2007). Such reforms are limited, though, by virtue of the very formats themselves, their structures and histories, as we have articulated. This is not reason for abandonment or dismissal. Indeed, as Casey and Dr. S demonstrate, performing ensembles can and do offer opportunities to move freely within their formats and sustain spaces of resonances for collaborative composition that is both musical and meaningful.

We must acknowledge, however, that systemic reform requires both some level of structural change as well as adaptive modification. This can be facilitated if we begin with professional and disciplinary policy guided by premises such as this, which we suggest as an example:

> Guiding action toward success and effectiveness within music education should be gauged by the ways in which curricular and programmatic diversity are aligned to the diversity of experience, socio-cultural needs, and learning interests of each given learning community.

While this may sound radical to some, if curricular policy in the field is to function in synchrony with local/regional complexities, then expanding the ways in which our professional practice is socially responsive and responsible is imperative. From a policy practice standpoint, we suggest the implementation of tactical goals of this sort can serve as significant starting points:

> Given historical deficits meeting standards of practice that address composition and improvisation, music practitioners in K–16 settings commit to the goal of enacting 20 percent of all curricular practice in the form of systemic and sustained engagements with music/sound as composition/creation/manipulation.

Leading Change

Higher education and music teacher education must be leaders in this process. While many individuals in higher education are doing this work, systemic and program-level re-structuring is yet to materialize regardless of much action by music teachers in the field. The troubling realization is that our diversity challenges are intrinsically linked to our programmatic homogeneity (Elpus, 2015; Burton, 2011). Much blame, at least in the US, is placed at the feet of National Association of Schools of Music (NASM). This is intriguing given that NASM's own General Principles (NASM Handbook 2019–20) articulate that "NASM affirms its special commitment to those principles of voluntary accreditation that encourage diversity among institutions and respect for operational integrity within institutions." At least nominally, this seems to establish a dialogical relationship which begins from the standpoints of institutions' needs and their curricular commitments and interests (see ibid., Standards and Guidelines, p. 53). Accreditation visits are at times led by individuals who might read NASM's guidelines in conservative ways, and the institution as a whole might indeed behave in a way whereby its soft policy directives supersede, and at times contradict, its own policy texts. Regardless, given NASM's ostensive commitment to "diversity among institutions and respect for operational integrity" (p. 53), the rush to the policy "middle" based on NASM principles alone seems unfounded. The question then is: Are efforts to maintain a middle point that is "generally characteristic" so strong as to create the widespread homogeneity we see? We find it doubtful.

We argue that a central hurdle may live in the rather *writerly* (Ball, 2015) manner in which policy is observed and a systemic hesitancy at the meso and micro level of schools of music to more *readerly* engage with program design and accreditation policy terms. Successful accounts of systemic program changes seem to suggest this as well—the creation of music education composition at Nebraska, renewal of the music education program at ASU, re-design of the core theory sequence at University of Miami, to cite a few. The challenges to our diversity seem more emic than etic.

From our vantage point, it is clear that NASM guidelines present a discursive traditionalism that could be amended:

- A repertory for study that includes various cultures and historical periods. (p. 95)
- Achieving a measurable degree of technical mastery in at least one of the traditional or innovative techniques appropriate to their area of study. (p. 86)
- The ability to hear, identify, and work conceptually with the elements of music such as rhythm, melody, harmony, structure, timbre, texture. (p. 99)

Often, however, NASM distinguishes "guidelines" from "standards" (regardless of individuals misreading both to mean the same thing) and as accreditors establish minimal parameters of practice, which while tendentious (toward content and structure) would not prevent other more ecumenical understandings of the terms. There is, importantly, much discursive opportunity to ground significant curricular and program diversity in the NASM document that is in line with suggestions articulated here. They remain under-explored from a policy standpoint by institutions of higher learning in music. To cite a few:

- Repeated opportunities for enacting in a variety of ways in roles such as listener, performer, composer, and scholar, and by responding to, interpreting, creating, analyzing, and evaluating music. (p. 96)
- An understanding of compositional processes, aesthetic properties of style, and the ways these shape and are shaped by artistic and cultural forces. (p. 98)

- Evaluation, planning, and making projections are a set of connected activities that relate to all aspects of a music unit's work. They include, but go well beyond numbers of students, personnel, or programs, lists of resource needs, or declarations of aspiration. They address strategies and contextual issues consistent with the purposes, size and scope, program offerings, and responsibilities of the music unit. (p. 76)
- There are many ways to achieve excellence. Innovative and carefully planned experimentation is encouraged. Experimentation might lead to programs of study not specifically indicated in Standards for Accreditation IV—XVI. (p. 86)

Differential Legitimacy

As this chapter aims to establish both a conceptual and pragmatic way to engage in change that might place composition/creation as a more present aspect of curricular policy, what we are able to offer here only begins to address the challenging dialogue and action needed today. Where might we start with simple, systemic, and effective action, tomorrow? In higher music education, taking credible steps to enact more inclusive and equitable curricular aims seems reasonable. To cite a few:

- Commit to expanding the rationale and pedagogical purpose of "core" curricular activities within music schools, aligning with a professional practice that innovatively approximates excellence to social responsibility, and artistry to equity and diversity.
- Amplify the aims of "methods" classes, placing creation as a critical element.
- Systemically expand co-teaching opportunities, intra and across department teaching.
- Expand the role of the co-curricular, structurally creating programs-within-programs, specifically eyeing integration, risk-taking, and diversification of practice
- For those institutions where that is possible (and related to the item above), facilitate graduate students as drivers for/of innovation.

As we see it, these tactical aims are the kind of foundational steps toward larger policy shifts. The Association of European Conservatoires offers a current example in a multi-year project named Strengthening Music in Society, which resonates with our argument and places renewed professionalism front and center, looking at "rethinking and opening curricula," "exploring the landscape for digitization," "embedding entrepreneurship in higher ed," and "contextualizing the admissions [process]" among others.[5] We also see the significance interdepartmental collaboration can have in realizing composition projects within community and local school settings (Edwards et. al, 2020; Veblen, 2022) as evinced at one Canadian university, thus fostering the fundamental idea that "creativity is a collaborative process (not an individual possession)" (Haiven,

2014, p. 192). A similar model of this that has been running for 15 years is *QuerKlang—Experimentelles Komponieren in der Schule*[6] created by composers and music pedagogy faculty at the Universität der Künste, Berlin (Edwards, in press). Faculty composers and their students partner with music education students designing and implementing composition curricula with/for local schoolteachers throughout the city. University sponsored workshops/conferences such as *Composing in the Classroom: Models and Designs for the Creative Music Teacher* are another example. This event offered local teachers an opportunity to engage with composition and music education faculty and to hear and see how teachers in their own districts integrated composition throughout their general, choral, and band programs, and fostered progressive framings for professional development.

These and myriad other curricular practices can be constitutive of how programs can better integrate multiple "peripheries" to establish programs that better use the curricular and the co-curricular, finding greater flexibility and establishing more dynamic program policies—characterizing efforts toward *differential legitimacy* within higher music education. Policy renewal only happens when changing values are expressed in actualizable ways. This is already emergent—so identifying models or practices is not the issue—systemic spread, however, will take strategic effort.

Concluding Thoughts

For quite some time, curricular policy imperatives have privileged standardization and reciprocity under equivocated notions of equality—the thinking was that if, say, band or math programs follow the same general curriculum, equivalent goals, and were delivered in comparable manner no matter where, *all students would have the same chances to learn*. This fallacy no longer holds. In fact, it is not difficult to see classism, racism, and coloniality all over these kinds of arguments. In a profession with a history of precarity, it seems clear to us that no amount of advocacy will prevent a decline in music education: a decline of relevance, of programs, in jobs, and for music as a curricular space in our schools. The outcomes are plain for all to see, if we fail to diversify who we are, how we educate future teachers, what our programs offer and to what ends (and for whom) they are designed that decline might become a foregone conclusion. Just as significantly, how the field frames its own positions (aims and priorities) and how it chooses to integrate into the fabric of communities are at the crux of its own health and impact. Lastly, and positively, disruption and renewal of pedagogical relationships between *music creation* itself and student/community members' learning opportunity through music are already afoot (Myers, 2016). This can be a central platform for diversification, it can significantly redirect our long-standing advocacy problems, and particularly in North America, could lead *school music* to further and better align with *music-in-the-world*.

Notes

1. We do not deny or dismiss the various pedagogical efforts in the last decade or so critiquing and changing ensemble-based practice in music education, leading practitioners to consider more robust dialogical, participative, and collaborative practices. For example, O'Toole (2005), and Koops (2013).
2. For details on this see the work of Ball, Maguire, & Braun, 2012.
3. Quotes are from a conversation with a US teacher.
4. We are currently seeing more and more discussions (although not full-on changes) such as this: https://thepostmillennial.com/oxford-university-may-stop-teaching-sheet-music-because-of-its-complicity-in-white-supremacy.
5. See https://www.aec-music.eu/about-aec/news/sms-strengthening-music-in-society-project---year-3-successfully-completed.
6. http://www.querklang.eu/documents/5416/QuerKlang_English_Version.pdf

References

Allsup, R. E. (2016). *Remixing the classroom: Toward an open philosophy of music education.* Indiana University Press.

Allsup, R. E., & Benedict, C. (2008). The problems of band: An inquiry into the future of instrumental music education. *Philosophy of Music Education Review, 16*(2), 156–173

Ball, S. J. (2003). The teacher's soul and the terrors of performativity. *Journal of Educational Policy, 18*(2), 215–228.

Ball, S. (2016). Following policy: Networks, network ethnography and education policy mobilities. *Journal of Education Policy, 31*(5), 549–566.

Ball, S. (2015) What is policy? 21 years later: reflections on the possibilities of policy research. *Discourse: Studies in the Cultural Politics of Education, 36*(3), 306–313.

Ball, S., Maguire, M., & Braun, A. (2012). *How schools do policy: Policy enactments in secondary schools.* London: Routledge.

Benedict, C. & Schmidt, P. (2011). Politics of not knowing: The disappearing act of an education in music. *Journal of Curriculum Theorizing, 27*(3), 134–148.

Benedict, C., Schmidt, P., Spruce, G., & Woodford, P. (Eds.). (2015). *Oxford handbook of music education and social justice.* Oxford University Press.

Berrett, J. (2004). Louis Armstrong & Paul Whiteman: Two kings of jazz. Yale University Press.

Bradley, D. (2012). Avoiding the "p" word: Political contexts and multicultural music education. *Theory into Practice, 51*(3), 188–195.

Bylica, K. (2020). Hearing my world: negotiating borders, porosity, and relationality through cultural production in middle school music classes. *Music Education Research, 22*(3), 331–345. doi.org/10.1080/14613808.2020.1759519

Burton, S. (2011) Perspective consciousness and cultural relevancy: Partnership considerations for the re-conceptualization of music teacher preparation. *Arts Education Policy Review, 112*(3), 122–129.

Carpenter, J. (2013). Thomas Jefferson and the ideology of democratic schooling. *Democracy and Education, 21* (2), Article 5. https://democracyeducationjournal.org/home/vol21/iss2/5

Cooper, M. (2019). The Met will stage its first opera by a Black composer. *New York Times*. Online: https://www.nytimes.com/2019/09/19/arts/music/metropolitan-opera-black-composers-terence-blanchard.html

Costa-Giomi, E., & Chappell, E. (2007). Characteristics of band programs in a large urban school district: diversity or inequality? *Journal of Band Research, 42*(2), 1–18.

Cox, C. (2017). "Sonic thought." In B. Herzogenrath (Ed.), *Sonic thinking: A media philosophical approach* (pp. 99–109). Bloomsbury Academic.

Dyndahl, P. (2013). Musical gentrification, socio-cultural diversities, and the accountability of academics. In P. Dyndahl (Ed.), *Perspectives in music and music education: No. 9. Intersection and interplay: Contributions to the cultural study of music in performance, education, and society* (pp. 173–88). Lund: Malmö Academy of Music, Lund University.

Edwards, J., Blumer, C., Gardner, D., von Wartburg, A., & Veblen, K. (2020). (Re)communing musical creativity and imagination in the public space: The sound sculpture park project. Accepted Paper. ISME World Conference.

Edwards, J. (in press). Improvisational encounters with the sonic lifeworld. In D. Fischlin & M. Lamanno (Eds.), *The improviser's classroom: Pedagogies for Cocreative Worldmaking*. Temple University Press

Elpus, K. (2015). Music teacher licensure candidates in the United States: A demographic profile and analysis of licensure examination scores. *Journal of Research in Music Education, 63*(3), 314–335.

Foucault, M. (1971). *Lectures on the will to know* (L'ordre du discours). St. Martin's Press.

Gaudry, A., & Lorenz, D. 2018. Indigenization as inclusion, reconciliation, and decolonization: Navigating the different visions for indigenizing the Canadian Academy. *AlterNative 14*(3), 218–227. https://doi.org/10.1177/1177180118785382.

Gaztambide-Fernández, R. (2020). The orders of cultural production. *Journal of Curriculum Theorizing, 35*(3), 1–24.

Georgii-Hemming, E., & Westvall, M. (2010). Music education: A personal matter? Examining the current discourses of music education in Sweden. *British Journal of Music Education, 27*(1), 21–33. doi:10.1017/S0265051709990179

Gould, E. (2007). Social justice in music education: The problematic of democracy. *Music Education Research, 9*(2), 229–240, https://doi.org/10.1080/14613800701384359

Grin, J., & Van De Graaf, H. (1996). Implementation as communicative action: An interpretive understanding of interactions between policy actors and target groups. *Policy Sciences, 29*(4), 291–319. https://doi.org/10.1007/BF00138406

Haiven, M., & Khasnabish, A. (2014). *The radical imagination: Social movement research in the age of austerity*. Fernwood.

Haiven, M. (2014). *Crisis of imagination, crisis of power: Capitalism, creativity and the commons*. Fernwood

Hay, C., & Wincott, D. (1998). Structure, agency, and historical institutionalism. *Political Studies, 46*(5), 951-957, https://doi.org/10.1111/1467-9248.00177

Hess, J. (2017). Equity and music education: Euphemisms, terminal naivety, and whiteness. *Action, Criticism, & Theory for Music Education, 16*(3), 15–47.

Hickey, M. (2012). *Music outside the lines: Ideas for composing in K–12 music classroom*. Oxford University Press. doi: 10.1080/14613808.2012.685458

Jefferson, T. (1982/1787). *Notes on the state of Virginia*. W. W. Norton & Company..

Jorgensen, E. (1997). *In search of music education*. University of Illinois Press.

Kallio, A. A., & Länsman, H. (2018). Sami re-imaginings of equality in/through extracurricular arts education in Finland. *International Journal of Education & the Arts, 19*(7), 225–239.

Karlsen, S., & Westerlund, H. (2010). Immigrant students' development of musical agency: exploring democracy in music education. *British Journal of Music Education, 27*(3): 225–239.

Kaschub, M., & Smith, J. (Eds.). (2013). *Composing our future: Preparing music educators to teach composition.* Oxford University Press.

Kaschub, M., & Smith, J. (2014). *Promising practices in 21st century music teacher education.* Oxford University Press.

Kaschub, M., & Smith, J. (2021). With "app" attention: Developing musical capacities in digital environments. In G. Greher & S. Burton (Eds.), *Creative music making at your fingertips: A mobile technology guide for music educators* (pp. 67–80). Oxford University Press.

Koops, A. (2013). Facilitating composition in instrumental settings. In M. Kaschub & J. Smith, (Eds.), *Composing our future: Preparing music educators to teach composition* (pp. 149–166). Oxford University Press.

Koznin, A. (1991). Changing of the guard. *Tower Records' Pulse Magazine.*

Laitz, S. G. (2012). *The complete musician: An integrated approach to tonal theory, analysis, and listening* (3rd ed.). Oxford University Press.

Mantie, R. (2012). Band and/as music education: Antinomies and the struggle for legitimacy. *Philosophy of Music Education Review, 20*(1), 63–81.

Marcho, T. (2020). *Socially responsible music repertoire: Composer gender diversity in instrumental ensembles.* (Electronic Thesis or Dissertation). Retrieved from https://etd.ohiolink.edu/

Martin, M., & Desoto, D. (2018). How Rhiannon Giddens reconstructs black pain with the banjo. *NPR, All Things Considered.* Online: https://www.npr.org/2018/04/22/604356508/how-rhiannon-giddens-reconstructs-black-pain-with-the-banjo

Miller, P., & N. Rose. (2008). *Governing the present: Administering economic, social and personal life.* Polity.

Myers, D. E. (2016). Creativity, diversity, and integration: Radical change in the bachelor of music curriculum. *Arts and Humanities in Higher Education, 15*(3–4), 293–307. https://doi.org/10.1177/1474022216647378

NASM (2019–20). Handbook. https://nasm.arts-accredit.org/wp-content/uploads/sites/2/2020/01/M-2019-20-Handbook-02-13-2020.pdf

O'Toole, P. (2005). I sing in a choir but "I have no voice!" *Visions of research in music education, 6.* Retrieved from http://www.rider.edu/~vrme/

Odland, B., & Auinger, S. (2009). Reflections on the sonic commons. *Leonardo Music Journal, 19,* 63–68.

Palkki, J., & Caldwell, P. (2018). "We are often invisible": A survey on safe space for LGBTQ students in secondary school choral programs. *Research Studies in Music Education, 40*(1), 28–49. https://doi.org/10.1177/1321103X17734973

Pemberton, H. (2003). Learning, governance and economic policy. *British Journal of Politics and International Relations, 5*(4), 500–524, https://doi.org/10.1111/1467-856x.00117

Piston, W., & Devoto, M. (1978/1941). Harmony. (4th ed.). New York: Norton

Prest, A., & Goble, J. S. (2021). Toward a sociology of music education informed by Indigenous perspectives. In R. Wright, P. Kanellopoulos, G. Johansen, & P. Schmidt (Eds.), *Routledge handbook of sociology of music education* (pp. 80-96). Routledge.

Recharte, M. (2019). De-centering Music: A "sound education." *Action, Criticism, and Theory for Music Education, 18*(1), 68–88. doi:10.22176/act18.1.68

Rosa, H. (2020/2016). *Resonance: A sociology of our relationship to the world* (J. C. Wagner, Trans.). Cambridge, UK: Polity.

Rosa, H. (2013/2005). *Social acceleration: A new theory of modernity* (J. Trejo-Mathys, Trans.). Columbia University Press.

Schmidt, P. (2020a). *Policy as concept and practice: A guide to music educators.* Oxford University Press.

Schmidt, P. (2020b). Developing our policy know-how: Why policy should be part of music educator identity. *Music Educators Journal, 107*(1), 24–30. https://doi.org/10.1177/002743212 0929072

Schmidt, P. (2018). Engaging in policy-making through community-oriented work. In L. Higgins & B. L. Bartleet (Eds.), *The Oxford handbook on community music* (pp. 403–420). Oxford University Press.

Schmidt, P. (2017). Why policy matters: Developing a policy vocabulary in music education. In P. Schmidt & R. Colwell (Eds.), *Policy and the political life of music education: Standpoints for understanding and action* (pp. 11–36). Oxford University Press.

Schmidt, P. (2009). Reinventing from within: Thinking spherically as a policy imperative in music education. *Arts Education Policy Review, 110*(4), 39–47.

Shaw J. T. (2015). "Knowing their world": Urban choral music educators' knowledge of context. *Journal of Research in Music Education, 63*(2), 198–223. doi:10.1177/0022429415584377

Shieh, E. (2020). Making practice into policy: Bridging, buffering, and building in our schools. *Music Educators Journal, 107*(1), 31–36.

Shlain, L. (1999). *The alphabet versus the goddess: The conflict between word and image.* Compass/Penguin.

Shouldice, H. (2014). Teachers' beliefs regarding composition in elementary general music: Definitions, values, and impediments. *Research Studies in Music Education, 36*(2), 215–230. doi: 10.1177/1321103X14556574

Stone, D. A. (2011). *Policy paradox: The art of political decision making* (3rd ed.). W. W. Norton.

Thompson, L. (2007). Considering beliefs in learning to teach music. *Music Educators Journal, 93*(3), 30–35.

Veblen, K. K. (2022) Toward school and community musical engagements. In C. Abril & B. Gault (Eds.). *Oxford handbook of teaching general music: Dimensions of practice.* (172–191). Oxford University Press.

Wallace, D. (2018/2009). *Das hier ist Wasser/This is water.* Köln, Deutschland: Kiepenheuer & Witsch.

Woodford, P. (2002). The social construction of music teacher identity in undergraduate music education majors. In R. Colwell & C. Richardson (Eds.), *Handbook of research on music teaching and learning* (pp. 675–694). Schirmer Books.

Wright, R. (2016/2010). Democracy, social exclusion and music education: Possibilities for change. In R. Wright (Ed.), *Sociology and music education* (pp. 263–281). Routledge.

CHAPTER 43

FUTURE FORWARD

Composition in Music Teacher Education

MICHELE KASCHUB

OPPORTUNITIES to create original music have never been as readily available to as many people as they are today. This fact has brought music composition—including songwriting and production—to the forefront of discussions around the world concerning 21st century music education curricula. Is composition instruction to reflect history or contemporary practices, or if it is to serve two masters, what is an appropriate balance of attention between the two? Should instruction follow the example of the giants of Western European traditions, or should it reflect practices indigenous to the local culture? Is composition truly for everyone or the province of the gifted, wealthy, or otherwise advantaged? These and other topics echo around the globe.

Music composition is a recent addition to music education systems historically focused on excellence in performance, such as those found in the United States (Mark, 2008). Given the exacting practices and performance standards that often dominate such programs in primary, middle, and high schools (Williams, 2007), it has been difficult for composition, with its open-ended outcomes and emergent curricular leanings, to find a foothold. Globally, the role of composition in formal music education tends to mirror cultural values. Indeed, composition is often caught in the crosshairs of culture wars as schools delivering Western-influenced curricula set aside autochthonic musics.

Despite these challenges, composition has much to offer to those seeking to nurture the musical development of young people. The act of composing:

- allows students to grow, discover, and create themselves through artistic and meaningful engagements with sound,
- invites students consider their understanding of the world in new ways as they exercise their creative potentials in music,

- draws singing, playing, improvising, and listening together as ways of knowing that inform and intensify all areas of personal and collaborative musicianship,
- provides a means through which students can explore and express their humanity as can only be done with music, and
- is an experience where personal joy and satisfaction in musical doing and being can be found.

Given an opportunity to compose, students learn to create meaning and make sense of the world through their exploration of musical sound-feeling relationships. Just as students practice writing to clarify their conceptions and share their thoughts, so can they engage in composing to clarify their perceptions and to gain a better understanding of their feelings.[1] This outcome does not happen by chance, but through the enactment of pedagogies that direct, challenge, and nurture students' artistry as they grow and develop as composers.

While music educators may agree with these ideas in principle, many find that teaching composition—even finding the time to include it in their classes—can be quite challenging. Adding further complication, music composition requires educators and students to approach teaching and learning from a different mindset than the one typically used in ensemble settings. With composition, it must be the students' artistry and full range of musical capacities (Kaschub & Smith, 2016) that are called upon as they imagine their pieces, set intentions, create and test material, and evaluate the music that they are inventing. Student-composers learn by assuming responsibility for the significant artistic decision made concerning their work. This requires the teacher to relinquish the dominant artistic role of director to engage in facilitation, guiding, and mentorship. Just as students benefit from adopting the perspectives of composer and listener in addition to that of performer, so too must educators consider new vantage points in defining good teaching.

To accomplish this task, music teachers and teacher-educators need access to information about new instructional practices. Teachers need to embrace diversity as it is found in the individual nature of each student-creator and in the broader community of composers. Through this lens, they can better understand the nature and value of individual and collaborative work as a function of artistic action. Presenting students with a wide range of experiential contexts allows them to embrace traditional and emerging musics alongside the tools and frameworks that support their bringing music into being. Teachers also must be willing to help students recognize, sustain, and extend their cultural heritages so that the traditional practices of their cultures are honored as equal to those which may be societally dominant. Additionally, for full artistry to be achieved, teachers must be prepared to help students produce work that can inhabit personal, physical, virtual, immediate, and asynchronous spaces. The demands of this work are high, but so is the potential that composition holds for the musical growth of every child. Thus, music teacher-educators must think critically and act intentionally to bring composition pedagogy into the curricula of initial and continuing music teacher preparation.

The Role of Music Teacher-Educators in Re-Centering Composition

With equal seriousness one might ask, "Where does the work of music teacher education begin?," and perhaps with an added measure of exasperation, "Where does the work of music teacher education end?" In consideration of the latter, it is easy to teach the longstanding and familiar, comfortably settled into a body of information masquerading as sufficient. Such practices absolutely mark the end of music education. It is in the answer to the former question, however, that the future lies. Music faculty constitute a body that must be committed to further educate itself if it is to keep pace with societal and musical evolution and prepare future generations to do the same.

Self-Education

In the 1980s and 1990s, practitioners and music teacher-educators could reasonably argue that few resources existed to address music composition in compulsory schooling. This is no longer the case. Research examining the compositional processes and products of children grew significantly across these and the following decades. These efforts brought forth a considerable collection of books and articles offering insights about the work of young composers as well as guidance for teachers seeking best practices across a range of settings. Entry into this literature might be found through the literature reviews of Wiggins (2007), Kaschub & Smith (2009), and Viig (2015), or in the selected list of composition-focused books featured in Figure 43.1. In addition to written resources, state, division, and national conferences now feature programming devoted to composition. These topic area strands often address composition, songwriting, and production across a range of ages and settings so that educators might tailor their inquiries to match their teaching responsibilities.

Addressing Curricular Challenges

Music teacher-educators analyzing current teaching practices and learning goals in PreK–12 education understand that there must be a link between those visions and the courses they design. In seeking modifications to existing curricula, they may encounter questions concerning why change is needed and exactly what changes should be made. These concerns require serious attention as curriculum represents how philosophical beliefs become realized within the boundaries established by accrediting bodies and specific institutions. Moreover, the curriculum that pre-service teachers experience in

Curricular Guidance Spanning K-12

- Hickey, M. (2012). *Music Outside the Lines: Ideas for Composing in K-12 Music Classrooms.* Oxford University Press.
- Kaschub, M. & Smith, J. (2009). *Minds on Music: Composition for Creative and Critical Thinking.* Rowman & Littlefield.

Elementary Music

- Glover, J. (2000). *Children composing 4-14.* Routledge.
- Kaschub, M. and Smith, J., (2016). *Experiencing Music Composition in Grades 3 – 5.* New York, NY: Oxford University Press.
- Kaschub, M. and Smith, J., (forthcoming). *Experiencing Music Composition in Grades K – 2.* Rowman & Littlefield.
- Composing under construction: Exploring the elements of Music Composition (Grades 3-6). GIA Publications.
- Wiggins, J. (1990). *Composition in the classroom: A tool for teaching. R&L Education.*
- Wilson, J. (2005) *Composition for young musicians: A fun way for kids to begin creating music.*

Middle & High School Music

- Kaschub, M. and Smith, J., (forthcoming). *Experiencing Music Composition in Middle School General Music.* Roman & Littlefield.
- van Rensburg, A. J. (2013). *Music Composition for Teens: A Graded First Course.* CreateSpace Independent Publishing Platform.
- Wilkins, M. L. (2006). *Creative Music Composition.* Routledge.

Choral Music

- *Musicianship: Composing in choir.* (2016). Jody Kerchner & Katherine Strand, Eds. GIA Publications, Inc.

Instrumental Music (Band and Orchestra)

- Klose, C. (2011). *Piano Teacher's Guide to Creative Composition.* Hal Leonard.
- *Musicianship: Composing in Band and Orchestra.* (2013). Clint Randles and David Stringham, Eds. GIA Publications, Inc.

Technology

- Freeman, B. (2013). *Teaching Music through Composition: A Curriculum Using Technology.* Oxford University Press.

Teacher Education

- *Composing Our Future: Preparing Music Educators to Teach Composition.* (2013). Kaschub, M. and Smith, J., Eds. Oxford University Press.

FIGURE 43.1. Select books addressing composition and composition pedagogy

their preparation programs constitutes a lived curriculum against which they measure their future curriculum design decisions.

Teacher education programs are necessarily shaped by credit hour limitations, scheduling, faculty availability, enrollment, and dozens of other influencing variables. In terms of curriculum implementation, these areas constitute logistical hurdles which often can be overcome with a commitment to problem-solving. The bigger challenges lie at the level of fundamental belief systems and concern three important questions: Who can be a composer? What is the value of composition? and What can be considered core foundations in the preparation of music educators?

Reconceptualizing the Composer

Despite evidence to the contrary, many musicians—even college faculty—hold a vision of the composer as a solitary figure, possessing a special talent rarely found in the general population. This mythological image has led to a world in which children, when asked to draw a composer, sketch a man with long white hair, sitting at a piano, feathered quill in hand, notating their masterpieces (Glover, 2002). While there is hope that conceptions have evolved following Glover's study, these ideas are so deeply entrenched within institutional practices that Campbell, Myers, and Sarath (2016) authored a manifesto arguing for the broad inclusion of composition within college music curriculums. This point cannot be made strongly enough: a manifesto was deemed necessary to advocate for teaching the very practice that brings music into existence. What music exists that does not have one or more originators?

To address the curricular marginalization and experiential exclusion that such beliefs have wrought, music teacher-educators must partner with composition and other faculty to design ways for pre-service teachers to gain personal and positive experiences in composing. These experiences must not be limited to the use of the instructional etudes that are often part-and-parcel of music theory coursework. While such activities highlight important historical practices and the foundations of modern composition, they are teacher-driven and limit students' imaginations. For composing experiences to be powerful contributors to the development of pre-service teachers' belief that they can compose, they must have artistic control over the design choices and musical decisions that shape their work.

The Value of Composition

As much of collegiate music study centers conservatory-styled education in the preparation of teachers (Kratus, 2015), questions arise concerning how composition can be used to develop musicianship—meaning to serve performance. This view is short-sighted. The value of composition is not limited to advancing performance knowledge and skills. Rather, the value of composition lies in its ability to allow people to communicate their musical ideas and imaginings rather than limiting their musical engagements to the interpretation and delivery of the work of others.

In this same vein, looping software and other methods of creating with technology are often attacked as being in some way lesser than *real composition* which is typically defined in the mind of the commentator as the use of musical notation of the European style. It may be possible to point out that these approaches require specific skills that take time to learn and develop, just like the forms of composition that predate these approaches. Additionally, while the tools used to carry out this type of composition differ from those used previously, looping and other production tools do require many of the same thought processes as the models as those found in earlier form of music composition.

Music Teaching: A Varied Vocation

Collegiate music education faculty, for the most part, have progressed through degree programs requiring the development of a particular set of performance skills associated with solo performance and participation in large choral or instrumental ensembles. While these requirements are certainly one way to prepare future music teachers, they are not the only way to do so. Other forms of music and musical practices seeking to enter the bastions of higher education face considerable challenges, primarily that they are outside the comfortable experience of those already inside the institutions.

As an example, for many years jazz was excluded from school classrooms and higher education (Mark, 1987). People preparing to become music teachers learned little, if anything, about jazz history – and they certainly were not allowed to specialize in its practice. Music teachers writing in response to the suggestion that jazz should be represented in music education programs in the United States offered derisive criticism:

> Training a group of student instrumentalists to perform trite and transient music in emulation of some of the more pretentious professionals seen and heard on recordings, radio, and television is not a particularly good example of a worthwhile educational project. (Feldman, 1964, p. 60)

At present, jazz has been fully assimilated into most collegiate music programs. National accrediting bodies urge its inclusion in history courses, through ensembles, and in other areas of study. In some programs, music education majors can declare jazz as their applied area of study or as the primary concentration within their degree program. While this evolution has advanced knowledge of the jazz idiom, there are other musical forms and practices now standing where jazz once waited. Changing acceptance status requires a lengthy journey as evidenced by a footnote from Feldman's 1964 work. Offering what he thought to be a seething condemnation of the popular music of the day, "rock'n'roll," he wrote, "It is, in effect, an oversimplified, primitive, and juvenile version of jazz" (p. 60).

Now modern band, hip-hop, popular music, and others are finding their way into tertiary music programs. These musical practices often are presented as topics of current interest rather than positioned as music education degree specializations or concentrations. Just as jazz once sat outside the comfort zone of music faculty trained and educated in other areas of music-making, so composition still sits. Recognition of the influences that shape the inclusion/exclusion conundrum suggest re-evaluation of the status quo. Composition, the activity that provides a foundation for the creation of much of the world's music, must be intentionally and meaningfully included in preparation of music educators.

COMPOSITION IN MUSIC TEACHER
PREPARATION: LEVELS OF CURRICULAR
COMMITMENT

Pre-service and practicing teachers acknowledge the value of composition while si-multaneously lamenting their lack of preparation to lead creative activities in their classrooms and rehearsal halls (Randles & Smith, 2012; Stringham, Thornton, & Shevock, 2015). To capitalize on existing belief and earnest interest, music teacher-educators can design meaningful opportunities for music educators to develop new skills. To maximize teaching and learning potentials, teachers must: 1) have direct per-sonal experiences with music composition, 2) establish a foundation of pedagogical knowledge derived from deconstructing their experiences within composition activi-ties, and 3) participate in an active composition community comprised of professional composers, educators, and students. Composition pedagogies developed within these structures foster the pairing of personal foundations with professional skills.

One and Not Done

Curriculum design and implementation is a balancing act. Music teacher-educators face a complicated challenge when called upon to make decisions involving content, time allocations, and preparation to teach material that may be new to them. Given the competing nature of these tasks, some faculty choose to designate a single day within an undergraduate course to consider composition in a specific setting or with a particular age group. Offerings for practicing teachers might take the form of conference sessions, day-long professional development workshops, or even brief and intensive summer courses.

These approaches have some merit, but also invite concern. While undergraduates may spend a single class addressing composition pedagogy, this experience is insuffi-cient for the creation of confidence with the topic (Piazza & Talbot, 2021). Perhaps even more concerning is the possibility that students' limited time on topic leads them to infer that composition is not really that important. Such inference would reveal an un-fortunate hidden curriculum.

Practitioners experience a similar time-based phenomenon. When professional ed-ucation is measured in hours—often just single day on a topic—teachers do not expe-rience the ongoing development and support needed to take new learning successfully into practice (Wei, Darling-Hammond, & Adamson, 2010). Even longer workshops may offer similar results. Hickey & Schmidt (2019) tracked teacher implementation of com-position and improvisation activities following a pedagogy workshop and found that while the intention to implement creative activities increased immediately following the event, intention and implementation declined at six weeks, six months, and nine months, respectively.

It is possible to design meaningful professional engagements for both pre-service and in-service teachers. Darling-Hammond, Hyler, & Gardner (2017) identified seven features of professional development as positively influencing teacher knowledge and practice: focus on content, active learning, support for collaboration, models of effective practice, coaching and expert support, feedback and reflection, and sustained duration (pp. 4–16). These features were applied across a series of summer courses within a tri-level program titled *Composing Together*. This program was initiated at the University of Southern Maine Dr. Alfred and D. Suzi Osher School of Music and the Aaron Copland School of Music at Queen's College/CUNY in 2007. Teachers in these programs studied composition through direct engagement in composing activities and took applied lessons with professional composers. Teachers of the same grade level or content area focus collaborated to develop lessons and units with the intent of implementation in the following school year. Teachers were provided feedback on their compositions and their lessons by course instructors, professional composers, and their peers. Additionally, teachers were encouraged to contact the course instructors between summer classes, and many invited the professional composers with whom they studied into their schools to work with their young students. By the end of the three-year course sequence, all participants comfortably identified themselves as composers (Kaschub & Smith, 2017).

Threads and Curricular Through-Lines

Undergraduate programs offer greater time flexibility than is typically found in graduate programs or summer professional development offerings. While one-and-done approaches leave pre-service teachers feeling underprepared, a spiralized approach that embeds composition in early course work and revisits it across multiple methods and techniques classes can build pre-service teacher confidence. This approach normalizes the presence of composition in music teaching and learning as it prepares teachers to support generative music making as part of elementary and secondary education.

Stringham, Thornton, & Shevock (2015) examined composition as an integral part of a secondary instrumental techniques class. They found music composition to be a valuable course component that offered insight into the thinking processes of beginning instrumentalists and served as an assessment tool for measuring pre-service teachers' grasp of specific course content. Applying this example across the general, choral, and instrumental music methods course triumvirate—or within the brass, guitar, percussion, piano, strings, voice, and woodwinds techniques course sequence—would prepare pre-service teachers to include composition in their future work. (Note: Information and materials supporting this approach can be found in the texts previously displayed in Figure 43.1.)

Dedicated Coursework

Another approach worthy of consideration is the creation of coursework specifically focusing on the development of compositional skills across elementary, middle, and high school. Like its partners in choral and instrumental music, composition methods courses would examine foundations in philosophy and research; explore the design and implementation of curriculum at the course, unit, and daily lesson plan levels; help students strategize about recruiting; offer guidance as to how to build and maintain such programs; and present ideas concerning how composition programs might best be evaluated. Dedicated coursework is most effective when it helps students develop skills as composers, addresses teaching and learning at different stages and across a range of settings, and experience applying their newly acquired knowledge and skills in interactions with school-age students.

Building a Base of Personal Composing Experiences

To grow confident in the ability to lead composition study, pre-service teachers must be comfortable with composing (Deemer, 2016). This comfort is established through experiences with a wide variety of projects spanning a variety of contexts and settings. Pre-service teachers benefit from participation in teacher-facilitated whole-class composition, small group and partnered work, and opportunities to compose on their own. They also need to compose music in different styles, exploring idiomatic writing in different genres. Work with both acoustic and digital instruments, as well as other sound sources, will serve to expand their sonic palettes and acquaint them with a range of compositional tools. Further, practice with the use of invented notations, graphic and iconic symbol systems, and traditional notation will allow them to understand the commonalities of representation and how each system has its place in learning to preserve compositional thought. The projects shown in Figure 43.2 are sequenced to scaffold the development of pre-service teachers' confidence in their composition skills and their skills in giving and receiving feedback.

Methods Courses Addressing Composition Pedagogy across PreK–12

Methods courses are typically designed to prepare pre-service teachers to be engaged and effective practitioners who can plan, implement, and assess instruction. Such courses should prepare students to articulate their educational philosophy and offer rationales for their pedagogical choices and decisions. Additionally, coursework should actively contribute to pre-service teachers' conception of their professional identity and their confidence to fulfill the role of teacher.

Within composition pedagogy, teachers need to familiarize themselves with specific facets of the creative process and how each is evidenced and best approached at different ages and levels of compositional skills. Teachers must understand finding inspiration, product planning, sound exploration, selection of materials, idea generation, idea testing, adopting/discarding ideas, notation/preservation, assembling sounds,

Project 1: Compose Anything

The creation of a safe and supportive space where each student can compose as they do, be recognized in their success, and positioned for future growth is critical to the self-actualization of "composer" as a facet of musical identity. Pre-service teachers are often at a loss as to what to do when they are invited to compose. If they have taken music theory courses, they may long for the exacting guidelines that compositional etudes often feature. One goal of this activity is to counter such boundaries by giving students a chance to shape their own products. For the purposes of this activity, it does not matter what students create and share, only that they create and share something.

  Another activity goal is for students to experience acceptance of who they are as composers. Begin by asking for a volunteer to start the in-class sharing process. Ask the composer to briefly describe what they have composed, why they chose to this work to share, and what they are proud of in their work or about their work. Have the composer perform or play a recording of their piece, then invite class members to offer *positive* feedback. This practice draws attention to those aspects of composition that are working and builds composer confidence.

Project 2: Composing for My Instrument

Creating a composition for their personal performance instrument or voice is a way to build a new experience atop a familiar one. Guidelines for this project can be very simple: compose for the instrument or voice you use when in the role of performer, create 60-90 minutes of music, notation is optional, be able to accurately repeat the piece. Once composers have had time to create their pieces, invite them to share their work using the same questioning and feedback processes as described in Project 1. This reinforces the feeling of being safe and supported within a community of composers.

Project 3: Compose for a Friend's Instrument

Composers work in pairs, interviewing each other about their instrument or voice. They take the information they gather from their partner and use it to guide the creation of a solo work for their partner's instrument. Composers should check in with each other periodically to gain the performer's perspective on the piece as it is created. This allows composers to learn about the specific features of an instrument as well as the preferences of a particular performer. Pieces need not be more that 60-90 seconds in length. This project introduces peer input and constructive criticism within the creation process. The in-class sharing portion of this project again focuses on positive comments only.

Project 4: Paired Trios

Divide the class into groups of three and then pair two groups together. Each team will compose a trio for its partner team. All instrument/voice groups are welcome as the core challenge – addressing the compositional capacities of feelingful intention, musical expressivity, and artistic craftsmanship[a] – remain constant. Teams should be encouraged to interview and consult with each other, as they did individually in Project 3.

  The sharing session for this project introduces two new approaches to feedback. First, a sharing session is scheduled while composers are in the process of creating their trios. This allows them to hear from the "audience" as they work. Second, peers are invited to offer positive comments and wishes. Wish statements are presented as "I" comments: "I wish that the melody introduced by the clarinet could be repeated by the tuba. I would like hear it in the lower octave." These statements are designed to give composers something to consider as they enter revision or consider their next project. Using 2 positive comments followed by 1 wish keeps the feedback session positively balanced.

FIGURE 43.2. Sequenced composition projects for pre-service teachers

[a] A brief description of compositional capacities can be found in Kaschub, M., & Smith, J. P. (2016). The big picture: Developing musical capacities. *Music Educators Journal*, 102(3), 33–40. A more thorough discussion of how compositional capacities can be developed appear in Kaschub, M. and Smith, J., (2016). *Experiencing Music Composition in Grades 3 – 5*. Oxford University Press.

> Project 5: My Project
> As any student learns to compose, it is important that they be given opportunities to design, undertake, and assess their own projects. This project allows composers to identify a musical product that they would like to create (e.g., a pop song, a piece for clarinet and piano, a music theater duet). They are then charged with drafting a work schedule and creating the criteria by which they will evaluate their piece.
>
> Sharing for these pieces can take place in-process or when compositions are completed, but the role of the composer shifts. During sharing, composers steer the feedback process by seeking specific feedback concerning spots in the composition that they are struggling to complete or where they would like to better understand how the audience is experiencing the music. This self-directed feedback allows composers to externalize their thinking processes and can provide insights that advance their work.

FIGURE 43.2. Continued

verifying compositional decisions, developing or extending ideas, re-visioning, editing, sharing, requesting and receiving feedback, organizing performance, evaluating products, and accepting/rejecting criticism to help their students master the specific skills associated with each step in the process. Further, it will be helpful for teachers to think of composers as novice, intermediate, and advanced in their skill development at each grade level rather than across all years of schooling. This framing allows teachers to consider what might be the best approach to developing the skills of idea generation with a novice nine-year-old as opposed to an experienced composer of advanced skills nearing high school graduation.

Most importantly, coursework must address the human element of composition. Composing is a highly personal act in which composers expose their musical thinking and personal feelings. Criticism delivered factually and with limited sensitivity will result in students with hurt feelings and perhaps who, with their musical confidence undercut, abandon composition. For this reason, it is crucial that pre-service teachers not only consider the psychological aspects of composition pedagogy, but also that they develop their language through first practicing with their peers and then move into school settings to work with young composers.

Composition-Focused Fieldwork: Developing Pedagogical Knowledge

Experiences based in classroom immersion may be the most critical component in the pre-service teacher's journey to identify themselves as real teachers (Conkling, 2007). Classroom experiences help pre-service teachers become adept at recognizing teachable moments, anticipating students' concerns, offering support without co-opting their students' artistic processes, and interpreting how students process new information or grapple with ongoing challenges. Active participation in classrooms allows pre-service teachers to observe experienced educators, to design lessons, and to interact with students in the composing process. Most importantly, novice teachers can critically reflect on their teaching practice so that their skills can evolve.

As many school-based mentors are not yet comfortable with or confident in their skills as composition teachers, it can be difficult to find field sites to support this work. Field work typically relies on a mentor-mentee relationship in which the pre-service teacher learns *from* the host-practitioner. To advance composition pedagogy, this relationship must be reframed as one of collaboration in which each partner possesses a particular expertise (Kaschub, 2019). Success requires an awareness of experiential boundaries. Pre-service teachers bring conceptual knowledge related to composition pedagogy to the partnership; host-practitioners bring their knowledge of the learner and an understanding of age-appropriate teaching strategies. Together, co-learners can design and implement lessons that allow students to experience composition. Through this work, pre-service teachers gain comfort in the classroom and become occupationally socialized, while host-practitioners learn new skills and extend their passion for teaching (Kruse, 2011).

Gaining Momentum

Creating opportunities for music education majors of all interests and specialty areas to experience composition and study composition pedagogy is an important first step toward advancing composition in music education. However, journeys are rarely completed in a single step. Just as there are students who wish to become music teachers because they are inspired by their experiences as performers and their interactions with their ensemble directors (Rickels, Hoffman, & Fredrickson, 2019), so too exist students who love composing music and wish to share that passion with others. How might music teacher education address these would-be teachers?

Composition Educators: Considering New Professional Identities

Identity is tied to the defining moments of life. It arises from experiences that inform and allow people to create themselves into purposeful, artistic, and expressive beings. Identity is a cognitive (Berzonsky, 2011), emotional, and embodied construct (Hodgen & Askew, 2007; Rajan-Rankin, 2014) that provides a personal frame of reference for processing self-relevant information, solving problems, and making decisions. It guides, and is shaped by, life's journey (Kroger, 2007; Zimmer-Gimbeck & Mortimer, 2006) and finds definition in affiliations with social and professional groups (Brewer & Hewstone, 2004).

In totality, identity might be described as an understanding of self that is fashioned through discourse and derived from the categories in which people are placed and in which they place themselves. These categories may be real and culturally evident, but they are not natural; they are constructed (Hall, 1990). As such, it is important to consider identity in music teacher education. For example: What categories of identity exist? Can people freely choose their affiliations or are some choices limited? What influence might music teacher identity have on the practices of music education?

A Troubling Dichotomy

The history of identity research in music teacher education finds root in the concept of *occupational identity*. This term refers to the conscious awareness of oneself as a worker (Skorikov & Vondracek, 2011) and denotes perception of occupational abilities, goals, interests, and values. Investigating the development of occupational identity in music education majors, Froelich & L'Roy (1985) noted that pre-service teachers self-identified as performers more strongly with each year of study, though they could not readily identify the broader aims of music education. These findings raised concern about the focus and quality of music teacher education and spurred numerous studies probing the balance between "performer" and "teacher" (Ballantyne et al., 2012; Bennett, 2013; Bernard, 2004; Beyon, 1998; Bouij, 1998; Chong et al., 2011; Cox, 1997; Dolloff, 2007; Gillespie & Hamann, 1999; Haston & Russell, 2012; Hargreaves et al., 2011; Isbell, 2008; Pellegrino, 2009; Roberts, 1991; Scheib, 2007).

While many different facets of identity are now recognized in the literature, early studies upheld this initial dichotomy. Polarization can be useful in the early stages of problem-defining, but the maintenance of this particular dichotomy as it plays out in teacher preparation programs is an impediment to music education's future. The problem is not that the dichotomy is unfounded, but that it was the only finding possible. Vocational aspects of identity develop during childhood and adolescence as preferences narrow (Beal & Crockett, 2010; Guichard, 2001; Holland, 1987; Savickas et al., 2009), and when children are presented with a singular option, preferences solidify very quickly. If school-age students are instructed by teachers who present music education as performance education while granting little attention to listening, composition, improvisation, and other musical engagements, those same students when seeking to become teachers will self-identify as performers (Rickels et al., 2013). In researching music teacher identity, music education has led the witness and marveled at the troubling testimony offered as if it came as a surprise. The deck, if music teacher education can be so characterized, was stacked—and so it remains. Sociology's focus on occupational identity has given way to a conception of identity that is multifaceted and increasingly nuanced. Yet, music education largely remains focused on a dichotomy of its own construction and validation while a bigger mystery remains to be solved: Where are other musical roles in the conception of music educator?

The Preservation of Dominance

In seeking to understand identity, sociologists have examined the evolution of dominant identities and how they are sustained. Over time, dominant roles acquire the appearance of common sense (Kumashiro, 2009) and thus remain unquestioned in practice. The application of objective interrogation to such practices often allows their roots to be better understood. For example, Kratus (2015) has traced a series of key influences that shape present practice throughout music education. First, in the European art music of the 1800s, the performer eclipsed the composer and captivated audiences with showy performances and dramatic flair. In response, conservatory training focused on creating more performers. When institutes of advanced study turned attention to teacher preparation, the model of performance training was already well-established and education a simple add-on. Subsequently, teachers translated their training into their work with school children to complete the trickle-down sequence.

The deeply entrenched performer role dominates nearly all areas of music education. Those who belong to this category wield considerable agency in maintaining their positions of power (Johnson, 2006; Kimmel & Ferber, 2010; Wildman, 2005). Dominant practices are insulated and protected through the construction of community-specific values, social classes, and other hierarchies (Goodman, 2011; Meyers & Gutman, 2011) and faculty whose primary musical backgrounds are in performance articulate and enforce the rights of entry and passage, as well as the rules of exclusion, for those seeking to join the ranks of music education. Entry-seekers and participants are limited to specified fields (performance) and instruments (often those of the Western classical tradition) along with their concomitant audition procedures, courses of study, and juried recitals. Every level of participation is designed to give senior level performers the opportunity to judge and approve or disapprove of all others—effectively enforcing a within-group hierarchy that completes the cycle of power.

"The Wages of Dominance Is Damage"

Damaged identities form when members of a powerful group view others as unworthy of full respect to the extent that less powerful groups are prevented from "occupying valuable social roles or entering into desirable relationships that are themselves constitutive of identity" (Nelson, 2001, p. xii). Within music teacher education the exclusion of would-be teachers who excel in composition—or at minimum, the requirement that they prioritize a performer-role, as is commonly the case—constitutes a "deprivation of opportunity" (p. xii). This prevents the profession of music education from developing a particular knowledge and pedagogy absent from, and under-utilized by, our profession (Berkley, 2001; Orman, 2002; Randles & Smith, 2012; Strand, 2006).

Moreover, the exclusion of composition as an accepted area of applied study within music teacher preparation programs may impinge on the identity formation of young composers as they put on a transient identity, that of performer, to gain access to education. Nelson writes, "a person's identity is damaged when she endorses, as part of her self-concept, a dominant group's dismissive or exploitative understanding of her group, and loses or fails to acquire a sense of herself as worthy of full moral respect" (2001, p. xii). In the case of the young composer who wants to be a music teacher, the admission fee at the gate of collegiate study is the forfeiture of the composer-self. How many would-be music teachers are composers until they are told at the point of auditioning for music school to identify their instrument or voice part? Why does the composer's journey to become music teacher begin with a requisite loss of musical identity and self-integrity?

Music teacher identity, at core, involves an affective stance dependent upon power and self-agency (Zembylas, 2003). When some musical identities are positioned as not worthy of attention and musical passions are negated, future teachers and music education as a field are limited to a closed-loop conception of music, music-making, and music teaching. Writing in opposition to this type of practice, Reimer states:

> All human beings require an education of sufficient depth and breadth to enable each to become as genuine, as distinctive, and as personally developed as possible. That necessary dimension of human becoming is smothered, often to extinction, by approaches to education stressing identicality rather than individuality (2014, p. 31).

The identicality the Reimer decries is not a natural order mandate; rather, it is one created by music teacher education. As such, music teacher education has the power to consider new options. What might composers bring to the field of music education? What insights do they possess that may differ from the viewpoints of performers? How might the presence of composers—with their unique ways of thinking about music, making music, and teaching music—expand conceptions of what music education might become and how music teaching and learning could evolve? These questions must be considered if music education's offerings and practices are to become truly inclusive.

Considering the Composer-Educator

Music teachers who pursue composition as their primary area of expertise can offer unique insights to the practice of music education. While pedagogies of composition and performance share concern for historical foundations, technical skills, and the acquisition of domain-specific vocabularies, they do differ in significant ways. Teachers of performance select repertoire, engage in score study, and consider the composer's intention in partnership with their own artistic interpretations as they guide students in preparing performances. The final product is one that the teacher can envision before instruction even begins.

Teachers of composition are faced with different challenges. The music that the teacher and students will study does not exist at the outset of instruction. The teacher does not have to develop a sense of the composer's intention from the score, because the composer is right there, beside the teacher, present as the authority on their own work. As the score is in a state of evolution for much of the process, the performance cannot be envisioned with any accuracy until it is eminent. These conditions change the act of music teaching and learning.

In practical terms, composers have a personal investment in the creation and performance of their music. As such, they may be more likely to construct a curriculum that places the generation of new music in balance with music-making activities sustaining historical traditions and practices (Elliott, 1995). They may also significantly alter their students' experiences of music through the inclusion of teacher-composed works (Lindroth, 2012; Randles, 2009). Moreover, as composers are educated to exercise generative creativity, they learn an open form of teaching where imagination and need drive learning. From the perspective of the composer, musical tradition is a point of departure—a visitor in the room, but not the master of what will be. By necessity, teaching is tailored to the learner because the learner controls nearly every aspect of the outcome. In such contexts, power structures between teacher and student are equalized and the educator's expertise is a tool to be used by the student rather than the driving force of instruction (Allsup, 2013).

The differences between performance-focused and composition-focused teaching and learning suggest that there are multiple pathways for engaging students in music education. Each is unique and its presence adds value to the experience of the learner. It is also true that each form of teaching and learning offers insights only made evident through comparison with the other. As such, it is imperative that music teacher-educators embrace the possibilities found in welcoming *composer* as a music teacher identity.

Curriculum Considerations

Students focusing their applied study in composition can be as equally prepared to lead music programs with ensembles as are their playing or singing focused peers. Just as a trumpet player takes a Woodwinds Techniques course to learn how to play and teach woodwind instruments, so too can a composer take an instrumental techniques course to learn how to teach those instruments to students. The same holds true for all other manner of music education coursework and, when considered in reverse, further highlights the inequity created when vocalists and instrumentalists do not have the opportunity to learn to compose and how to teach students to do the same.

Most music education students training in the United States undertake the study of history, theory, aural skills, and conducting, along with other recommended courses adhering to the accreditation guidelines set forth music and teacher accrediting bodies. One approach to preparing music teachers within these frameworks would be to create parallel opportunities for composers to enroll in lessons and ensembles as shown in Figure 43.3. This single model is but one approach and is well-suited to institutions that address K–12 music. The model could be adapted in any number of ways for schools organizing teacher training programs by sub-specializations in band, choral, general music, jazz, or orchestra.

Area	Composition	Instrumental (Classical)	Instrumental (Jazz)	Vocal (Classical)	Vocal (Jazz)
Professional Courses	Professional & Philosophical Foundations, Research & Evaluation				
Methods Classes	Teaching Music Listening K–12, Teaching Vocal Music K–12, Teaching Instrumental Music K–12, Teaching Music Improvisation K–12, Teaching Music Composition K–12				
Techniques Courses	Brass, Guitar, Strings, Percussion, Piano, Voice, and Woodwinds				
Applied Lessons	7 semesters composition	7 semesters classical instrument	7 semesters jazz instrument	7 semesters classical voice	7 semesters jazz voice
Primary Ensemble	7 semesters composers' ensemble	7 semesters band or orchestra	7 semesters big band or combo	7 semesters chorale or chamber singers	7 semesters vocal jazz ensemble
Supporting Ensemble/ Secondary Area	4 semesters, student choice (band, chorus, orchestra, jazz ensembles)	4 semesters, student choice (chorus, jazz ensembles, composers' ensemble)	4 semesters, student choice (chorus, band, orchestra, composers' ensemble)	4 semesters, student choice (band, orchestra, jazz ensembles, composers' ensemble)	4 semesters, student choice (chorus, band, orchestra, composers' ensemble)
Additional Required Experiences	1 semester each: chamber music, jazz ensemble, composers' workshop				

FIGURE 43.3. Music education–specific coursework with possible applied area and ensemble requirement adaptations

In the Words of Composer-Educators

Composer-educators already exist and their voices, though few in number, should be heard. Featured in this section are the thoughts shared in personal communication (January 26, 2022) by Saigelyn (a second-year teacher in an elementary general music and beginning band position in Vermont), Jonathan and Katie (seniors completing their student teaching internships), Blaine (a junior), and Michael (a sophomore). Saigelyn earned a music education degree with an applied area emphasis in composition; the other four interviewees are in various stages of earning their undergraduate degrees as MUE/Comp students at the University of Southern Maine.

> Question 1: *What advice would you give to college music education professors concerning how composition is represented within the totality of their music teacher preparation programs? How should composition be addressed in MUE?*
>
> Saigelyn: The full compositional experience should be addressed and presented in all music teacher preparation programs, including opportunities to compose, to workshop those compositions, to receive feedback, and to perform those compositions in concerts.
>
> Jonathan: Composition is the process of creating meaningful and emotional products that can be shared and developed. Understanding how that happens creates better music and better musicians. Composition can be included in nearly every lesson. It doesn't take much effort to bring it in and doing so makes learning to teach more personal.
>
> Katie: Composition should be viewed as equal to vocal and instrumental concentrations. In composition, students [are still judged on their performance skills and] may be seen as "behind" in comparison to vocalists or instrumentalists. This is because they most likely haven't had ensembles or composition specific classes/lessons in a K–12 setting to refine their skills. Composers shouldn't be required to show proficiency on an instrument or voice to be accepted into a program. It is unfair to expect composers to be performance-proficient while not expecting vocalists or instrumentalists to be composition-proficient.
>
> Blaine: The most important part of teaching composition is to instill in pre-service teachers that all composition is valid. Composition should be held to the same level of appreciation as the other important aspects of music. Singing, playing, composing, improvising, and listening are of equal value. Teachers should find ways to incorporate composition into all aspects of their class as a way to connect students to the things they listen to and perform all the time. These experiences help students establish a personal and meaningful connection to the art.
>
> Question 2: *What advice would you give to young composers who want to teach music, as they shop for college programs?*

Saigelyn: Reach out to students in the programs you find. Ask if it's a program that you can help shape into what works for you—all composers are different and might want/need different, unique qualities in a program. Ask if the professors are people who are open to different genres, and what specializations they might have. Ask about the community and support of peers in the music program; those will likely be the people who perform the music you write. Professors that help lift up their composition students and create opportunities for them to hear and share their music are the professors who set examples for how you can help your own students later on.

Blaine: Any program that offers a music education degree with a concentration in composition values the importance of the medium. Finding schools that are as invested in the thing that you love as much as you are should be a priority for every student.

Michael: When visiting schools, meet with the music education professors and ask if you'd be able to teach composition-based activities or lessons as well as maybe write pieces for when you are peer teaching. Being a composer, you bring an insightful angle to dissecting the components of music. You have the ability to teach people *why* the music achieves its ability to speak to human emotions.

Question 3: *What composition opportunities do you provide or hope to provide (if you are a pre-service teacher) to your students?*

Saigelyn: In addition to projects with my elementary band students and general music classes, I'm facilitating a student-led Composition Club. It was started by two of my band students who put up signs all around the school and got 11 other students to join. They meet after school and I've made it clear that I'm there to help only when needed. The instigators are taking on a leadership role and I'm excited to see what kinds of compositions they create. Their goal is to make recordings to share during our school-wide "pack time," a school-community SEL-based morning meeting that happens twice a week.

Katie: I hope to provide group composition opportunities in my ensembles as well as to teach a songwriting/composition class. Many songwriting classes require students to write lyrics which may discourage instrumentalists from enrolling in the course. I believe offering composition as an option would encourage more students to explore creating music.

Jonathan: I regularly include composition in my classes. I like to start every day with active listening exercises, and I want my students to be able to create their parts just as well as they can perform them.

Michael: I hope to provide ways for students to build their connection with music by finding activities that allow them to grow their musicality, to share what music speaks to them, and to develop their compositional voice. I will facilitate listening activities where students dissect the pieces they like and share what musical components they believe make the piece effective in communicating its feeling or meaning. Students can then take the components they like and use them as starting points for creating their own compositions.

Question 4: *Are there any other thoughts about composition in music education (or other thoughts) that you would like to share?*

Saigelyn: Speaking as a composer, composition gives me a sense of control. It helps me understand myself and have compassion for others. It also helps me feel accomplished and empowered, and gets me excited and joyful about teaching, music, the people around me, and life in general. I write music because I truly can't imagine my life without it. I want every child to have the opportunity to discover that for themselves.

Blaine: I can't wait to give my students the opportunity to feel the way I feel when I start a new project or finally finish a massive work.

Michael: Composition can be a way to expand one's musicality and ability to make musical connections. It can allow an individual to have a deeper, more personal understanding of music' potential to enliven a feeling or idea. I believe there is value in teaching people how to conceptualize and assign meaning to the components of a piece of music. It is valuable to be able to assign a feeling, no matter how deep or broad, to a sorrowful Chopin melody or to understand why Coldplay adds more dense textures and increases their dynamic level during an Instrumental break. The questions I want my students to be able to answer are, "What is being communicated?" and "How is it being communicated?" If a student is able conceptualize a feeling, action, or idea from certain musical components when listening to, performing, and composing music, then they will be able to effectively communicate the music they imagine.

Conclusion

Future music educators are the direct result of the meaningful engagements that they experience with music. For some, these powerful experiences lie in singing and playing instruments; for others, joy is found in the creating music for others to sing, play, and hear. Music teacher education no longer needs to limit its membership to the historic roles, programs, and the curricula that exclude some students in favor of others based on how they connect with music. In welcoming students who push musical, pedagogical, social, and cultural boundaries, music education will find strength in its wealth of diversity (Fitzpatrick, Henninger, & Taylor, 2014; Rowley & Dunbar-Hall, 2013; Talbot, 2018) and new ways to engage students of differing musical passions and interests. No matter what our preferred mode of musical connection—singing, performing, composing, improvising, or listening—our musicking reveals our humanity, a humanity that must honor and value the music in every human as a central tenet in the education of future music teachers.

NOTE

1. See Bennett Reimer's discussion of "Music Education and the Education of Feeling," in Reimer, 2003, pp. 89–94.

REFERENCES

Allsup, R. (2013). The compositional turn in music education: From closed forms to open texts. In Kaschub, M., & Smith, J. (Eds), *Composing our future: Preparing music educators to teach composition*, (pp. 57–70). Oxford University Press.

Ballantyne, J., Kerchner, J. L., & Aróstegui, J. L. (2012). Developing music teacher identities: An international multi-site study. *International Journal of Music Education, 30*(3), 211–226.

Beal, S. J., & Crockett, L. J. (2010). Adolescents' occupational and educational aspirations and expectations: Links to high school activities and adult educational attainment. *Developmental psychology, 46*(1), 258.

Bennett, D. (2013). The use of learner-generated drawings in the development of music students' teacher identities. *International Journal of Music Education, 31*(1), 53–67.

Berkley, R. (2001). Why is teaching composing so challenging? A survey of classroom observation and teachers' opinions. *British Journal of Music Education, 18*(2), 119–138.

Bernard, R. (2004). *Striking a chord: Elementary general music teachers' expressions of their identities as musician-teachers* (Doctoral dissertation). *Retrieved from Proquest Dissertations and Theses.* (Publication No. AAT 3134467).

Berzonsky, M. D. (2011). A social-cognitive perspective on identity construction. In Schwartz, S., Luyckx, K. & Vignoles, V. (Eds), *Handbook of identity theory and research* (pp. 55–76). Springer.

Beynon, C. (1998). From music student to music teacher: Negotiating an identity. In P. Woodford (Ed.), *Critical thinking in music: Theory and practice* (pp. 83–105). University of Western Ontario Press.

Bouij, Christer. (1998). Swedish music teachers in training and professional life. *International Journal of Music Education, 32*, 24–31.

Brewer, M. B., & Hewstone, M. E. (2004). *Self and social identity*. Blackwell Publishing.

Campbell, P. S., Myers, D. E., & Sarath, E. W. (2016). Transforming music study from its foundations: A manifesto for progressive change in the undergraduate preparation of music majors. Routledge.

Chong, S., Low, E. L., & Goh, K. C. (2011). Emerging professional teacher identity of pre-service teachers. *Australian Journal of Teacher Education, 36*(8), 50–64.

Conkling, S. W. (2007). The possibilities of situated learning for teacher preparation: The professional development partnership. *Music Educators Journal, 93*(3), 44–48.

Cox, P. (1997). The professional socialization of music teachers as musicians and educators. In R. Rideout (Ed.), *On the sociology of music education* (pp. 112–120). University of Oklahoma.

Darling-Hammond, L., Hyler, M. E., & Gardner, M. (2017). *Effective teacher professional development*. Learning Policy Institute. Retrieved from https://learningpolicyinstitute.org/sites/default/files/product-files/Effective_Teacher_Professional_Development_REPORT.pdf

Deemer, R. (2016). Reimagining the role of composition in music teacher education. *Music Educators Journal, 102*(3), 41–45.

Dolloff, L. (2007). All the things we are: Balancing our multiple identities in music teaching. *Action, Criticism, and Theory for Music Education*, 6(2), 1–21.

Elliott, D. (1995). *Music matters: a new philosophy of music education*. Oxford University Press.

Feldman, H. A. (1964). Jazz: A place in music education? *Music Educators Journal*, 50(6), 60–64.

Fitzpatrick, K. R., Henninger, J. C., & Taylor, D. M. (2014). Access and retention of marginalized populations within undergraduate music education degree programs. *Journal of Research in Music Education*, 62(2), 105–127.

Froehlich, H. & L'Roy, D. (1985). An investigation of occupational identity in undergraduate music education majors. *Bulletin of the Council for Research in Music Education*, 85, 65–75.

Gillespie, R., & Hamann, D. L. (1999). Career choice among string music education students in American colleges and universities. *Journal of Research in Music Education*, 47(3), 266–278.

Glover, J. (2002). *Children composing 4–14*. Routledge.

Goodman, D. J. (2011). *Promoting diversity and social justice: Educating people from privileged groups*. Routledge.

Guichard, J. (2001). Adolescents' scholastic field, identity frames, and future projects. In Nurmi, J-E, (Ed). *Navigating through adolescence: European Perspectives* (pp. 279–306). Routledge.

Hall, S. (1990). *Cultural identity and diaspora*. Lawrence and Wishart.

Haston, W., & Russell, J. A. (2012). Turning into teachers influences of authentic context learning experiences on occupational identity development of preservice music teachers. *Journal of Research in Music Education*, 59(4), 369–392.

Hargreaves, D., Purves, R., Welch, G., & Marshall, N. (2011). Developing identities and attitudes in musicians and classroom music teachers. *British Journal of Educational Psychology*, 77(3), 665–682. DOI: 10.1348/000709906X154676.

Hickey, M., & Schmidt, C. (2019). The effect of professional development on music teachers' improvisation and composition activities. *Bulletin of the Council for Research in Music Education* (222), 27–43.

Hodgen, J., & Askew, M. (2007). Emotion, identity, and teacher learning: Becoming a primary mathematics teacher. *Oxford Review of Education*, 33(4), 469–487.

Holland, J. L. (1987). Current status of Holland's theory of careers: Another perspective. *Career Development Quarterly*, 36(1), 24–30.

Isbell, D. (2008). Musicians and teachers: The socialization and occupational identity of pre-service music teachers. *Journal of Research in Music Education*, 56(2), 162–178.

Johnson, A. (2006). *Privilege, power and difference* (2nd ed.). Mayfield.

Kaschub, M. (2019). Music composition and *Kyosei*: Advancing practice through teaching-learning partnerships. In *Cases on Kyosei practice in music education* (pp. 194–213). IGI Global.

Kaschub, M., & Smith, J. (2009). *Minds on music: Composition for creative and critical thinking*. Rowman & Littlefield.

Kaschub, M., & Smith, J. P. (2016). The big picture: Developing musical capacities. *Music Educators Journal*, 102(3), 33–40.

Kaschub, M., & Smith, J. (2017). *An examination of composer identity formation within Composing Together*. Unpublished program review. University of Southern Maine.

Kimmel, M., & A. Ferber. (2010). *Privilege: A reader* (2nd ed.). Westview Press.

Kratus, J. (2015). The role of subversion in changing music education. In Music education: Navigating the future (pp. 340–346).

Kroger, J. (2007). *Identity development: Adolescence through adulthood*. Sage.

Kruse, N. B. (2011). Navigating on-site teaching experiences: Multiple perspectives from two school-university partnerships. *Visions of Research in Music Education, 19*, 1–21.

Kumashiro, K. (2009). *Against common sense: Teaching and learning toward social justice.* Taylor & Francis.

Lindroth, J. T. (2012). *The impact of arranging music for the large ensemble on the teacher: A phenomenological exploration* (Doctoral dissertation, University of South Florida).

Mark, M. L. (1987). The acceptance of jazz in the music education curriculum: A model for interpreting a historical process. *Bulletin of the Council for Research in Music Education*, 15–21.

Mark, M. (2008). *A concise history of American music education.* R&L Education.

Myers, J. H., & Gutman, J. (2011). *Life style and psychographics.* Marketing Classics Press.

Nelson, H. L. (2001). *Damaged identities, narrative repair.* Cornell University Press.

Orman, E. K. (2002). Comparison of the national standards for music education and elementary music specialists' use of class time. *Journal of Research in Music Education, 50*(2), 155–164.

Pellegrino, K. (2009). Connections between performer and teacher identities in music teachers: Setting an agenda for research. *Journal of Music Teacher Education, 19*(1), 39–55.

Piazza, E. S., & Talbot, B. C. (2021). Creative Musical Activities in Undergraduate Music Education Curricula. *Journal of Music Teacher Education, 30*(2), 37–50.

Randles, C. (2009). "That's my piece, that's my signature, and it means more . . .": Creative identity and the ensemble teacher/arranger. *Research Studies in Music Education, 31*(1), 52–68.

Randles, C., & Smith, G. D. (2012). A first comparison of pre-service music teachers' identities as creative musicians in the United States and England. *Research Studies in Music Education, 34*(2), 173–187.

Rajan-Rankin, S. (2014). Self-identity, embodiment and the development of emotional resilience. *British Journal of Social Work, 44*(8), 2426–2442.

Reimer, B. (2003). *A philosophy of music education: Advancing the vision* (3rd ed.). Prentice Hall.

Reimer, B. (2014). Reflections on *Music Educators Journal* in its centennial year. *Music Educators Journal, 100*(3), 27–32.

Rickels, D. A., Brewer, W. D., Councill, K. H., Fredrickson, W. E., Hairston, M., Perry, D. L., & Schmidt, M. (2013). Career influences of music education audition candidates. *Journal of Research in Music Education, 61*(1), 115–134.

Rickels, D. A., Hoffman III, E. C., & Fredrickson, W. E. (2019). A comparative analysis of influences on choosing a music teaching occupation. *Journal of Research in Music Education, 67*(3), 286–303.

Roberts, B. (1991). Music teacher education as identity construction. *International Journal of Music Education, 18*, 30–39.

Rowley, J., & Dunbar-Hall, P. (2013). Cultural diversity in music learning: Developing identity as a music teacher and learner. *Pacific-Asian Education, 25*(2), 41–50.

Savickas, M. L., Nota, L., Rossier, J., Dauwalder, J. P., Duarte, M. E., Guichard, J., Soresi, S., Van Esbroeck, R., & Van Vianen, A. E. M., (2009). Life designing: A paradigm for career construction in the 21st century. *Journal of Vocational Behavior, 75*(3), 239–250.

Scheib, J. W. (2007). Music teacher socialization and identity formation: Redesigning teacher education and professional development to enhance career satisfaction. In *2nd Biennial Symposium on Music Teacher Education, Greensboro, NC.* National Association for Music Education: Society for Music Teacher Education.

Skorikov, V. B., & Vondracek, F. W. (2011). Occupational identity. In Schwartz, S., Luyckx, K., Vignoles, V. (Eds), *Handbook of identity theory and research* (pp. 693–714). Springer.

Strand, K. (2006). Survey of Indiana music teachers on using composition in the classroom. *Journal of Research in Music Education, 54*(2), 154–167.

Stringham, D. A., Thornton, L. C., & Shevock, D. J. (2015). Composition and improvisation in instrumental methods courses: Instrumental music teacher educators' perspectives. *Bulletin of the Council for Research in Music Education* (205), 7–25.

Talbot, B. C. (Ed.). (2018). *Marginalized voices in music education*. Routledge.

Viig, T. G. (2015) Composition in music education: A literature review of 10 years of research articles published in music education journals. *Nordic Research in Music Education Yearbook, 16*, 227–257.

Wei, R. C., Darling-Hammond, L., & Adamson, F. (2010). *Professional development in the United States: Trends and challenges* (28). National Staff Development Council.

Wiggins, J. (2007). Compositional process in music. In *International handbook of research in arts education* (pp. 453–476). Springer.

Wildman, S. M. (2005). Persistence of white privilege. Washington University Journal of Law and Policy, *18*, 245.

Williams, D. A. (2007). What are music educators doing and how well are we doing it? *Music Educators Journal, 94*(1), 18–23.

Zembylas, M. (2003). Emotions and teacher identity: A poststructural perspective. *Teachers and Teaching: Theory and Practice, 3*, 213–235.

Zimmer-Gembeck, M. J., & Mortimer, J. T. (2006). Selection processes and vocational development: A multi-method approach. In R. Macmillan (Ed.), *Constructing adulthood: Agency and subjectivity in adolescence and adulthood* (Vol. 11). Elsevier.

Index

For the benefit of digital users, indexed terms that span two pages (e.g., 52–53) may, on occasion, appear on only one of those pages.

Figures are indicated by *f* following the page number